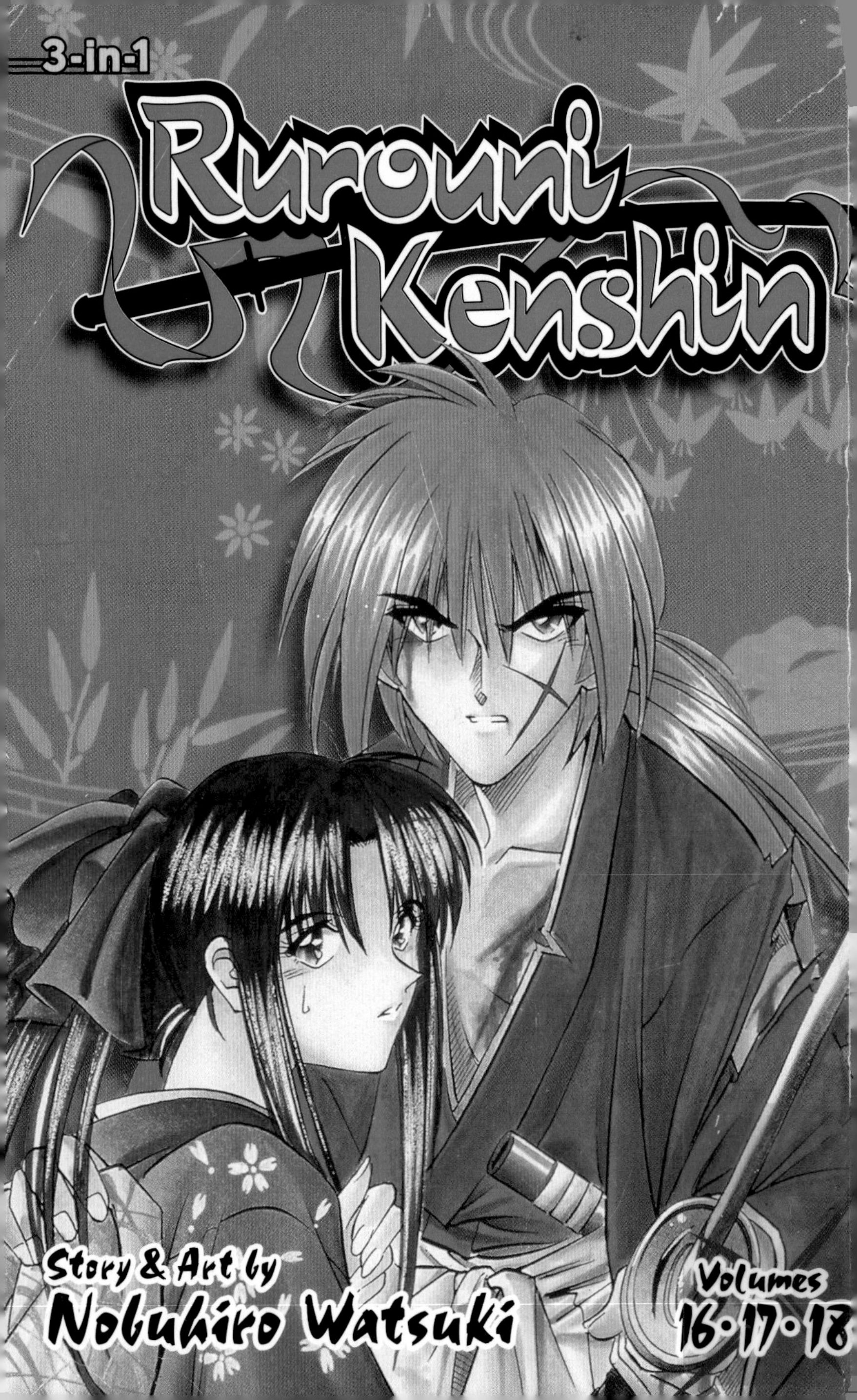
3-in-1
Rurouni Kenshin
Story & Art by
Nobuhiro Watsuki
Volumes
16•17•18

RUROUNI KENSHIN
3-in-1 Edition Volume 6
A compilation of the graphic novel volumes 16-17-18

STORY AND ART BY
NOBUHIRO WATSUKI

Translation/Kenichiro Yagi
English Adaptation/Gerard Jones
Touch-Up Art & Lettering/Steve Dutro
Design/Sean Lee (Manga Edition)
Design/Izumi Evers (Omnibus Edition)
Editor/Avery Gotoh (Manga Edition)
Editor/Shaenon Garrity (Omnibus Edition)

RUROUNI KENSHIN © 1994 by Nobuhiro Watsuki
All rights reserved.
First published in Japan in 1994 by SHUEISHA Inc., Tokyo.
English translation rights arranged by SHUEISHA Inc.

Printed in the U.S.A.

Published by VIZ Media, LLC
P.O. Box 77010
San Francisco, CA 94107

10 9 8 7 6 5 4 3 2 1
Omnibus edition first printing, April 2018

www.viz.com   www.shonenjump.com

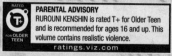

"RUROKEN" CHARACTERS ARE KIND OF PLAIN, SO MAKING THEM INTO ACTION FIGURES MIGHT NOT WORK (ESPECIALLY THE FEMALES)...
OH, LIKE THAT'S OUR FAULT?! HOW 'BOUT YOU JUST SUCK AT DRAWING CUTE GIRLS?!
IT'S WHY THE FANS SAY YOU CAN'T DO FEMALE CHARACTERS, DUH!!

和 月 伸 宏

NOBUHIRO WATSUKI

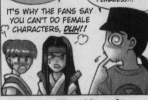

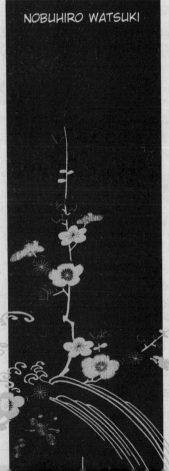

FIGURE BOOM

...OR SO THEY SAY. IT'S ALL *GOOD*—FOR WATSUKI, ANYWAY, WHO STARTED COLLECTING "X-MEN" FIGURES THREE YEARS AGO. AND THE BOOM'S NOT JUST IN WESTERN ACTION FIGURES, EITHER—EVEN THE GARAGE KITS FOR TRULY OLD-SCHOOL JAPANESE HEROES AND HEROINES ARE SEEING NEW POPULARITY. YOU DON'T EVEN HAVE TO ***BUY*** THE ACTION FIGURES TO APPRECIATE THEM: WATSUKI, THE KIND OF GUY WHO'S BROUGHT TO TEARS BY THE *KIN'NIKU SHŌJO-TAI* SONG, "OMOCHA-YA MEGURI (TOY-STORE TRAWLER)," FINDS THAT HIS HEART JUST WON'T STOP POUNDING. THIS SPRING'S REALLY GETTING STARTED WITH A BANG!

Rurouni Kenshin, which has found fans not only in Japan but around the world, first made its appearance in 1992, as an original short story in ***Weekly Shonen Jump Special.*** Later rewritten and published as a regular, continuing ***Jump*** series in 1994, ***Rurouni Kenshin*** ended serialization in 1999 but continued in popularity, as evidenced by the 2000 publication of ***Yahiko no Sakabatô*** ("Yahiko's Reversed-Edge Sword") in ***Weekly Shonen Jump.*** His most current work, ***Busô Renkin*** ("Armored Alchemist"), began publication in June 2003, also in ***Jump***.

Rurouni Kenshin™

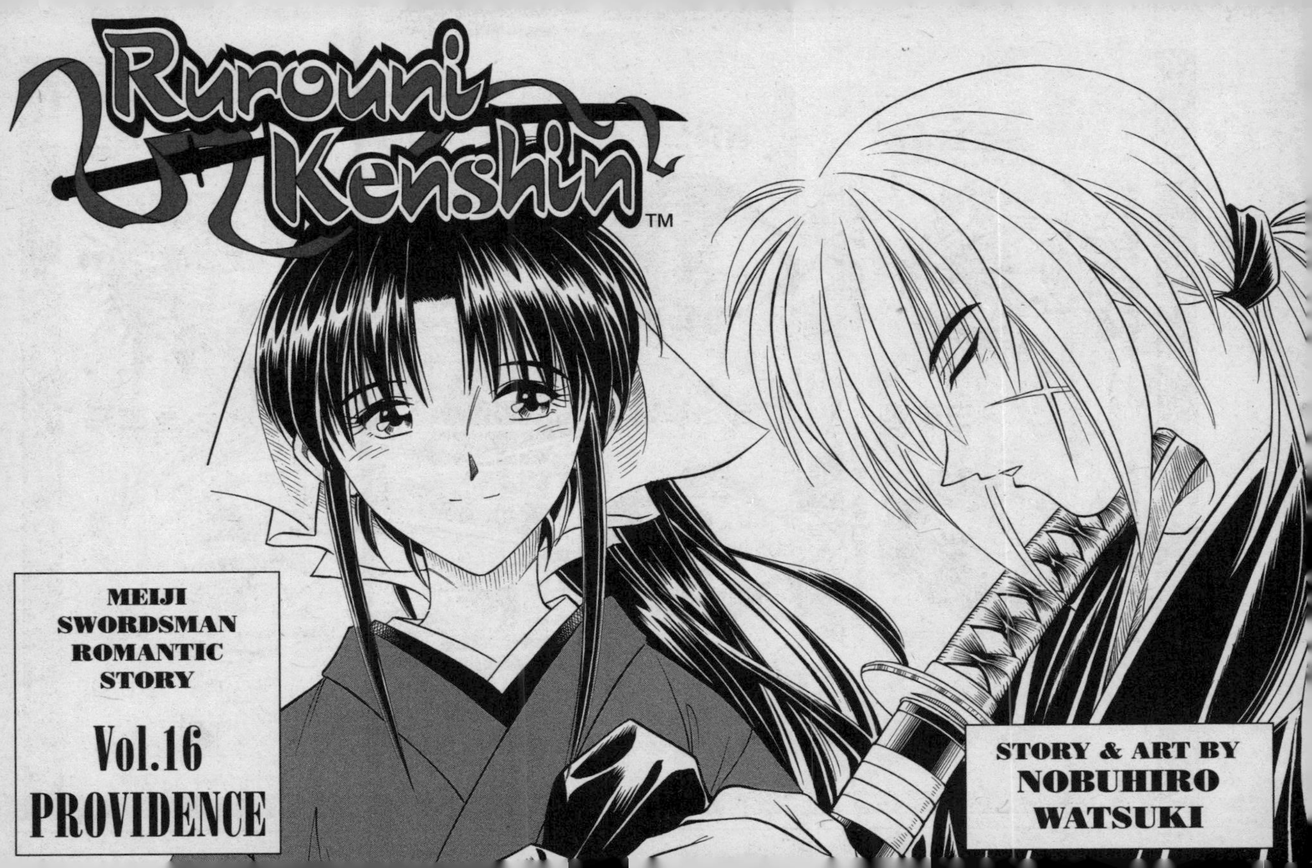

MEIJI SWORDSMAN ROMANTIC STORY

Vol.16 PROVIDENCE

STORY & ART BY NOBUHIRO WATSUKI

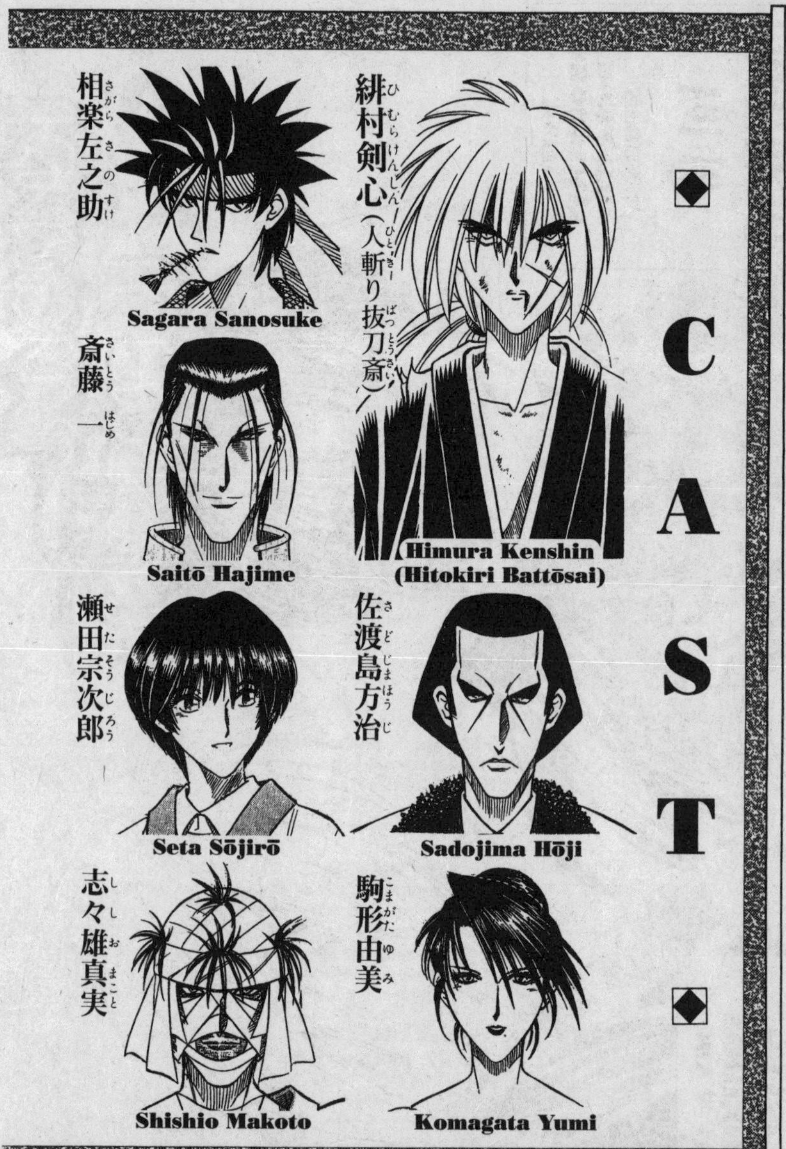
CAST
緋村剣心（人斬り抜刀斎）
Himura Kenshin (Hitokiri Battōsai)
相楽左之助
Sagara Sanosuke
斎藤一
Saitō Hajime
佐渡島方治
Sadojima Hōji
瀬田宗次郎
Seta Sōjirō
駒形由美
Komagata Yumi
志々雄真実
Shishio Makoto

Once he was *hitokiri*, an assassin, called Battōsai. His name was legend among the pro-Imperialist or "patriot" warriors who launched the Meiji Era. Now, Himura Kenshin is *rurouni*, a wanderer, and carries a reversed-edge *sakabatō* to prohibit himself from killing.

THUS FAR

Kenshin has journeyed to Kyoto to block the machinations of Shishio Makoto, the man who took Kenshin's place as *hitokiri* or government-sanctioned slayer of men. Along the way, Kenshin falls in with a girl—Misao, who intensely admires Shinomori Aoshi—and eventually fights a duel with Sōjirō, one of Shishio's *Juppongatana* or "Ten Swords." With his first *sakabatō* broken and new *sakabatō*, "Shinuchi," in hand, Kenshin seeks out Hiko Seijūrō, master of Hiten Mitsurugi-ryū, to obtain the ultimate secret of that school: *Amakakeru Ryū no Hirameki*. Together with Sanosuke and Saitō, Kenshin heads off Shishio's plans to burn down Kyoto and attack Tokyo by cannon from a battleship, leading to a final battle at Shishio's lair...a battle to which Kenshin goes, promising Misao that he'll bring back Aoshi. First, Sanosuke fights the fallen priest, "Bright King" Anji, defeating him with the newly learned "Mastery of Three Layers"—only for Anji to reveal that, while Kenshin is being distracted, most of the *Juppongatana* are attacking Aoi-Ya, the inn where Misao and the others are mounting a desperate stand. Leaving Saitō to battle "Blind Sword" Usui, Kenshin hurries to dispatch the next opponent, Sōjirō...but now Aoshi stands in Kenshin's way. After a fierce battle, Kenshin is able to defeat Aoshi...without reverting to his suppressed *hitokiri* self.

Meanwhile, back at Aoi-Ya, Yahiko and the others defeat "Flighted" Henya and "Giant Scythe" Kamatari and, just when the menace of *Hagun* or "Army of Destruction" Fuji seems most overwhelming, Hiko appears and challenges the giant to a duel, granting his opponent long-yearned-for recognition as a fellow samurai. Eventually defeated by Hiko's *Kuzu-Ryūsen*, Fuji is nonetheless better for the experience, and Hiko's status as a "great" man is revealed. Back with Kenshin and Sōjirō, their battle begins, once news of Aoi-Ya's victory is revealed. In the end, the *Shukuchi* or "Reduced Earth" technique of Sōjirō proves superior to the "God-Speed" of Kenshin...leaving the former *hitokiri* to wonder what comes next.

CONTENTS

RUROUNI KENSHIN
Meiji Swordsman Romantic Story
BOOK SIXTEEN: PROVIDENCE

**ACT 130
Sōjirō's Story:
Moonlight Encounter
7**

**ACT 131
Sōjirō's Story:
Feast of Thunder
25**

**ACT 132
Sōjirō's Story:
Smile in the Frozen Rain
43**

**ACT 133
Destruction of the Soul
63**

**ACT 134
The Second Secret
83**

**ACT 135
Those Who Gather,
Those Who Part
103**

**ACT 136
When Did the Battle Begin?
123**

**ACT 137
Fuel
143**

**ACT 138
Providence
163**

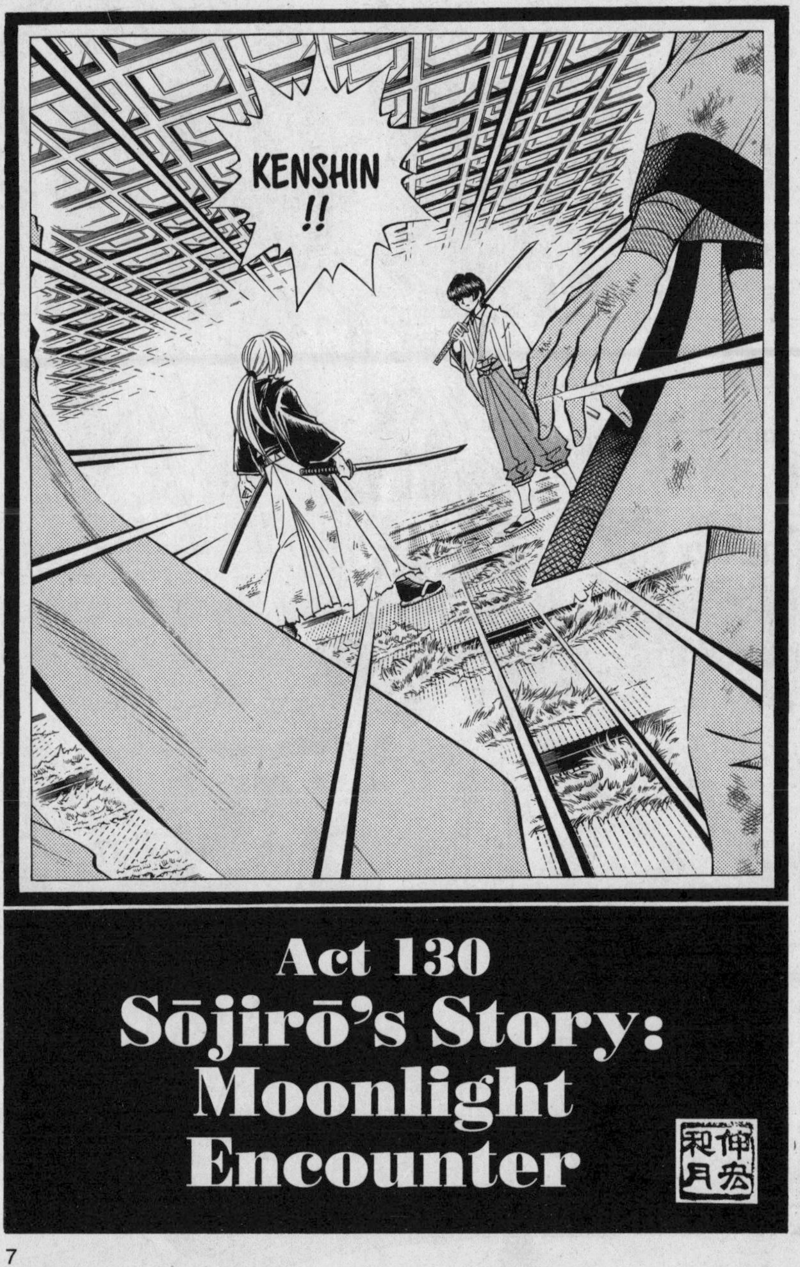
KENSHIN !!

Act 130
Sōjirō's Story: Moonlight Encounter

伸宏和月

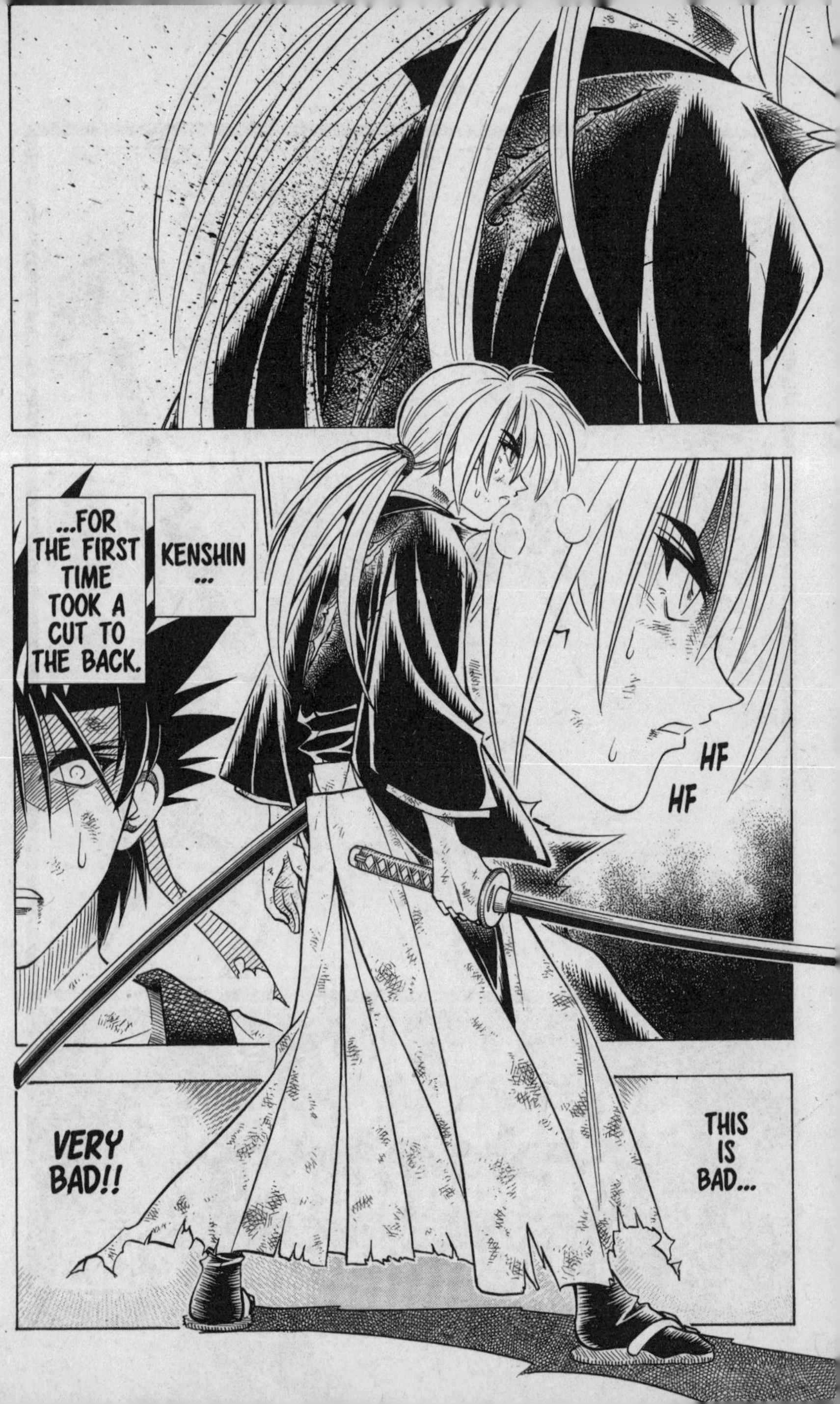
HF
HF
KENSHIN...
...FOR THE FIRST TIME TOOK A CUT TO THE BACK.
THIS IS BAD...
VERY BAD!!

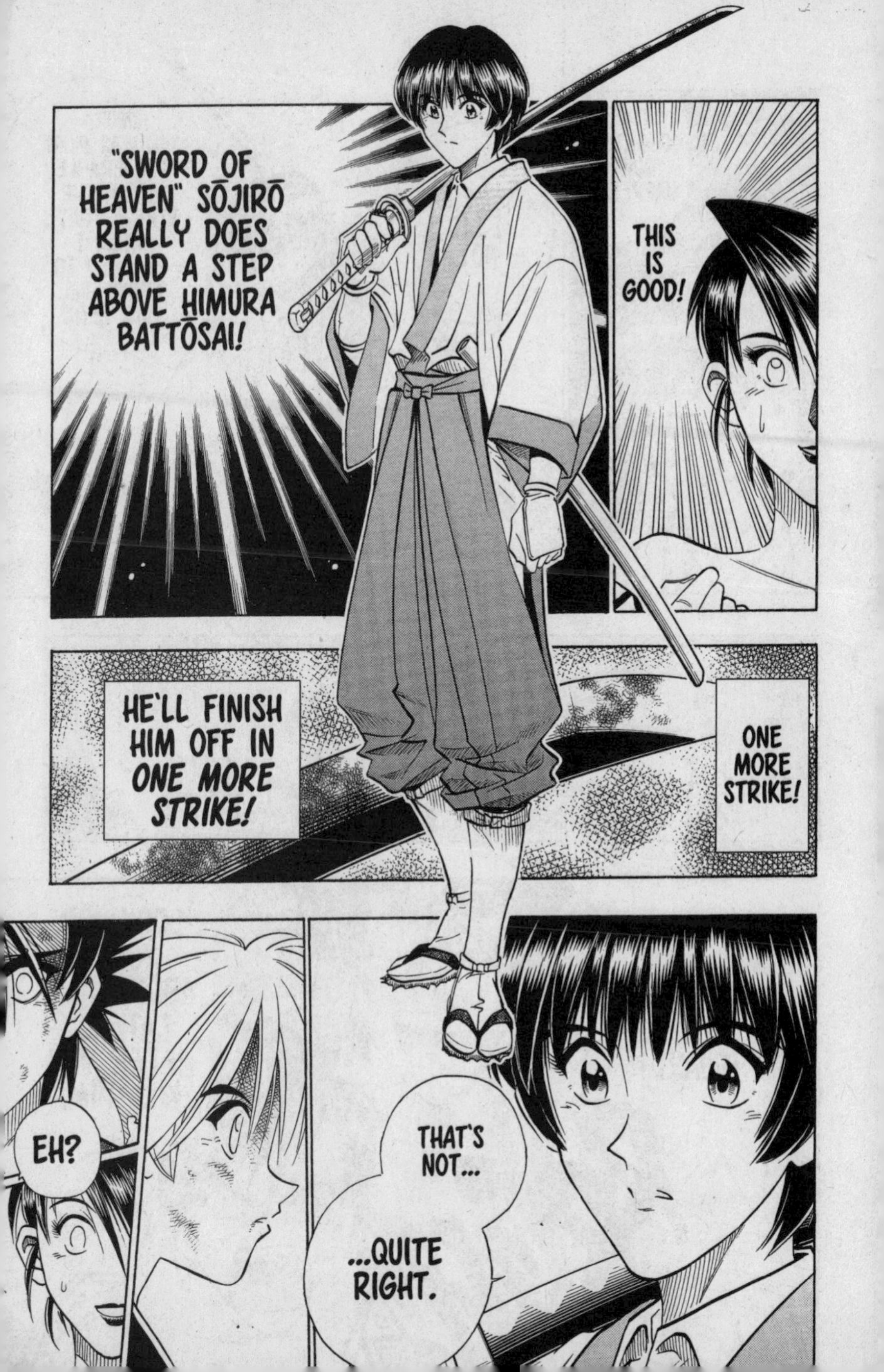
THIS IS GOOD!
"SWORD OF HEAVEN" SŌJIRŌ REALLY DOES STAND A STEP ABOVE HIMURA BATTŌSAI!
ONE MORE STRIKE!
HE'LL FINISH HIM OFF IN ONE MORE STRIKE!
THAT'S NOT...
...QUITE RIGHT.
EH?

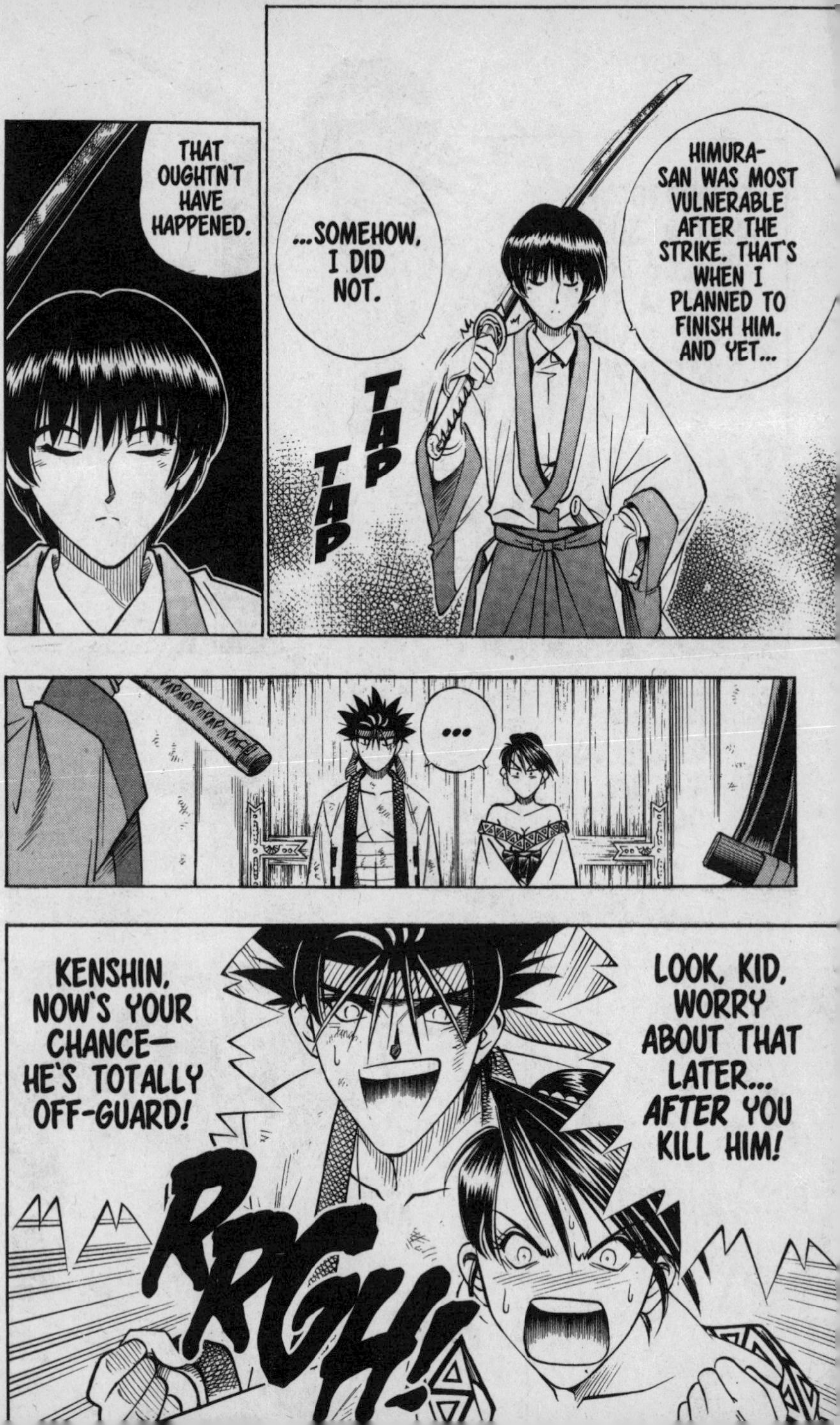
HIMURA-SAN WAS MOST VULNERABLE AFTER THE STRIKE. THAT'S WHEN I PLANNED TO FINISH HIM. AND YET...
...SOMEHOW, I DID NOT.
TAP TAP
THAT OUGHTN'T HAVE HAPPENED.
...
LOOK, KID, WORRY ABOUT THAT LATER... AFTER YOU KILL HIM!
KENSHIN, NOW'S YOUR CHANCE— HE'S TOTALLY OFF-GUARD!
RRGH!!

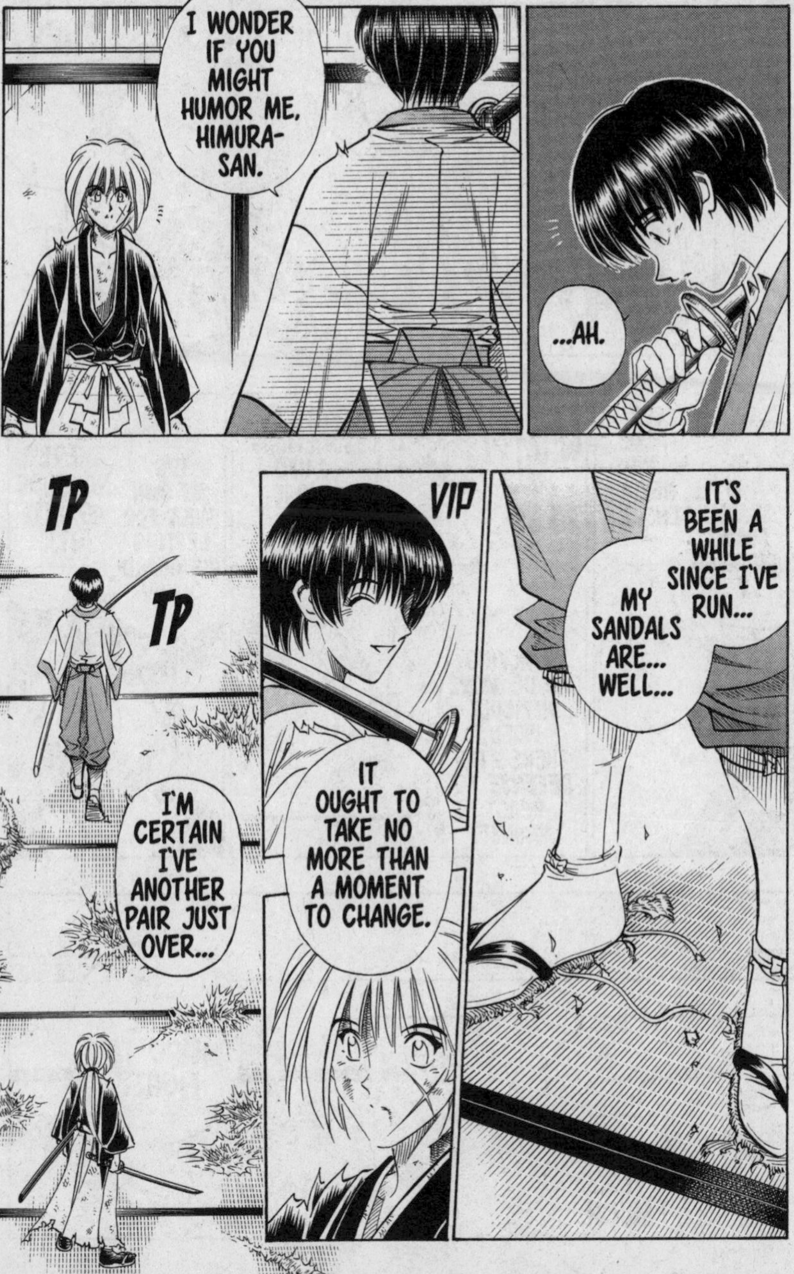
...AH.
I WONDER IF YOU MIGHT HUMOR ME, HIMURA-SAN.
IT'S BEEN A WHILE SINCE I'VE RUN...
MY SANDALS ARE... WELL...
VIP
IT OUGHT TO TAKE NO MORE THAN A MOMENT TO CHANGE.
TP
TP
I'M CERTAIN I'VE ANOTHER PAIR JUST OVER...

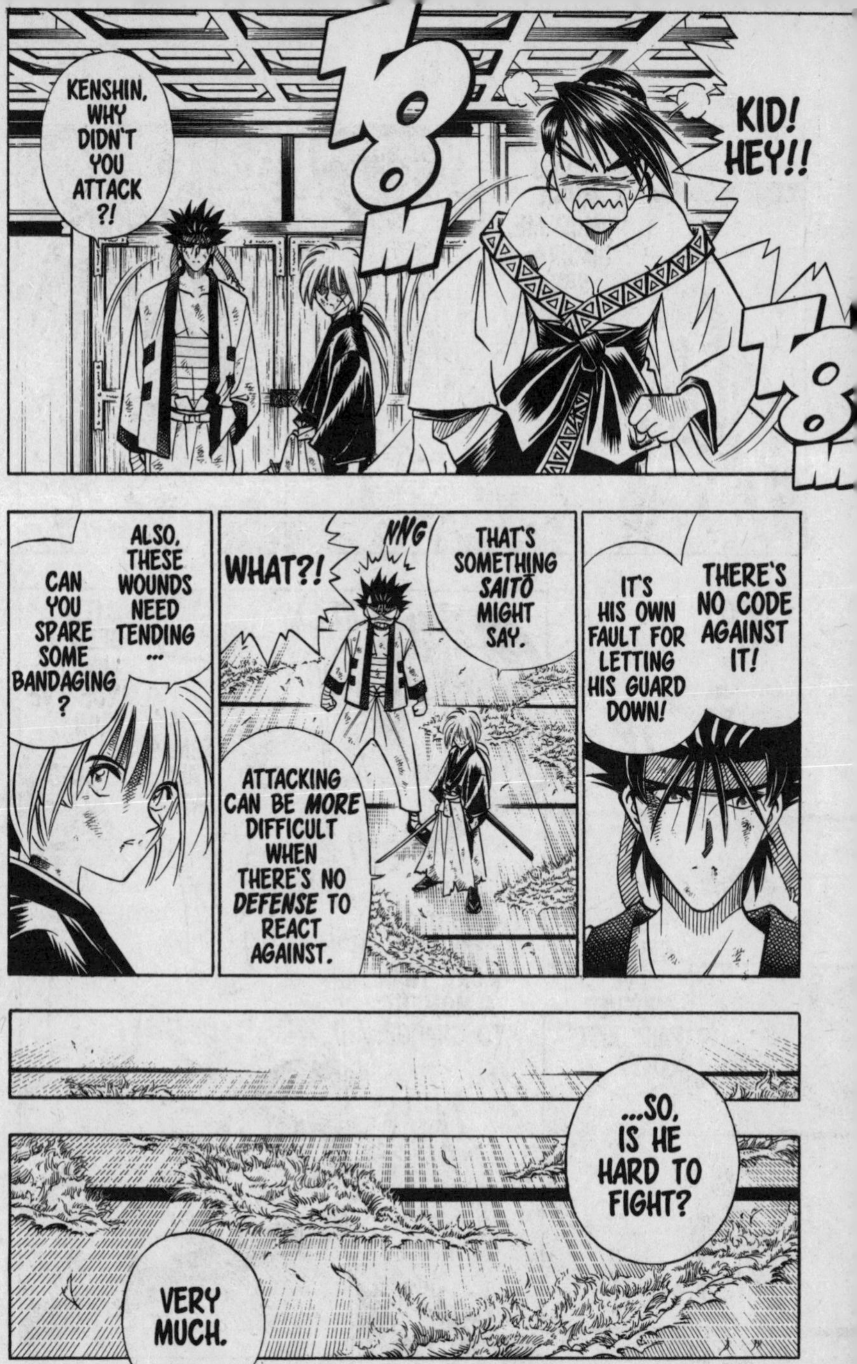
TOM
KID! HEY!!
TOM
KENSHIN, WHY DIDN'T YOU ATTACK?!
THERE'S NO CODE AGAINST IT!
IT'S HIS OWN FAULT FOR LETTING HIS GUARD DOWN!
THAT'S SOMETHING *SAITŌ* MIGHT SAY.
NNG
WHAT?!
ATTACKING CAN BE *MORE* DIFFICULT WHEN THERE'S NO *DEFENSE* TO REACT AGAINST.
ALSO, THESE WOUNDS NEED TENDING...
CAN YOU SPARE SOME BANDAGING?
...SO, IS HE HARD TO FIGHT?
VERY MUCH.

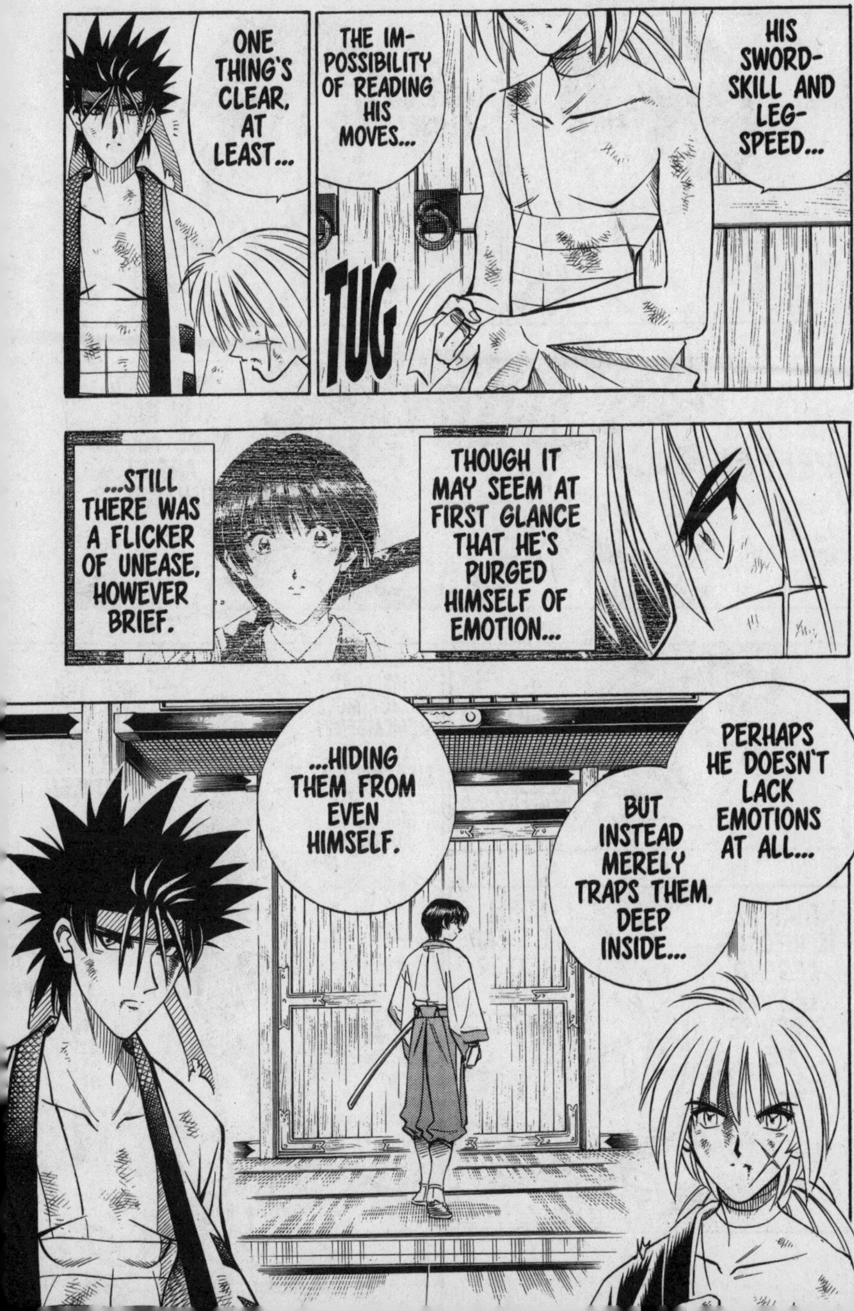
HIS SWORD-SKILL AND LEG-SPEED...
THE IMPOSSIBILITY OF READING HIS MOVES...
TUG
ONE THING'S CLEAR, AT LEAST...
THOUGH IT MAY SEEM AT FIRST GLANCE THAT HE'S PURGED HIMSELF OF EMOTION...
...STILL THERE WAS A FLICKER OF UNEASE, HOWEVER BRIEF.
PERHAPS HE DOESN'T LACK EMOTIONS AT ALL...
BUT INSTEAD MERELY TRAPS THEM, DEEP INSIDE...
...HIDING THEM FROM EVEN HIMSELF.

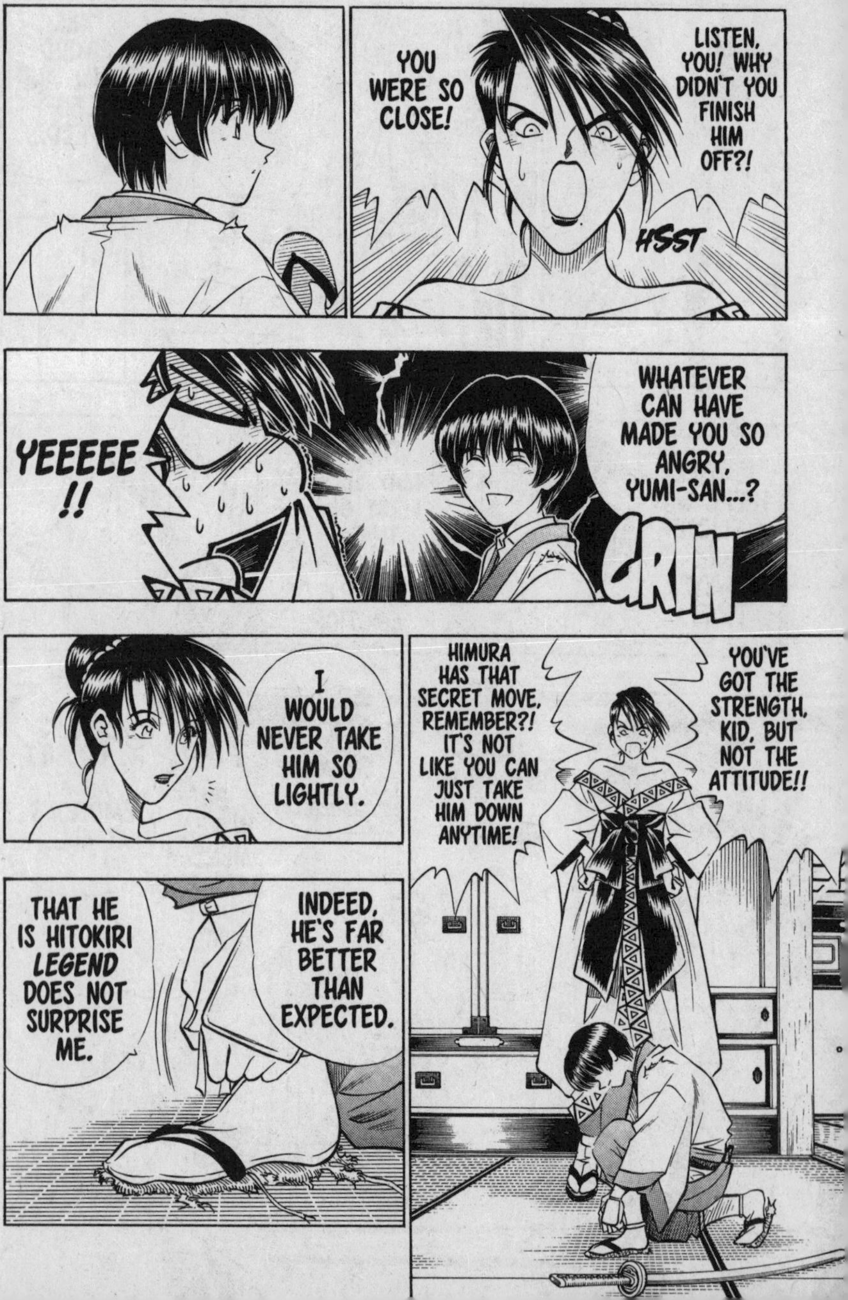
LISTEN, YOU! WHY DIDN'T YOU FINISH HIM OFF?!
YOU WERE SO CLOSE!
HSST
WHATEVER CAN HAVE MADE YOU SO ANGRY, YUMI-SAN...?
GRIN
YEEEEE!!
YOU'VE GOT THE STRENGTH, KID, BUT NOT THE ATTITUDE!!
HIMURA HAS THAT SECRET MOVE, REMEMBER?! IT'S NOT LIKE YOU CAN JUST TAKE HIM DOWN ANYTIME!
I WOULD NEVER TAKE HIM SO LIGHTLY.
INDEED, HE'S FAR BETTER THAN EXPECTED.
THAT HE IS HITOKIRI *LEGEND* DOES NOT SURPRISE ME.

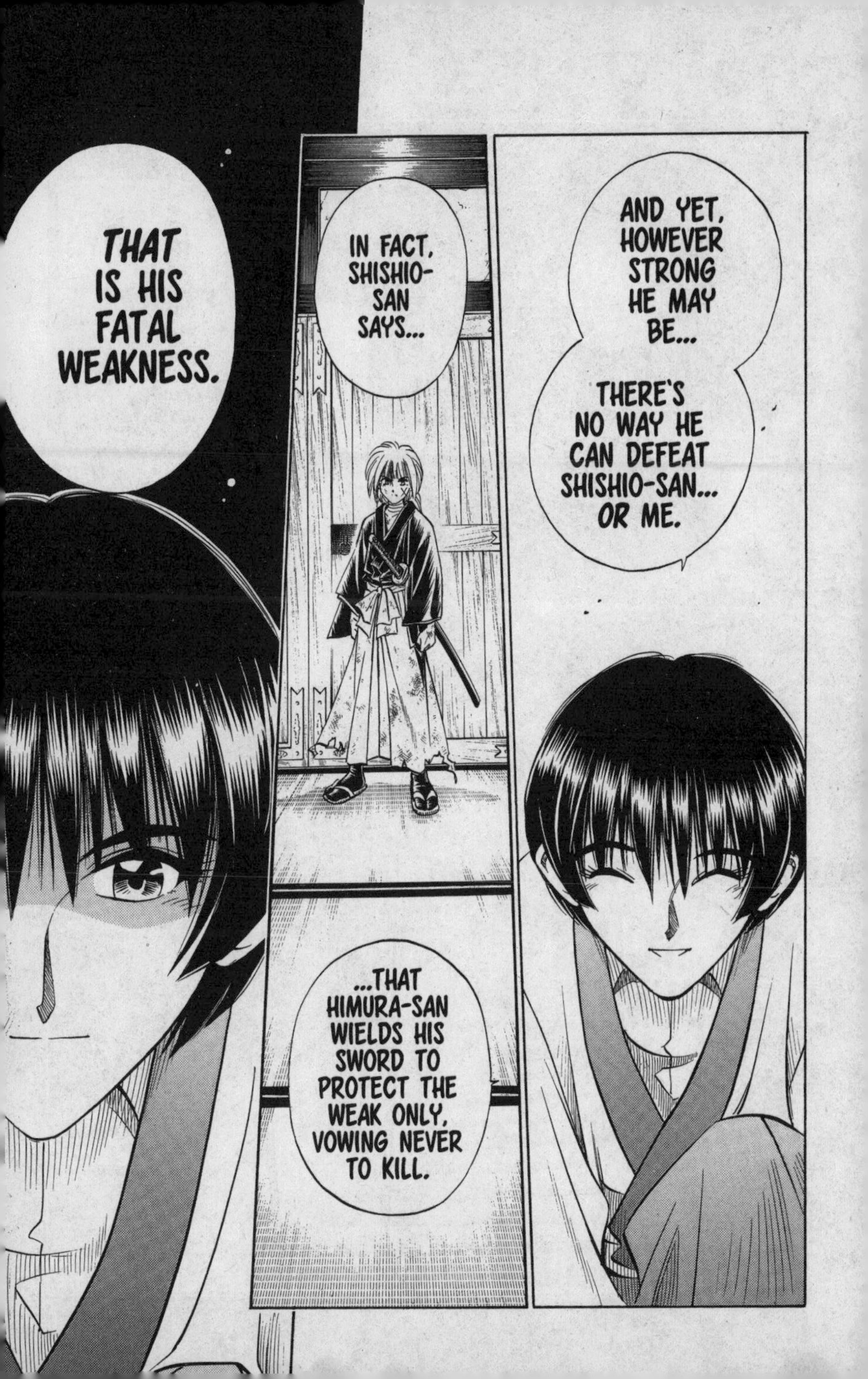
AND YET, HOWEVER STRONG HE MAY BE...
THERE'S NO WAY HE CAN DEFEAT SHISHIO-SAN... OR ME.
IN FACT, SHISHIO-SAN SAYS...
...THAT HIMURA-SAN WIELDS HIS SWORD TO PROTECT THE WEAK ONLY, VOWING NEVER TO KILL.
THAT IS HIS FATAL WEAKNESS.

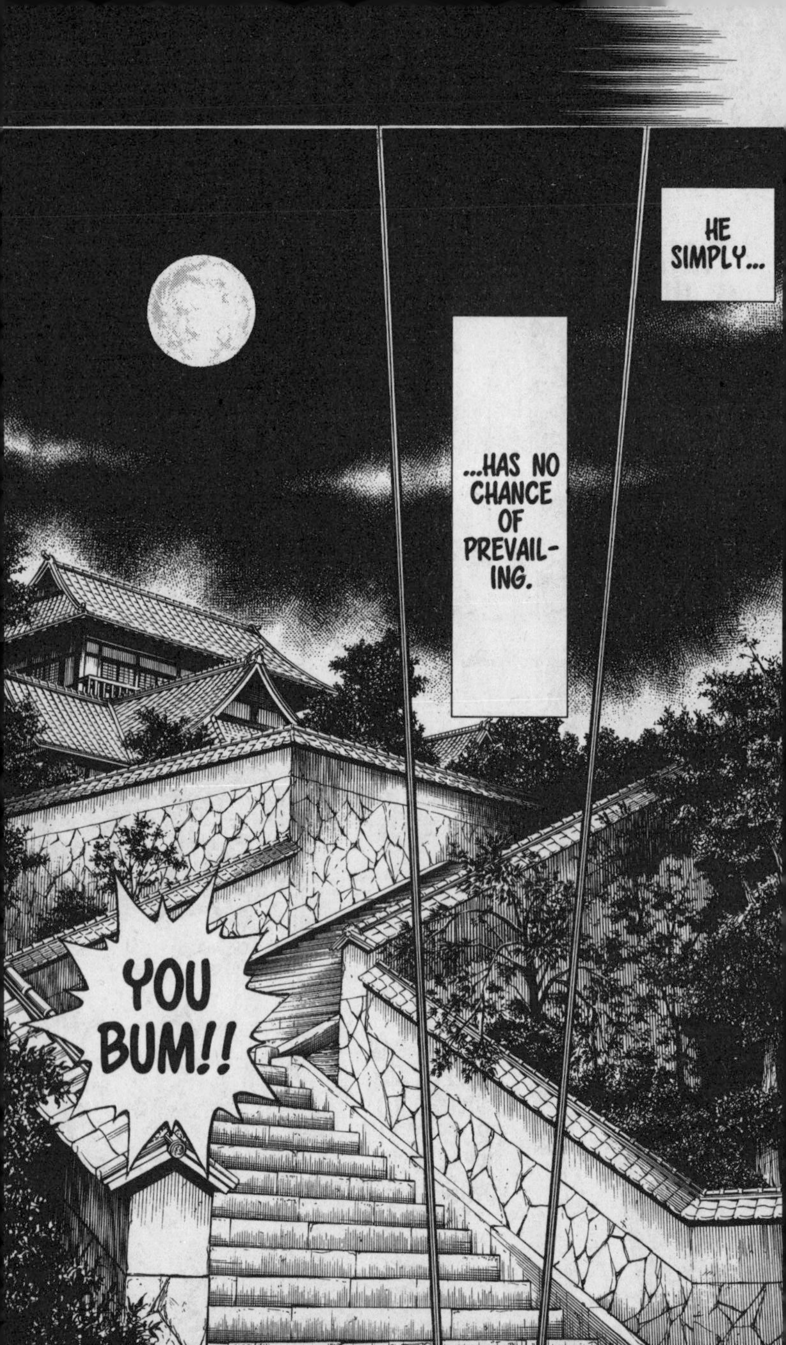
HE SIMPLY...
...HAS NO CHANCE OF PREVAIL-ING.
YOU BUM!!

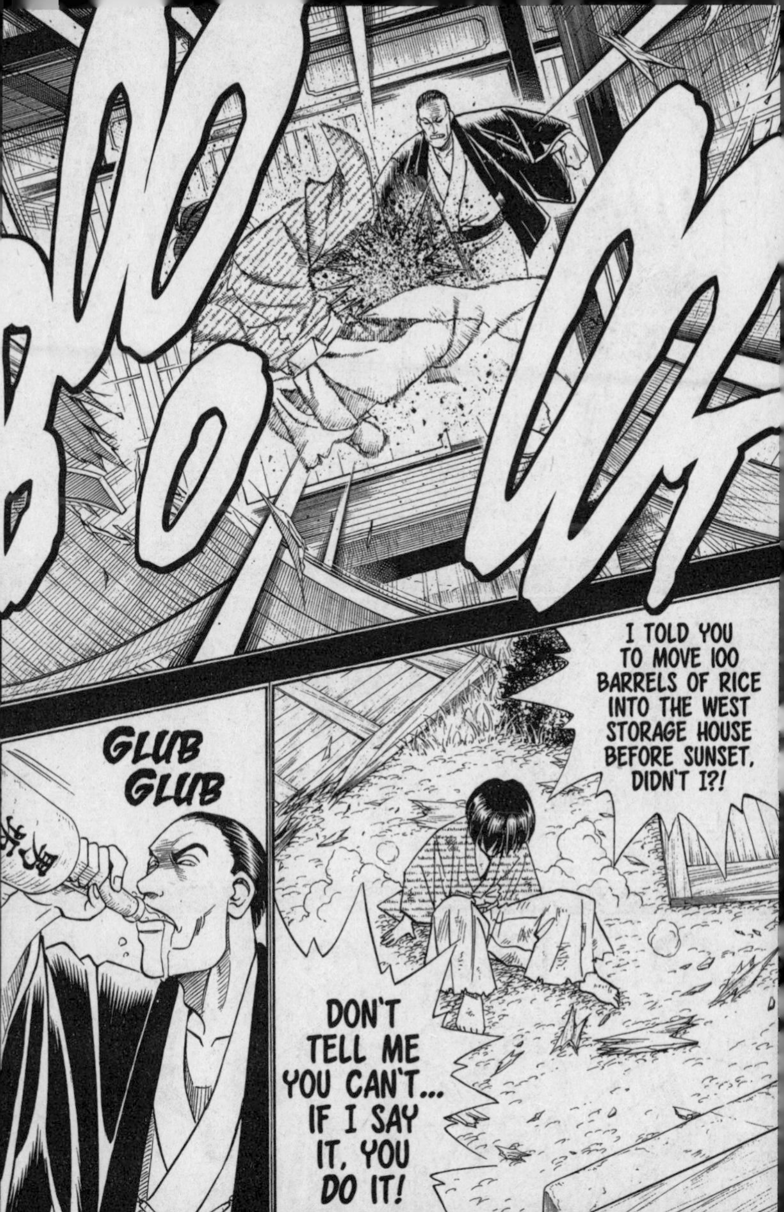
I TOLD YOU TO MOVE 100 BARRELS OF RICE INTO THE WEST STORAGE HOUSE BEFORE SUNSET, DIDN'T I?!
DON'T TELL ME YOU CAN'T... IF I SAY IT, YOU DO IT!
GLUB GLUB

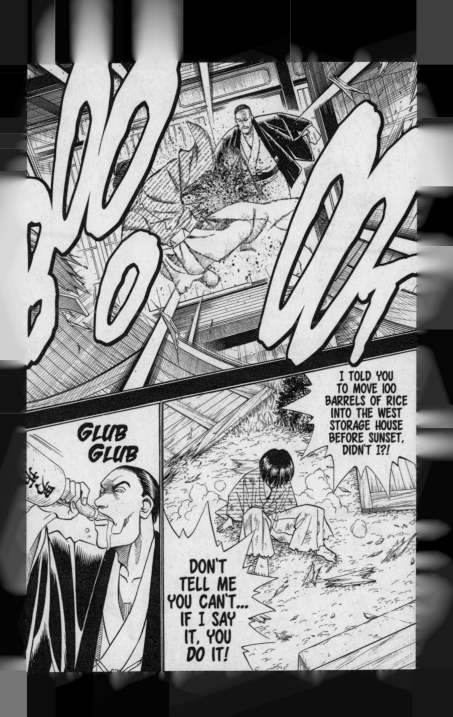

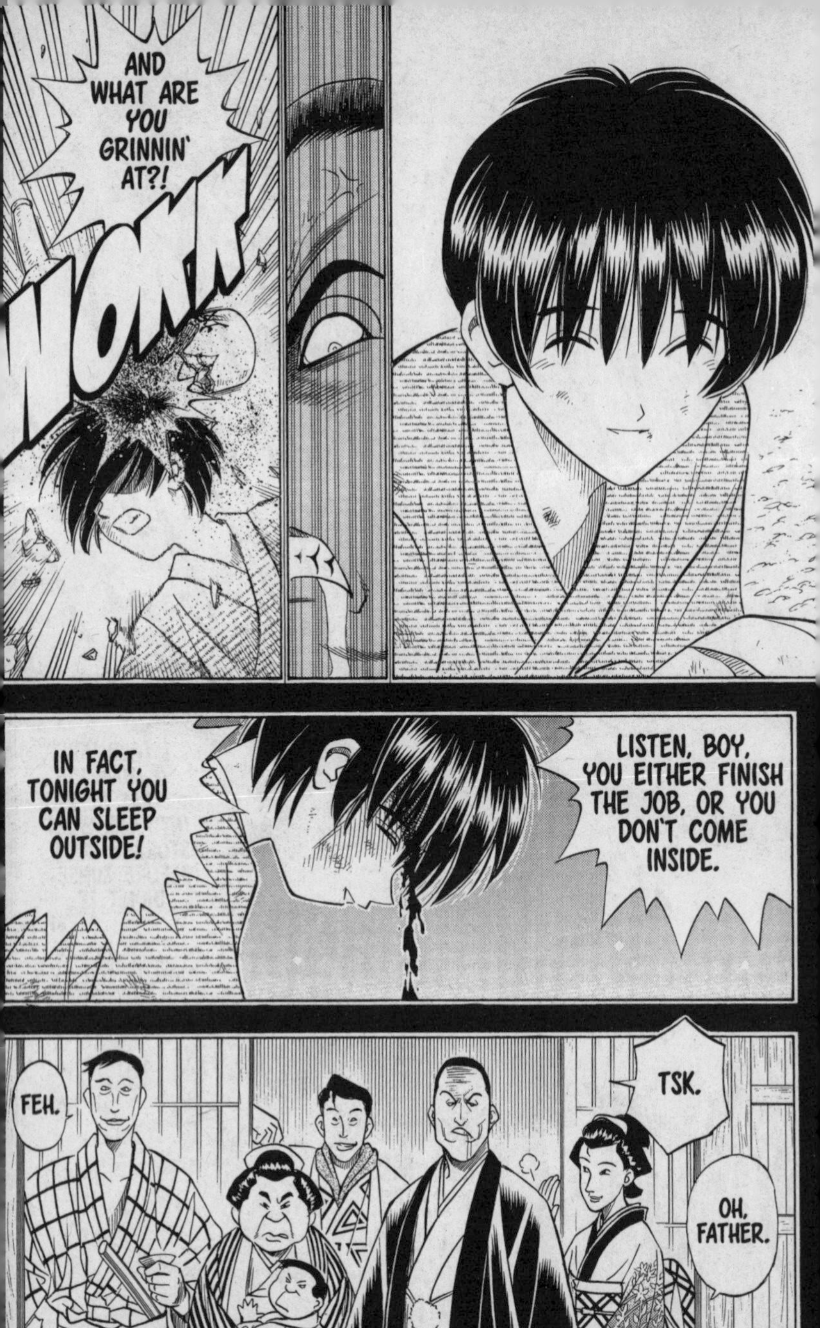
AND WHAT ARE YOU GRINNIN' AT?!
WONK
LISTEN, BOY, YOU EITHER FINISH THE JOB, OR YOU DON'T COME INSIDE.
IN FACT, TONIGHT YOU CAN SLEEP OUTSIDE!
TSK.
OH, FATHER.
FEH.

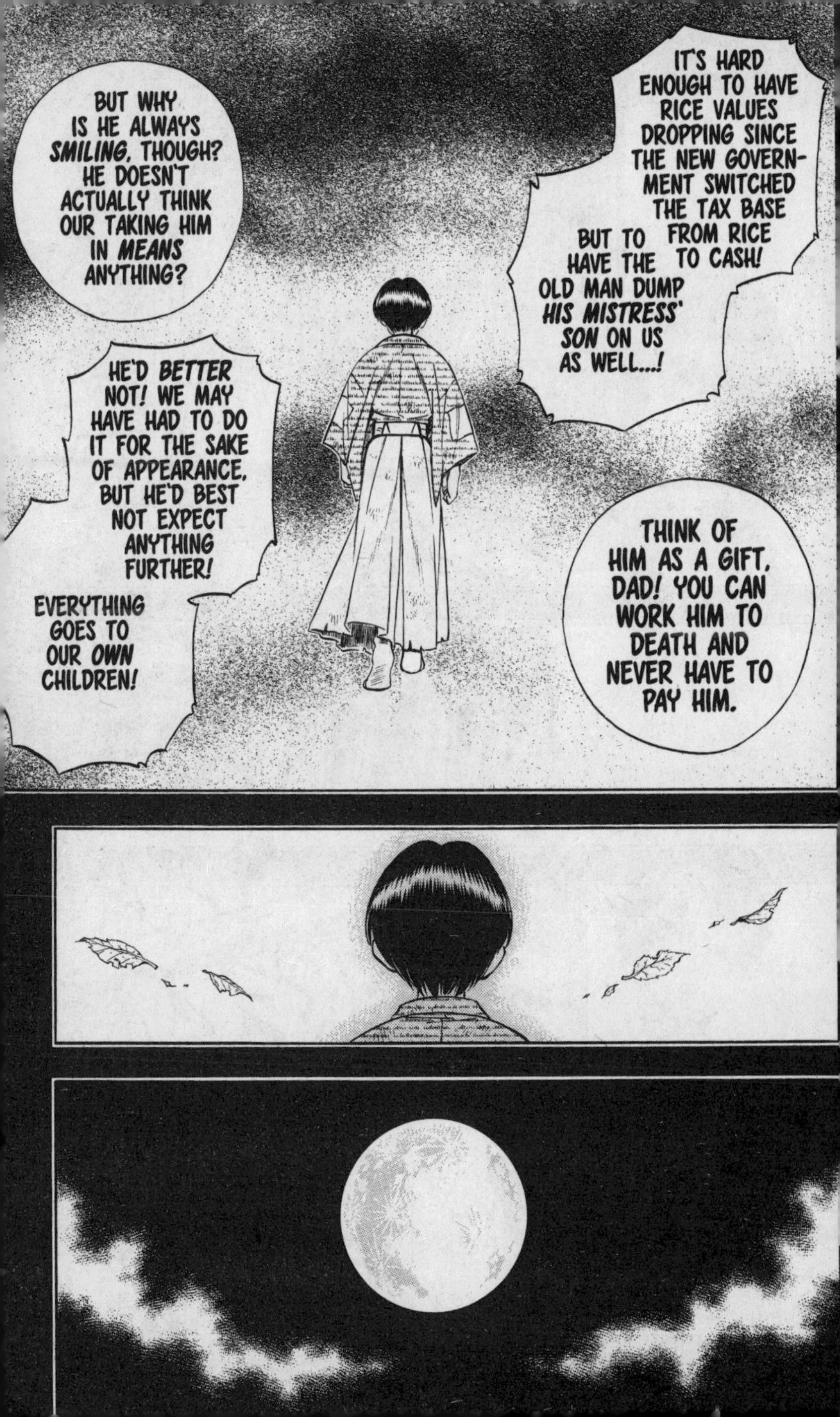
IT'S HARD ENOUGH TO HAVE RICE VALUES DROPPING SINCE THE NEW GOVERNMENT SWITCHED THE TAX BASE FROM RICE TO CASH!
BUT TO HAVE THE OLD MAN DUMP *HIS MISTRESS' SON* ON US AS WELL...!
BUT WHY IS HE ALWAYS *SMILING*, THOUGH? HE DOESN'T ACTUALLY THINK OUR TAKING HIM IN *MEANS* ANYTHING?
HE'D *BETTER* NOT! WE MAY HAVE HAD TO DO IT FOR THE SAKE OF APPEARANCE, BUT HE'D BEST NOT EXPECT ANYTHING FURTHER!
EVERYTHING GOES TO OUR *OWN* CHILDREN!
THINK OF HIM AS A GIFT, DAD! YOU CAN WORK HIM TO DEATH AND NEVER HAVE TO PAY HIM.

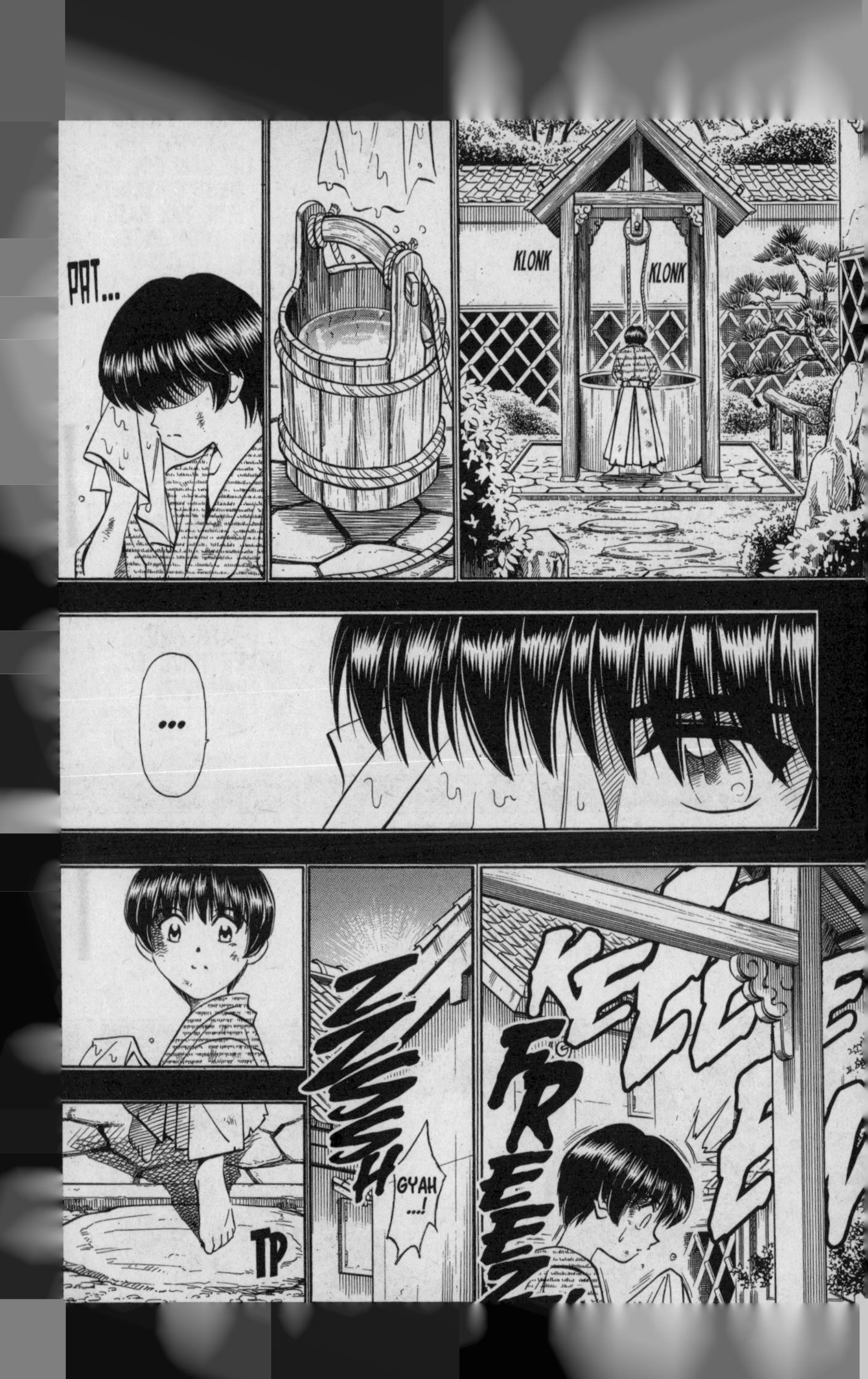
KLONK
KLONK
PAT...
...
GYAH ...!
TP

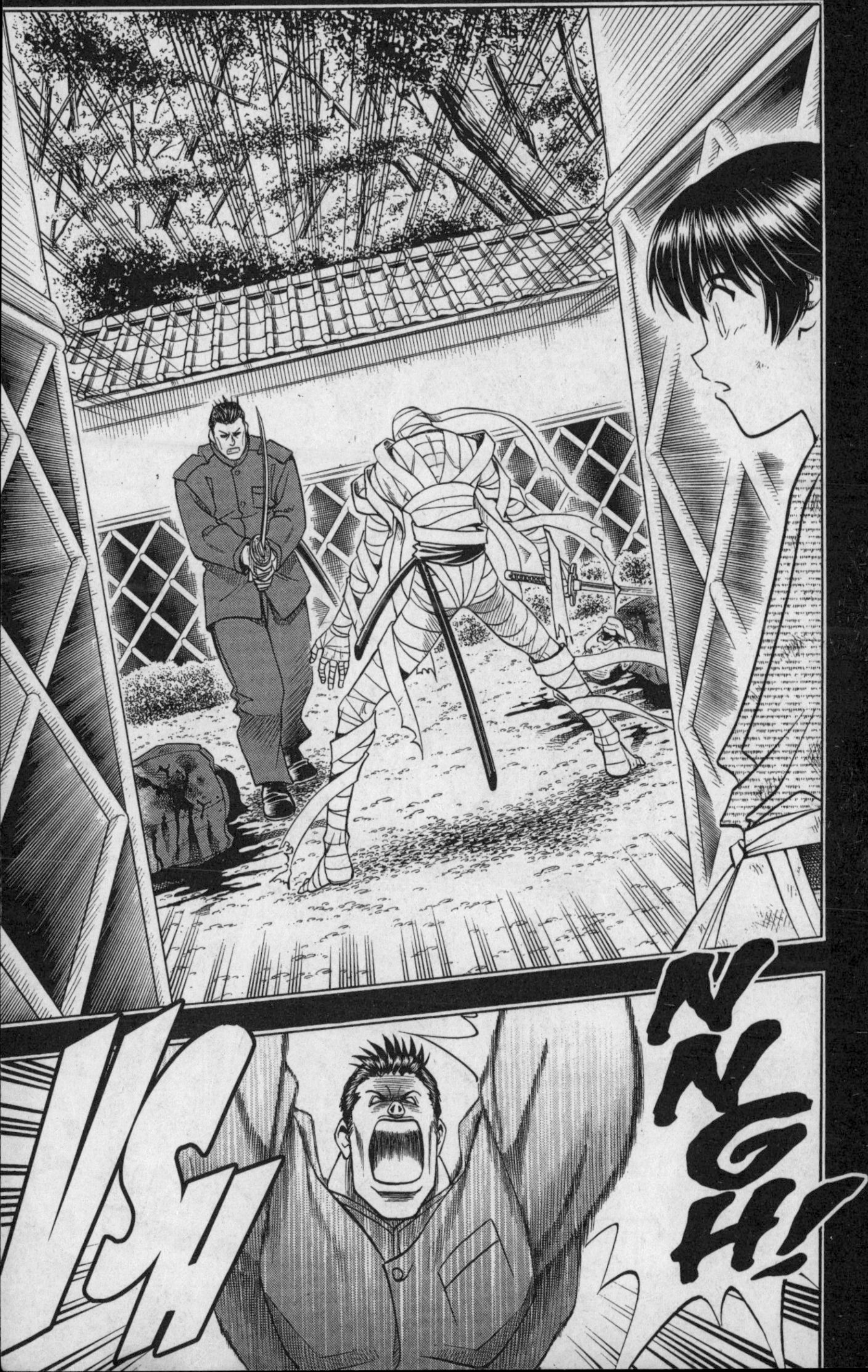

NNGH!
UGH

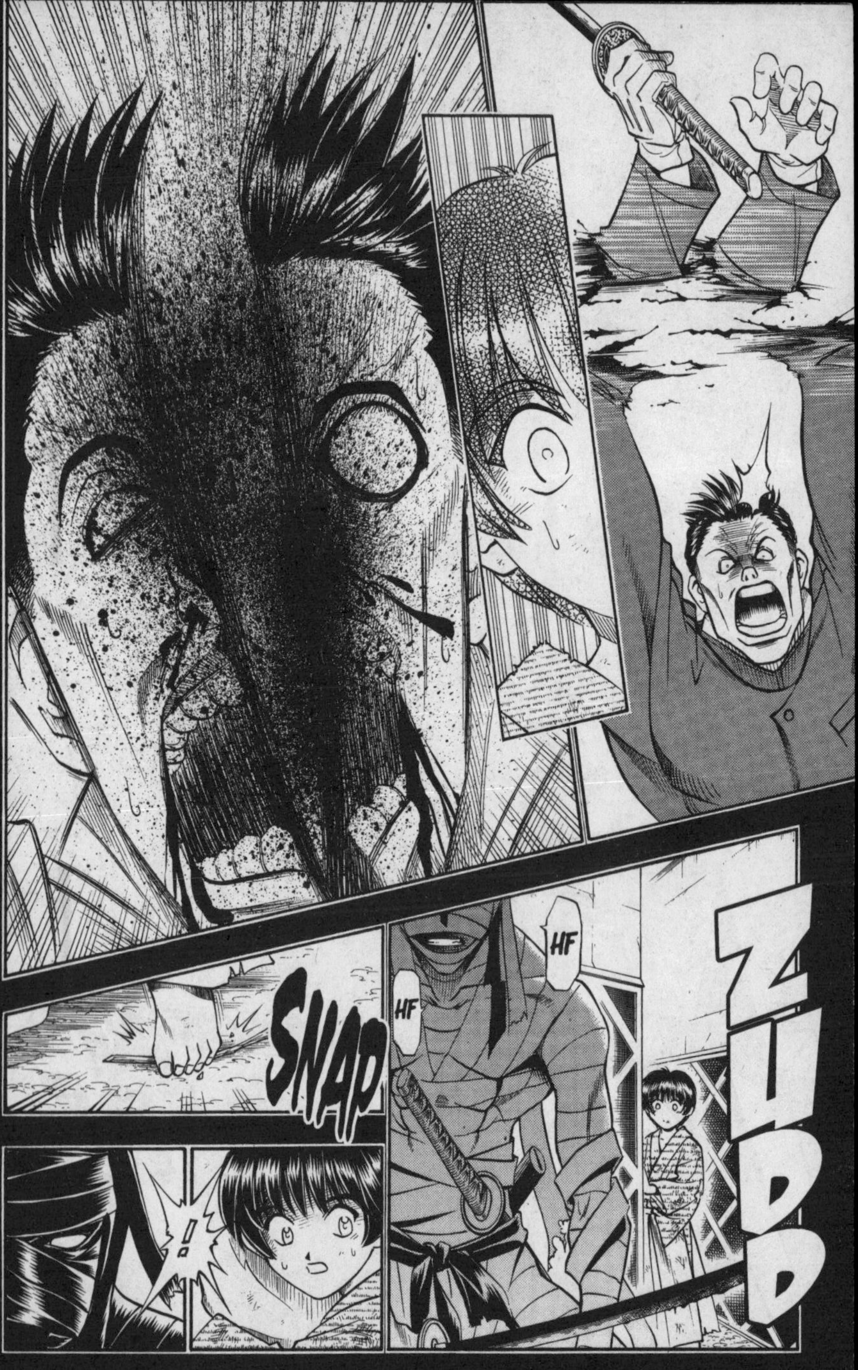
ZUDD
HF
HF
SNAP
!

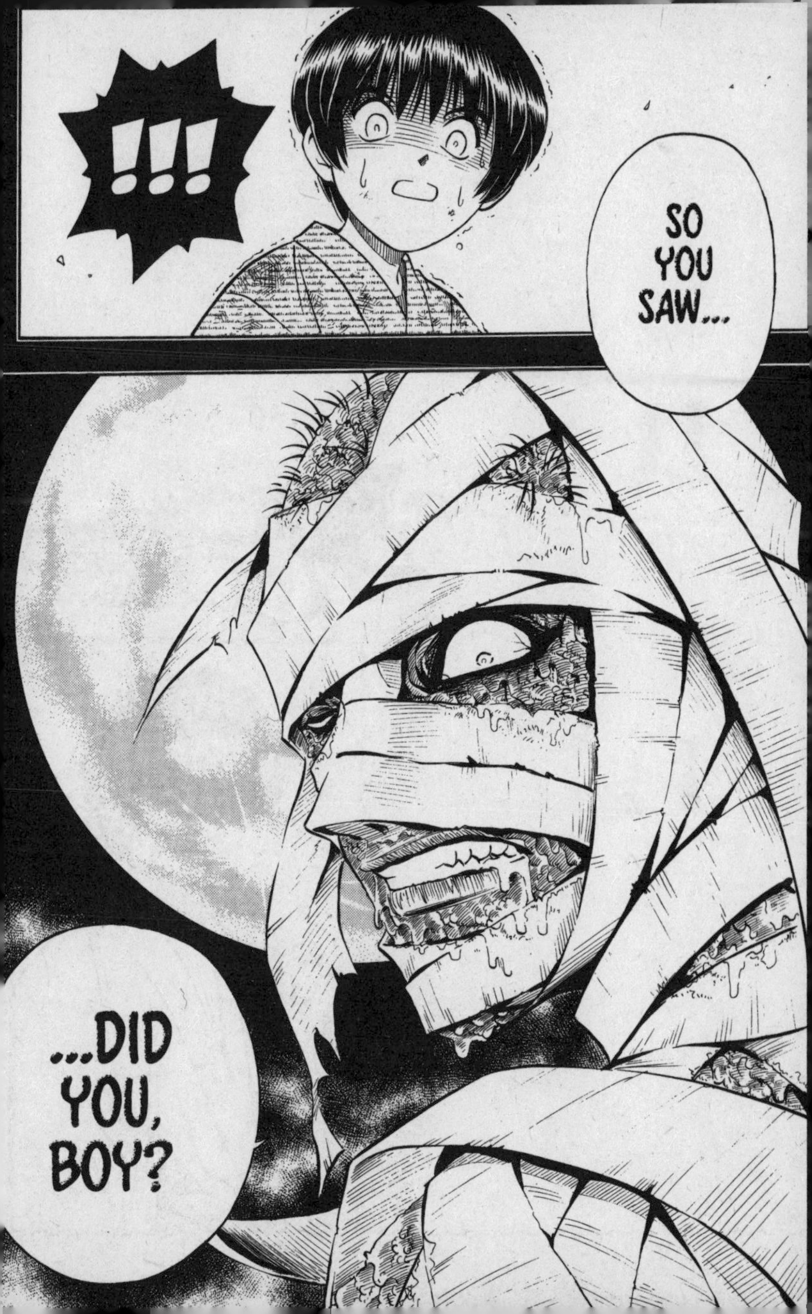
!!!
SO YOU SAW...
...DID YOU, BOY?

Rurouni Kenshin

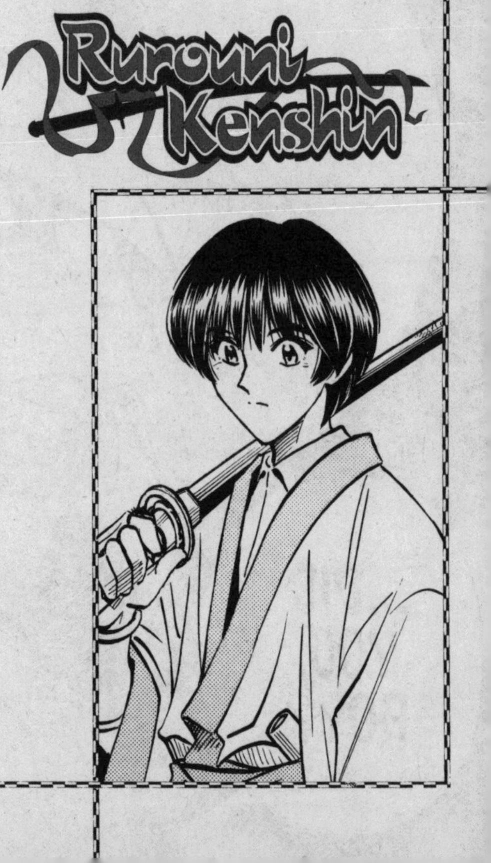

Act 131—Sōjirō's Story: Feast of Thunder

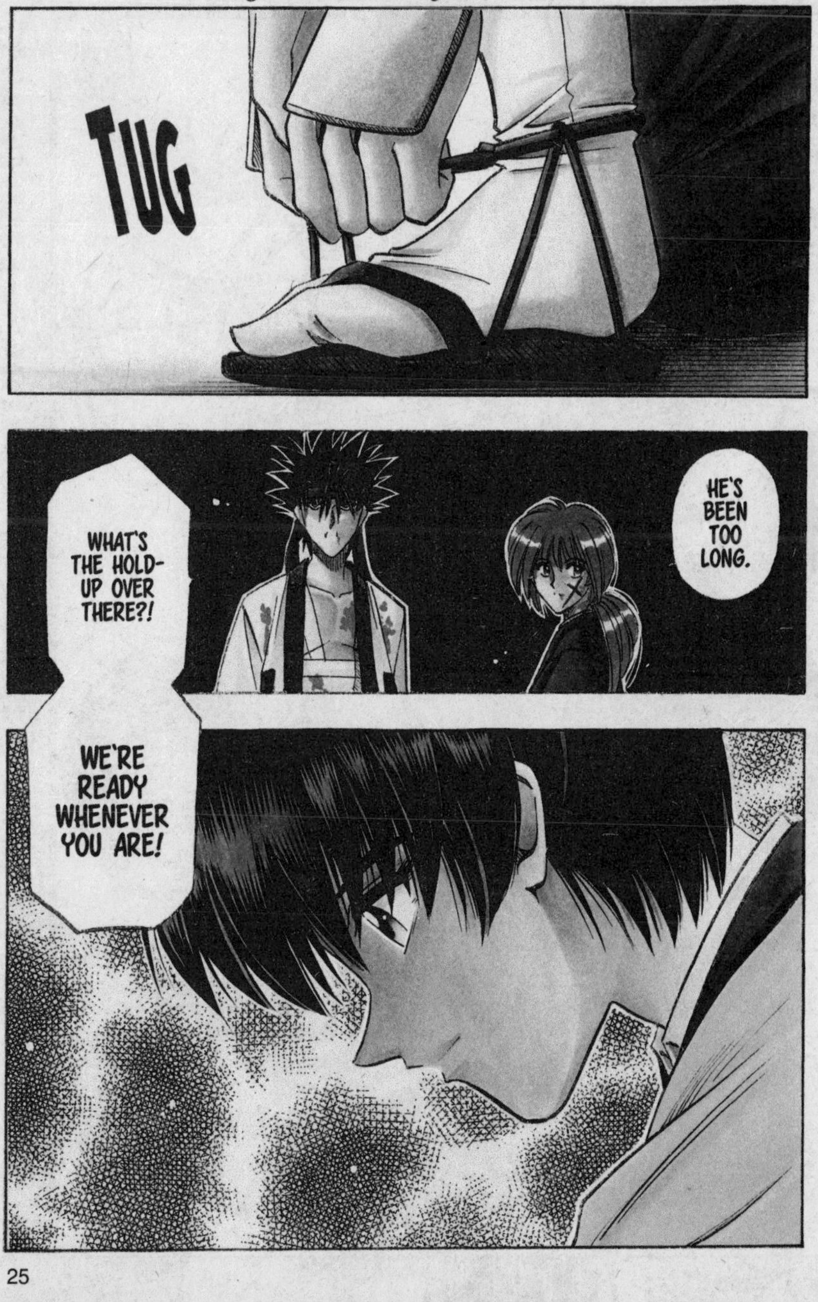
TUG
HE'S BEEN TOO LONG.
WHAT'S THE HOLD-UP OVER THERE?!
WE'RE READY WHENEVER YOU ARE!

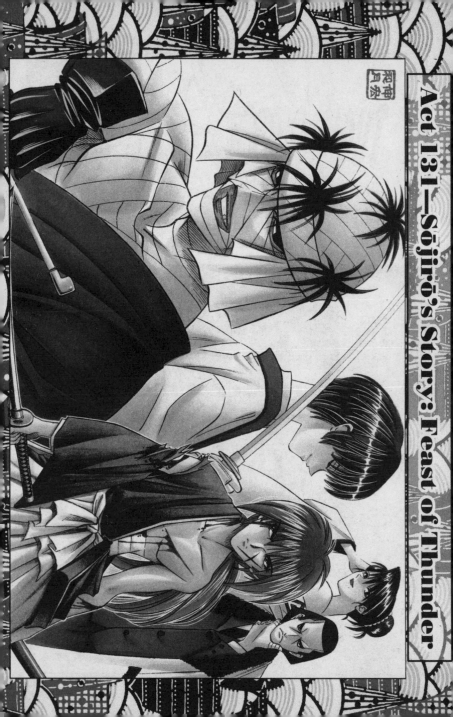

Act 131—Sōjirō's Story: Feast of Thunder

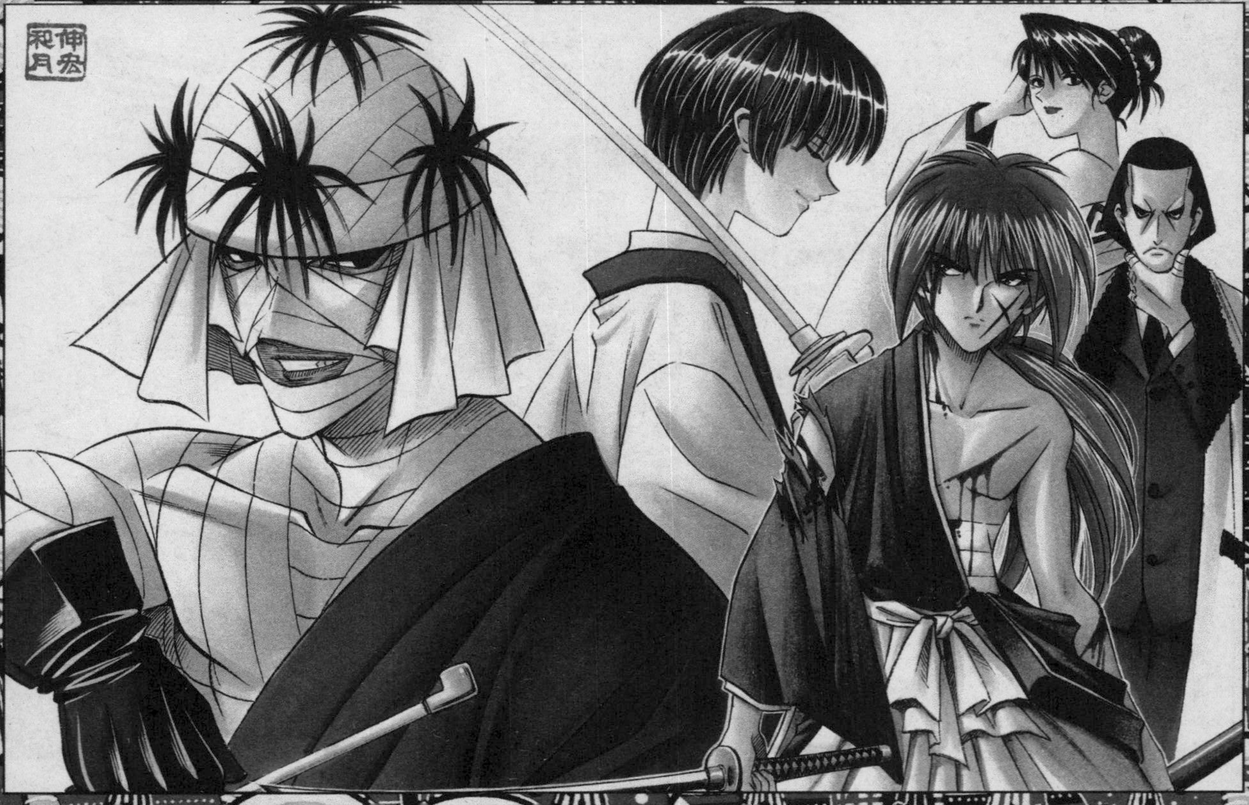

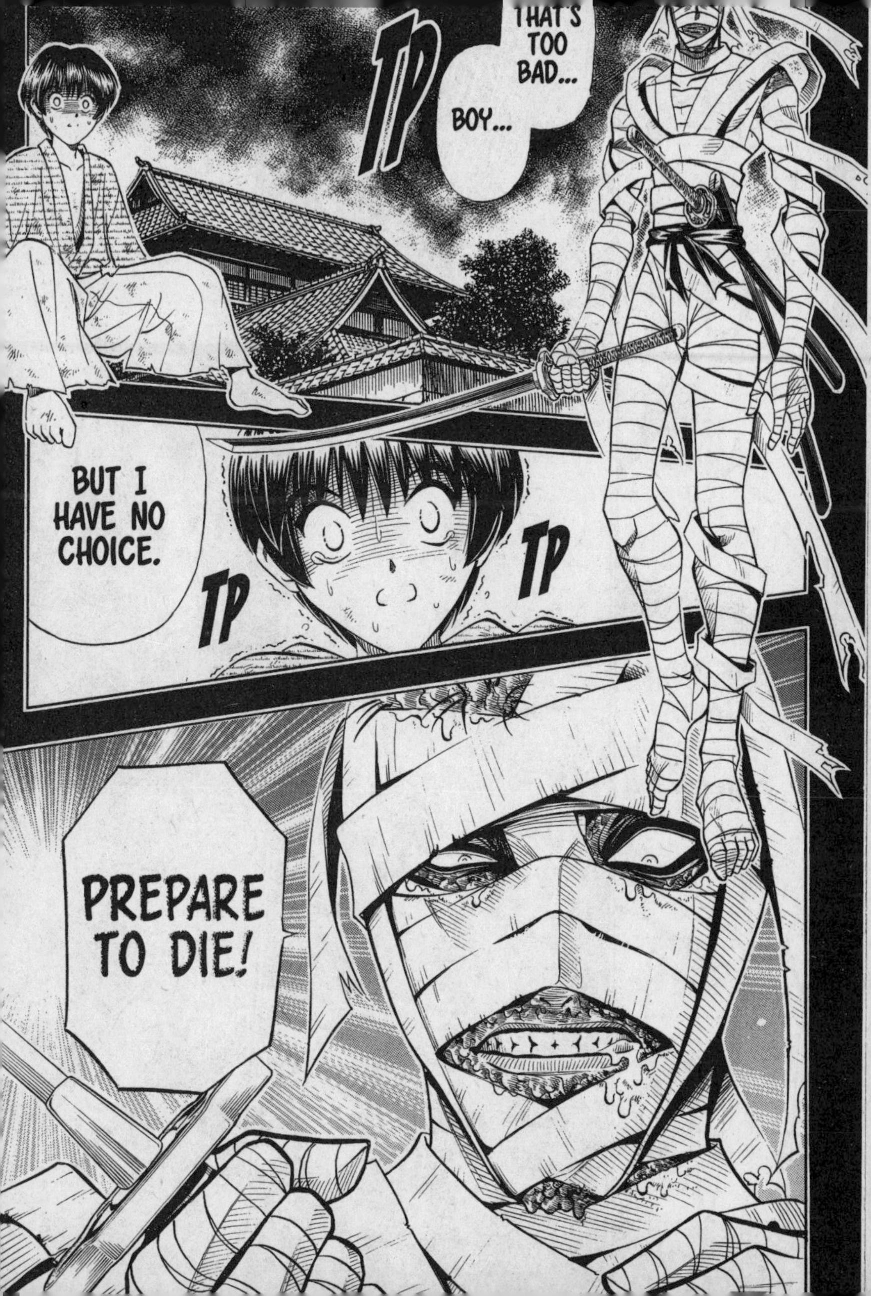
THAT'S TOO BAD...
BOY...
TP
TP
BUT I HAVE NO CHOICE.
TP
PREPARE TO DIE!

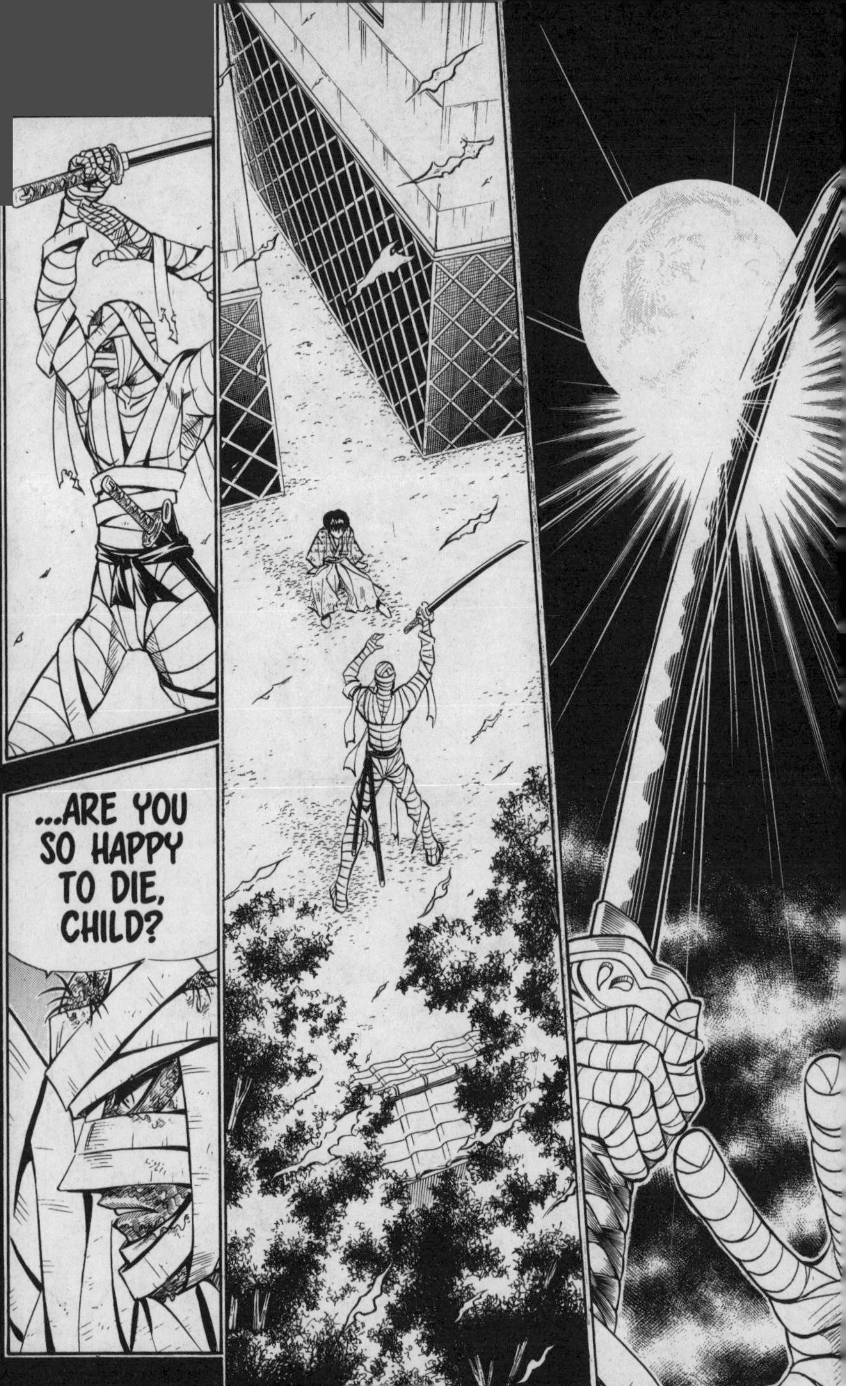
...ARE YOU SO HAPPY TO DIE, CHILD?

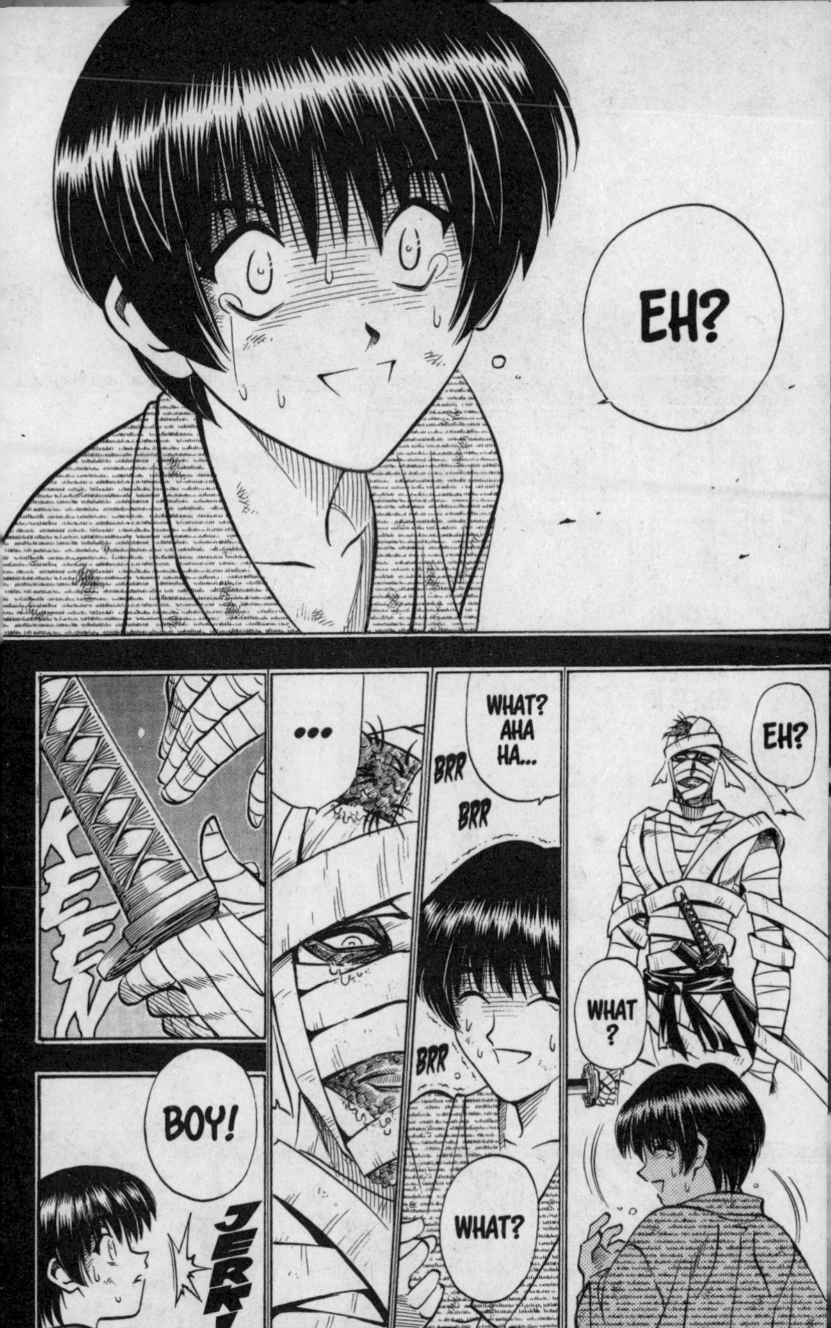
EH?
EH?
WHAT?
WHAT? AHA HA...
BRR
BRR
BRR
WHAT?
...
BOY!
JERK!

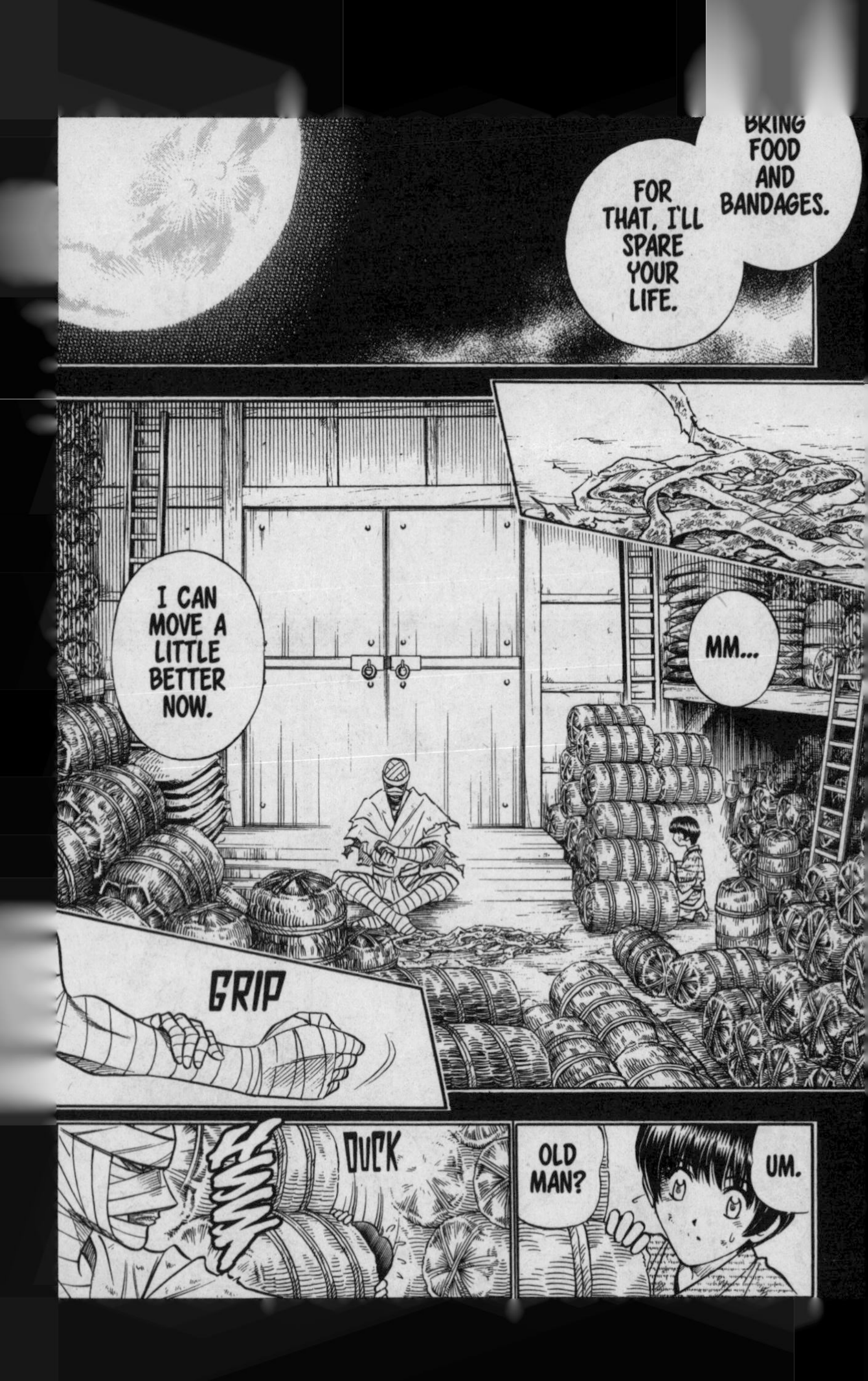
BRING FOOD AND BANDAGES.
FOR THAT, I'LL SPARE YOUR LIFE.
MM...
I CAN MOVE A LITTLE BETTER NOW.
GRIP
UM.
OLD MAN?
DUCK

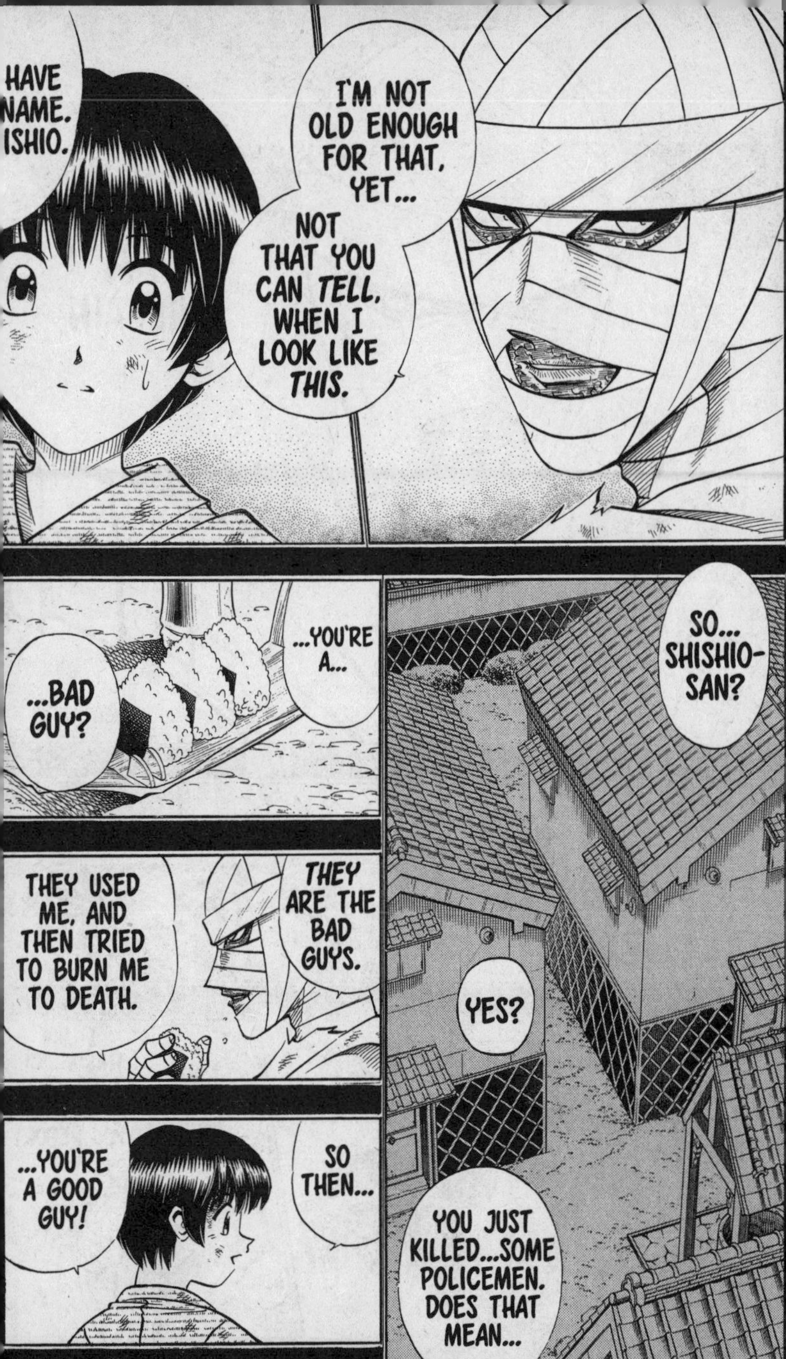
I'M NOT OLD ENOUGH FOR THAT, YET...
NOT THAT YOU CAN *TELL*, WHEN I LOOK LIKE *THIS*.
HAVE
NAME.
ISHIO.
SO... SHISHIO-SAN?
YES?
YOU JUST KILLED...SOME POLICEMEN. DOES THAT MEAN...
...YOU'RE A...
...BAD GUY?
THEY ARE THE BAD GUYS.
THEY USED ME, AND THEN TRIED TO BURN ME TO DEATH.
SO THEN...
...YOU'RE A GOOD GUY!

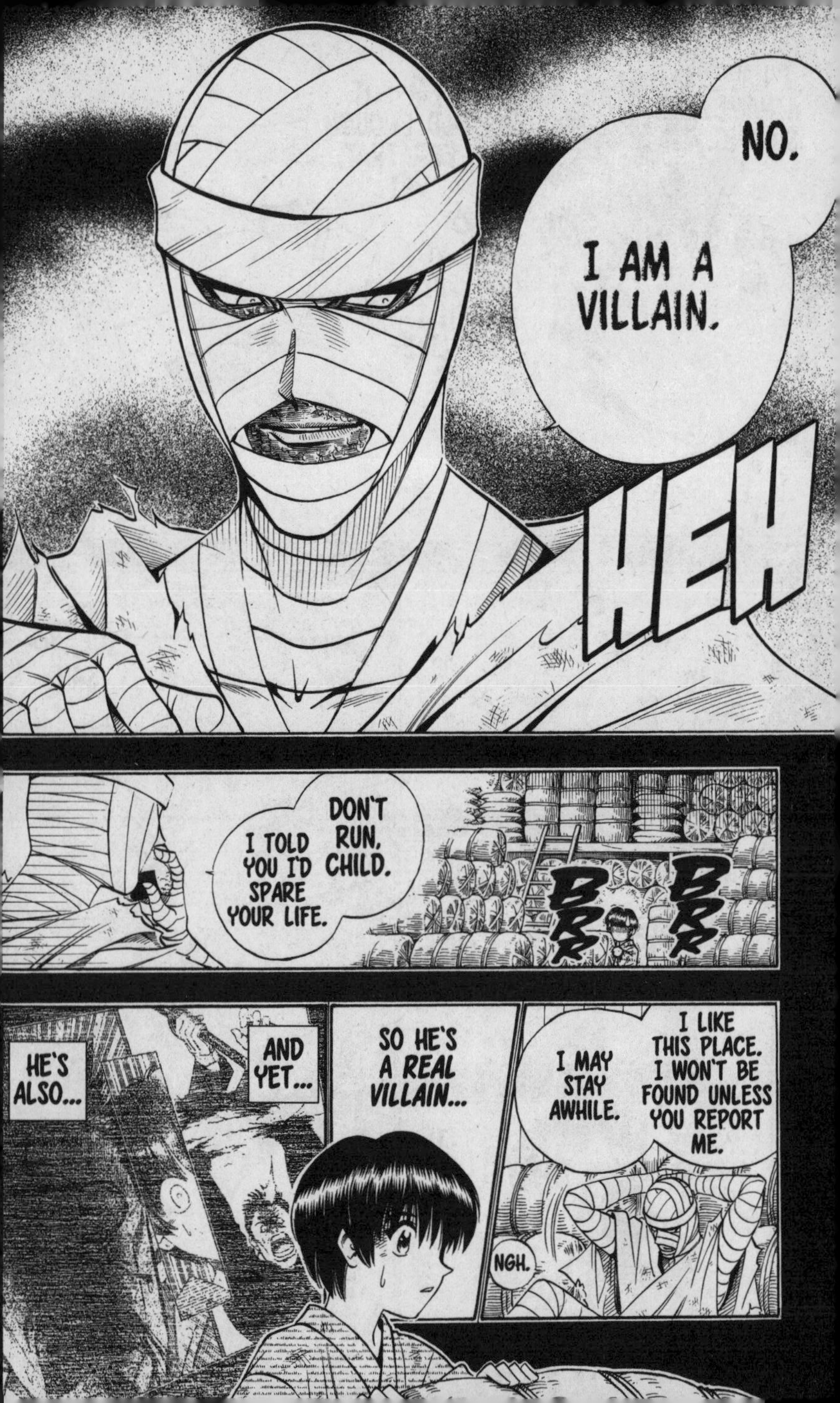
NO.
I AM A VILLAIN.
HEH
DON'T RUN, CHILD.
I TOLD YOU I'D SPARE YOUR LIFE.
I LIKE THIS PLACE. I WON'T BE FOUND UNLESS YOU REPORT ME.
I MAY STAY AWHILE.
NGH.
SO HE'S A *REAL* VILLAIN...
AND YET...
HE'S ALSO...

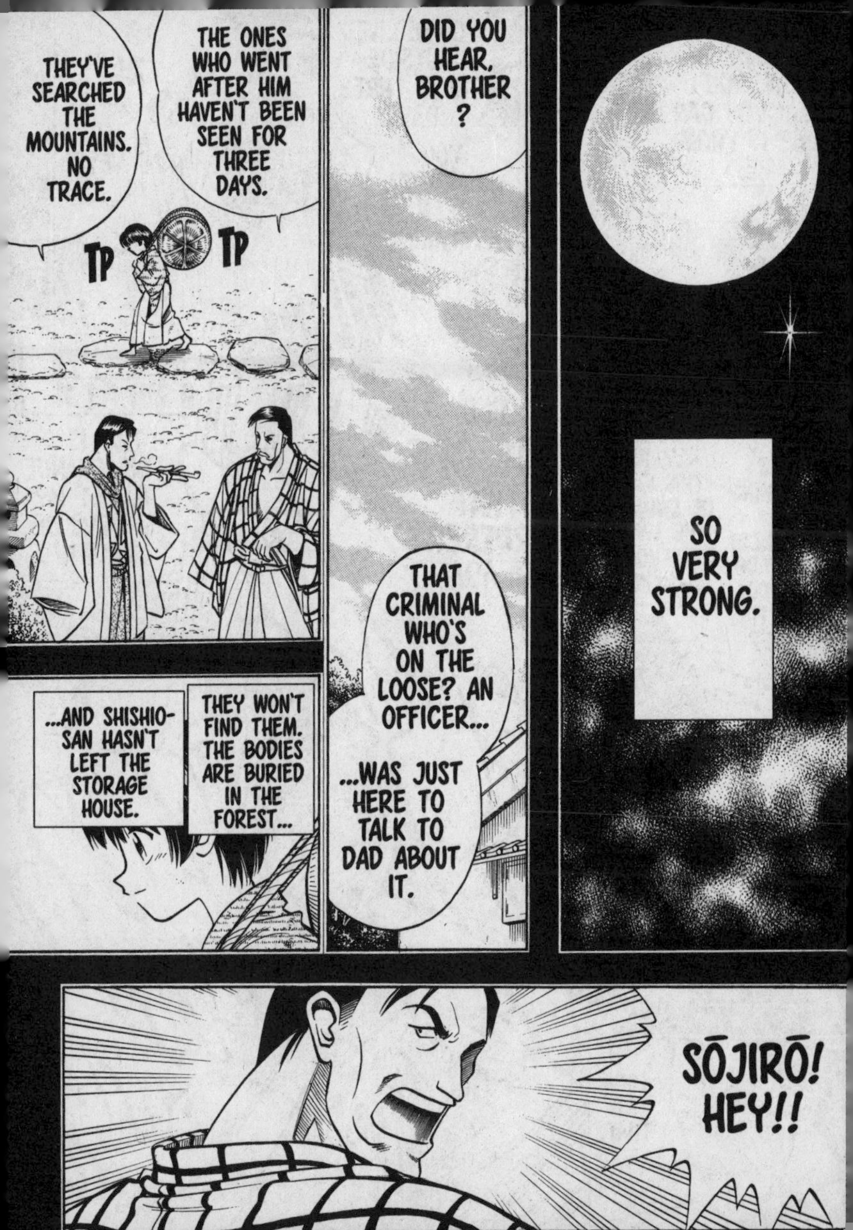
SO VERY STRONG.
DID YOU HEAR, BROTHER?
THAT CRIMINAL WHO'S ON THE LOOSE? AN OFFICER...
...WAS JUST HERE TO TALK TO DAD ABOUT IT.
THE ONES WHO WENT AFTER HIM HAVEN'T BEEN SEEN FOR THREE DAYS.
THEY'VE SEARCHED THE MOUNTAINS. NO TRACE.
TP
TP
THEY WON'T FIND THEM. THE BODIES ARE BURIED IN THE FOREST...
...AND SHISHIO-SAN HASN'T LEFT THE STORAGE HOUSE.
SŌJIRŌ! HEY!!

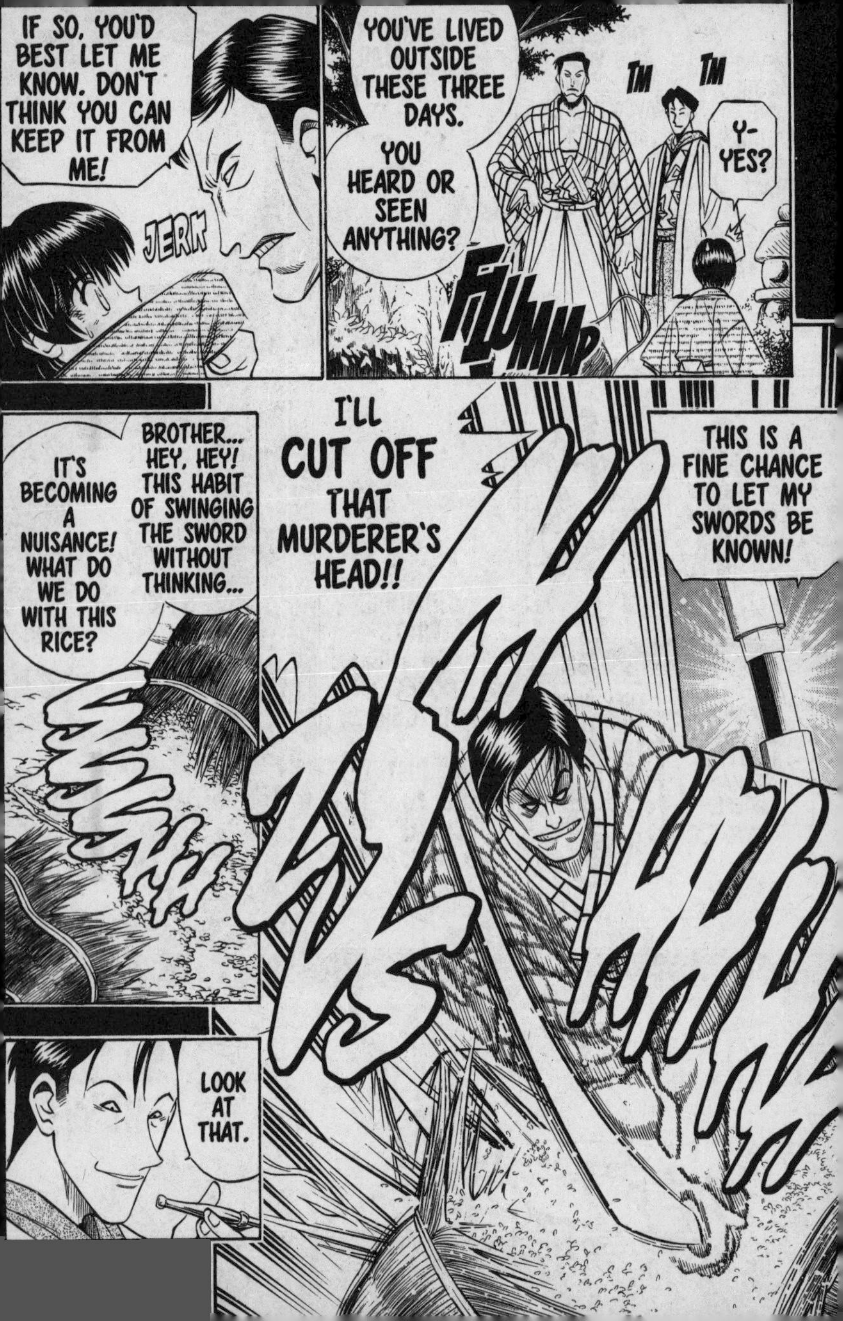
YOU'VE LIVED OUTSIDE THESE THREE DAYS.
YOU HEARD OR SEEN ANYTHING?
TM
TM
Y-YES?
FLUMMP
IF SO, YOU'D BEST LET ME KNOW. DON'T THINK YOU CAN KEEP IT FROM ME!
JERK
THIS IS A FINE CHANCE TO LET MY SWORDS BE KNOWN!
I'LL CUT OFF THAT MURDERER'S HEAD!!
BROTHER... HEY, HEY! THIS HABIT OF SWINGING THE SWORD WITHOUT THINKING...
IT'S BECOMING A NUISANCE! WHAT DO WE DO WITH THIS RICE?
LOOK AT THAT.

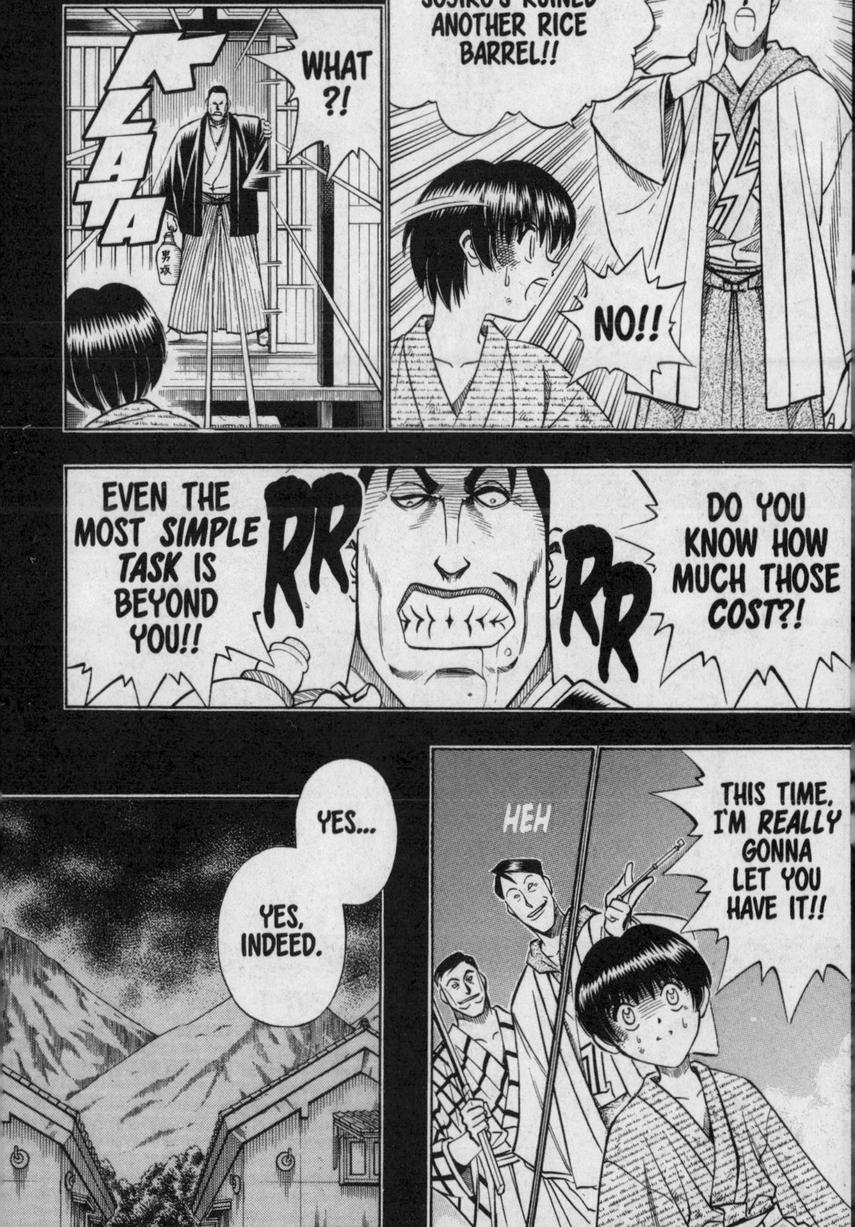
UH-OH! SŌJIRŌ'S RUINED ANOTHER RICE BARREL!!
NO!!
WHAT ?!
KATA
DO YOU KNOW HOW MUCH THOSE COST?!
RR
RR
EVEN THE MOST SIMPLE TASK IS BEYOND YOU!!
THIS TIME, I'M REALLY GONNA LET YOU HAVE IT!!
HEH
YES...
YES, INDEED.

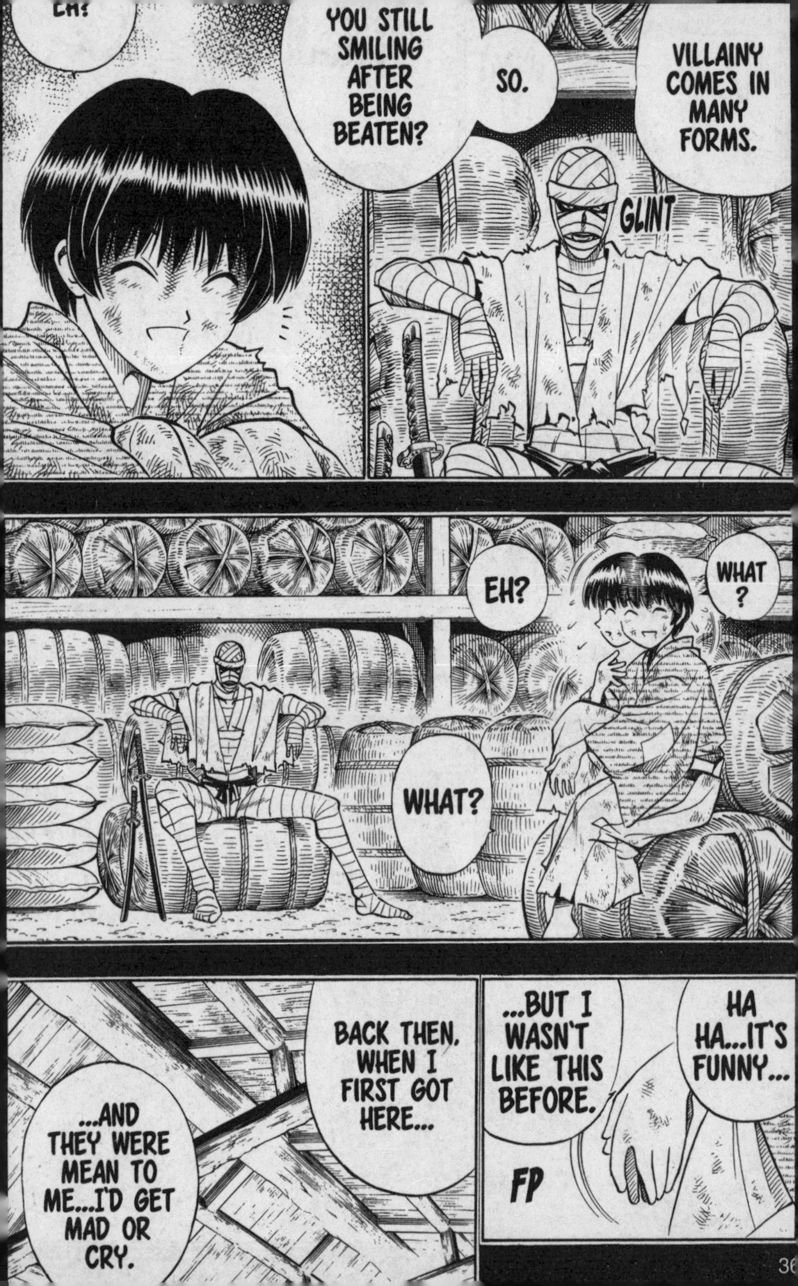
VILLAINY COMES IN MANY FORMS.
GLINT
SO.
YOU STILL SMILING AFTER BEING BEATEN?
WHAT ?
EH?
WHAT?
HA HA...IT'S FUNNY...
...BUT I WASN'T LIKE THIS BEFORE.
FP
BACK THEN, WHEN I FIRST GOT HERE...
...AND THEY WERE MEAN TO ME...I'D GET MAD OR CRY.

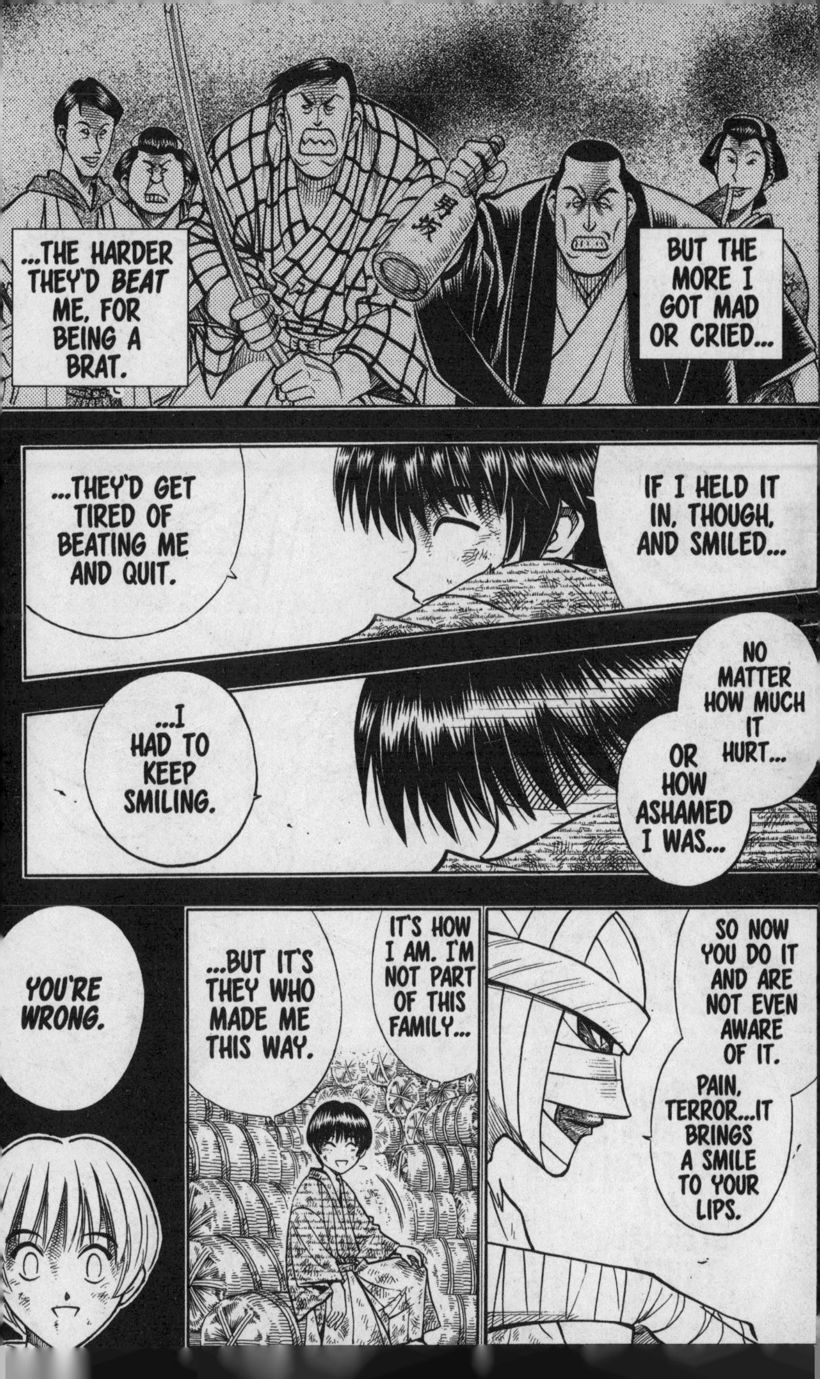
BUT THE MORE I GOT MAD OR CRIED...
男坂
...THE HARDER THEY'D BEAT ME, FOR BEING A BRAT.
IF I HELD IT IN, THOUGH, AND SMILED...
...THEY'D GET TIRED OF BEATING ME AND QUIT.
NO MATTER HOW MUCH IT HURT...
OR HOW ASHAMED I WAS...
...I HAD TO KEEP SMILING.
SO NOW YOU DO IT AND ARE NOT EVEN AWARE OF IT.
PAIN, TERROR...IT BRINGS A SMILE TO YOUR LIPS.
IT'S HOW I AM. I'M NOT PART OF THIS FAMILY...
...BUT IT'S THEY WHO MADE ME THIS WAY.
YOU'RE WRONG.

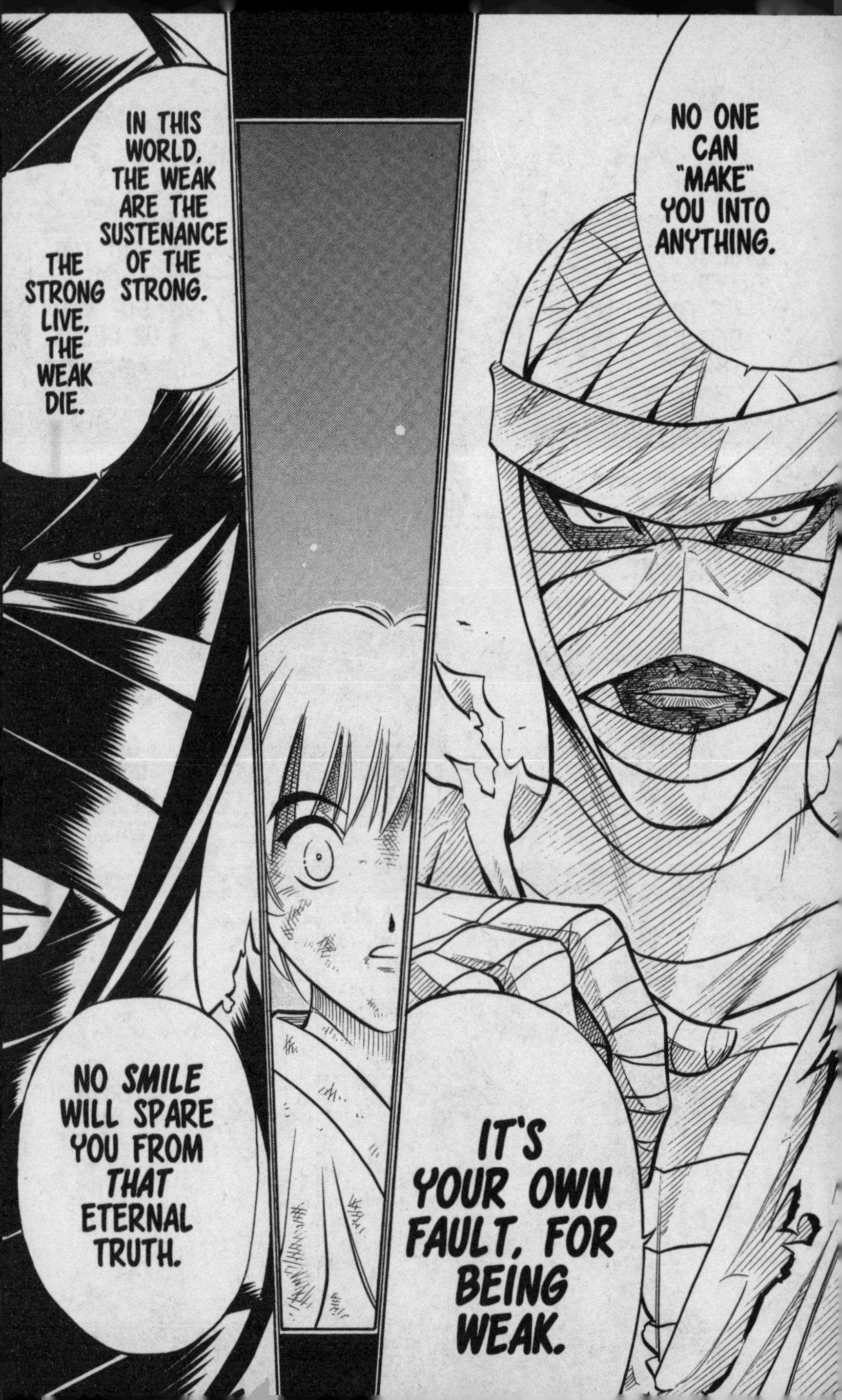
NO ONE CAN "MAKE" YOU INTO ANYTHING.
IT'S YOUR OWN FAULT, FOR BEING WEAK.
IN THIS WORLD, THE WEAK ARE THE SUSTENANCE OF THE STRONG.
THE STRONG LIVE, THE WEAK DIE.
NO *SMILE* WILL SPARE YOU FROM *THAT* ETERNAL TRUTH.

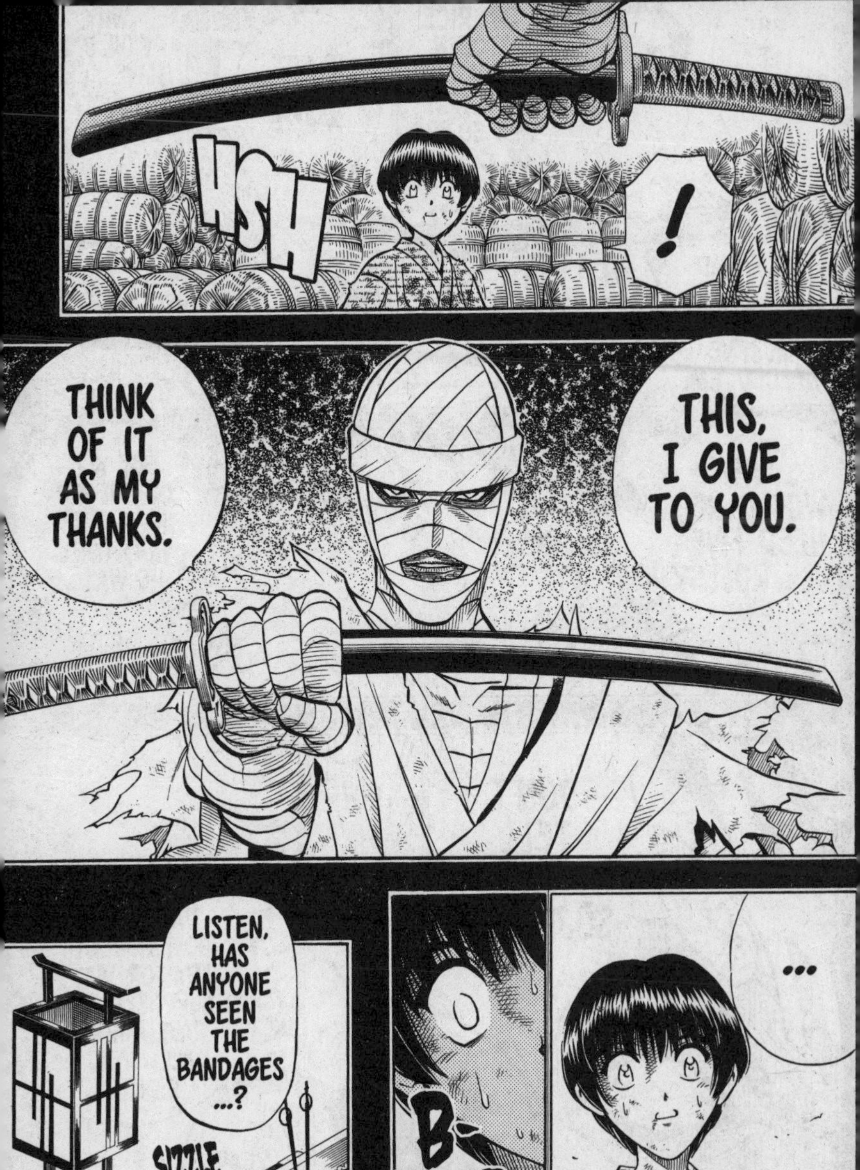
!
HSH
THIS, I GIVE TO YOU.
THINK OF IT AS MY THANKS.
...
B-BMP
LISTEN, HAS ANYONE SEEN THE BANDAGES ...?
SIZZLE

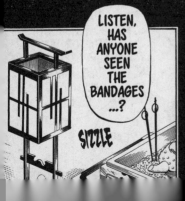

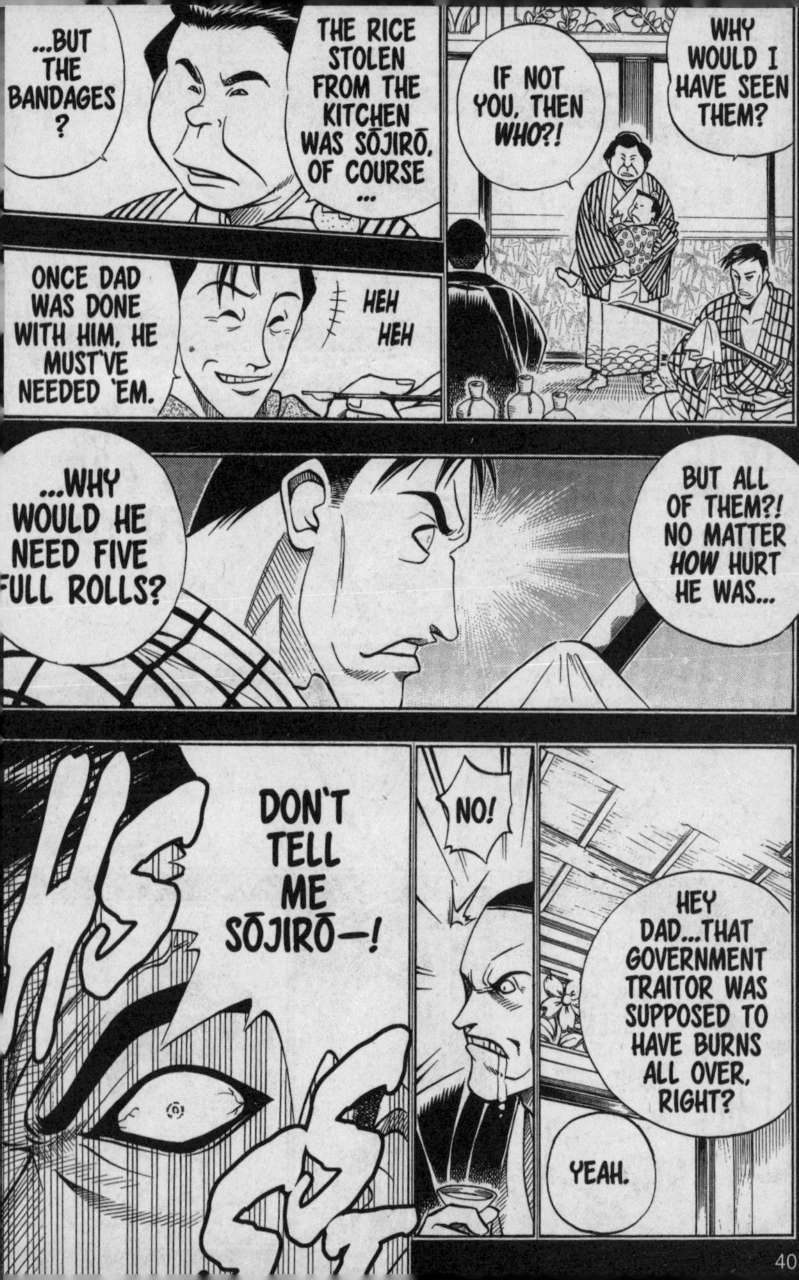
WHY WOULD I HAVE SEEN THEM?
IF NOT YOU, THEN *WHO?!*
THE RICE STOLEN FROM THE KITCHEN WAS SŌJIRŌ, OF COURSE...
...BUT THE BANDAGES?
HEH HEH
ONCE DAD WAS DONE WITH HIM, HE MUST'VE NEEDED 'EM.
BUT ALL OF THEM?! NO MATTER *HOW* HURT HE WAS...
...WHY WOULD HE NEED FIVE FULL ROLLS?
HEY DAD...THAT GOVERNMENT TRAITOR WAS SUPPOSED TO HAVE BURNS ALL OVER, RIGHT?
YEAH.
NO!
DON'T TELL ME SŌJIRŌ—!

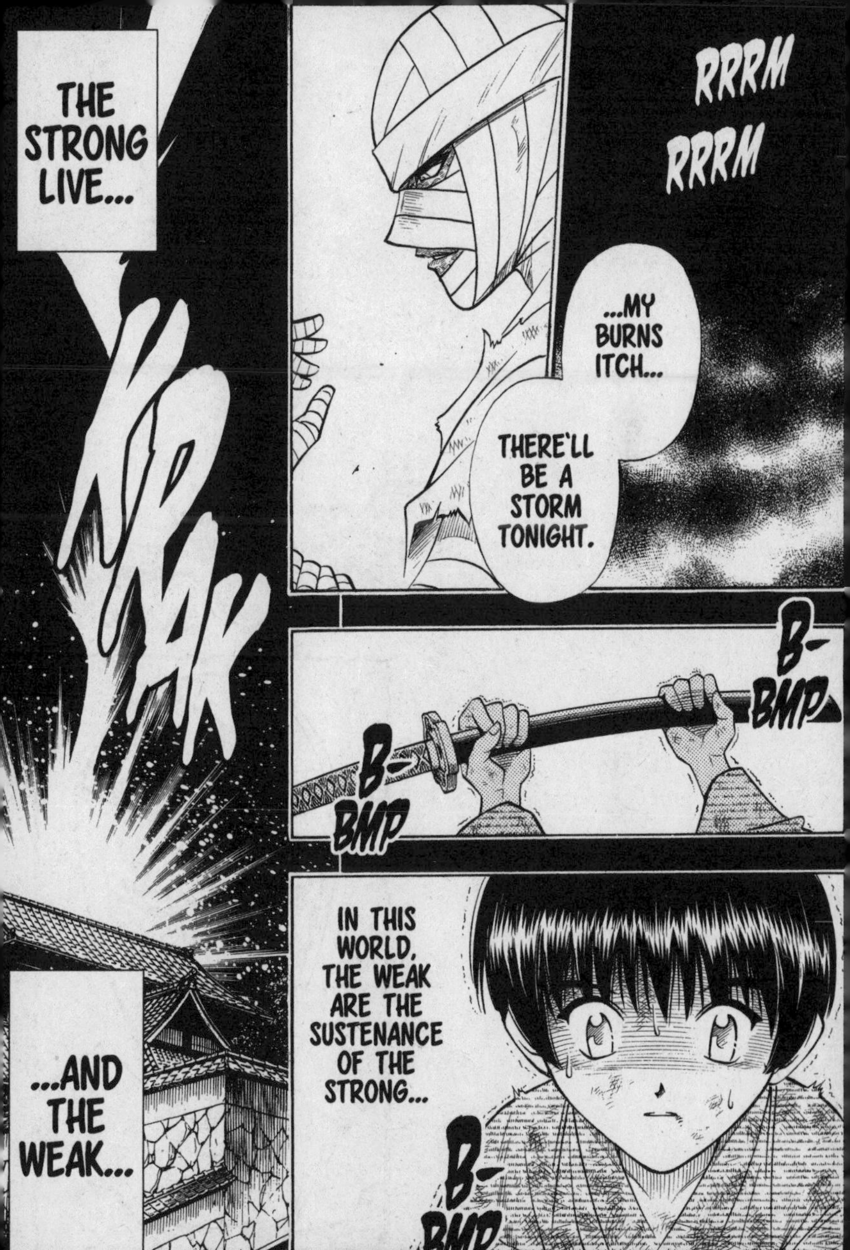
RRRM
RRRM
...MY BURNS ITCH...
THERE'LL BE A STORM TONIGHT.
B-BMP
B-BMP
IN THIS WORLD, THE WEAK ARE THE SUSTENANCE OF THE STRONG...
B-BMP
THE STRONG LIVE...
KRAK
...AND THE WEAK...

Rurouni Kenshin

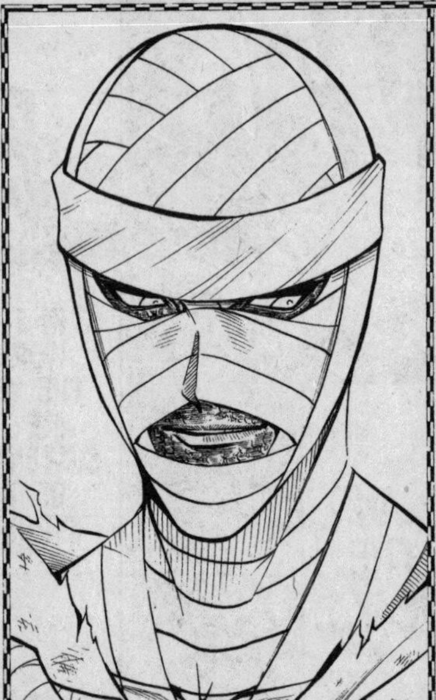

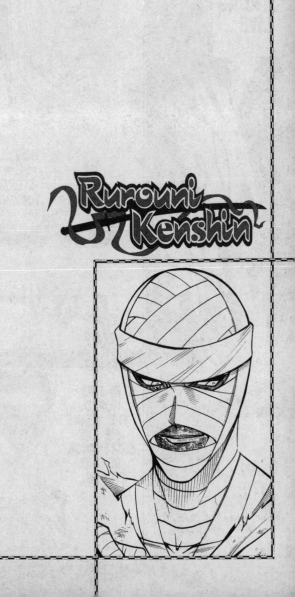

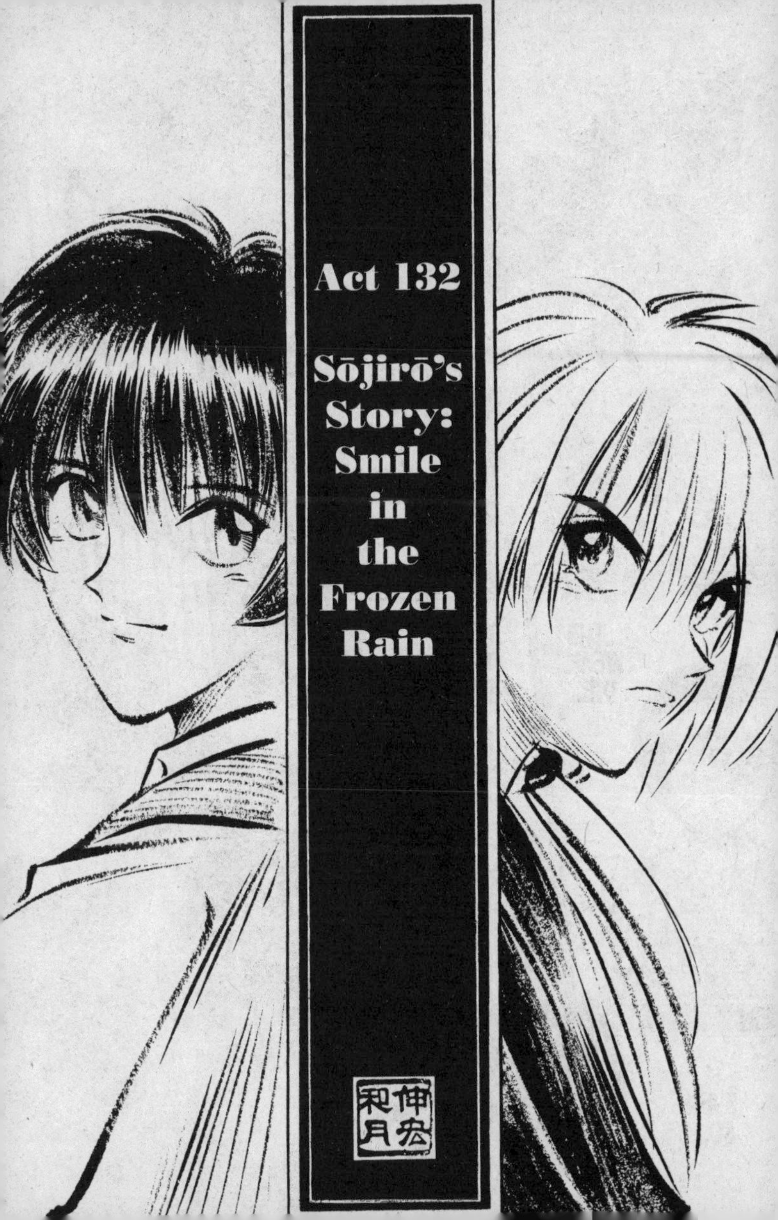
Act 132
Sōjirō's Story: Smile in the Frozen Rain
伸宏
和月

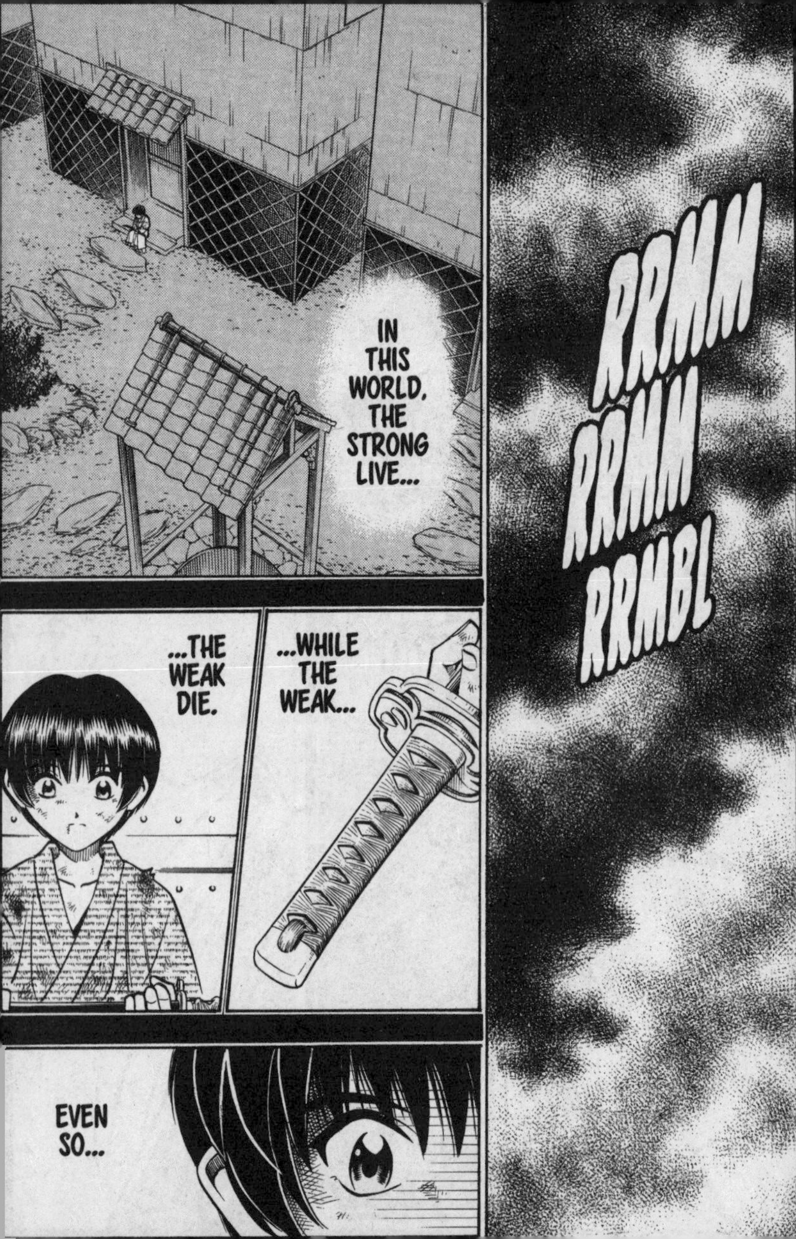
RRMM
RRMM
RRMBL
IN THIS WORLD, THE STRONG LIVE...
...WHILE THE WEAK...
...THE WEAK DIE.
EVEN SO...

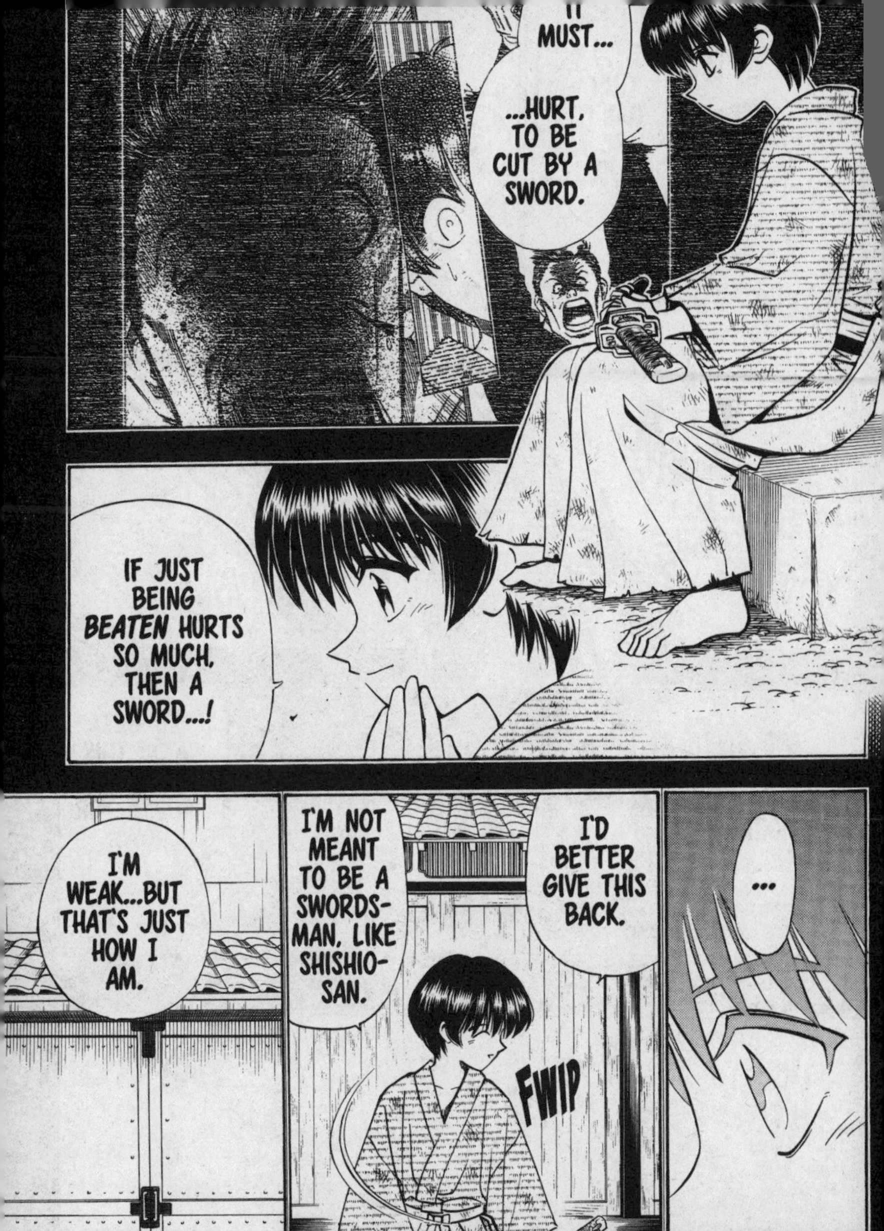
MUST...
...HURT, TO BE CUT BY A SWORD.
IF JUST BEING BEATEN HURTS SO MUCH, THEN A SWORD...!
...
I'D BETTER GIVE THIS BACK.
FWIP
I'M NOT MEANT TO BE A SWORDSMAN, LIKE SHISHIO-SAN.
I'M WEAK...BUT THAT'S JUST HOW I AM.

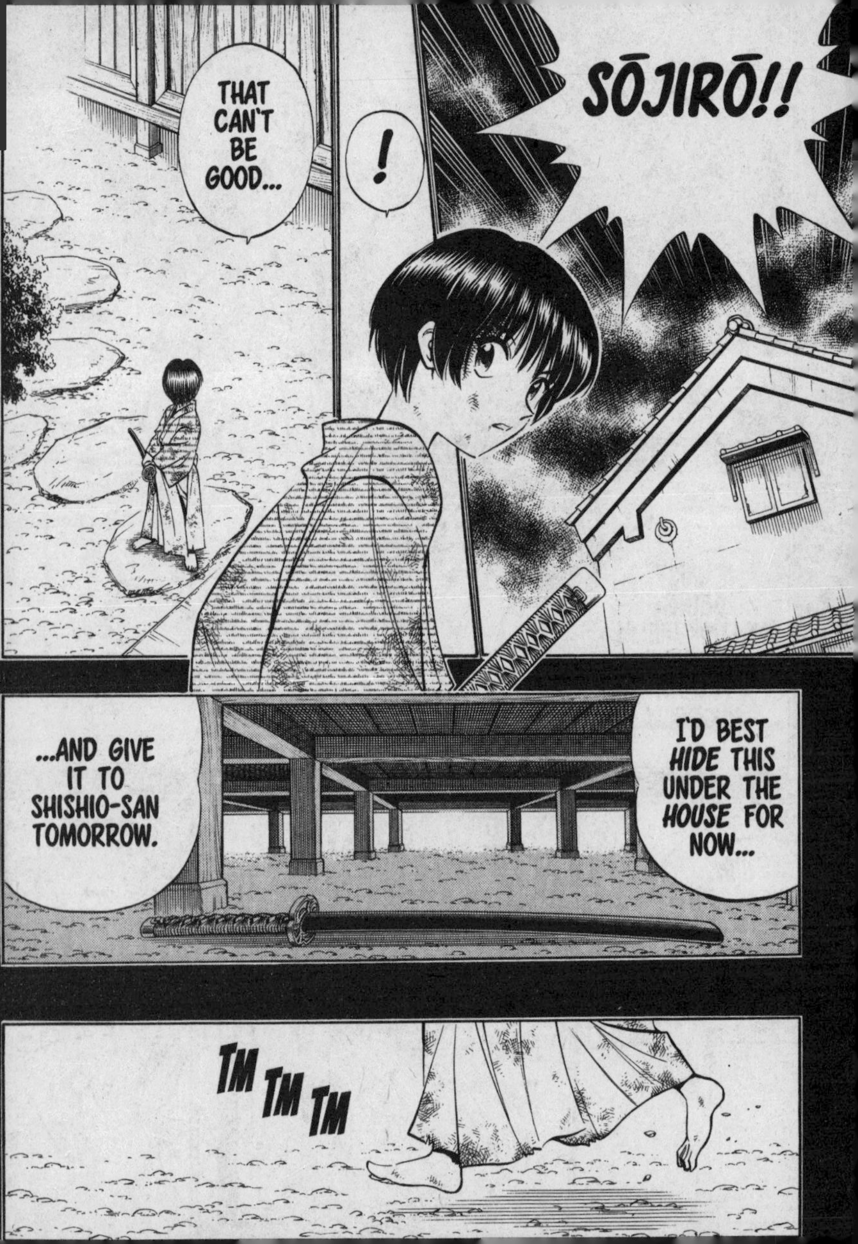
SŌJIRŌ!!
!
THAT CAN'T BE GOOD...
I'D BEST HIDE THIS UNDER THE HOUSE FOR NOW...
...AND GIVE IT TO SHISHIO-SAN TOMORROW.
TM TM TM

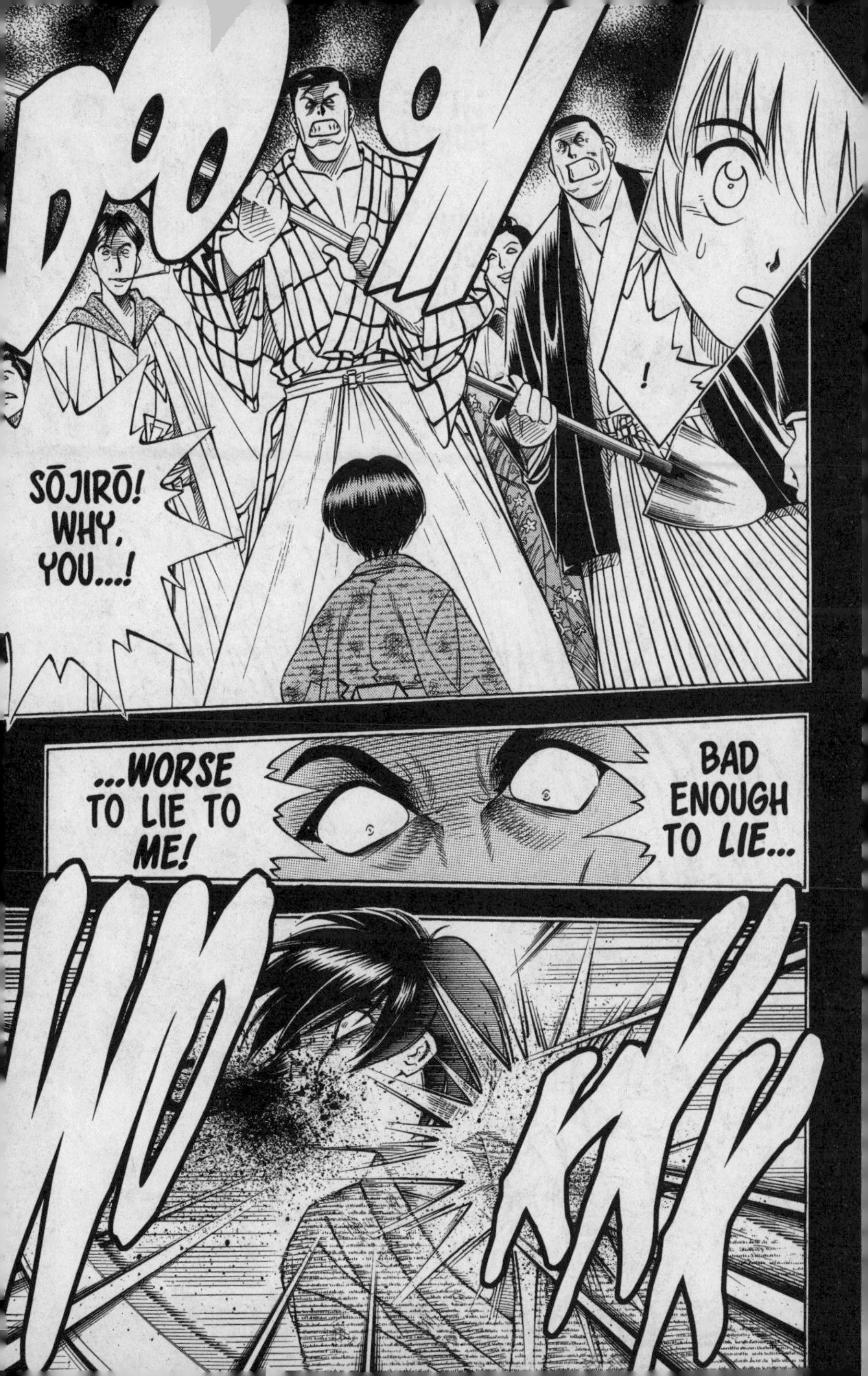
!
SŌJIRŌ! WHY, YOU...!
BAD ENOUGH TO LIE...
...WORSE TO LIE TO ME!

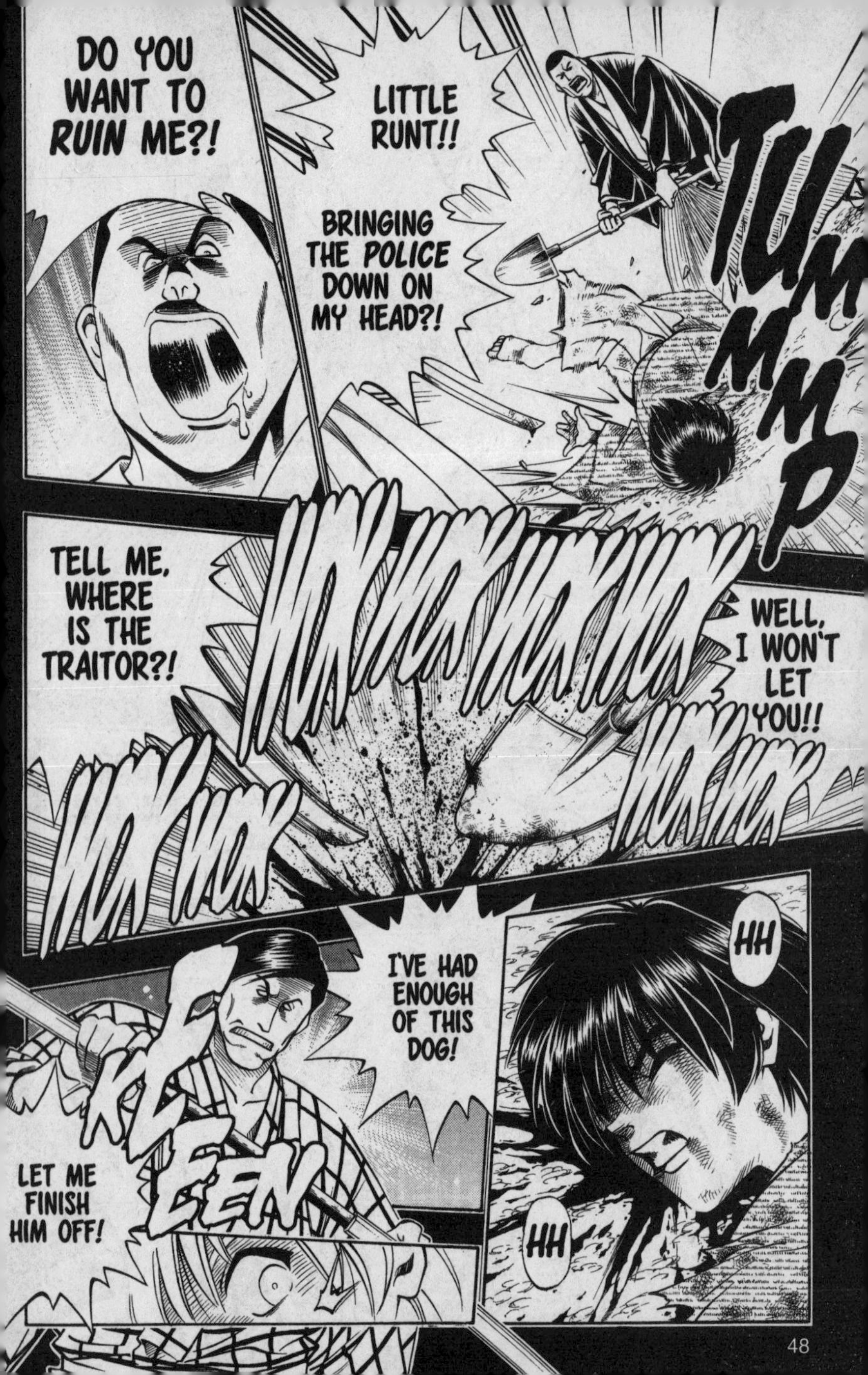
TUMMMP
LITTLE RUNT!!
BRINGING THE POLICE DOWN ON MY HEAD?!
DO YOU WANT TO RUIN ME?!
WELL, I WON'T LET YOU!!
TELL ME, WHERE IS THE TRAITOR?!
HH
HH
I'VE HAD ENOUGH OF THIS DOG!
LET ME FINISH HIM OFF!

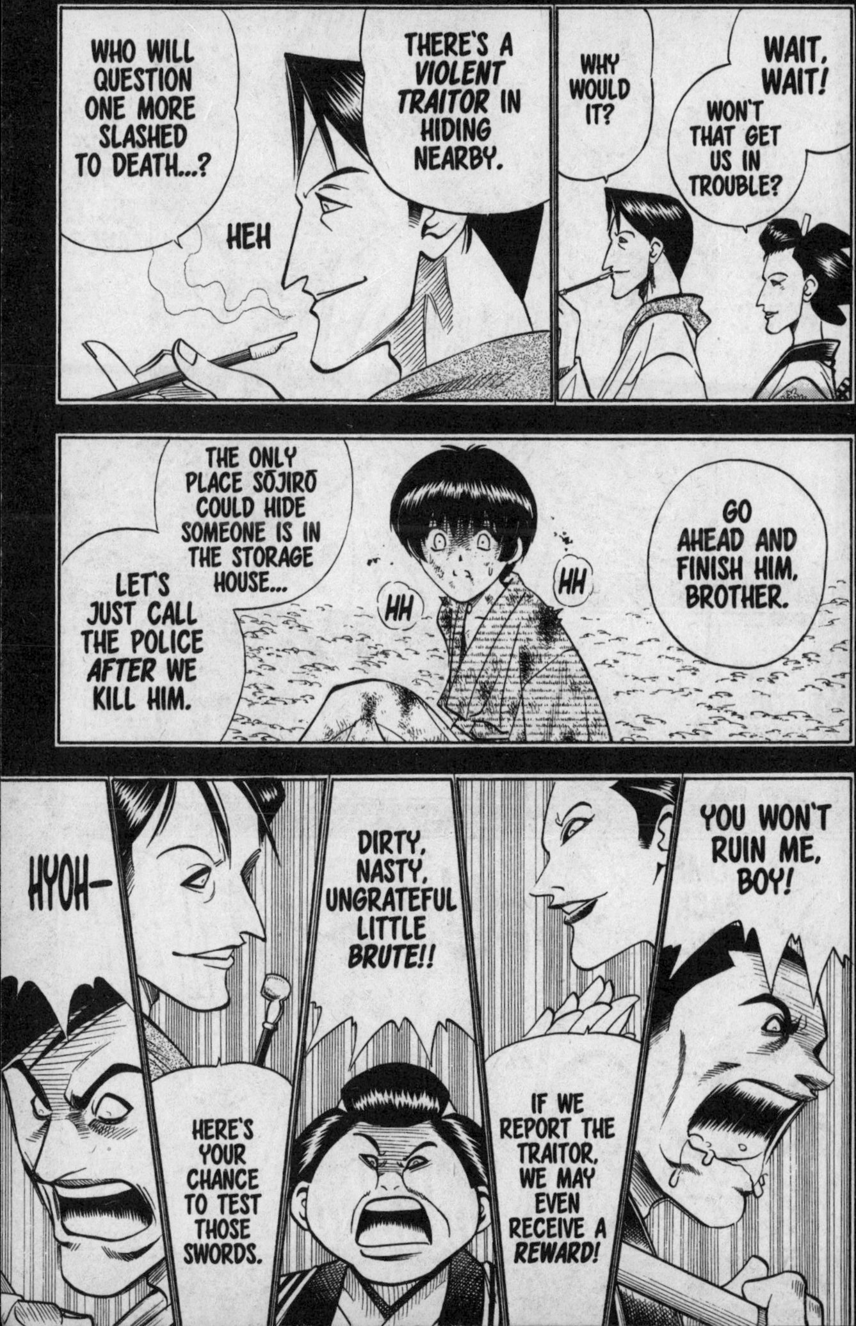

WAIT, WAIT!
WON'T THAT GET US IN TROUBLE?
WHY WOULD IT?
THERE'S A *VIOLENT TRAITOR* IN HIDING NEARBY.
WHO WILL QUESTION ONE MORE SLASHED TO DEATH...?
HEH
GO AHEAD AND FINISH HIM, BROTHER.
HH
HH
THE ONLY PLACE SŌJIRŌ COULD HIDE SOMEONE IS IN THE STORAGE HOUSE...
LET'S JUST CALL THE POLICE *AFTER* WE KILL HIM.
YOU WON'T RUIN ME, BOY!
IF WE REPORT THE TRAITOR, WE MAY EVEN RECEIVE A *REWARD!*
DIRTY, NASTY, UNGRATEFUL LITTLE *BRUTE!!*
HERE'S YOUR CHANCE TO TEST THOSE SWORDS.
HYOH-

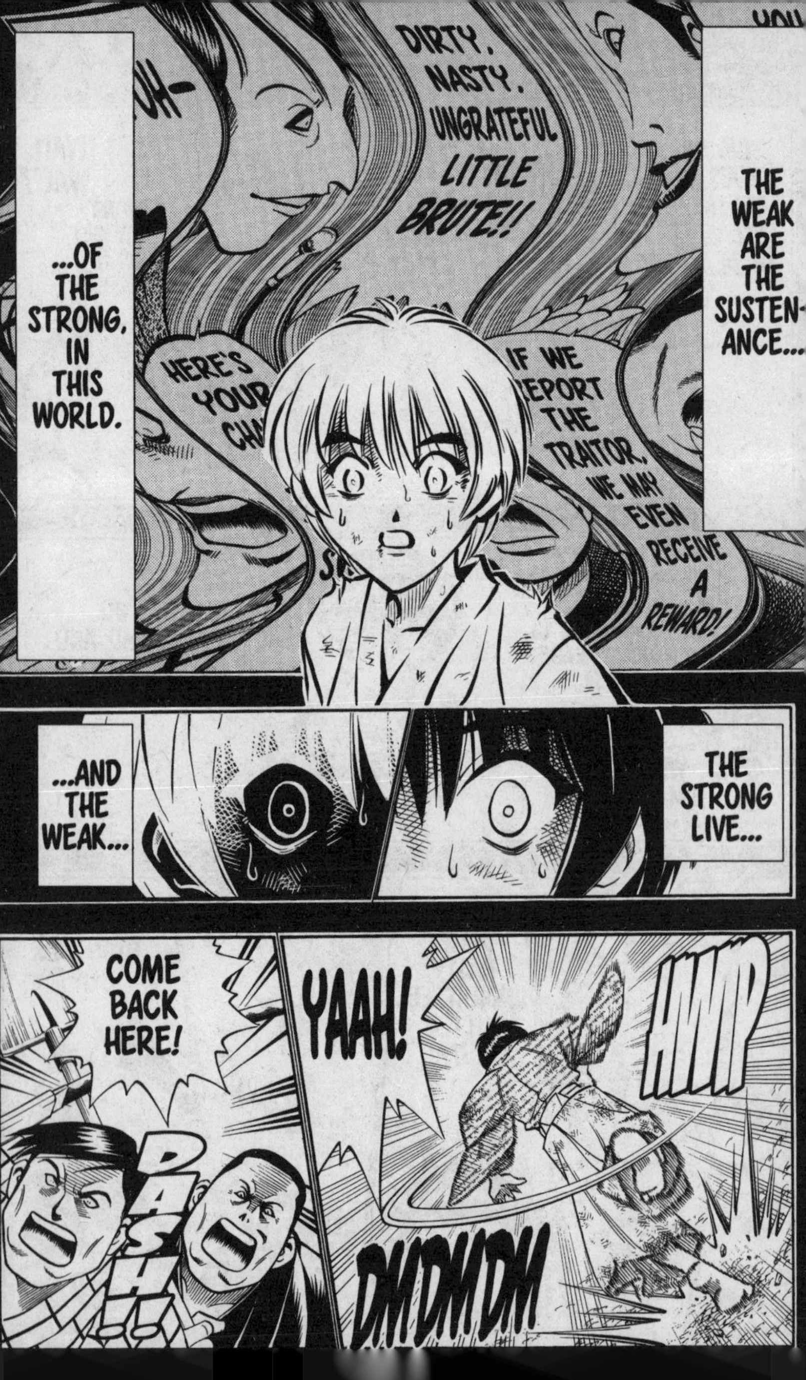
THE WEAK ARE THE SUSTENANCE...
DIRTY, NASTY, UNGRATEFUL LITTLE BRUTE!!
IF WE REPORT THE TRAITOR, WE MAY EVEN RECEIVE A REWARD!
HERE'S YOUR
...OF THE STRONG, IN THIS WORLD.
THE STRONG LIVE...
...AND THE WEAK...
HMMP
YAAH!
DMDMDM
COME BACK HERE!
DASH...

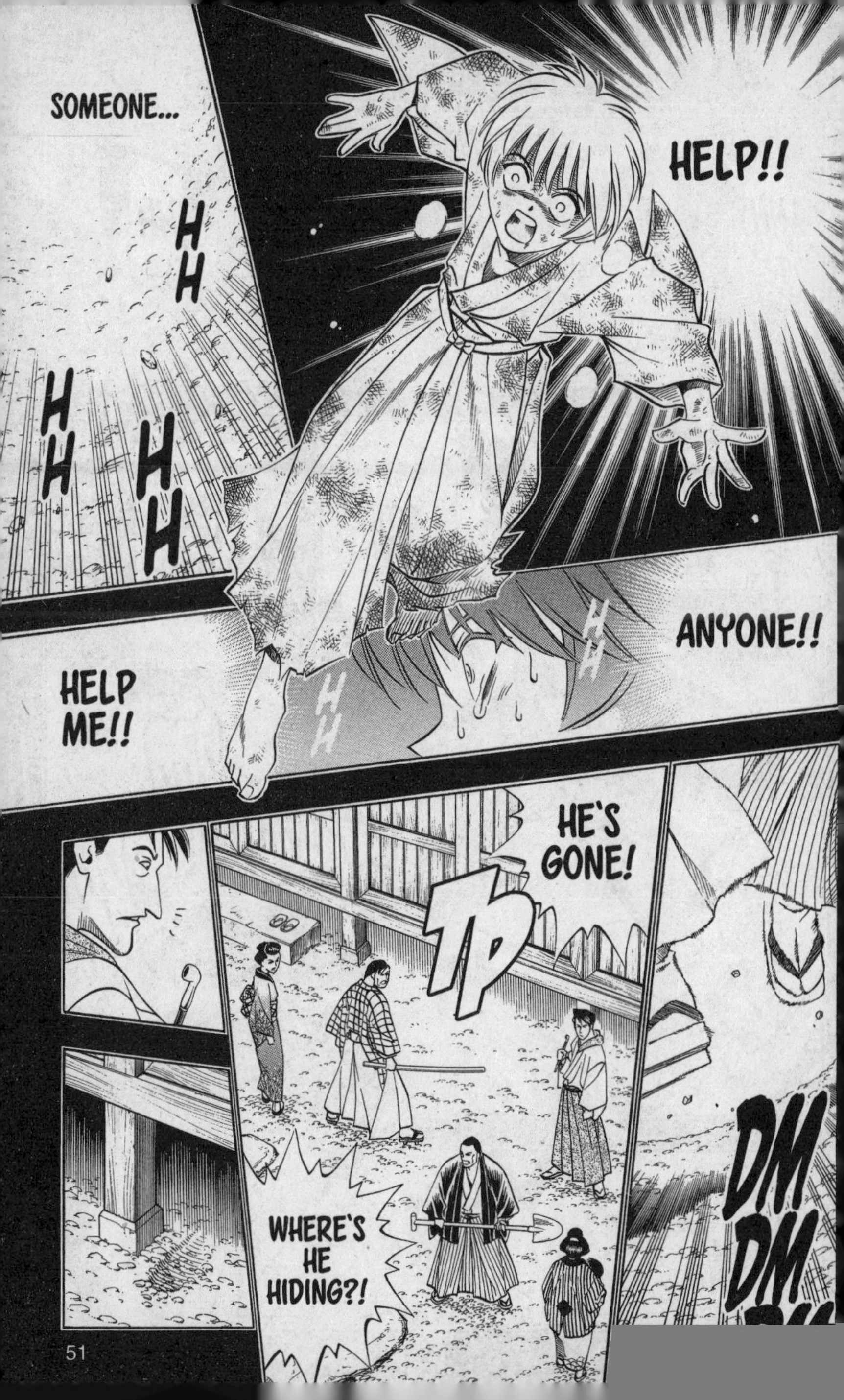
SOMEONE...
HELP!!
HH
HH
HH
ANYONE!!
HELP ME!!
HH
HH
DM
DM
HE'S GONE!
WHERE'S HE HIDING?!

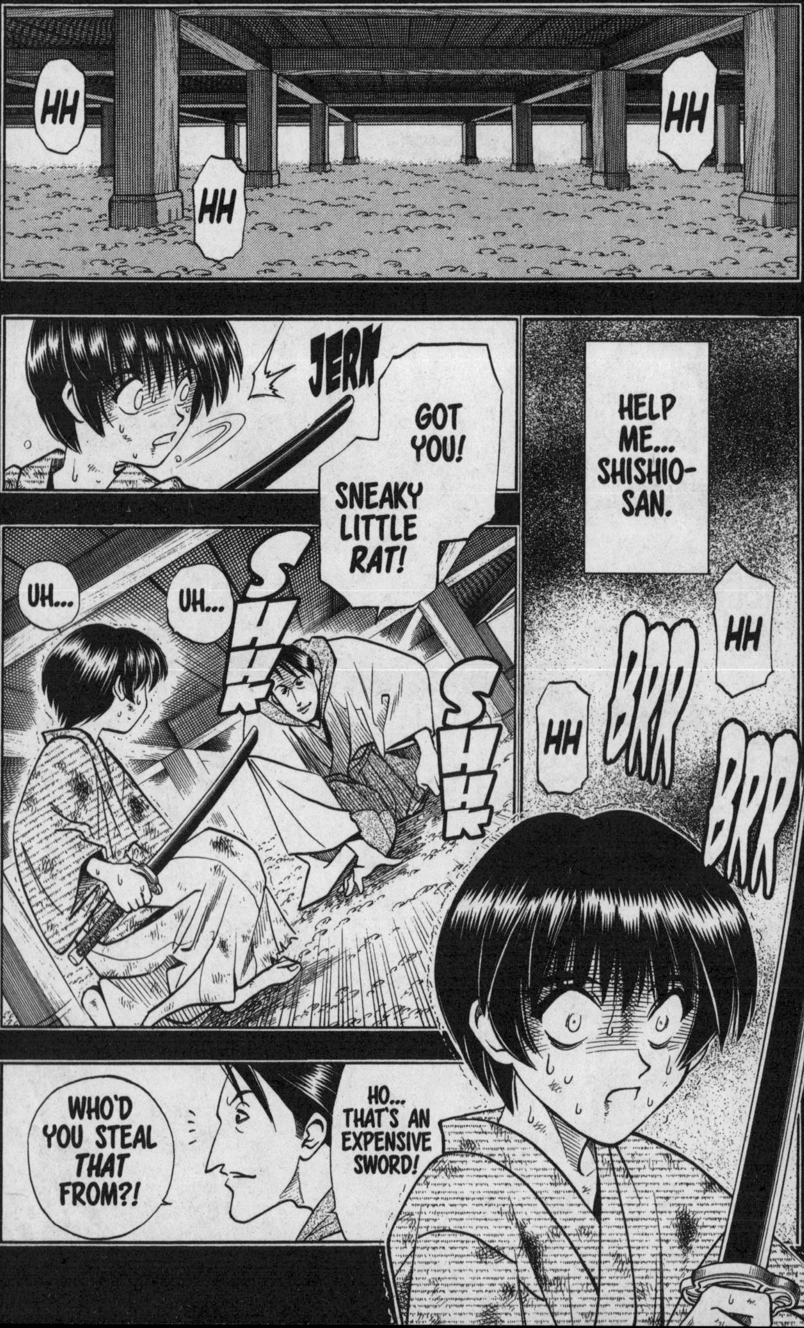
HH
HH
HH
HELP ME... SHISHIO-SAN.
HH
BRR
HH
BRR
JERK
GOT YOU!
SNEAKY LITTLE RAT!
SHUK
SHUK
UH...
UH...
HO... THAT'S AN EXPENSIVE SWORD!
WHO'D YOU STEAL *THAT* FROM?!

GIVE IT TO ME!

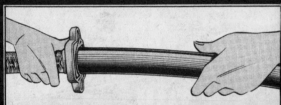

IN THIS WORLD, THE STRONG LIVE...

AND THE WEAK...

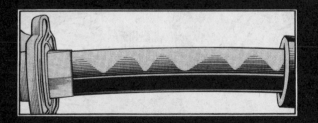

DIE!

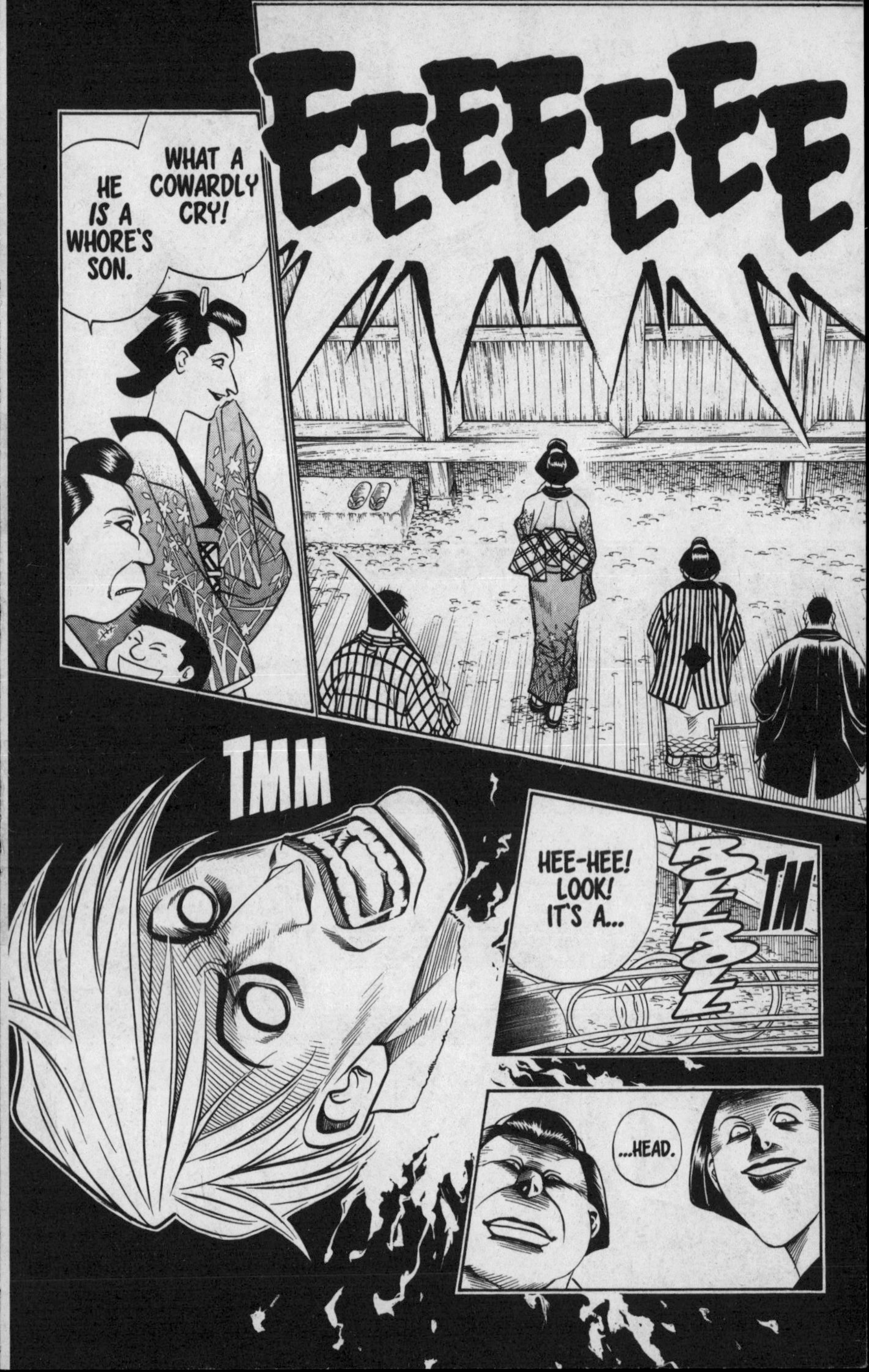
EEEEEE
WHAT A COWARDLY CRY!
HE IS A WHORE'S SON.
TM
BOLBOLL
HEE-HEE! LOOK! IT'S A...
...HEAD.
TMM

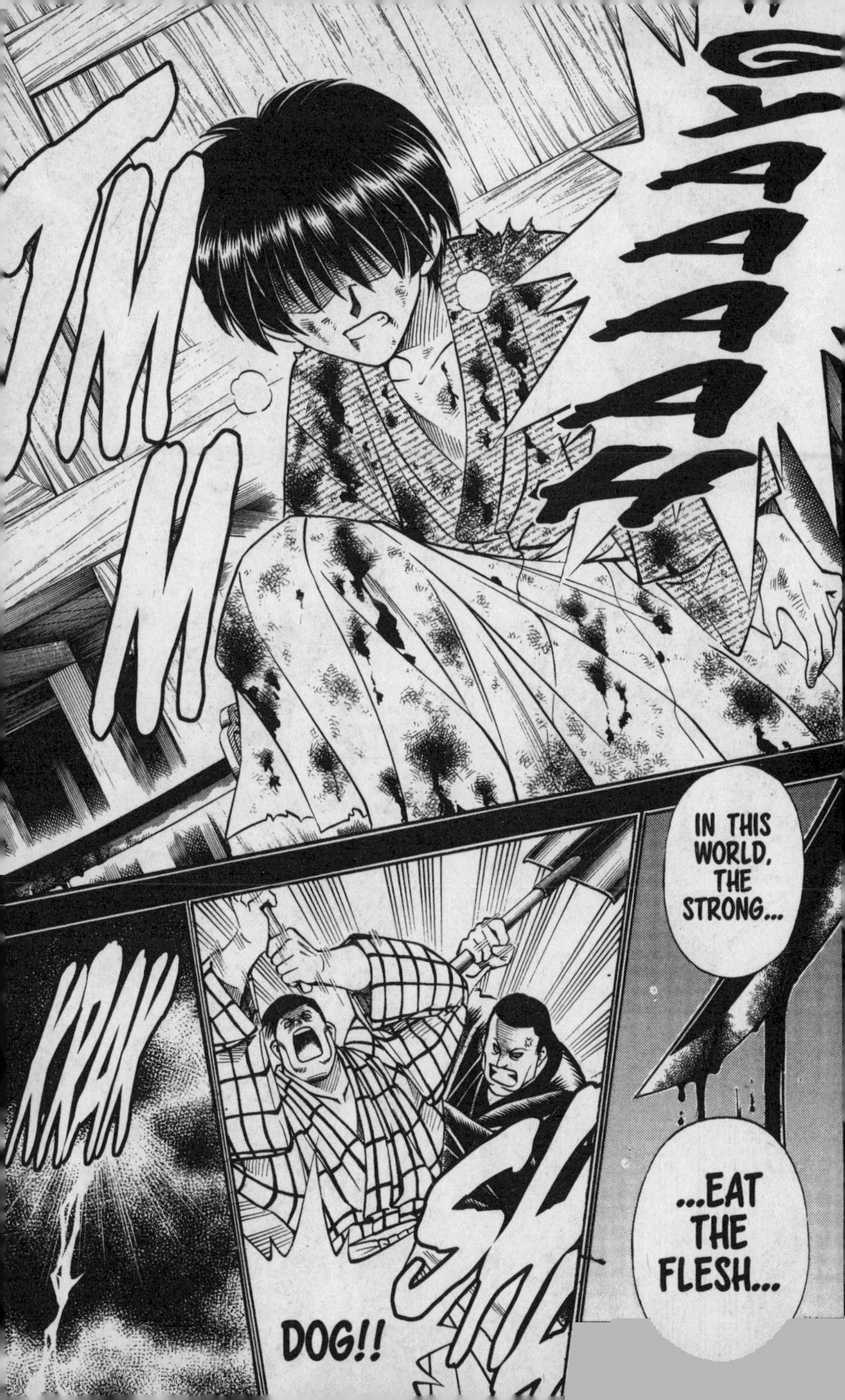
IN THIS WORLD, THE STRONG...
...EAT THE FLESH...
DOG!!

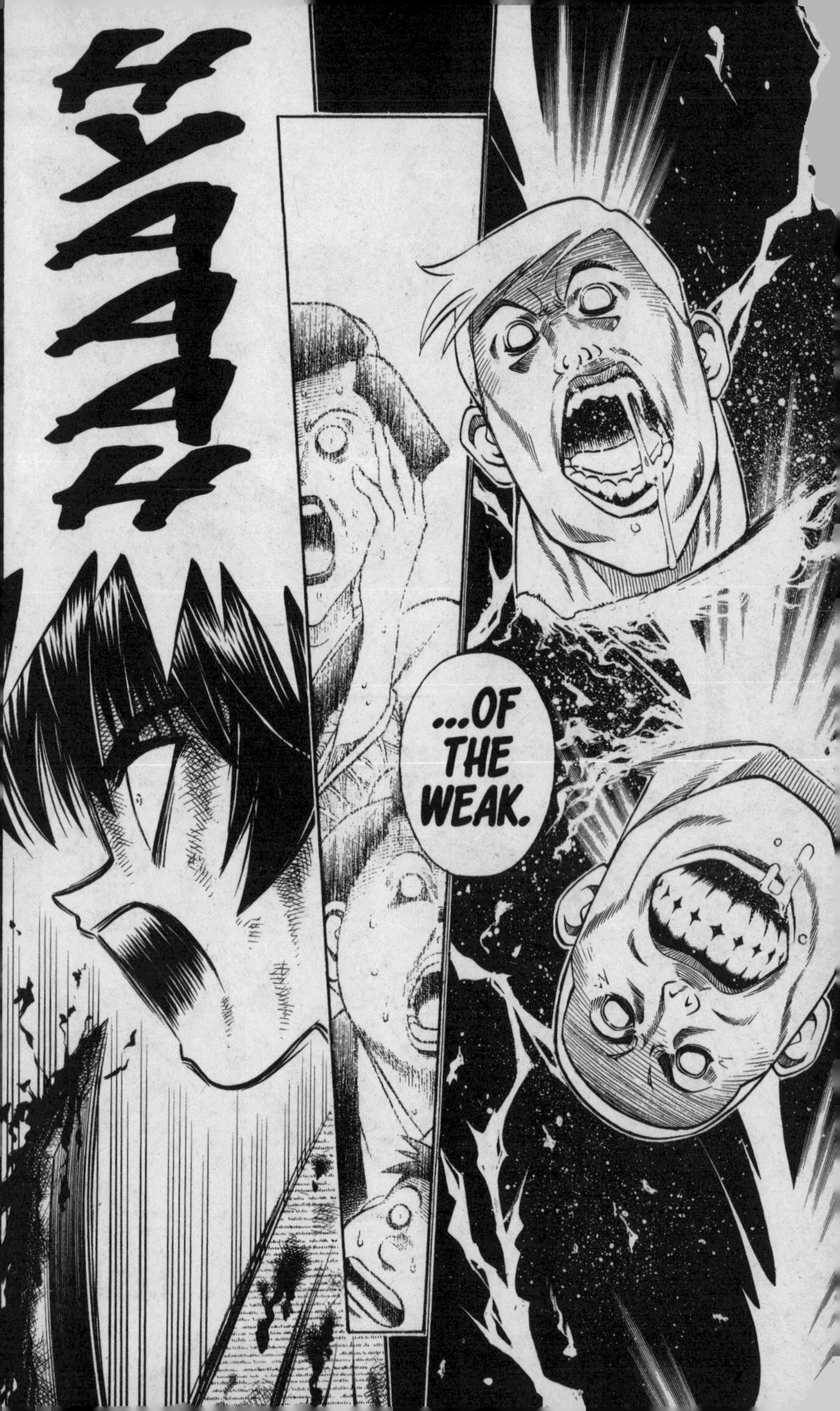
...OF THE WEAK.
HYAAAH

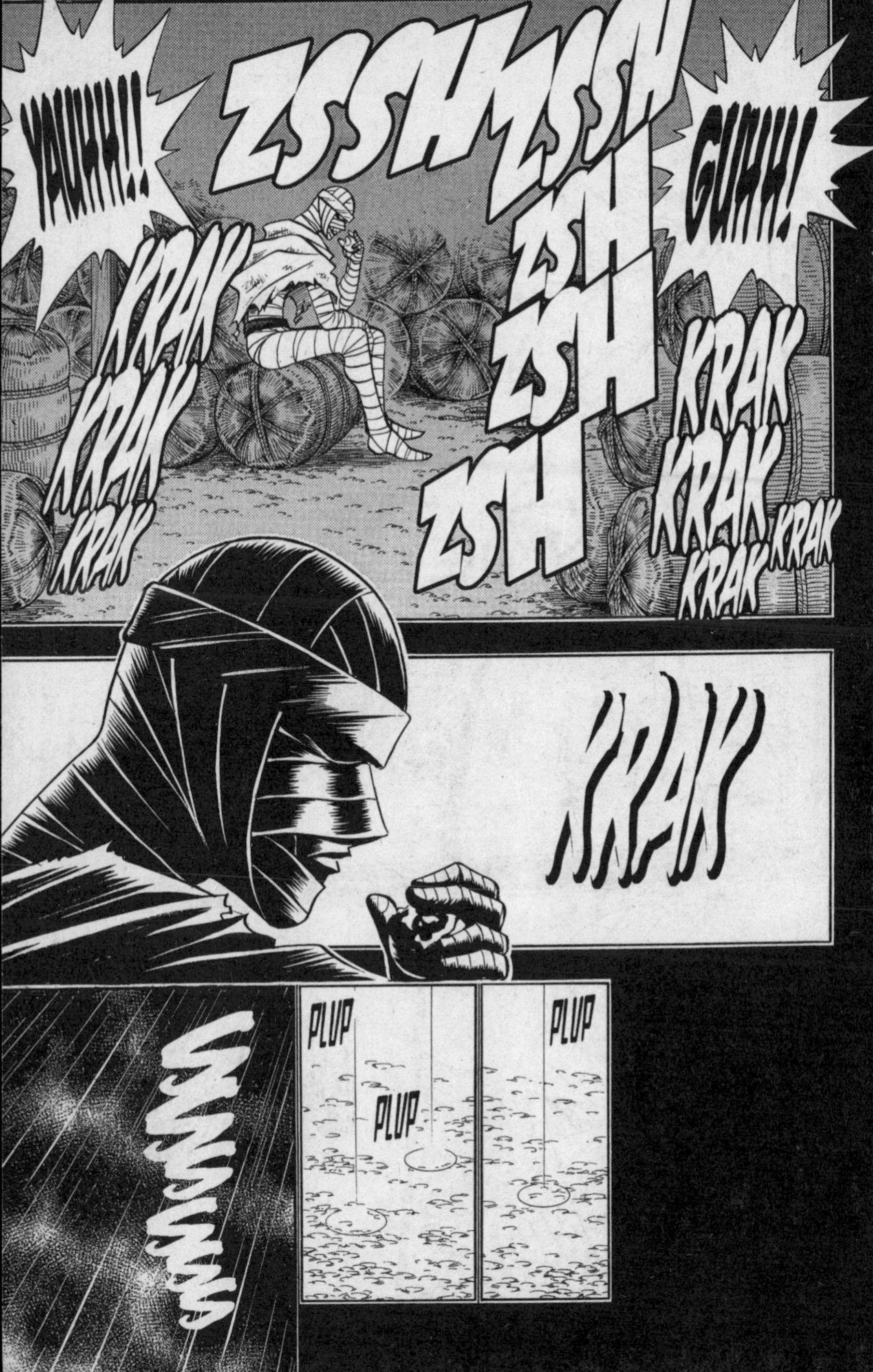
GUHH!
ZSSH ZSSH
ZSH
ZSH
ZSH
KRAK
KRAK
KRAK
KRAK
KRAK
YAUHH!!
KRAK
KRAK
KRAK
KRAK
PLUP
PLUP
PLUP

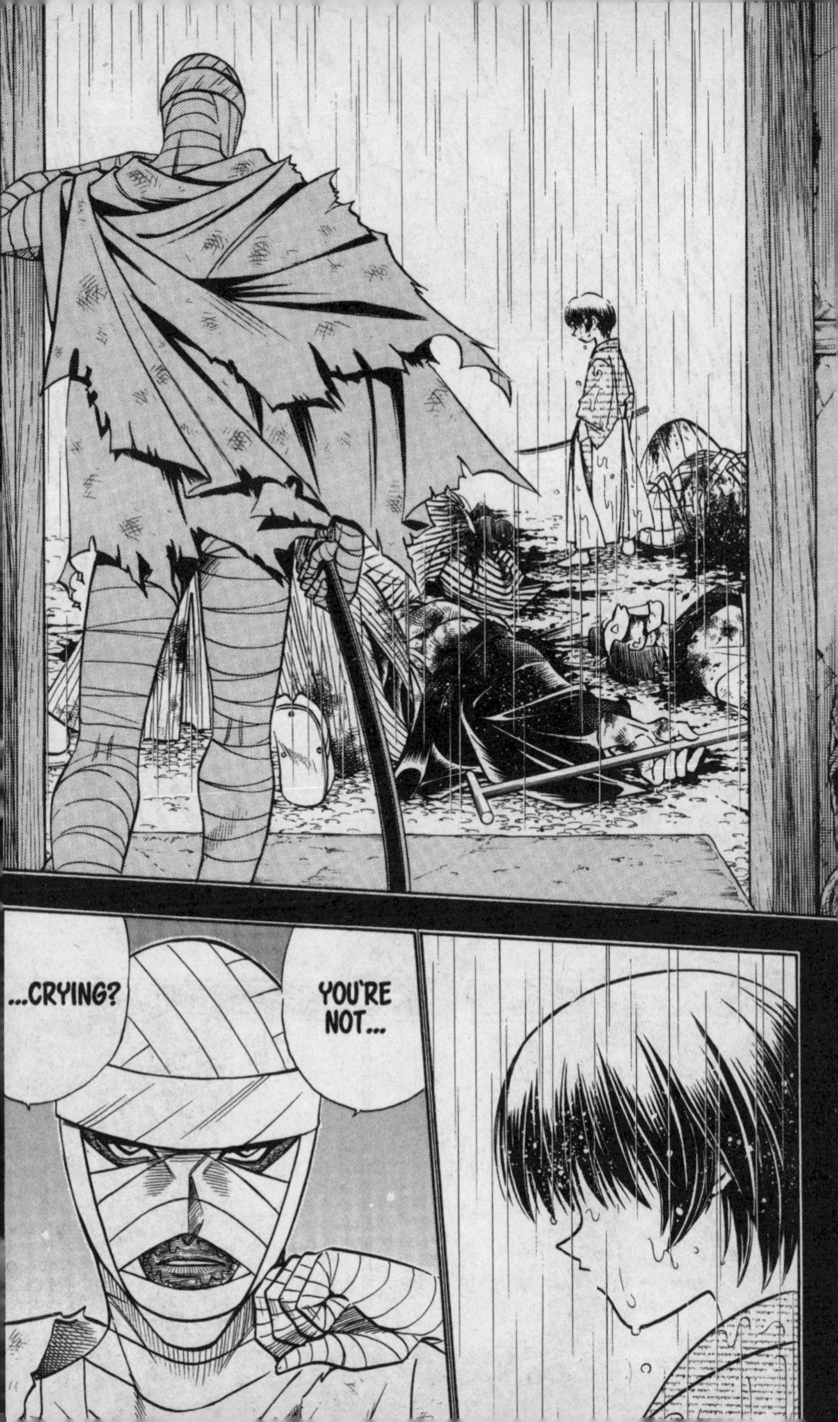
YOU'RE NOT...
...CRYING?

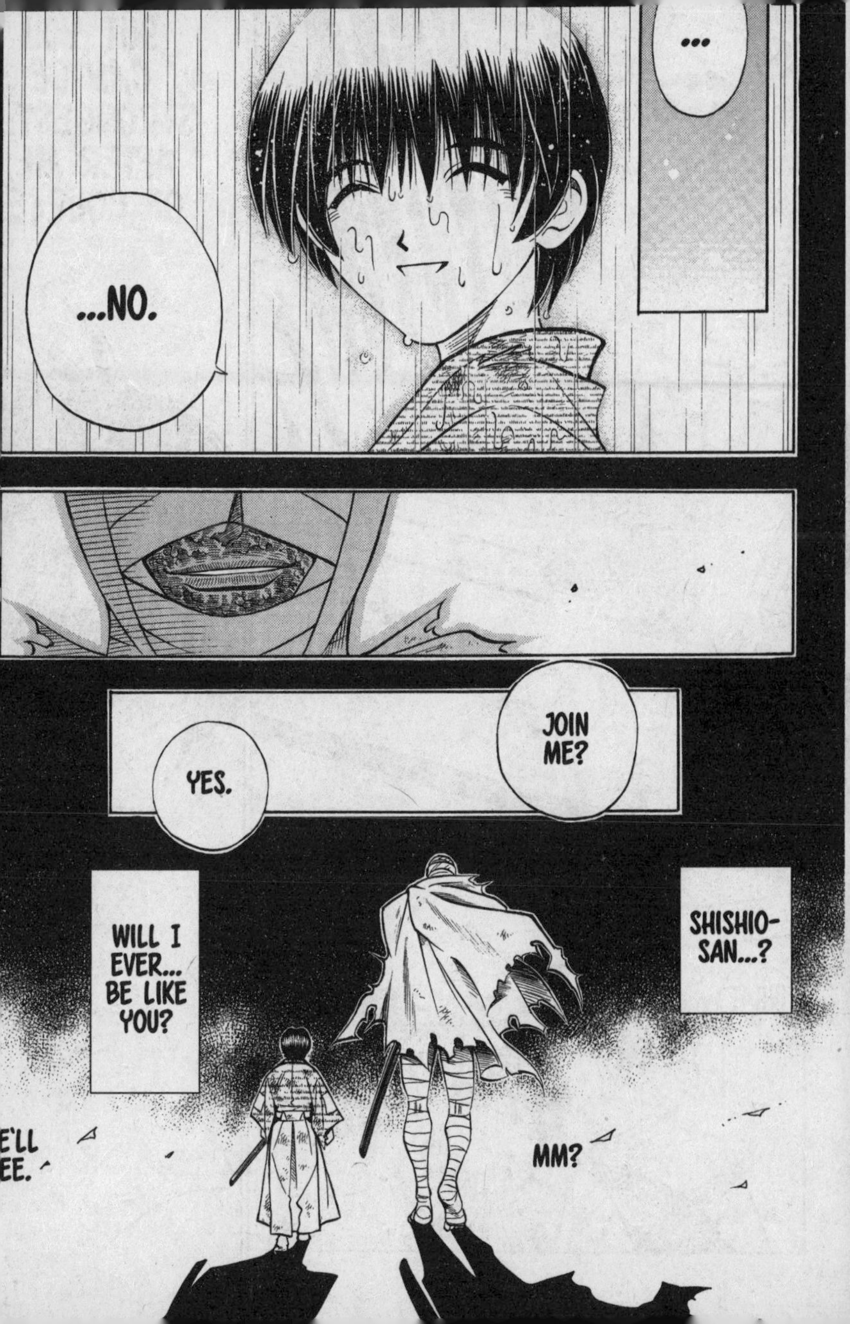
...
...NO.
JOIN ME?
YES.
SHISHIO-SAN...?
MM?
WILL I EVER... BE LIKE YOU?
E'LL EE.

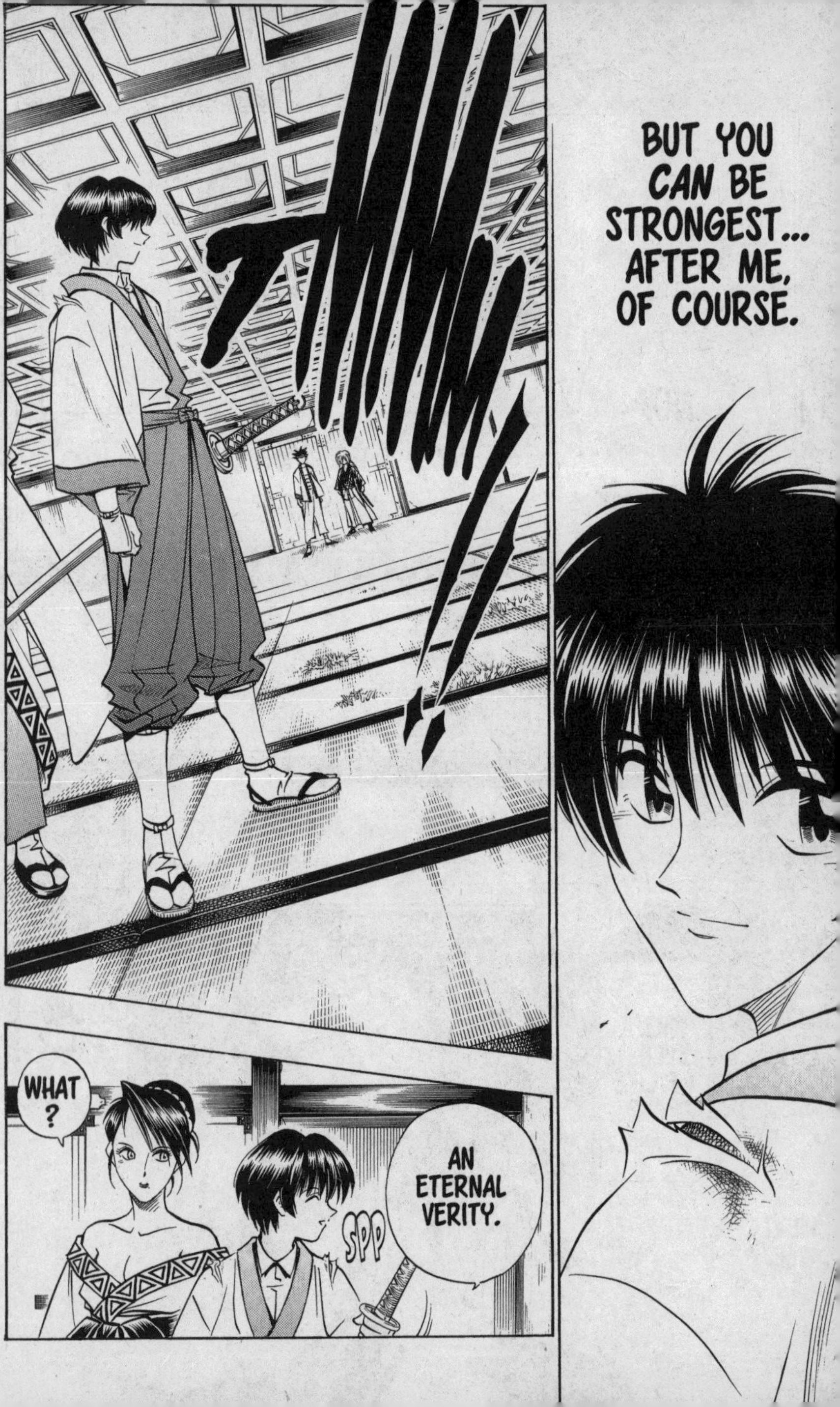
BUT YOU CAN BE STRONGEST... AFTER ME, OF COURSE.
AN ETERNAL VERITY.
SPP
WHAT?

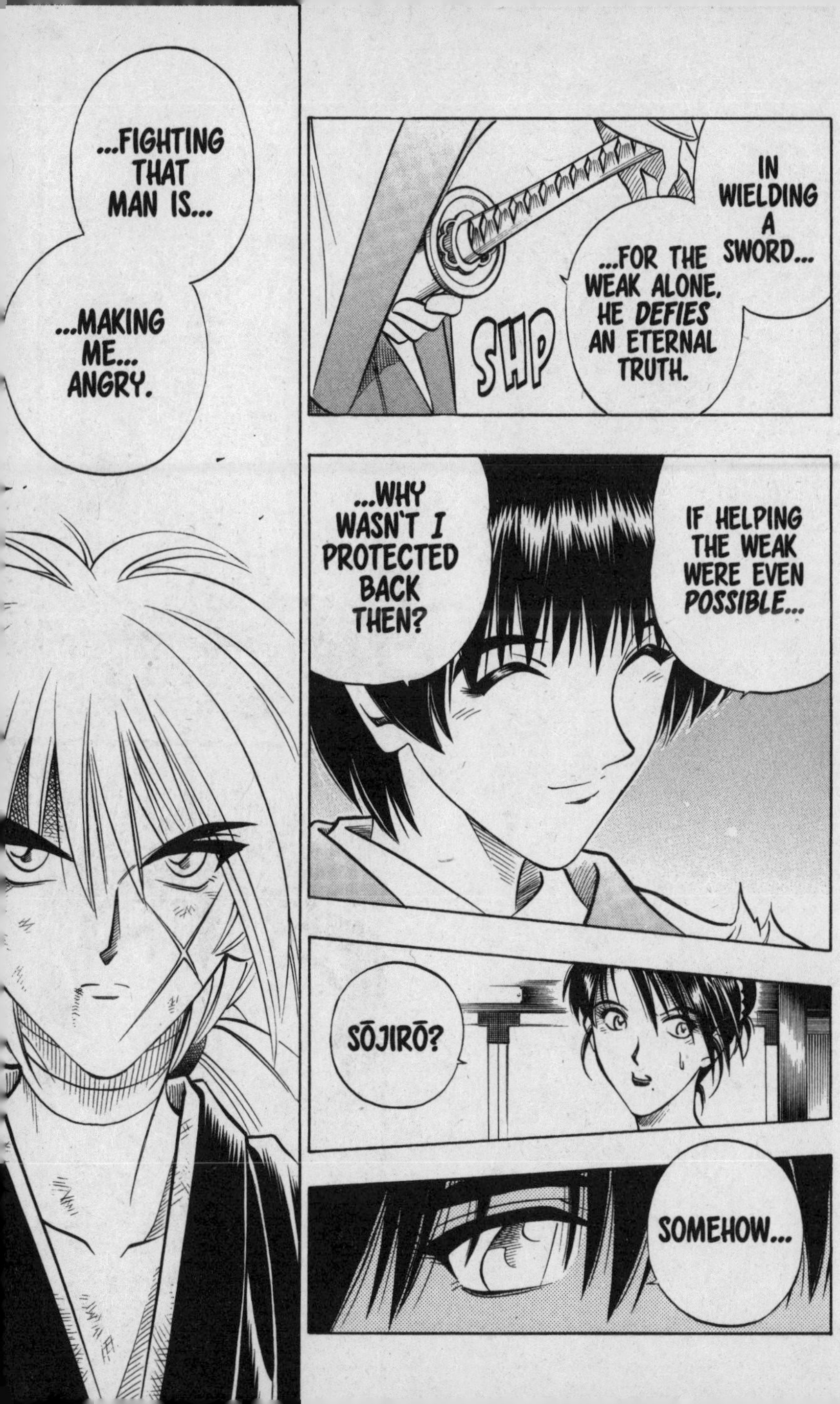
IN WIELDING A SWORD...
...FOR THE WEAK ALONE, HE DEFIES AN ETERNAL TRUTH.
SHP
IF HELPING THE WEAK WERE EVEN POSSIBLE...
...WHY WASN'T I PROTECTED BACK THEN?
SŌJIRŌ?
SOMEHOW...
...FIGHTING THAT MAN IS...
...MAKING ME... ANGRY.

Rurouni Kenshin

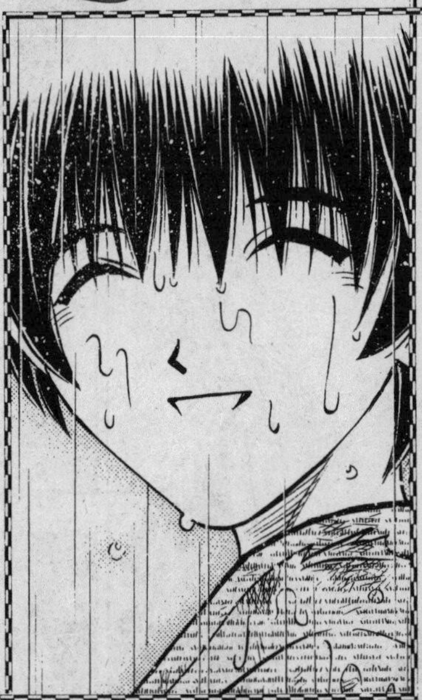

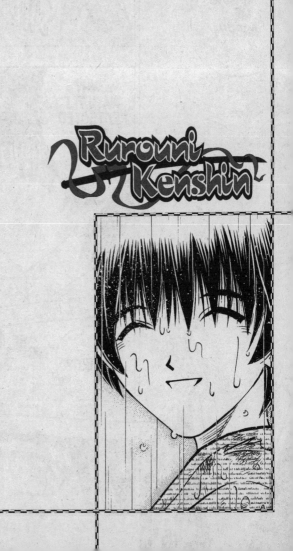

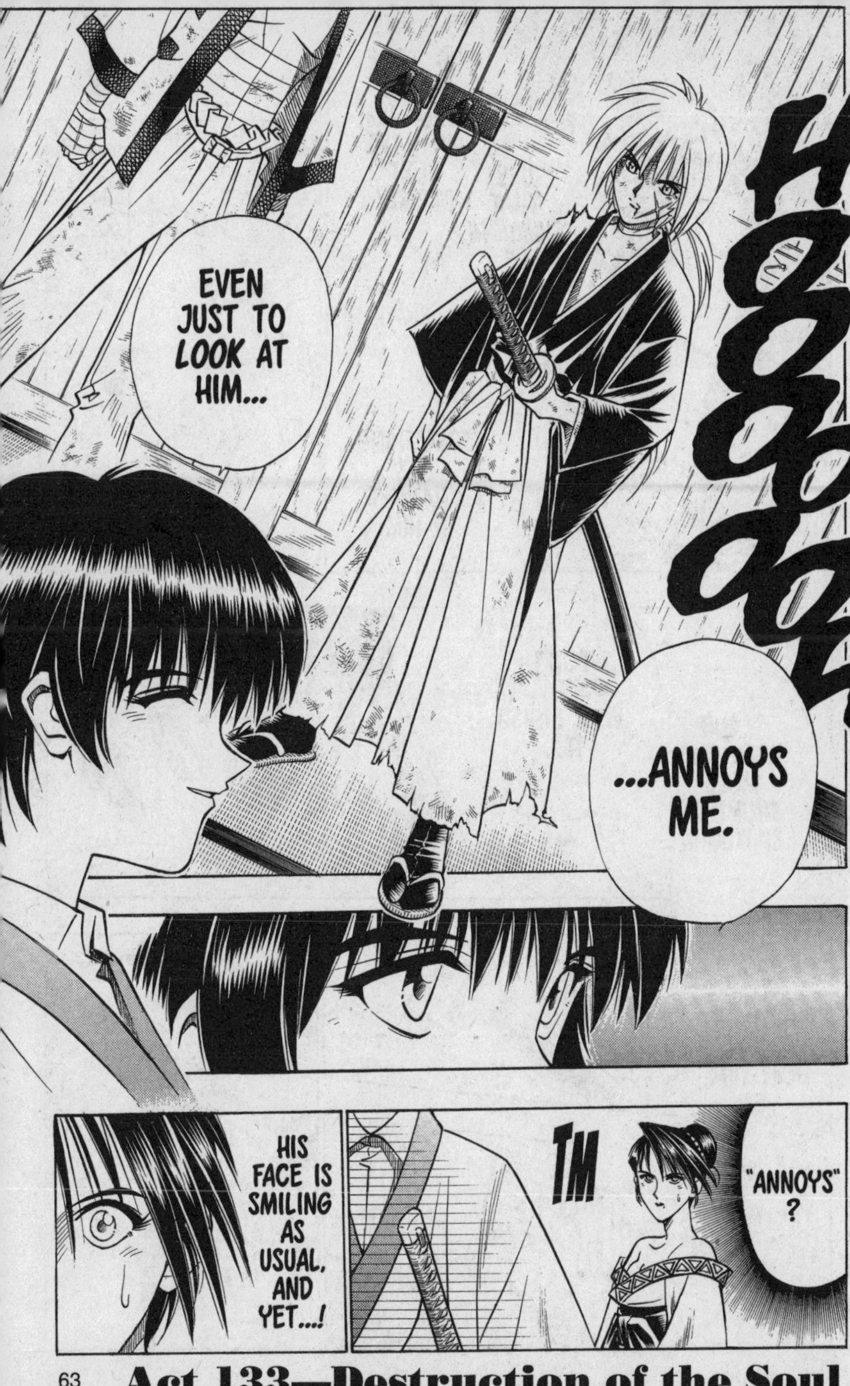
EVEN JUST TO LOOK AT HIM...
...ANNOYS ME.
"ANNOYS" ?
TM
HIS FACE IS SMILING AS USUAL, AND YET...!

Act 133—Destruction of the Soul

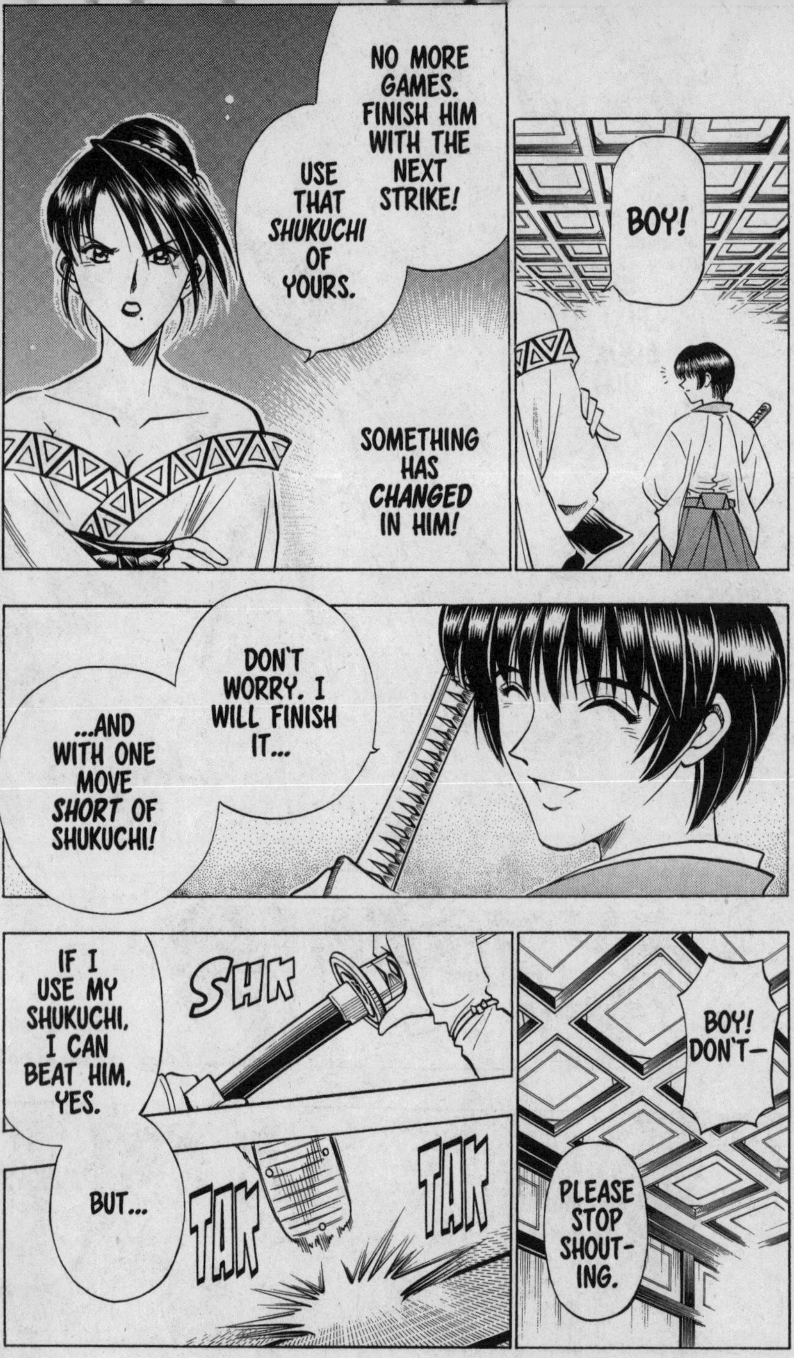
BOY!
NO MORE GAMES. FINISH HIM WITH THE NEXT STRIKE!
USE THAT SHUKUCHI OF YOURS.
SOMETHING HAS CHANGED IN HIM!
DON'T WORRY. I WILL FINISH IT...
...AND WITH ONE MOVE SHORT OF SHUKUCHI!
BOY! DON'T—
PLEASE STOP SHOUT-ING.
SHK
IF I USE MY SHUKUCHI, I CAN BEAT HIM, YES.
TAK
TAK
BUT...

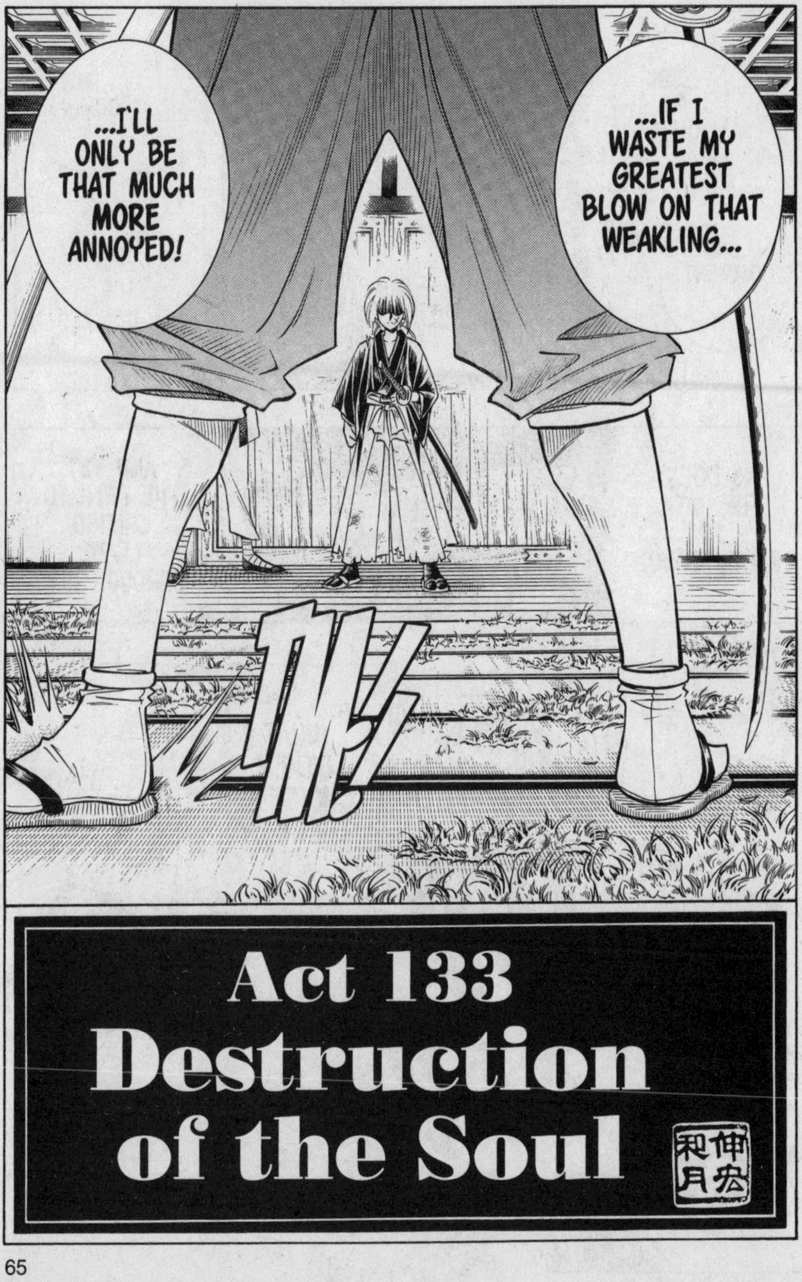
...IF I WASTE MY GREATEST BLOW ON THAT WEAKLING...
...I'LL ONLY BE THAT MUCH MORE ANNOYED!
TM!

Act 133 Destruction of the Soul

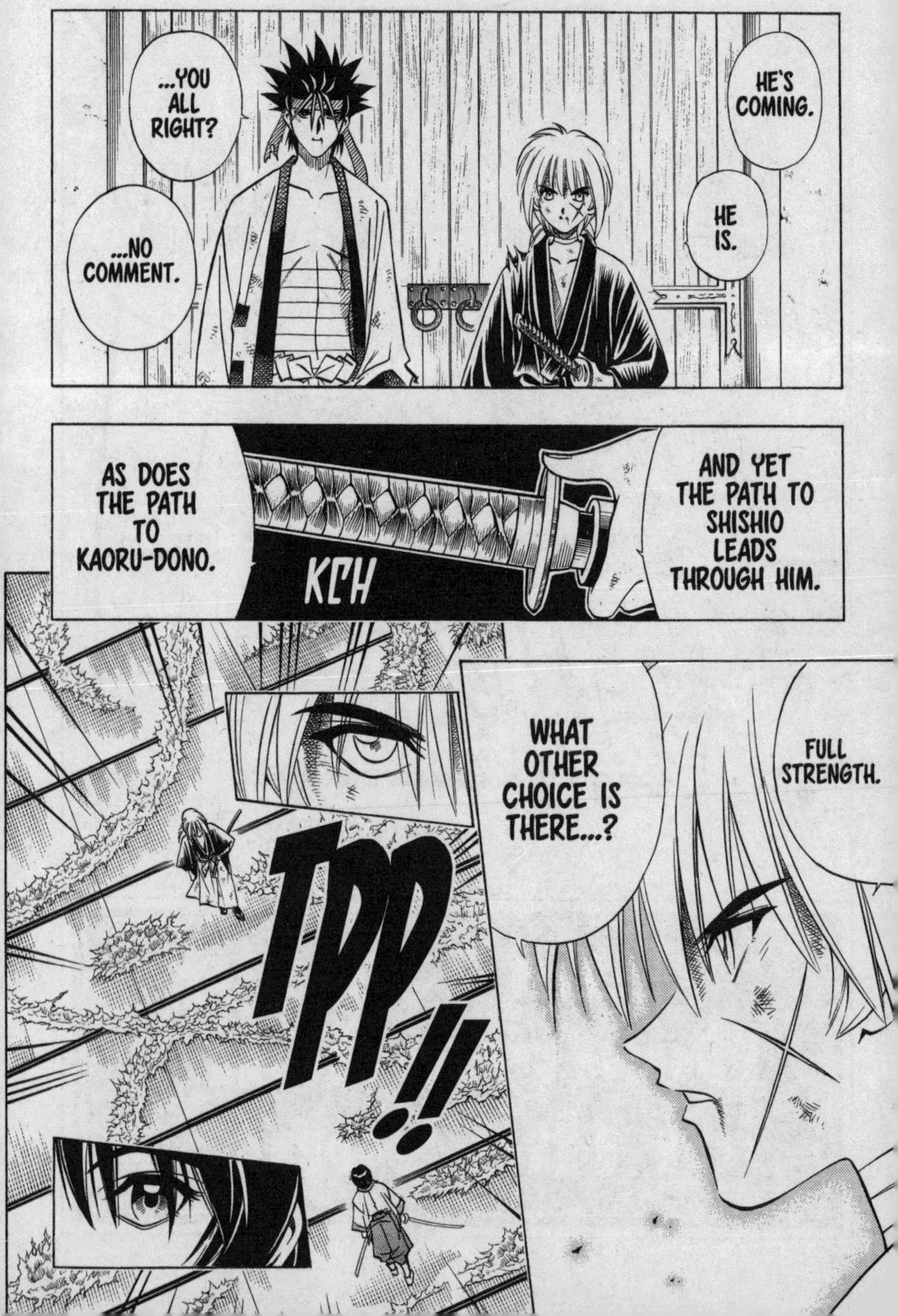
HE'S COMING.
HE IS.
...YOU ALL RIGHT?
...NO COMMENT.
AND YET THE PATH TO SHISHIO LEADS THROUGH HIM.
KCH
AS DOES THE PATH TO KAORU-DONO.
FULL STRENGTH.
WHAT OTHER CHOICE IS THERE...?
TPP!!

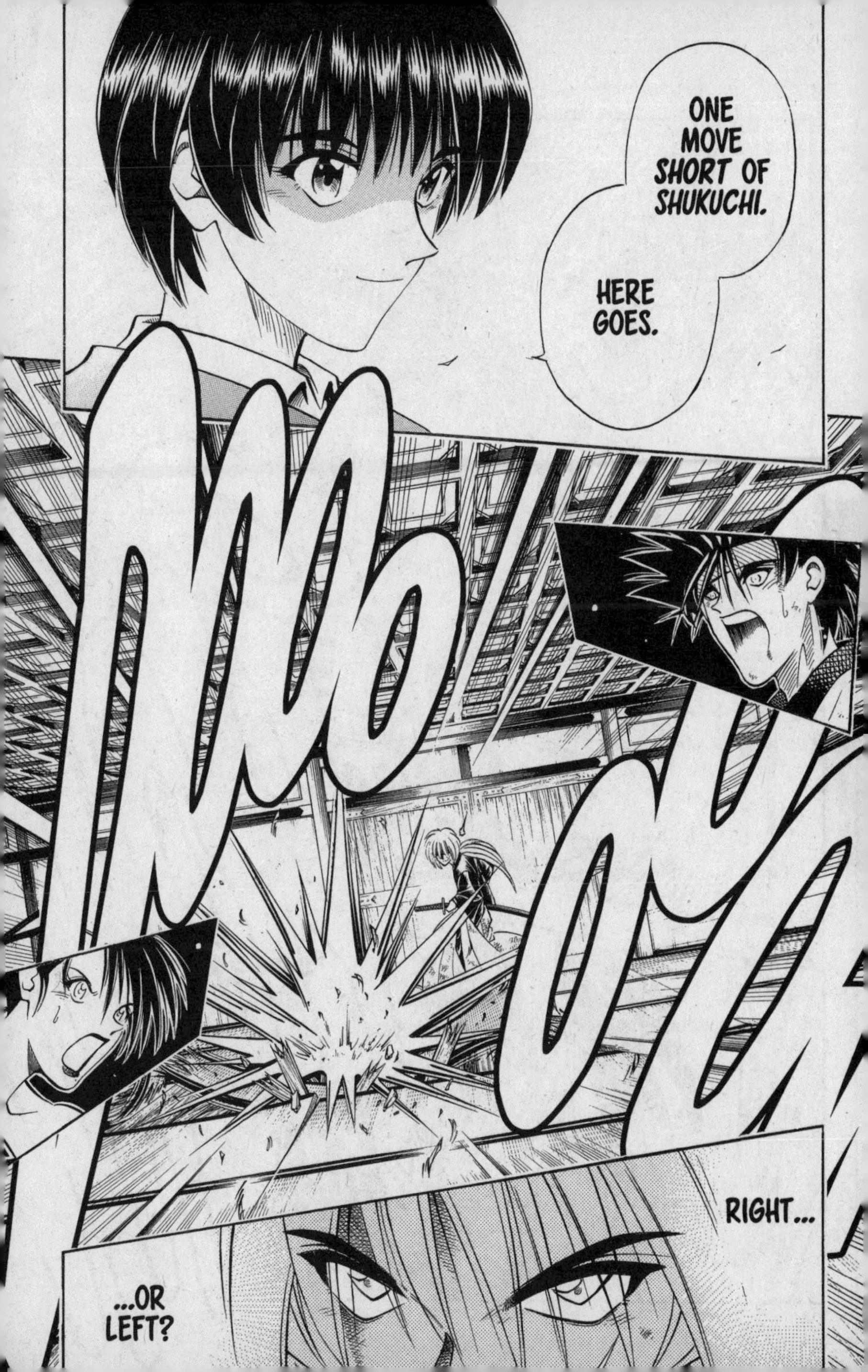
ONE MOVE SHORT OF SHUKUCHI.
HERE GOES.
RIGHT...
...OR LEFT?

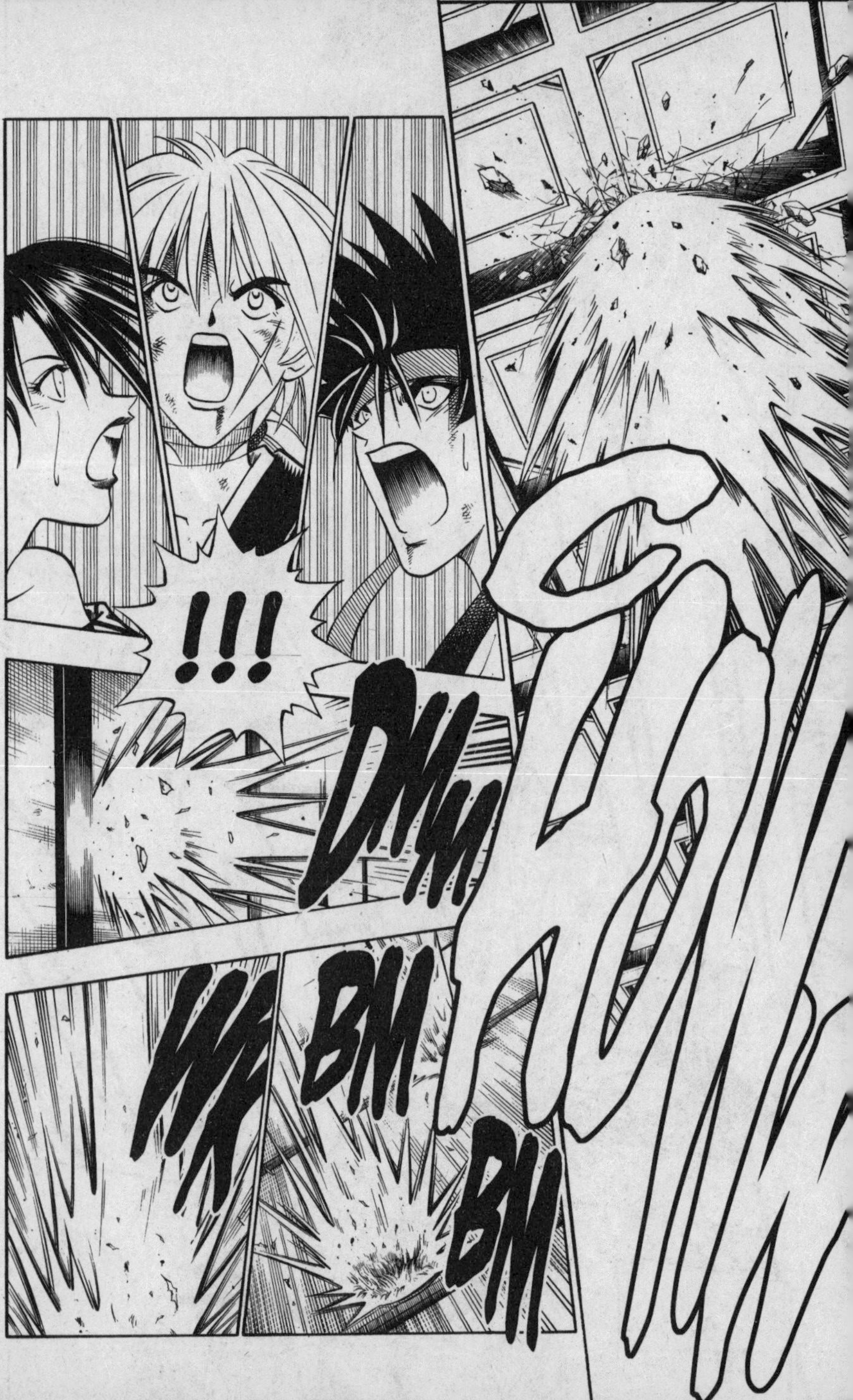
!!!
BM
BM
BM

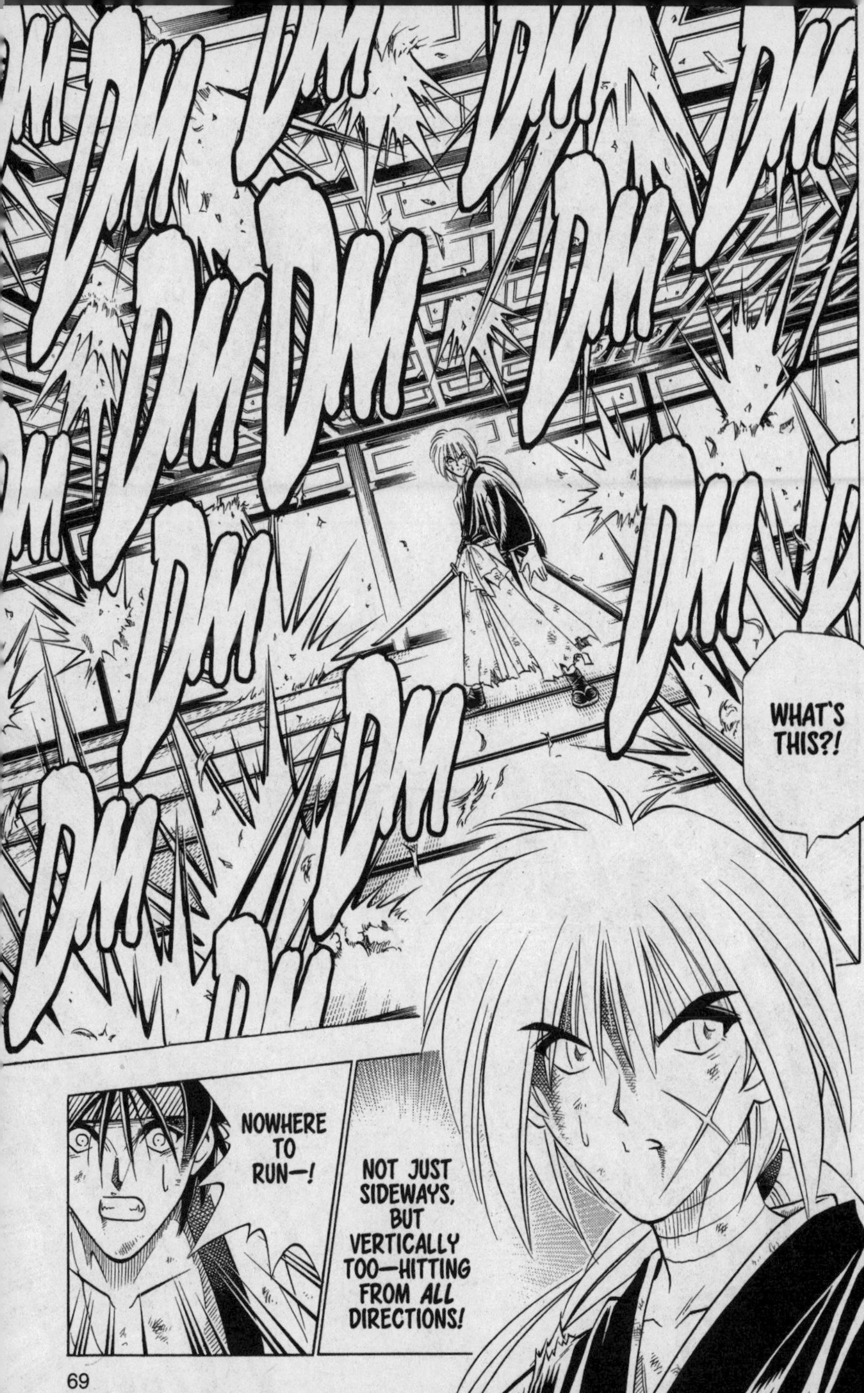
DM DM DM DM DM DM DM DM DM DM DM DM DM DM
WHAT'S THIS?!
NOT JUST SIDEWAYS, BUT VERTICALLY TOO—HITTING FROM ALL DIRECTIONS!
NOWHERE TO RUN—!

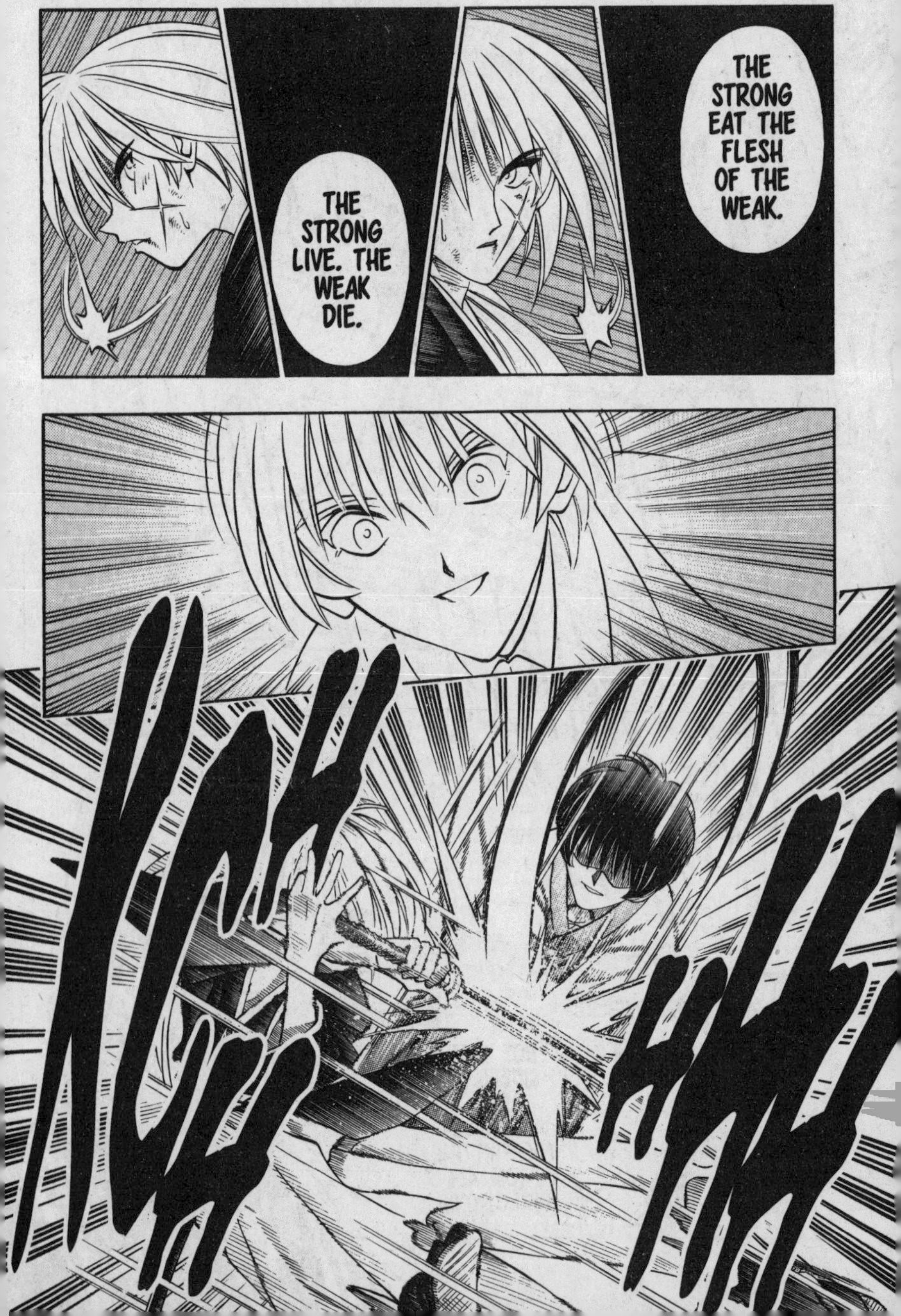
THE STRONG EAT THE FLESH OF THE WEAK.
THE STRONG LIVE. THE WEAK DIE.

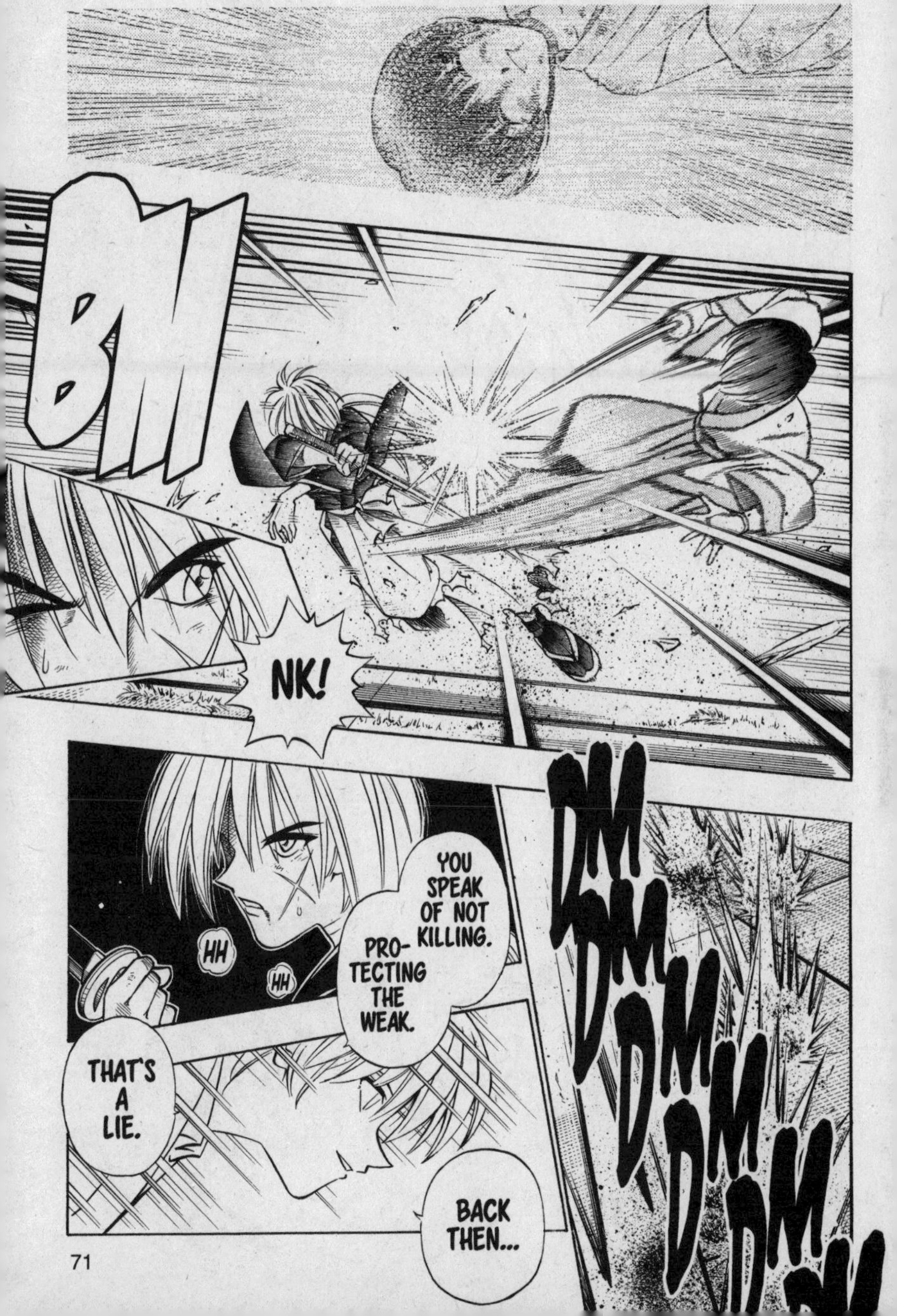
BM
NK!
DM DM DM DM DM DM DM
YOU SPEAK OF NOT KILLING.
PROTECTING THE WEAK.
HH
HH
THAT'S A LIE.
BACK THEN...

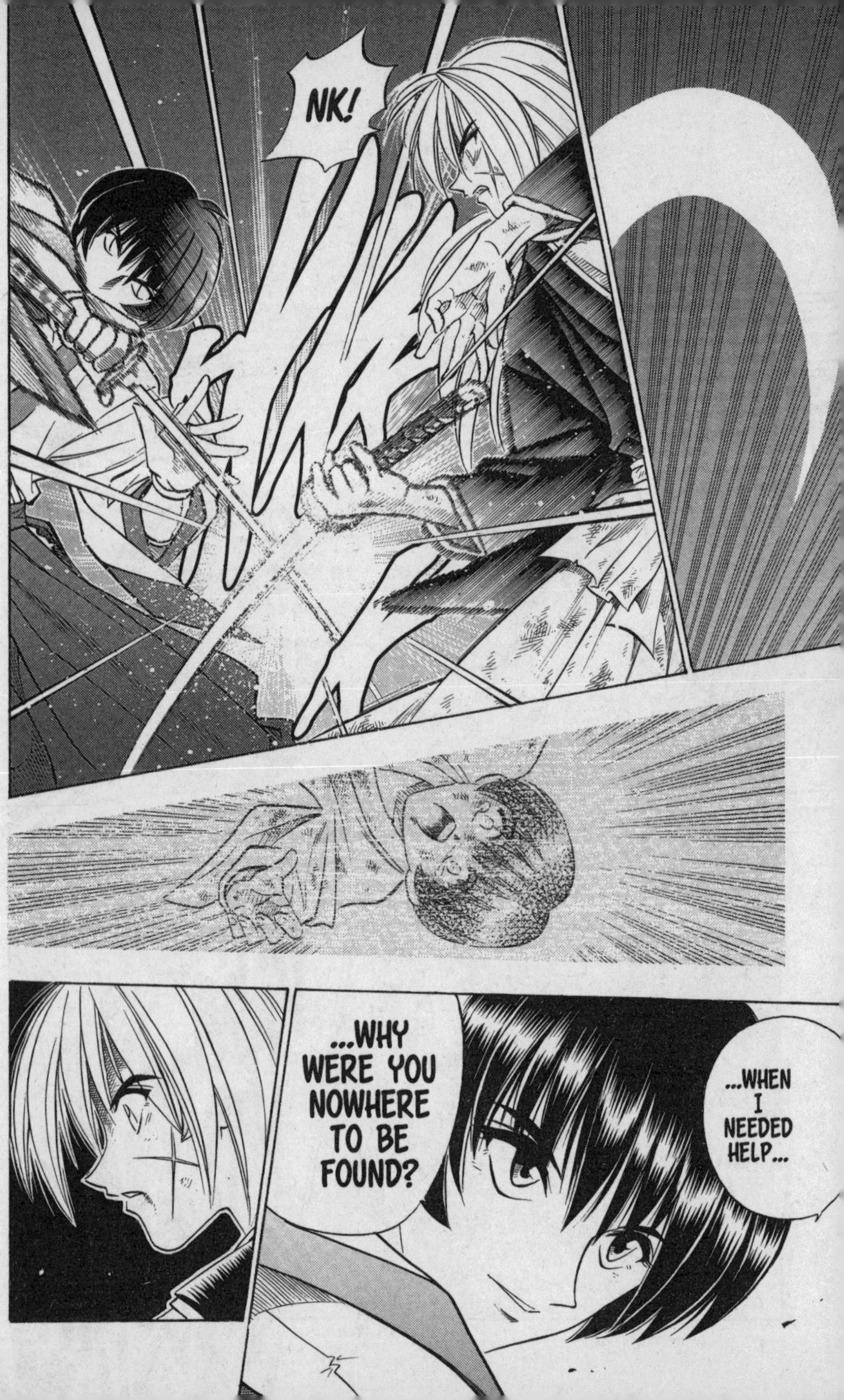
NK!
...WHEN I NEEDED HELP...
...WHY WERE YOU NOWHERE TO BE FOUND?

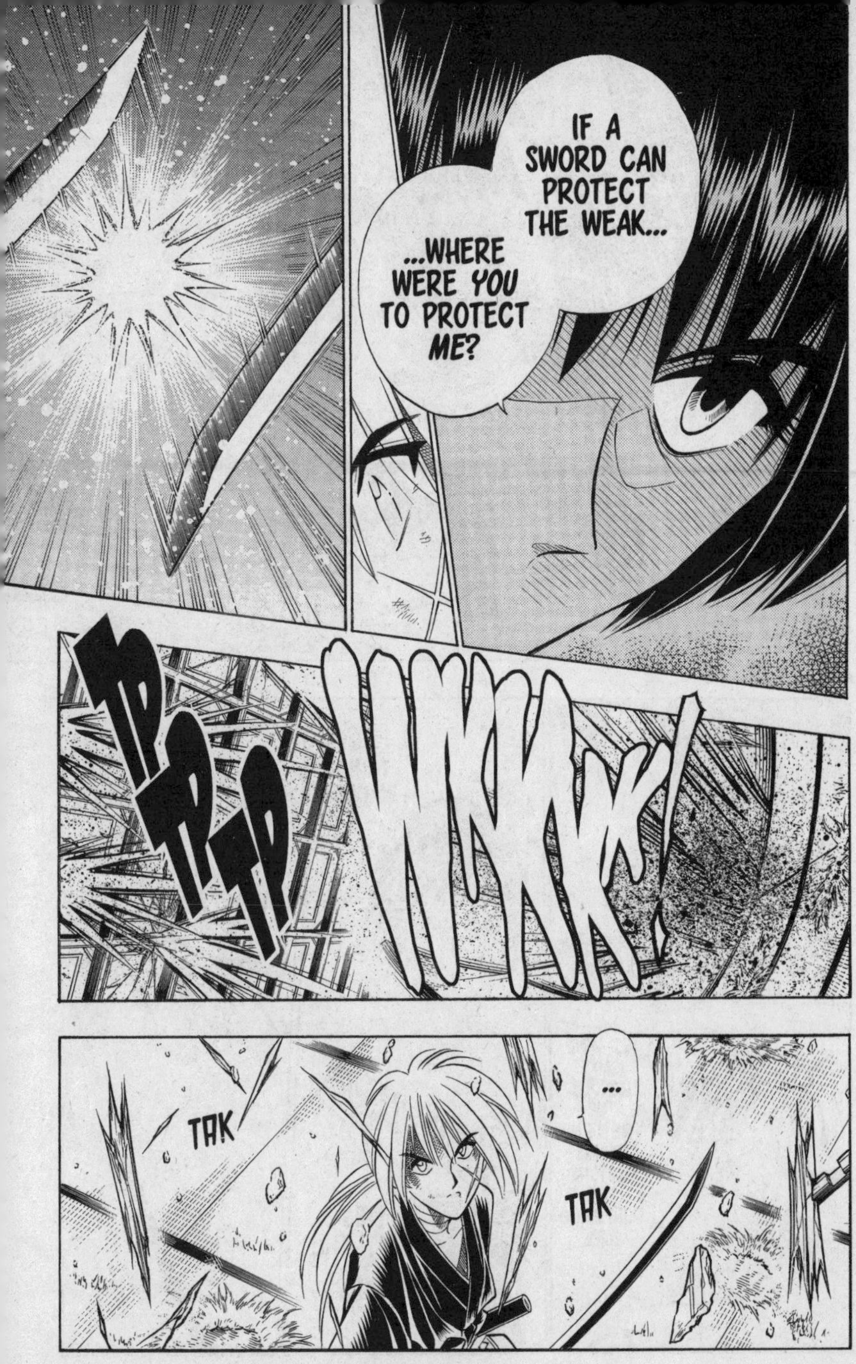
IF A SWORD CAN PROTECT THE WEAK...
...WHERE WERE YOU TO PROTECT ME?
...
TAK
TAK

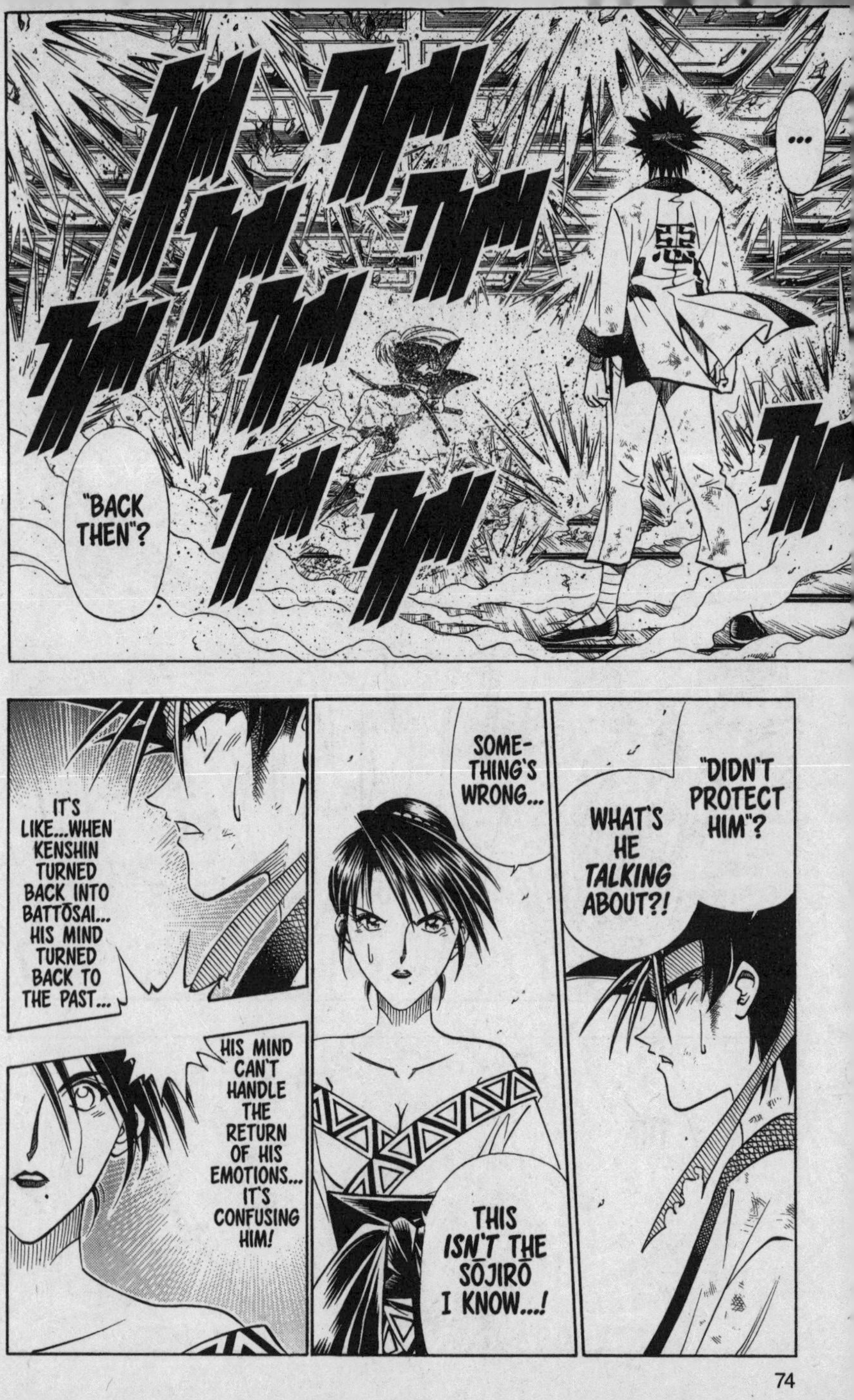
...
"BACK THEN"?
"DIDN'T PROTECT HIM"?
WHAT'S HE *TALKING* ABOUT?!
SOME-THING'S WRONG...
THIS *ISN'T* THE SŌJIRŌ I KNOW...!
IT'S LIKE...WHEN KENSHIN TURNED BACK INTO BATTŌSAI... HIS MIND TURNED BACK TO THE PAST...
HIS MIND CAN'T HANDLE THE RETURN OF HIS EMOTIONS... IT'S CONFUSING HIM!

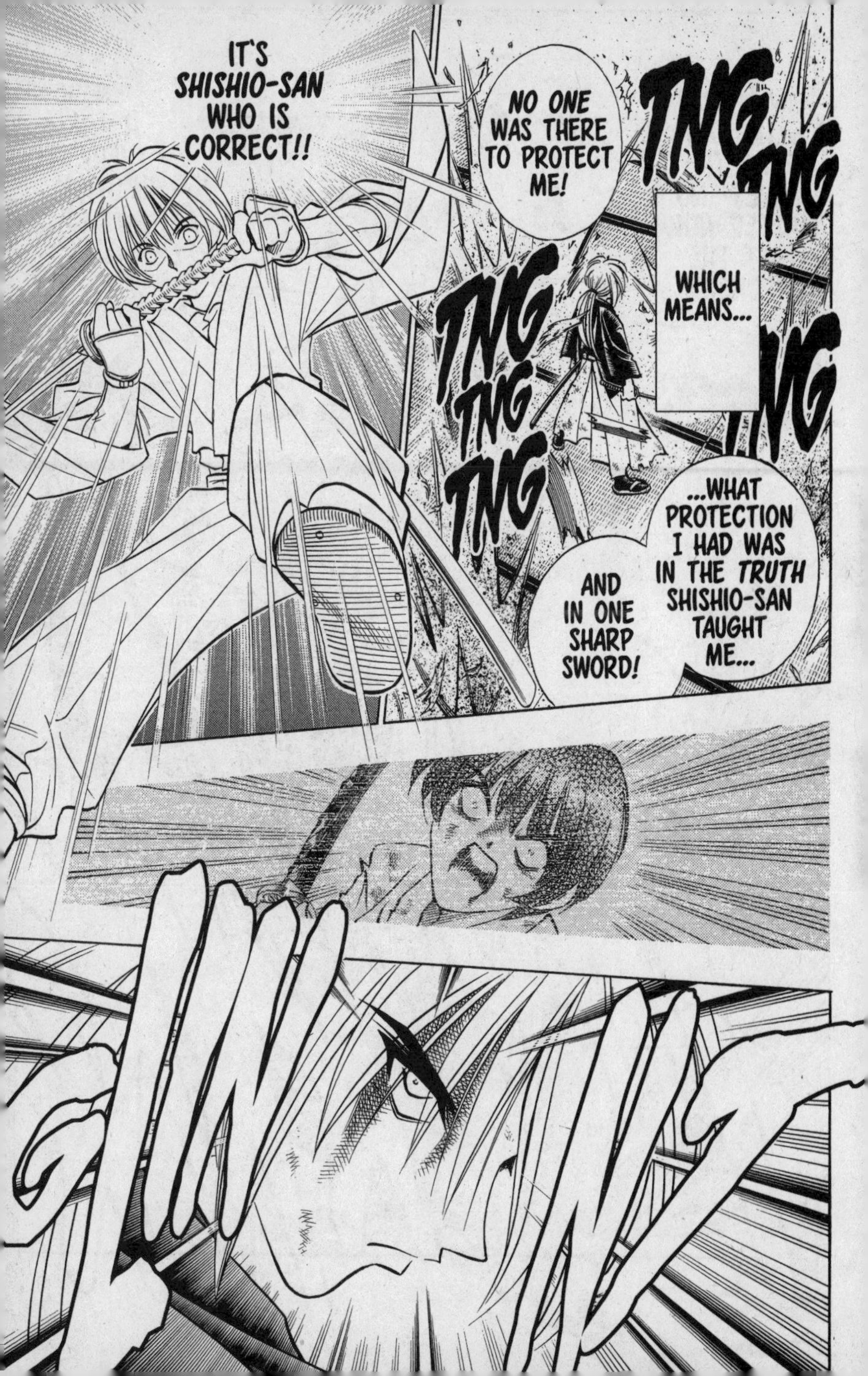
NO ONE WAS THERE TO PROTECT ME!
TNG TNG TNG
WHICH MEANS...
TNG TNG TNG
...WHAT PROTECTION I HAD WAS IN THE *TRUTH* SHISHIO-SAN TAUGHT ME...
AND IN ONE SHARP SWORD!
IT'S SHISHIO-SAN WHO IS CORRECT!!

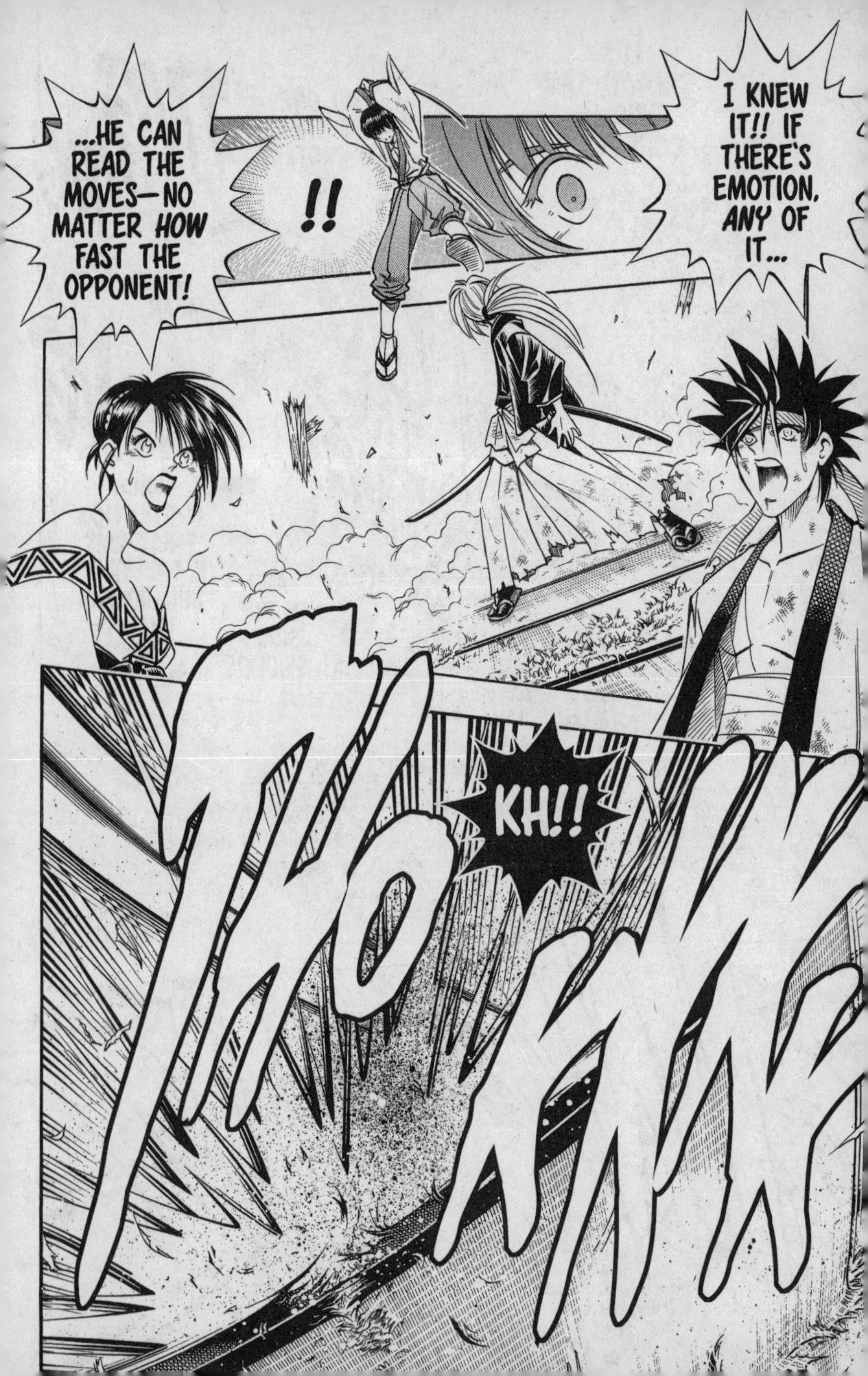
I KNEW IT!! IF THERE'S EMOTION, ANY OF IT...
!!
...HE CAN READ THE MOVES—NO MATTER *HOW* FAST THE OPPONENT!
KH!!

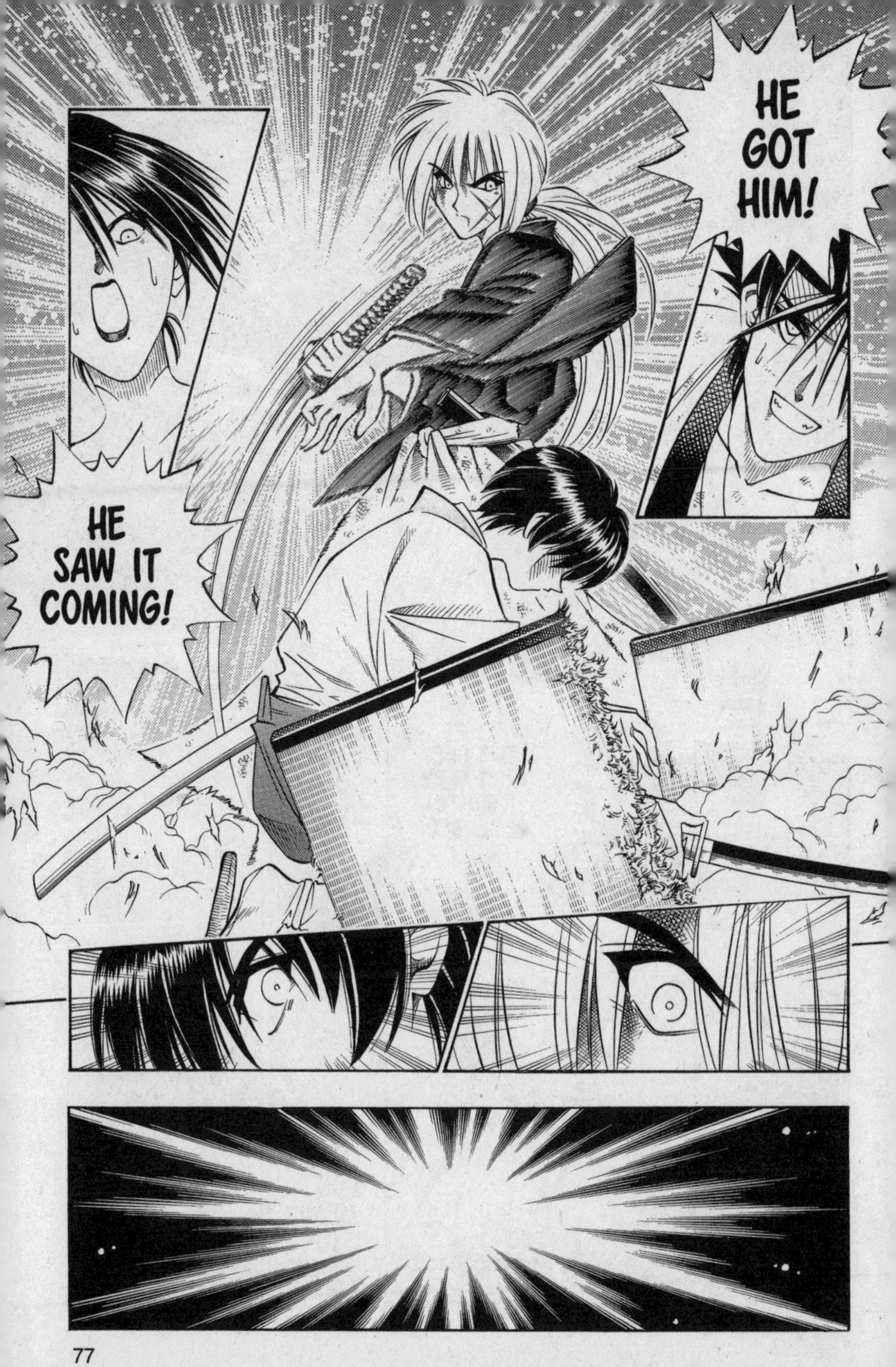
HE GOT HIM!
HE SAW IT COMING!

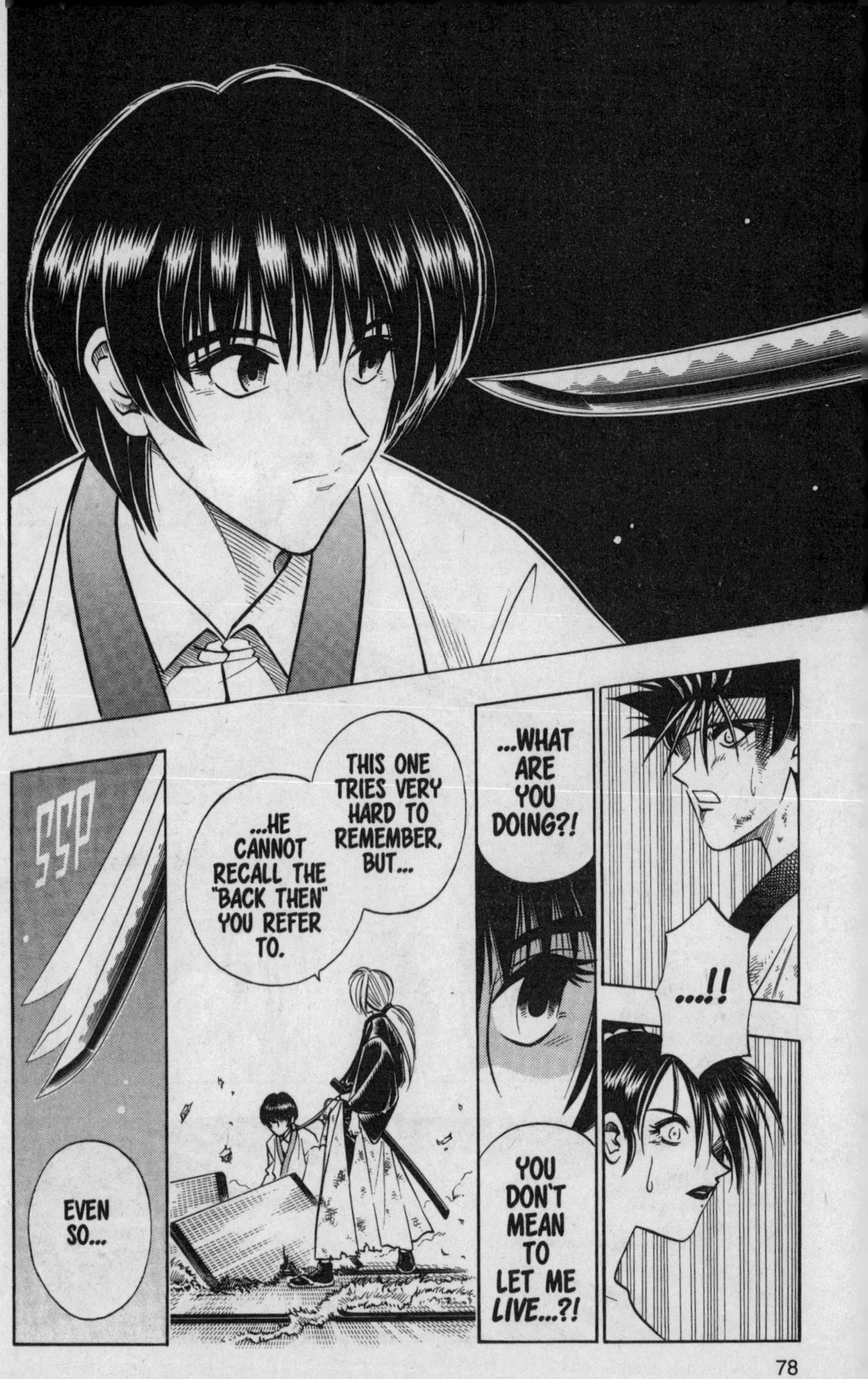
...WHAT ARE YOU DOING?!
...!!
YOU DON'T MEAN TO LET ME LIVE...?!
THIS ONE TRIES VERY HARD TO REMEMBER, BUT...
...HE CANNOT RECALL THE "BACK THEN" YOU REFER TO.
SSP
EVEN SO...

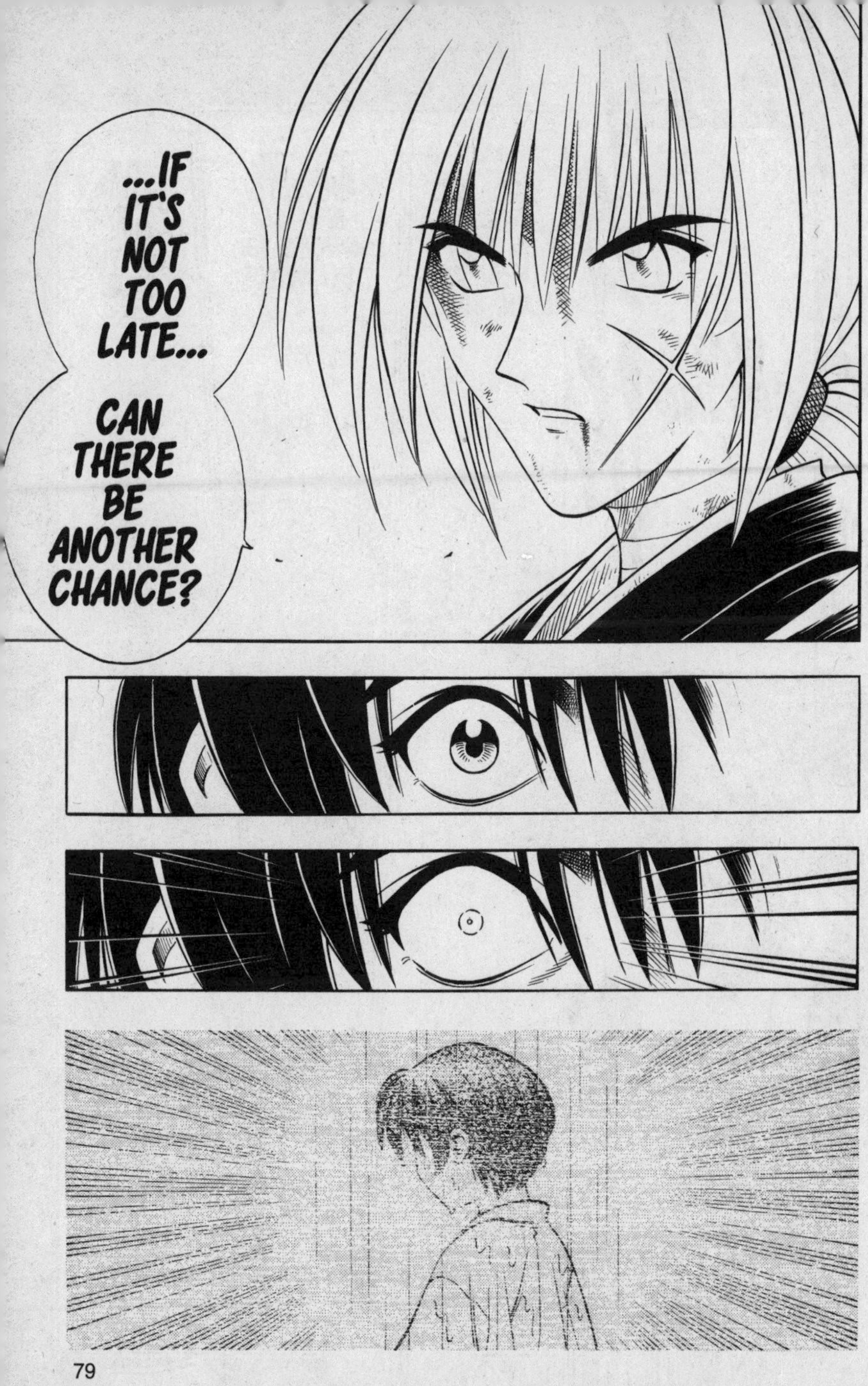
...IF IT'S NOT TOO LATE...
CAN THERE BE ANOTHER CHANCE?

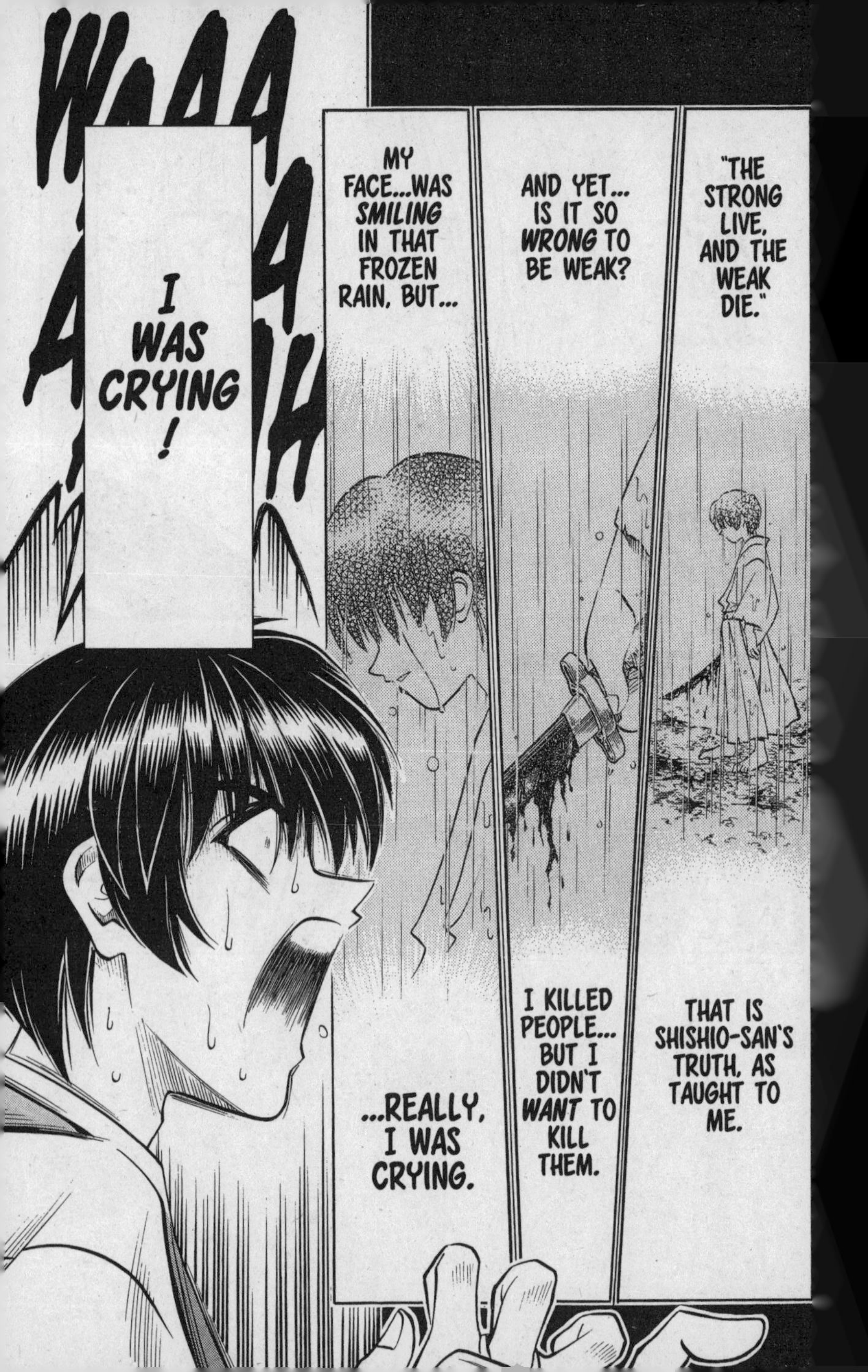
"THE STRONG LIVE, AND THE WEAK DIE."
THAT IS SHISHIO-SAN'S TRUTH, AS TAUGHT TO ME.
AND YET... IS IT SO *WRONG* TO BE WEAK?
I KILLED PEOPLE... BUT I DIDN'T *WANT* TO KILL THEM.
MY FACE...WAS *SMILING* IN THAT FROZEN RAIN, BUT...
...REALLY, I WAS CRYING.
I WAS CRYING!

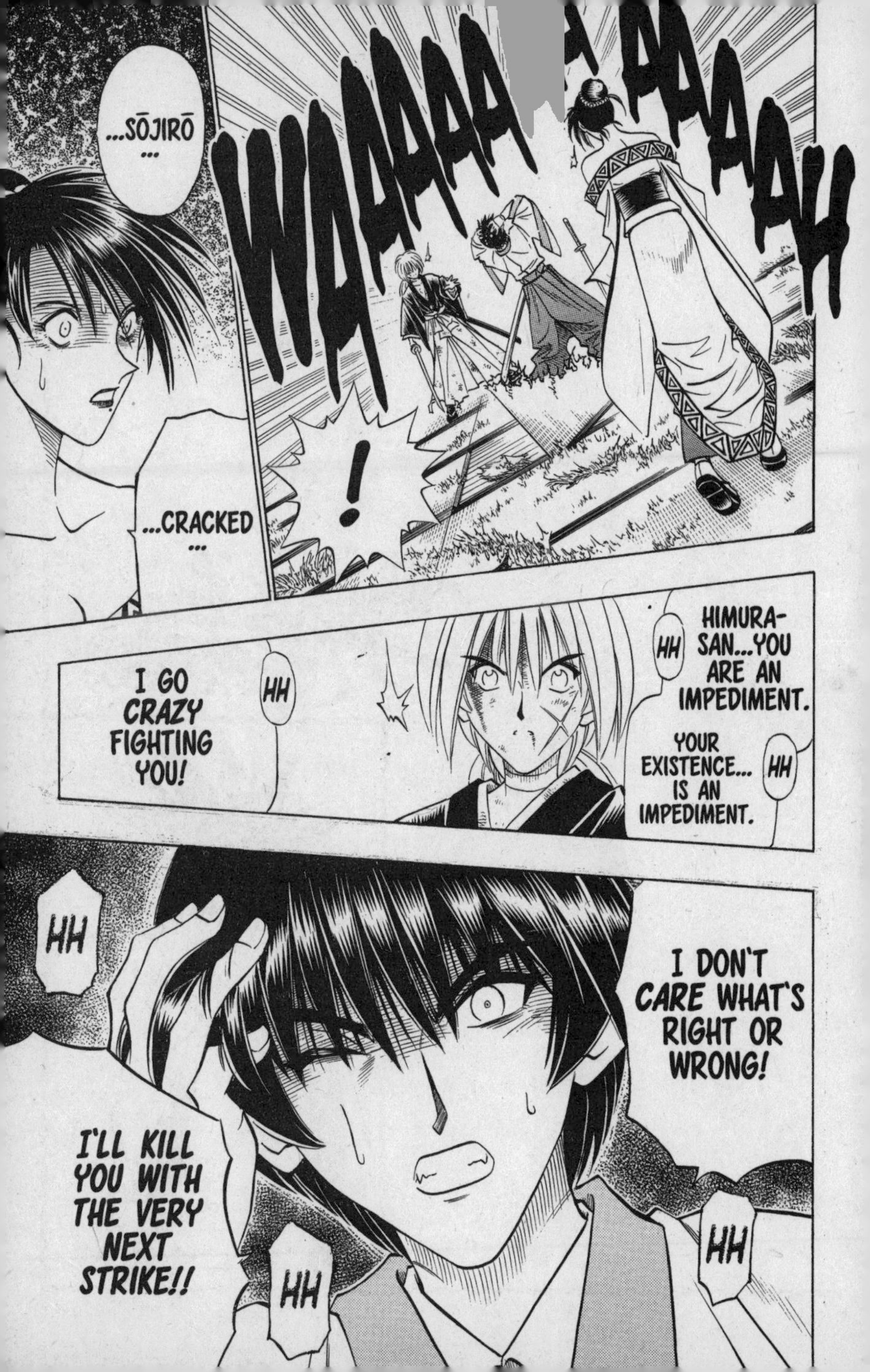
WAAAAA
AAAAH
!
...SŌJIRŌ ...
...CRACKED ...
HH
HIMURA-SAN...YOU ARE AN IMPEDIMENT.
YOUR EXISTENCE... IS AN IMPEDIMENT.
HH
HH
I GO CRAZY FIGHTING YOU!
I DON'T CARE WHAT'S RIGHT OR WRONG!
HH
HH
I'LL KILL YOU WITH THE VERY NEXT STRIKE!!
HH

Rurouni Kenshin

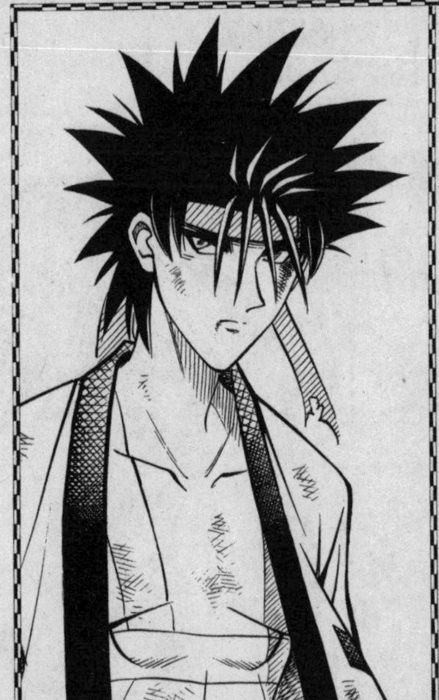

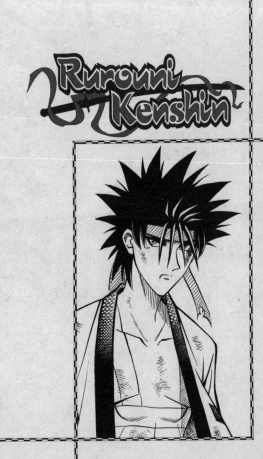

Act 134—The Second Secret

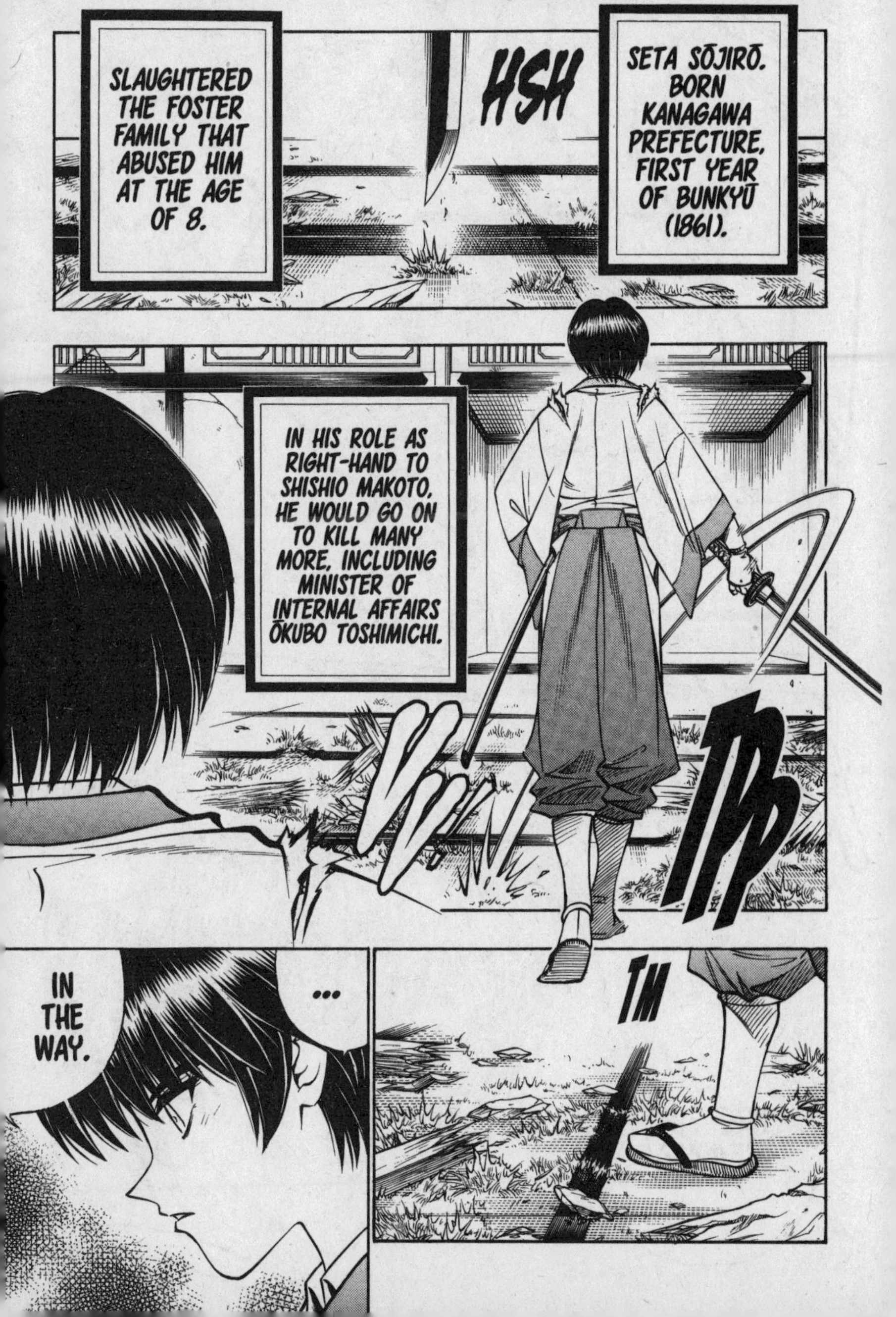
SETA SŌJIRŌ. BORN KANAGAWA PREFECTURE, FIRST YEAR OF BUNKYŪ (1861).
HSH
SLAUGHTERED THE FOSTER FAMILY THAT ABUSED HIM AT THE AGE OF 8.
TP
IN HIS ROLE AS RIGHT-HAND TO SHISHIO MAKOTO, HE WOULD GO ON TO KILL MANY MORE, INCLUDING MINISTER OF INTERNAL AFFAIRS ŌKUBO TOSHIMICHI.
TM
...
IN THE WAY.

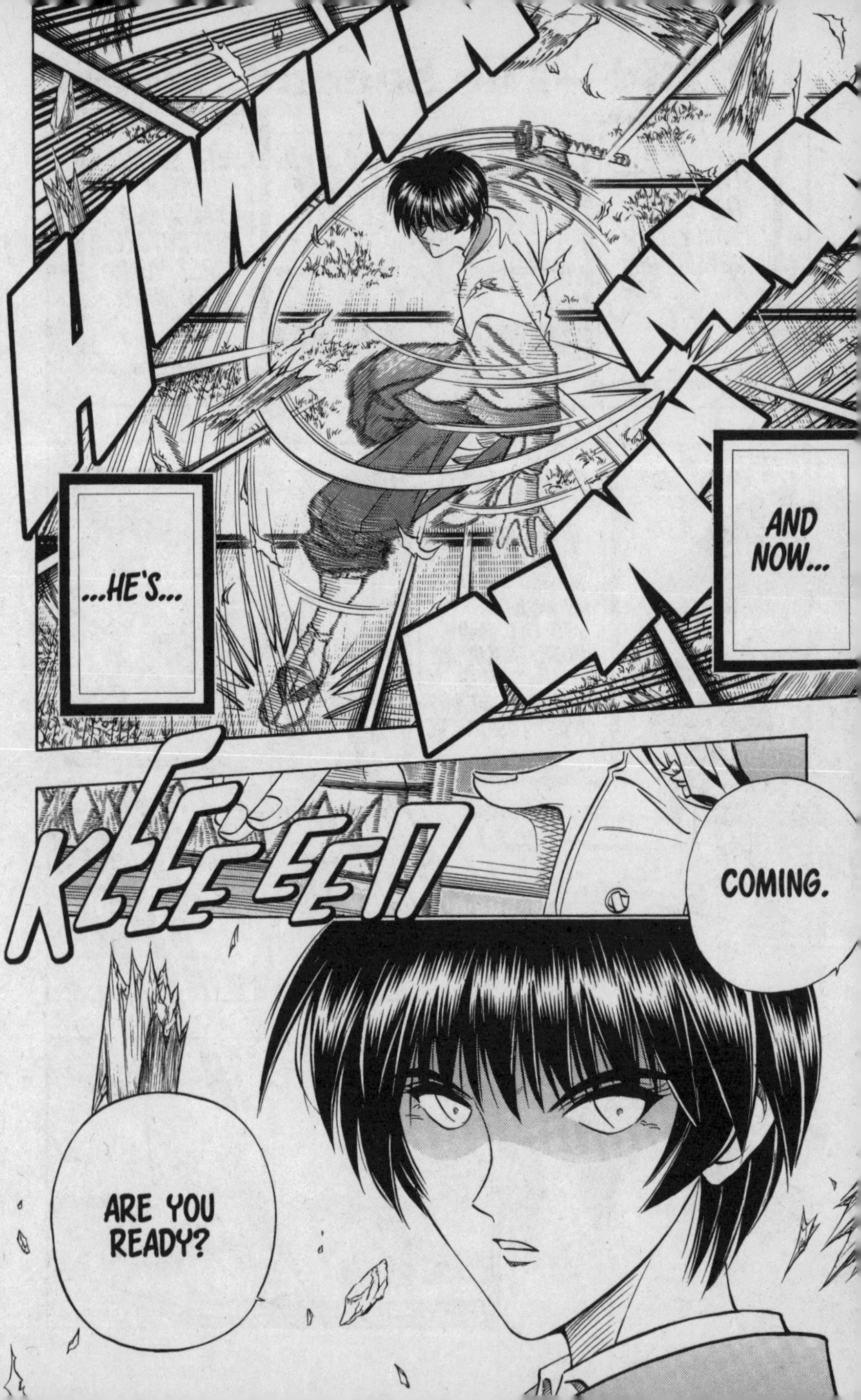
AND NOW...
...HE'S...
COMING.
ARE YOU READY?

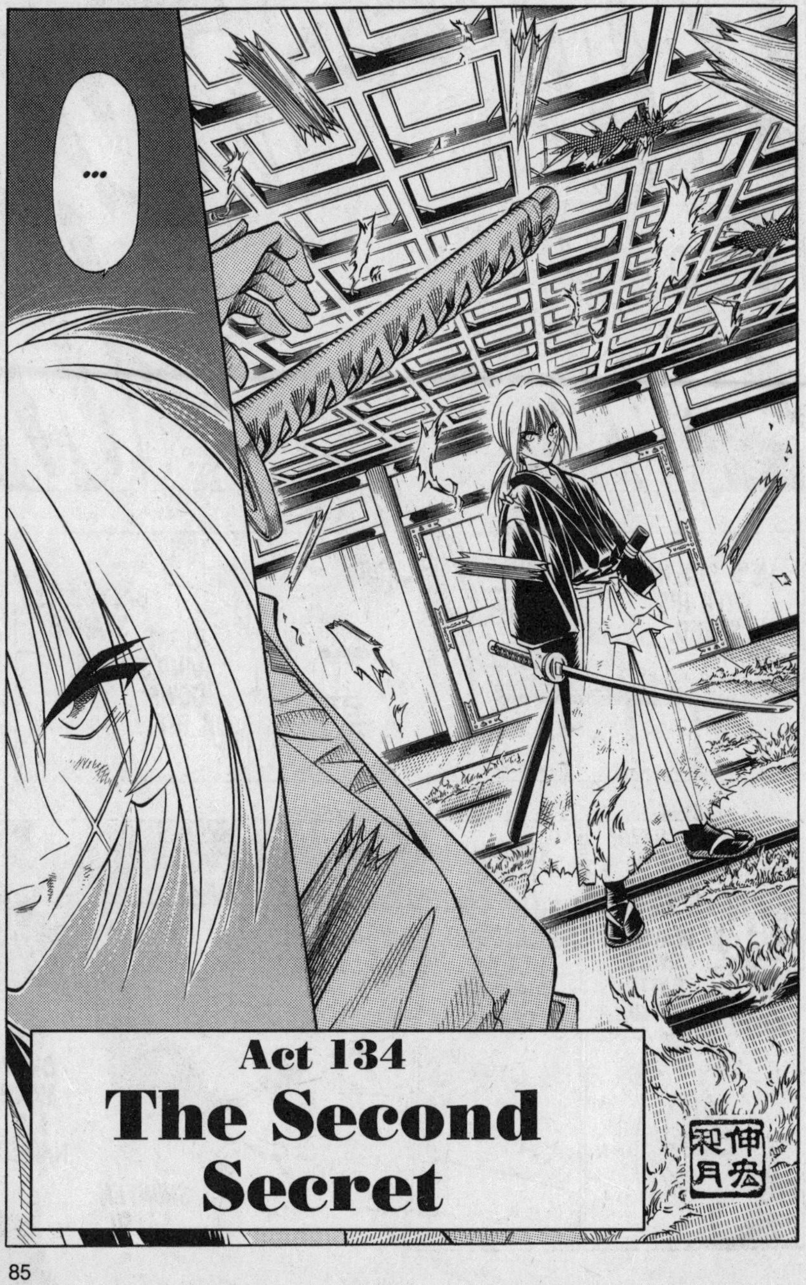
...
Act 134
The Second Secret
伸宏
和月

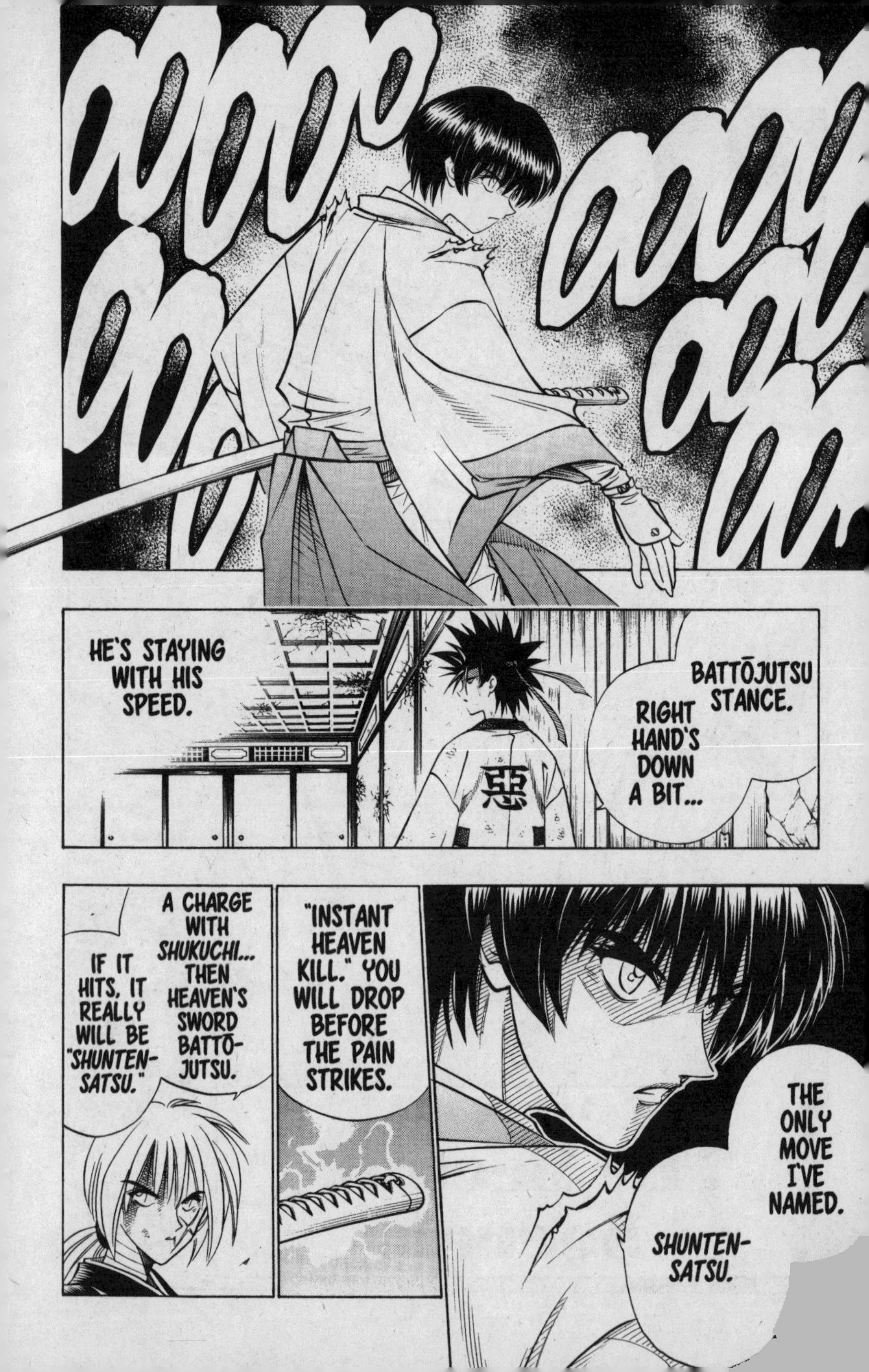
BATTŌJUTSU STANCE.
RIGHT HAND'S DOWN A BIT...
HE'S STAYING WITH HIS SPEED.
THE ONLY MOVE I'VE NAMED.
SHUNTEN-SATSU.
"INSTANT HEAVEN KILL." YOU WILL DROP BEFORE THE PAIN STRIKES.
A CHARGE WITH SHUKUCHI... THEN HEAVEN'S SWORD BATTŌ-JUTSU.
IF IT HITS, IT REALLY WILL BE "SHUNTEN-SATSU."

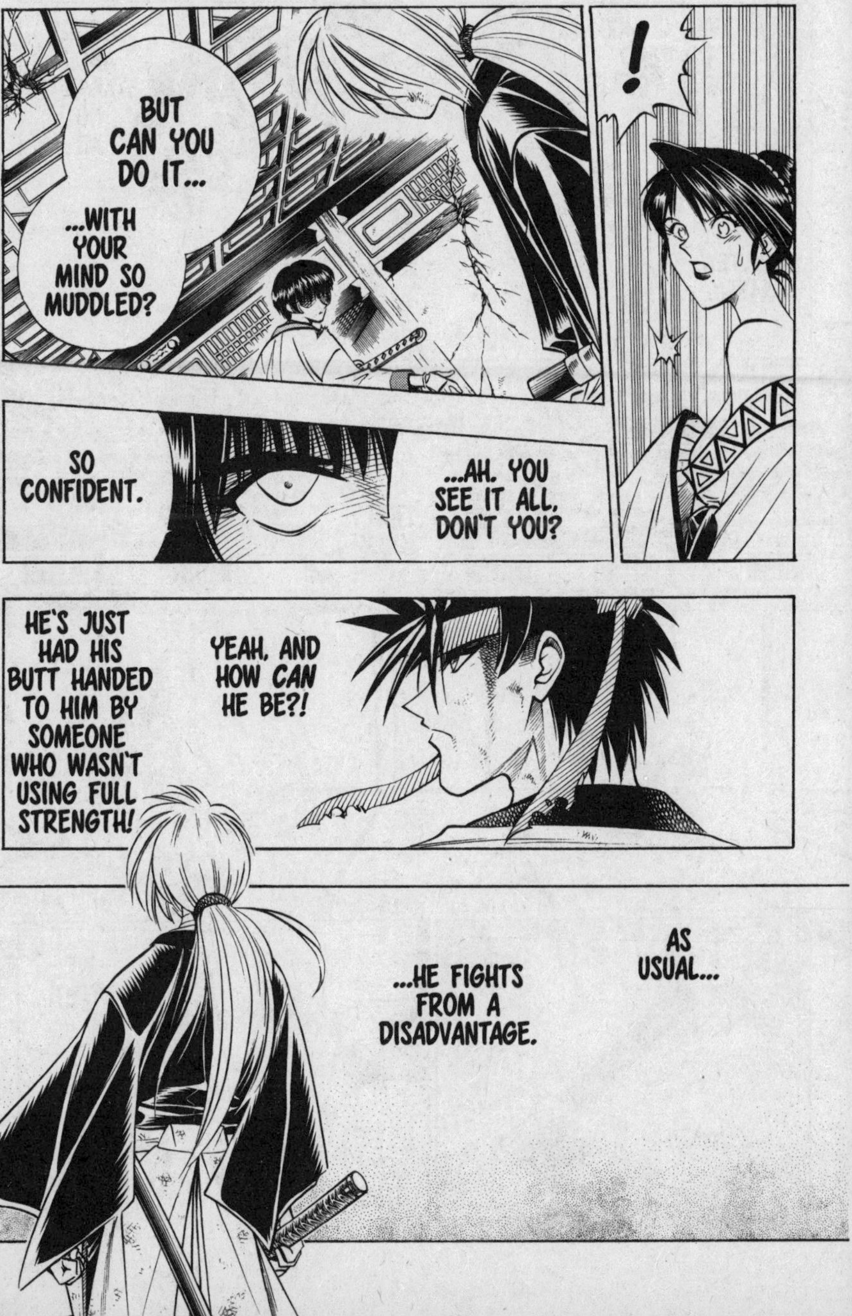
!
BUT CAN YOU DO IT...
...WITH YOUR MIND SO MUDDLED?
...AH. YOU SEE IT ALL, DON'T YOU?
SO CONFIDENT.
YEAH, AND HOW *CAN* HE BE?!
HE'S JUST HAD HIS BUTT HANDED TO HIM BY SOMEONE WHO WASN'T USING FULL STRENGTH!
AS USUAL...
...HE FIGHTS FROM A DISADVANTAGE.

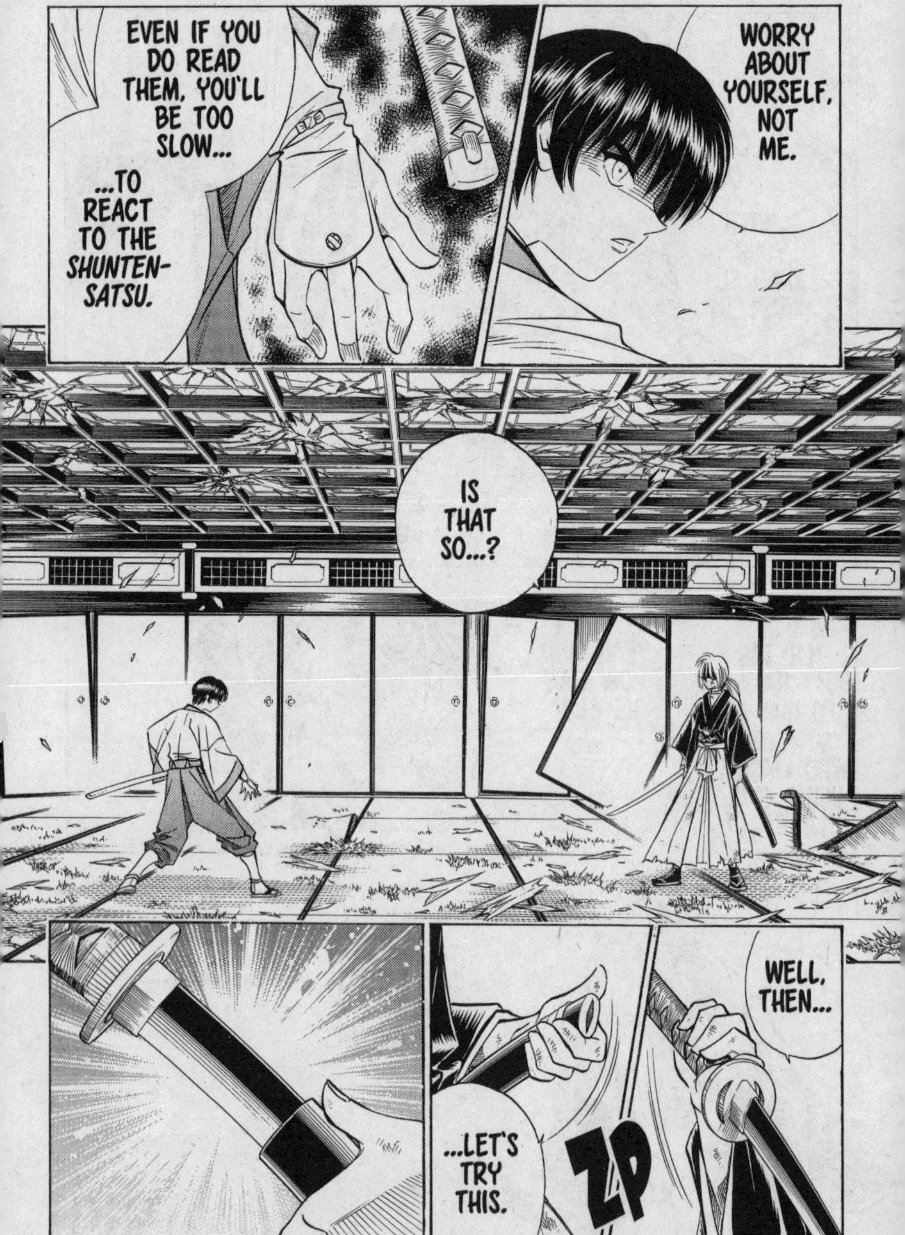
WORRY ABOUT YOURSELF, NOT ME.
EVEN IF YOU DO READ THEM, YOU'LL BE TOO SLOW...
...TO REACT TO THE SHUNTEN-SATSU.
IS THAT SO...?
WELL, THEN...
...LET'S TRY THIS.
ZP

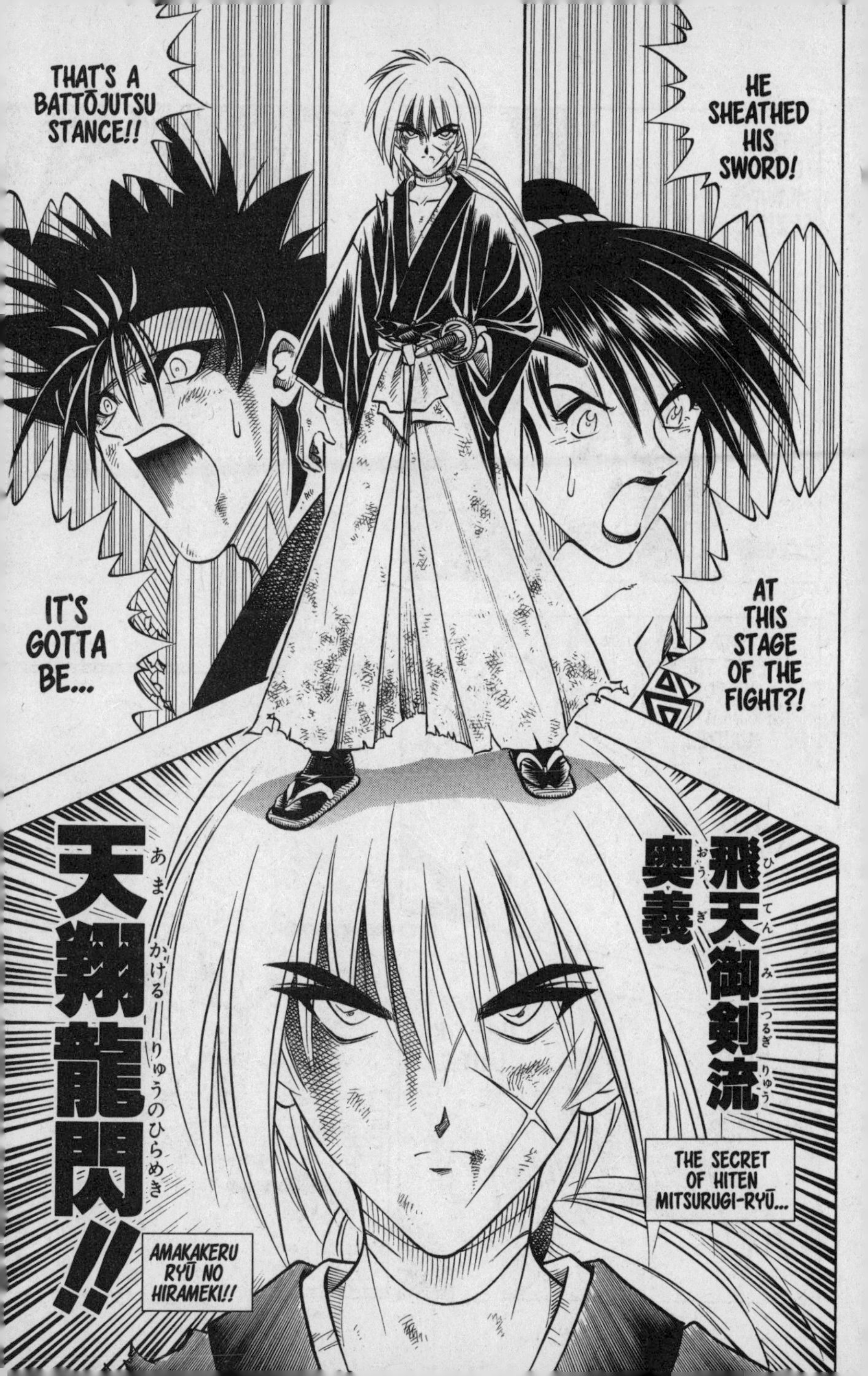
HE SHEATHED HIS SWORD!
THAT'S A BATTŌJUTSU STANCE!!
AT THIS STAGE OF THE FIGHT?!
IT'S GOTTA BE...
飛天御剣流 奥義
THE SECRET OF HITEN MITSURUGI-RYŪ...
天翔龍閃!!
AMAKAKERU RYŪ NO HIRAMEKI!!

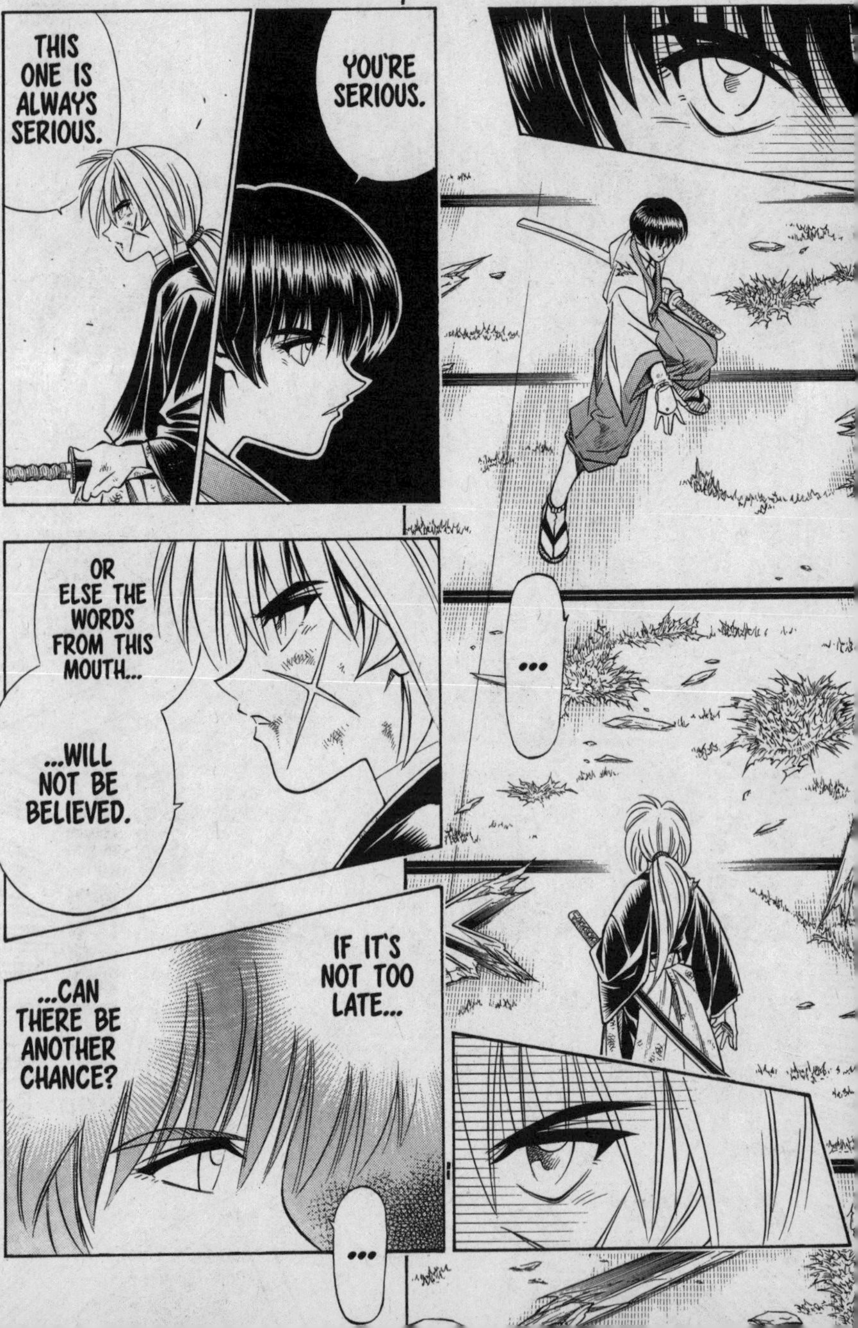
YOU'RE SERIOUS.
THIS ONE IS ALWAYS SERIOUS.
...
OR ELSE THE WORDS FROM THIS MOUTH...
...WILL NOT BE BELIEVED.
IF IT'S NOT TOO LATE...
...CAN THERE BE ANOTHER CHANCE?
...

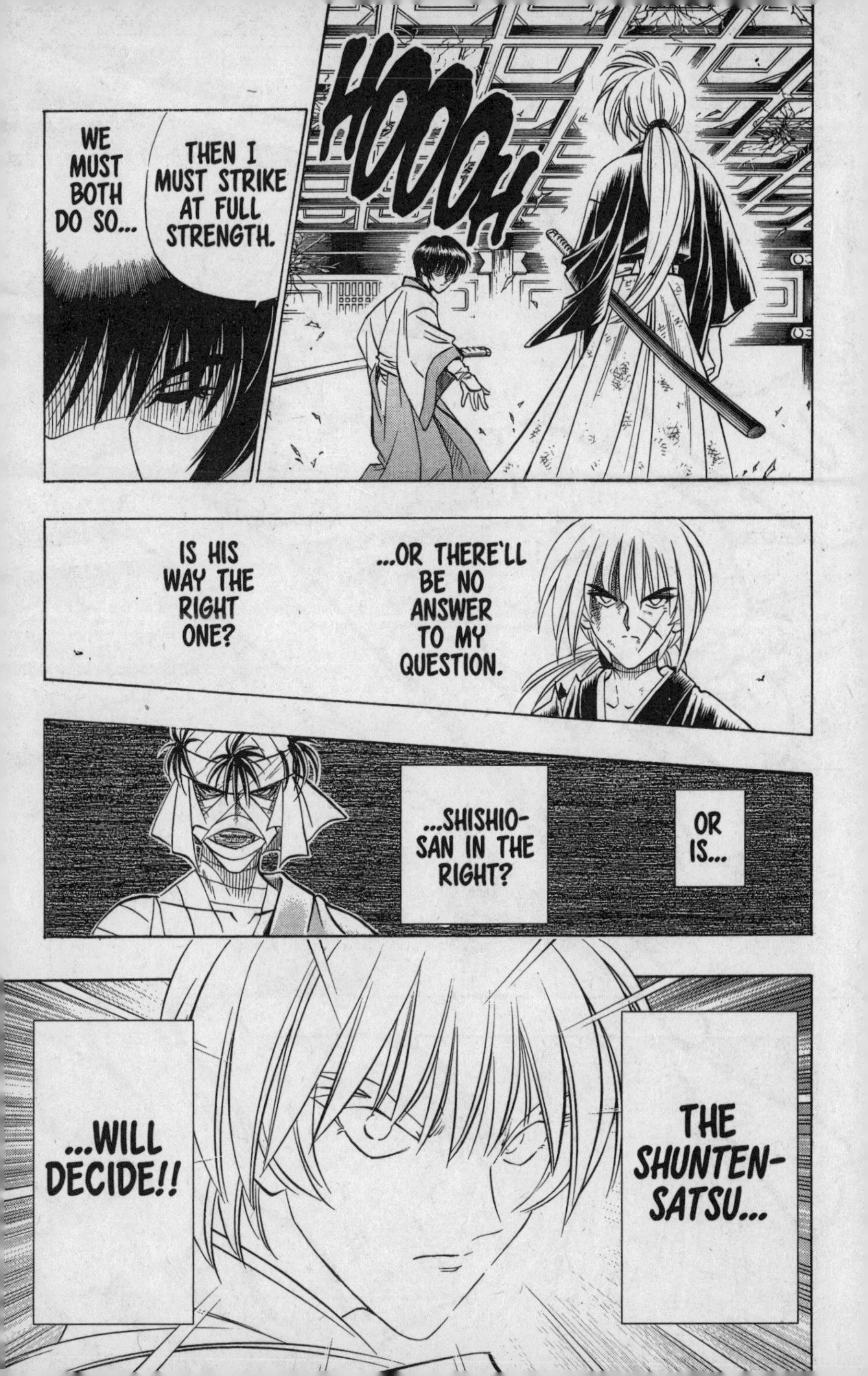
HOOOH
THEN I MUST STRIKE AT FULL STRENGTH.
WE MUST BOTH DO SO...
...OR THERE'LL BE NO ANSWER TO MY QUESTION.
IS HIS WAY THE RIGHT ONE?
OR IS...
...SHISHIO-SAN IN THE RIGHT?
THE SHUNTEN-SATSU...
...WILL DECIDE!!

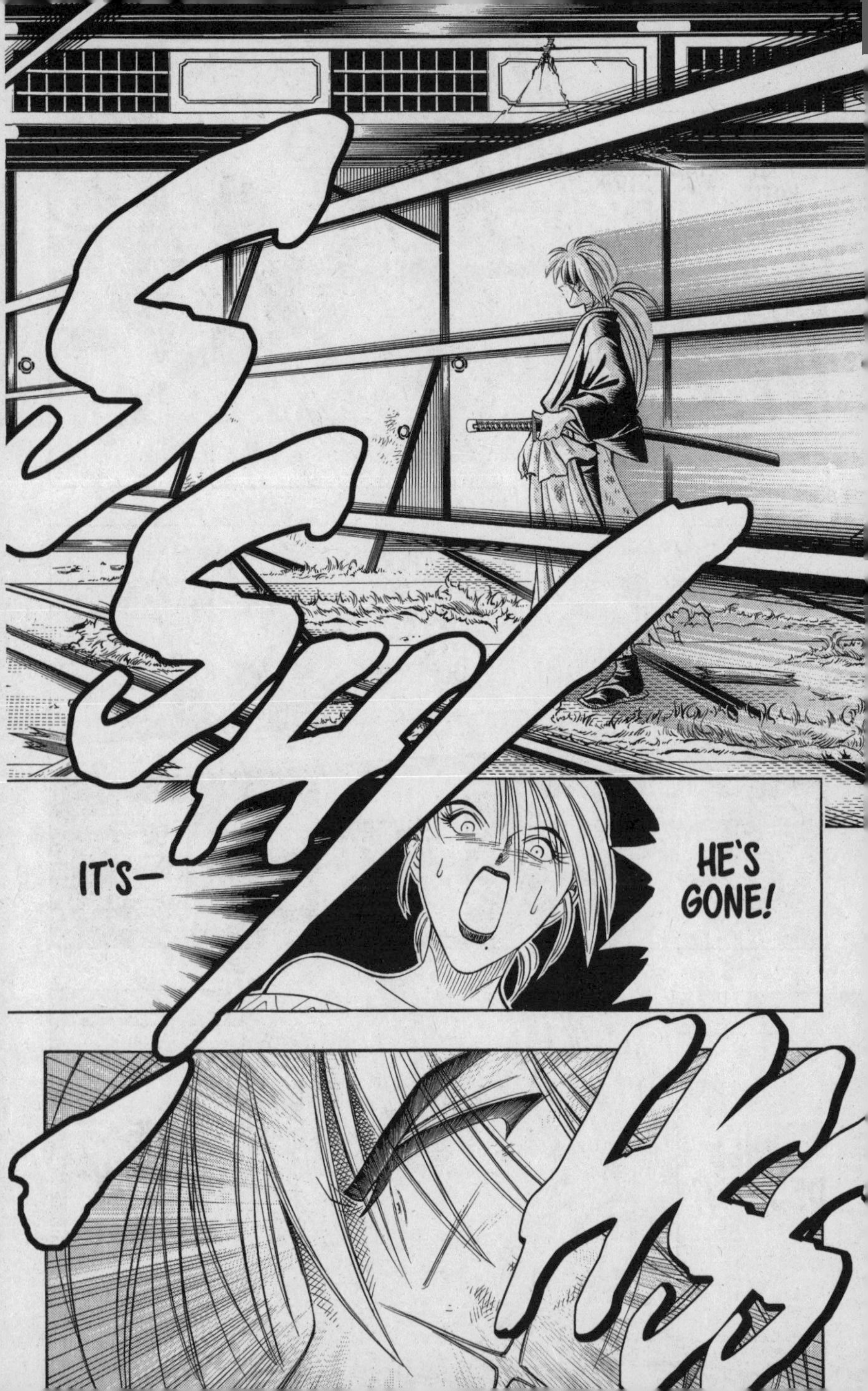
HE'S GONE!
IT'S—

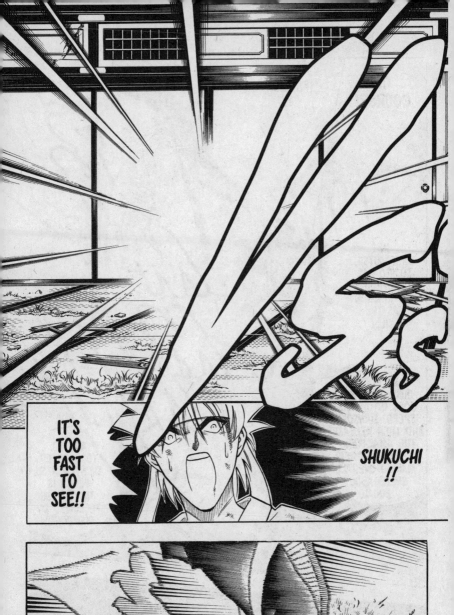

IT'S TOO FAST TO SEE!!

SHUKUCHI !!

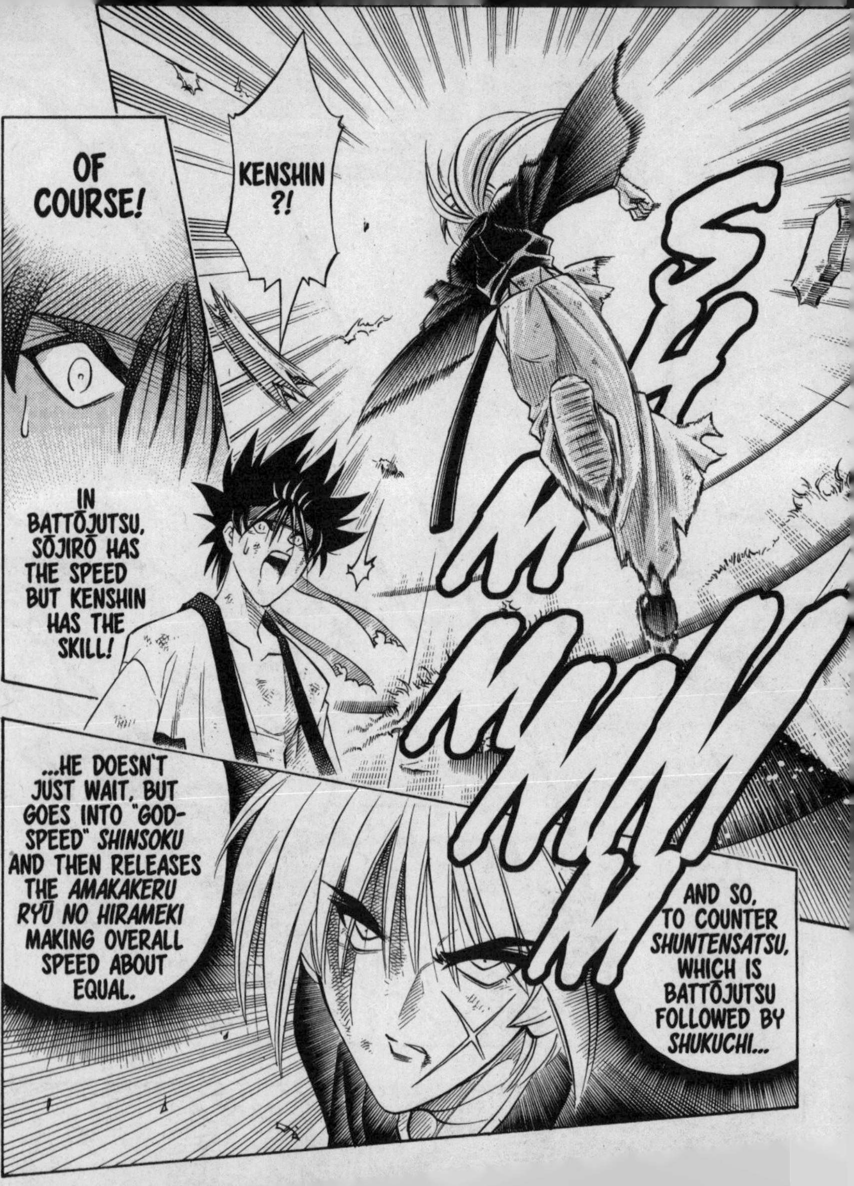
KENSHIN ?!
OF COURSE!
IN BATTŌJUTSU, SŌJIRŌ HAS THE SPEED BUT KENSHIN HAS THE SKILL!
AND SO, TO COUNTER SHUNTENSATSU, WHICH IS BATTŌJUTSU FOLLOWED BY SHUKUCHI...
...HE DOESN'T JUST WAIT, BUT GOES INTO "GOD-SPEED" SHINSOKU AND THEN RELEASES THE AMAKAKERU RYŪ NO HIRAMEKI MAKING OVERALL SPEED ABOUT EQUAL.

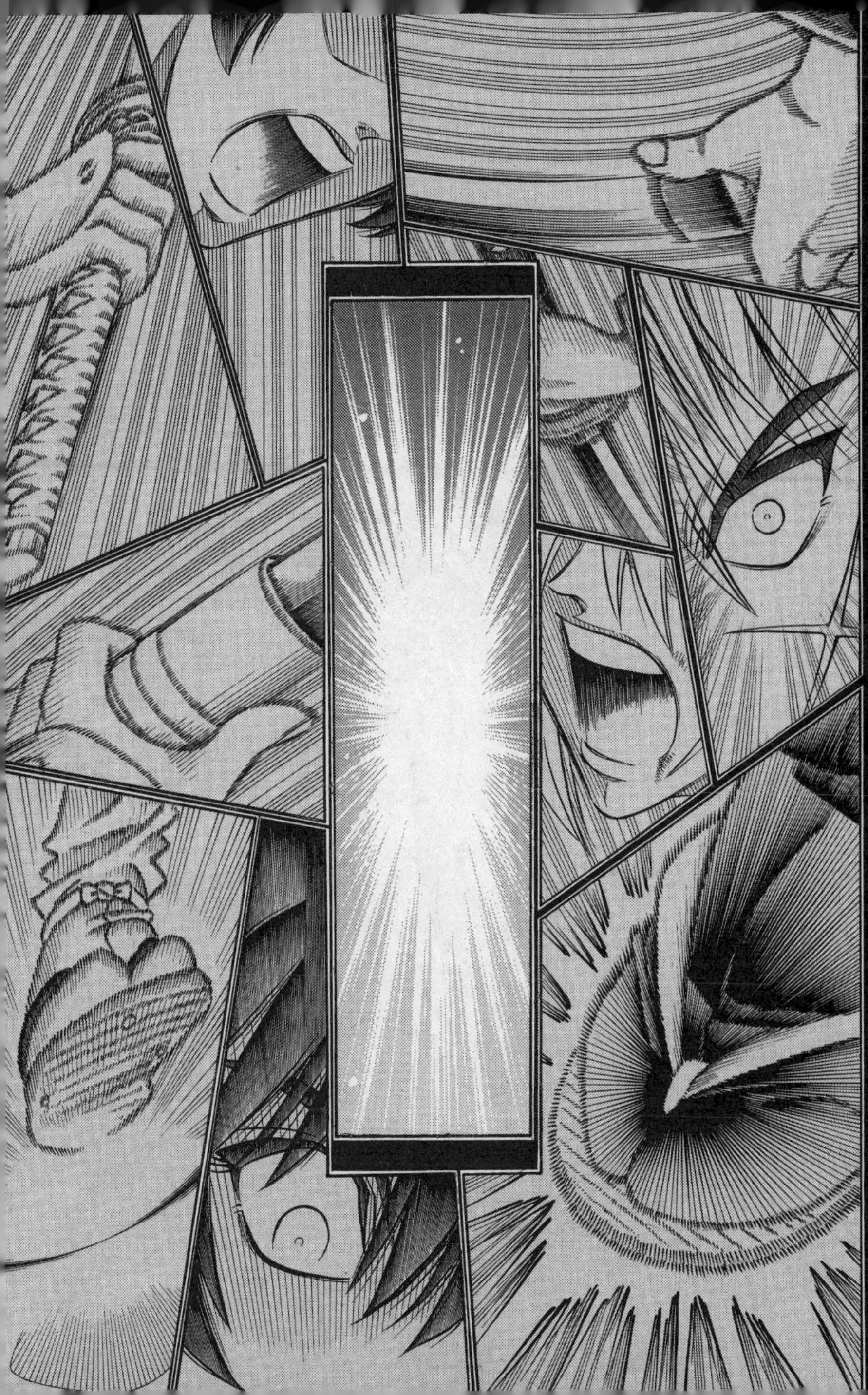

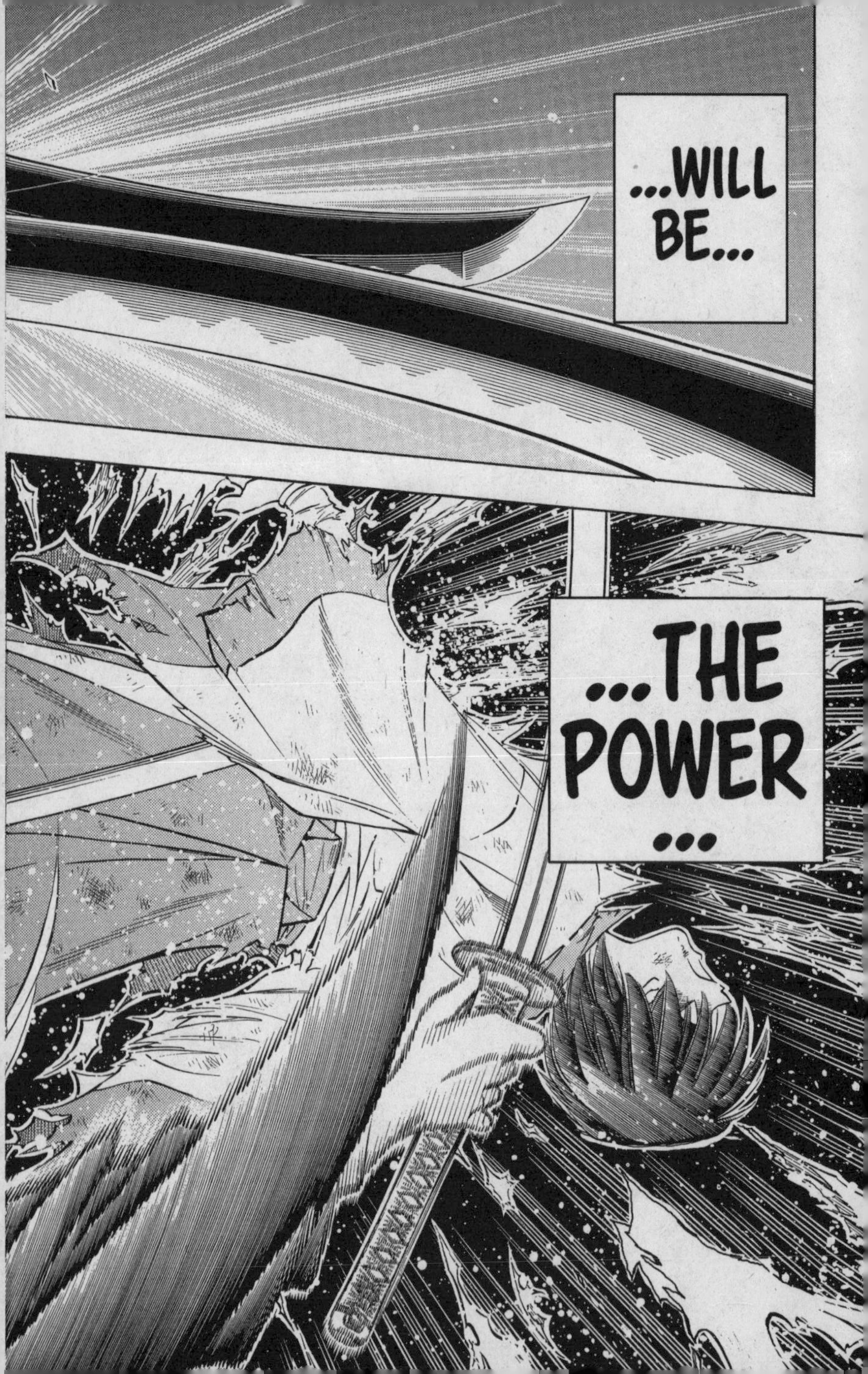
...WILL BE...
...THE POWER ...

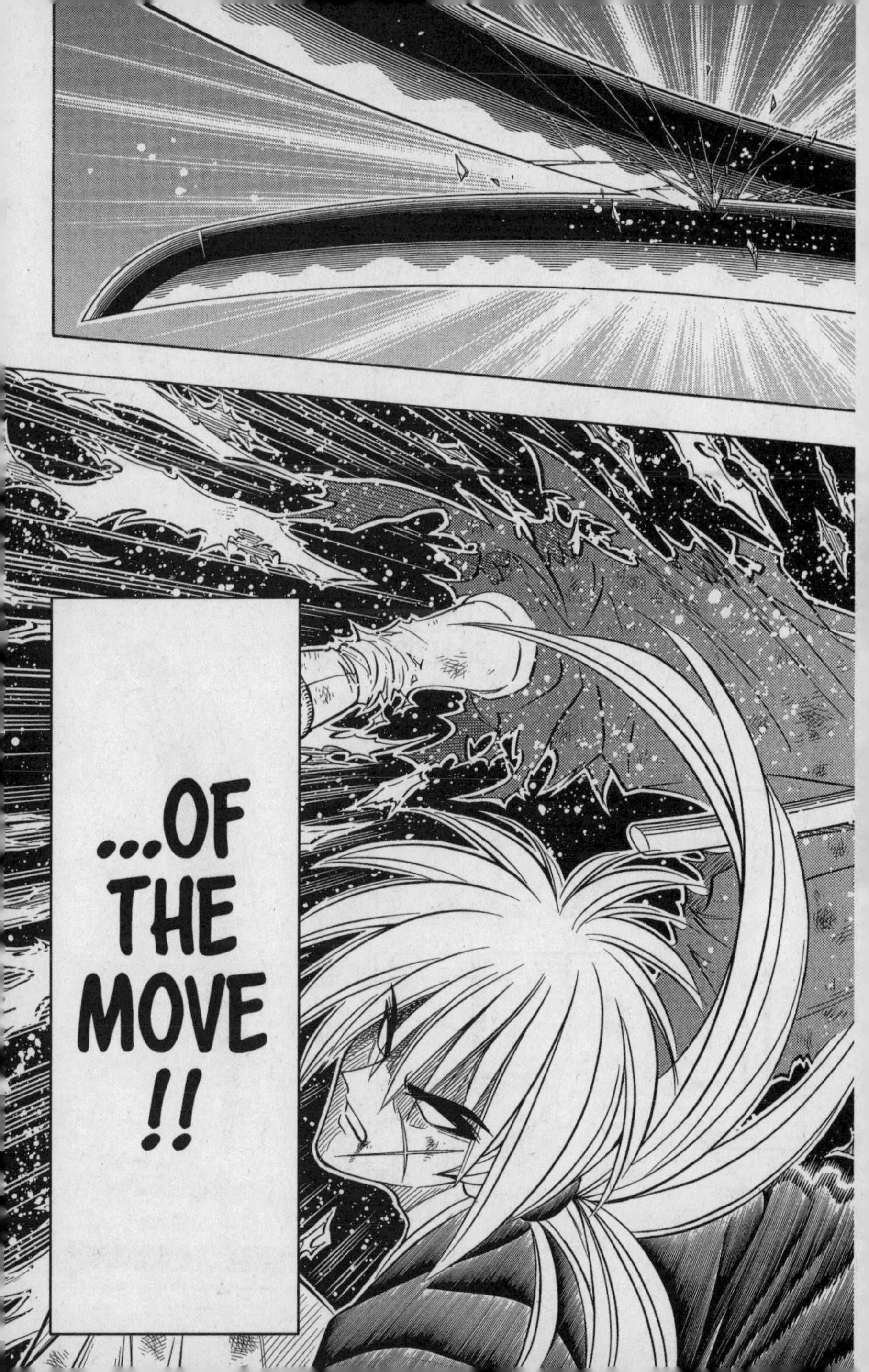
...OF THE MOVE !!

...BARELY.

HH

HH

HEY. YOU ALL RIGHT?

HOW'S SŌJIRŌ?

NOD

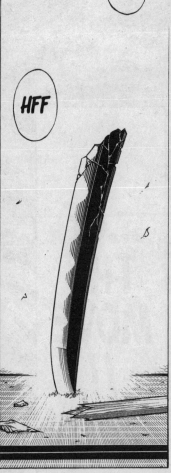

HFF

HFF

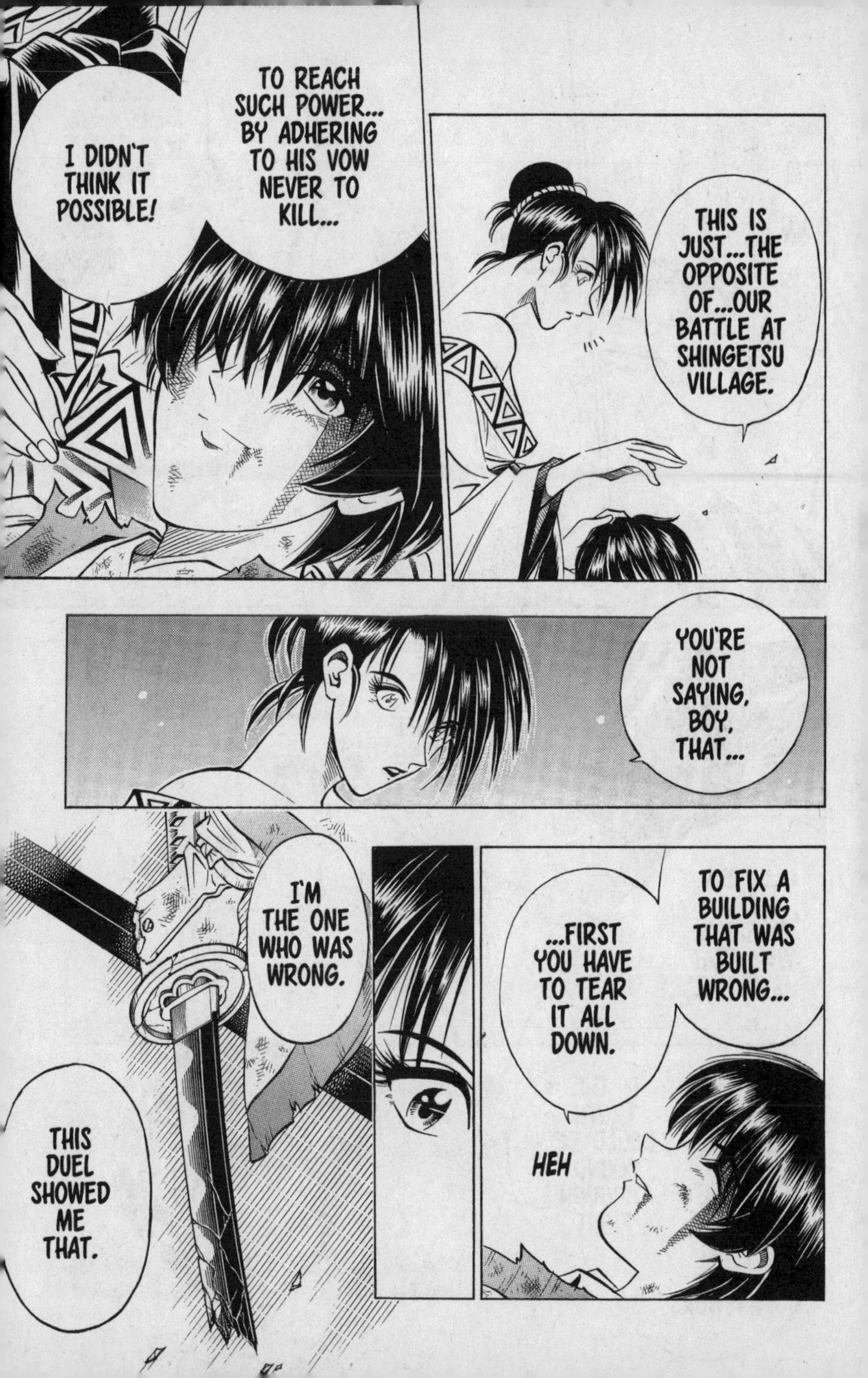
THIS IS JUST...THE OPPOSITE OF...OUR BATTLE AT SHINGETSU VILLAGE.
TO REACH SUCH POWER... BY ADHERING TO HIS VOW NEVER TO KILL...
I DIDN'T THINK IT POSSIBLE!
YOU'RE NOT SAYING, BOY, THAT...
TO FIX A BUILDING THAT WAS BUILT WRONG...
...FIRST YOU HAVE TO TEAR IT ALL DOWN.
HEH
I'M THE ONE WHO WAS WRONG.
THIS DUEL SHOWED ME THAT.

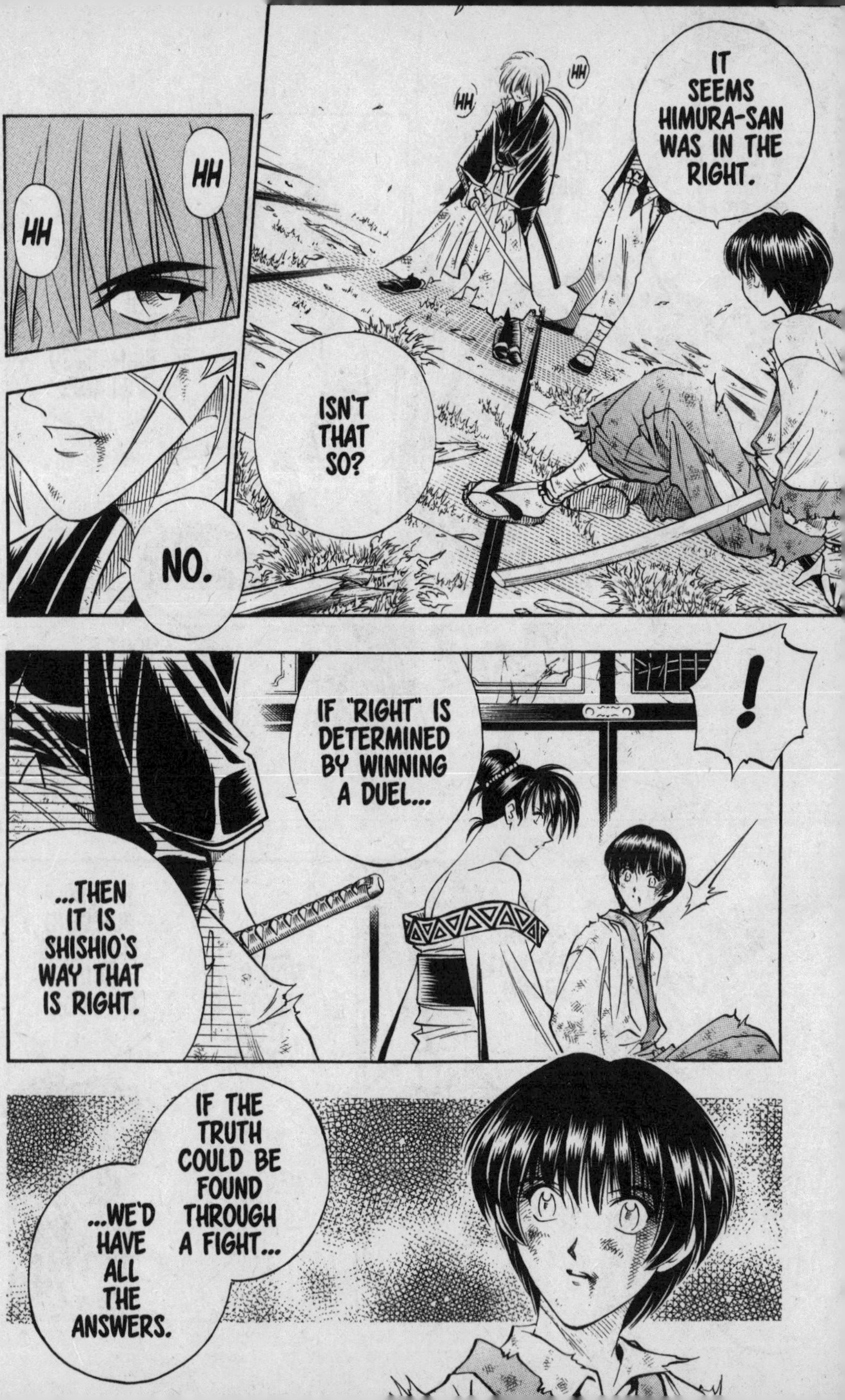
HH
HH
IT SEEMS HIMURA-SAN WAS IN THE RIGHT.
ISN'T THAT SO?
HH
HH
NO.
!
IF "RIGHT" IS DETERMINED BY WINNING A DUEL...
...THEN IT IS SHISHIO'S WAY THAT IS RIGHT.
IF THE TRUTH COULD BE FOUND THROUGH A FIGHT...
...WE'D HAVE ALL THE ANSWERS.

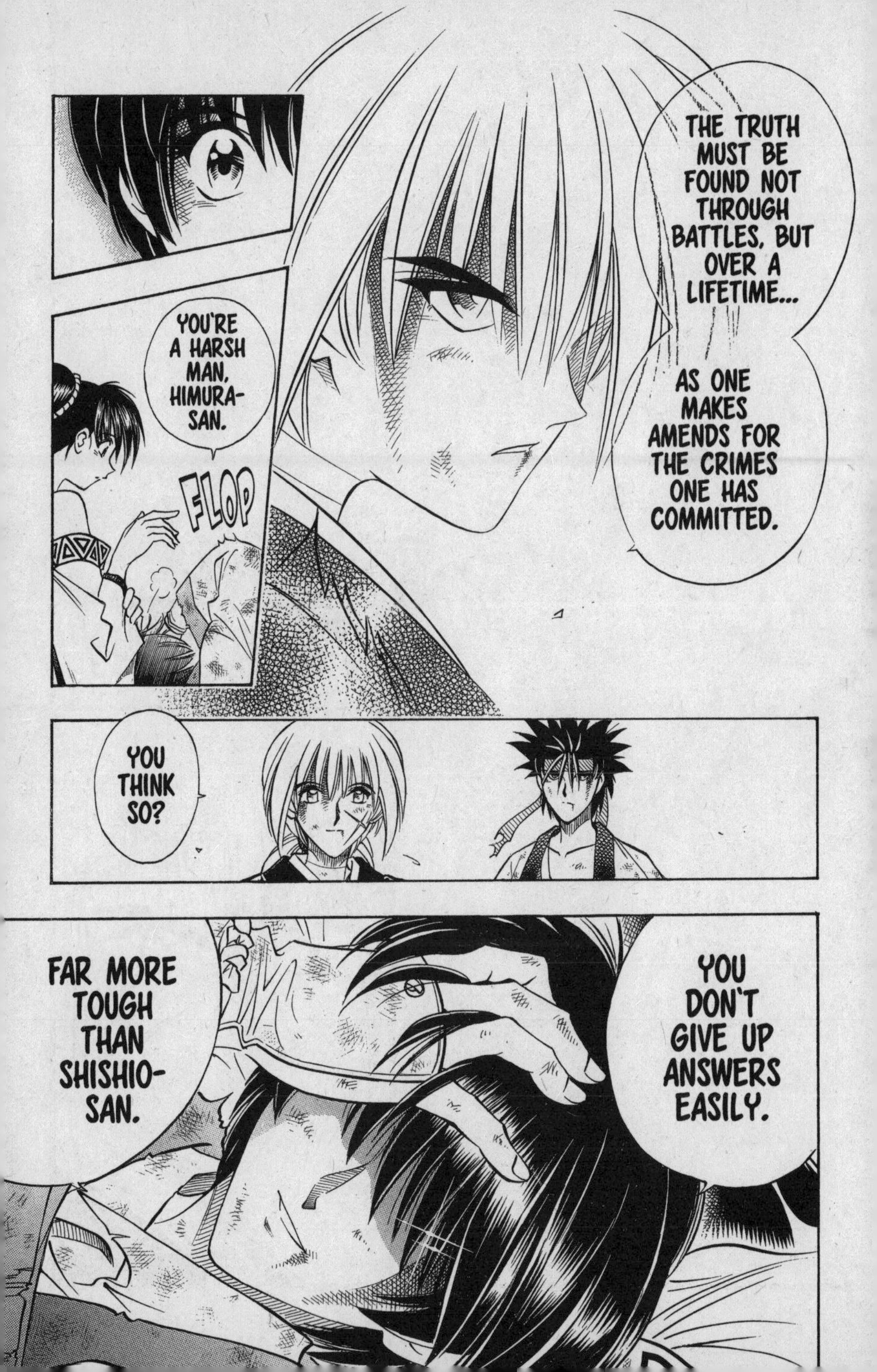
THE TRUTH MUST BE FOUND NOT THROUGH BATTLES, BUT OVER A LIFETIME...
AS ONE MAKES AMENDS FOR THE CRIMES ONE HAS COMMITTED.
YOU'RE A HARSH MAN, HIMURA-SAN.
FLOP
YOU THINK SO?
YOU DON'T GIVE UP ANSWERS EASILY.
FAR MORE TOUGH THAN SHISHIO-SAN.

Rurouni Kenshin

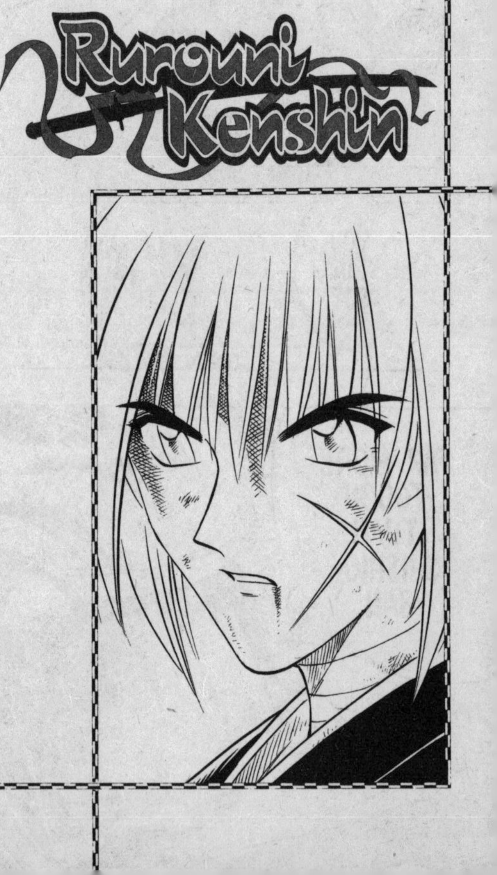

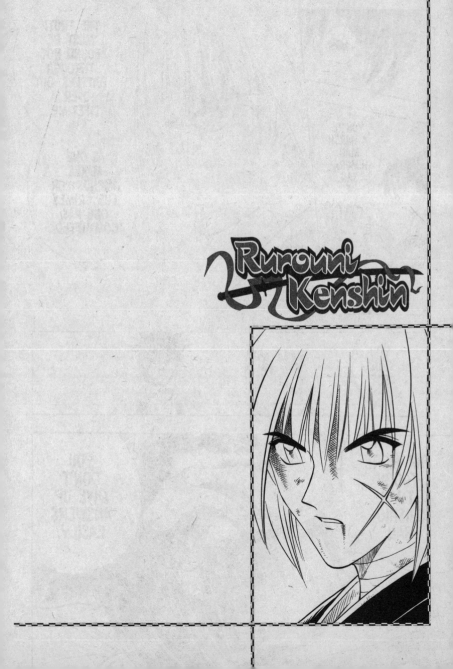

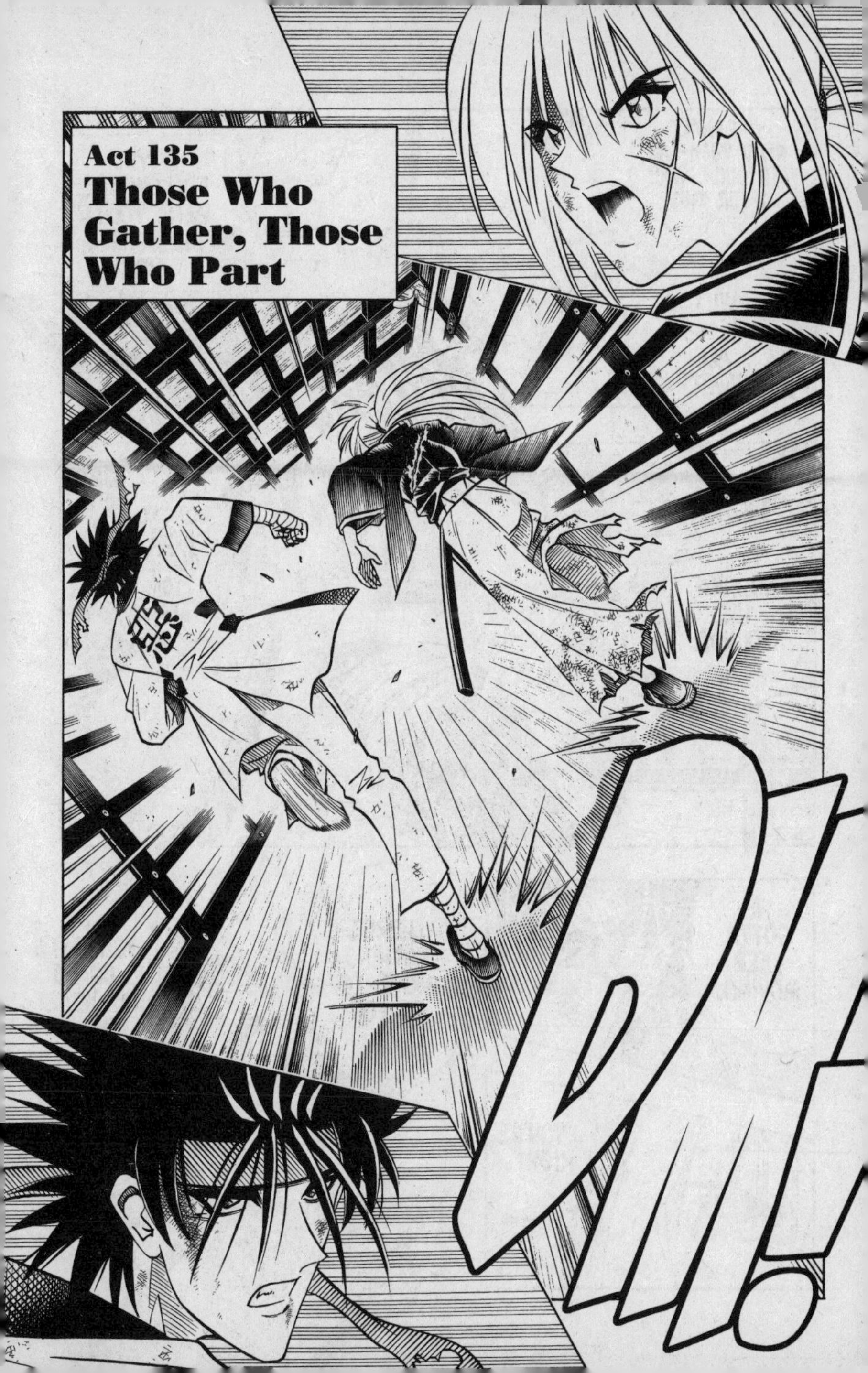
Act 135
Those Who Gather, Those Who Part

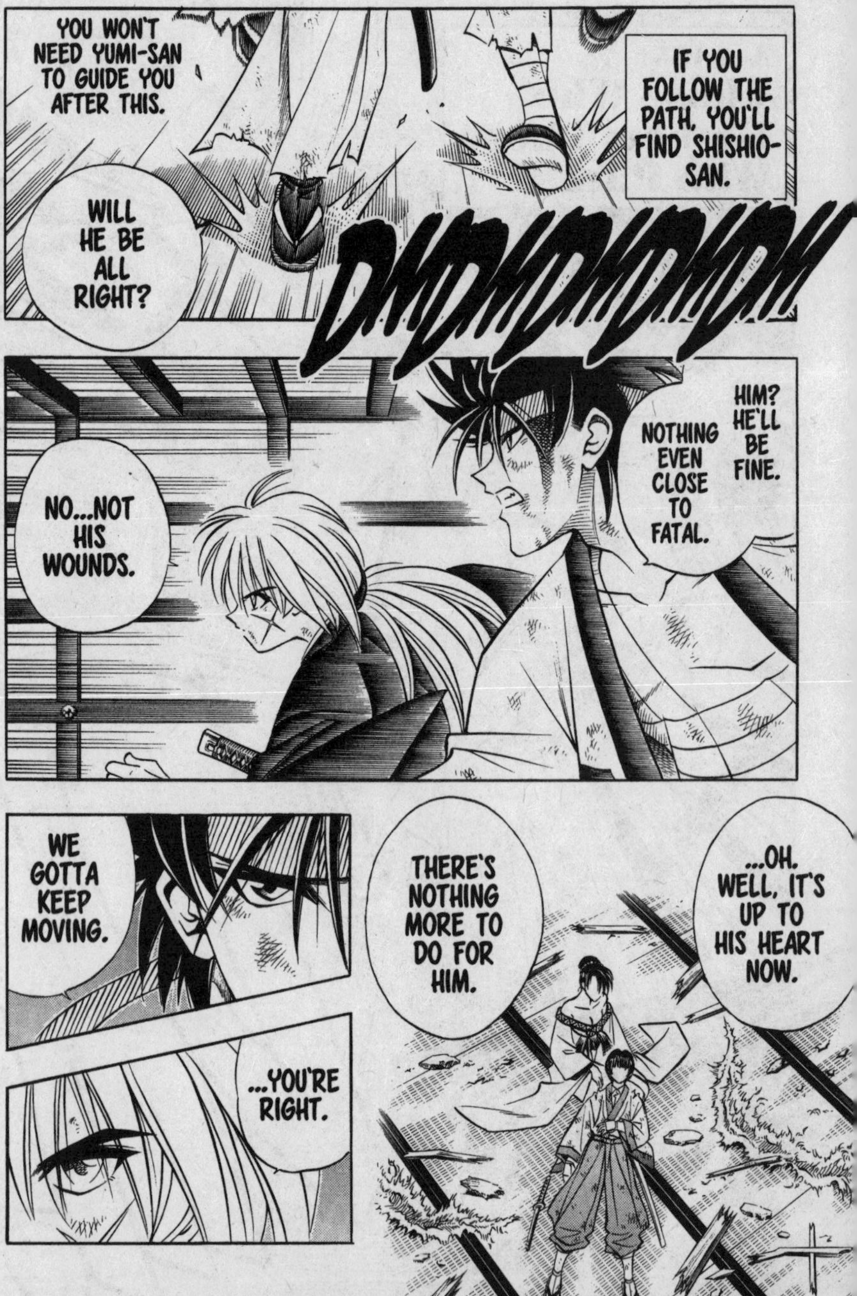
IF YOU FOLLOW THE PATH, YOU'LL FIND SHISHIO-SAN.
YOU WON'T NEED YUMI-SAN TO GUIDE YOU AFTER THIS.
WILL HE BE ALL RIGHT?
HIM? HE'LL BE FINE.
NOTHING EVEN CLOSE TO FATAL.
NO...NOT HIS WOUNDS.
...OH. WELL, IT'S UP TO HIS HEART NOW.
THERE'S NOTHING MORE TO DO FOR HIM.
WE GOTTA KEEP MOVING.
...YOU'RE RIGHT.

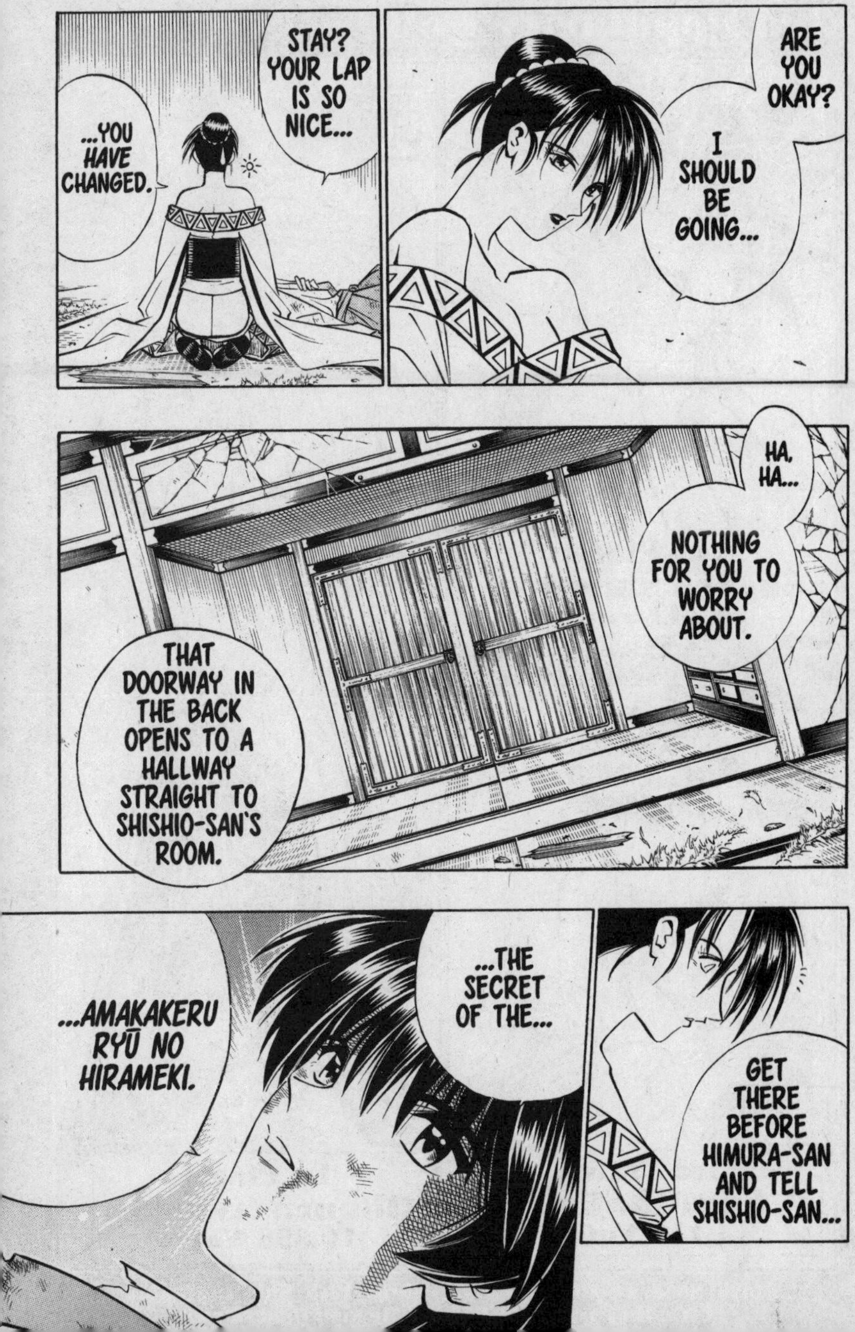
ARE YOU OKAY?
I SHOULD BE GOING...
STAY? YOUR LAP IS SO NICE...
...YOU HAVE CHANGED.
HA, HA...
NOTHING FOR YOU TO WORRY ABOUT.
THAT DOORWAY IN THE BACK OPENS TO A HALLWAY STRAIGHT TO SHISHIO-SAN'S ROOM.
GET THERE BEFORE HIMURA-SAN AND TELL SHISHIO-SAN...
...THE SECRET OF THE...
...AMAKAKERU RYŪ NO HIRAMEKI.

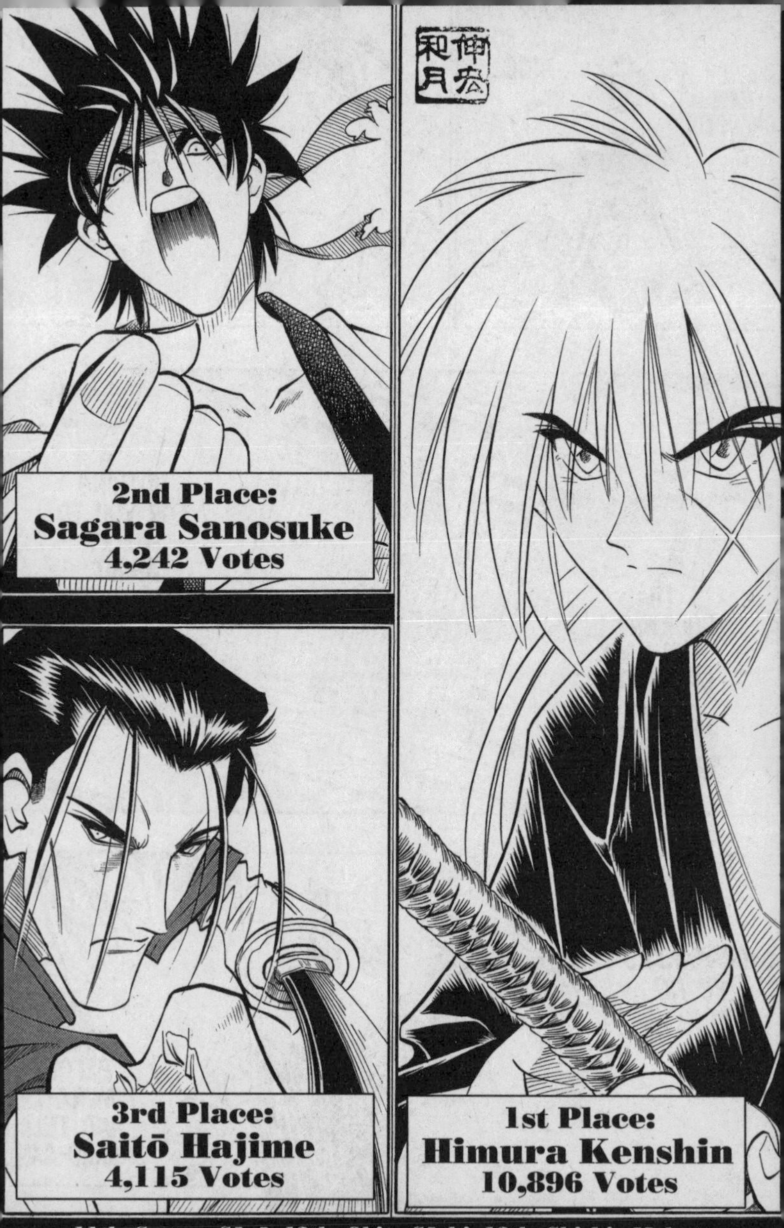
1st Place:
Himura Kenshin
10,896 Votes
2nd Place:
Sagara Sanosuke
4,242 Votes
3rd Place:
Saitō Hajime
4,115 Votes

11th: Sagara Sōzō 12th: Okita Sōshi 13th: Shishio Makoto
14th: Han'nya 15th: Takani Megumi (and so on...)

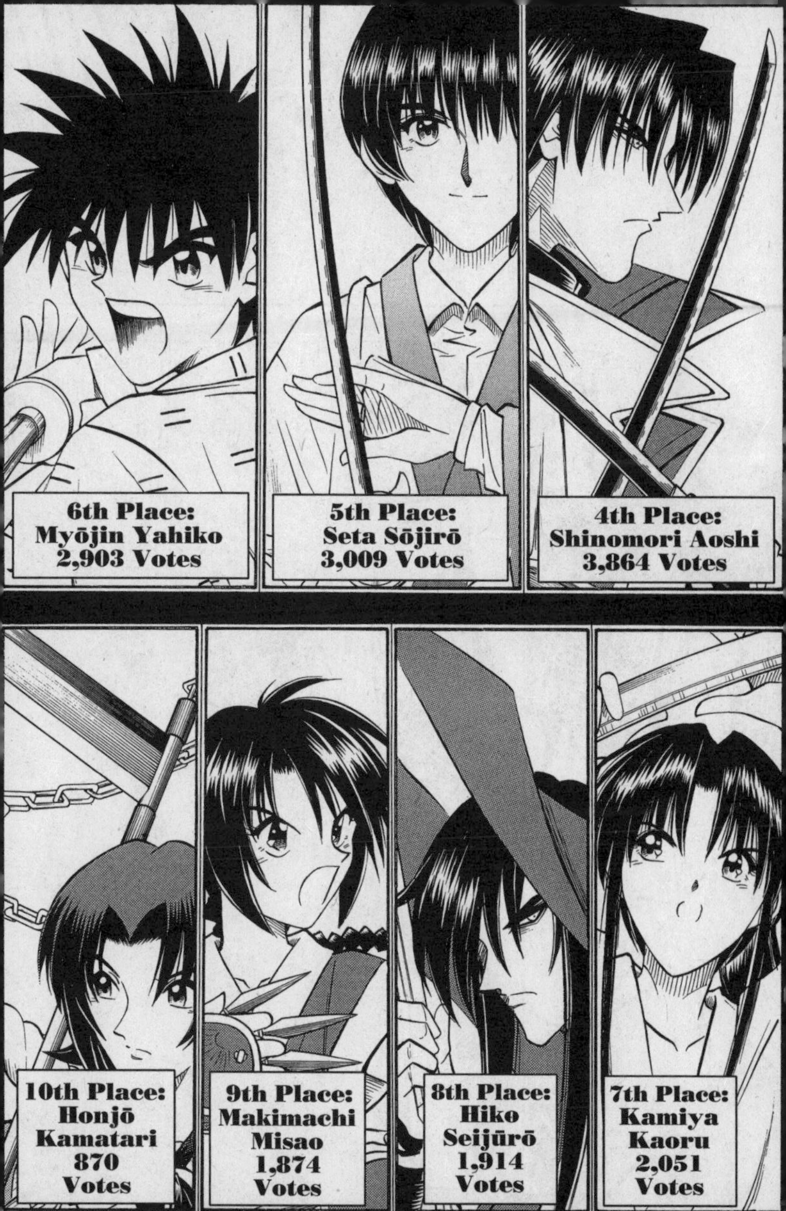
4th Place: Shinomori Aoshi 3,864 Votes
5th Place: Seta Sōjirō 3,009 Votes
6th Place: Myōjin Yahiko 2,903 Votes
7th Place: Kamiya Kaoru 2,051 Votes
8th Place: Hiko Seijūrō 1,914 Votes
9th Place: Makimachi Misao 1,874 Votes
10th Place: Honjō Kamatari 870 Votes

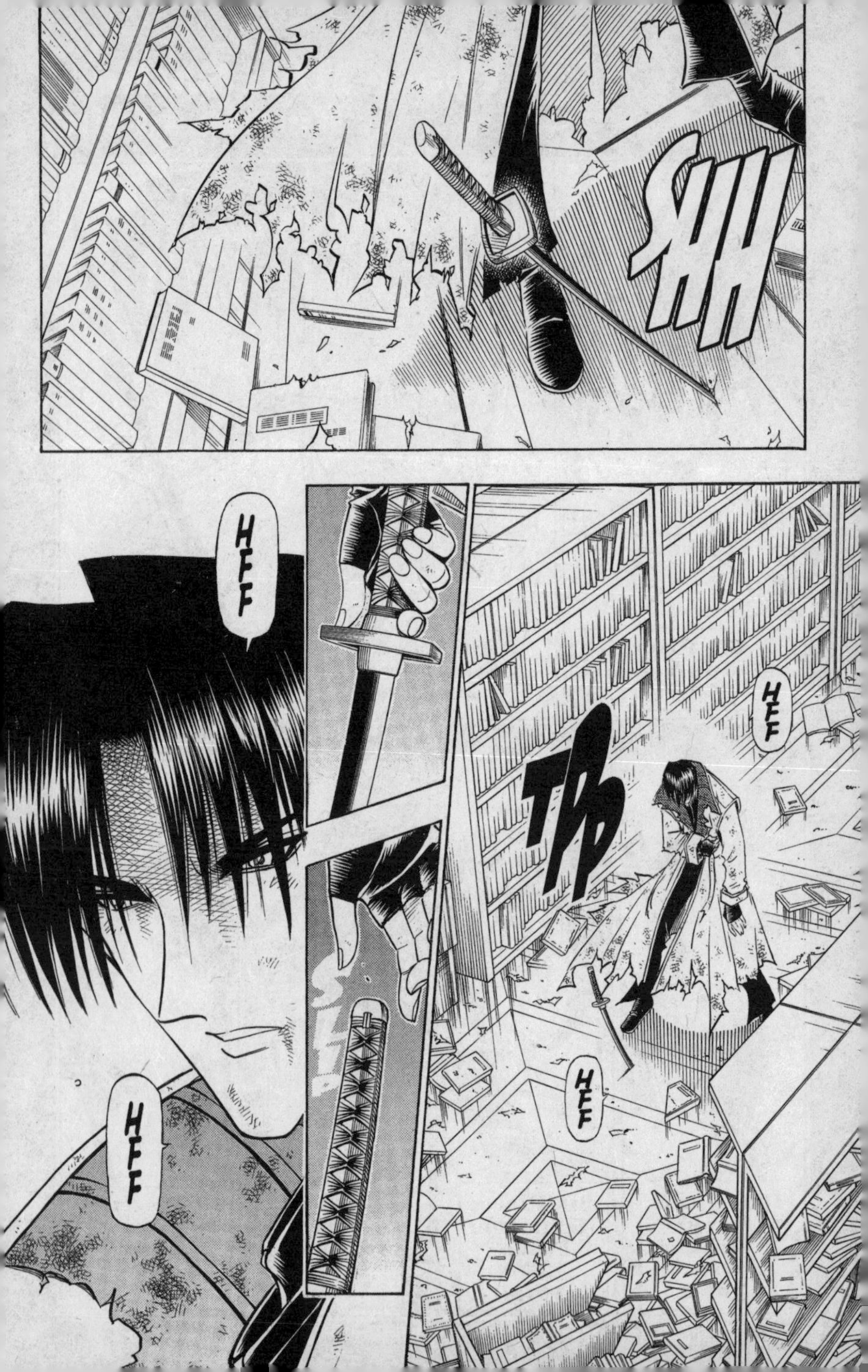
SHH
HFF
TP
HFF
HFF
HFF

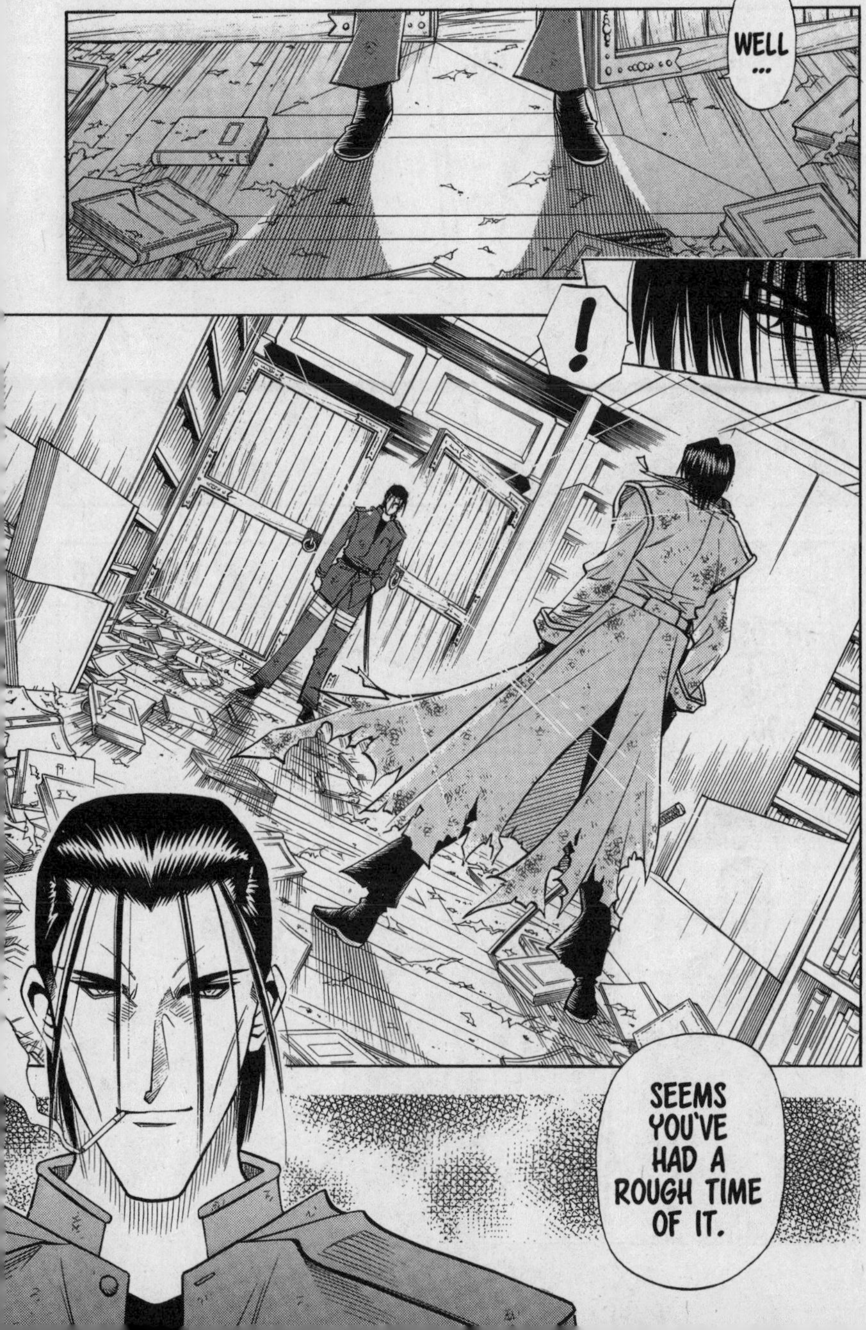
WELL...
!
SEEMS YOU'VE HAD A ROUGH TIME OF IT.

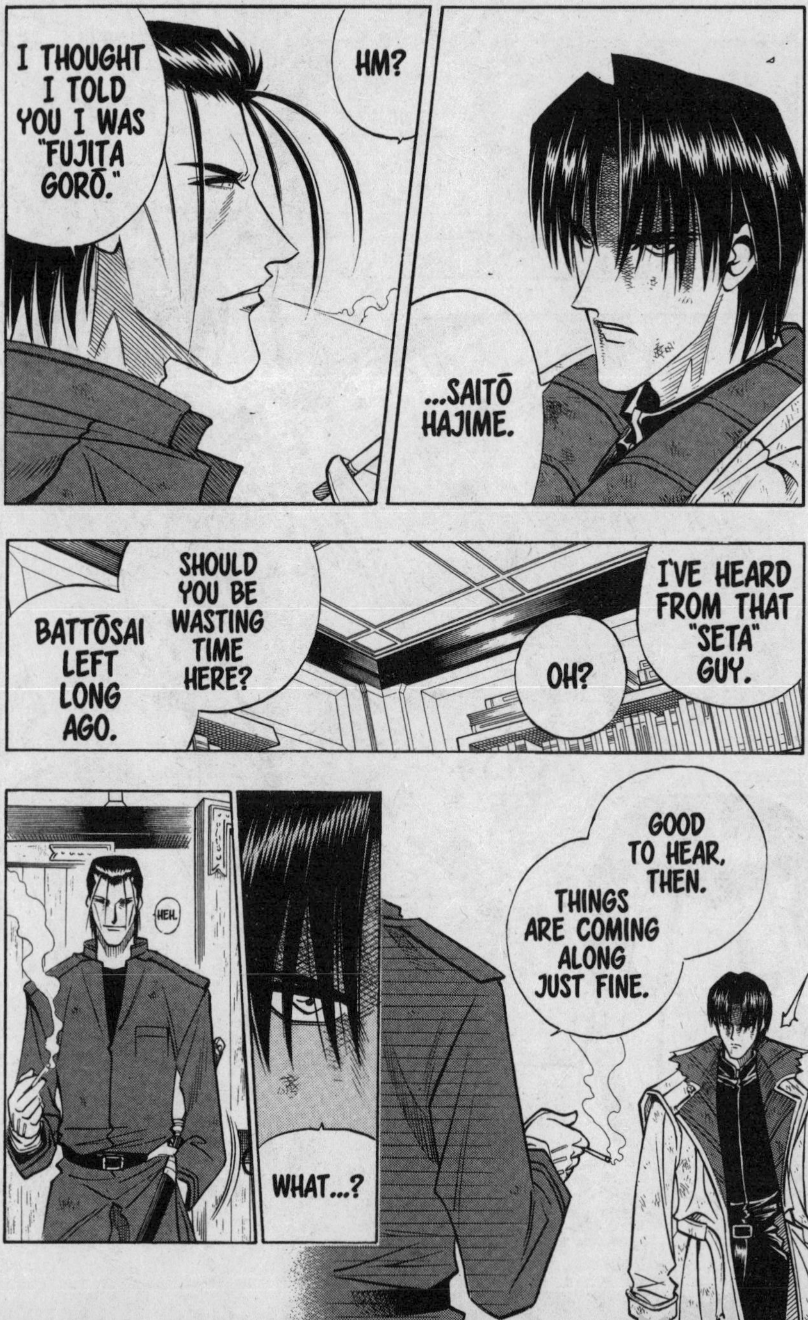
...SAITŌ HAJIME.
HM?
I THOUGHT I TOLD YOU I WAS "FUJITA GORŌ."
I'VE HEARD FROM THAT "SETA" GUY.
OH?
SHOULD YOU BE WASTING TIME HERE?
BATTŌSAI LEFT LONG AGO.
GOOD TO HEAR, THEN.
THINGS ARE COMING ALONG JUST FINE.
WHAT...?
HEH.

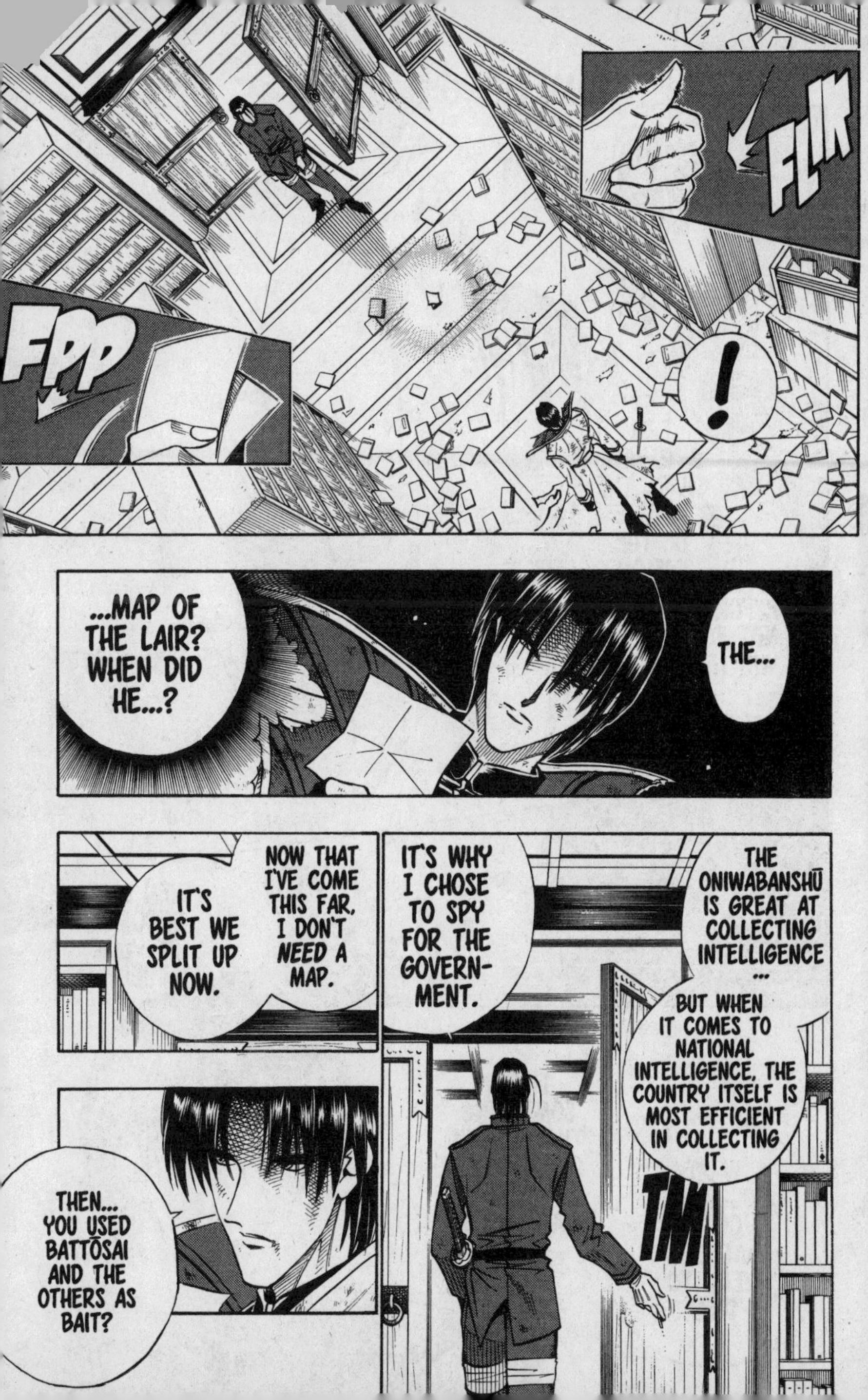
FLIK
!
FPP
THE...
...MAP OF THE LAIR? WHEN DID HE...?
THE ONIWABANSHŪ IS GREAT AT COLLECTING INTELLIGENCE ...
BUT WHEN IT COMES TO NATIONAL INTELLIGENCE, THE COUNTRY ITSELF IS MOST EFFICIENT IN COLLECTING IT.
IT'S WHY I CHOSE TO SPY FOR THE GOVERNMENT.
TM
NOW THAT I'VE COME THIS FAR, I DON'T NEED A MAP.
IT'S BEST WE SPLIT UP NOW.
THEN... YOU USED BATTŌSAI AND THE OTHERS AS BAIT?

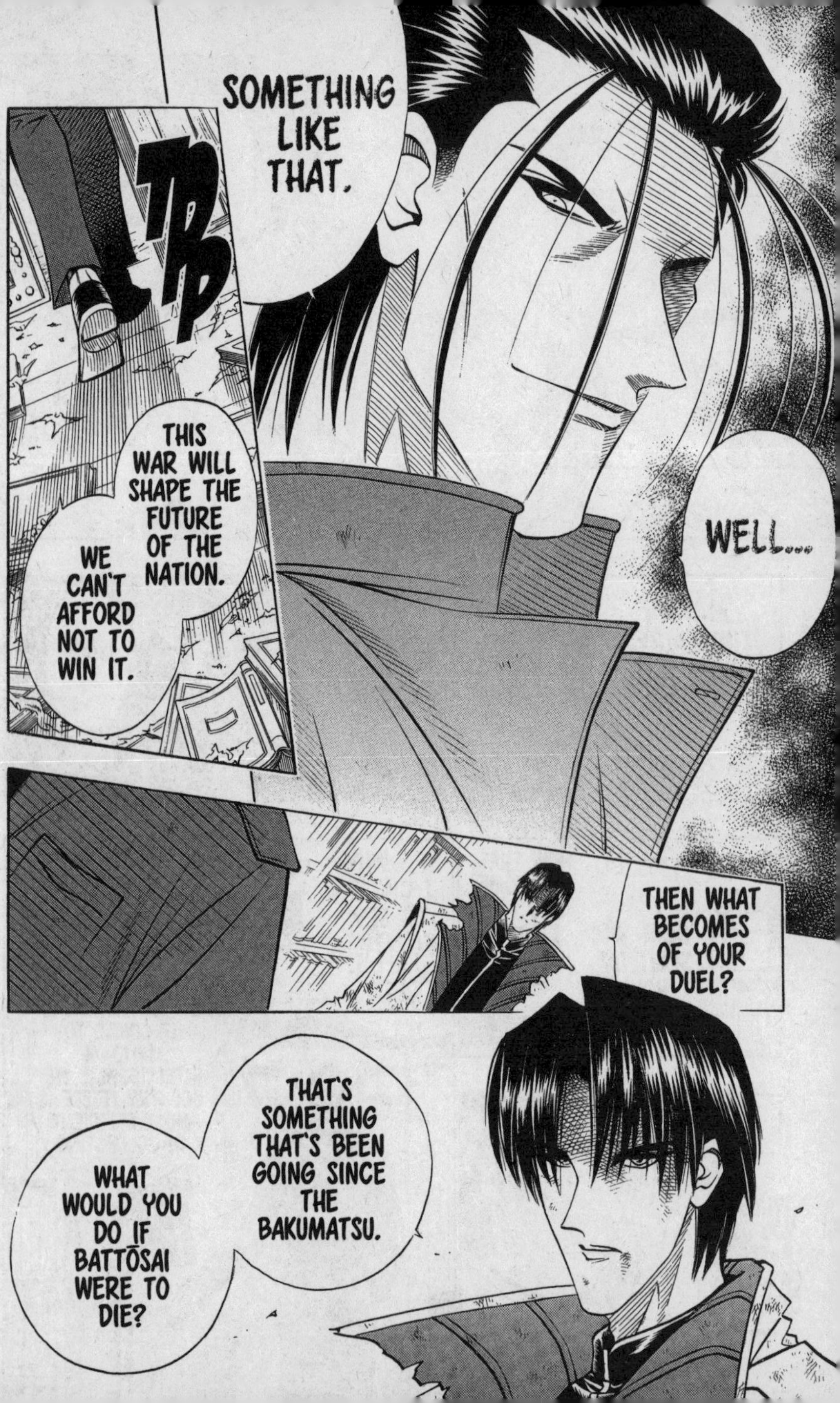
WELL...
SOMETHING LIKE THAT.
TP
THIS WAR WILL SHAPE THE FUTURE OF THE NATION.
WE CAN'T AFFORD NOT TO WIN IT.
THEN WHAT BECOMES OF YOUR DUEL?
THAT'S SOMETHING THAT'S BEEN GOING SINCE THE BAKUMATSU.
WHAT WOULD YOU DO IF BATTŌSAI WERE TO DIE?

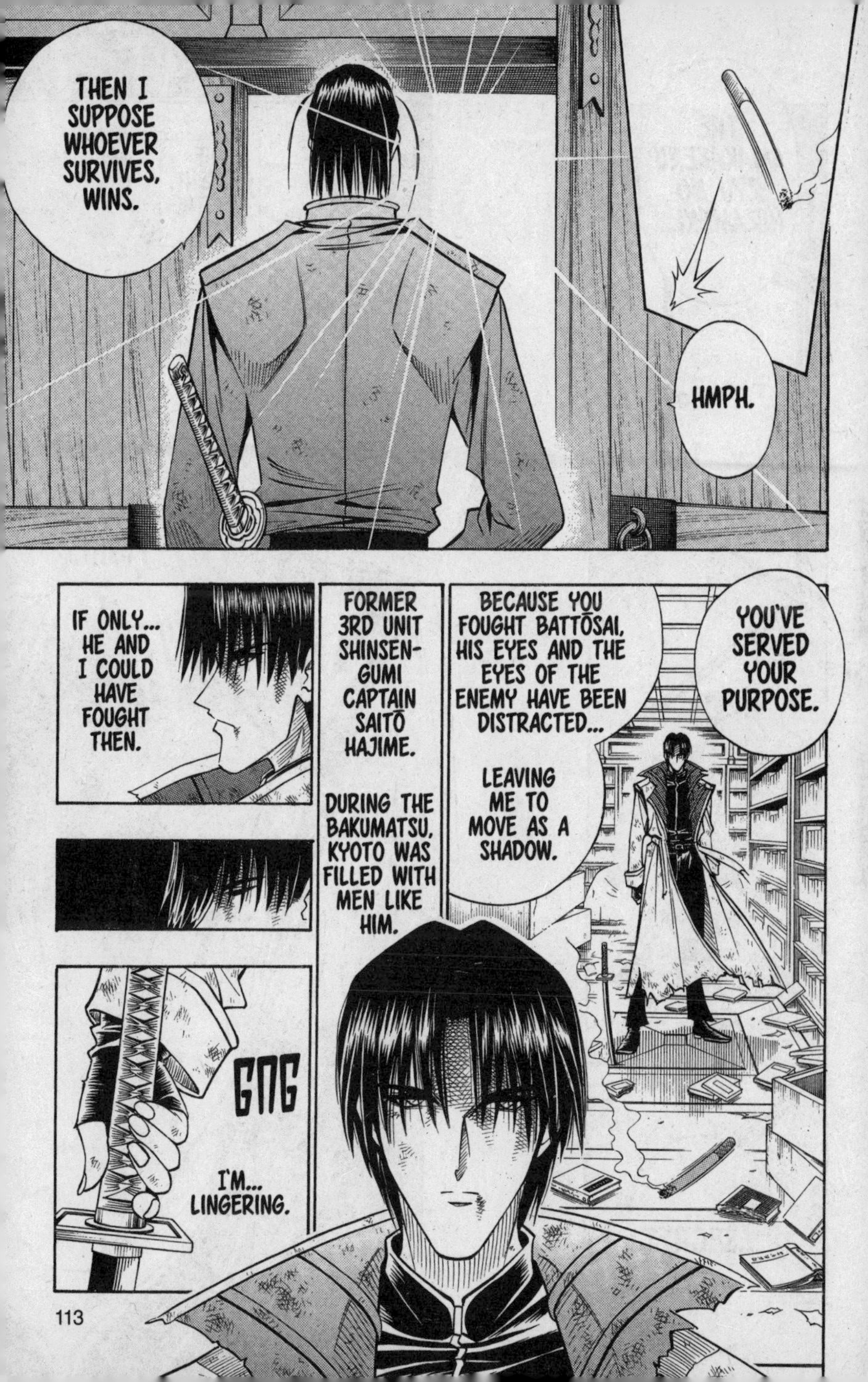
THEN I SUPPOSE WHOEVER SURVIVES, WINS.
HMPH.
YOU'VE SERVED YOUR PURPOSE.
BECAUSE YOU FOUGHT BATTŌSAI, HIS EYES AND THE EYES OF THE ENEMY HAVE BEEN DISTRACTED...
LEAVING ME TO MOVE AS A SHADOW.
FORMER 3RD UNIT SHINSEN-GUMI CAPTAIN SAITŌ HAJIME.
DURING THE BAKUMATSU, KYOTO WAS FILLED WITH MEN LIKE HIM.
IF ONLY... HE AND I COULD HAVE FOUGHT THEN.
GNG
I'M... LINGERING.

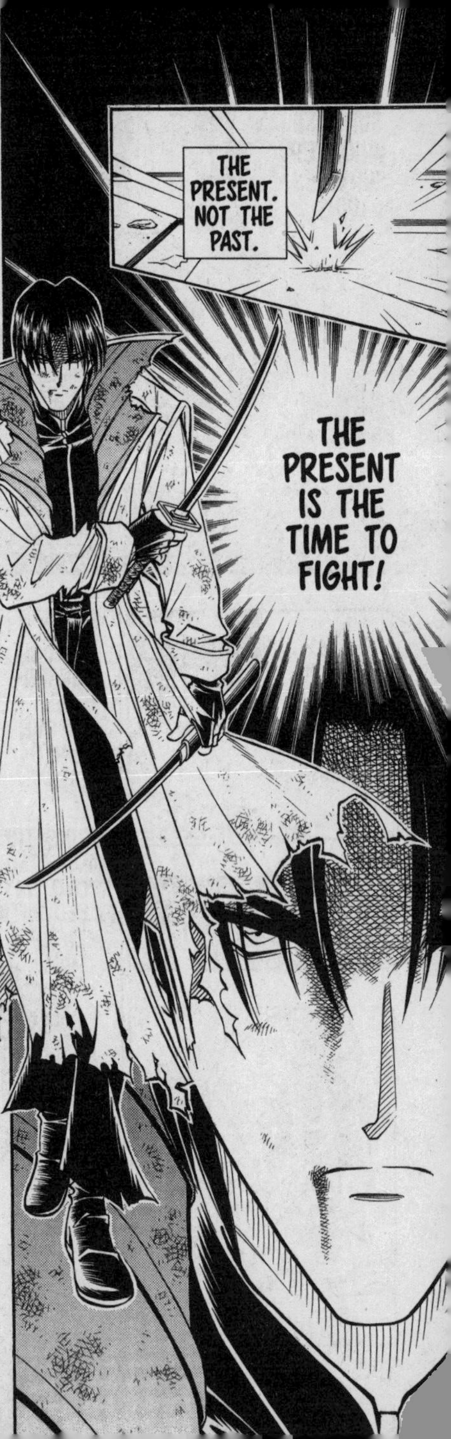
THE PRESENT. NOT THE PAST.
THE PRESENT IS THE TIME TO FIGHT!
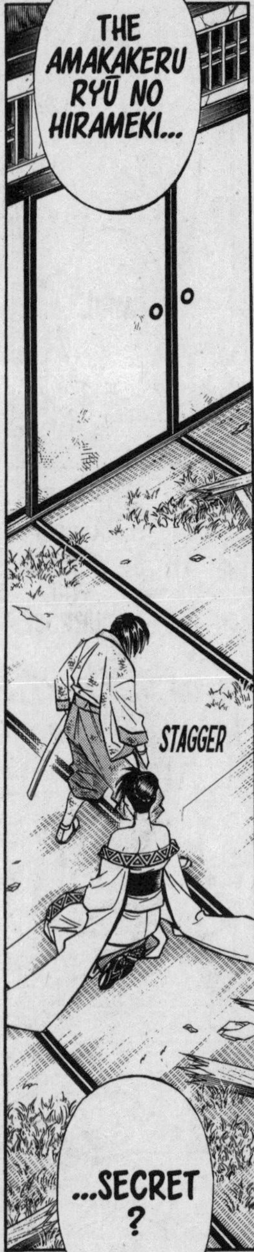
THE AMAKAKERU RYŪ NO HIRAMEKI...
STAGGER
...SECRET?

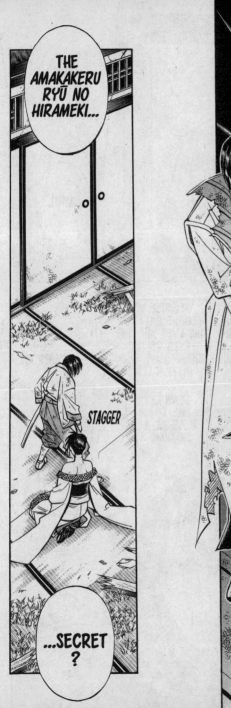

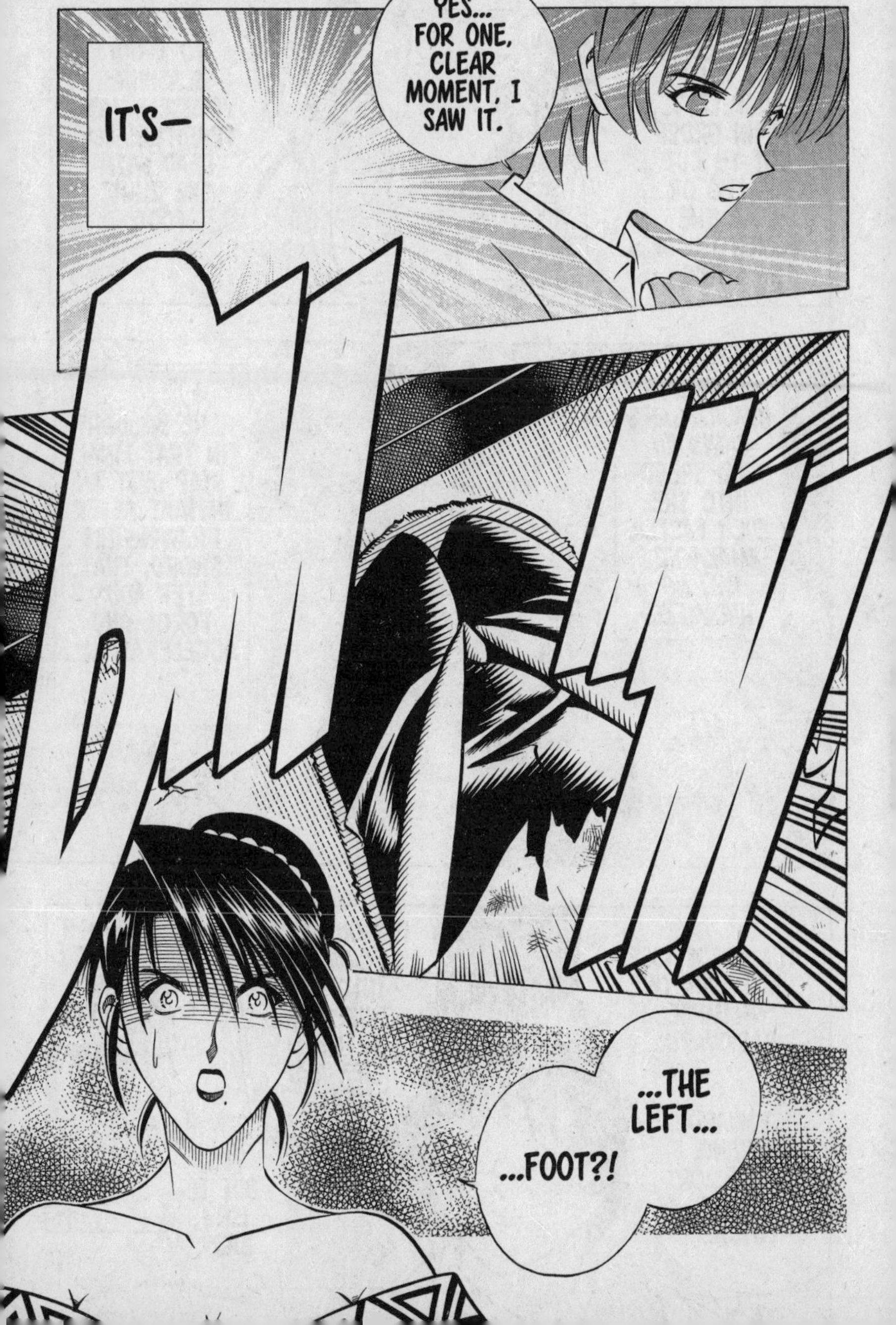
YES... FOR ONE, CLEAR MOMENT, I SAW IT.
IT'S—
...THE LEFT... ...FOOT?!

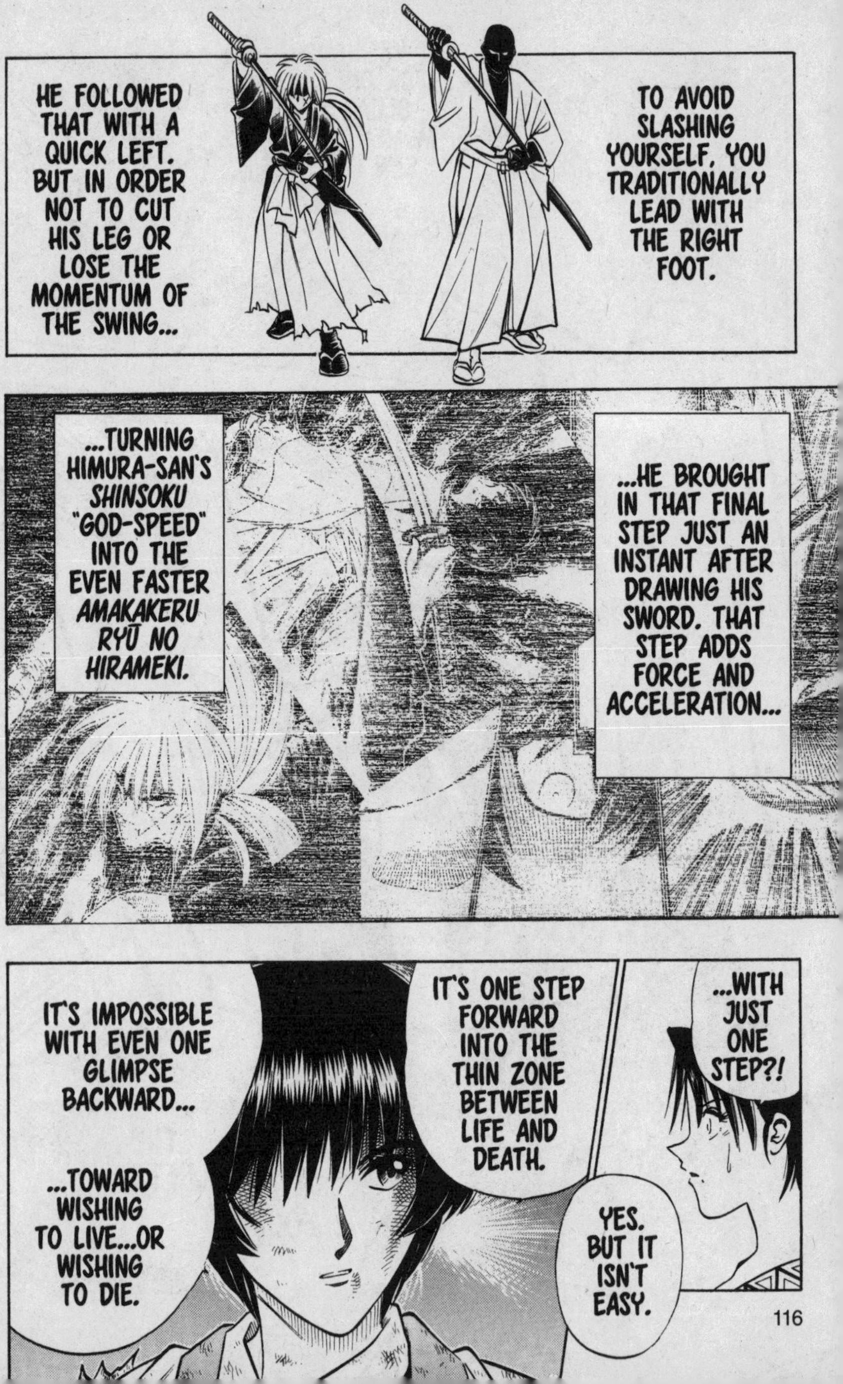

TO AVOID SLASHING YOURSELF, YOU TRADITIONALLY LEAD WITH THE RIGHT FOOT.
HE FOLLOWED THAT WITH A QUICK LEFT. BUT IN ORDER NOT TO CUT HIS LEG OR LOSE THE MOMENTUM OF THE SWING...
...HE BROUGHT IN THAT FINAL STEP JUST AN INSTANT AFTER DRAWING HIS SWORD. THAT STEP ADDS FORCE AND ACCELERATION...
...TURNING HIMURA-SAN'S *SHINSOKU* "GOD-SPEED" INTO THE EVEN FASTER *AMAKAKERU RYŪ NO HIRAMEKI*.
...WITH JUST ONE STEP?!
YES. BUT IT ISN'T EASY.
IT'S ONE STEP FORWARD INTO THE THIN ZONE BETWEEN LIFE AND DEATH.
IT'S IMPOSSIBLE WITH EVEN ONE GLIMPSE BACKWARD...
...TOWARD WISHING TO LIVE...OR WISHING TO DIE.

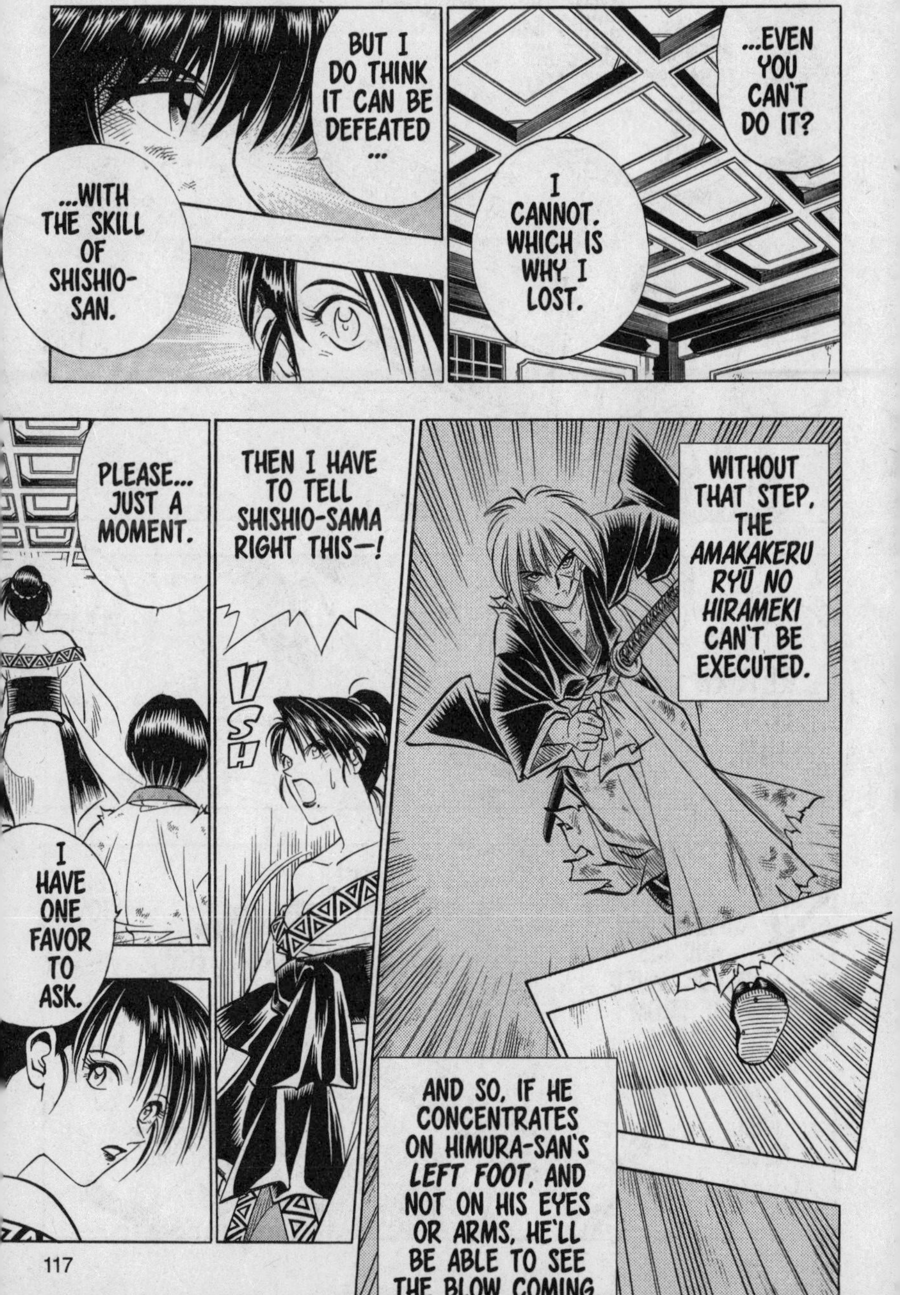
...EVEN YOU CAN'T DO IT?
I CANNOT. WHICH IS WHY I LOST.
BUT I DO THINK IT CAN BE DEFEATED ...
...WITH THE SKILL OF SHISHIO-SAN.
WITHOUT THAT STEP, THE *AMAKAKERU RYŪ NO HIRAMEKI* CAN'T BE EXECUTED.
AND SO, IF HE CONCENTRATES ON HIMURA-SAN'S *LEFT FOOT*, AND NOT ON HIS EYES OR ARMS, HE'LL BE ABLE TO SEE THE BLOW COMING.
THEN I HAVE TO TELL SHISHIO-SAMA RIGHT THIS—!
VSH
PLEASE... JUST A MOMENT.
I HAVE ONE FAVOR TO ASK.

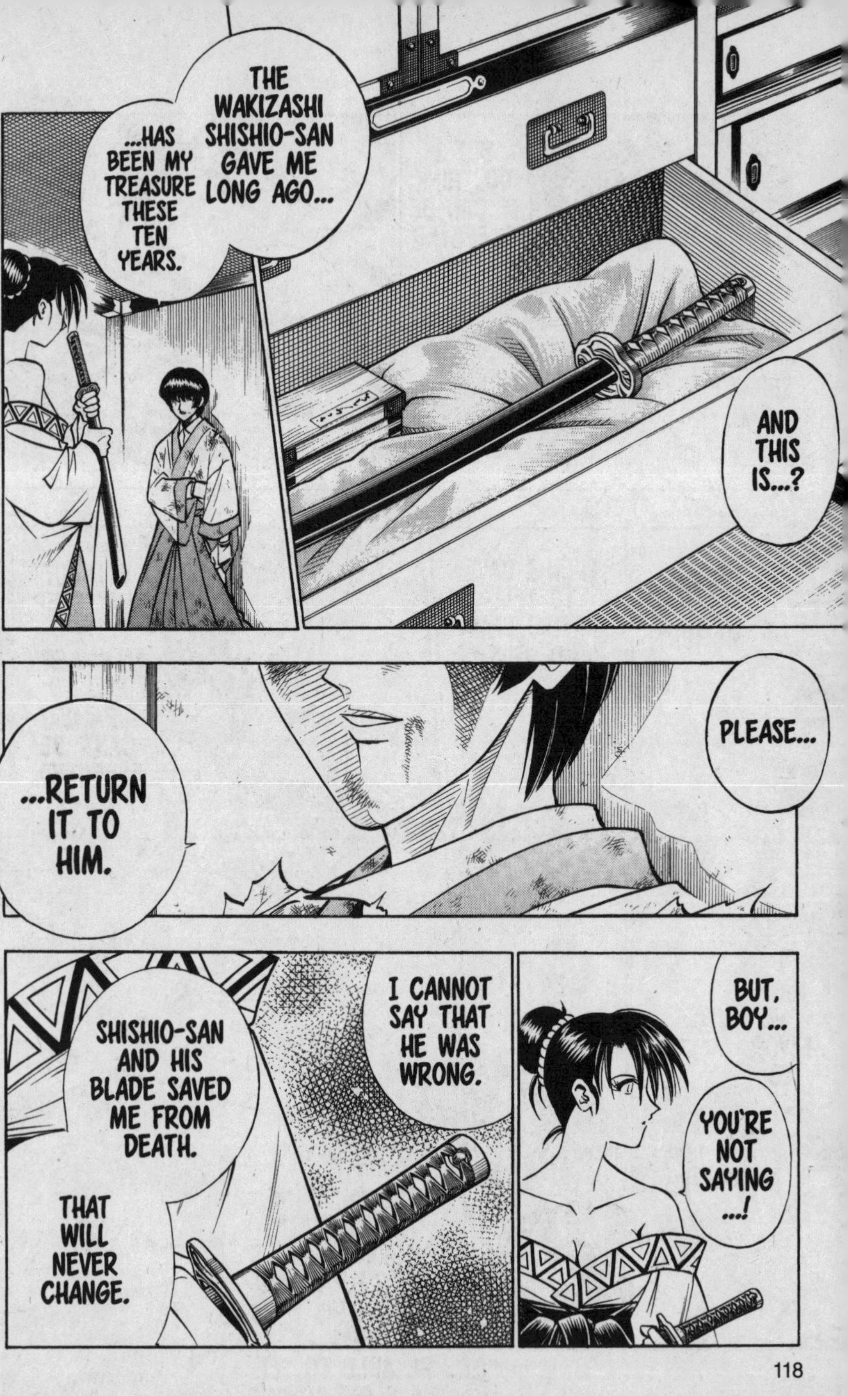
AND THIS IS...?
THE WAKIZASHI SHISHIO-SAN GAVE ME LONG AGO...
...HAS BEEN MY TREASURE THESE TEN YEARS.
PLEASE...
...RETURN IT TO HIM.
BUT, BOY...
YOU'RE NOT SAYING ...!
I CANNOT SAY THAT HE WAS WRONG.
SHISHIO-SAN AND HIS BLADE SAVED ME FROM DEATH.
THAT WILL NEVER CHANGE.

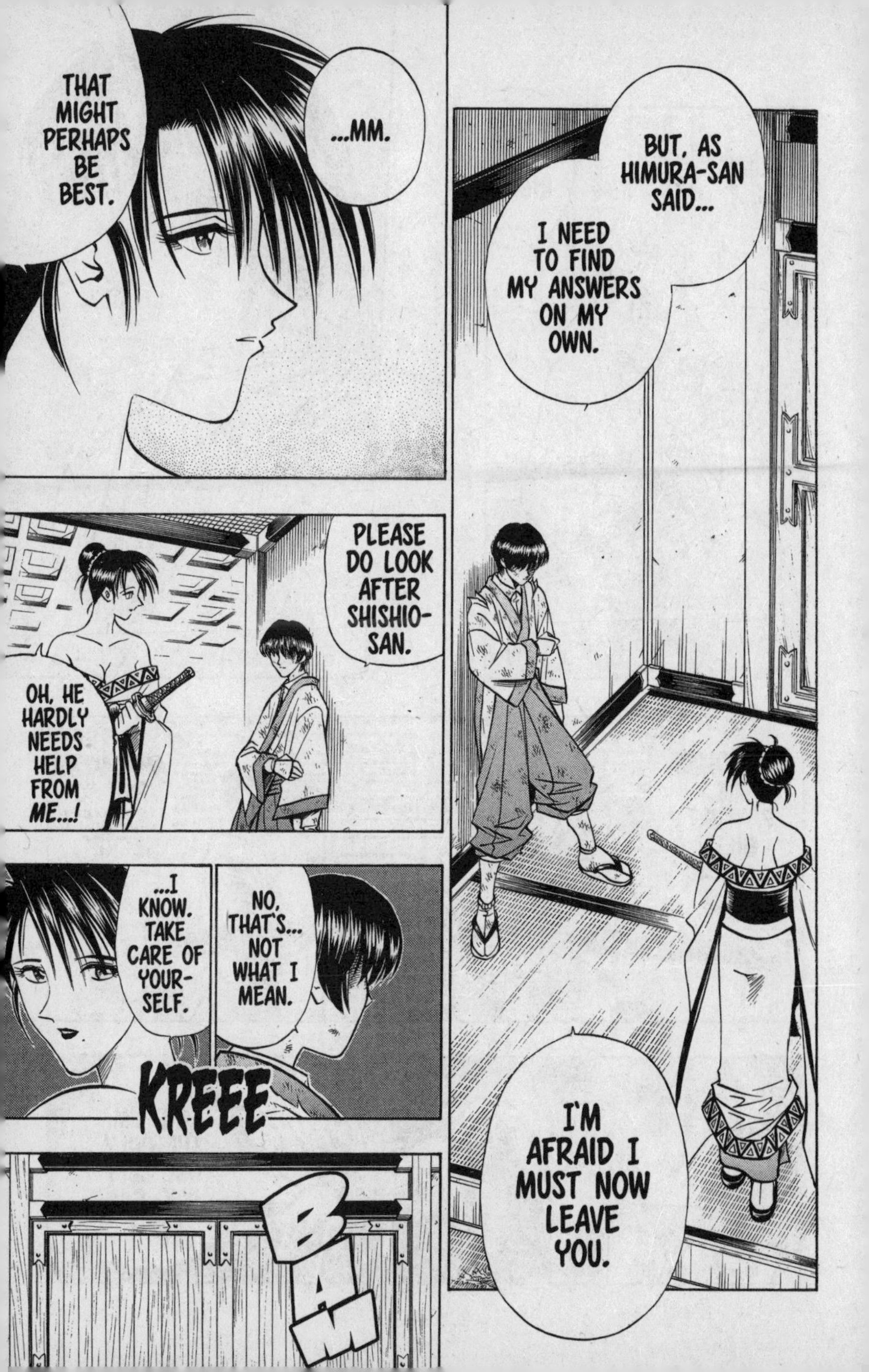
BUT, AS HIMURA-SAN SAID...
I NEED TO FIND MY ANSWERS ON MY OWN.
I'M AFRAID I MUST NOW LEAVE YOU.
...MM.
THAT MIGHT PERHAPS BE BEST.
PLEASE DO LOOK AFTER SHISHIO-SAN.
OH, HE HARDLY NEEDS HELP FROM ME...!
NO, THAT'S... NOT WHAT I MEAN.
...I KNOW. TAKE CARE OF YOURSELF.
KREEE
BAM

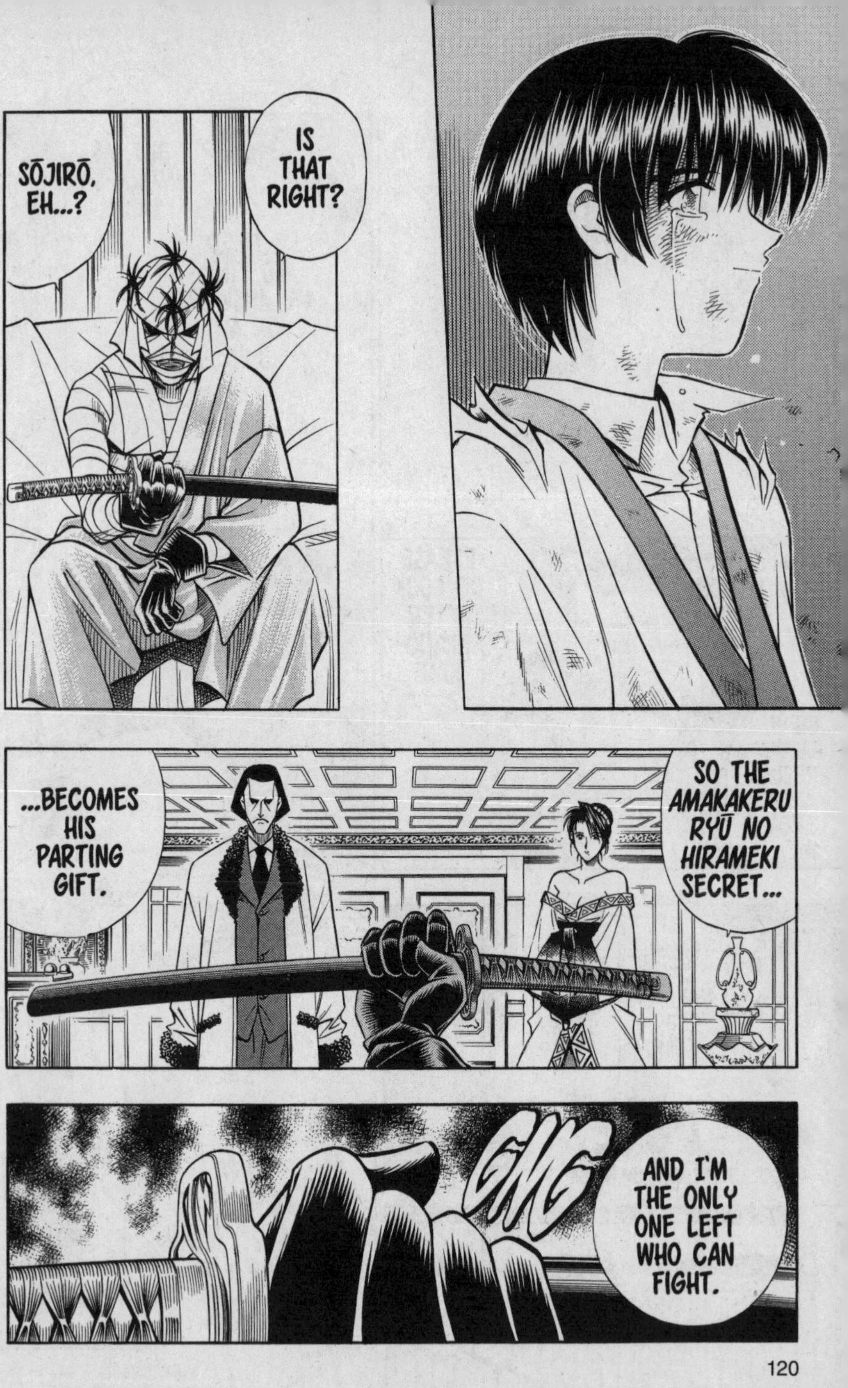
IS THAT RIGHT?
SŌJIRŌ, EH...?
SO THE AMAKAKERU RYŪ NO HIRAMEKI SECRET...
...BECOMES HIS PARTING GIFT.
AND I'M THE ONLY ONE LEFT WHO CAN FIGHT.
GNG

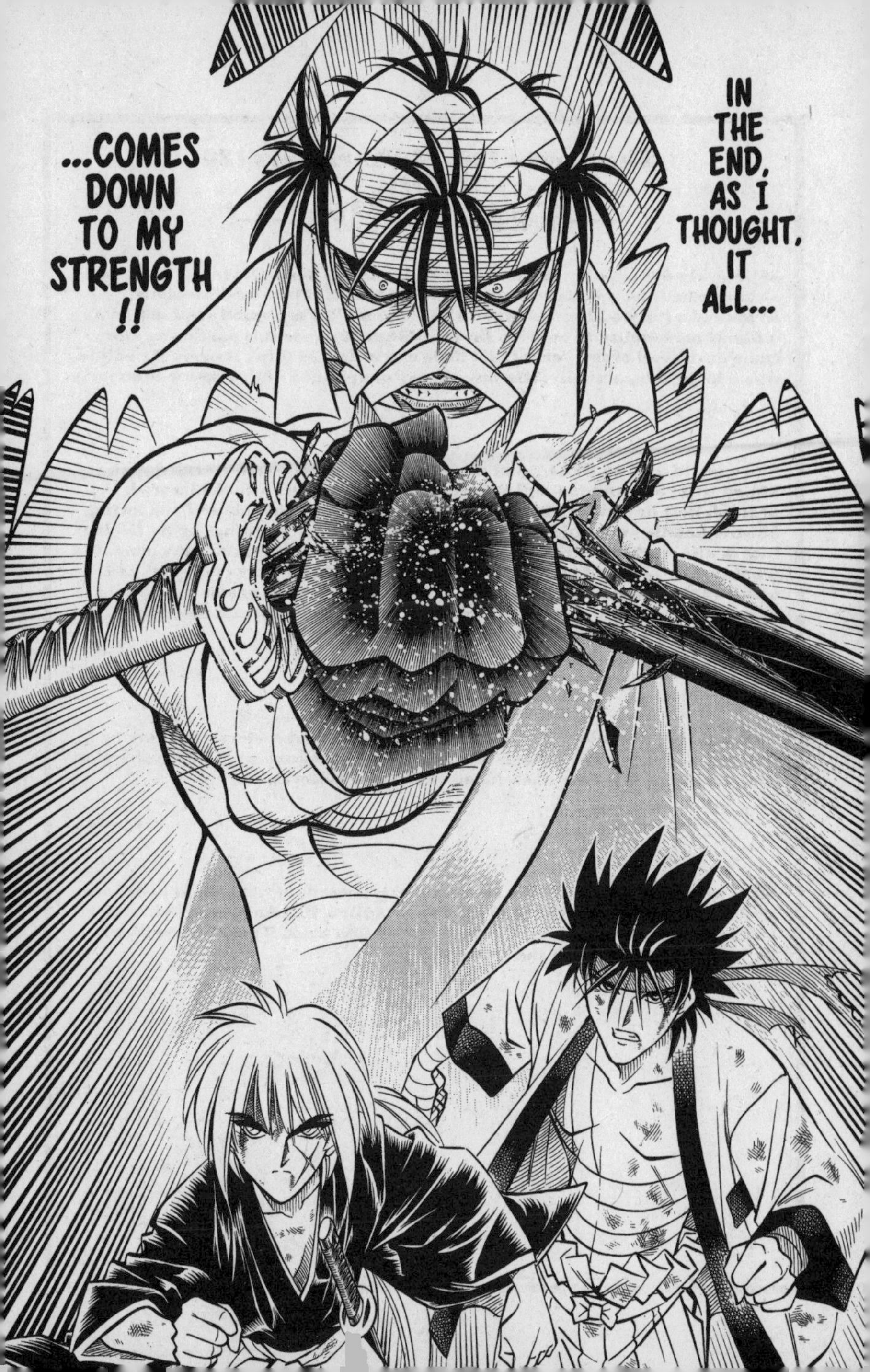
IN THE END, AS I THOUGHT, IT ALL...
...COMES DOWN TO MY STRENGTH !!

The Secret Life of Characters (26)
AMENDMENT
—Seta Sōjirō—

Sōjirō—always popular, always a struggle. As has been previously mentioned, although he is based on the Okita Sōshi of Shiba Ryōtarō's *Shinsengumi Keppuroku* ("Blood-Record of the Shinsengumi"), I personally found him a difficult personality to convey. On top of that, because this particular story came at the end of the year, I had little extra time to think it over. My editor was a huge help, actually. (He has always understood Sōjirō better than me.)

Since the historical Okita Sōshi died young, many fans have worried that Sōjirō will go young too, but it's always been my plan to have him stick around. Despite having abandoned all efforts to think for himself and letting Shishio handle everything, Sōjirō's not the type to wrap things up by fleeing into death—rather, he'll suffer through life, atoning for all that he's done. It's a harsh way of thinking, but as a human being, it's the only choice he *can* make. (Think of Shishio as a leader of a radical religious group and Sōjirō as a believer filled with crazed devotion, as though he's just handed over his brain. Does that put it in a different perspective?)

Although, for whatever reasons (including family and society), life may be a struggle, so long as one is born into the human race, one must never abandon one's efforts to think for oneself...or so Watsuki believes.

Still, whatever it is *I* may say about Sōjirō's personality, no doubt he'll keep smiling and living that life of indifference. Sōjirō, like Anji, is a character I feel I haven't fully realized; I'd like to bring him back, if possible. Not that any plans are in place at the moment....

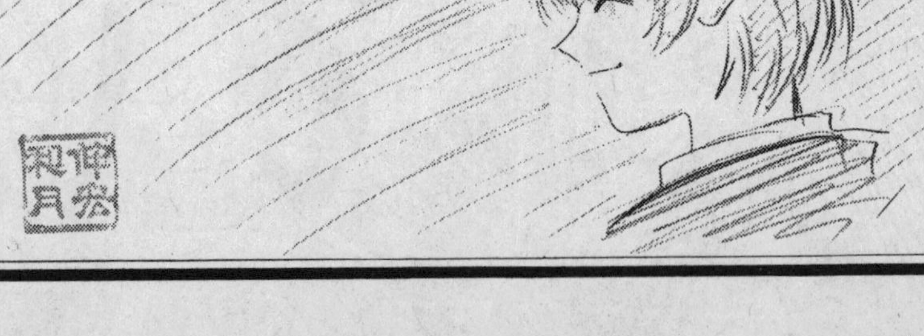
伸宏
和月

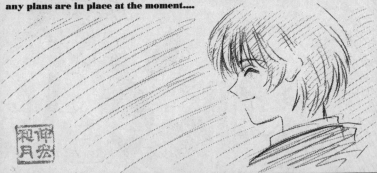

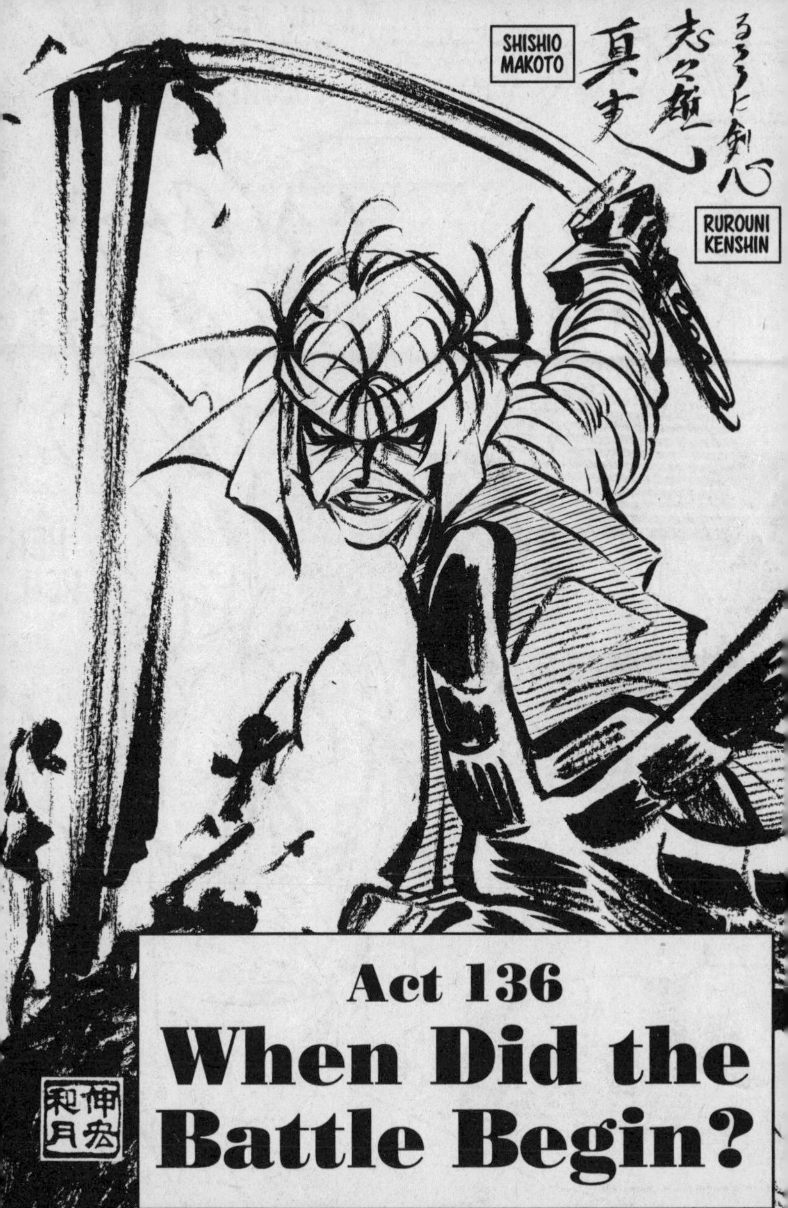
るろうに剣心
RUROUNI KENSHIN
志々雄真実
SHISHIO MAKOTO

Act 136
When Did the Battle Begin?

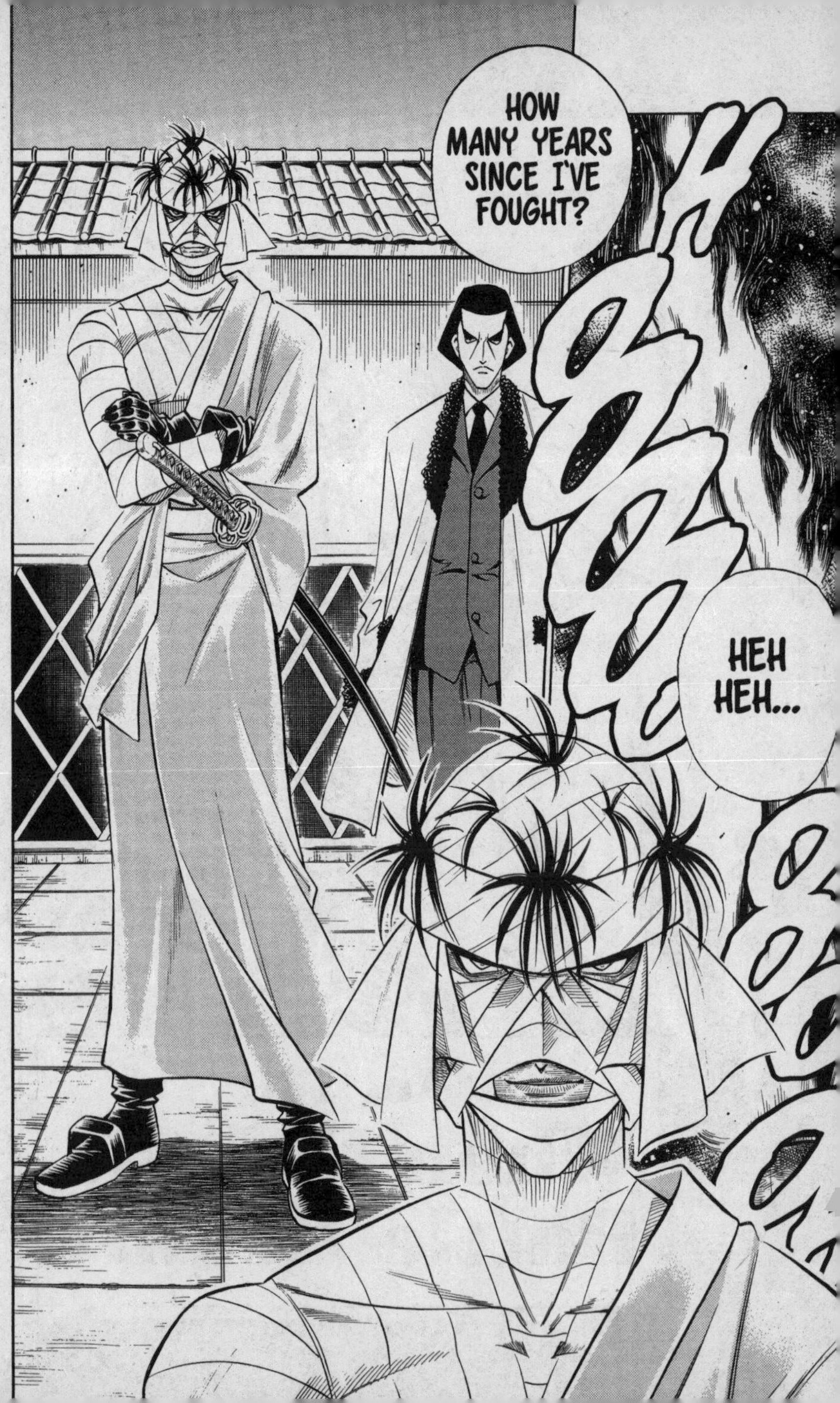
HOW MANY YEARS SINCE I'VE FOUGHT?
HEH HEH...

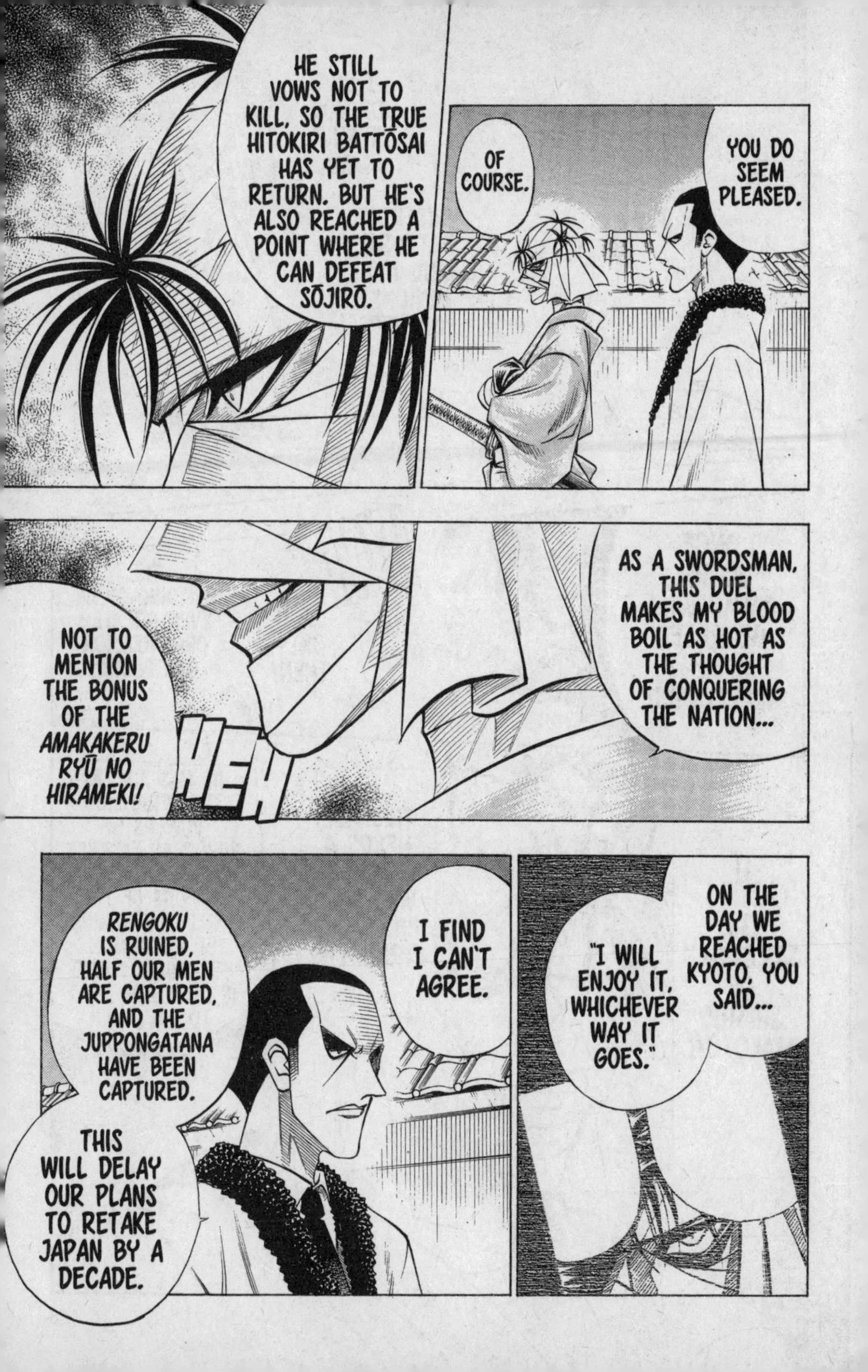
YOU DO SEEM PLEASED.
OF COURSE.
HE STILL VOWS NOT TO KILL, SO THE TRUE HITOKIRI BATTŌSAI HAS YET TO RETURN. BUT HE'S ALSO REACHED A POINT WHERE HE CAN DEFEAT SŌJIRŌ.
AS A SWORDSMAN, THIS DUEL MAKES MY BLOOD BOIL AS HOT AS THE THOUGHT OF CONQUERING THE NATION...
HEH
NOT TO MENTION THE BONUS OF THE AMAKAKERU RYŪ NO HIRAMEKI!
ON THE DAY WE REACHED KYOTO, YOU SAID...
"I WILL ENJOY IT, WHICHEVER WAY IT GOES."
I FIND I CAN'T AGREE.
RENGOKU IS RUINED, HALF OUR MEN ARE CAPTURED, AND THE JUPPONGATANA HAVE BEEN CAPTURED.
THIS WILL DELAY OUR PLANS TO RETAKE JAPAN BY A DECADE.

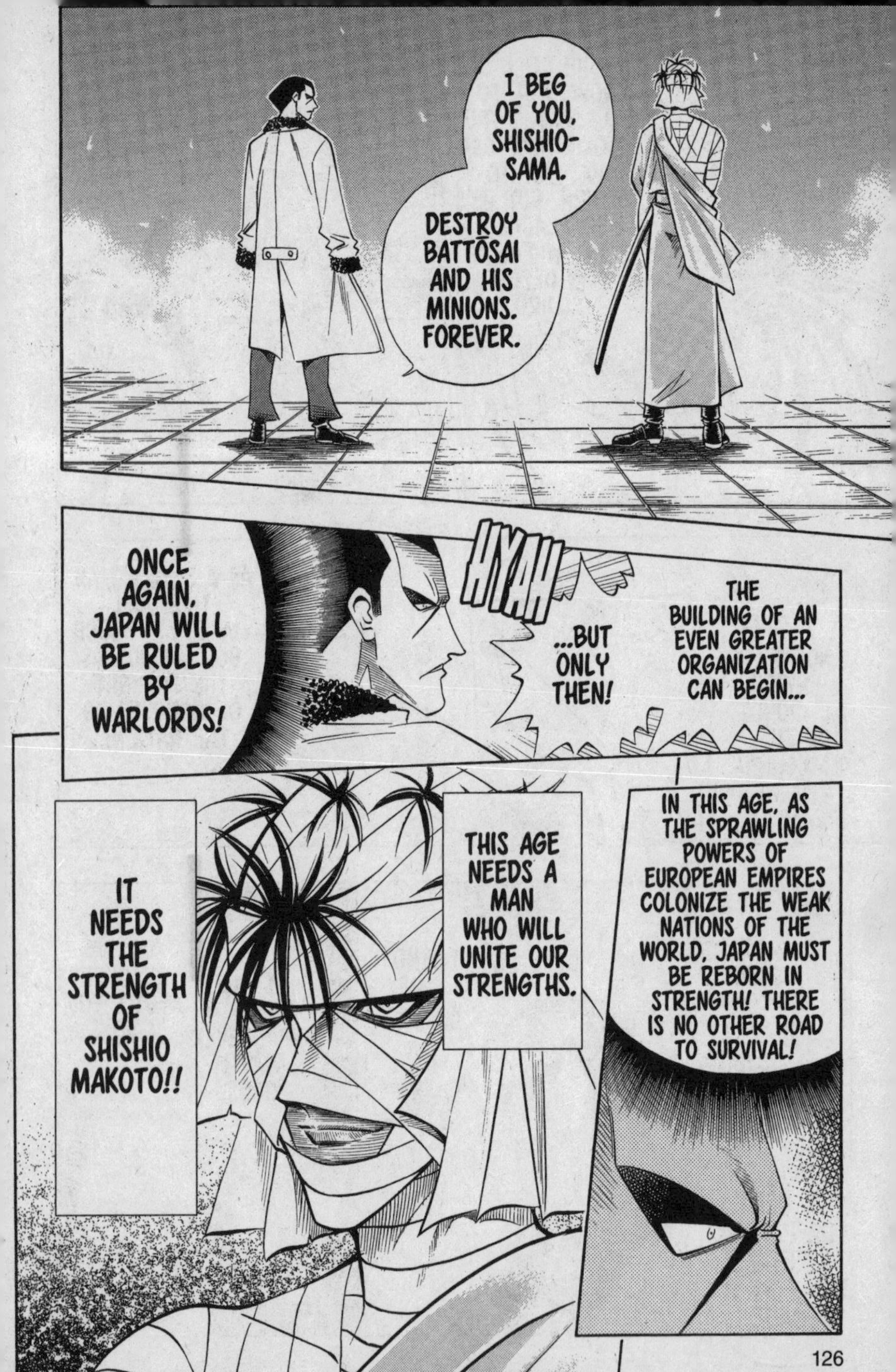
I BEG OF YOU, SHISHIO-SAMA.
DESTROY BATTŌSAI AND HIS MINIONS. FOREVER.
THE BUILDING OF AN EVEN GREATER ORGANIZATION CAN BEGIN...
...BUT ONLY THEN!
HYAH
ONCE AGAIN, JAPAN WILL BE RULED BY WARLORDS!
IN THIS AGE, AS THE SPRAWLING POWERS OF EUROPEAN EMPIRES COLONIZE THE WEAK NATIONS OF THE WORLD, JAPAN MUST BE REBORN IN STRENGTH! THERE IS NO OTHER ROAD TO SURVIVAL!
THIS AGE NEEDS A MAN WHO WILL UNITE OUR STRENGTHS.
IT NEEDS THE STRENGTH OF SHISHIO MAKOTO!!

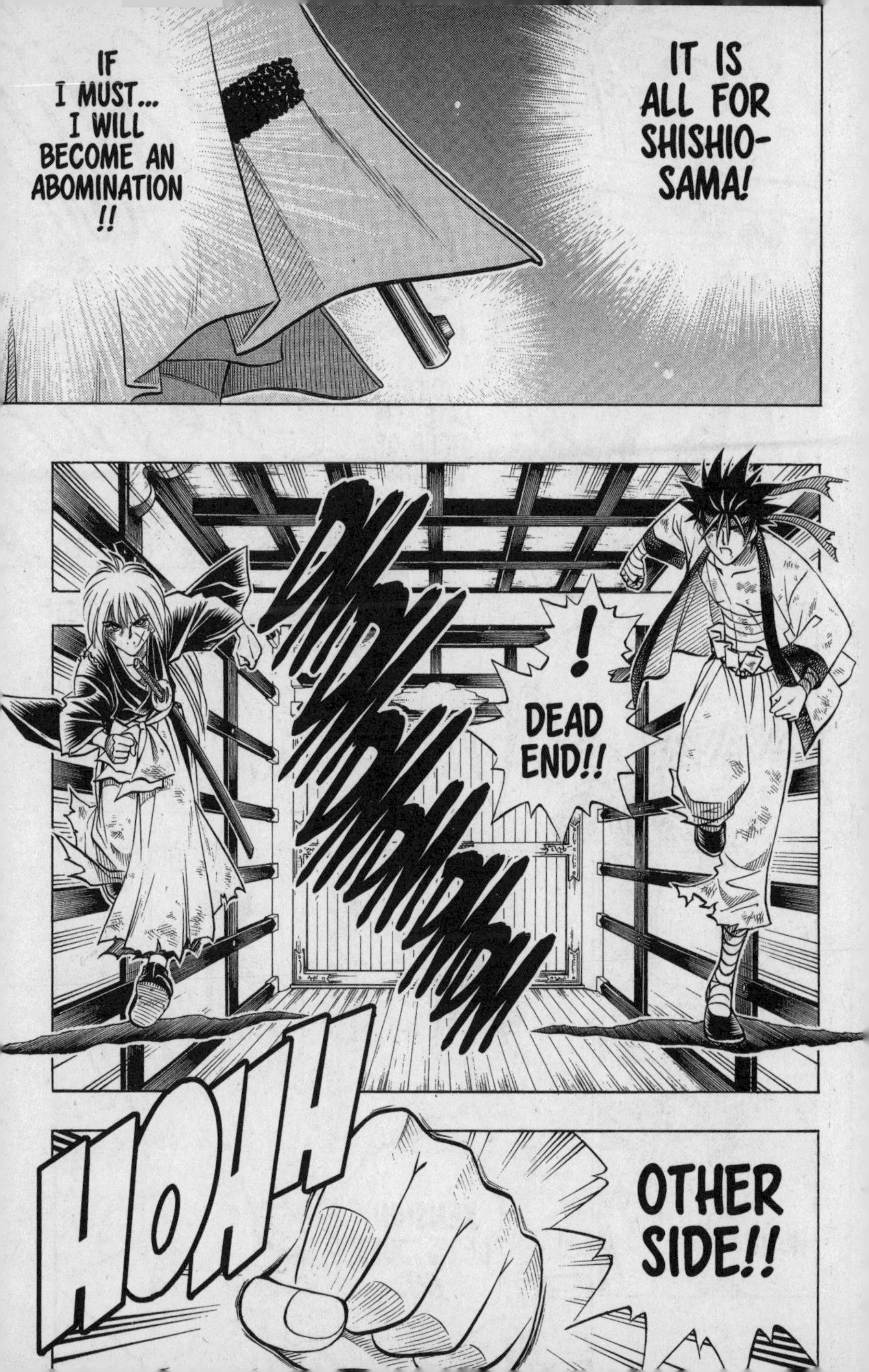
IT IS ALL FOR SHISHIO-SAMA!
IF I MUST... I WILL BECOME AN ABOMINATION!!
!
DEAD END!!
OTHER SIDE!!
HOH

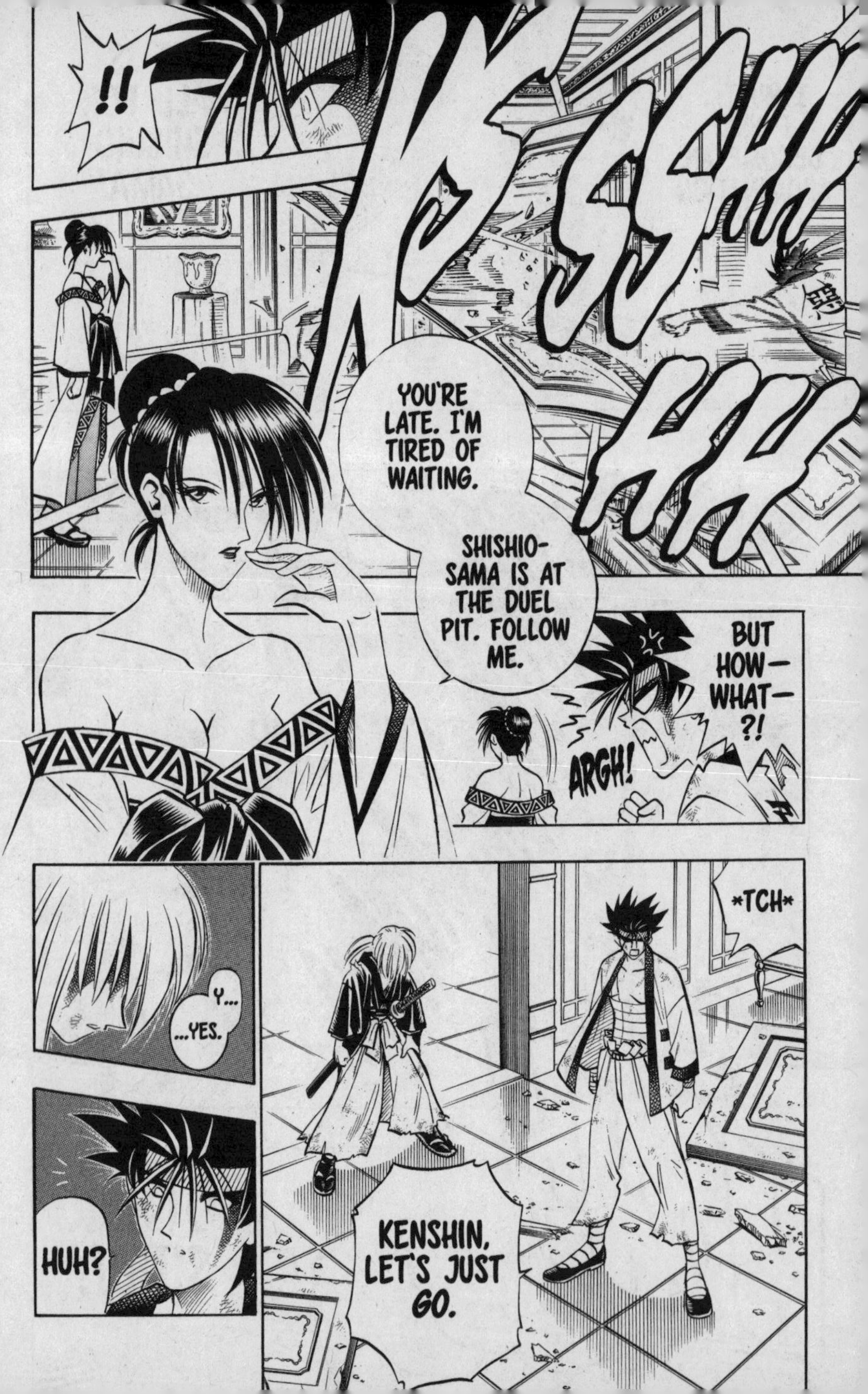
!!
YOU'RE LATE. I'M TIRED OF WAITING.
SHISHIO-SAMA IS AT THE DUEL PIT. FOLLOW ME.
BUT HOW— WHAT—?!
ARGH!
TCH
KENSHIN, LET'S JUST GO.
Y... ...YES.
HUH?

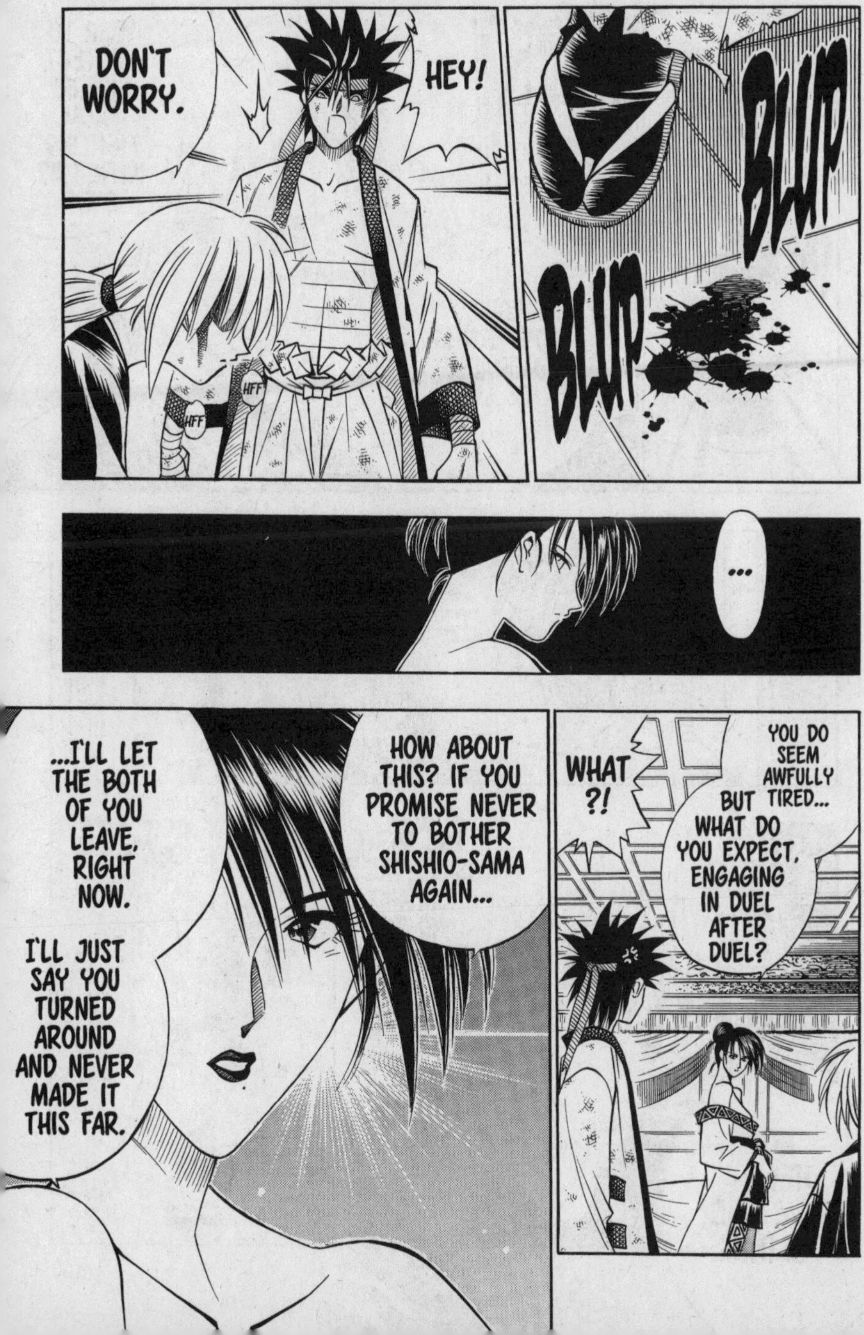
BLUP
BLUP
HEY!
DON'T WORRY.
HFF
HFF
...
YOU DO SEEM AWFULLY TIRED... BUT WHAT DO YOU EXPECT, ENGAGING IN DUEL AFTER DUEL?
WHAT ?!
HOW ABOUT THIS? IF YOU PROMISE NEVER TO BOTHER SHISHIO-SAMA AGAIN...
...I'LL LET THE BOTH OF YOU LEAVE, RIGHT NOW.
I'LL JUST SAY YOU TURNED AROUND AND NEVER MADE IT THIS FAR.

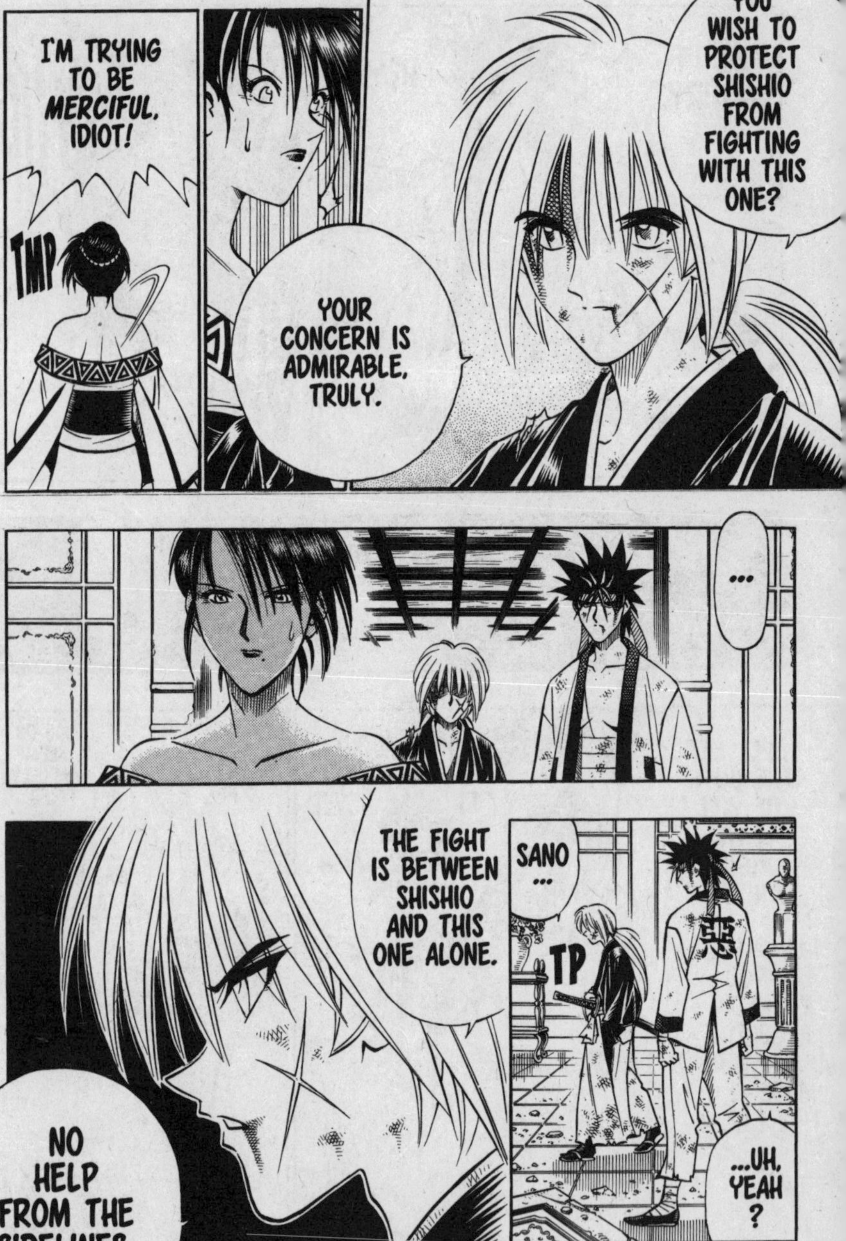
YOU WISH TO PROTECT SHISHIO FROM FIGHTING WITH THIS ONE?
YOUR CONCERN IS ADMIRABLE, TRULY.
I'M TRYING TO BE MERCIFUL, IDIOT!
TMP
...
SANO...
TP
...UH, YEAH?
THE FIGHT IS BETWEEN SHISHIO AND THIS ONE ALONE.
NO HELP FROM THE SIDELINES.

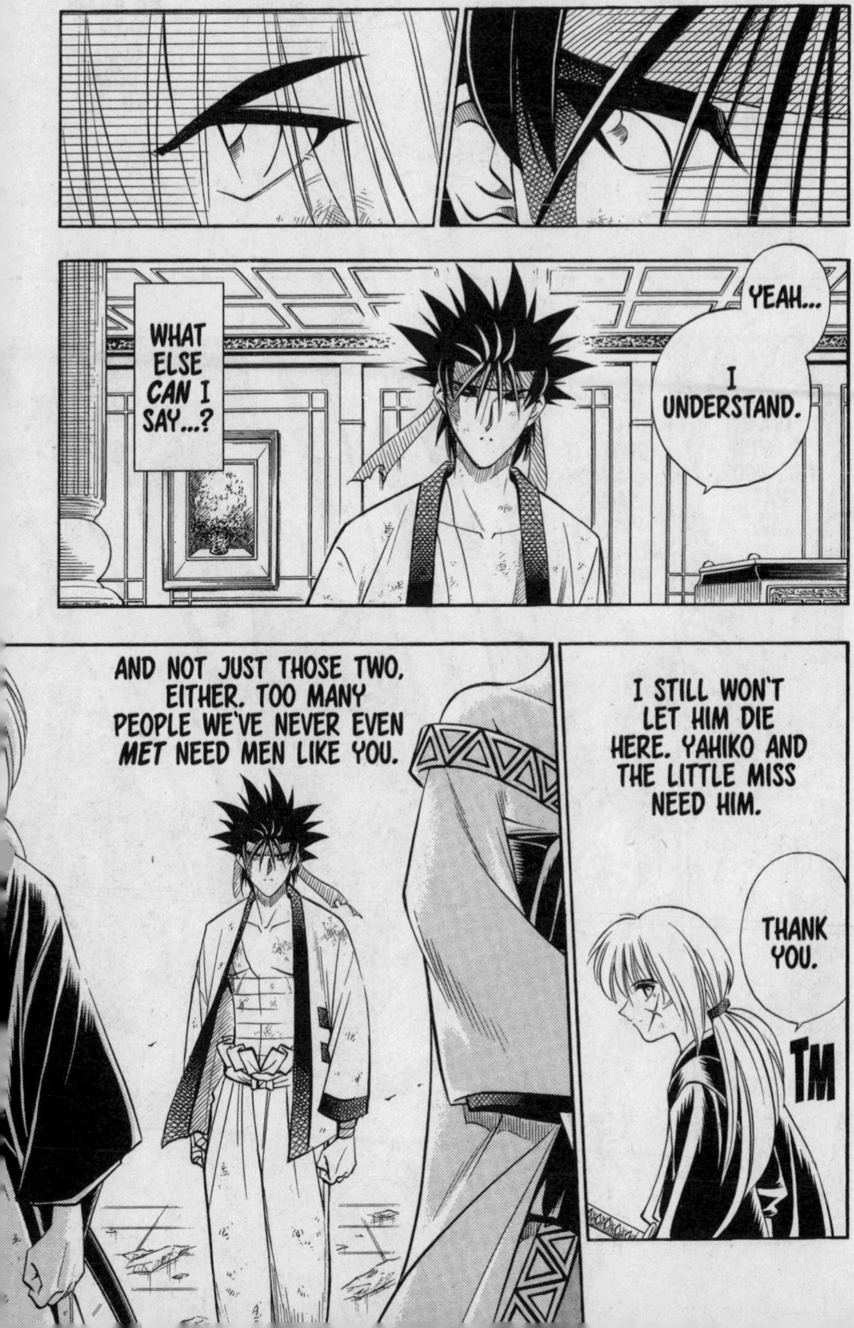
YEAH...
I UNDERSTAND.
WHAT ELSE *CAN* I SAY...?
I STILL WON'T LET HIM DIE HERE. YAHIKO AND THE LITTLE MISS NEED HIM.
THANK YOU.
TM
AND NOT JUST THOSE TWO, EITHER. TOO MANY PEOPLE WE'VE NEVER EVEN *MET* NEED MEN LIKE YOU.

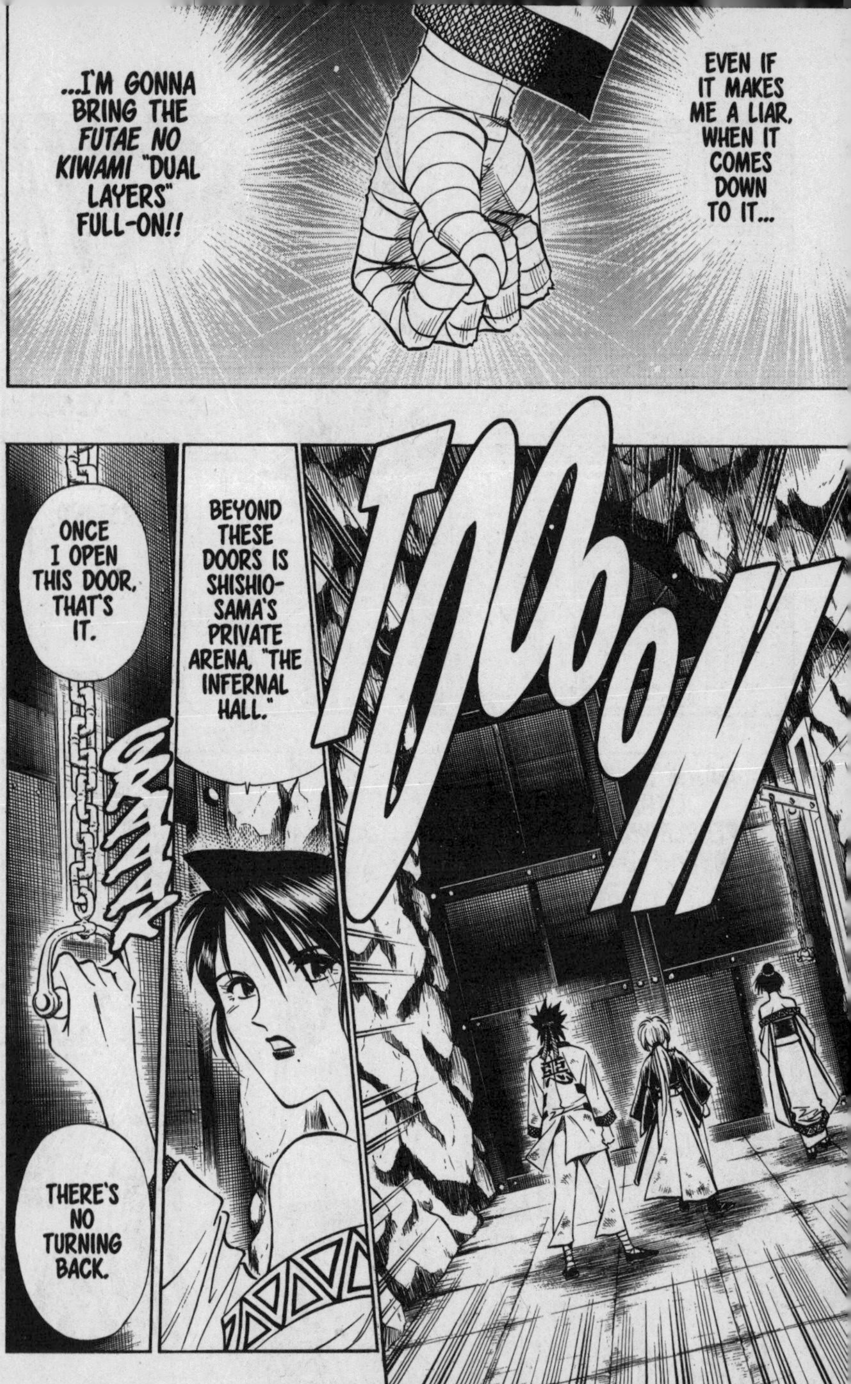
EVEN IF IT MAKES ME A LIAR, WHEN IT COMES DOWN TO IT...
...I'M GONNA BRING THE *FUTAE NO KIWAMI* "DUAL LAYERS" FULL-ON!!
BEYOND THESE DOORS IS SHISHIO-SAMA'S PRIVATE ARENA, "THE INFERNAL HALL."
ONCE I OPEN THIS DOOR, THAT'S IT.
THERE'S NO TURNING BACK.

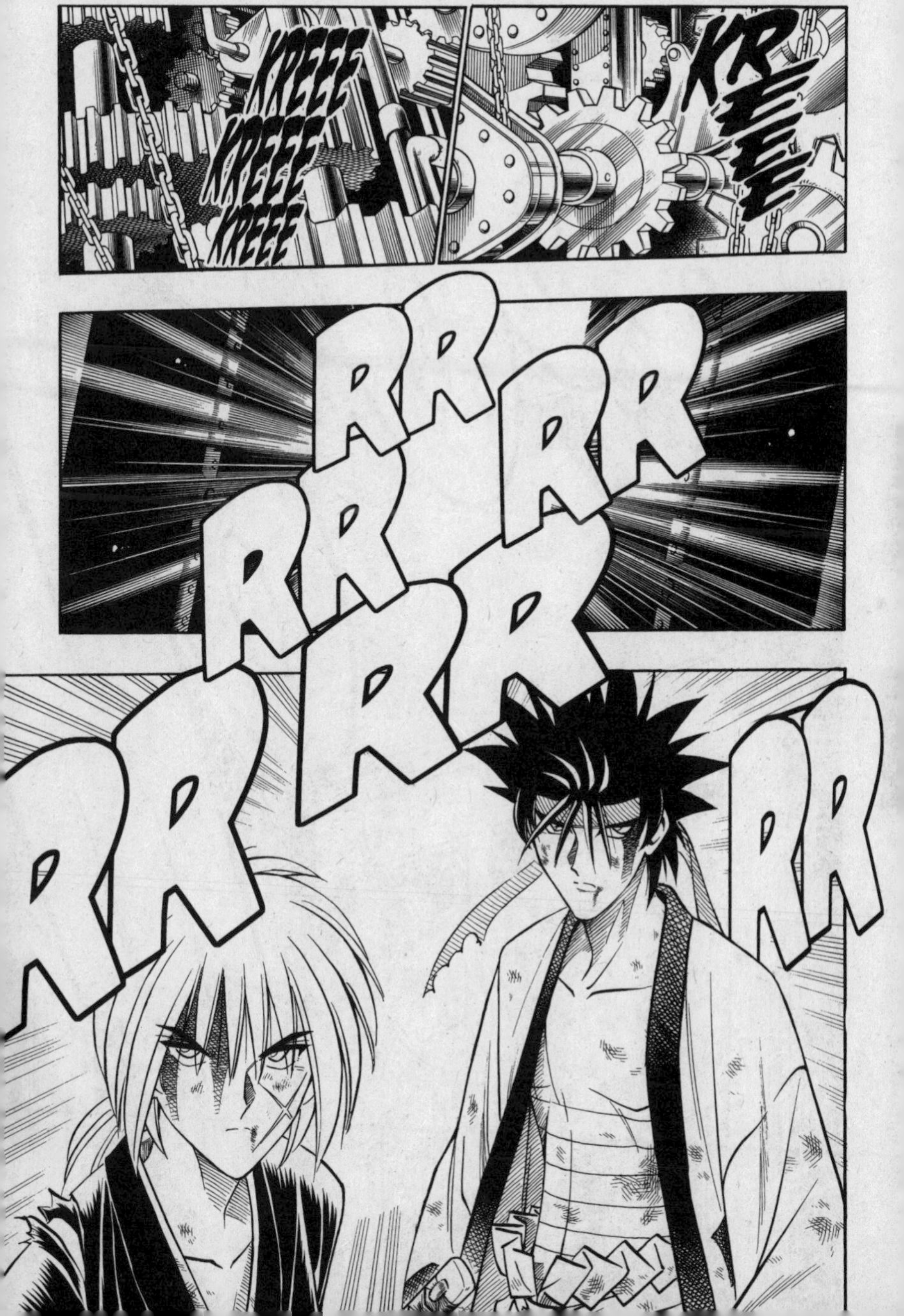
KREEEE
KREEE
KREEE
KREEE
RRRRRRRRRRRR

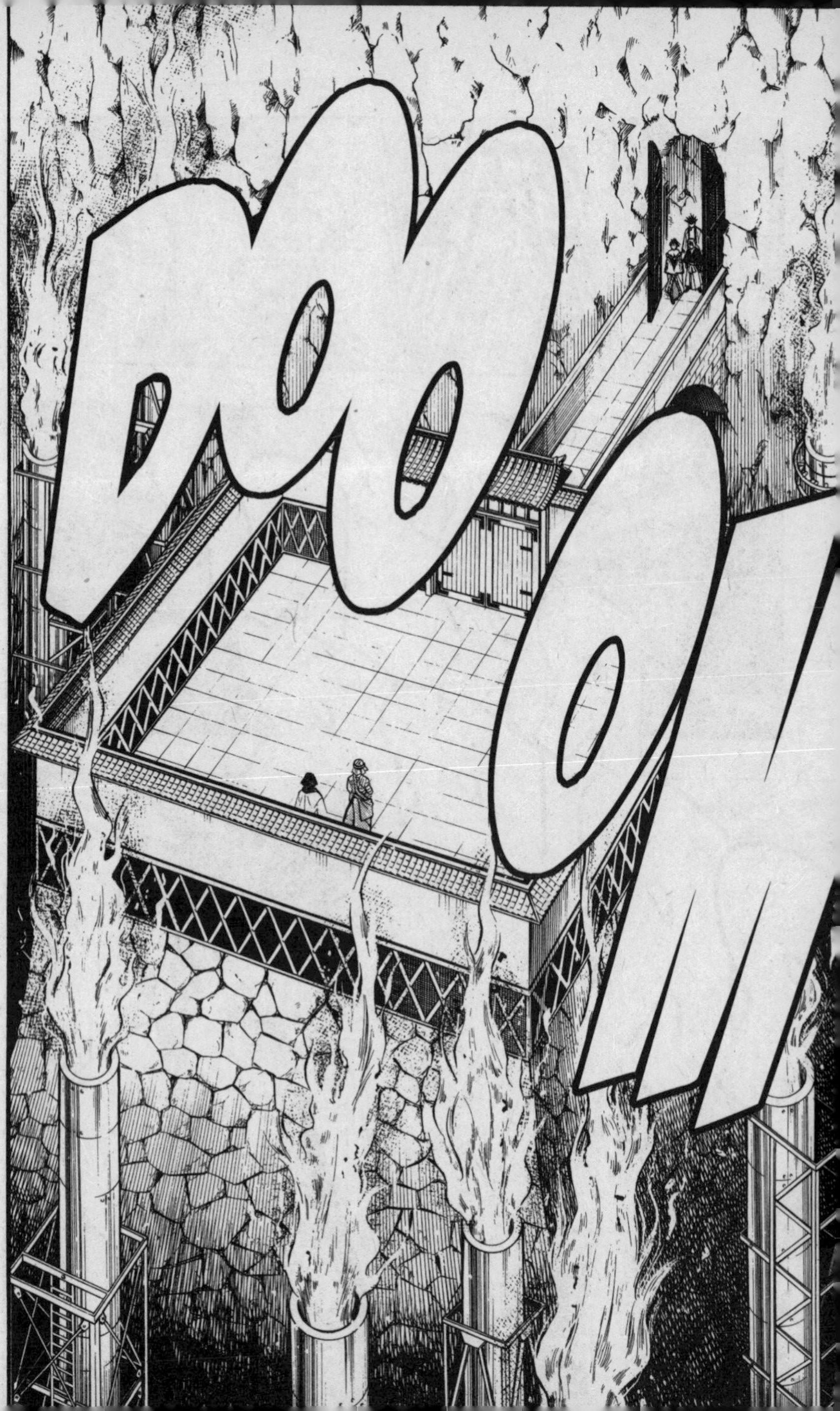
DOOON

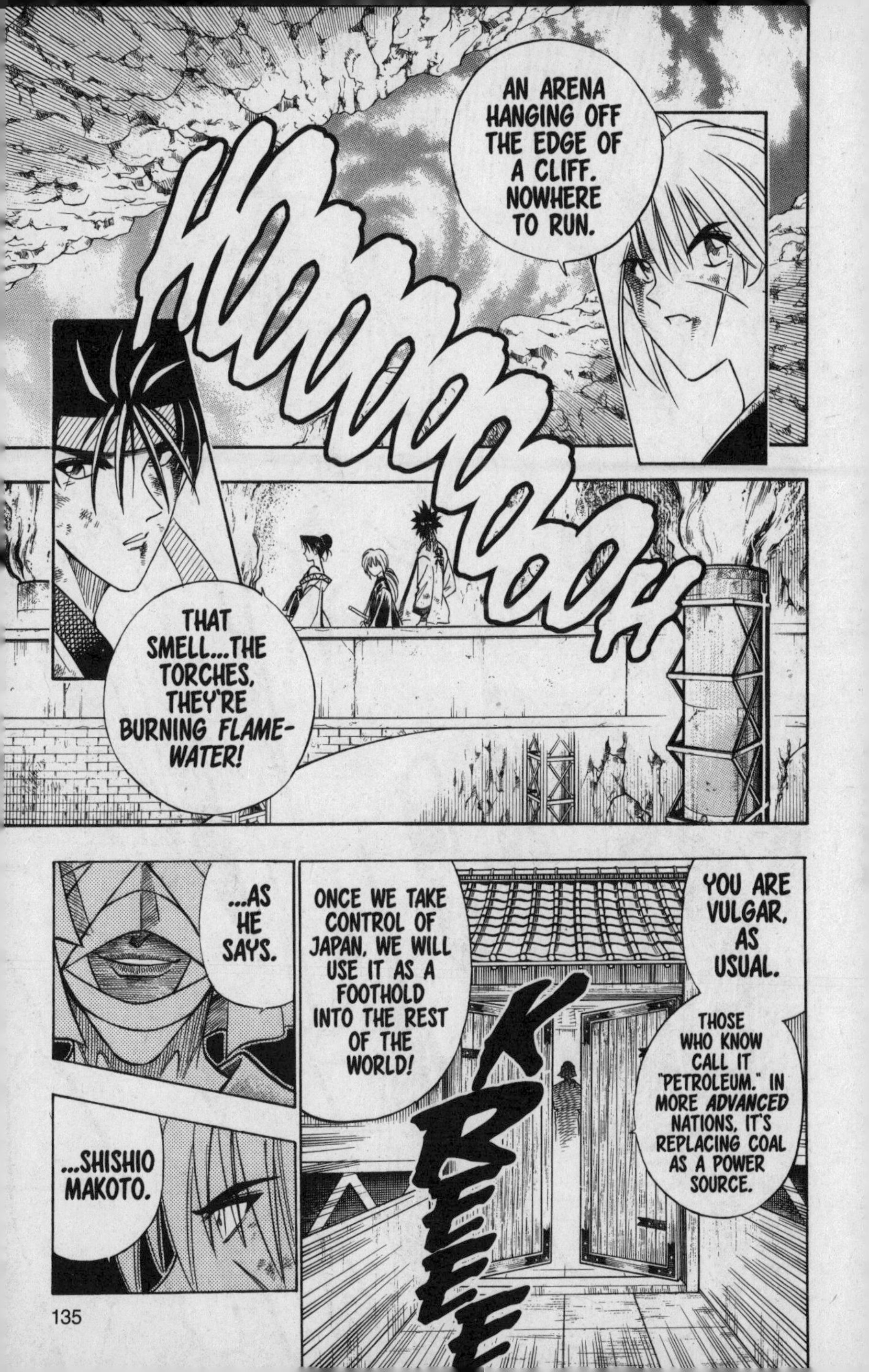
AN ARENA HANGING OFF THE EDGE OF A CLIFF. NOWHERE TO RUN.
THAT SMELL...THE TORCHES, THEY'RE BURNING *FLAME-WATER!*
YOU ARE VULGAR, AS USUAL.
THOSE WHO KNOW CALL IT "PETROLEUM." IN MORE *ADVANCED* NATIONS, IT'S REPLACING COAL AS A POWER SOURCE.
ONCE WE TAKE CONTROL OF JAPAN, WE WILL USE IT AS A FOOTHOLD INTO THE REST OF THE WORLD!
...AS HE SAYS.
...SHISHIO MAKOTO.

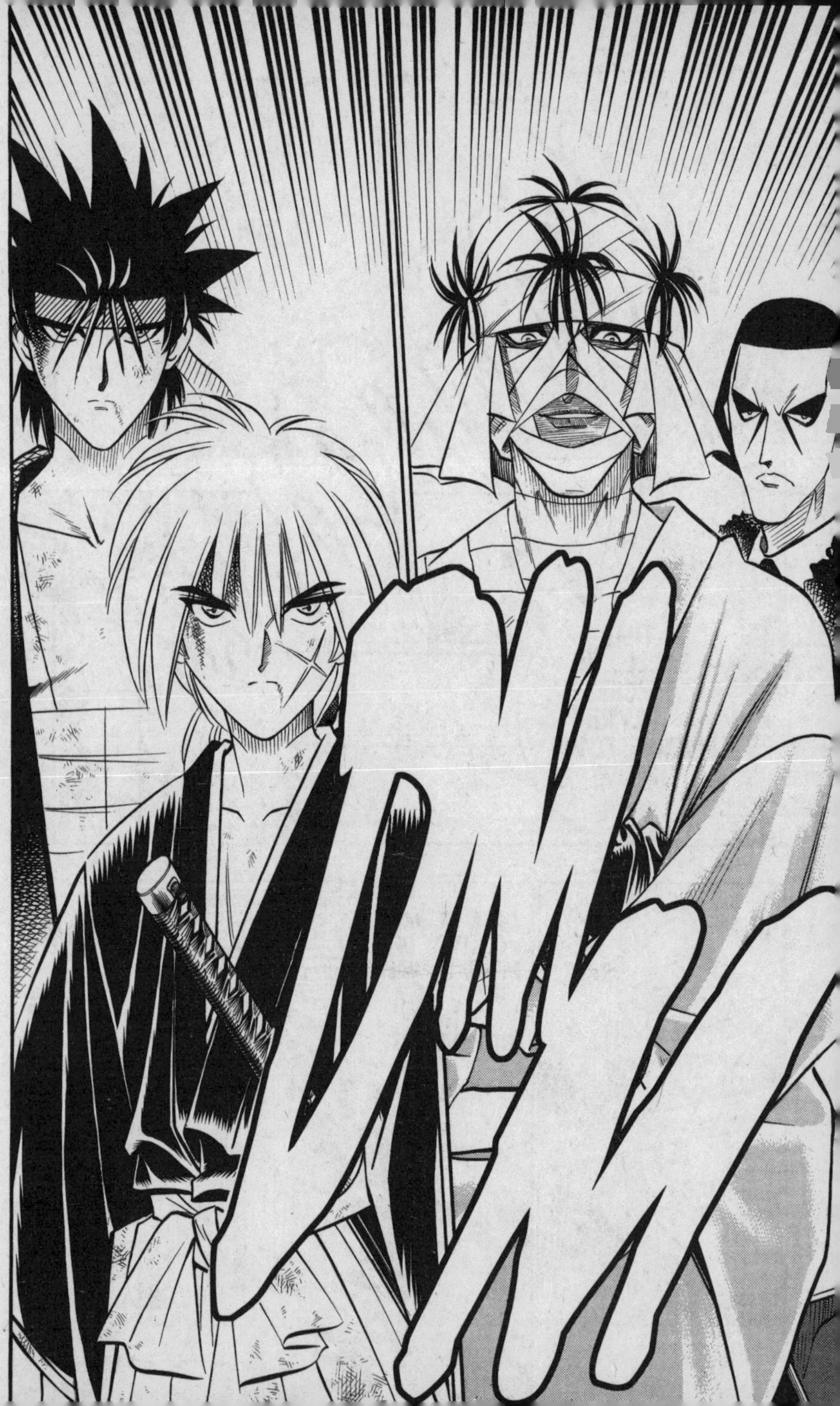

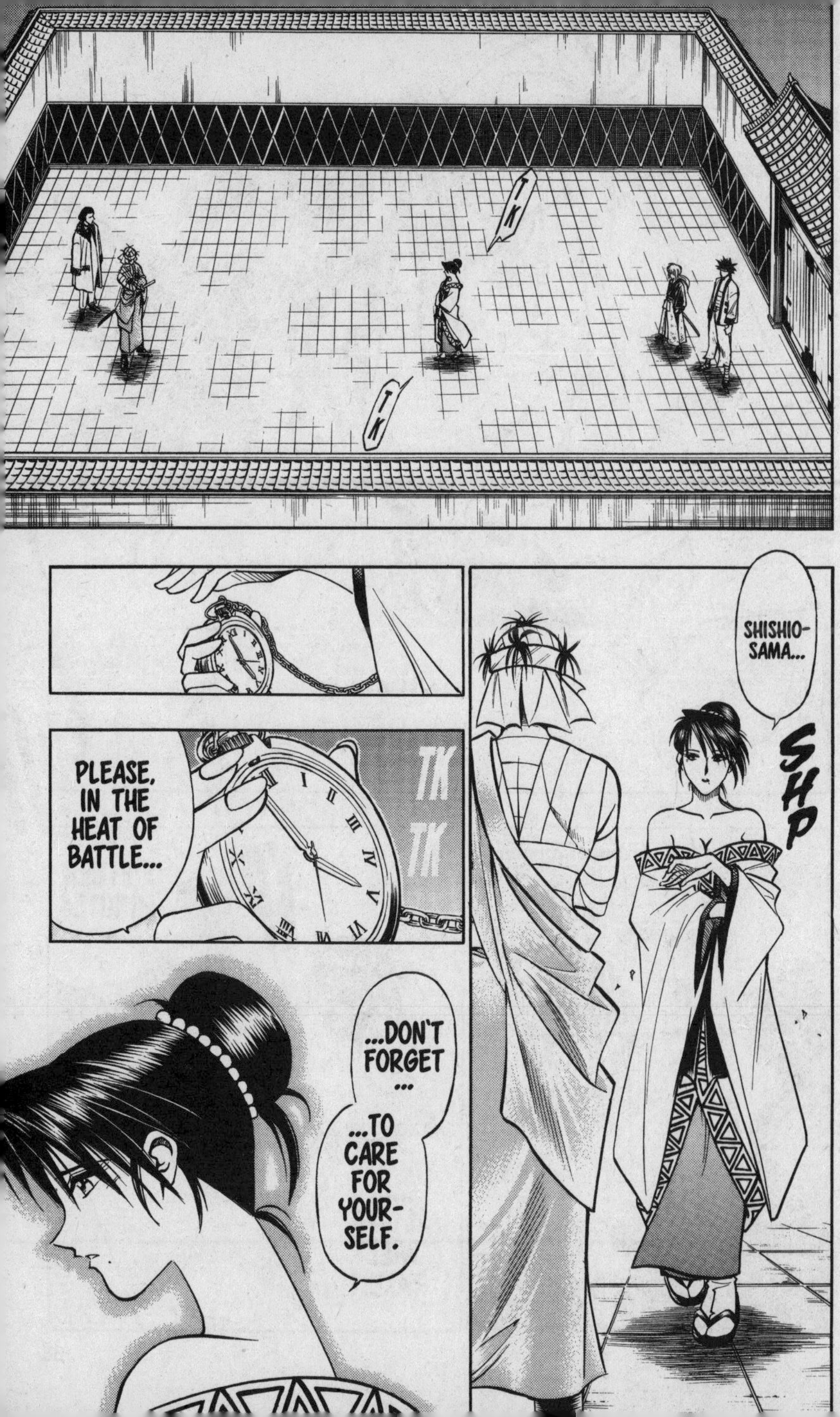
TK
TK
SHISHIO-SAMA...
SHP
PLEASE, IN THE HEAT OF BATTLE...
TK TK
...DON'T FORGET ...
...TO CARE FOR YOUR-SELF.

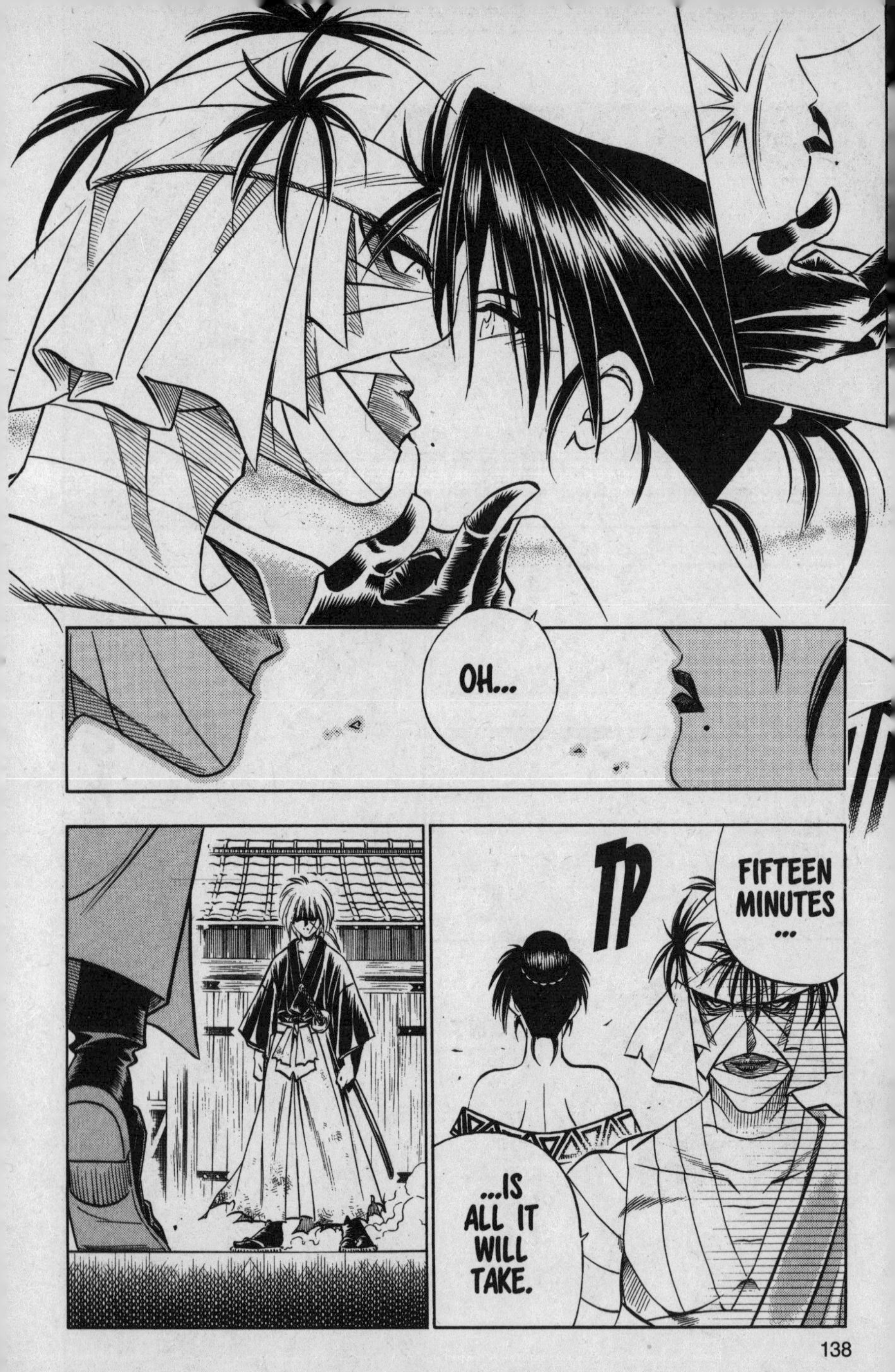
OH...
TP
FIFTEEN MINUTES ...
...IS ALL IT WILL TAKE.

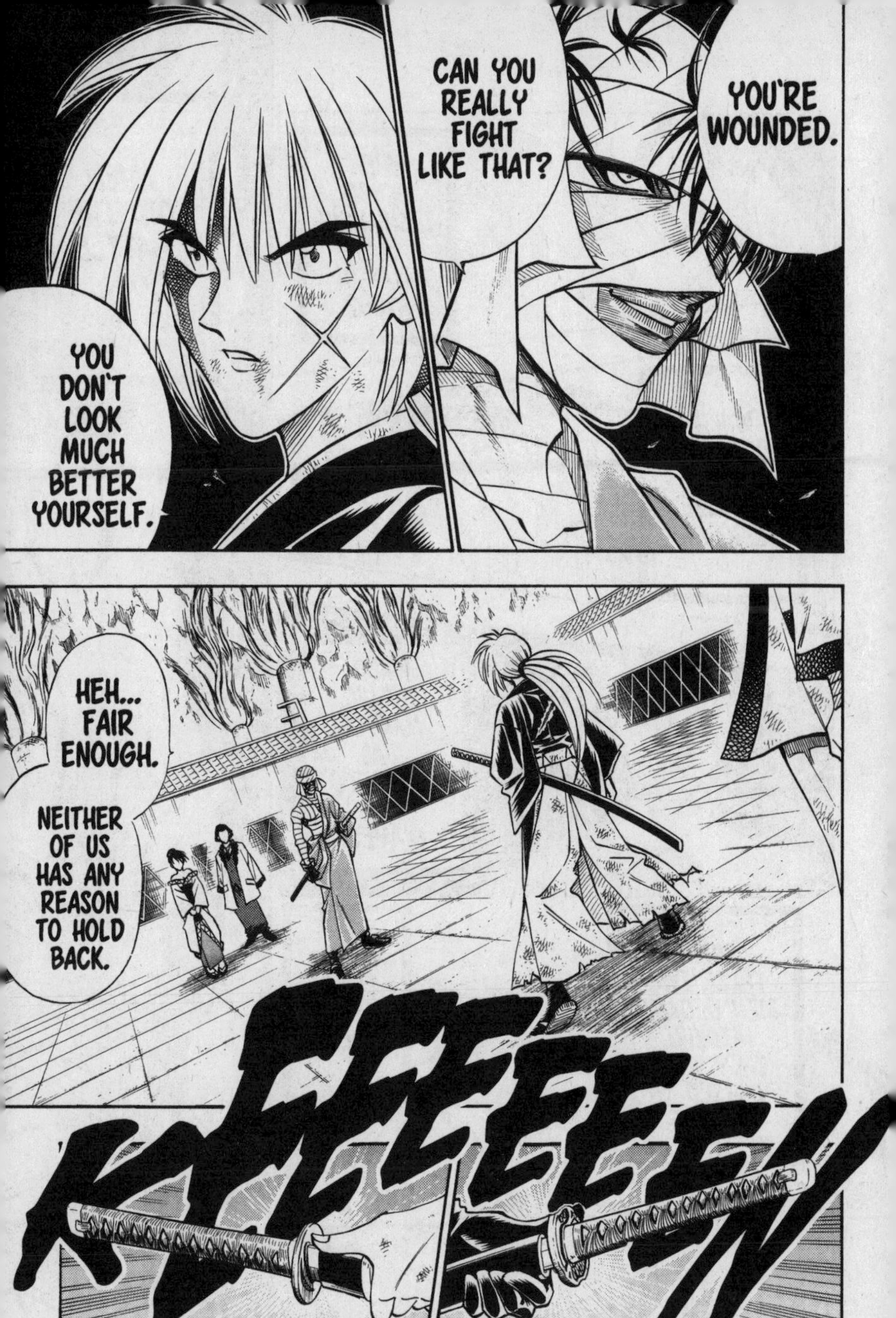
YOU'RE WOUNDED.
CAN YOU REALLY FIGHT LIKE THAT?
YOU DON'T LOOK MUCH BETTER YOURSELF.
HEH... FAIR ENOUGH.
NEITHER OF US HAS ANY REASON TO HOLD BACK.

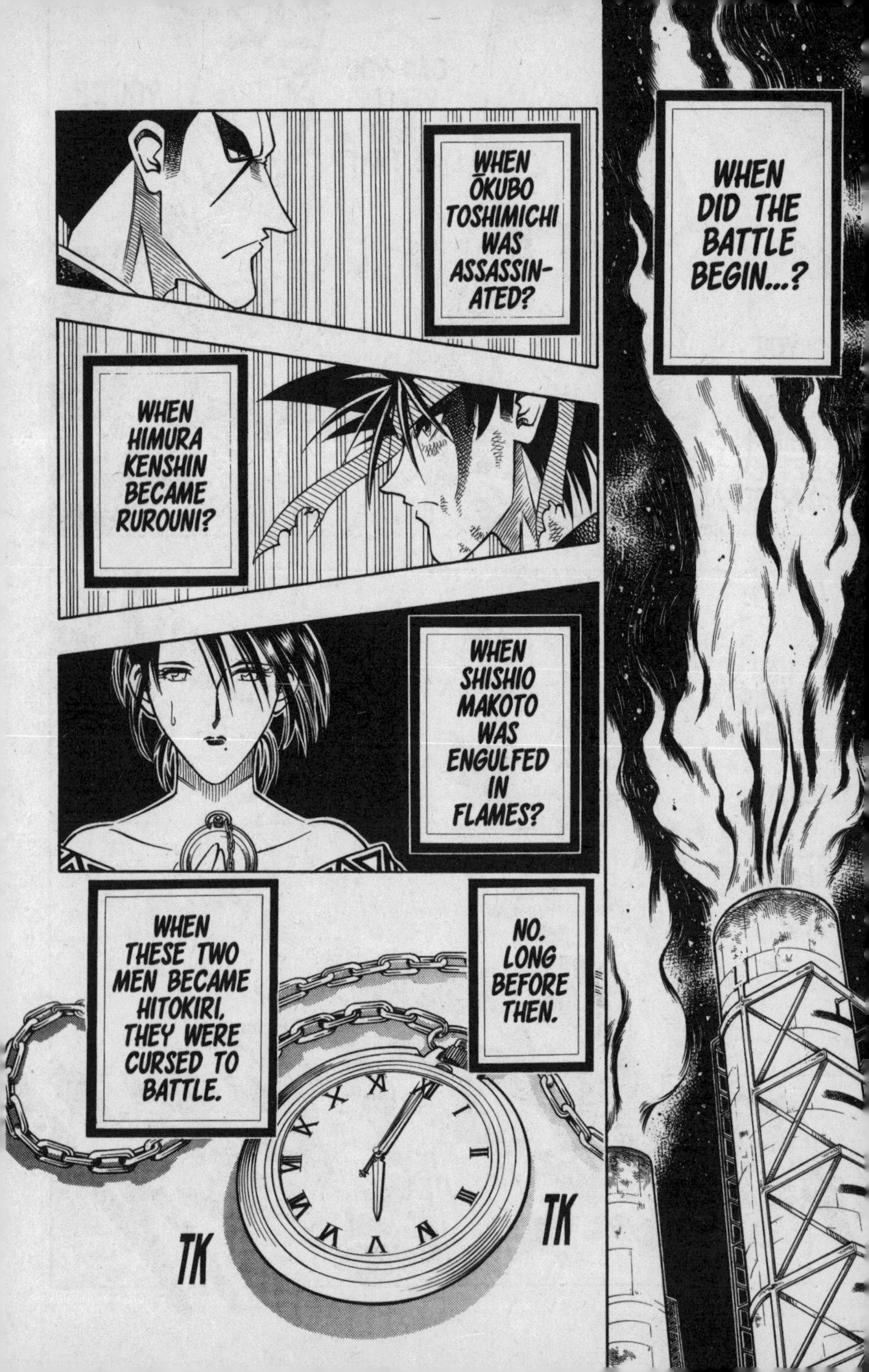
WHEN DID THE BATTLE BEGIN...?
WHEN ŌKUBO TOSHIMICHI WAS ASSASSIN-ATED?
WHEN HIMURA KENSHIN BECAME RUROUNI?
WHEN SHISHIO MAKOTO WAS ENGULFED IN FLAMES?
NO. LONG BEFORE THEN.
WHEN THESE TWO MEN BECAME HITOKIRI, THEY WERE CURSED TO BATTLE.
TK
TK

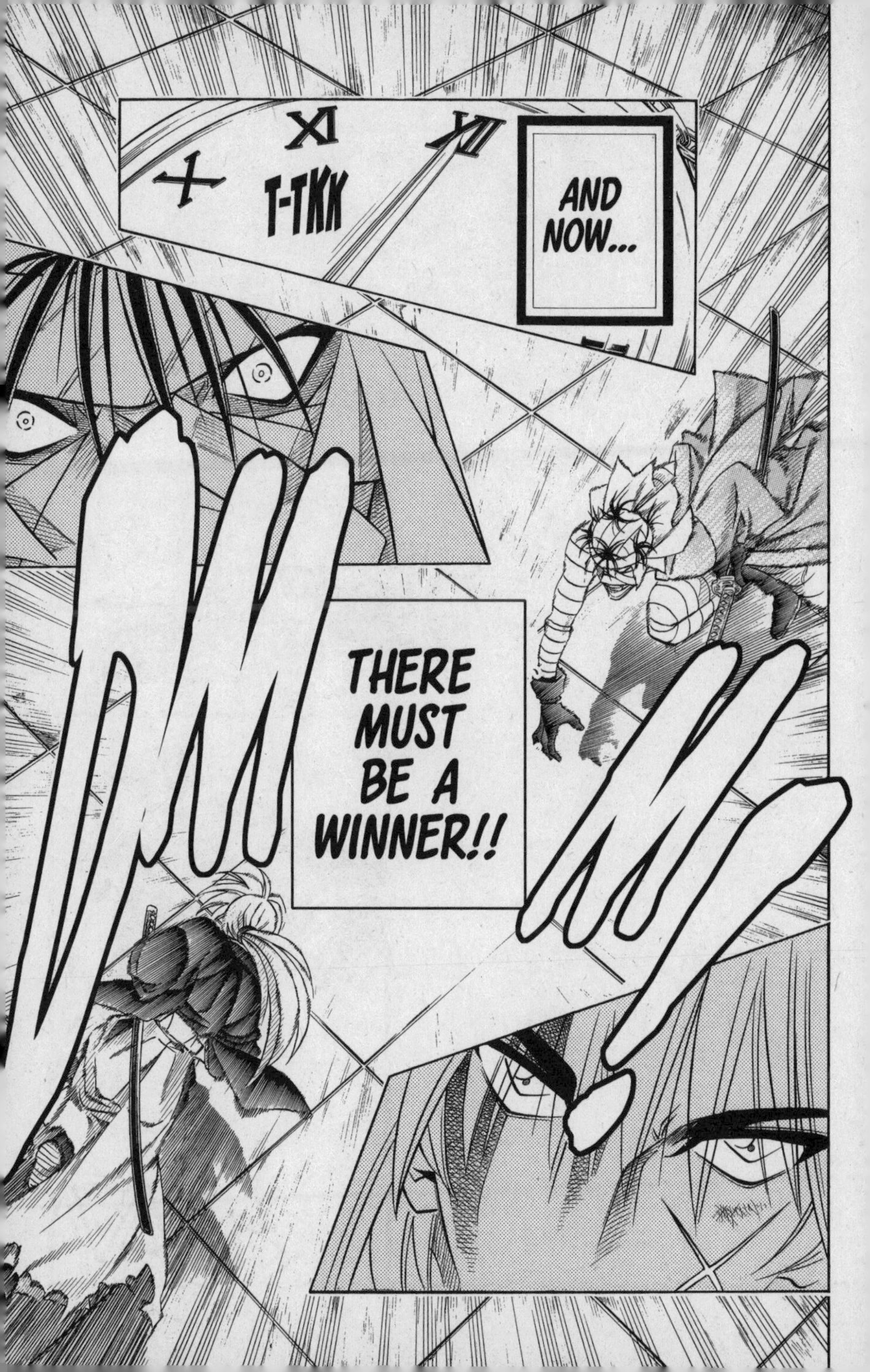
AND NOW...
T-TKK
THERE MUST BE A WINNER!!

Rurouni Kenshin

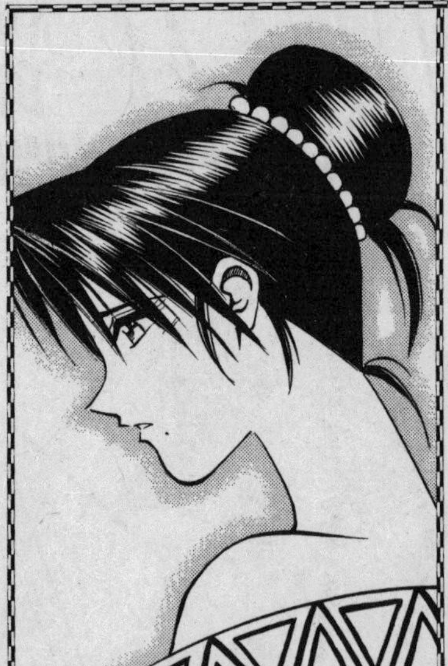

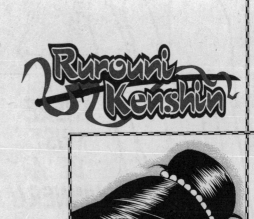

Act 137—Fuel

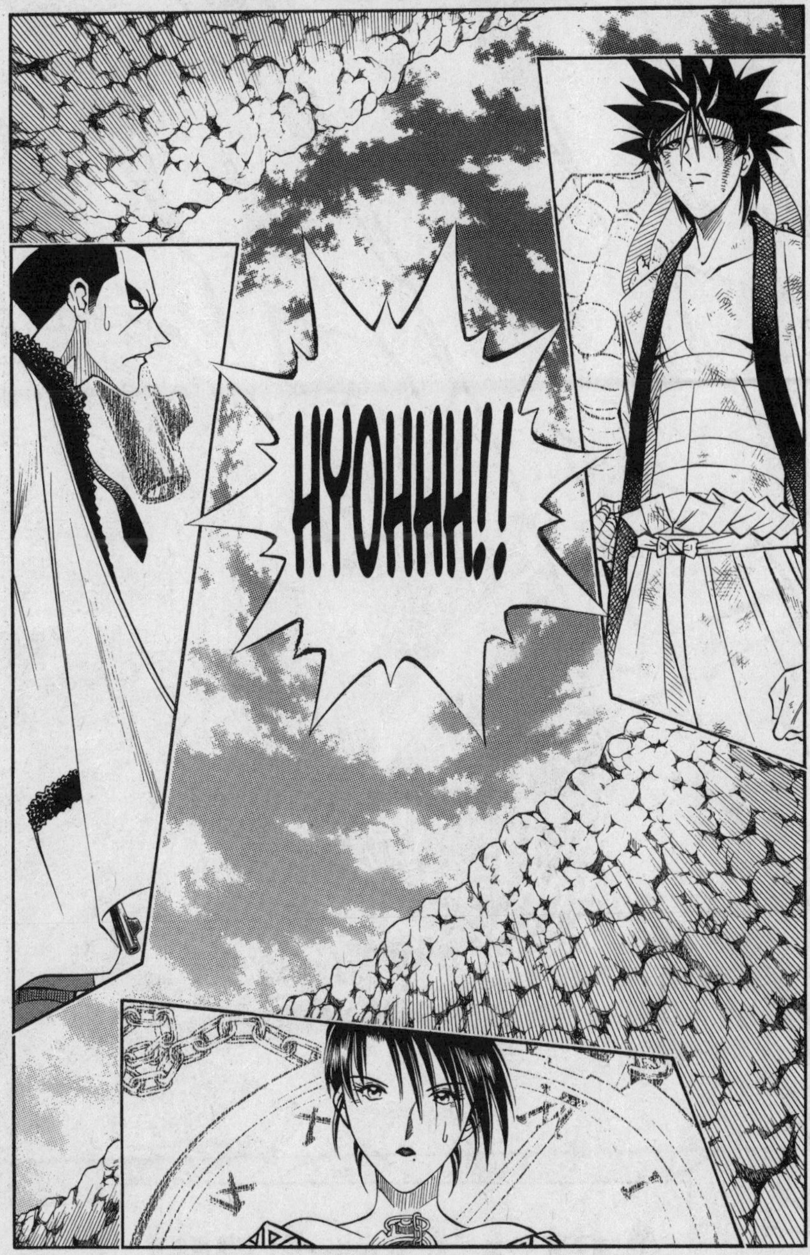
HYOHHH!!

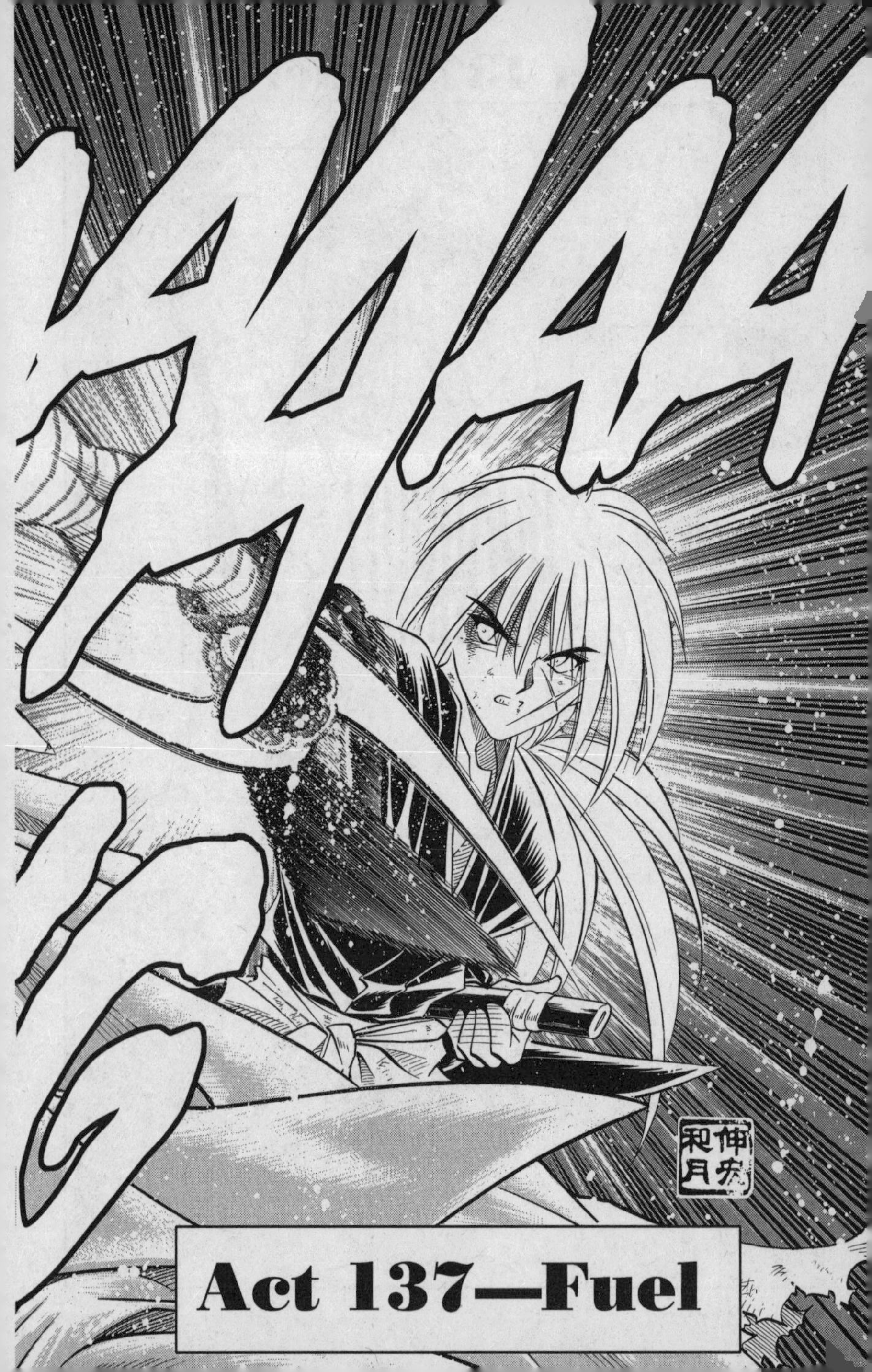
Act 137—Fuel

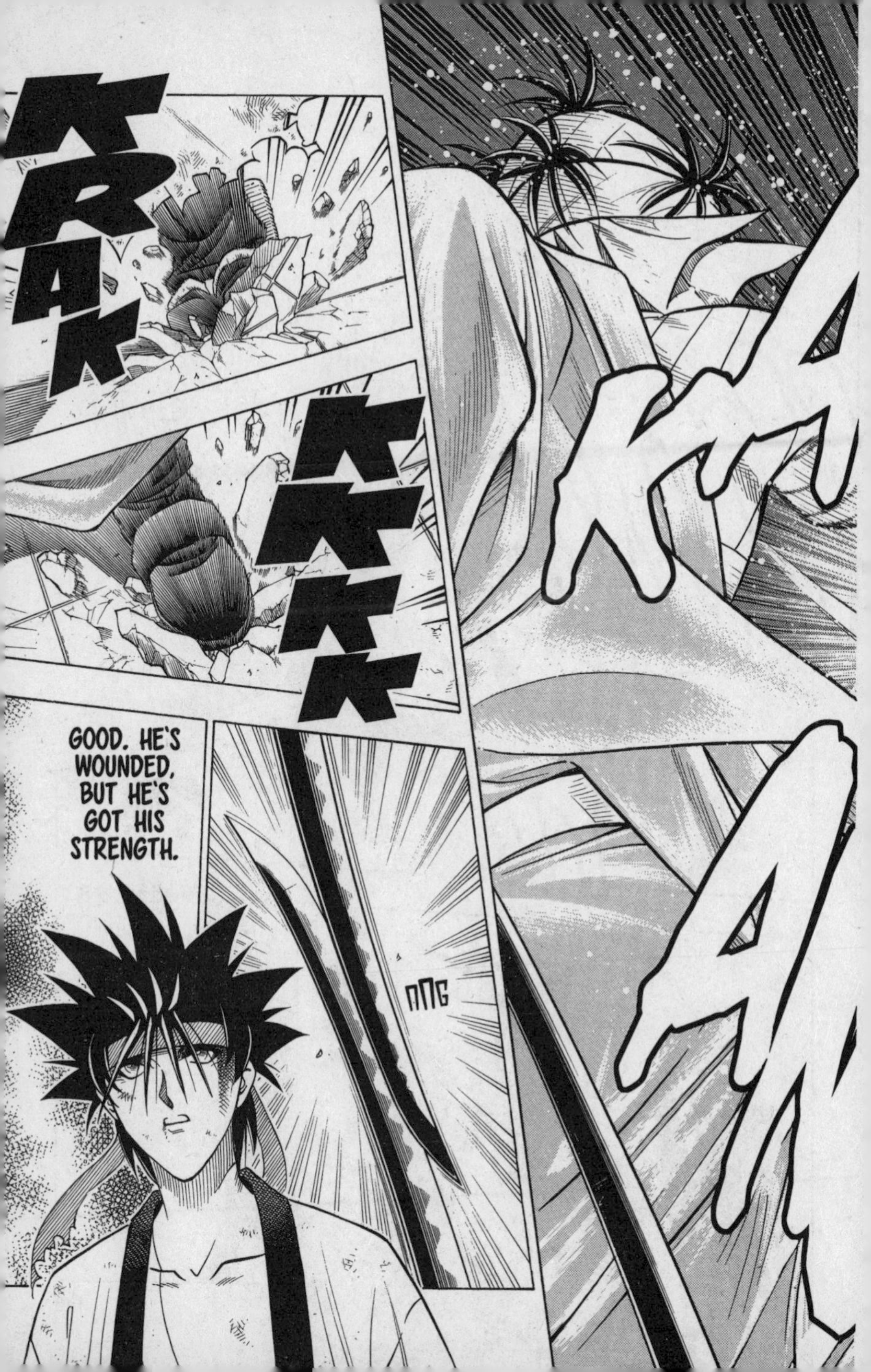
KRAK
KKKK
NNG
GOOD. HE'S WOUNDED, BUT HE'S GOT HIS STRENGTH.

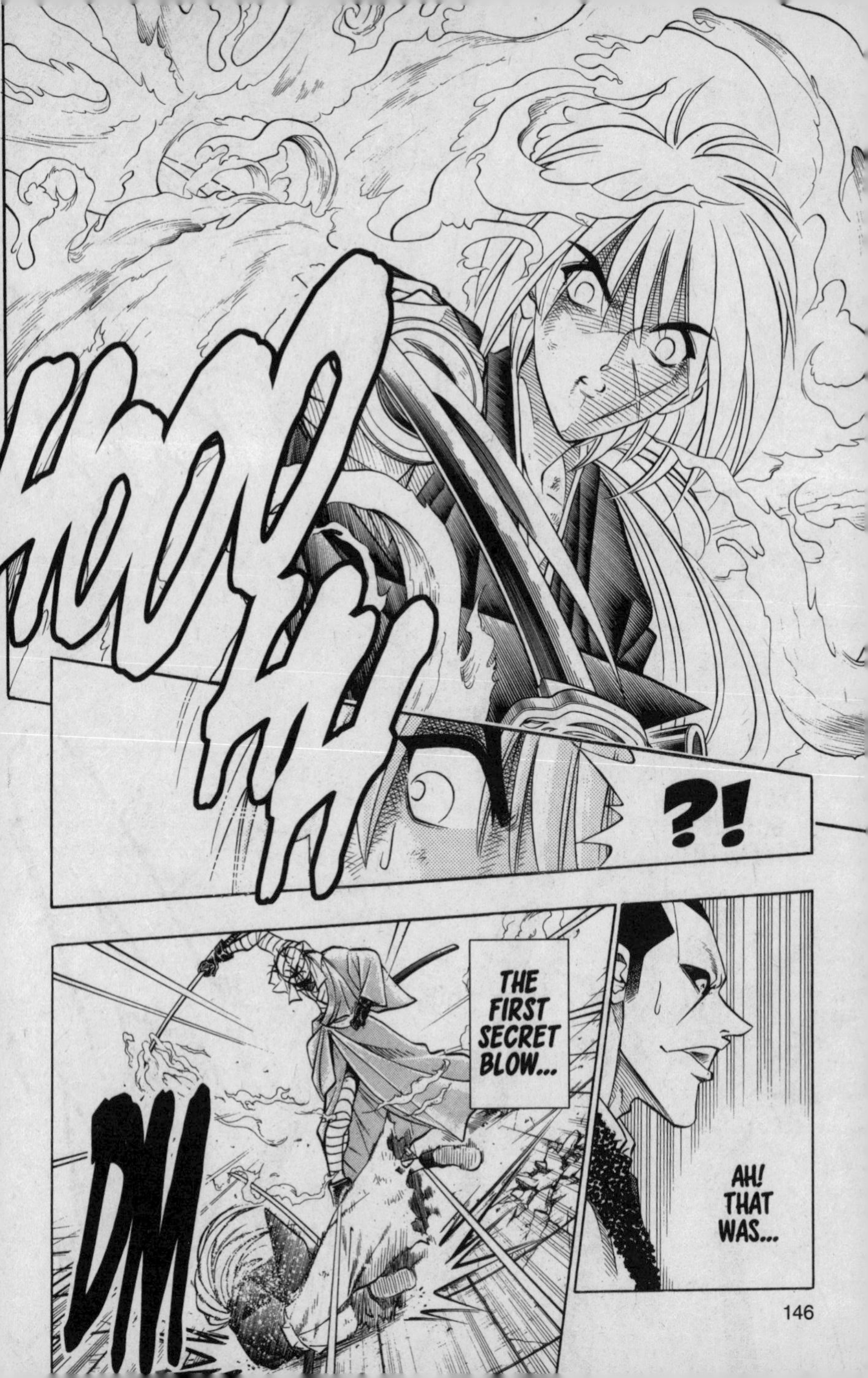
?!
AH! THAT WAS...
THE FIRST SECRET BLOW...

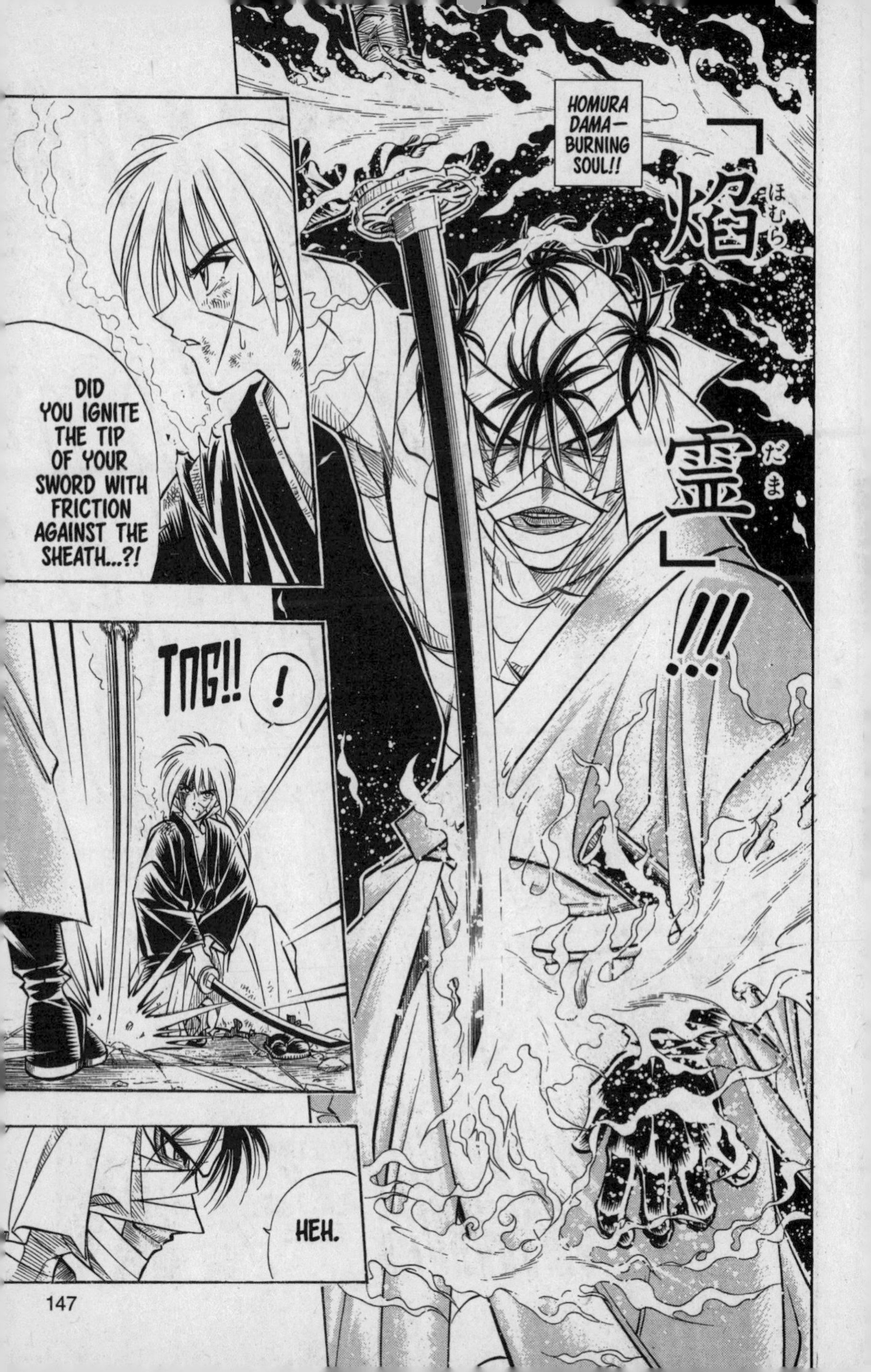
HOMURA DAMA— BURNING SOUL!!
「焔霊」!!!
DID YOU IGNITE THE TIP OF YOUR SWORD WITH FRICTION AGAINST THE SHEATH...?!
TNG!!
!
HEH.

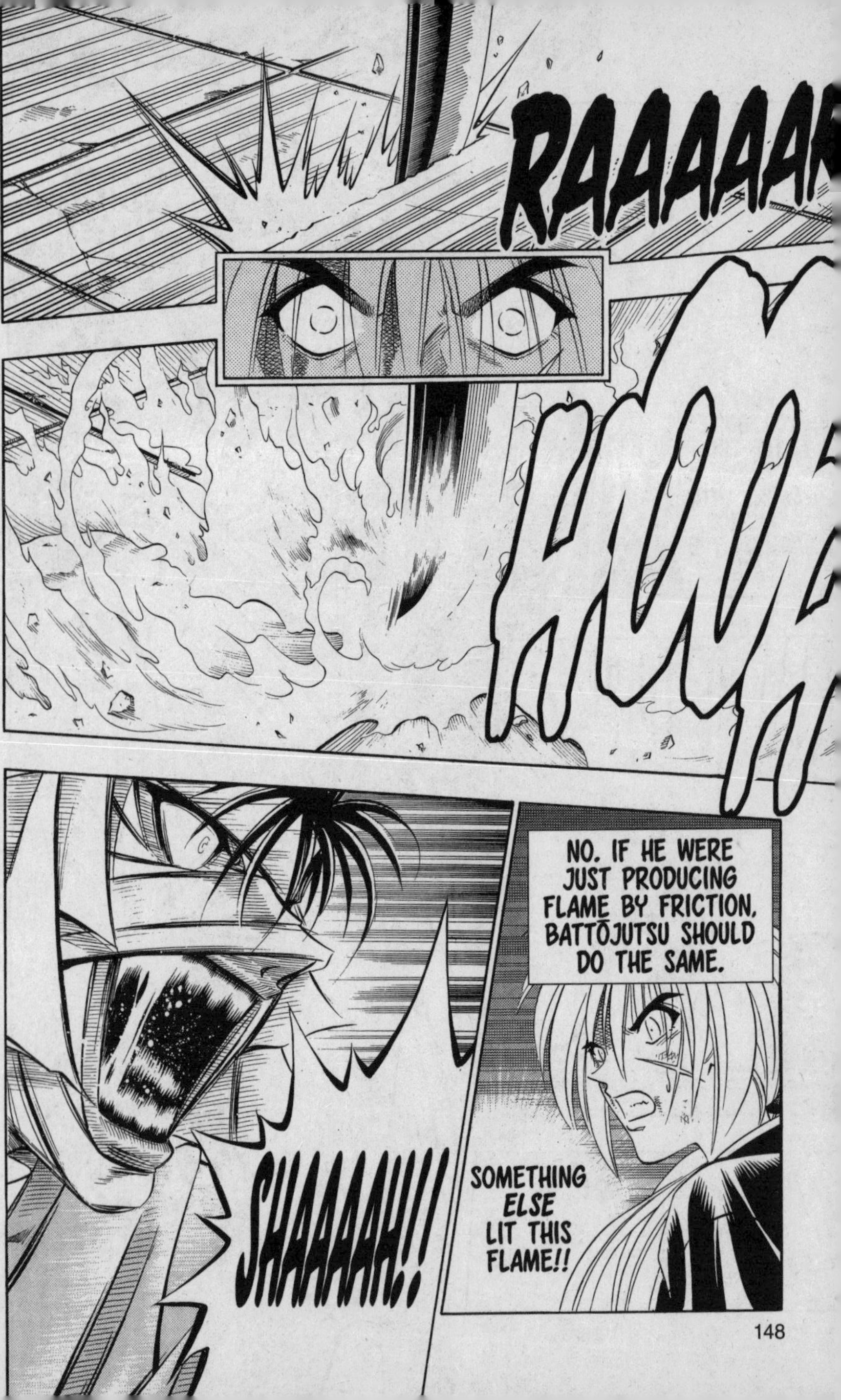
RAAAAAR
NO. IF HE WERE JUST PRODUCING FLAME BY FRICTION, BATTŌJUTSU SHOULD DO THE SAME.
SOMETHING *ELSE* LIT THIS FLAME!!
SHAAAAH!!

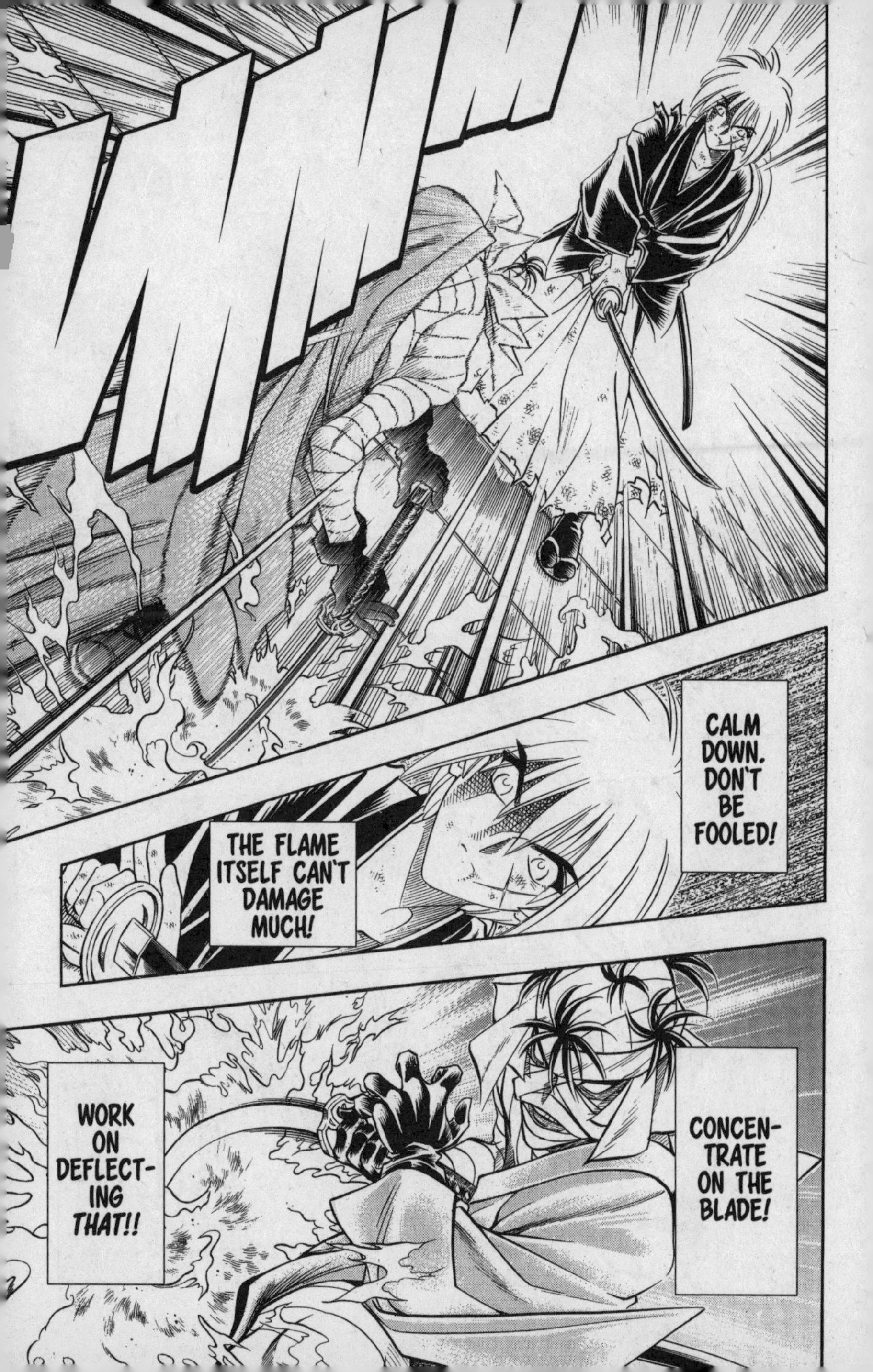
CALM DOWN. DON'T BE FOOLED!
THE FLAME ITSELF CAN'T DAMAGE MUCH!
CONCEN-TRATE ON THE BLADE!
WORK ON DEFLECT-ING THAT!!

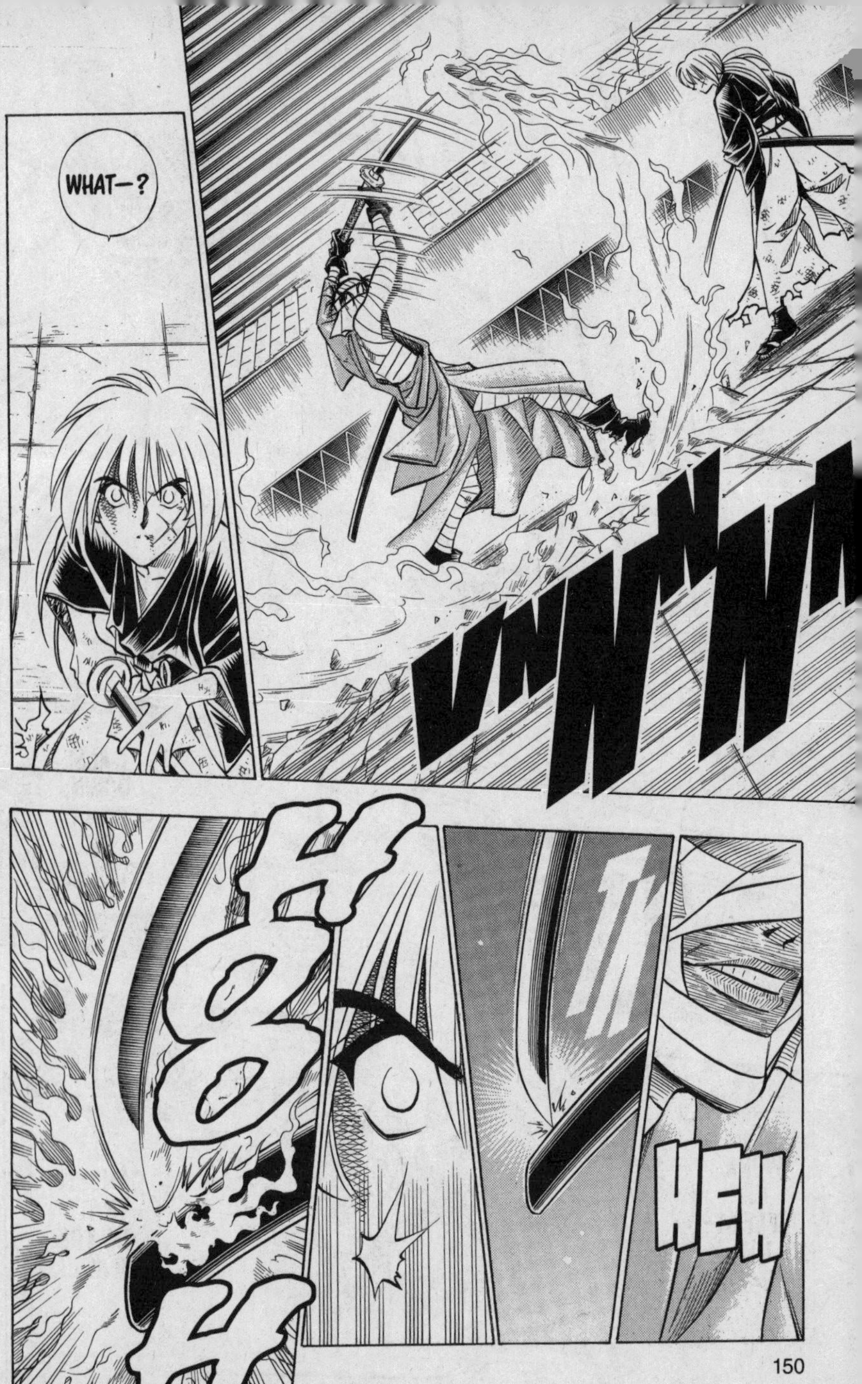
HEH
WHAT—?

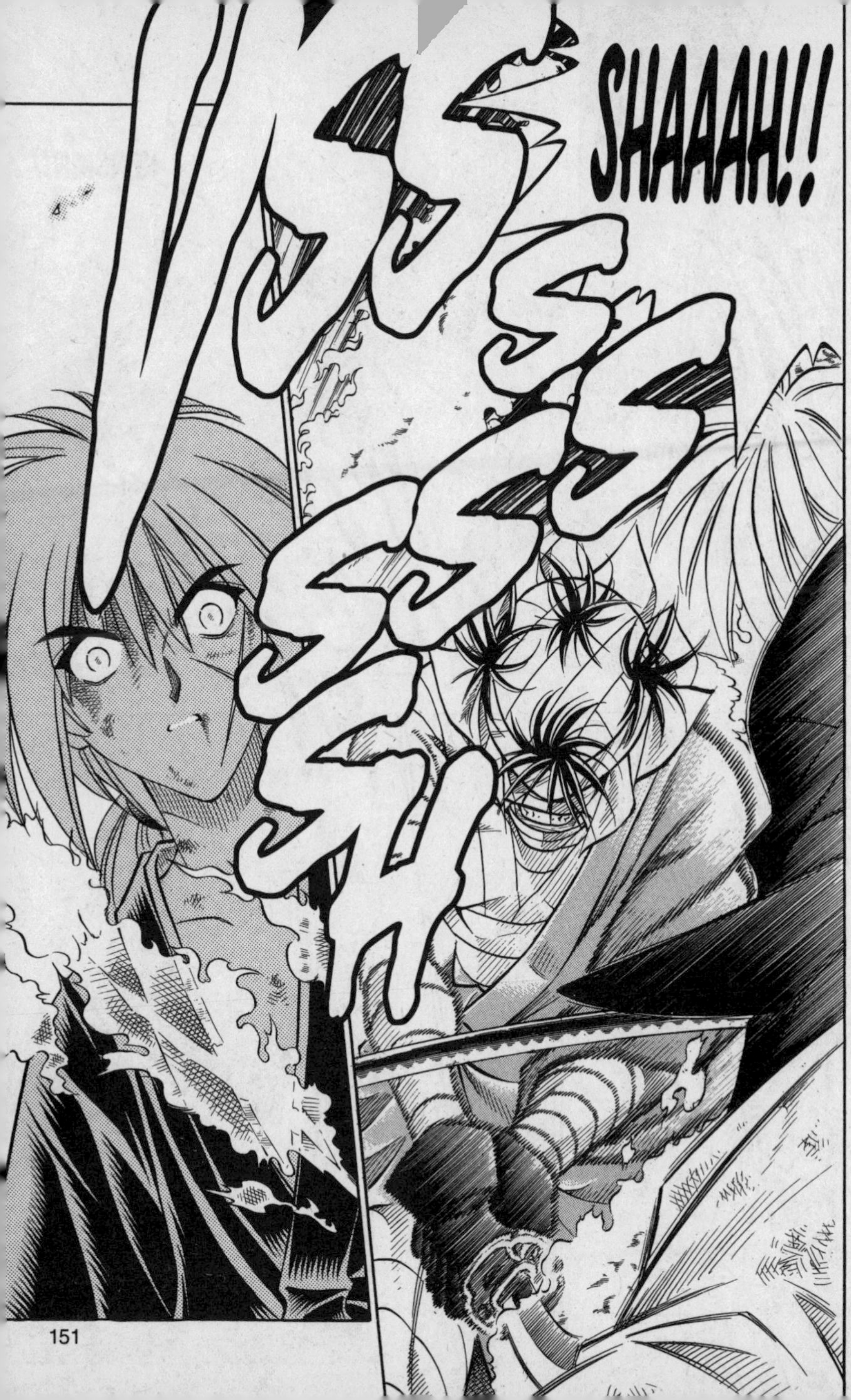
SHAAAH!!
ZSSSH

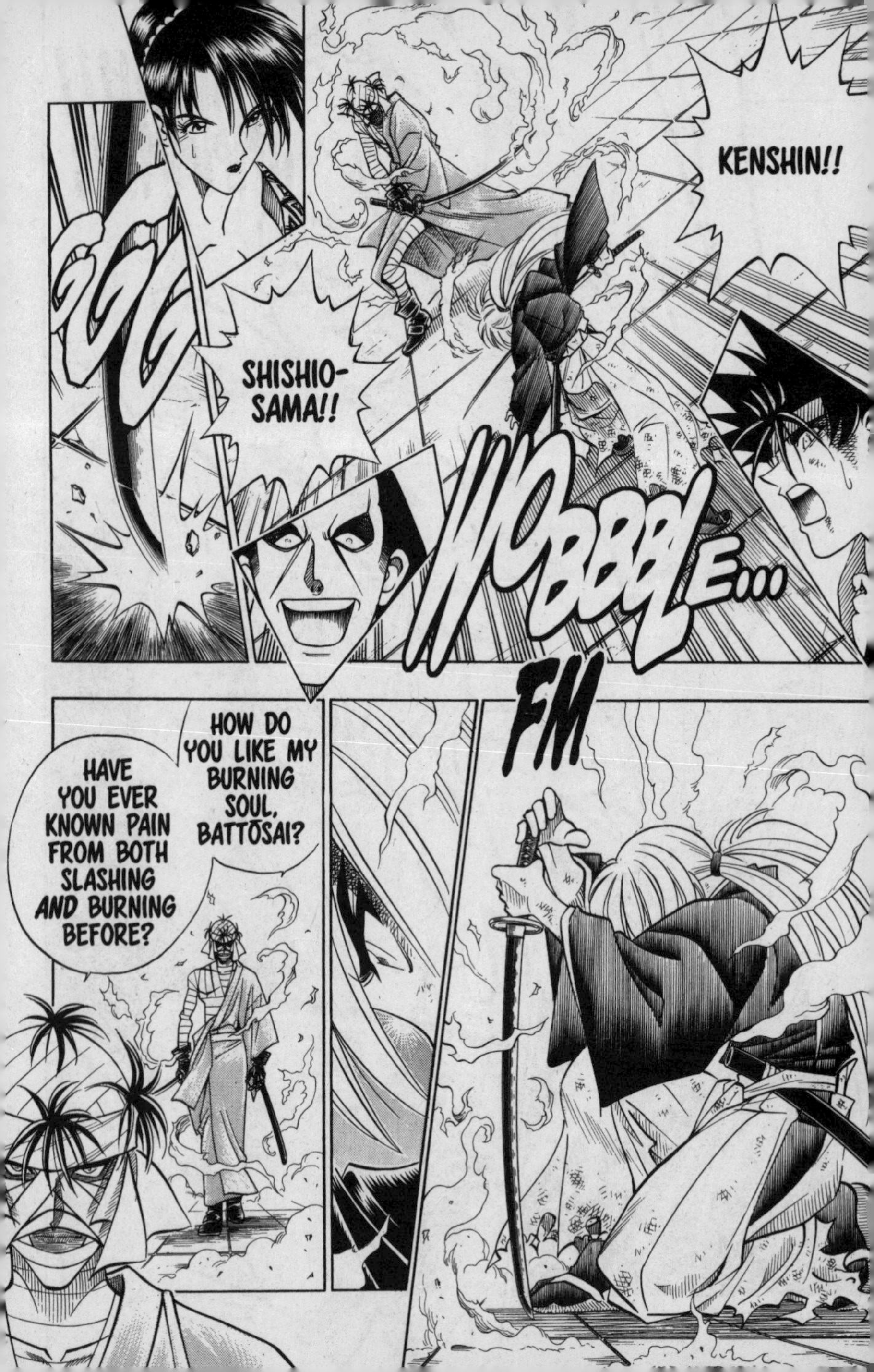
KENSHIN!!
SHISHIO-SAMA!!
WOBBBLE...
FM
HOW DO YOU LIKE MY BURNING SOUL, BATTŌSAI?
HAVE YOU EVER KNOWN PAIN FROM BOTH SLASHING AND BURNING BEFORE?

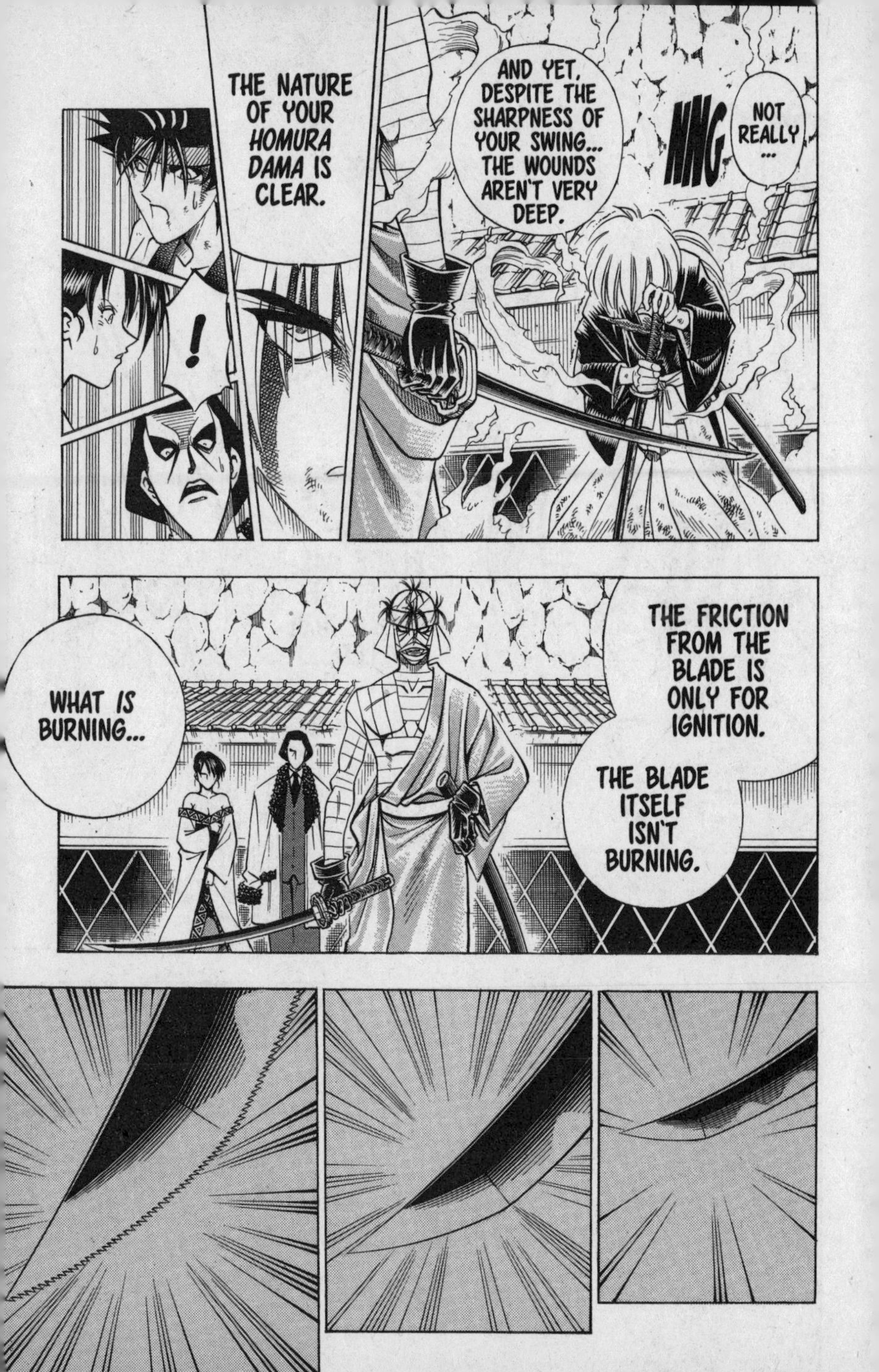

NNG
NOT REALLY...
AND YET, DESPITE THE SHARPNESS OF YOUR SWING... THE WOUNDS AREN'T VERY DEEP.
THE NATURE OF YOUR *HOMURA DAMA* IS CLEAR.
!
THE FRICTION FROM THE BLADE IS ONLY FOR IGNITION.
THE BLADE ITSELF ISN'T BURNING.
WHAT IS BURNING...

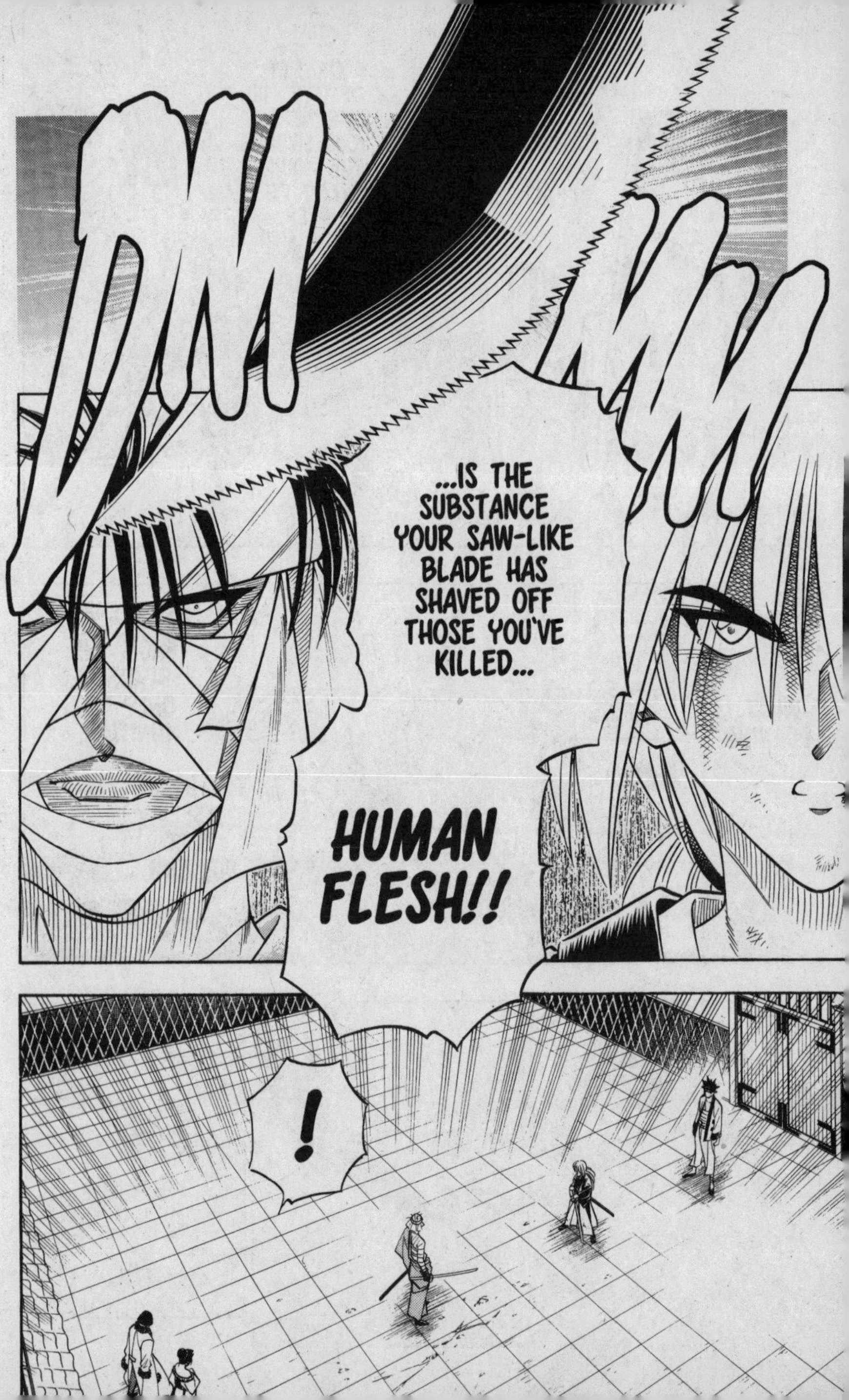
DMMM
...IS THE SUBSTANCE YOUR SAW-LIKE BLADE HAS SHAVED OFF THOSE YOU'VE KILLED...
HUMAN FLESH!!
!

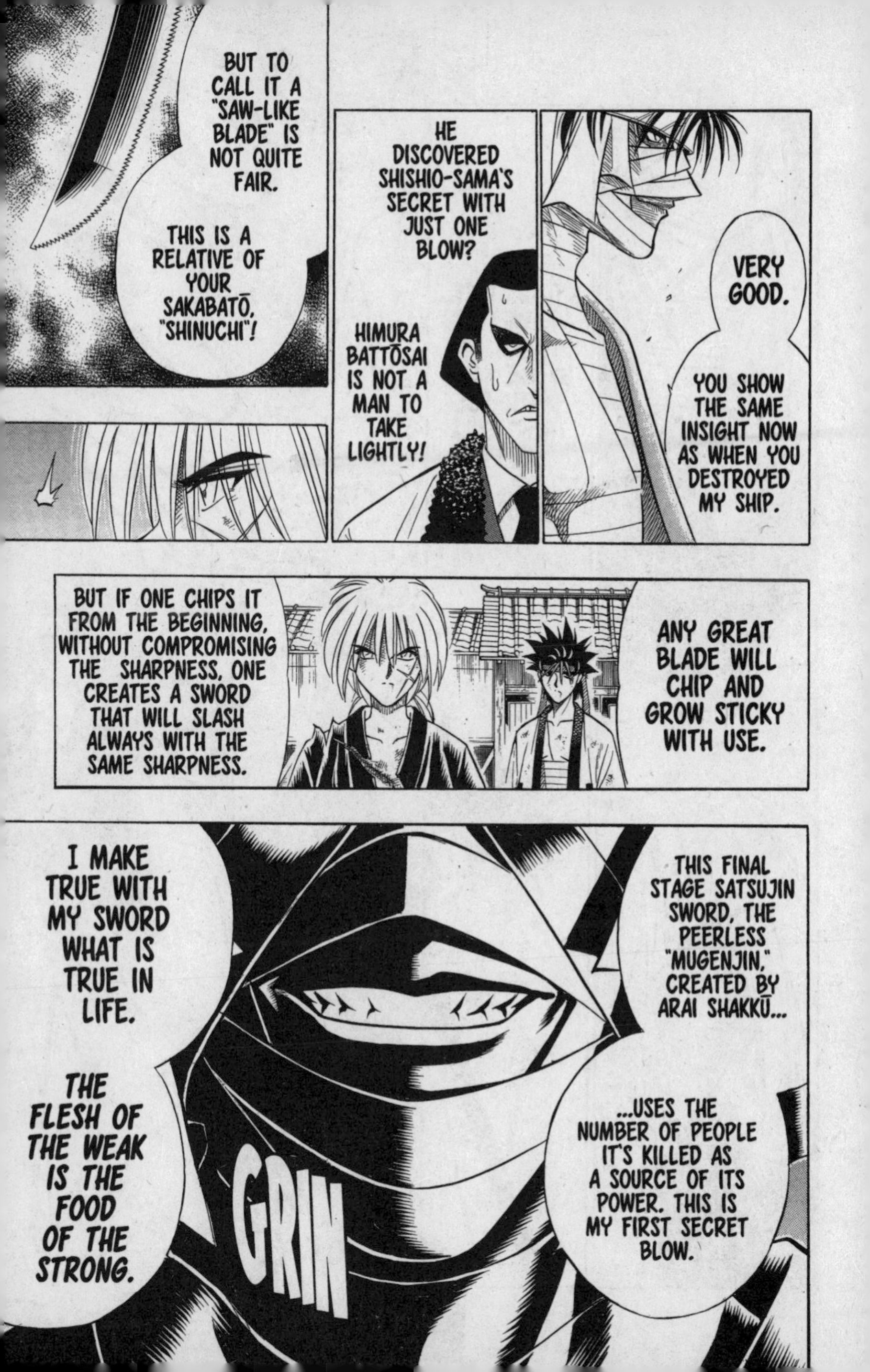
VERY GOOD.
YOU SHOW THE SAME INSIGHT NOW AS WHEN YOU DESTROYED MY SHIP.
HE DISCOVERED SHISHIO-SAMA'S SECRET WITH JUST ONE BLOW?
HIMURA BATTŌSAI IS NOT A MAN TO TAKE LIGHTLY!
BUT TO CALL IT A "SAW-LIKE BLADE" IS NOT QUITE FAIR.
THIS IS A RELATIVE OF YOUR SAKABATŌ, "SHINUCHI"!
ANY GREAT BLADE WILL CHIP AND GROW STICKY WITH USE.
BUT IF ONE CHIPS IT FROM THE BEGINNING, WITHOUT COMPROMISING THE SHARPNESS, ONE CREATES A SWORD THAT WILL SLASH ALWAYS WITH THE SAME SHARPNESS.
THIS FINAL STAGE SATSUJIN SWORD, THE PEERLESS "MUGENJIN," CREATED BY ARAI SHAKKŪ...
...USES THE NUMBER OF PEOPLE IT'S KILLED AS A SOURCE OF ITS POWER. THIS IS MY FIRST SECRET BLOW.
I MAKE TRUE WITH MY SWORD WHAT IS TRUE IN LIFE.
THE FLESH OF THE WEAK IS THE FOOD OF THE STRONG.
GRIN

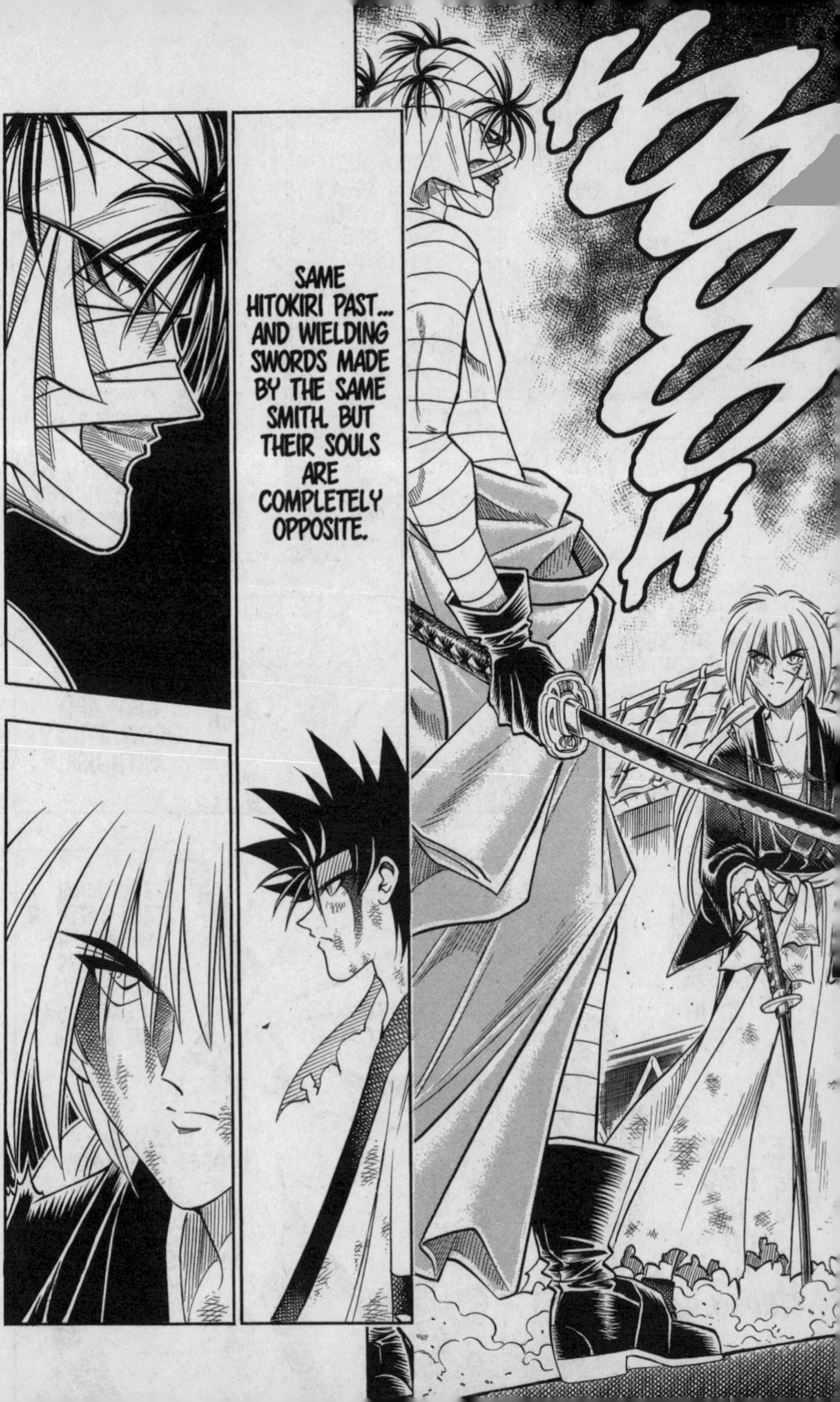
SAME HITOKIRI PAST... AND WIELDING SWORDS MADE BY THE SAME SMITH. BUT THEIR SOULS ARE COMPLETELY OPPOSITE.

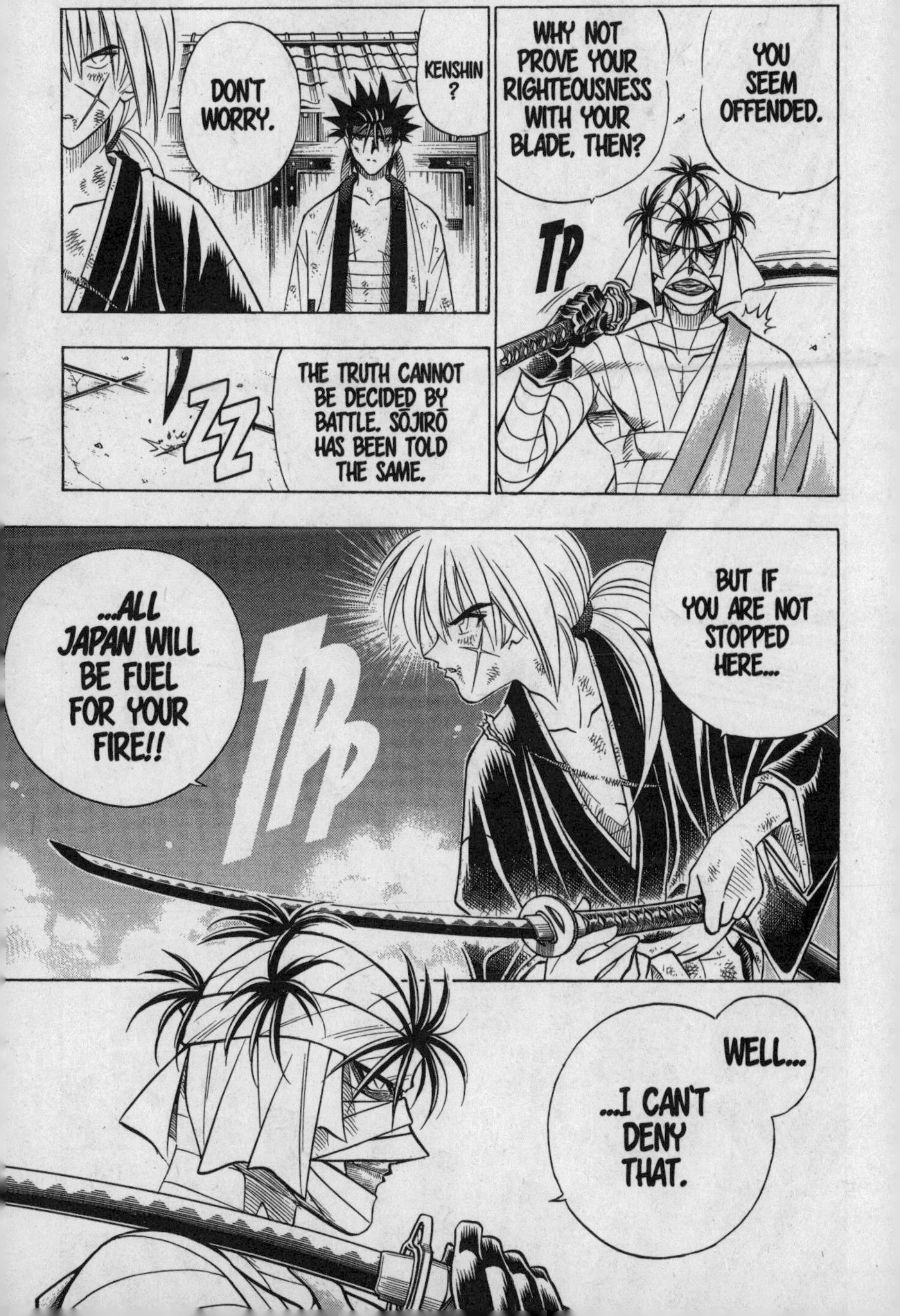
YOU SEEM OFFENDED.
WHY NOT PROVE YOUR RIGHTEOUSNESS WITH YOUR BLADE, THEN?
TP
KENSHIN ?
DON'T WORRY.
THE TRUTH CANNOT BE DECIDED BY BATTLE. SŌJIRŌ HAS BEEN TOLD THE SAME.
ZZ
BUT IF YOU ARE NOT STOPPED HERE...
...ALL JAPAN WILL BE FUEL FOR YOUR FIRE!!
TP
WELL...
...I CAN'T DENY THAT.

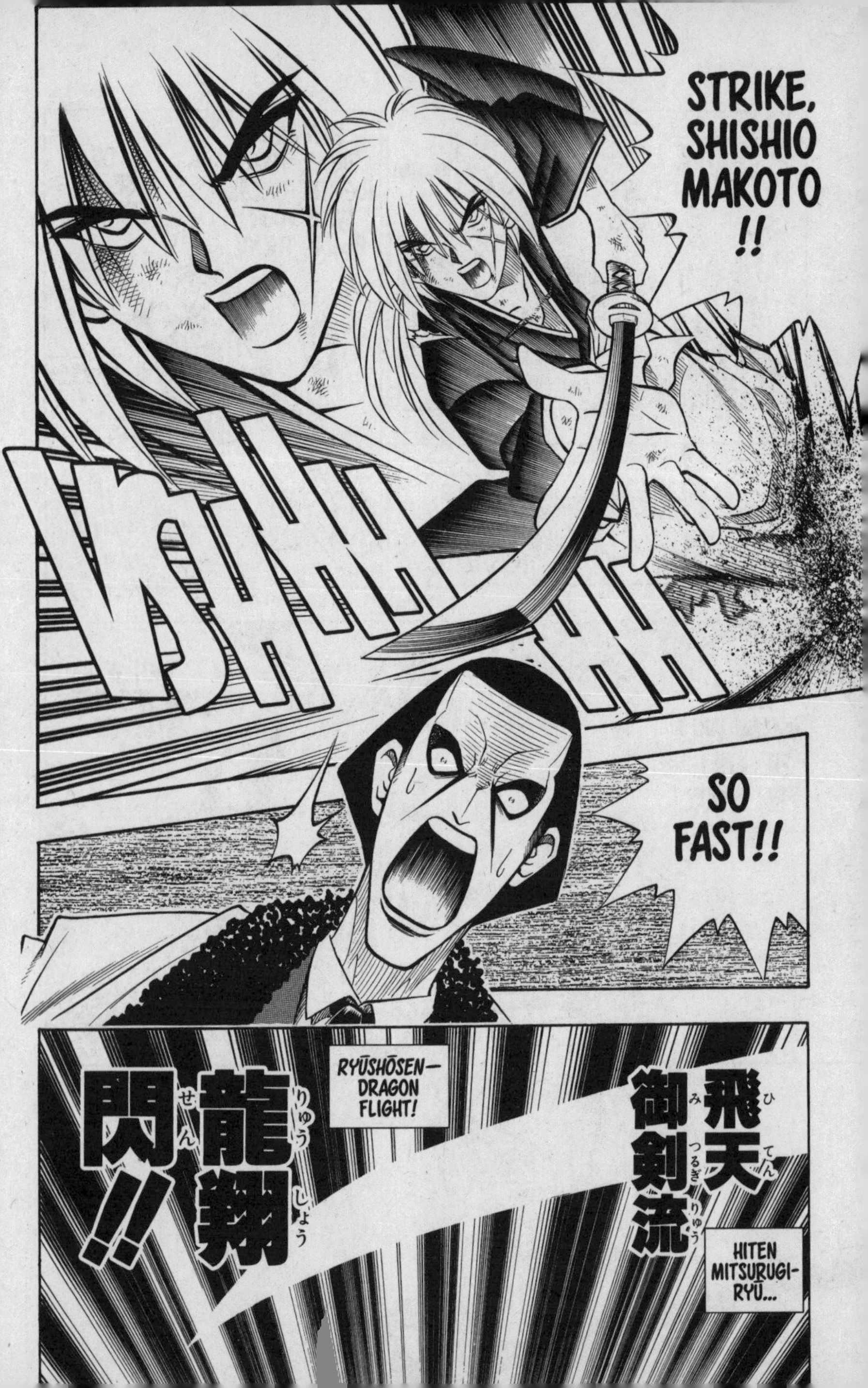
STRIKE, SHISHIO MAKOTO!!
SO FAST!!
飛天御剣流
HITEN MITSURUGI-RYŪ...
龍翔閃!!
RYŪSHŌSEN—DRAGON FLIGHT!

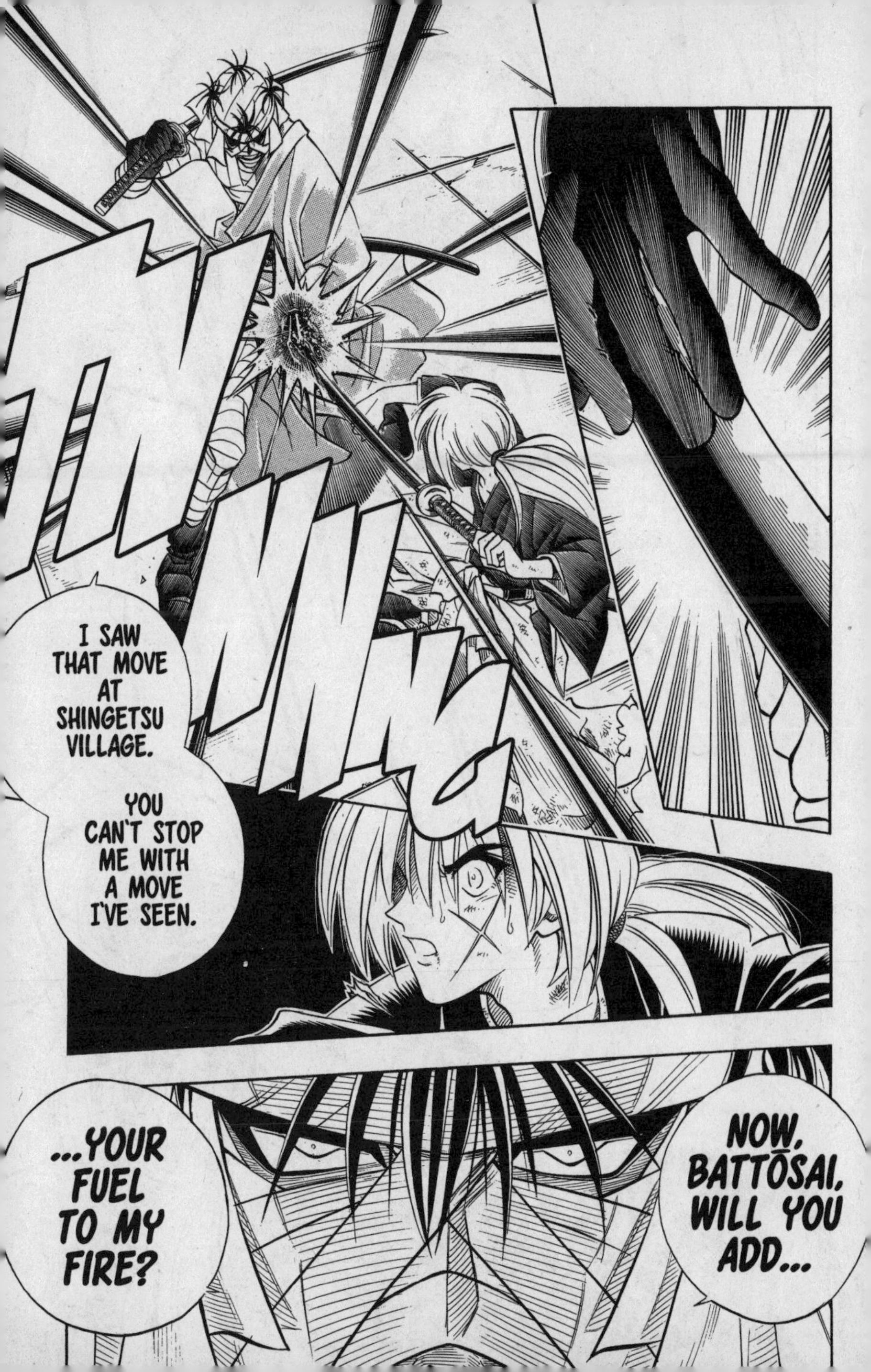
I SAW THAT MOVE AT SHINGETSU VILLAGE.
YOU CAN'T STOP ME WITH A MOVE I'VE SEEN.
NOW, BATTŌSAI, WILL YOU ADD...
...YOUR FUEL TO MY FIRE?

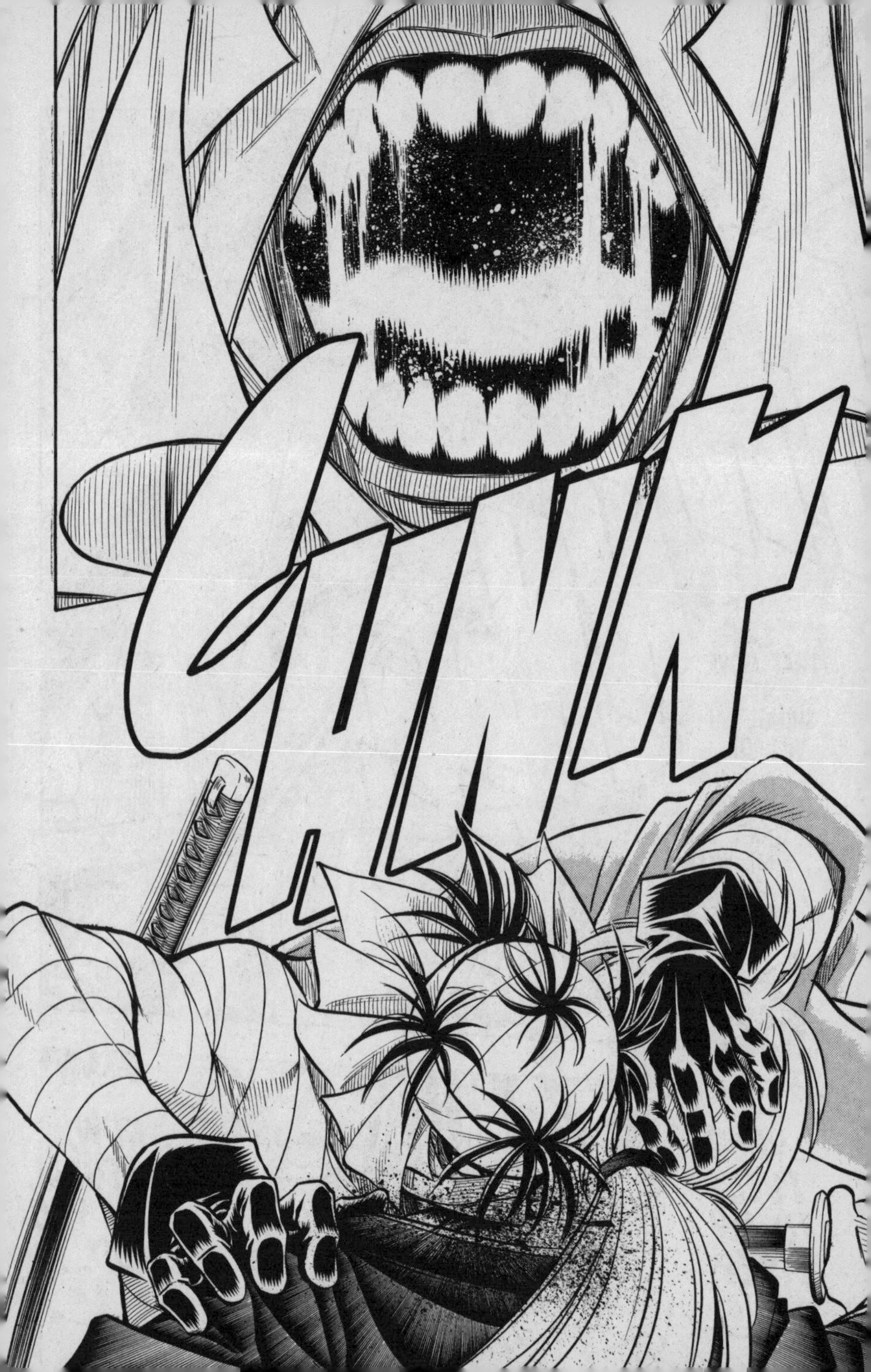

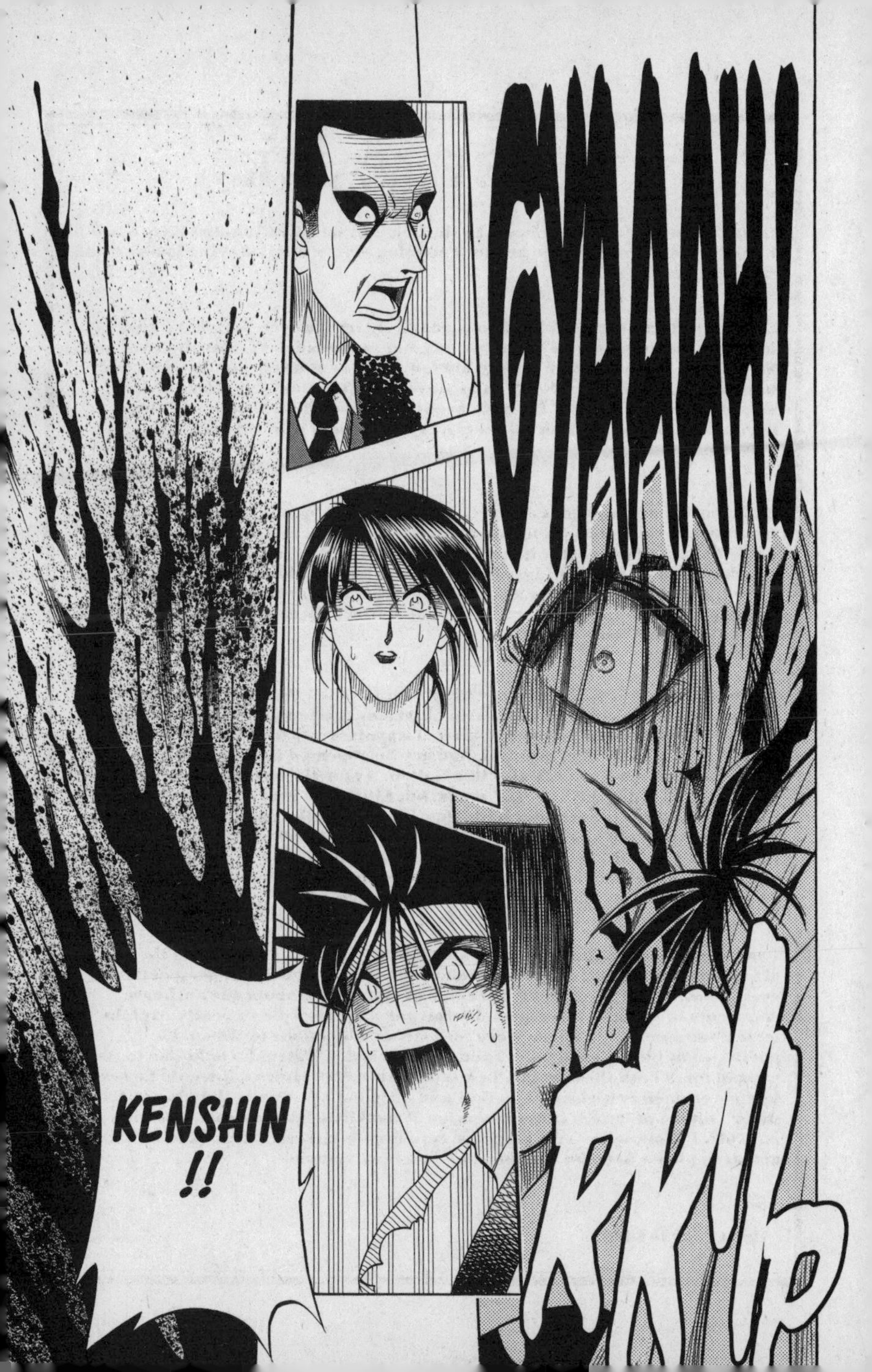
GYAAAH!!
KENSHIN !!

"FREE TALK"

Long time no see. Watsuki here. In the original serialization, the Kyoto arc has ended and the new arc begun. I'm doing pretty okay, staying healthy and working hard.

I'd like to start off by talking about action figures (as you may have guessed from my author's note). They're totally hot at the moment. How hot, you ask? So hot that Watsuki's own deeply hidden otaku soul has begun to stir! (And how lame a sentence is that?) In any event, by the time this (compiled) volume is out (in Japan), I'll have acquired the original Getter 1. If they decide to issue Getter 2 and Getter 3, my happiness will be that much more complete.

As far as import toys go, I still pick up *X-Men* and *Spawn* figures from a few other series I like, along the way. Despite the craze, I try to remind myself about the choosing carefully thing. Maybe it's just me, but shelling out 30,000 to 40,000 yen* just for one figure isn't my kind of hobby. I do hope it's not a fad that'll go away, though, and that action figures eventually become a legitimate toy genre. (For that matter, I'm hoping American comics aren't just a fad here either!)

As for games...let's talk about the highly anticipated *Dark Stalkers* sequel *Vampire Savior*. As I write this, I've played only a few times, but Morrigan seems to have become weaker, which disappoints me. Watsuki was nevertheless charmed by her, as usual, and getting defeated in "versus" mode is fine so long as it's by her. I also like Gallon. As for the new characters, Loligan—okay, not the "Lolita" mode, but Lilith, the real character—is interesting—her relationship with Morrigan, if not the character herself. Since I already play so many characters, though, I had to pass. I'll get to them once I'm a bit more settled in. All the fighting games Watsuki gets hooked on seem to have samurai or robots or monsters...no normal humans. Should I be worried?

Changing the topic, thank you for all your fan letters...and not just the letters of support, either, but the critical ones, too. I get a new bit of perspective every time I read one. There were lots of complaints about the author's comments in Volume 14—especially the parts where I didn't really explain myself—so I'm sorry. There were also strong objections to Watsuki's portrayal of the Shinsengumi Yamanami Keisuke. Watsuki would like to expand upon both these points in a later volume. Of course, it would be best to answer each criticism, objection and question personally, but due to the sheer volume of letters (not to mention Watsuki's schedule) that's just not possible. I suppose my best response is to create interesting work as a manga artist, so please keep on reading. See you next volume!

*About $300 to $400.

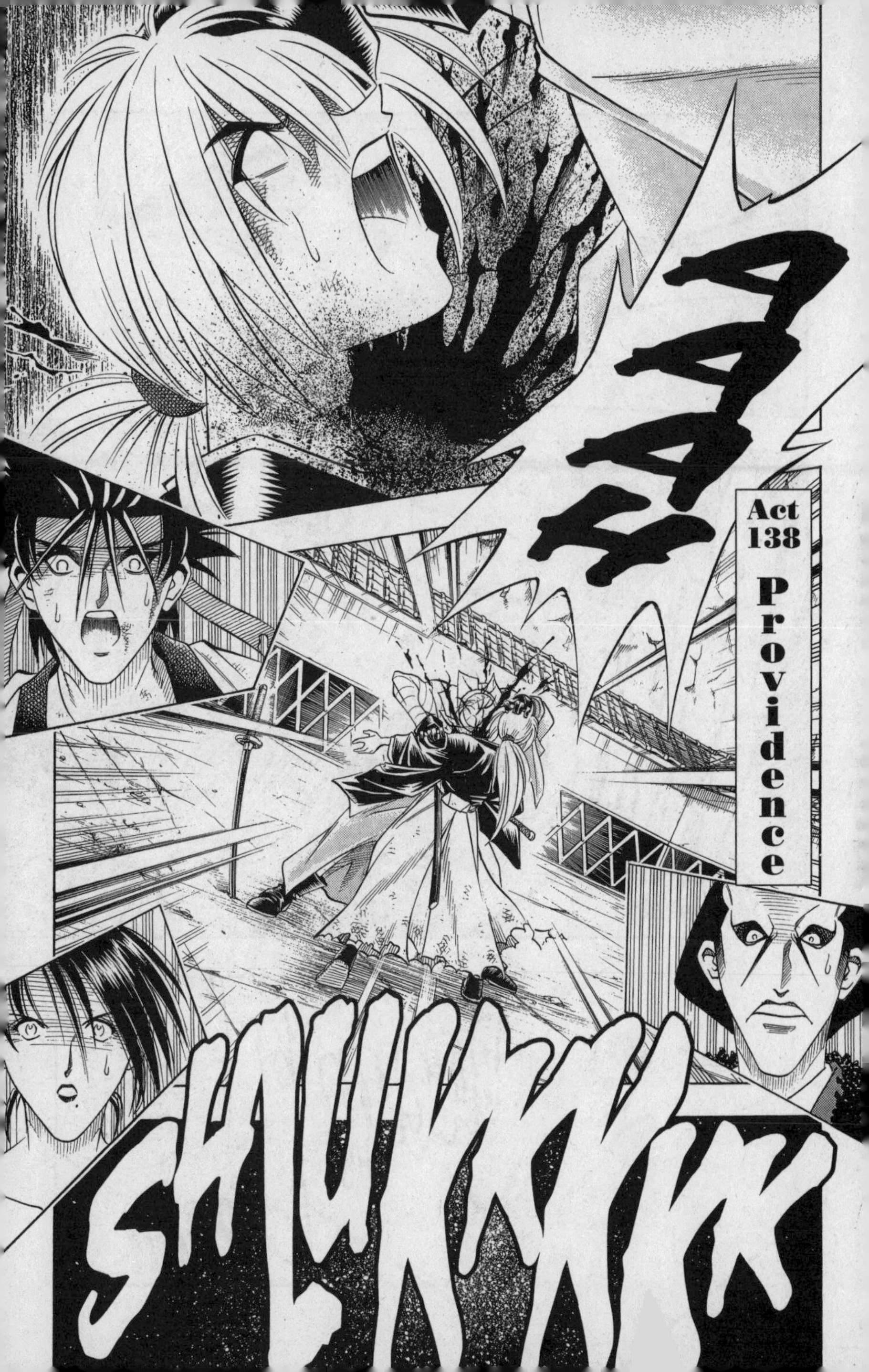
AAAH
Act 138
Providence
SHUNNNK

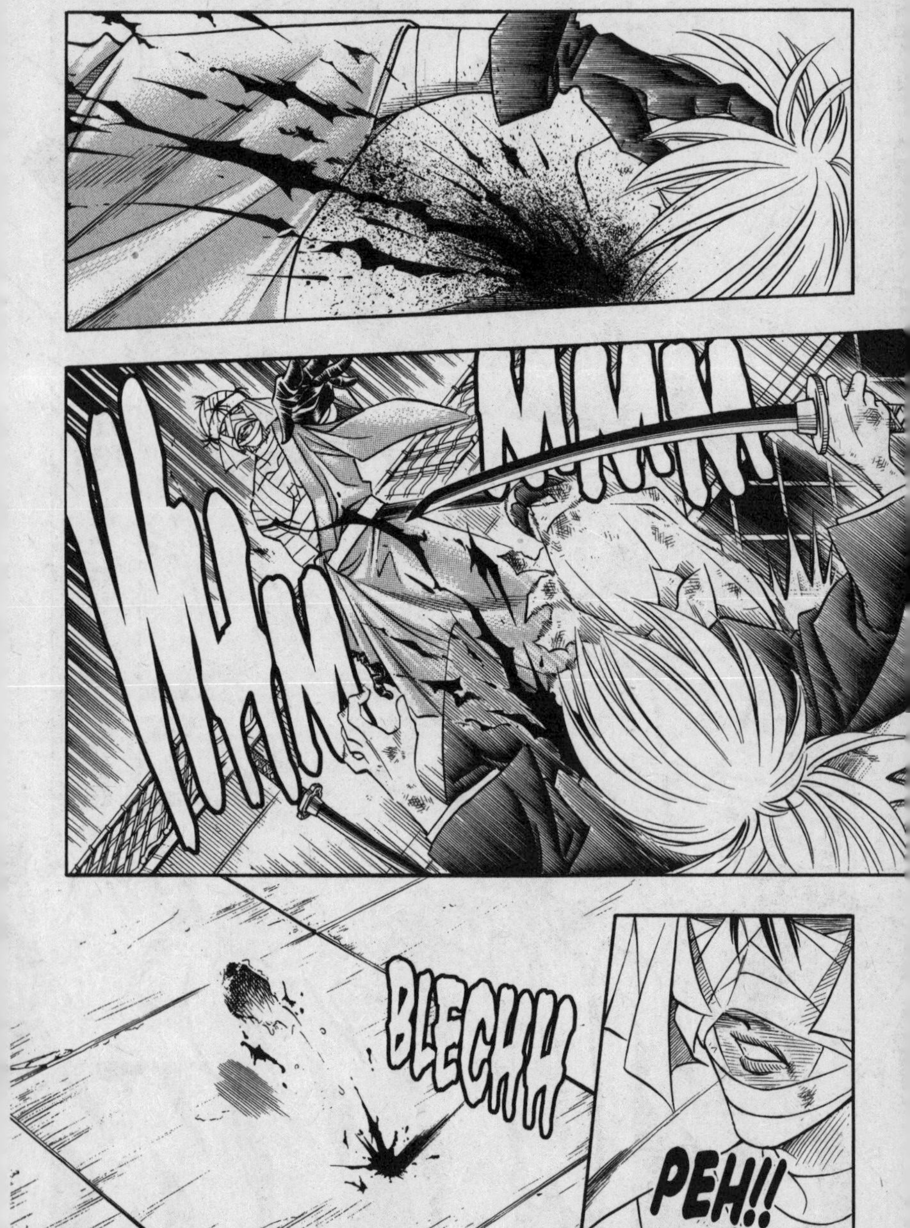

WHAM
MMMM
PEH!!
BLECHH

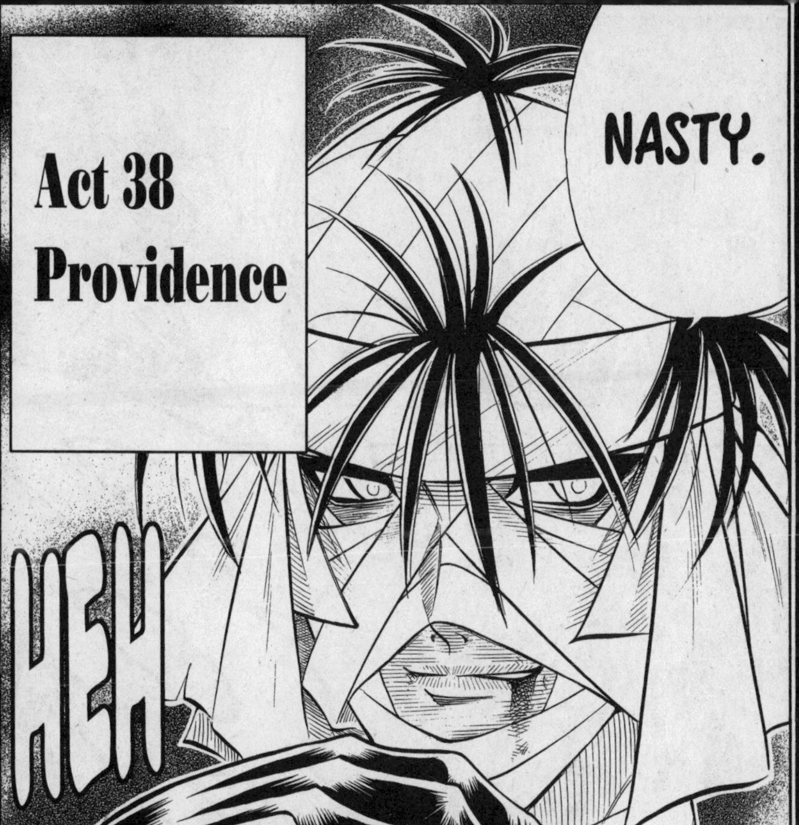
NASTY.
Act 38 Providence
HEH
NEITHER POISON NOR MEDICINE.

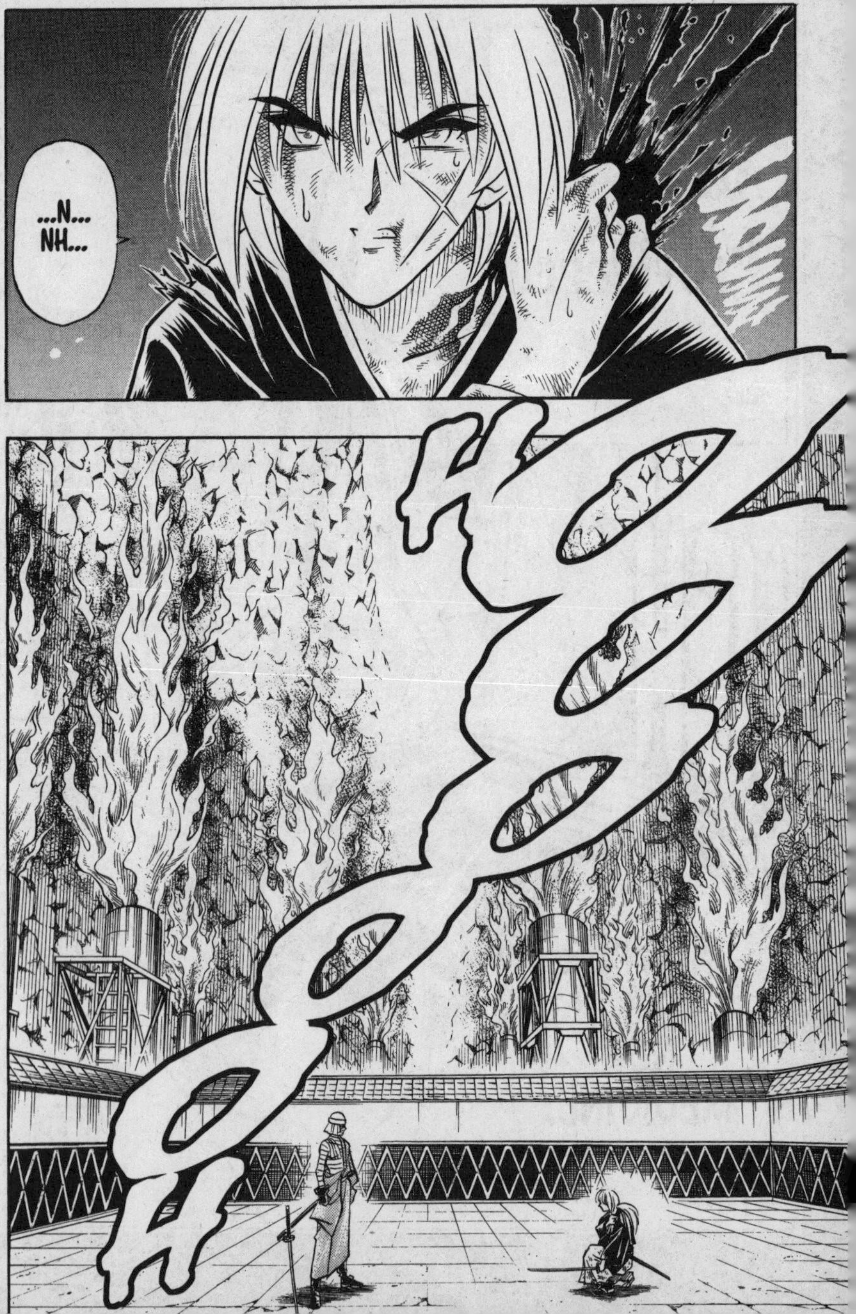
...N... NH...

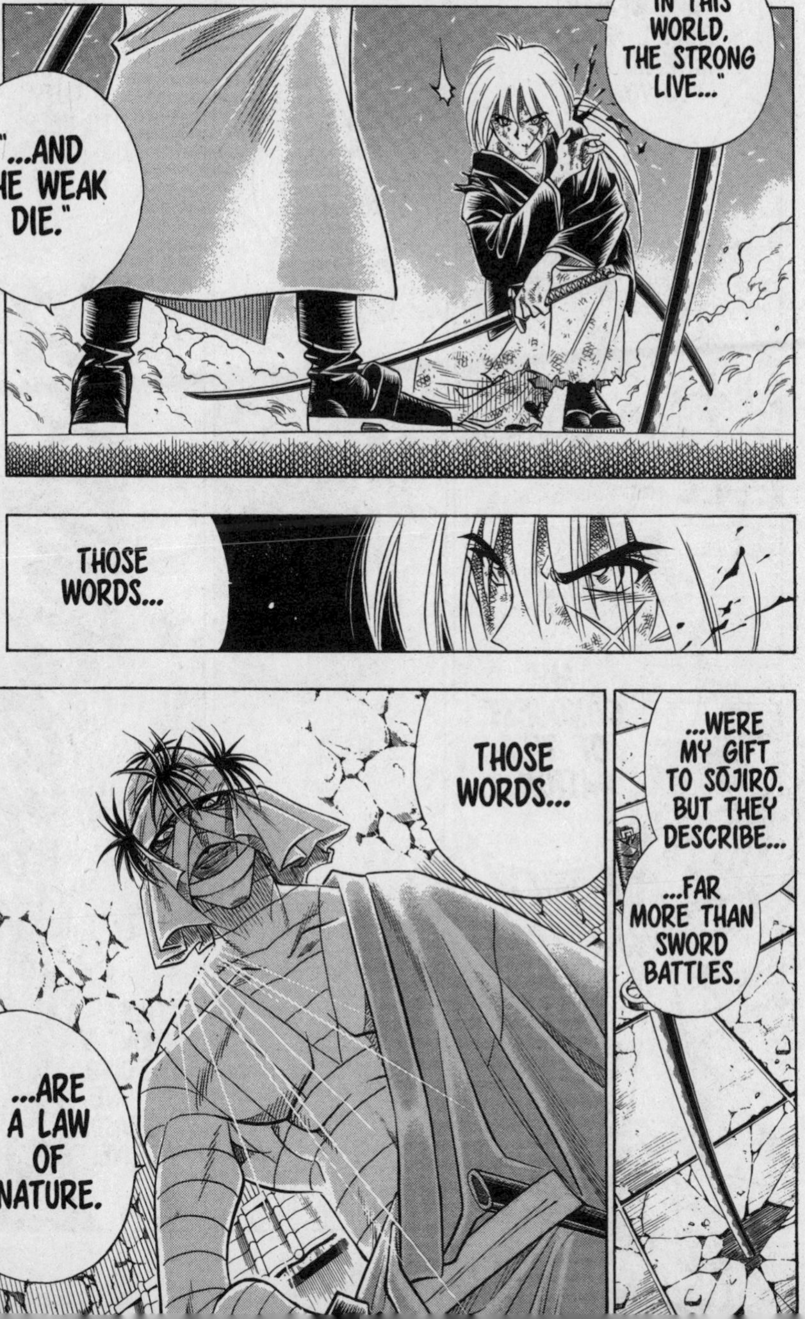
"IN THIS WORLD, THE STRONG LIVE..."
"...AND THE WEAK DIE."
THOSE WORDS...
...WERE MY GIFT TO SŌJIRŌ. BUT THEY DESCRIBE...
...FAR MORE THAN SWORD BATTLES.
THOSE WORDS...
...ARE A LAW OF NATURE.

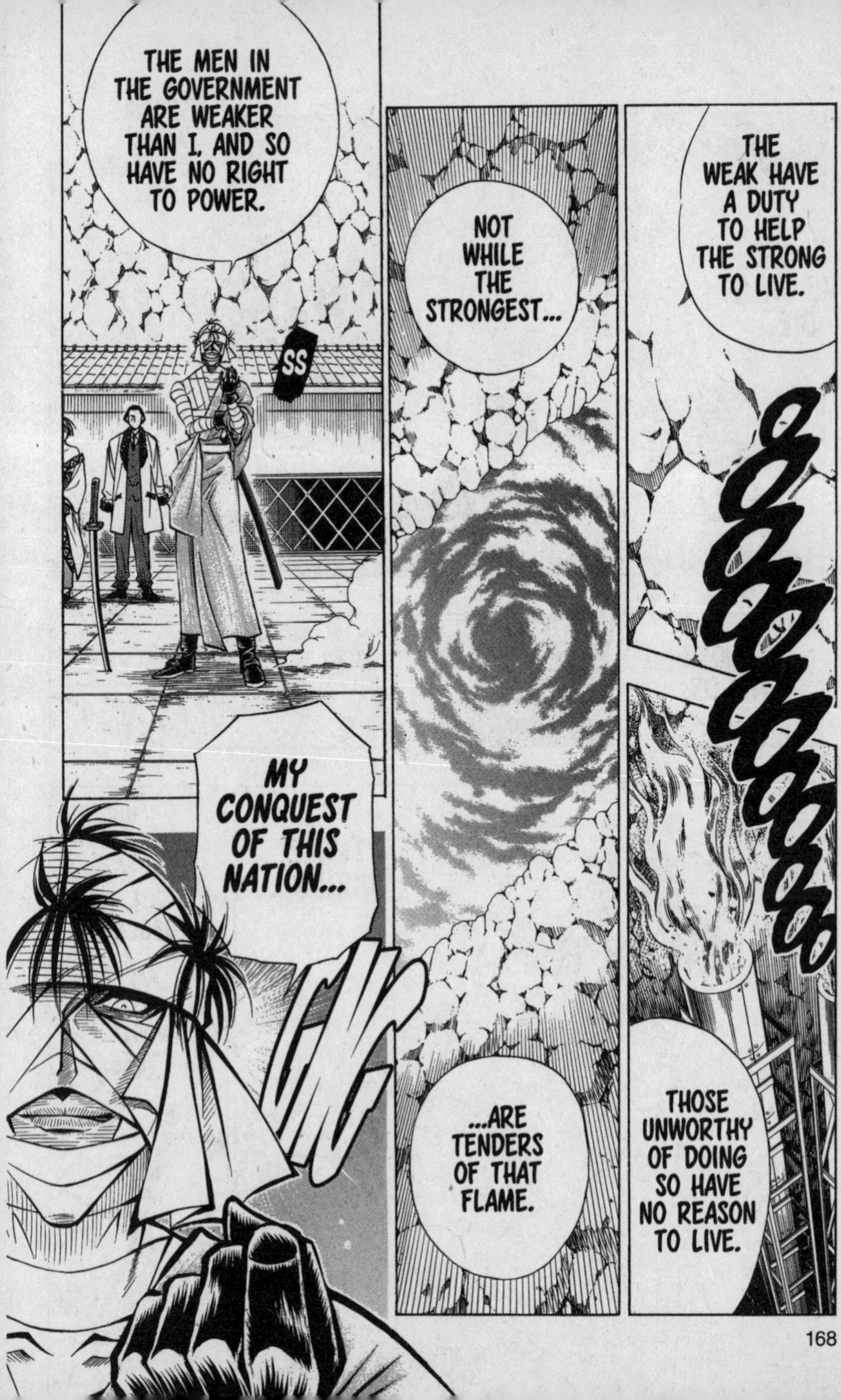
THE WEAK HAVE A DUTY TO HELP THE STRONG TO LIVE.
THOSE UNWORTHY OF DOING SO HAVE NO REASON TO LIVE.
NOT WHILE THE STRONGEST...
...ARE TENDERS OF THAT FLAME.
THE MEN IN THE GOVERNMENT ARE WEAKER THAN I, AND SO HAVE NO RIGHT TO POWER.
SS
MY CONQUEST OF THIS NATION...

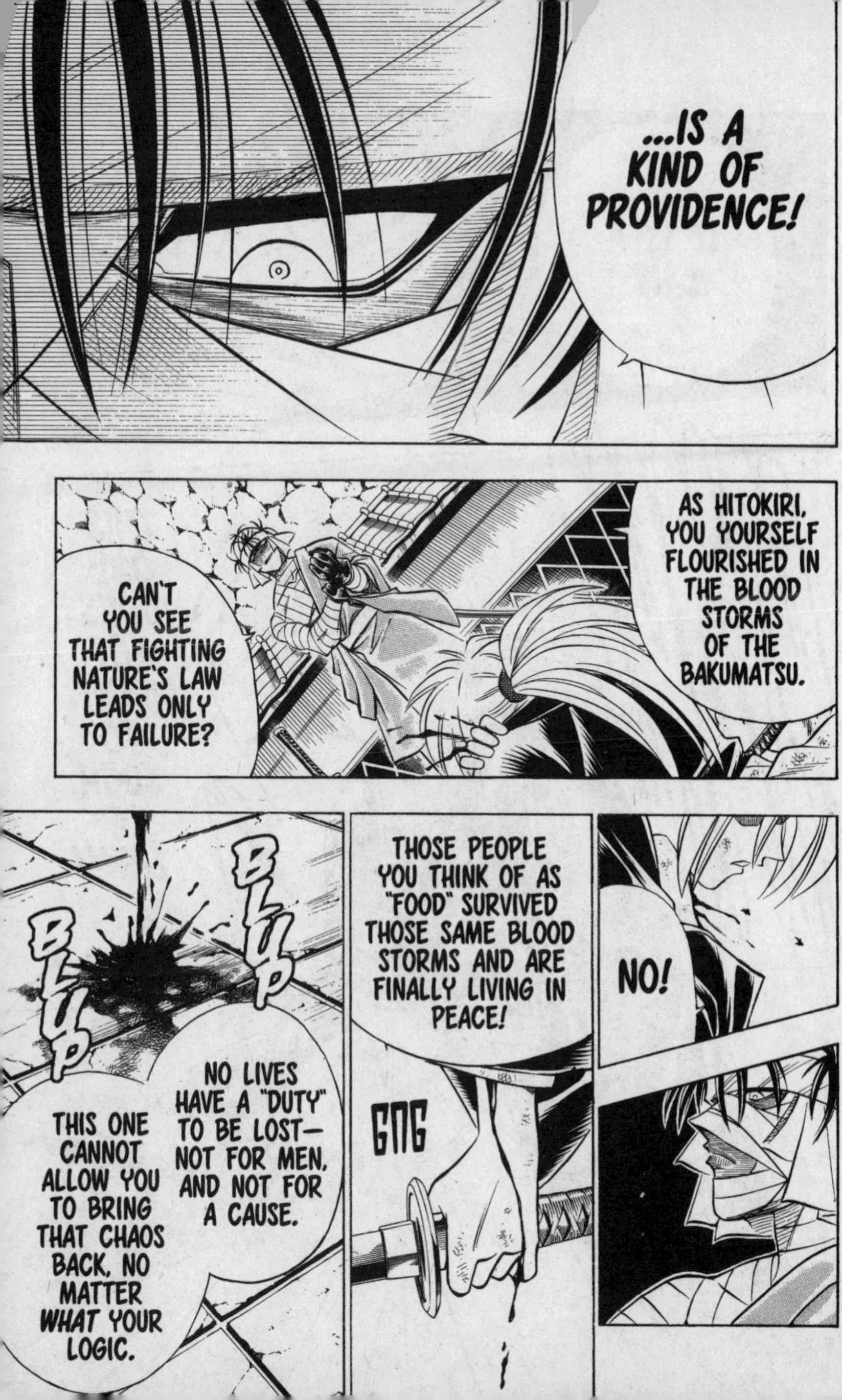
...IS A KIND OF PROVIDENCE!
AS HITOKIRI, YOU YOURSELF FLOURISHED IN THE BLOOD STORMS OF THE BAKUMATSU.
CAN'T YOU SEE THAT FIGHTING NATURE'S LAW LEADS ONLY TO FAILURE?
NO!
THOSE PEOPLE YOU THINK OF AS "FOOD" SURVIVED THOSE SAME BLOOD STORMS AND ARE FINALLY LIVING IN PEACE!
GNG
BLUP
BLUP
NO LIVES HAVE A "DUTY" TO BE LOST—NOT FOR MEN, AND NOT FOR A CAUSE.
THIS ONE CANNOT ALLOW YOU TO BRING THAT CHAOS BACK, NO MATTER *WHAT* YOUR LOGIC.

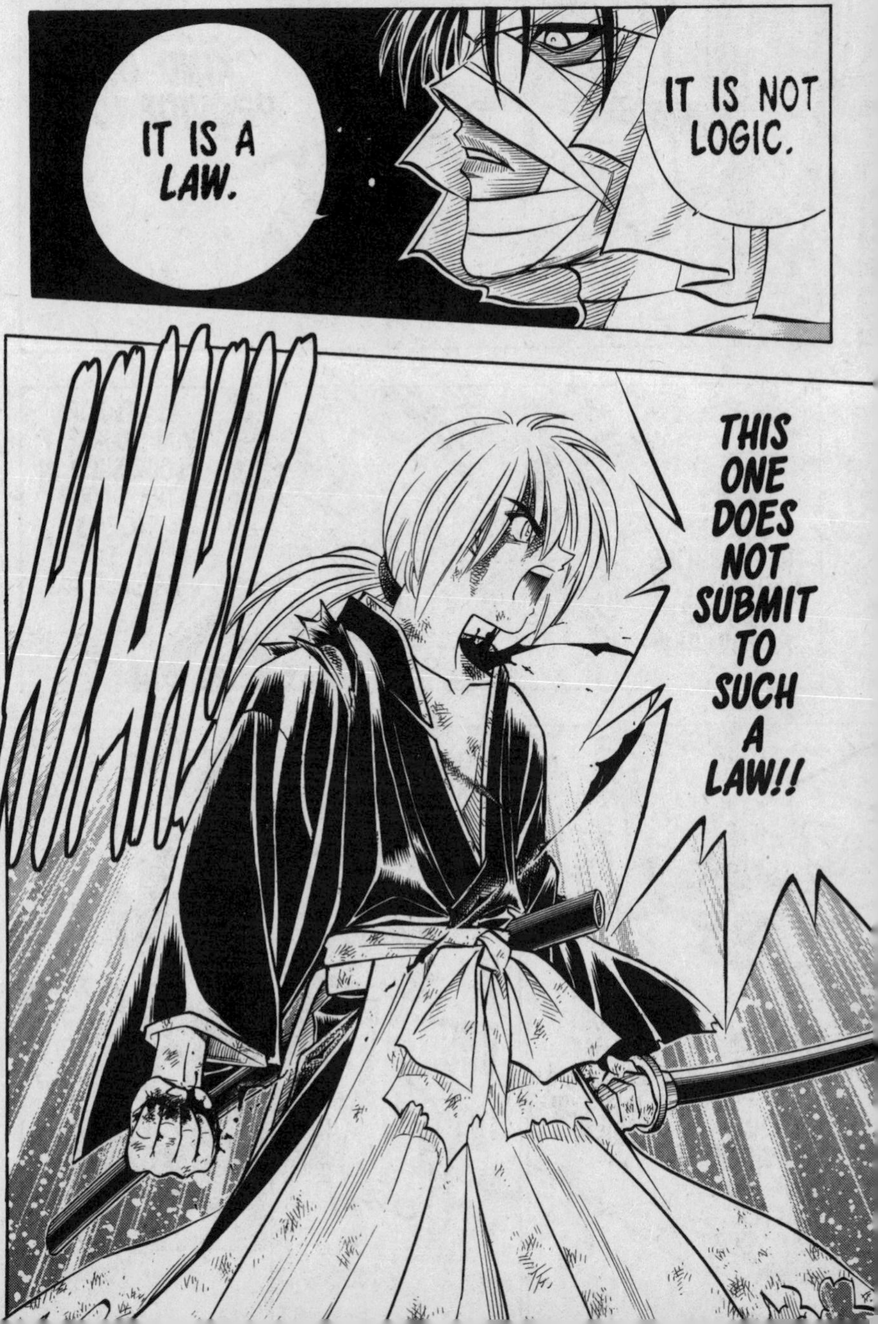
IT IS NOT LOGIC.
IT IS A LAW.
THIS ONE DOES NOT SUBMIT TO SUCH A LAW!!

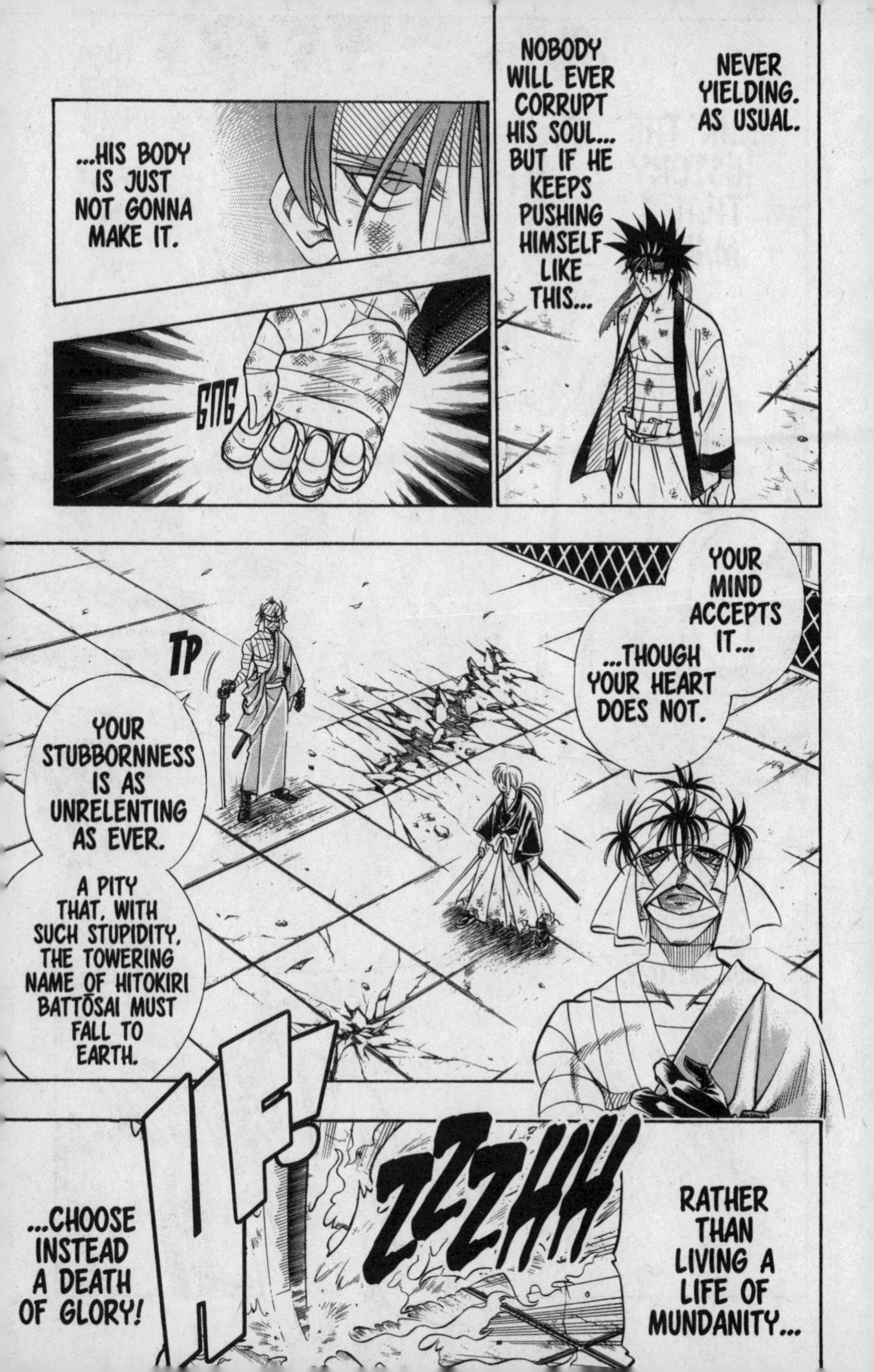
NEVER YIELDING. AS USUAL.
NOBODY WILL EVER CORRUPT HIS SOUL... BUT IF HE KEEPS PUSHING HIMSELF LIKE THIS...
...HIS BODY IS JUST NOT GONNA MAKE IT.
YOUR MIND ACCEPTS IT...
...THOUGH YOUR HEART DOES NOT.
TP
YOUR STUBBORNNESS IS AS UNRELENTING AS EVER.
A PITY THAT, WITH SUCH STUPIDITY, THE TOWERING NAME OF HITOKIRI BATTŌSAI MUST FALL TO EARTH.
RATHER THAN LIVING A LIFE OF MUNDANITY...
ZZZHH
HF
...CHOOSE INSTEAD A DEATH OF GLORY!

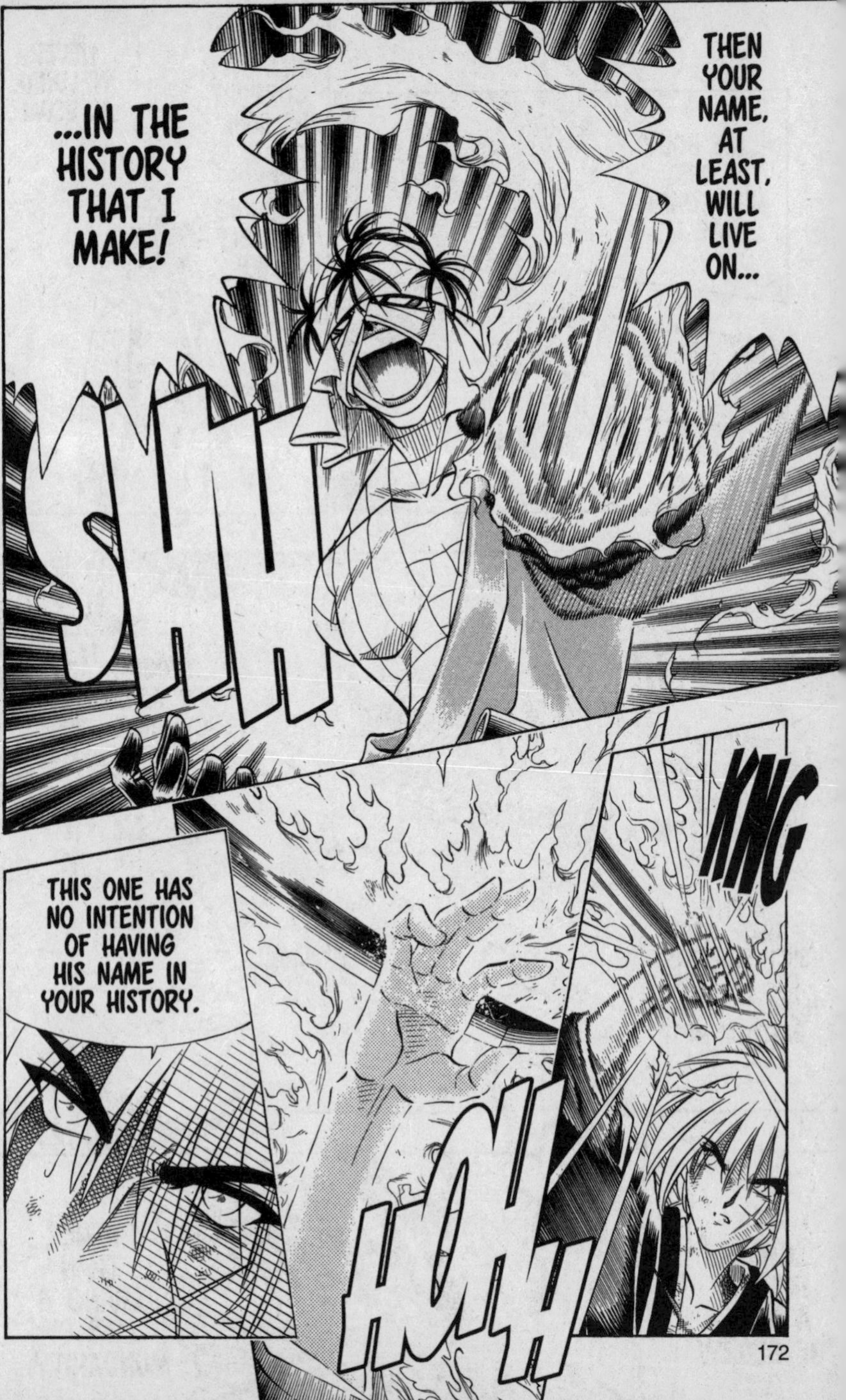
THEN YOUR NAME, AT LEAST, WILL LIVE ON...
...IN THE HISTORY THAT I MAKE!
SHH
KNG
THIS ONE HAS NO INTENTION OF HAVING HIS NAME IN YOUR HISTORY.
HOH

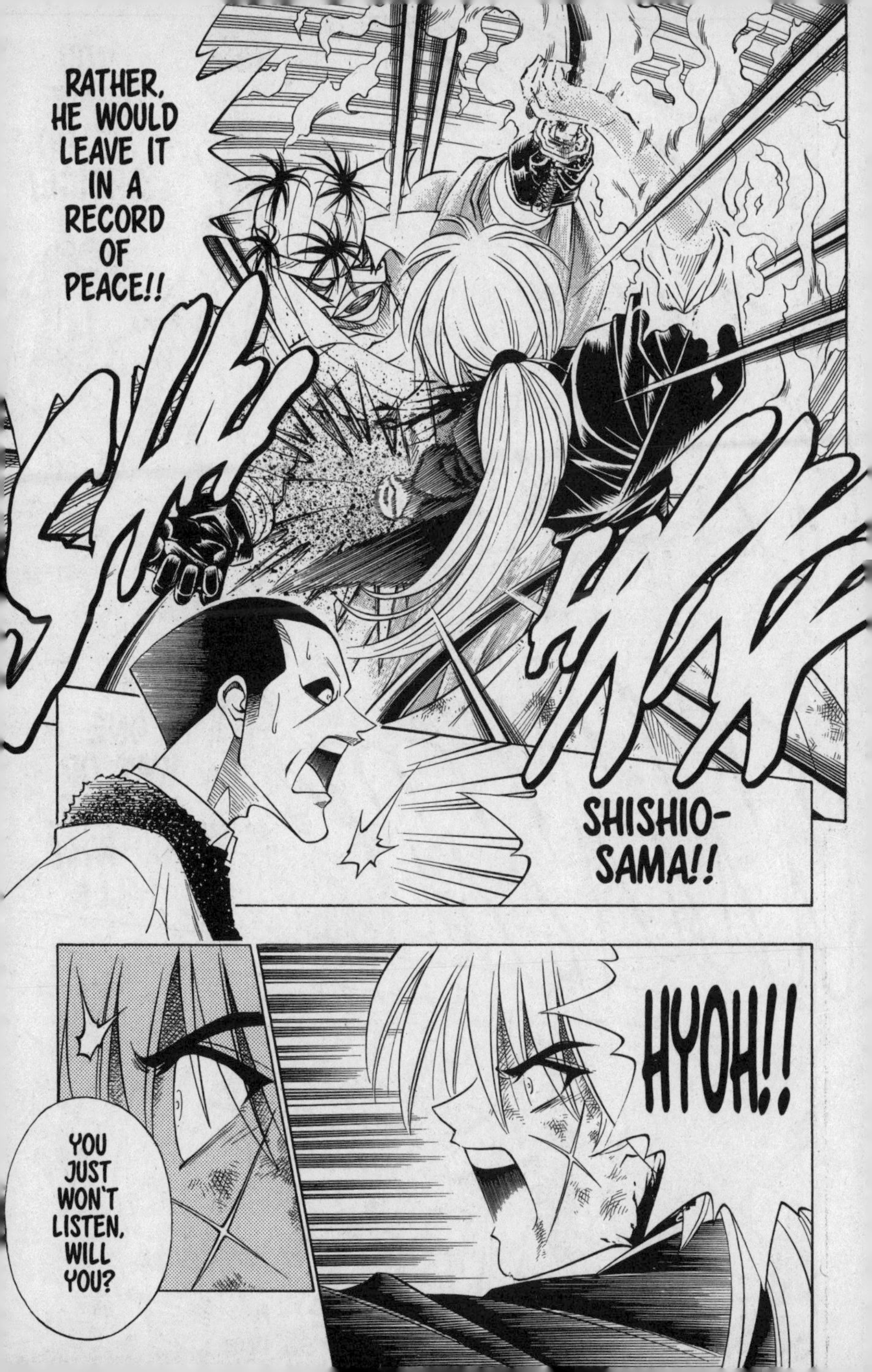
RATHER, HE WOULD LEAVE IT IN A RECORD OF PEACE!!
SHISHIO-SAMA!!
HYOH!!
YOU JUST WON'T LISTEN, WILL YOU?

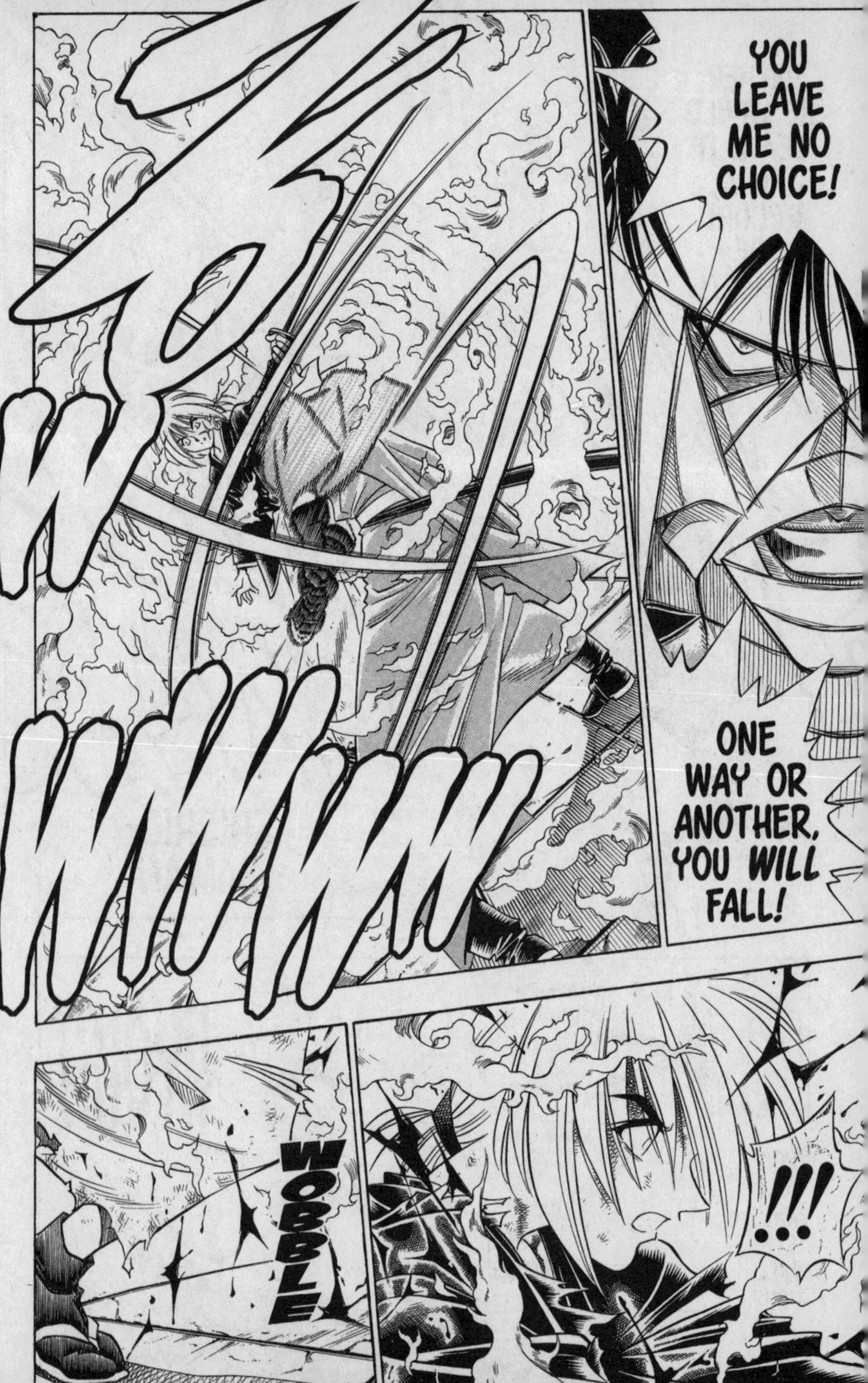
YOU LEAVE ME NO CHOICE!
ONE WAY OR ANOTHER, YOU WILL FALL!
!!!
WOBBLE

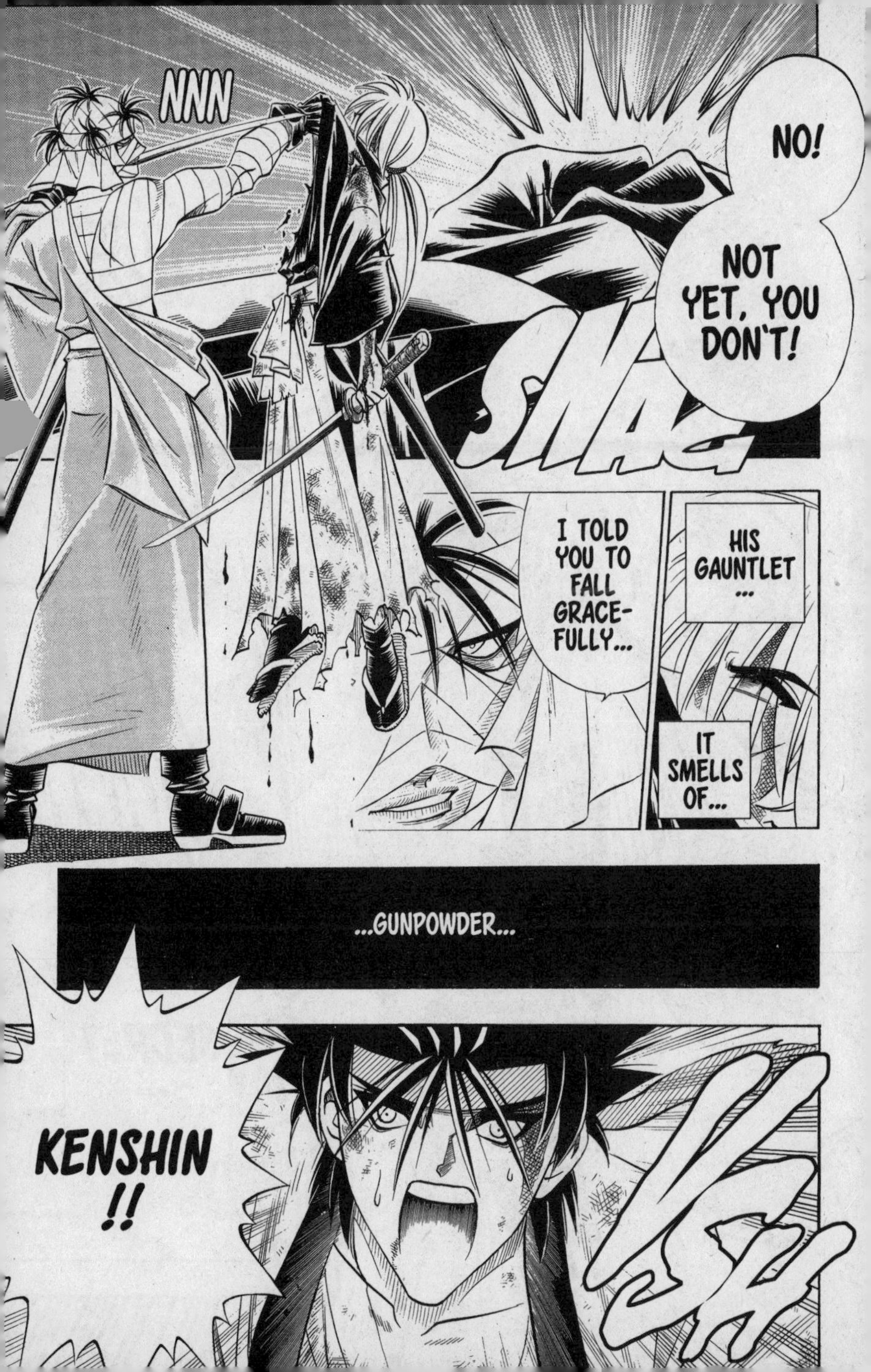
NO!
NOT YET, YOU DON'T!
SHAG
NNN
HIS GAUNTLET ...
IT SMELLS OF...
I TOLD YOU TO FALL GRACE-FULLY...
...GUNPOWDER...
KENSHIN !!

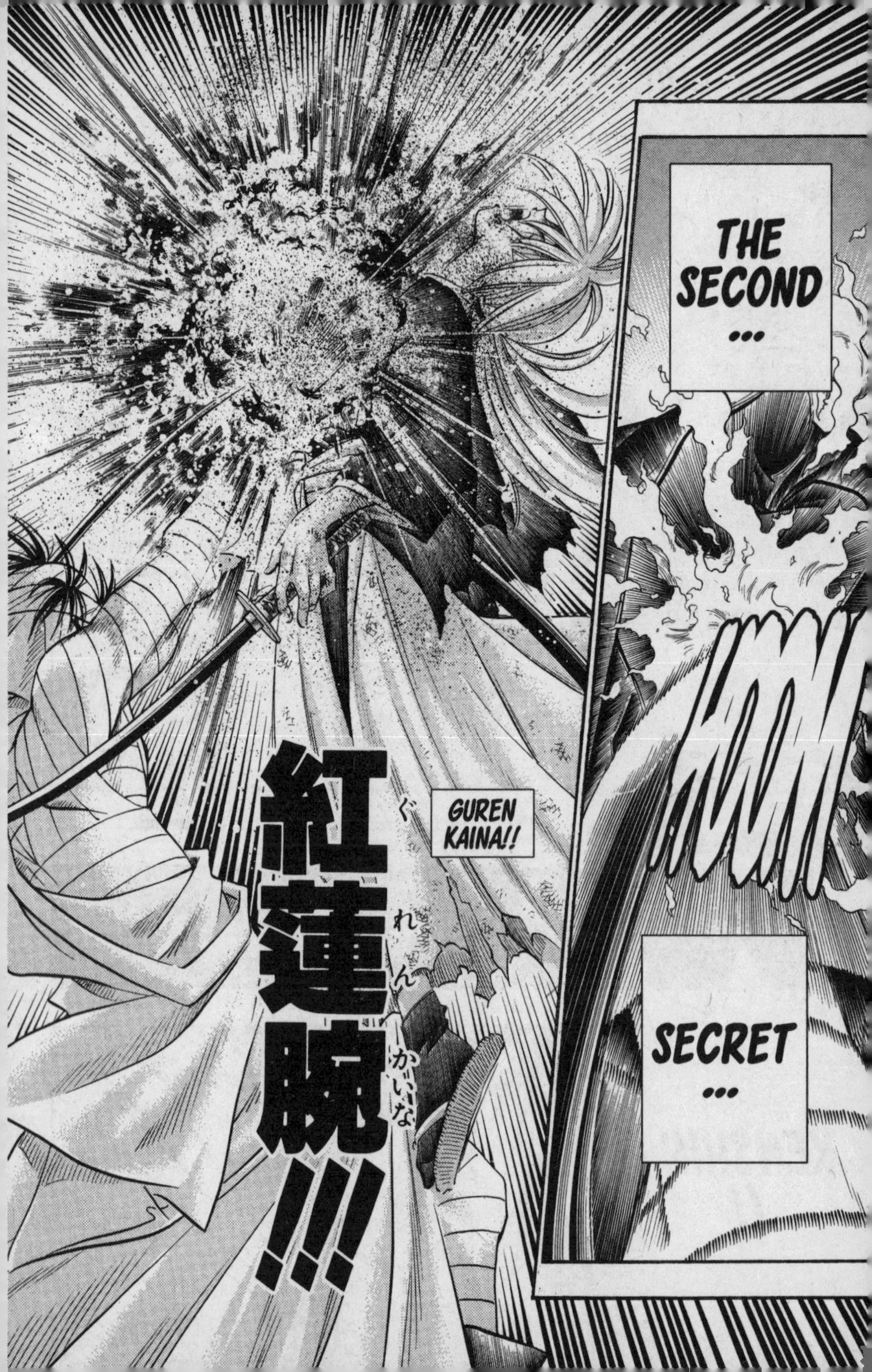
THE SECOND ...
SECRET ...
紅蓮腕!!!
GUREN KAINA!!

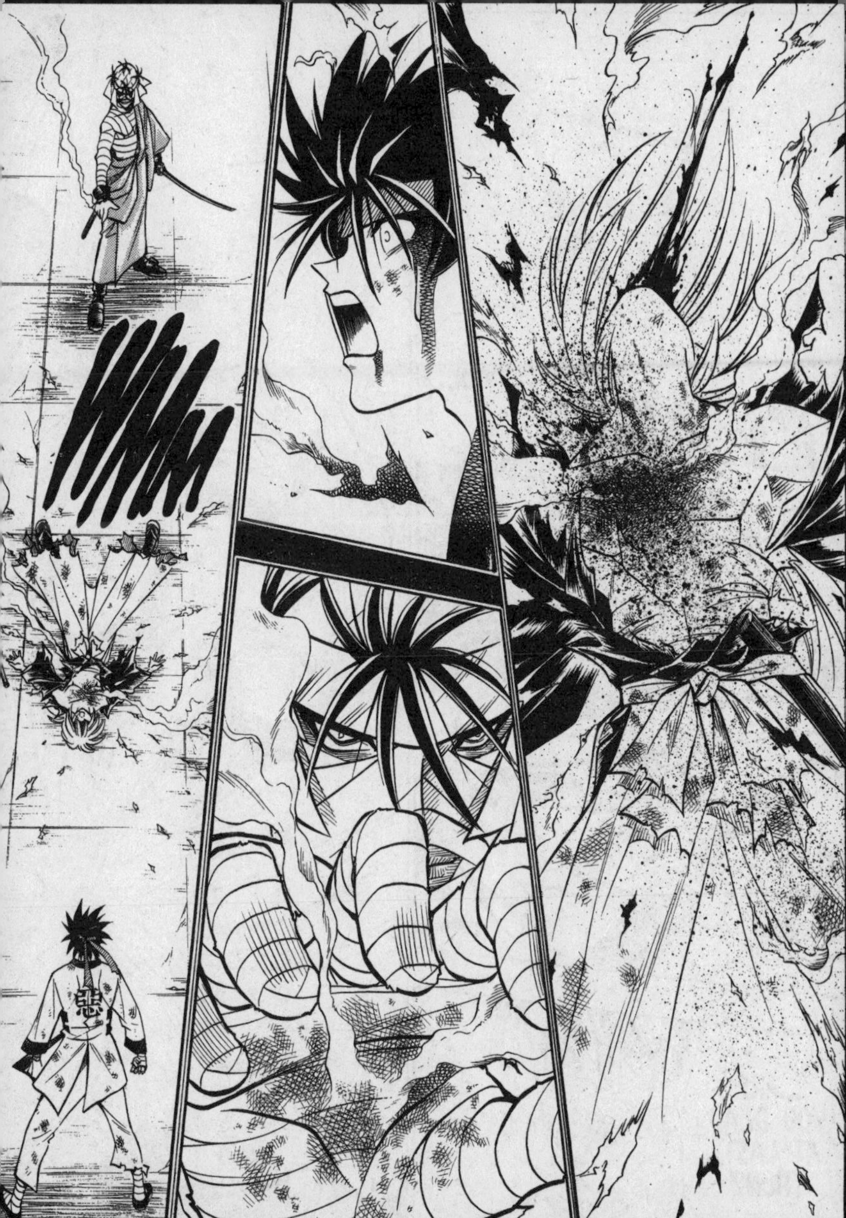

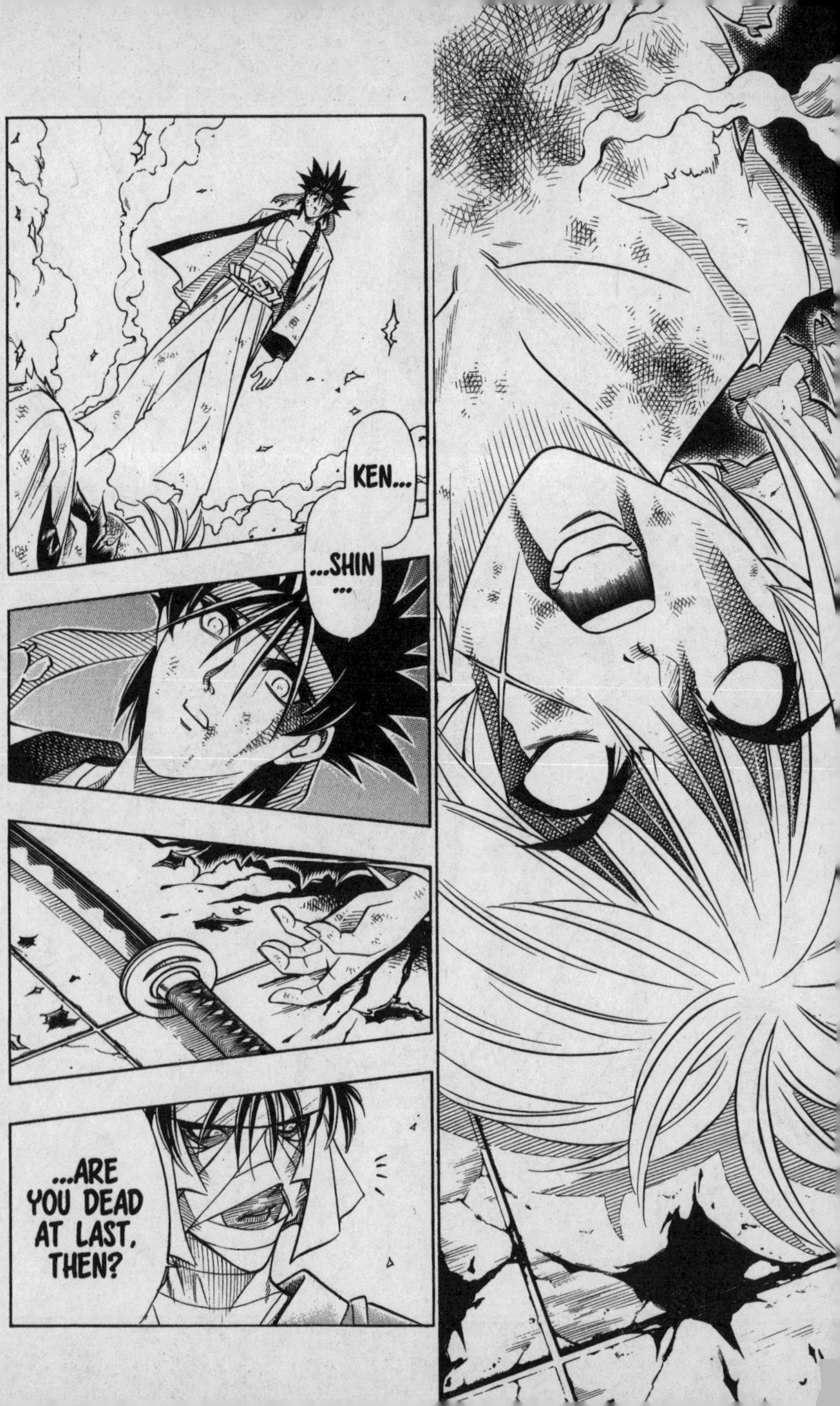
KEN...
...SHIN ...
...ARE YOU DEAD AT LAST, THEN?

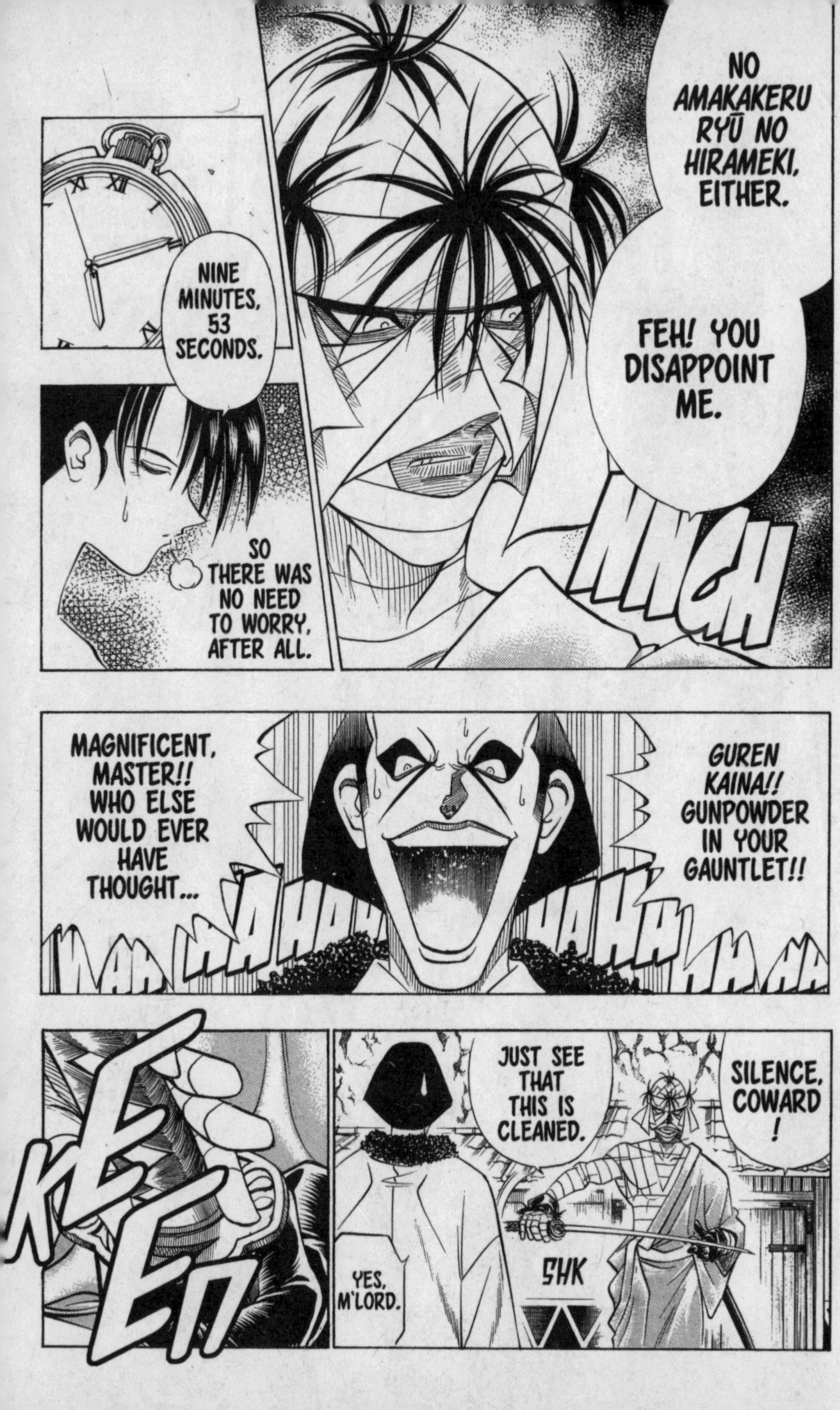
NO AMAKAKERU RYŪ NO HIRAMEKI, EITHER.
FEH! YOU DISAPPOINT ME.
NNGH
NINE MINUTES, 53 SECONDS.
SO THERE WAS NO NEED TO WORRY, AFTER ALL.
GUREN KAINA!! GUNPOWDER IN YOUR GAUNTLET!!
MAGNIFICENT, MASTER!! WHO ELSE WOULD EVER HAVE THOUGHT...
SILENCE, COWARD!
JUST SEE THAT THIS IS CLEANED.
SHK
YES, M'LORD.
KEEN

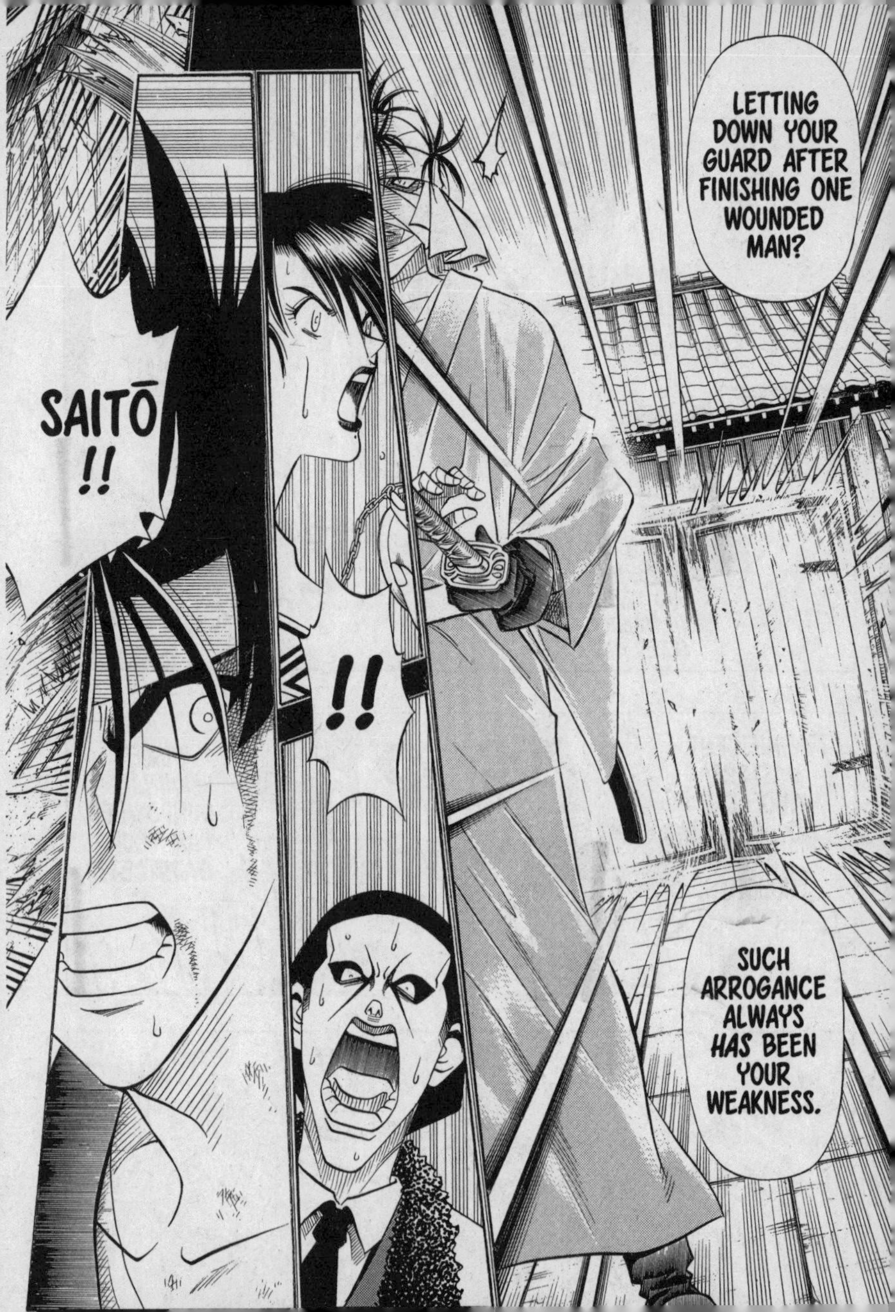
LETTING DOWN YOUR GUARD AFTER FINISHING ONE WOUNDED MAN?
SUCH ARROGANCE ALWAYS HAS BEEN YOUR WEAKNESS.
!!
SAITŌ !!

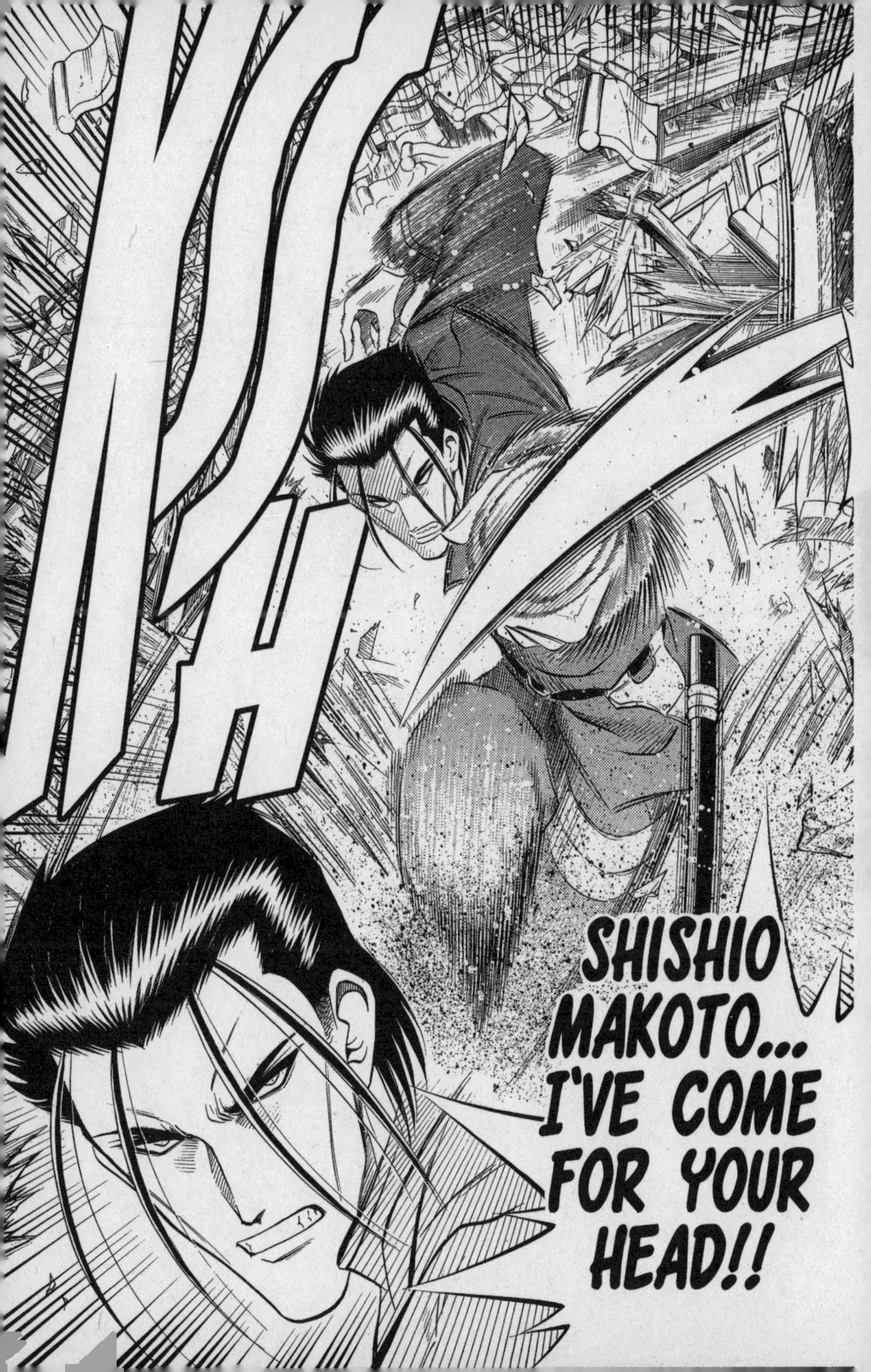
SHISHIO MAKOTO... I'VE COME FOR YOUR HEAD!!

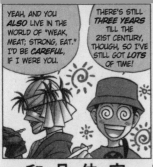

THERE'S STILL THREE YEARS TILL THE 21ST CENTURY, THOUGH, SO I'VE STILL GOT LOTS OF TIME!
YEAH, AND YOU ALSO LIVE IN THE WORLD OF "WEAK, MEAT; STRONG, EAT." I'D BE CAREFUL, IF I WERE YOU.

和 月 伸 宏

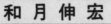

NOBUHIRO WATSUKI

NEXT GENERATION

LOOKING AT HOW THINGS ARE GOING IN THE WORLD, AND LOOKING AT THE EVENTS GOING ON AROUND ME, RECENTLY THESE WORDS HAVE COME TO TAKE ON NEW RESONANCE. ALTHOUGH IT MAY FEEL TO ME LIKE TIME HAS STOPPED SINCE I TOOK ON THIS SERIES, HERE IT IS, ALREADY CLOSE TO BEING THE 21ST CENTURY...AND ME COMING UP FAST ON THE BIG 3-0. I'M STARTING TO FEEL PRETTY STRONGLY THAT IT'S WELL PAST TIME I CHARTED SOME NEW DIRECTIONS FOR MYSELF.

Rurouni Kenshin, which has found fans not only in Japan but around the world, first made its appearance in 1992, as an original short story in ***Weekly Shonen Jump Special***. Later rewritten and published as a regular, continuing ***Jump*** series in 1994, ***Rurouni Kenshin*** ended serialization in 1999 but continued in popularity, as evidenced by the 2000 publication of ***Yahiko no Sakabatô*** ("Yahiko's Reversed-Edge Sword") in ***Weekly Shonen Jump***. His most current work, ***Busô Renkin*** ("Armored Alchemist"), began publication in June 2003, also in ***Jump***.

Rurouni Kenshin

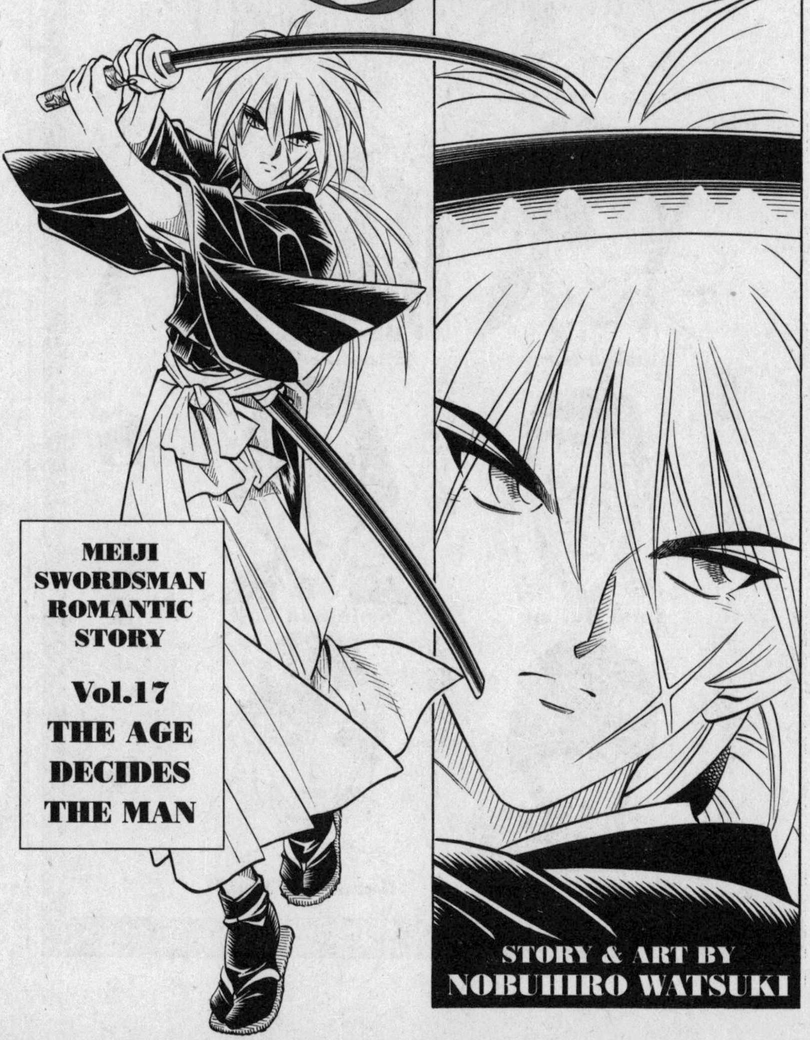

MEIJI SWORDSMAN ROMANTIC STORY

Vol.17

THE AGE DECIDES THE MAN

STORY & ART BY

NOBUHIRO WATSUKI

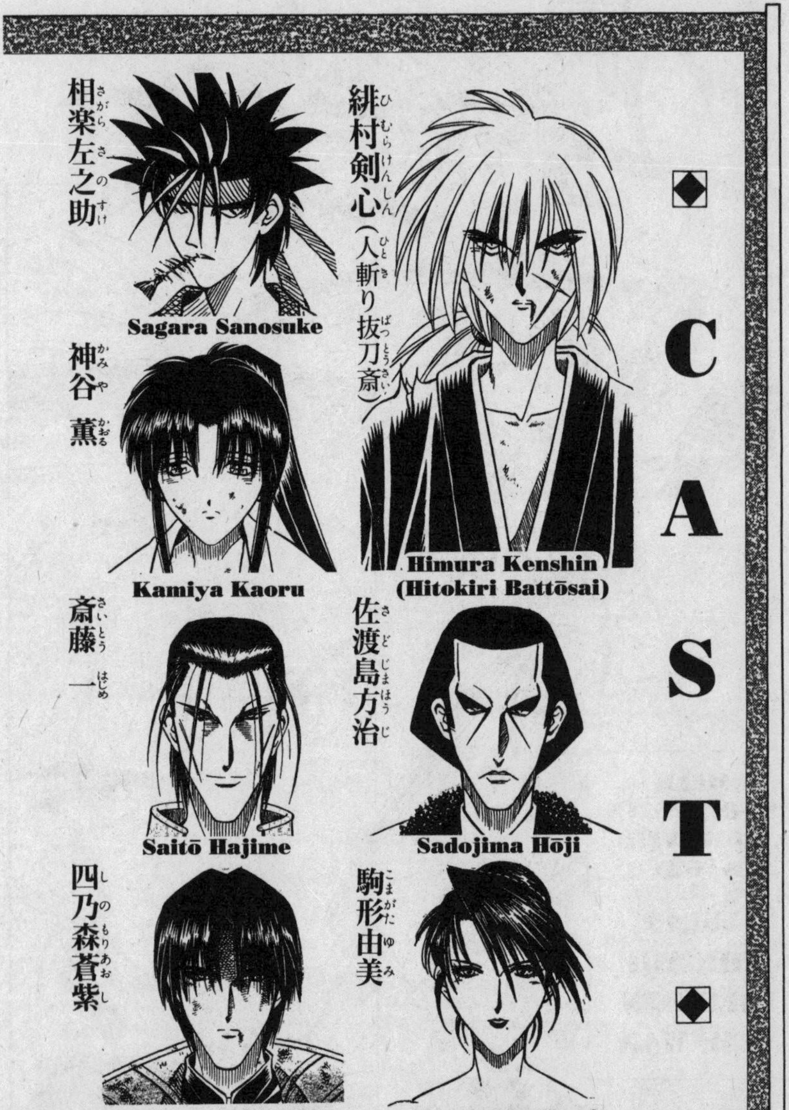
CAST
緋村剣心(人斬り抜刀斎)
Himura Kenshin (Hitokiri Battōsai)
佐渡島方治
Sadojima Hōji
駒形由美
Komagata Yumi
相楽左之助
Sagara Sanosuke
神谷 薫
Kamiya Kaoru
斎藤 一
Saitō Hajime
四乃森蒼紫
Shinomori Aoshi

Once he was *hitokiri*, an assassin, called Battōsai. His name was legend among the pro-Imperialist or "patriot" warriors who launched the Meiji Era. Now, Himura Kenshin is *rurouni*, a wanderer, and carries a reversed-edge *sakabatō* to prohibit himself from killing.

志々雄真実

Shishio Makoto

THUS FAR

Kenshin has journeyed to Kyoto to block the machinations of Shishio Makoto, the man who took Kenshin's place as *hitokiri* or government-sanctioned slayer of men. In a duel with Sōjirō, one of the madman Shishio's *Juppongatana* "Ten Sword" assassins, Kenshin's former blade is broken and a new one is acquired—"Shinuchi," a *sakabatō* like the first.

Newly armed (and after an edge-of-death battle with his former *Hiten Mitsurugi* master, Hiko Seijūrō), Kenshin joins up with Sanosuke and Saitō so that they may foil the plans of Shishio to burn down Tokyo and attack it by cannon. Arriving at Shishio's lair at last, the three are met by Shishio's three best: "Bright King" Anji, "Blind Sword" Usui, and the ever-smiling Sōjirō. After fierce battles, Anji is defeated by Sanosuke, and Usui dies against Saitō. Sōjirō, defeated by Kenshin despite the latter's vow never to kill, decides he must leave Shishio's side and seek the truth on his own terms.

Kenshin, already wounded from his duels with Aoshi and Sōjirō, finally reaches the "Infernal Hall" and challenges its madman owner, who still is insisting that it is nature's law that the "weak become the sustenance of the strong." As Kenshin lies unconscious, struck down by Shishio's second "secret sword," *Guren Kaina*, who should burst in on the scene but Saitō....

RUROUNI KENSHIN
Meiji Swordsman Romantic Story
BOOK SEVENTEEN: THE AGE DECIDES THE MAN

Act 139
Howling Laugh
189

Act 140
Thread of Life
209

Act 141
Double-Edged Flame
229

Act 142
Final Encounter
249

Act 143
The Third Secret
267

Act 144
Shape of Love
287

Act 145
Duel of an Era
307

Act 146
The Passion of Hōji
327

Act 147
Kyoto Epilogue
Fate of the Juppongatana (Part I)
345

Act 148
Kyoto Epilogue
Fate of the Juppongatana (Part II)
363

Act 139
Howling Laugh

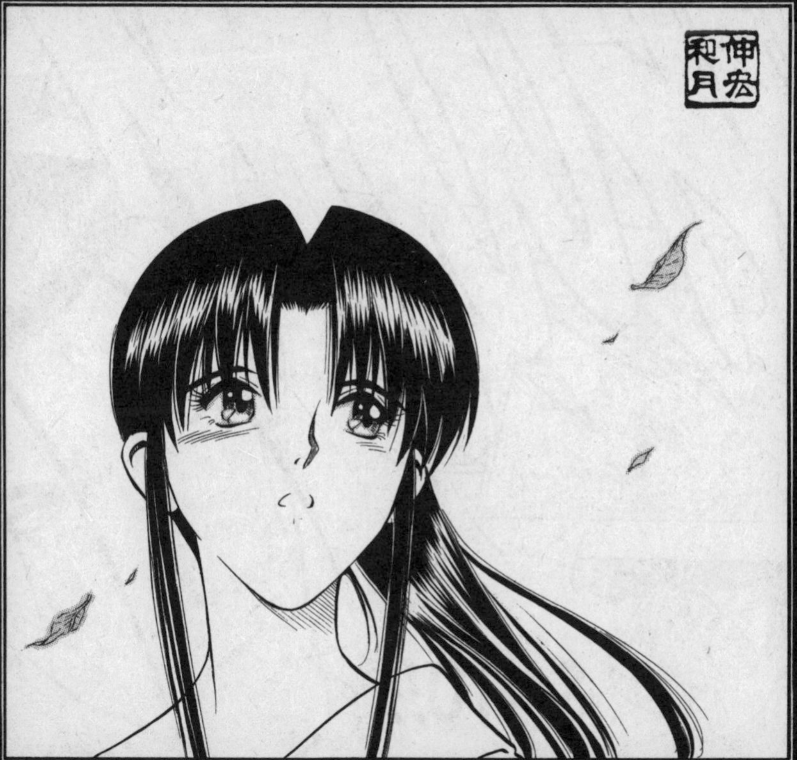
伸宏和月

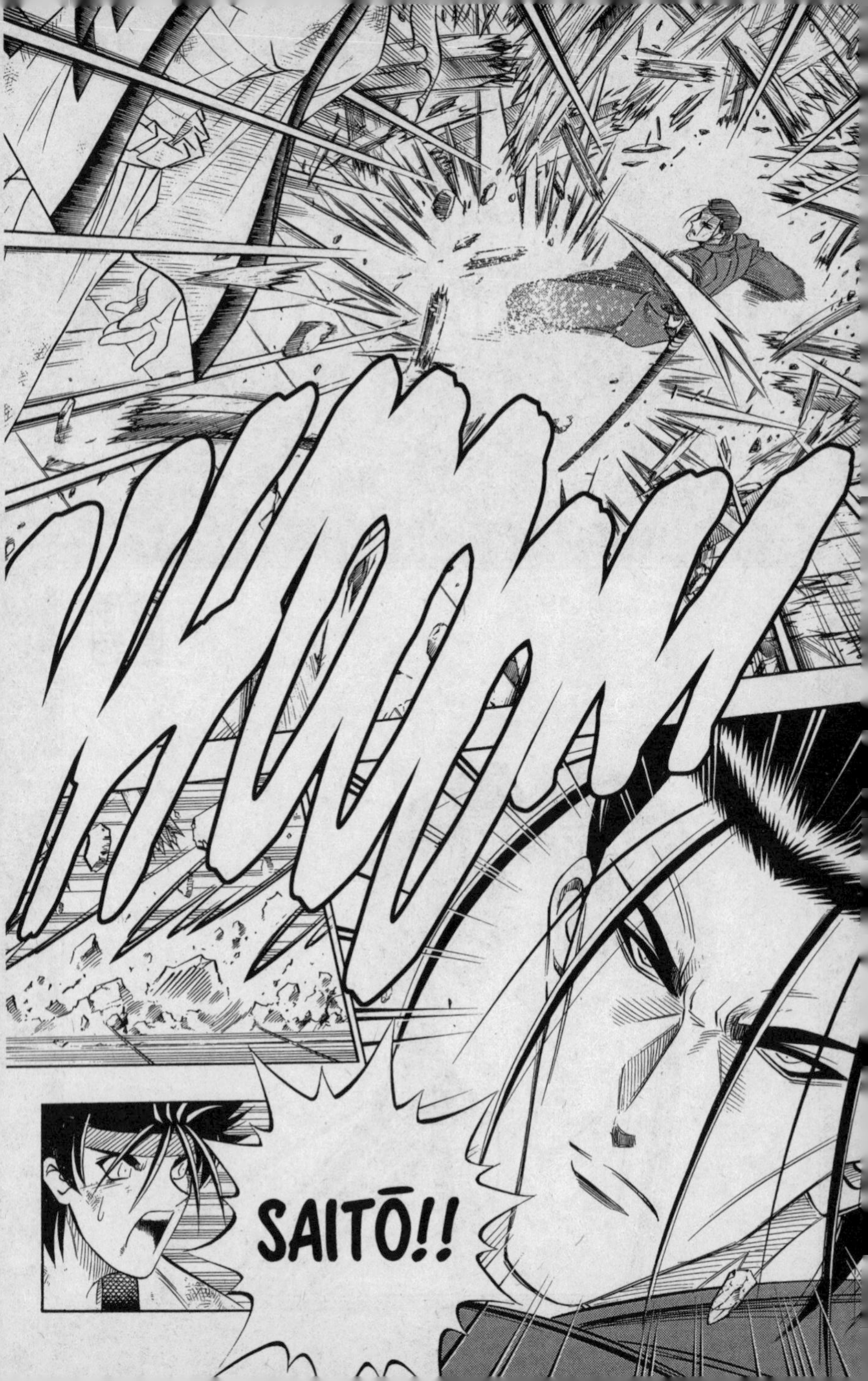
SAITŌ!!

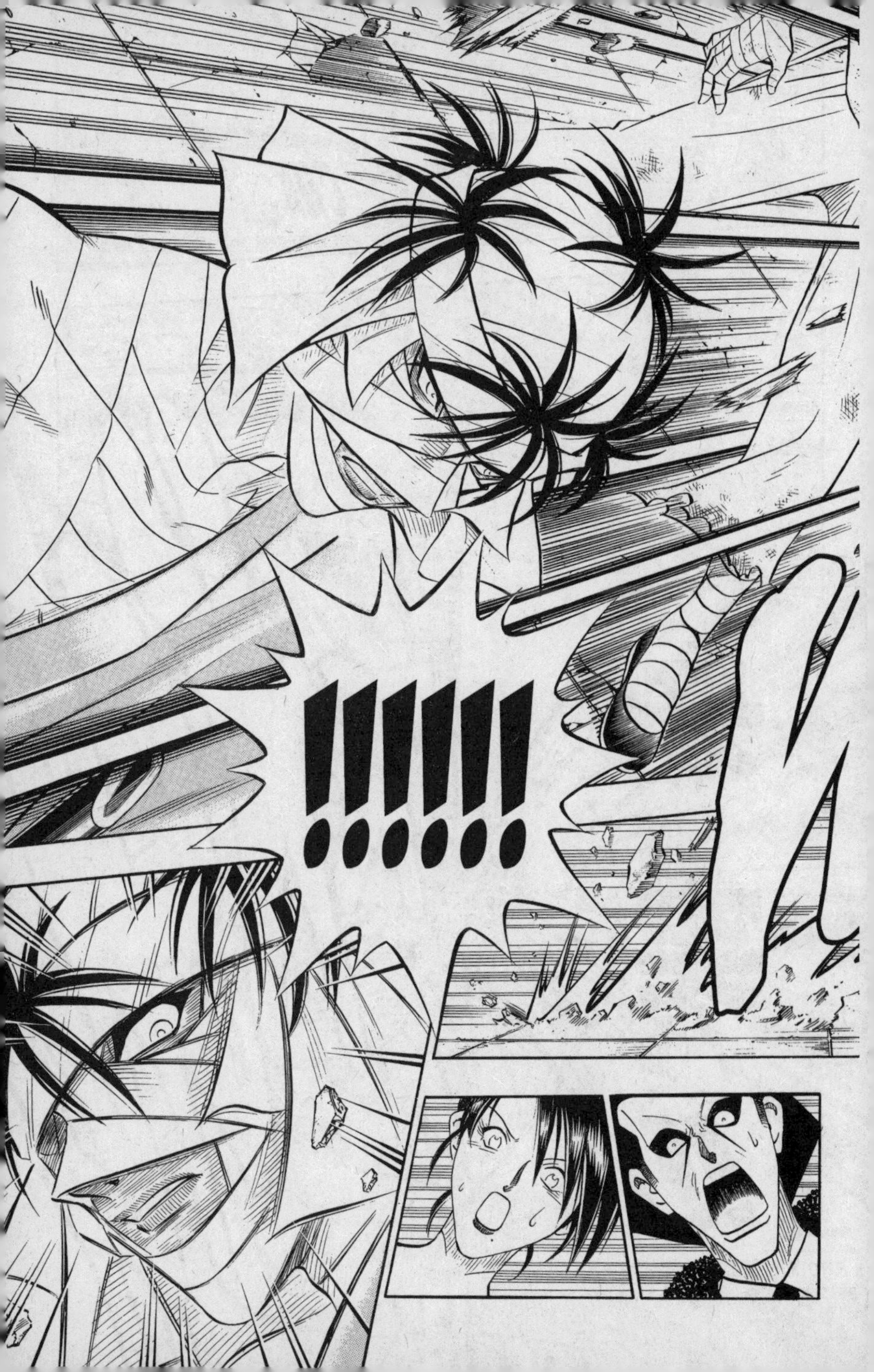
!!!!!!

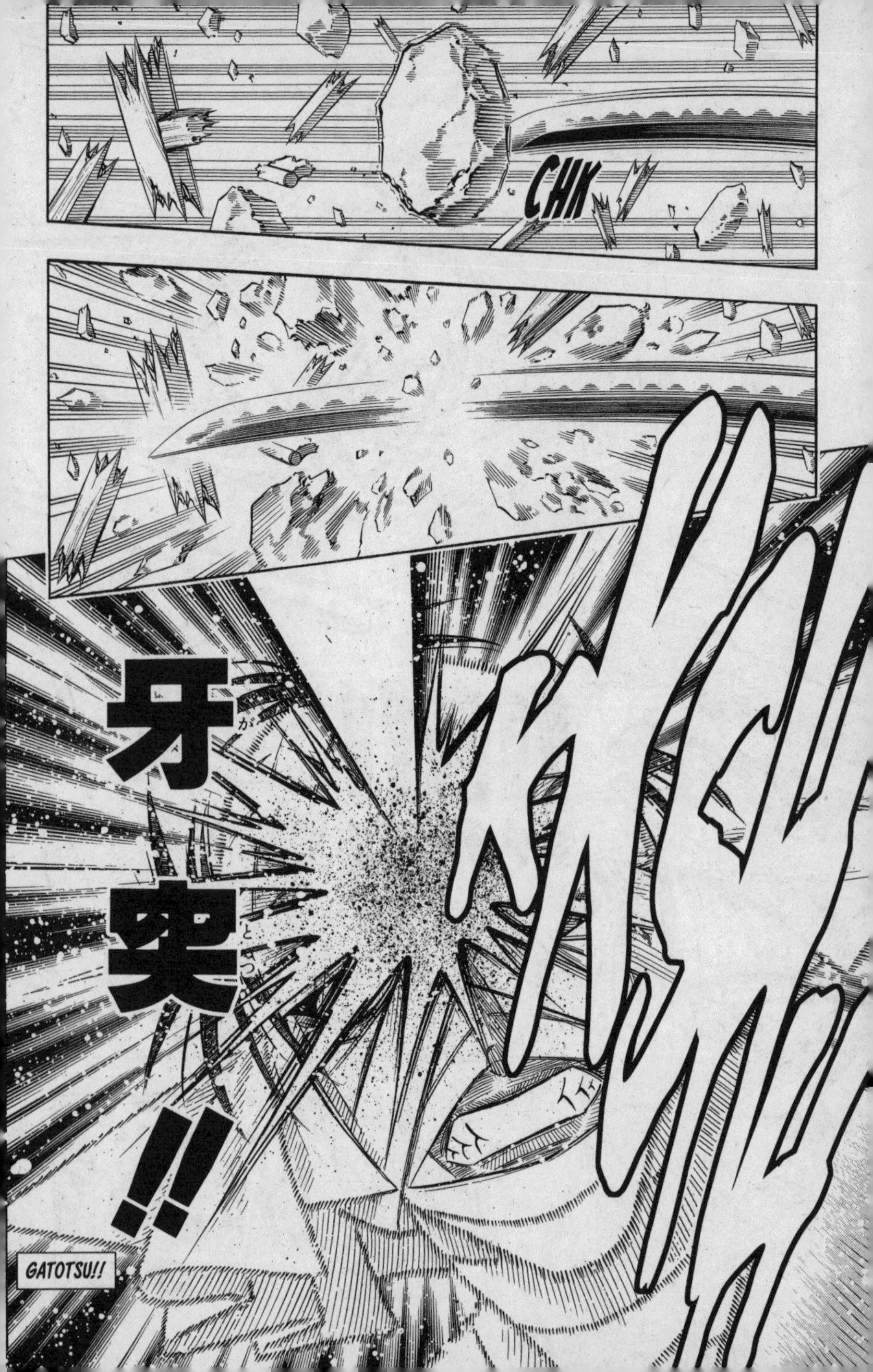
CHK
牙突!!
GATOTSU!!

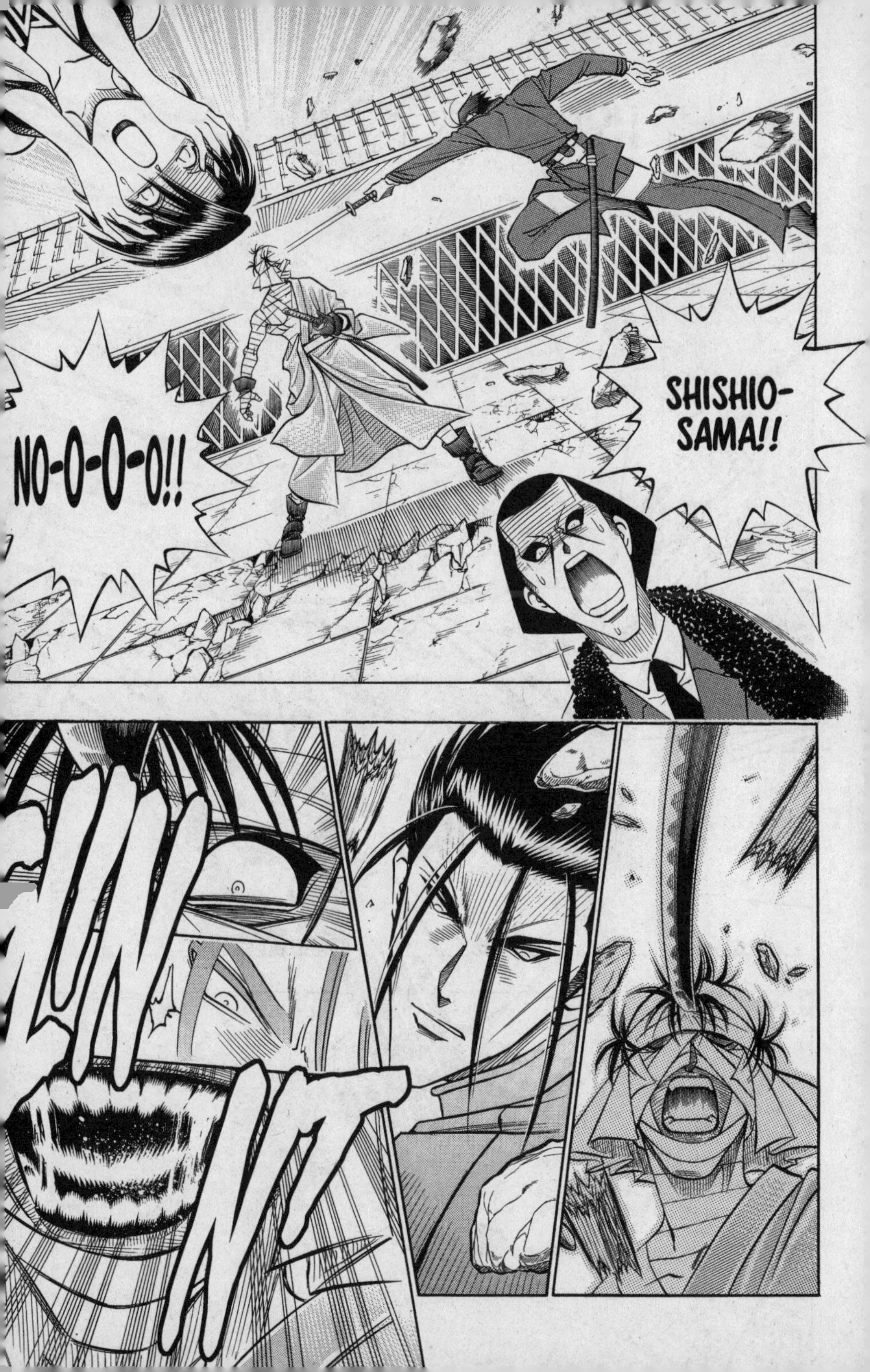
SHISHIO-SAMA!!
NO-O-O-O!!

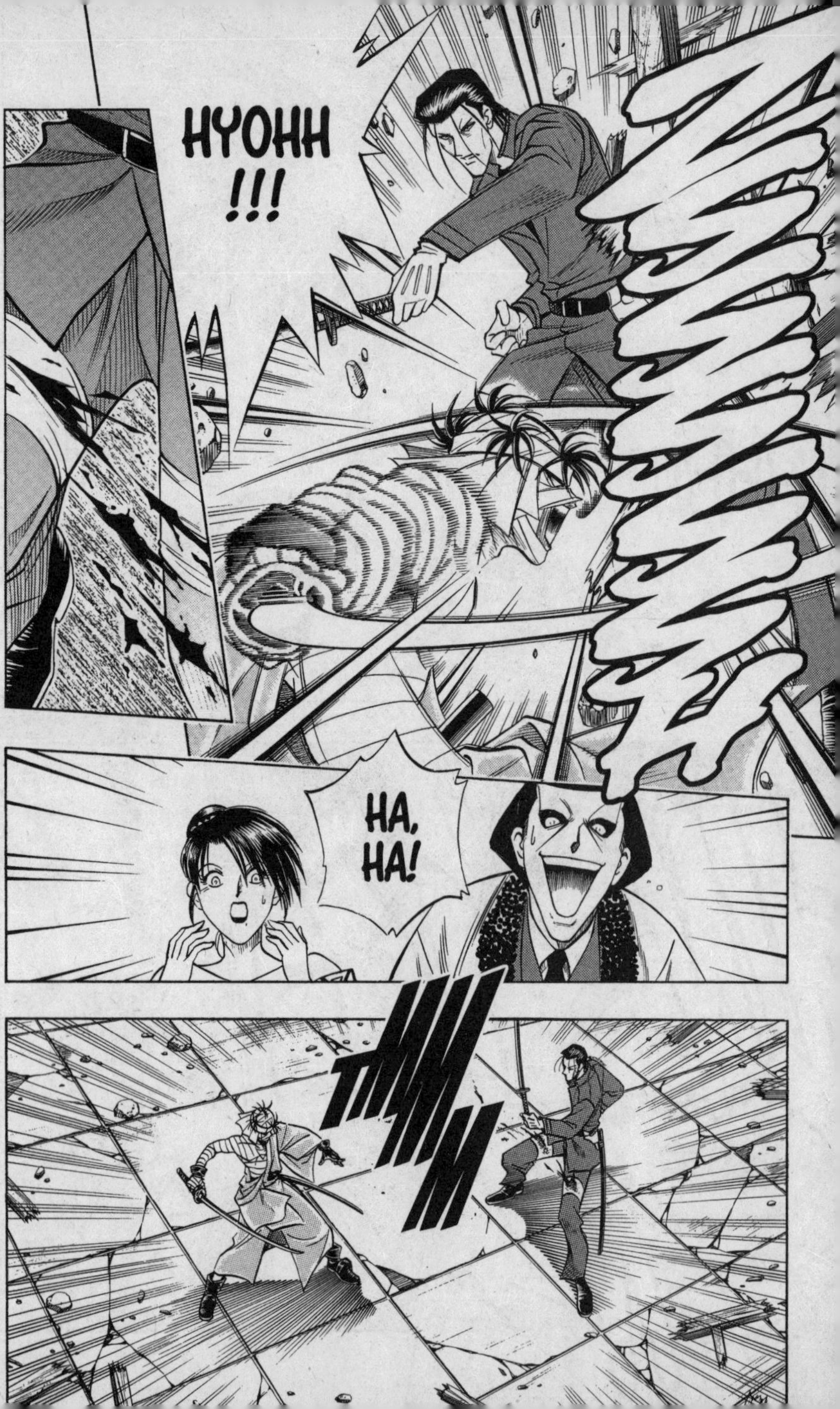
HYOHH !!!
HA, HA!

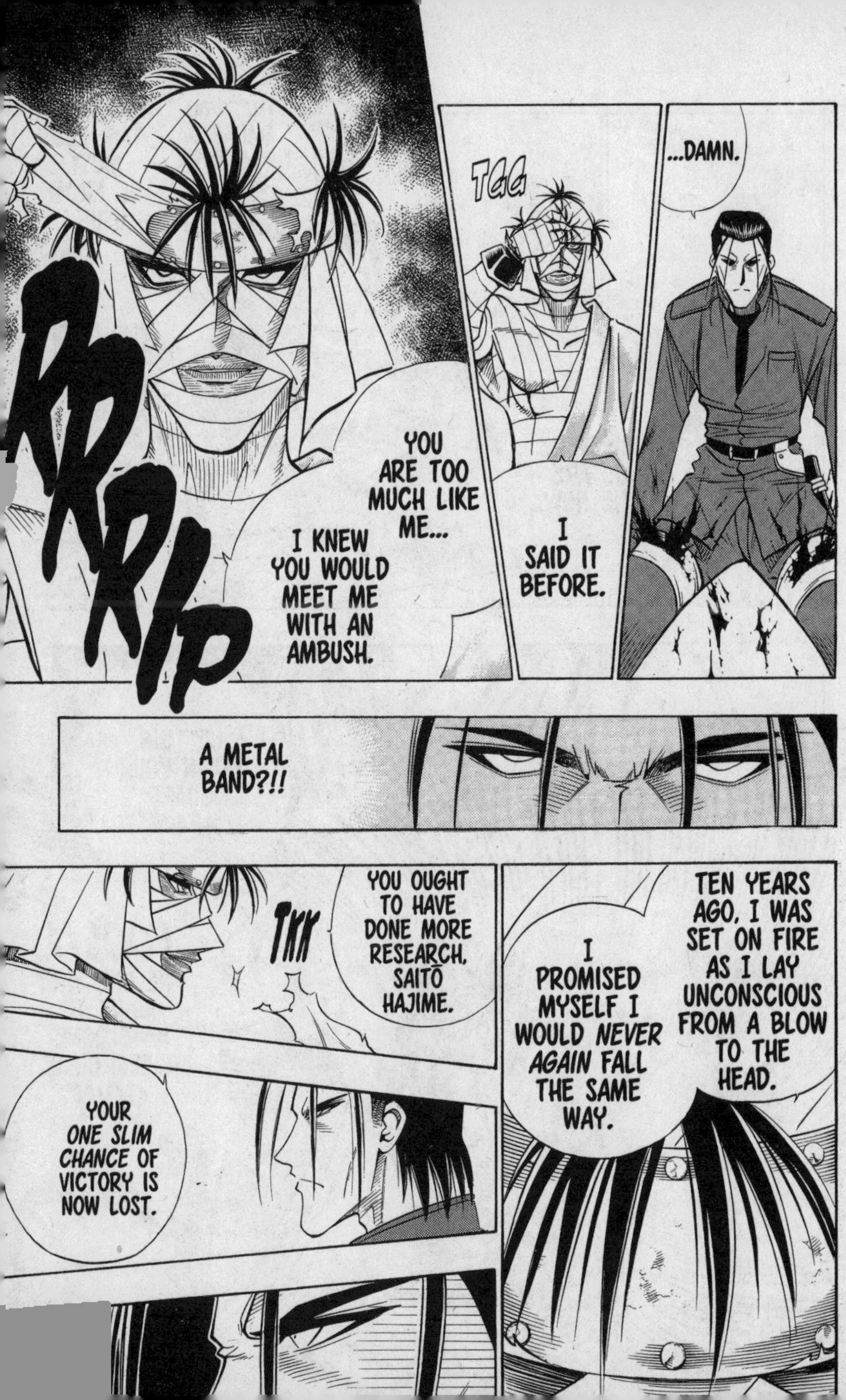
...DAMN.
TAG
I SAID IT BEFORE.
YOU ARE TOO MUCH LIKE ME...
I KNEW YOU WOULD MEET ME WITH AN AMBUSH.
RRRIP
A METAL BAND?!!
TEN YEARS AGO, I WAS SET ON FIRE AS I LAY UNCONSCIOUS FROM A BLOW TO THE HEAD.
I PROMISED MYSELF I WOULD *NEVER AGAIN* FALL THE SAME WAY.
YOU OUGHT TO HAVE DONE MORE RESEARCH, SAITŌ HAJIME.
TKK
YOUR ONE SLIM CHANCE OF VICTORY IS NOW LOST.

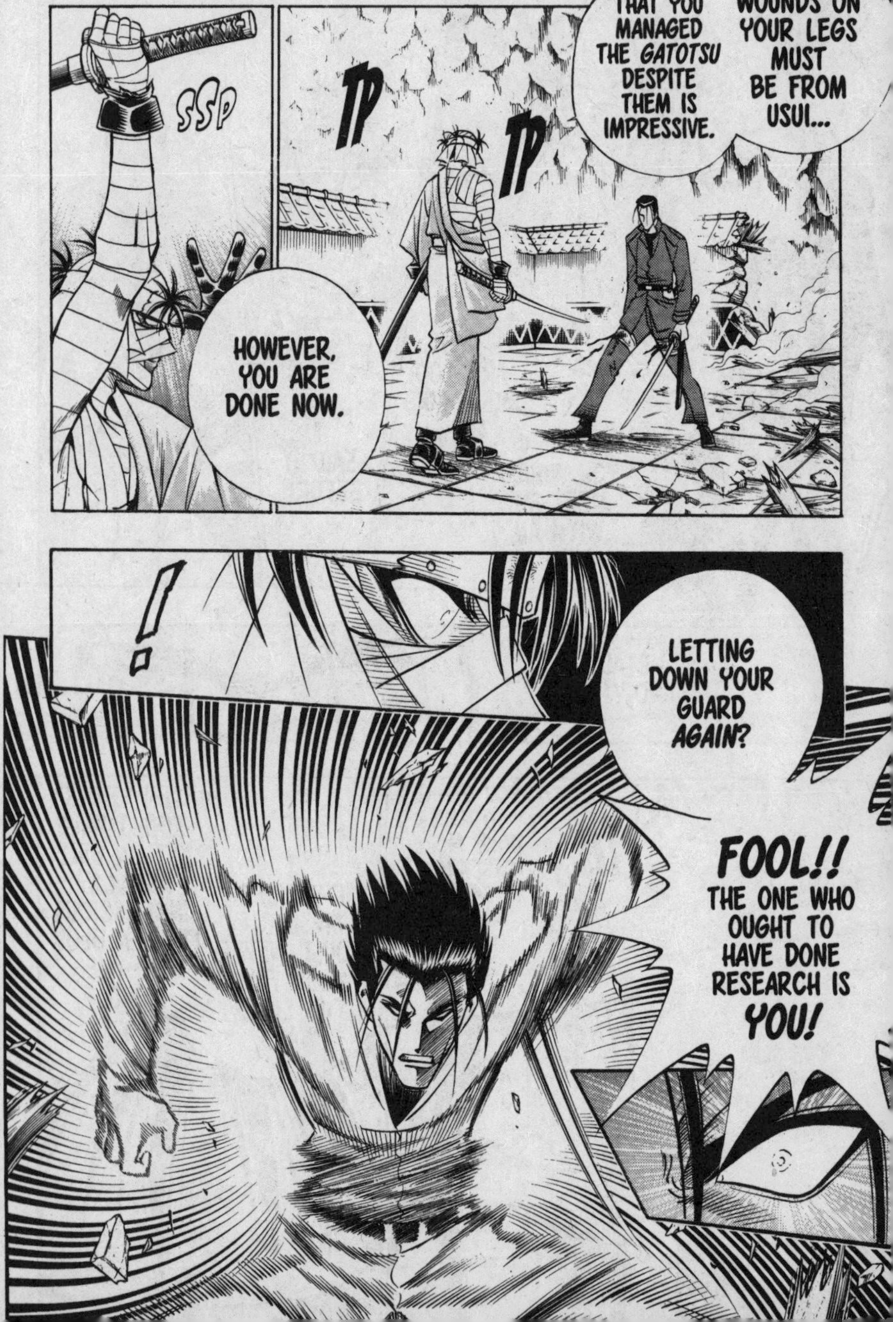
THOSE WOUNDS ON YOUR LEGS MUST BE FROM USUI...
THAT YOU MANAGED THE *GATOTSU* DESPITE THEM IS IMPRESSIVE.
TP
TP
SSP
HOWEVER, YOU ARE DONE NOW.
LETTING DOWN YOUR GUARD *AGAIN*?
!
FOOL!! THE ONE WHO OUGHT TO HAVE DONE RESEARCH IS ***YOU!***

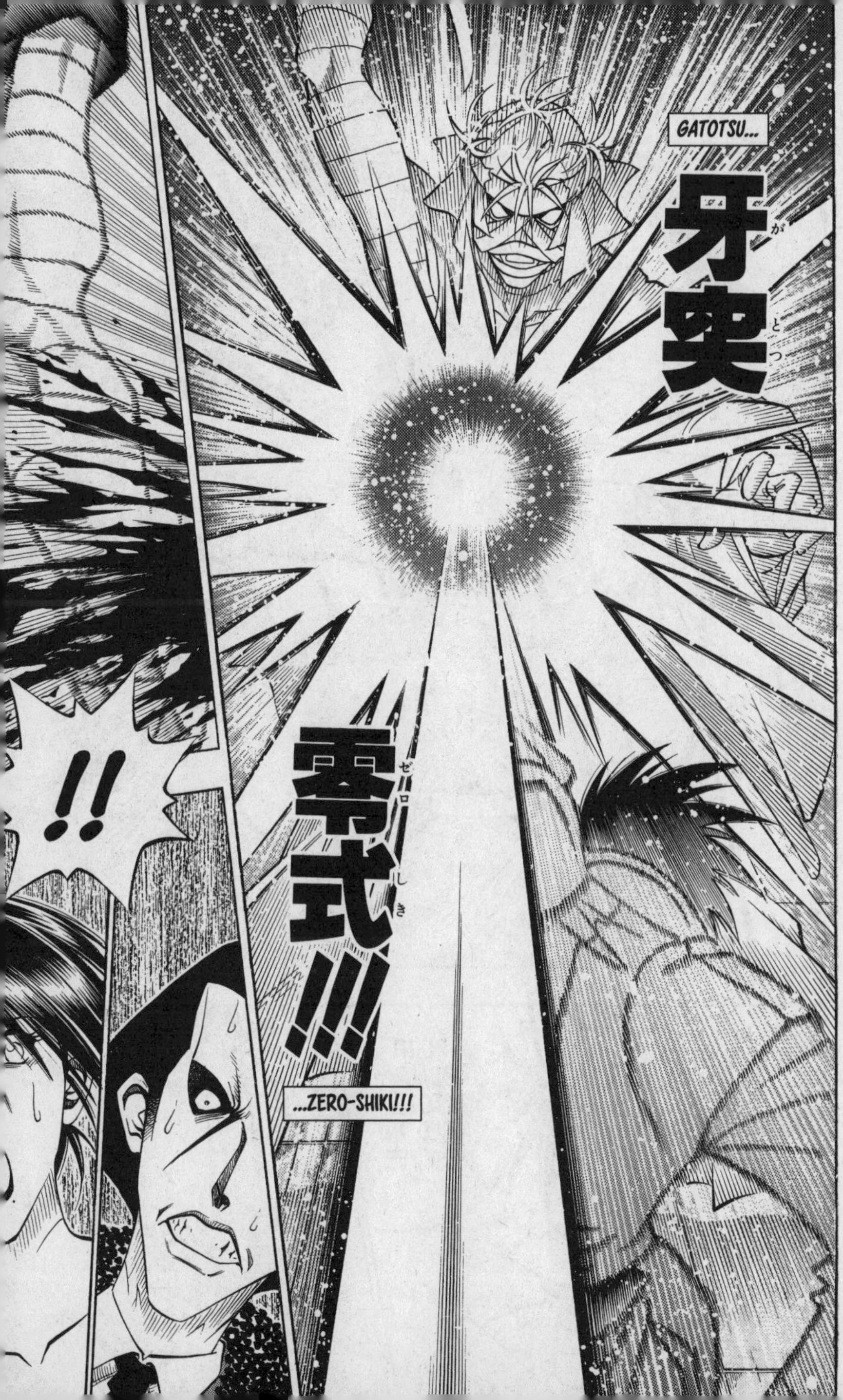
GATOTSU...
牙突
零式!!!
...ZERO-SHIKI!!!
!!

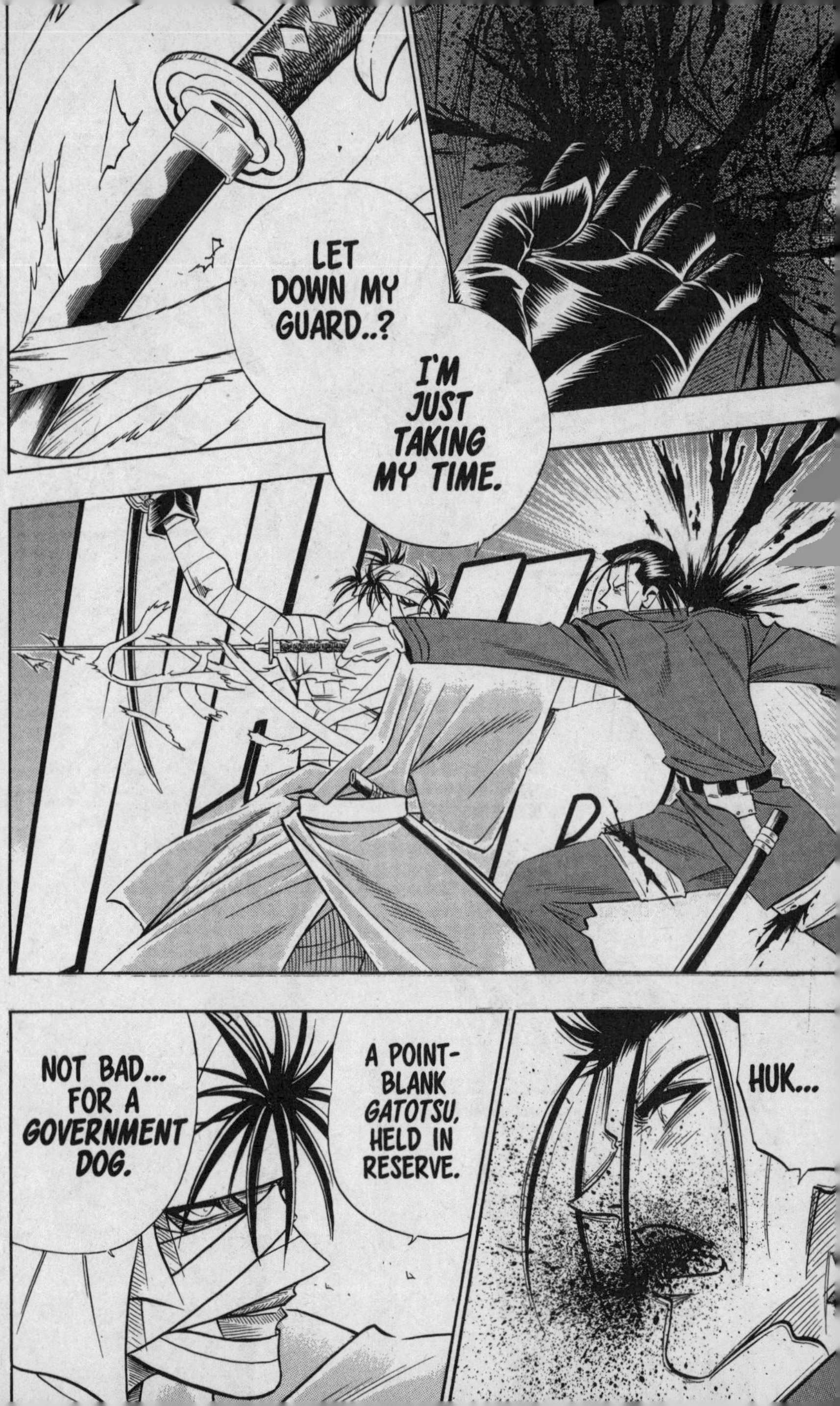
LET DOWN MY GUARD..?
I'M JUST TAKING MY TIME.
HUK...
A POINT-BLANK GATOTSU, HELD IN RESERVE.
NOT BAD... FOR A GOVERNMENT DOG.

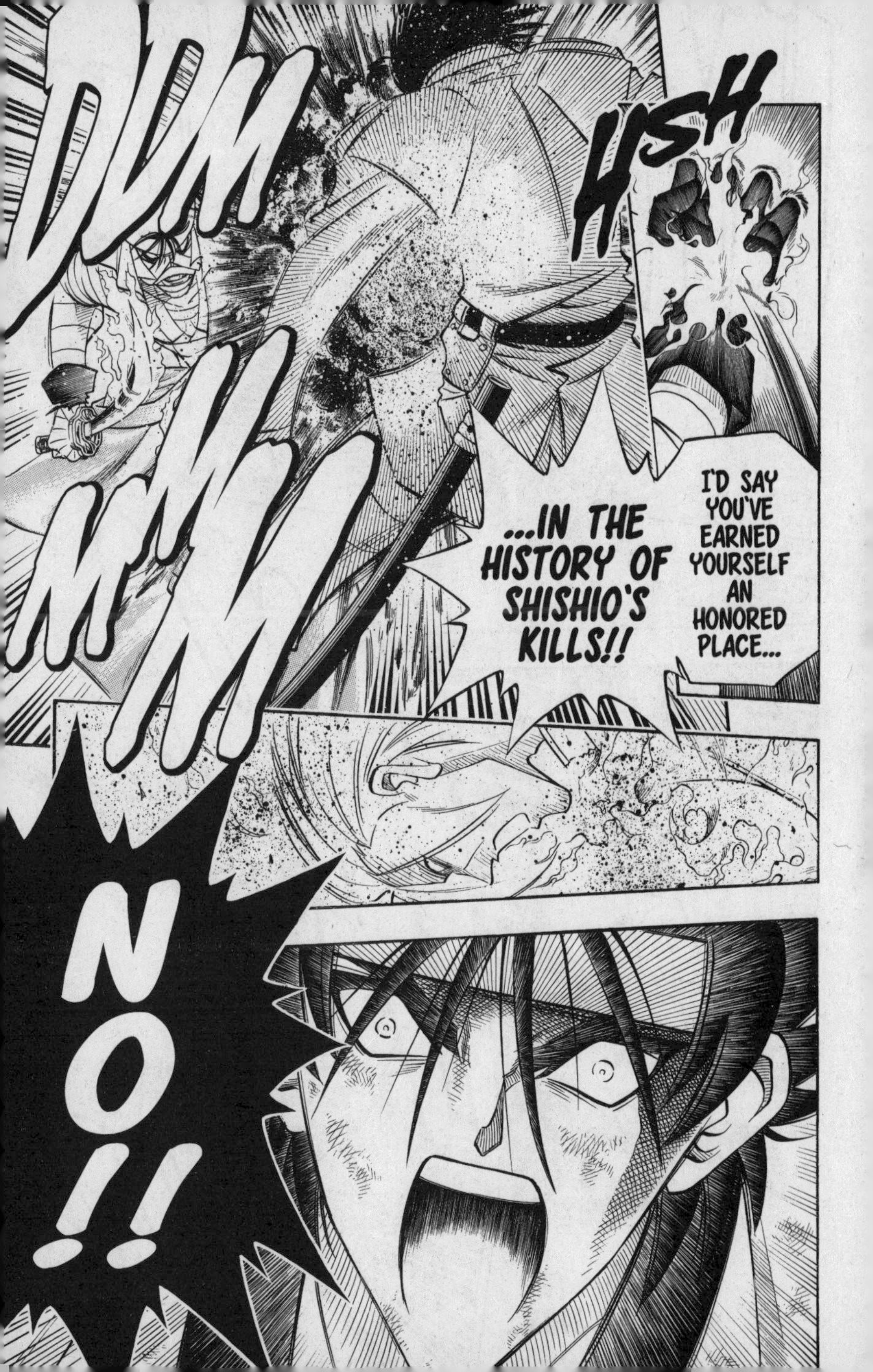
HSH
I'D SAY YOU'VE EARNED YOURSELF AN HONORED PLACE...
...IN THE HISTORY OF SHISHIO'S KILLS!!
NO!!

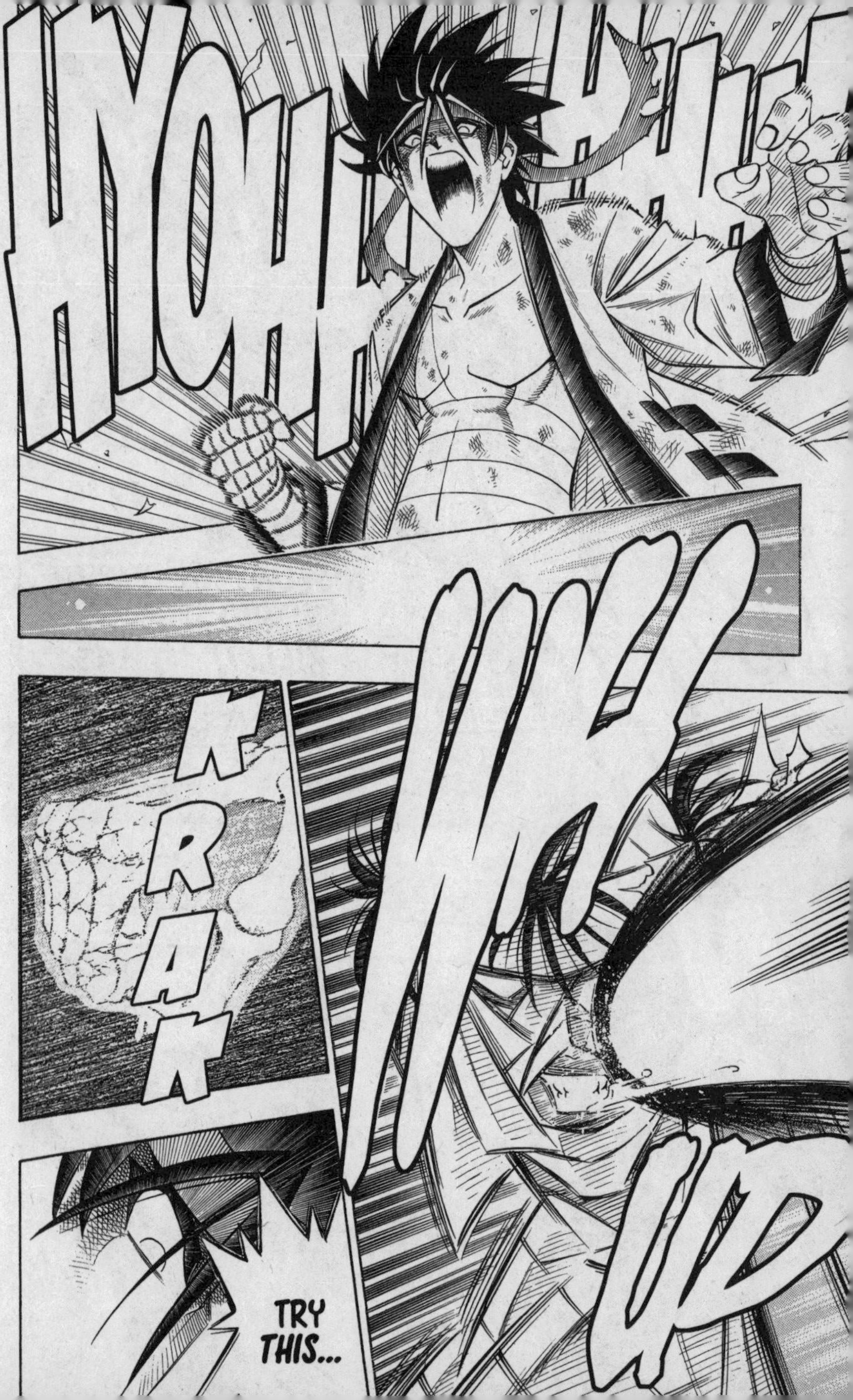
KRAK
TRY THIS...

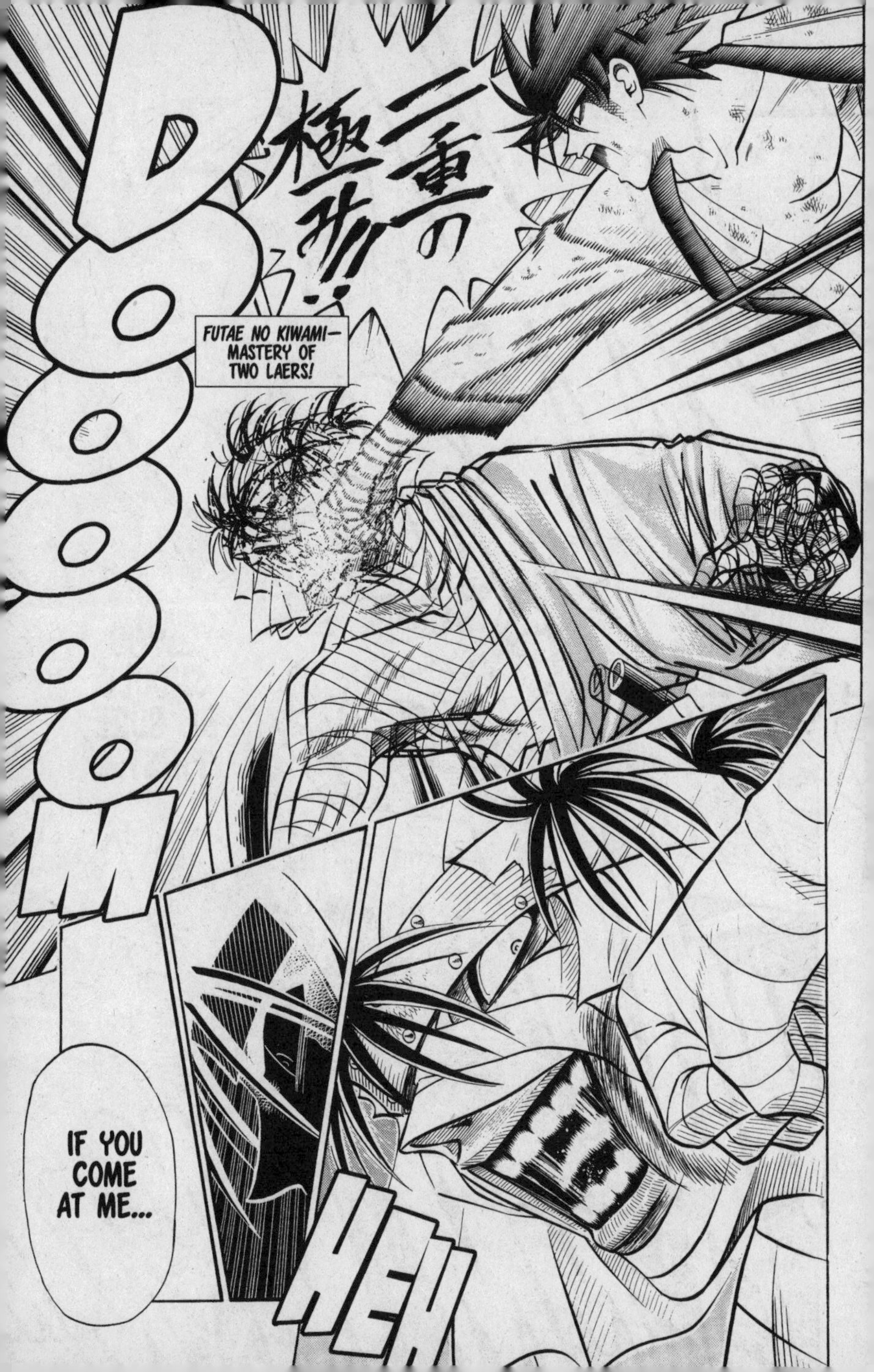
二重の極み!!
FUTAE NO KIWAMI—MASTERY OF TWO LAERS!
DOOOOOOM
HEH
IF YOU COME AT ME...

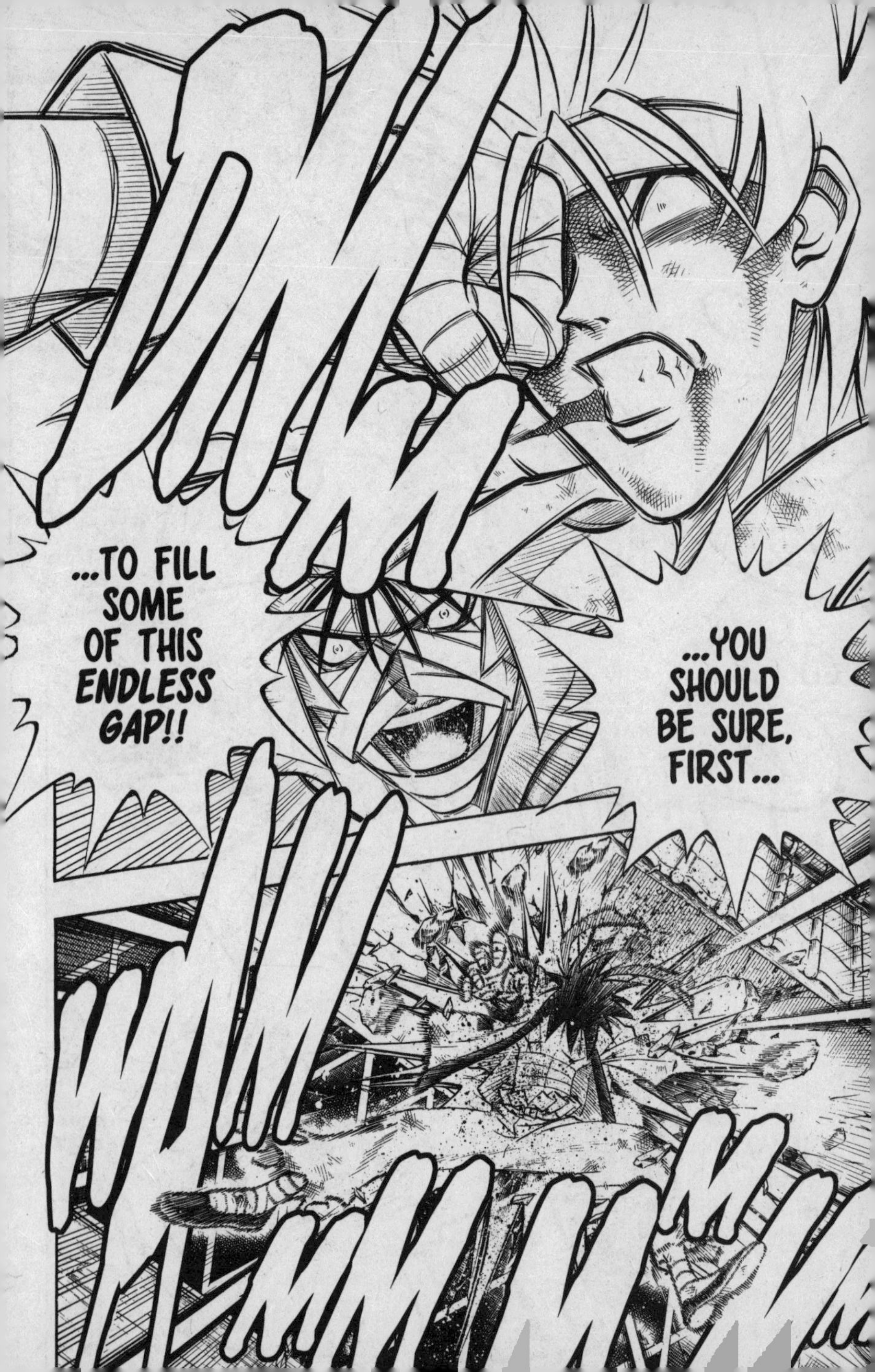
...YOU SHOULD BE SURE, FIRST...
...TO FILL SOME OF THIS ENDLESS GAP!!

YOU...

...SCUM...

PSSSHH

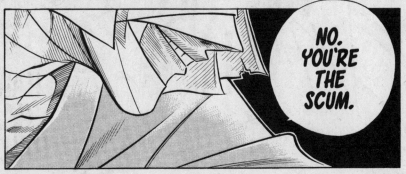

NO. YOU'RE THE SCUM.

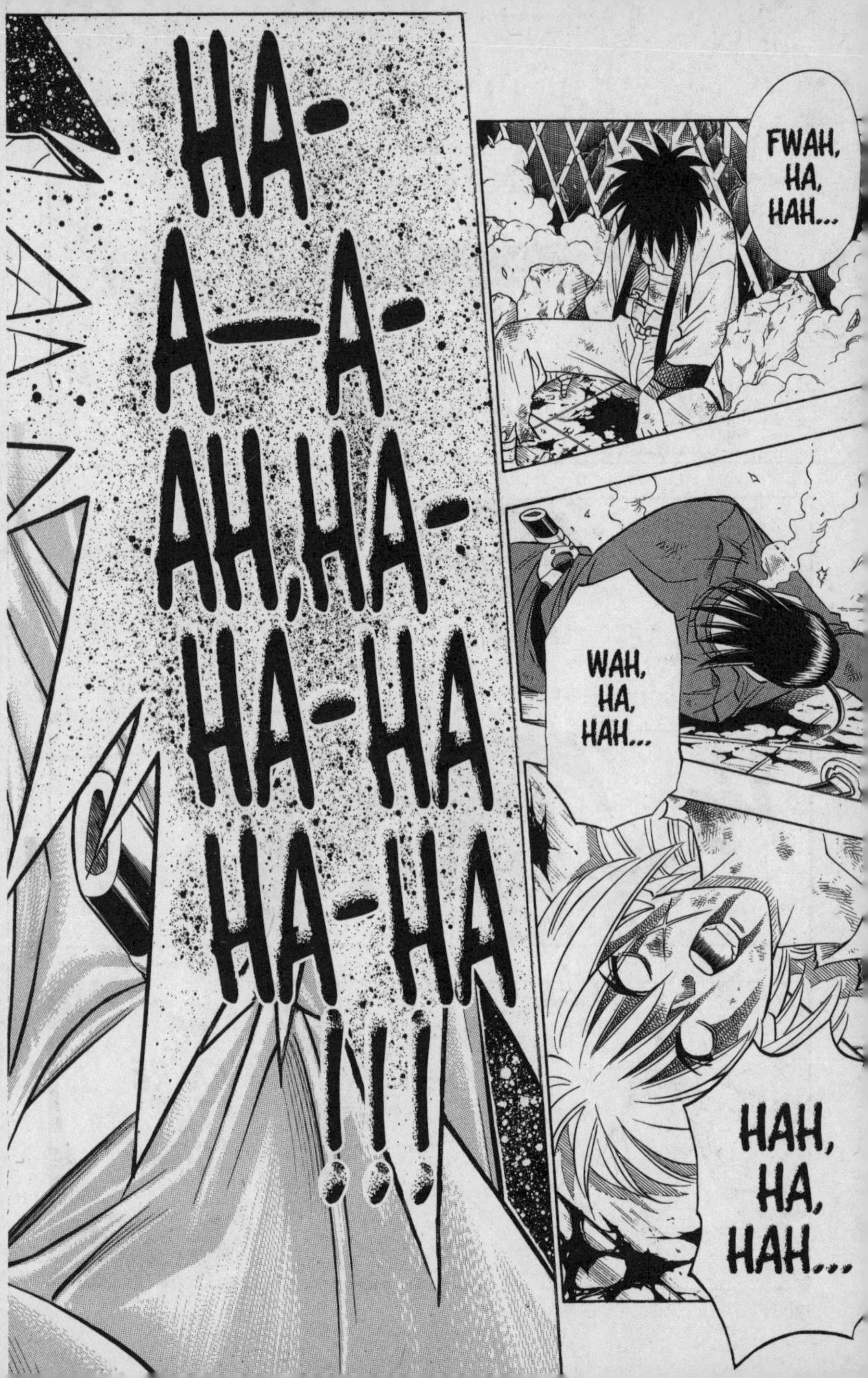
FWAH, HA, HAH...
WAH, HA, HAH...
HAH, HA, HAH...
HA-A—A-A AH,HA-HA-HA HA-HA!!!

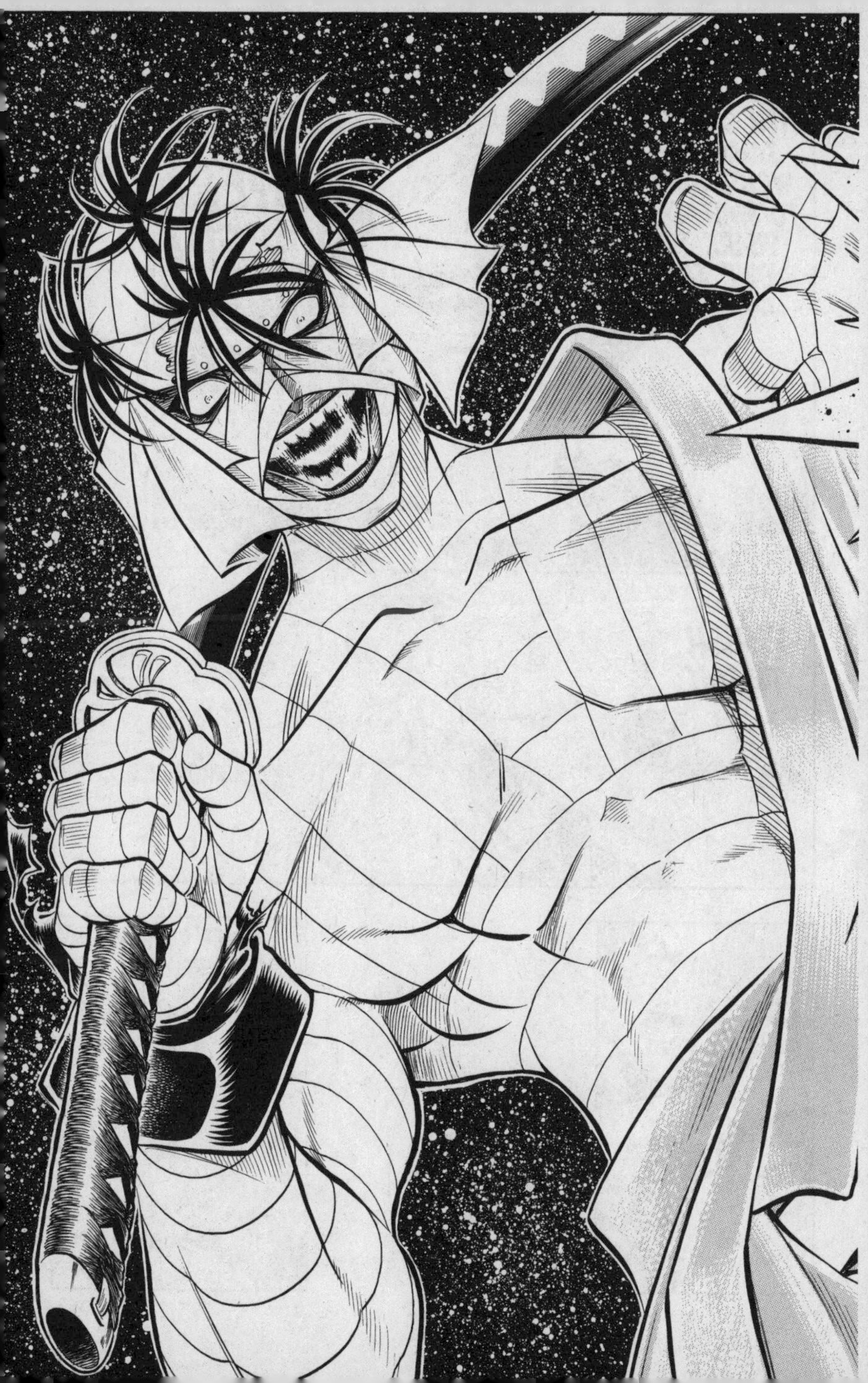

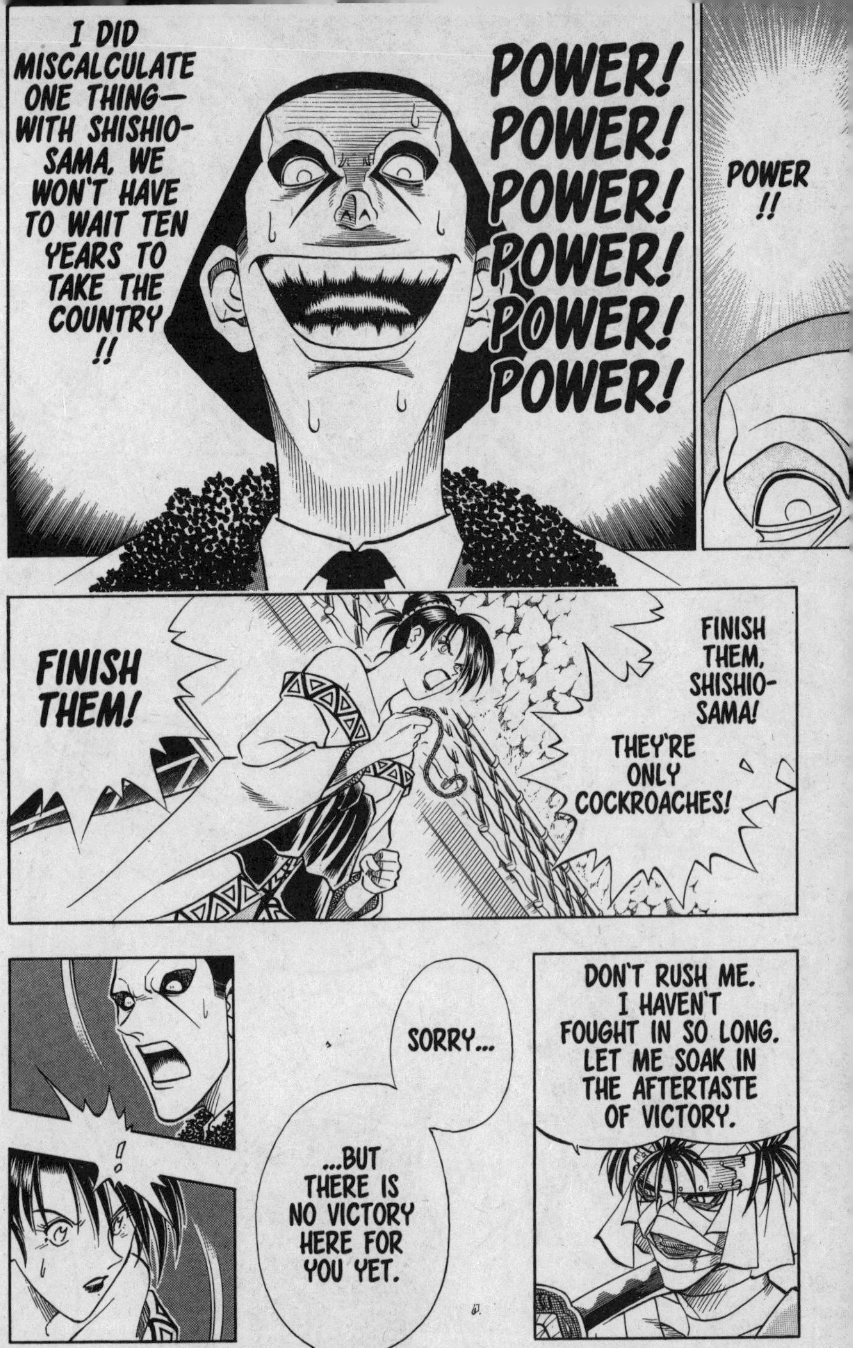
POWER !!
POWER! POWER! POWER! POWER! POWER! POWER!
I DID MISCALCULATE ONE THING— WITH SHISHIO-SAMA, WE WON'T HAVE TO WAIT TEN YEARS TO TAKE THE COUNTRY !!
FINISH THEM, SHISHIO-SAMA!
THEY'RE ONLY COCKROACHES!
FINISH THEM!
DON'T RUSH ME. I HAVEN'T FOUGHT IN SO LONG. LET ME SOAK IN THE AFTERTASTE OF VICTORY.
SORRY...
...BUT THERE IS NO VICTORY HERE FOR YOU YET.
!

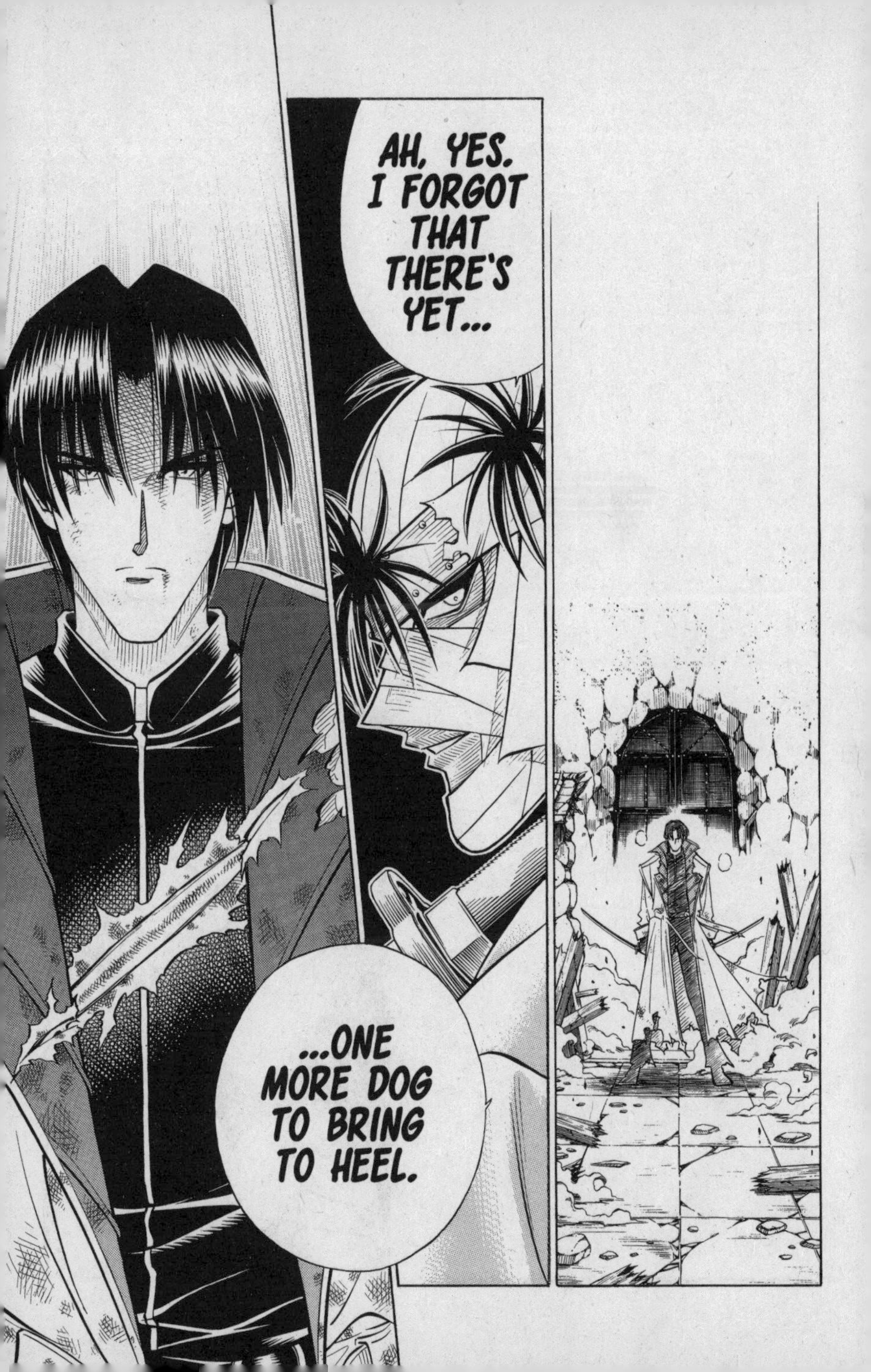
AH, YES. I FORGOT THAT THERE'S YET...
...ONE MORE DOG TO BRING TO HEEL.

Rurouni Kenshin

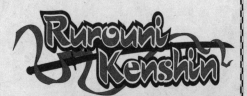

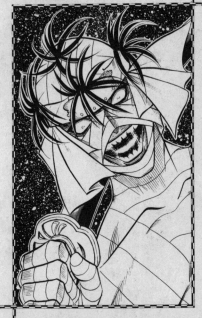

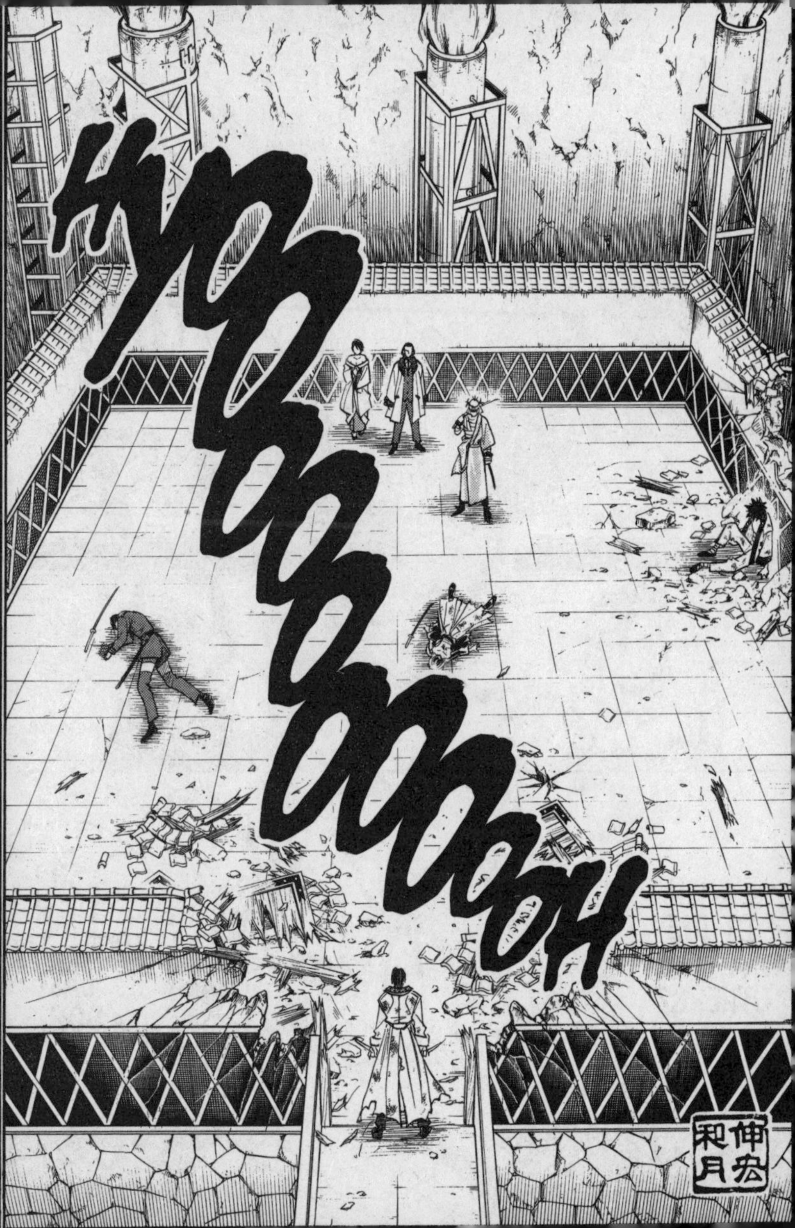
伸宏和月

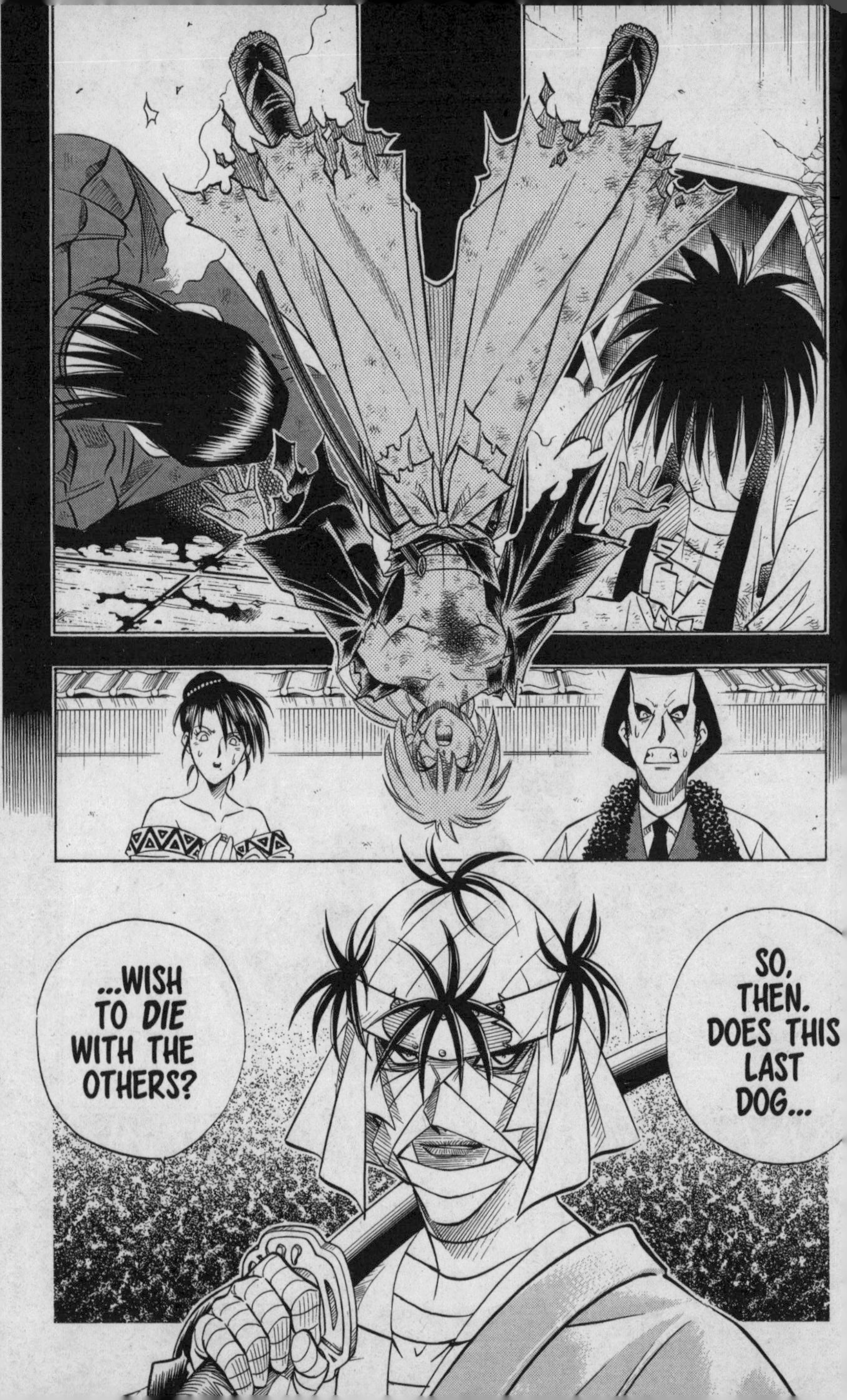
SO, THEN. DOES THIS LAST DOG...
...WISH TO *DIE* WITH THE OTHERS?

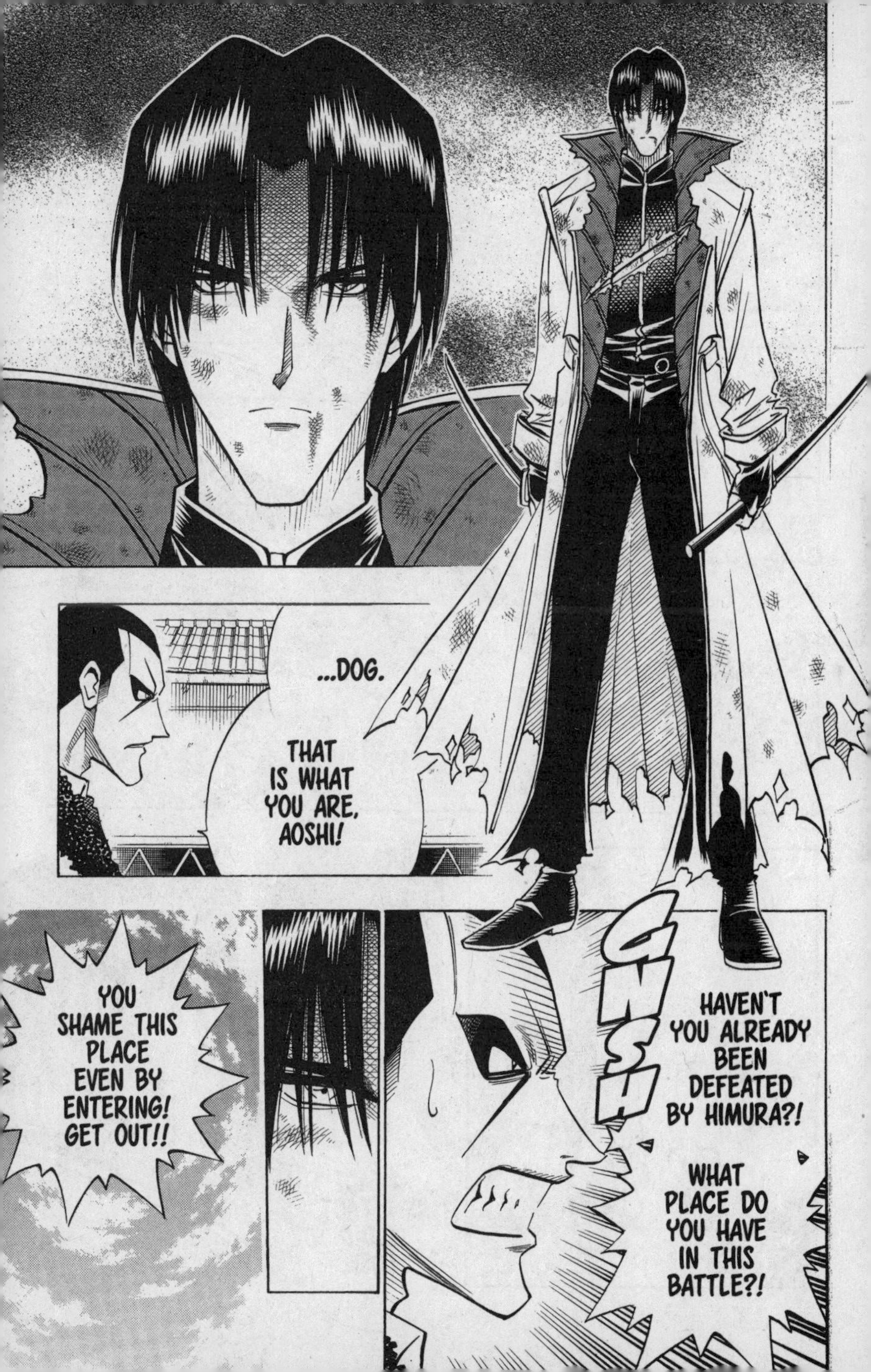
...DOG.
THAT IS WHAT YOU ARE, AOSHI!
GNSH
HAVEN'T YOU ALREADY BEEN DEFEATED BY HIMURA?!
WHAT PLACE DO YOU HAVE IN THIS BATTLE?!
YOU SHAME THIS PLACE EVEN BY ENTERING! GET OUT!!

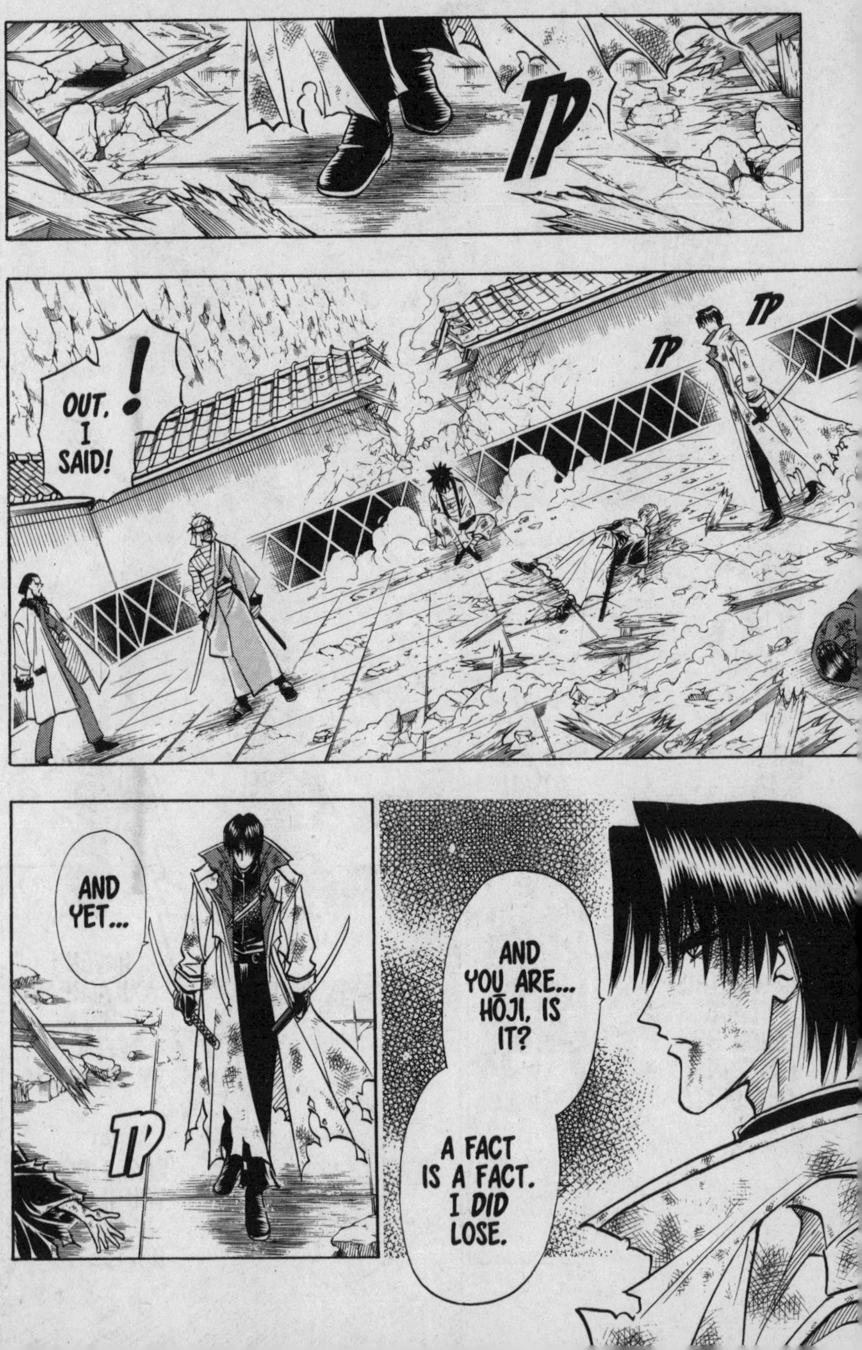
TP
TP
TP
OUT, I SAID!
!
AND YOU ARE... HŌJI, IS IT?
A FACT IS A FACT. I DID LOSE.
AND YET...
TP

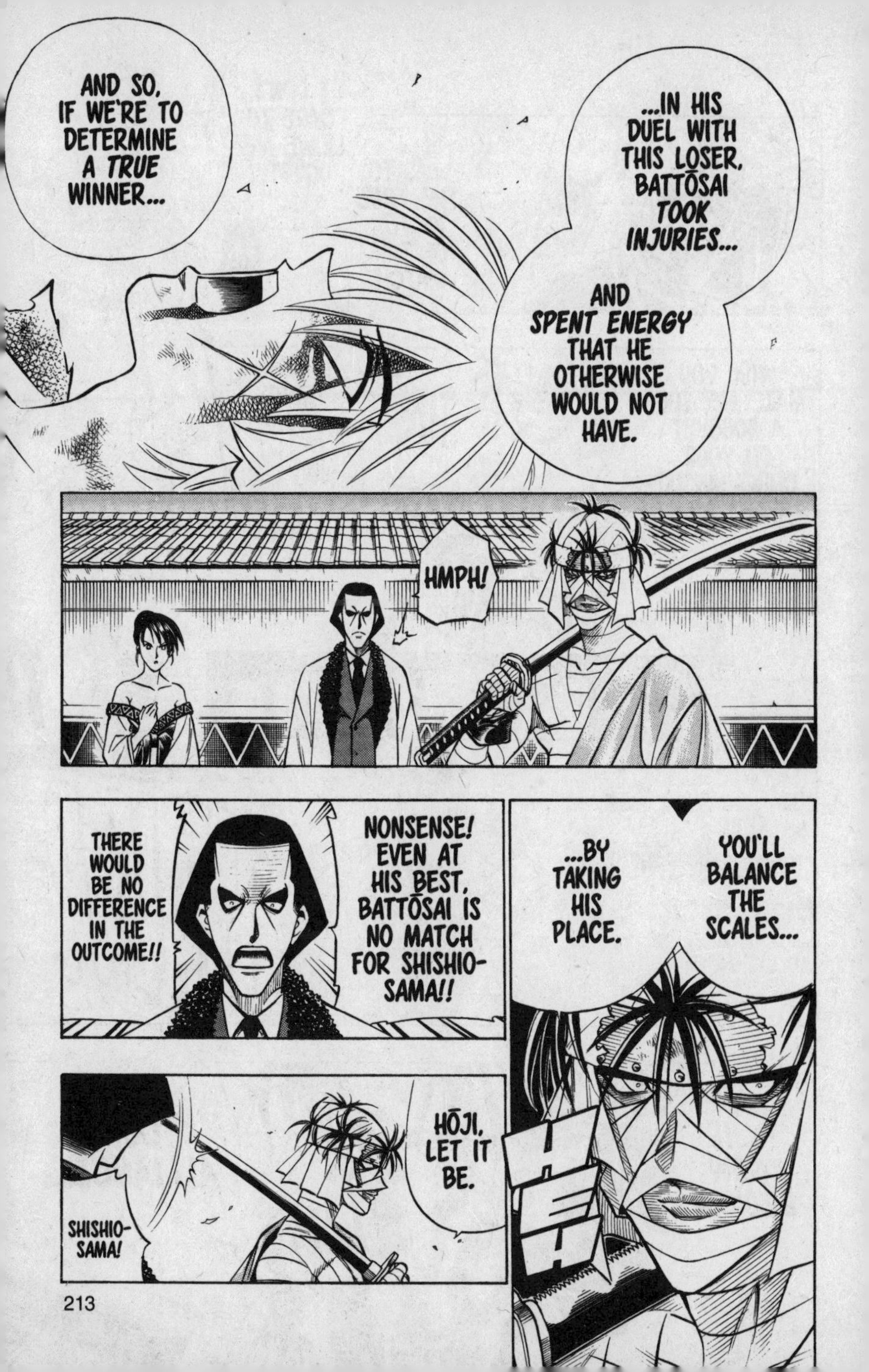
...IN HIS DUEL WITH THIS LOSER, BATTŌSAI *TOOK INJURIES*...
AND *SPENT ENERGY* THAT HE OTHERWISE WOULD NOT HAVE.
AND SO, IF WE'RE TO DETERMINE A *TRUE* WINNER...
HMPH!
YOU'LL BALANCE THE SCALES...
...BY TAKING HIS PLACE.
HEH
NONSENSE! EVEN AT HIS BEST, BATTŌSAI IS NO MATCH FOR SHISHIO-SAMA!!
THERE WOULD BE NO DIFFERENCE IN THE OUTCOME!!
HŌJI, LET IT BE.
SHISHIO-SAMA!

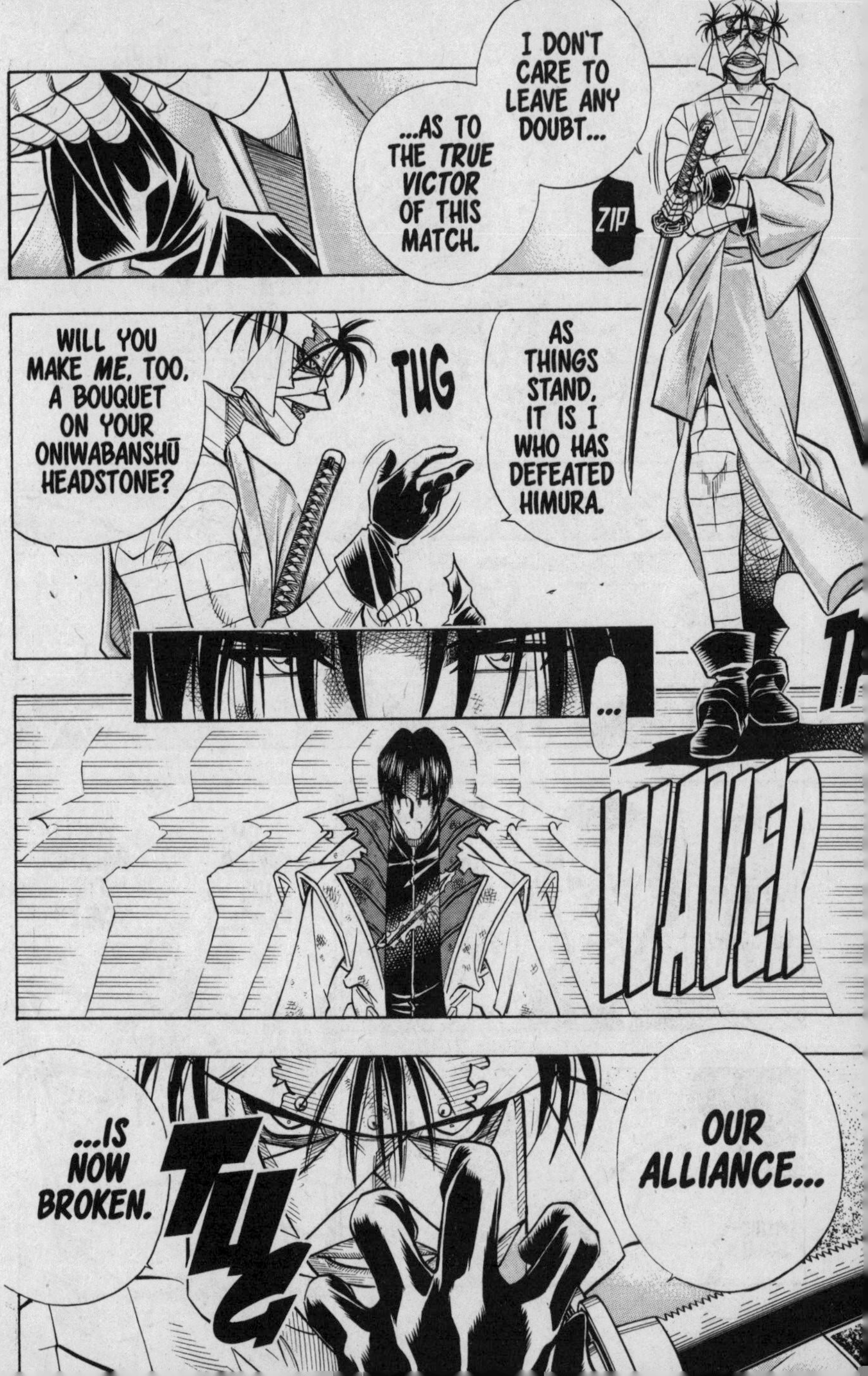
I DON'T CARE TO LEAVE ANY DOUBT...
...AS TO THE *TRUE VICTOR* OF THIS MATCH.
ZIP
AS THINGS STAND, IT IS I WHO HAS DEFEATED HIMURA.
TUG
WILL YOU MAKE *ME*, TOO, A BOUQUET ON YOUR ONIWABANSHŪ HEADSTONE?
...
WAVER
OUR ALLIANCE...
...IS NOW BROKEN.

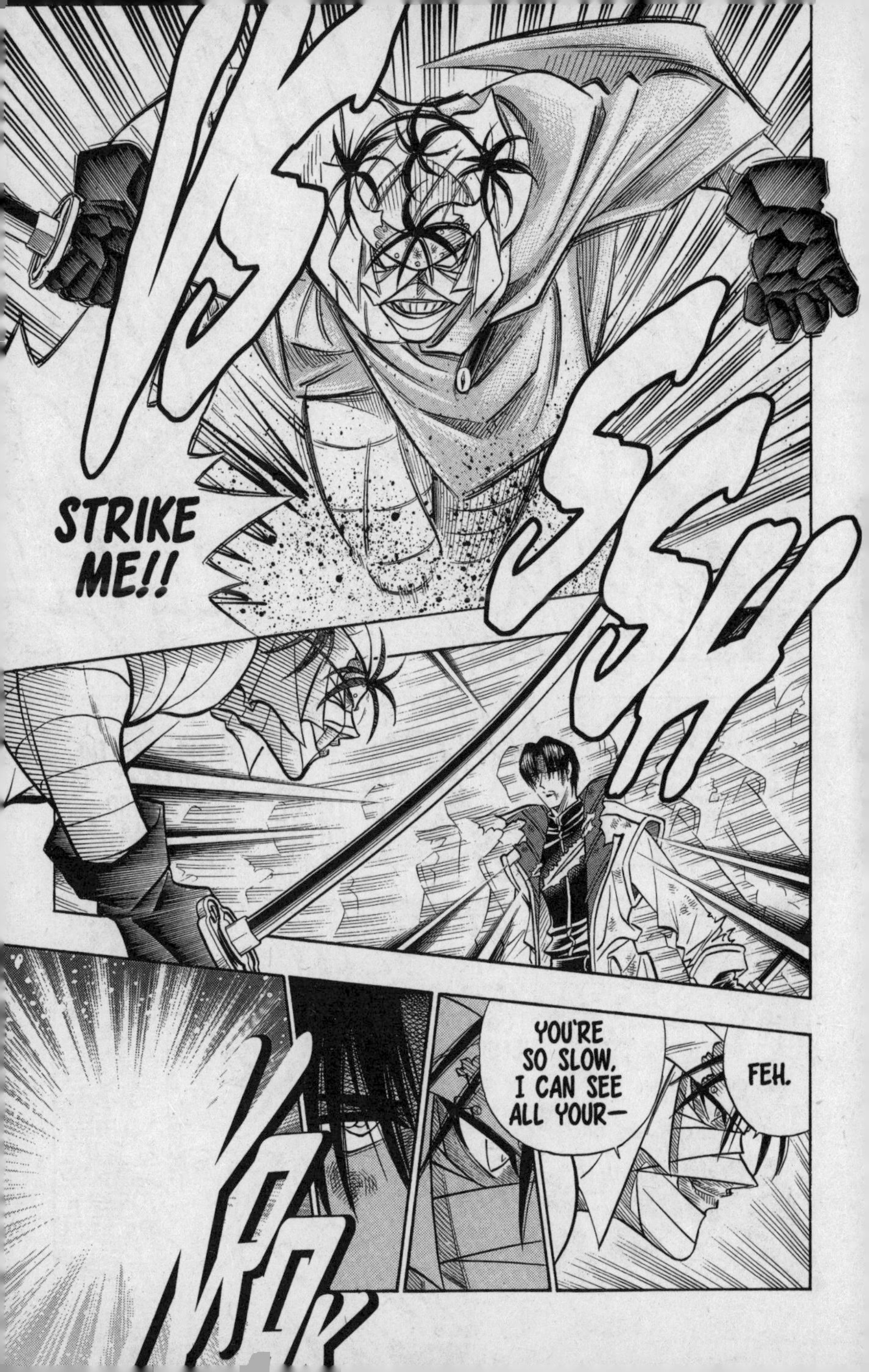
STRIKE ME!!
FEH.
YOU'RE SO SLOW, I CAN SEE ALL YOUR—

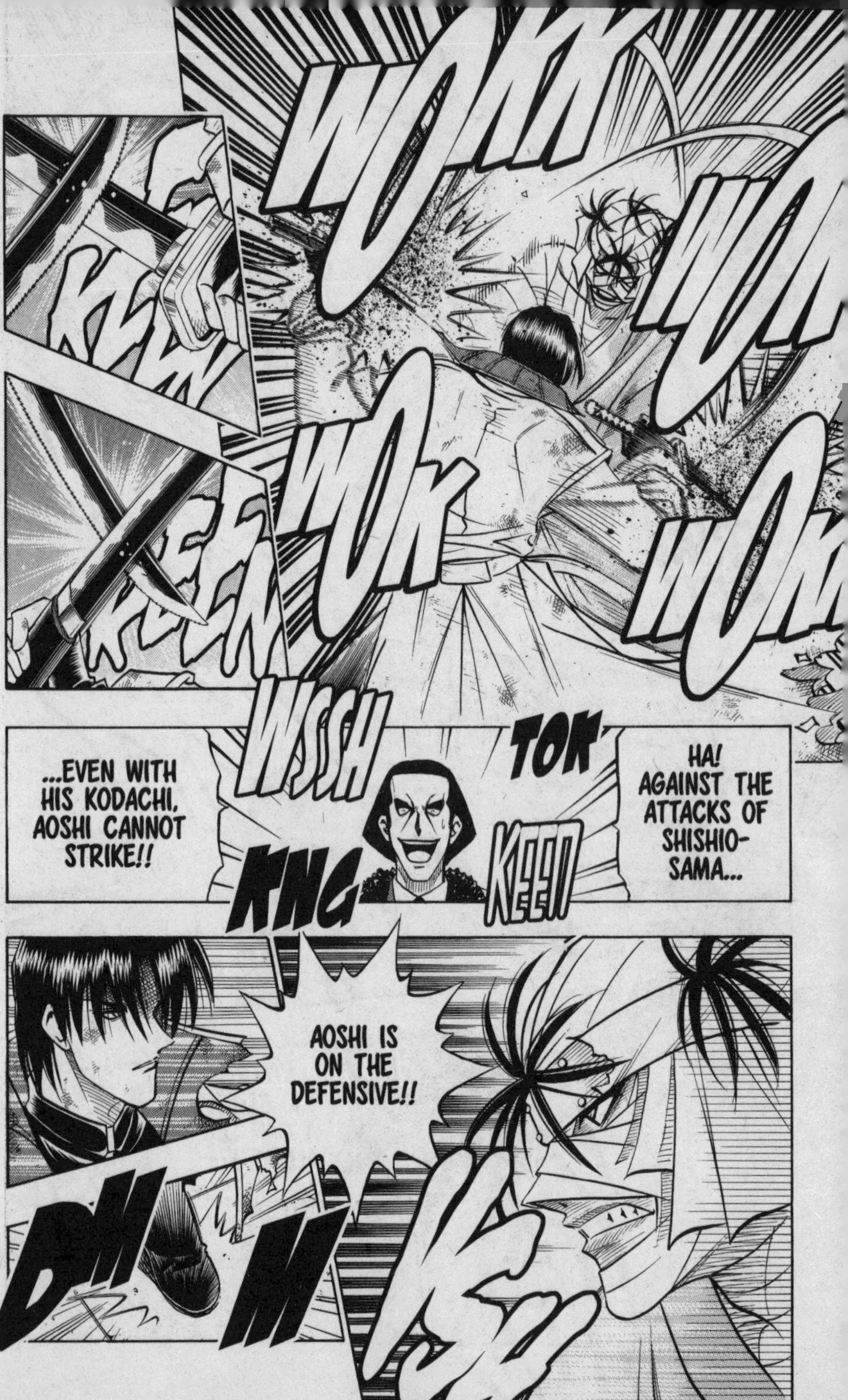
HA! AGAINST THE ATTACKS OF SHISHIO-SAMA...
TOK
KEEN
...EVEN WITH HIS KODACHI, AOSHI CANNOT STRIKE!!
KNG
AOSHI IS ON THE DEFENSIVE!!

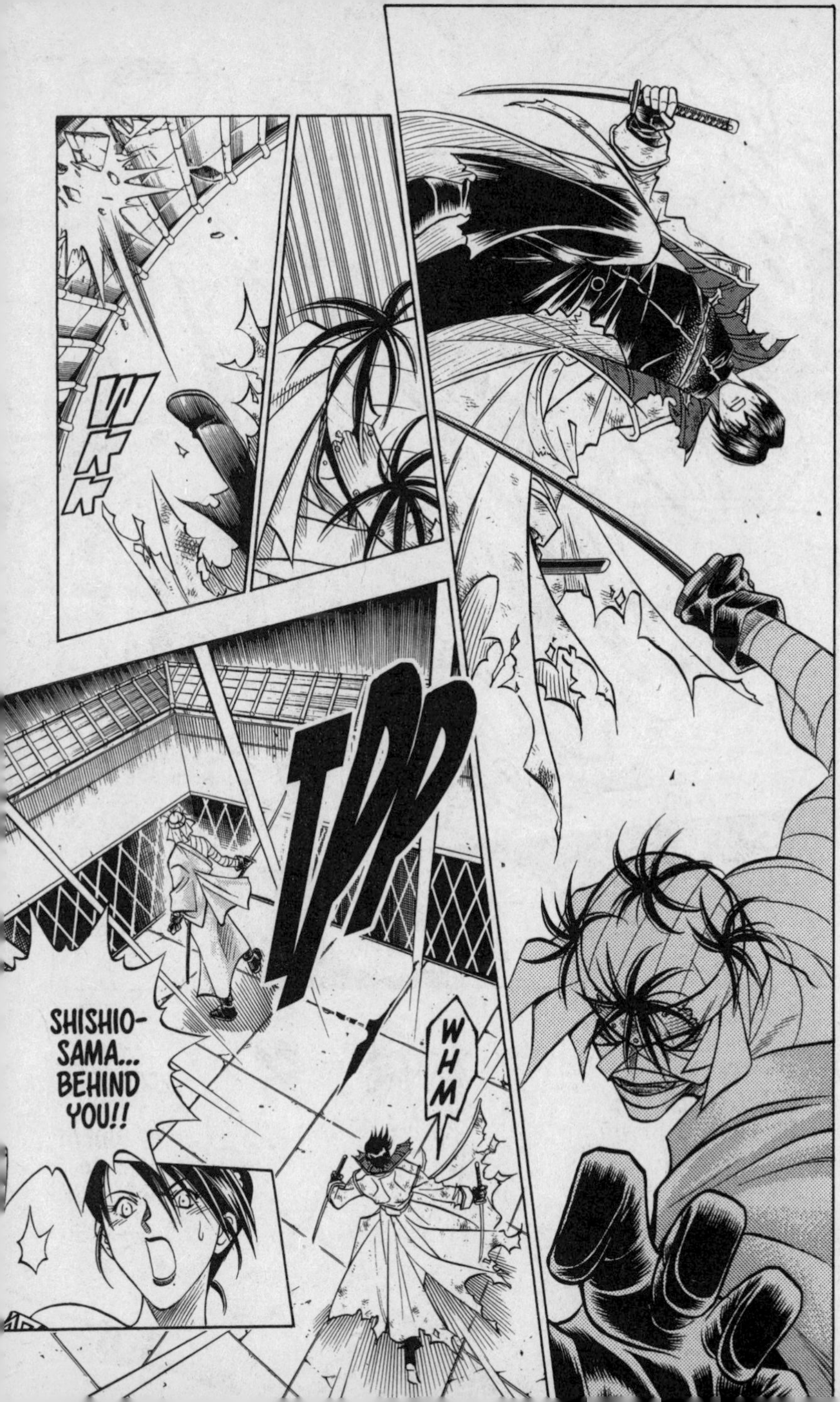
WHM
SHISHIO-SAMA... BEHIND YOU!!

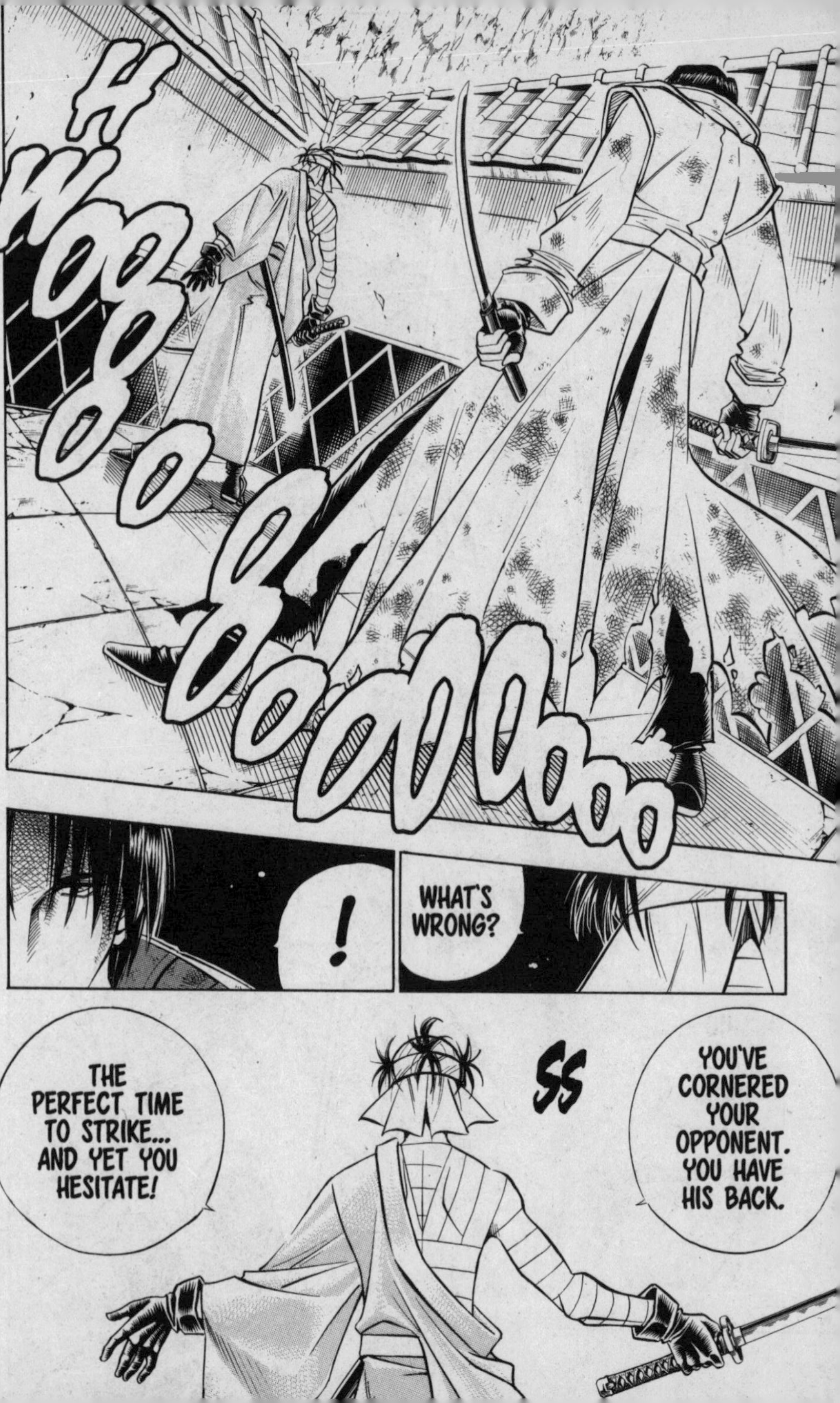
HWOOOOOOOOOOOOOO
WHAT'S WRONG?
!
YOU'VE CORNERED YOUR OPPONENT. YOU HAVE HIS BACK.
SS
THE PERFECT TIME TO STRIKE... AND YET YOU HESITATE!

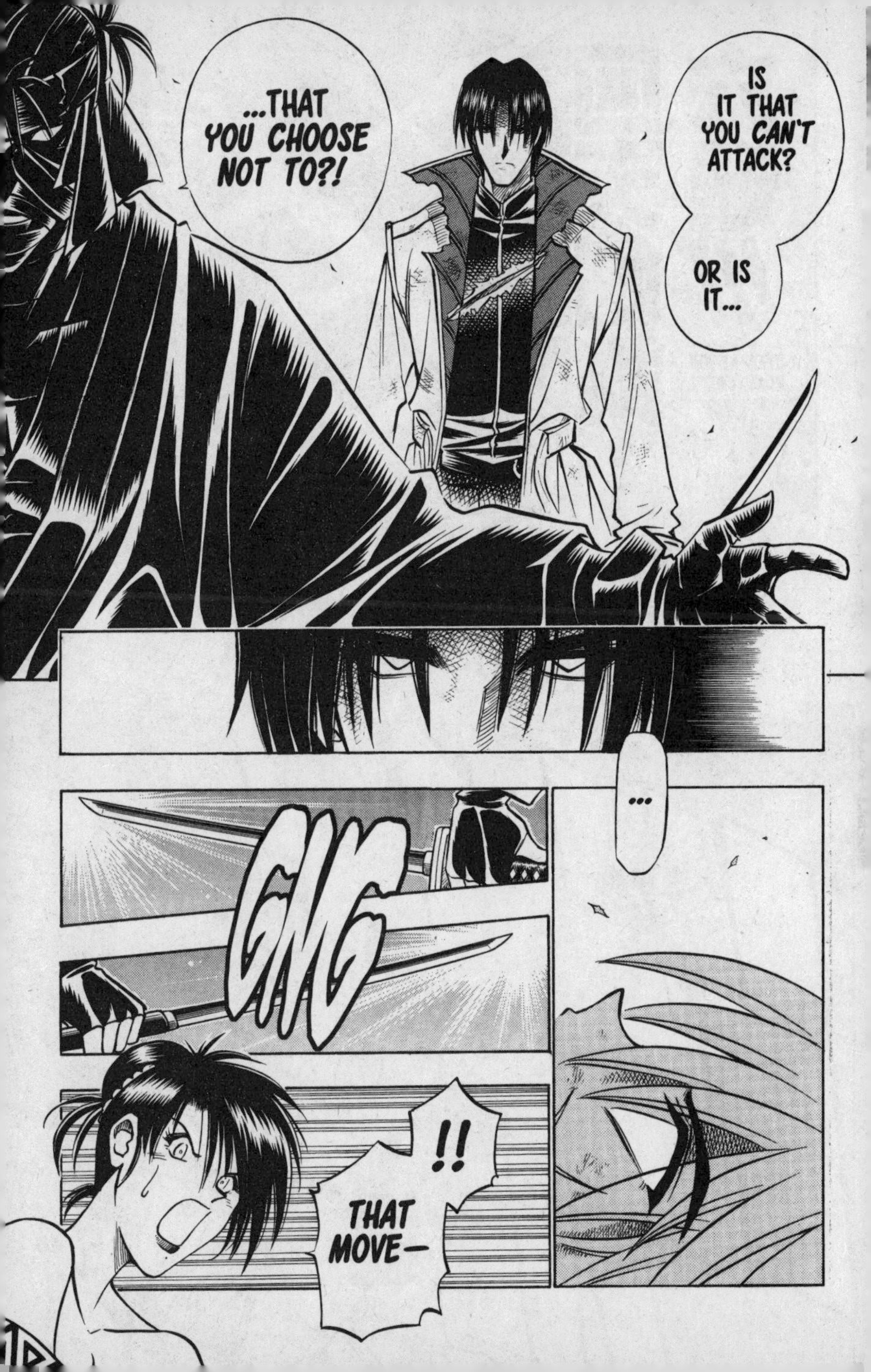
IS IT THAT YOU CAN'T ATTACK?
OR IS IT...
...THAT YOU CHOOSE NOT TO?!
...
!!
THAT MOVE—

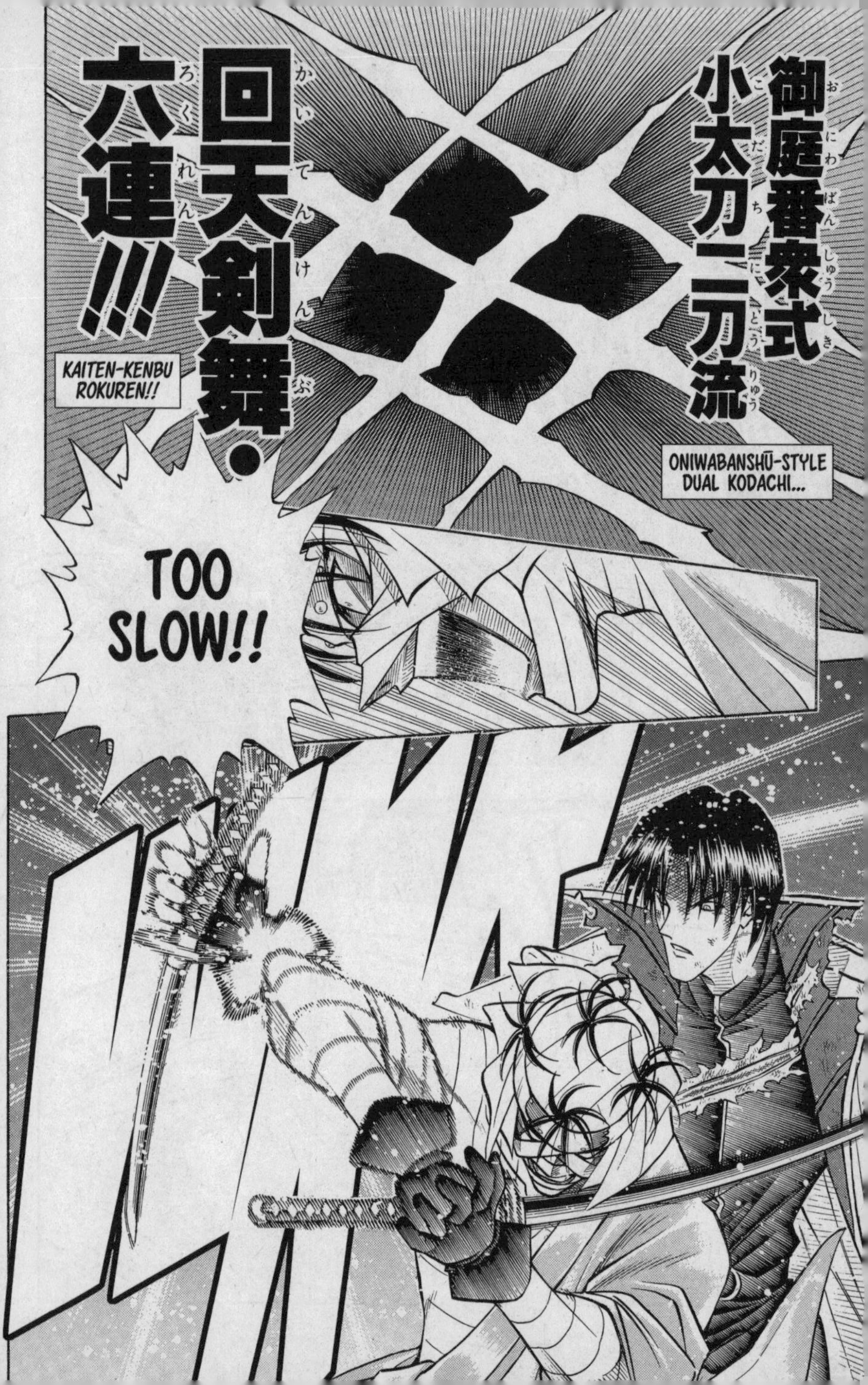
御庭番衆式小太刀二刀流
ONIWABANSHŪ-STYLE DUAL KODACHI...
回天剣舞・六連!!
KAITEN-KENBU ROKUREN!!
TOO SLOW!!

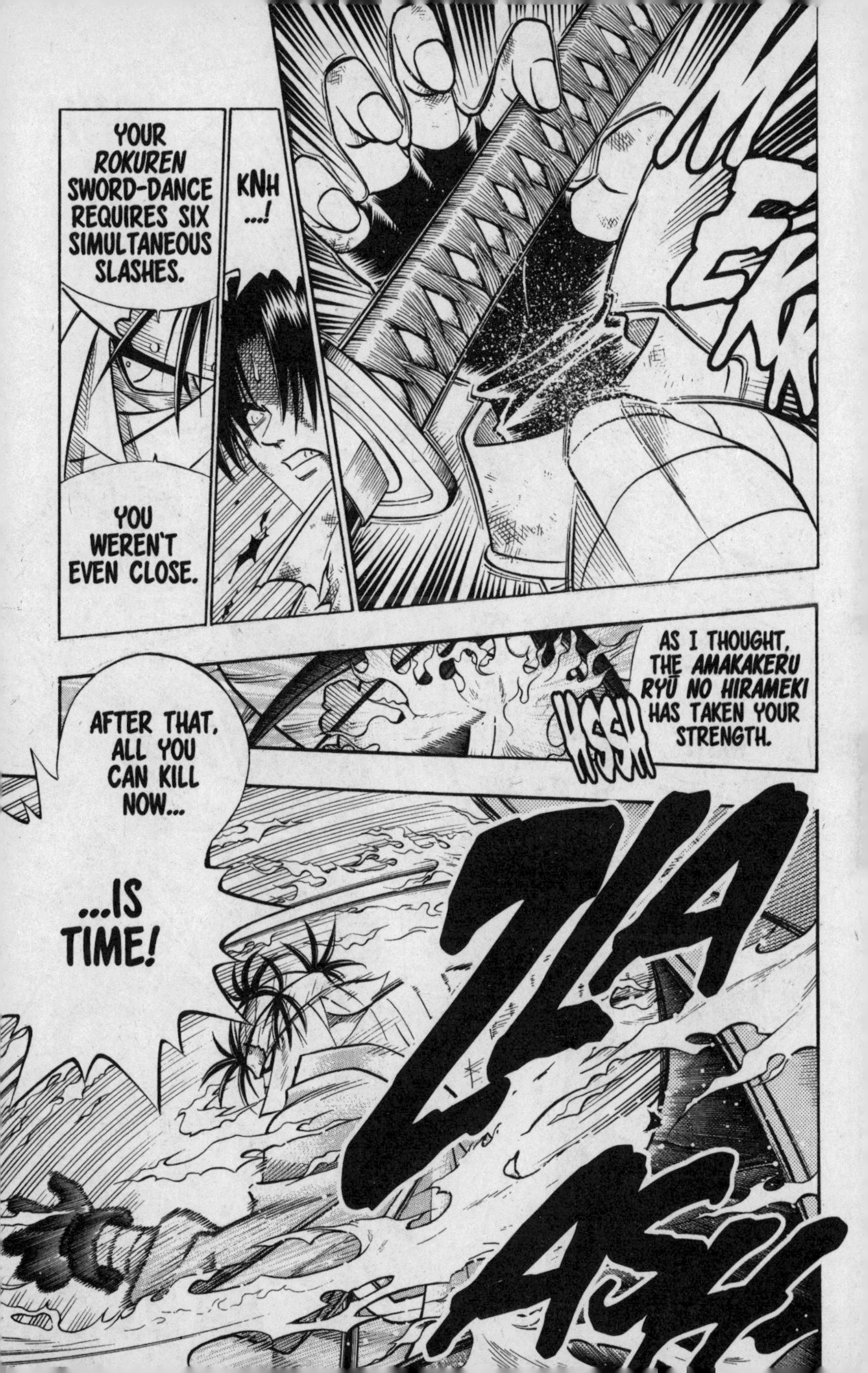
KNH ...!
YOUR ROKUREN SWORD-DANCE REQUIRES SIX SIMULTANEOUS SLASHES.
YOU WEREN'T EVEN CLOSE.
AS I THOUGHT, THE AMAKAKERU RYŪ NO HIRAMEKI HAS TAKEN YOUR STRENGTH.
AFTER THAT, ALL YOU CAN KILL NOW...
...IS TIME!

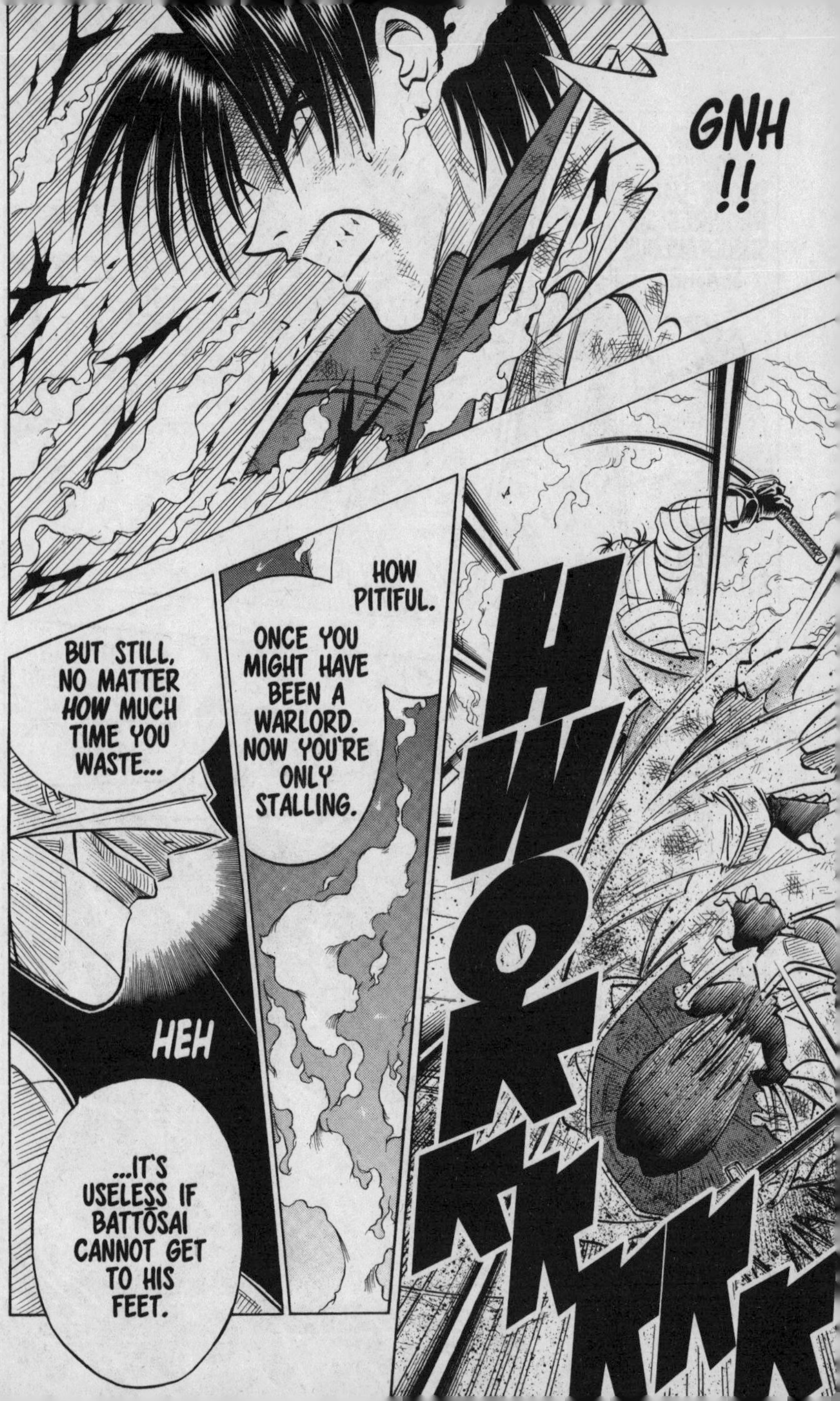
GNH !!
HWOKKKK
HOW PITIFUL.
ONCE YOU MIGHT HAVE BEEN A WARLORD. NOW YOU'RE ONLY STALLING.
BUT STILL, NO MATTER *HOW* MUCH TIME YOU WASTE...
HEH
...IT'S USELESS IF BATTŌSAI CANNOT GET TO HIS FEET.

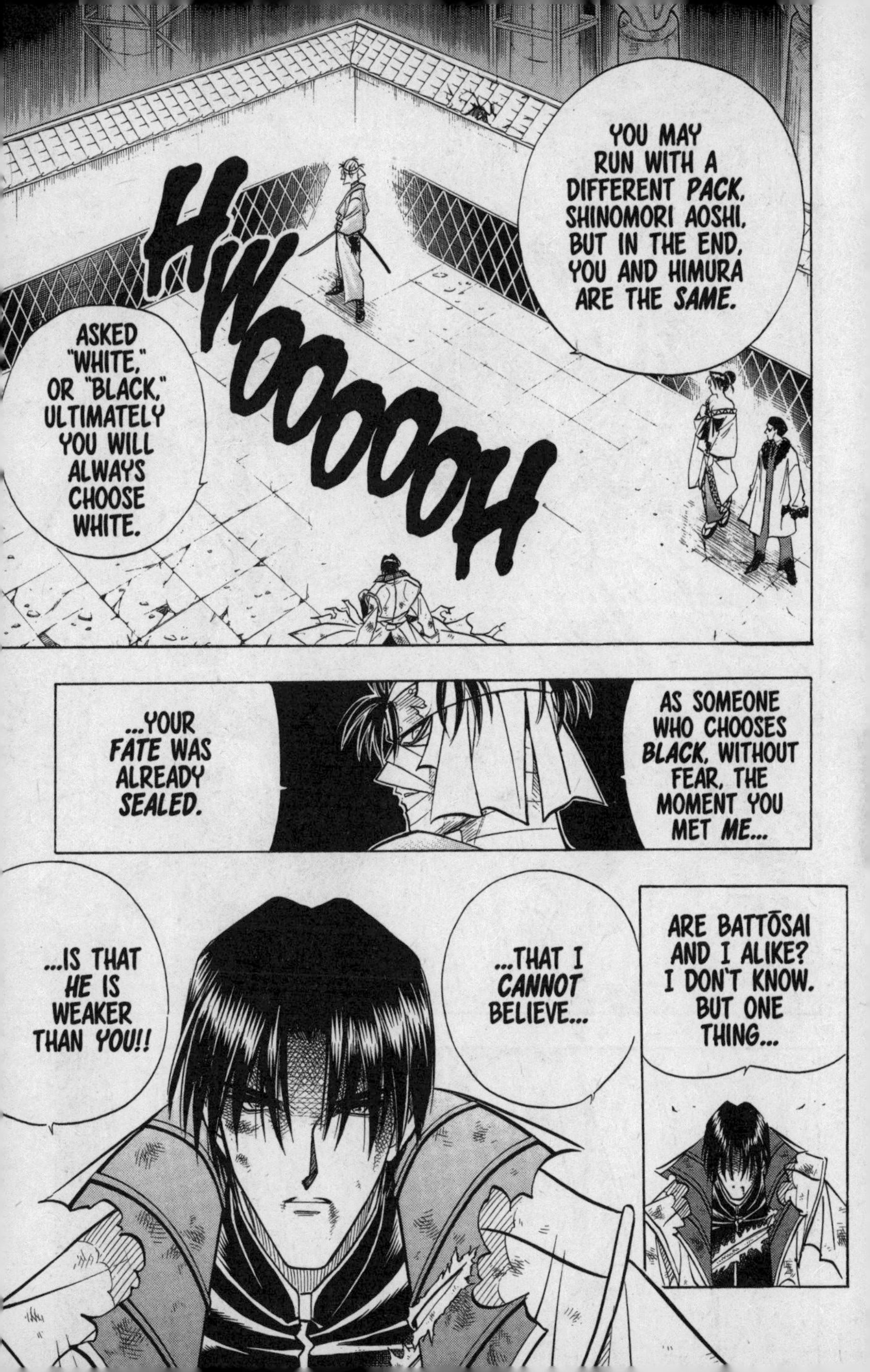
YOU MAY RUN WITH A DIFFERENT PACK, SHINOMORI AOSHI, BUT IN THE END, YOU AND HIMURA ARE THE SAME.
HWOOOOOH
ASKED "WHITE," OR "BLACK," ULTIMATELY YOU WILL ALWAYS CHOOSE WHITE.
AS SOMEONE WHO CHOOSES BLACK, WITHOUT FEAR, THE MOMENT YOU MET ME...
...YOUR FATE WAS ALREADY SEALED.
ARE BATTŌSAI AND I ALIKE? I DON'T KNOW. BUT ONE THING...
...THAT I CANNOT BELIEVE...
...IS THAT HE IS WEAKER THAN YOU!!

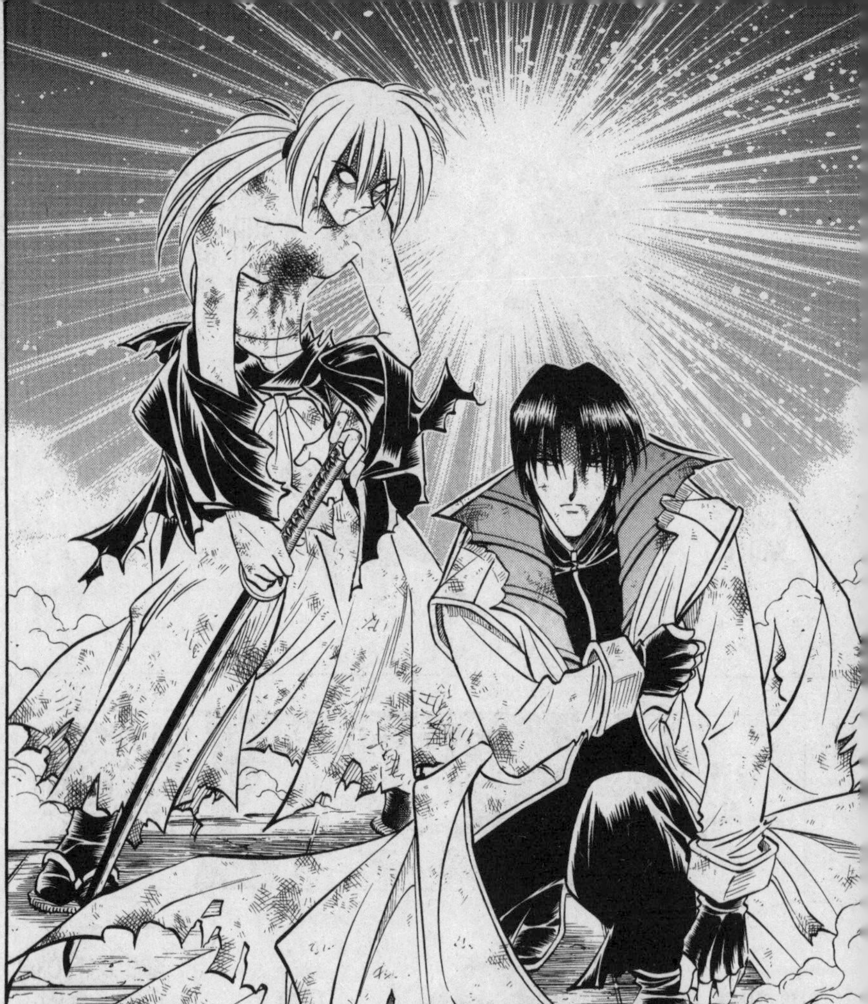
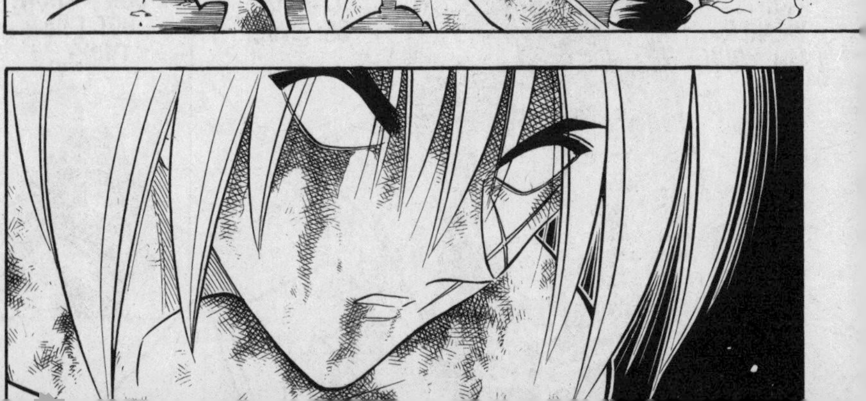

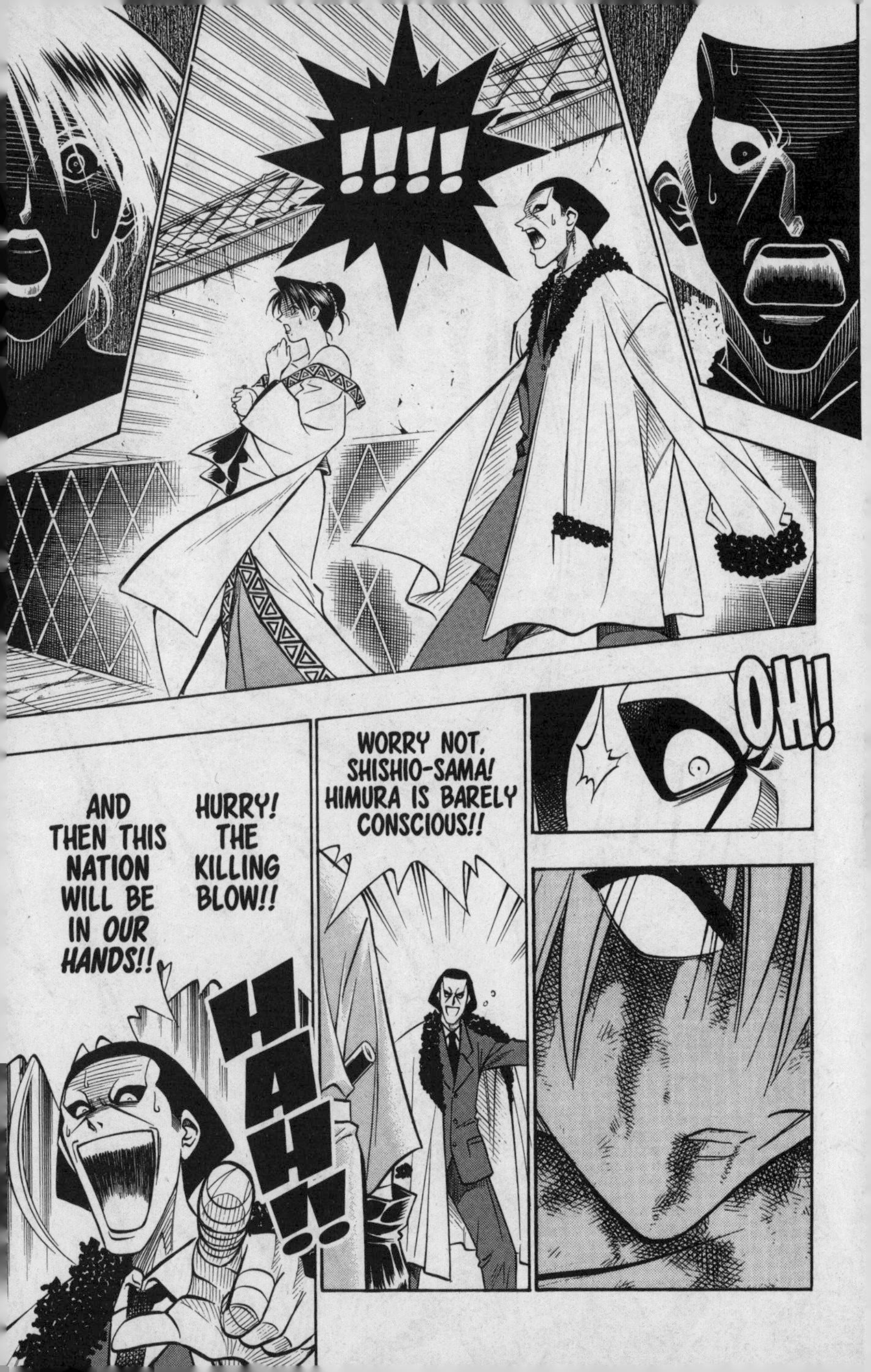
!!!!
OH!
WORRY NOT, SHISHIO-SAMA! HIMURA IS BARELY CONSCIOUS!!
HURRY! THE KILLING BLOW!!
AND THEN THIS NATION WILL BE IN OUR HANDS!!
HAH!!

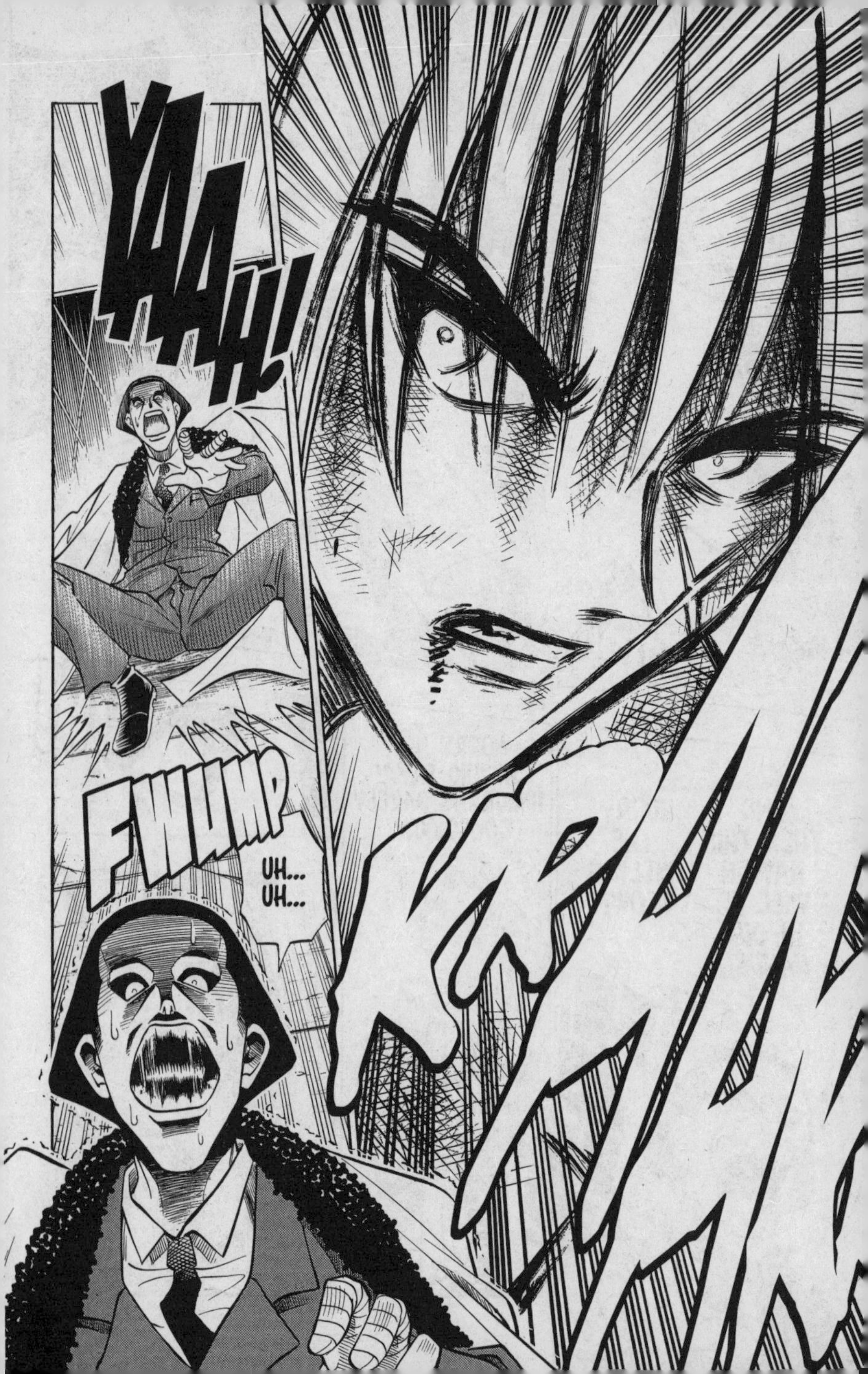
YAAH!!
FWUMP
UH...
UH...

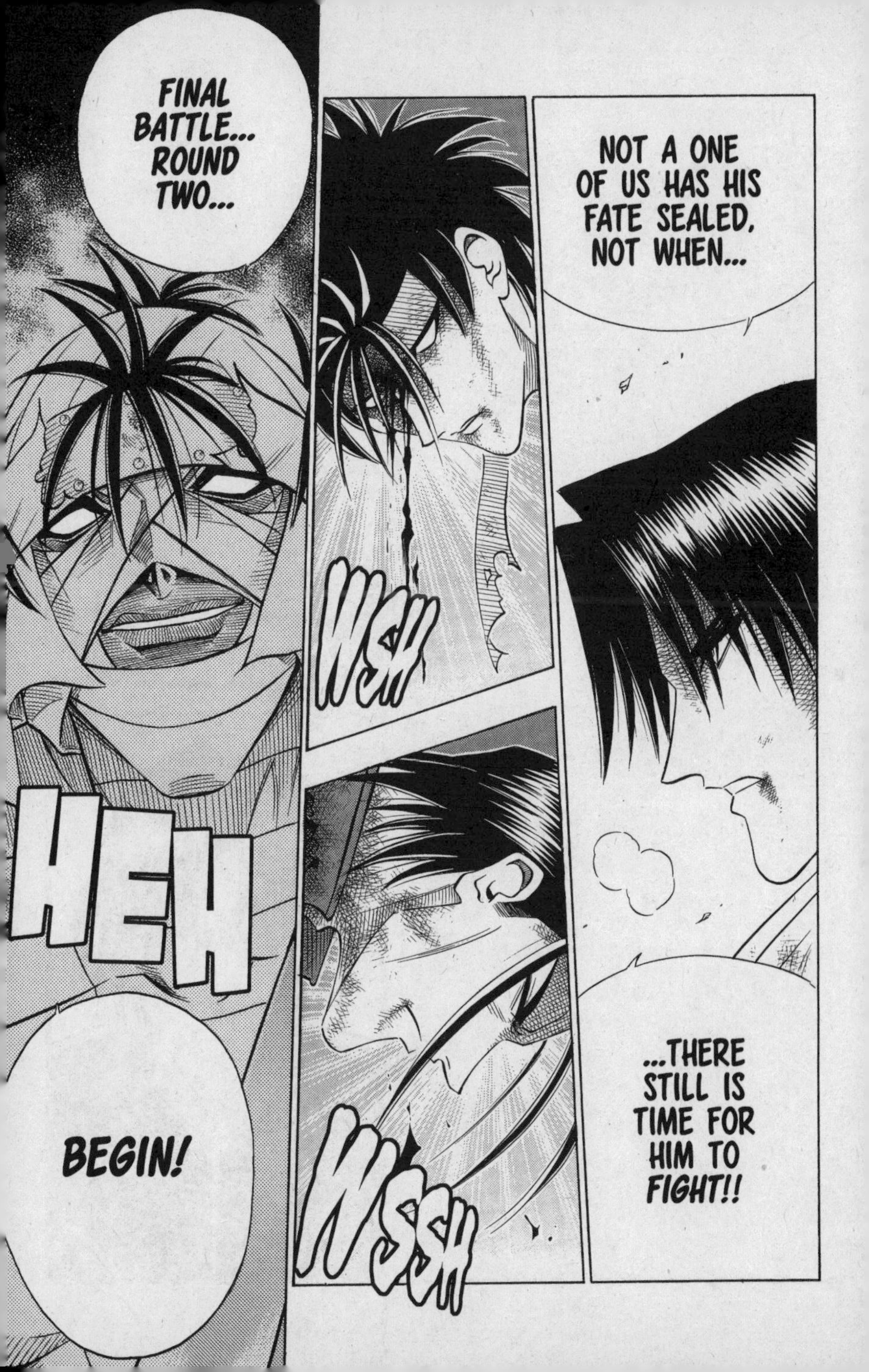
NOT A ONE OF US HAS HIS FATE SEALED, NOT WHEN...
...THERE STILL IS TIME FOR HIM TO FIGHT!!
WSH
WSSH
FINAL BATTLE... ROUND TWO...
HEH
BEGIN!

Rurouni Kenshin

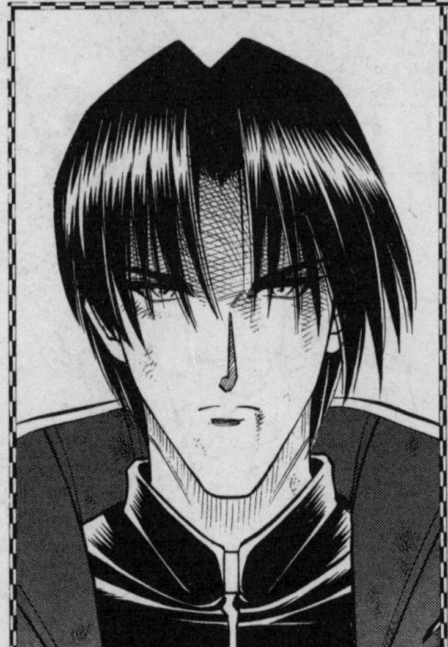

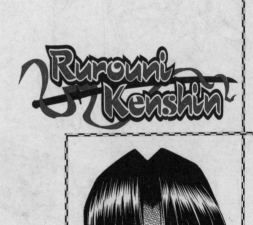

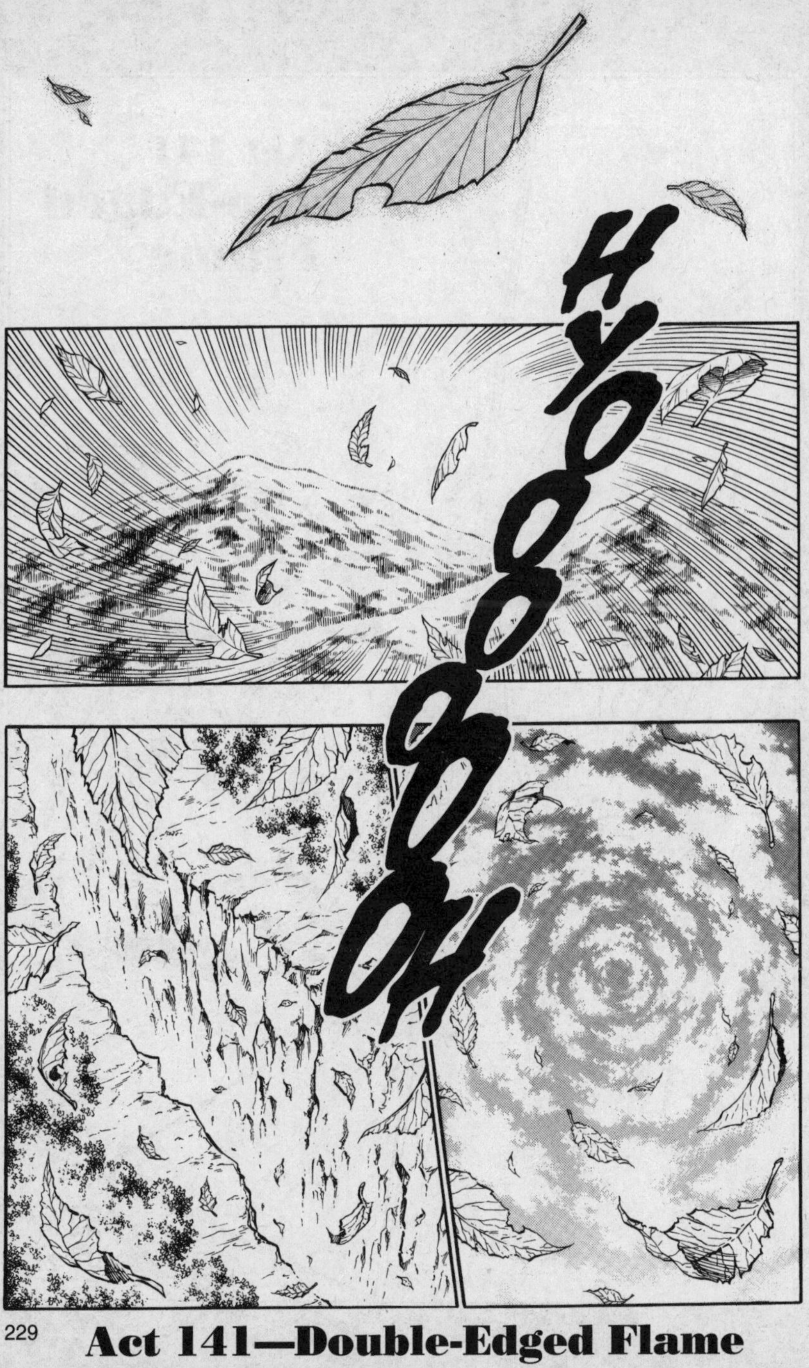
HYOOOOOOOH

Act 141—Double-Edged Flame

Act 141
Double-Edged Flame

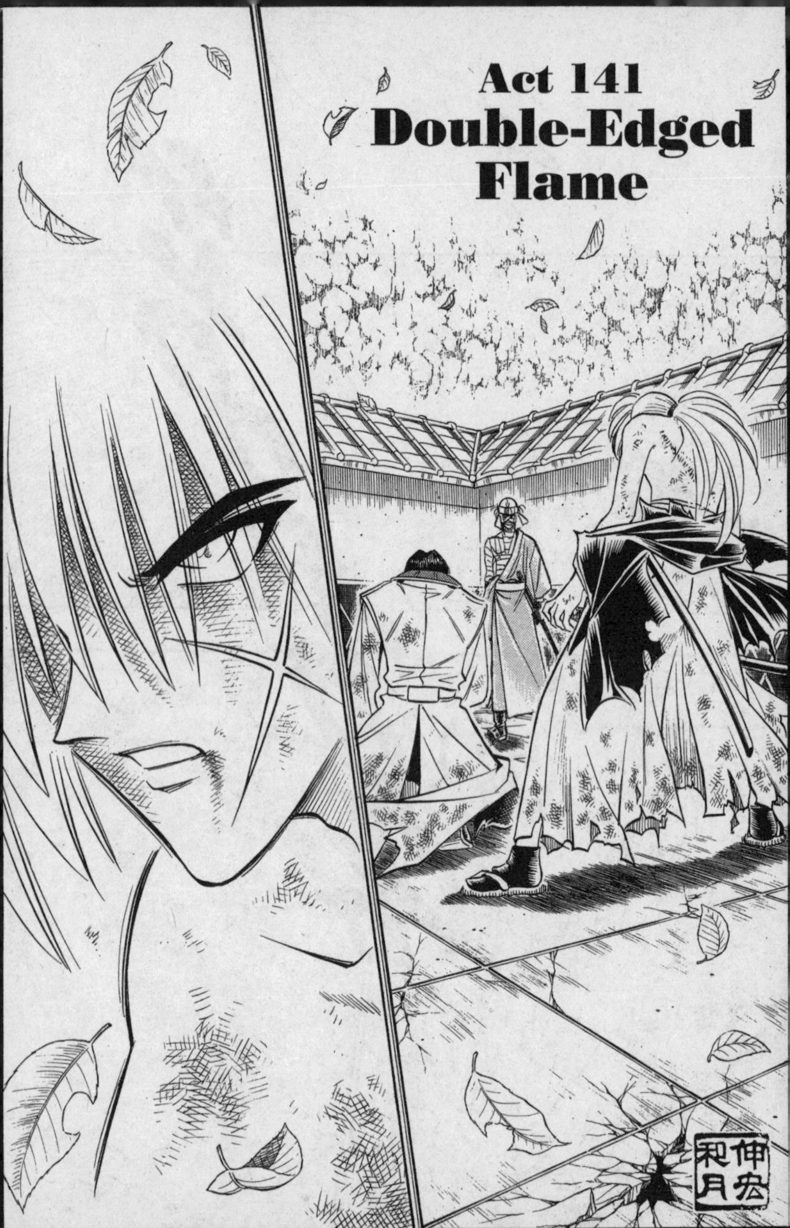
伸宏和月

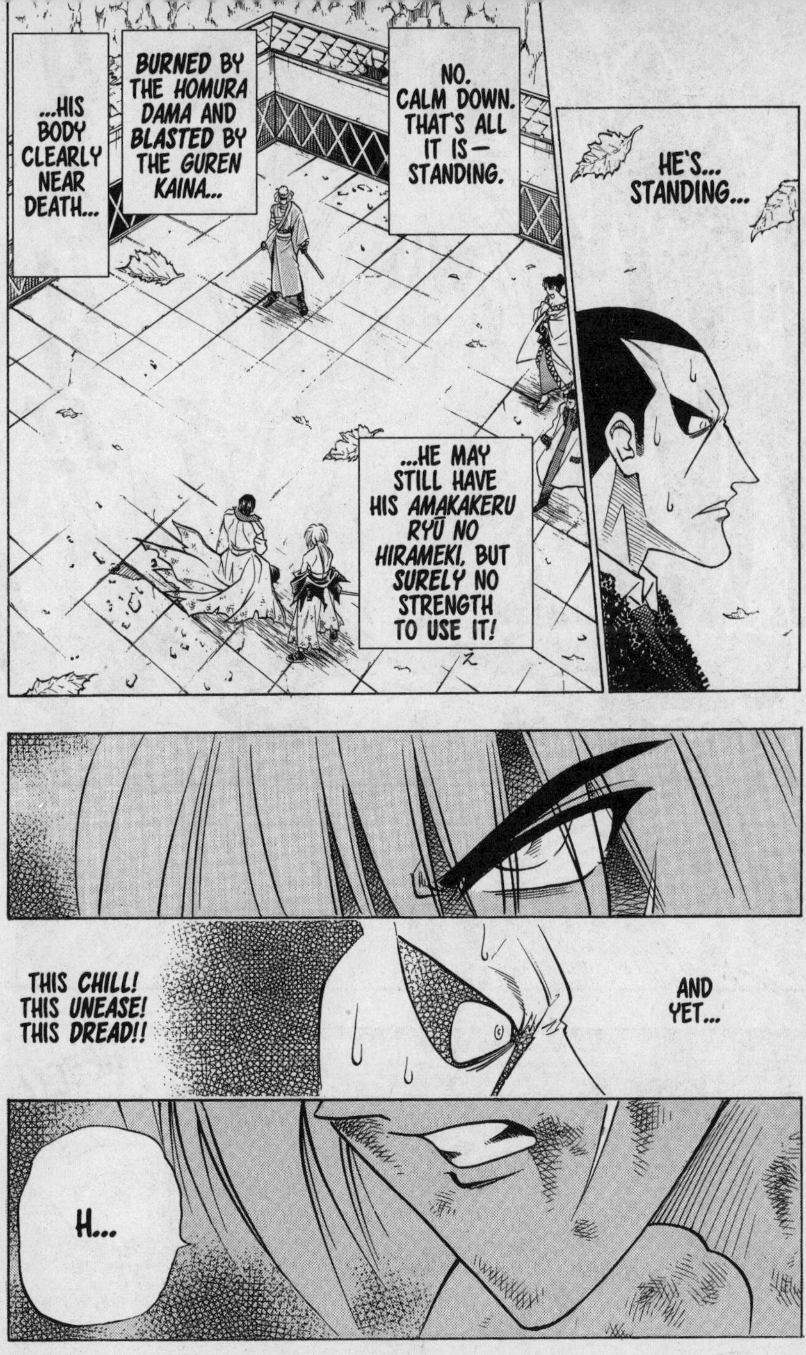
HE'S... STANDING...
NO. CALM DOWN. THAT'S ALL IT IS— STANDING.
BURNED BY THE HOMURA DAMA AND BLASTED BY THE GUREN KAINA...
...HIS BODY CLEARLY NEAR DEATH...
...HE MAY STILL HAVE HIS AMAKAKERU RYŪ NO HIRAMEKI, BUT SURELY NO STRENGTH TO USE IT!
AND YET...
THIS CHILL! THIS UNEASE! THIS DREAD!!
H...

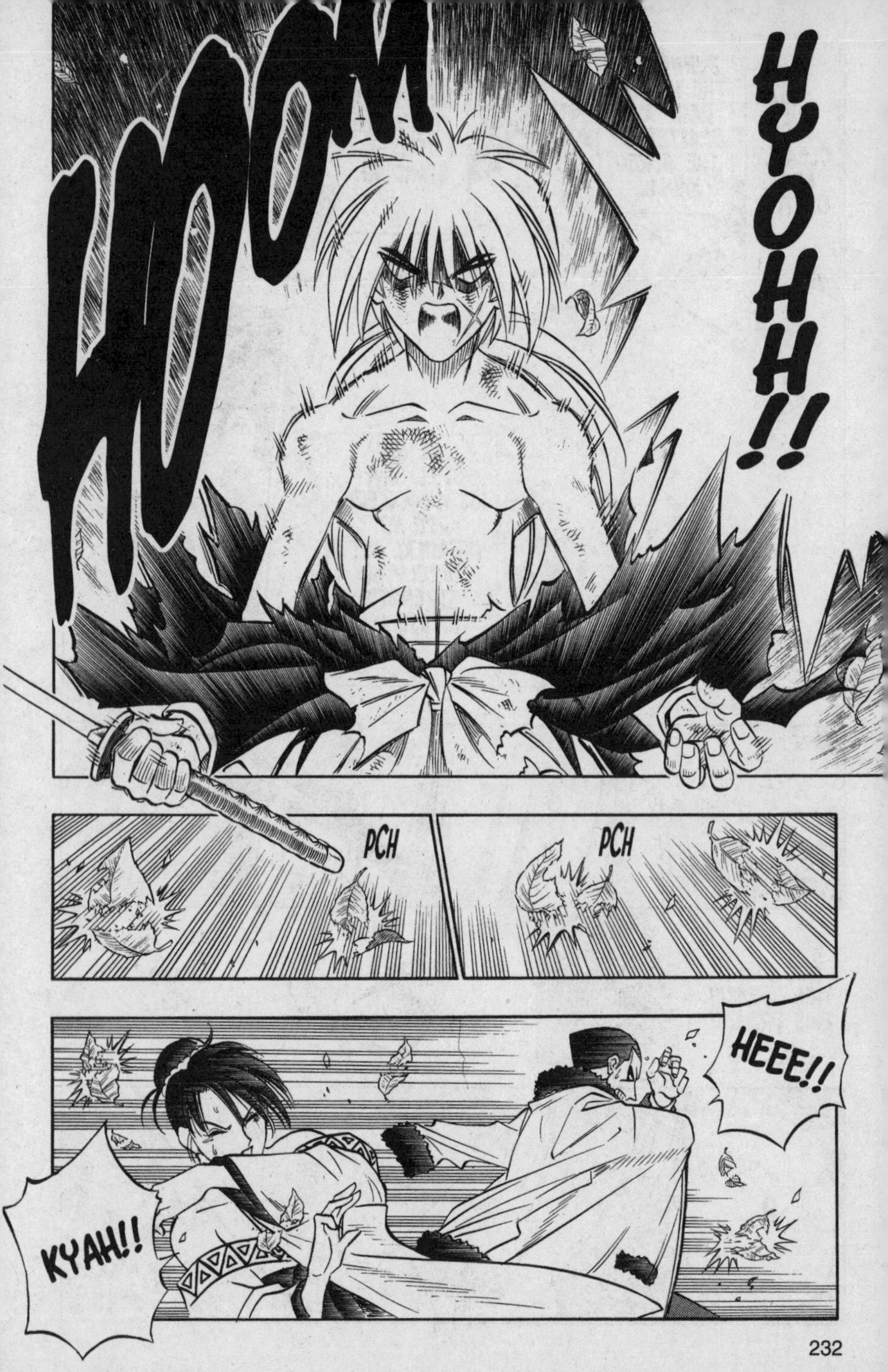
HYOHHH!!
HOOOM
PCH
PCH
HEEE!!
KYAH!!

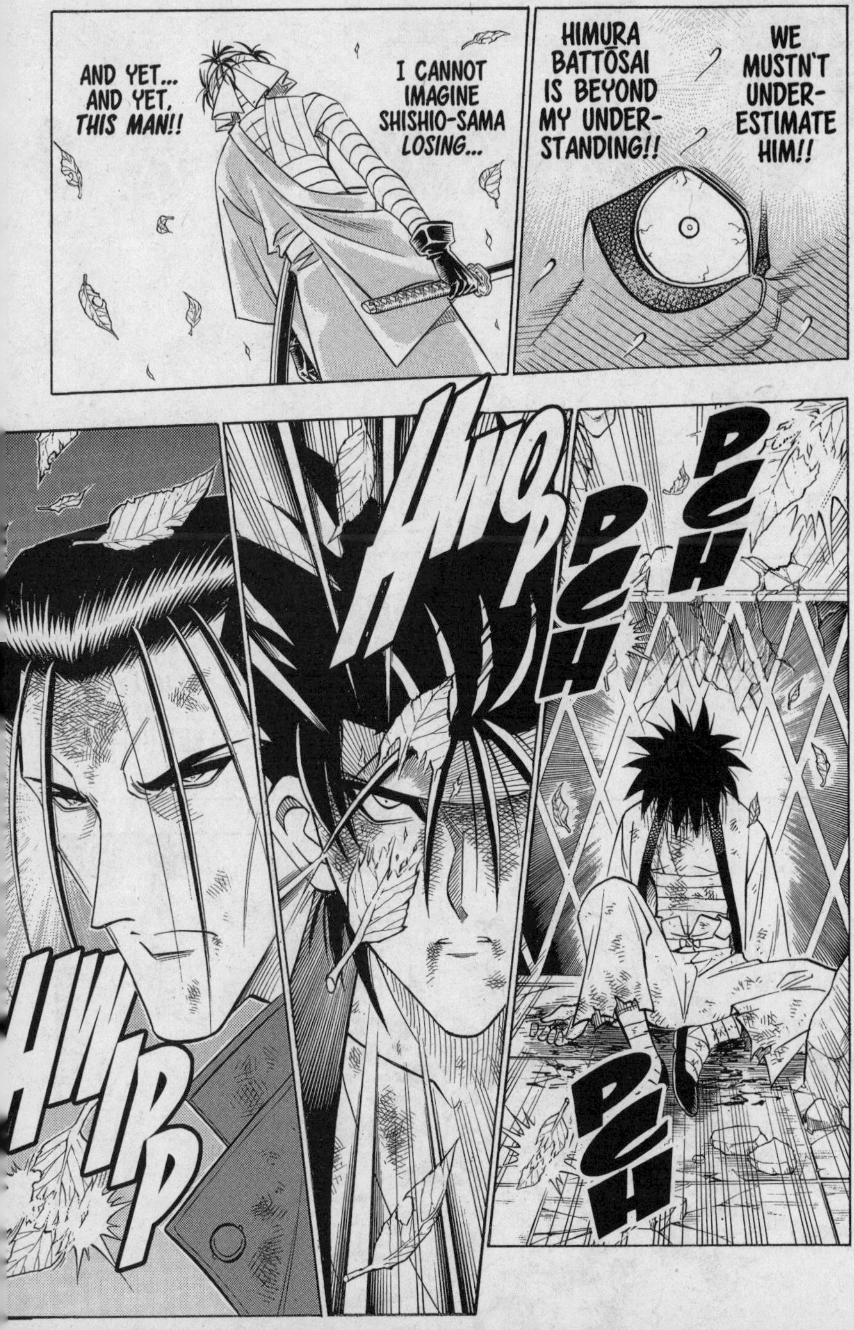
WE MUSTN'T UNDER-ESTIMATE HIM!!
HIMURA BATTŌSAI IS BEYOND MY UNDER-STANDING!!
I CANNOT IMAGINE SHISHIO-SAMA LOSING...
AND YET... AND YET, THIS MAN!!
PCH
PCH
PCH

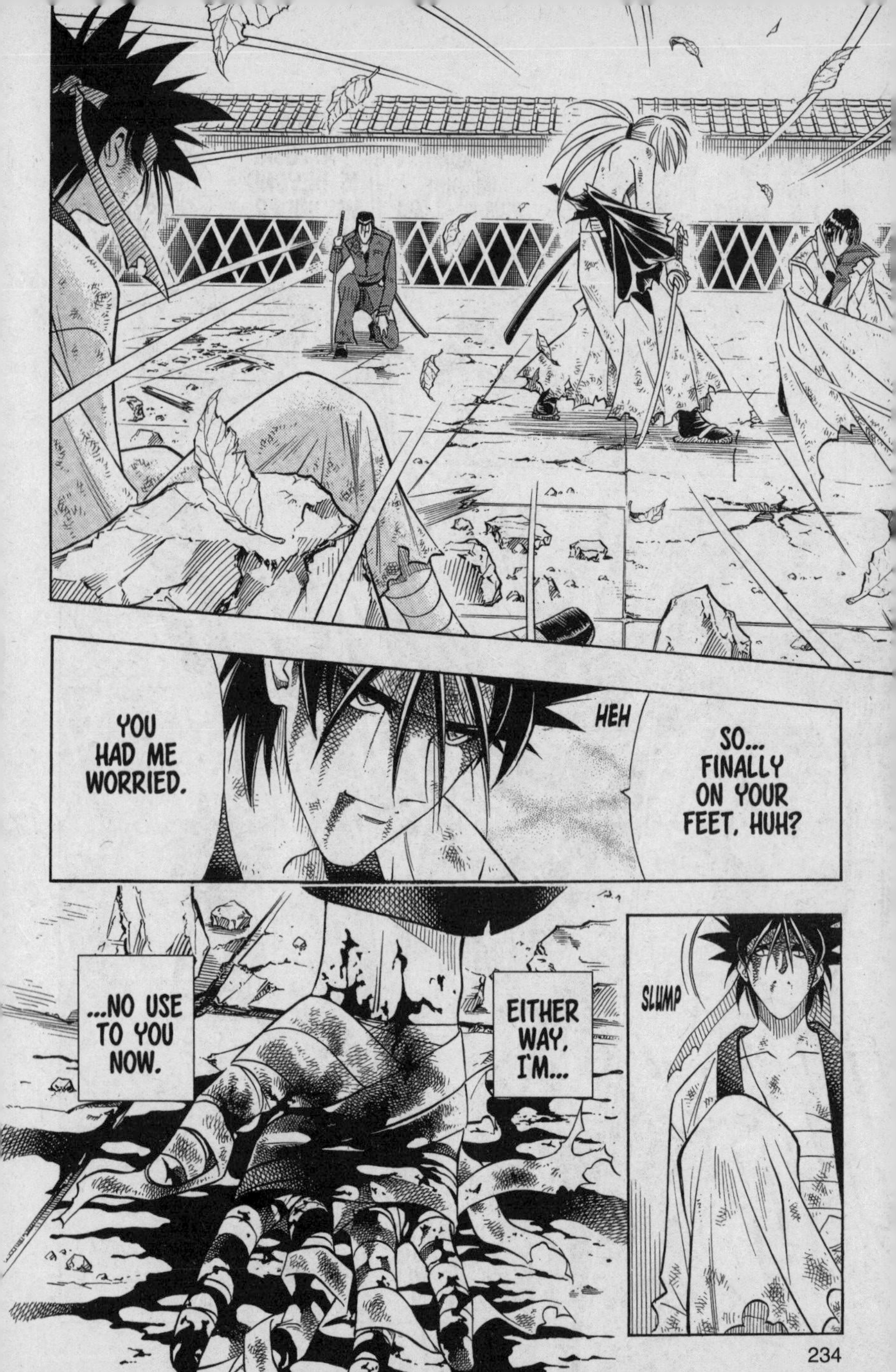
SO... FINALLY ON YOUR FEET, HUH?
HEH
YOU HAD ME WORRIED.
SLUMP
EITHER WAY, I'M...
...NO USE TO YOU NOW.

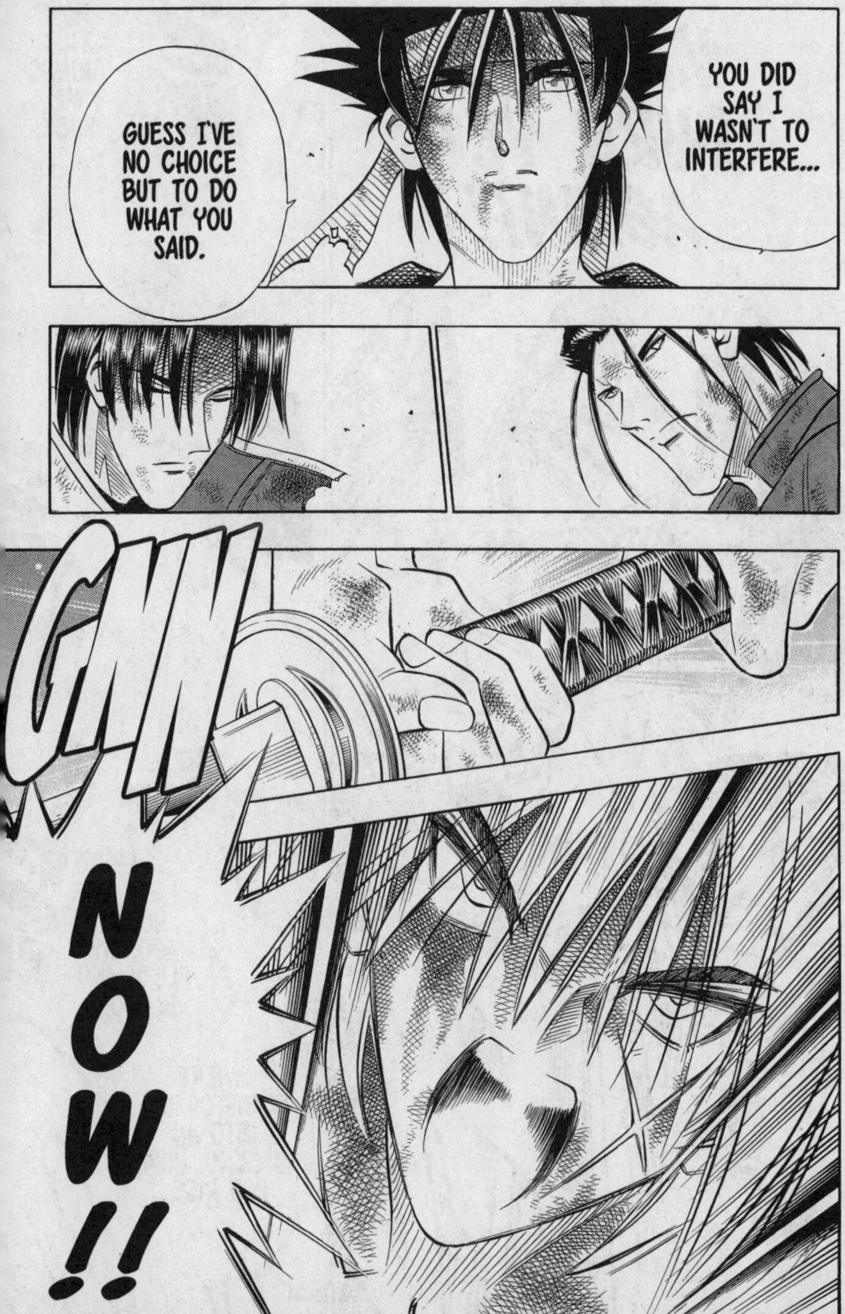
YOU DID SAY I WASN'T TO INTERFERE...
GUESS I'VE NO CHOICE BUT TO DO WHAT YOU SAID.
GNN
NOW!!

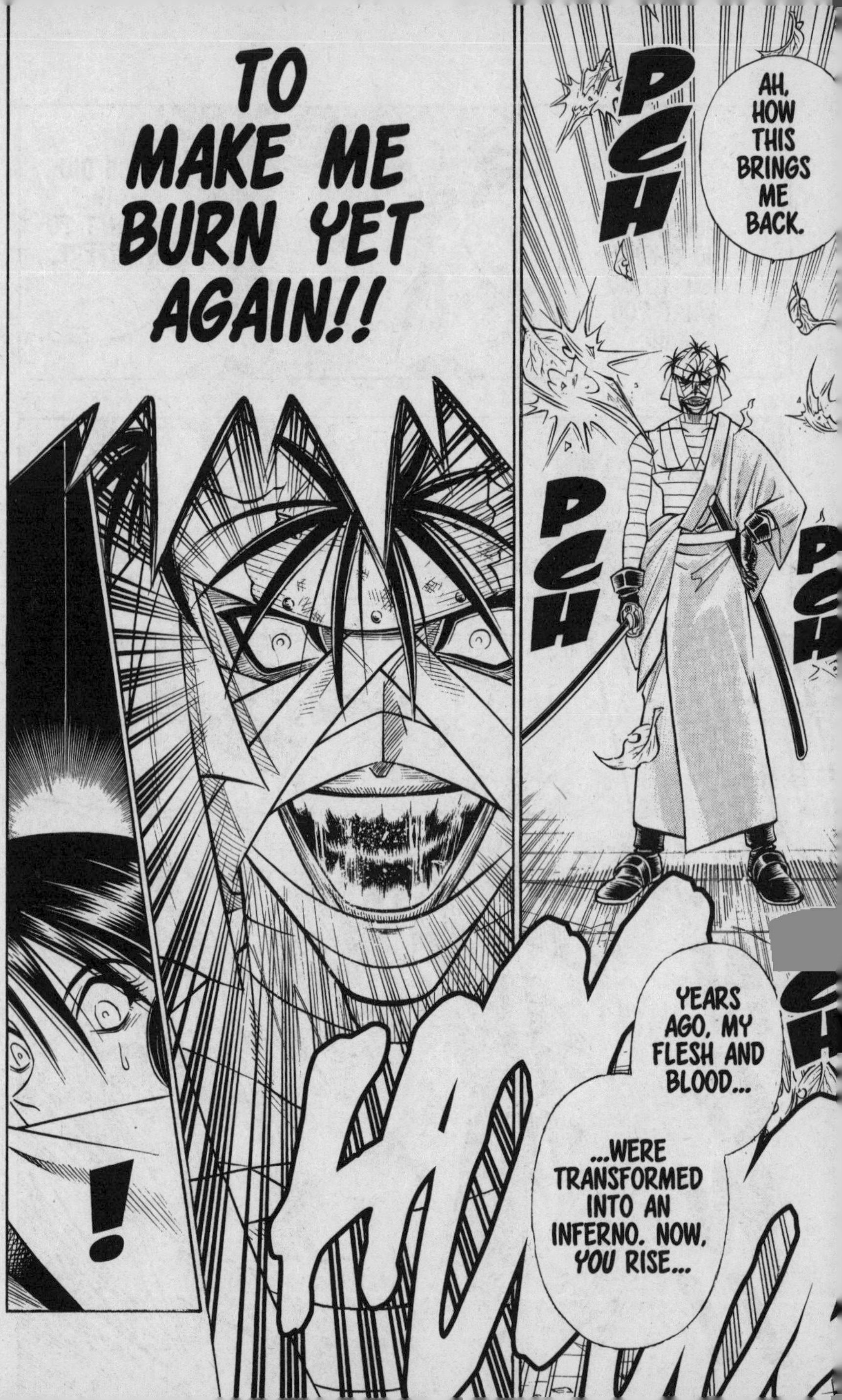
PCH
AH, HOW THIS BRINGS ME BACK.
PCH
PCH
YEARS AGO, MY FLESH AND BLOOD...
...WERE TRANSFORMED INTO AN INFERNO. NOW, YOU RISE...
TO MAKE ME BURN YET AGAIN!!
!

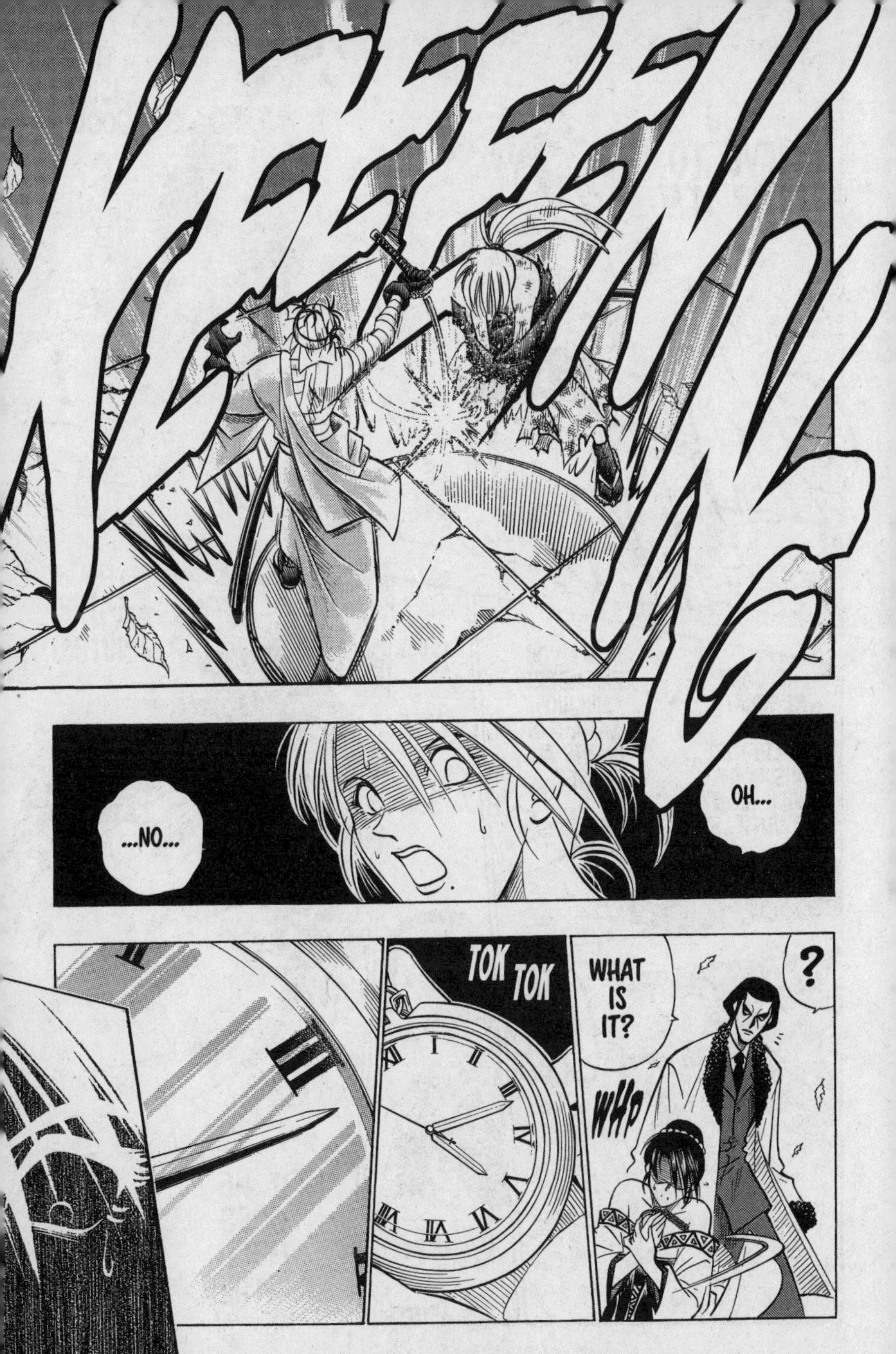
OH...
...NO...
?
WHAT IS IT?
WHP
TOK TOK

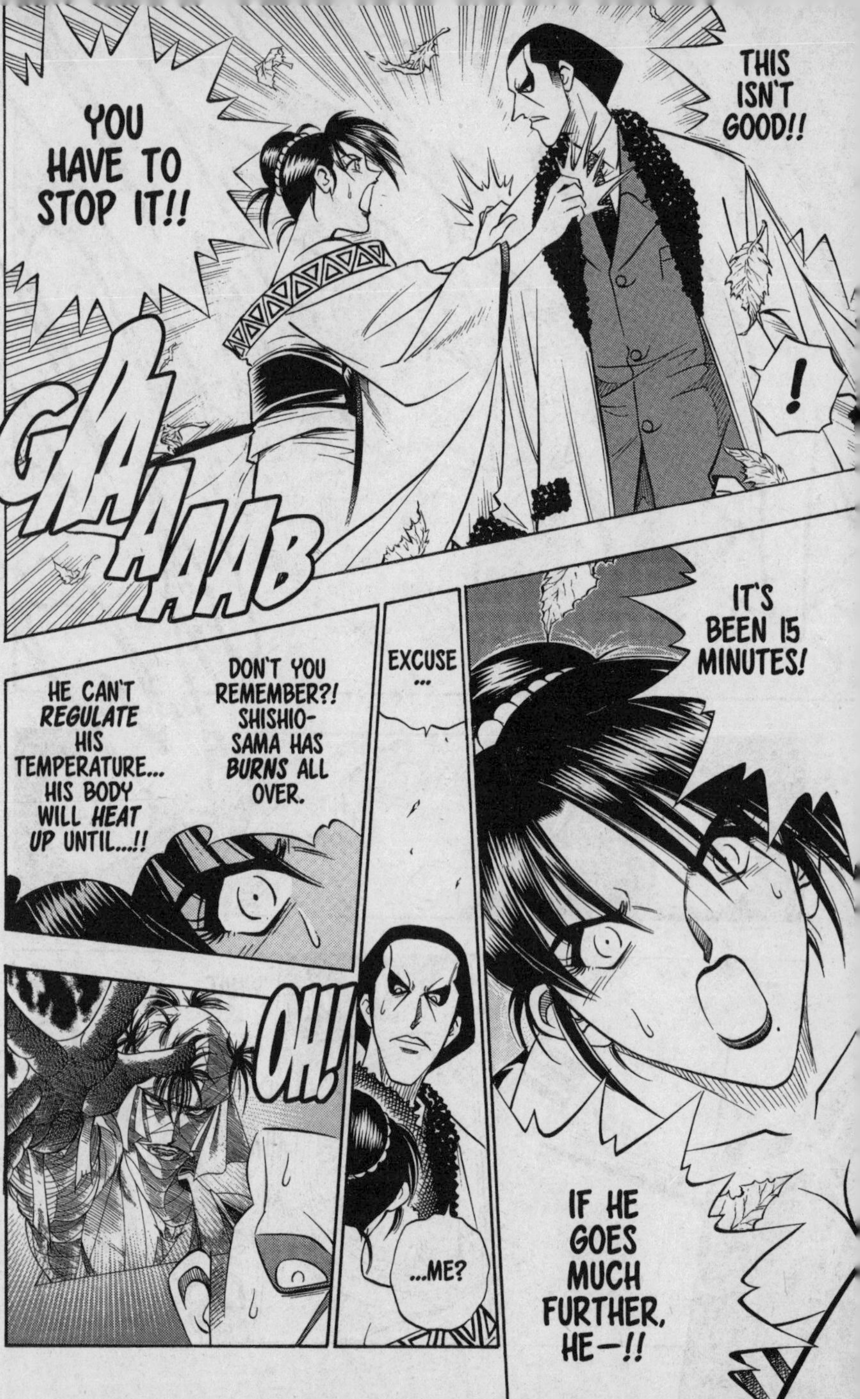
THIS ISN'T GOOD!!
!
YOU HAVE TO STOP IT!!
GAAAAB
IT'S BEEN 15 MINUTES!
IF HE GOES MUCH FURTHER, HE—!!
EXCUSE ...
...ME?
DON'T YOU REMEMBER?! SHISHIO-SAMA HAS *BURNS* ALL OVER.
HE CAN'T *REGULATE* HIS TEMPERATURE... HIS BODY WILL *HEAT UP* UNTIL...!!
OH!

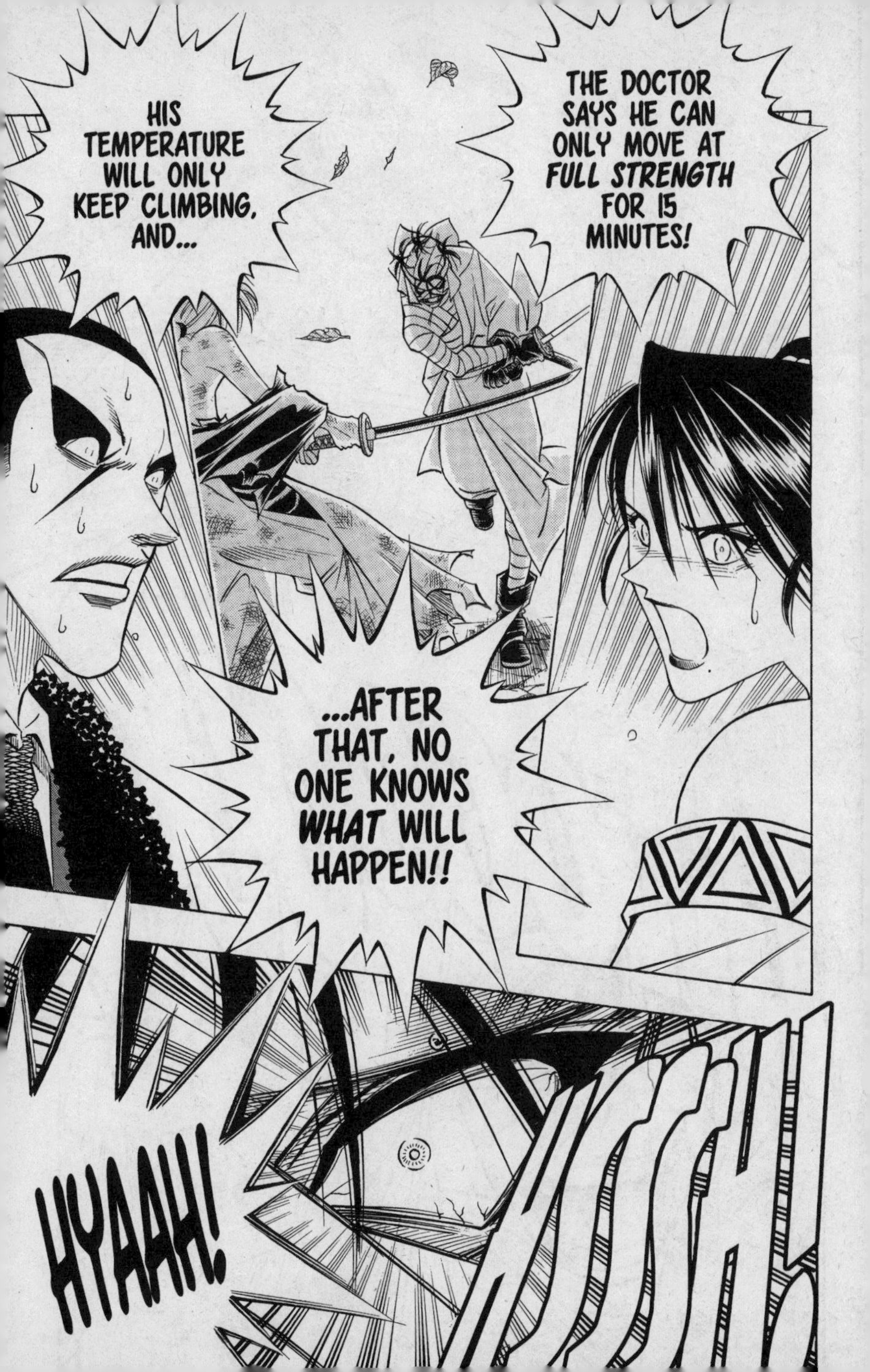
THE DOCTOR SAYS HE CAN ONLY MOVE AT *FULL STRENGTH* FOR 15 MINUTES!
HIS TEMPERATURE WILL ONLY KEEP CLIMBING, AND...
...AFTER THAT, NO ONE KNOWS *WHAT* WILL HAPPEN!!
HYAAH!

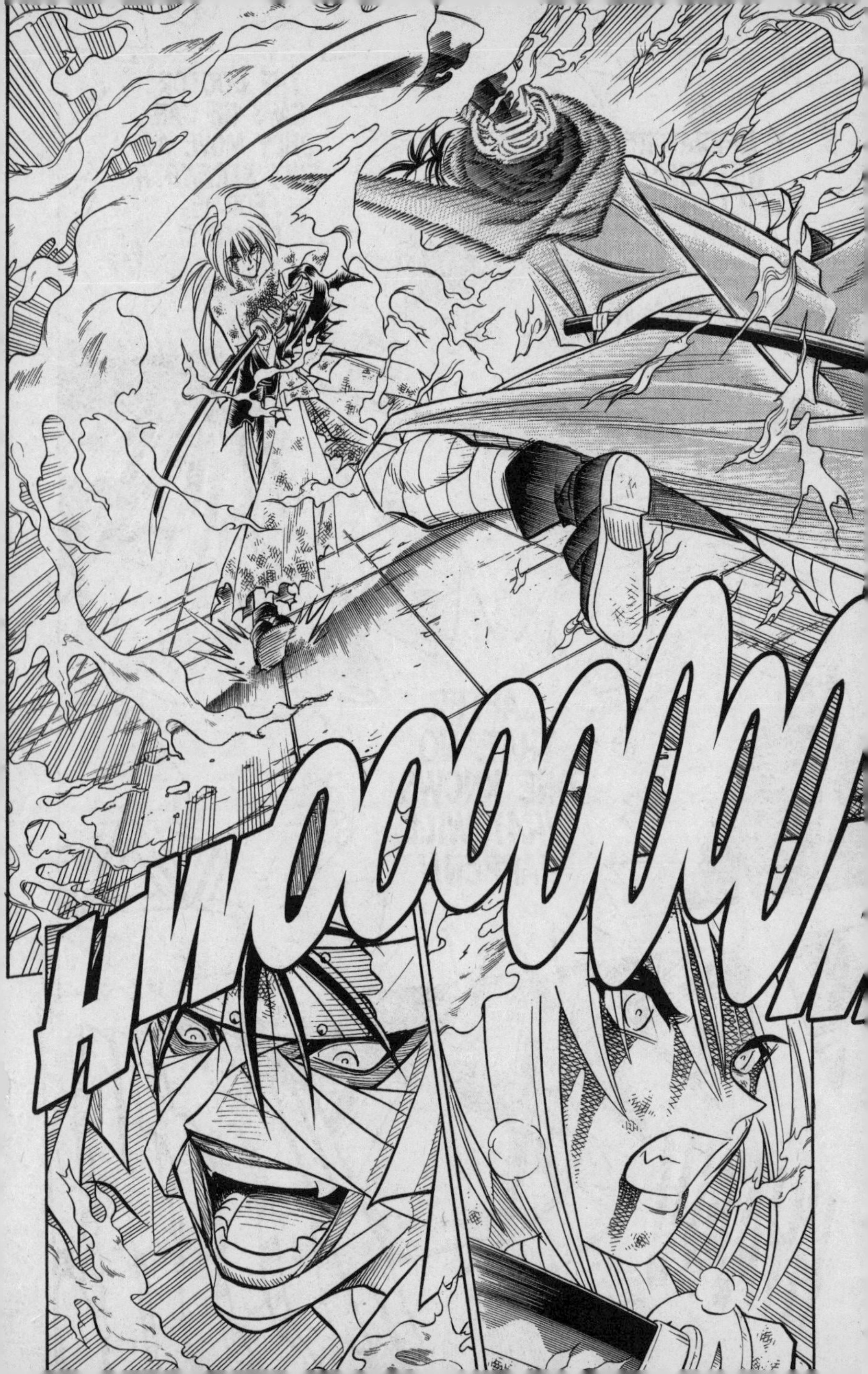
HWAAAAAA

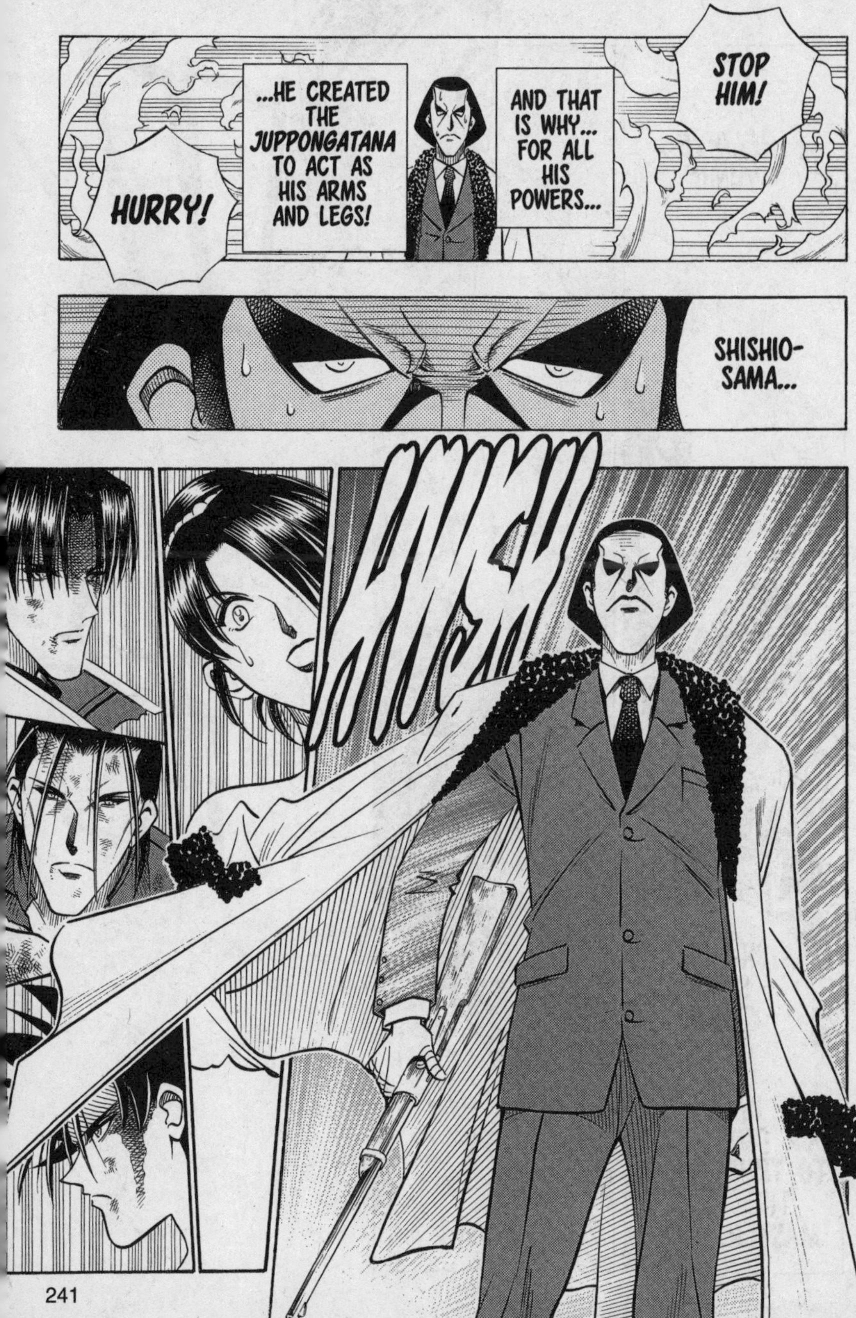
STOP HIM!
AND THAT IS WHY... FOR ALL HIS POWERS...
...HE CREATED THE JUPPONGATANA TO ACT AS HIS ARMS AND LEGS!
HURRY!
SHISHIO-SAMA...

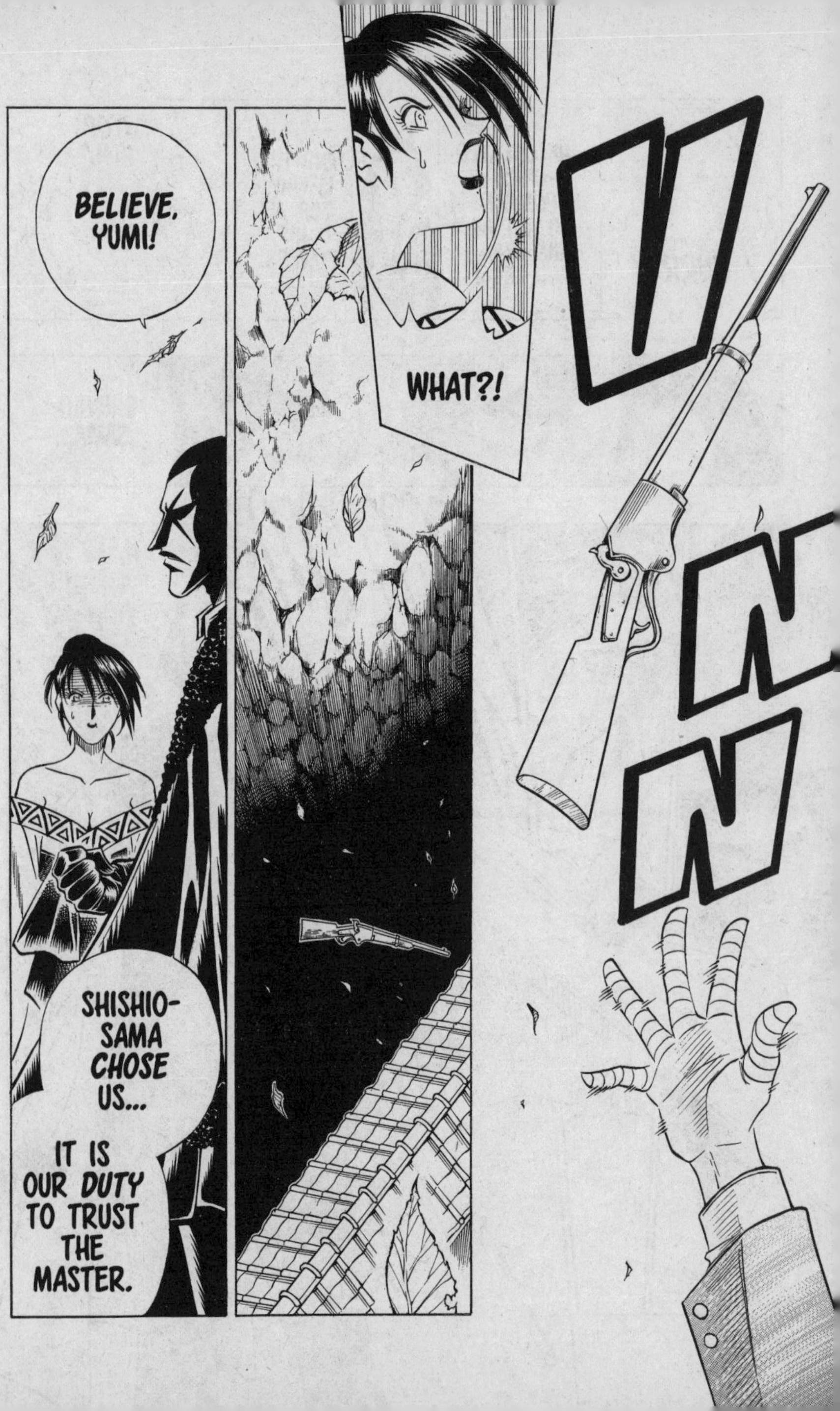
VNN
WHAT?!
BELIEVE, YUMI!
SHISHIO-SAMA CHOSE US...
IT IS OUR DUTY TO TRUST THE MASTER.

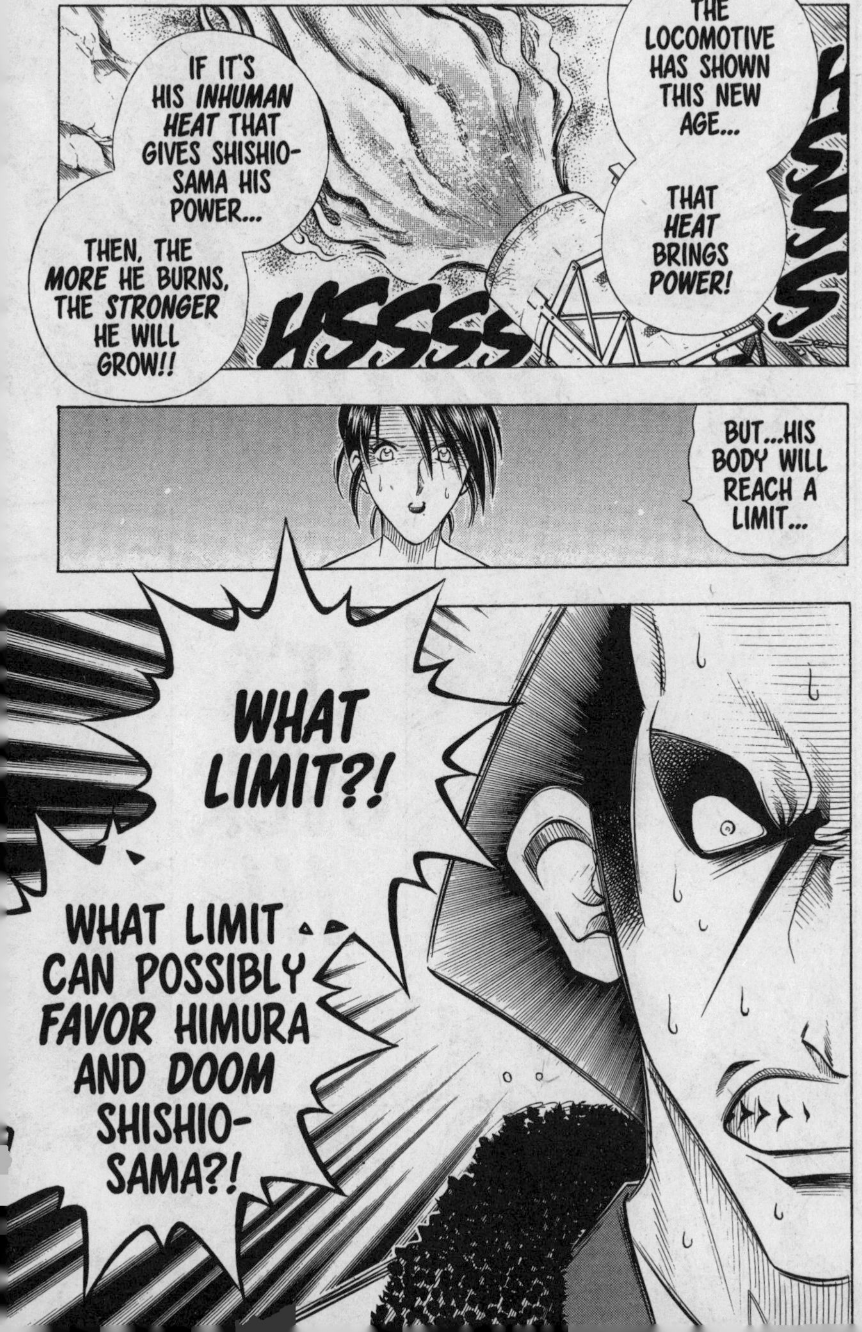
HSSSS
THE LOCOMOTIVE HAS SHOWN THIS NEW AGE...
THAT HEAT BRINGS POWER!
IF IT'S HIS INHUMAN HEAT THAT GIVES SHISHIO-SAMA HIS POWER...
THEN, THE MORE HE BURNS, THE STRONGER HE WILL GROW!!
HSSSS
BUT...HIS BODY WILL REACH A LIMIT...
WHAT LIMIT?!
WHAT LIMIT CAN POSSIBLY FAVOR HIMURA AND DOOM SHISHIO-SAMA?!

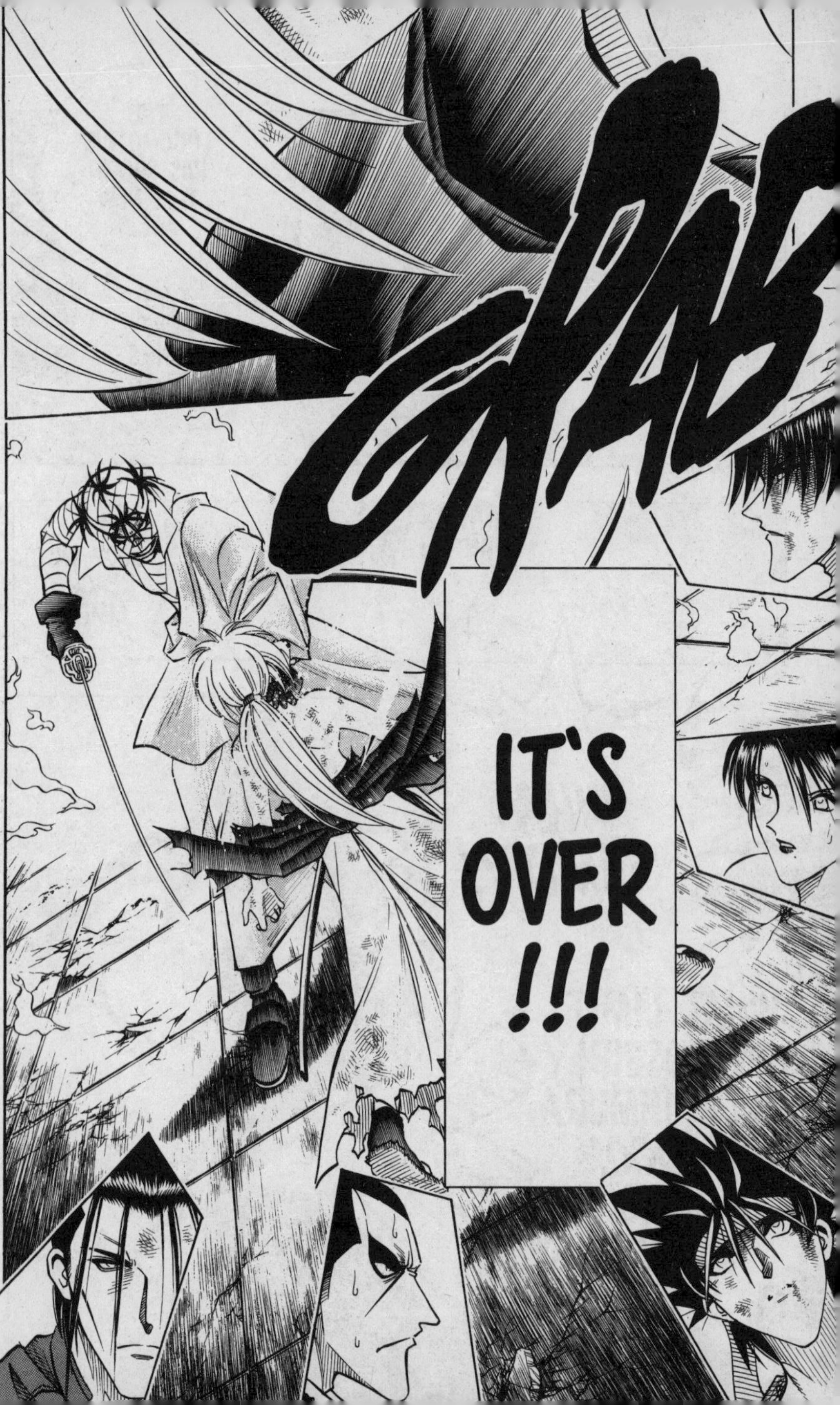
SHAK
IT'S OVER !!!

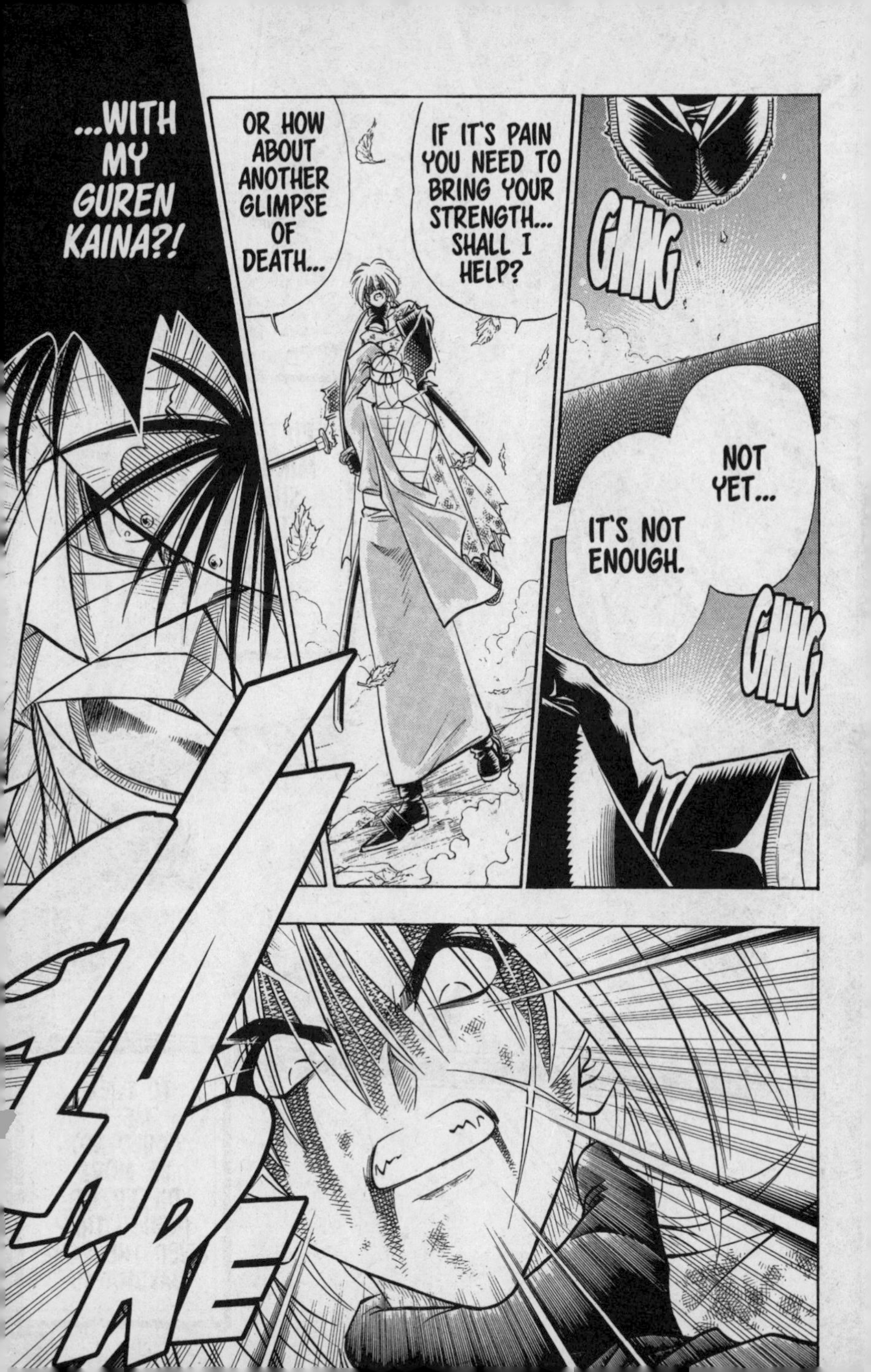
GNNG
NOT YET...
IT'S NOT ENOUGH.
GNNG
IF IT'S PAIN YOU NEED TO BRING YOUR STRENGTH... SHALL I HELP?
OR HOW ABOUT ANOTHER GLIMPSE OF DEATH...
...WITH MY GUREN KAINA?!

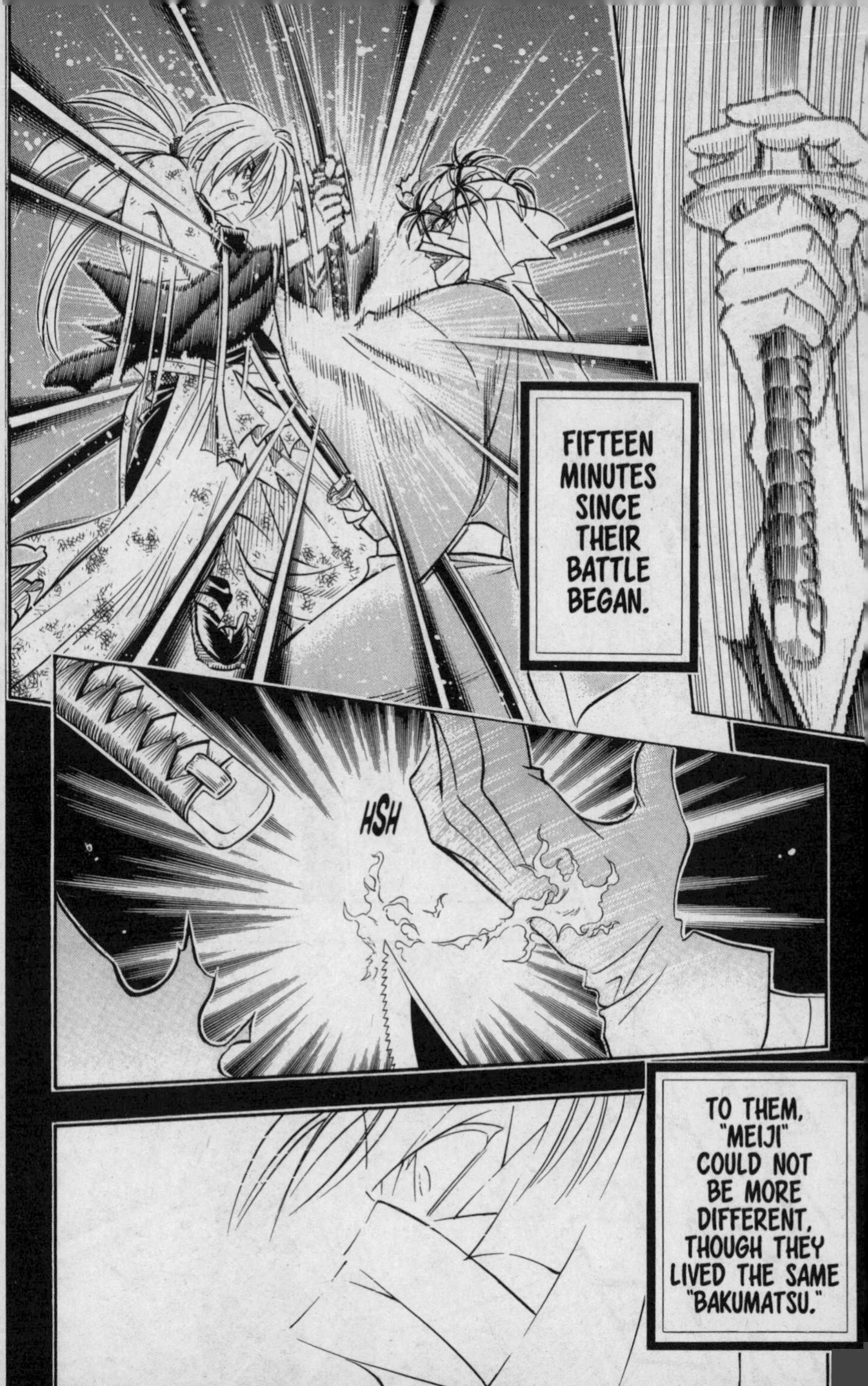
FIFTEEN MINUTES SINCE THEIR BATTLE BEGAN.
HSH
TO THEM, "MEIJI" COULD NOT BE MORE DIFFERENT, THOUGH THEY LIVED THE SAME "BAKUMATSU."

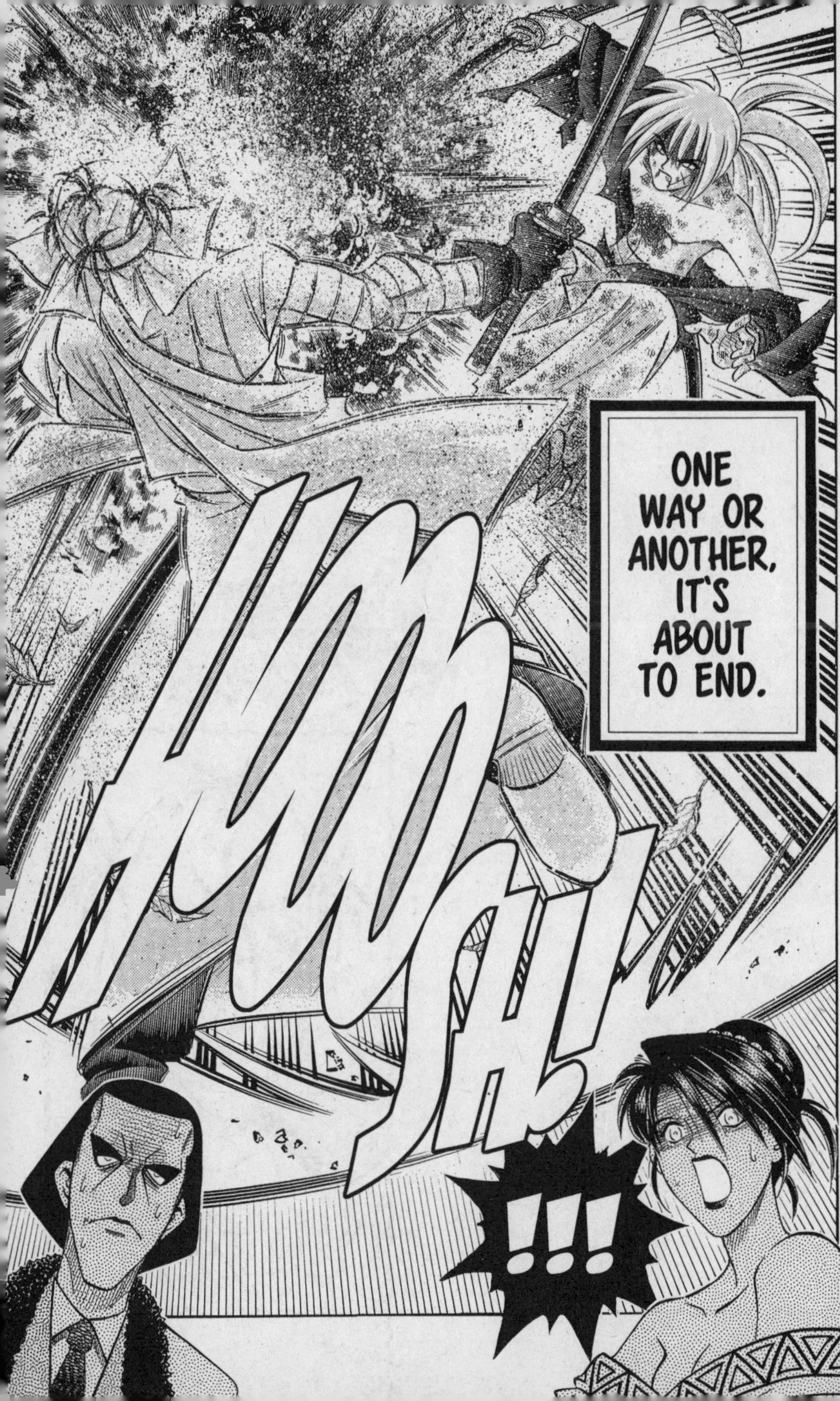
ONE WAY OR ANOTHER, IT'S ABOUT TO END.
!!!

Rurouni Kenshin

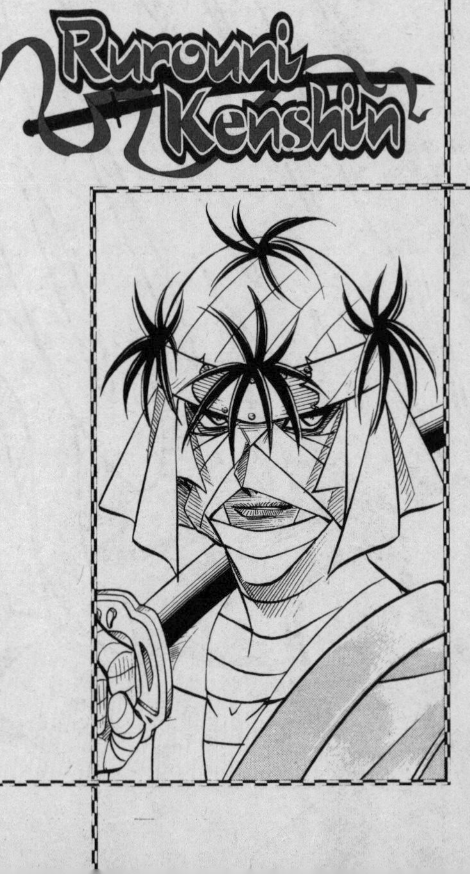

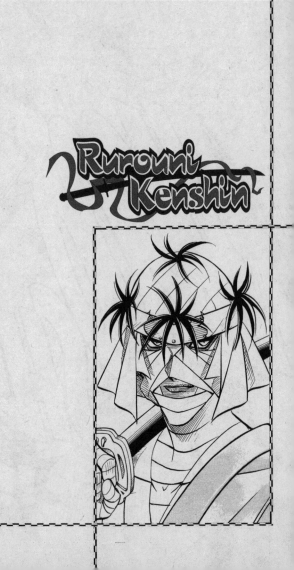

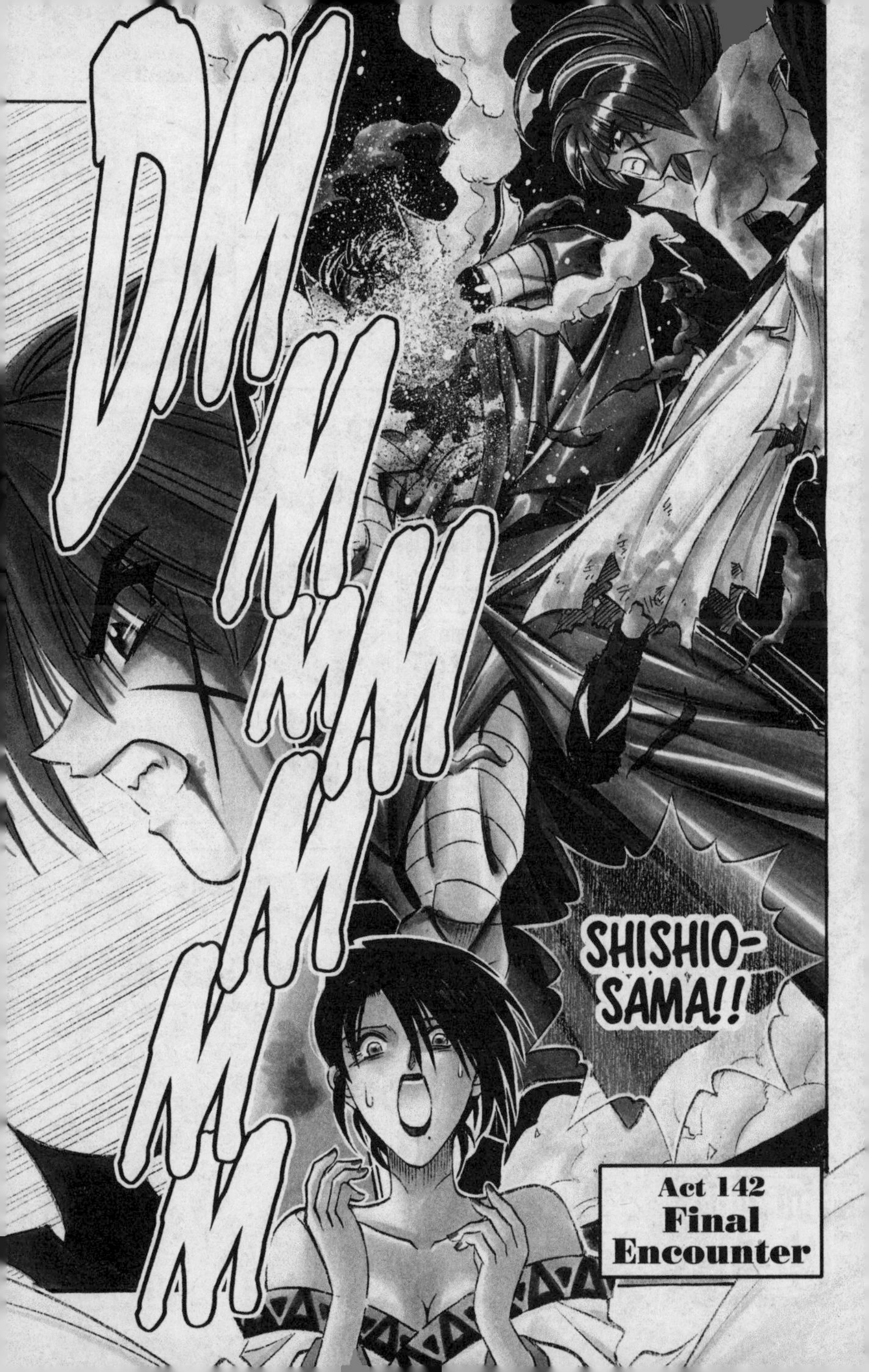
SHISHIO-SAMA!!
Act 142
Final Encounter

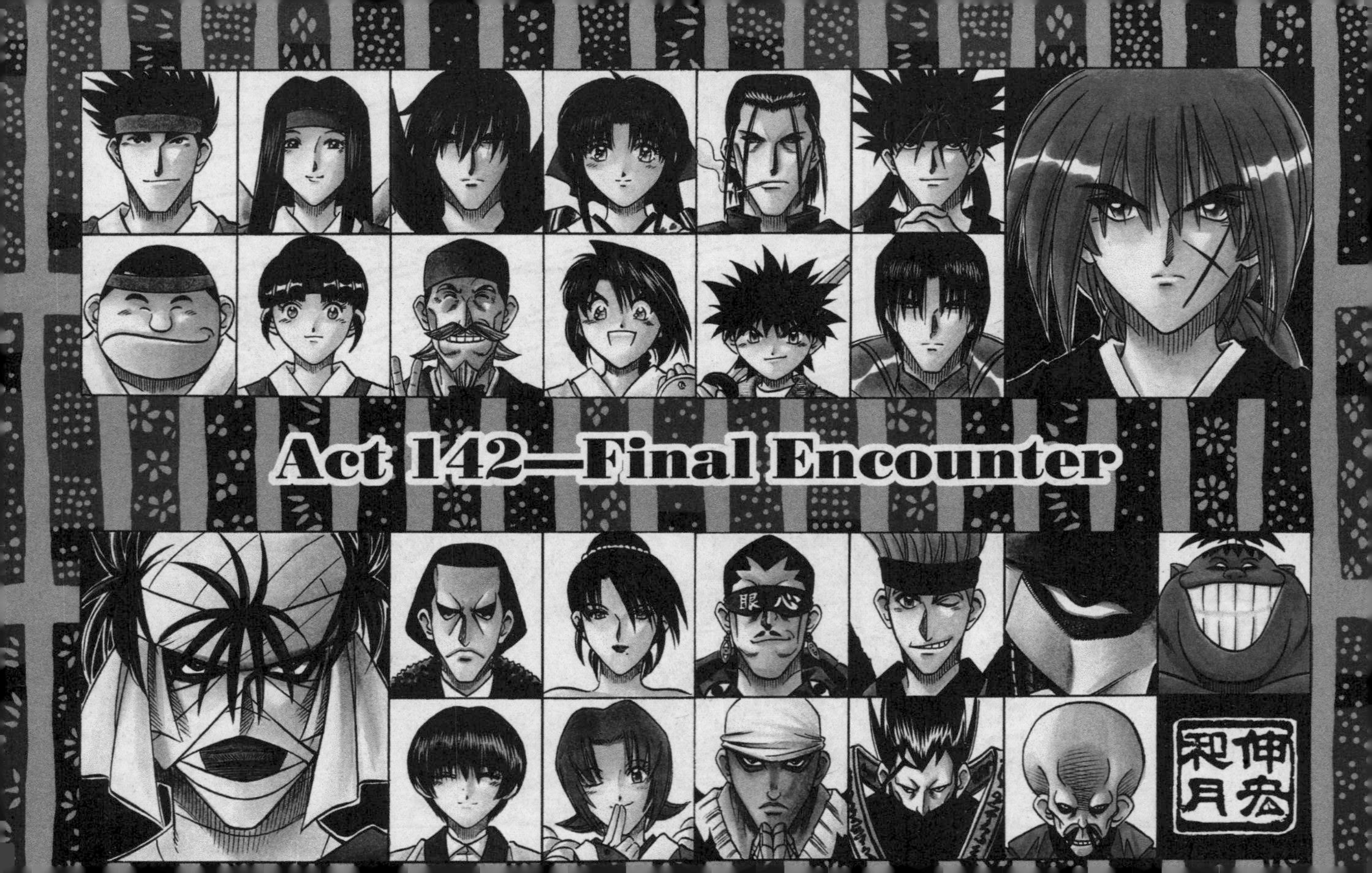
Act 142—Final Encounter
和月伸宏

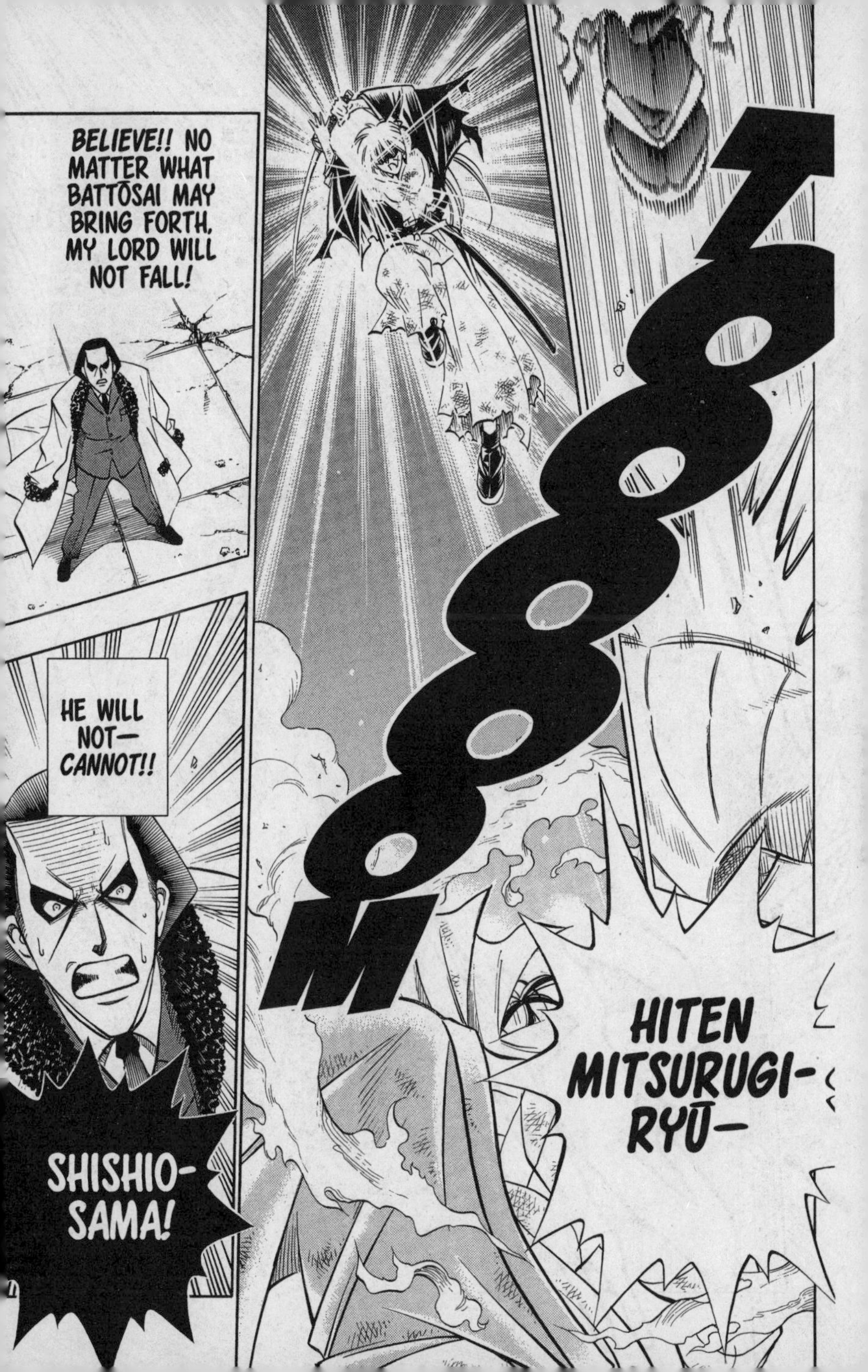
HITEN MITSURUGI-RYŪ-
BELIEVE!! NO MATTER WHAT BATTŌSAI MAY BRING FORTH, MY LORD WILL NOT FALL!
HE WILL NOT— CANNOT!!
SHISHIO-SAMA!

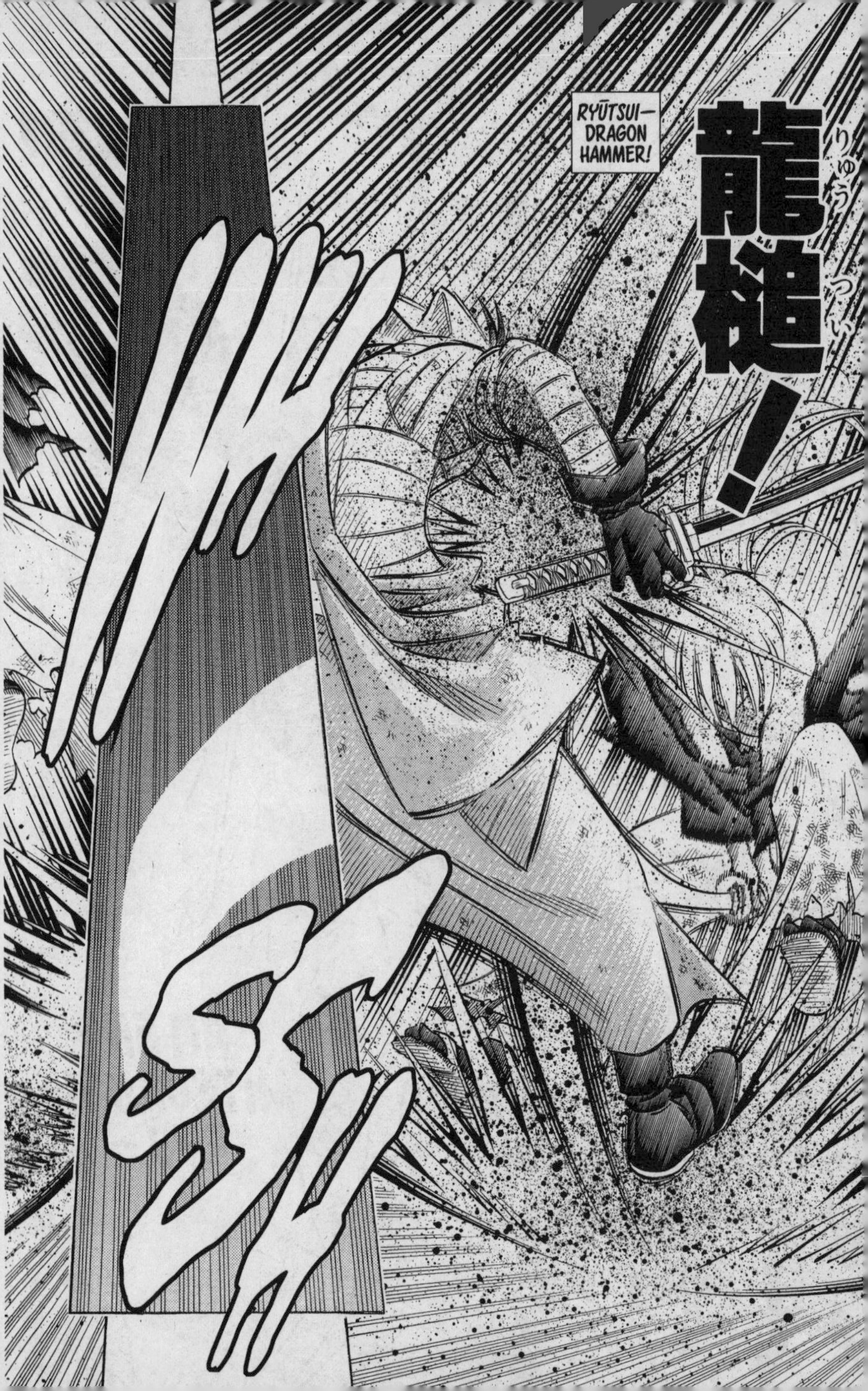
龍槌！
りゅうつい
RYŪTSUI—DRAGON HAMMER!

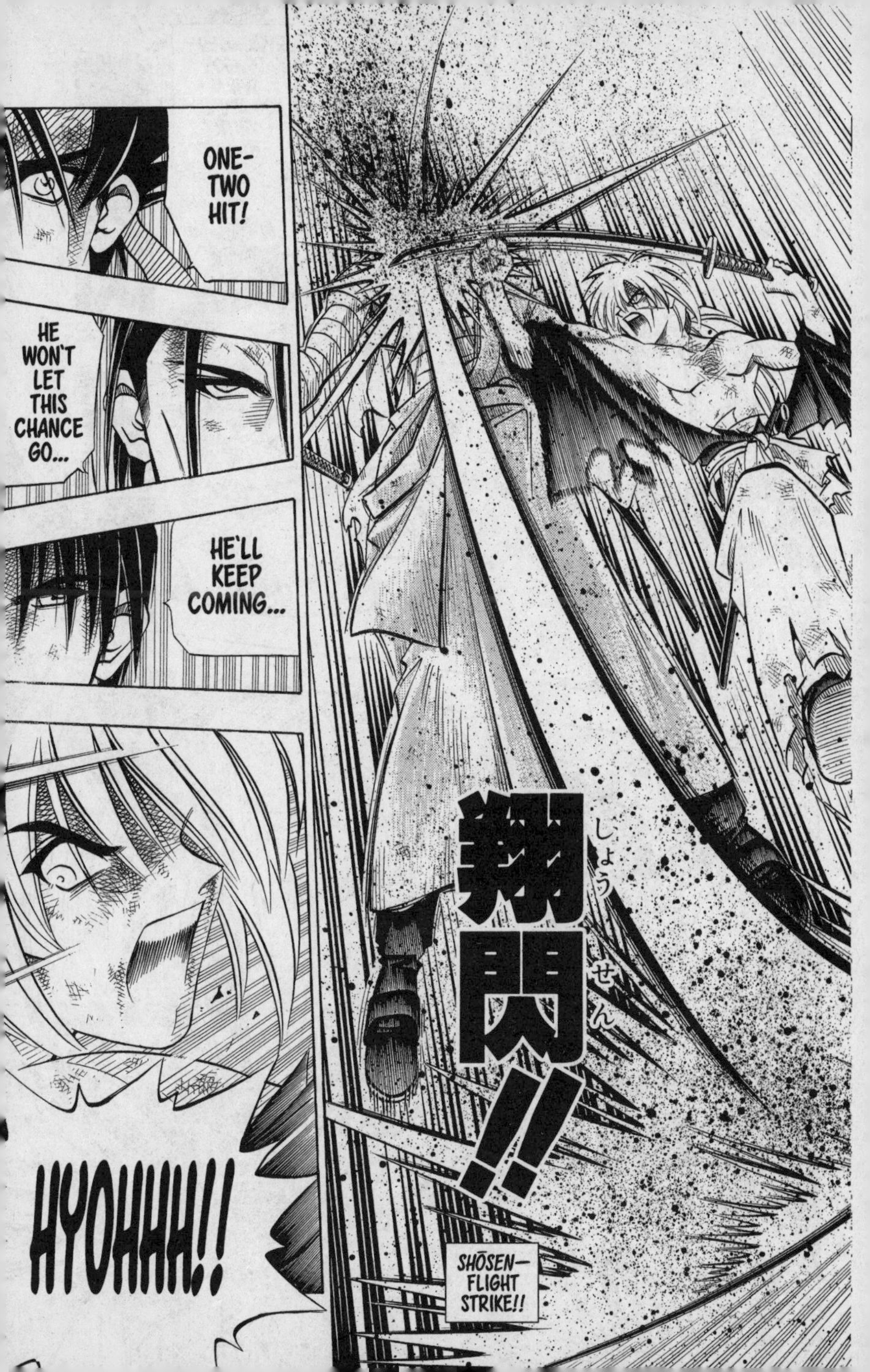
翔閃!!
SHŌSEN—FLIGHT STRIKE!!
ONE-TWO HIT!
HE WON'T LET THIS CHANCE GO...
HE'LL KEEP COMING...
HYOHHH!!

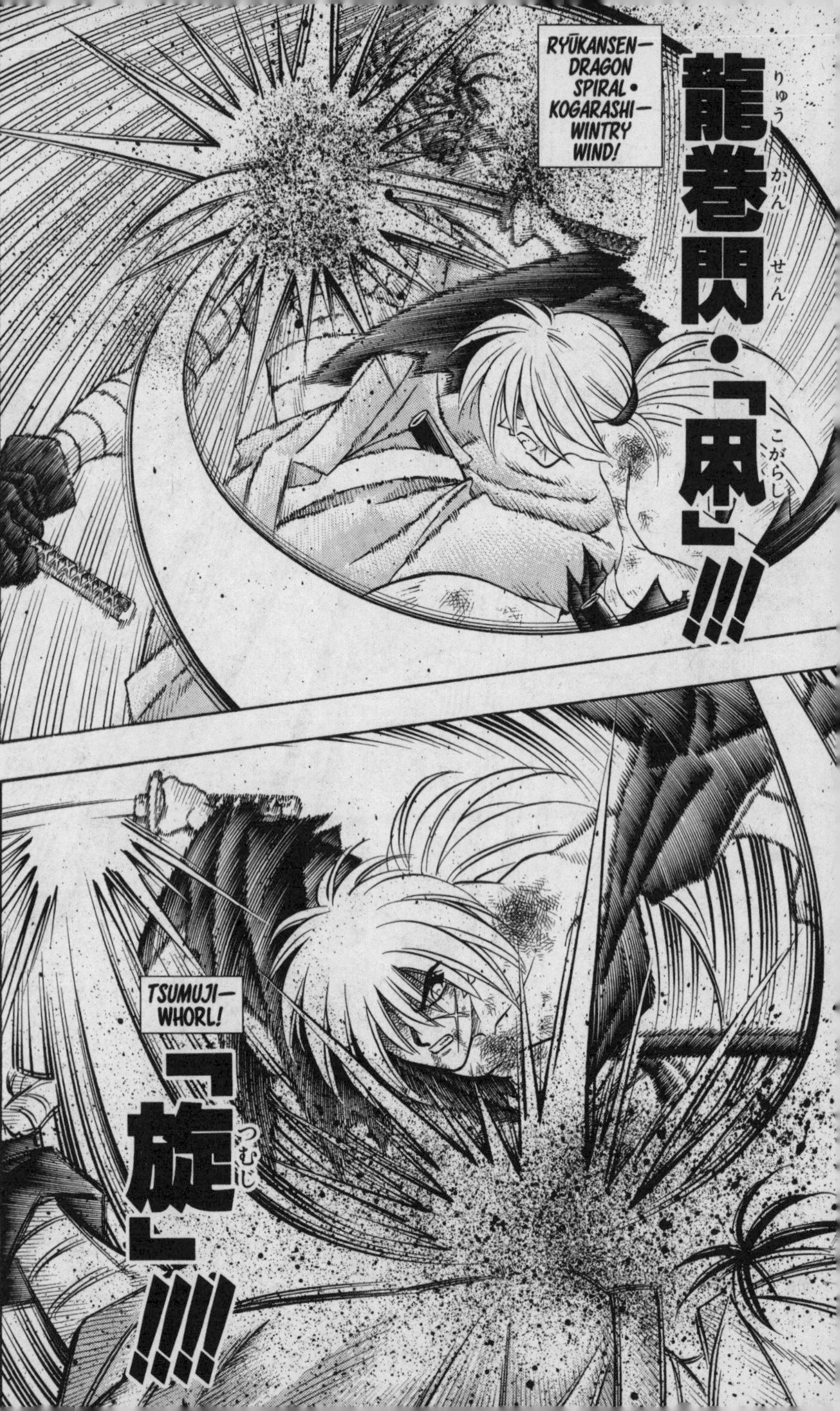
RYŪKANSEN—DRAGON SPIRAL • KOGARASHI—WINTRY WIND!
龍巻閃・「凩」!!!
TSUMUJI—WHORL!
「旋」!!!!

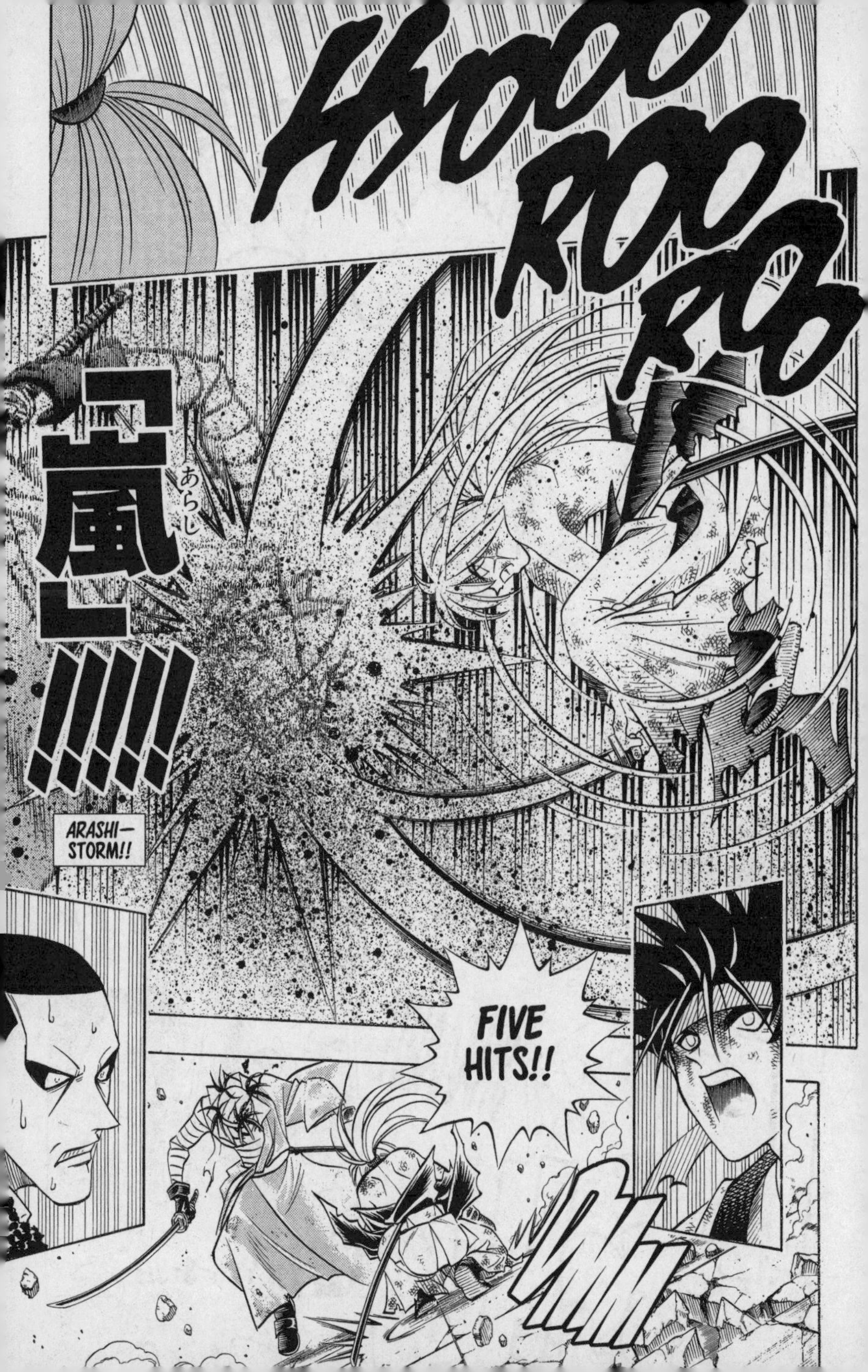
HYOO
ROO
ROO
嵐(あらし)!!!!!
ARASHI—STORM!!
FIVE HITS!!

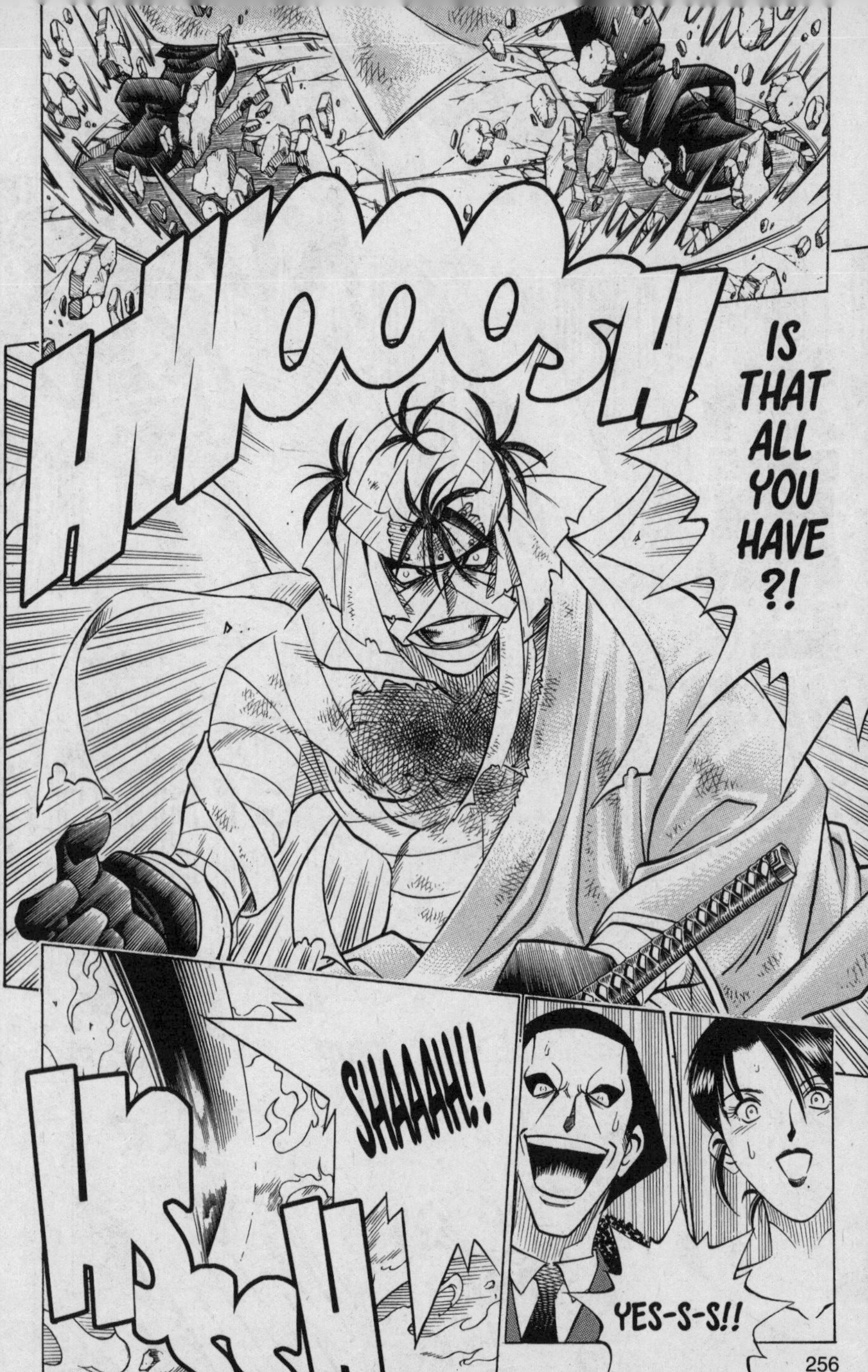
IS THAT ALL YOU HAVE?!
YES-S-S!!
SHAAAH!!

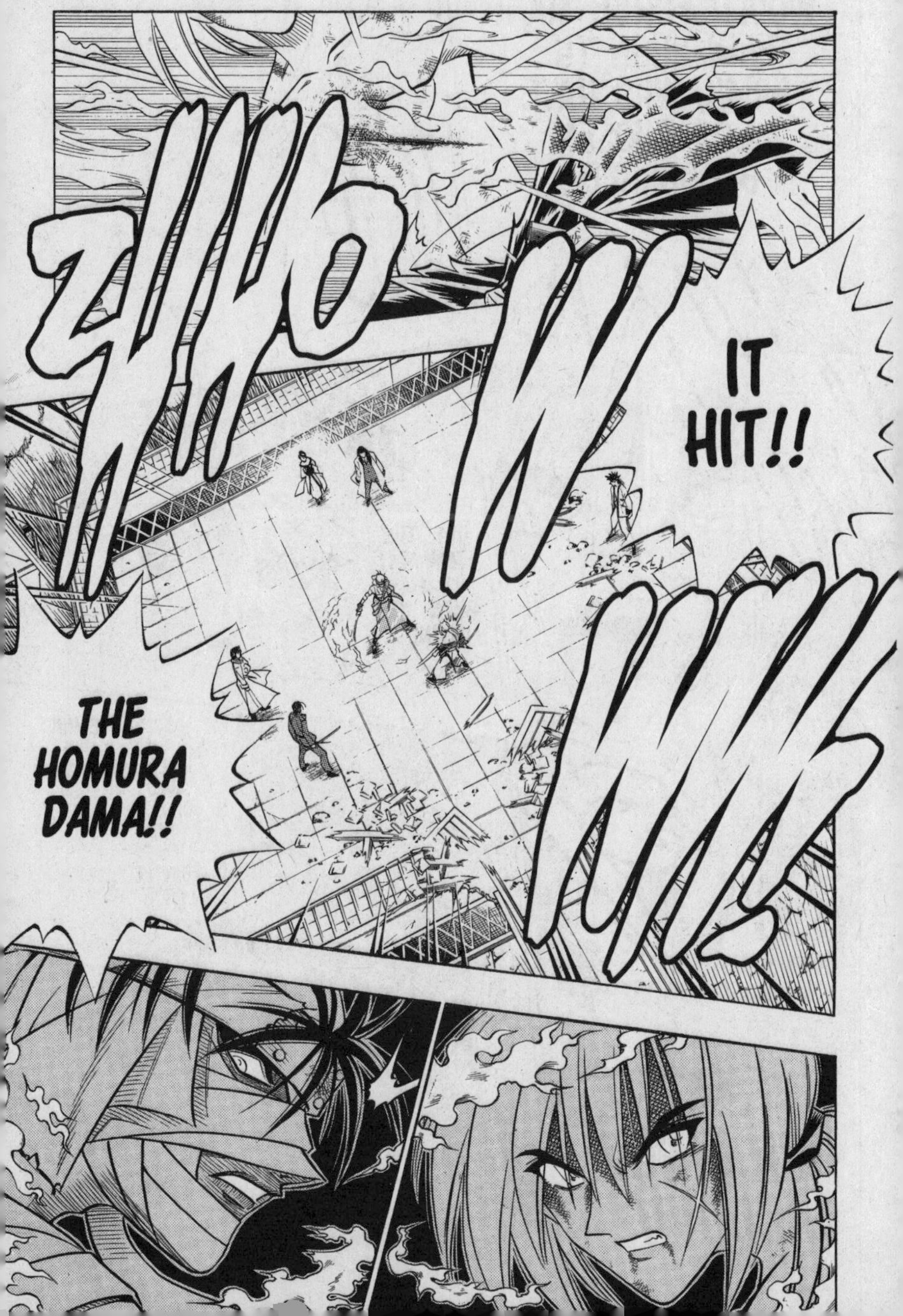
IT HIT!!
THE HOMURA DAMA!!

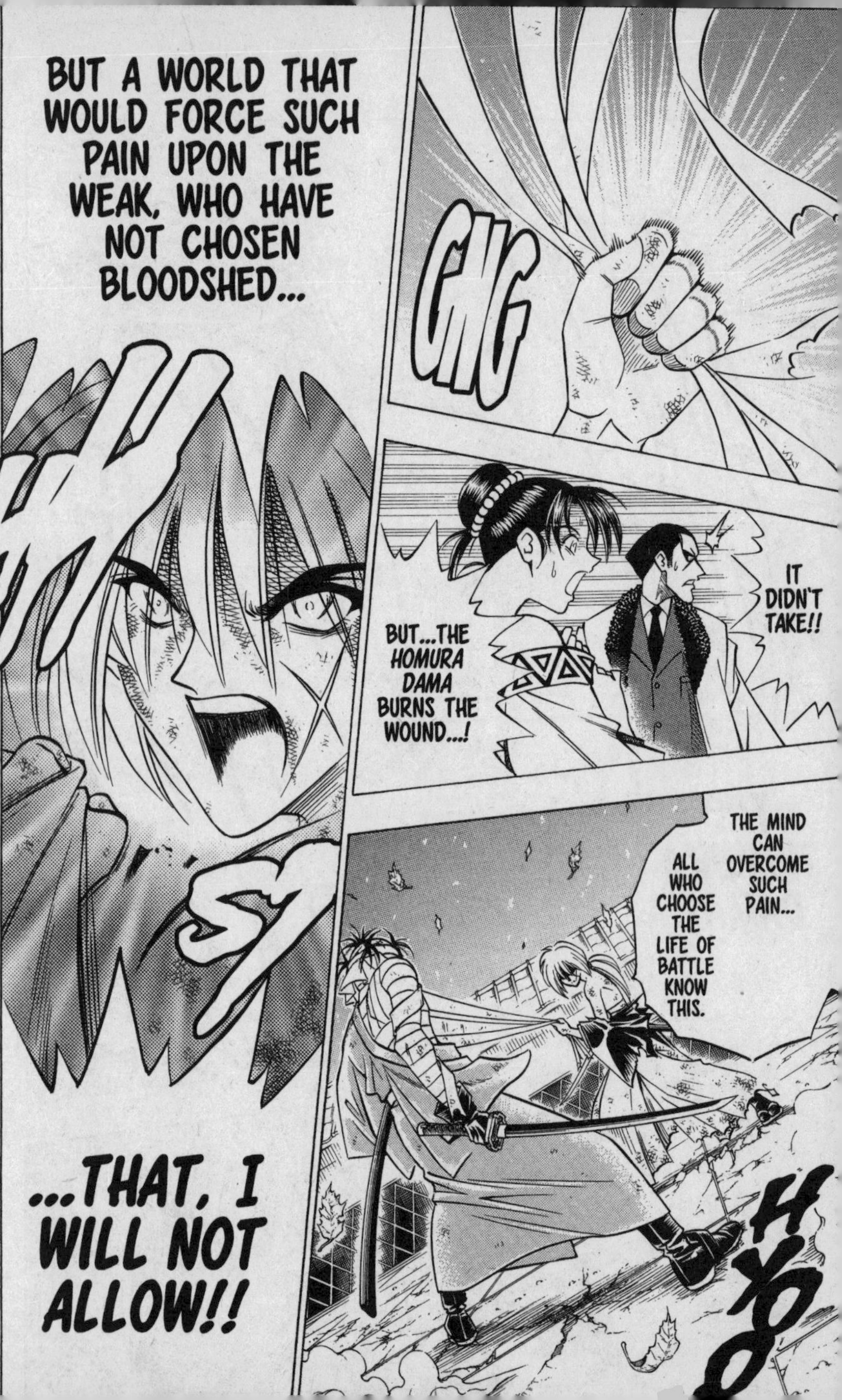
CMG
IT DIDN'T TAKE!!
BUT...THE HOMURA DAMA BURNS THE WOUND...!
THE MIND CAN OVERCOME SUCH PAIN...
ALL WHO CHOOSE THE LIFE OF BATTLE KNOW THIS.
BUT A WORLD THAT WOULD FORCE SUCH PAIN UPON THE WEAK, WHO HAVE NOT CHOSEN BLOODSHED...
...THAT, I WILL NOT ALLOW!!

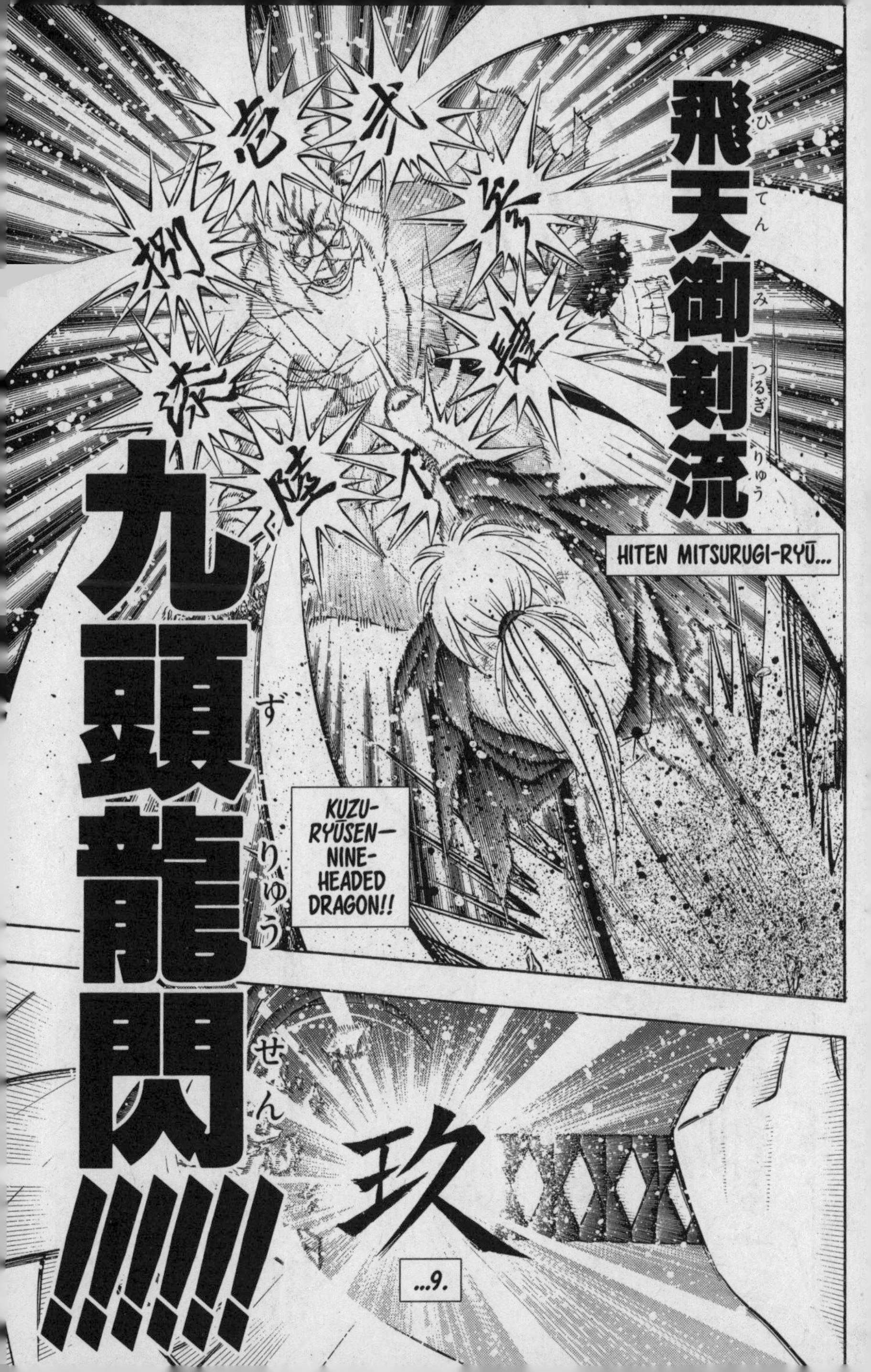

飛天御剣流
HITEN MITSURUGI-RYŪ...
九頭龍閃!!!!!!
KUZU-RYŪSEN—NINE-HEADED DRAGON!!
玖
...9.

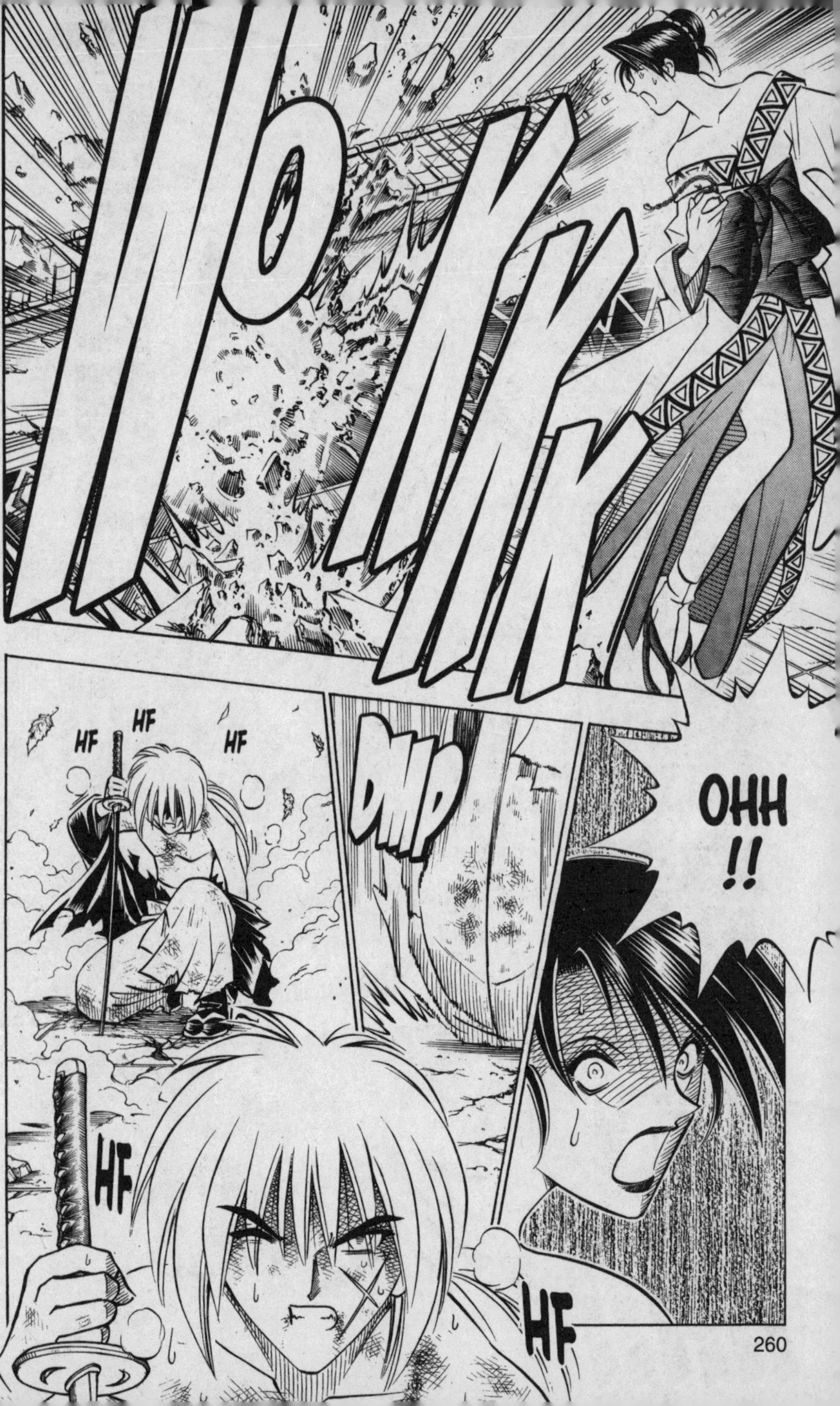
OHH
!!
DMP
HF
HF
HF
HF
HF

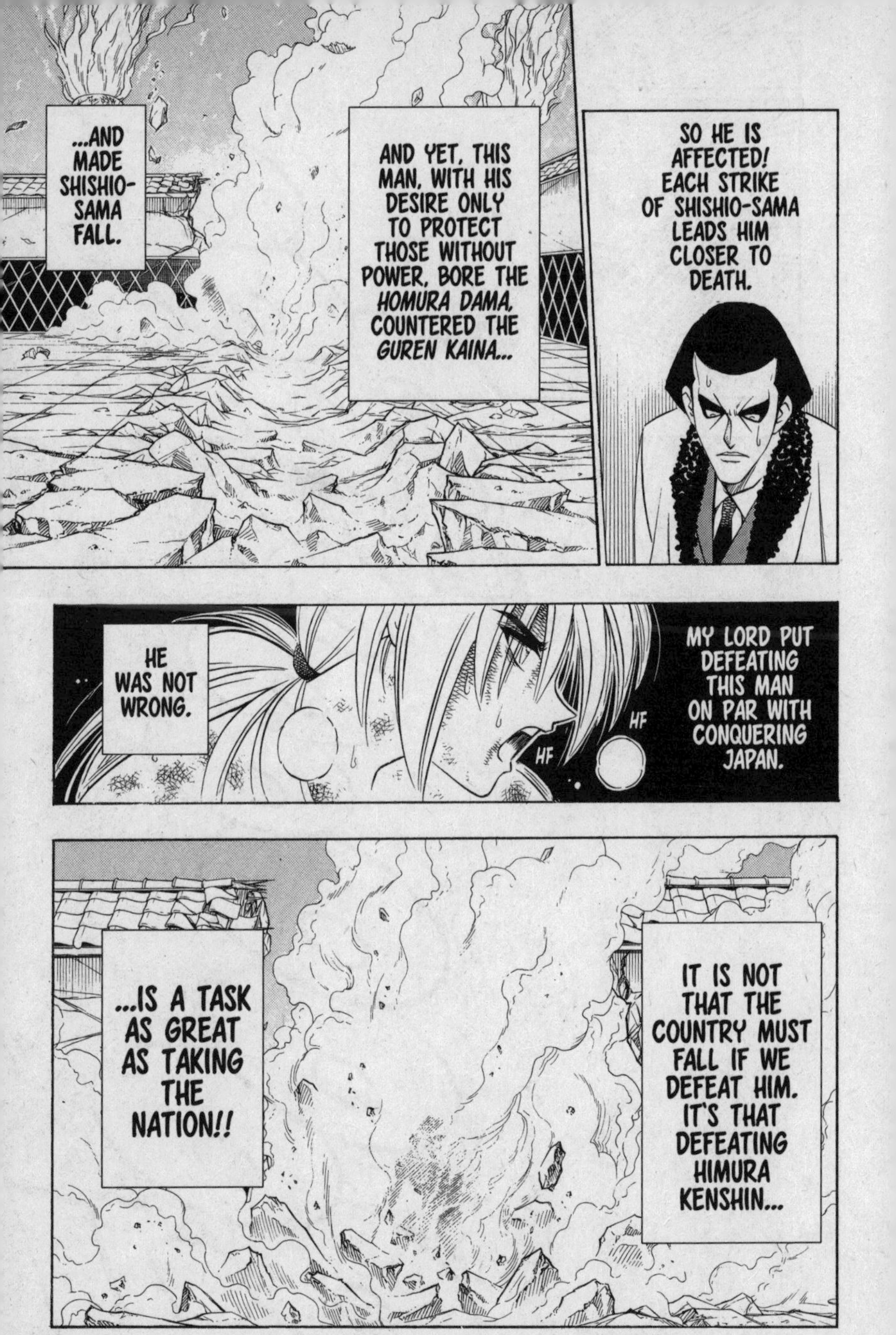
SO HE IS AFFECTED! EACH STRIKE OF SHISHIO-SAMA LEADS HIM CLOSER TO DEATH.
AND YET, THIS MAN, WITH HIS DESIRE ONLY TO PROTECT THOSE WITHOUT POWER, BORE THE *HOMURA DAMA*, COUNTERED THE *GUREN KAINA*...
...AND MADE SHISHIO-SAMA FALL.
MY LORD PUT DEFEATING THIS MAN ON PAR WITH CONQUERING JAPAN.
HF
HF
HE WAS NOT WRONG.
IT IS NOT THAT THE COUNTRY MUST FALL IF WE DEFEAT HIM. IT'S THAT DEFEATING HIMURA KENSHIN...
...IS A TASK AS GREAT AS TAKING THE NATION!!

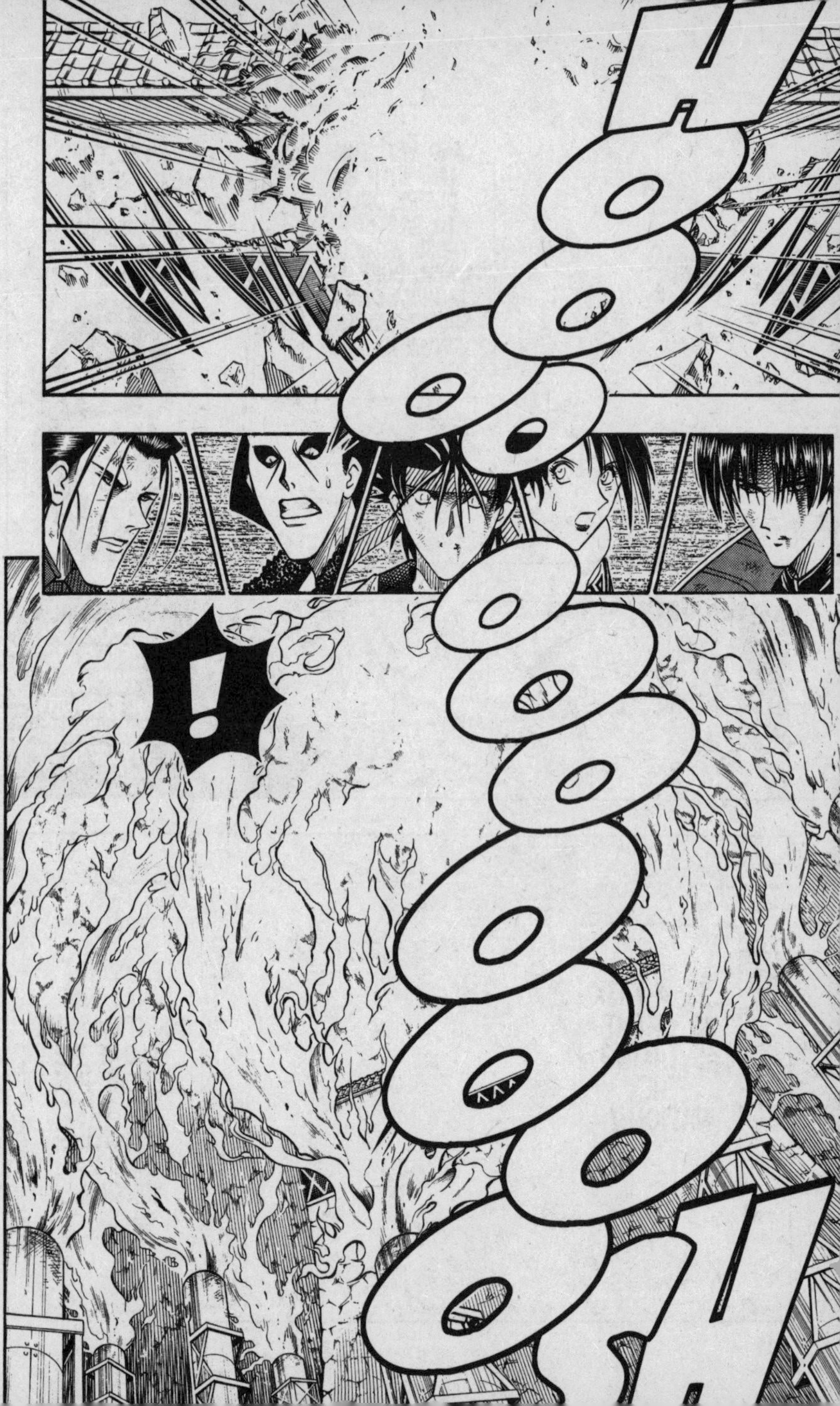
HOOOOOOOOOOOH!
!

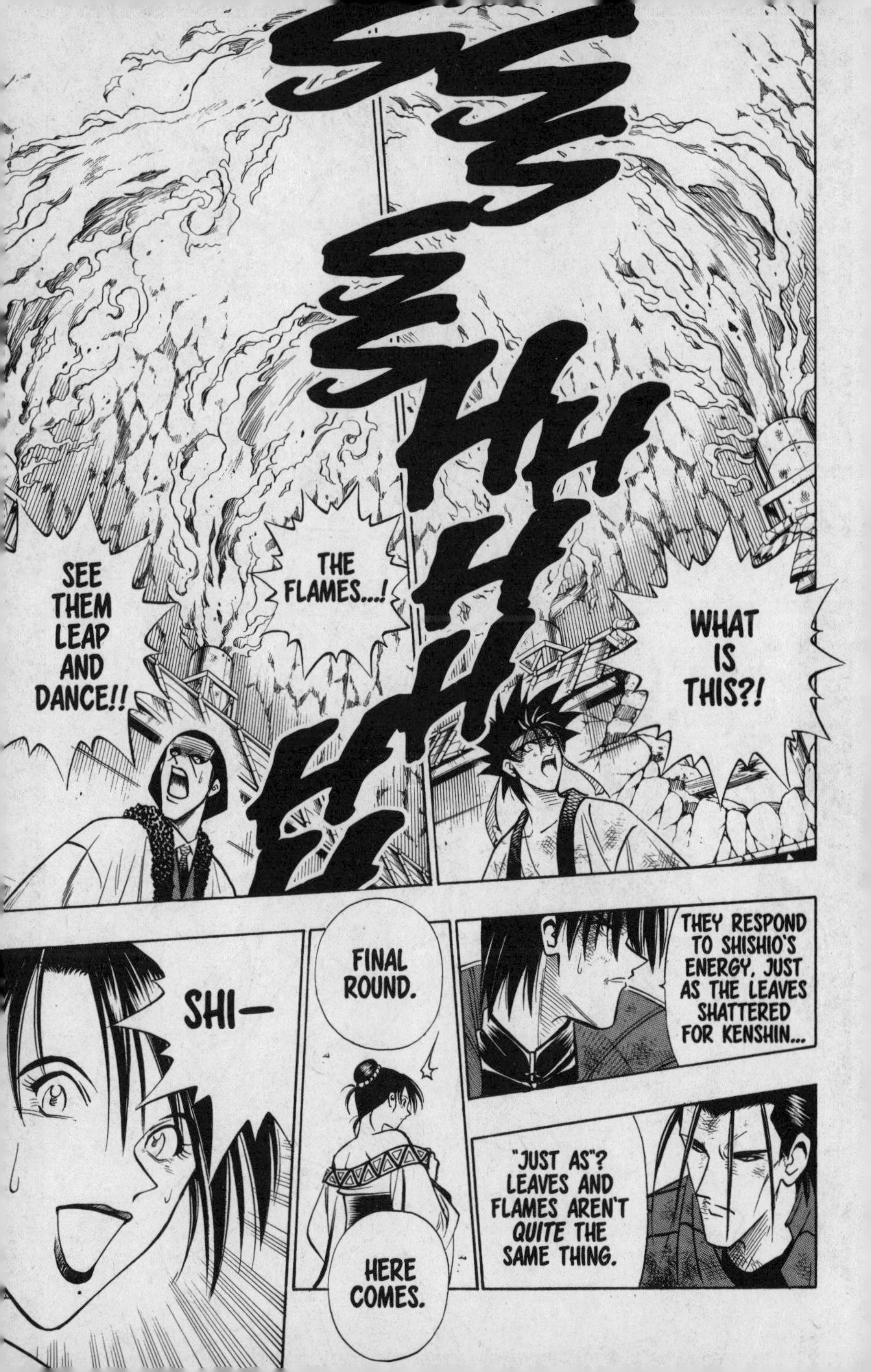
WHAT IS THIS?!
THE FLAMES...!
SEE THEM LEAP AND DANCE!!
THEY RESPOND TO SHISHIO'S ENERGY, JUST AS THE LEAVES SHATTERED FOR KENSHIN...
"JUST AS"? LEAVES AND FLAMES AREN'T *QUITE* THE SAME THING.
FINAL ROUND.
HERE COMES.
SHI—

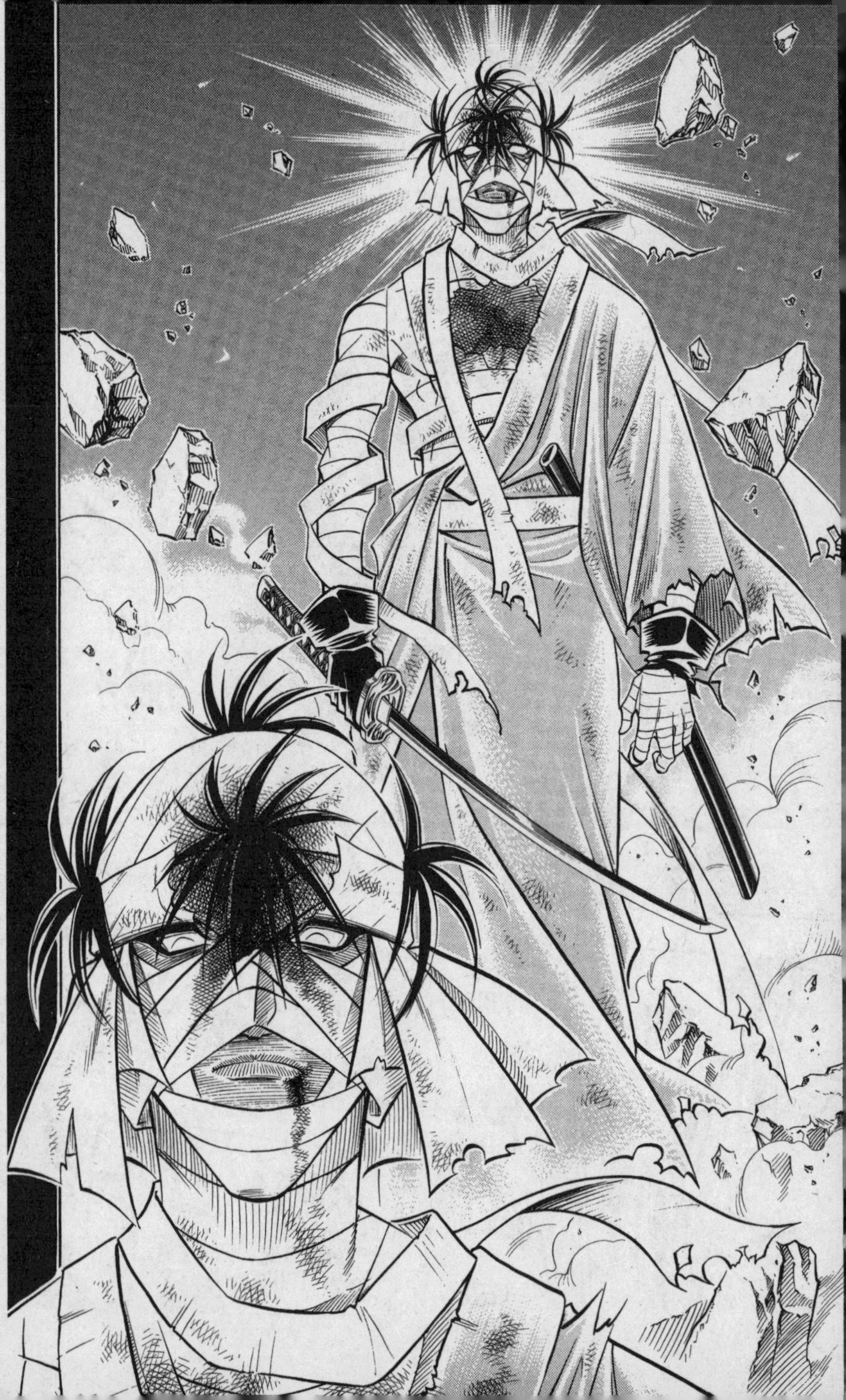

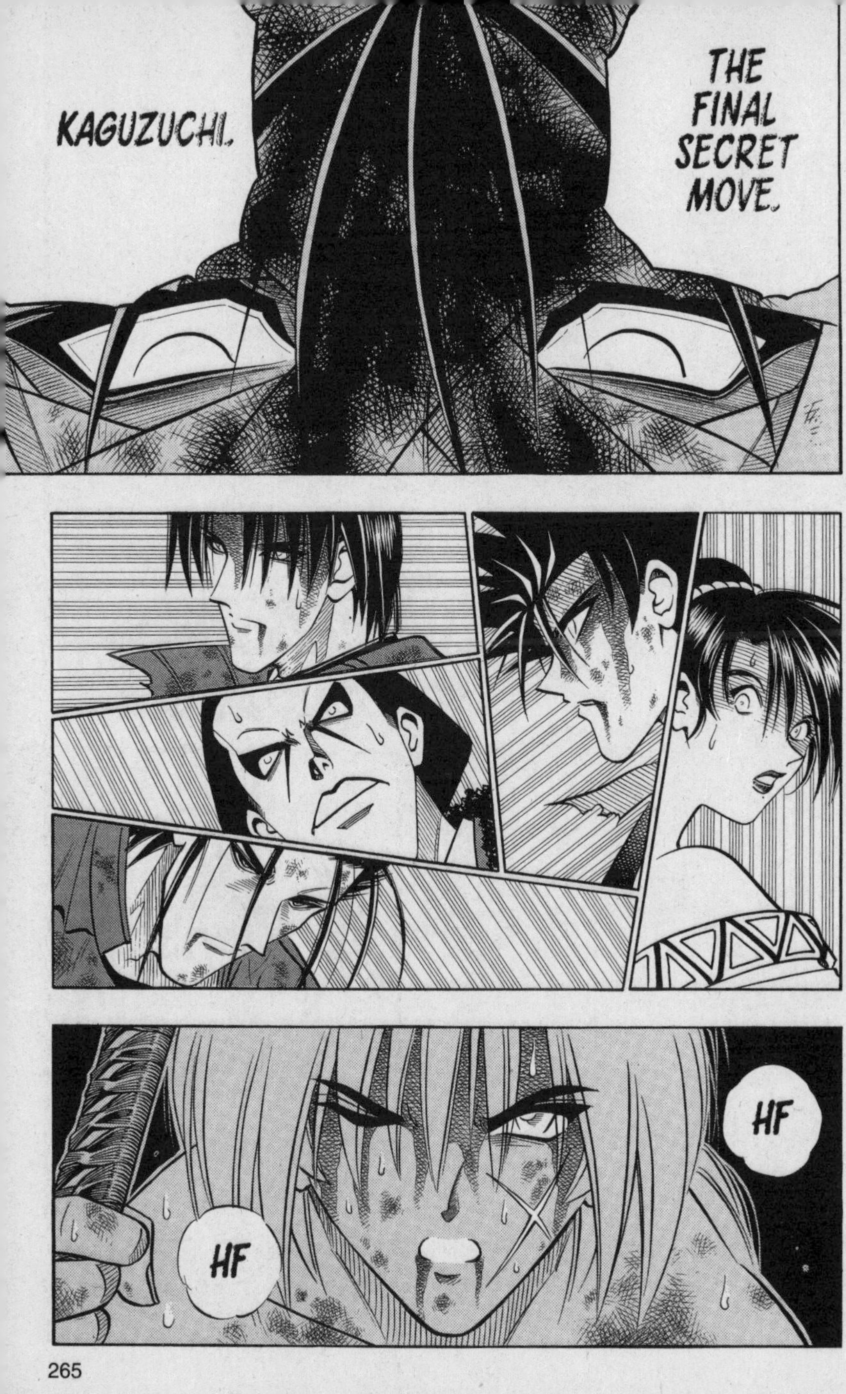
THE FINAL SECRET MOVE...
KAGUZUCHI...
HF
HF

Rurouni Kenshin

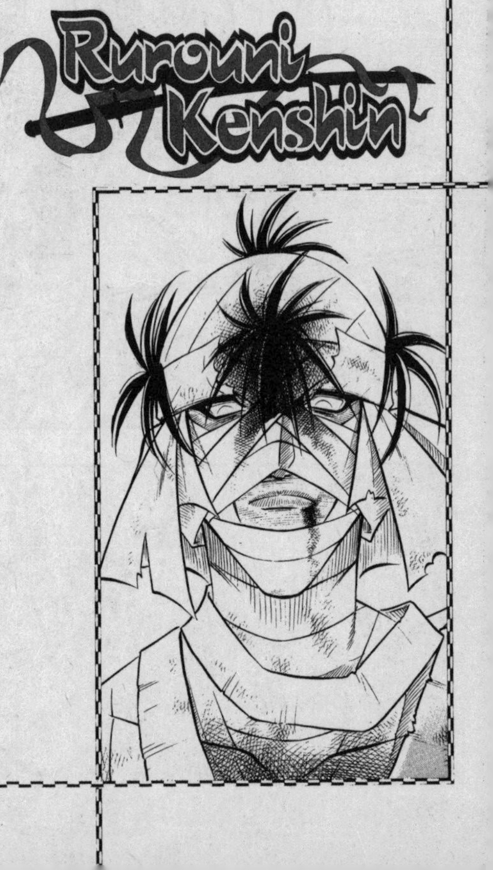

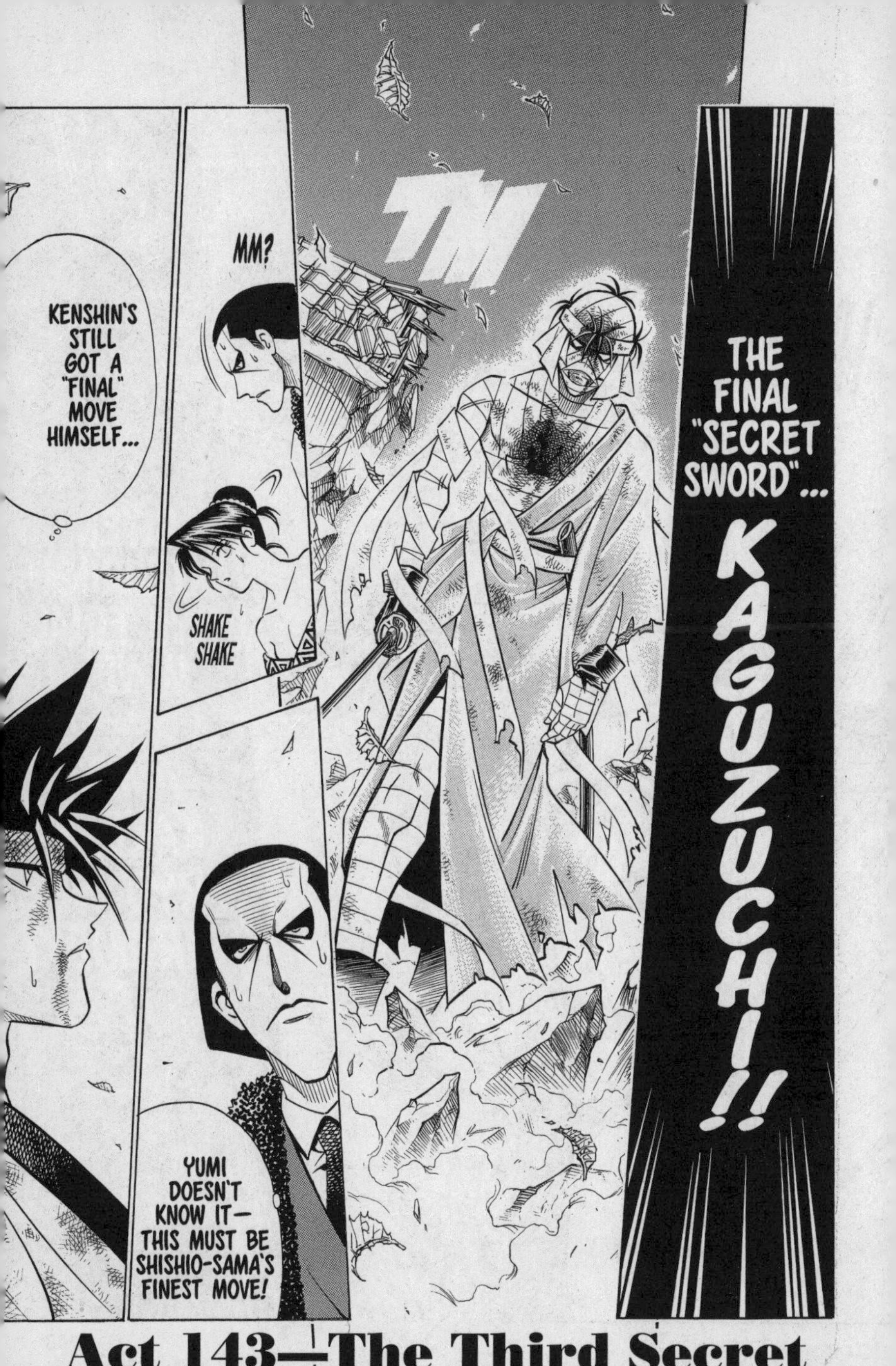
TM
THE FINAL "SECRET SWORD"...
KAGUZUCHI!!
MM?
SHAKE SHAKE
YUMI DOESN'T KNOW IT— THIS MUST BE SHISHIO-SAMA'S FINEST MOVE!
KENSHIN'S STILL GOT A "FINAL" MOVE HIMSELF...

Act 143—The Third Secret

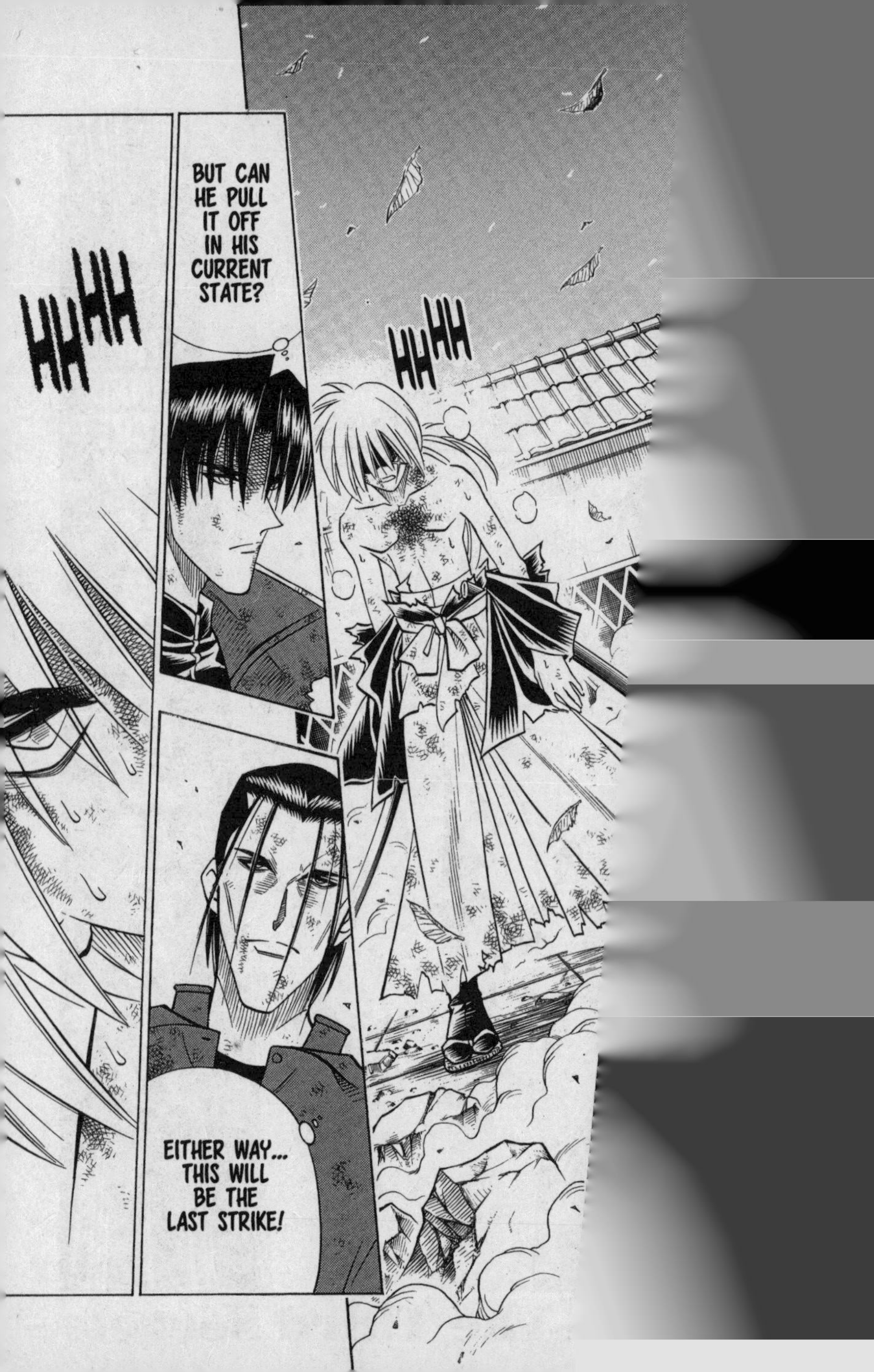
HHHH
BUT CAN HE PULL IT OFF IN HIS CURRENT STATE?
EITHER WAY... THIS WILL BE THE LAST STRIKE!
HHHH

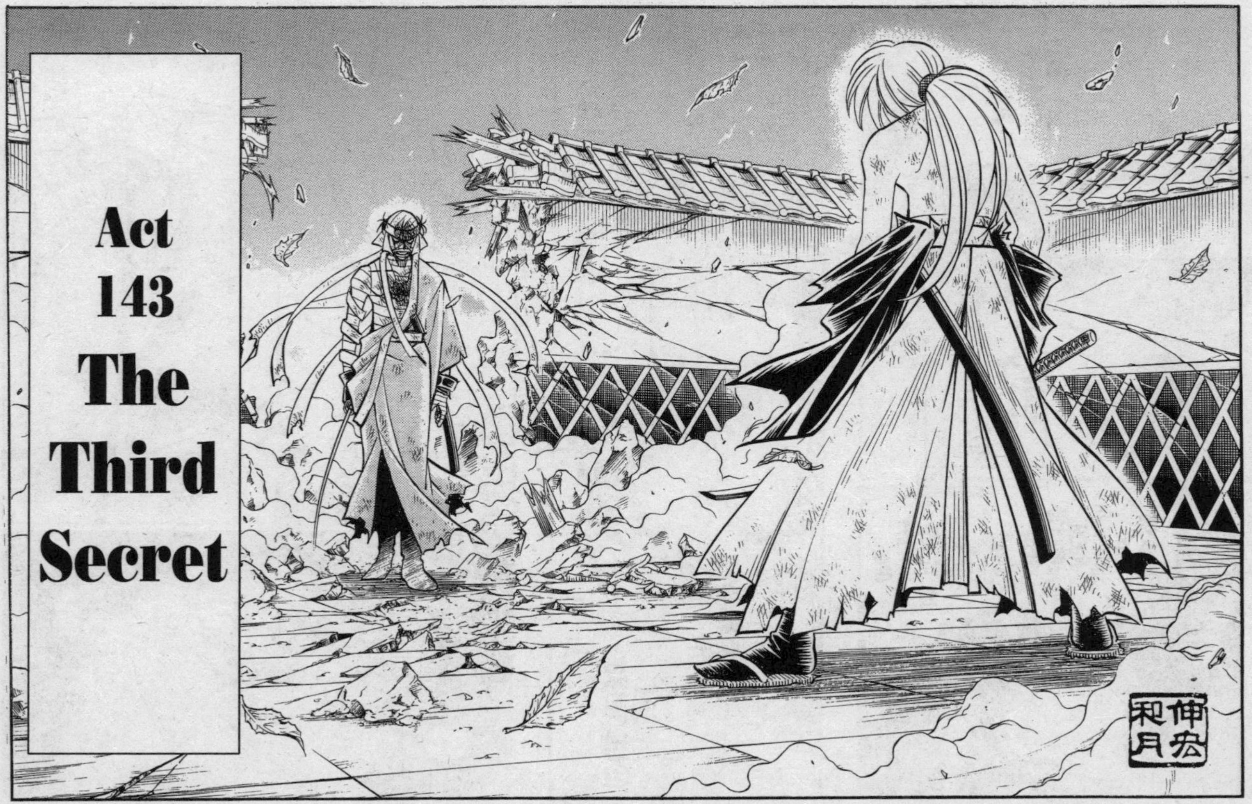
Act 143 The Third Secret
伸宏
和月

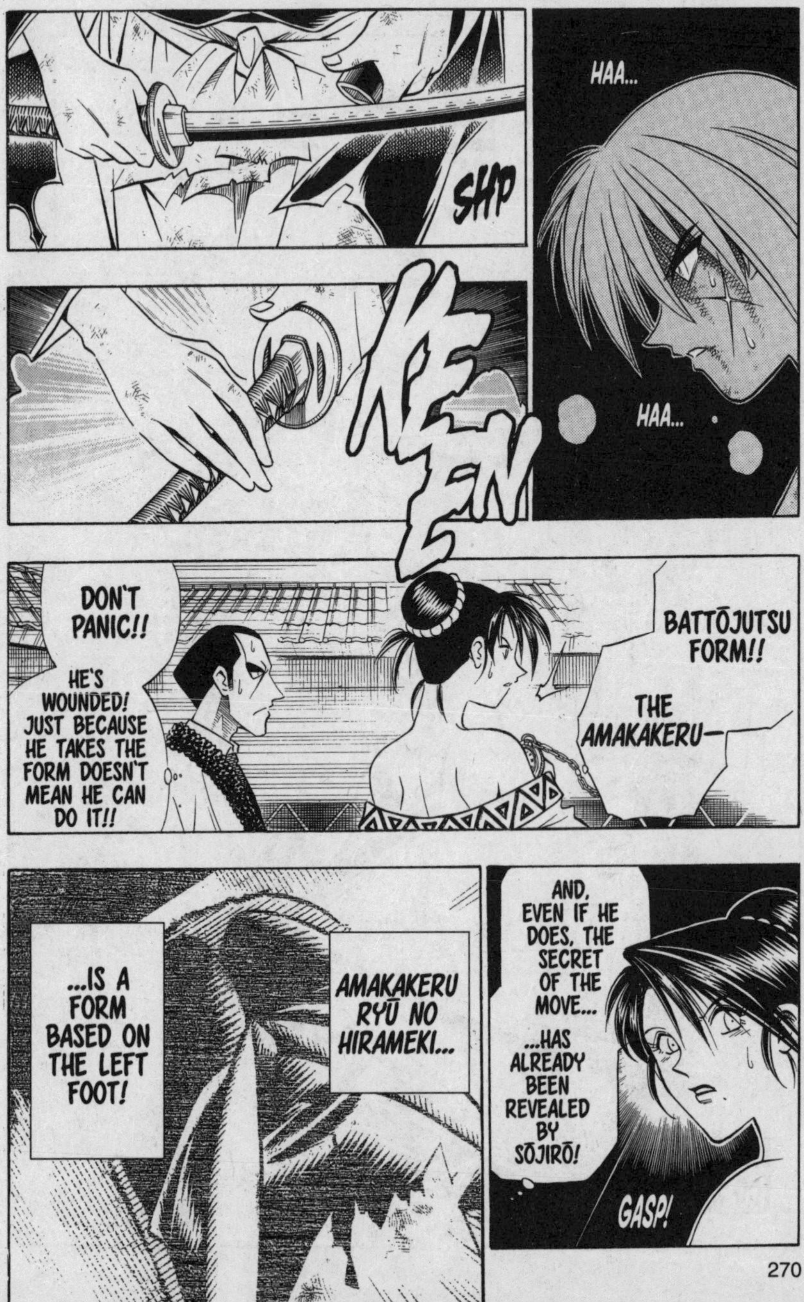
HAA...
HAA...
SHP
KEEN
BATTŌJUTSU FORM!!
THE AMAKAKERU—
DON'T PANIC!!
HE'S WOUNDED! JUST BECAUSE HE TAKES THE FORM DOESN'T MEAN HE CAN DO IT!!
AND, EVEN IF HE DOES, THE SECRET OF THE MOVE...
...HAS ALREADY BEEN REVEALED BY SŌJIRŌ!
GASP!
AMAKAKERU RYŪ NO HIRAMEKI...
...IS A FORM BASED ON THE LEFT FOOT!

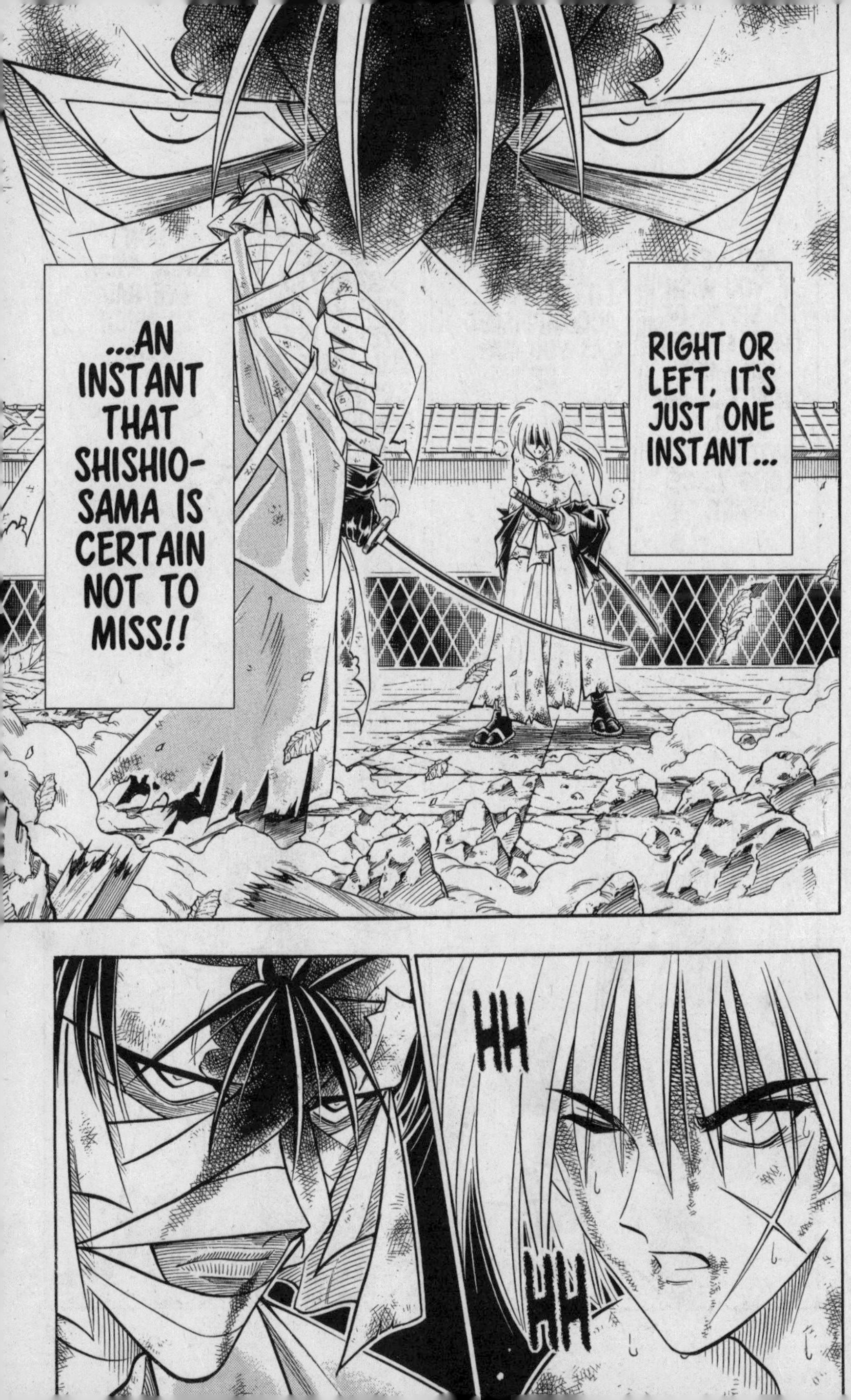
RIGHT OR LEFT, IT'S JUST ONE INSTANT...
...AN INSTANT THAT SHISHIO-SAMA IS CERTAIN NOT TO MISS!!
HH
HH

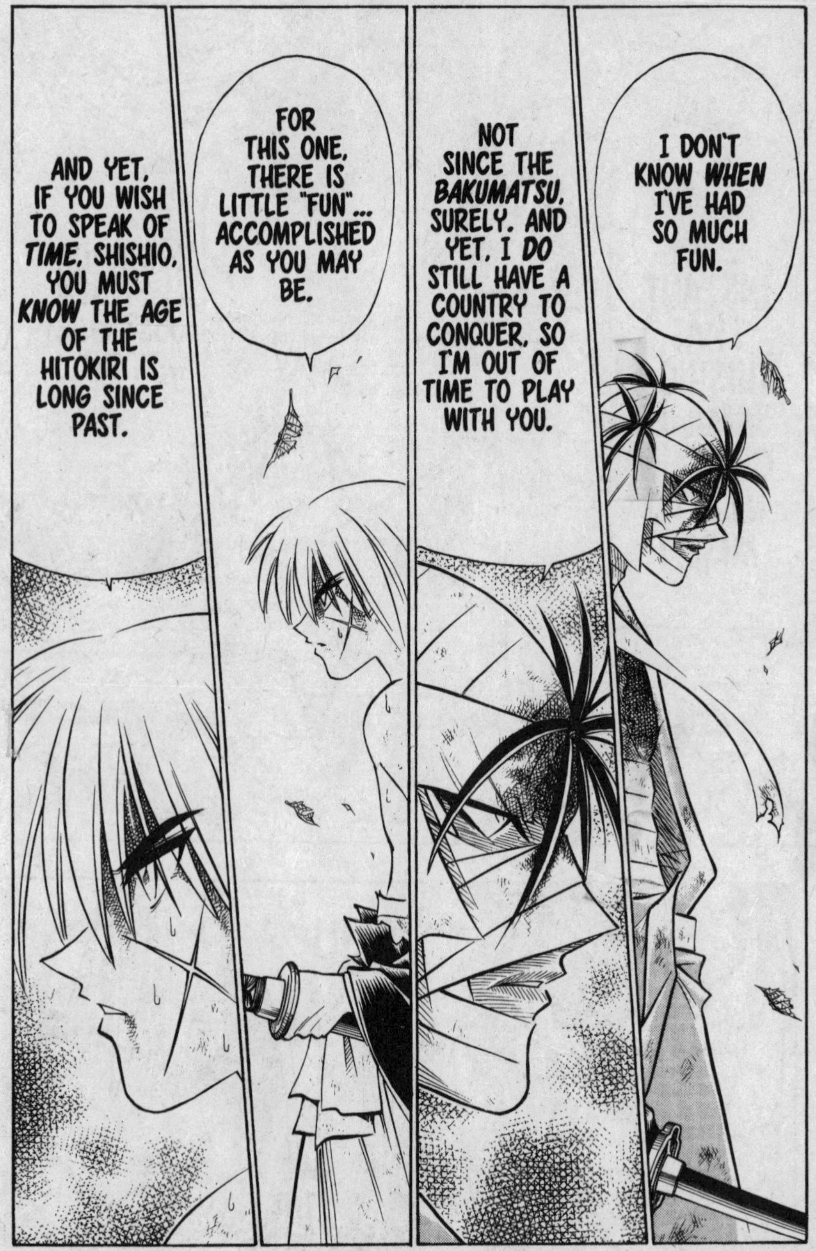
I DON'T KNOW *WHEN* I'VE HAD SO MUCH FUN.
NOT SINCE THE *BAKUMATSU*, SURELY. AND YET, I *DO* STILL HAVE A COUNTRY TO CONQUER, SO I'M OUT OF TIME TO PLAY WITH YOU.
FOR THIS ONE, THERE IS LITTLE "FUN"... ACCOMPLISHED AS YOU MAY BE.
AND YET, IF YOU WISH TO SPEAK OF *TIME*, SHISHIO, YOU MUST *KNOW* THE AGE OF THE HITOKIRI IS LONG SINCE PAST.

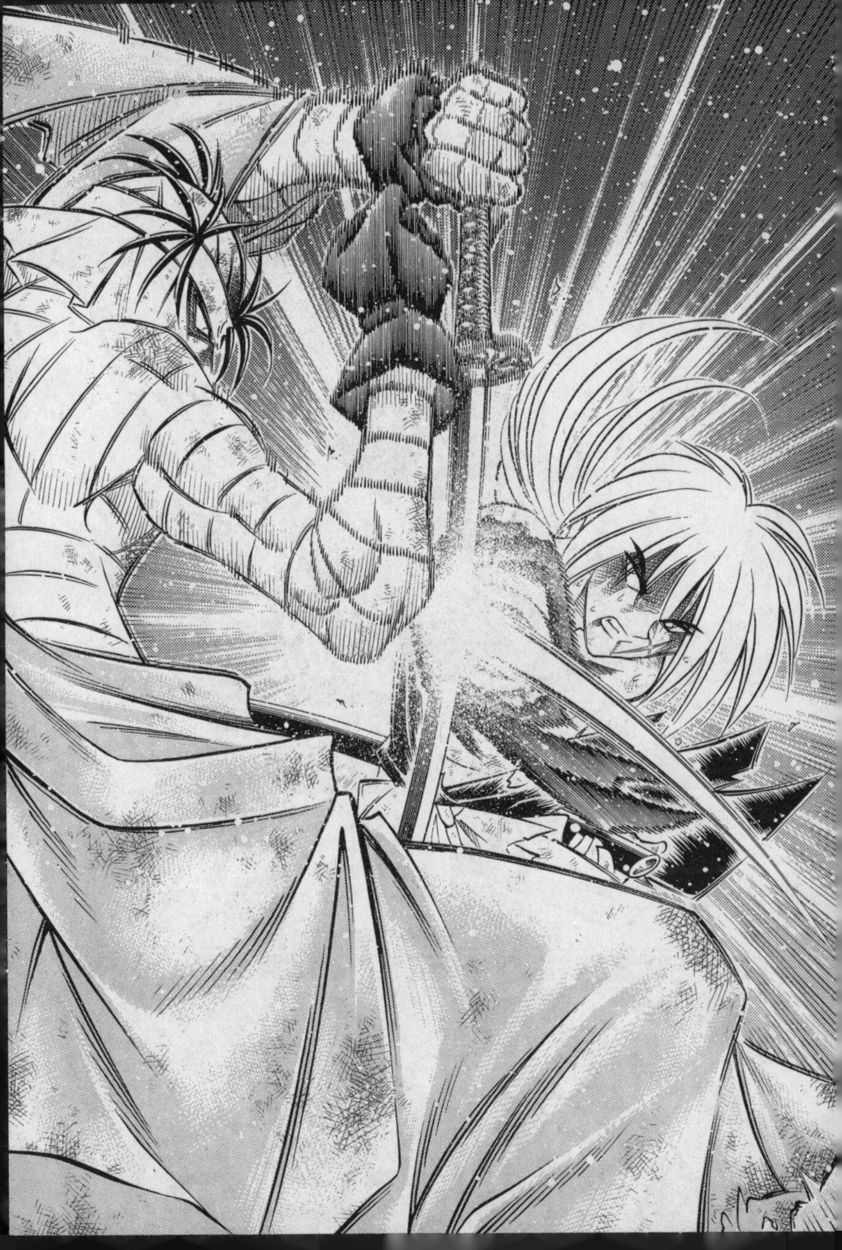

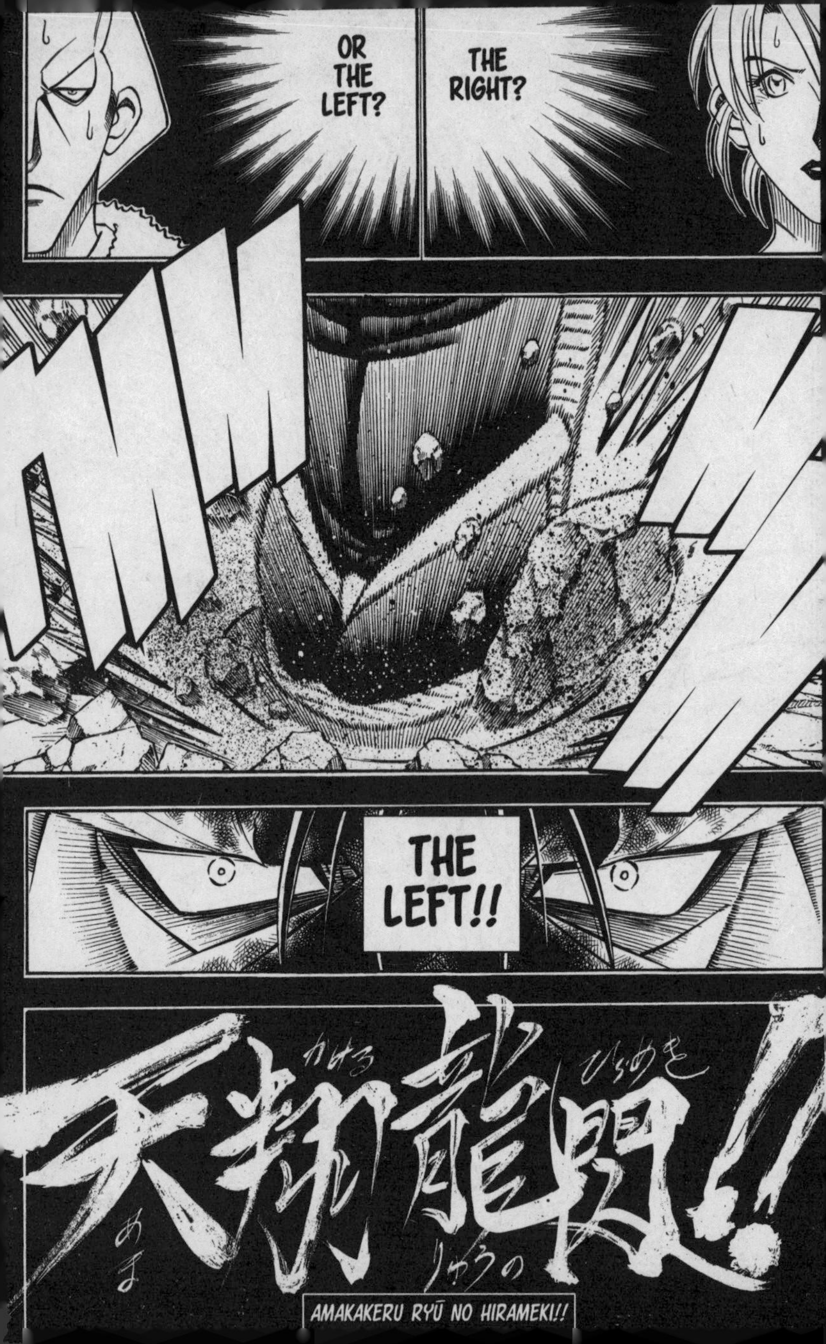
THE RIGHT?
OR THE LEFT?
THE LEFT!!
天翔龍閃!!
AMAKAKERU RYŪ NO HIRAMEKI!!

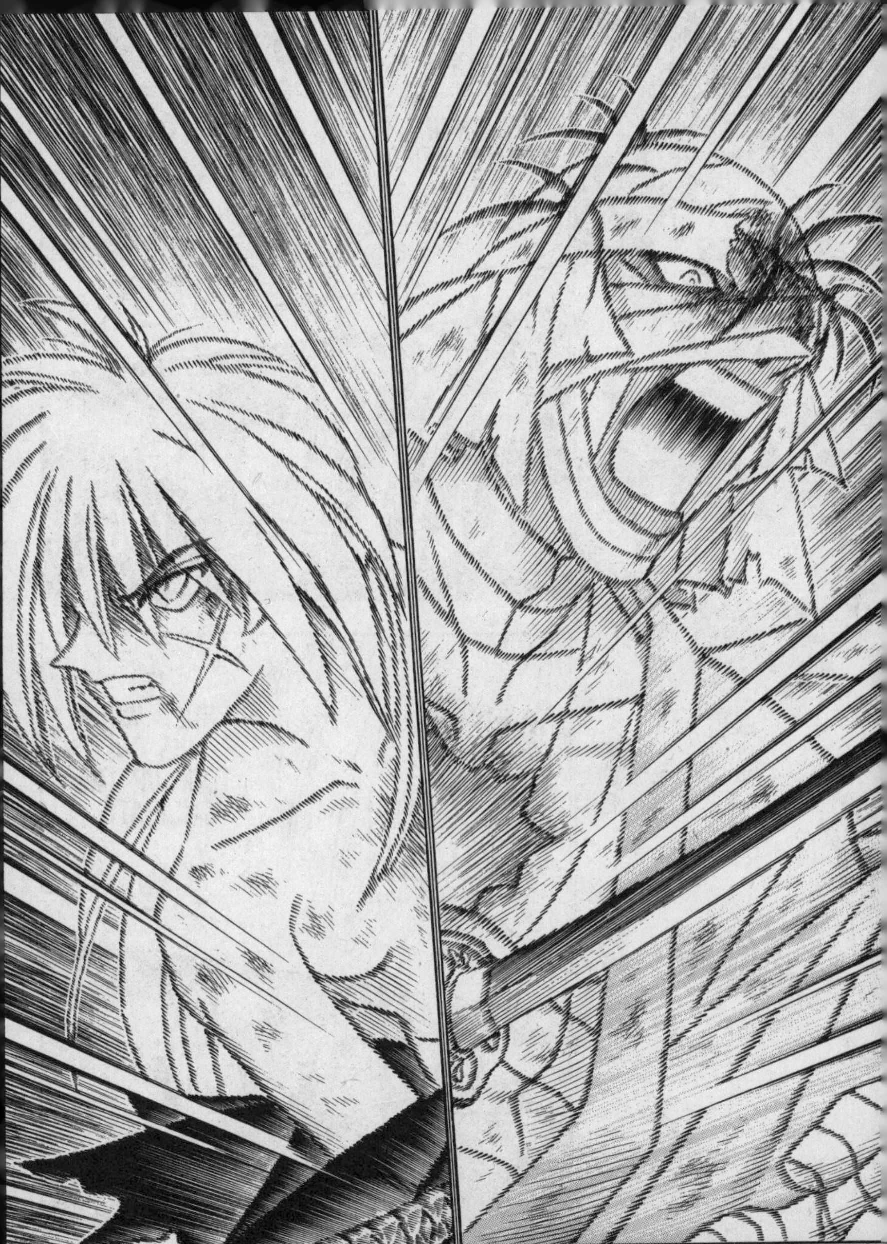

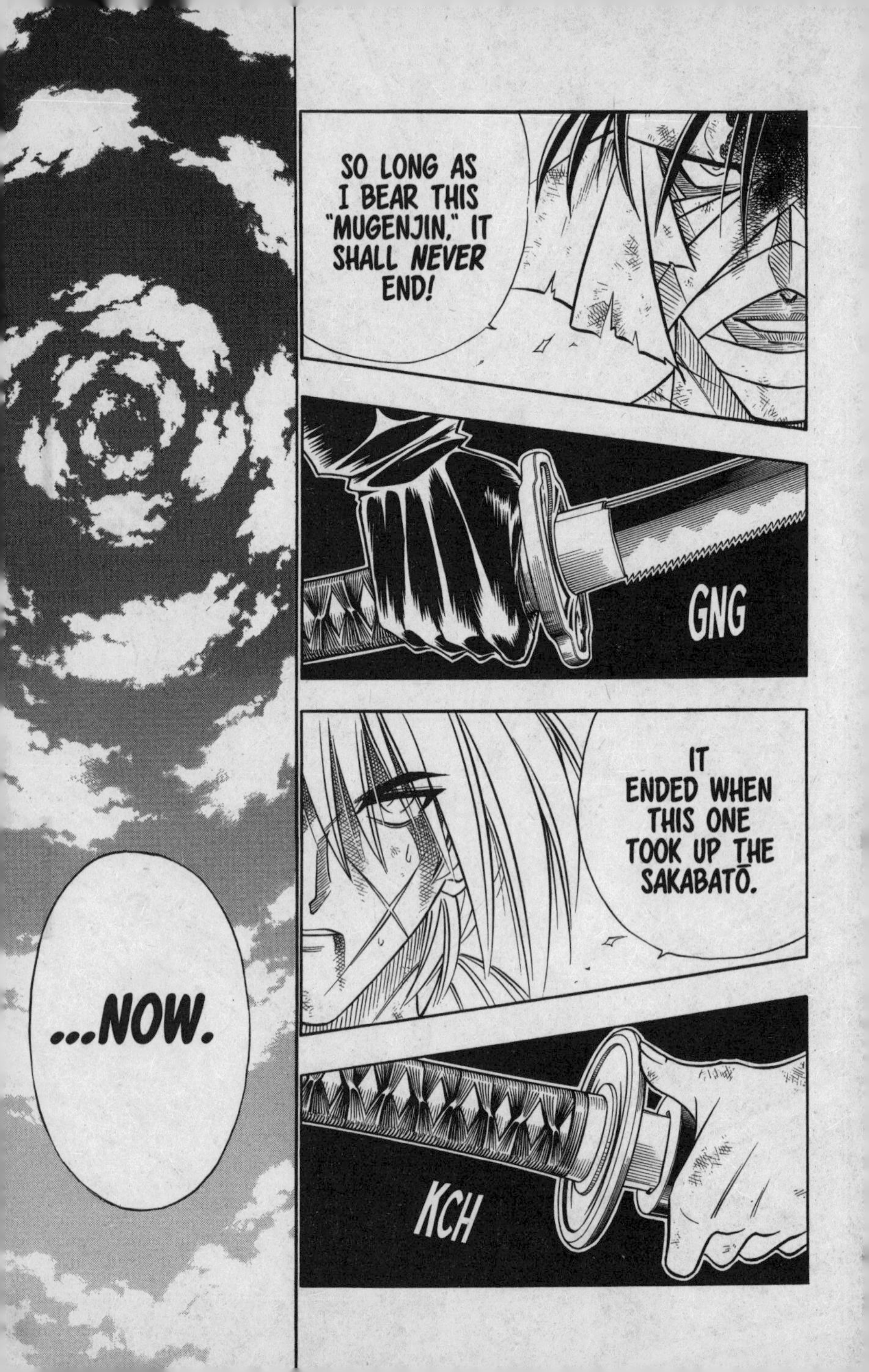
SO LONG AS I BEAR THIS "MUGENJIN," IT SHALL *NEVER* END!
GNG
IT ENDED WHEN THIS ONE TOOK UP THE SAKABATŌ.
KCH
...NOW.

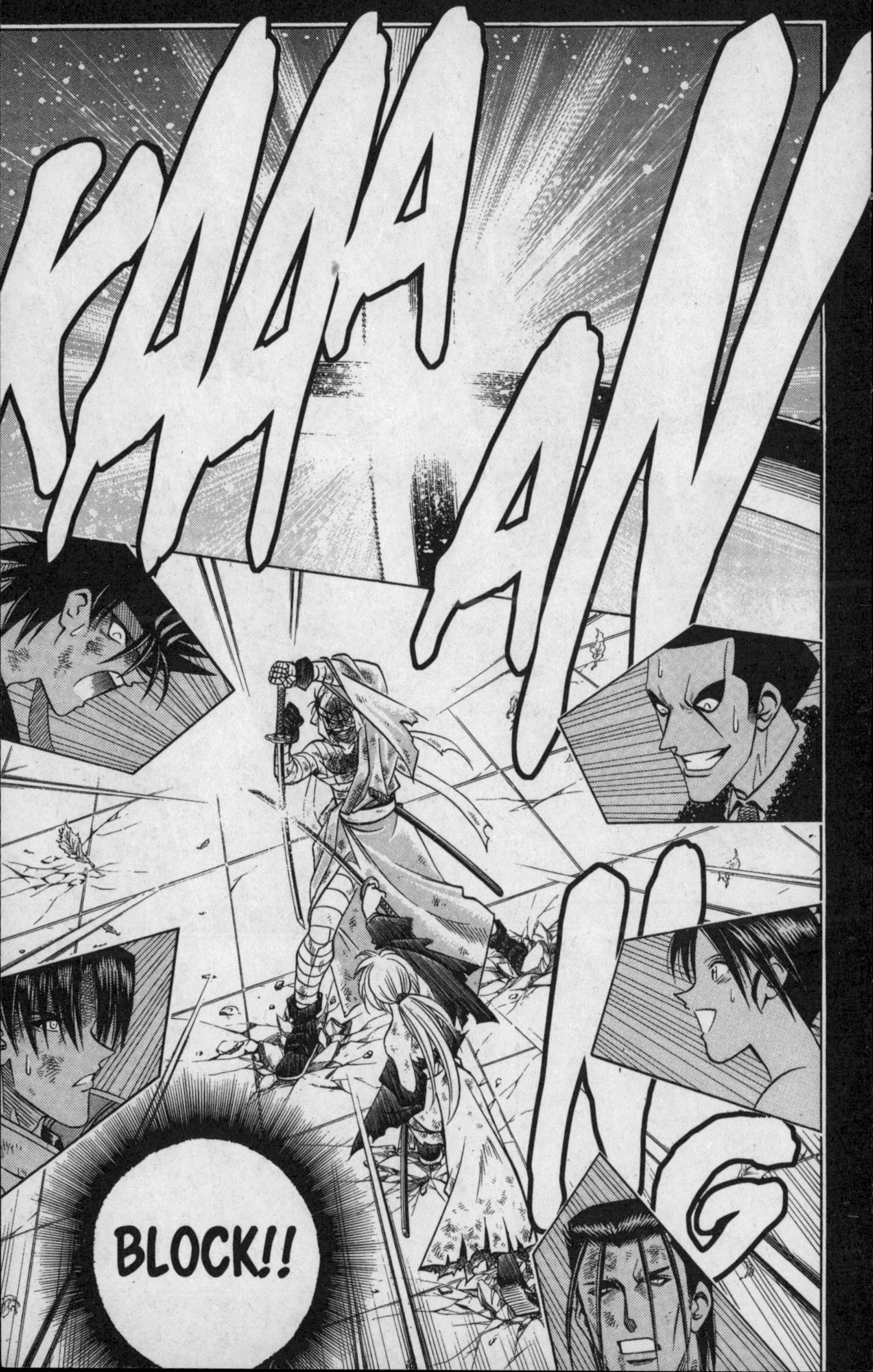
SHAAAANNG
BLOCK!!

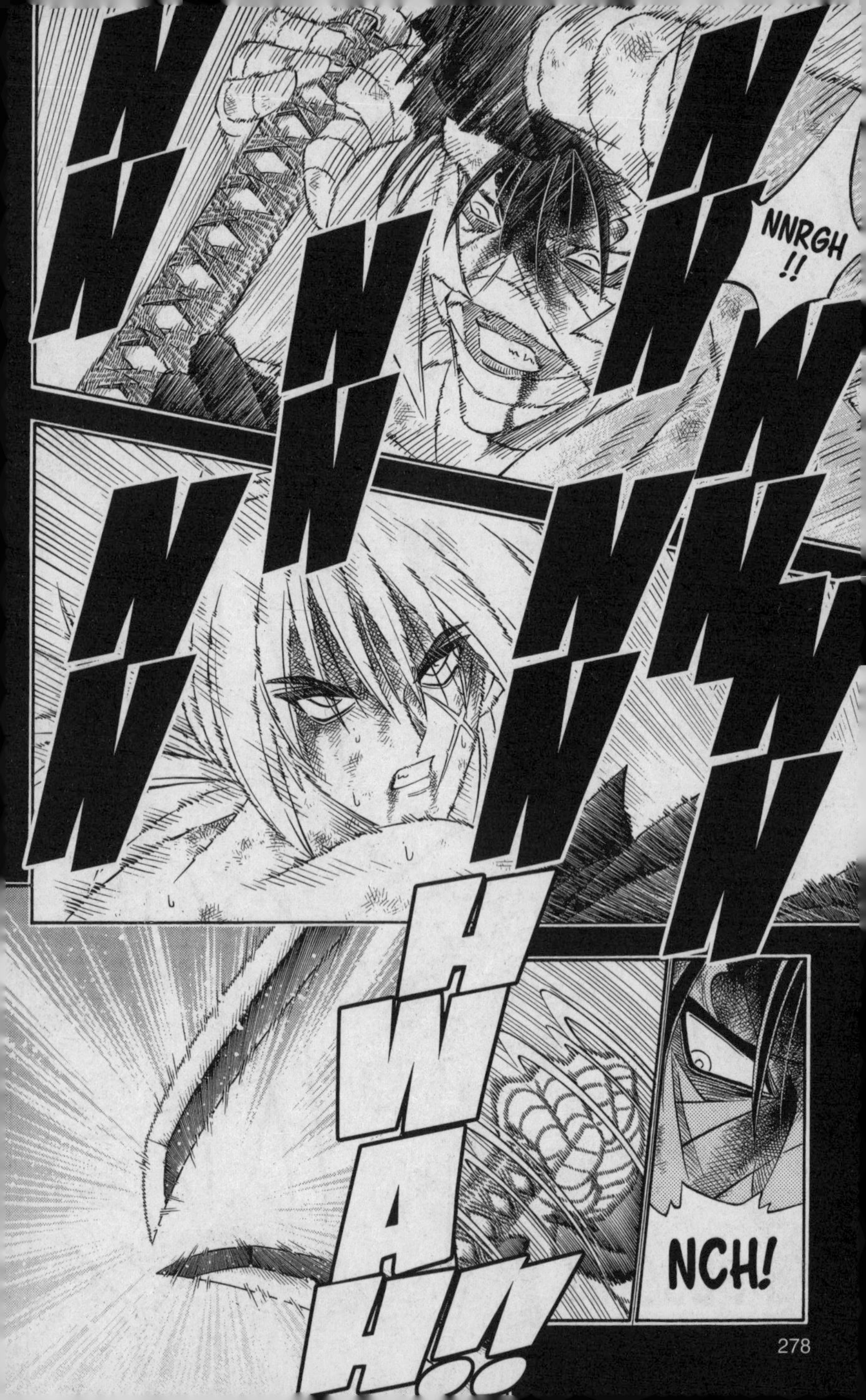
NNRGH !!
NCH!
HWAH!!

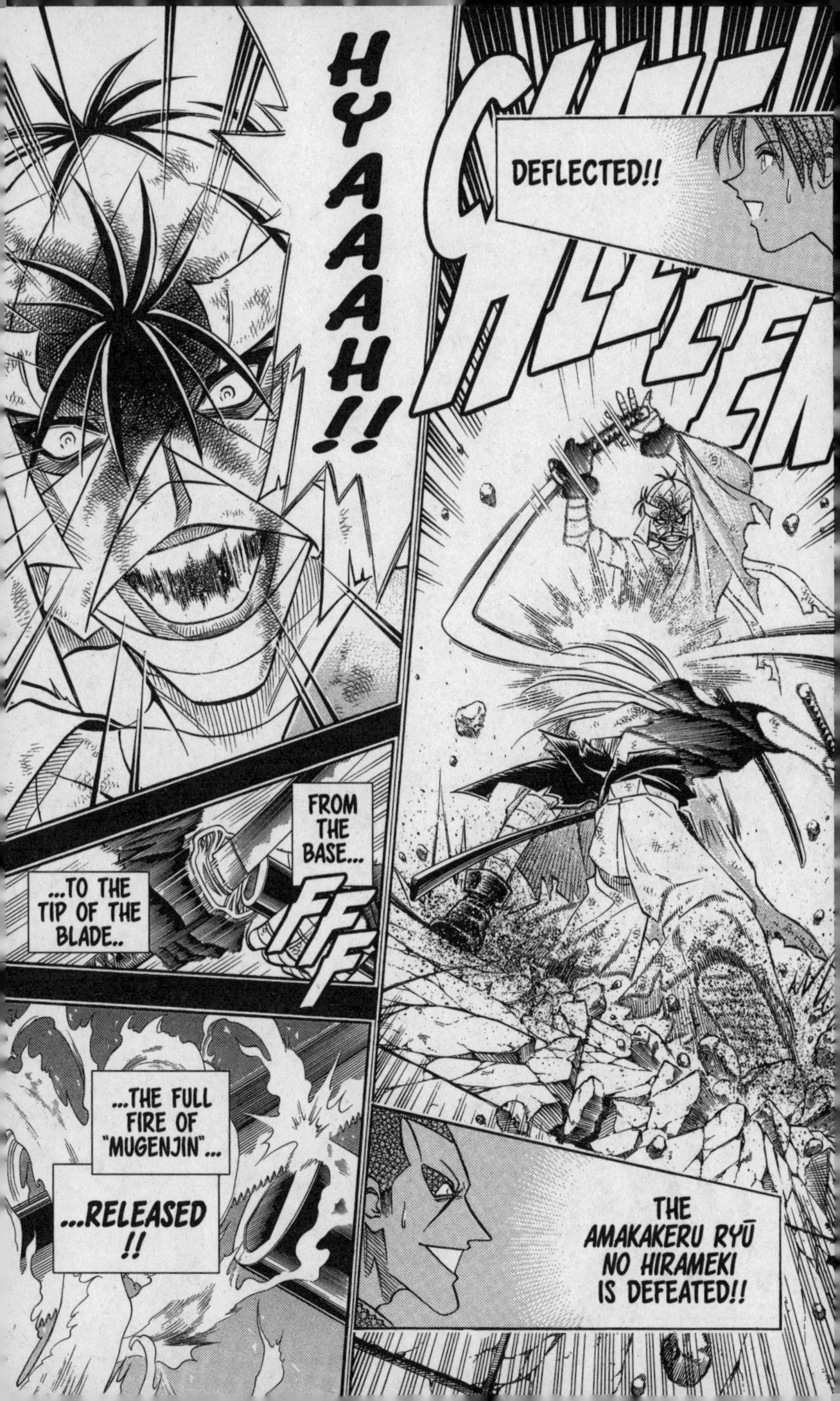
DEFLECTED!!
THE AMAKAKERU RYŪ NO HIRAMEKI IS DEFEATED!!
HYAAAAH!!
FROM THE BASE...
...TO THE TIP OF THE BLADE..
FFF
...THE FULL FIRE OF "MUGENJIN"...
...RELEASED !!

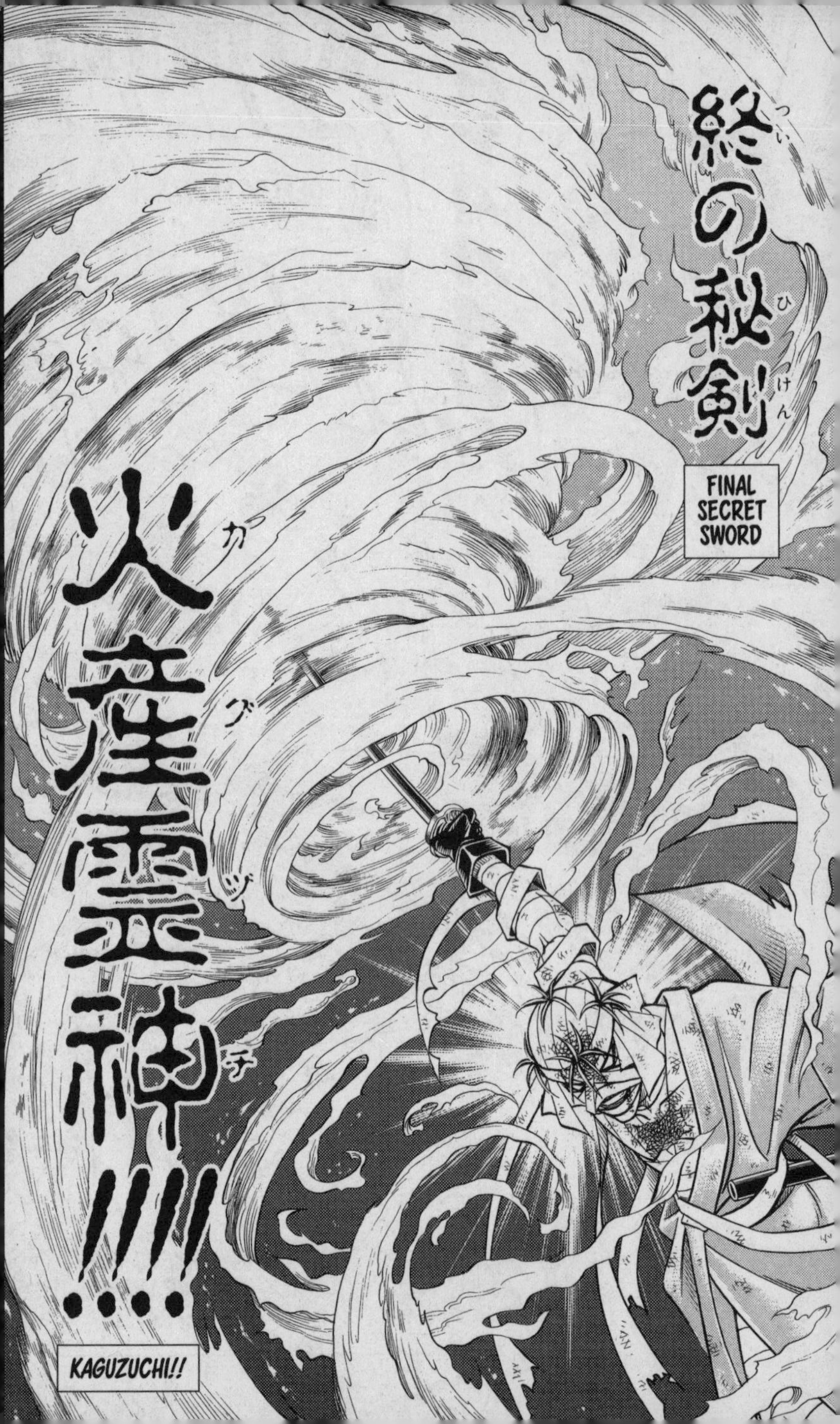
終の秘剣
FINAL SECRET SWORD
火産霊神!!!!
KAGUZUCHI!!

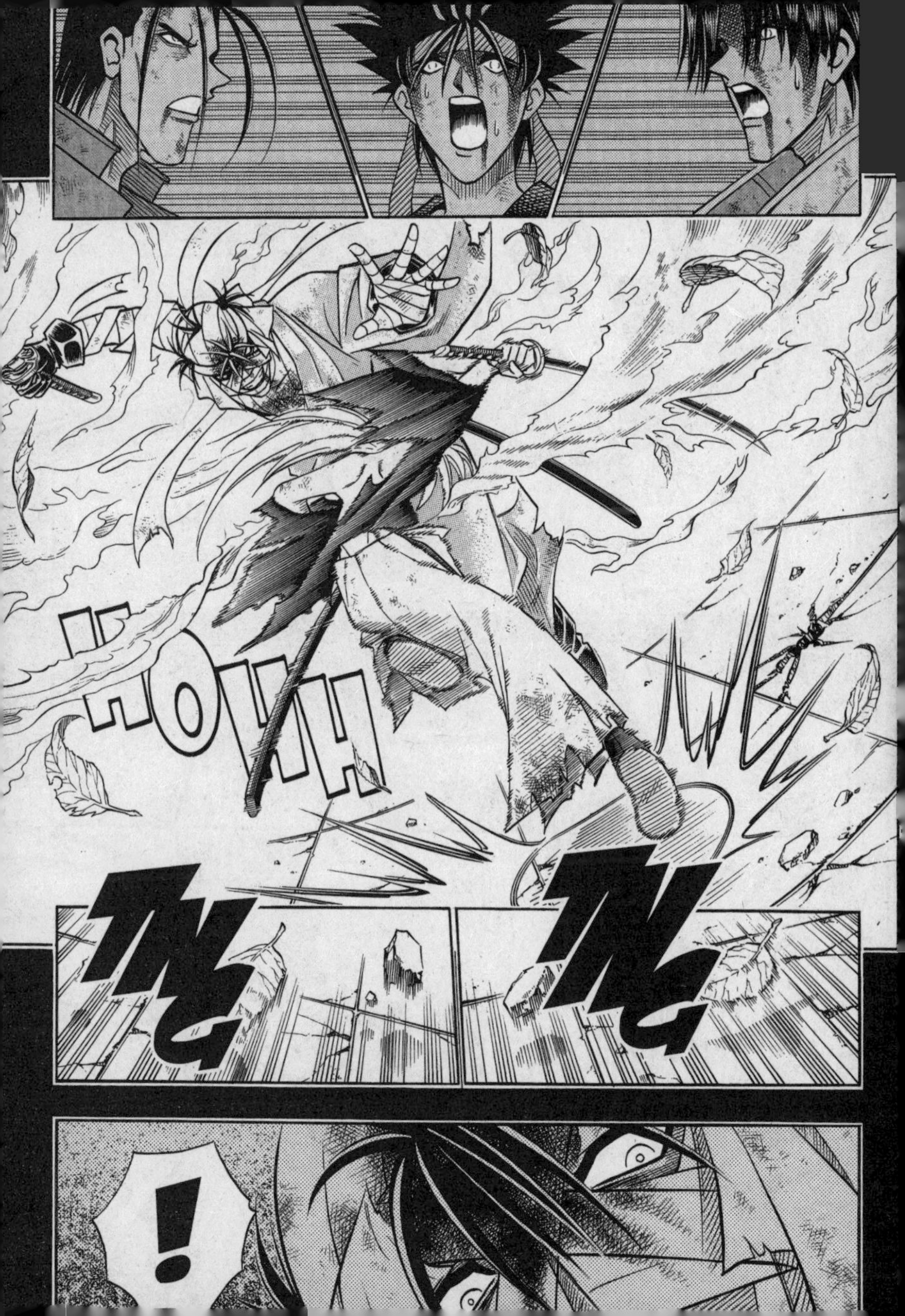
!

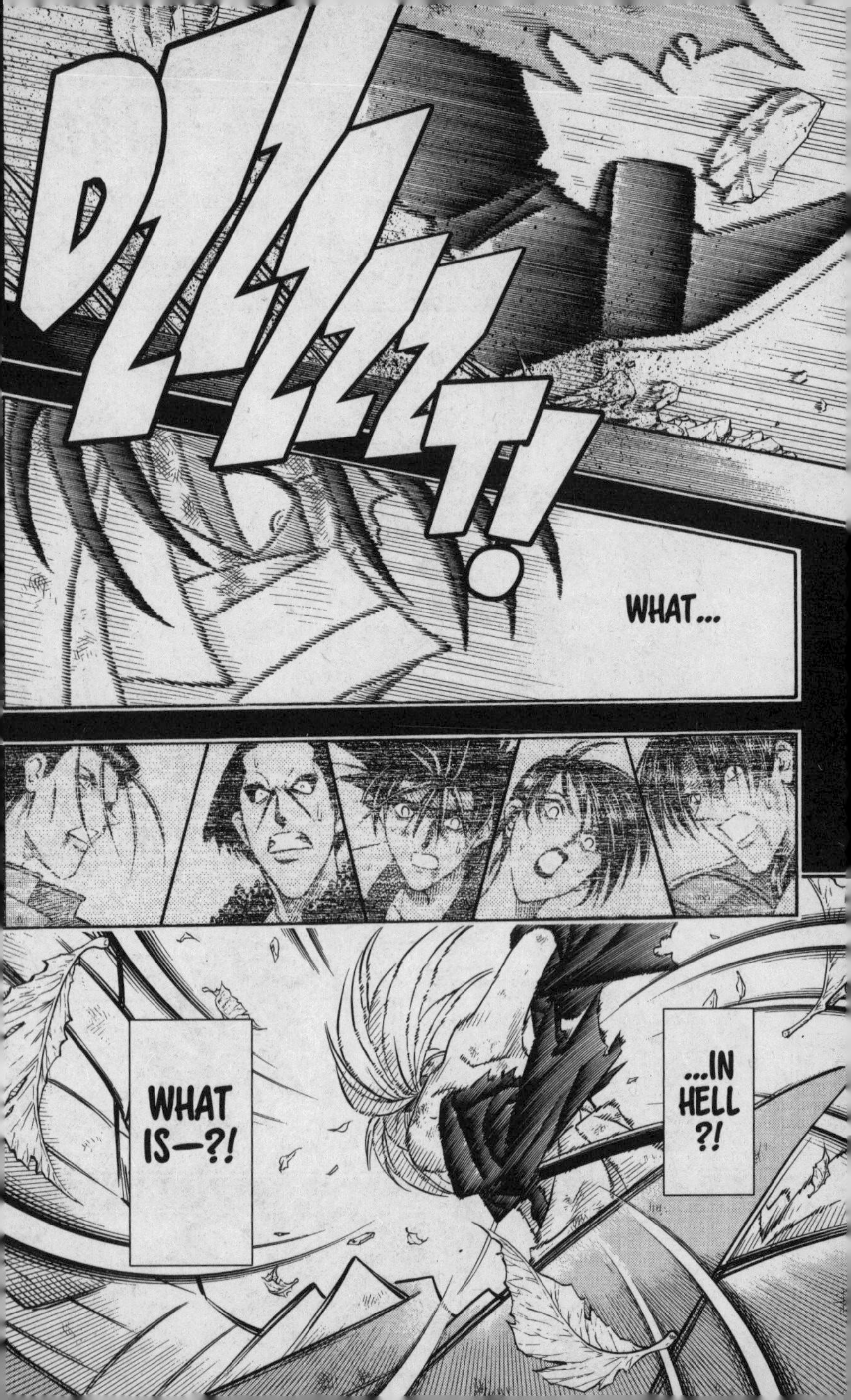
DZZZT!
WHAT...
...IN HELL?!
WHAT IS—?!

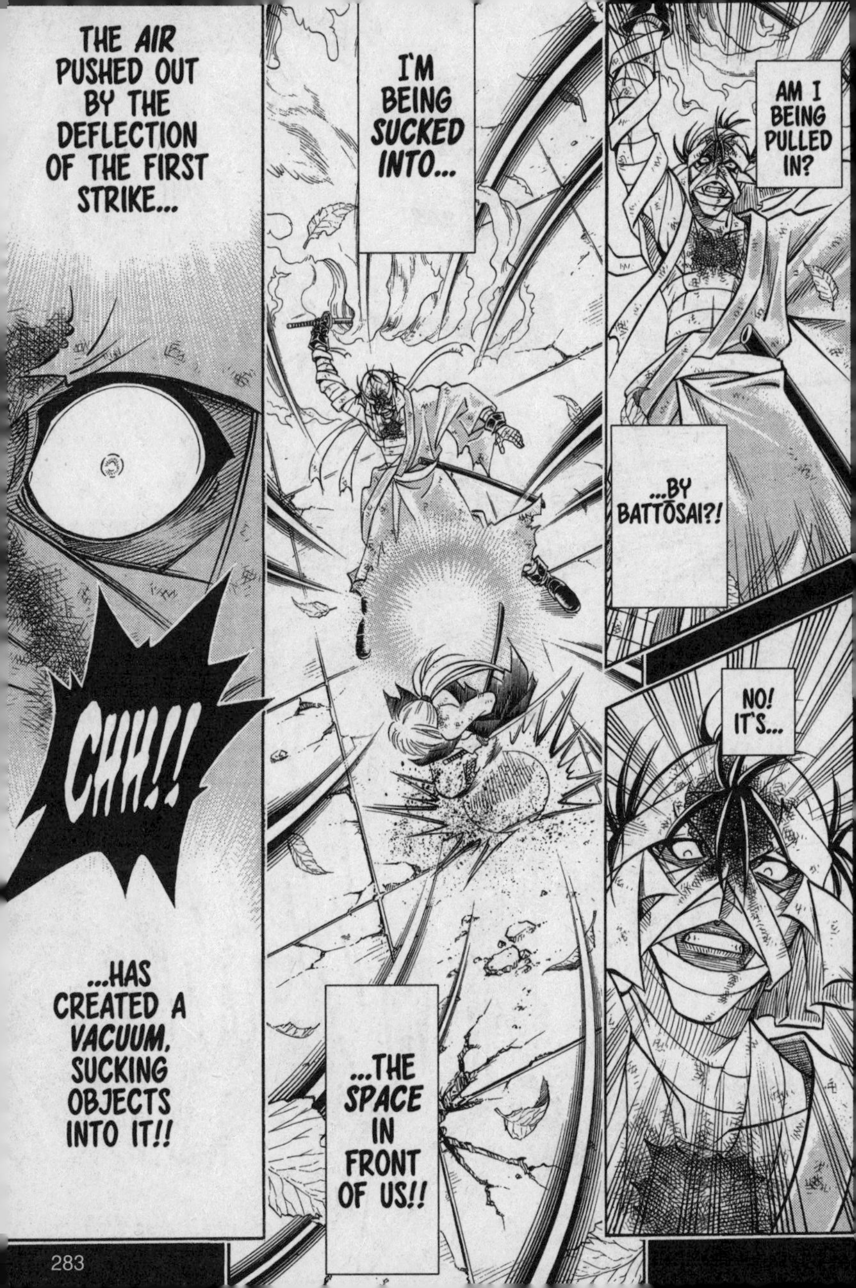
AM I BEING PULLED IN?
...BY BATTOSAI?!
NO! IT'S...
I'M BEING SUCKED INTO...
...THE SPACE IN FRONT OF US!!
THE AIR PUSHED OUT BY THE DEFLECTION OF THE FIRST STRIKE...
CHH!!
...HAS CREATED A VACUUM, SUCKING OBJECTS INTO IT!!

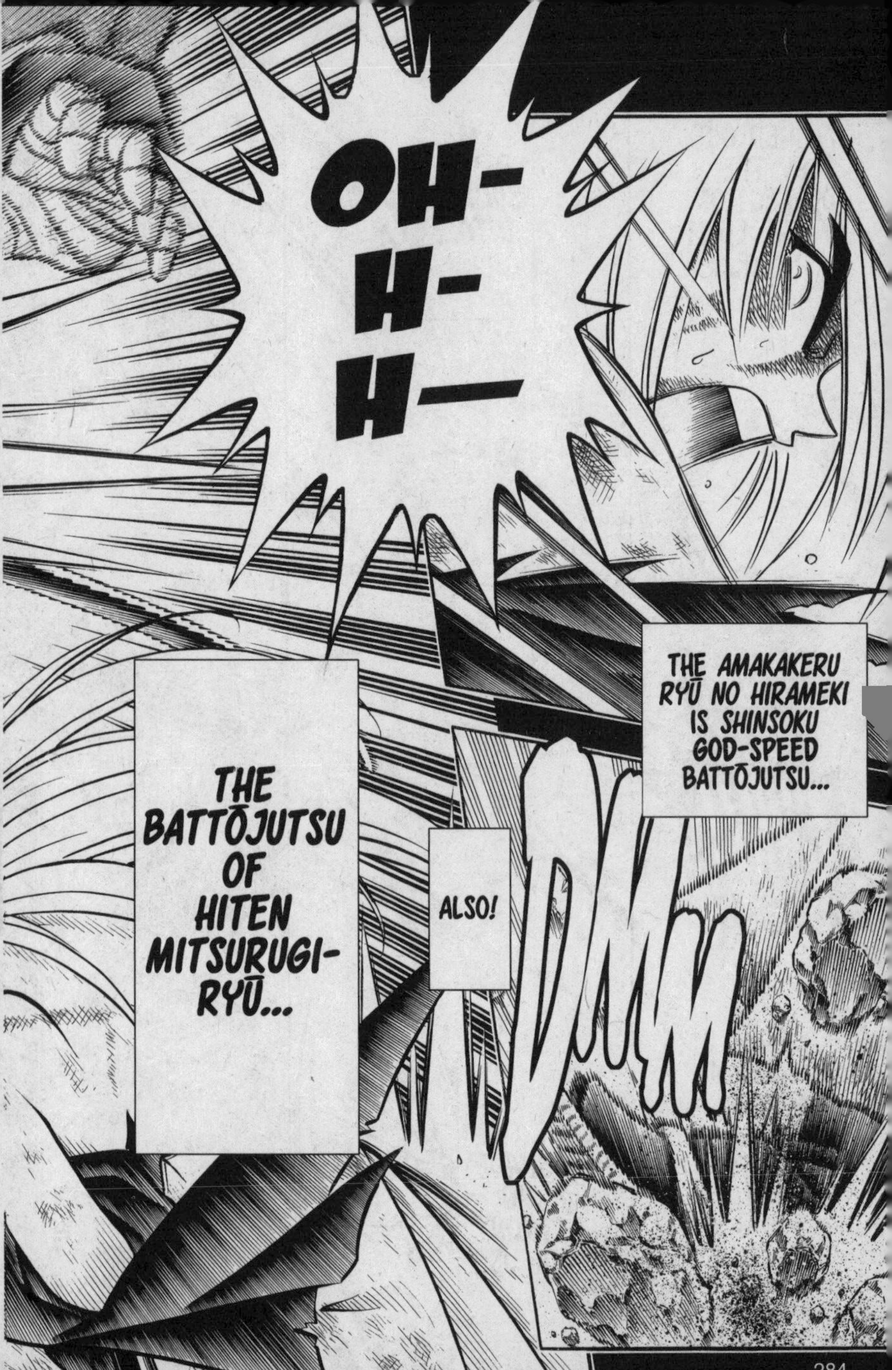
OH-H-H—
THE AMAKAKERU RYŪ NO HIRAMEKI IS SHINSOKU GOD-SPEED BATTŌJUTSU...
ALSO!
THE BATTŌJUTSU OF HITEN MITSURUGI-RYŪ...

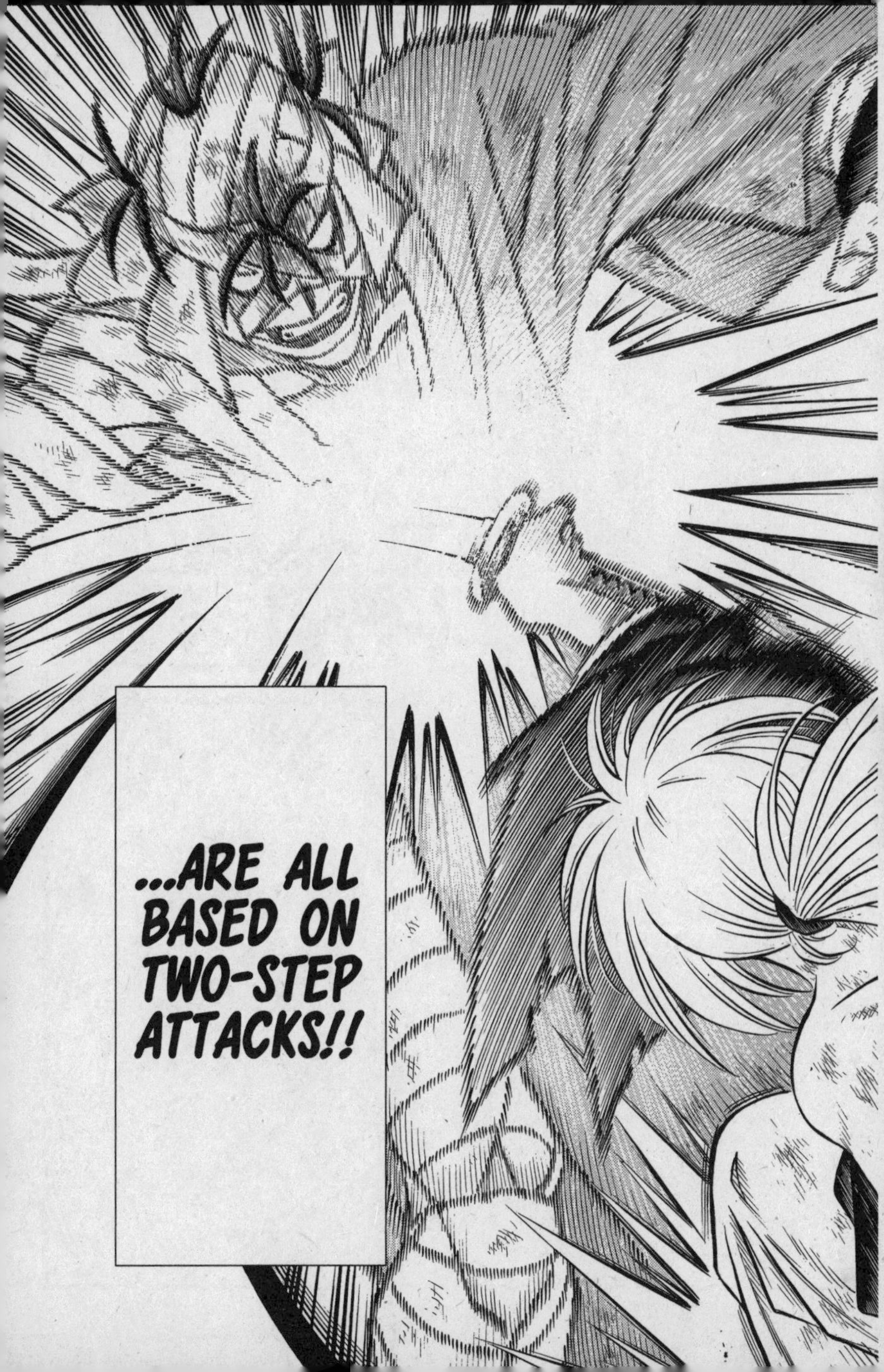
...ARE ALL BASED ON TWO-STEP ATTACKS!!

Rurouni Kenshin

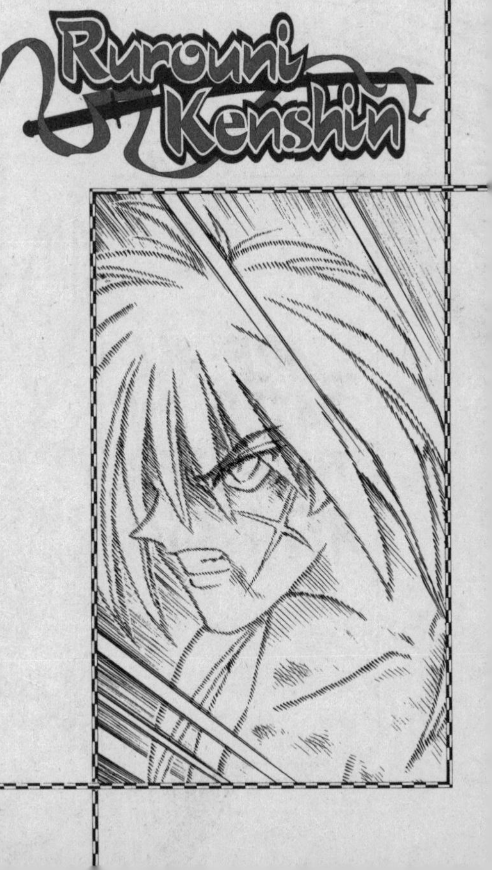

Act 144—Shape of Love

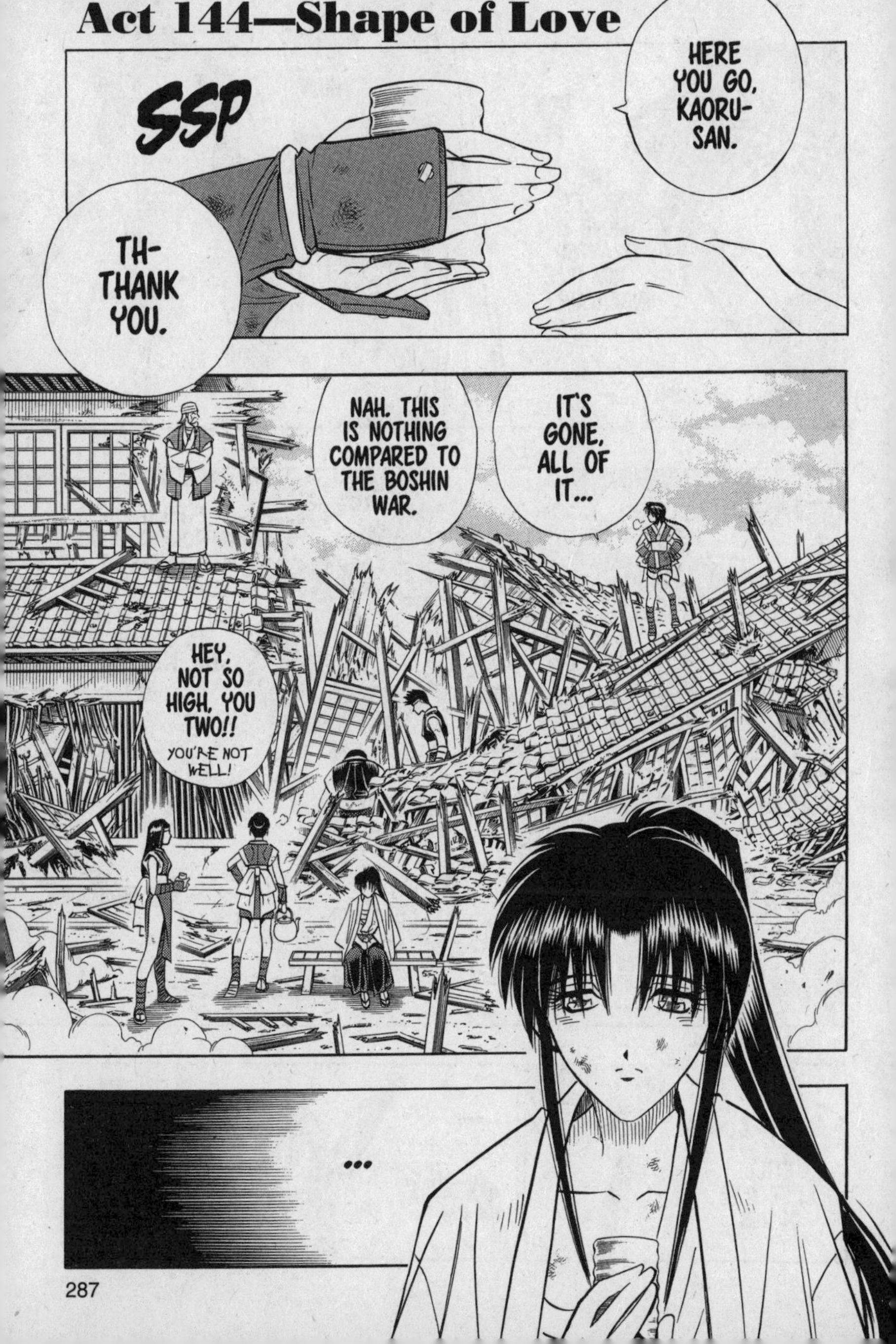
HERE YOU GO, KAORU-SAN.
SSP
TH-THANK YOU.
IT'S GONE, ALL OF IT...
NAH. THIS IS NOTHING COMPARED TO THE BOSHIN WAR.
HEY, NOT SO HIGH, YOU TWO!!
YOU'RE NOT WELL!
...

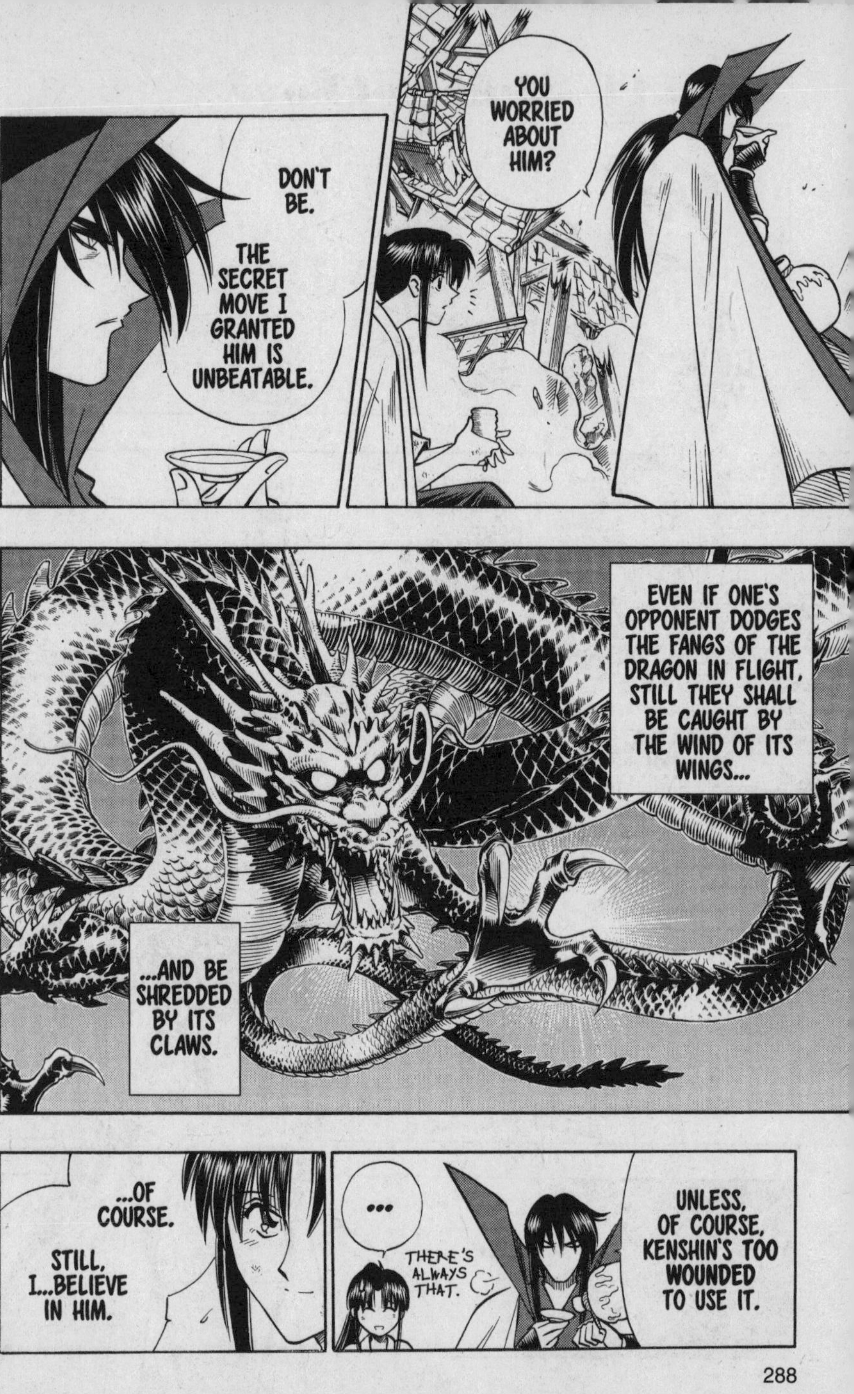
YOU WORRIED ABOUT HIM?
DON'T BE.
THE SECRET MOVE I GRANTED HIM IS UNBEATABLE.
EVEN IF ONE'S OPPONENT DODGES THE FANGS OF THE DRAGON IN FLIGHT, STILL THEY SHALL BE CAUGHT BY THE WIND OF ITS WINGS...
...AND BE SHREDDED BY ITS CLAWS.
UNLESS, OF COURSE, KENSHIN'S TOO WOUNDED TO USE IT.
THERE'S ALWAYS THAT.
...
...OF COURSE.
STILL, I...BELIEVE IN HIM.

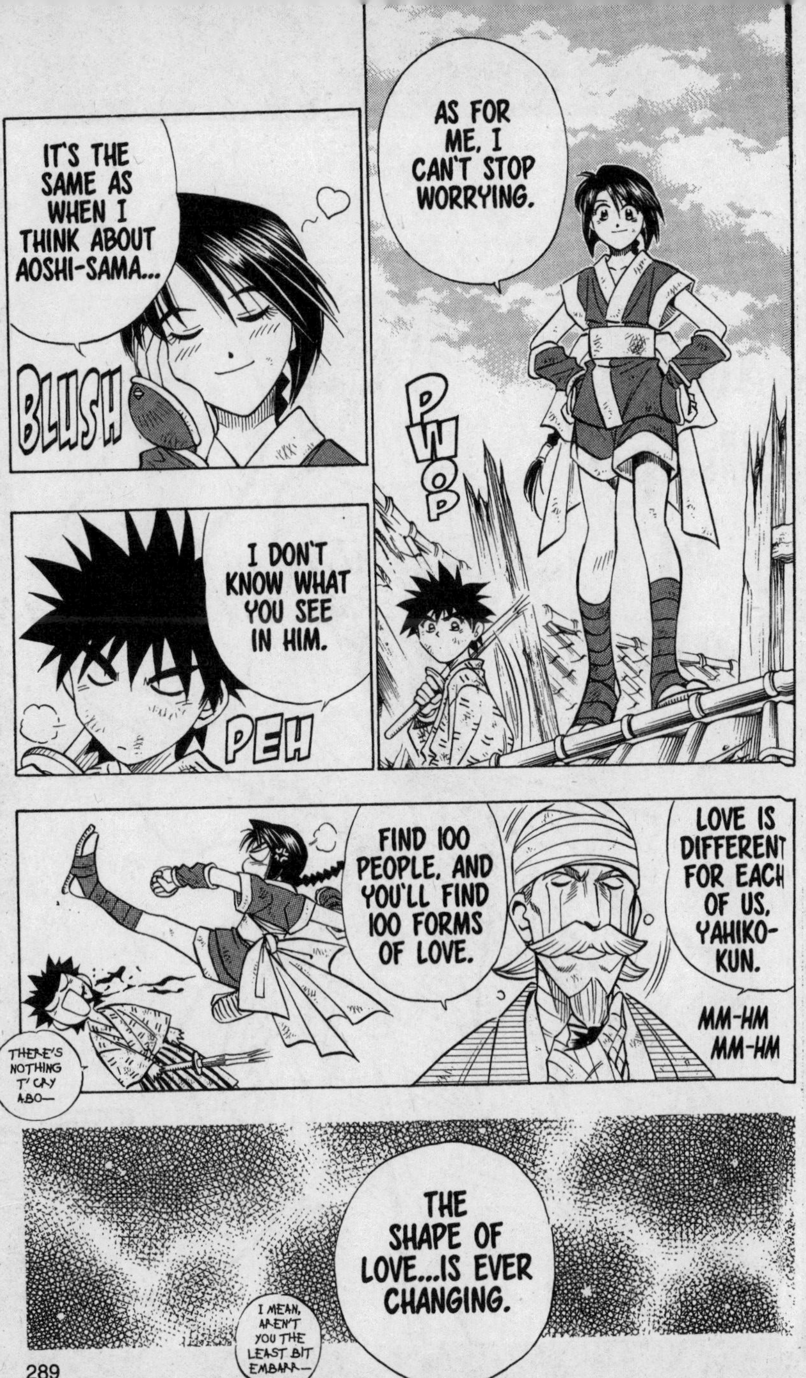
AS FOR ME, I CAN'T STOP WORRYING.
PWOP
IT'S THE SAME AS WHEN I THINK ABOUT AOSHI-SAMA...
BLUSH
I DON'T KNOW WHAT YOU SEE IN HIM.
PEH
LOVE IS DIFFERENT FOR EACH OF US, YAHIKO-KUN.
MM-HM MM-HM
FIND 100 PEOPLE, AND YOU'LL FIND 100 FORMS OF LOVE.
THERE'S NOTHING T' CRY ABO—
THE SHAPE OF LOVE...IS EVER CHANGING.
I MEAN, AREN'T YOU THE LEAST BIT EMBARR—

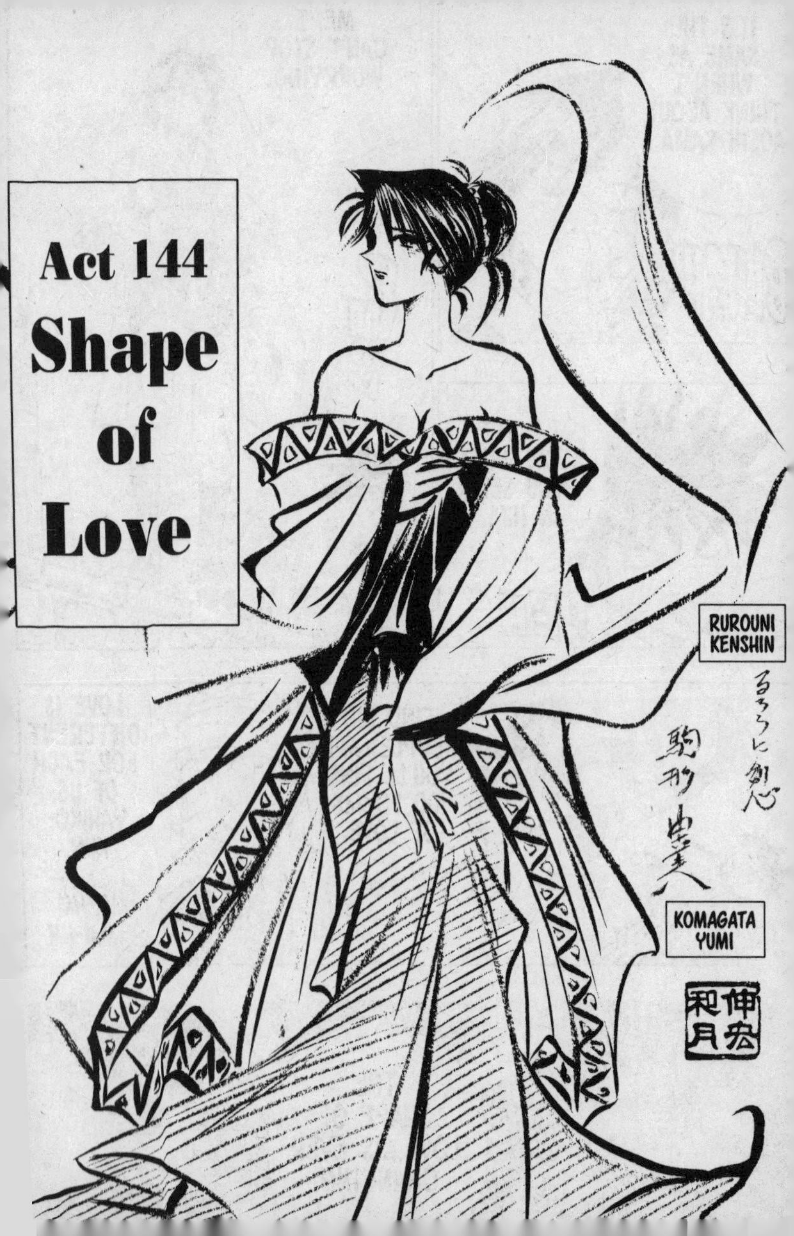
Act 144
Shape of Love
RUROUNI KENSHIN
るろうに剣心
駒形由美
KOMAGATA YUMI
伸宏
和月

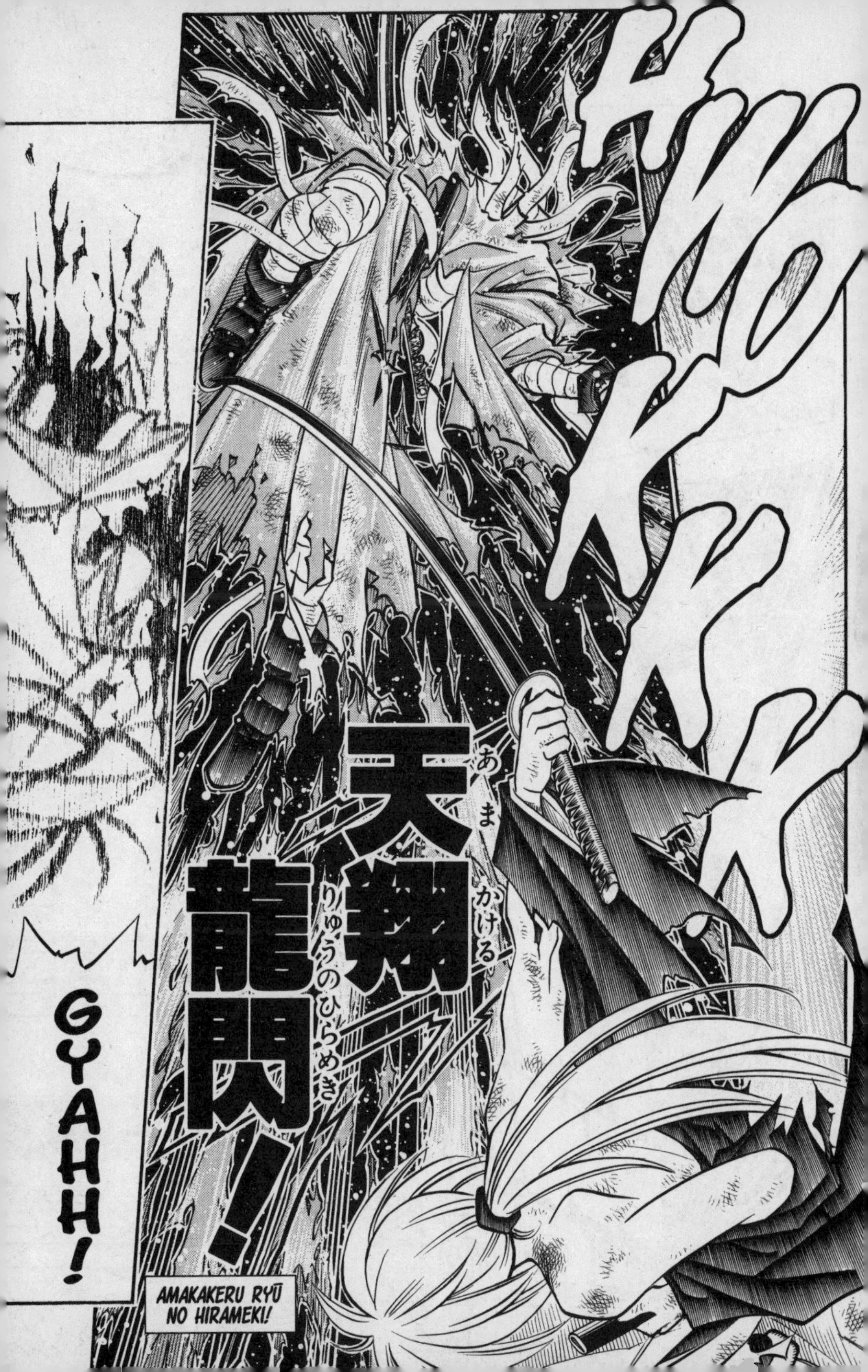
天翔龍閃！
AMAKAKERU RYŪ NO HIRAMEKI!
GYAHH!

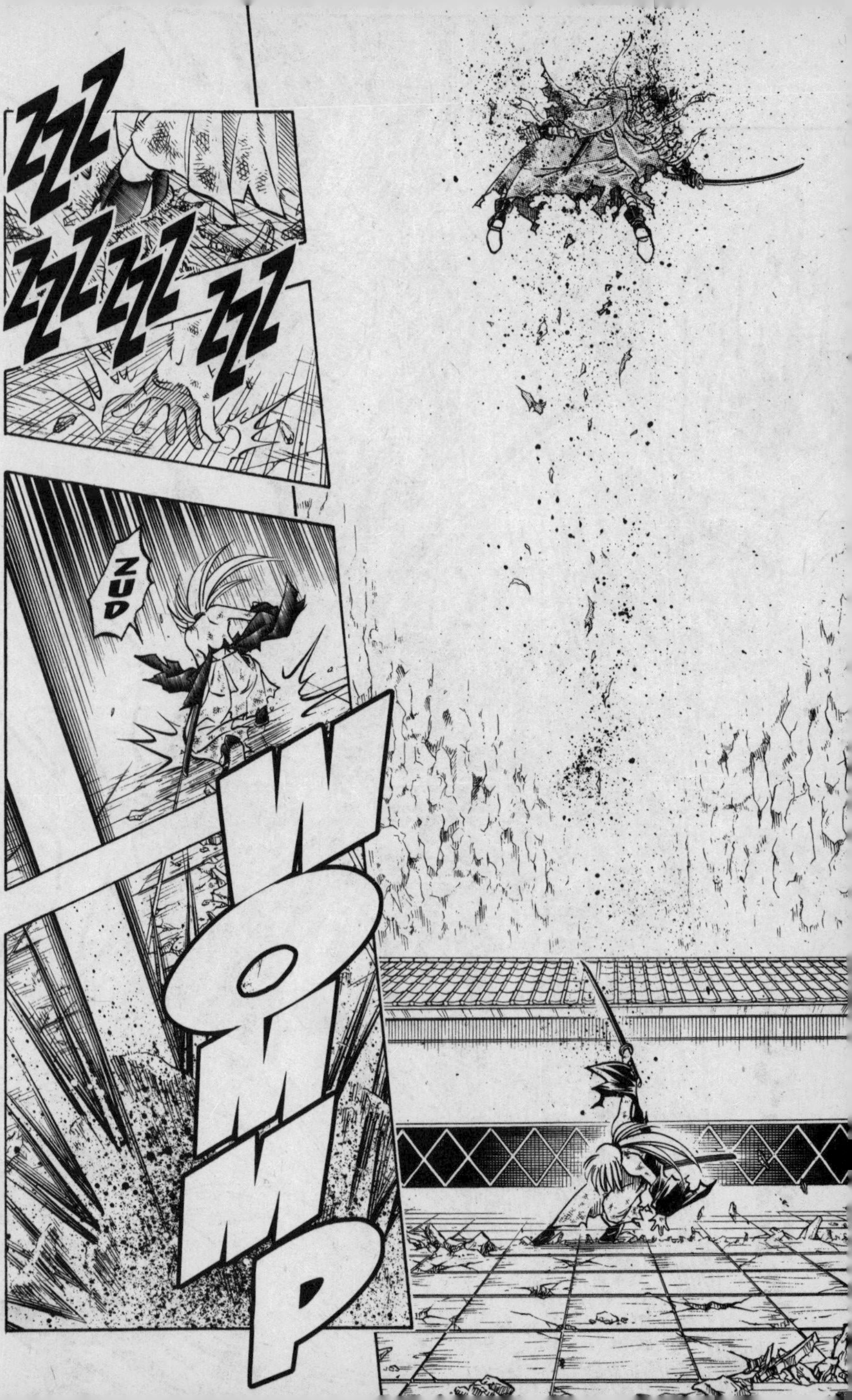
ZZZ
ZZZZZ
ZZZ
ZUD
WOMMP

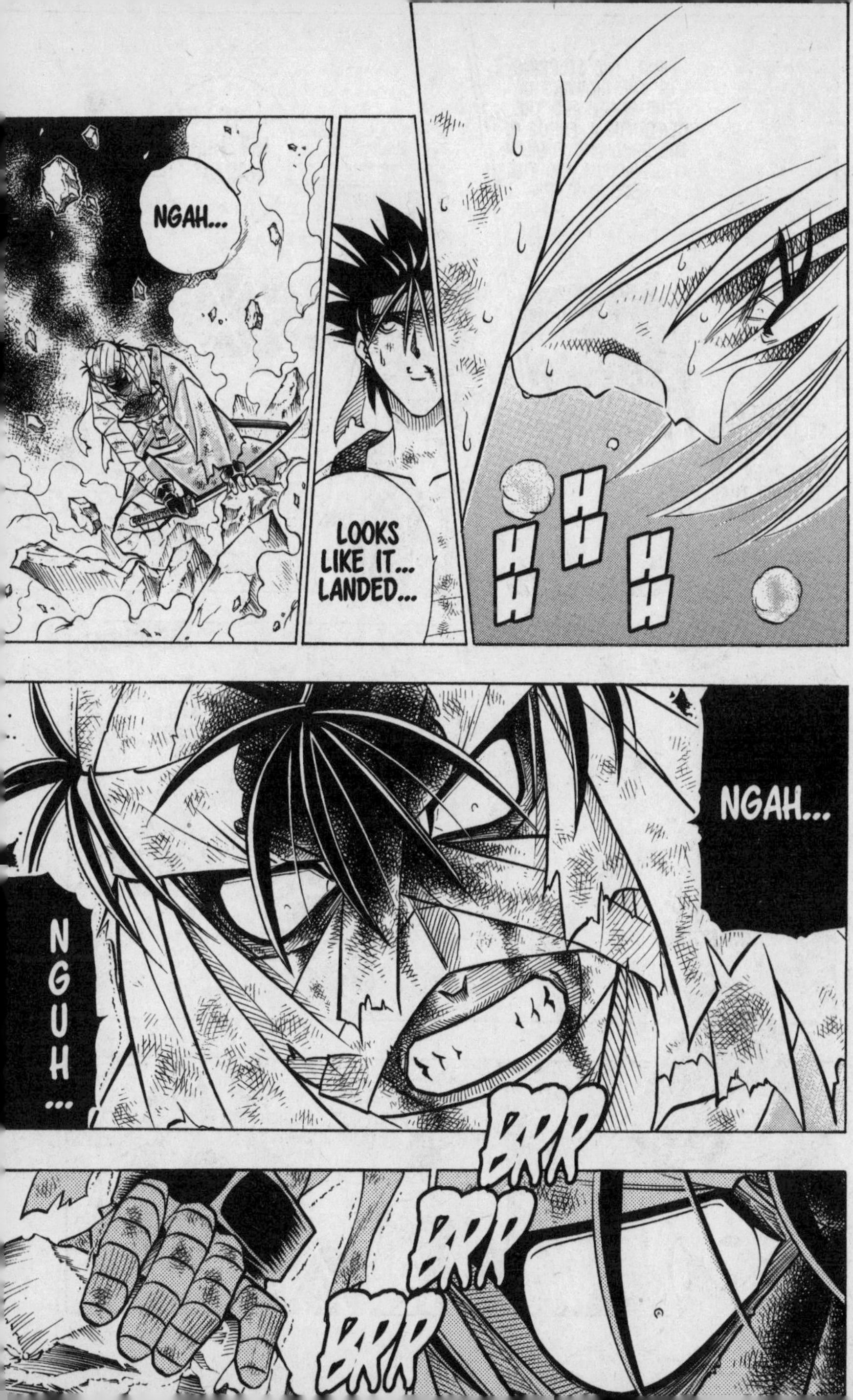
HH
HH
HH
LOOKS LIKE IT... LANDED...
NGAH...
NGAH...
NGUH...
BRR
BRR
BRR

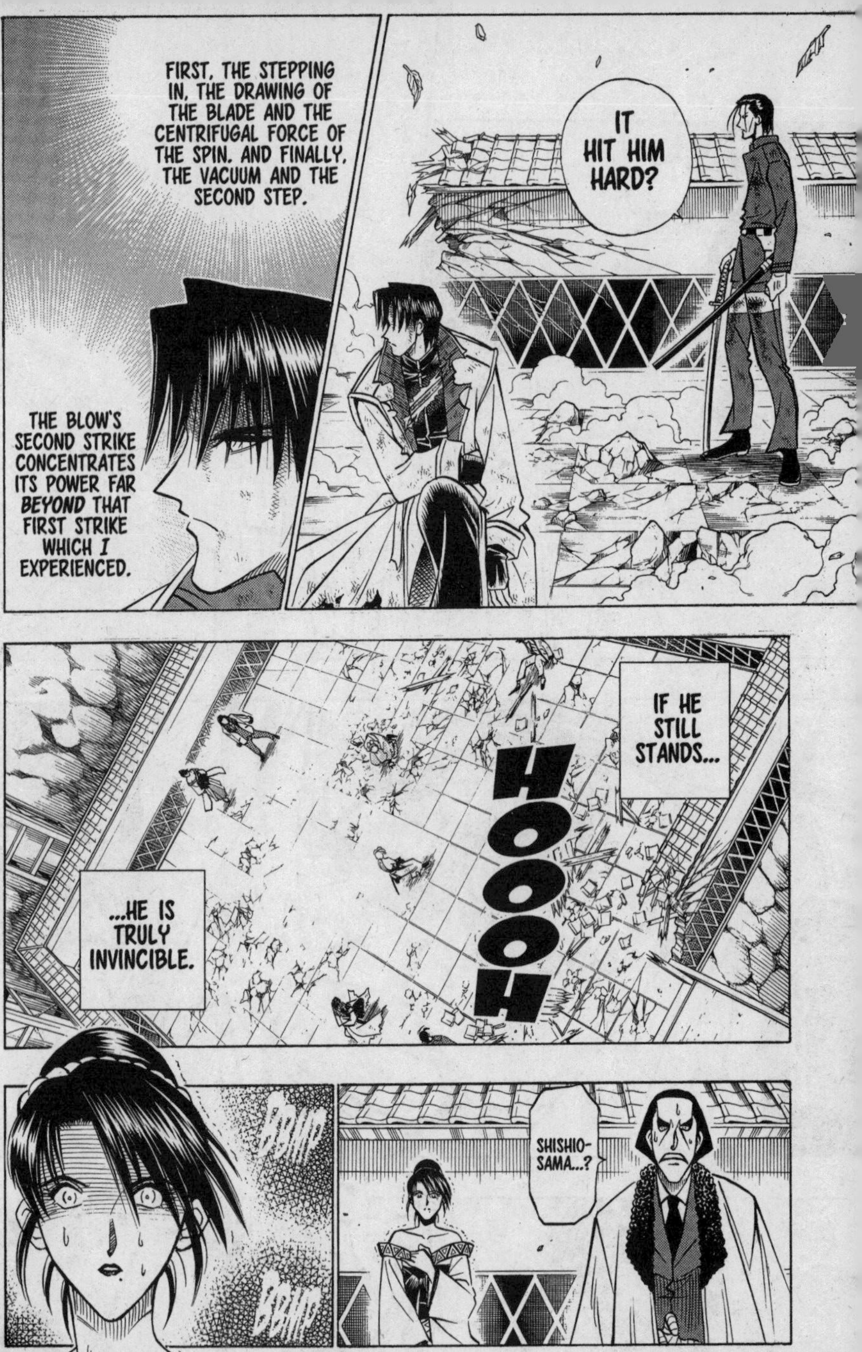
IT HIT HIM HARD?
FIRST, THE STEPPING IN, THE DRAWING OF THE BLADE AND THE CENTRIFUGAL FORCE OF THE SPIN. AND FINALLY, THE VACUUM AND THE SECOND STEP.
THE BLOW'S SECOND STRIKE CONCENTRATES ITS POWER FAR *BEYOND* THAT FIRST STRIKE WHICH *I* EXPERIENCED.
IF HE STILL STANDS...
HOOOOH
...HE IS TRULY INVINCIBLE.
SHISHIO-SAMA...?

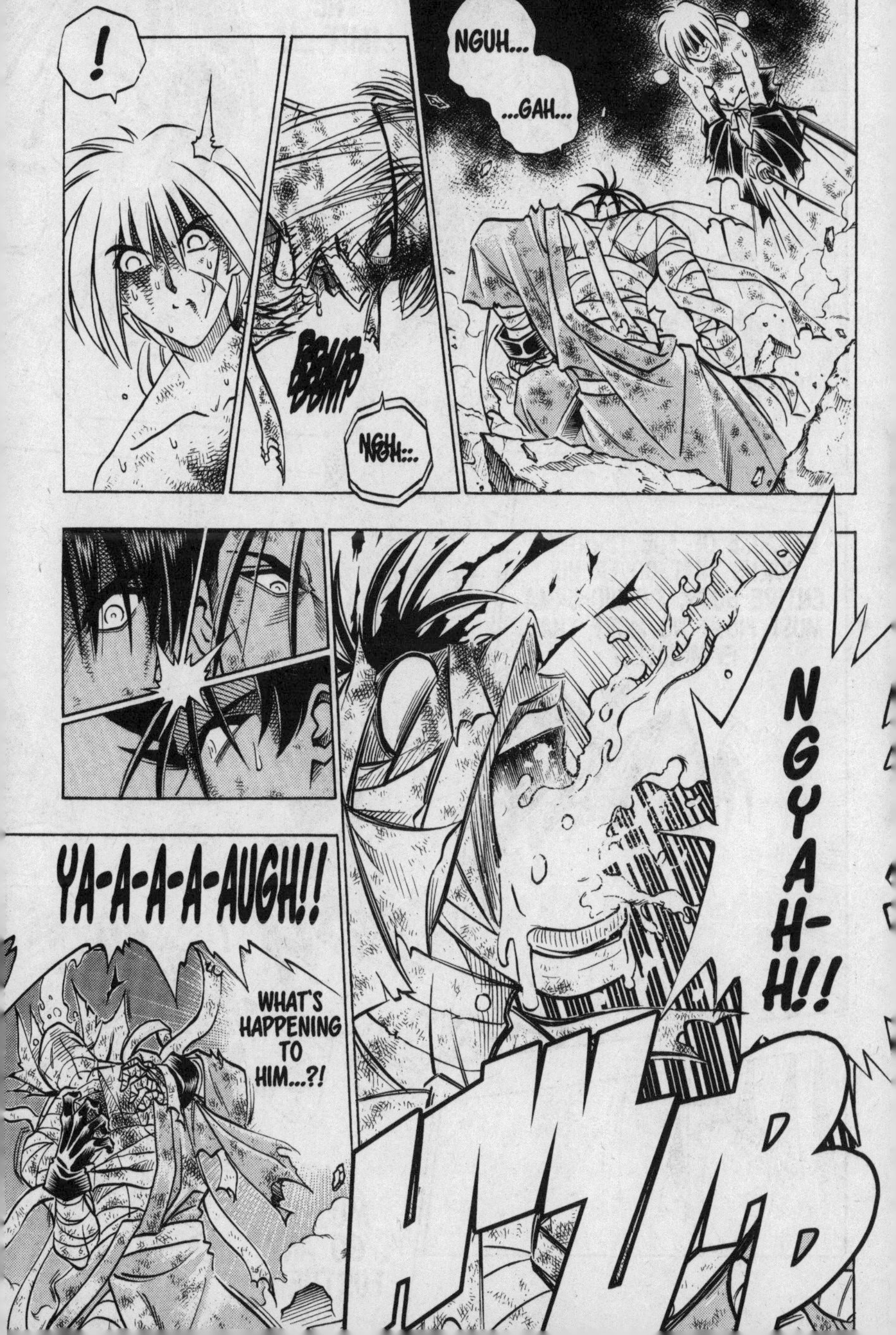
NGUH...
...GAH...
NGH NGH...
BBUMP BBUMP
!
NGYAH-H!!
YA-A-A-A-AUGH!!
WHAT'S HAPPENING TO HIM...?!

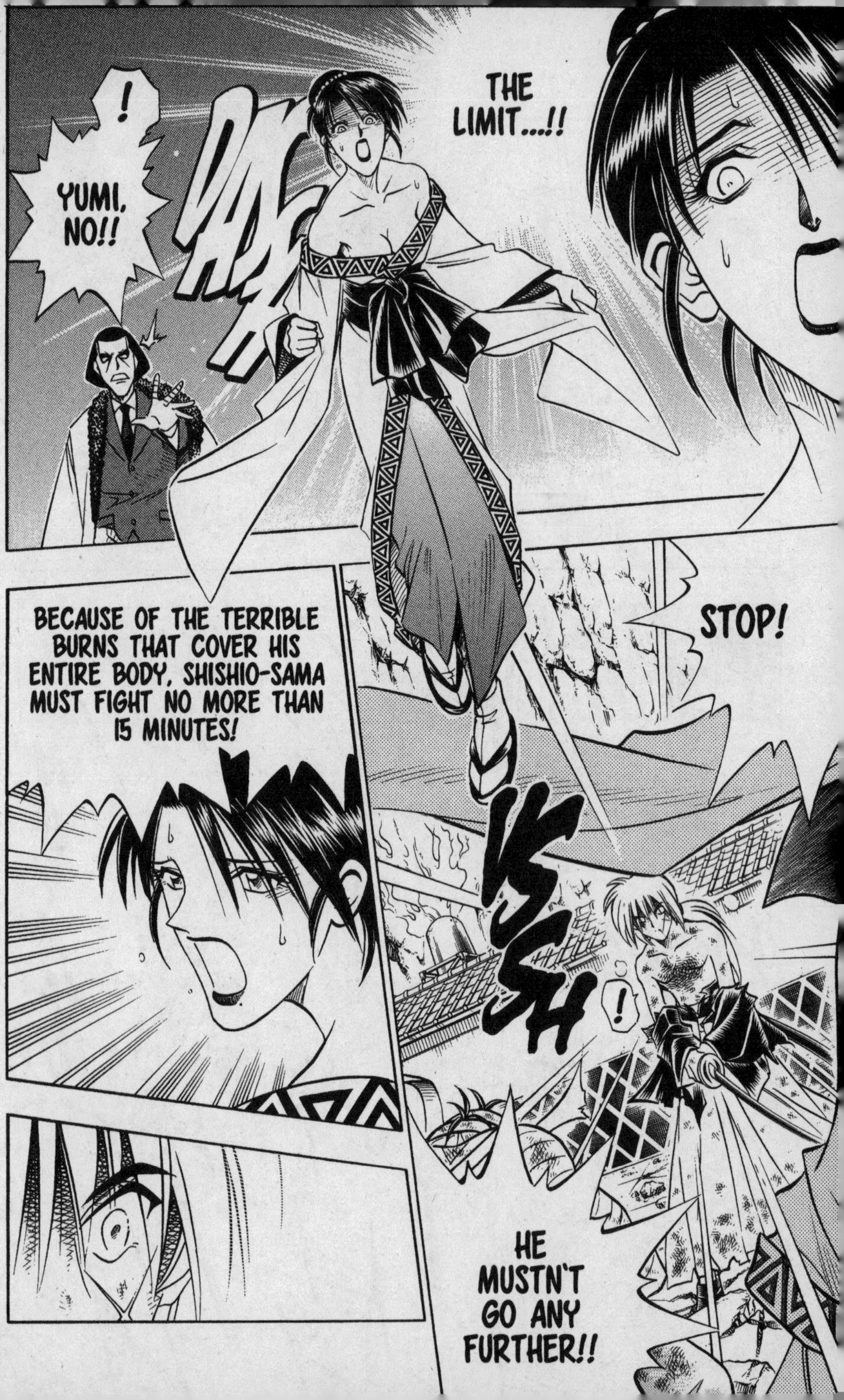
THE LIMIT...!!
!
YUMI, NO!!
STOP!
!
BECAUSE OF THE TERRIBLE BURNS THAT COVER HIS ENTIRE BODY, SHISHIO-SAMA MUST FIGHT NO MORE THAN 15 MINUTES!
HE MUSTN'T GO ANY FURTHER!!

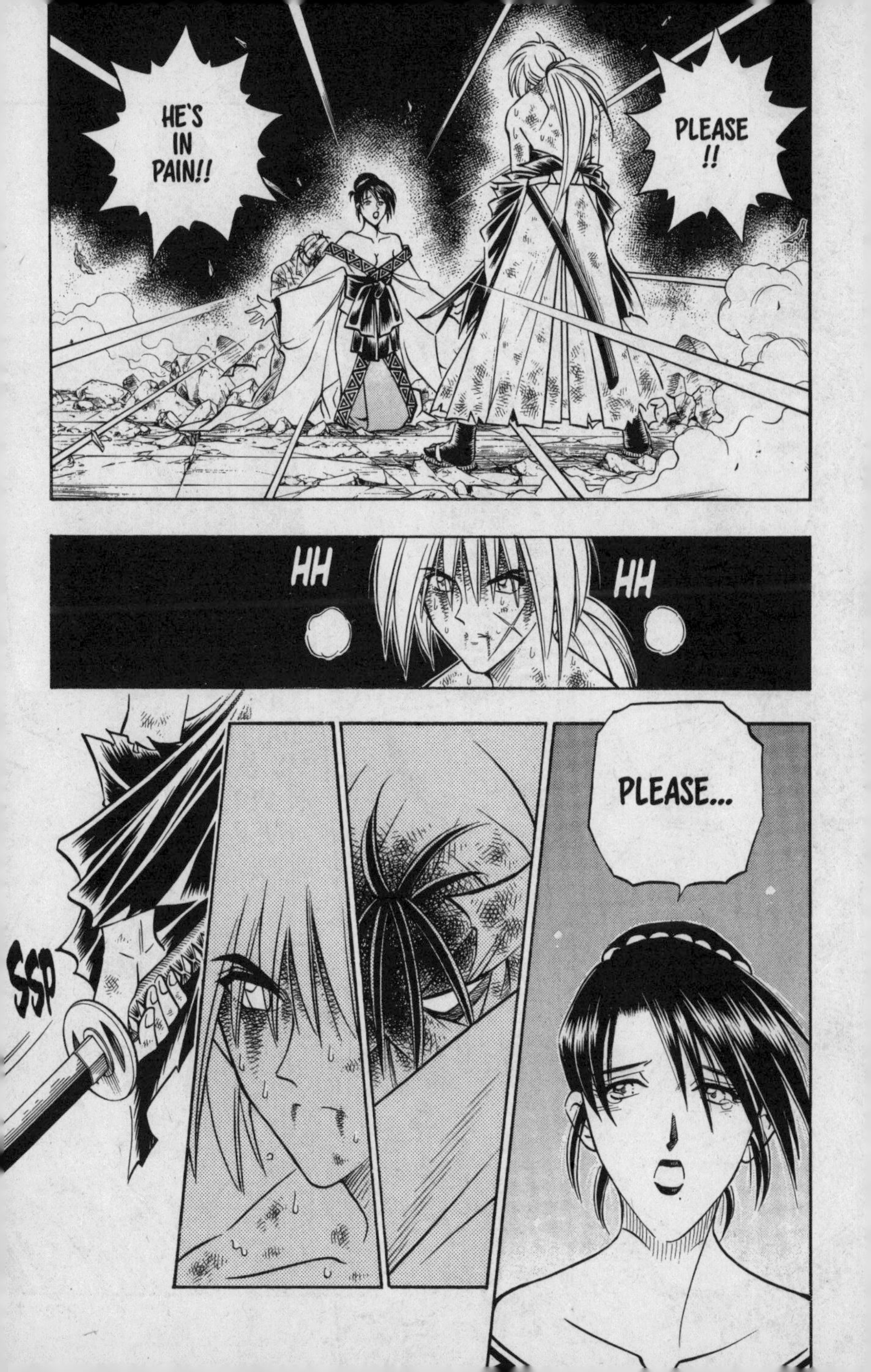
PLEASE !!
HE'S IN PAIN!!
HH
HH
PLEASE...
SSP

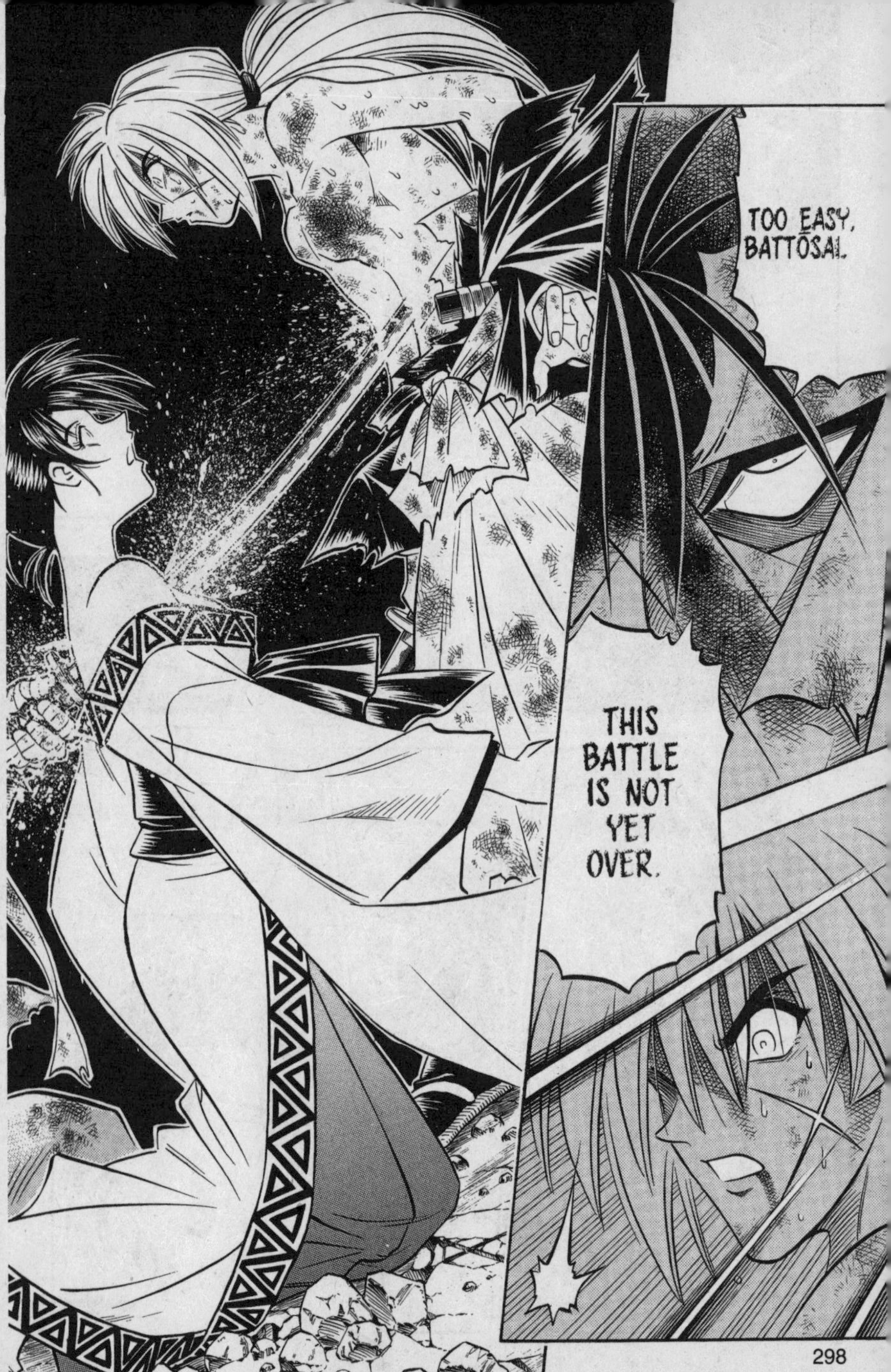
TOO EASY, BATTŌSAI.
THIS BATTLE IS NOT YET OVER.

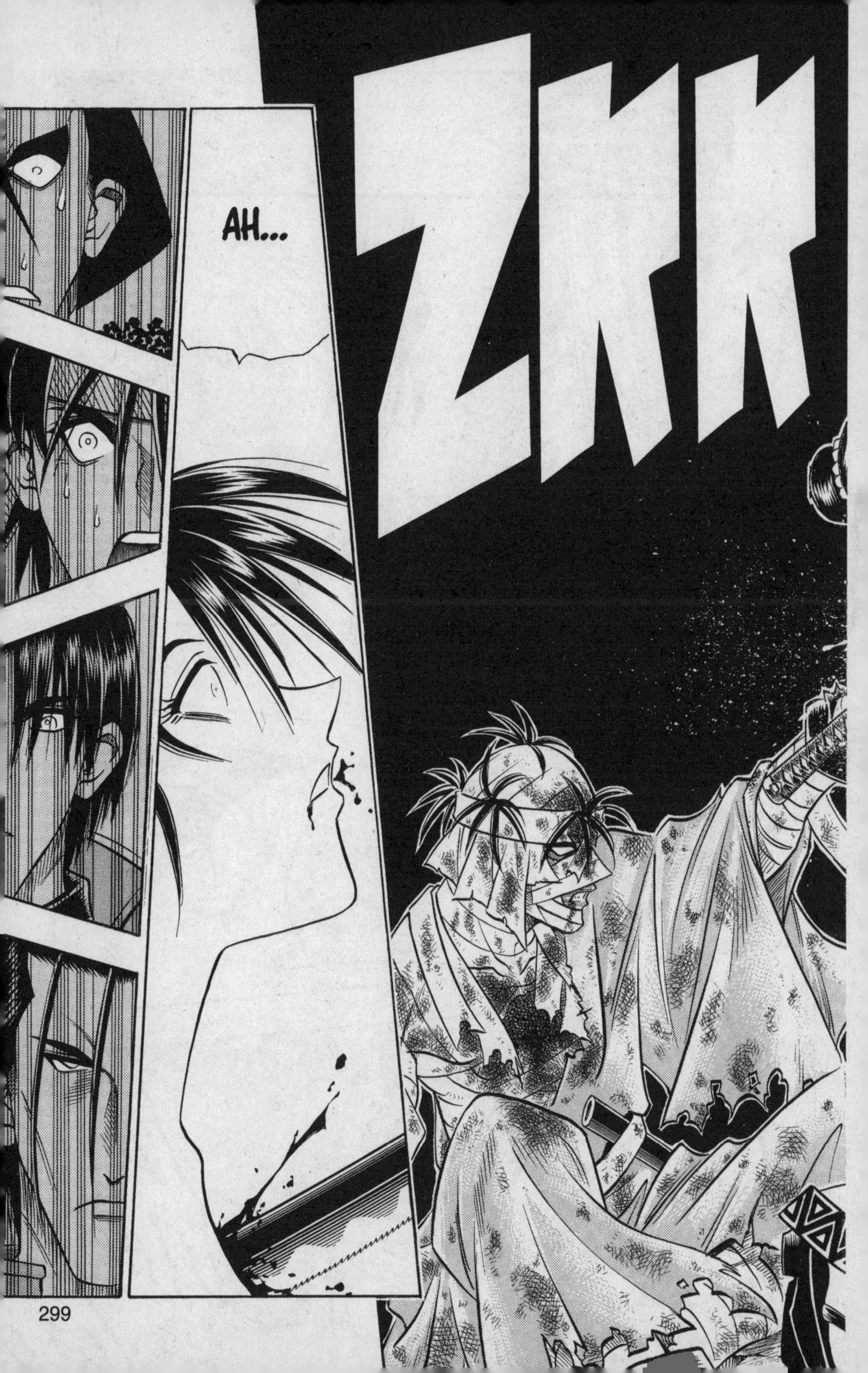
ZKK
AH...

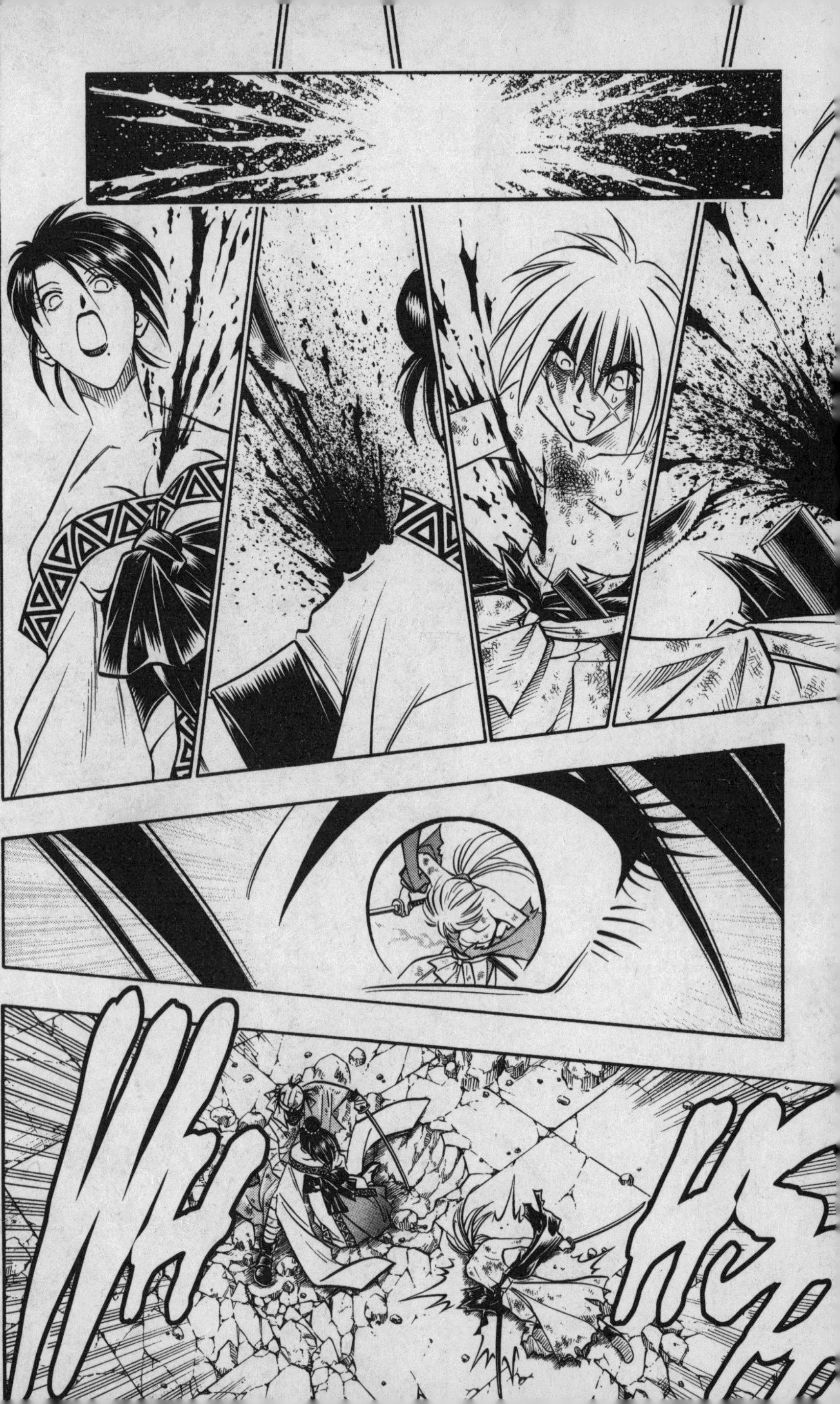

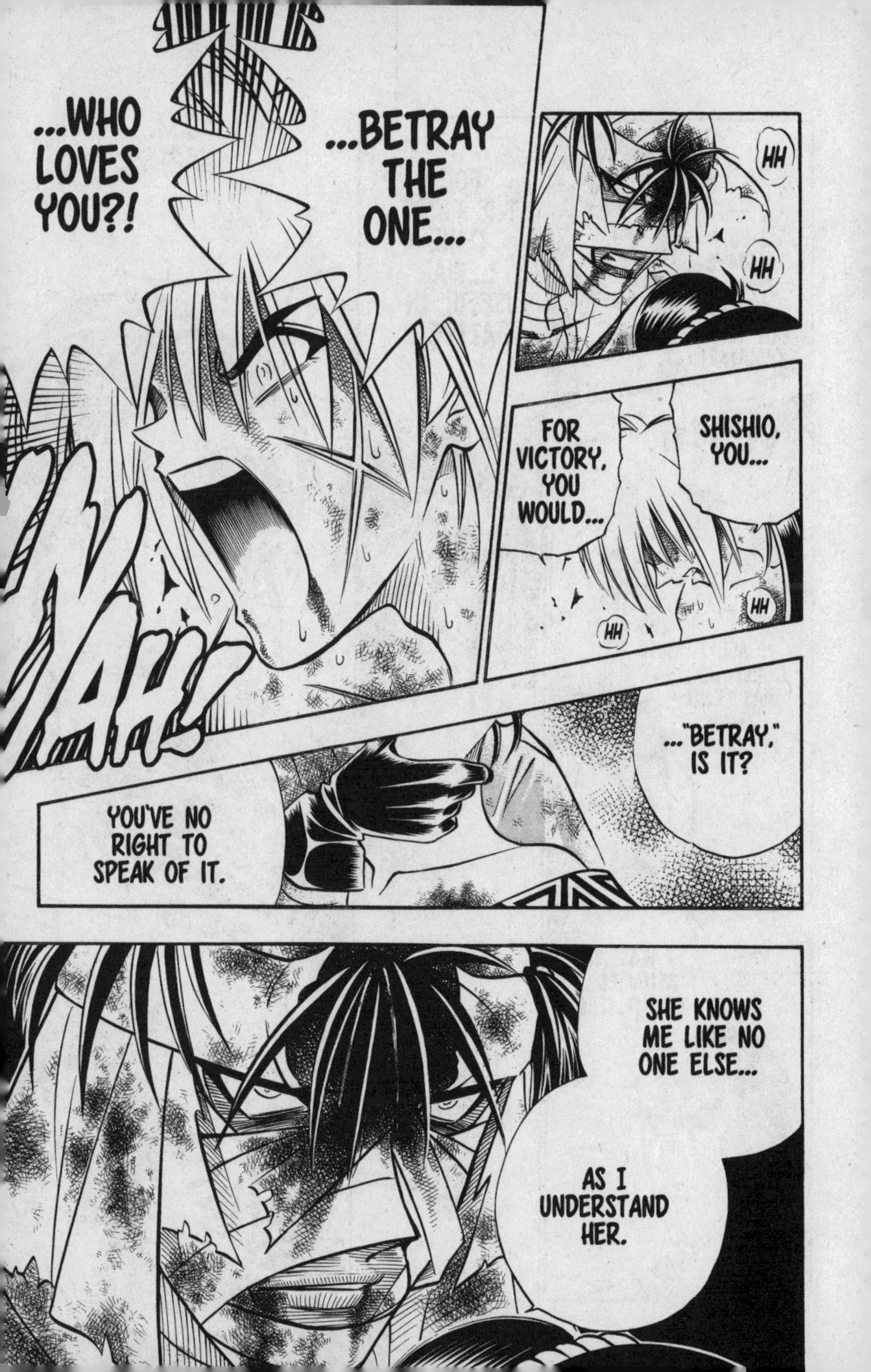
HH
HH
SHISHIO, YOU...
FOR VICTORY, YOU WOULD...
HH
HH
...BETRAY THE ONE...
...WHO LOVES YOU?!
NAH!
..."BETRAY," IS IT?
YOU'VE NO RIGHT TO SPEAK OF IT.
SHE KNOWS ME LIKE NO ONE ELSE...
AS I UNDERSTAND HER.

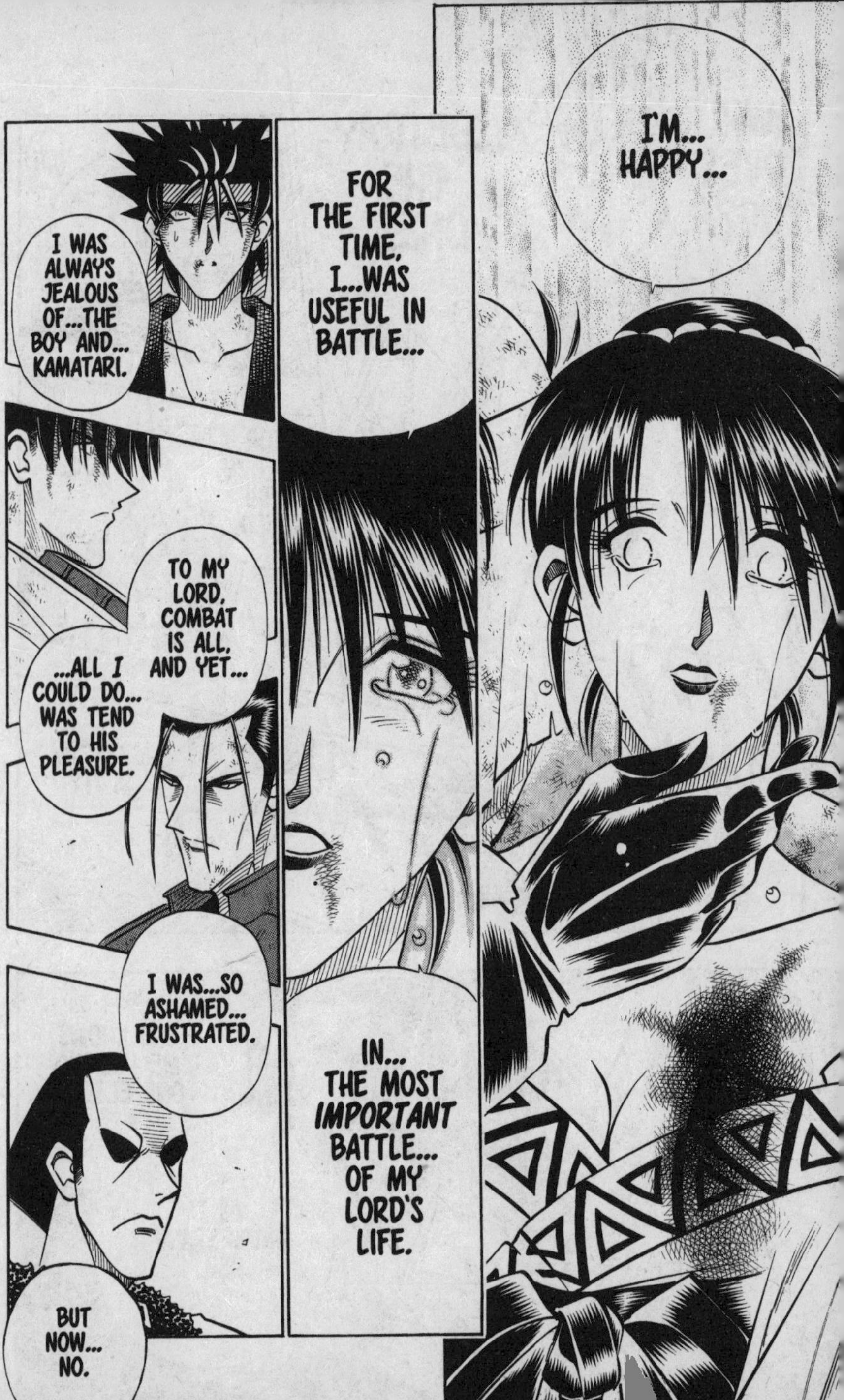
I WAS ALWAYS JEALOUS OF...THE BOY AND... KAMATARI.
TO MY LORD, COMBAT IS ALL, AND YET...
...ALL I COULD DO... WAS TEND TO HIS PLEASURE.
I WAS...SO ASHAMED... FRUSTRATED.
BUT NOW... NO.
FOR THE FIRST TIME, I...WAS USEFUL IN BATTLE...
IN... THE MOST *IMPORTANT* BATTLE... OF MY LORD'S LIFE.
I'M... HAPPY...

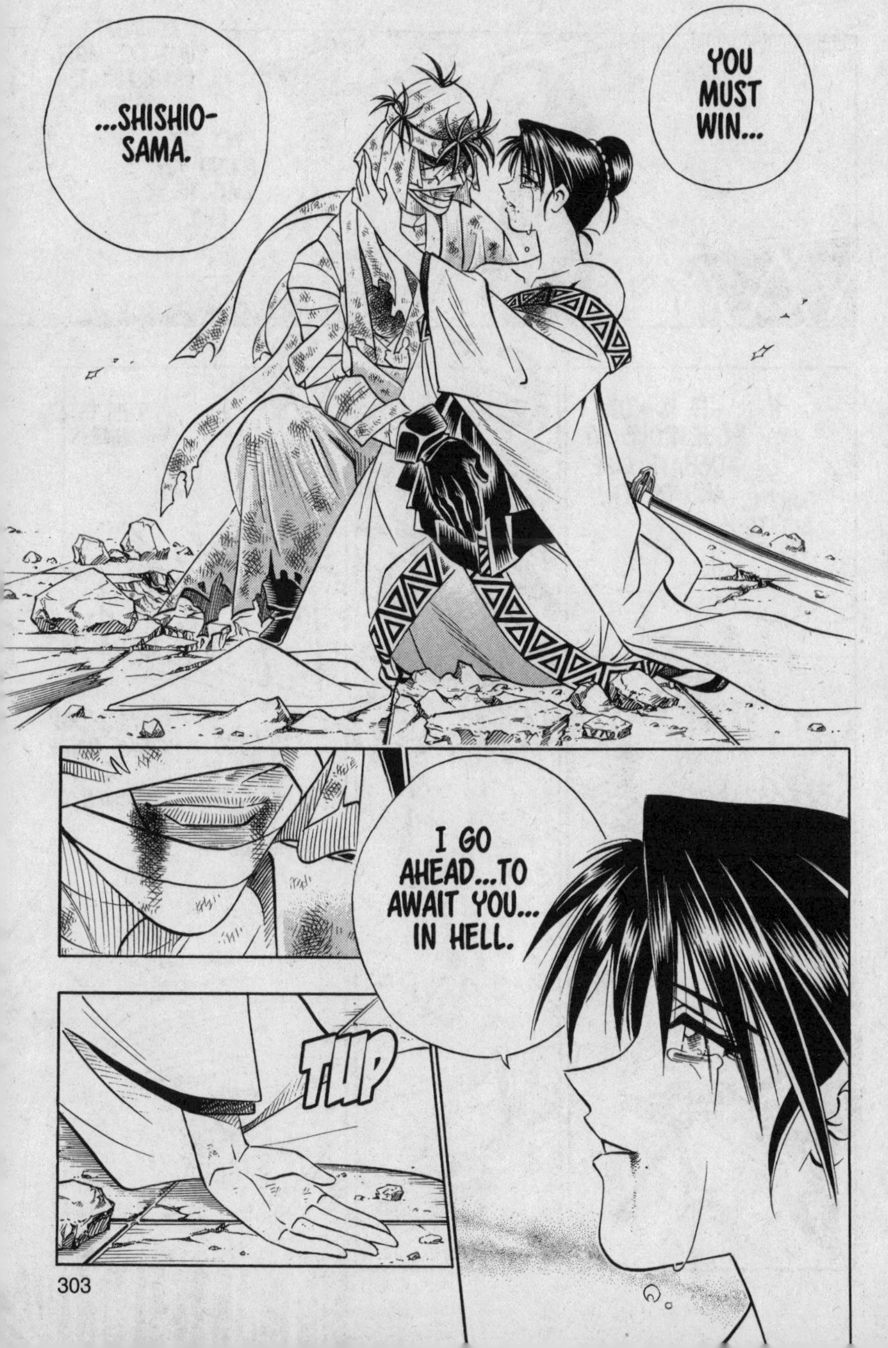
YOU MUST WIN...
...SHISHIO-SAMA.
I GO AHEAD...TO AWAIT YOU... IN HELL.
TUP

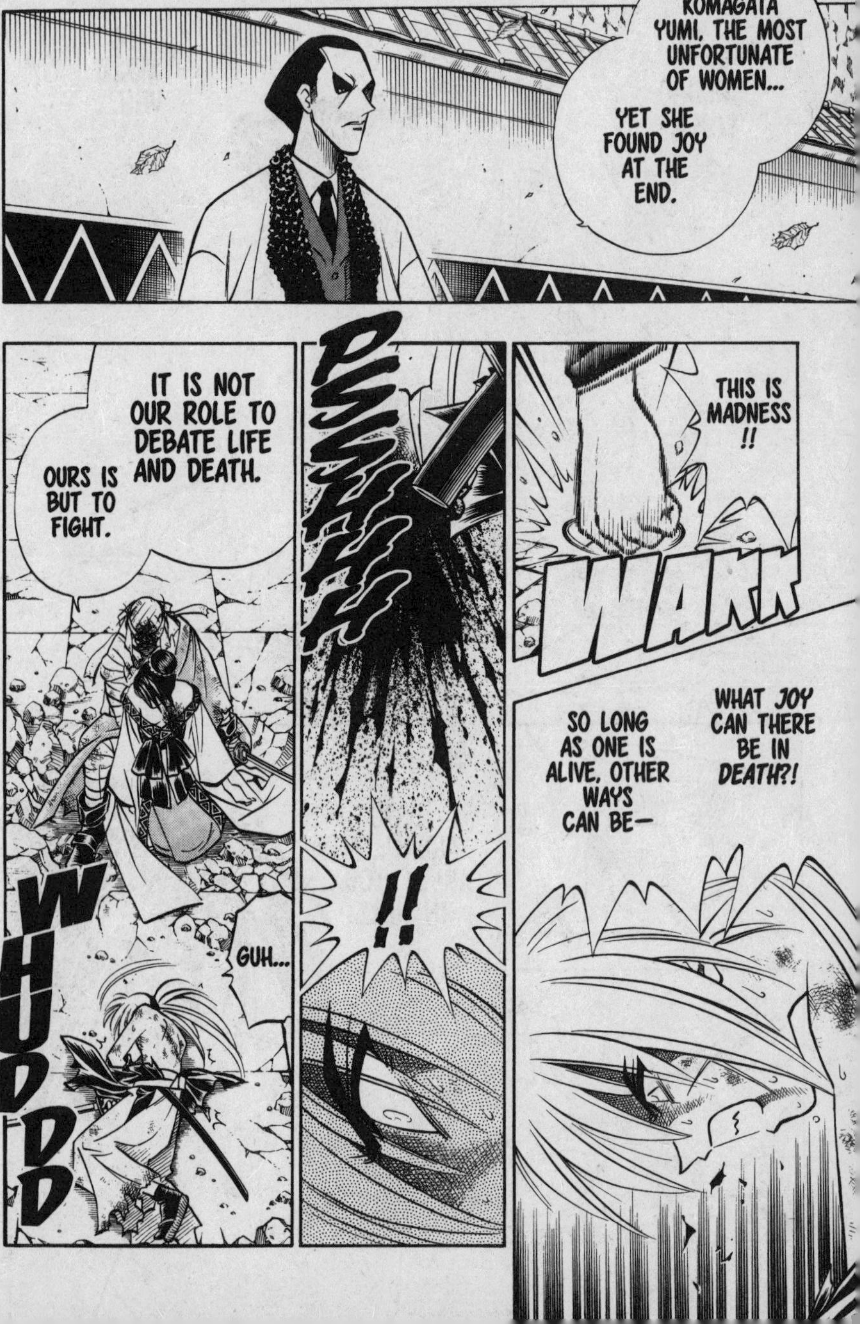
KOMAGATA YUMI, THE MOST UNFORTUNATE OF WOMEN...
YET SHE FOUND JOY AT THE END.
THIS IS MADNESS !!
WAKK
WHAT JOY CAN THERE BE IN DEATH?!
SO LONG AS ONE IS ALIVE, OTHER WAYS CAN BE—
PSSHHH
!!
IT IS NOT OUR ROLE TO DEBATE LIFE AND DEATH.
OURS IS BUT TO FIGHT.
WHUDDD
GUH...

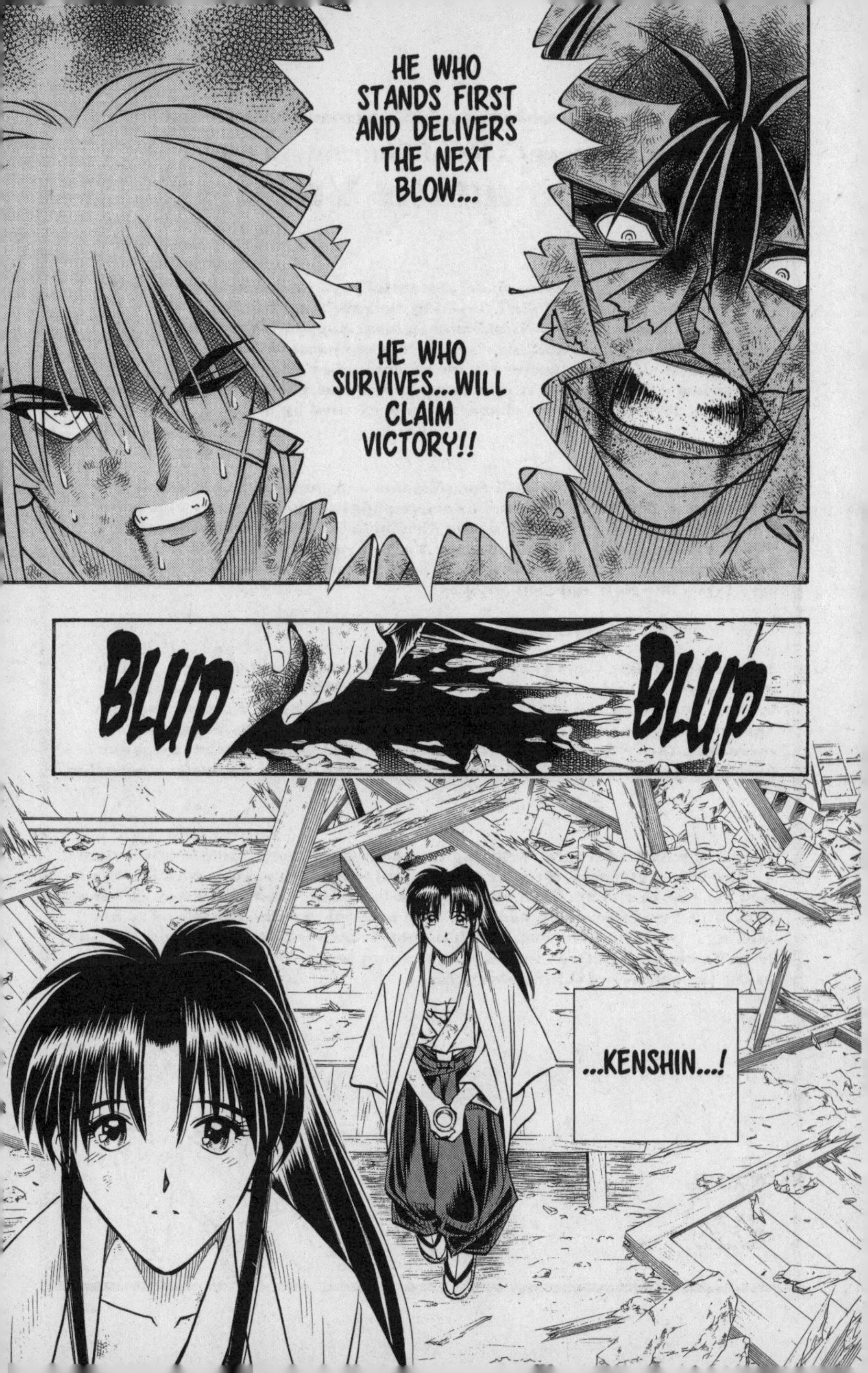
HE WHO STANDS FIRST AND DELIVERS THE NEXT BLOW...
HE WHO SURVIVES...WILL CLAIM VICTORY!!
BLUP
BLUP
...KENSHIN...!

The Secret Life of Characters (40)
—Komagata Yumi—

Personality-wise, she has no model. Essentially, as her name suggests, she's a version of the character Ogin (played by actress Yumi Kaoru) in the *Mitokōmon* spin-off series, *Mitokōmon Gaiden: Kagerō Ninpō-Chō*. Initially created to be sexy and nothing else, one might almost say she wasn't a character at all, but an accessory for Shishio; after all, a proper villain always has a temptress or two hanging off his arm, right? Imagine my surprise to see her developing into a character so motivated by love....

The way she died brought both compliments and complaints, but as I had conceived of happiness for Yumi as accompanying Shishio everywhere, it struck me that "everywhere" would also include Hell. (Kenshin may say, "What joy is there in death?," but for Yumi the point isn't death, it's being with her love.) And how boring for Shishio to be surrounded only by middle-aged types like Hōji and Usui anyway!

In terms of design, I can't say there's a model. As I've said, her only function was to be sexy, so I designed her on the spot. Halfway through, though, I became hooked on the character Morrigan from *Vampire Hunter*, and thus kept exposing more and more of the shoulders and cleavage, eventually increasing the sexiness by about 120%. I've heard that fans who try and dress as her for "cosplay" have a difficult time keeping the top up; sorry about that.

I always have had trouble drawing women and, honestly speaking, this time I'd just about given up. What drawing Yumi helped me realize was, fun can be had not just in making them cute but also in making them seductive, or even evil. With Yumi's sexed-up body, messing up even one line could lead to her looking downright indecent, which taught its own lessons...while also driving home to me my relative inexperience. In that sense, Yumi was quite a tutor in the importance of skillful sketching.

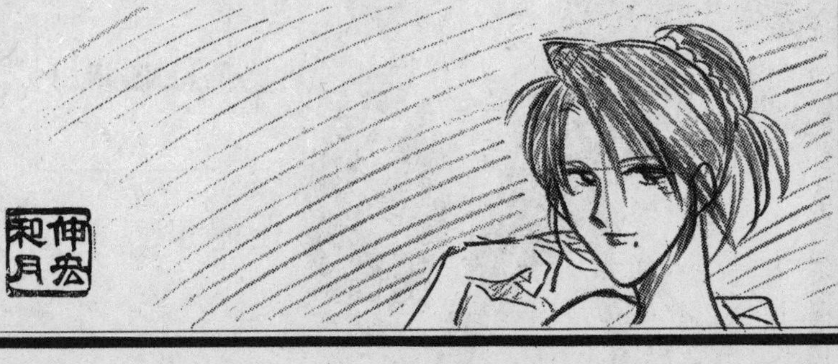
伸宏
和月

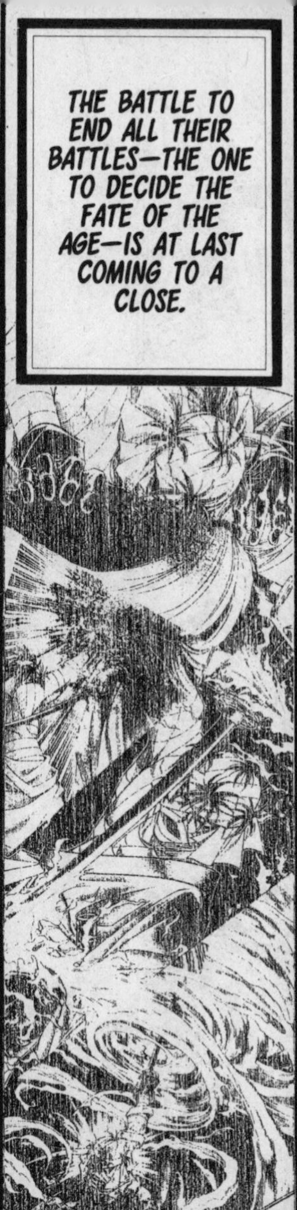
THE BATTLE TO END ALL THEIR BATTLES—THE ONE TO DECIDE THE FATE OF THE AGE—IS AT LAST COMING TO A CLOSE.

Act 145
Duel of an Era

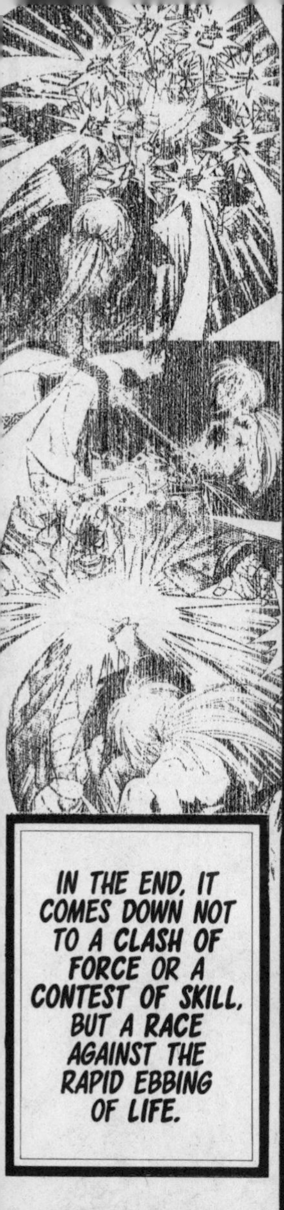
IN THE END, IT COMES DOWN NOT TO A CLASH OF FORCE OR A CONTEST OF SKILL, BUT A RACE AGAINST THE RAPID EBBING OF LIFE.

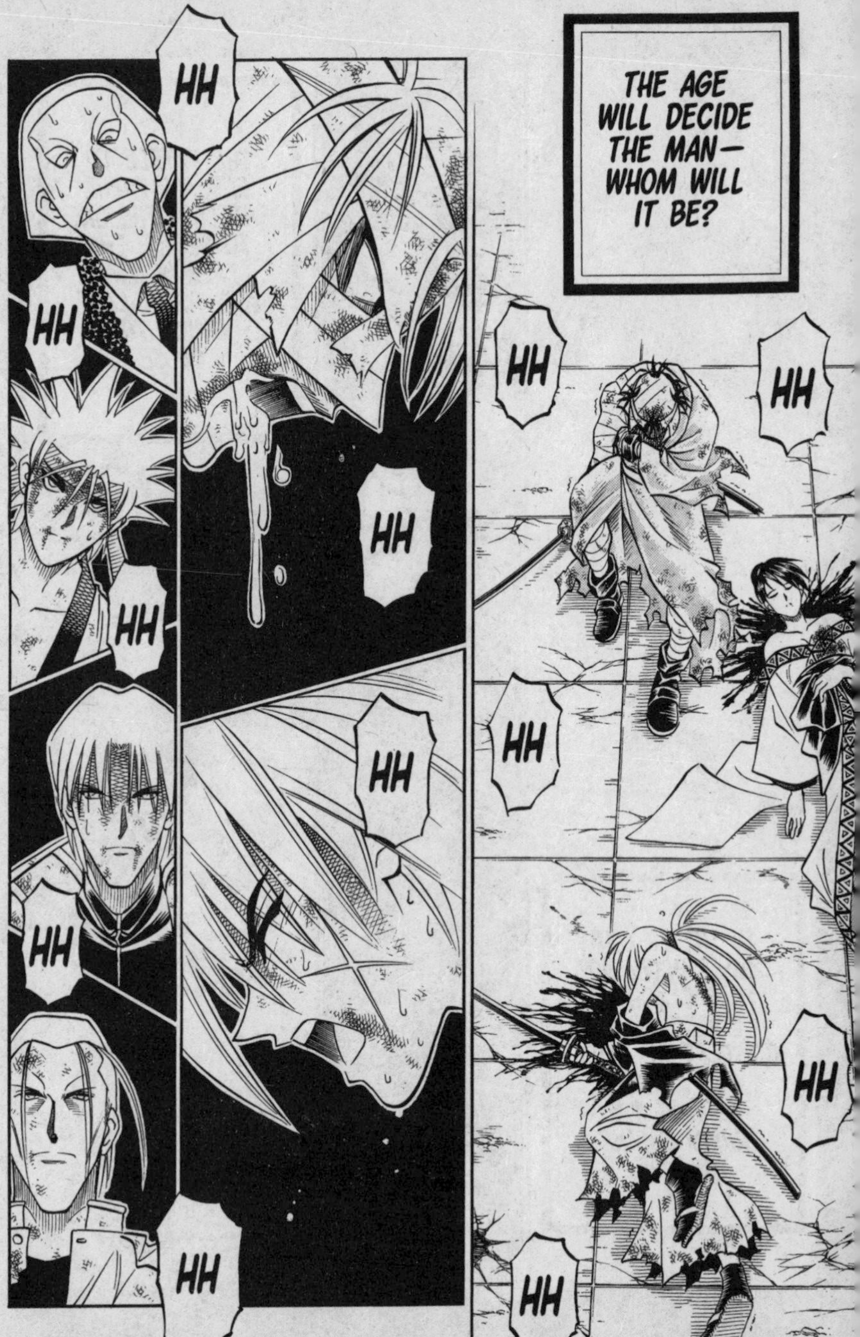
THE AGE WILL DECIDE THE MAN—WHOM WILL IT BE?
HH
HH
HH
HH
HH
HH
HH
HH
HH
HH
HH
HH

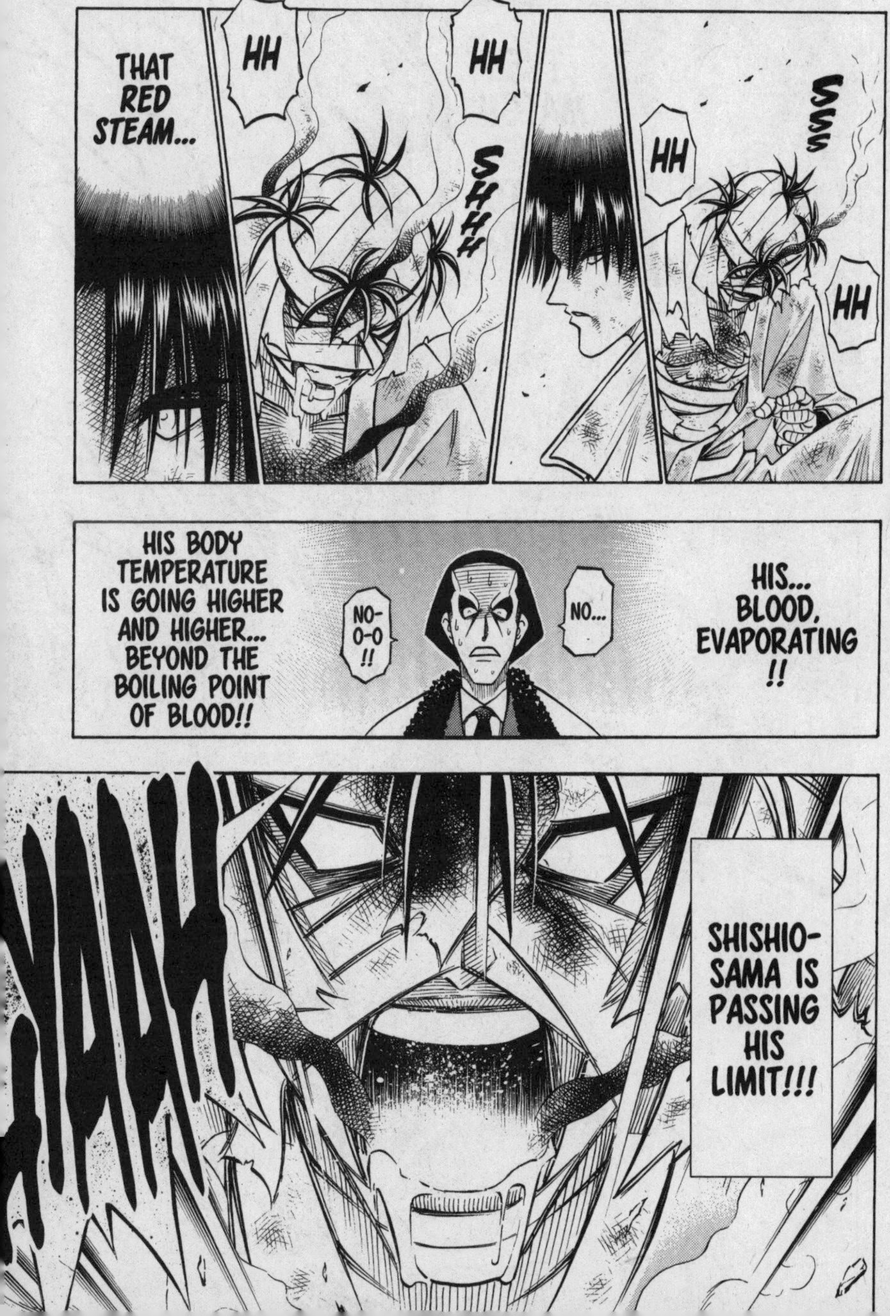
SSS
HH
HH
HH
SHHHH
HH
THAT RED STEAM...
HIS... BLOOD, EVAPORATING!!
NO...
NO-O-O!!
HIS BODY TEMPERATURE IS GOING HIGHER AND HIGHER... BEYOND THE BOILING POINT OF BLOOD!!
SHISHIO-SAMA IS PASSING HIS LIMIT!!!

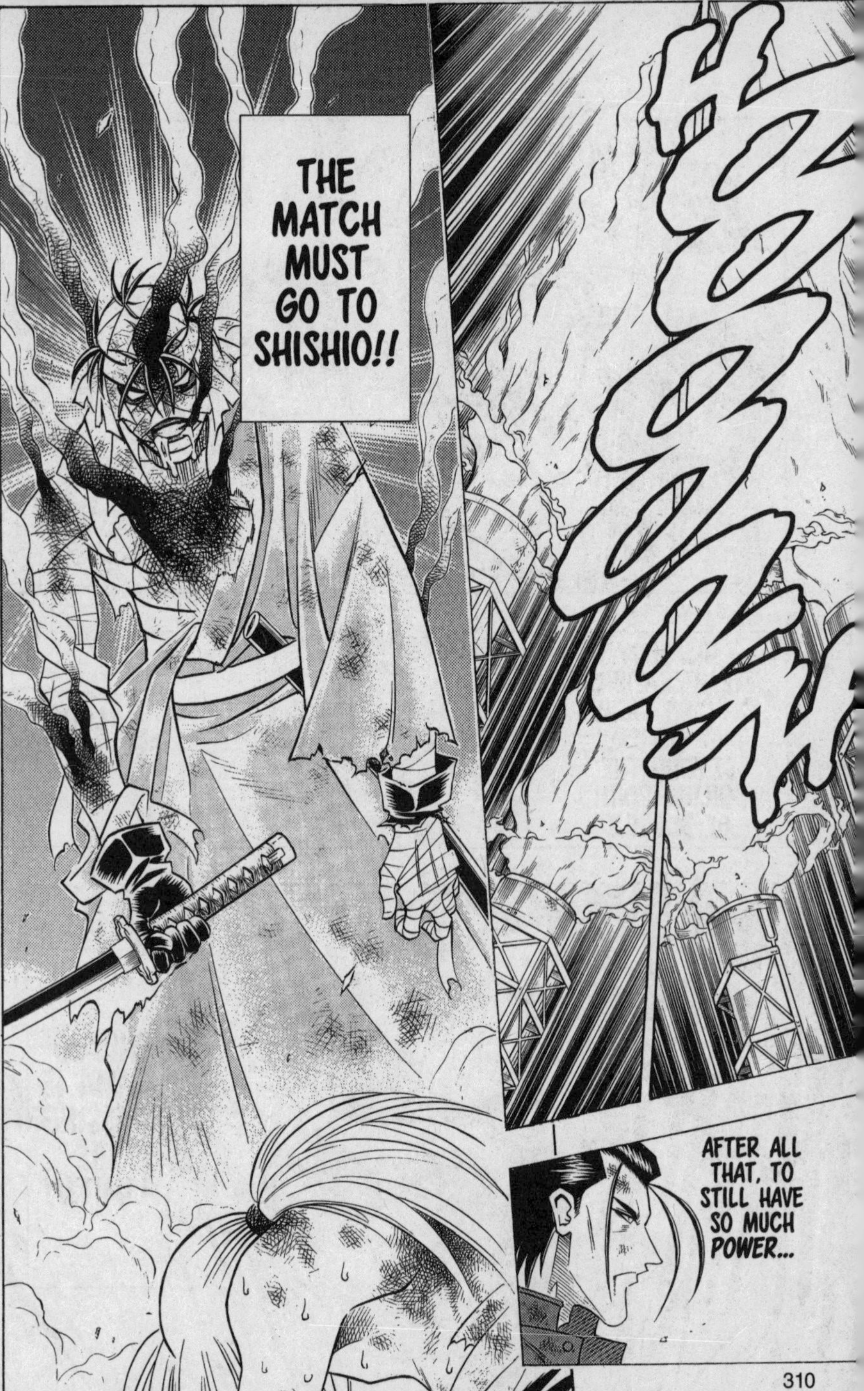
AFTER ALL THAT, TO STILL HAVE SO MUCH POWER...
THE MATCH MUST GO TO SHISHIO!!

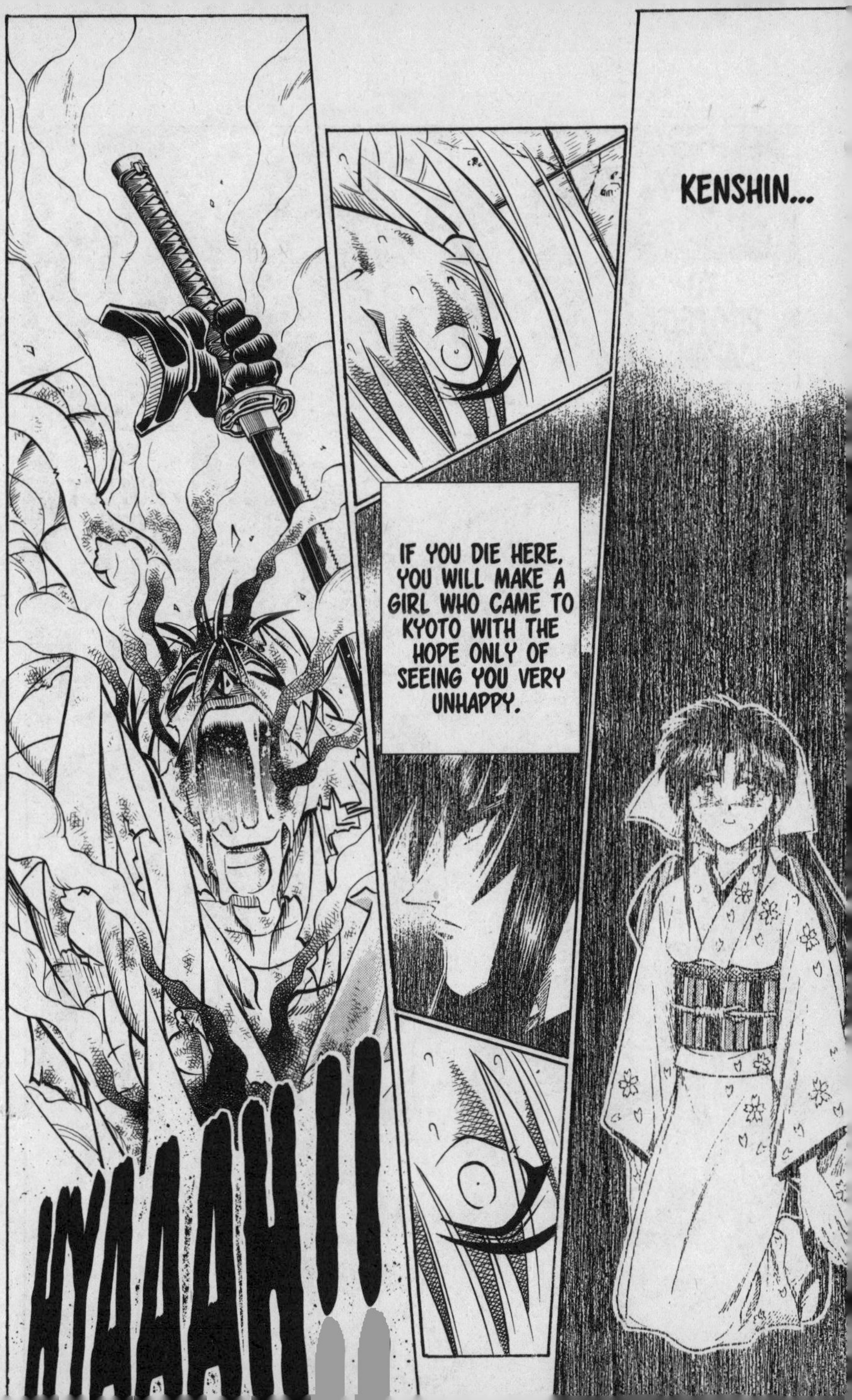
KENSHIN...
IF YOU DIE HERE, YOU WILL MAKE A GIRL WHO CAME TO KYOTO WITH THE HOPE ONLY OF SEEING YOU VERY UNHAPPY.
HYAAAH!!

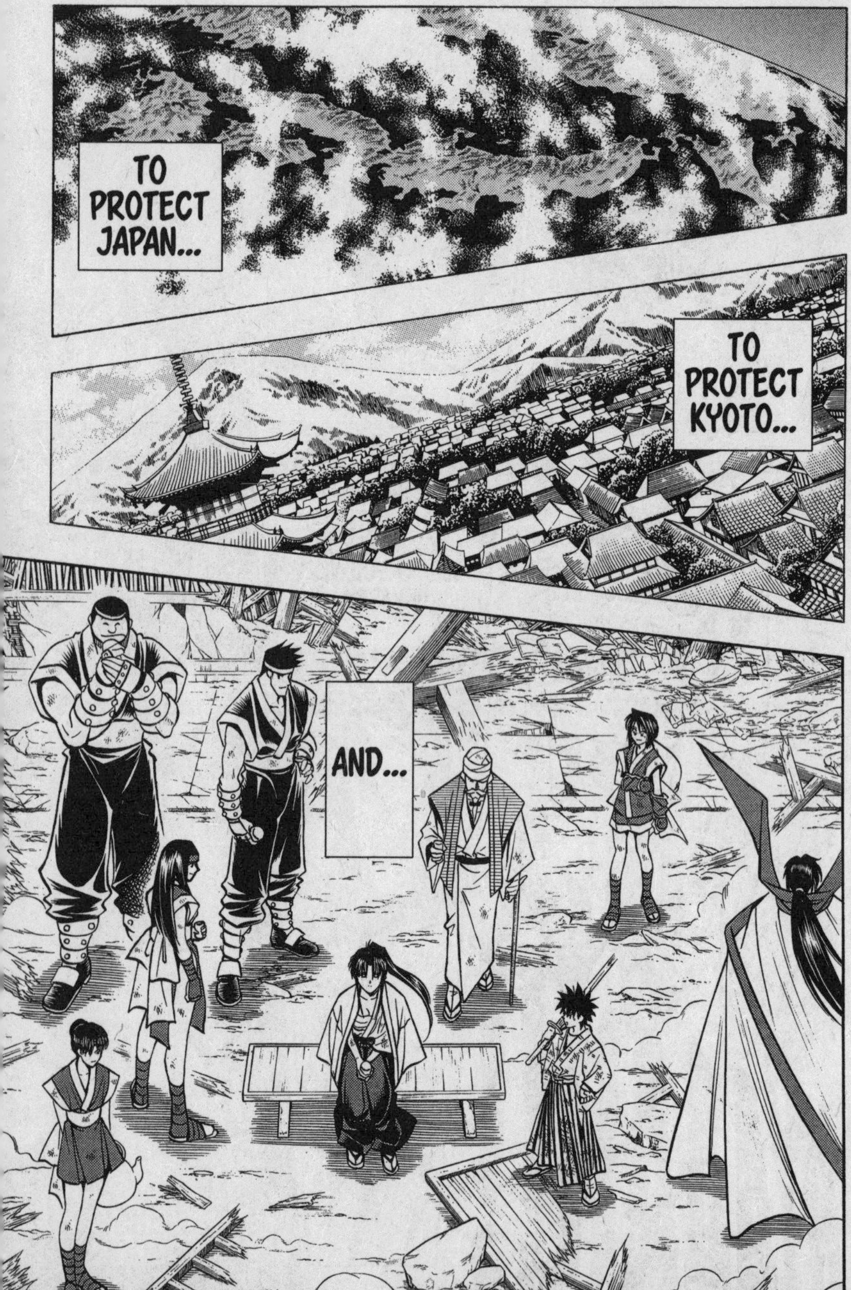
TO PROTECT JAPAN...
TO PROTECT KYOTO...
AND...

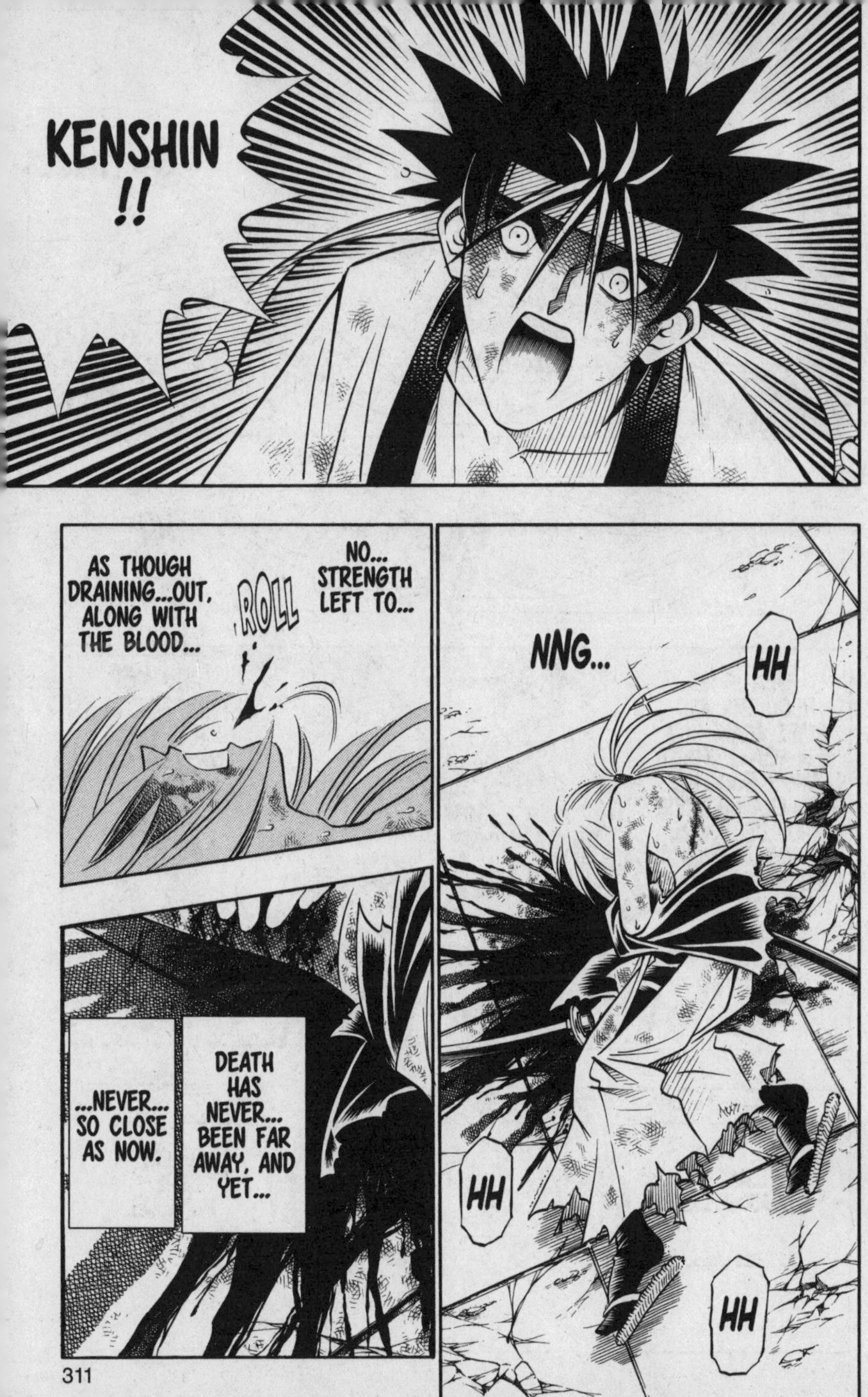
KENSHIN !!
HH
NNG...
HH
HH
NO... STRENGTH LEFT TO...
ROLL
AS THOUGH DRAINING...OUT, ALONG WITH THE BLOOD...
DEATH HAS NEVER... BEEN FAR AWAY, AND YET...
...NEVER... SO CLOSE AS NOW.

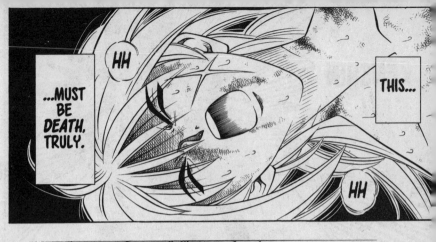

THIS...
HH
...MUST BE DEATH, TRULY.
HH
HH
AND YET, THIS BATTLE... HAS COST SHISHIO MOST OF HIS POWER, AS WELL.
EVEN IF HE RECOVERS AND RISES AGAIN IN A FEW YEARS...THOSE WHO CARRY THE NEW ERA ON THEIR SHOULDERS WILL HAVE GROWN STRONGER, TOO... AND WILL STOP HIM.
SURELY THE MISSION...
...HAS BEEN ACCOMPLISHED.

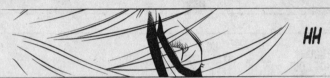

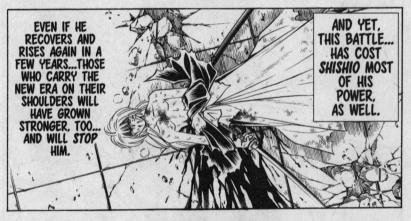

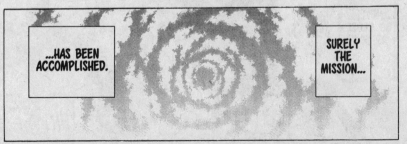

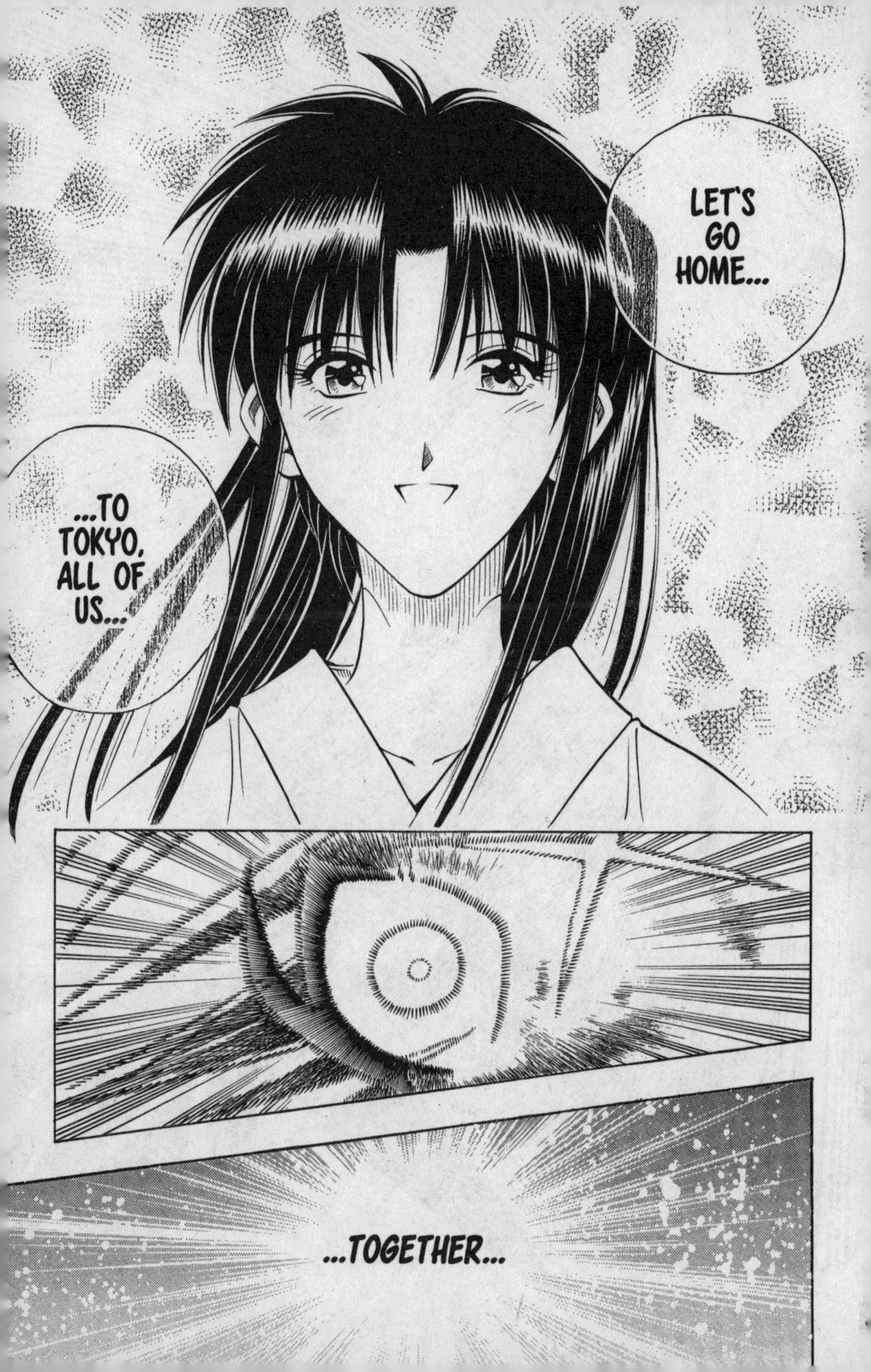
LET'S GO HOME...
...TO TOKYO, ALL OF US...
...TOGETHER...

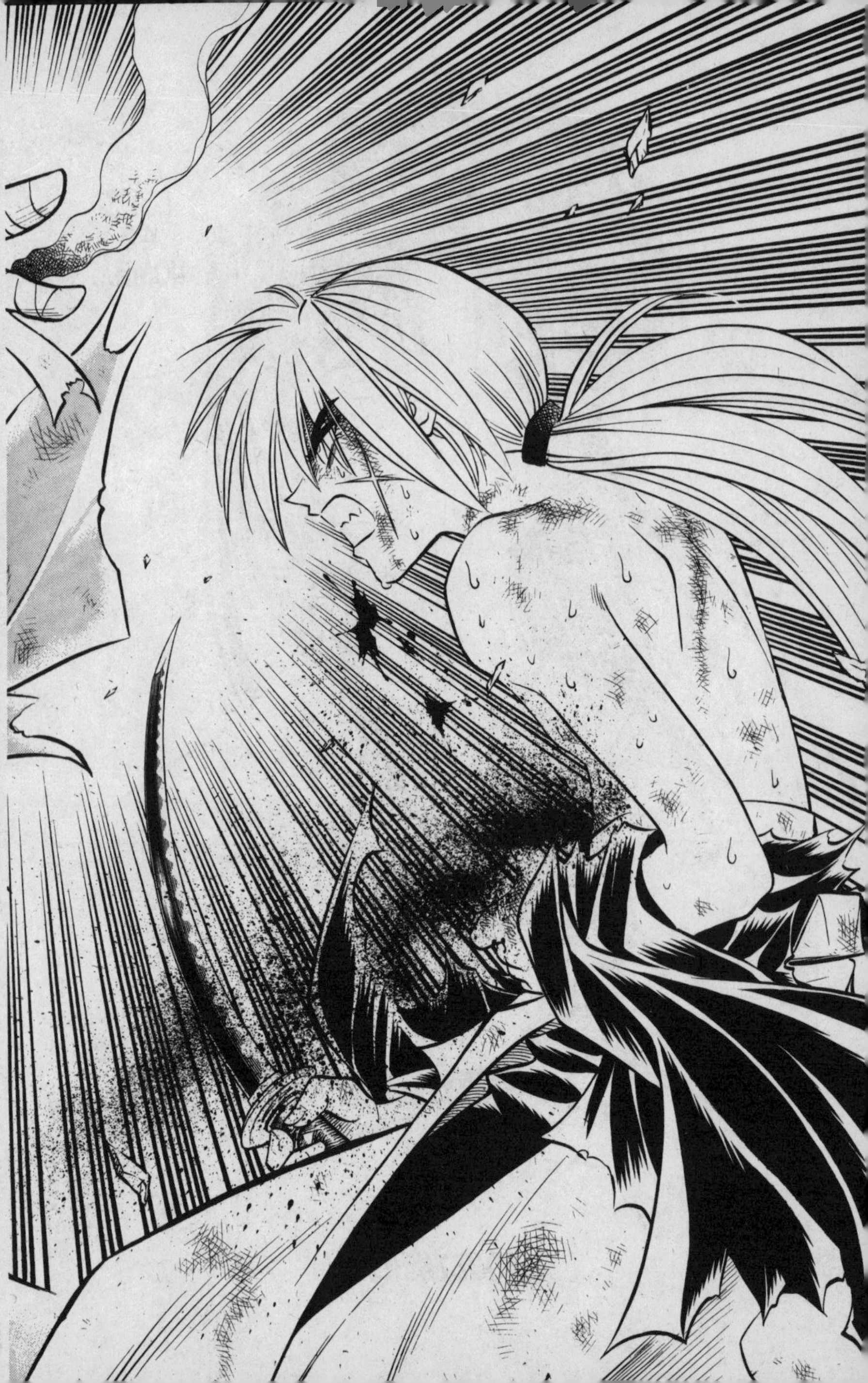

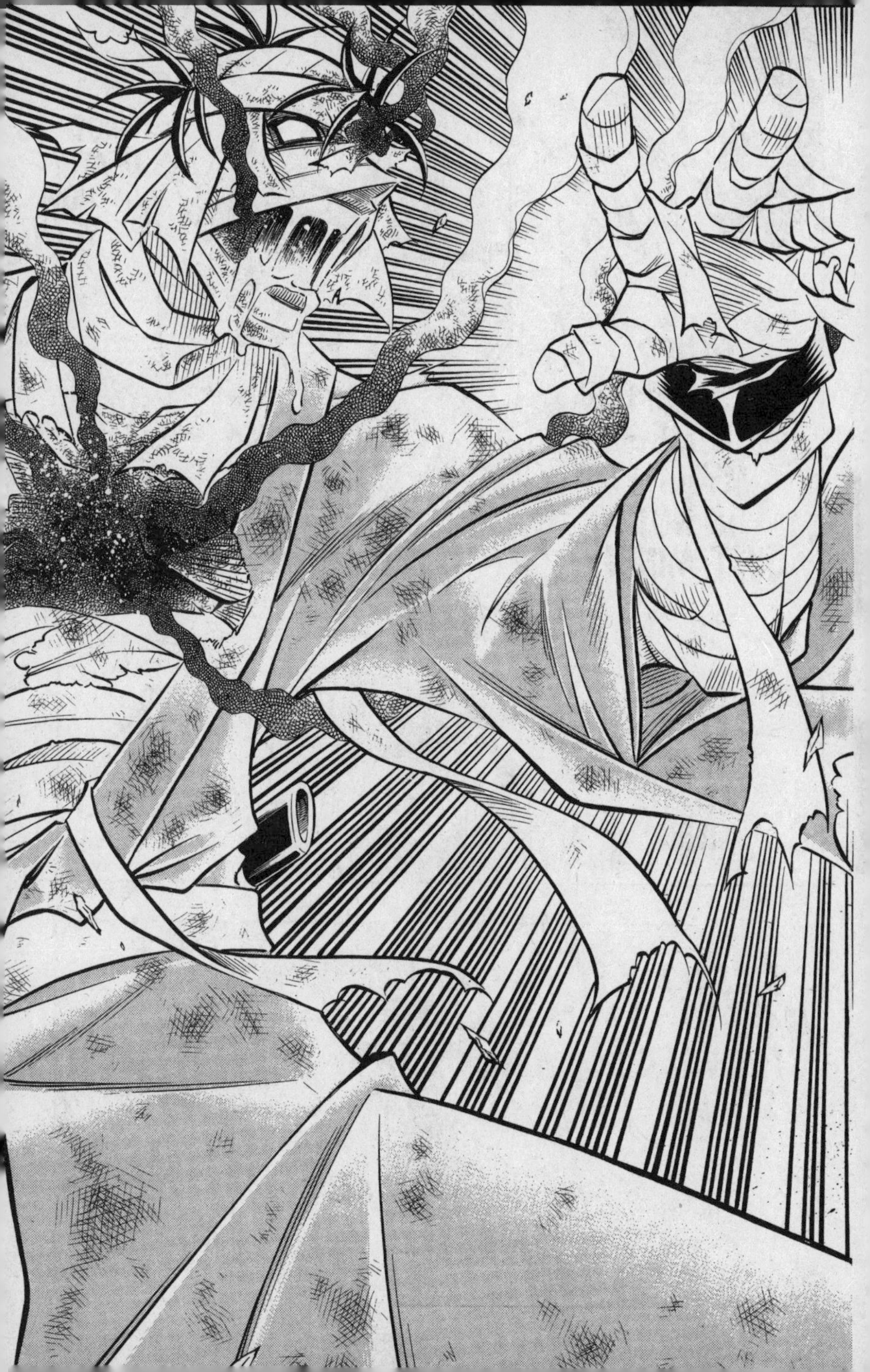

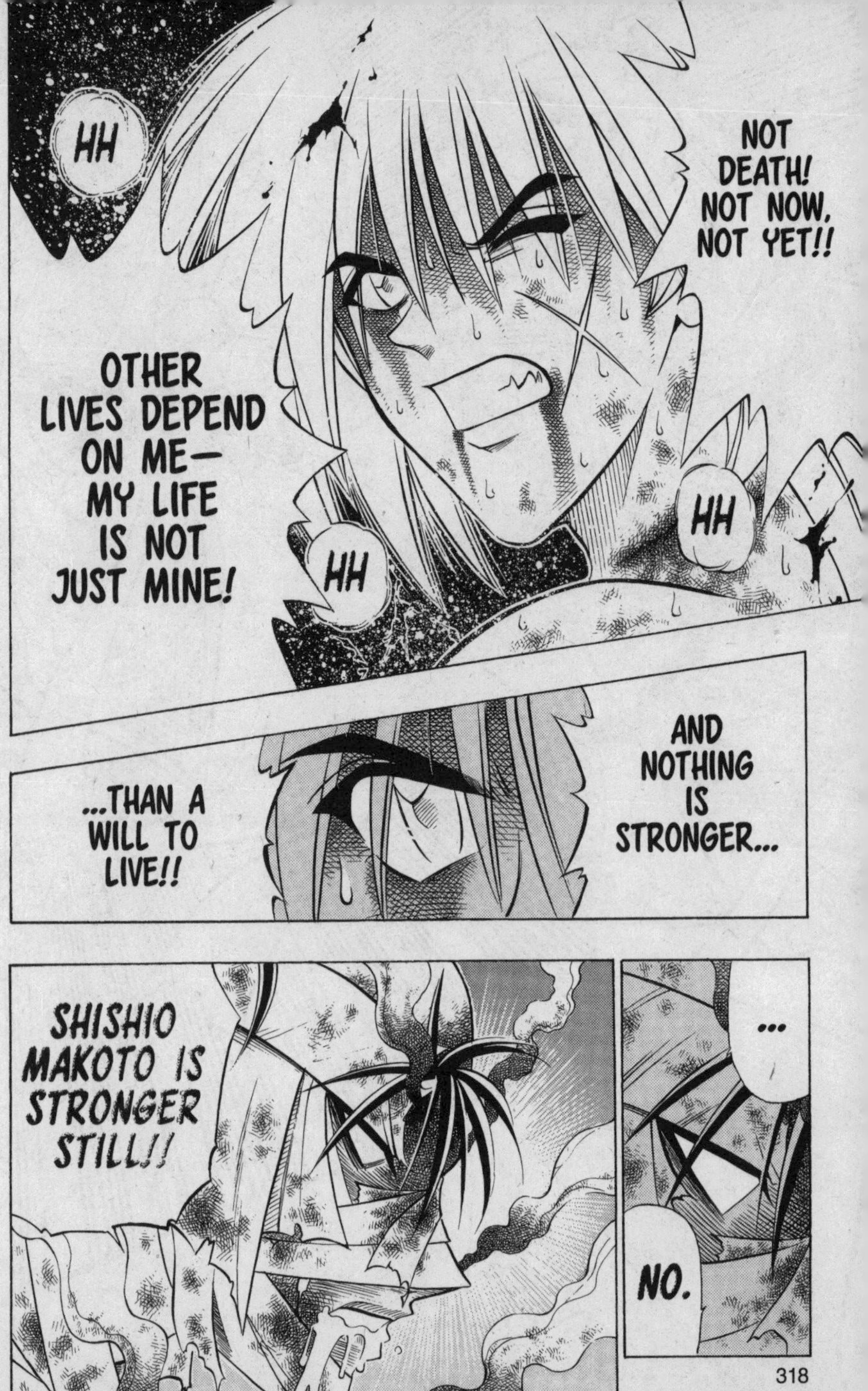
NOT DEATH! NOT NOW, NOT YET!!
HH
HH
OTHER LIVES DEPEND ON ME— MY LIFE IS NOT JUST MINE!
HH
AND NOTHING IS STRONGER...
...THAN A WILL TO LIVE!!
...
NO.
SHISHIO MAKOTO IS STRONGER STILL!!

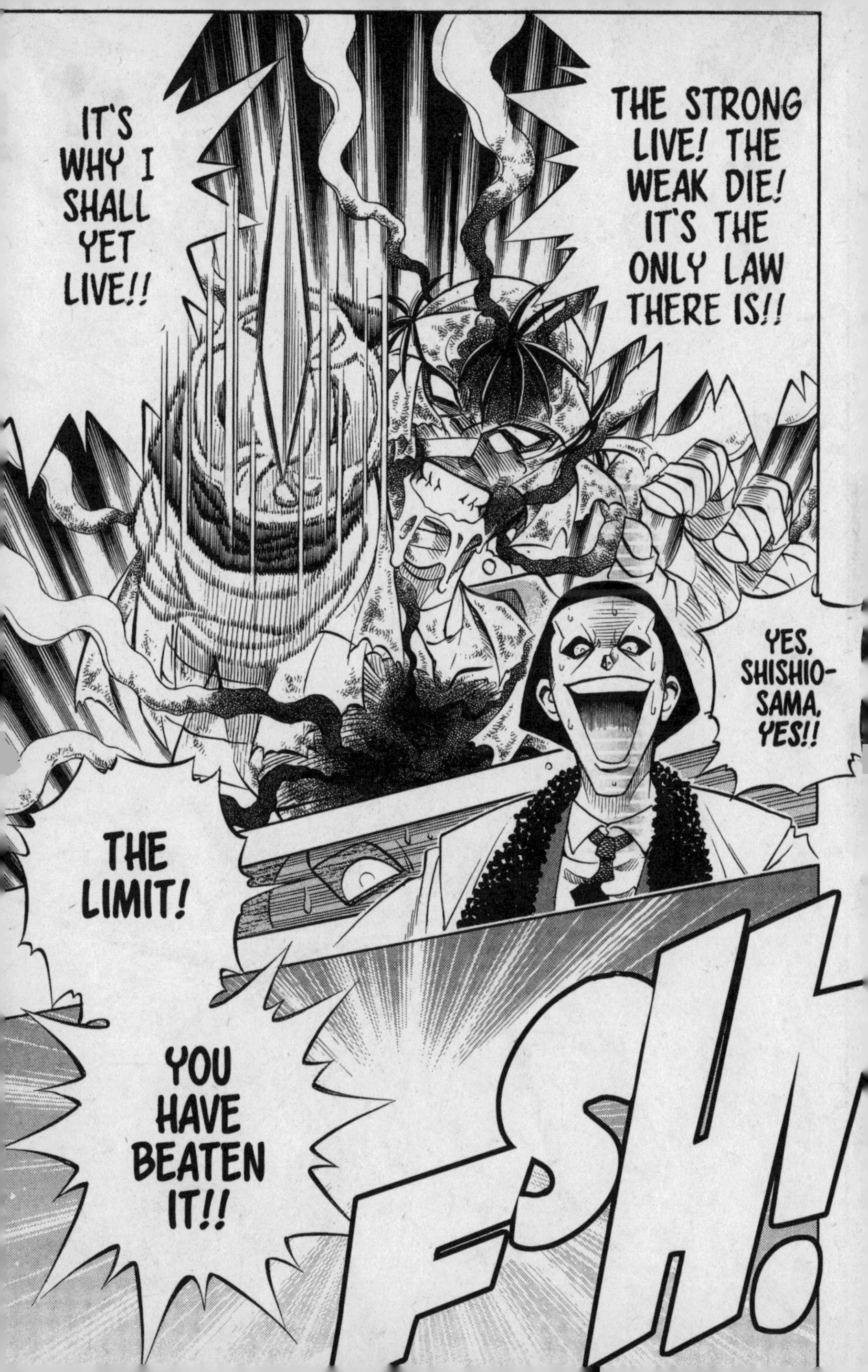
THE STRONG LIVE! THE WEAK DIE! IT'S THE ONLY LAW THERE IS!!
IT'S WHY I SHALL YET LIVE!!
YES, SHISHIO-SAMA, YES!!
THE LIMIT!
YOU HAVE BEATEN IT!!
FSH!

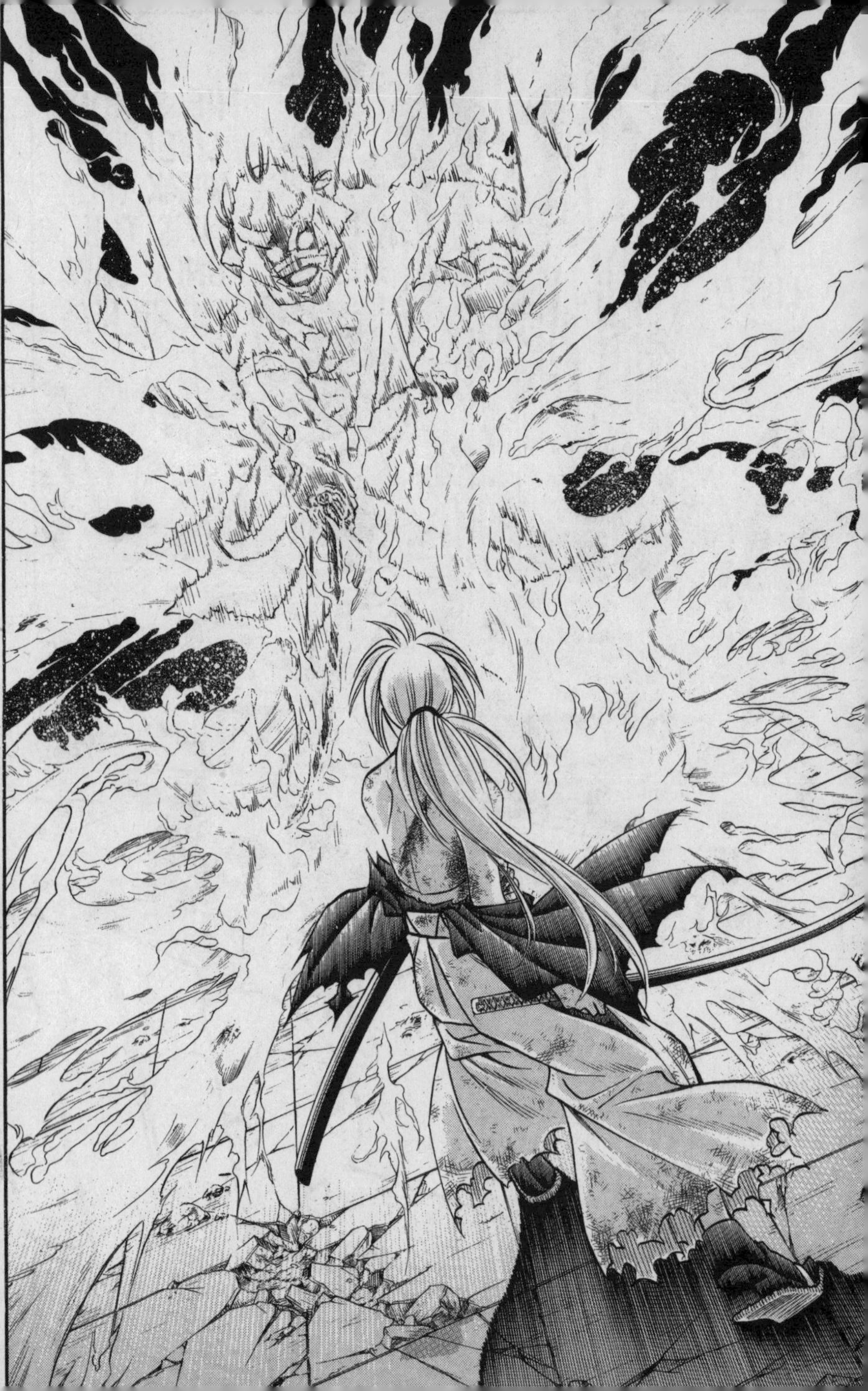

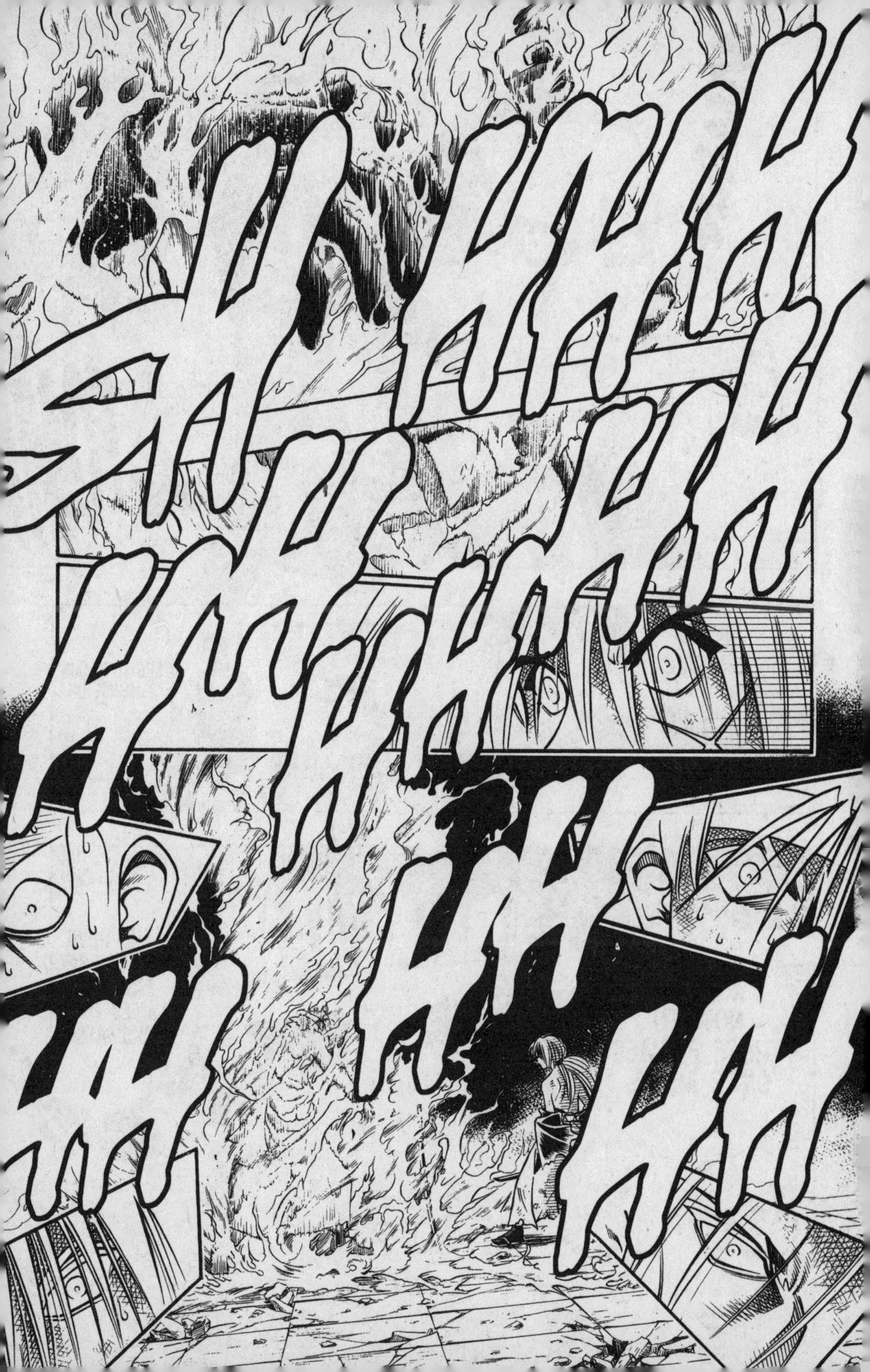

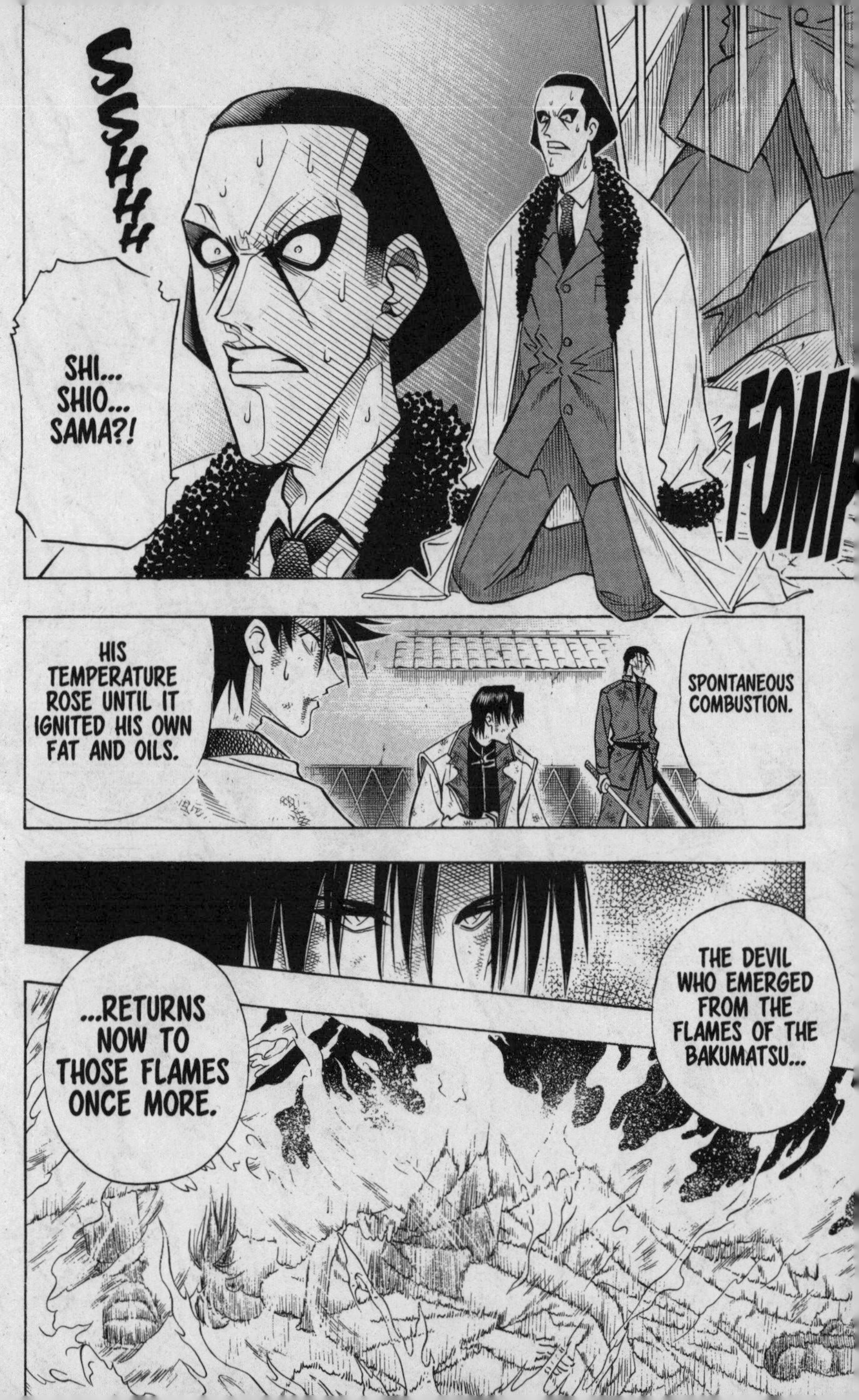
FOMP
SSHHH
SHI... SHIO... SAMA?!
SPONTANEOUS COMBUSTION.
HIS TEMPERATURE ROSE UNTIL IT IGNITED HIS OWN FAT AND OILS.
THE DEVIL WHO EMERGED FROM THE FLAMES OF THE BAKUMATSU...
...RETURNS NOW TO THOSE FLAMES ONCE MORE.

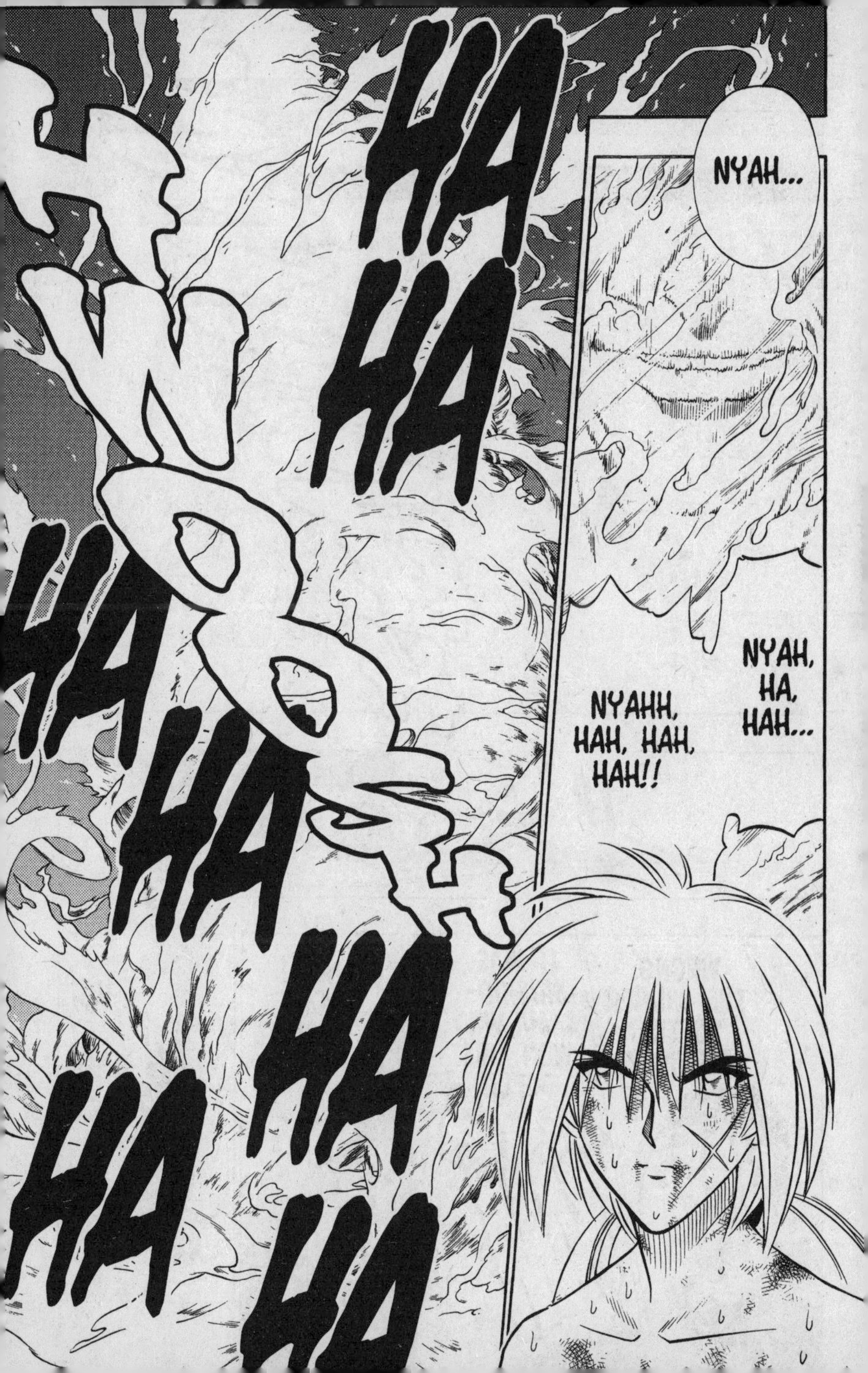
NYAH...
NYAH, HA, HAH...
NYAHH, HAH, HAH, HAH!!

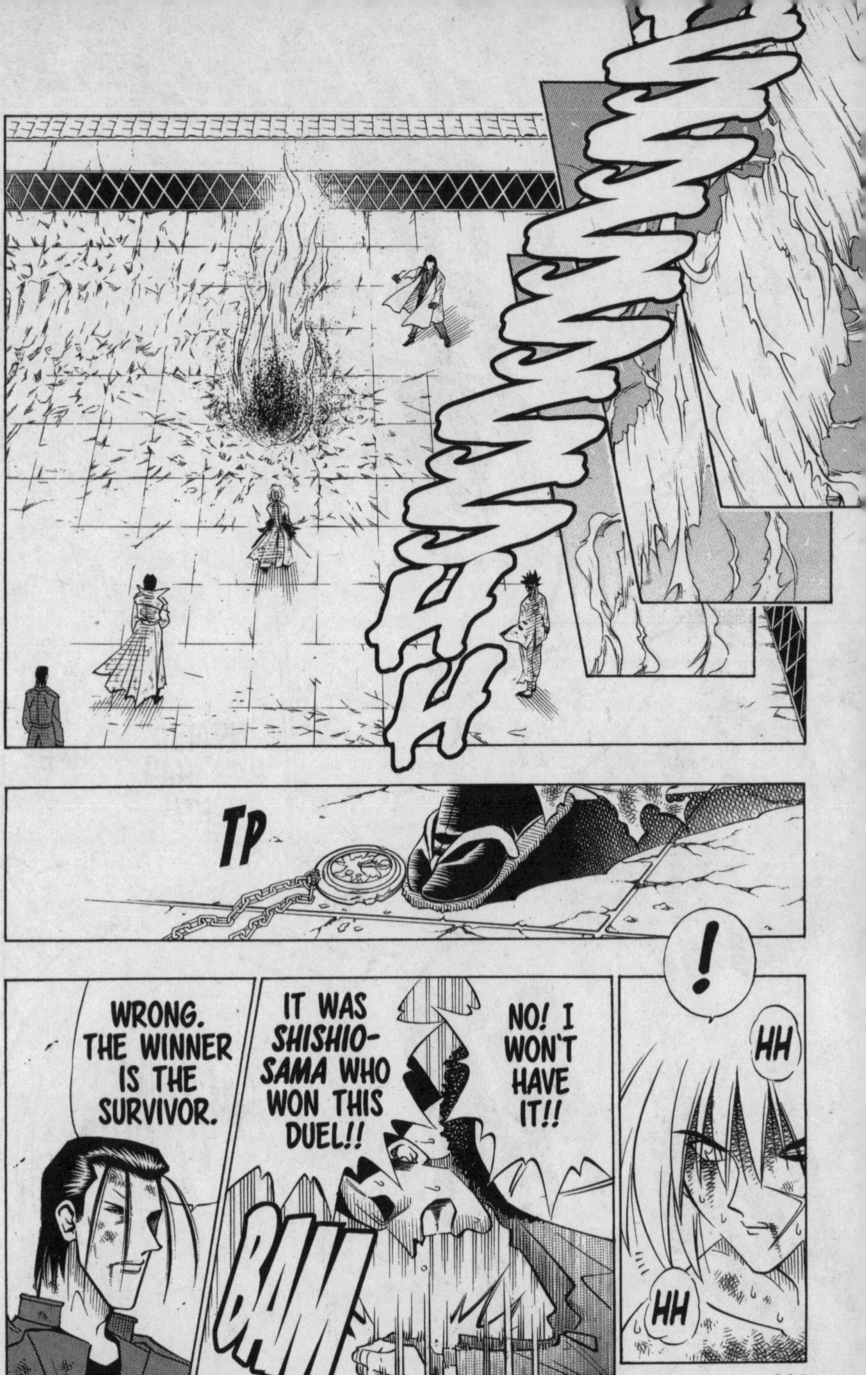
TP
!
HH
HH
NO! I WON'T HAVE IT!!
IT WAS SHISHIO-SAMA WHO WON THIS DUEL!!
BAM
WRONG. THE WINNER IS THE SURVIVOR.

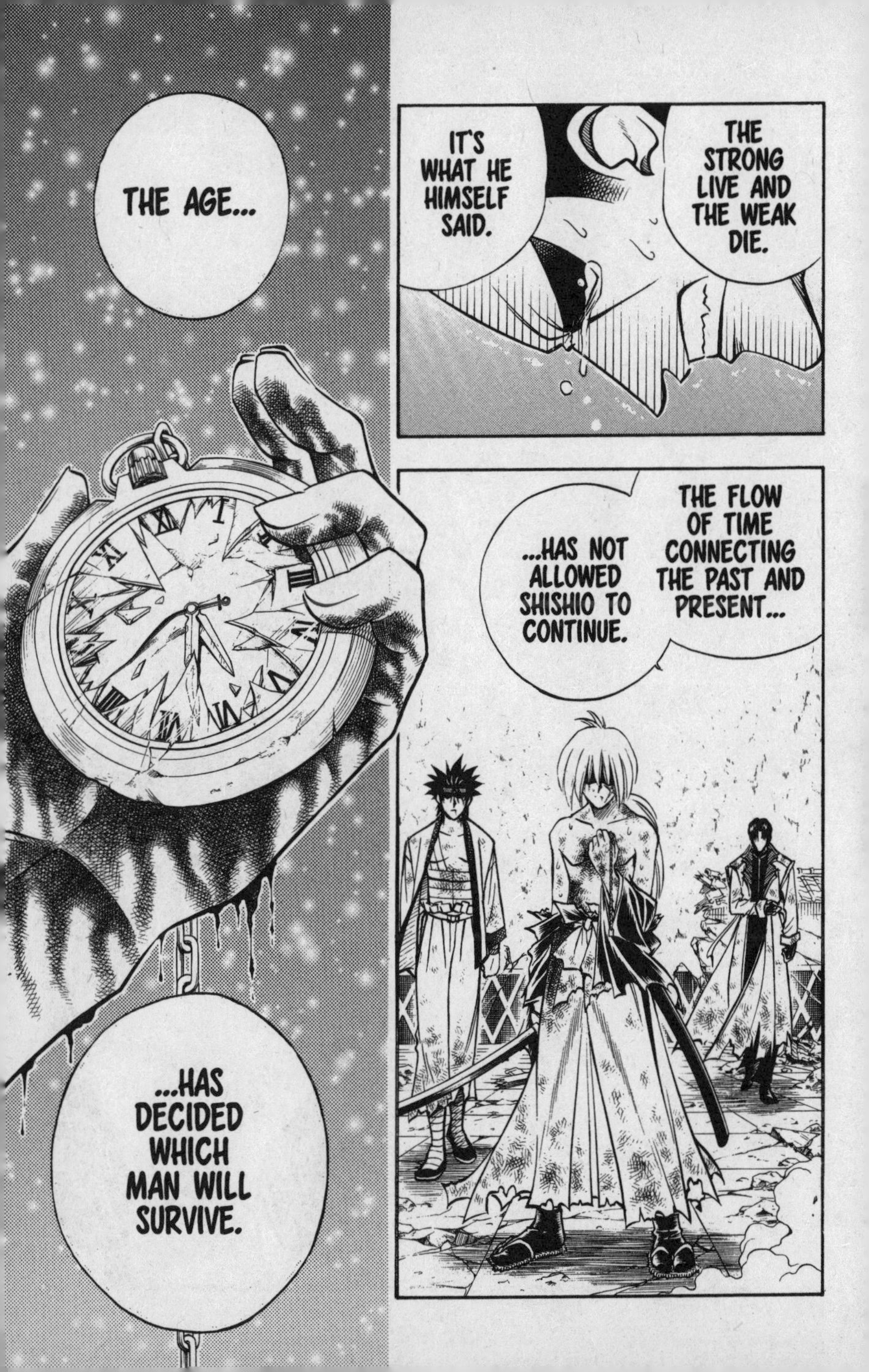
THE STRONG LIVE AND THE WEAK DIE.
IT'S WHAT HE HIMSELF SAID.
THE FLOW OF TIME CONNECTING THE PAST AND PRESENT...
...HAS NOT ALLOWED SHISHIO TO CONTINUE.
THE AGE...
...HAS DECIDED WHICH MAN WILL SURVIVE.

Rurouni Kenshin

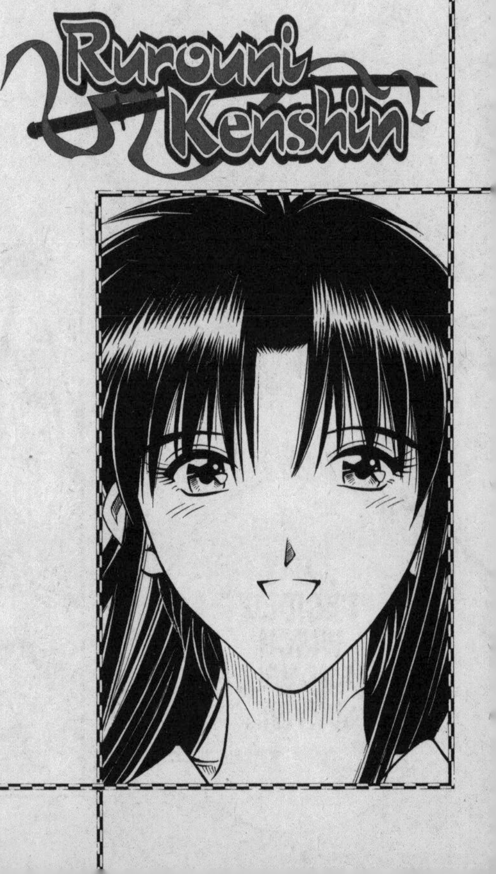

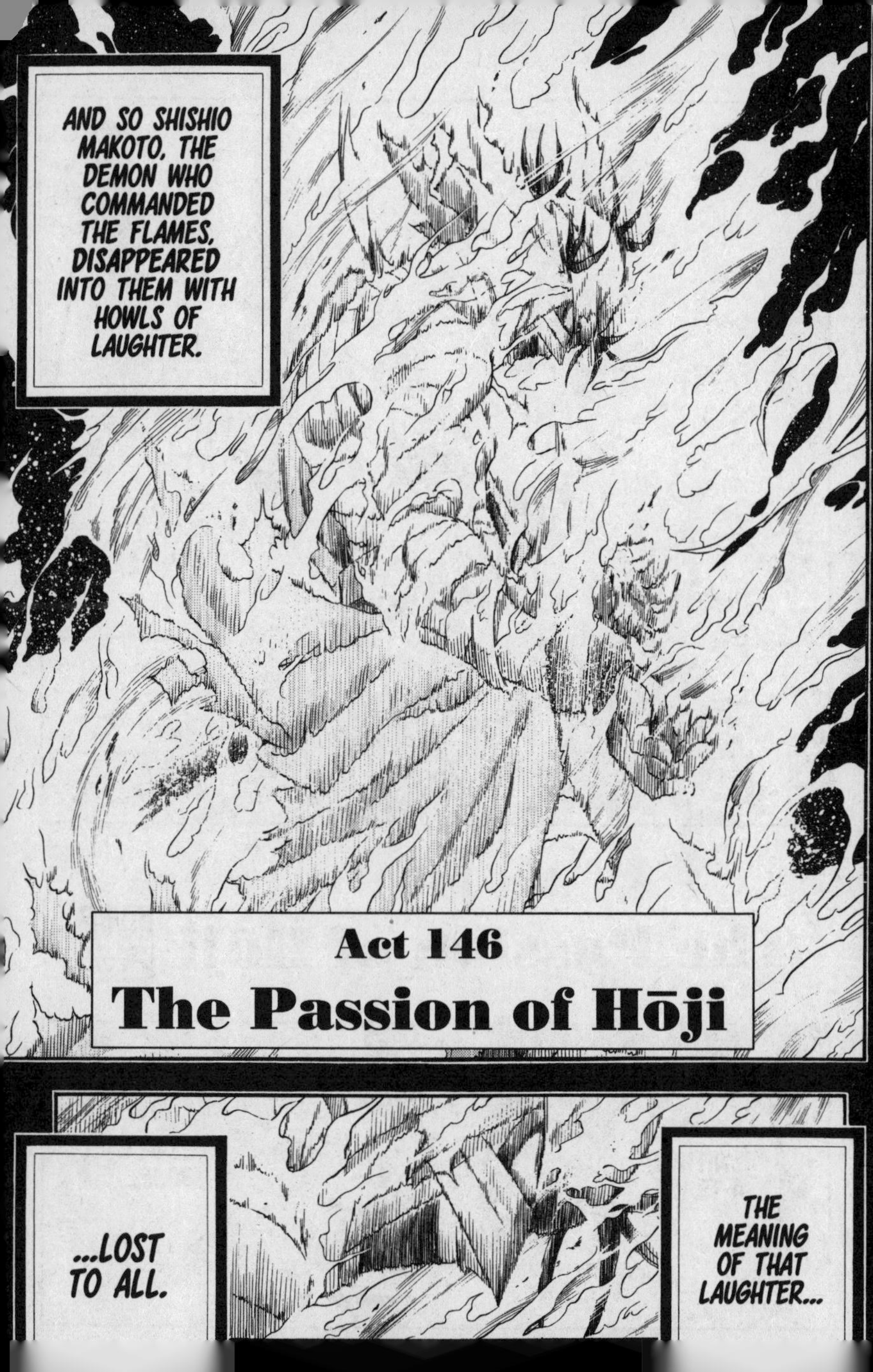
AND SO SHISHIO MAKOTO, THE DEMON WHO COMMANDED THE FLAMES, DISAPPEARED INTO THEM WITH HOWLS OF LAUGHTER.
Act 146
The Passion of Hōji
THE MEANING OF THAT LAUGHTER...
...LOST TO ALL.

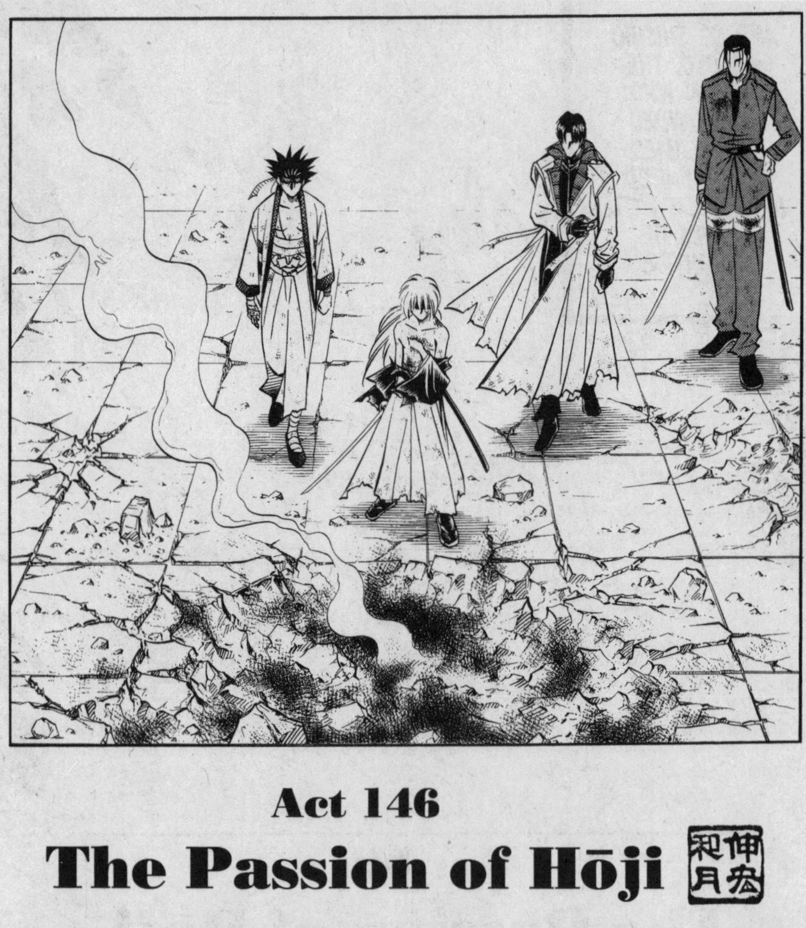

Act 146

The Passion of Hōji

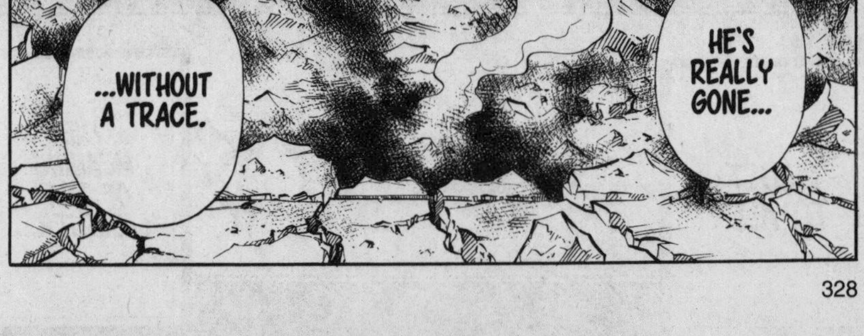
HE'S REALLY GONE...
...WITHOUT A TRACE.

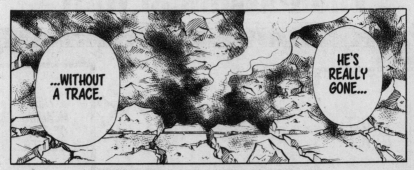

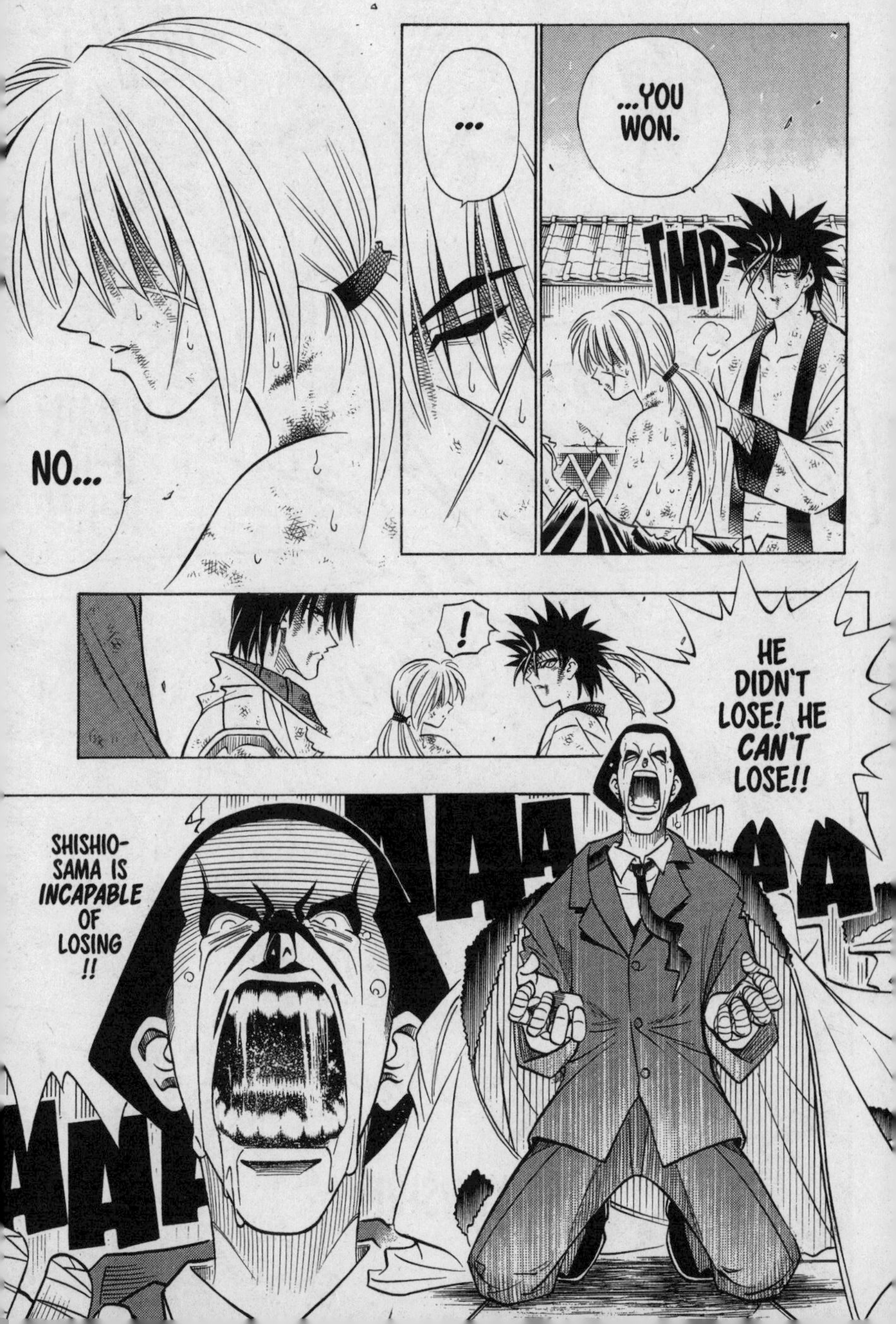
...YOU WON.
TMP
...
NO...
!
HE DIDN'T LOSE! HE CAN'T LOSE!!
SHISHIO-SAMA IS INCAPABLE OF LOSING!!
AAA
AAA

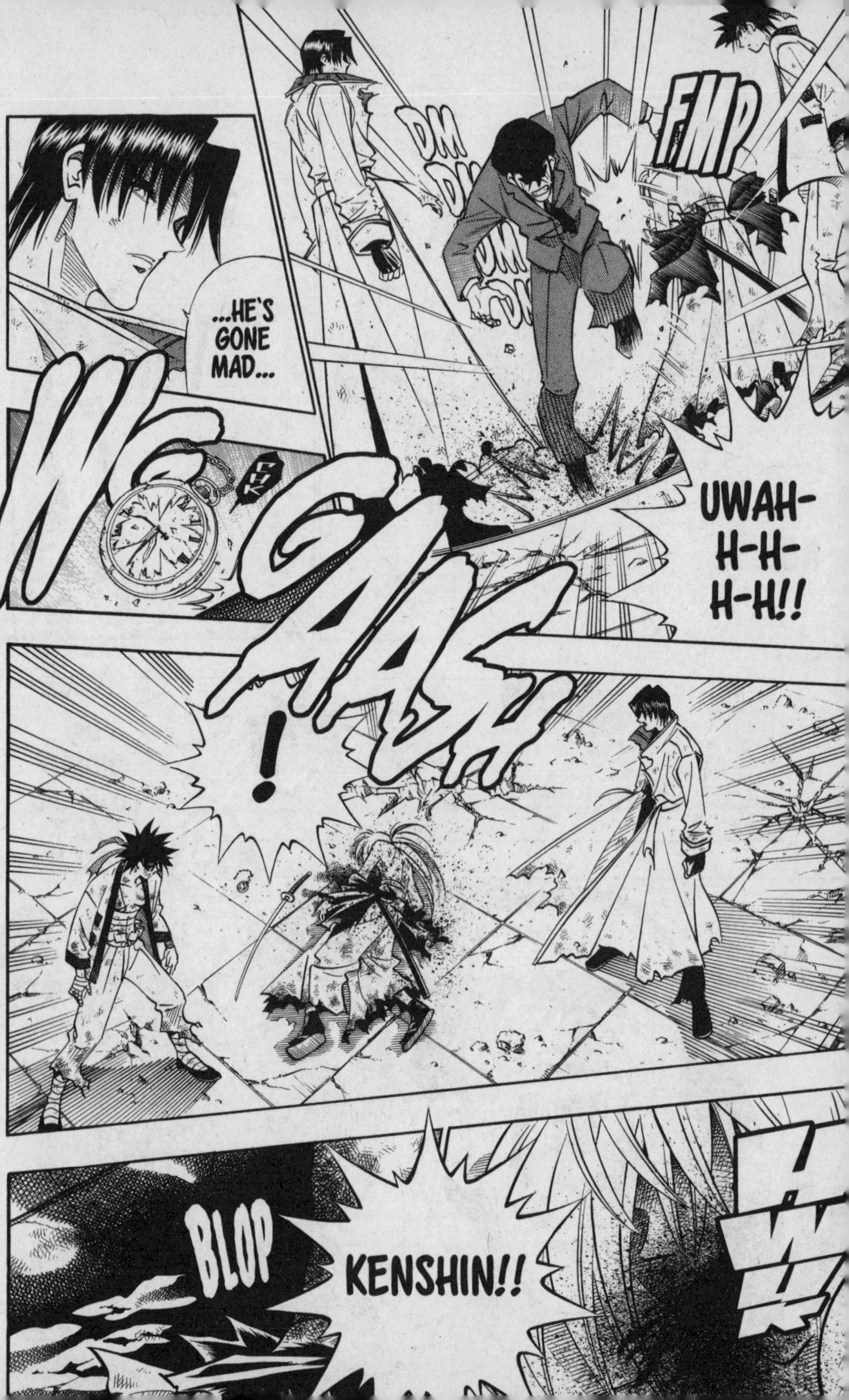

FMP
DM
DM
DM
DM
UWAH-H-H-H-H!!
...HE'S GONE MAD...
CHK
KENSHIN!!
BLOP

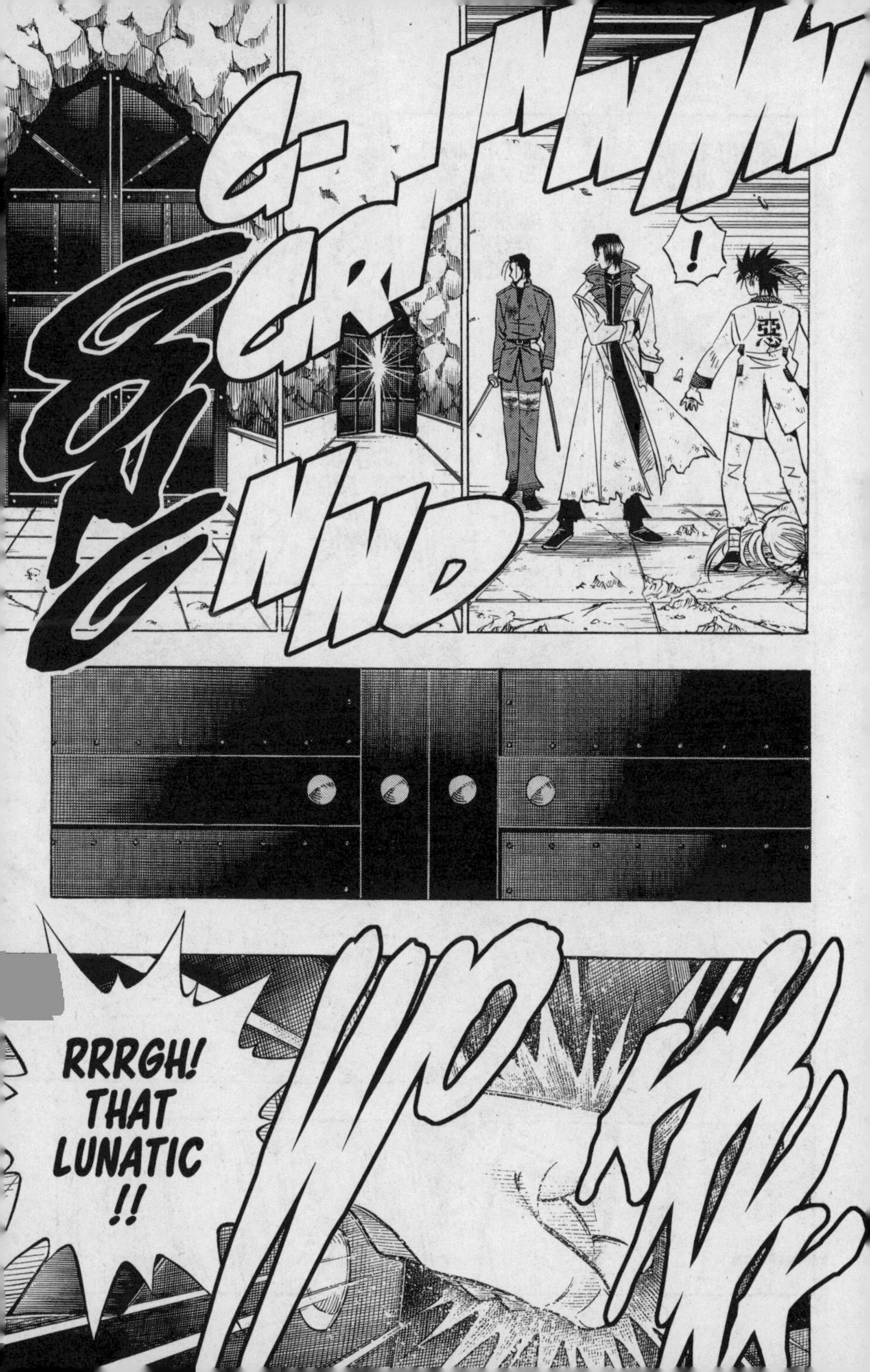
!
RRRGH! THAT LUNATIC !!

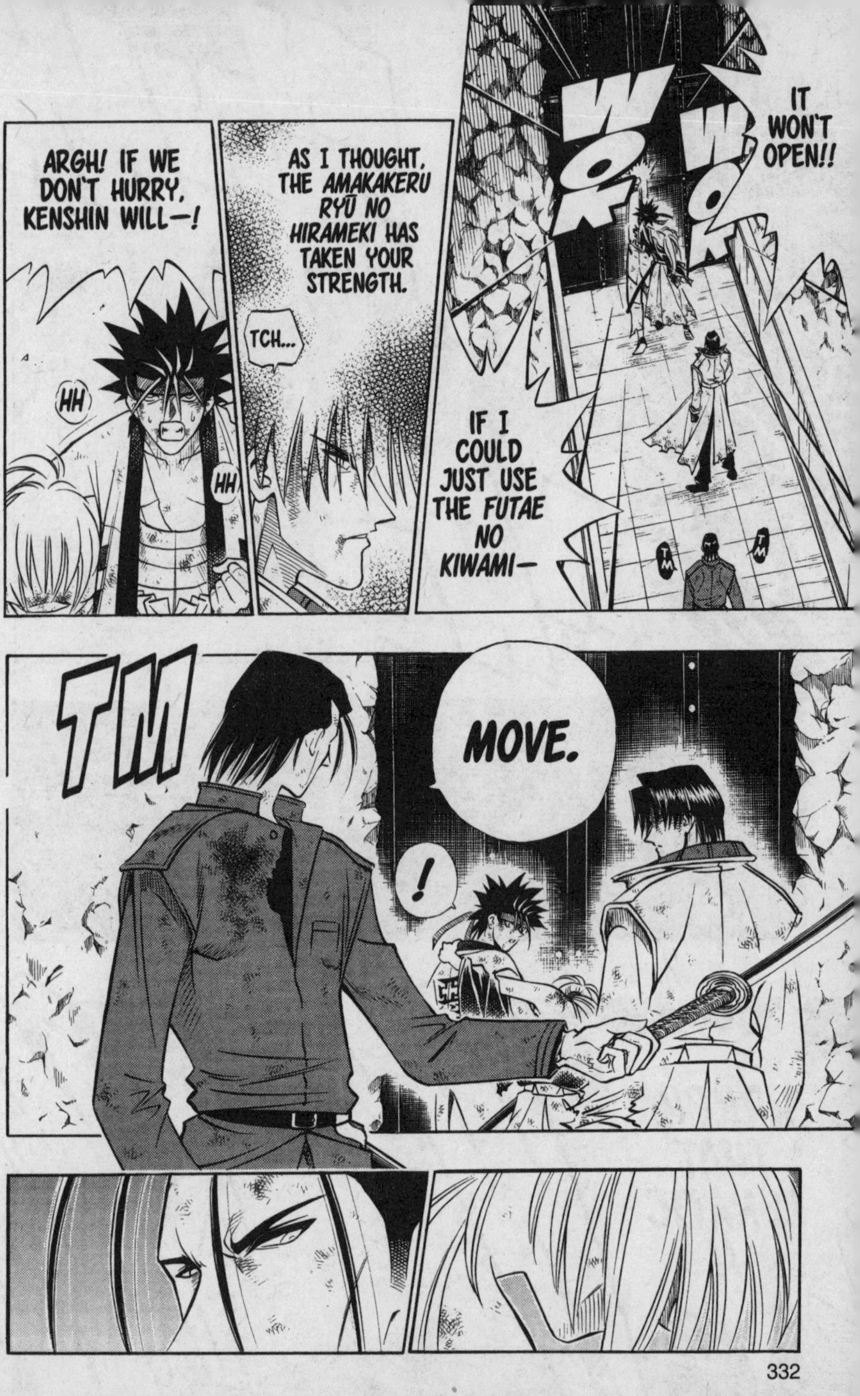
IT WON'T OPEN!!
WOK WOK
IF I COULD JUST USE THE *FUTAE NO KIWAMI*—
TM TM
AS I THOUGHT, THE *AMAKAKERU RYŪ NO HIRAMEKI* HAS TAKEN YOUR STRENGTH.
TCH...
ARGH! IF WE DON'T HURRY, KENSHIN WILL—!
HH
HH
MOVE.
TM
!

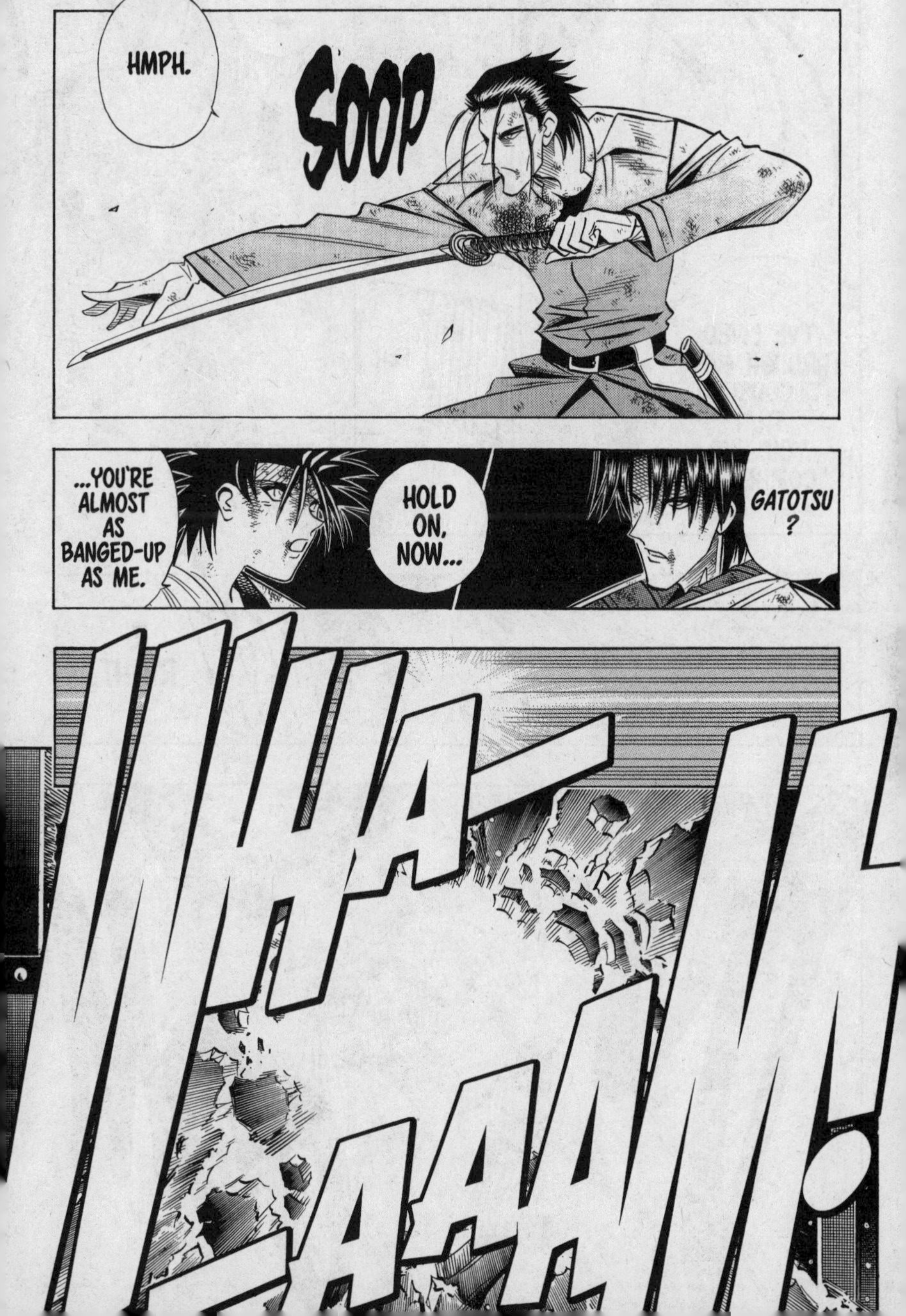
HMPH.
SOOP
GATOTSU?
HOLD ON, NOW...
...YOU'RE ALMOST AS BANGED-UP AS ME.

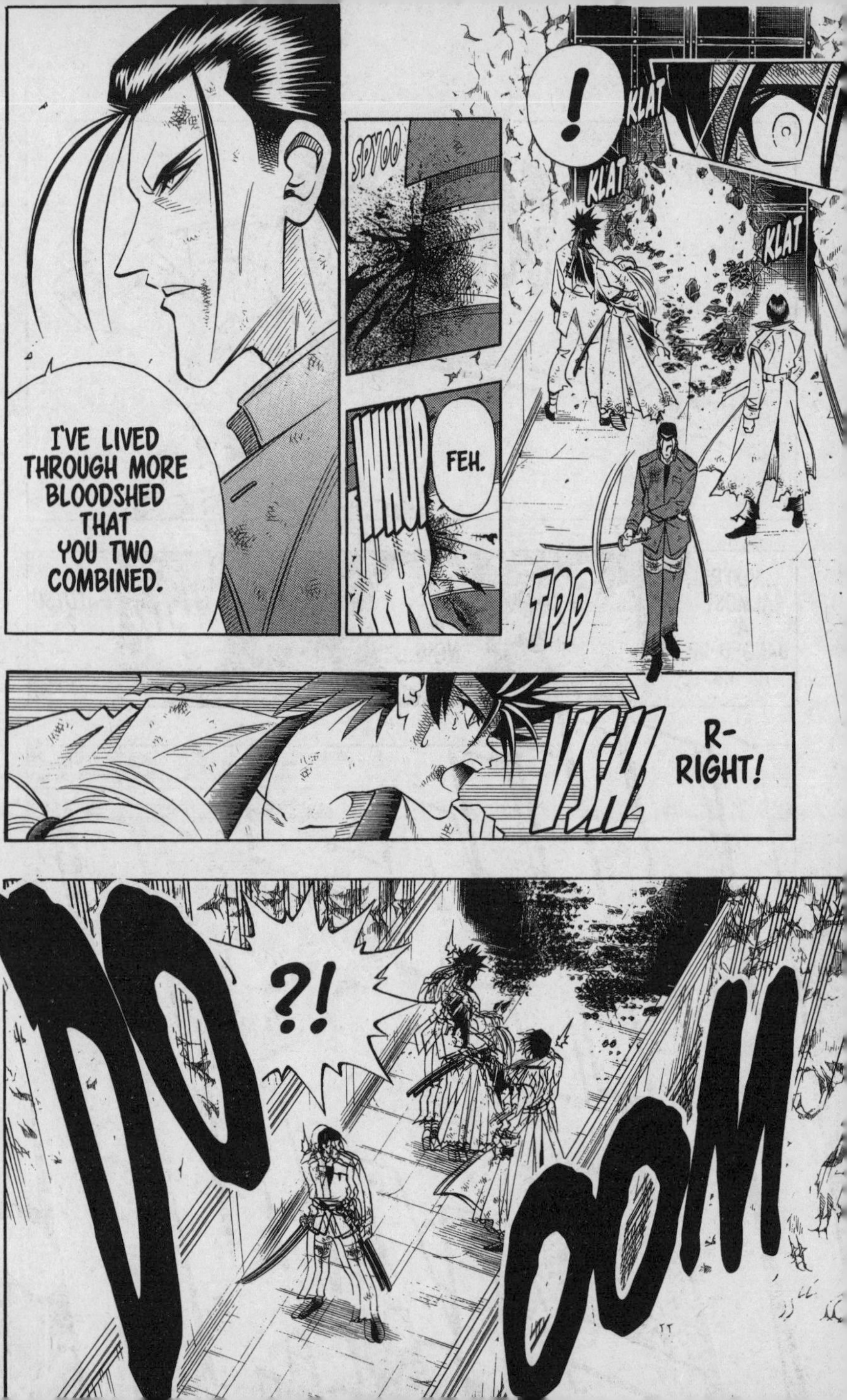
KLAT
!
KLAT
KLAT
TPP
SPYOO
FEH.
WHUP
I'VE LIVED THROUGH MORE BLOODSHED THAT YOU TWO COMBINED.
R-RIGHT!
VSH
?!
DOOM

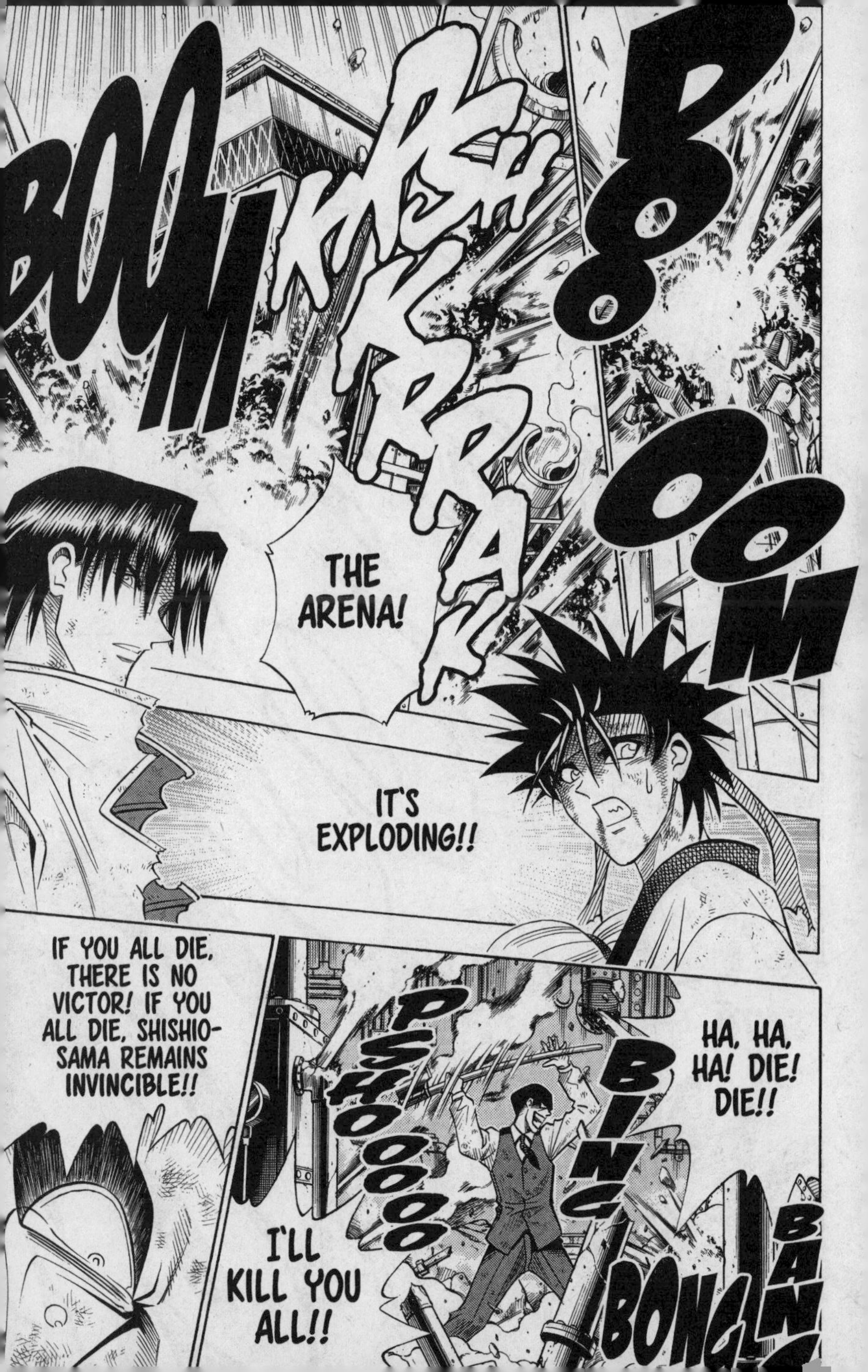
BOOOOM
BOOM
THE ARENA!
IT'S EXPLODING!!
HA, HA, HA! DIE! DIE!!
BING
PSHOOOOO
I'LL KILL YOU ALL!!
BAN
BONG
IF YOU ALL DIE, THERE IS NO VICTOR! IF YOU ALL DIE, SHISHIO-SAMA REMAINS INVINCIBLE!!

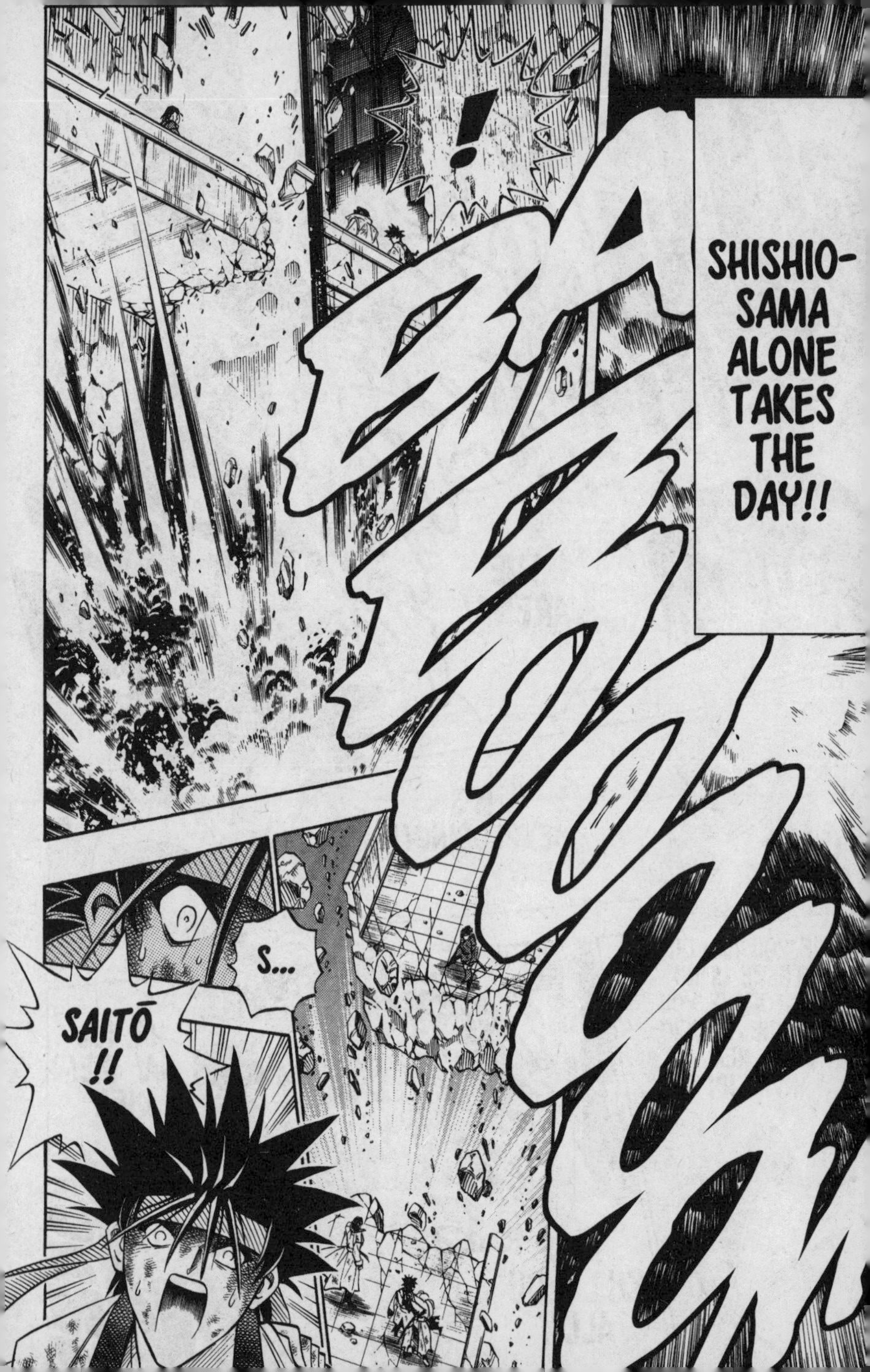
!
SHISHIO-SAMA ALONE TAKES THE DAY!!
S...
SAITŌ!!

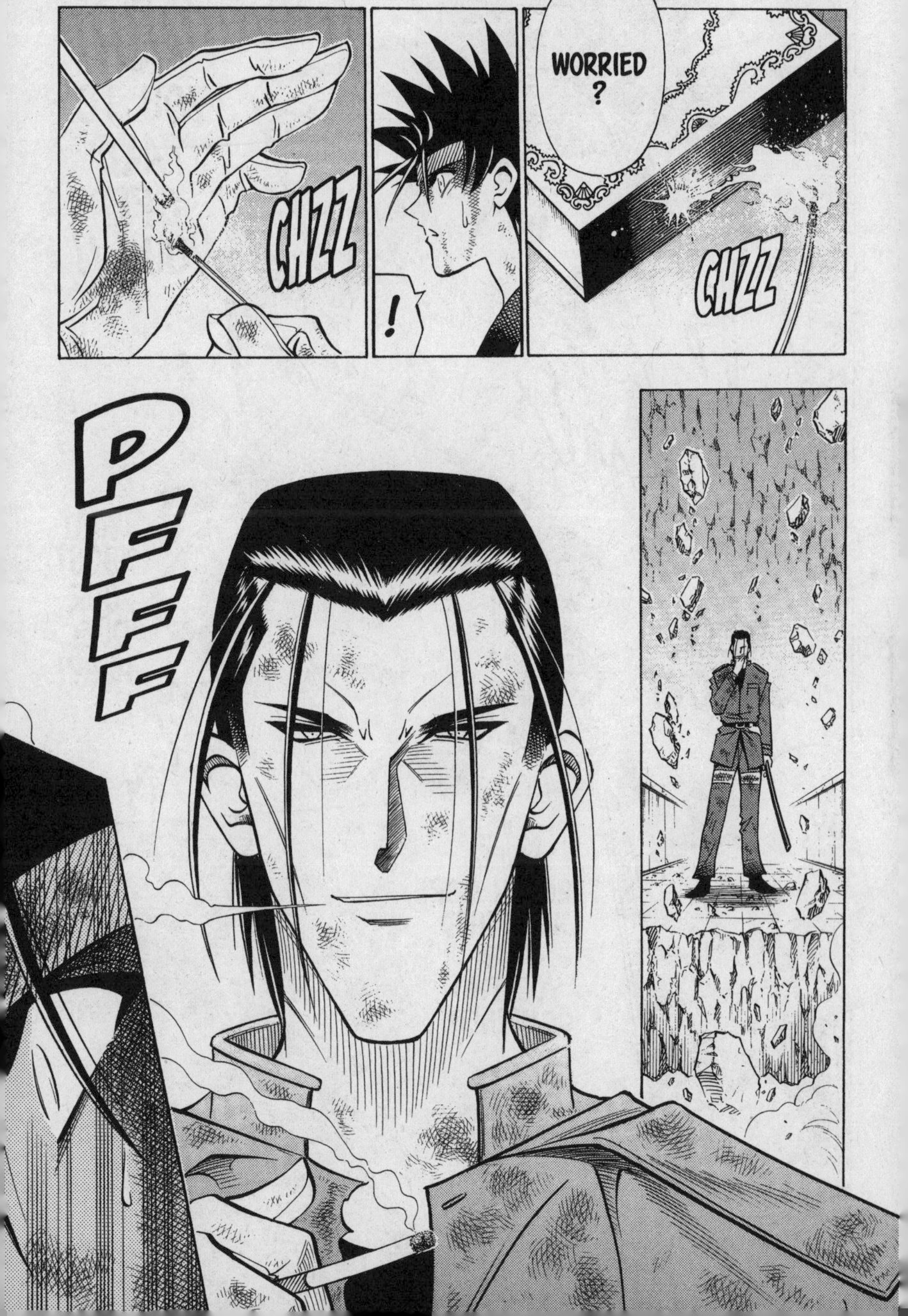
WORRIED ?
CHZZ
!
CHZZ
PFFFF

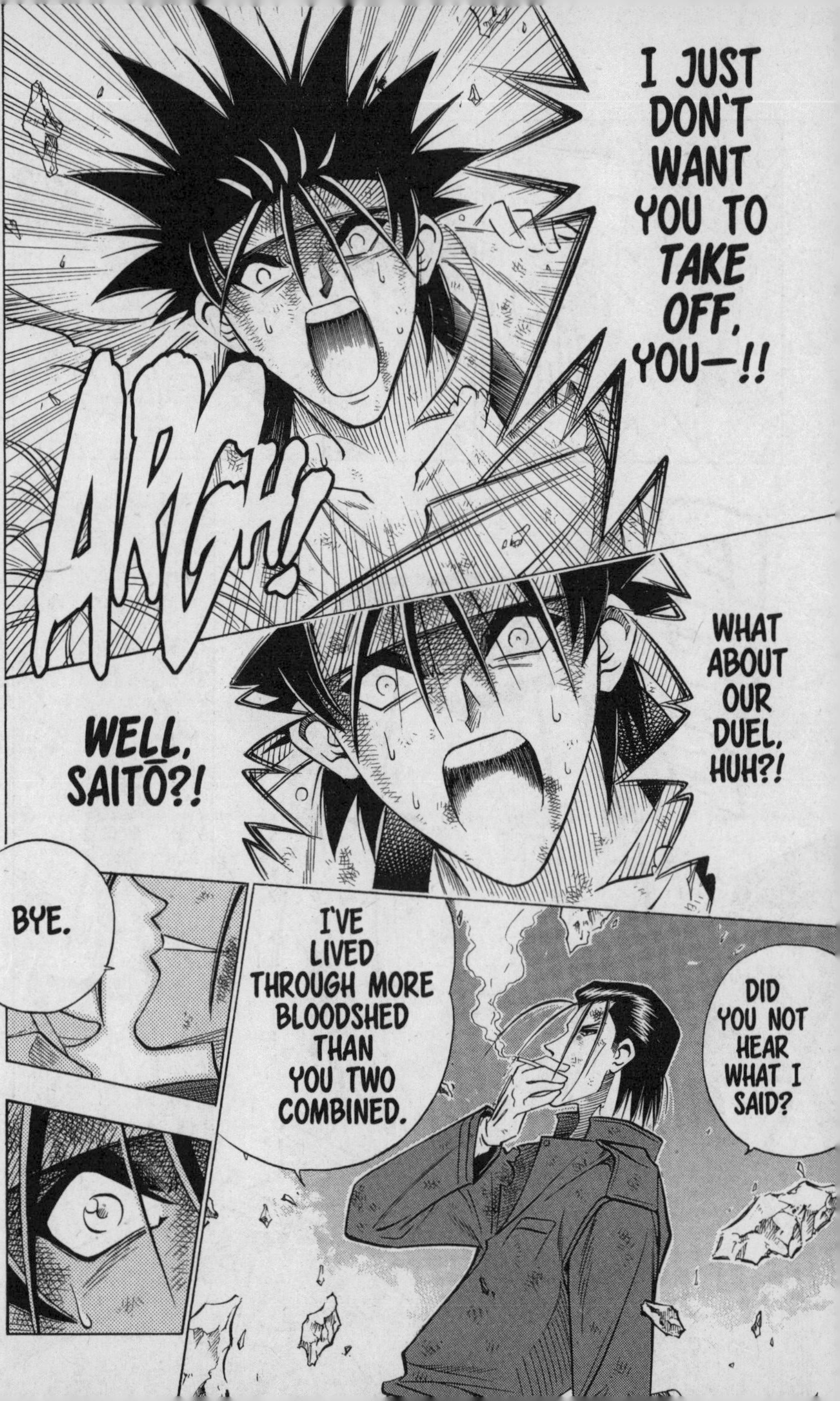
I JUST DON'T WANT YOU TO TAKE OFF, YOU—!!
ARGH!
WHAT ABOUT OUR DUEL, HUH?!
WELL, SAITŌ?!
DID YOU NOT HEAR WHAT I SAID?
I'VE LIVED THROUGH MORE BLOODSHED THAN YOU TWO COMBINED.
BYE.

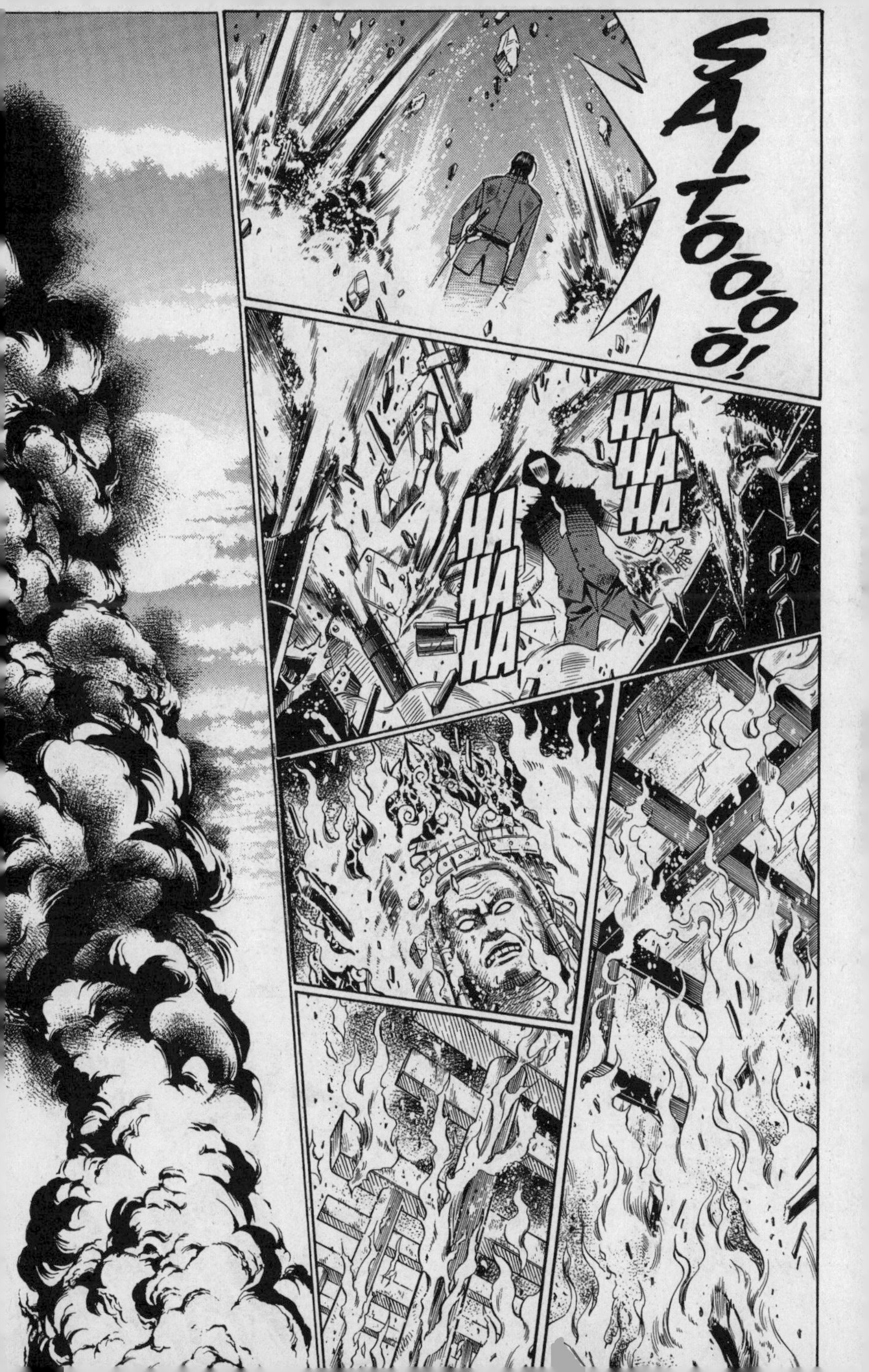
SAITO-O-O-O-O!
HA HA HA HA
HA HA HA HA

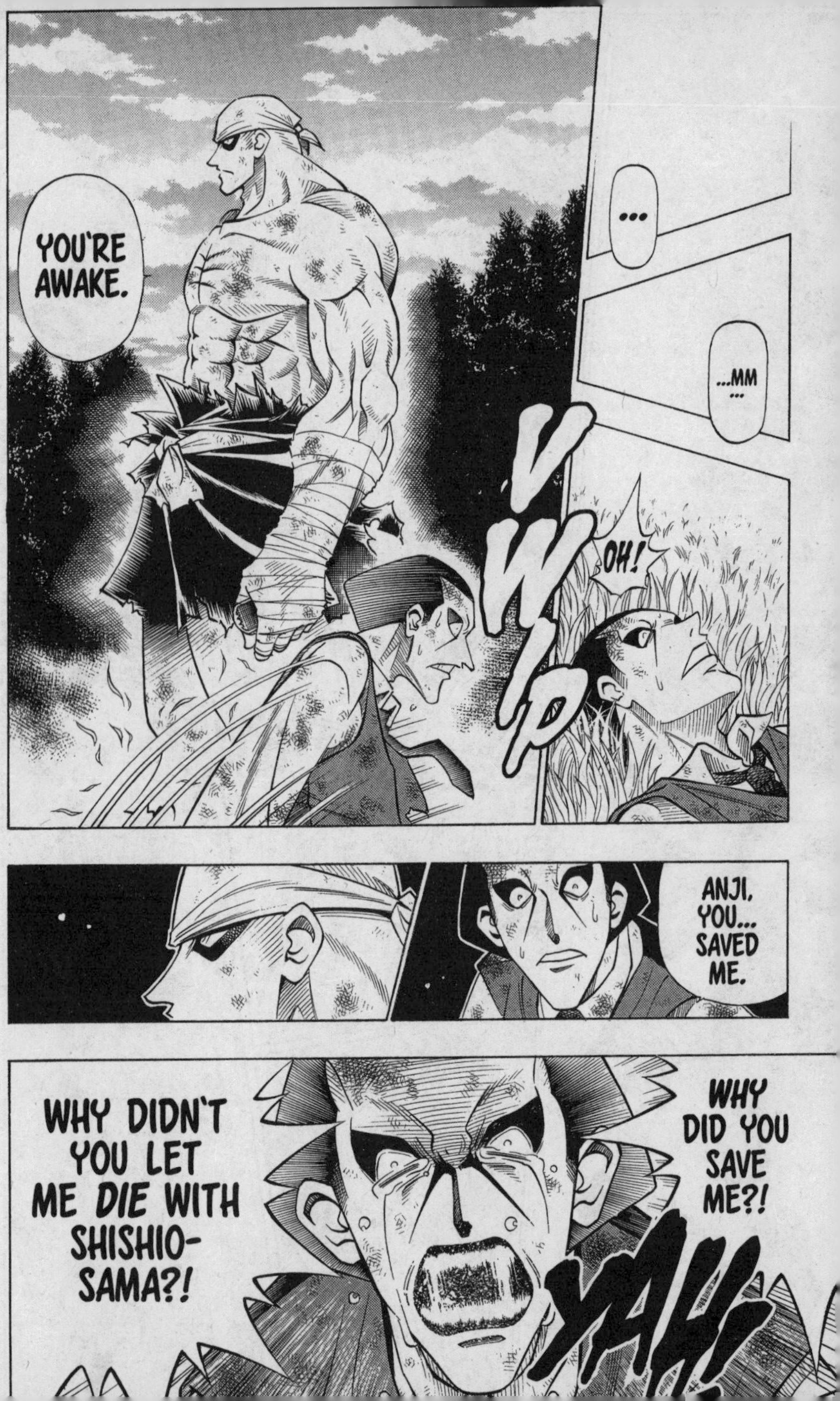
...
...MM ...
OH!
VWIP
YOU'RE AWAKE.
ANJI, YOU... SAVED ME.
WHY DID YOU SAVE ME?!
WHY DIDN'T YOU LET ME *DIE* WITH SHISHIO-SAMA?!
YAH!

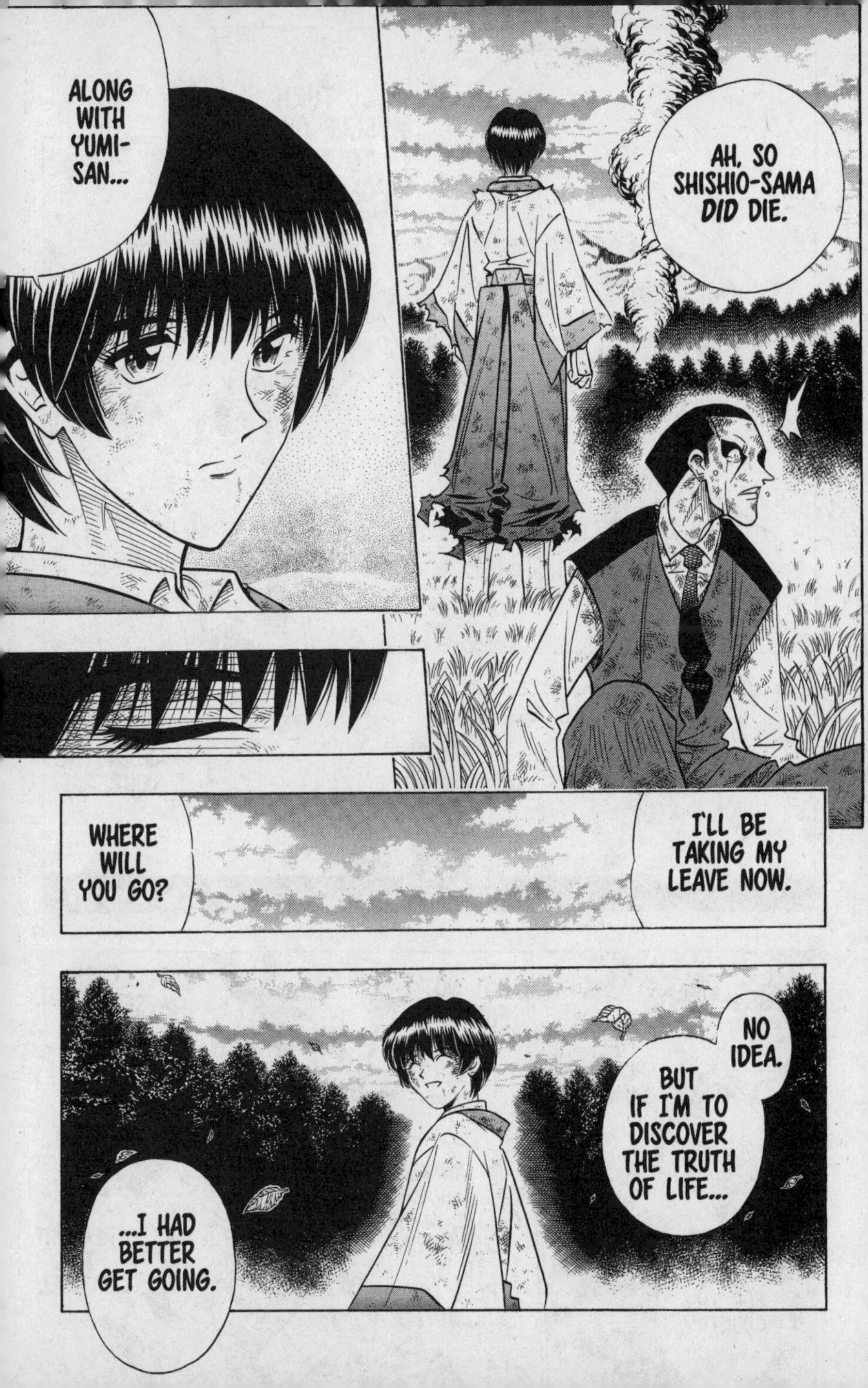
AH, SO SHISHIO-SAMA *DID* DIE.
ALONG WITH YUMI-SAN...
I'LL BE TAKING MY LEAVE NOW.
WHERE WILL YOU GO?
NO IDEA.
BUT IF I'M TO DISCOVER THE TRUTH OF LIFE...
...I HAD BETTER GET GOING.

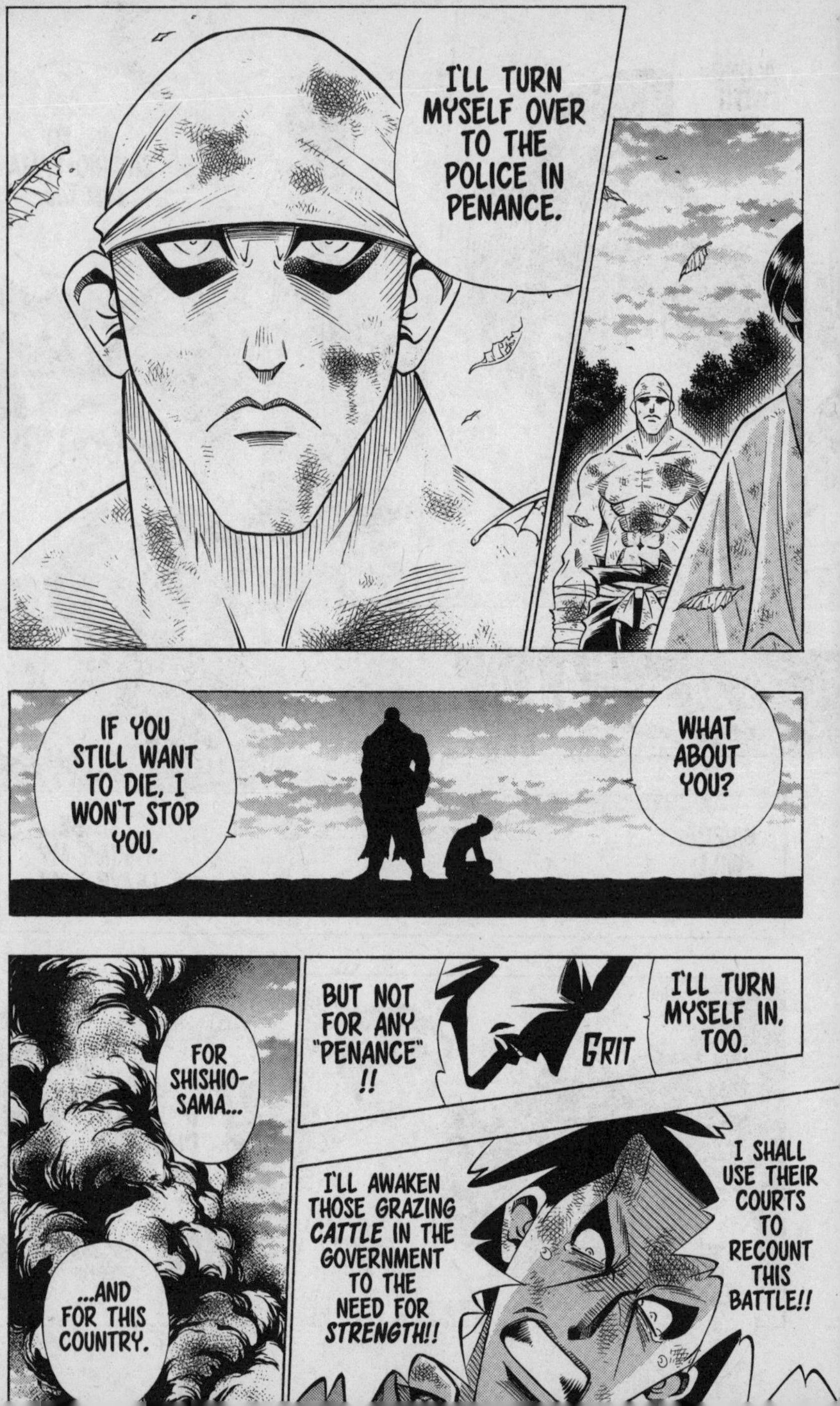
I'LL TURN MYSELF OVER TO THE POLICE IN PENANCE.
WHAT ABOUT YOU?
IF YOU STILL WANT TO DIE, I WON'T STOP YOU.
I'LL TURN MYSELF IN, TOO.
GRIT
BUT NOT FOR ANY "PENANCE"!!
I SHALL USE THEIR COURTS TO RECOUNT THIS BATTLE!!
I'LL AWAKEN THOSE GRAZING CATTLE IN THE GOVERNMENT TO THE NEED FOR STRENGTH!!
FOR SHISHIO-SAMA...
...AND FOR THIS COUNTRY.

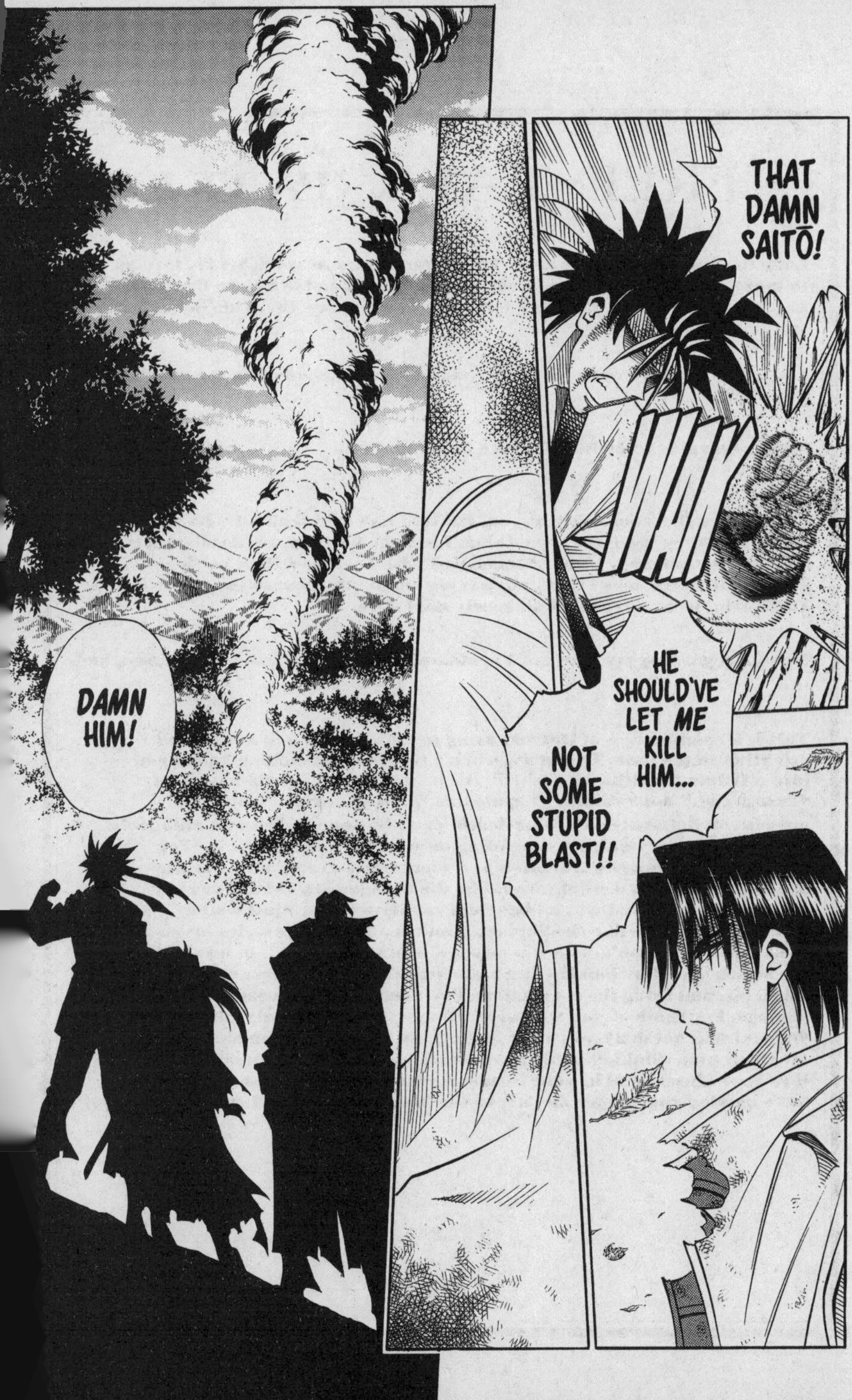
THAT DAMN SAITŌ!
HE SHOULD'VE LET *ME* KILL HIM...
NOT SOME STUPID BLAST!!
DAMN HIM!

"FREE TALK"⟨PART I⟩

Long time no see! Watsuki here. The water heater at work broke, forcing us to move again, and my repainted version of the Zombie Spawn figure is nowhere to be found. Despite such perils of everyday life, I am doing fairly well. Somehow.

I want to say more about the two complaints I touched on in the previous Free Talk.

First, regarding something I wrote in volume 14...

I received a few complaints saying Watsuki had talked about wives and maids as if they were the same thing. I can see how my words might have been taken that way. I was preoccupied with keeping a limit on the number of characters I used, not paying much attention to the subtleties. Those who were offended, I sincerely apologize.

Second, regarding my views of Yamanami Keisuke, the leader of Shinsengumi.

This is a combination of Watsuki using too few words and not paying attention to the tone. To clarify, when I wrote about making Yamanami into a villain for Hijikata Toshizō, the protagonist, I should have said "antagonist," not "villain." I apologize. Writing stories especially ones involving battles of life or death, can't be done without an antagonist. This changes very quickly depending on who the protagonist is. (For example, if we rewrite *RuroKen* as a picaresque drama with Shishio as the protagonist, Kenshin would be the antagonist). Even if you say that the Shinsengumi was a historical reality and not "just a story," you can't deny that we like the Shinsengumi because of the stories involving them. (Watsuki hasn't once met anyone who said they fell in love with the Shinsengumi by looking at a historical timeline!) Please think about this a bit, and using the corrections I've made above, reread the original passage. For those of you who are still upset, I can't do anything more. Watsuki will not deny you your feelings, so please move on and forget all about him, thinking of his words as the mumblings of an idiot, and love the Shinsengumi in your own separate ways. But those of you who have quelled your anger...let's love the Shinsengumi together!

Act 147
Kyoto Epilogue
Fate of the Juppongatana (Part I)

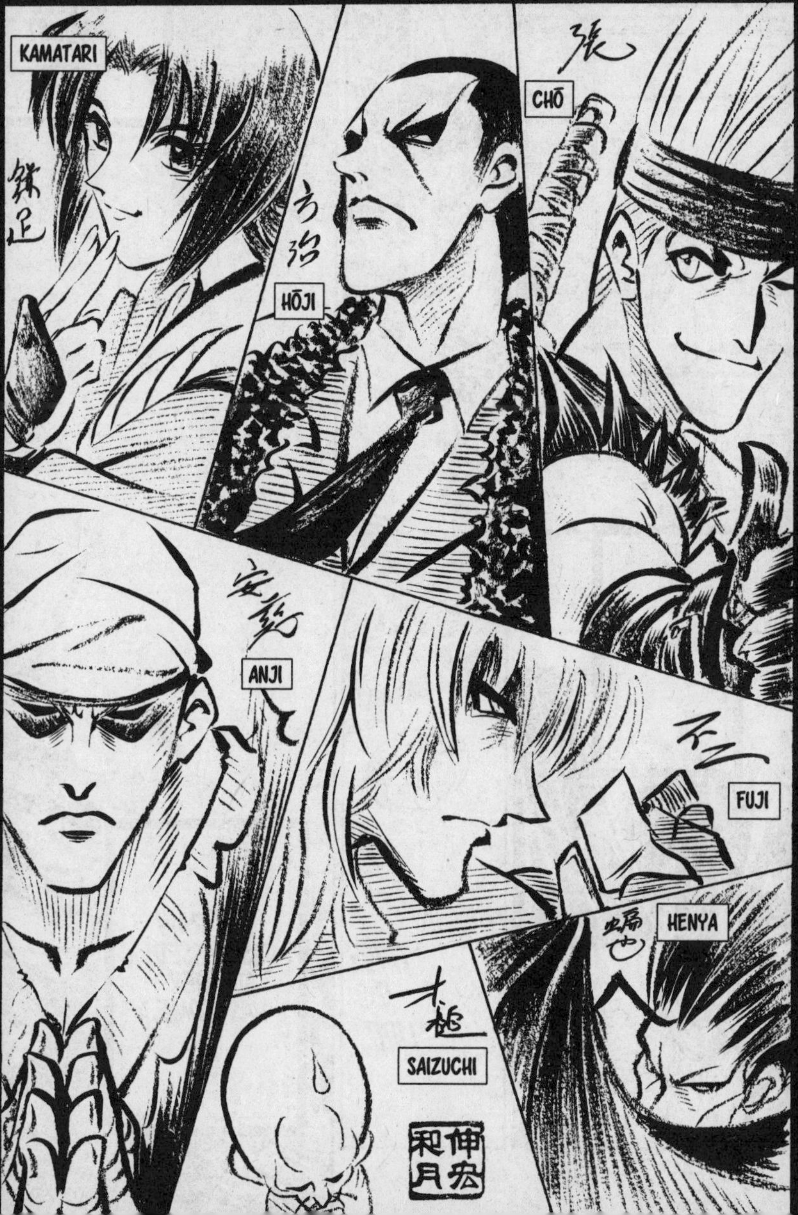
CHŌ
HŌJI
KAMATARI
FUJI
ANJI
HENYA
SAIZUCHI

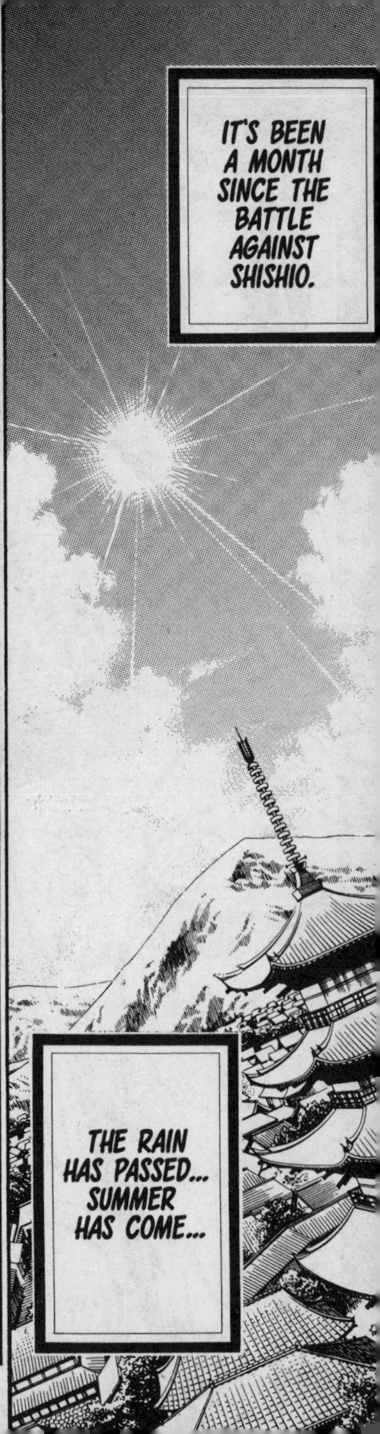
IT'S BEEN A MONTH SINCE THE BATTLE AGAINST SHISHIO.
THE RAIN HAS PASSED... SUMMER HAS COME...

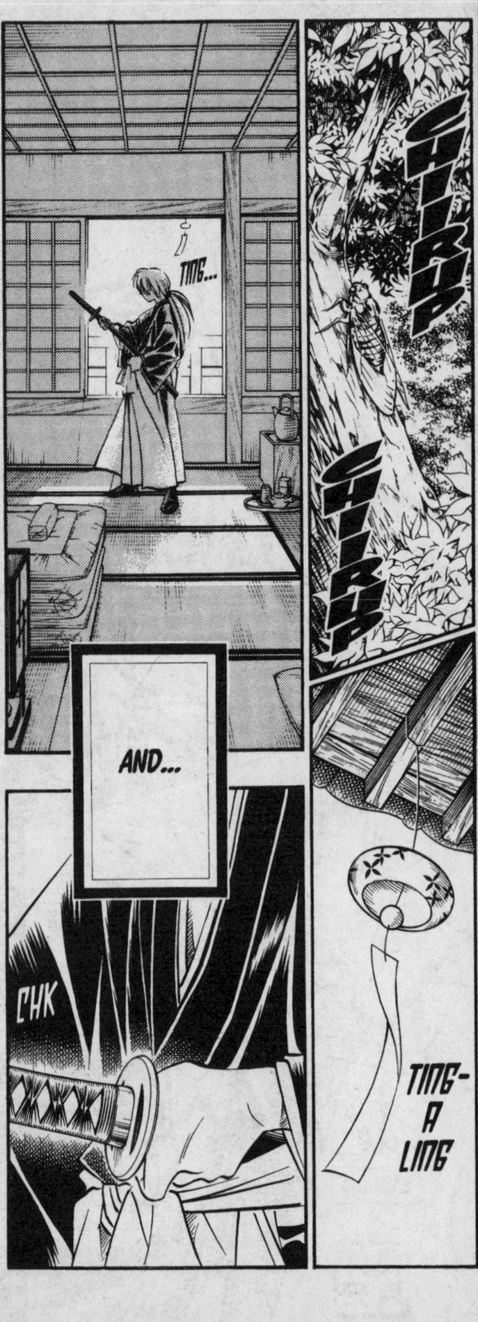
CHIRP
CHIRP
TING...
TING-A LING
AND...
CHK

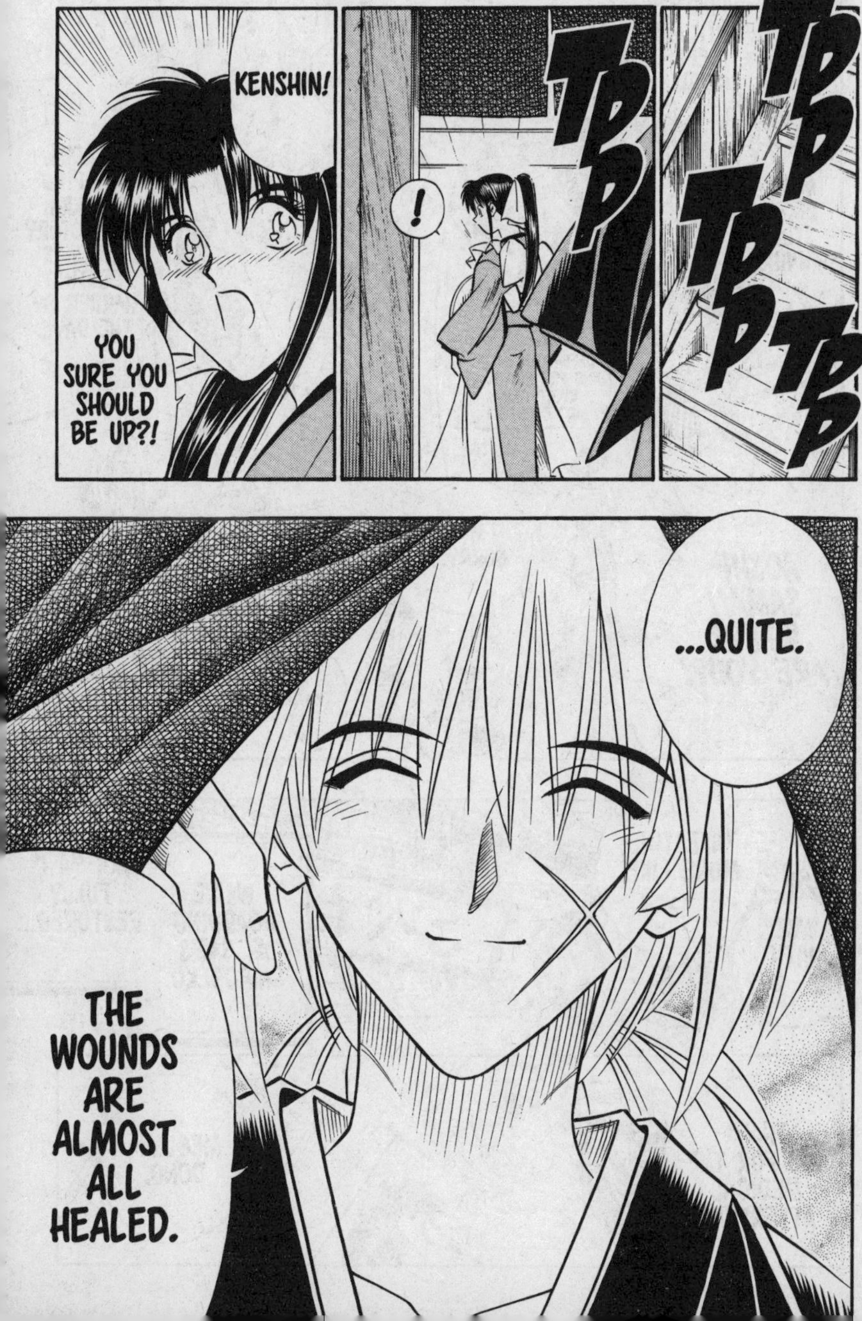
TP TP TP TP
TP
!
KENSHIN!
YOU SURE YOU SHOULD BE UP?!
...QUITE.
THE WOUNDS ARE ALMOST ALL HEALED.

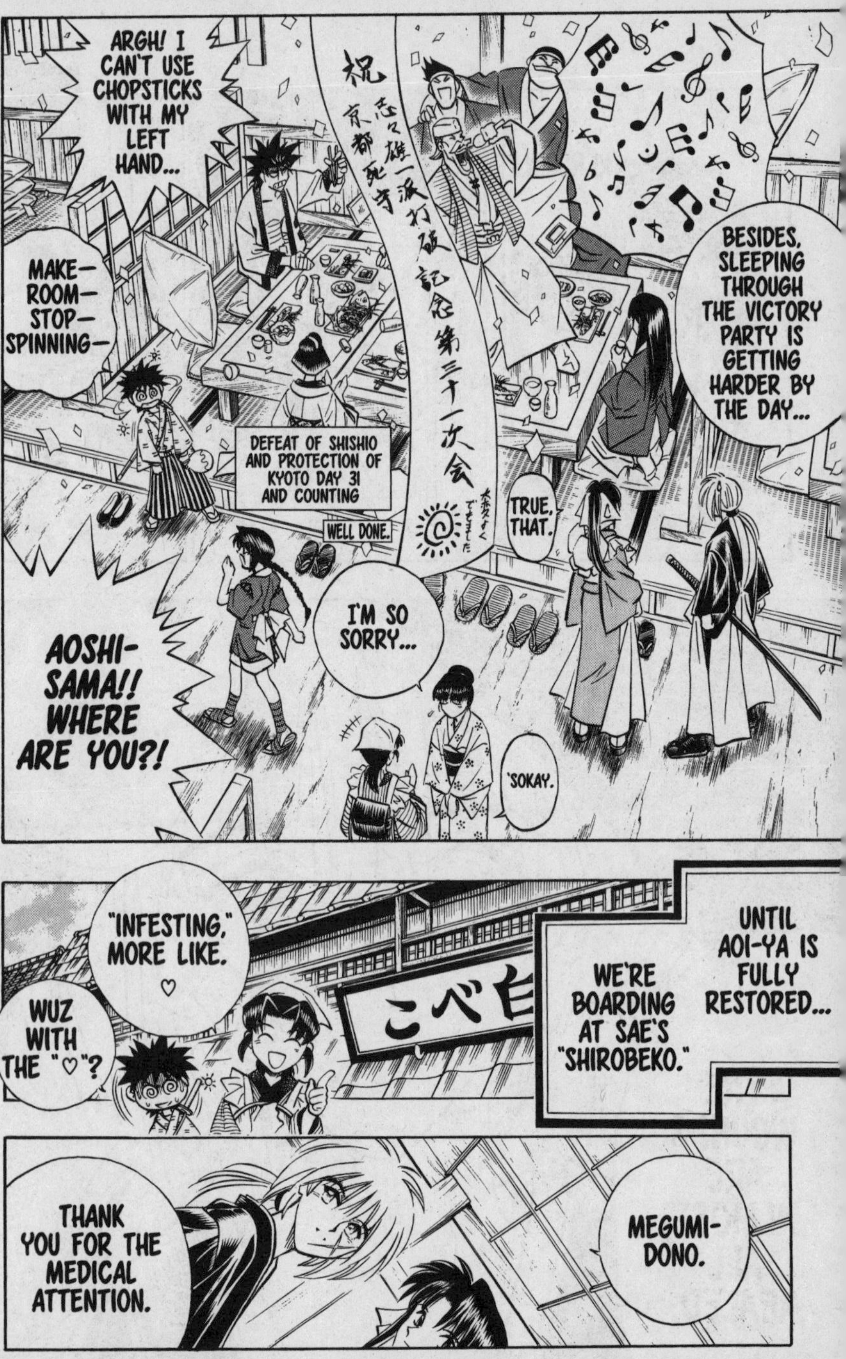
BESIDES, SLEEPING THROUGH THE VICTORY PARTY IS GETTING HARDER BY THE DAY...
祝
志々雄一派打破記念第三十一次会
京都死守
ARGH! I CAN'T USE CHOPSTICKS WITH MY LEFT HAND...
MAKE— ROOM— STOP— SPINNING—
DEFEAT OF SHISHIO AND PROTECTION OF KYOTO DAY 31 AND COUNTING
大変よくできました
WELL DONE.
TRUE, THAT.
I'M SO SORRY...
AOSHI-SAMA!! WHERE ARE YOU?!
'SOKAY.
UNTIL AOI-YA IS FULLY RESTORED...
WE'RE BOARDING AT SAE'S "SHIROBEKO."
"INFESTING," MORE LIKE. ♡
WUZ WITH THE "♡"?
MEGUMI-DONO.
THANK YOU FOR THE MEDICAL ATTENTION.

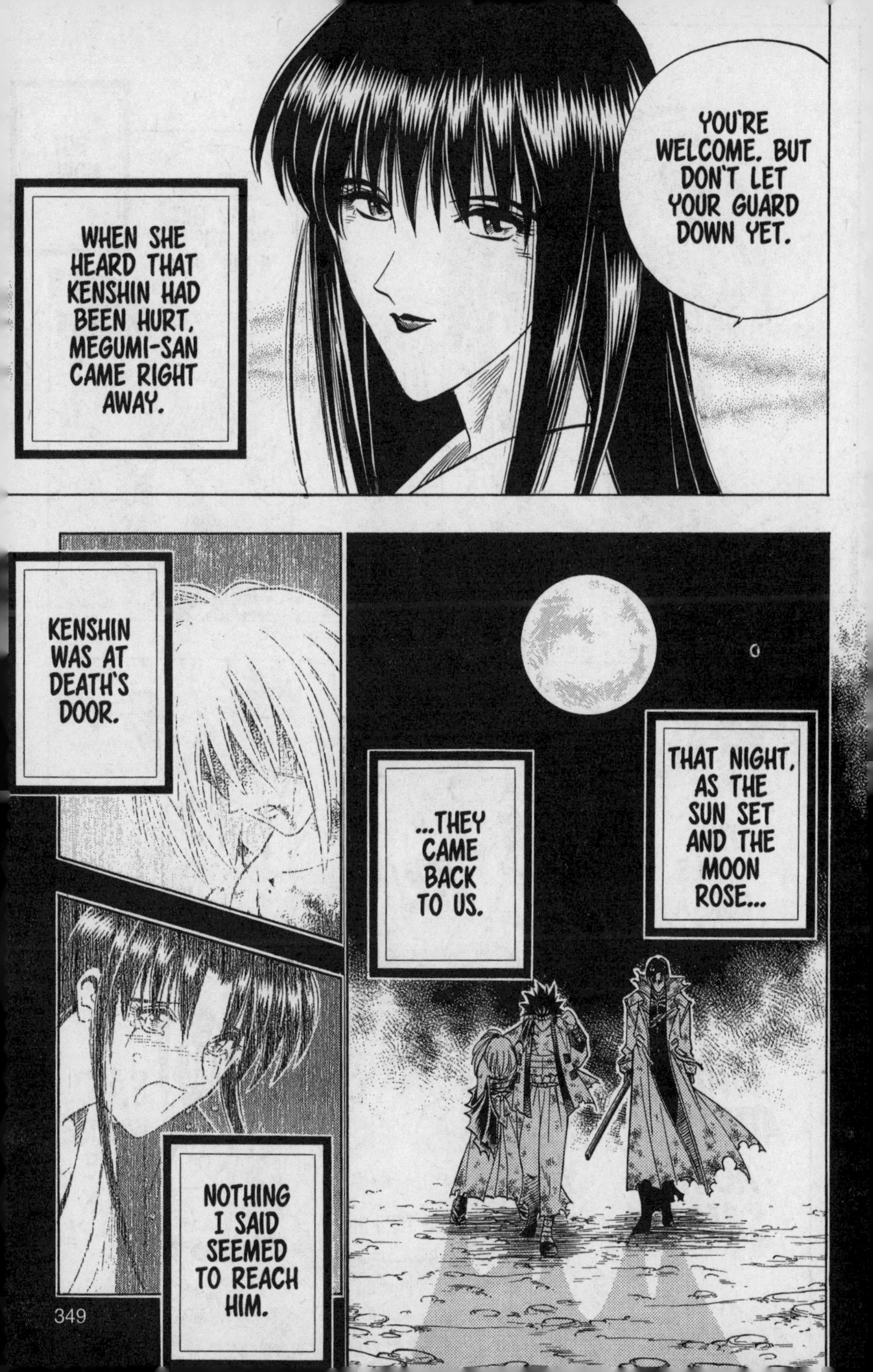
YOU'RE WELCOME. BUT DON'T LET YOUR GUARD DOWN YET.
WHEN SHE HEARD THAT KENSHIN HAD BEEN HURT, MEGUMI-SAN CAME RIGHT AWAY.
THAT NIGHT, AS THE SUN SET AND THE MOON ROSE...
...THEY CAME BACK TO US.
KENSHIN WAS AT DEATH'S DOOR.
NOTHING I SAID SEEMED TO REACH HIM.

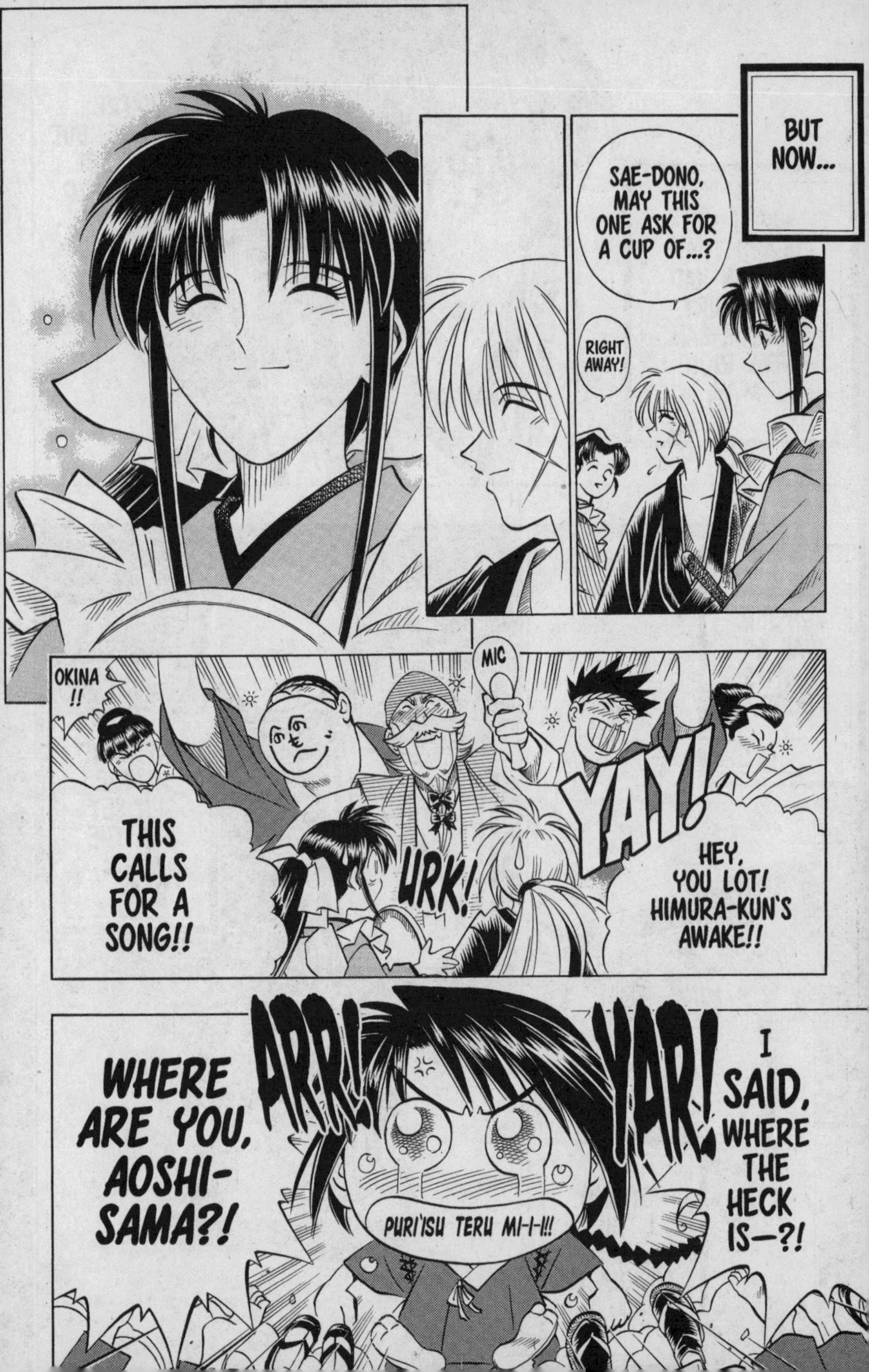
BUT NOW...
SAE-DONO, MAY THIS ONE ASK FOR A CUP OF...?
RIGHT AWAY!
HEY, YOU LOT! HIMURA-KUN'S AWAKE!!
YAY!
MIC
URK!
THIS CALLS FOR A SONG!!
OKINA !!
I SAID, WHERE THE HECK IS—?!
YAR!
ARR-R!
PURI'ISU TERU MI-I-I!!
WHERE ARE YOU, AOSHI-SAMA?!

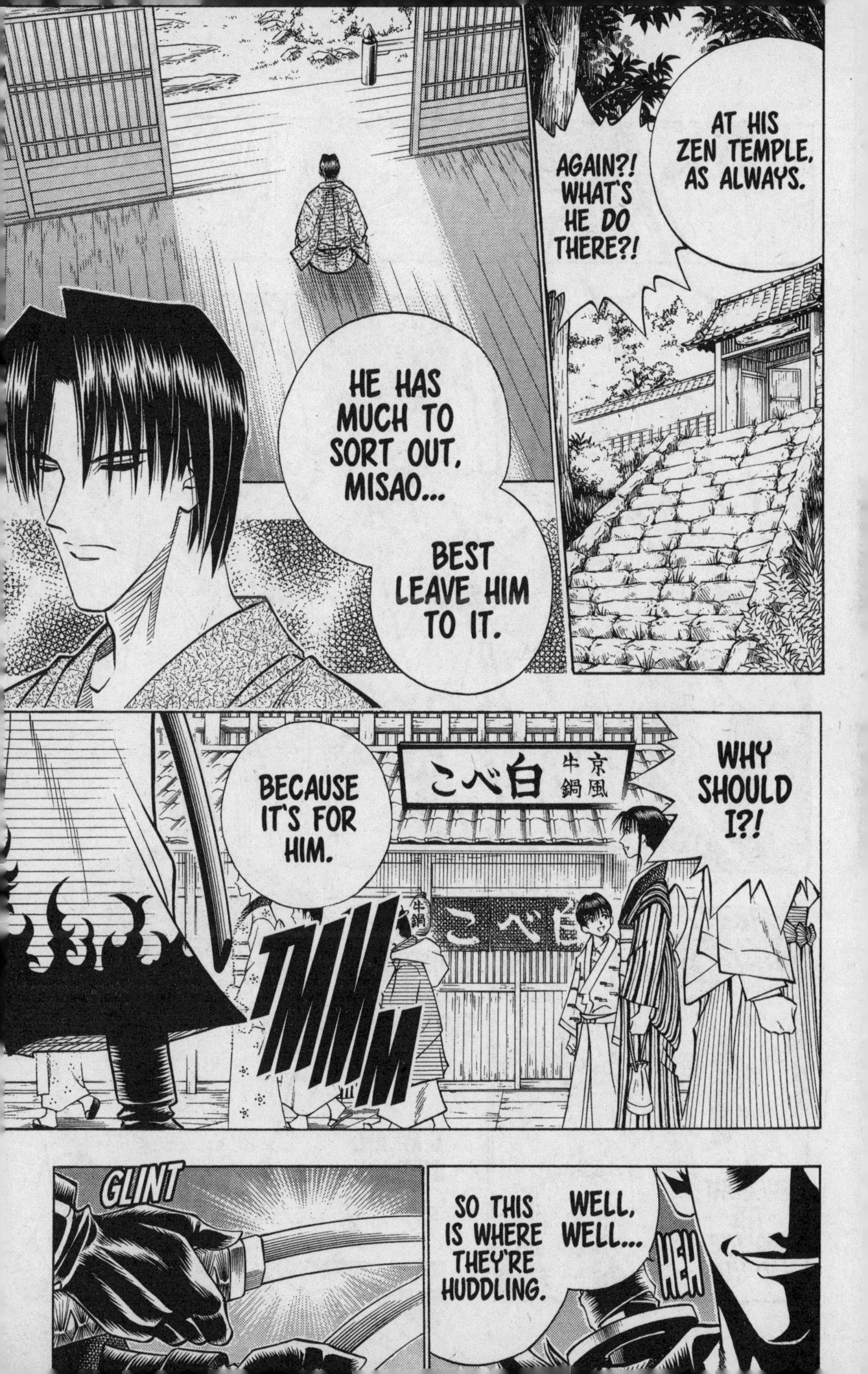
AT HIS ZEN TEMPLE, AS ALWAYS.
AGAIN?! WHAT'S HE DO THERE?!
HE HAS MUCH TO SORT OUT, MISAO...
BEST LEAVE HIM TO IT.
WHY SHOULD I?!
京風 牛鍋
白べこ
BECAUSE IT'S FOR HIM.
牛鍋
TMMM
WELL, WELL...
SO THIS IS WHERE THEY'RE HUDDLING.
HEH
GLINT

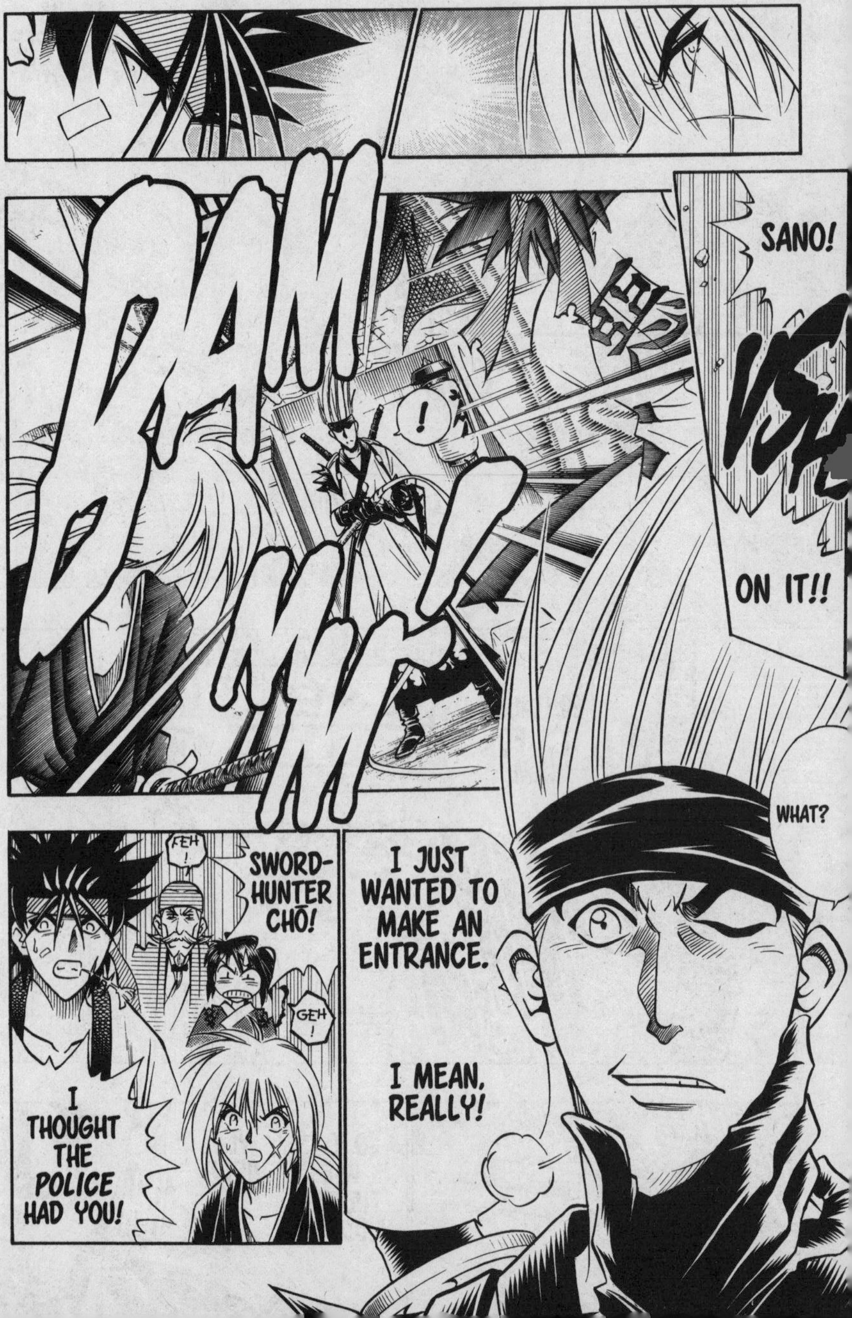
SANO!
ON IT!!
!
WHAT?
I JUST WANTED TO MAKE AN ENTRANCE.
I MEAN, REALLY!
SWORD-HUNTER CHŌ!
FEH!
GEH!
I THOUGHT THE POLICE HAD YOU!

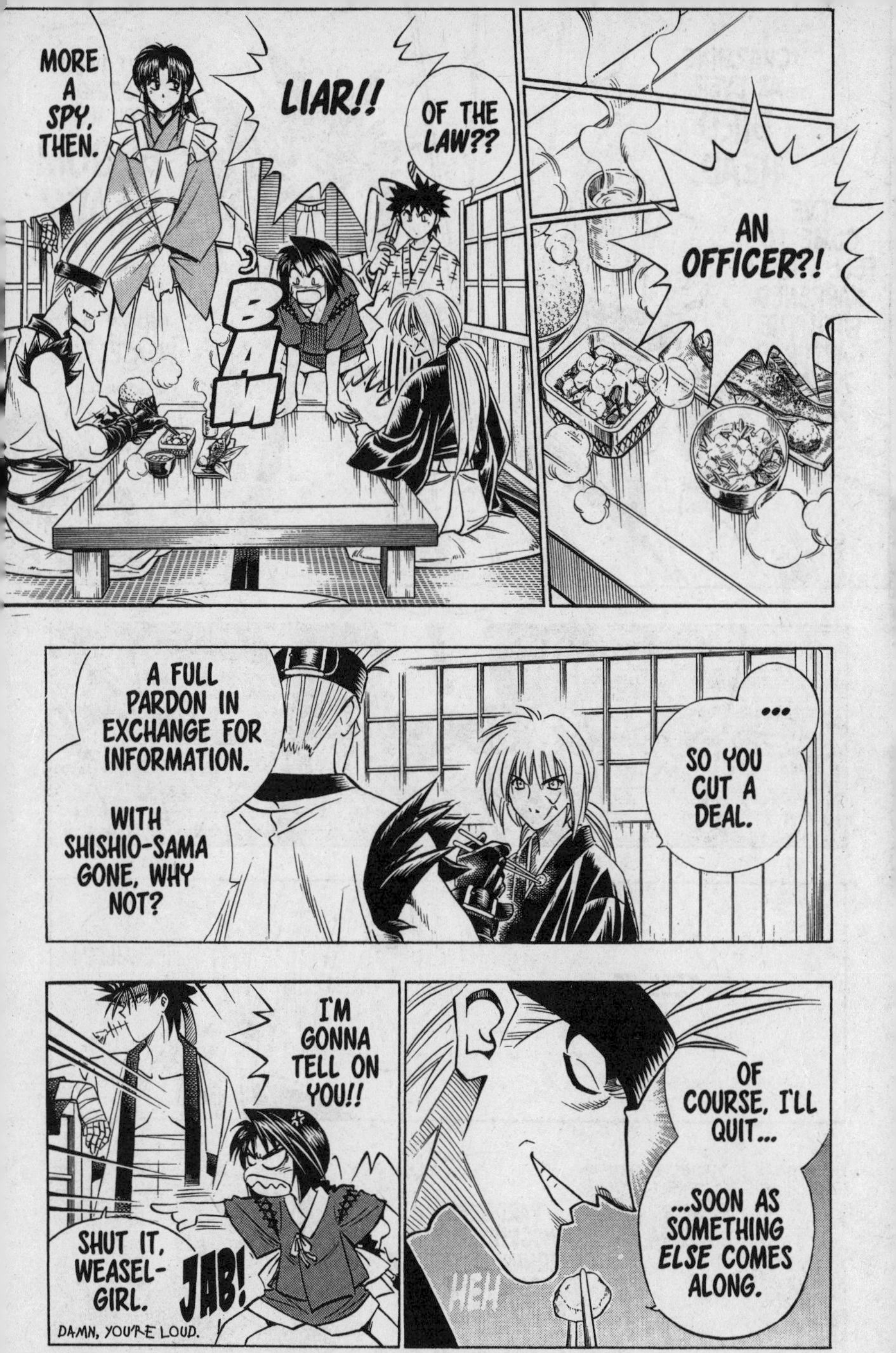
AN OFFICER?!
OF THE LAW??
LIAR!!
MORE A SPY, THEN.
BAM
...
SO YOU CUT A DEAL.
A FULL PARDON IN EXCHANGE FOR INFORMATION.
WITH SHISHIO-SAMA GONE, WHY NOT?
OF COURSE, I'LL QUIT...
...SOON AS SOMETHING ELSE COMES ALONG.
HEH
I'M GONNA TELL ON YOU!!
SHUT IT, WEASEL-GIRL.
JAB!
DAMN, YOU'RE LOUD.

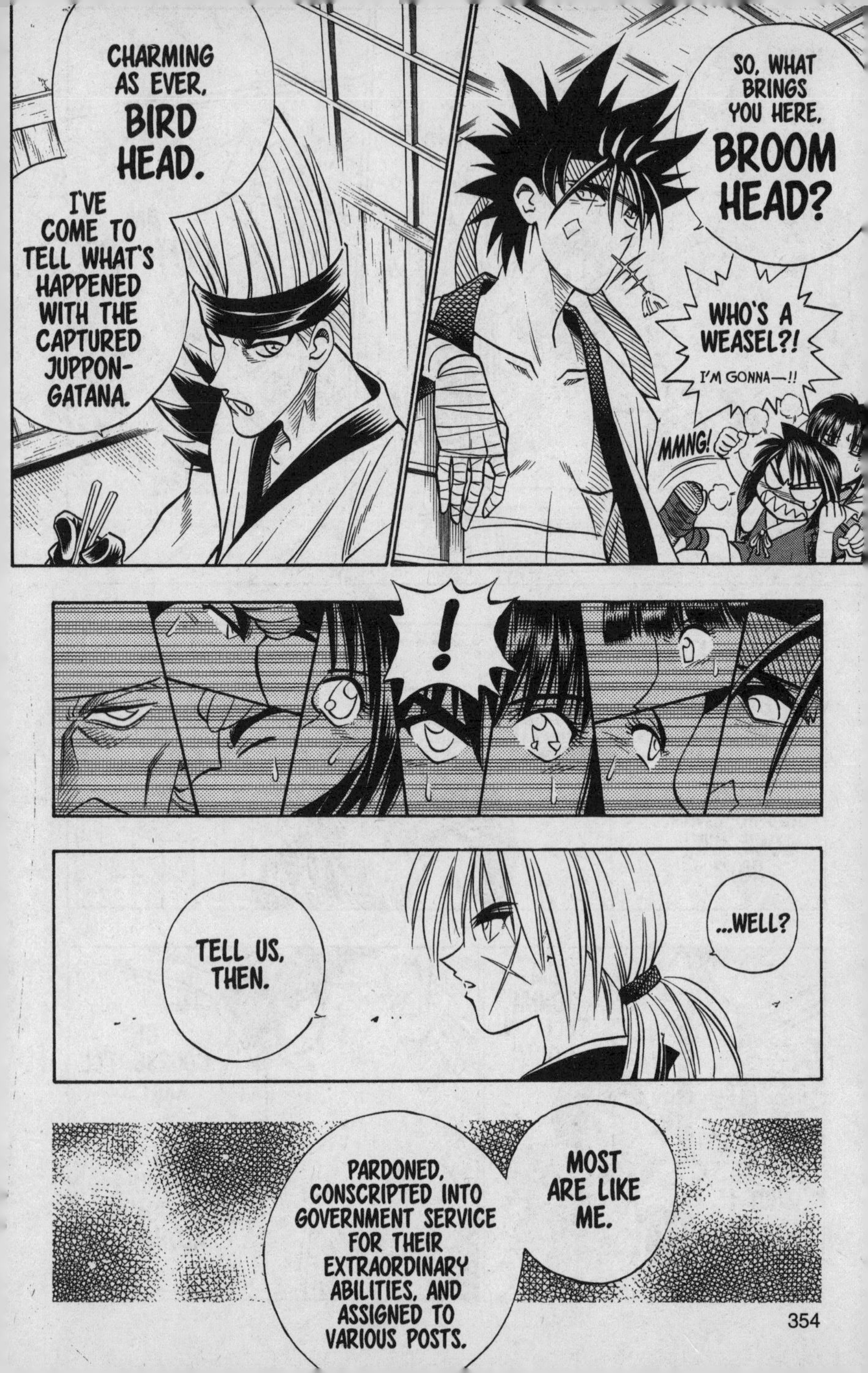
SO, WHAT BRINGS YOU HERE, BROOM HEAD?
WHO'S A WEASEL?!
I'M GONNA—!!
MMNG!
CHARMING AS EVER, BIRD HEAD.
I'VE COME TO TELL WHAT'S HAPPENED WITH THE CAPTURED JUPPON-GATANA.
!
...WELL?
TELL US, THEN.
MOST ARE LIKE ME.
PARDONED, CONSCRIPTED INTO GOVERNMENT SERVICE FOR THEIR EXTRAORDINARY ABILITIES, AND ASSIGNED TO VARIOUS POSTS.

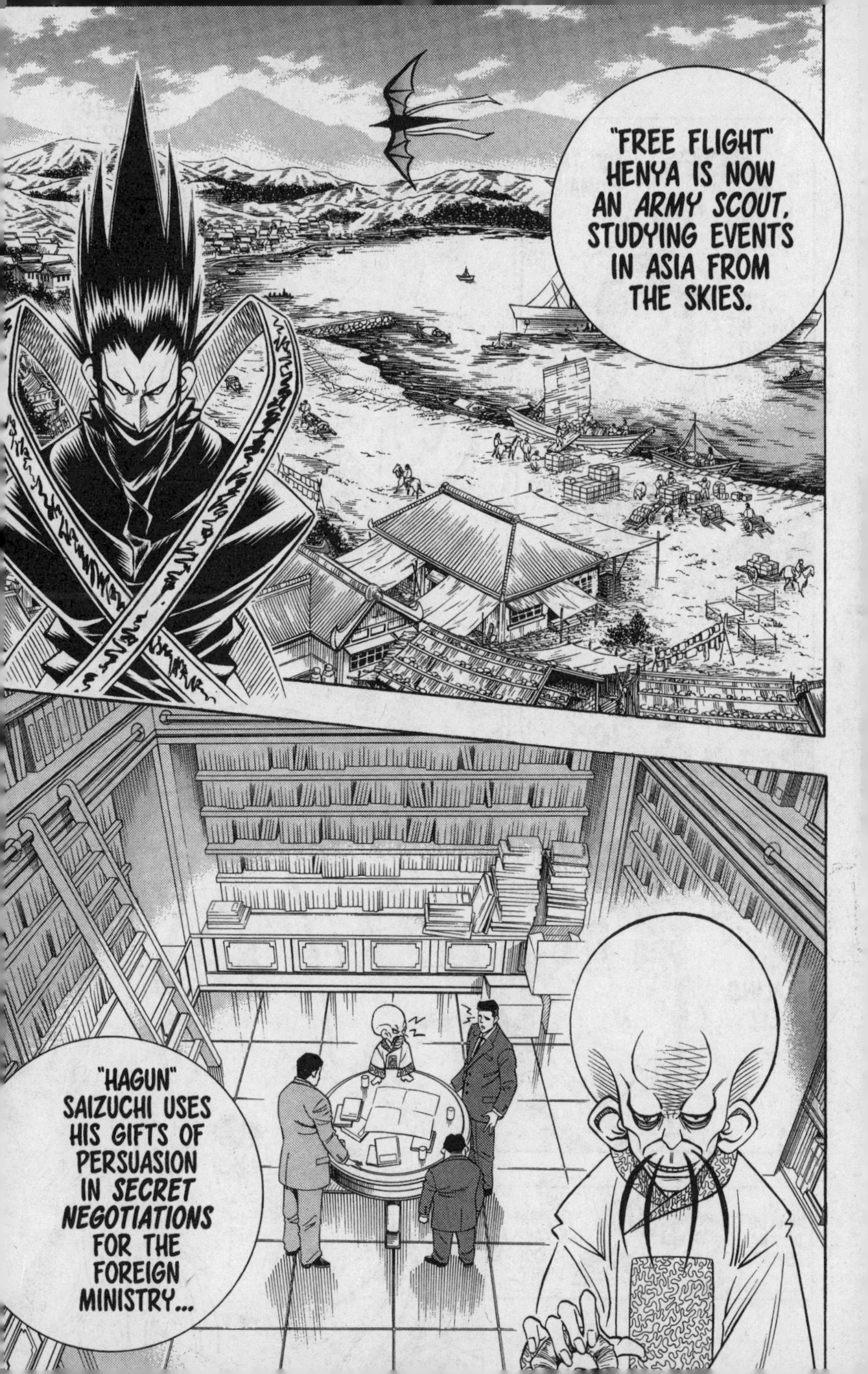
"FREE FLIGHT" HENYA IS NOW AN ARMY SCOUT, STUDYING EVENTS IN ASIA FROM THE SKIES.
"HAGUN" SAIZUCHI USES HIS GIFTS OF PERSUASION IN SECRET NEGOTIATIONS FOR THE FOREIGN MINISTRY...

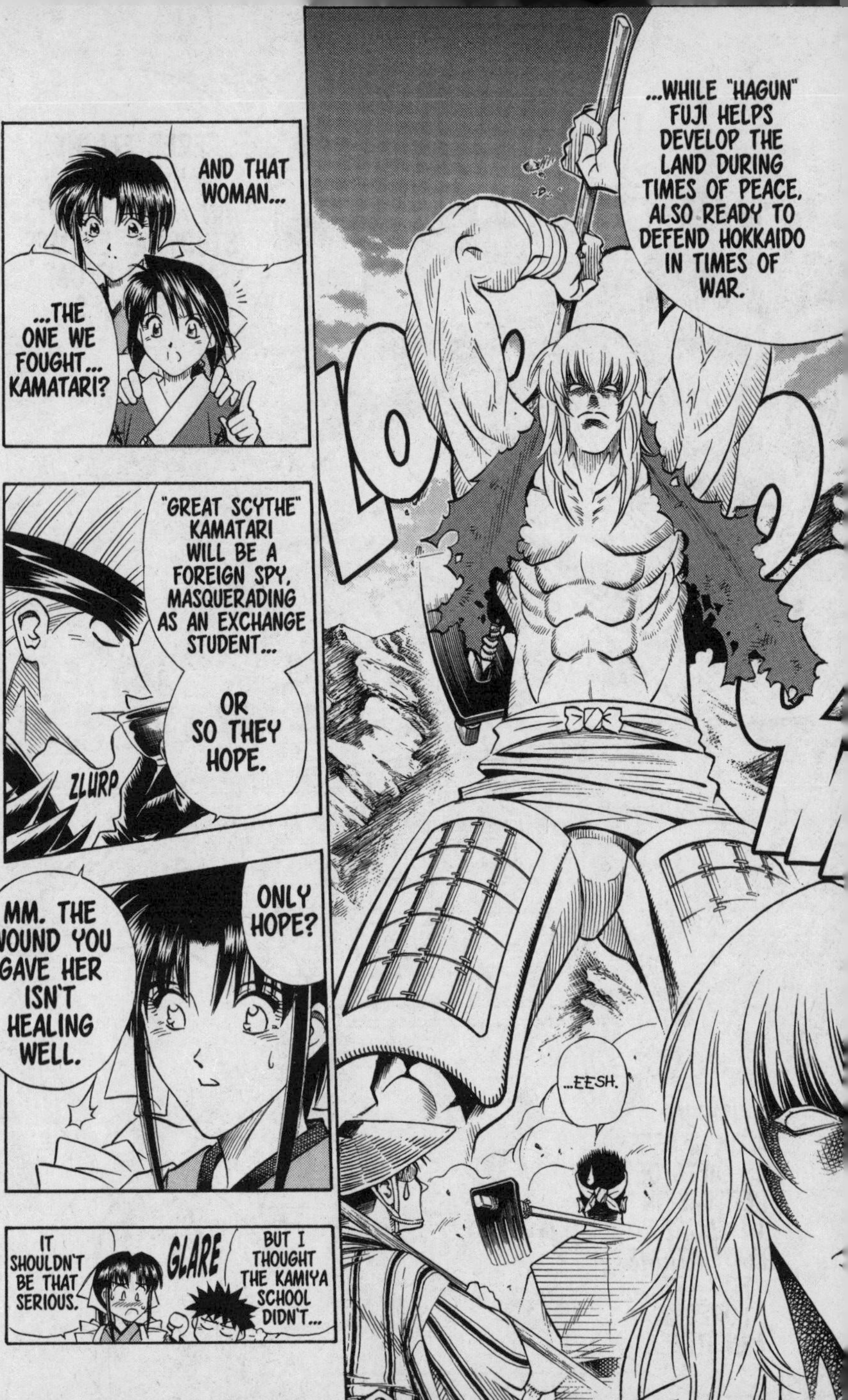
...WHILE "HAGUN" FUJI HELPS DEVELOP THE LAND DURING TIMES OF PEACE, ALSO READY TO DEFEND HOKKAIDO IN TIMES OF WAR.
...EESH.
AND THAT WOMAN...
...THE ONE WE FOUGHT... KAMATARI?
"GREAT SCYTHE" KAMATARI WILL BE A FOREIGN SPY, MASQUERADING AS AN EXCHANGE STUDENT...
OR SO THEY HOPE.
ZLURP
ONLY HOPE?
MM. THE WOUND YOU GAVE HER ISN'T HEALING WELL.
BUT I THOUGHT THE KAMIYA SCHOOL DIDN'T...
GLARE
IT SHOULDN'T BE THAT SERIOUS.

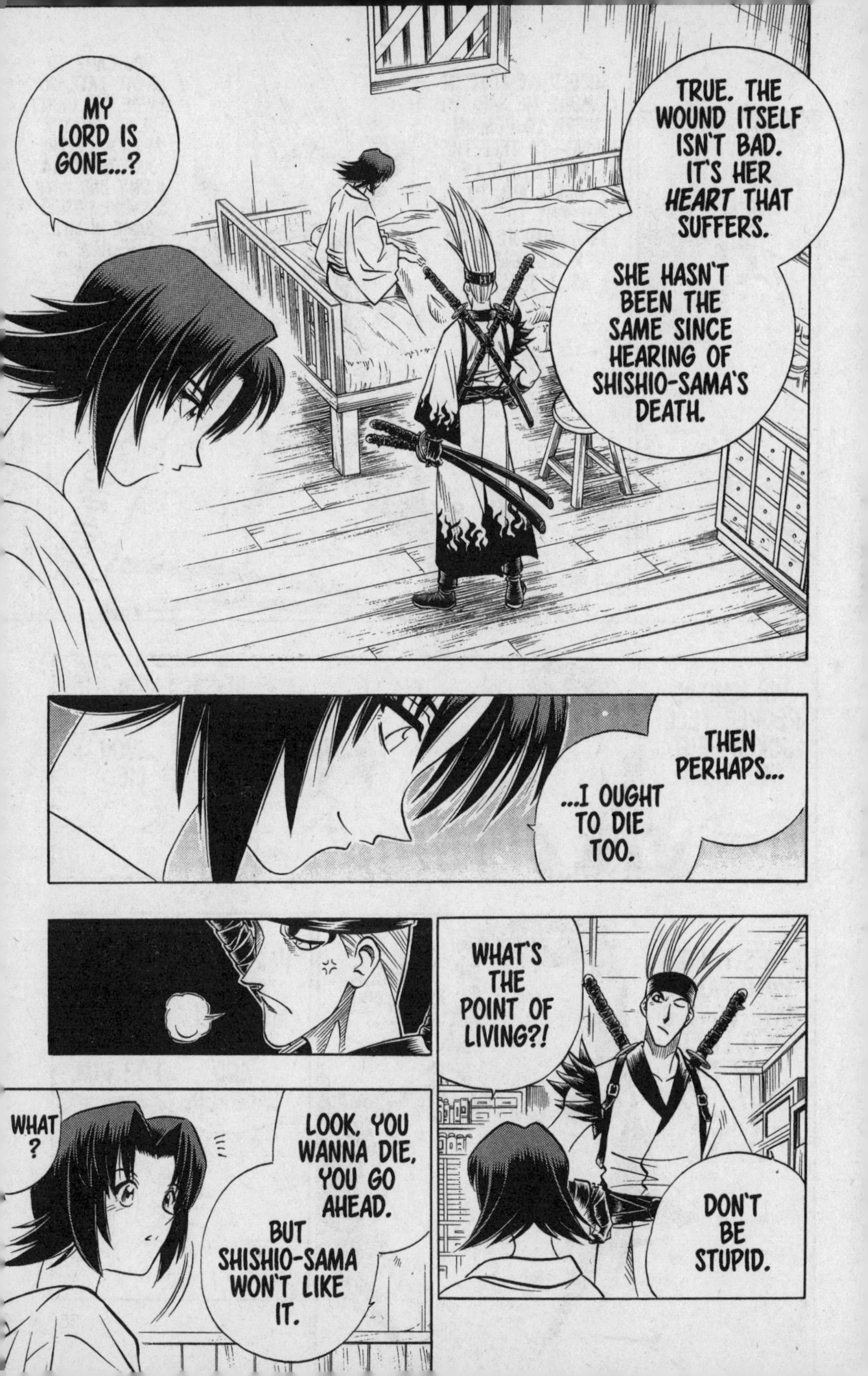
TRUE. THE WOUND ITSELF ISN'T BAD. IT'S HER *HEART* THAT SUFFERS.
SHE HASN'T BEEN THE SAME SINCE HEARING OF SHISHIO-SAMA'S DEATH.
MY LORD IS GONE...?
THEN PERHAPS...
...I OUGHT TO DIE TOO.
WHAT'S THE POINT OF LIVING?!
DON'T BE STUPID.
LOOK, YOU WANNA DIE, YOU GO AHEAD.
BUT SHISHIO-SAMA WON'T LIKE IT.
WHAT?

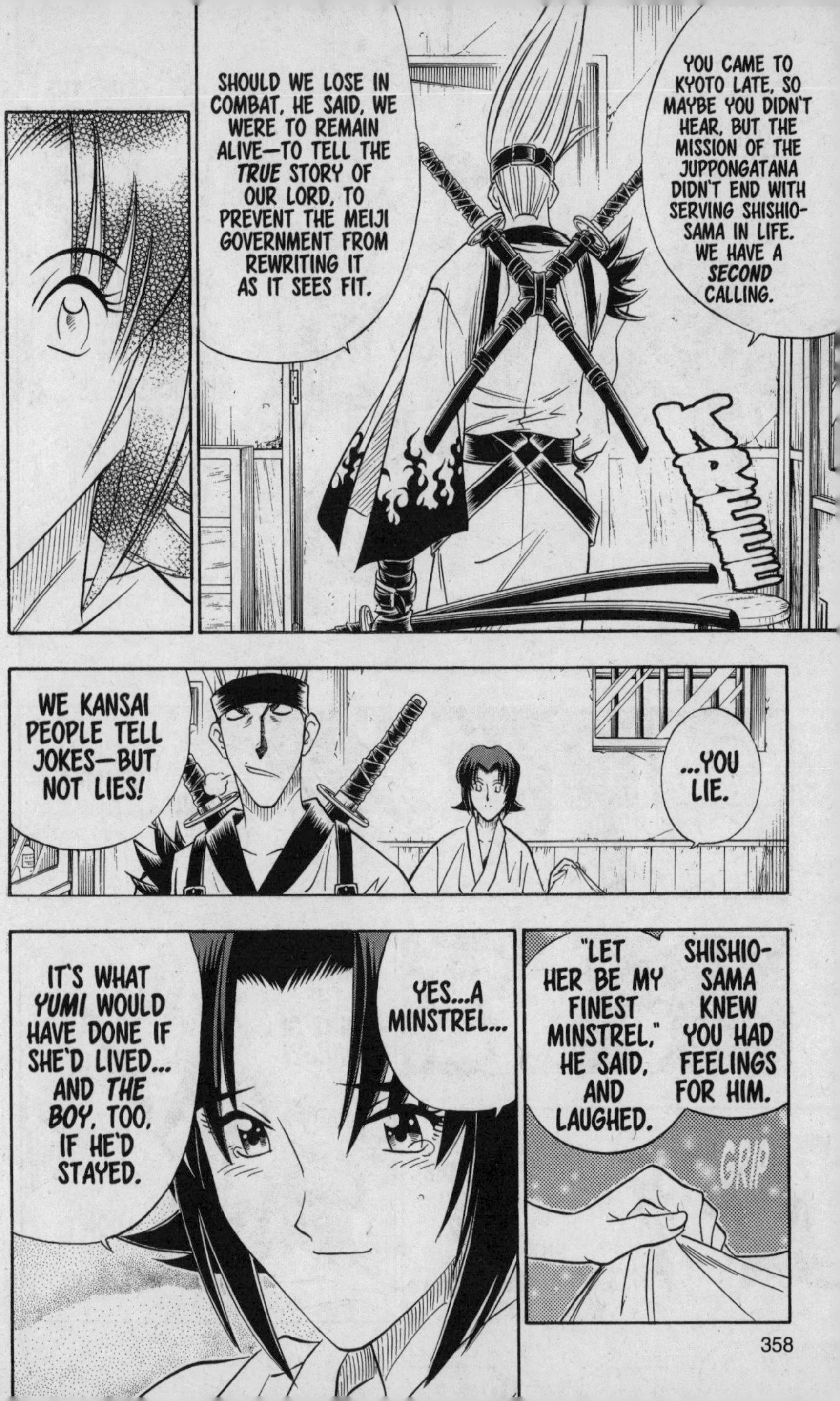
YOU CAME TO KYOTO LATE, SO MAYBE YOU DIDN'T HEAR, BUT THE MISSION OF THE JUPPONGATANA DIDN'T END WITH SERVING SHISHIO-SAMA IN LIFE. WE HAVE A *SECOND* CALLING.
SHOULD WE LOSE IN COMBAT, HE SAID, WE WERE TO REMAIN ALIVE—TO TELL THE *TRUE* STORY OF OUR LORD, TO PREVENT THE MEIJI GOVERNMENT FROM REWRITING IT AS IT SEES FIT.
...YOU LIE.
WE KANSAI PEOPLE TELL JOKES—BUT NOT LIES!
SHISHIO-SAMA KNEW YOU HAD FEELINGS FOR HIM.
"LET HER BE MY FINEST MINSTREL," HE SAID, AND LAUGHED.
GRIP
YES...A MINSTREL...
IT'S WHAT *YUMI* WOULD HAVE DONE IF SHE'D LIVED... AND *THE BOY*, TOO, IF HE'D STAYED.

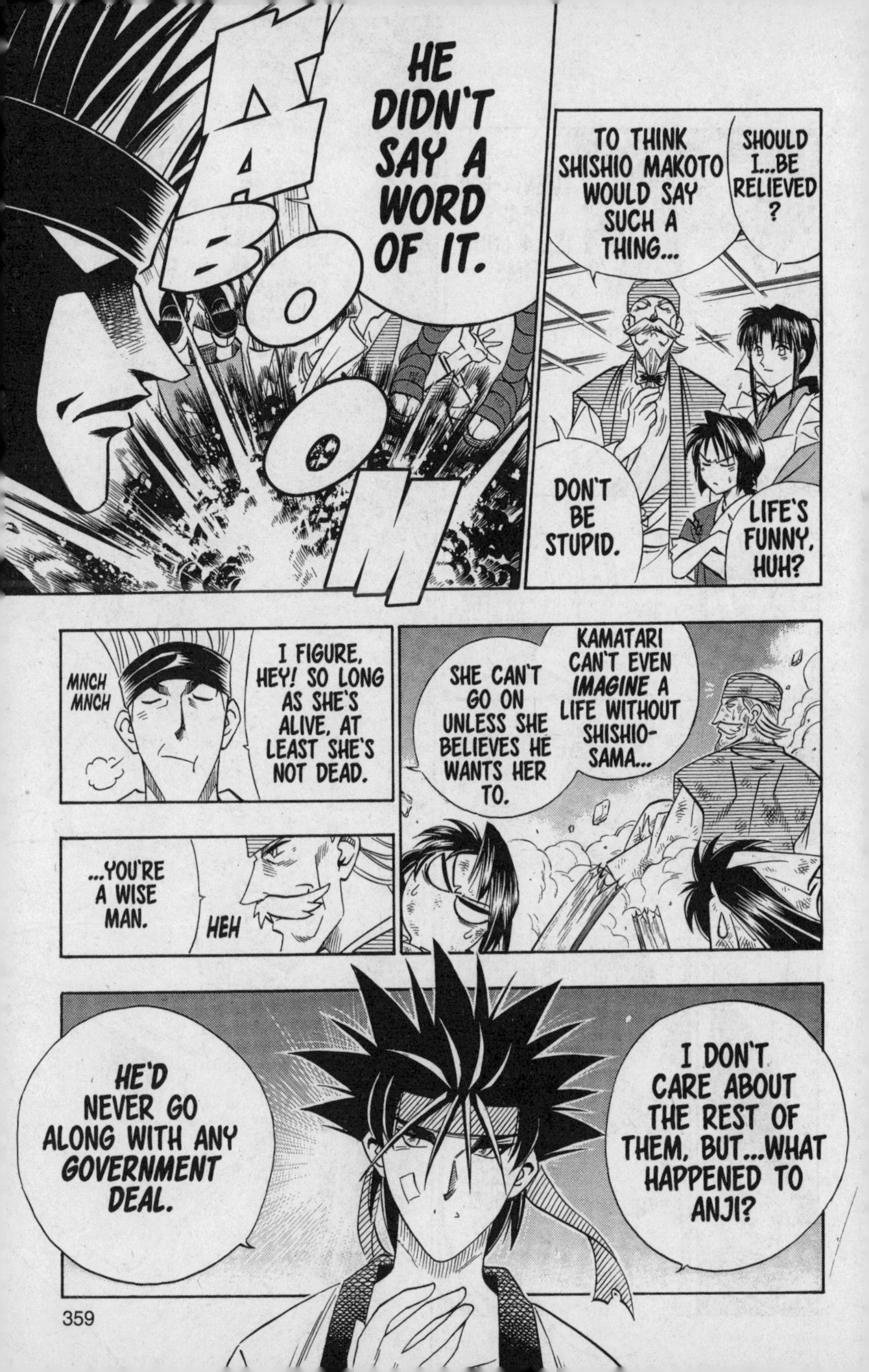
SHOULD I...BE RELIEVED?
TO THINK SHISHIO MAKOTO WOULD SAY SUCH A THING...
LIFE'S FUNNY, HUH?
DON'T BE STUPID.
HE DIDN'T SAY A WORD OF IT.
BOOM
KAMATARI CAN'T EVEN *IMAGINE* A LIFE WITHOUT SHISHIO-SAMA...
SHE CAN'T GO ON UNLESS SHE BELIEVES HE WANTS HER TO.
I FIGURE, HEY! SO LONG AS SHE'S ALIVE, AT LEAST SHE'S NOT DEAD.
MNCH MNCH
HEH
...YOU'RE A WISE MAN.
I DON'T CARE ABOUT THE REST OF THEM, BUT...WHAT HAPPENED TO ANJI?
HE'D NEVER GO ALONG WITH ANY GOVERNMENT DEAL.

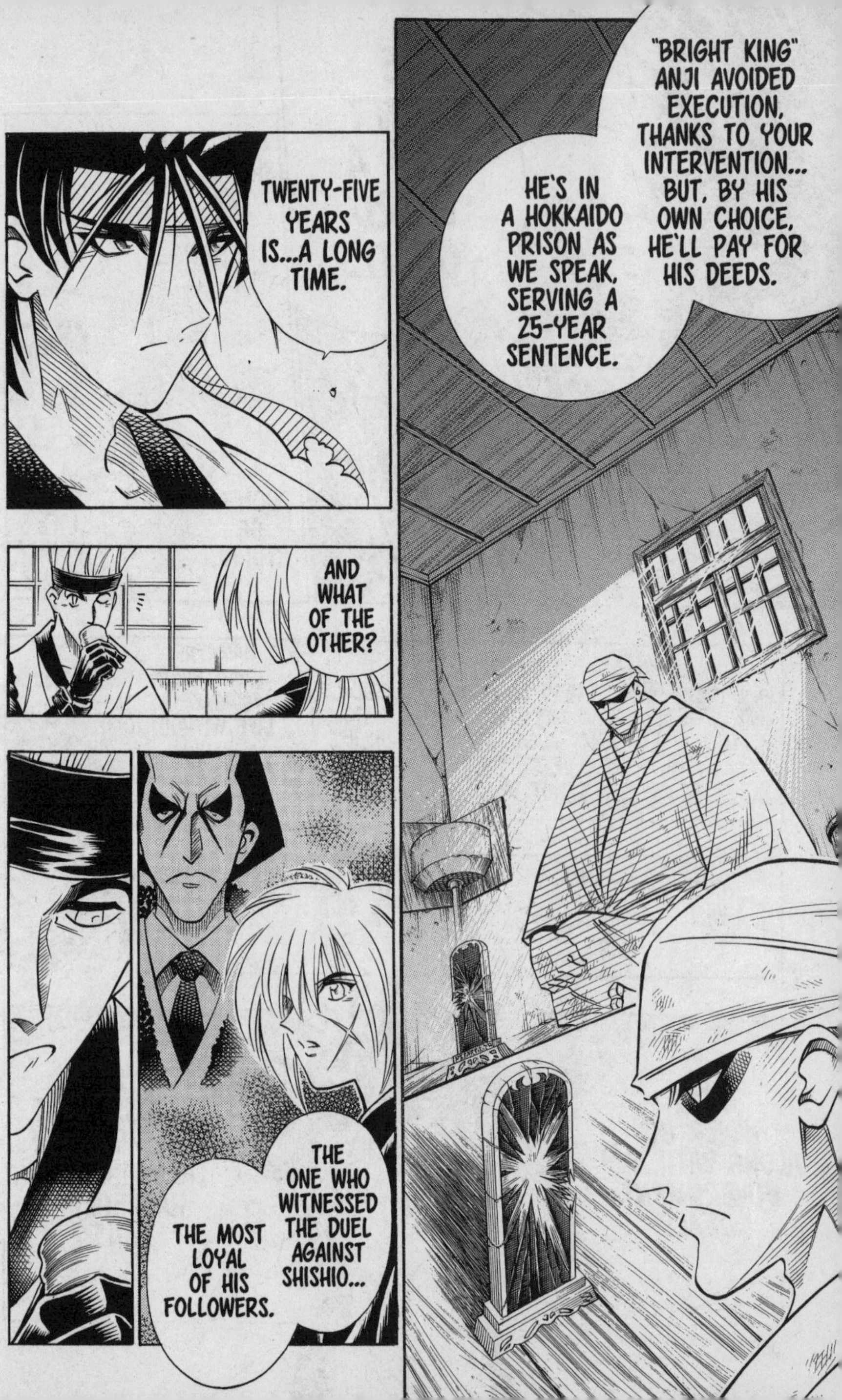
"BRIGHT KING" ANJI AVOIDED EXECUTION, THANKS TO YOUR INTERVENTION... BUT, BY HIS OWN CHOICE, HE'LL PAY FOR HIS DEEDS.
HE'S IN A HOKKAIDO PRISON AS WE SPEAK, SERVING A 25-YEAR SENTENCE.
TWENTY-FIVE YEARS IS...A LONG TIME.
AND WHAT OF THE OTHER?
THE ONE WHO WITNESSED THE DUEL AGAINST SHISHIO...
THE MOST LOYAL OF HIS FOLLOWERS.

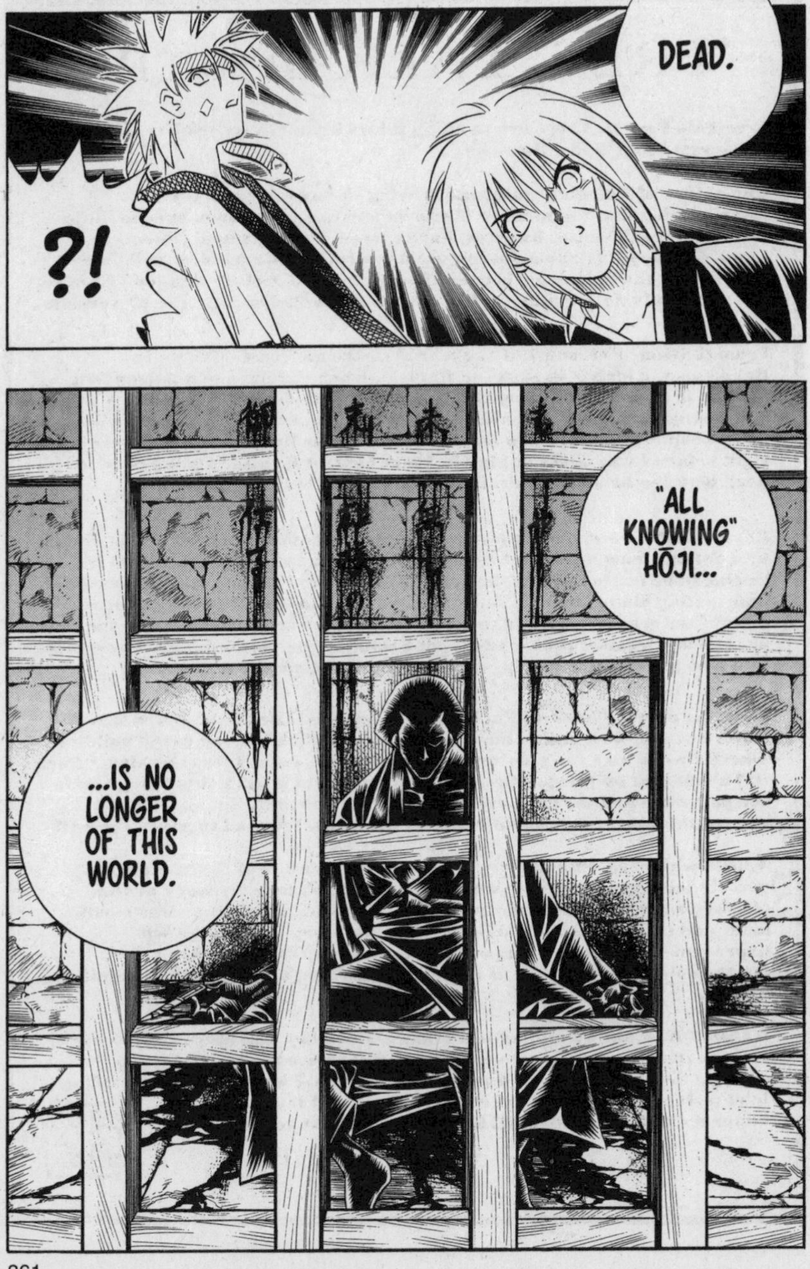
DEAD.
?!
"ALL KNOWING" HŌJI...
...IS NO LONGER OF THIS WORLD.

"FREE TALK"〈PART II〉

Free Talk Part II. There are so many things I want to write about (all stupid, of course) that I'll just list them.

The nature of *Polygon Samu Supi* is being slowly revealed. It's a bit disappointing that the number of characters has gone down, but the Ninja (Hanzō, Garu, Sōgetsu, Kagetsu) have exceeded the Samurai (Haōmaru, Ukyō, Genjūrō)!! (Hanma doesn't use a sword, and is excluded. Shiki uses swords, but the hair color is too different, so we'll exclude him too.) Even so, I'm still really anticipating it. Oh, but I'm still anticipating... the 2D version...

From the same SNK suddenly appeared *Gekka no Kenshi*. It's set in Bakumatsu, which is enough for Watsuki, who's dreamed of a Bakumatsu version of *Samu Supi*. (I literally had a dream. Haōmaru's descendant was a Shinsengumi member, Genjūrō's descendant was a hitokiri who'd killed 1,000 people, and Nakoruru for some reason was just Nakoruru. I woke up right before I was going to play it. I was heartbroken.) It's going head to head with the *Samu Supi* series...I hope they're both fun games.

Recently, I've received fan letters with "print club" photos on them. When I first got one from a friend, I thought, "What's so fun about this?" But it's getting to be fun looking at them. Still, I'd hate having one taken of myself. I hate getting photos taken... But I do have some interest in taking photos. People and scenery can add to my drawing experience. I don't have the time or the knowledge at the moment, but I think I'll get hooked soon. Those of you who have confidence in your looks, contact me about modeling!

Speaking of being hooked, I'm hooked on sunsets. I never get bored watching them. But they just built a huge apartment building in front of the building where I work, so I can't see any sunsets now. Then, as I was thinking, "Darn it!" about that building, I discovered that at night it has lights that go on in the pathways and the gate, creating a very nice effect. But as soon as I started thinking, "The world balances itself out," we had to move. Darn it!

A little while ago, I finally saw the theatrical version of *Evangelion*. It was obvious that the people who created it didn't love the story or the characters, so I'm a little disappointed. But the dramatization, the movement and the editing were superb. When the story led into the self-improvement seminar, I was nearly fooled for an instant. I don't know if most people enjoyed it, but as a writer I was able to take home something from it.

Rurouni Kenshin is building to a climax. The story digs deeper and deeper now, so it's not easy for me as a writer. But I have to get over that if I'm going to develop themes in *RuroKen* like I want. I believe in happy endings in entertainment, and I'm working hard toward that, so please honor me with your support! See you in the next volume!

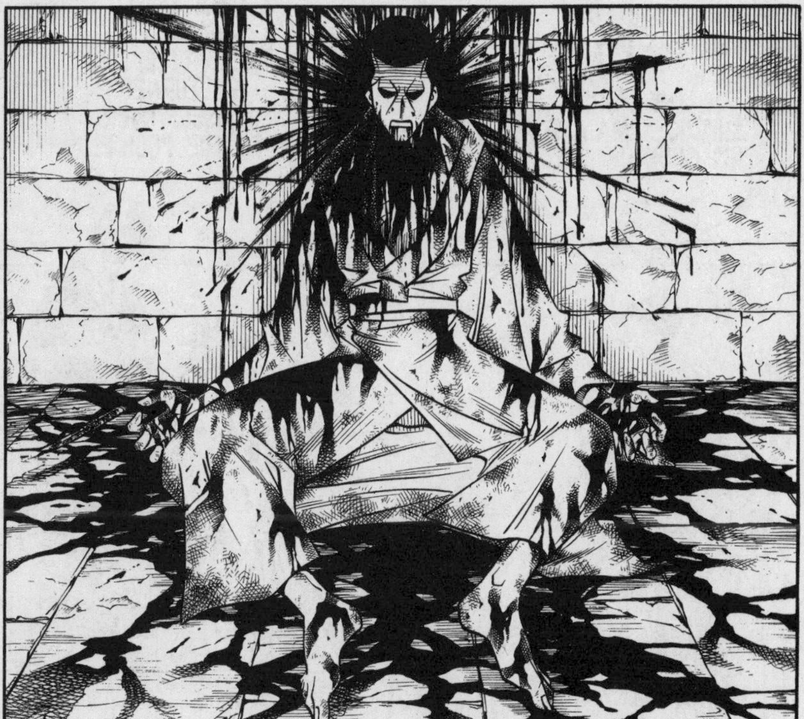

Act 148
Kyoto Epilogue Fate of the Juppongatana (Part II)

伸宏和月

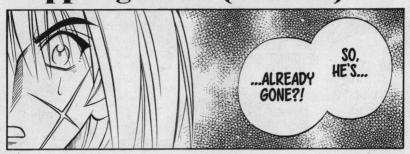

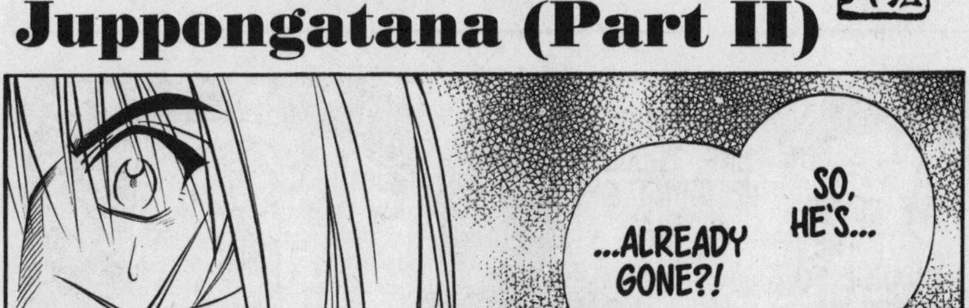
SO, HE'S...
...ALREADY GONE?!

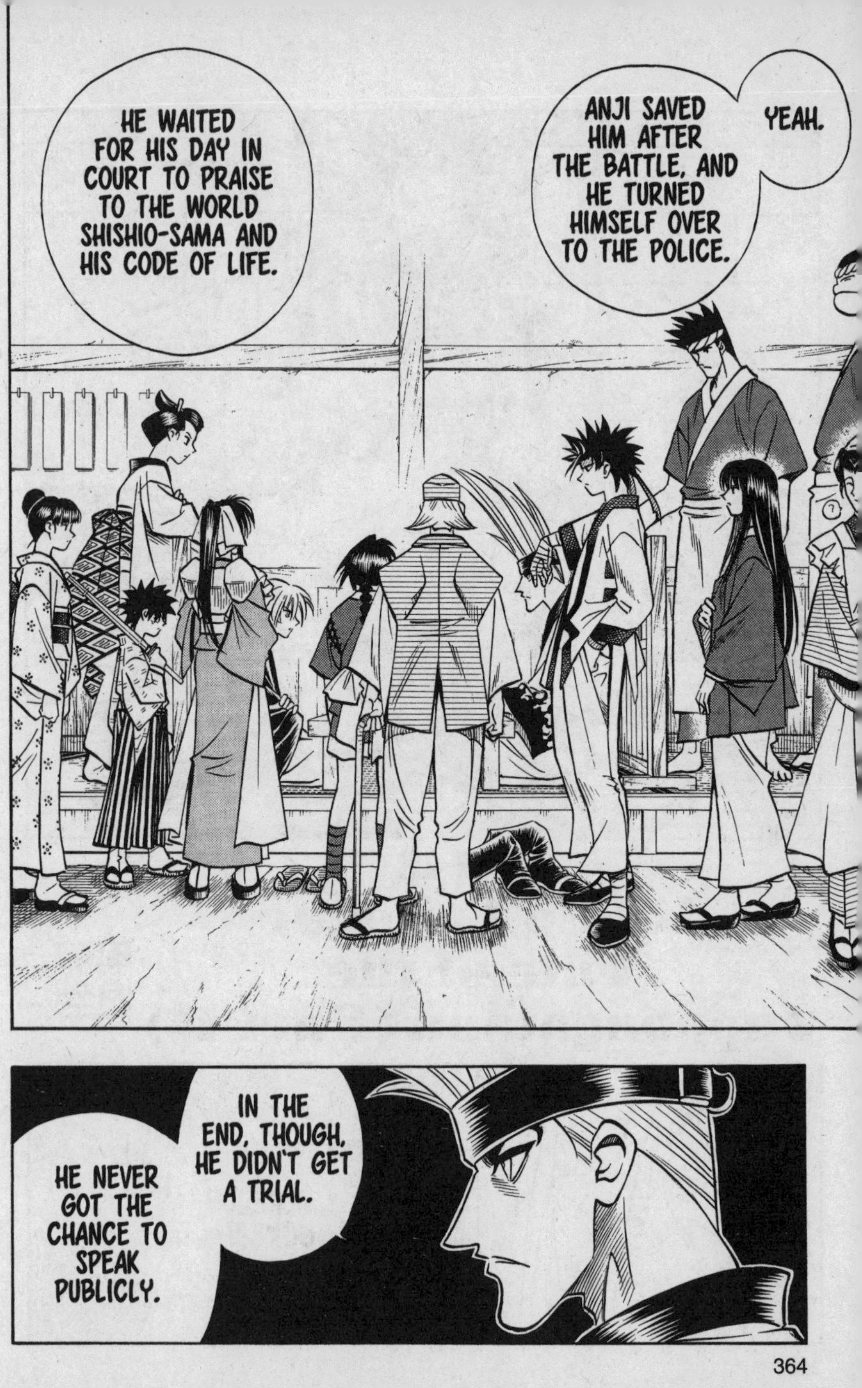
YEAH.
ANJI SAVED HIM AFTER THE BATTLE, AND HE TURNED HIMSELF OVER TO THE POLICE.
HE WAITED FOR HIS DAY IN COURT TO PRAISE TO THE WORLD SHISHIO-SAMA AND HIS CODE OF LIFE.
IN THE END, THOUGH, HE DIDN'T GET A TRIAL.
HE NEVER GOT THE CHANCE TO SPEAK PUBLICLY.

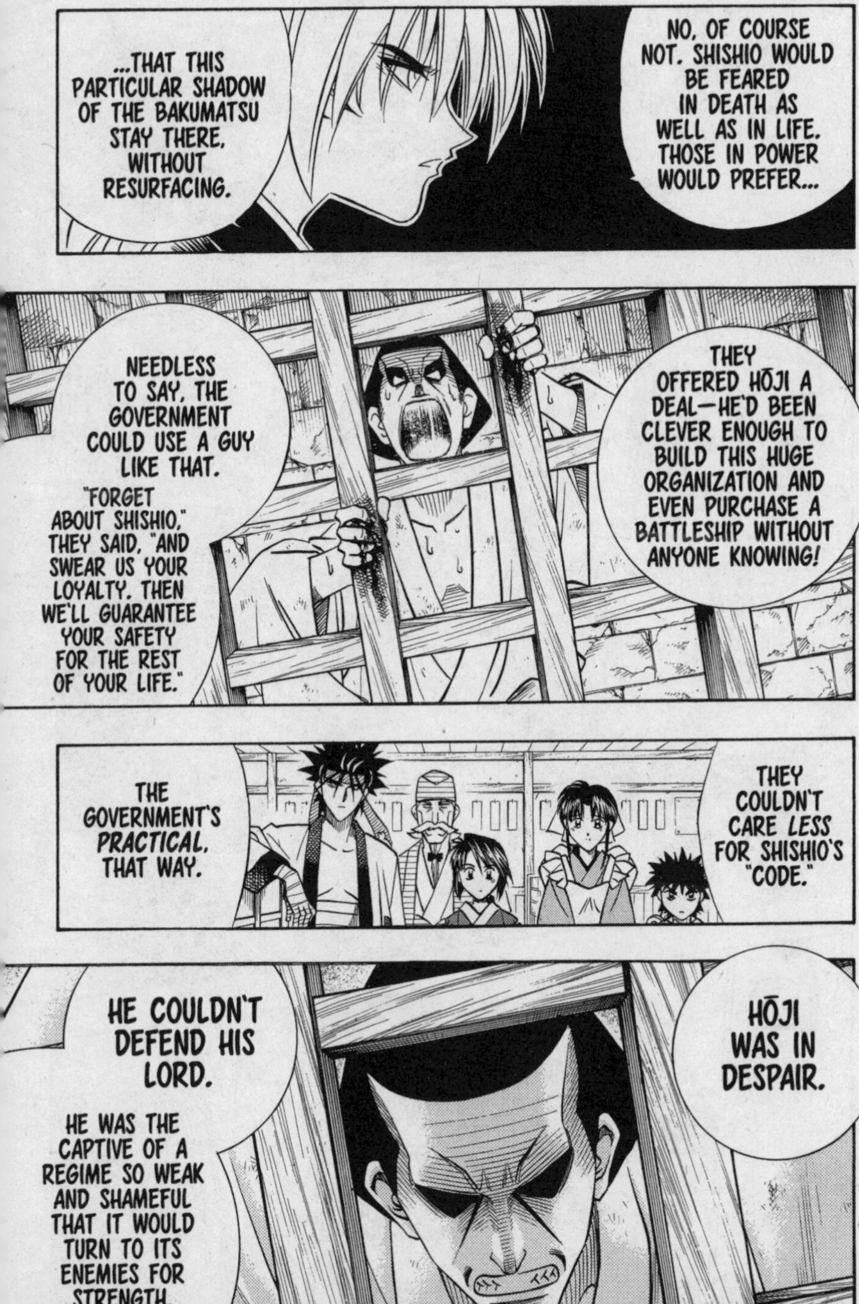
NO, OF COURSE NOT. SHISHIO WOULD BE FEARED IN DEATH AS WELL AS IN LIFE. THOSE IN POWER WOULD PREFER...
...THAT THIS PARTICULAR SHADOW OF THE BAKUMATSU STAY THERE, WITHOUT RESURFACING.
THEY OFFERED HŌJI A DEAL—HE'D BEEN CLEVER ENOUGH TO BUILD THIS HUGE ORGANIZATION AND EVEN PURCHASE A BATTLESHIP WITHOUT ANYONE KNOWING!
NEEDLESS TO SAY, THE GOVERNMENT COULD USE A GUY LIKE THAT.
"FORGET ABOUT SHISHIO," THEY SAID, "AND SWEAR US YOUR LOYALTY. THEN WE'LL GUARANTEE YOUR SAFETY FOR THE REST OF YOUR LIFE."
THEY COULDN'T CARE *LESS* FOR SHISHIO'S "CODE."
THE GOVERNMENT'S *PRACTICAL*, THAT WAY.
HŌJI WAS IN DESPAIR.
HE COULDN'T DEFEND HIS LORD.
HE WAS THE CAPTIVE OF A REGIME SO WEAK AND SHAMEFUL THAT IT WOULD TURN TO ITS ENEMIES FOR STRENGTH.

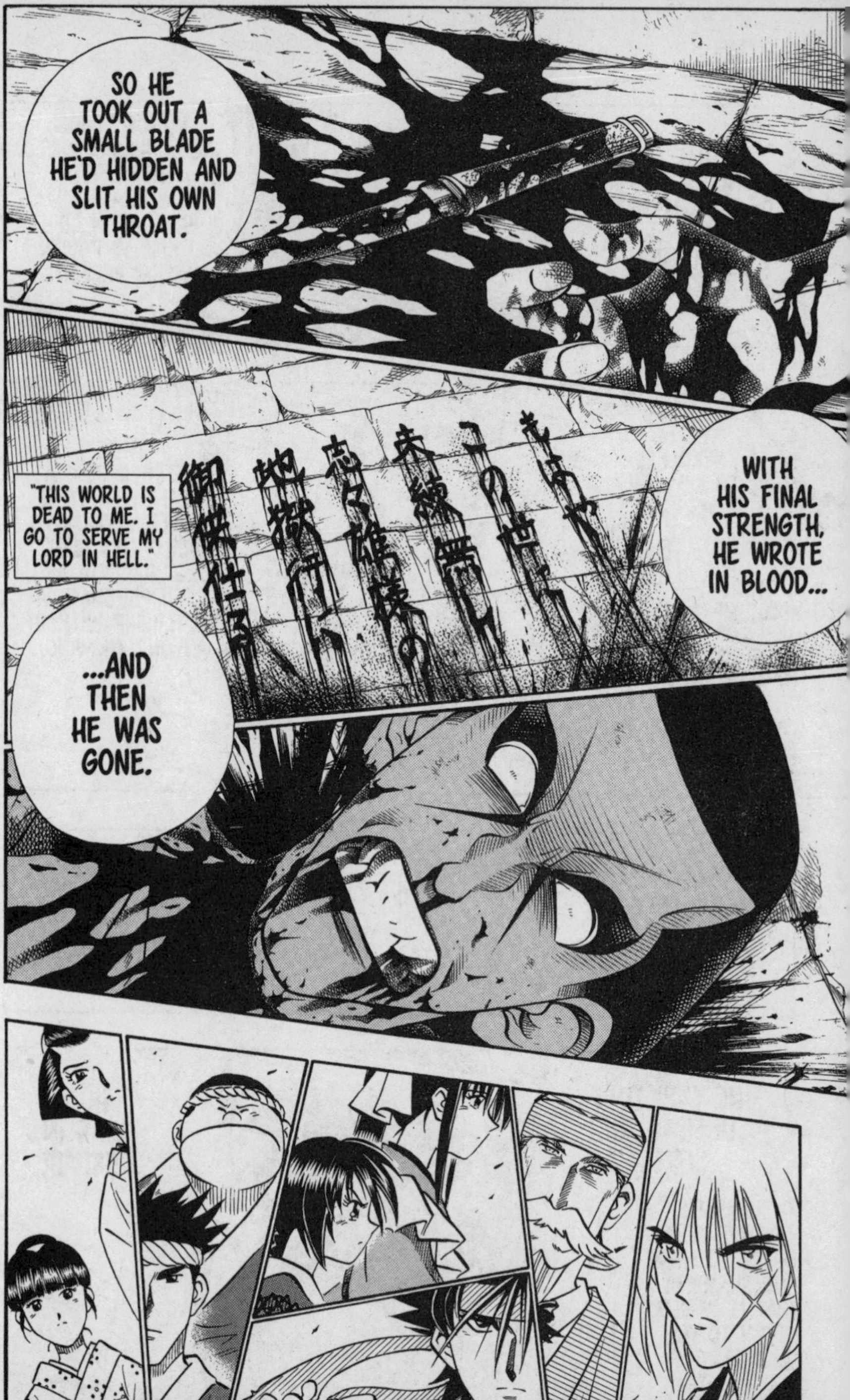
SO HE TOOK OUT A SMALL BLADE HE'D HIDDEN AND SLIT HIS OWN THROAT.
WITH HIS FINAL STRENGTH, HE WROTE IN BLOOD...
"THIS WORLD IS DEAD TO ME. I GO TO SERVE MY LORD IN HELL."
...AND THEN HE WAS GONE.

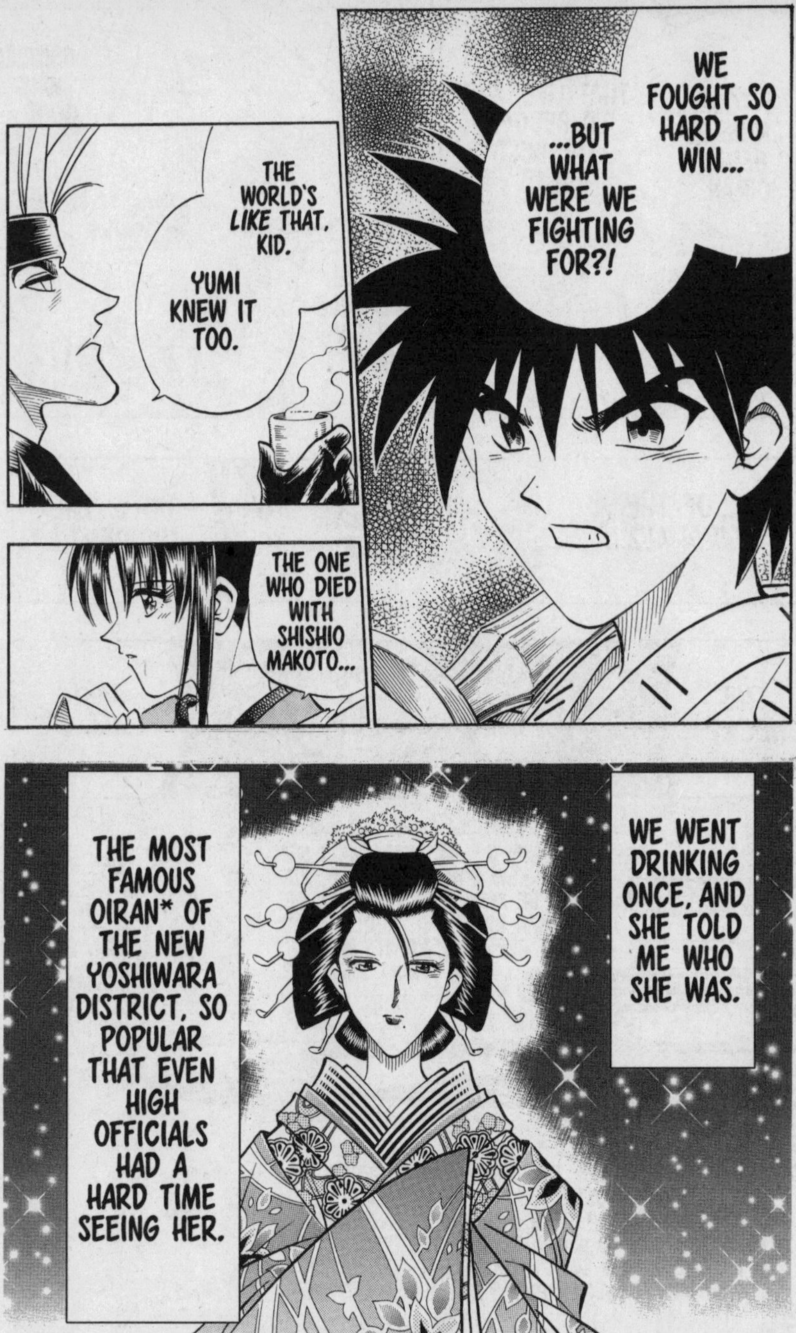
WE FOUGHT SO HARD TO WIN...
...BUT WHAT WERE WE FIGHTING FOR?!
THE WORLD'S *LIKE* THAT, KID.
YUMI KNEW IT TOO.
THE ONE WHO DIED WITH SHISHIO MAKOTO...
WE WENT DRINKING ONCE, AND SHE TOLD ME WHO SHE WAS.
THE MOST FAMOUS OIRAN* OF THE NEW YOSHIWARA DISTRICT, SO POPULAR THAT EVEN HIGH OFFICIALS HAD A HARD TIME SEEING HER.

*IN THE LEGAL BROTHELS OF THE DAY KNOWN AS *YŪKAKU*, AN *OIRAN* HELD THE HIGHEST RANK.

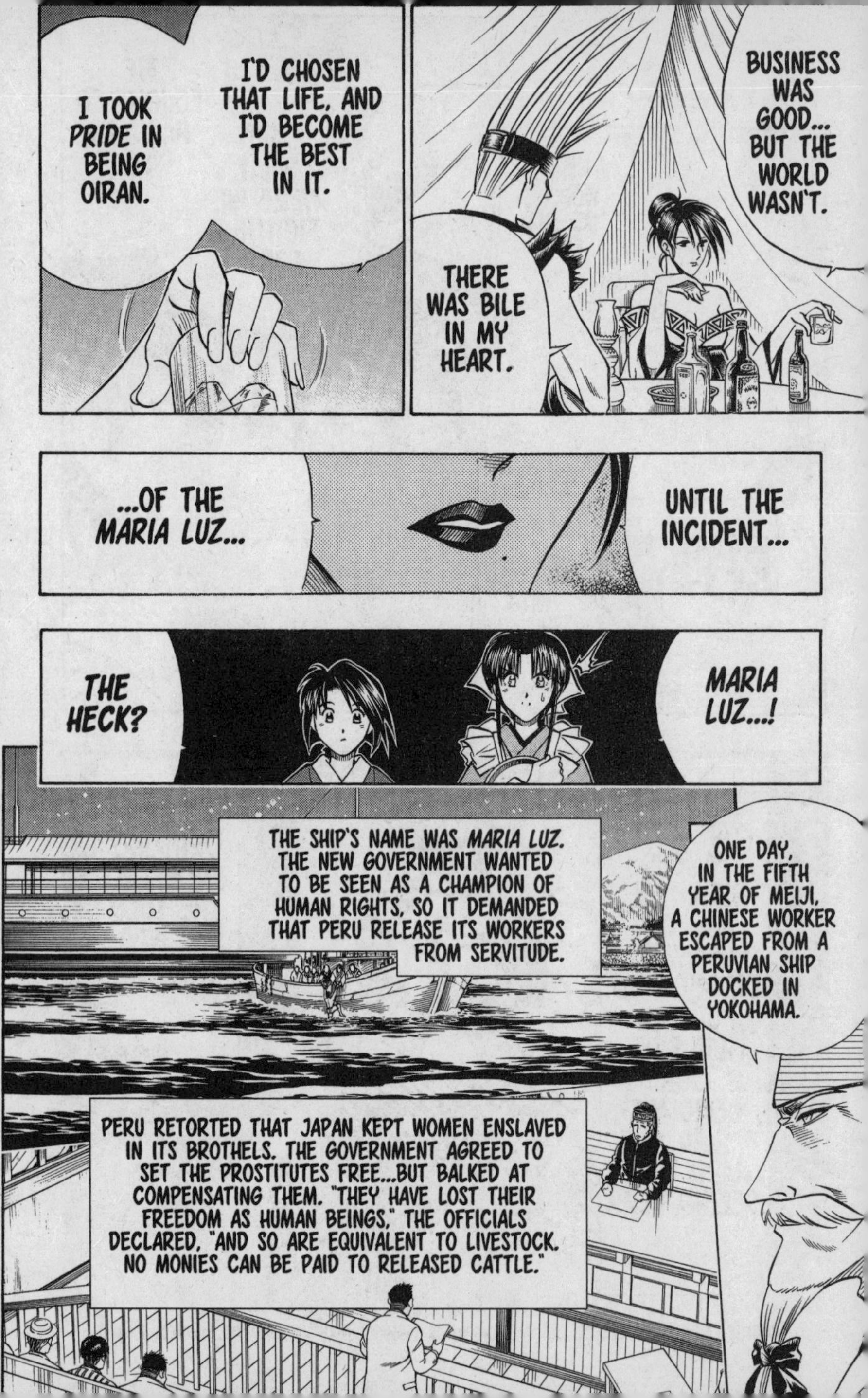
BUSINESS WAS GOOD... BUT THE WORLD WASN'T.
THERE WAS BILE IN MY HEART.
I'D CHOSEN THAT LIFE, AND I'D BECOME THE BEST IN IT.
I TOOK *PRIDE* IN BEING OIRAN.
UNTIL THE INCIDENT...
...OF THE *MARIA LUZ*...
MARIA LUZ...!
THE HECK?
ONE DAY, IN THE FIFTH YEAR OF MEIJI, A CHINESE WORKER ESCAPED FROM A PERUVIAN SHIP DOCKED IN YOKOHAMA.
THE SHIP'S NAME WAS *MARIA LUZ*. THE NEW GOVERNMENT WANTED TO BE SEEN AS A CHAMPION OF HUMAN RIGHTS, SO IT DEMANDED THAT PERU RELEASE ITS WORKERS FROM SERVITUDE.
PERU RETORTED THAT JAPAN KEPT WOMEN ENSLAVED IN ITS BROTHELS. THE GOVERNMENT AGREED TO SET THE PROSTITUTES FREE...BUT BALKED AT COMPENSATING THEM. "THEY HAVE LOST THEIR FREEDOM AS HUMAN BEINGS," THE OFFICIALS DECLARED, "AND SO ARE EQUIVALENT TO LIVESTOCK. NO MONIES CAN BE PAID TO RELEASED CATTLE."

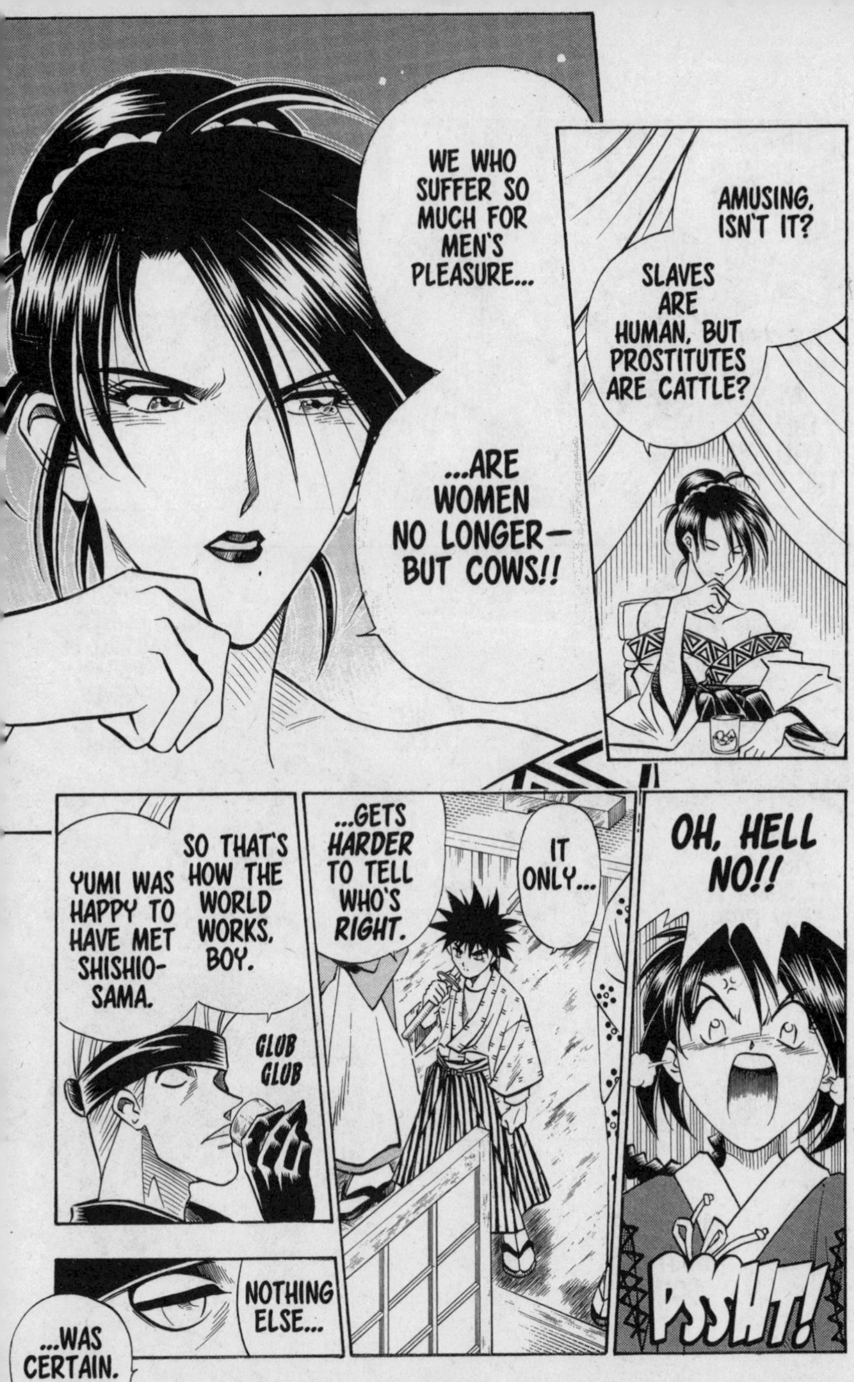
AMUSING, ISN'T IT?
SLAVES ARE HUMAN, BUT PROSTITUTES ARE CATTLE?
WE WHO SUFFER SO MUCH FOR MEN'S PLEASURE...
...ARE WOMEN NO LONGER—BUT COWS!!
OH, HELL NO!!
PSSHT!
IT ONLY...
...GETS HARDER TO TELL WHO'S RIGHT.
SO THAT'S HOW THE WORLD WORKS, BOY.
YUMI WAS HAPPY TO HAVE MET SHISHIO-SAMA.
GLUB GLUB
NOTHING ELSE...
...WAS CERTAIN.

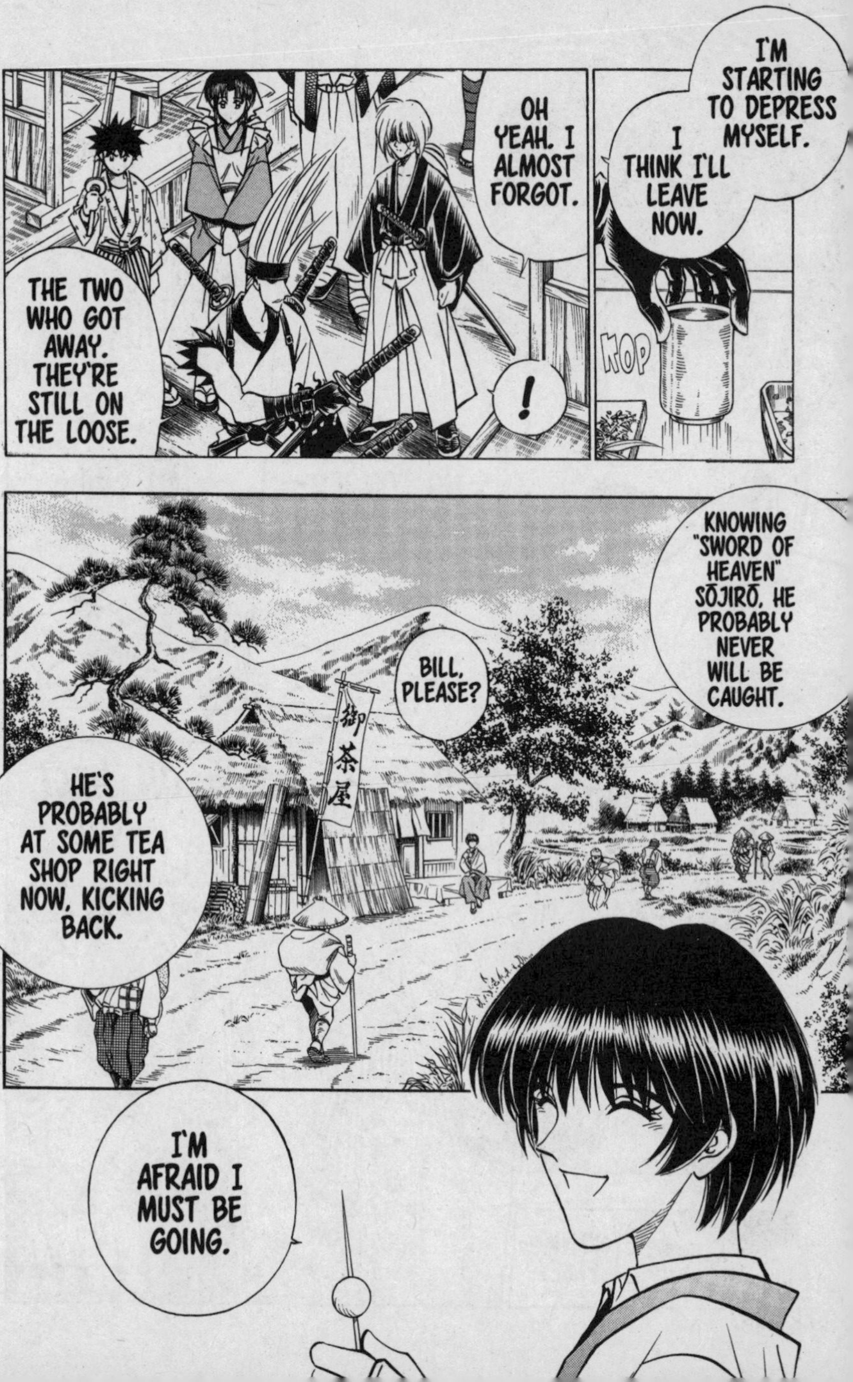
I'M STARTING TO DEPRESS MYSELF.
I THINK I'LL LEAVE NOW.
KOP
OH YEAH. I ALMOST FORGOT.
!
THE TWO WHO GOT AWAY. THEY'RE STILL ON THE LOOSE.
KNOWING "SWORD OF HEAVEN" SŌJIRŌ, HE PROBABLY NEVER WILL BE CAUGHT.
BILL, PLEASE?
御茶屋
HE'S PROBABLY AT SOME TEA SHOP RIGHT NOW, KICKING BACK.
I'M AFRAID I MUST BE GOING.

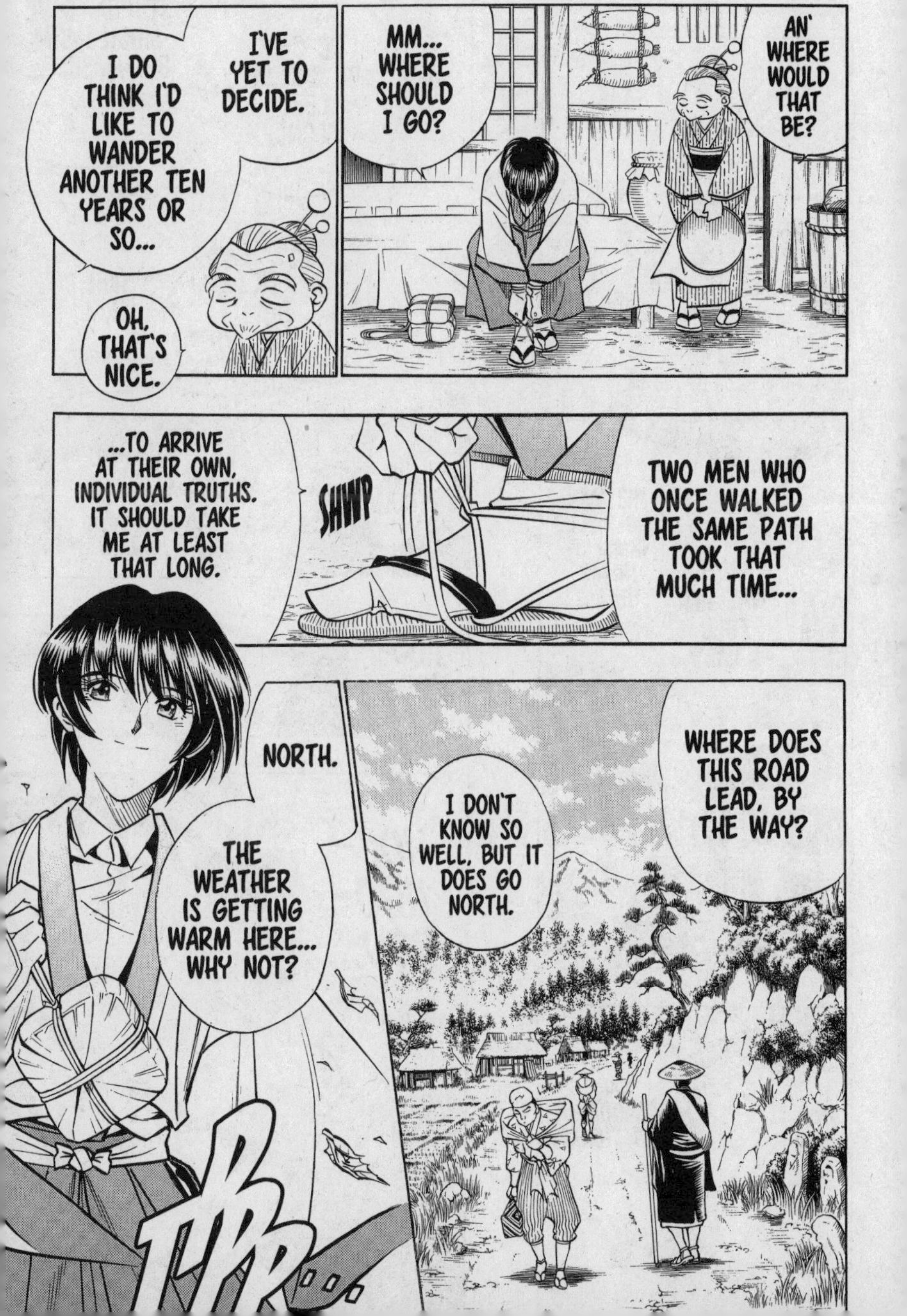
AN' WHERE WOULD THAT BE?
MM... WHERE SHOULD I GO?
I'VE YET TO DECIDE.
I DO THINK I'D LIKE TO WANDER ANOTHER TEN YEARS OR SO...
OH, THAT'S NICE.
TWO MEN WHO ONCE WALKED THE SAME PATH TOOK THAT MUCH TIME...
SHWP
...TO ARRIVE AT THEIR OWN, INDIVIDUAL TRUTHS. IT SHOULD TAKE ME AT LEAST THAT LONG.
WHERE DOES THIS ROAD LEAD, BY THE WAY?
I DON'T KNOW SO WELL, BUT IT DOES GO NORTH.
NORTH.
THE WEATHER IS GETTING WARM HERE... WHY NOT?
TPP...

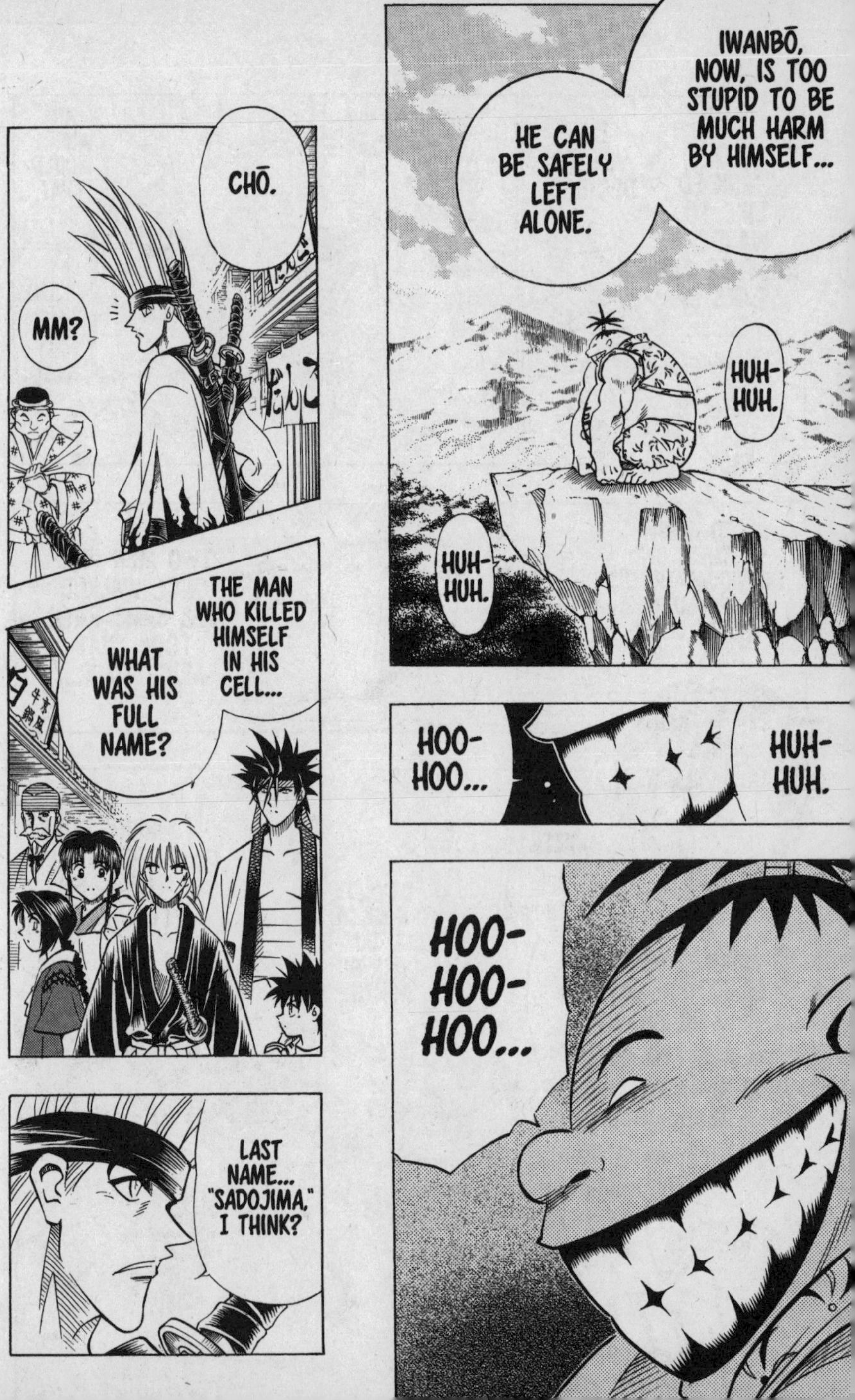
IWANBŌ, NOW, IS TOO STUPID TO BE MUCH HARM BY HIMSELF...
HE CAN BE SAFELY LEFT ALONE.
HUH-HUH.
HUH-HUH.
HUH-HUH.
HOO-HOO...
HOO-HOO-HOO...
CHŌ.
MM?
THE MAN WHO KILLED HIMSELF IN HIS CELL...
WHAT WAS HIS FULL NAME?
LAST NAME... "SADOJIMA," I THINK?

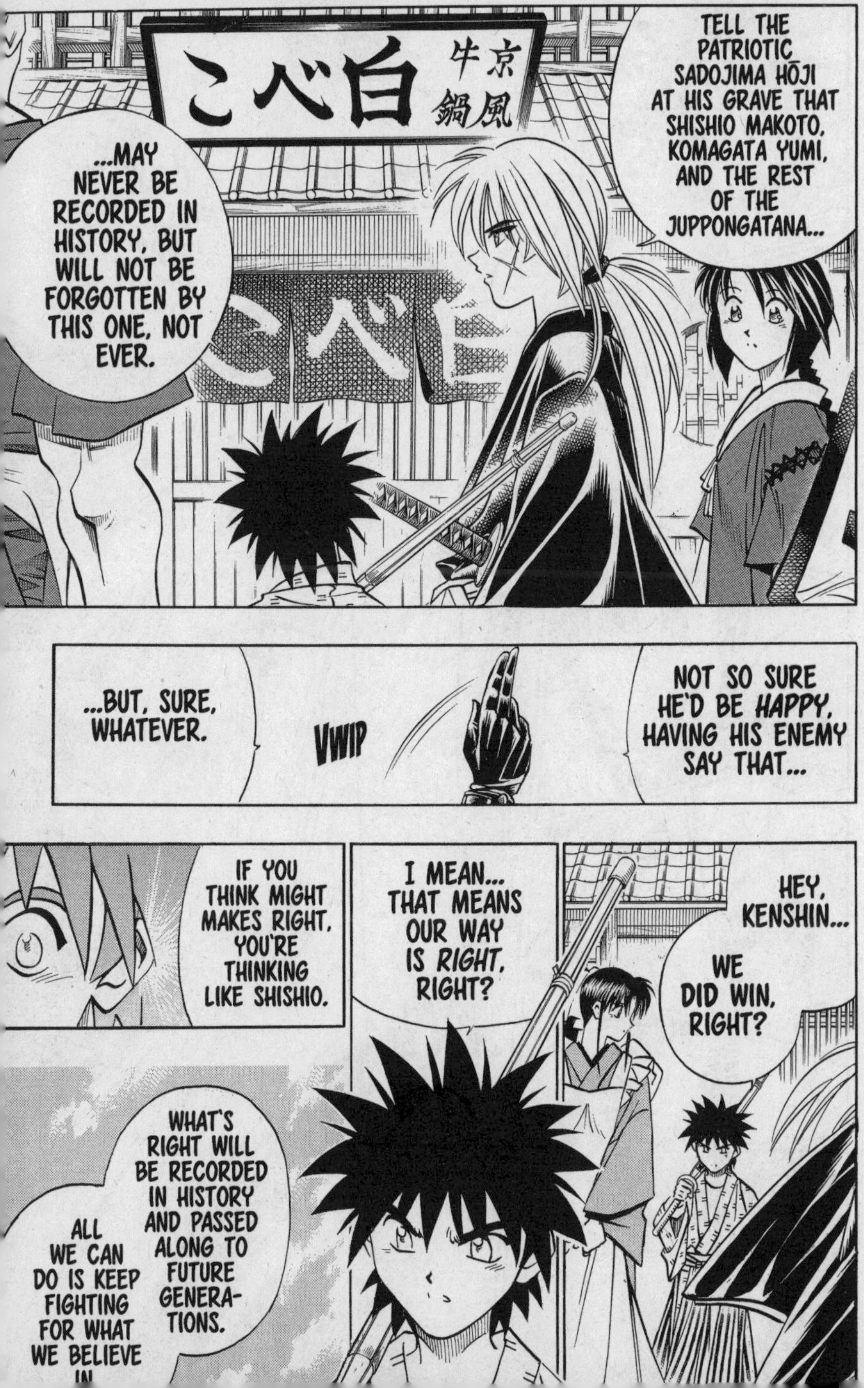
白べこ
京風
牛鍋
TELL THE PATRIOTIC SADOJIMA HŌJI AT HIS GRAVE THAT SHISHIO MAKOTO, KOMAGATA YUMI, AND THE REST OF THE JUPPONGATANA...
...MAY NEVER BE RECORDED IN HISTORY, BUT WILL NOT BE FORGOTTEN BY THIS ONE, NOT EVER.
NOT SO SURE HE'D BE *HAPPY*, HAVING HIS ENEMY SAY THAT...
VWIP
...BUT, SURE, WHATEVER.
HEY, KENSHIN...
WE DID WIN, RIGHT?
I MEAN... THAT MEANS OUR WAY IS *RIGHT*, RIGHT?
IF YOU THINK MIGHT MAKES RIGHT, YOU'RE THINKING LIKE SHISHIO.
WHAT'S RIGHT WILL BE RECORDED IN HISTORY AND PASSED ALONG TO FUTURE GENERATIONS.
ALL WE CAN DO IS KEEP FIGHTING FOR WHAT WE BELIEVE

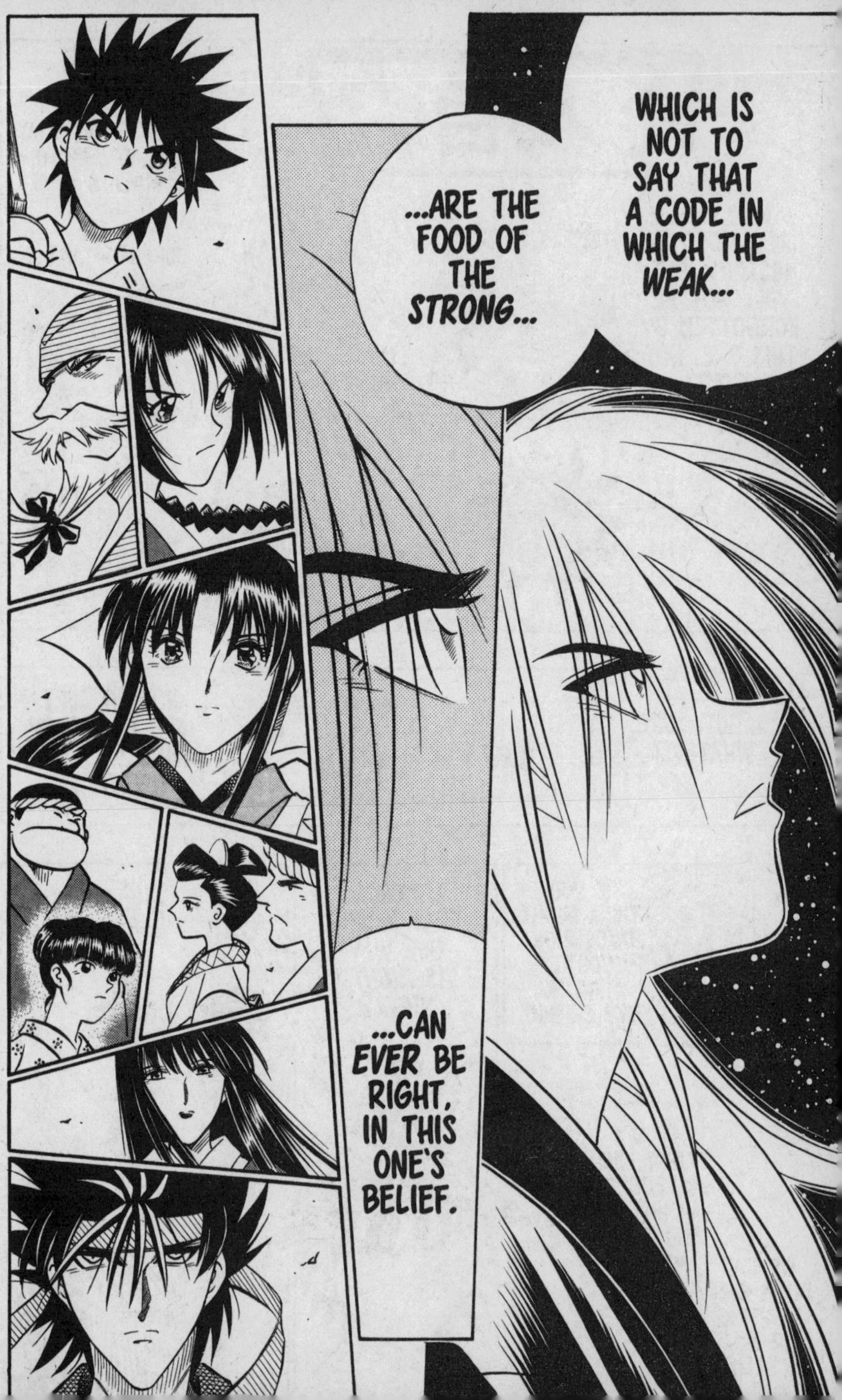
WHICH IS NOT TO SAY THAT A CODE IN WHICH THE WEAK...
...ARE THE FOOD OF THE STRONG...
...CAN EVER BE RIGHT, IN THIS ONE'S BELIEF.

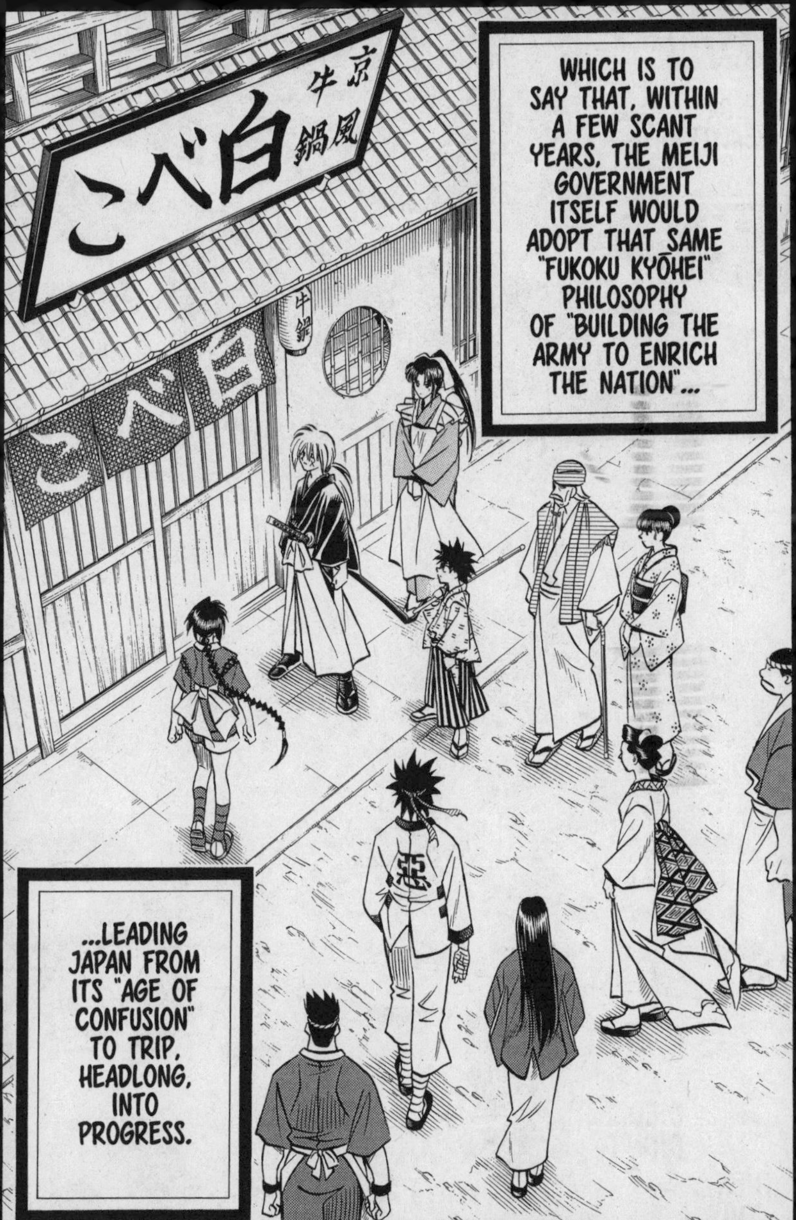
京風牛鍋
WHICH IS TO SAY THAT, WITHIN A FEW SCANT YEARS, THE MEIJI GOVERNMENT ITSELF WOULD ADOPT THAT SAME "FUKOKU KYŌHEI" PHILOSOPHY OF "BUILDING THE ARMY TO ENRICH THE NATION"...
...LEADING JAPAN FROM ITS "AGE OF CONFUSION" TO TRIP, HEADLONG, INTO PROGRESS.

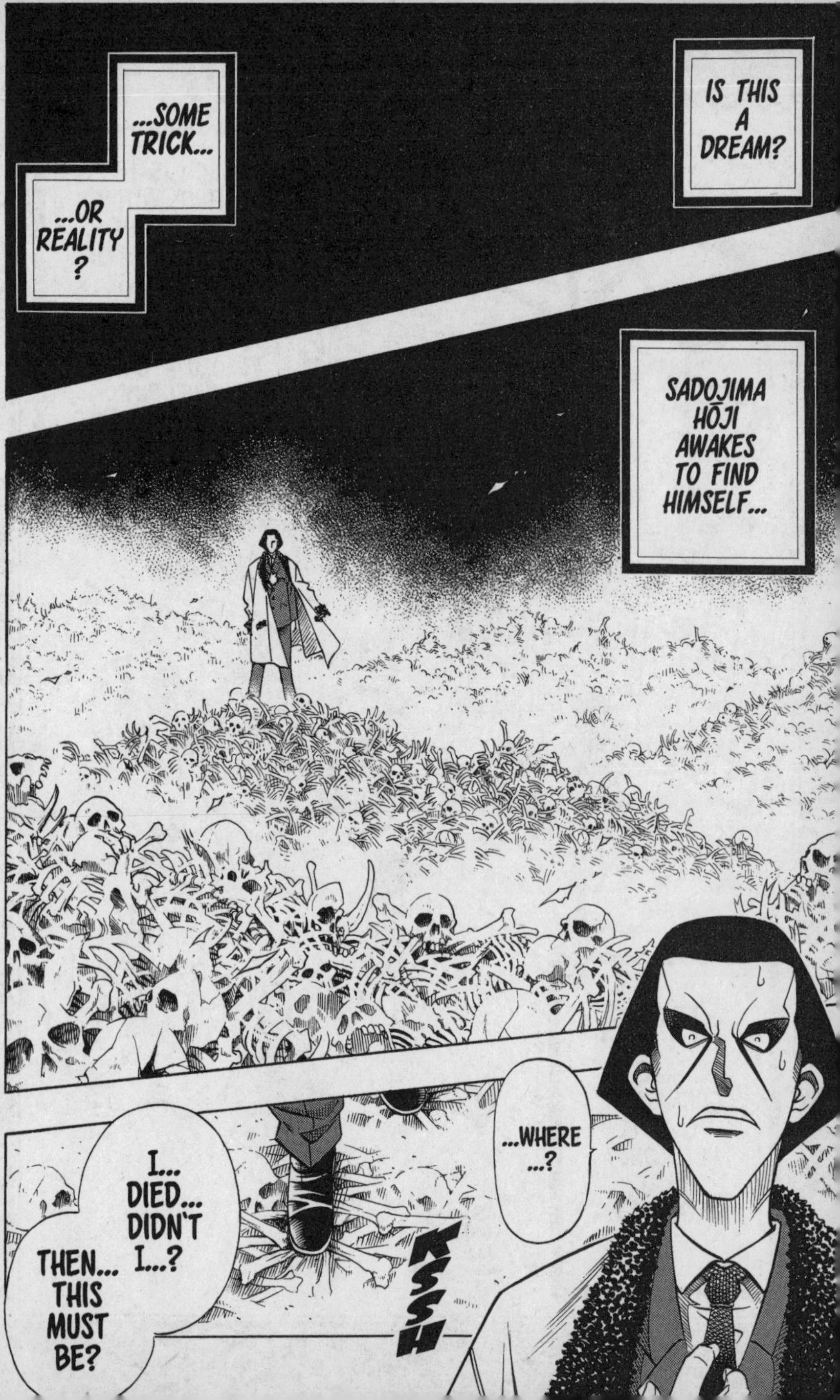
IS THIS A DREAM?
...SOME TRICK...
...OR REALITY?
SADOJIMA HŌJI AWAKES TO FIND HIMSELF...
...WHERE ...?
KSSH
I... DIED... DIDN'T I...?
THEN... THIS MUST BE?

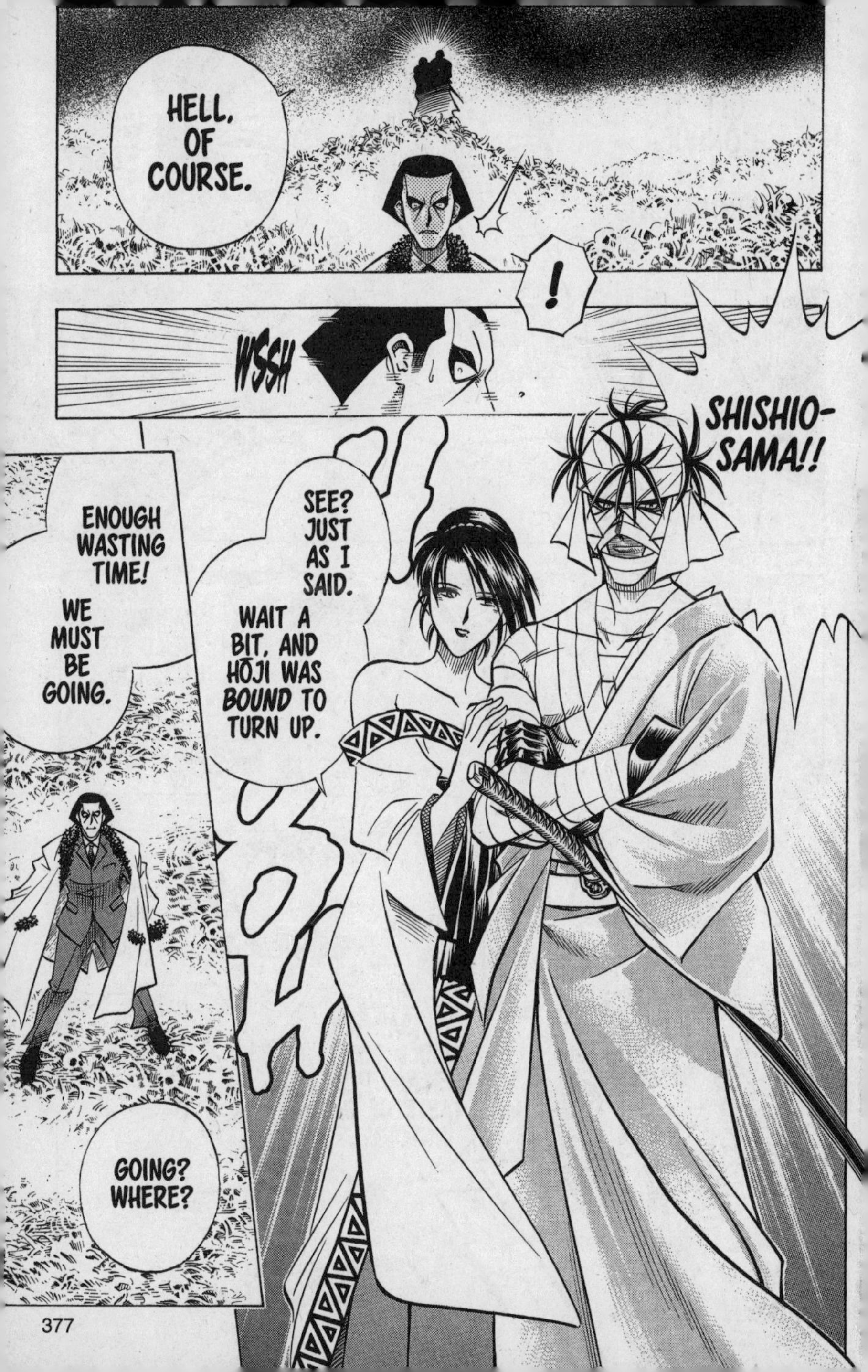
HELL, OF COURSE.
!
WSSH
SHISHIO-SAMA!!
SEE? JUST AS I SAID.
WAIT A BIT, AND HŌJI WAS **BOUND** TO TURN UP.
ENOUGH WASTING TIME!
WE MUST BE GOING.
GOING? WHERE?

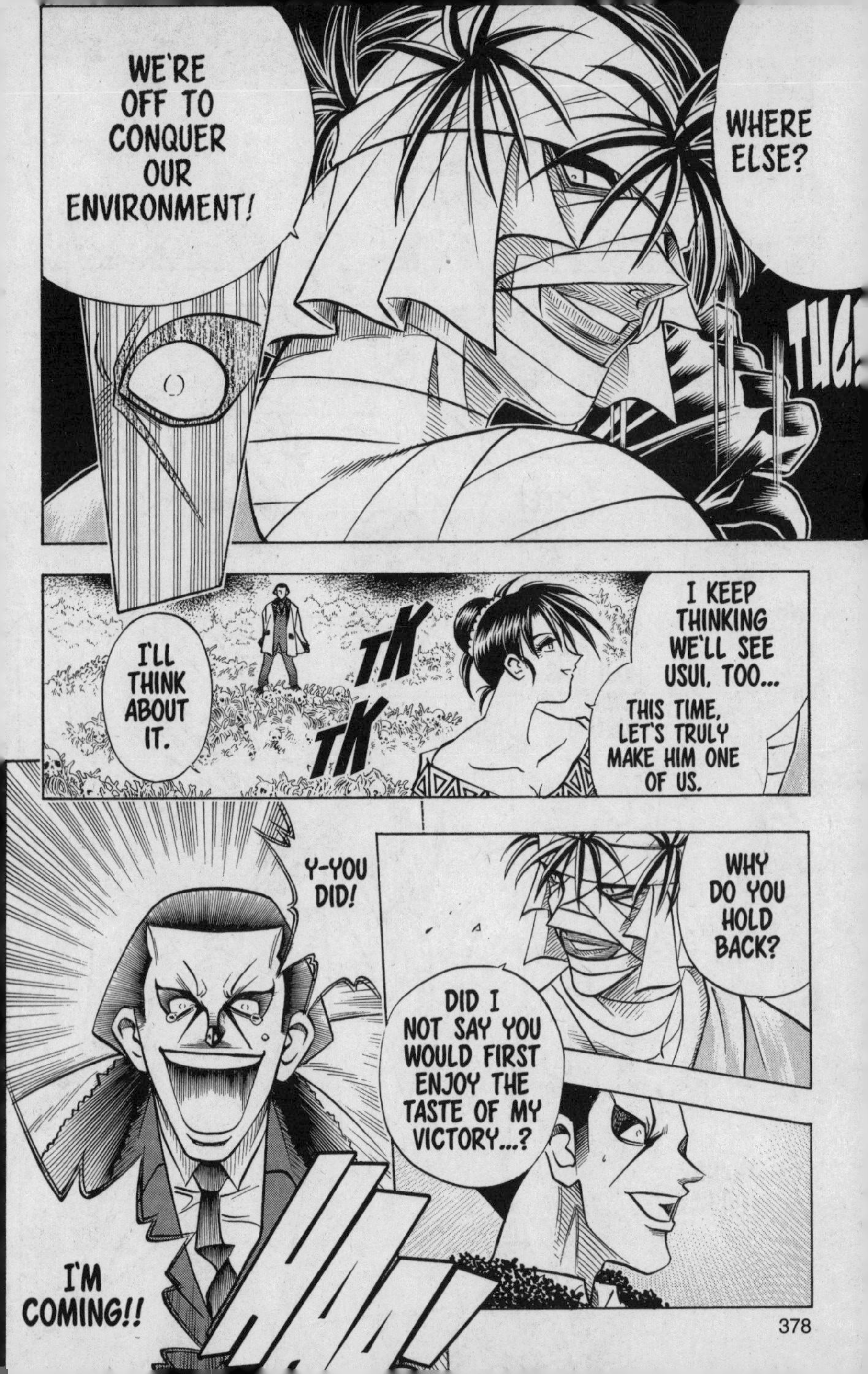
WHERE ELSE?
TUG!
WE'RE OFF TO CONQUER OUR ENVIRONMENT!
I KEEP THINKING WE'LL SEE USUI, TOO...
THIS TIME, LET'S TRULY MAKE HIM ONE OF US.
TK
TK
I'LL THINK ABOUT IT.
WHY DO YOU HOLD BACK?
DID I NOT SAY YOU WOULD FIRST ENJOY THE TASTE OF MY VICTORY...?
Y-YOU DID!
I'M COMING!!

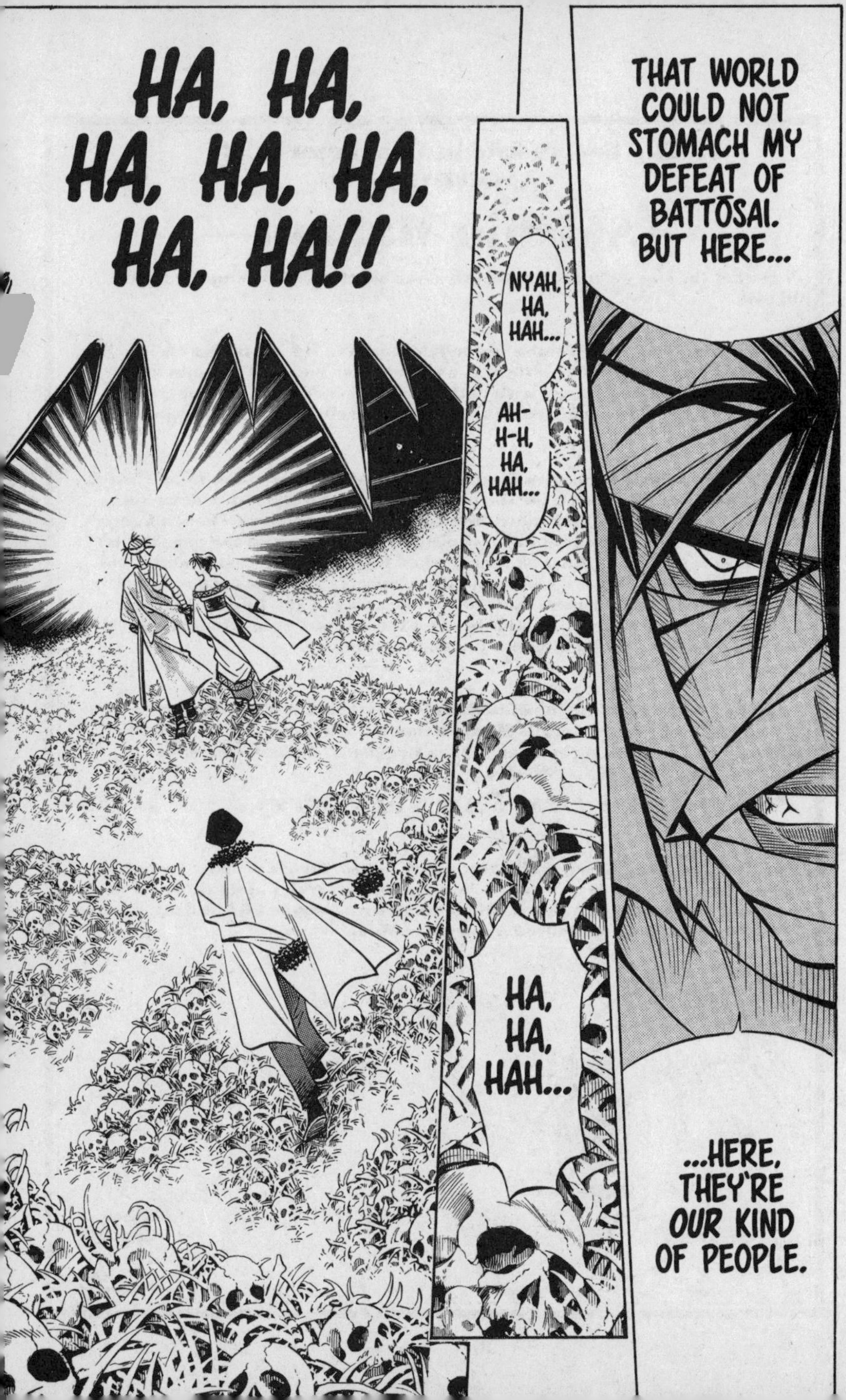
THAT WORLD COULD NOT STOMACH MY DEFEAT OF BATTŌSAI. BUT HERE...
...HERE, THEY'RE *OUR* KIND OF PEOPLE.
NYAH, HA, HAH...
AH-H-H, HA, HAH...
HA, HA, HAH...
HA, HA, HA, HA, HA, HA, HA!!

The Secret Life of Characters (24)
AMENDMENT

—Shishio Makoto—

Now that the story's done, I'm thinking Shishio was my take on the appeal of evil.

Shishio will never compromise his beliefs, not even if it costs him his life. He cares not one bit for using others as a means to an end, and pursues his objective—absolute power—with ruthless abandon. Shishio is the perfect opposite to Kenshin, aside from that one key overlap in their approaches.

In his way, Shishio is his own kind of ideal. I think, somewhere in our hearts, we all have an admiration for the perfect anti-hero. I *did* enjoy drawing Shishio in his final battle against Kenshin—I must be honest. Though I regret that I'll never be able to get across Shishio's death-scene on the page the way I see it in my head, in that last scene, when he walks over that mountain of skeletons...that, I can say with some confidence, is about as good a dramatization of a villain in *RuroKen* that we're ever going to get. I doubt I'll ever write another character like this in all of the series, but in whatever next series I do after this, I'd like to try something similar.

...Oh, and while I'm thinking of it, there's something I'd like to apologize for. It's about Shishio's moves. His *Homura Dama* is one thing, but his *Guren Kaina* is pretty much a rip from "Shura Kagetsu's" *Daibaku-Satsu* in *TenSamu*. To those of you at SNK...

Please know that I am very sorry.

I'm disgusted with myself—all right?—and, worse, I can't promise I won't do it again. I am so-o-o in love with the *Samurai Spirits* series...I do think I'll be carrying it with me into the afterlife, along with NeoGeo CDZ and my Jim Lee 500-yen coin. Yes, I am indeed a Very Bad Man.

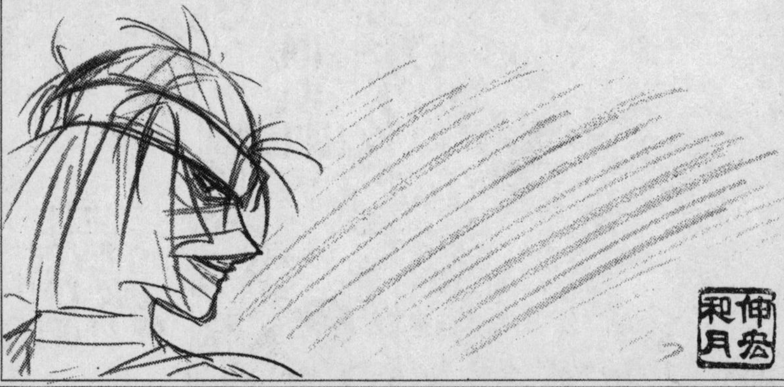
伸宏
和月

Rurouni Kenshin

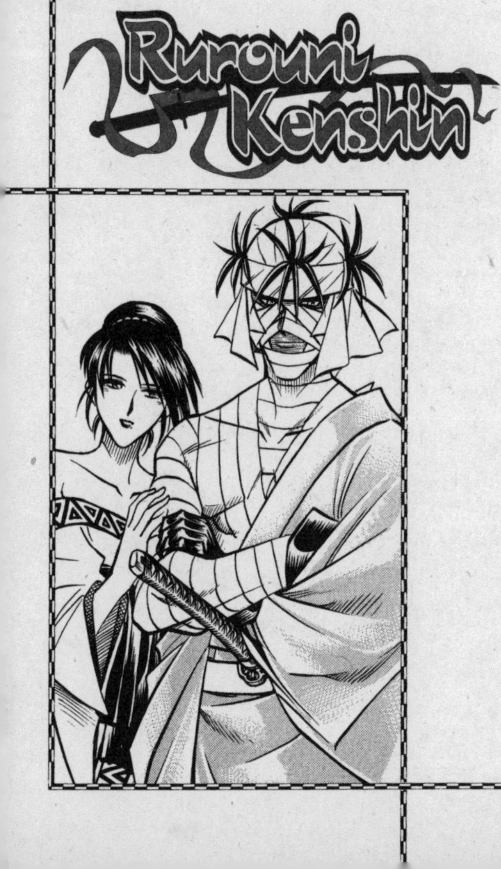

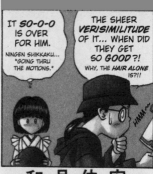

THE SHEER VERISIMILITUDE OF IT... WHEN DID THEY GET SO GOOD?!
WHY, THE HAIR ALONE IS?!!
IT SO-O-O IS OVER FOR HIM.
NINGEN SHIKKAKU... "GOING THRU THE MOTIONS."
HMM~

和月伸宏

NOBUHIRO WATSUKI

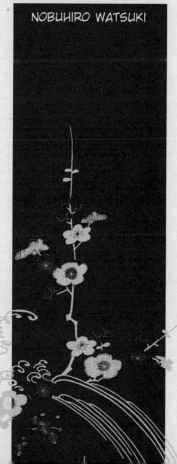

ACTION DOLL

I DID IT, I FINALLY DID IT-A SHOJO (FEMALE-BODY) ACTION FIGURE! THO' I SWORE I NEVER WOULD, NAKORURU—RIMURURU—POSABLE JOINTS—O, THE POSABLE JOINTS!! "NOBUHIRO WATSUKI" HAS FOUND HIMSELF HAVING TO CATCH 'EM ALL, OLD SCHOOL POKEMON-STYLE! IF THEY WERE TO RELEASE A "TWO-PLAYER" VERSION OF NAKO/RIMU, NOW...OH, MAN. OHMANOHMANOHMAN!!

ACTION DOLLS, THOUGH... WAIT!! THIS ISN'T THE "NEW DIRECTION" I TALKED ABOUT LAST TIME, IS IT?! BECAUSE, IF IT WERE, THAT WOULD BE JUST TOO SAD....

Rurouni Kenshin, which has found fans not only in Japan but around the world, first made its appearance in 1992, as an original short story in ***Weekly Shonen Jump Special***. Later rewritten and published as a regular, continuing ***Jump*** series in 1994, ***Rurouni Kenshin*** ended serialization in 1999 but continued in popularity, as evidenced by the 2000 publication of ***Yahiko no Sakabatô*** ("Yahiko's Reversed-Edge Sword") in ***Weekly Shonen Jump***. His most current work, ***Busô Renkin*** ("Armored Alchemist"), began publication in June 2003, also in ***Jump***.

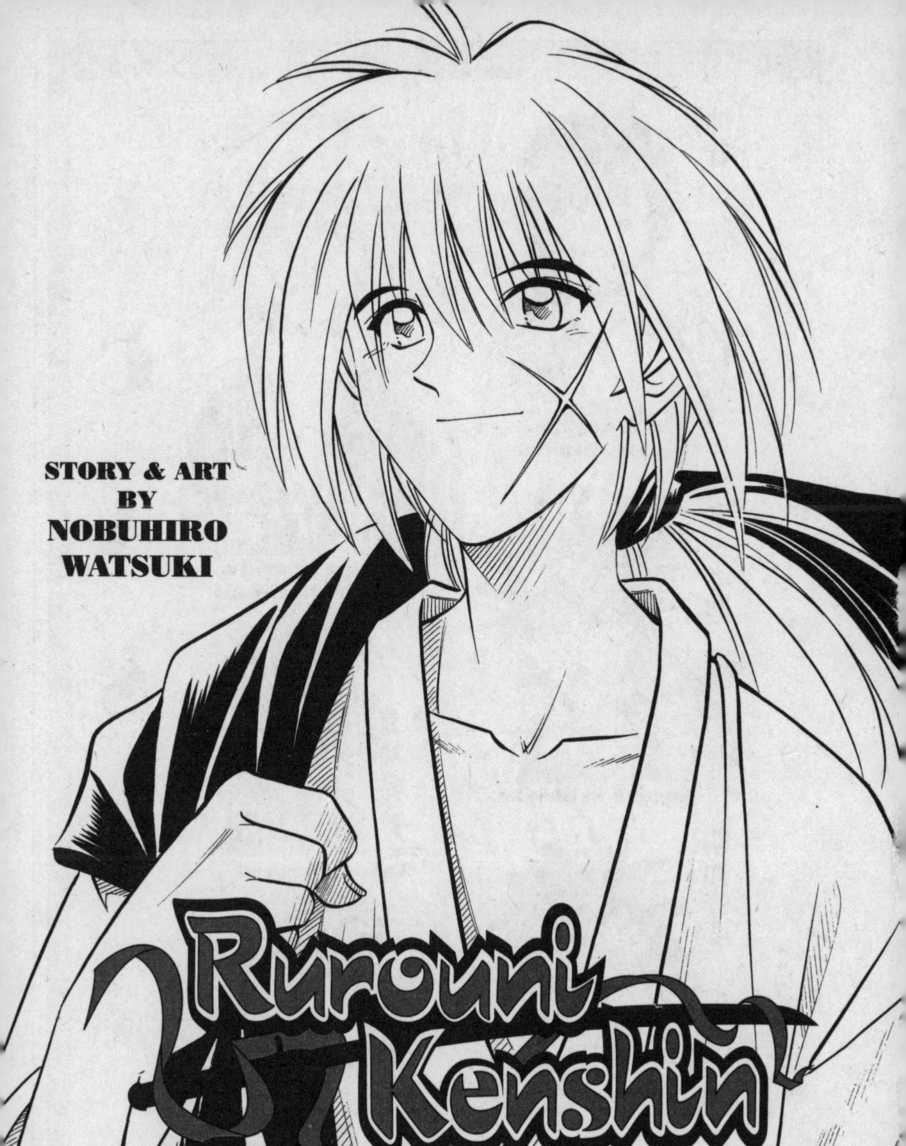

Rurouni Kenshin

STORY & ART
BY
NOBUHIRO
WATSUKI

MEIJI SWORDSMAN ROMANTIC STORY

Vol. 18: DO YOU STILL BEAR THE SCAR?

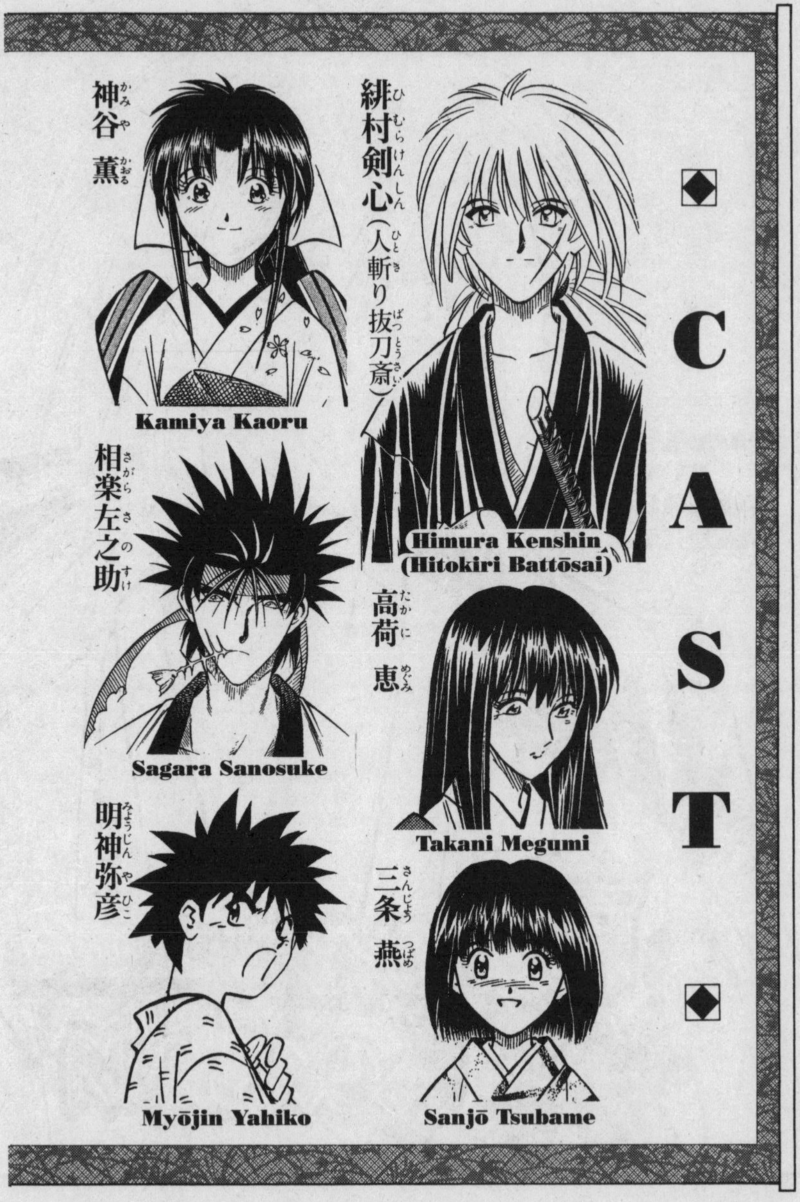
CAST
緋村剣心（人斬り抜刀斎）
Himura Kenshin
(Hitokiri Battōsai)
神谷薫
Kamiya Kaoru
相楽左之助
Sagara Sanosuke
高荷恵
Takani Megumi
明神弥彦
Myōjin Yahiko
三条燕
Sanjō Tsubame

Once he was *hitokiri*, an assassin, called Battōsai.
His name was legend among the pro-Imperialist or
"patriot" warriors who launched the Meiji Era.
Now, Himura Kenshin is *rurouni*, a wanderer, and
carries a reversed-edge *sakabatō* to prohibit himself from killing.

THUS FAR

Kenshin has journeyed to Kyoto to block the
machinations of Shishio Makoto, the man who
took Kenshin's place as *hitokiri*, a government-
sanctioned slayer of men. In a duel with Sōjirō,
one of the madman Shishio's *Juppongatana* "Ten
Sword" assassins, Kenshin's former blade is
broken and a new one is acquired—"Shinuchi,"
a *sakabatō* like the first.

Newly armed (and after an edge-of-death battle
with his former *Hiten Mitsurugi* master, Hiko
Seijūrō), Kenshin joins up with Sanosuke and
Saitō so that they may foil the plans of Shishio to
burn down Kyoto and attack Tokyo by cannon.
Arriving at Shishio's lair at last, the three are
met by Shishio's three best: "Bright King" Anji,
"Blind Sword" Usui, and the ever-smiling Sōjirō.
After fierce battles, Anji is defeated by Sanosuke,
and Usui dies against Saitō. Sōjirō, defeated by
Kenshin despite the latter's vow never to kill,
decides he must leave Shishio's side and seek the
truth on his own terms.

Finally Kenshin reaches the "Infernal Hall" and
challenges its madman owner, beginning a terrible
battle in which Yumi dies at Shishio's hand, and
the overheated body of Shishio himself ignites and
disappears into flame. A month goes by, Kenshin's
wounds heal, and drinking binges occur daily at
Shirobeko, where everyone stays during the
rebuilding of Aoi-Ya. Just then, "Sword Hunter"
Chō, now an intelligence officer, drops by and tells
of the fates of the remaining *Juppongatana*....

CONTENTS

RUROUNI KENSHIN
Meiji Swordsman Romantic Story
BOOK EIGHTEEN: DO YOU STILL BEAR THE SCAR?

ACT 149
Kyoto Epilogue
Early Summer Morning
389

ACT 150
Kyoto Epilogue
Early Summer Day
407

ACT 151
Kyoto Epilogue
In the Blue Sky
427

ACT 152
Cross-Shaped Scar
447

ACT 153
The One-Handed Man
467

ACT 154
The Signal Fire of Revenge
487

ACT 155
Jinchū
509

ACT 156
Comrades
529

ACT 157
Yahiko's Desperation
547

ACT 158
Twin Storms Blow!
560

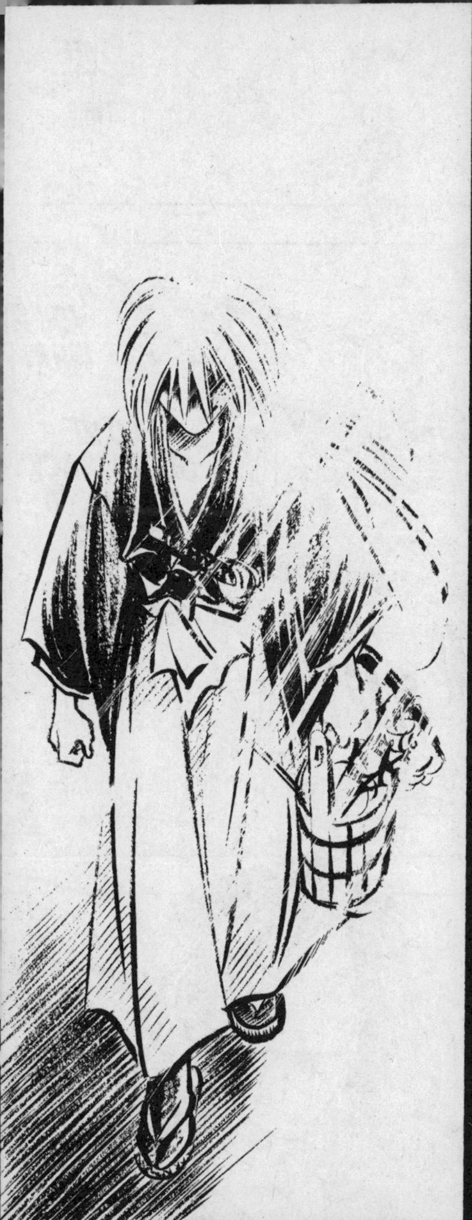

ACT 149
Kyoto Epilogue
Early Summer Morning

伸宏 和月

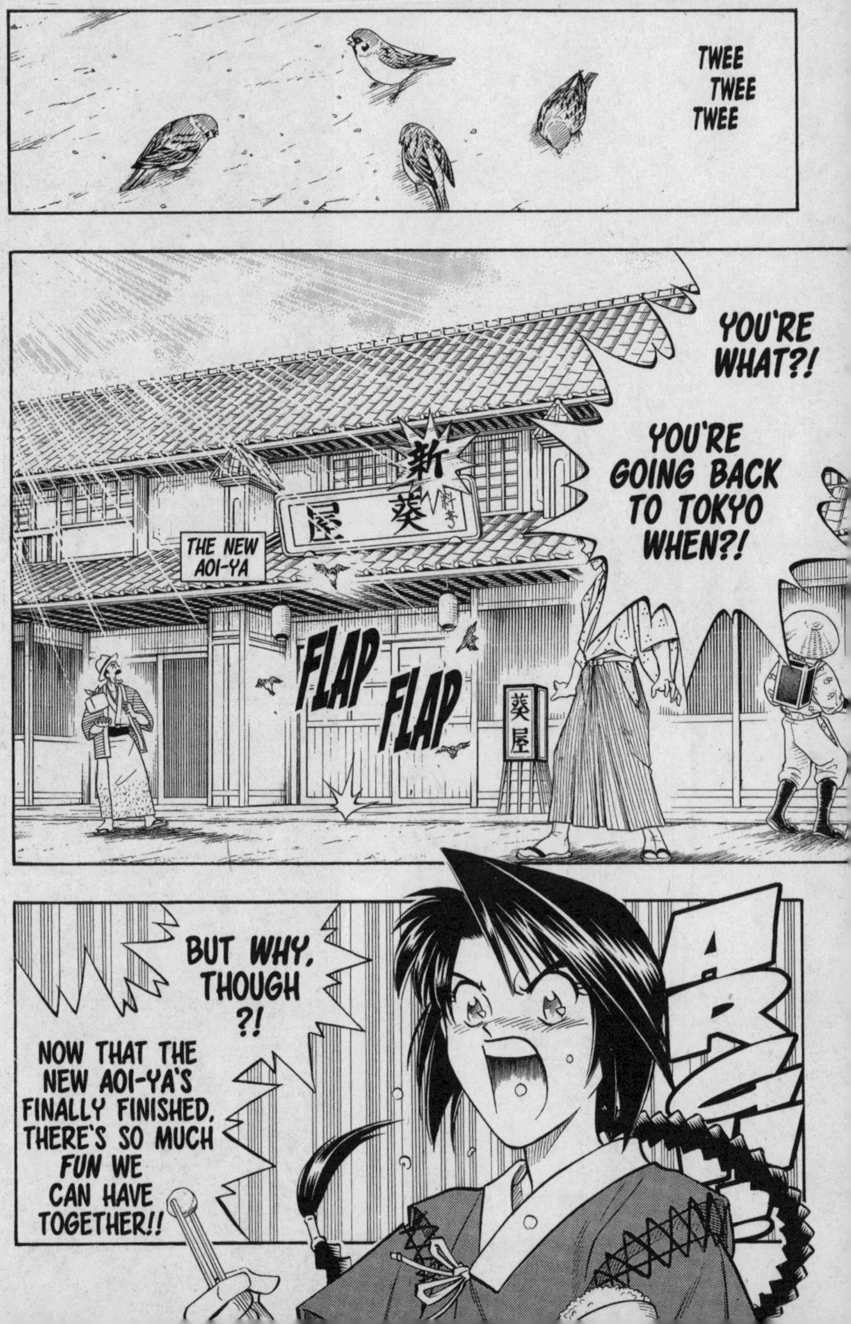
TWEE
TWEE
TWEE
YOU'RE WHAT?!
YOU'RE GOING BACK TO TOKYO WHEN?!
新
葵屋
料亭
THE NEW AOI-YA
FLAP
FLAP
葵屋
BUT WHY, THOUGH?!
NOW THAT THE NEW AOI-YA'S FINALLY FINISHED, THERE'S SO MUCH FUN WE CAN HAVE TOGETHER!!

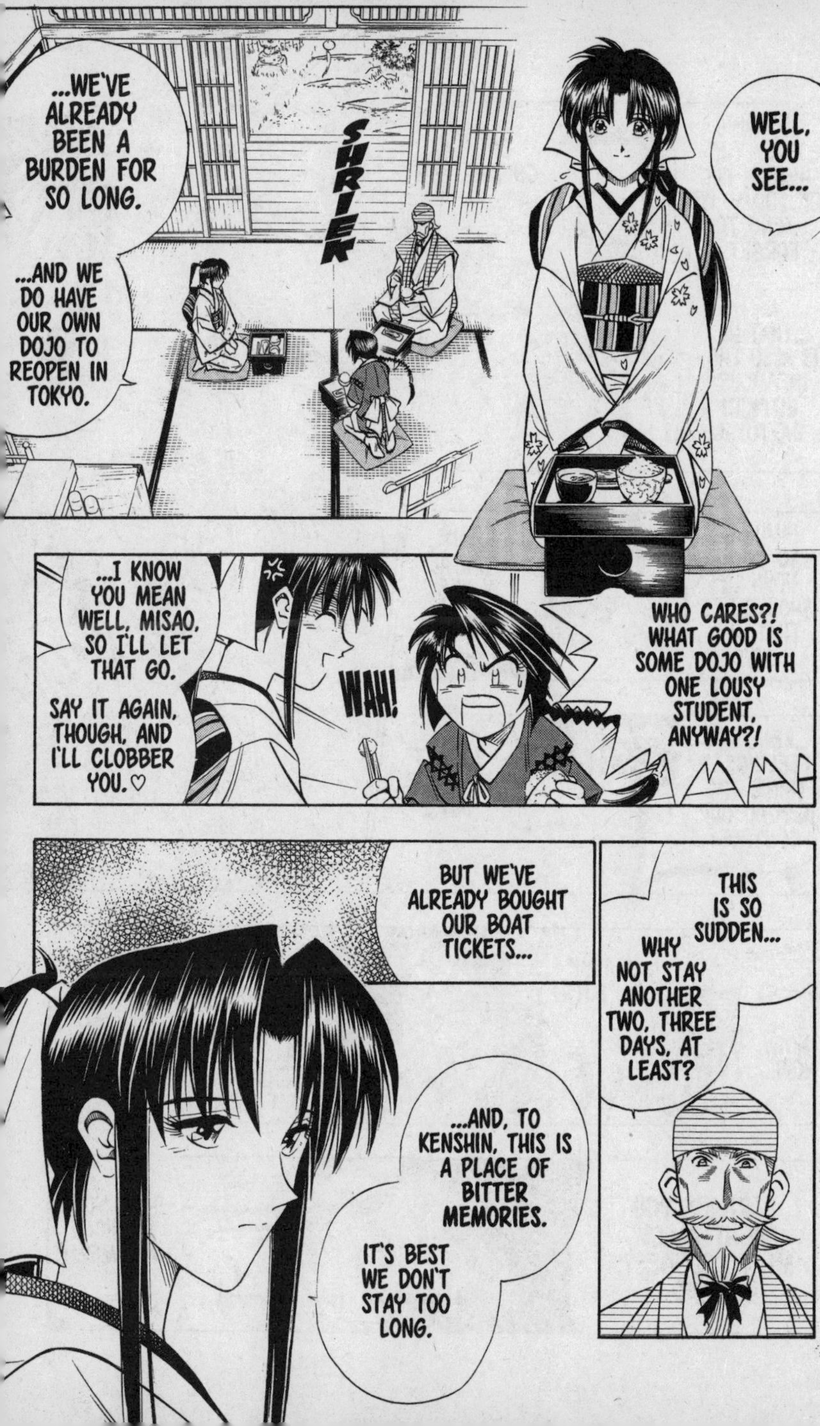
WELL, YOU SEE...
...WE'VE ALREADY BEEN A BURDEN FOR SO LONG.
SHRIEK
...AND WE DO HAVE OUR OWN DOJO TO REOPEN IN TOKYO.
WHO CARES?! WHAT GOOD IS SOME DOJO WITH ONE LOUSY STUDENT, ANYWAY?!
WAH!
...I KNOW YOU MEAN WELL, MISAO, SO I'LL LET THAT GO.
SAY IT AGAIN, THOUGH, AND I'LL CLOBBER YOU.♡
THIS IS SO SUDDEN...
WHY NOT STAY ANOTHER TWO, THREE DAYS, AT LEAST?
BUT WE'VE ALREADY BOUGHT OUR BOAT TICKETS...
...AND, TO KENSHIN, THIS IS A PLACE OF BITTER MEMORIES.
IT'S BEST WE DON'T STAY TOO LONG.

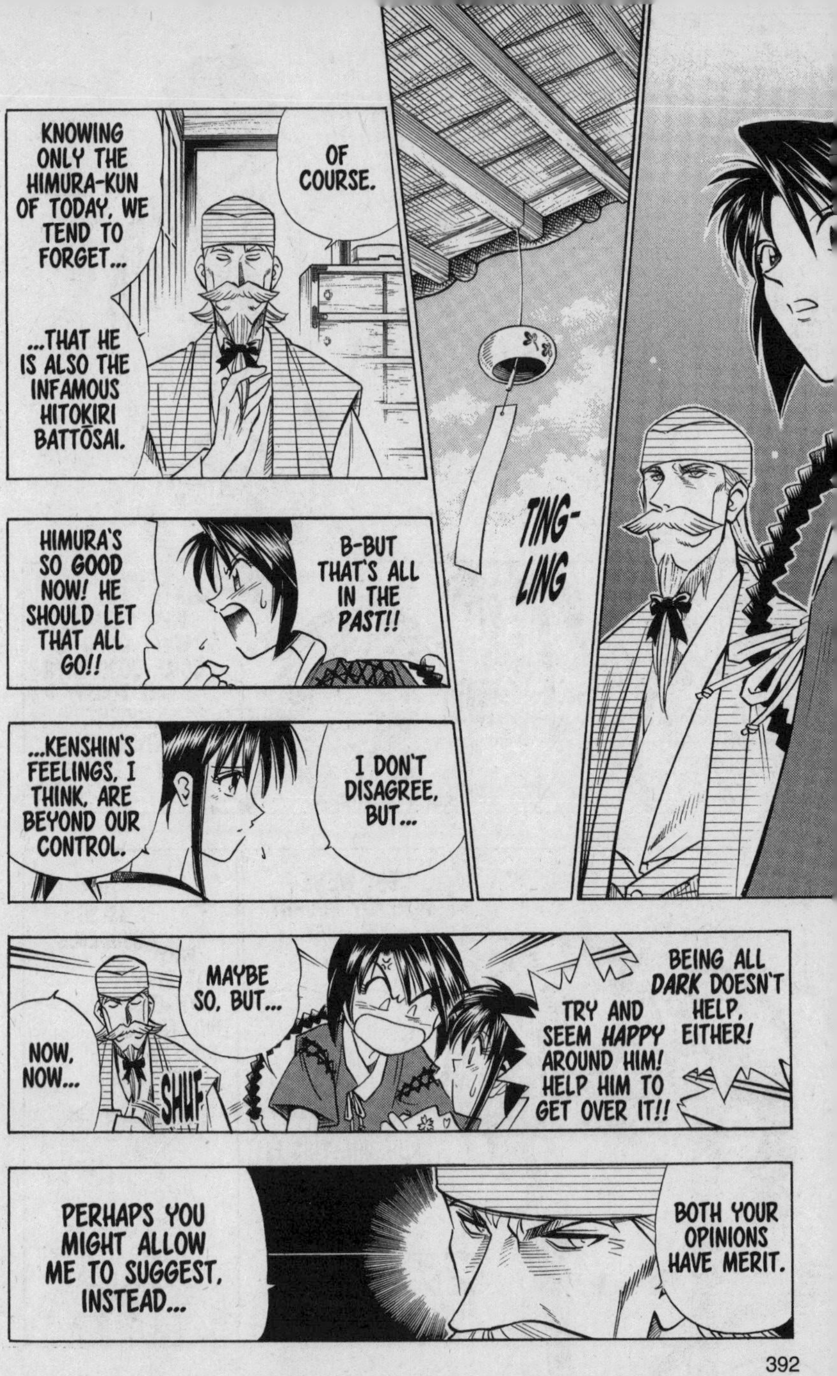
TING-LING
OF COURSE.
KNOWING ONLY THE HIMURA-KUN OF TODAY, WE TEND TO FORGET...
...THAT HE IS ALSO THE INFAMOUS HITOKIRI BATTŌSAI.
B-BUT THAT'S ALL IN THE PAST!!
HIMURA'S SO GOOD NOW! HE SHOULD LET THAT ALL GO!!
I DON'T DISAGREE, BUT...
...KENSHIN'S FEELINGS, I THINK, ARE BEYOND OUR CONTROL.
BEING ALL DARK DOESN'T HELP, EITHER!
TRY AND SEEM HAPPY AROUND HIM! HELP HIM TO GET OVER IT!!
MAYBE SO, BUT...
NOW, NOW...
SHUF
BOTH YOUR OPINIONS HAVE MERIT.
PERHAPS YOU MIGHT ALLOW ME TO SUGGEST, INSTEAD...

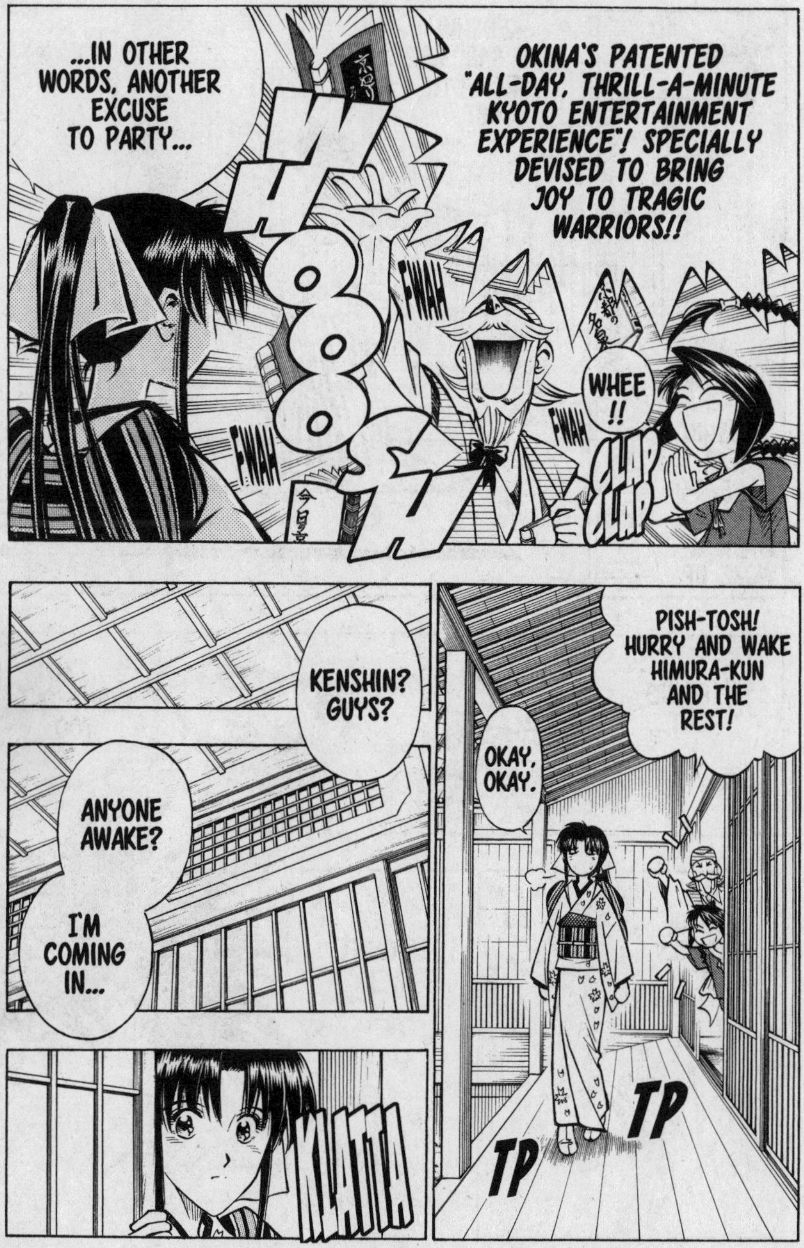
OKINA'S PATENTED "ALL-DAY, THRILL-A-MINUTE KYOTO ENTERTAINMENT EXPERIENCE"! SPECIALLY DEVISED TO BRING JOY TO TRAGIC WARRIORS!!
WHOOOSH
FWAH
FWAH
FWAH
WHEE !!
CLAP CLAP
...IN OTHER WORDS, ANOTHER EXCUSE TO PARTY...
PISH-TOSH! HURRY AND WAKE HIMURA-KUN AND THE REST!
OKAY, OKAY.
TP
TP
KENSHIN? GUYS?
ANYONE AWAKE?
I'M COMING IN...
KLATTA

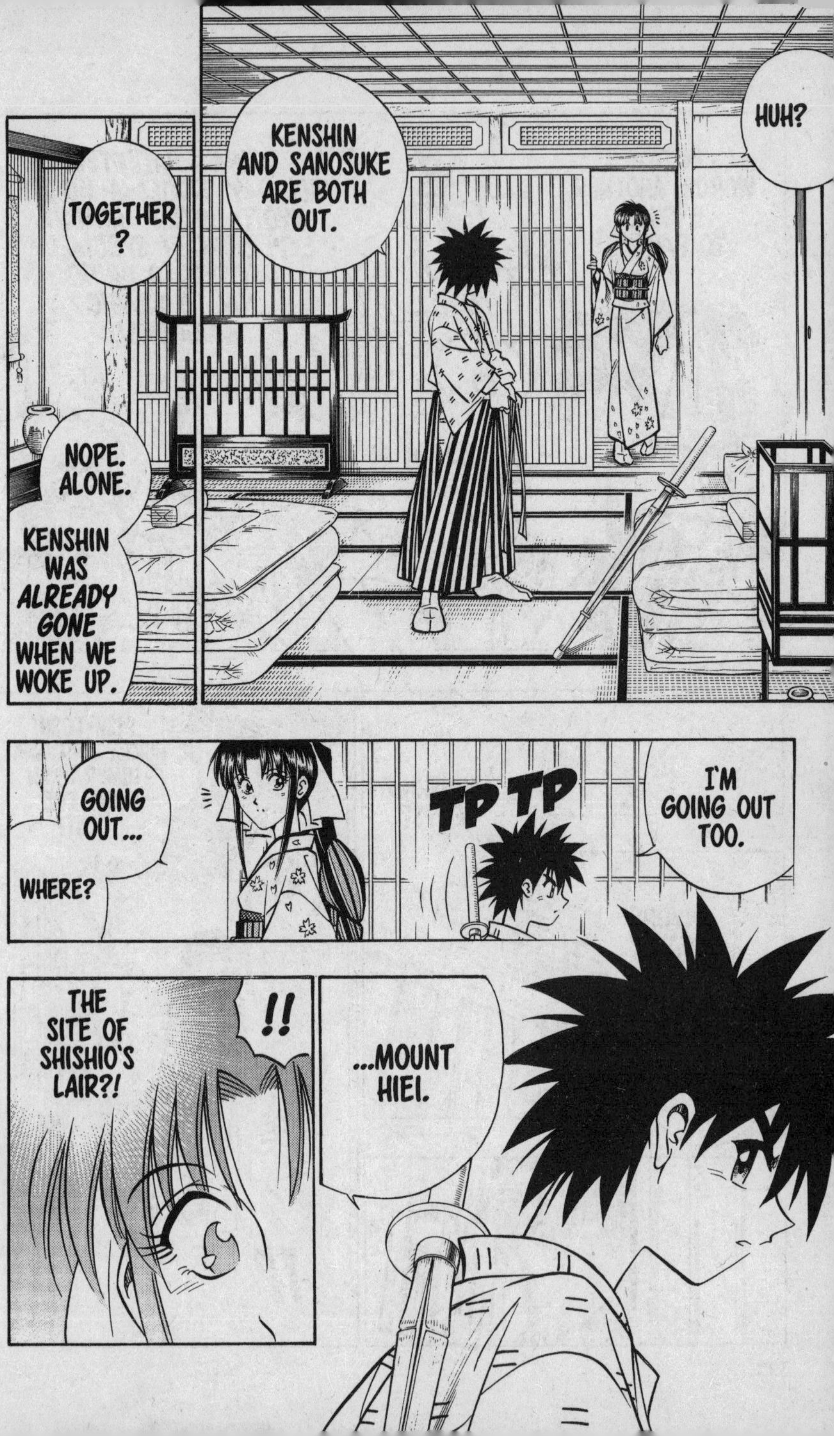
HUH?
KENSHIN AND SANOSUKE ARE BOTH OUT.
TOGETHER ?
NOPE. ALONE.
KENSHIN WAS ALREADY GONE WHEN WE WOKE UP.
I'M GOING OUT TOO.
TP TP
GOING OUT...
WHERE?
...MOUNT HIEI.
!!
THE SITE OF SHISHIO'S LAIR?!

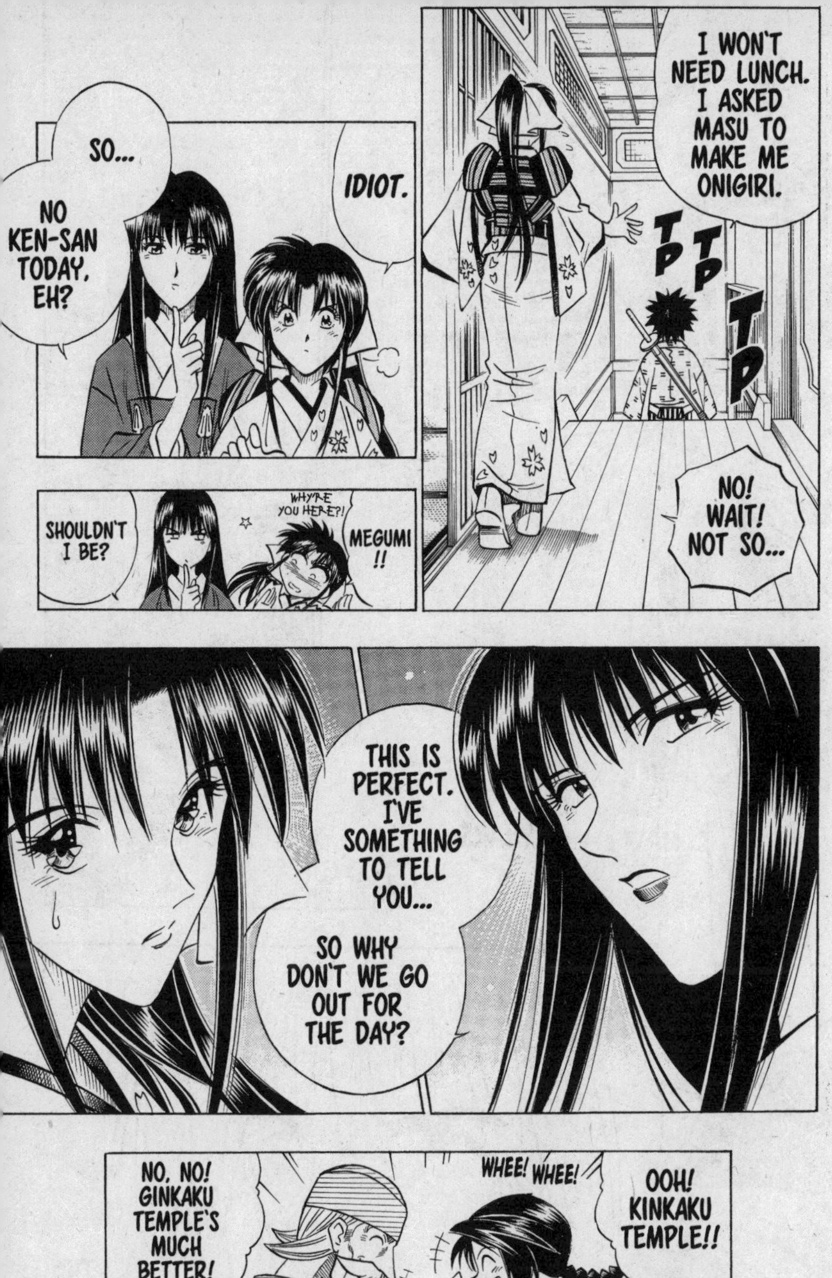

I WON'T NEED LUNCH. I ASKED MASU TO MAKE ME ONIGIRI.
TP TP TP
NO! WAIT! NOT SO...
IDIOT.
SO...
NO KEN-SAN TODAY, EH?
MEGUMI!!
WHY'RE YOU HERE?!
SHOULDN'T I BE?
THIS IS PERFECT. I'VE SOMETHING TO TELL YOU...
SO WHY DON'T WE GO OUT FOR THE DAY?
OOH! KINKAKU TEMPLE!!
WHEE! WHEE!
NO, NO! GINKAKU TEMPLE'S MUCH BETTER!

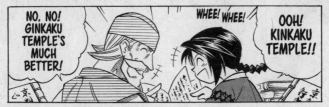

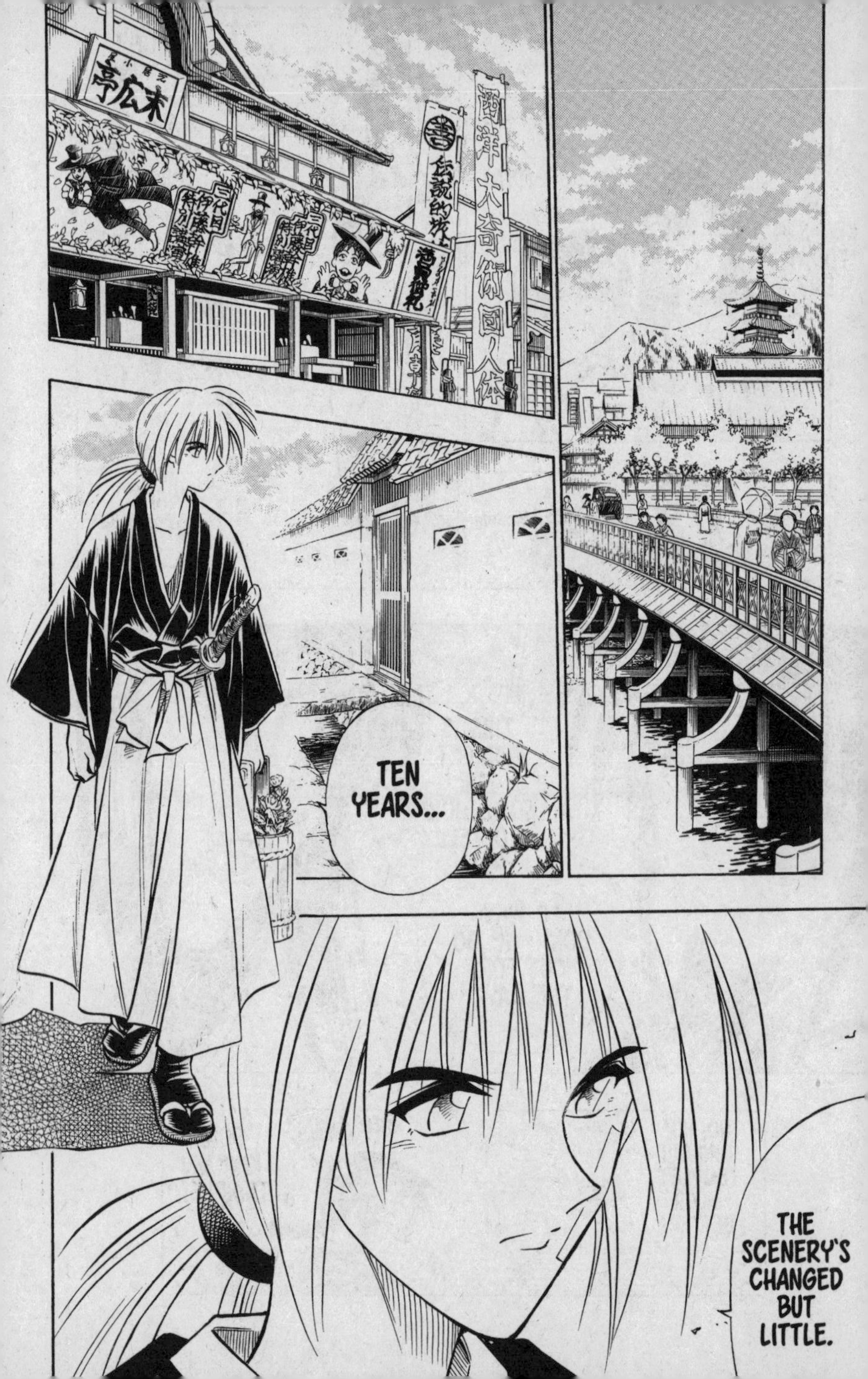
TEN YEARS...
THE SCENERY'S CHANGED BUT LITTLE.

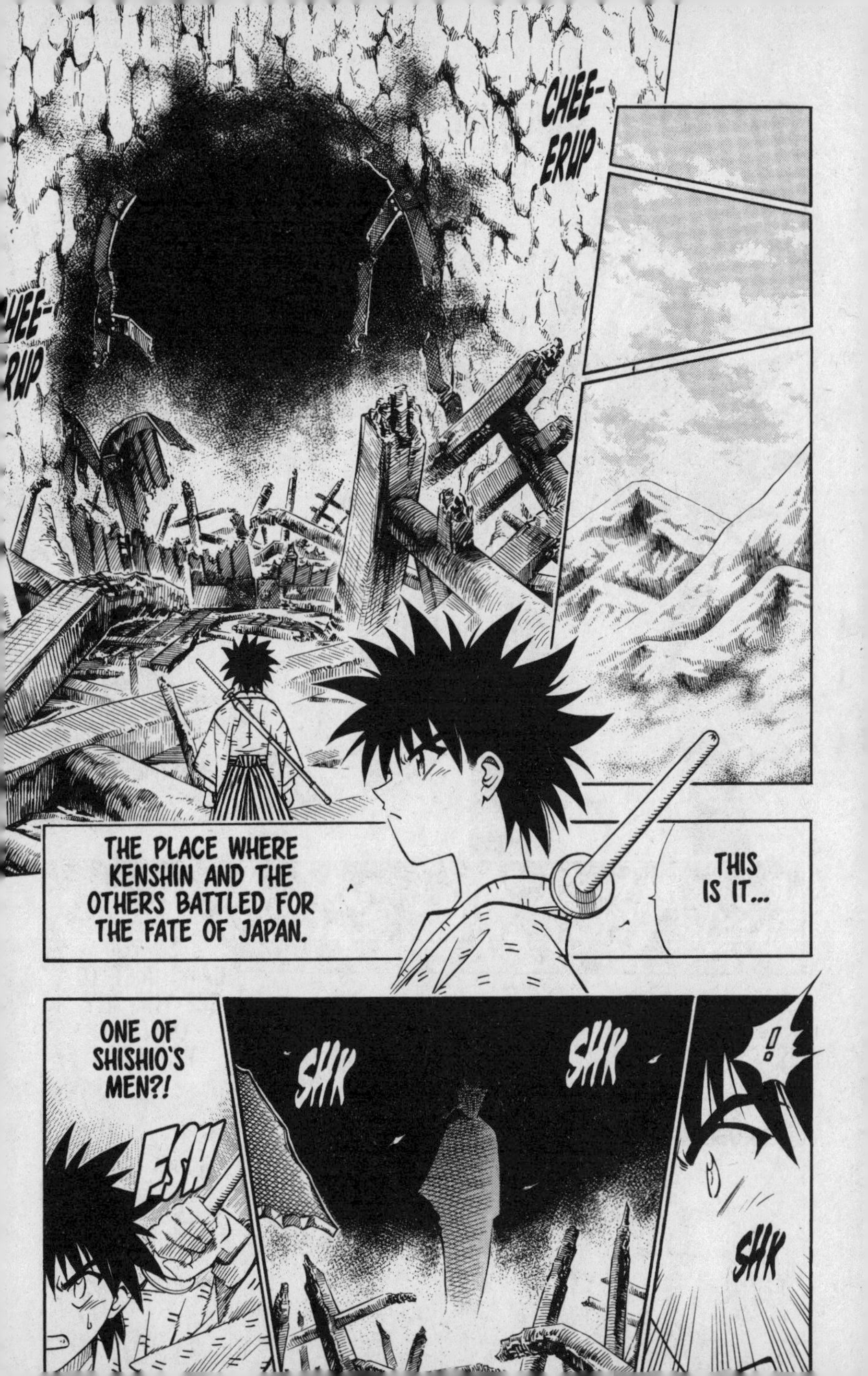
CHEE-ERUP
HEE-RUP
THIS IS IT...
THE PLACE WHERE KENSHIN AND THE OTHERS BATTLED FOR THE FATE OF JAPAN.
!
SHK
SHK
SHK
ONE OF SHISHIO'S MEN?!
FSH

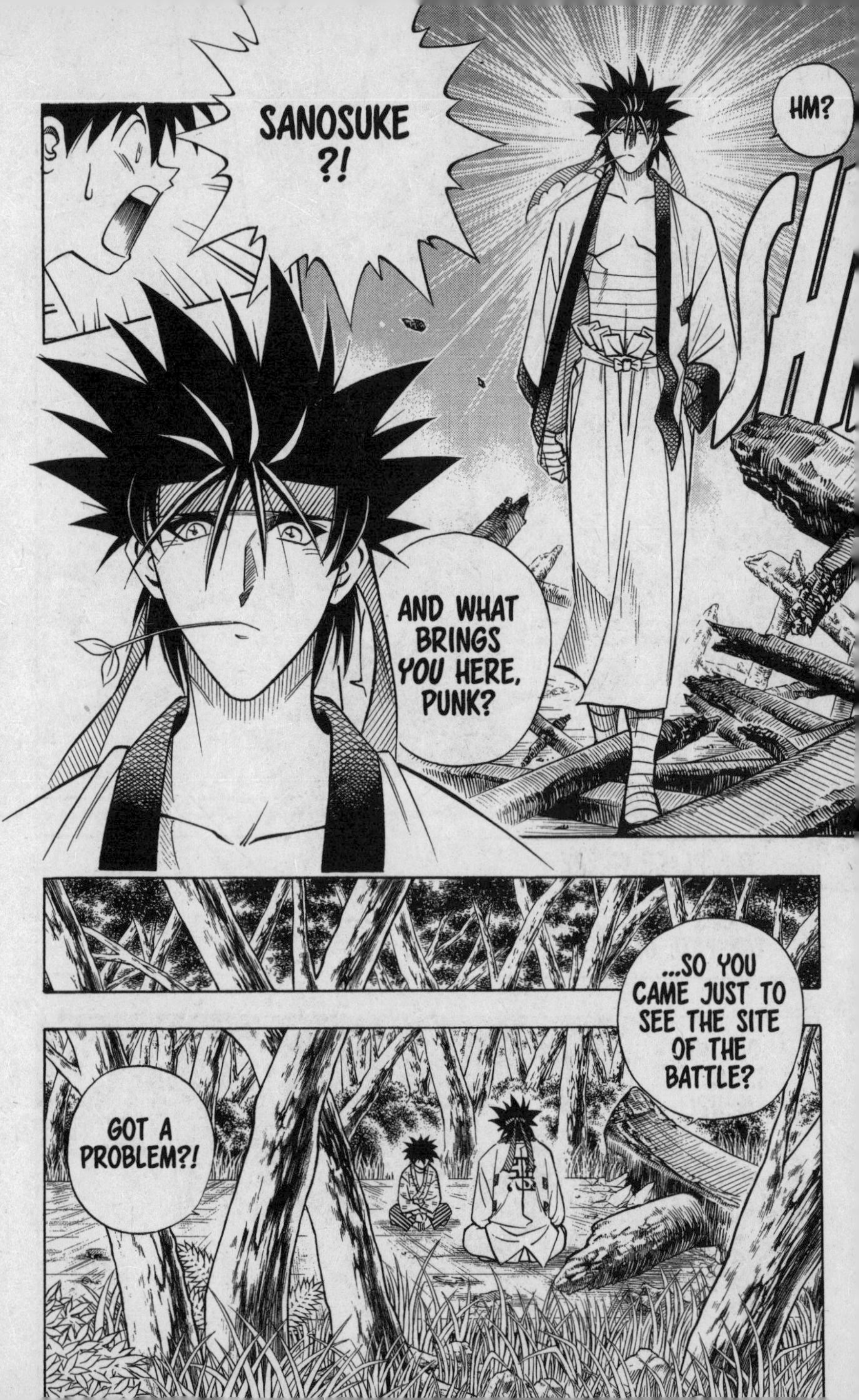
HM?
SANOSUKE ?!
AND WHAT BRINGS YOU HERE, PUNK?
...SO YOU CAME JUST TO SEE THE SITE OF THE BATTLE?
GOT A PROBLEM?!

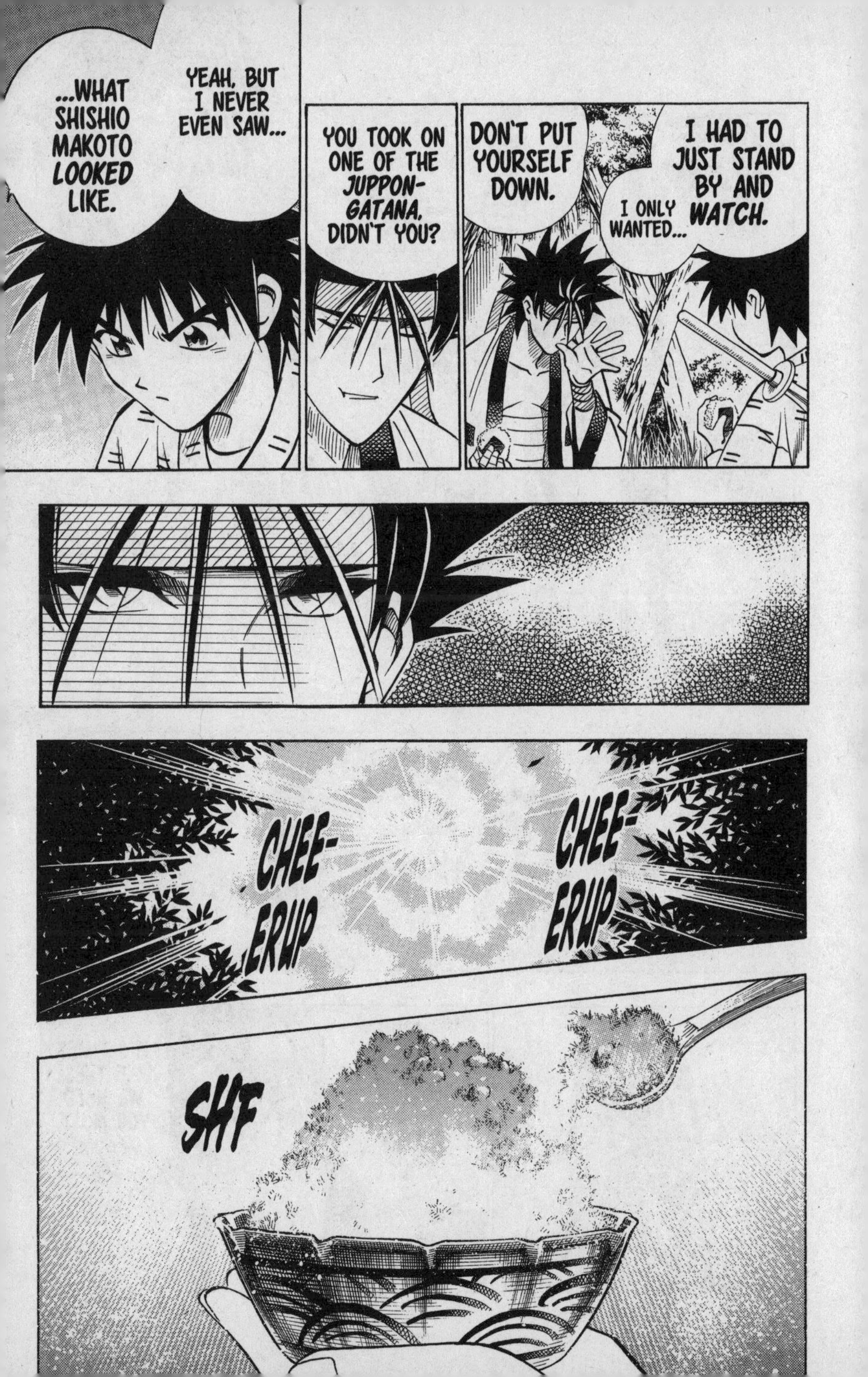
I HAD TO JUST STAND BY AND WATCH.
I ONLY WANTED...
DON'T PUT YOURSELF DOWN.
YOU TOOK ON ONE OF THE JUPPON-GATANA, DIDN'T YOU?
YEAH, BUT I NEVER EVEN SAW...
...WHAT SHISHIO MAKOTO LOOKED LIKE.
CHEE-ERUP
CHEE-ERUP
SHF

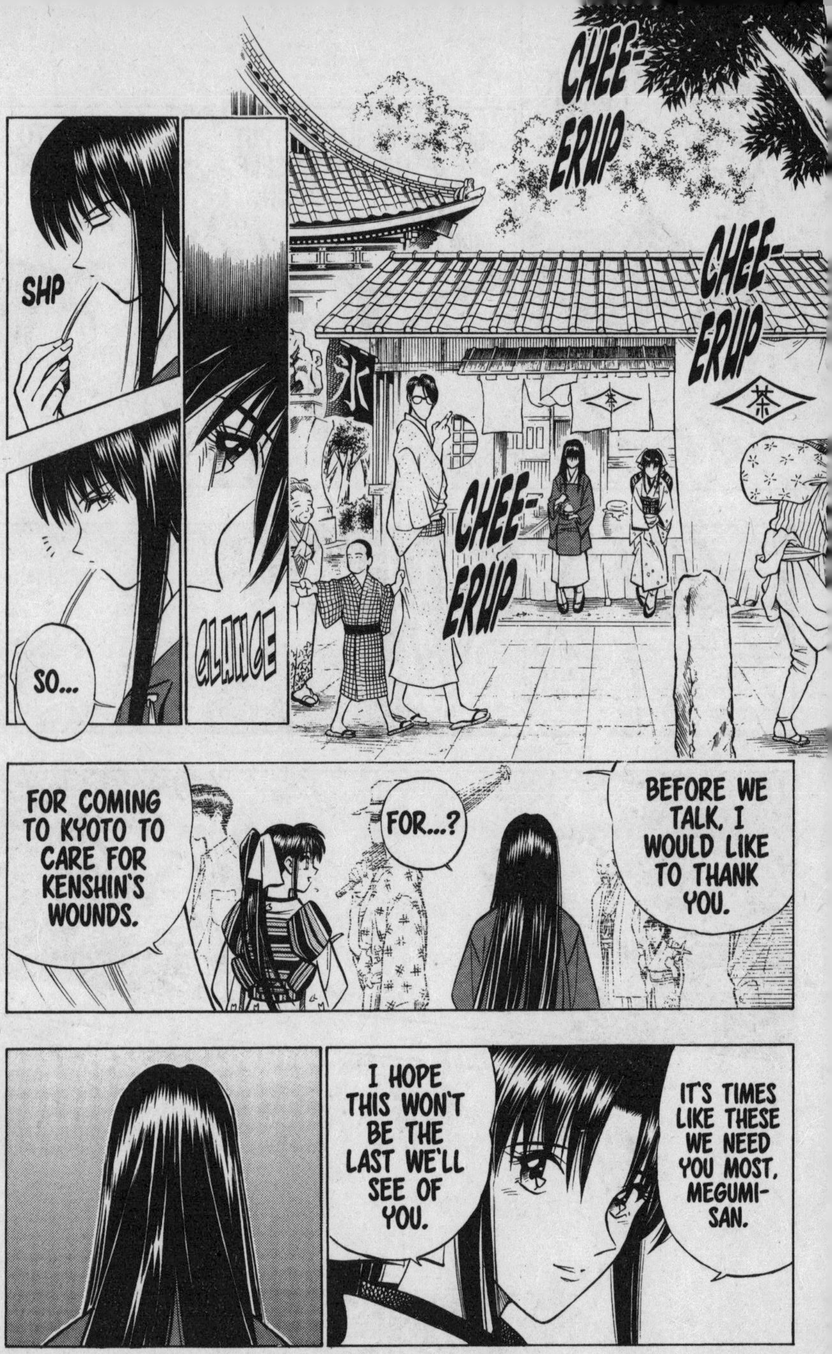
CHEE-ERUP
CHEE-ERUP
CHEE-ERUP
GLANCE
SHP
SO...
BEFORE WE TALK, I WOULD LIKE TO THANK YOU.
FOR...?
FOR COMING TO KYOTO TO CARE FOR KENSHIN'S WOUNDS.
IT'S TIMES LIKE THESE WE NEED YOU MOST, MEGUMI-SAN.
I HOPE THIS WON'T BE THE LAST WE'LL SEE OF YOU.

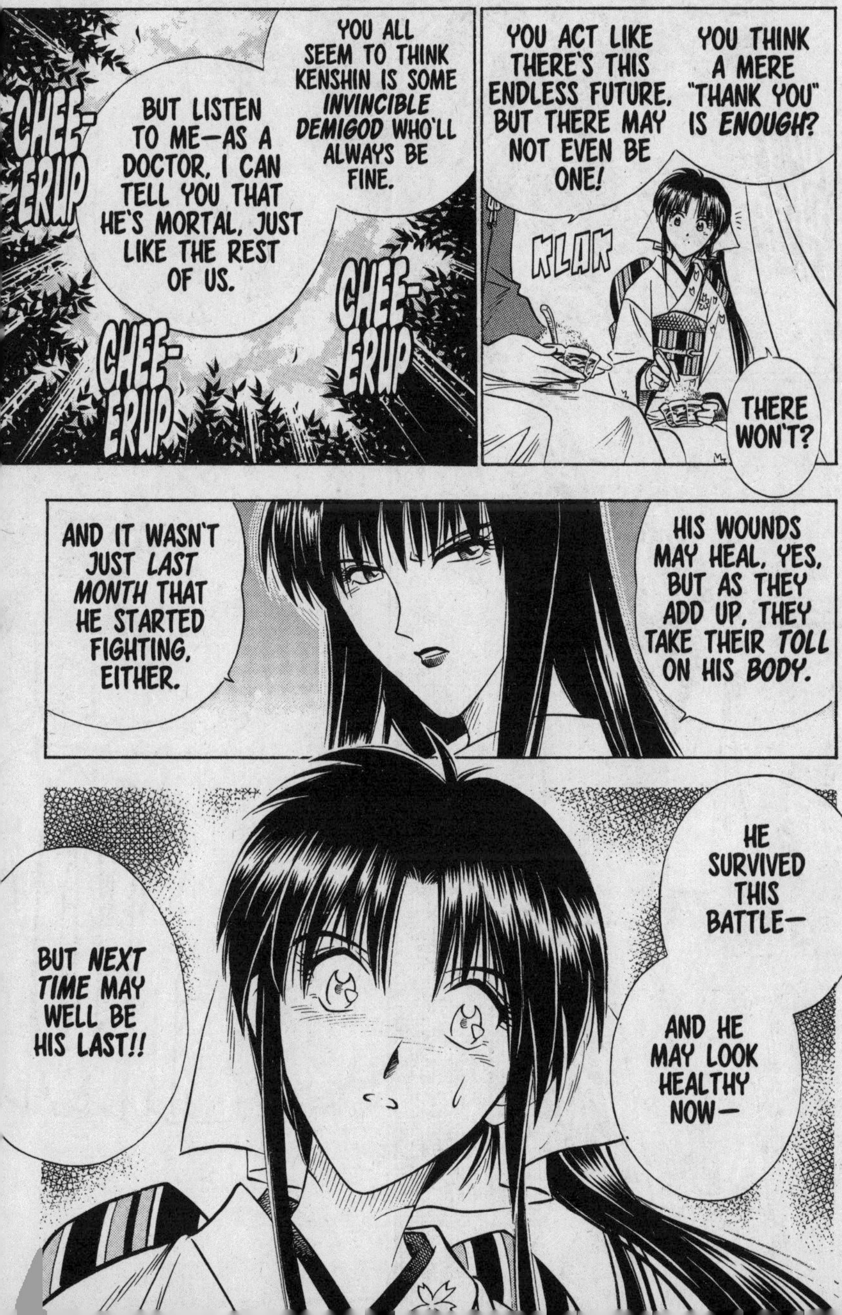
YOU THINK A MERE "THANK YOU" IS ENOUGH?
YOU ACT LIKE THERE'S THIS ENDLESS FUTURE, BUT THERE MAY NOT EVEN BE ONE!
KLAK
THERE WON'T?
YOU ALL SEEM TO THINK KENSHIN IS SOME INVINCIBLE DEMIGOD WHO'LL ALWAYS BE FINE.
BUT LISTEN TO ME—AS A DOCTOR, I CAN TELL YOU THAT HE'S MORTAL, JUST LIKE THE REST OF US.
CHEE-ERUP
CHEE-ERUP
CHEE-ERUP
HIS WOUNDS MAY HEAL, YES, BUT AS THEY ADD UP, THEY TAKE THEIR TOLL ON HIS BODY.
AND IT WASN'T JUST LAST MONTH THAT HE STARTED FIGHTING, EITHER.
HE SURVIVED THIS BATTLE—
AND HE MAY LOOK HEALTHY NOW—
BUT NEXT TIME MAY WELL BE HIS LAST!!

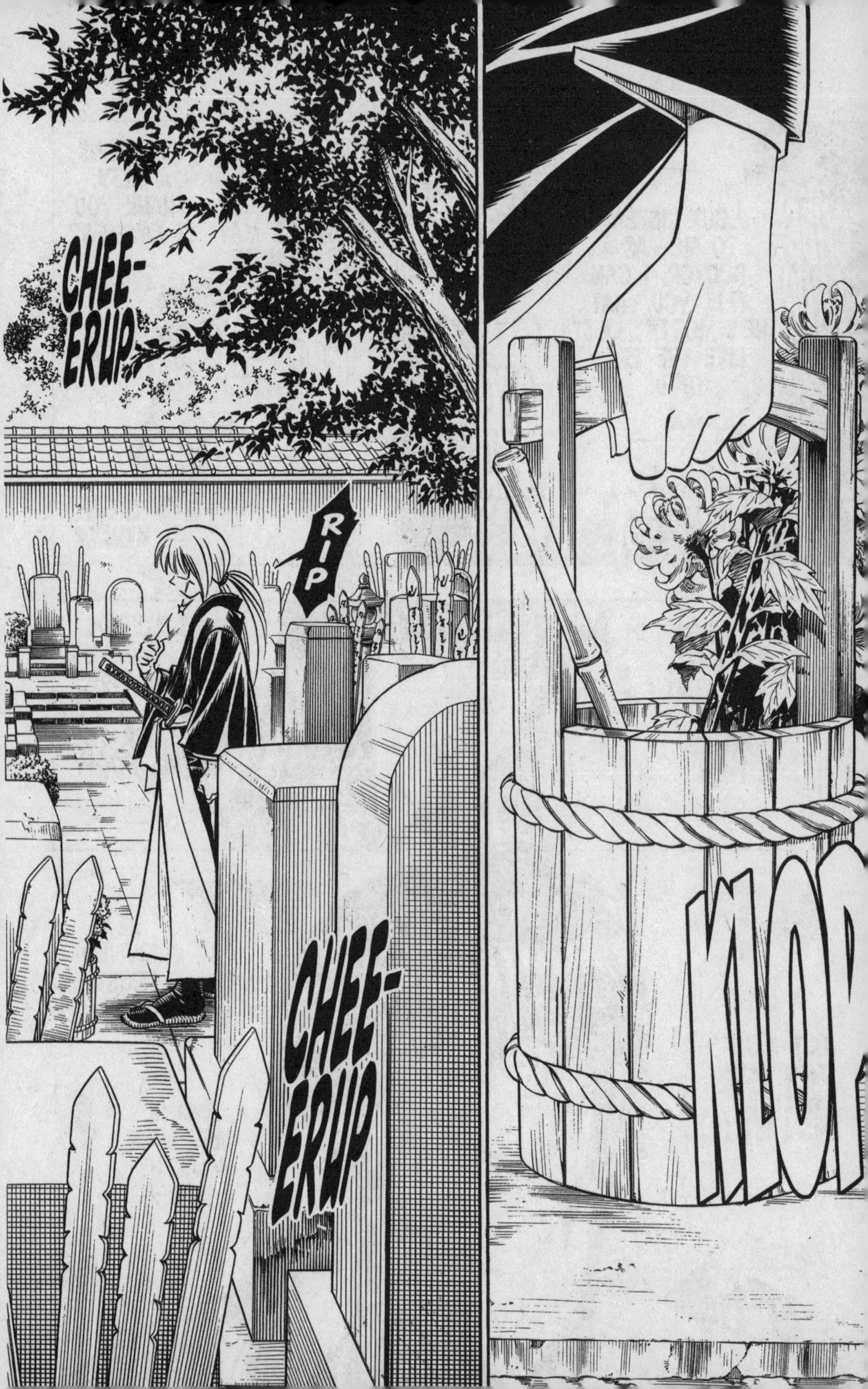
KLOP
CHEE-ERUP
RIP
CHEE-ERUP

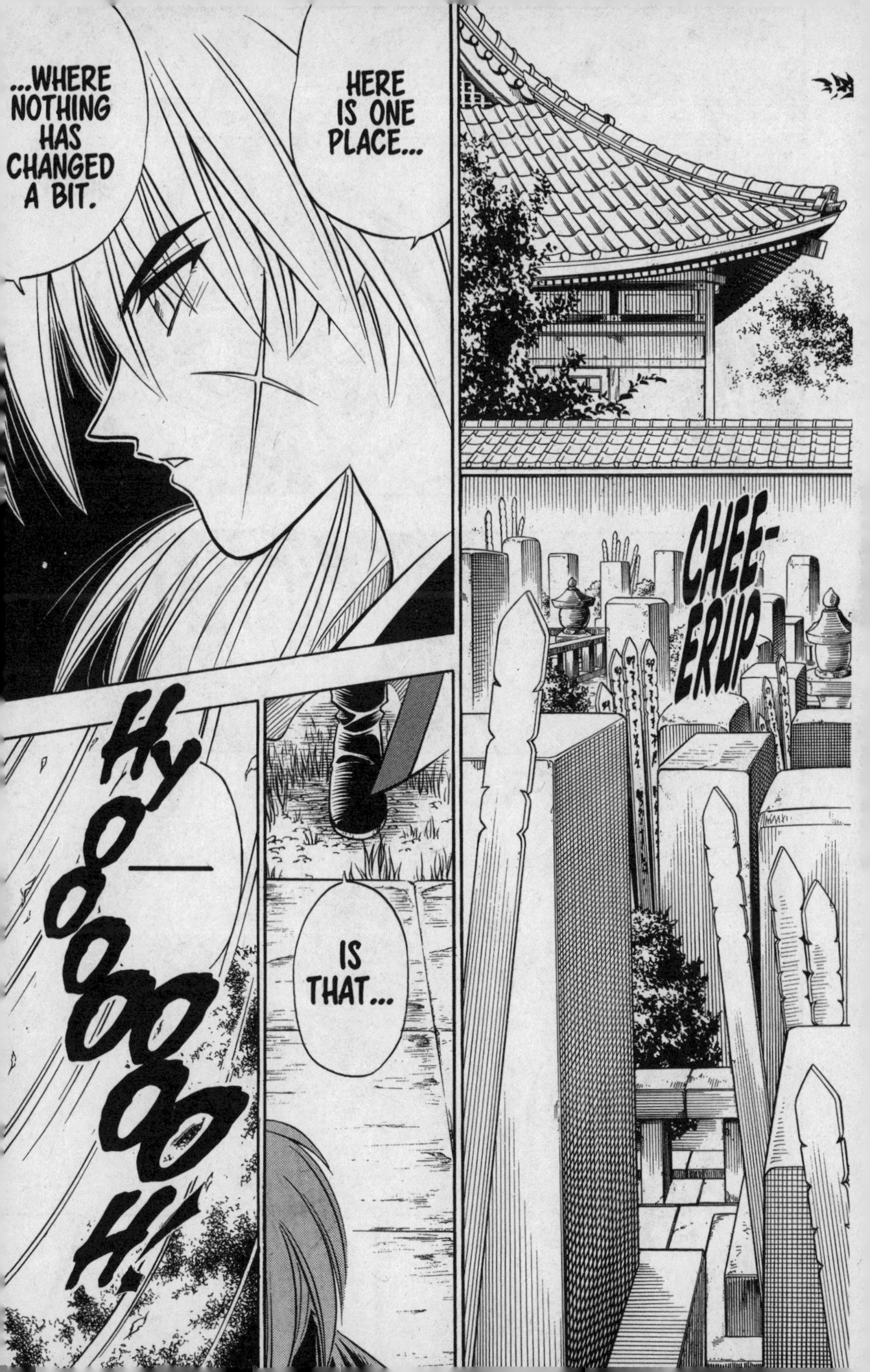
CHEE-ERUP
HERE IS ONE PLACE...
...WHERE NOTHING HAS CHANGED A BIT.
IS THAT...
HYOOOOOOH!

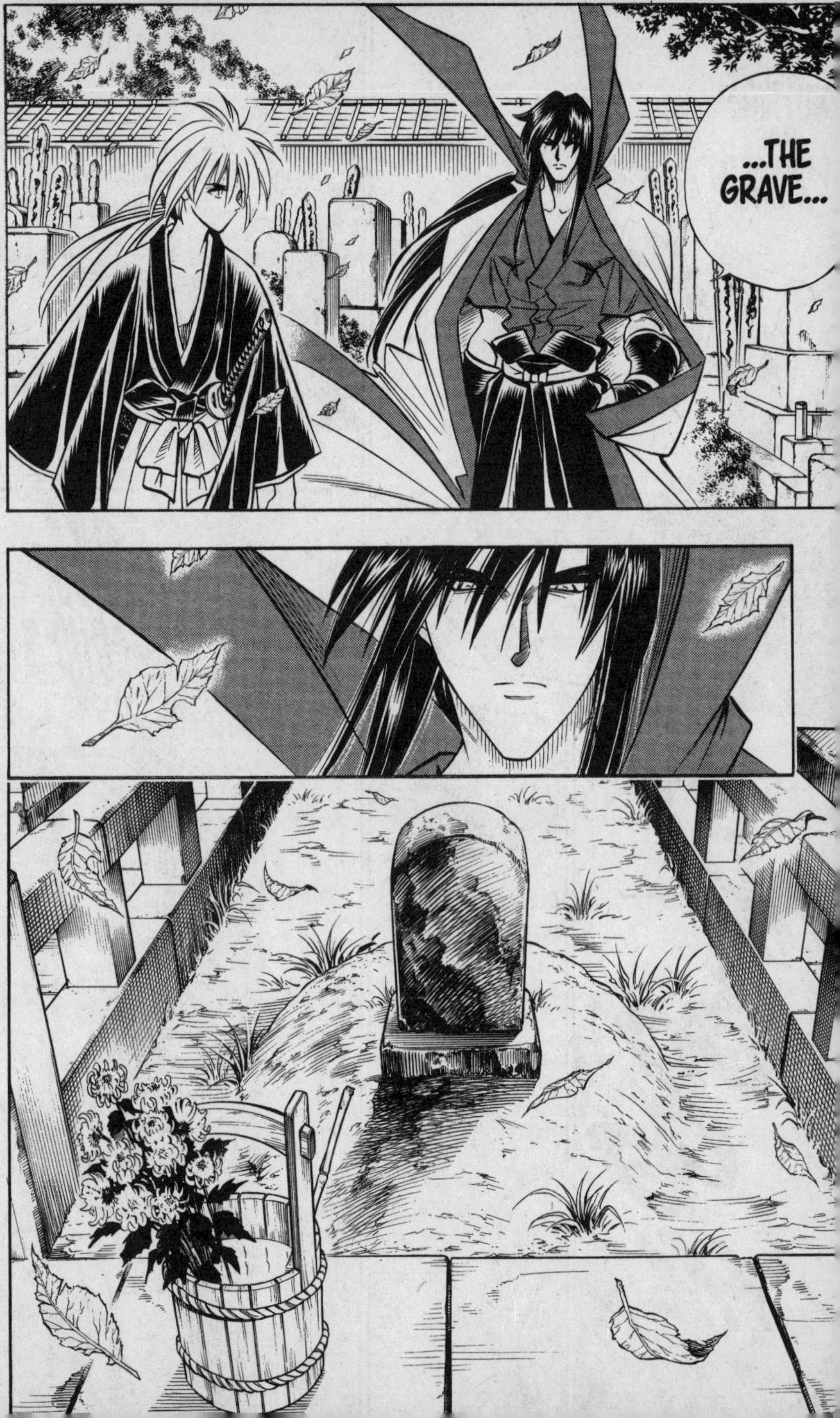
...THE GRAVE...

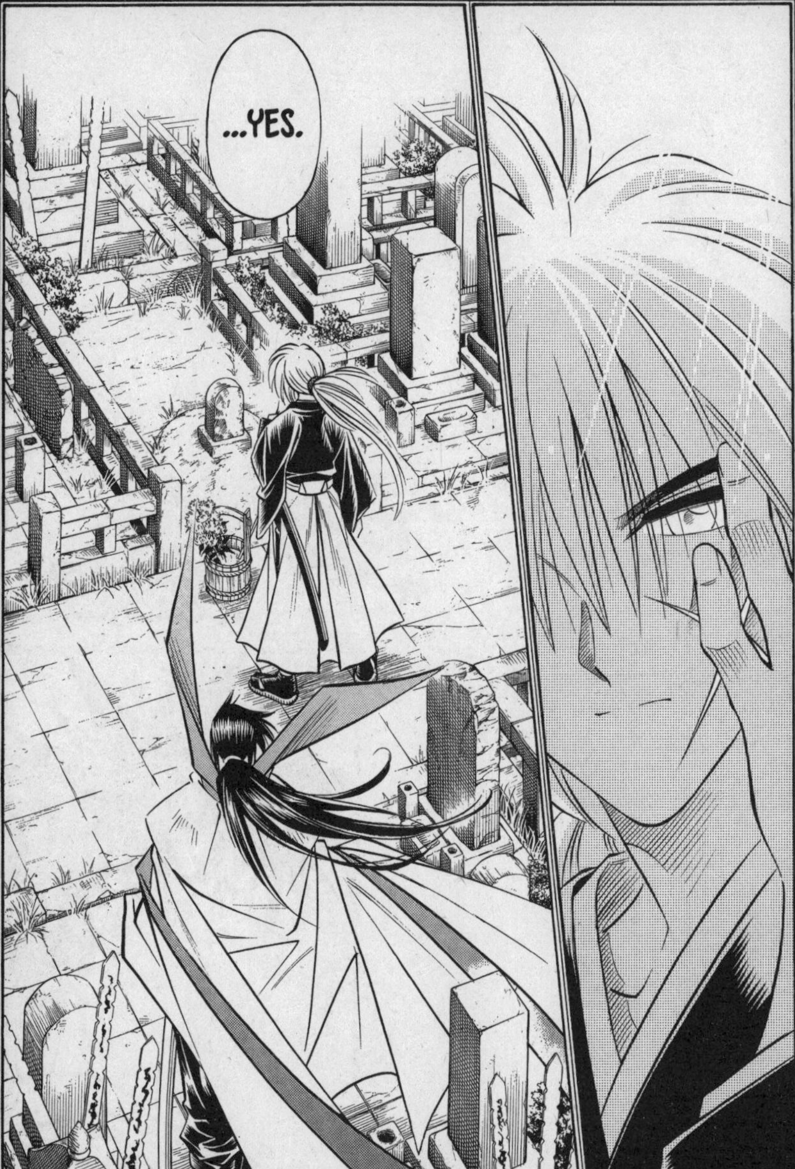
...YES.

Rurouni Kenshin

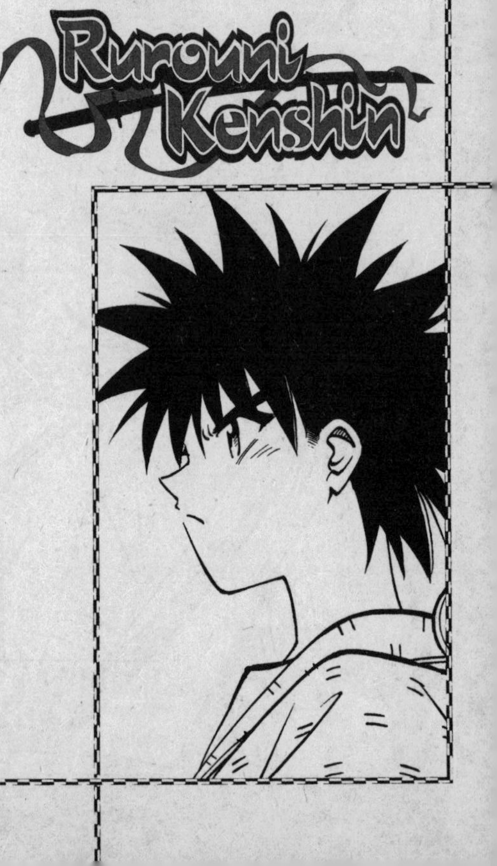

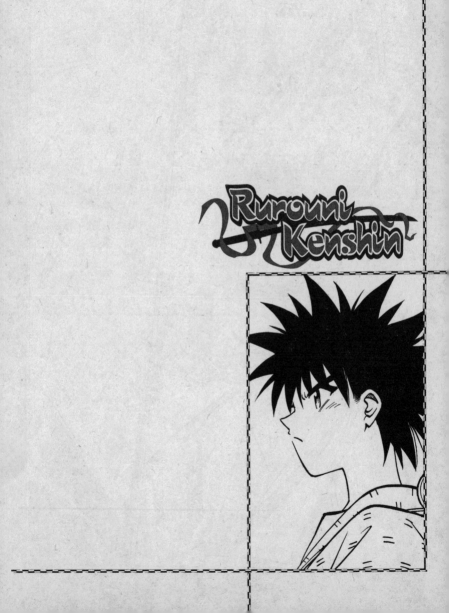

Act 150—Kyoto Epilogue
Early Summer Day

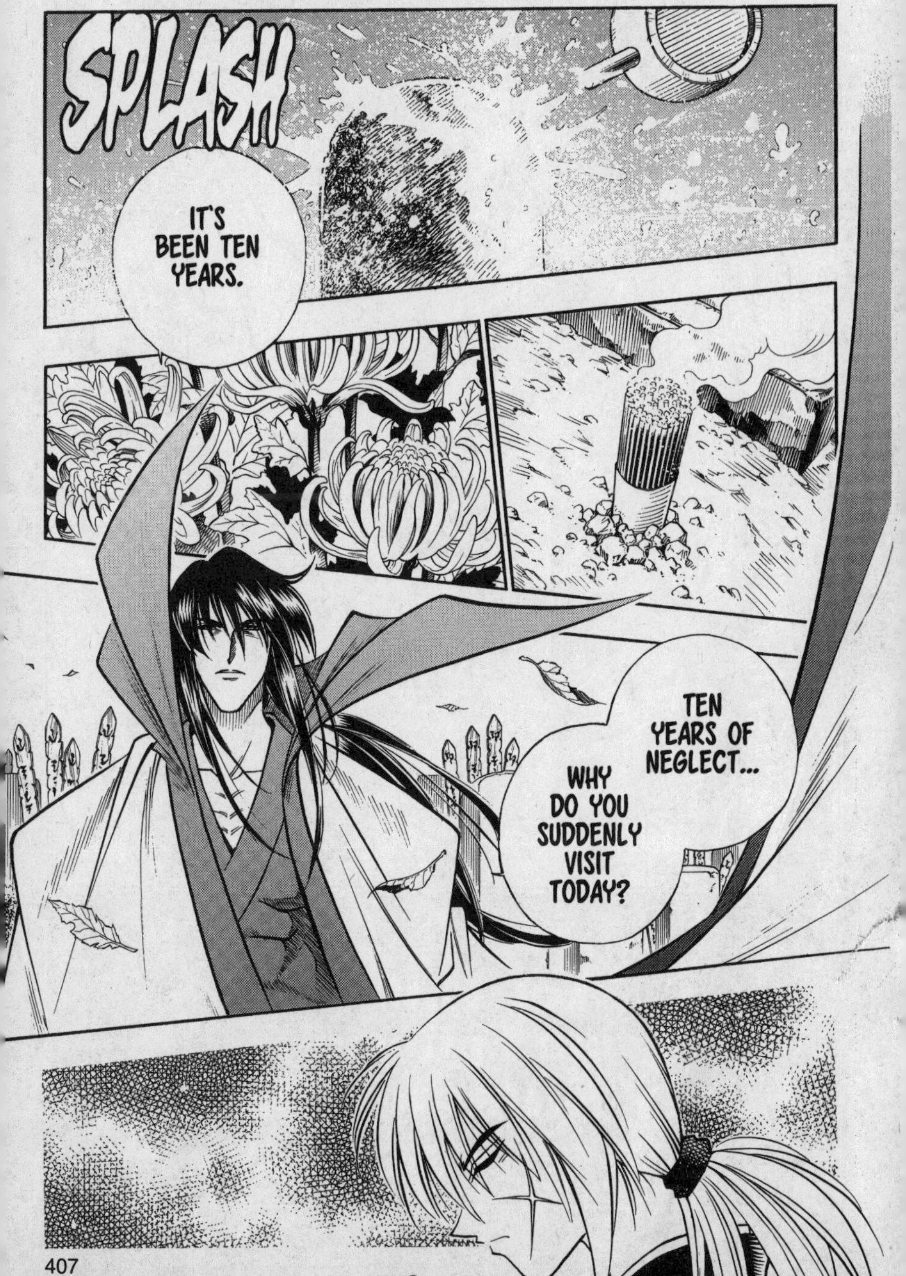
SPLASH
IT'S BEEN TEN YEARS.
TEN YEARS OF NEGLECT...
WHY DO YOU SUDDENLY VISIT TODAY?

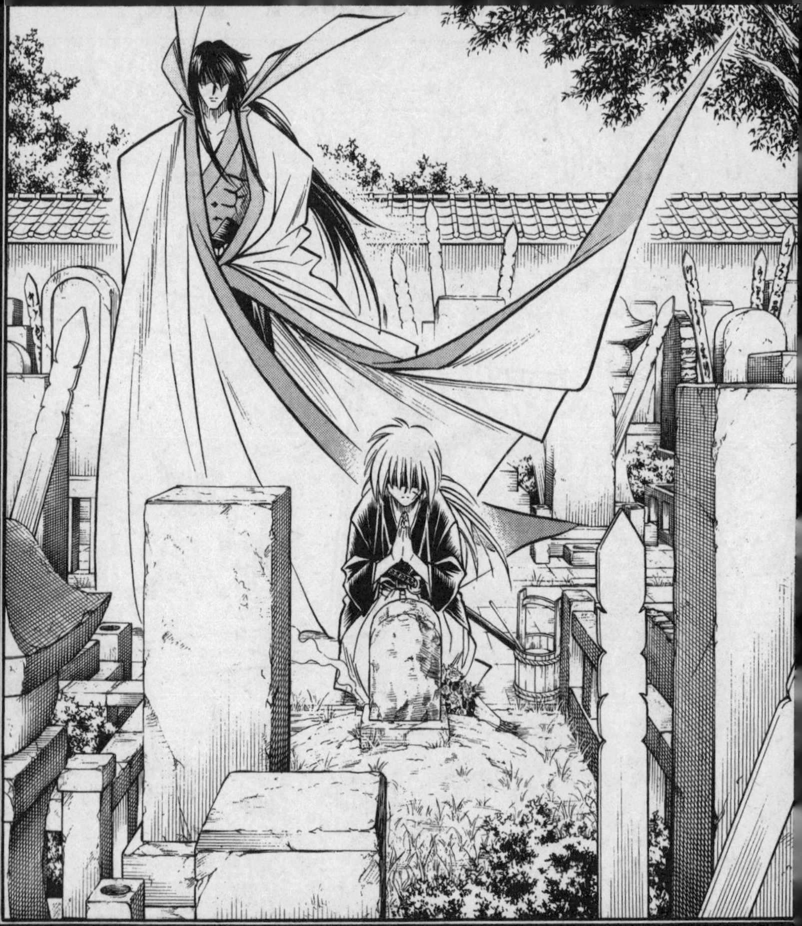

Act 150
Kyoto Epilogue
Early Summer Day

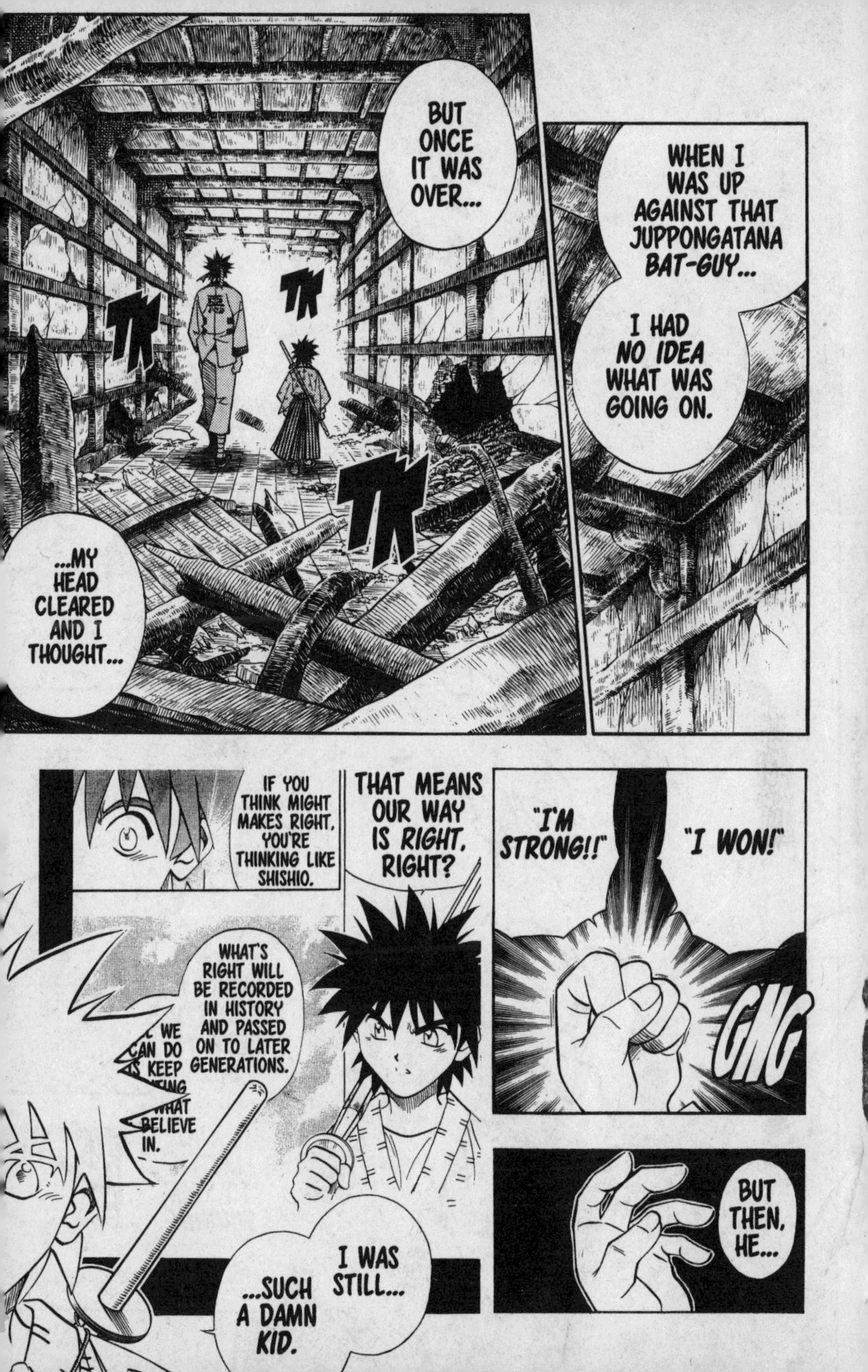
WHEN I WAS UP AGAINST THAT JUPPONGATANA BAT-GUY...
I HAD NO IDEA WHAT WAS GOING ON.
BUT ONCE IT WAS OVER...
TK
TK
TK
...MY HEAD CLEARED AND I THOUGHT...
"I'M STRONG!!"
"I WON!"
GNG
BUT THEN, HE...
THAT MEANS OUR WAY IS RIGHT, RIGHT?
IF YOU THINK MIGHT MAKES RIGHT, YOU'RE THINKING LIKE SHISHIO.
WHAT'S RIGHT WILL BE RECORDED IN HISTORY AND PASSED ON TO LATER GENERATIONS.
WE CAN DO KEEP WHAT BELIEVE IN.
I WAS STILL...
...SUCH A DAMN KID.

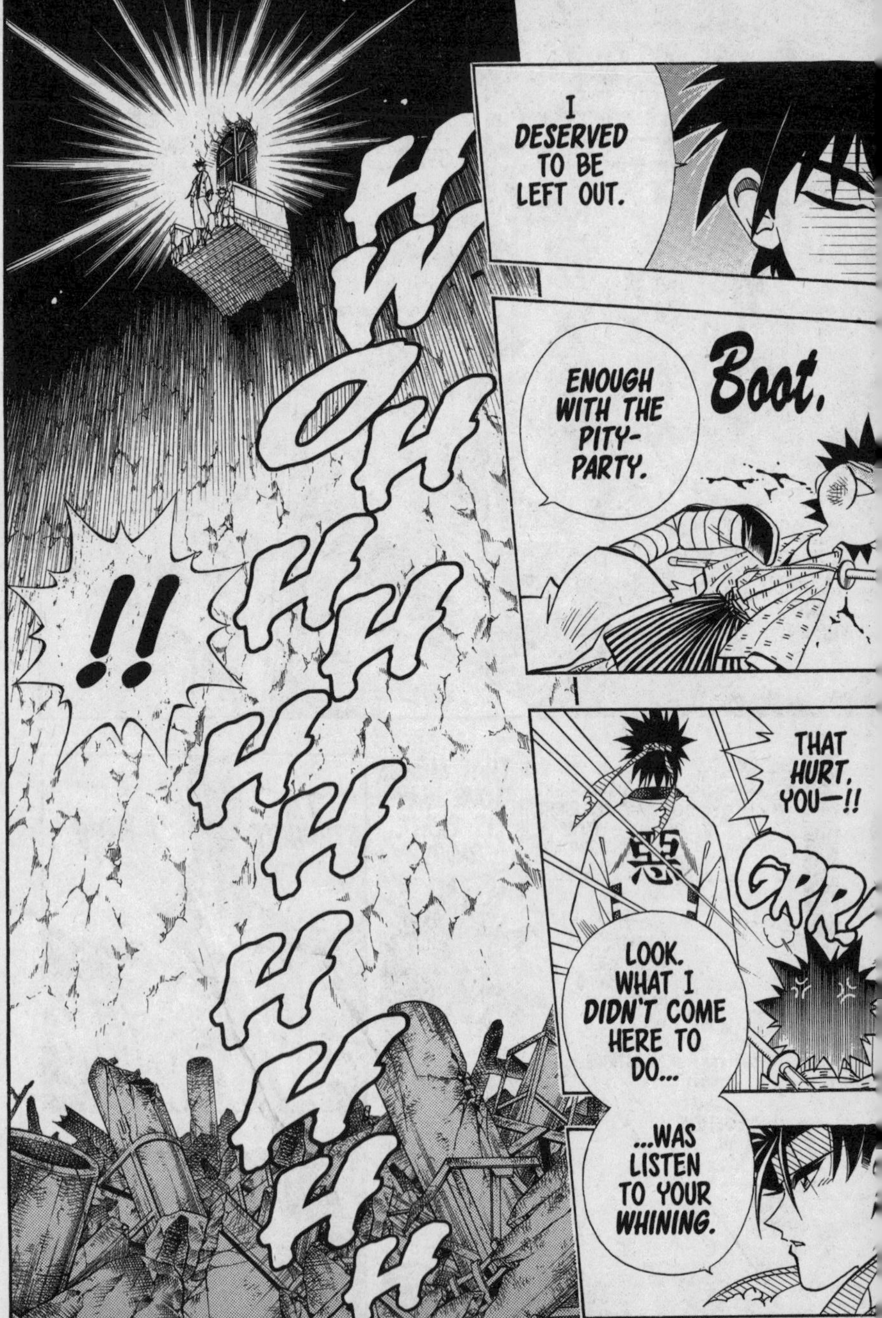
I DESERVED TO BE LEFT OUT.
ENOUGH WITH THE PITY-PARTY.
Boot.
THAT HURT, YOU—!!
GRR
LOOK. WHAT I DIDN'T COME HERE TO DO...
...WAS LISTEN TO YOUR WHINING.
!!

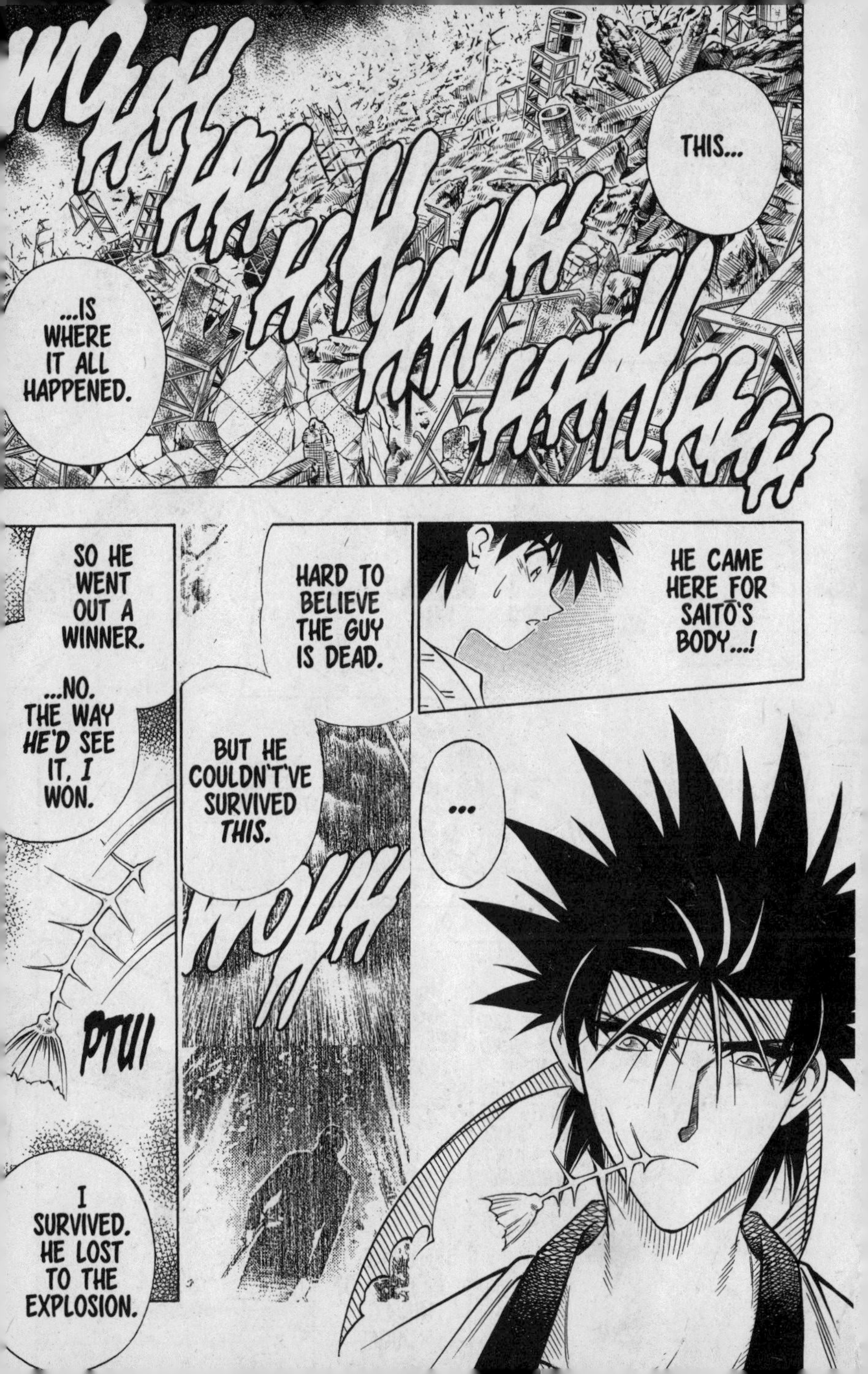
THIS...
...IS WHERE IT ALL HAPPENED.
HE CAME HERE FOR SAITŌ'S BODY...!
...
HARD TO BELIEVE THE GUY IS DEAD.
BUT HE COULDN'T'VE SURVIVED THIS.
SO HE WENT OUT A WINNER.
...NO. THE WAY HE'D SEE IT, I WON.
PTUI
I SURVIVED. HE LOST TO THE EXPLOSION.

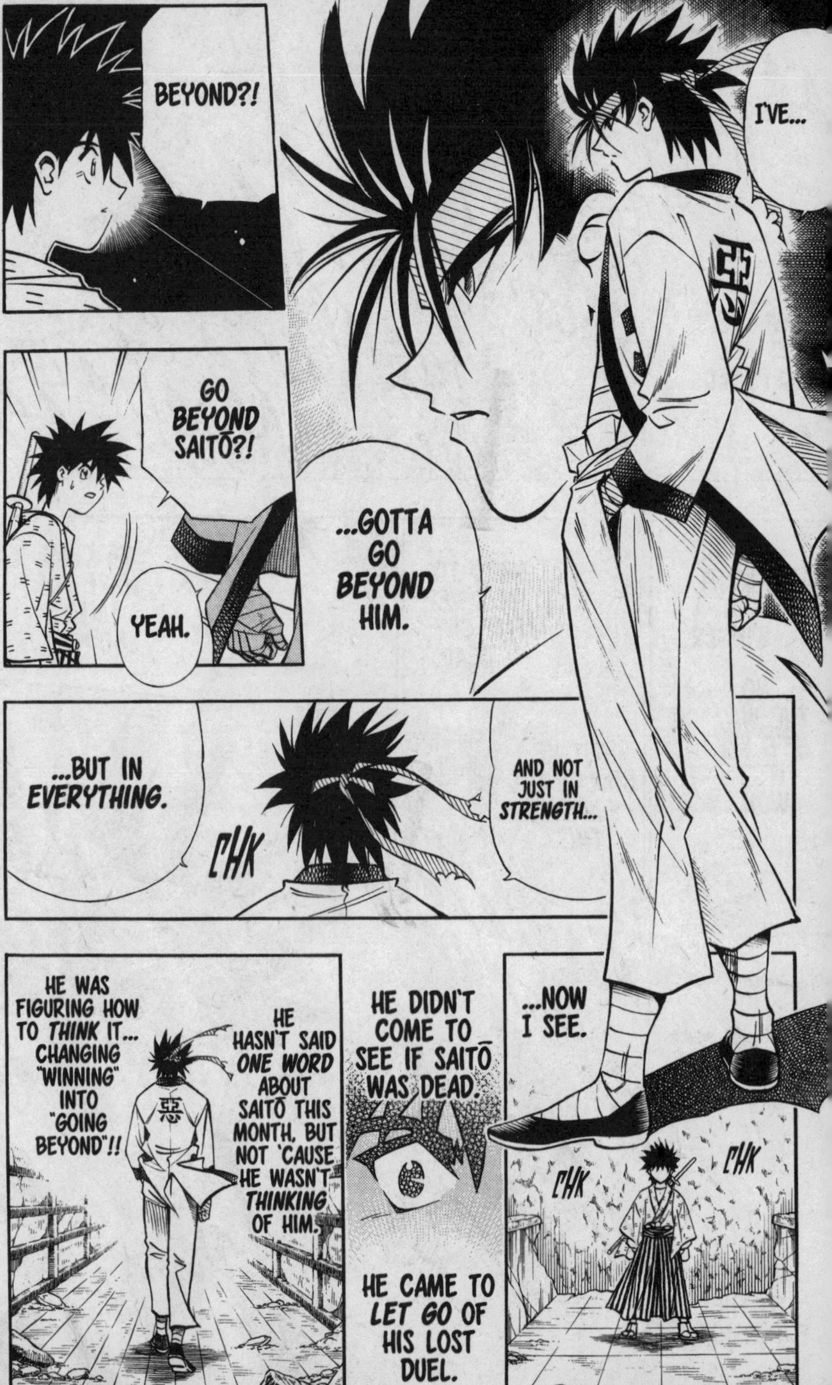
I'VE...
...GOTTA GO BEYOND HIM.
BEYOND?!
GO BEYOND SAITŌ?!
YEAH.
AND NOT JUST IN STRENGTH...
CHK
...BUT IN EVERYTHING.
...NOW I SEE.
CHK
CHK
HE DIDN'T COME TO SEE IF SAITŌ WAS DEAD.
HE CAME TO LET GO OF HIS LOST DUEL.
HE HASN'T SAID ONE WORD ABOUT SAITŌ THIS MONTH, BUT NOT 'CAUSE HE WASN'T THINKING OF HIM.
HE WAS FIGURING HOW TO THINK IT... CHANGING "WINNING" INTO "GOING BEYOND"!!

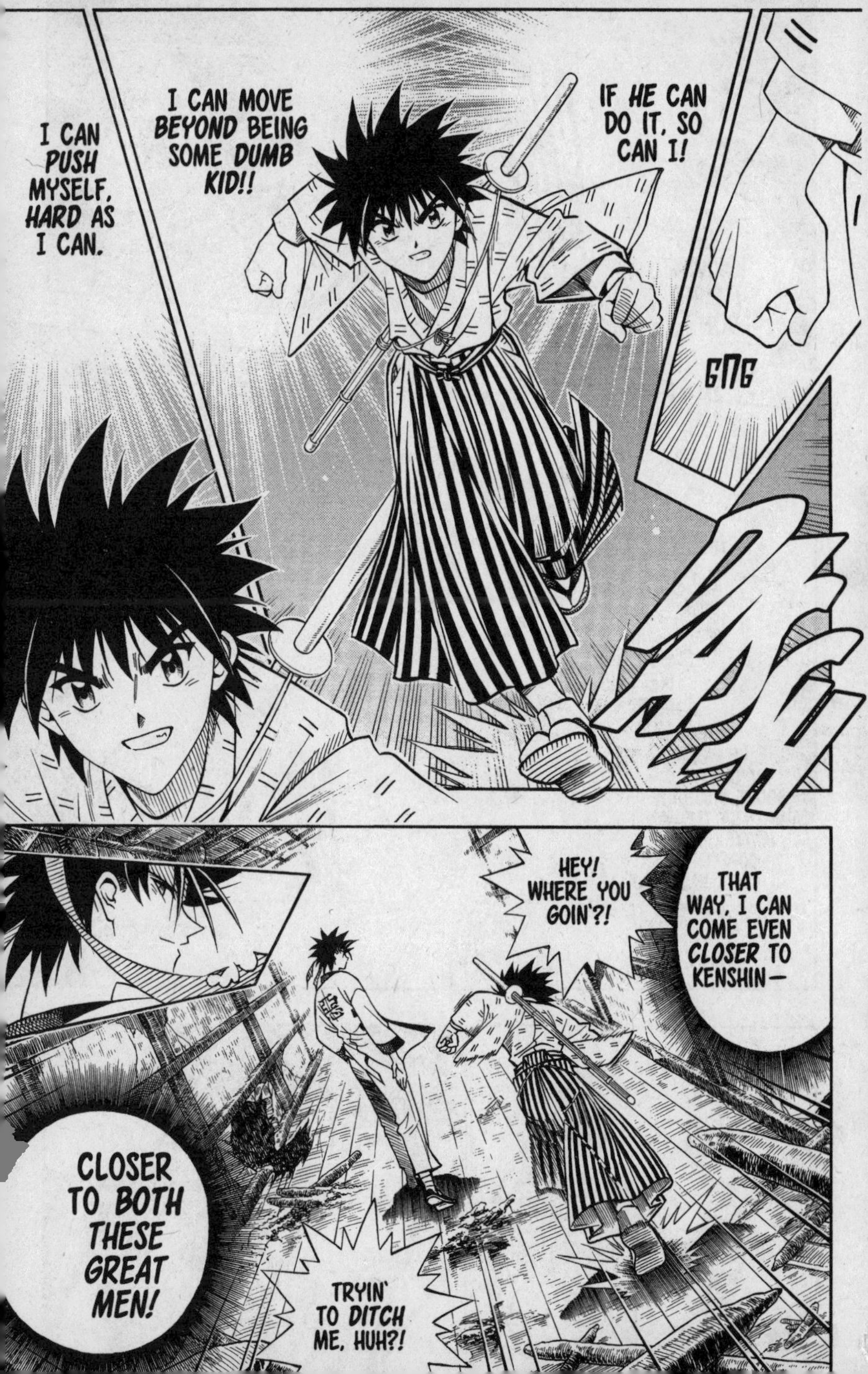
GNG
IF HE CAN DO IT, SO CAN I!
I CAN MOVE BEYOND BEING SOME DUMB KID!!
I CAN PUSH MYSELF, HARD AS I CAN.
DASH
THAT WAY, I CAN COME EVEN CLOSER TO KENSHIN—
HEY! WHERE YOU GOIN'?!
CLOSER TO BOTH THESE GREAT MEN!
TRYIN' TO DITCH ME, HUH?!

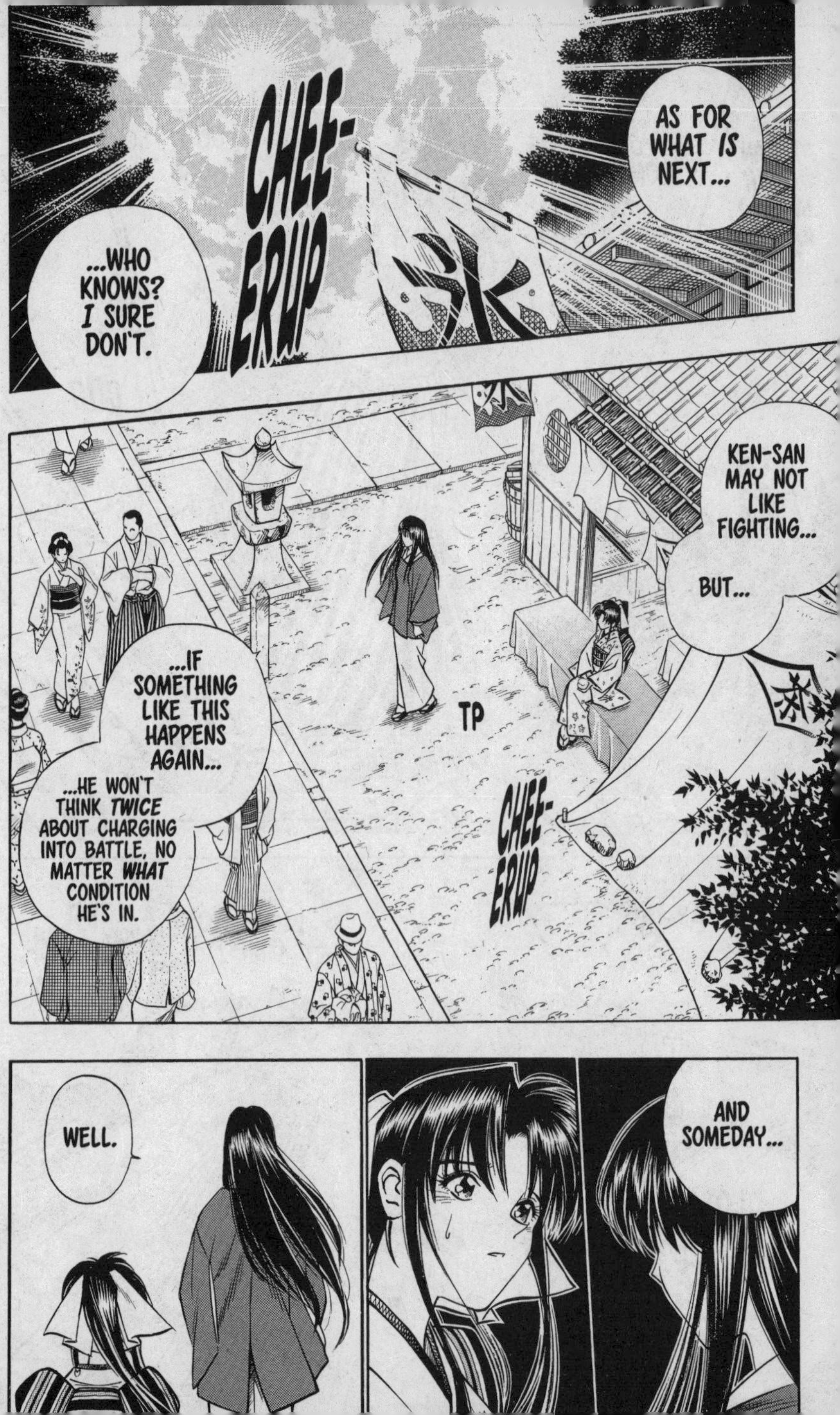
AS FOR WHAT IS NEXT...
CHEE-ERUP
...WHO KNOWS? I SURE DON'T.
KEN-SAN MAY NOT LIKE FIGHTING...
BUT...
...IF SOMETHING LIKE THIS HAPPENS AGAIN...
...HE WON'T THINK TWICE ABOUT CHARGING INTO BATTLE, NO MATTER WHAT CONDITION HE'S IN.
TP
CHEE-ERUP
AND SOMEDAY...
WELL.

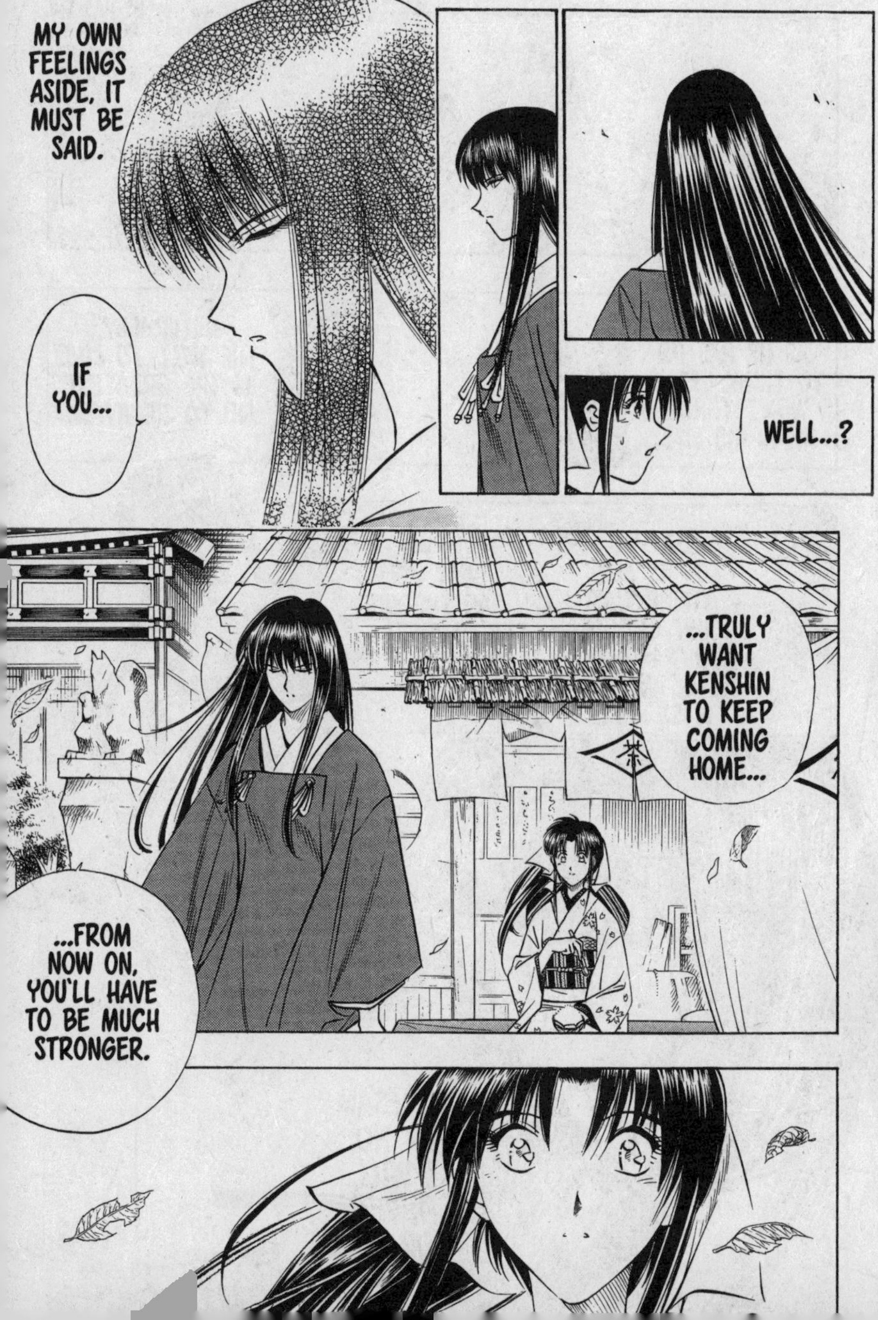
WELL...?
MY OWN FEELINGS ASIDE, IT MUST BE SAID.
IF YOU...
...TRULY WANT KENSHIN TO KEEP COMING HOME...
...FROM NOW ON, YOU'LL HAVE TO BE MUCH STRONGER.

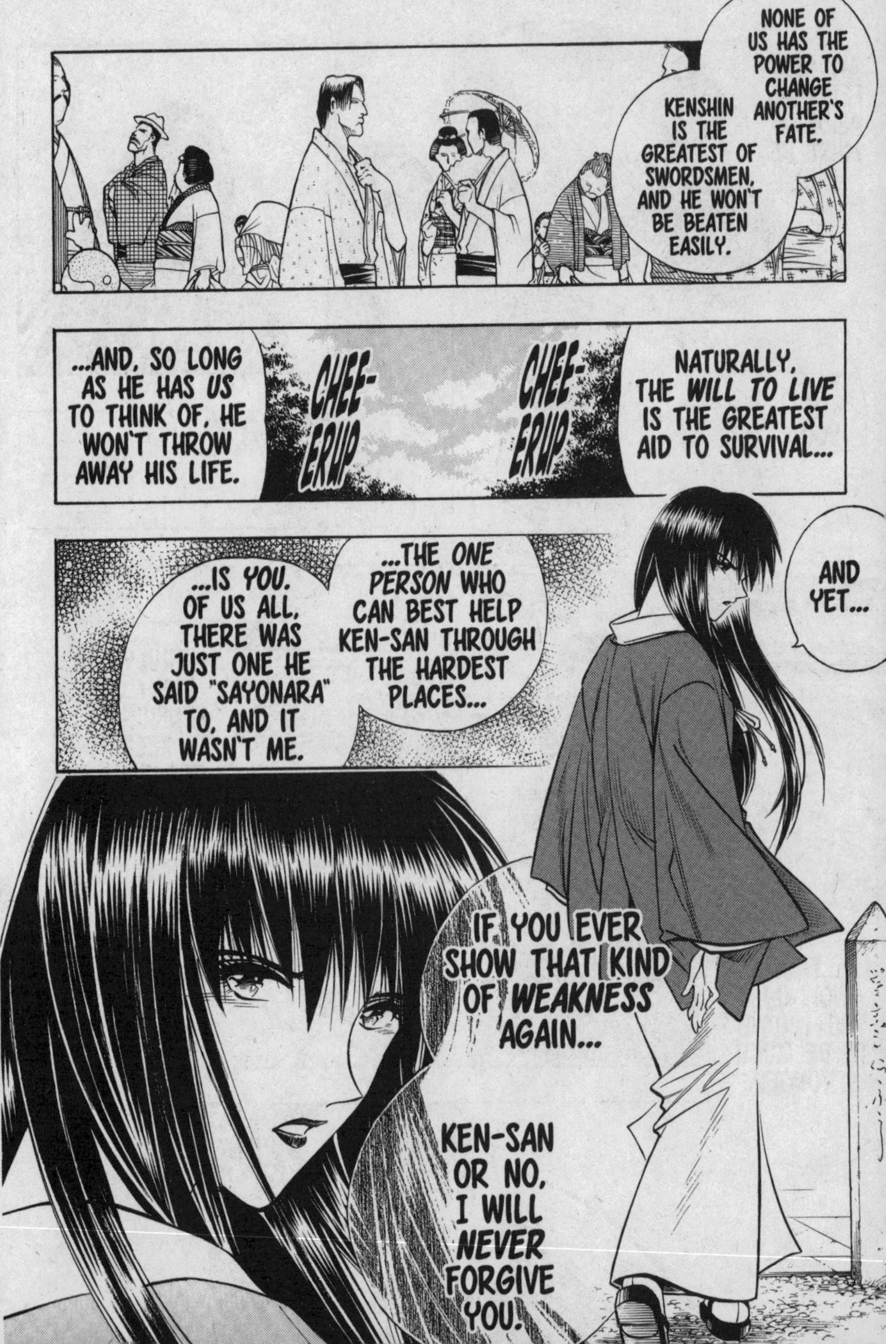
NONE OF US HAS THE POWER TO CHANGE ANOTHER'S FATE.
KENSHIN IS THE GREATEST OF SWORDSMEN, AND HE WON'T BE BEATEN EASILY.
NATURALLY, THE WILL TO LIVE IS THE GREATEST AID TO SURVIVAL...
CHEE-ERUP
CHEE-ERUP
...AND, SO LONG AS HE HAS US TO THINK OF, HE WON'T THROW AWAY HIS LIFE.
AND YET...
...THE ONE PERSON WHO CAN BEST HELP KEN-SAN THROUGH THE HARDEST PLACES...
...IS YOU. OF US ALL, THERE WAS JUST ONE HE SAID "SAYONARA" TO, AND IT WASN'T ME.
IF YOU EVER SHOW THAT KIND OF WEAKNESS AGAIN...
KEN-SAN OR NO, I WILL NEVER FORGIVE YOU.

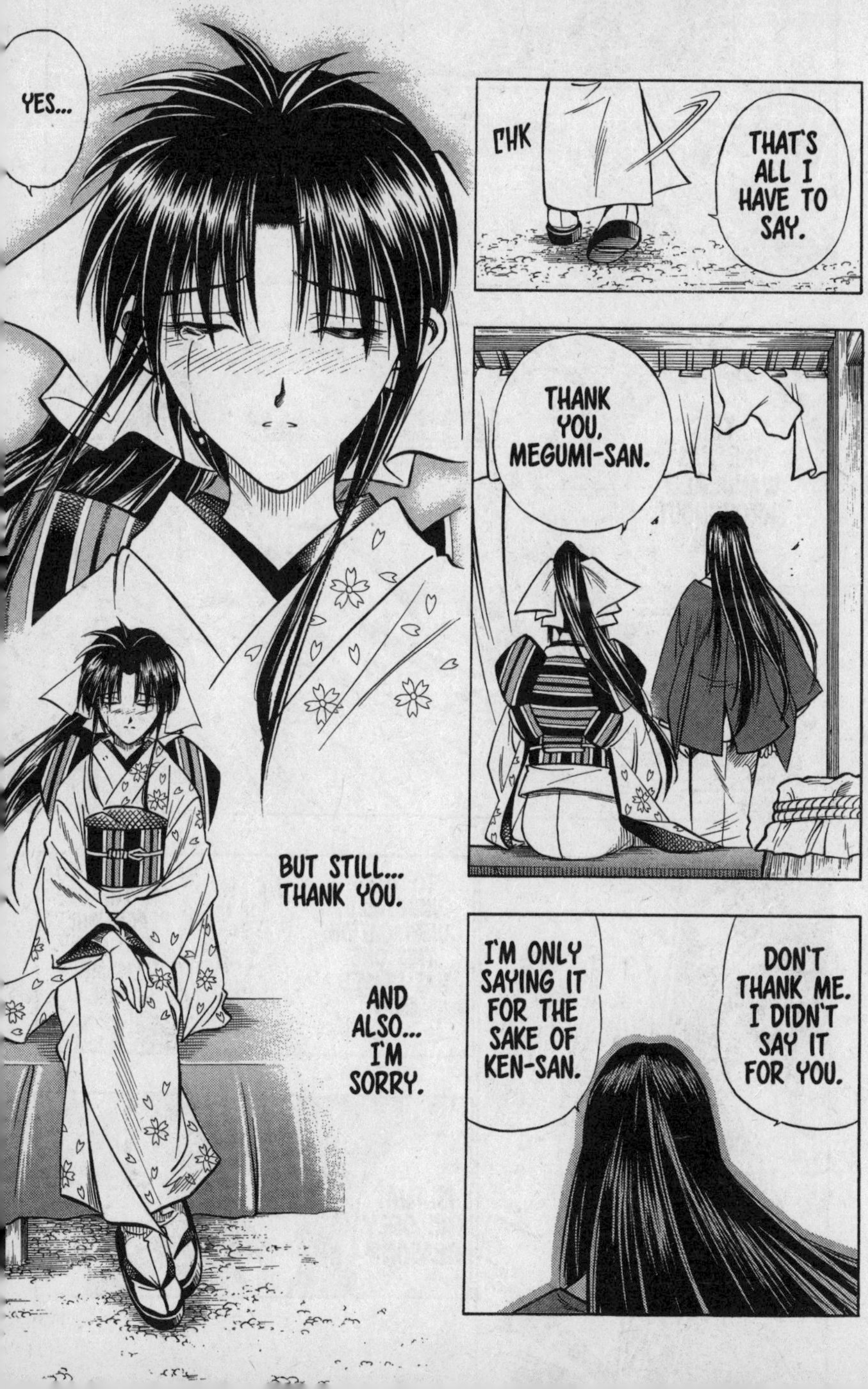
THAT'S ALL I HAVE TO SAY.
CHK
THANK YOU, MEGUMI-SAN.
DON'T THANK ME. I DIDN'T SAY IT FOR YOU.
I'M ONLY SAYING IT FOR THE SAKE OF KEN-SAN.
YES...
BUT STILL... THANK YOU.
AND ALSO... I'M SORRY.

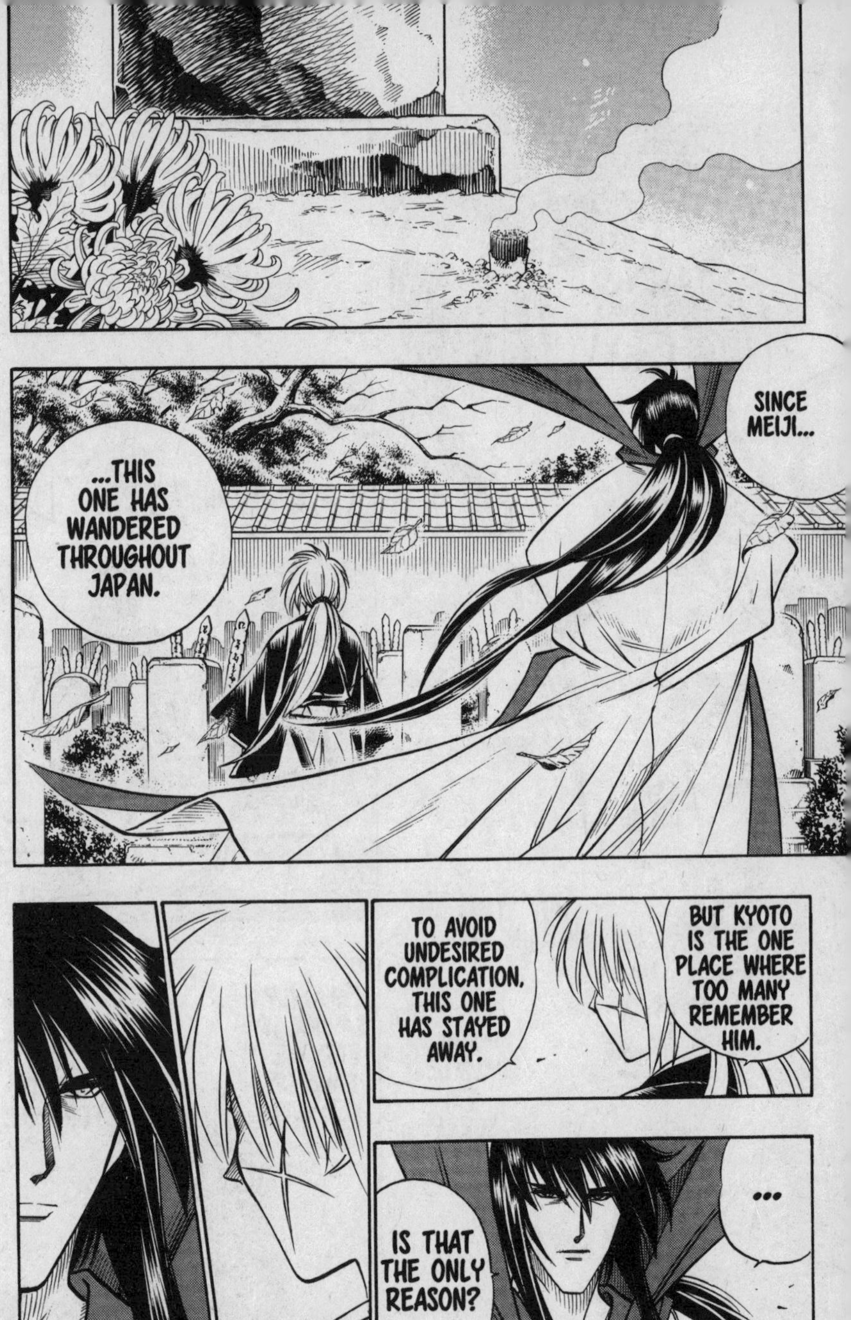
SINCE MEIJI...
...THIS ONE HAS WANDERED THROUGHOUT JAPAN.
BUT KYOTO IS THE ONE PLACE WHERE TOO MANY REMEMBER HIM.
TO AVOID UNDESIRED COMPLICATION, THIS ONE HAS STAYED AWAY.
...
IS THAT THE ONLY REASON?

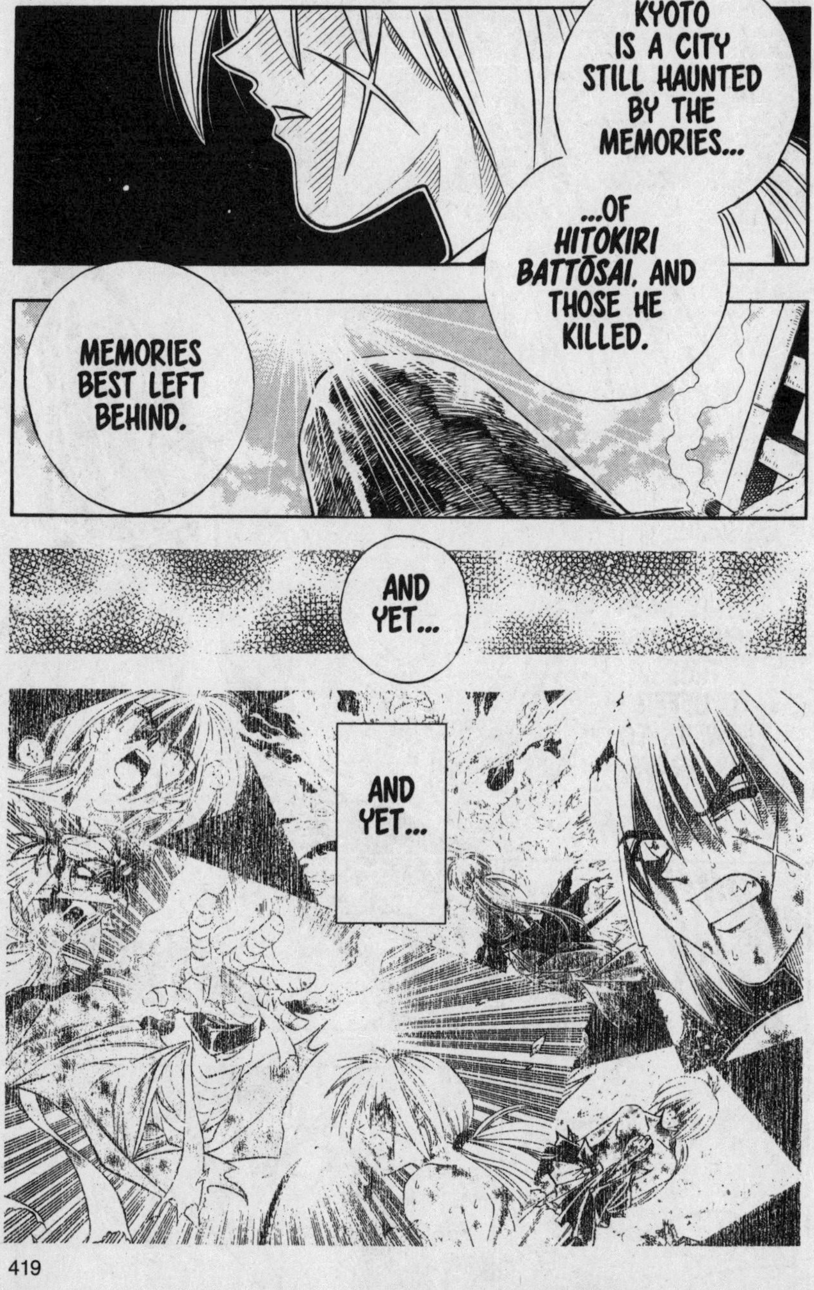
KYOTO IS A CITY STILL HAUNTED BY THE MEMORIES...
...OF HITOKIRI BATTŌSAI, AND THOSE HE KILLED.
MEMORIES BEST LEFT BEHIND.
AND YET...
AND YET...

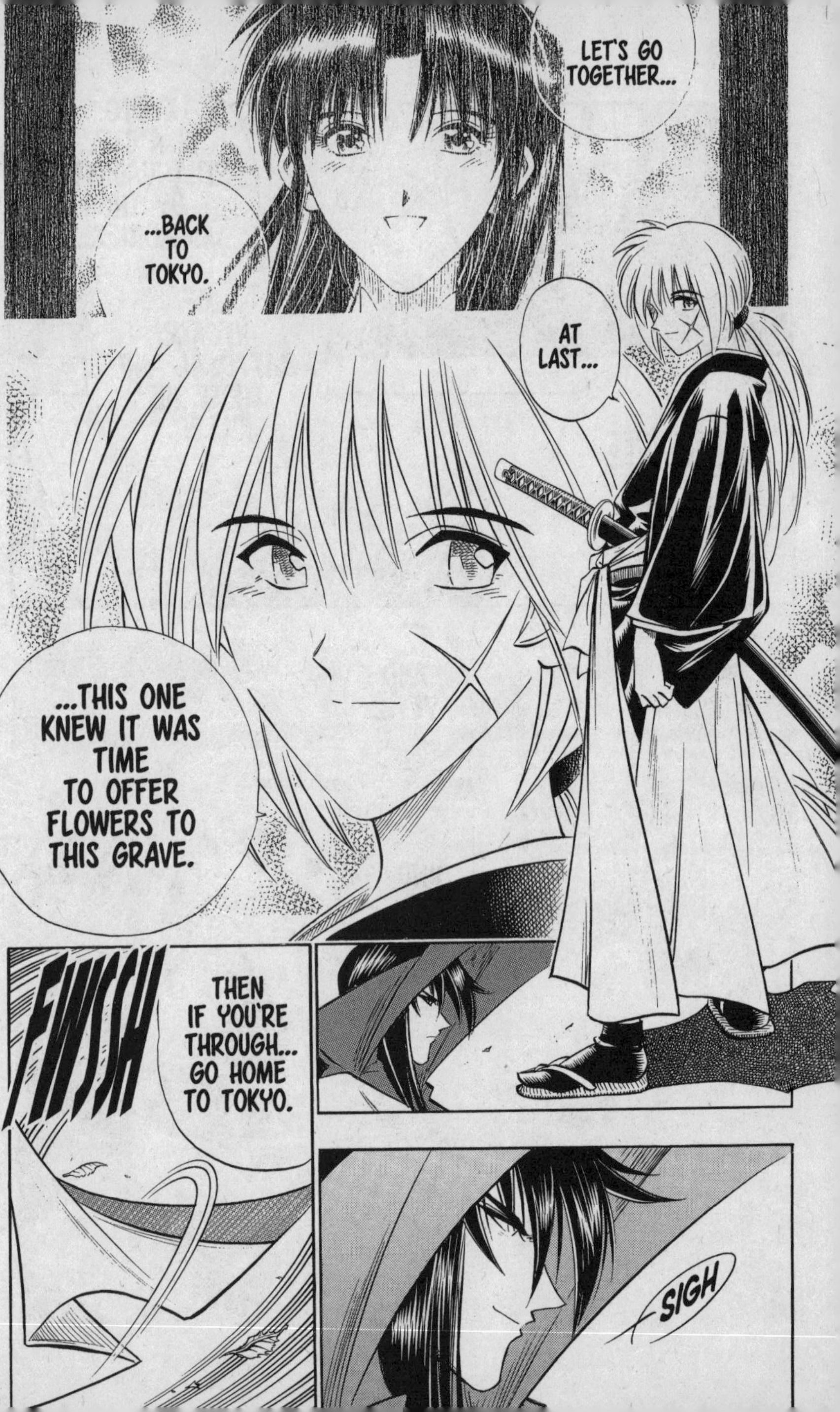
LET'S GO TOGETHER...
...BACK TO TOKYO.
AT LAST...
...THIS ONE KNEW IT WAS TIME TO OFFER FLOWERS TO THIS GRAVE.
THEN IF YOU'RE THROUGH... GO HOME TO TOKYO.
FWSH
SIGH

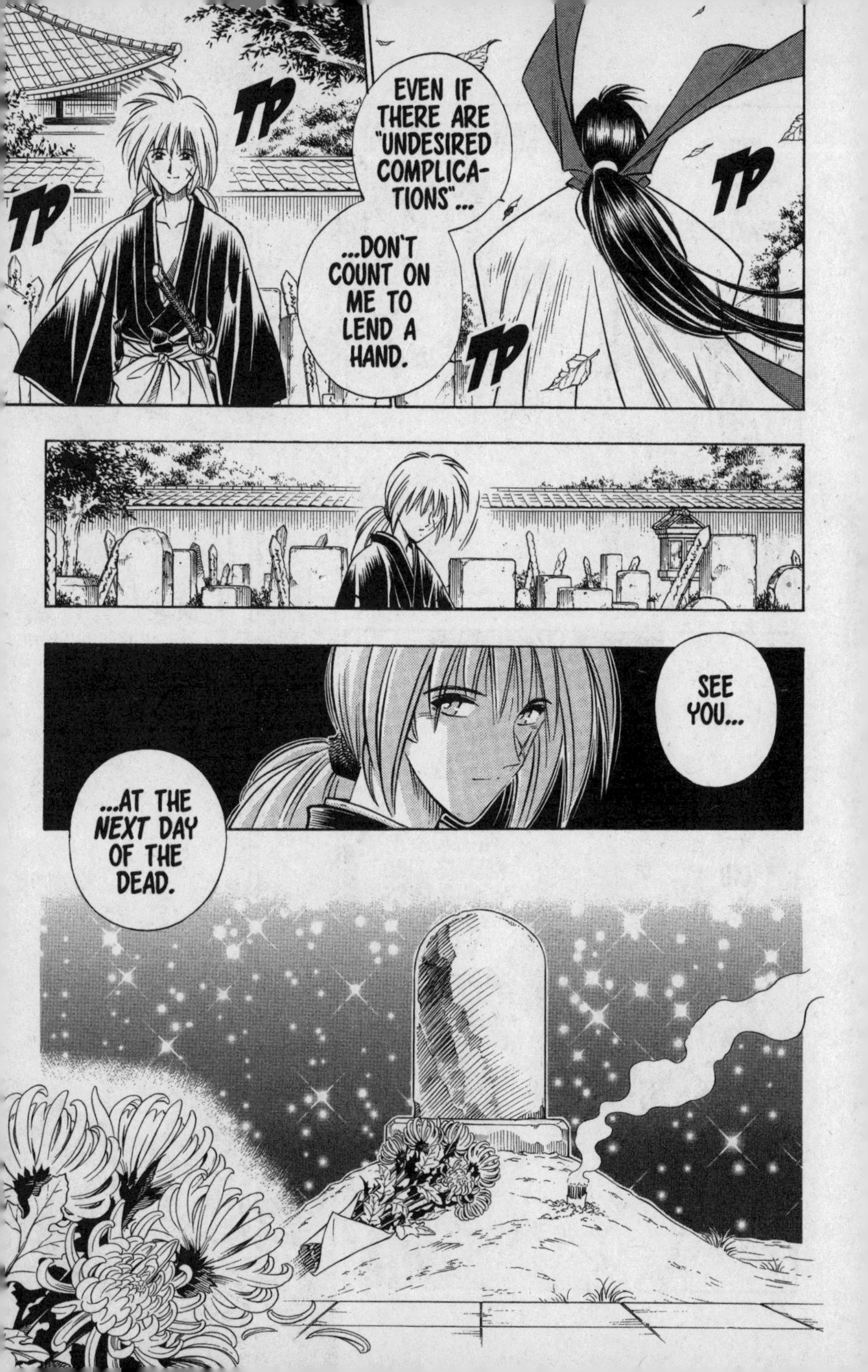
TP
TP
EVEN IF THERE ARE "UNDESIRED COMPLICATIONS"...
...DON'T COUNT ON ME TO LEND A HAND.
TP
TP
SEE YOU...
...AT THE NEXT DAY OF THE DEAD.

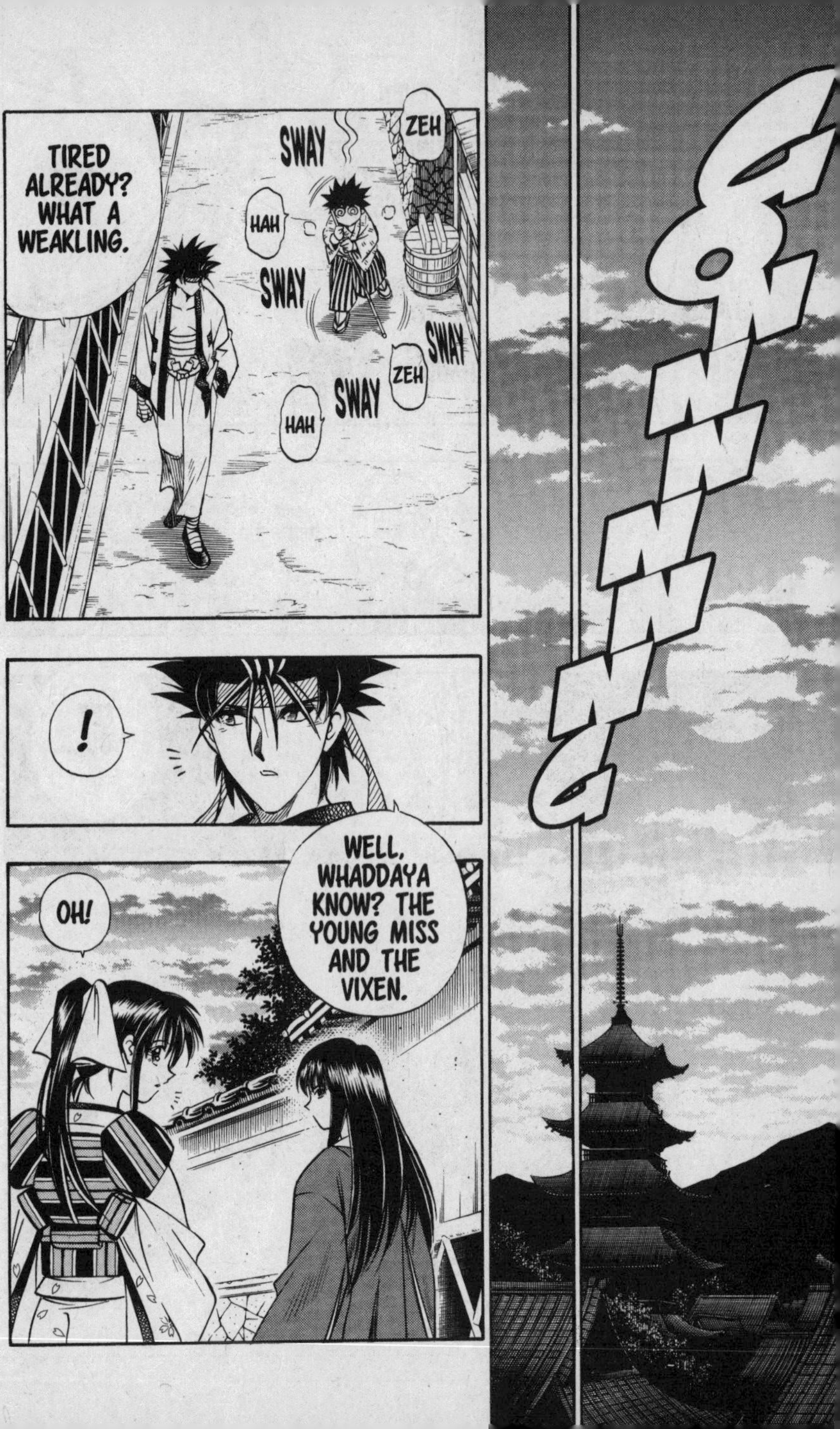
GONNNNNNG
ZEH
SWAY
HAH
SWAY
SWAY
ZEH
SWAY
HAH
TIRED ALREADY? WHAT A WEAKLING.
!
WELL, WHADDAYA KNOW? THE YOUNG MISS AND THE VIXEN.
OH!

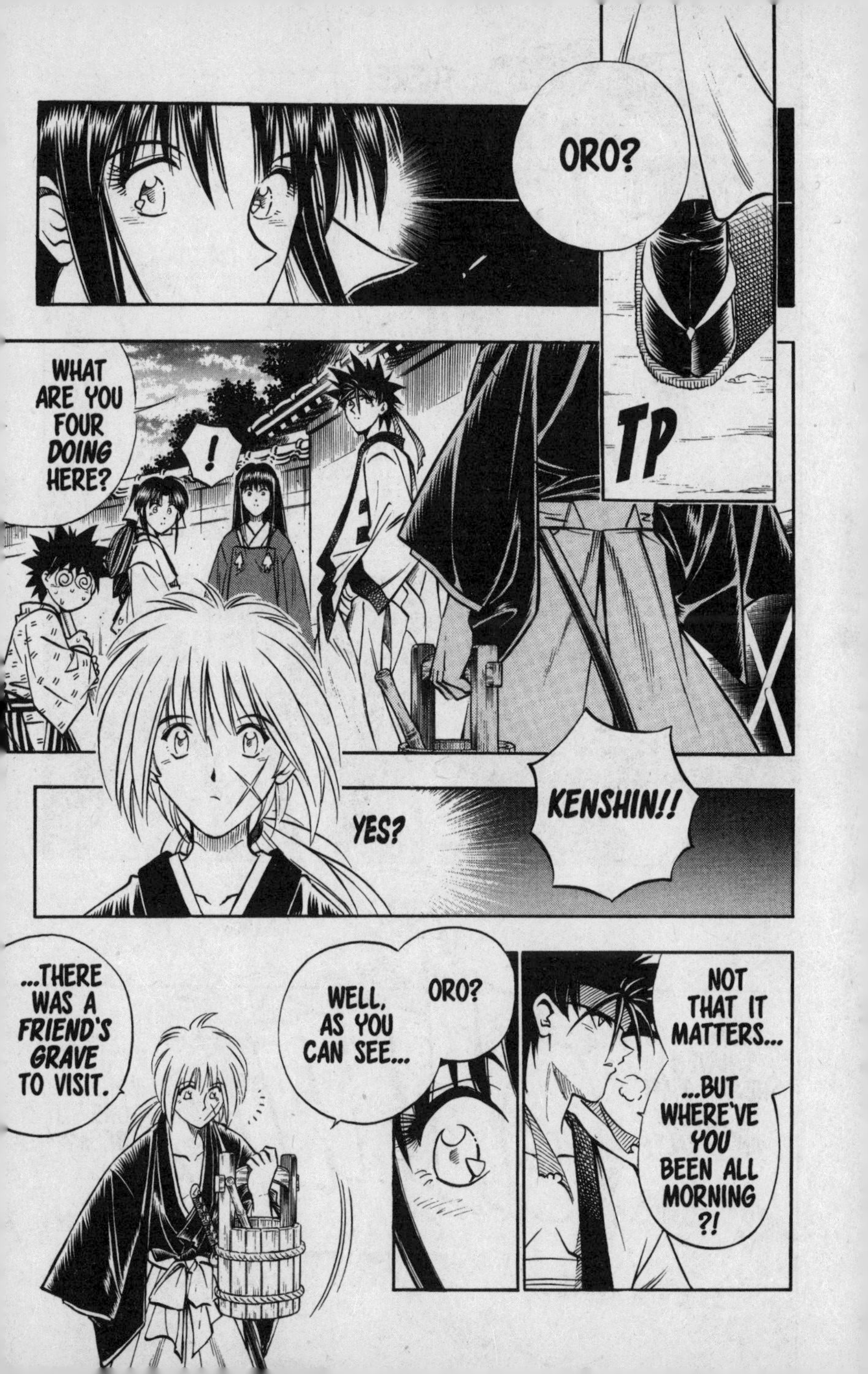
ORO?
TP
WHAT ARE YOU FOUR DOING HERE?
!
KENSHIN!!
YES?
NOT THAT IT MATTERS...
...BUT WHERE'VE YOU BEEN ALL MORNING?!
ORO?
WELL, AS YOU CAN SEE...
...THERE WAS A FRIEND'S GRAVE TO VISIT.

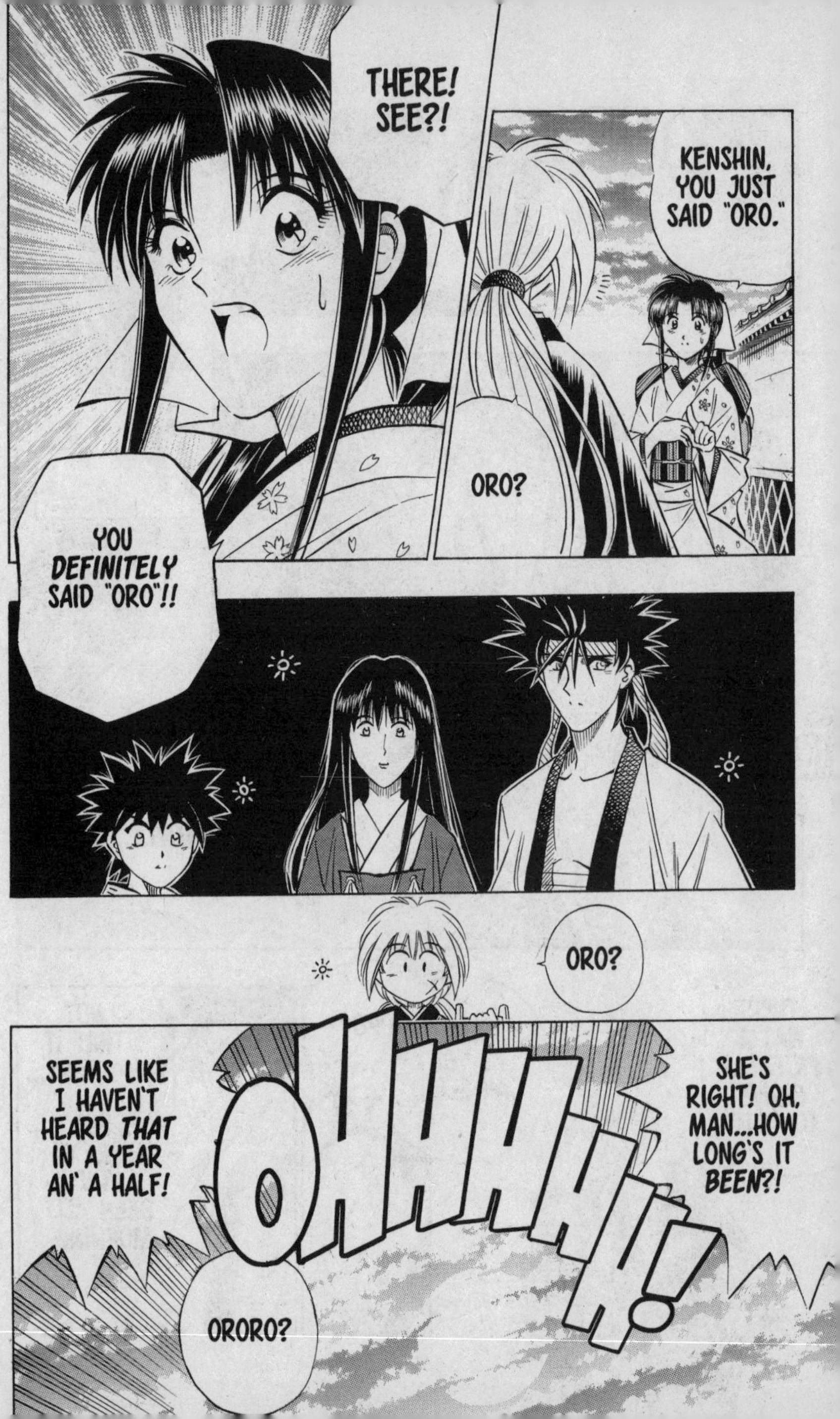
KENSHIN, YOU JUST SAID "ORO."
ORO?
THERE! SEE?!
YOU *DEFINITELY* SAID "ORO"!!
ORO?
SHE'S RIGHT! OH, MAN...HOW LONG'S IT BEEN?!
OHHHHH!!
SEEMS LIKE I HAVEN'T HEARD *THAT* IN A YEAR AN' A HALF!
ORORO?

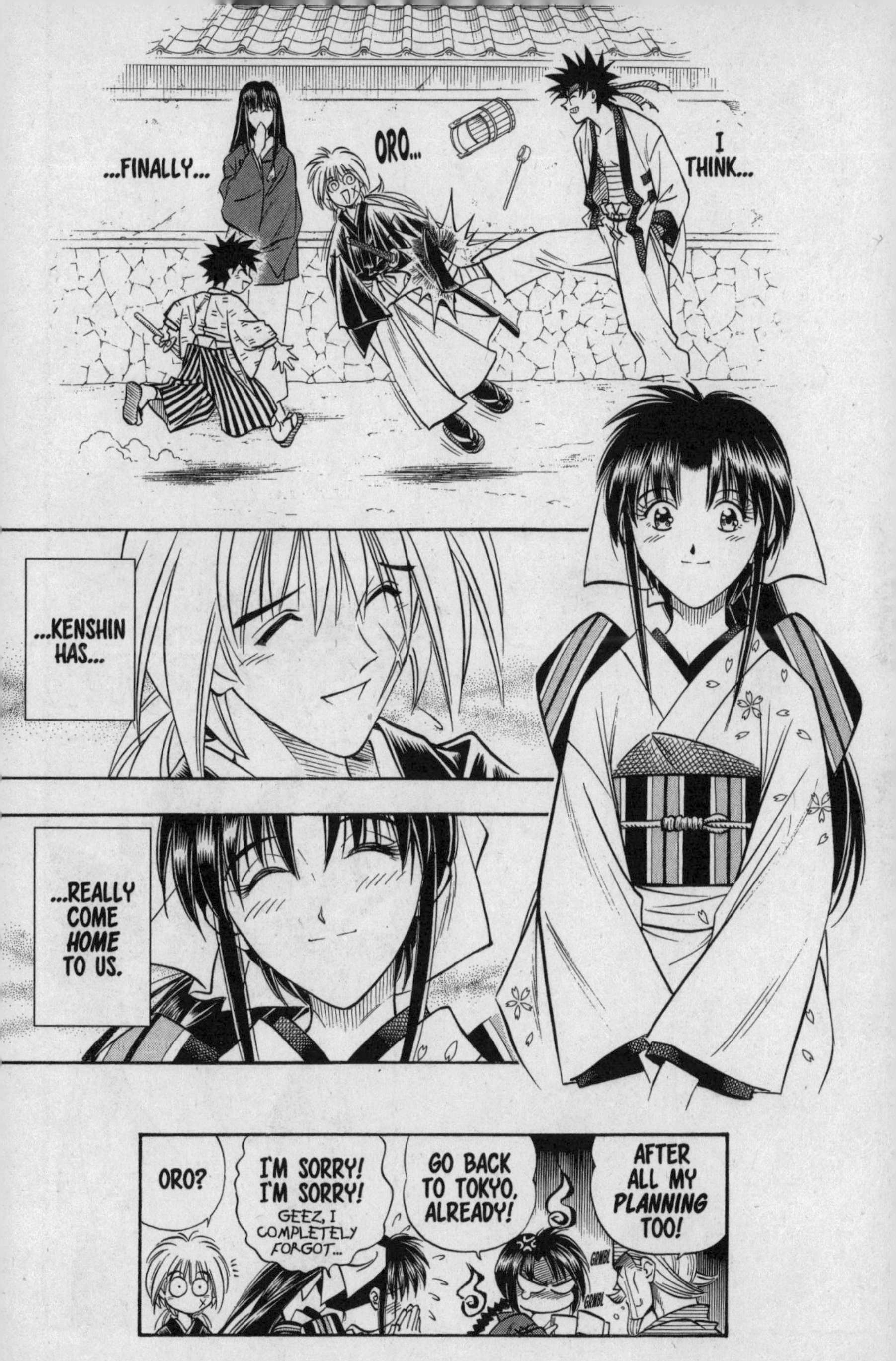
I THINK...
ORO...
...FINALLY...
...KENSHIN HAS...
...REALLY COME HOME TO US.
AFTER ALL MY PLANNING TOO!
GRMBL
GRMBL
GO BACK TO TOKYO, ALREADY!
I'M SORRY! I'M SORRY!
GEEZ, I COMPLETELY FORGOT...
ORO?

Rurouni Kenshin

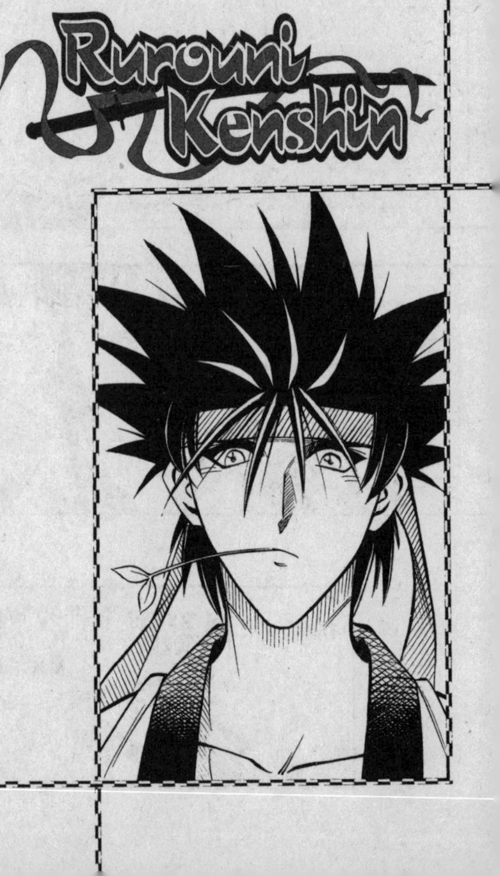

Act 151—Kyoto Epilogue

In the Blue Sky

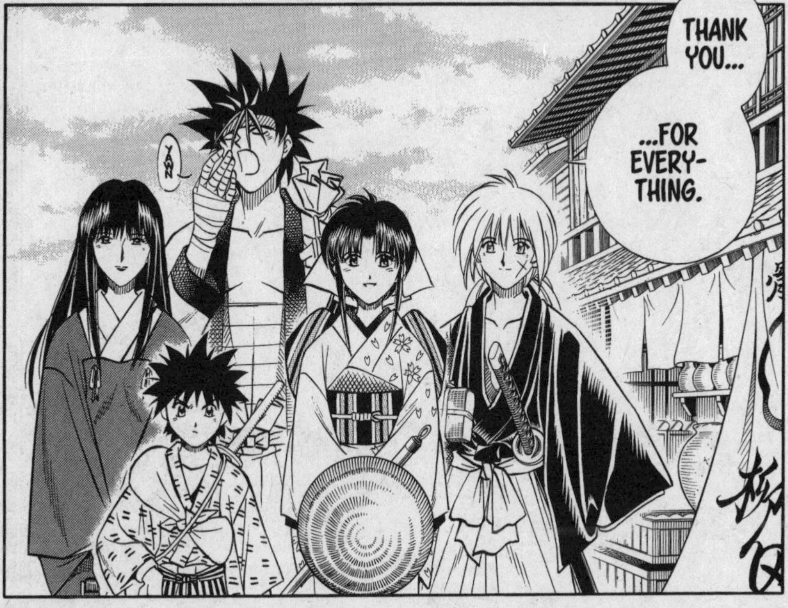
THANK YOU...
...FOR EVERY-THING.
YAWN

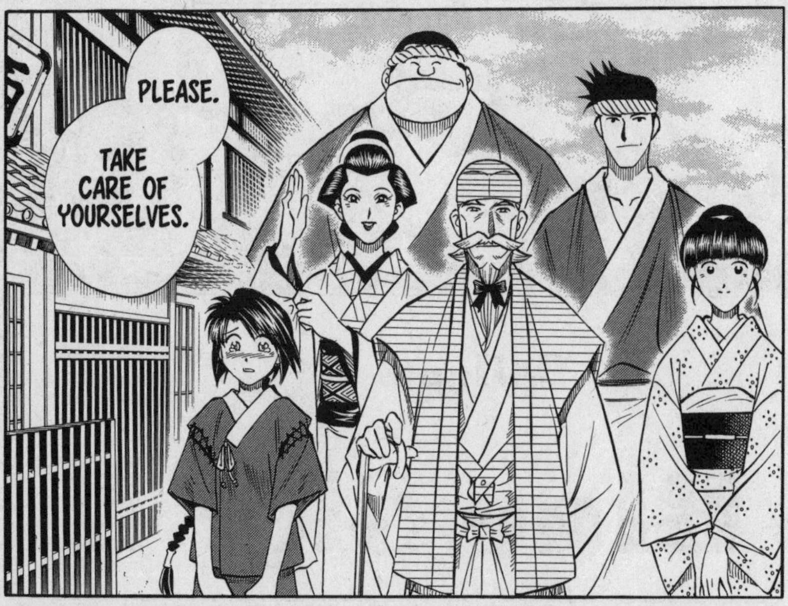
PLEASE.
TAKE CARE OF YOURSELVES.

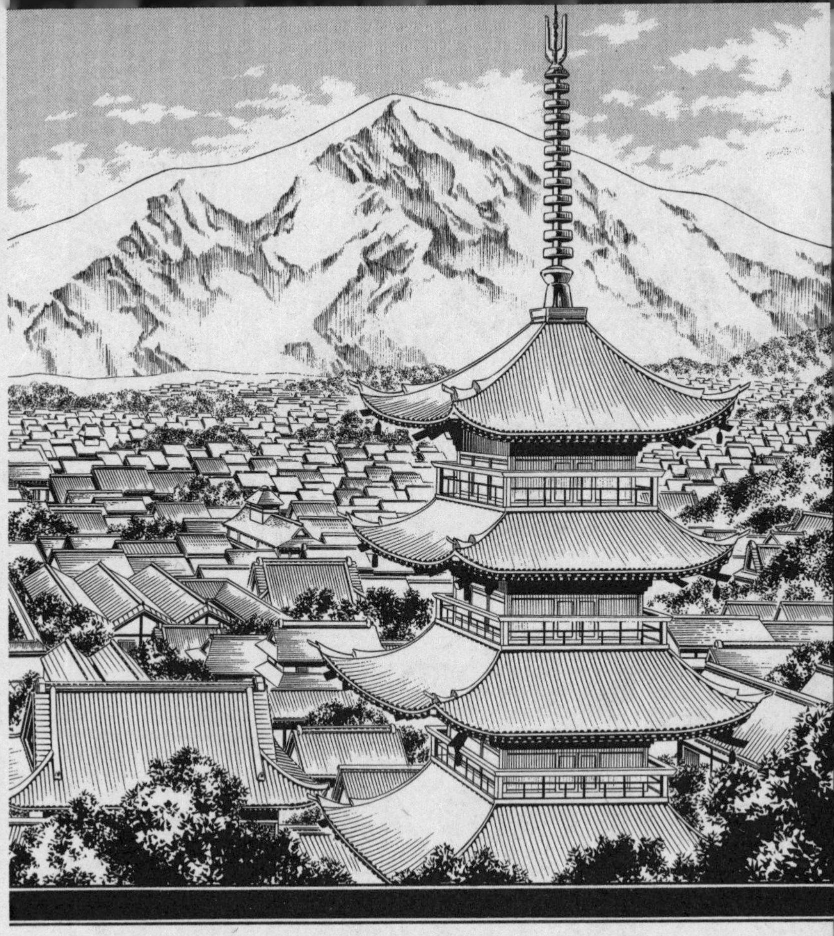

Epilogue

Blue Sky

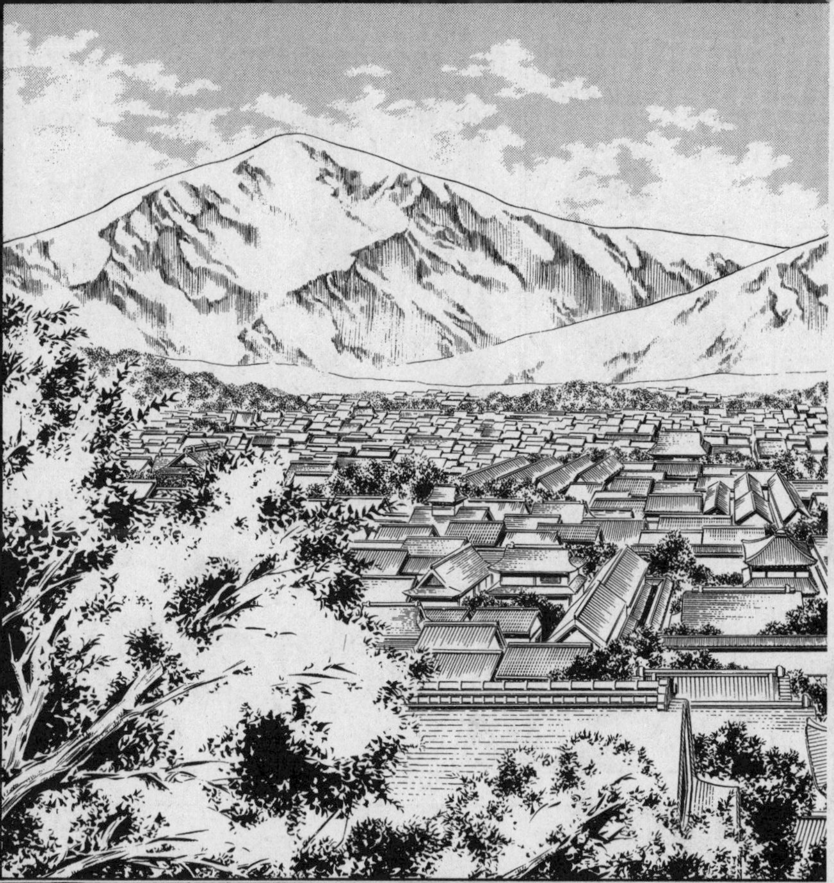

Act 151 Kyoto

In the

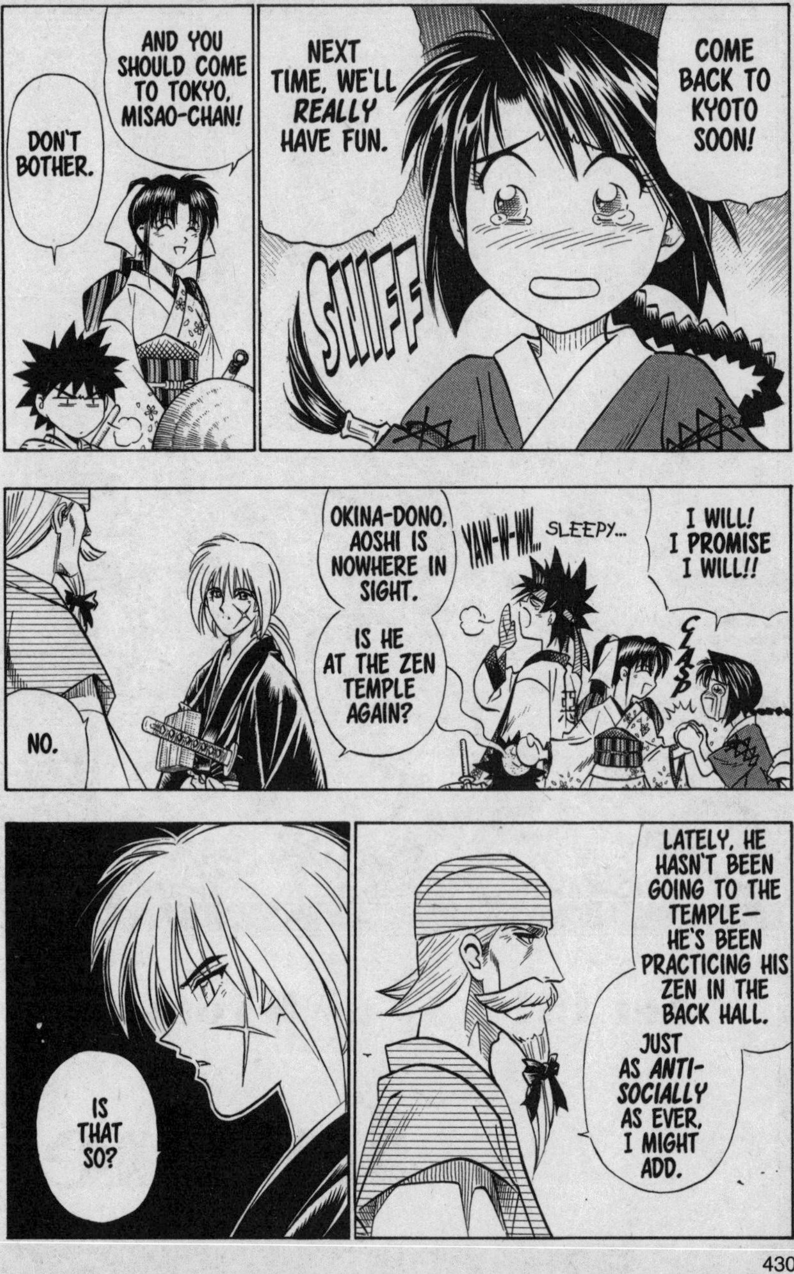
COME BACK TO KYOTO SOON!
NEXT TIME, WE'LL *REALLY* HAVE FUN.
SNIFF
AND YOU SHOULD COME TO TOKYO, MISAO-CHAN!
DON'T BOTHER.
I WILL! I PROMISE I WILL!!
CLASP
SLEEPY...
YAW-W-WN...
OKINA-DONO, AOSHI IS NOWHERE IN SIGHT.
IS HE AT THE ZEN TEMPLE AGAIN?
NO.
LATELY, HE HASN'T BEEN GOING TO THE TEMPLE—HE'S BEEN PRACTICING HIS ZEN IN THE BACK HALL.
JUST AS *ANTI-SOCIALLY* AS EVER, I MIGHT ADD.
IS THAT SO?

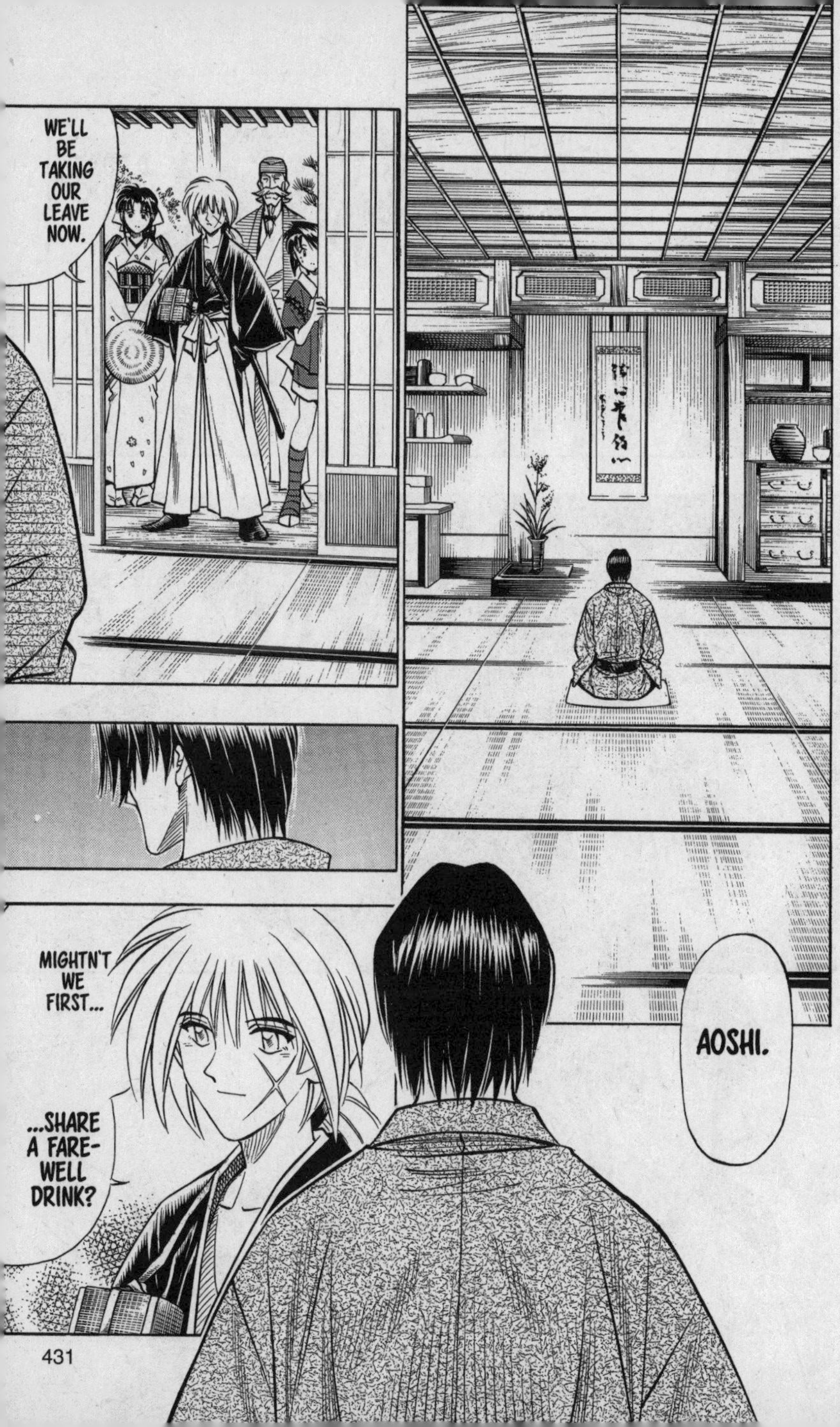
WE'LL BE TAKING OUR LEAVE NOW.
AOSHI.
MIGHTN'T WE FIRST...
...SHARE A FARE-WELL DRINK?

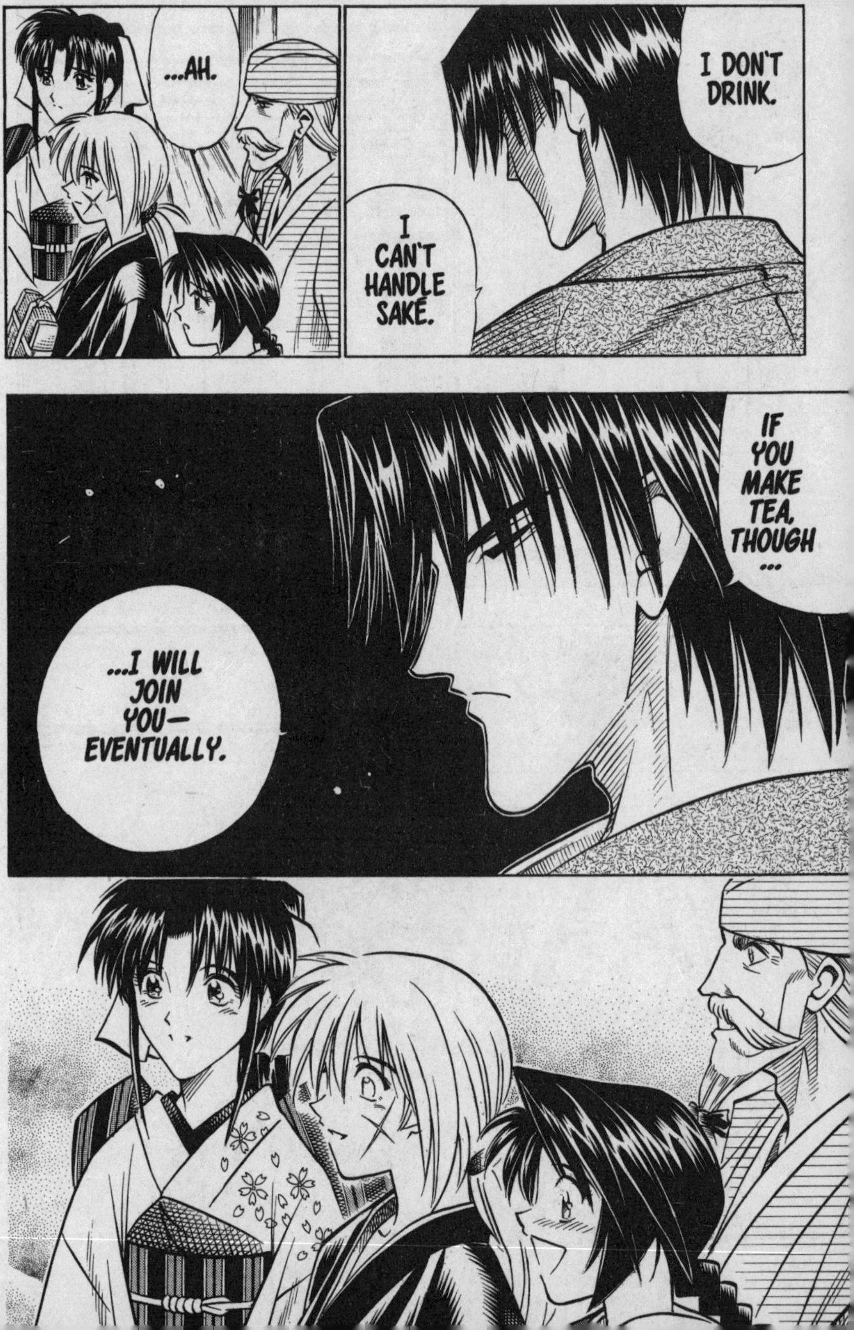
I DON'T DRINK.
I CAN'T HANDLE SAKÉ.
...AH.
IF YOU MAKE TEA, THOUGH...
...I WILL JOIN YOU—EVENTUALLY.

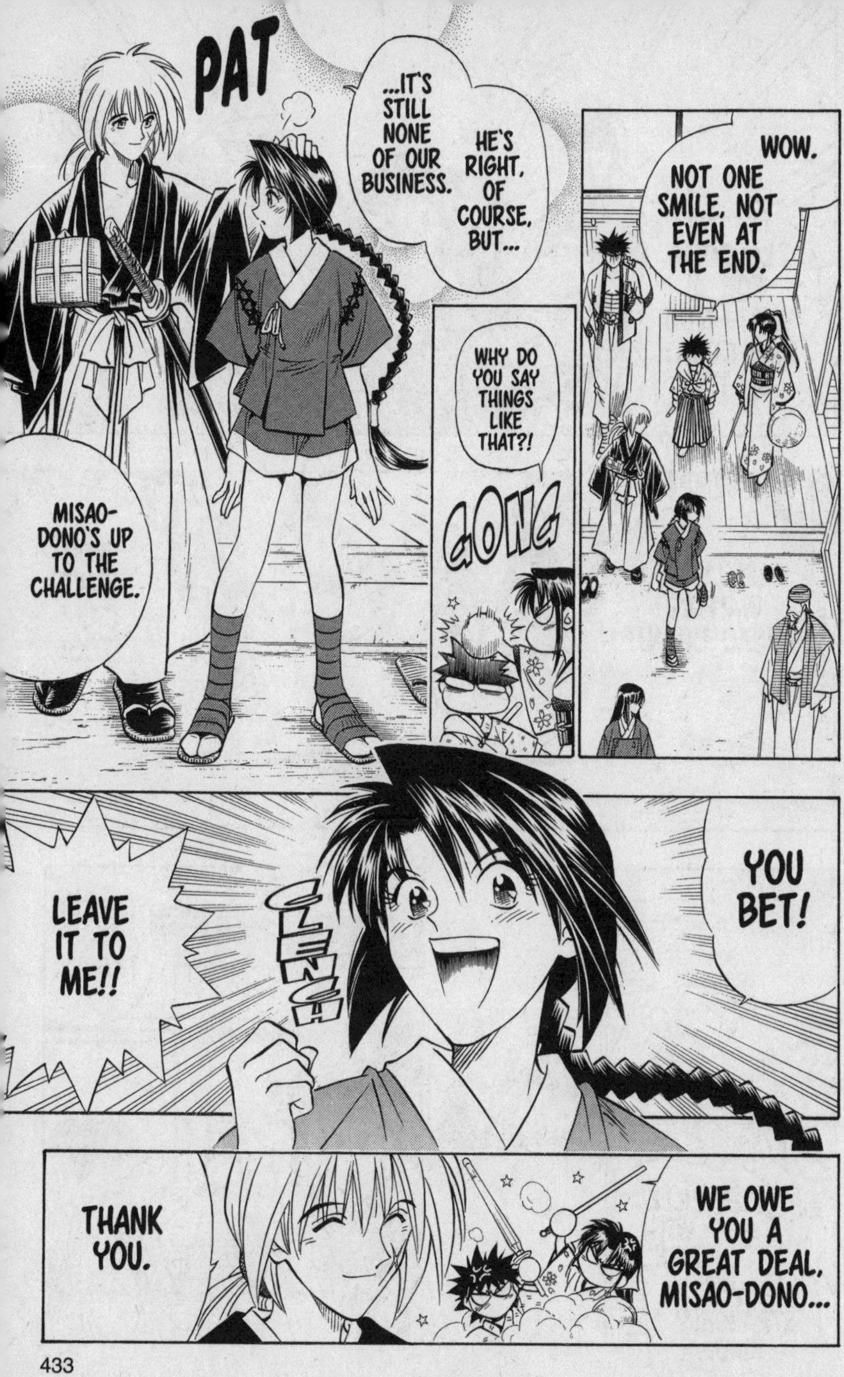
WOW.
NOT ONE SMILE, NOT EVEN AT THE END.
WHY DO YOU SAY THINGS LIKE THAT?!
GONG
PAT
HE'S RIGHT, OF COURSE, BUT...
...IT'S STILL NONE OF OUR BUSINESS.
MISAO-DONO'S UP TO THE CHALLENGE.
YOU BET!
CLENCH
LEAVE IT TO ME!!
WE OWE YOU A GREAT DEAL, MISAO-DONO...
THANK YOU.

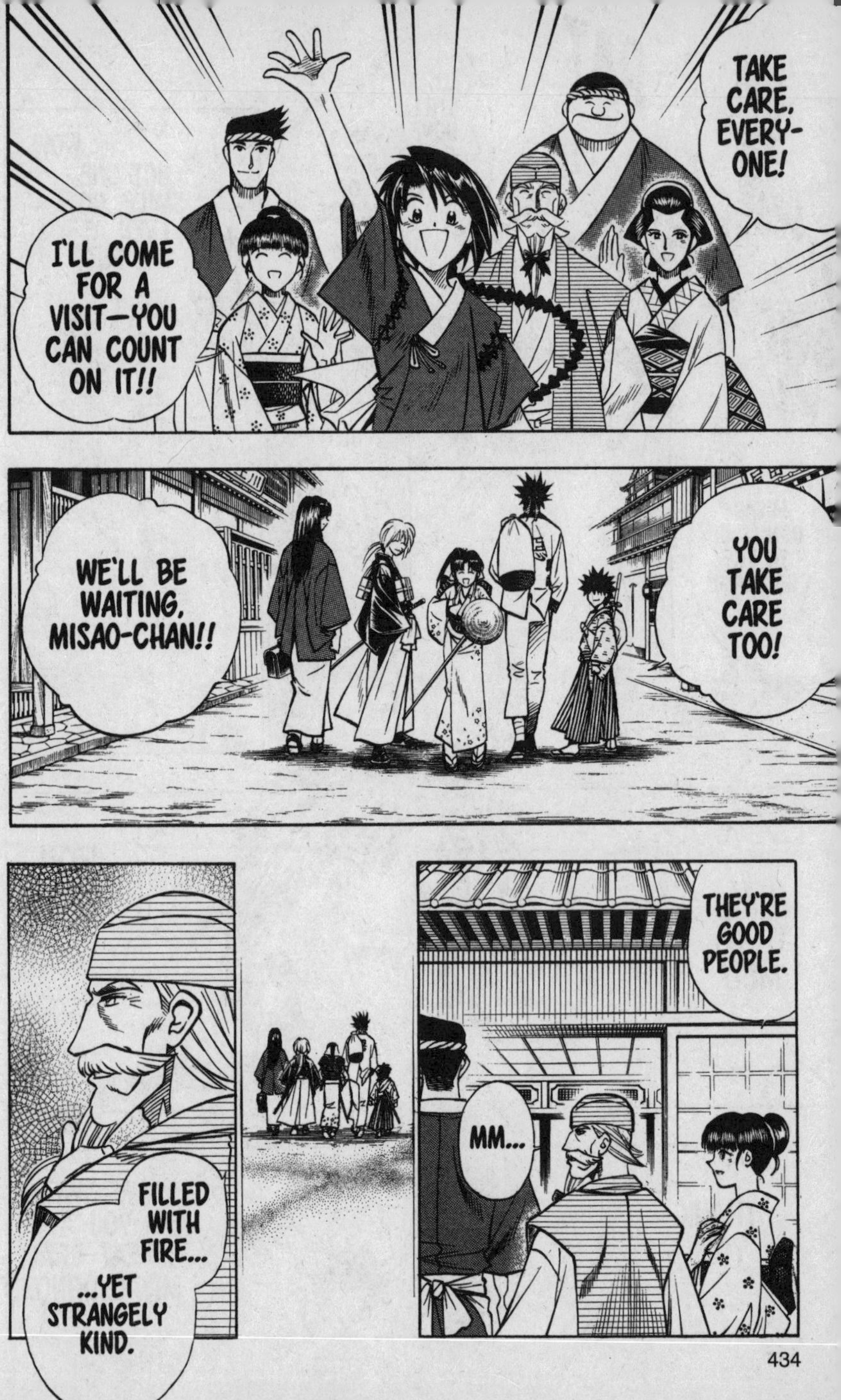
TAKE CARE, EVERYONE!
I'LL COME FOR A VISIT—YOU CAN COUNT ON IT!!
YOU TAKE CARE TOO!
WE'LL BE WAITING, MISAO-CHAN!!
THEY'RE GOOD PEOPLE.
MM...
FILLED WITH FIRE...
...YET STRANGELY KIND.

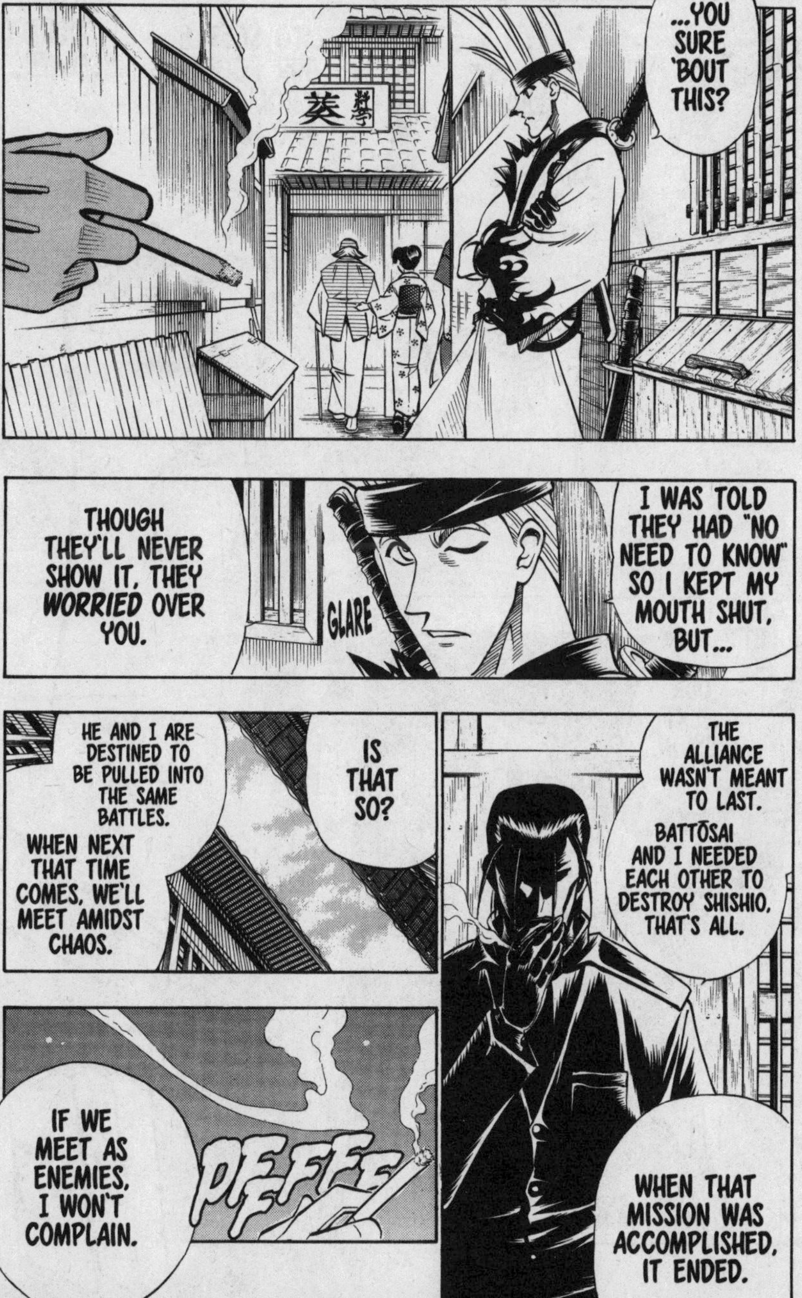
...YOU SURE 'BOUT THIS?
料亭 葵
I WAS TOLD THEY HAD "NO NEED TO KNOW" SO I KEPT MY MOUTH SHUT, BUT...
GLARE
THOUGH THEY'LL NEVER SHOW IT, THEY *WORRIED* OVER YOU.
THE ALLIANCE WASN'T MEANT TO LAST.
BATTŌSAI AND I NEEDED EACH OTHER TO DESTROY SHISHIO, THAT'S ALL.
WHEN THAT MISSION WAS ACCOMPLISHED, IT ENDED.
IS THAT SO?
HE AND I ARE DESTINED TO BE PULLED INTO THE SAME BATTLES.
WHEN NEXT THAT TIME COMES, WE'LL MEET AMIDST CHAOS.
PFFFFF
IF WE MEET AS ENEMIES, I WON'T COMPLAIN.

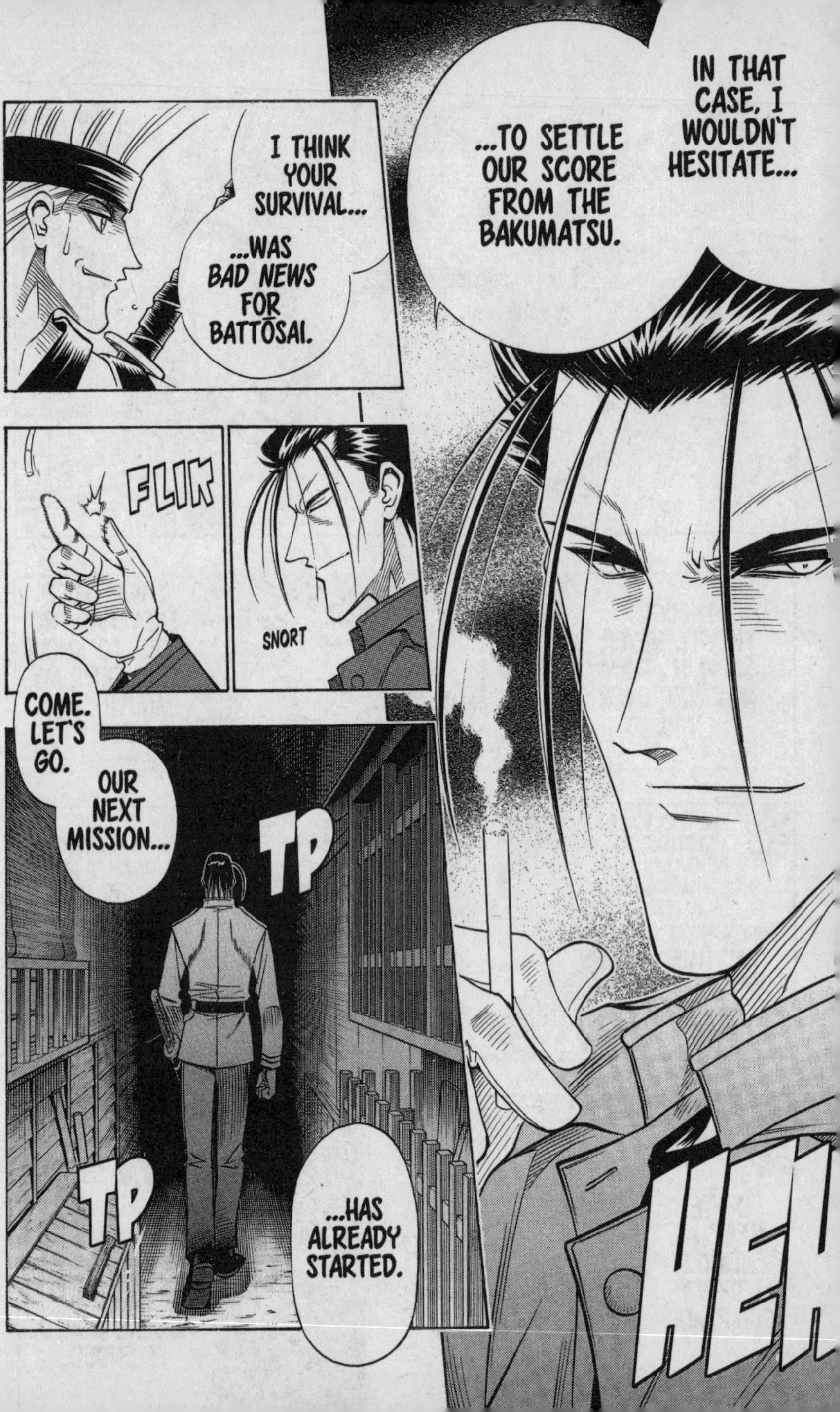
IN THAT CASE, I WOULDN'T HESITATE...
...TO SETTLE OUR SCORE FROM THE BAKUMATSU.
HEH
I THINK YOUR SURVIVAL...
...WAS BAD NEWS FOR BATTŌSAI.
SNORT
FLIK
COME. LET'S GO.
OUR NEXT MISSION...
TP
TP
...HAS ALREADY STARTED.

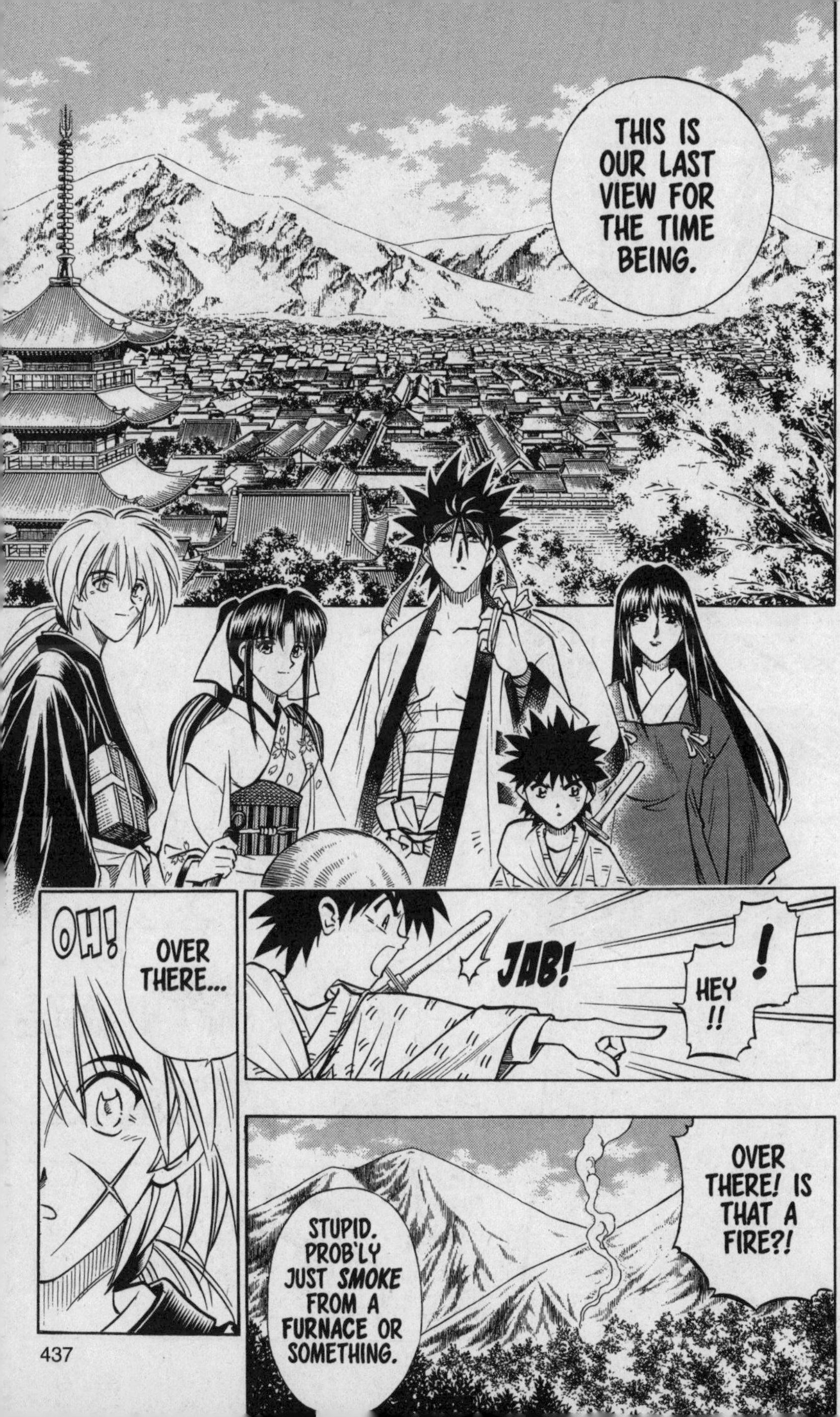
THIS IS OUR LAST VIEW FOR THE TIME BEING.
HEY !!
!
JAB!
OVER THERE! IS THAT A FIRE?!
STUPID. PROB'LY JUST SMOKE FROM A FURNACE OR SOMETHING.
OH!
OVER THERE...

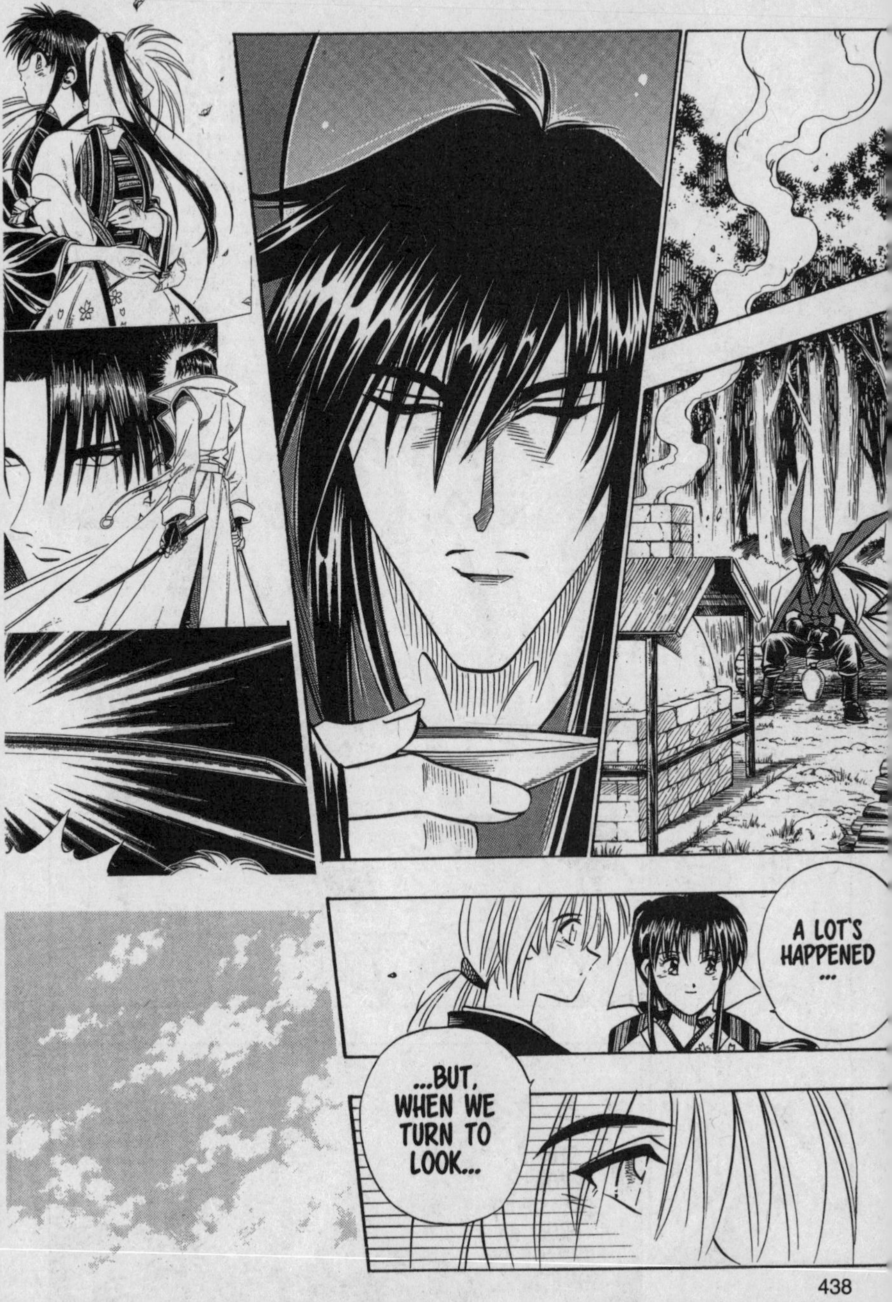
A LOT'S HAPPENED ...
...BUT, WHEN WE TURN TO LOOK...

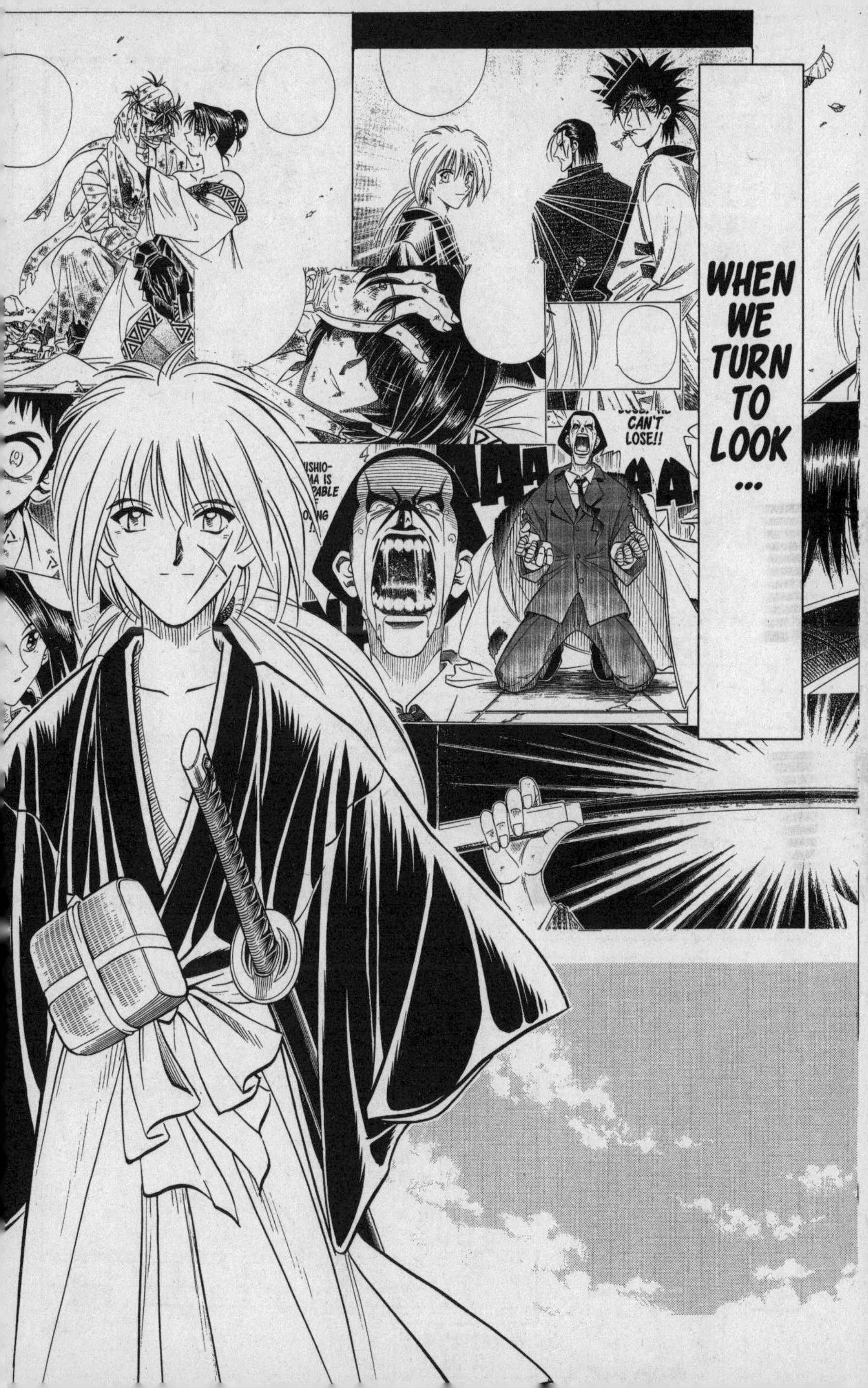
WHEN WE TURN TO LOOK ...
CAN'T LOSE!!
MA IS

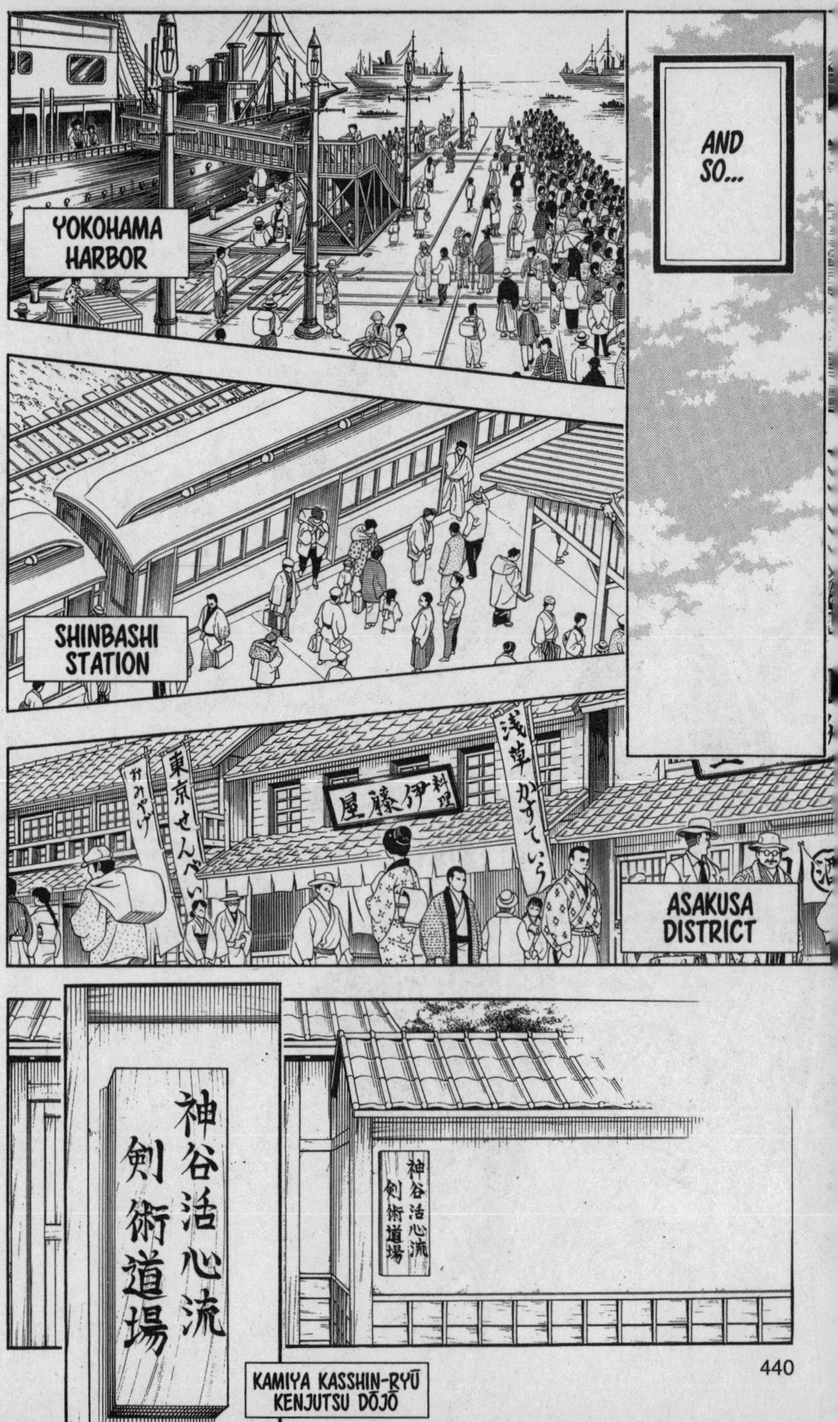
AND SO...
YOKOHAMA HARBOR
SHINBASHI STATION
浅草かすていら
料理
伊藤屋
東京せんべい
おみやげ
ASAKUSA DISTRICT
神谷活心流剣術道場
神谷活心流剣術道場
KAMIYA KASSHIN-RYŪ KENJUTSU DŌJŌ

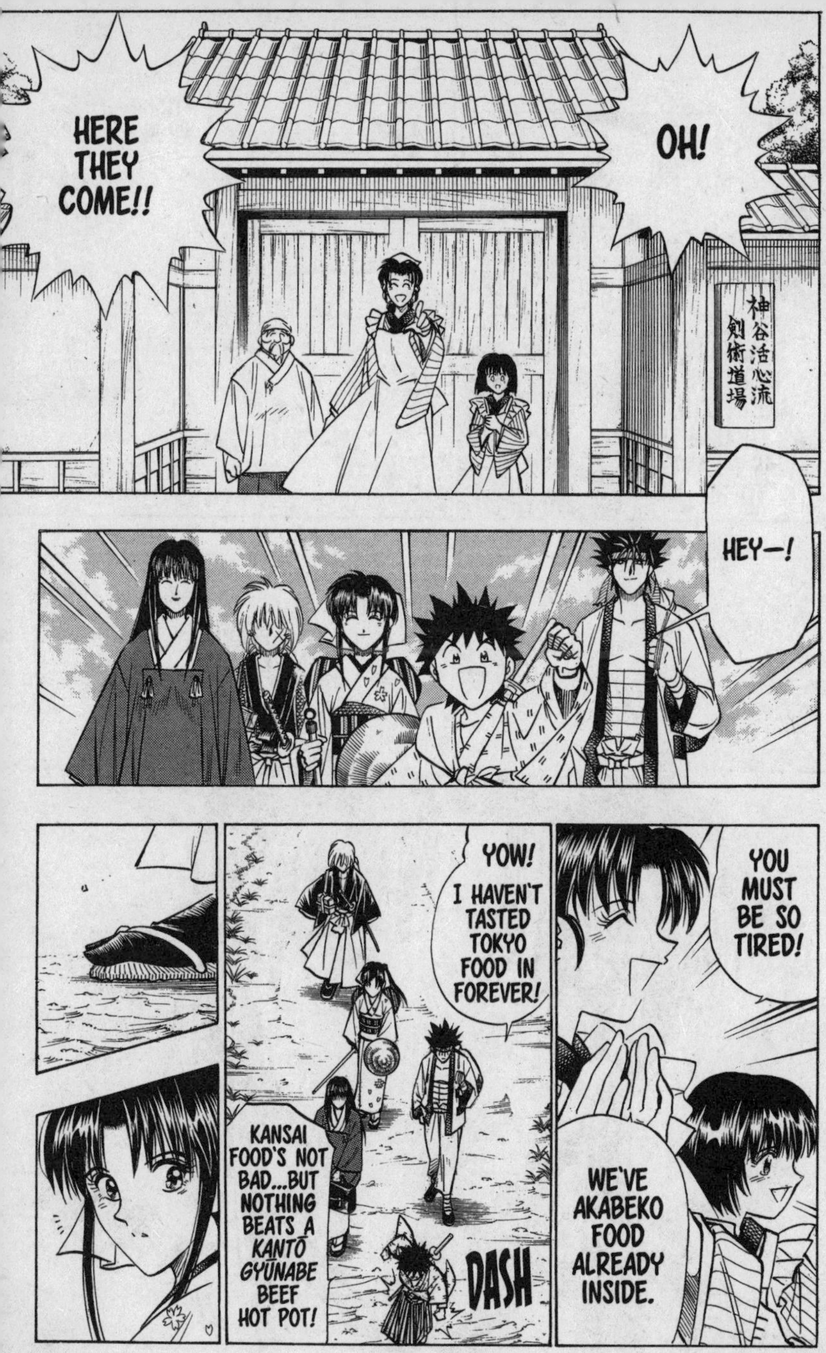
OH!
HERE THEY COME!!
神谷活心流
剣術道場
HEY—!
YOU MUST BE SO TIRED!
WE'VE AKABEKO FOOD ALREADY INSIDE.
YOW!
I HAVEN'T TASTED TOKYO FOOD IN FOREVER!
DASH
KANSAI FOOD'S NOT BAD...BUT NOTHING BEATS A KANTŌ GYŪNABE BEEF HOT POT!

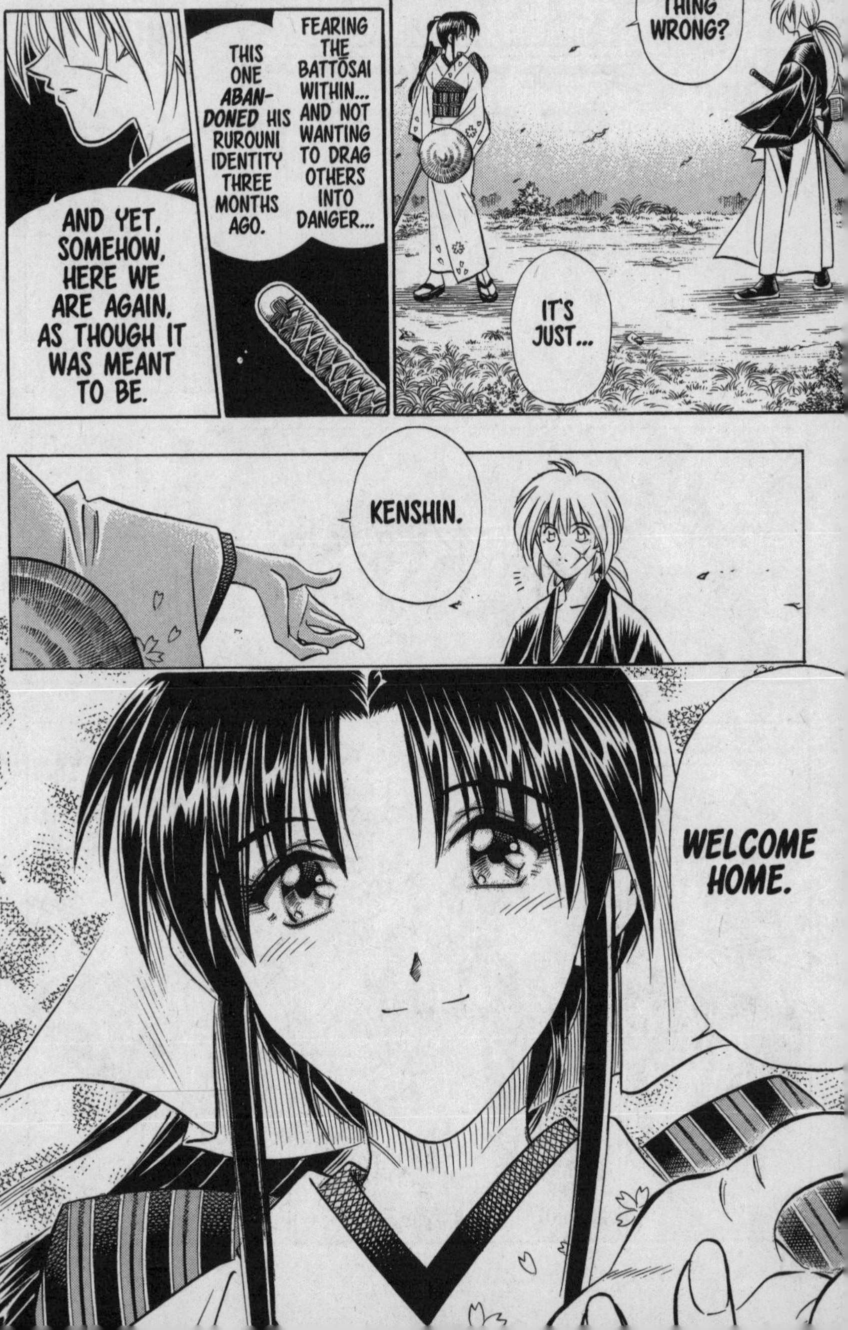
IS SOME-THING WRONG?
IT'S JUST...
FEARING THE BATTOSAI WITHIN... AND NOT WANTING TO DRAG OTHERS INTO DANGER...
THIS ONE *ABANDONED* HIS RUROUNI IDENTITY THREE MONTHS AGO.
AND YET, SOMEHOW, HERE WE ARE AGAIN, AS THOUGH IT WAS MEANT TO BE.
KENSHIN.
WELCOME HOME.

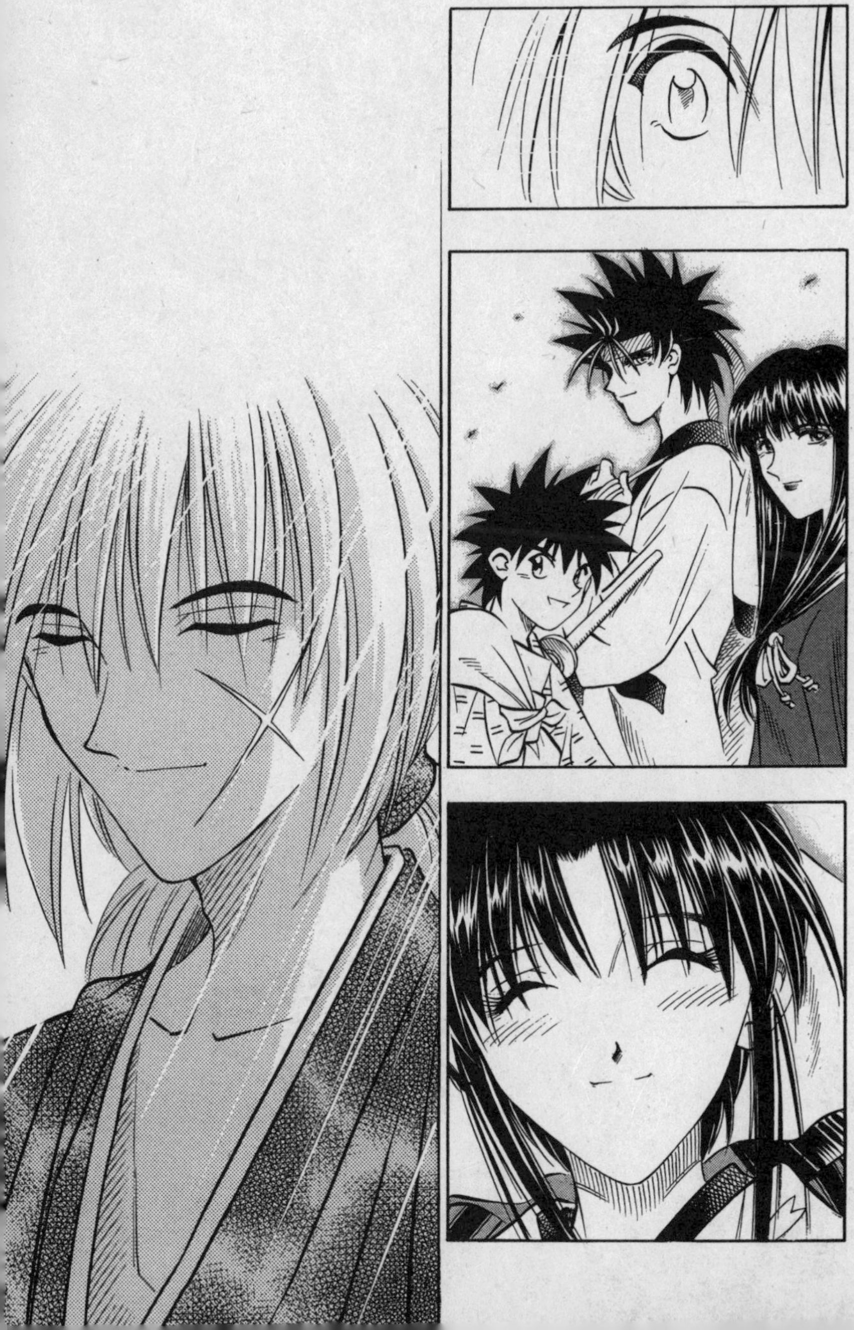

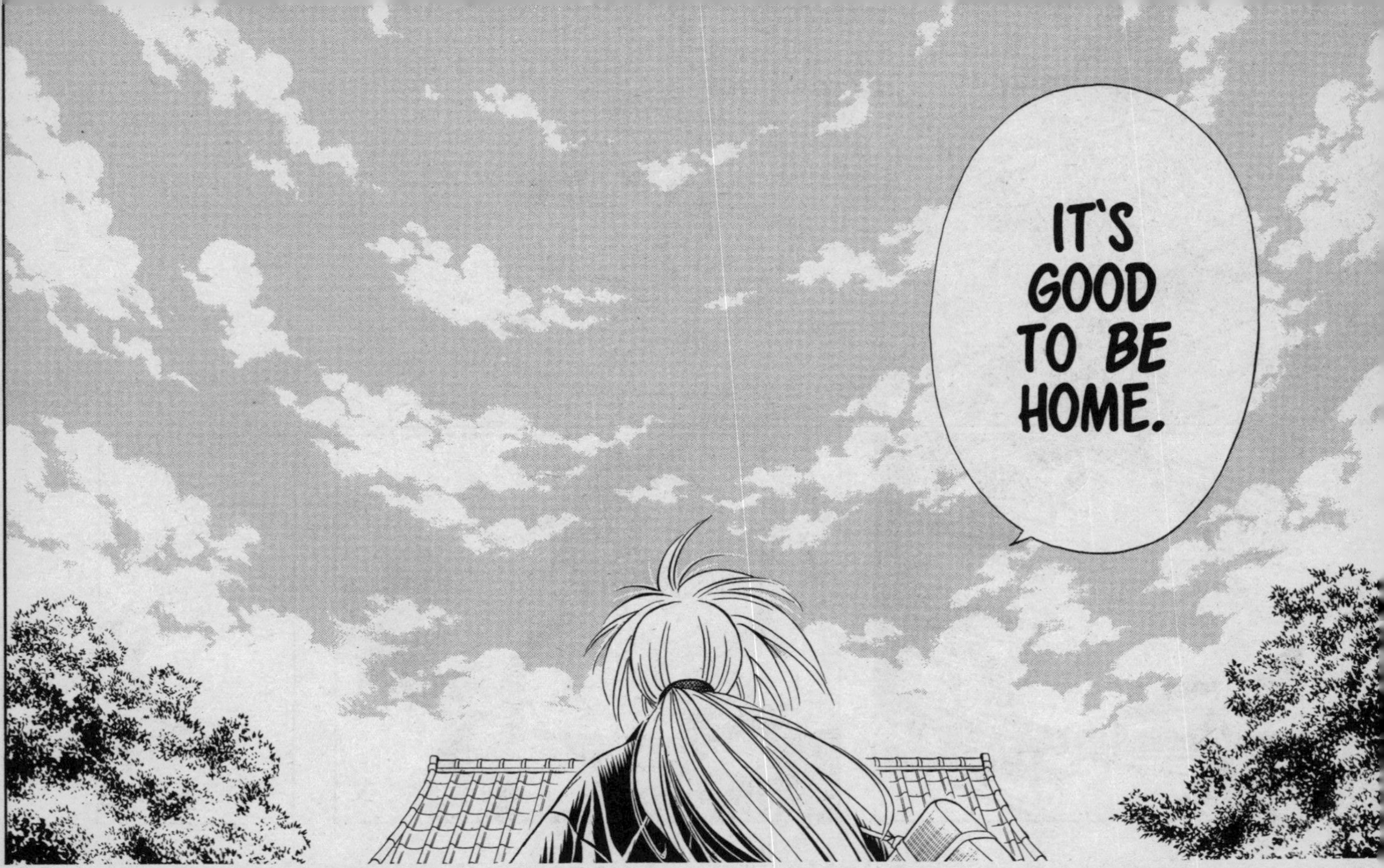
IT'S GOOD TO BE HOME.

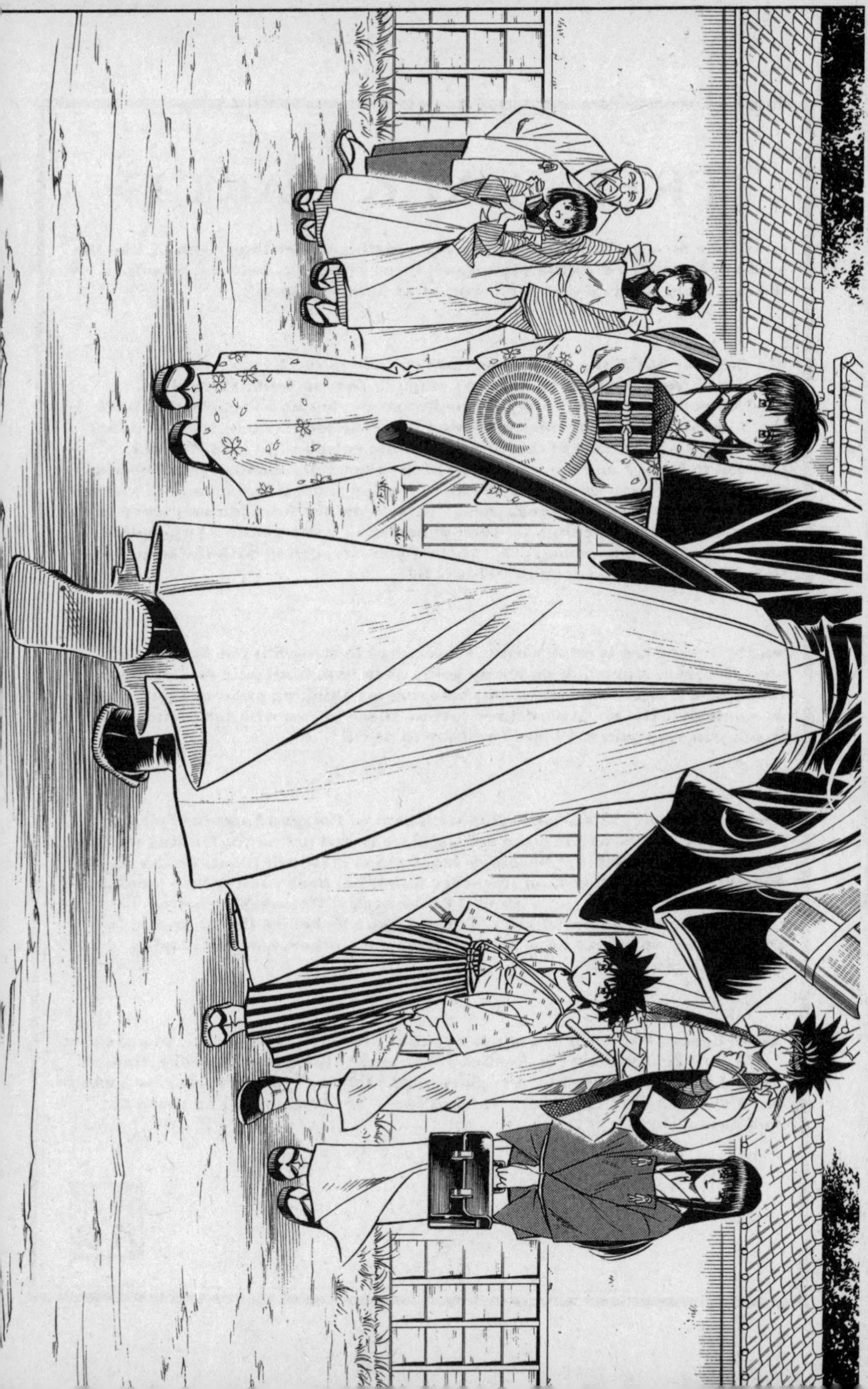

"FREE TALK" ⟨PART I⟩

Long time no see. Watsuki here. It's been getting colder lately—and I *like* the cold—so I've started shifting into gear. Or so I thought, but now here it is, the end of the year. My life's passing by at lightning speed.

"In the Blue Sky," the title of the final episode in the Kyoto Arc, was borrowed from the BGM of Temjin's stage in *Den'nō Senki Virtual On*. I used it because of the blue sky in the last scene, but also because this BGM (or, I should say, the arranged version from the soundtrack) is a piece that perfectly fits my image of the *Kenshin* Kyoto episodes. In that Watsuki listened to it over and over while writing—especially during the "Kenshin vs. Shishio" scenes—it seemed the ideal closing title. Also, as many of you may have noticed, that last (manga) scene came from the final (anime) scene of the original TV series opening. I'd been planning to wrap up the Kyoto episodes with "It's good to be home," but there I was, struggling with the scene, and then I saw *that*, and thought, "This is it."

So, the Kyoto Arc is finally over. I'd planned to stretch it out over a year, but once the ideas started, it ended up going over two. It all paid off in the end, though, as it *was* a turning point, bringing my thinking processes and abilities as a manga artist up two or three levels. Those of you who supported me, thank you very much. Please continue to do so!

And now for the silliness, starting with games. *Polygon Samurai Spirits:* At the time of this writing, the release date is still unknown. Waiting for it is hard, but for something this much fun, I guess I'll tough it out. *Gekka no Kenshi* (The Last Blade), on the other hand, has been coming into focus...no! Let's not *talk* about it, let's *play* it! Incidentally, Watsuki's favorite character—or so he anticipates—is Washizuka Kei'chirō (heh). As said in the previous volume, I hope they sharpen each other, both developing into great games.

To be honest, I've been so busy lately that I haven't played much of anything. I *did* play *TenSamu* on the NeoGeo CD so much that the stick broke, though. (Now I have to wait to buy a replacement.) I'm not really a gamer, so I can't say I'm experiencing withdrawal, but there are good days, and there are bad days...

Act 152
Cross-Shaped Scar

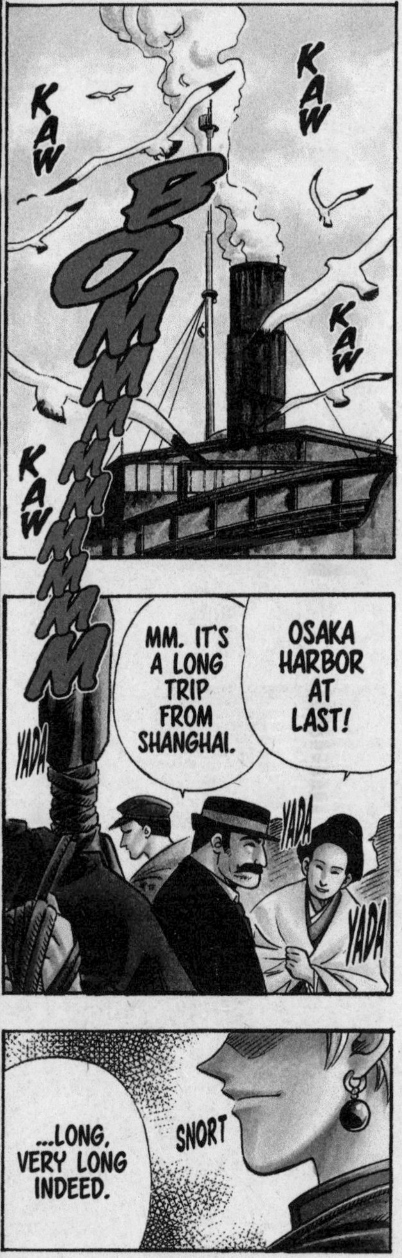
KAW
KAW
KAW
KAW
BOMMMMMMMMMMM
OSAKA HARBOR AT LAST!
MM. IT'S A LONG TRIP FROM SHANGHAI.
YADA
YADA
YADA
...LONG, VERY LONG INDEED.
SNORT

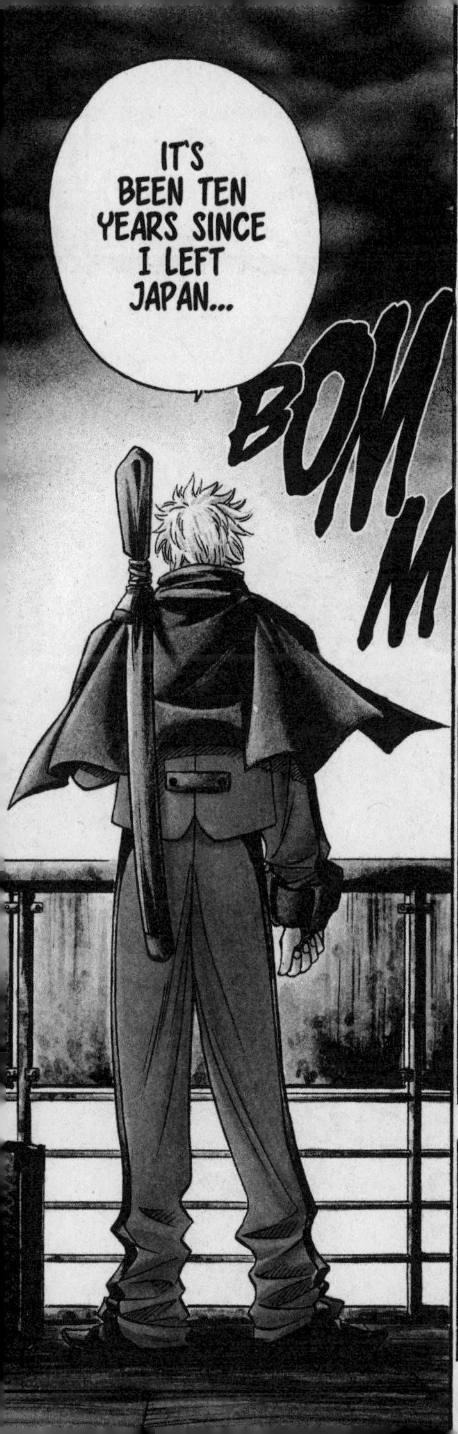
IT'S BEEN TEN YEARS SINCE I LEFT JAPAN...
BOMM

Act 152
Cross-Shaped Scar

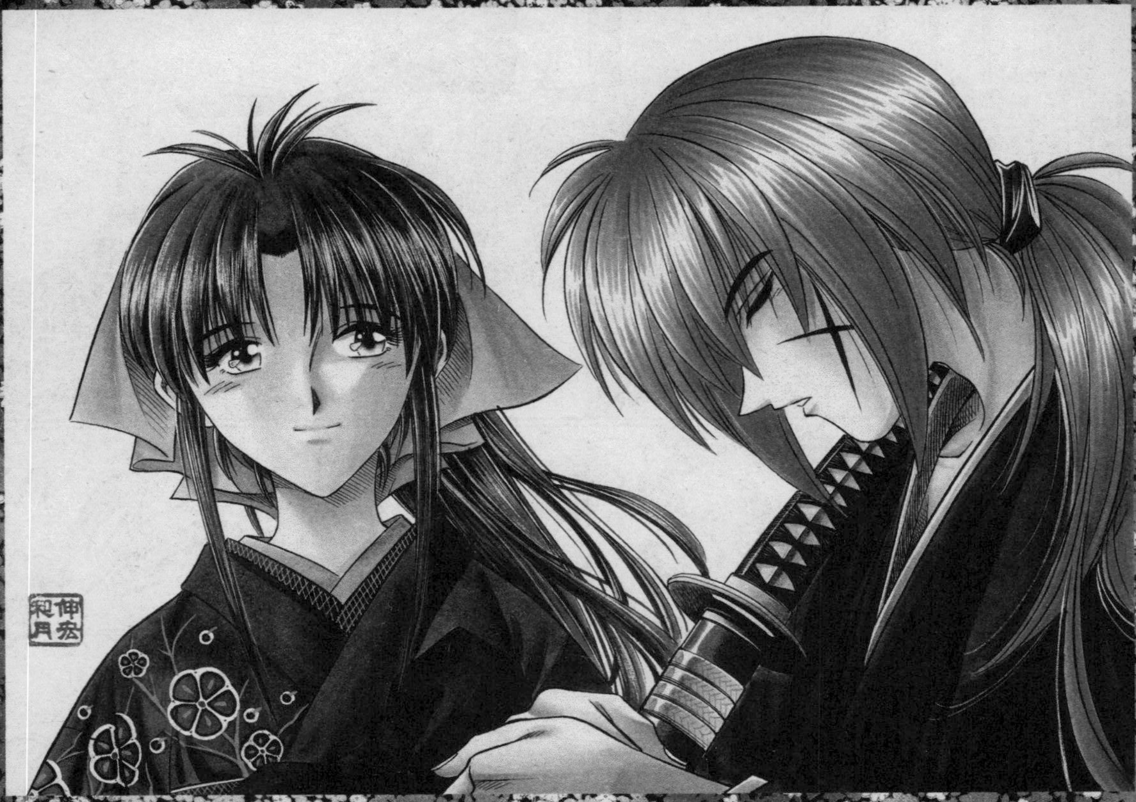

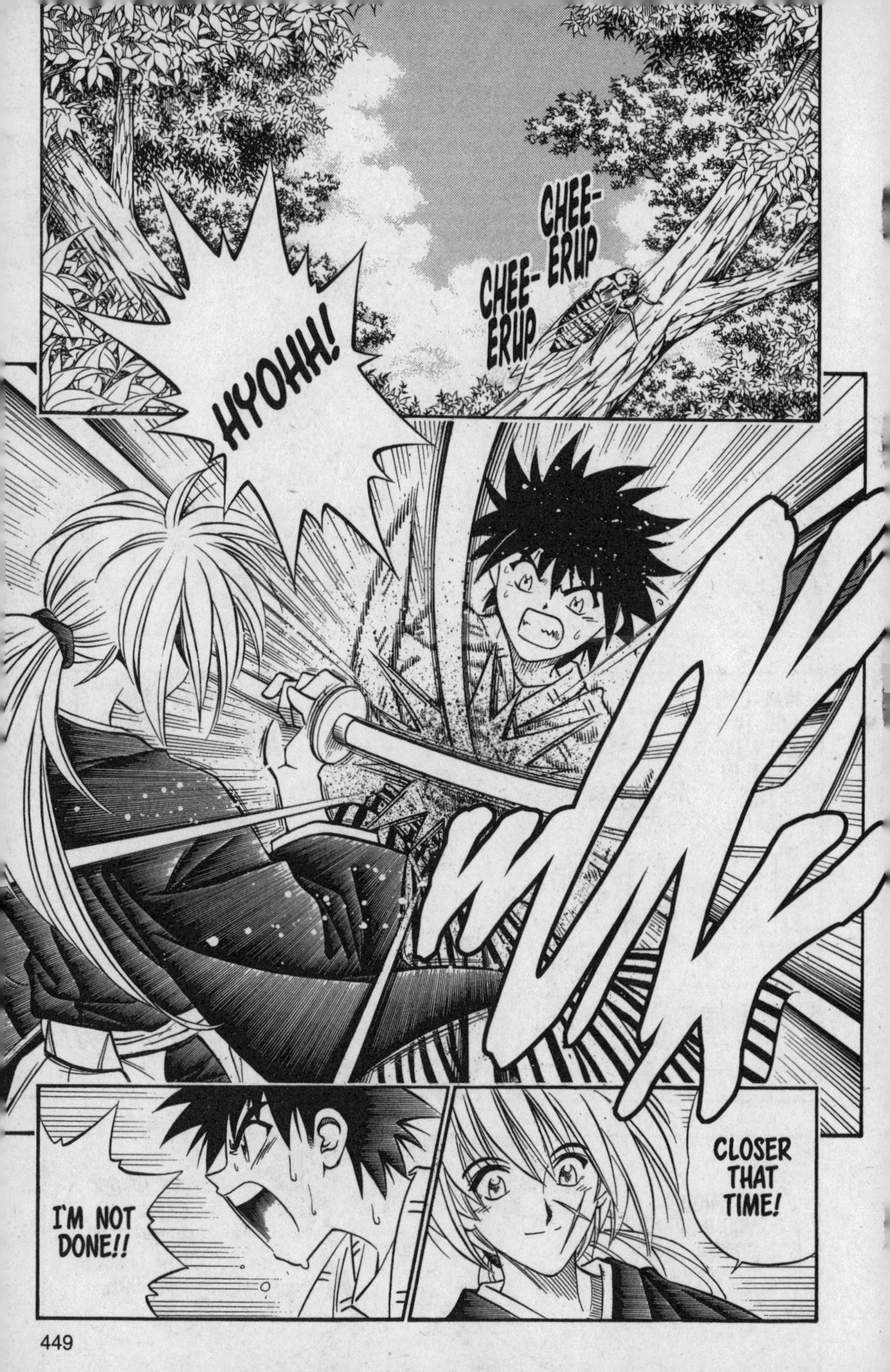
CHEE-ERUP
CHEE-ERUP
HYOHH!
CLOSER THAT TIME!
I'M NOT DONE!!

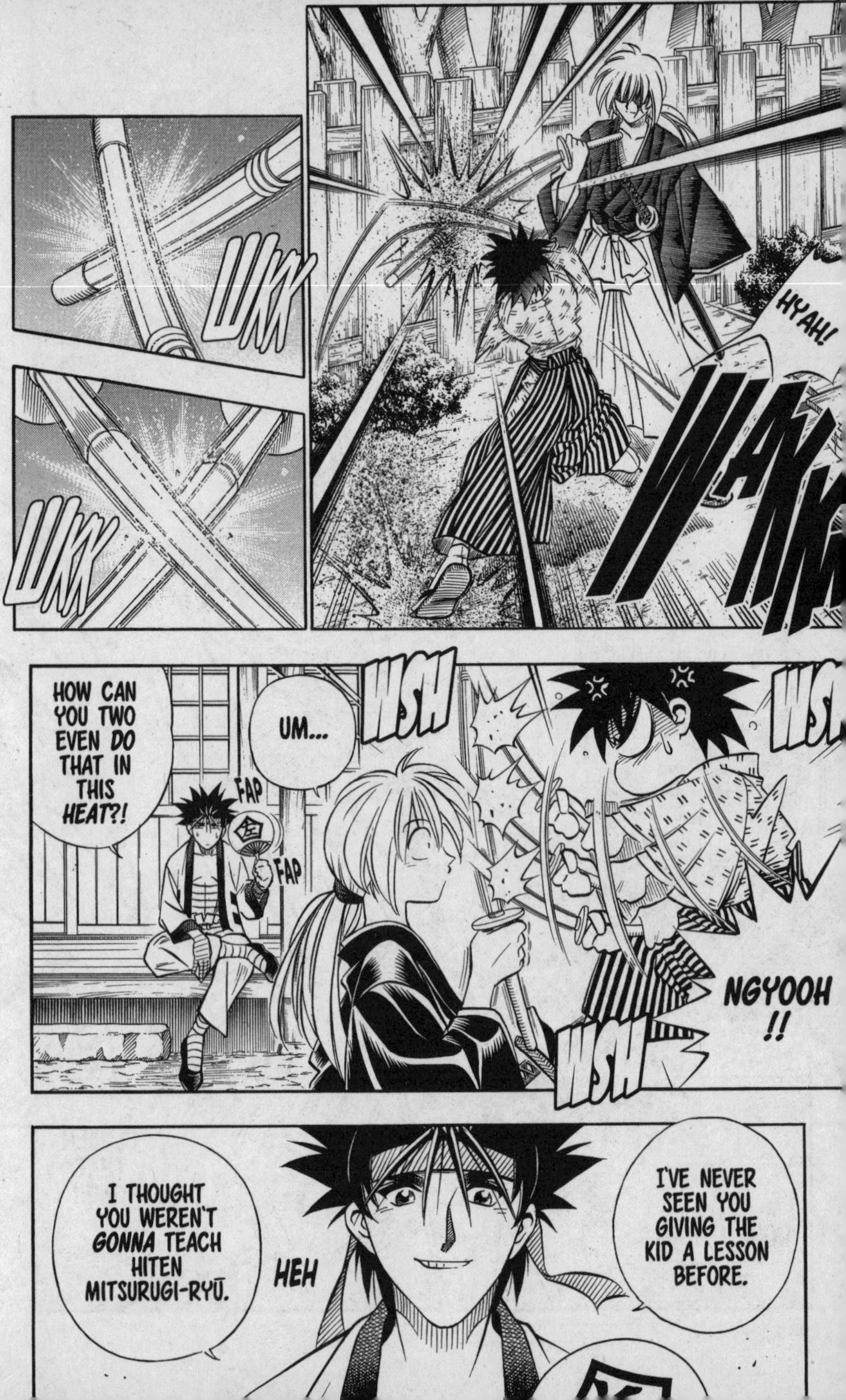
HYAH!
WAKK
WKK
WKK
NGYOOH !!
WSH
UM...
WSH
HOW CAN YOU TWO EVEN DO THAT IN THIS HEAT?!
FAP
FAP
I'VE NEVER SEEN YOU GIVING THE KID A LESSON BEFORE.
HEH
I THOUGHT YOU WEREN'T GONNA TEACH HITEN MITSURUGI-RYŪ.

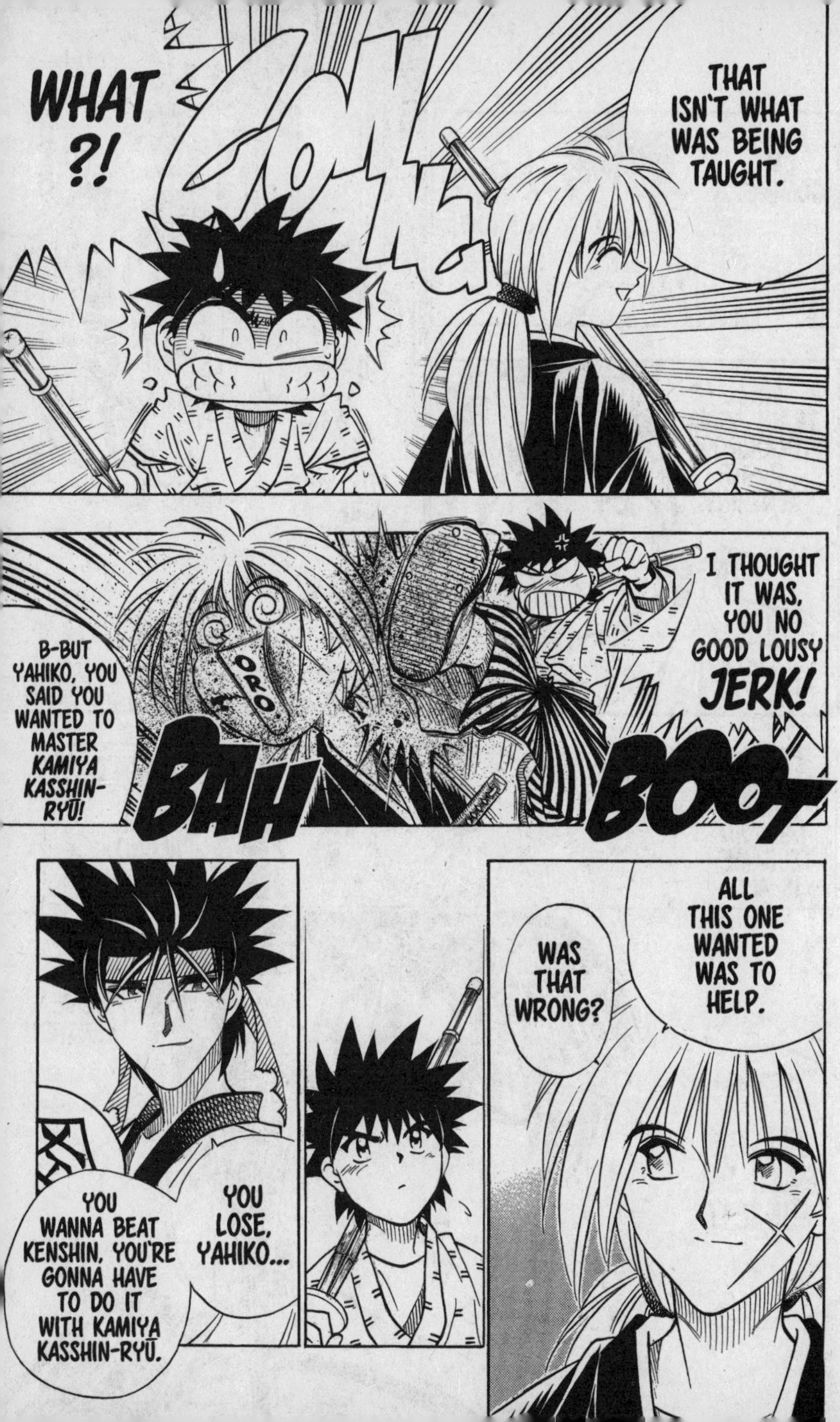
THAT ISN'T WHAT WAS BEING TAUGHT.
WHAT ?!
I THOUGHT IT WAS, YOU NO GOOD LOUSY JERK!
BOOT
BAH
ORO
B-BUT YAHIKO, YOU SAID YOU WANTED TO MASTER KAMIYA KASSHIN-RYŪ!
ALL THIS ONE WANTED WAS TO HELP.
WAS THAT WRONG?
YOU LOSE, YAHIKO...
YOU WANNA BEAT KENSHIN, YOU'RE GONNA HAVE TO DO IT WITH KAMIYA KASSHIN-RYŪ.

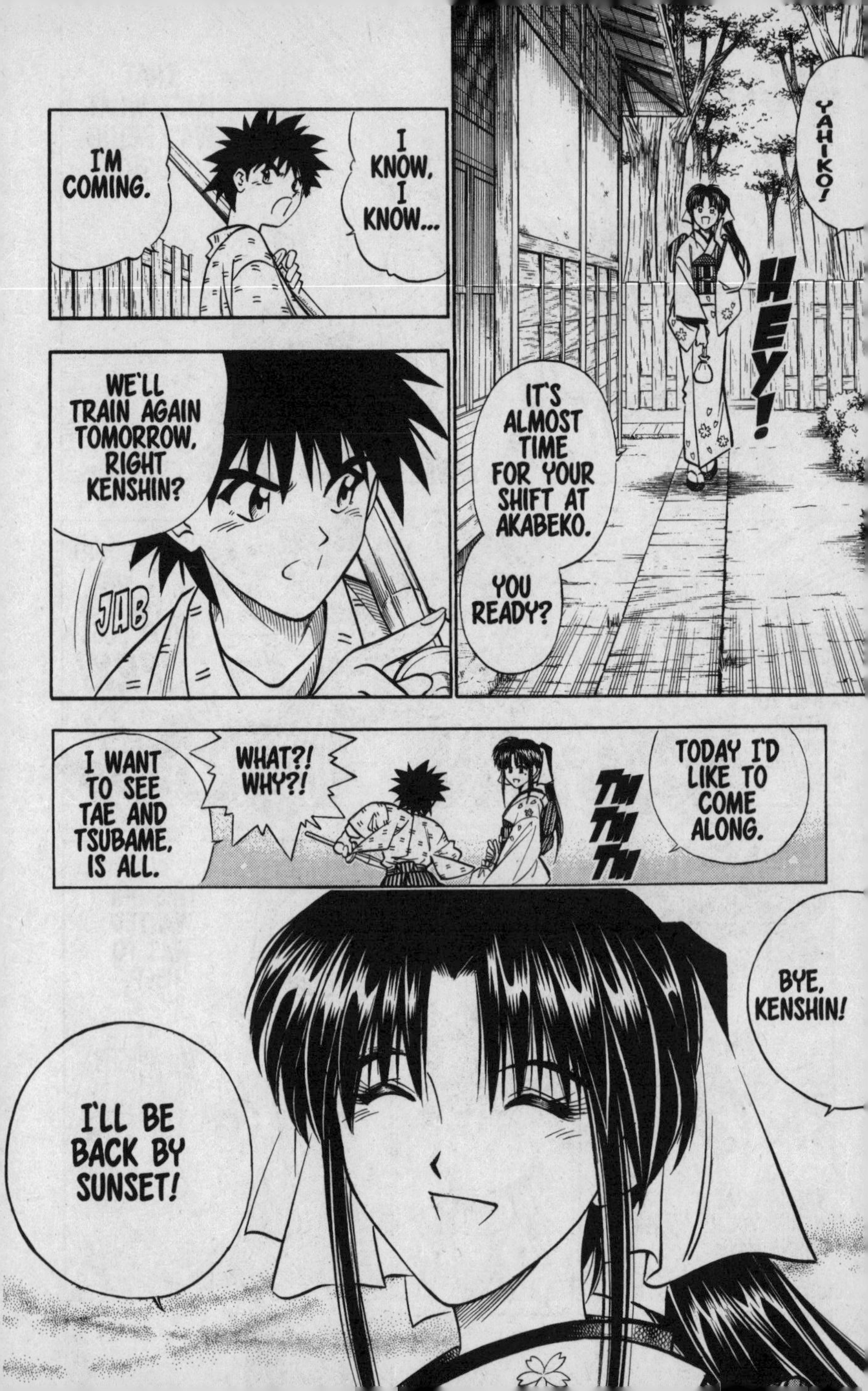
YAHIKO!
HEY!
IT'S ALMOST TIME FOR YOUR SHIFT AT AKABEKO.
YOU READY?
I KNOW, I KNOW...
I'M COMING.
WE'LL TRAIN AGAIN TOMORROW, RIGHT KENSHIN?
JAB
TODAY I'D LIKE TO COME ALONG.
TM TM TM
WHAT?! WHY?!
I WANT TO SEE TAE AND TSUBAME, IS ALL.
BYE, KENSHIN!
I'LL BE BACK BY SUNSET!

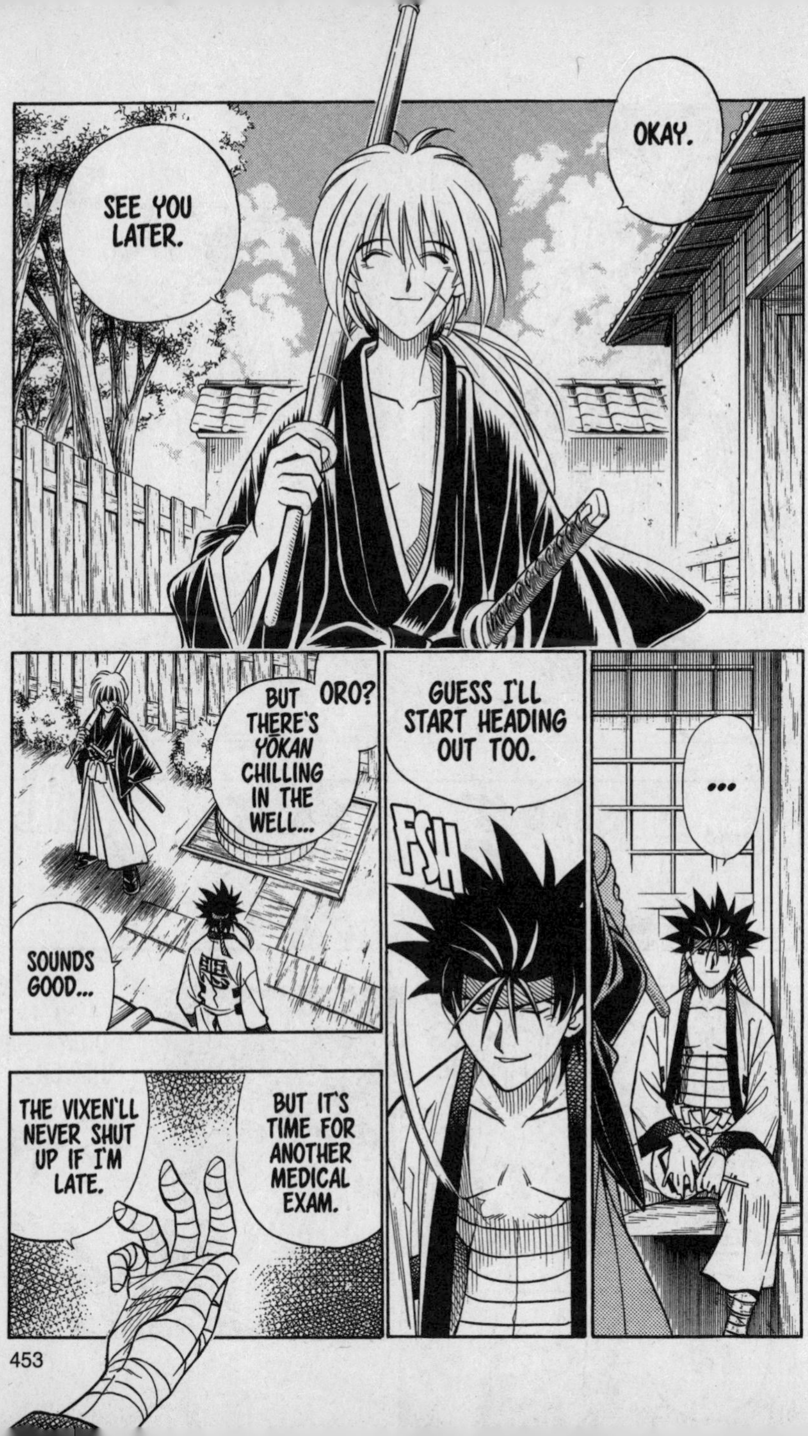
OKAY.
SEE YOU LATER.
...
GUESS I'LL START HEADING OUT TOO.
FSH
ORO?
BUT THERE'S YŌKAN CHILLING IN THE WELL...
SOUNDS GOOD...
BUT IT'S TIME FOR ANOTHER MEDICAL EXAM.
THE VIXEN'LL NEVER SHUT UP IF I'M LATE.

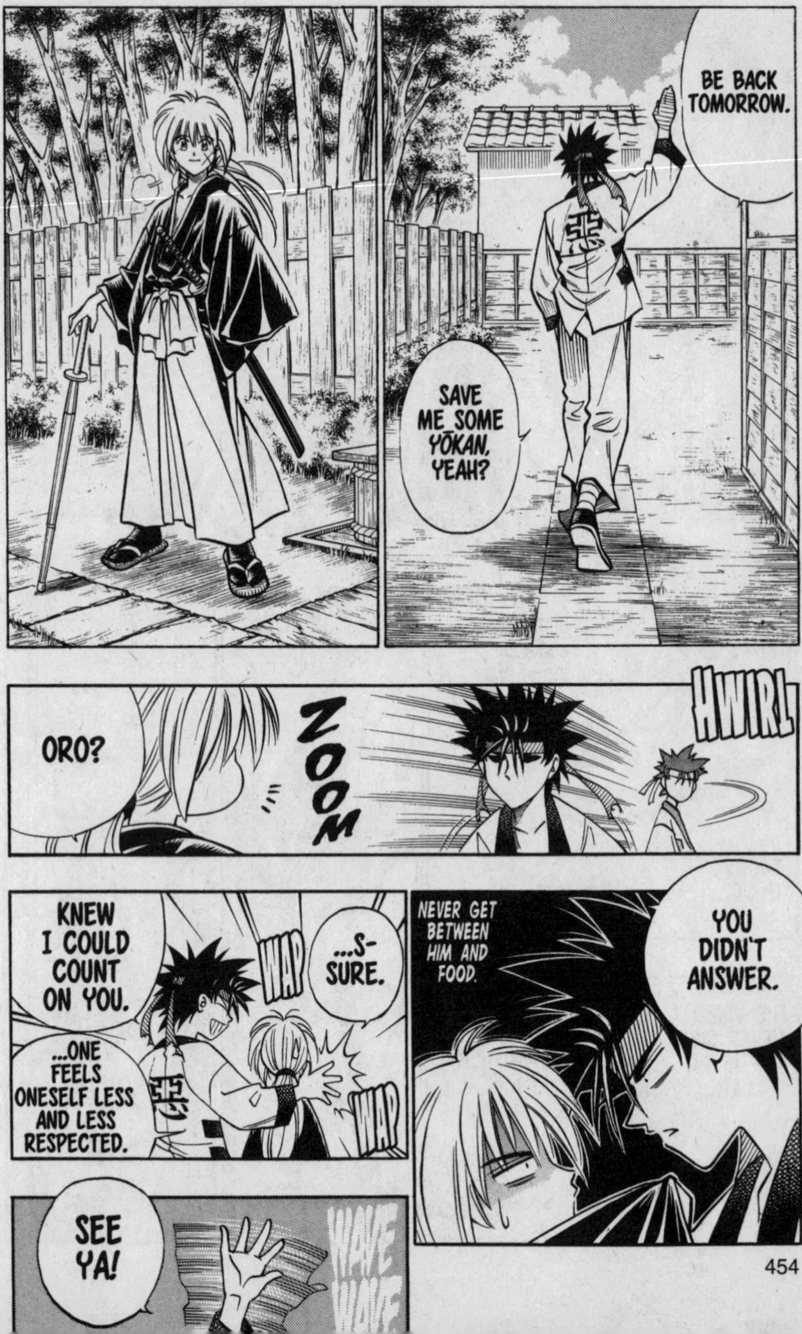
BE BACK TOMORROW.
SAVE ME SOME YŌKAN, YEAH?
HWIRL
ZOOM
ORO?
YOU DIDN'T ANSWER.
NEVER GET BETWEEN HIM AND FOOD.
...S-SURE.
WAP
KNEW I COULD COUNT ON YOU.
WAP
...ONE FEELS ONESELF LESS AND LESS RESPECTED.
WAVE WAVE
SEE YA!

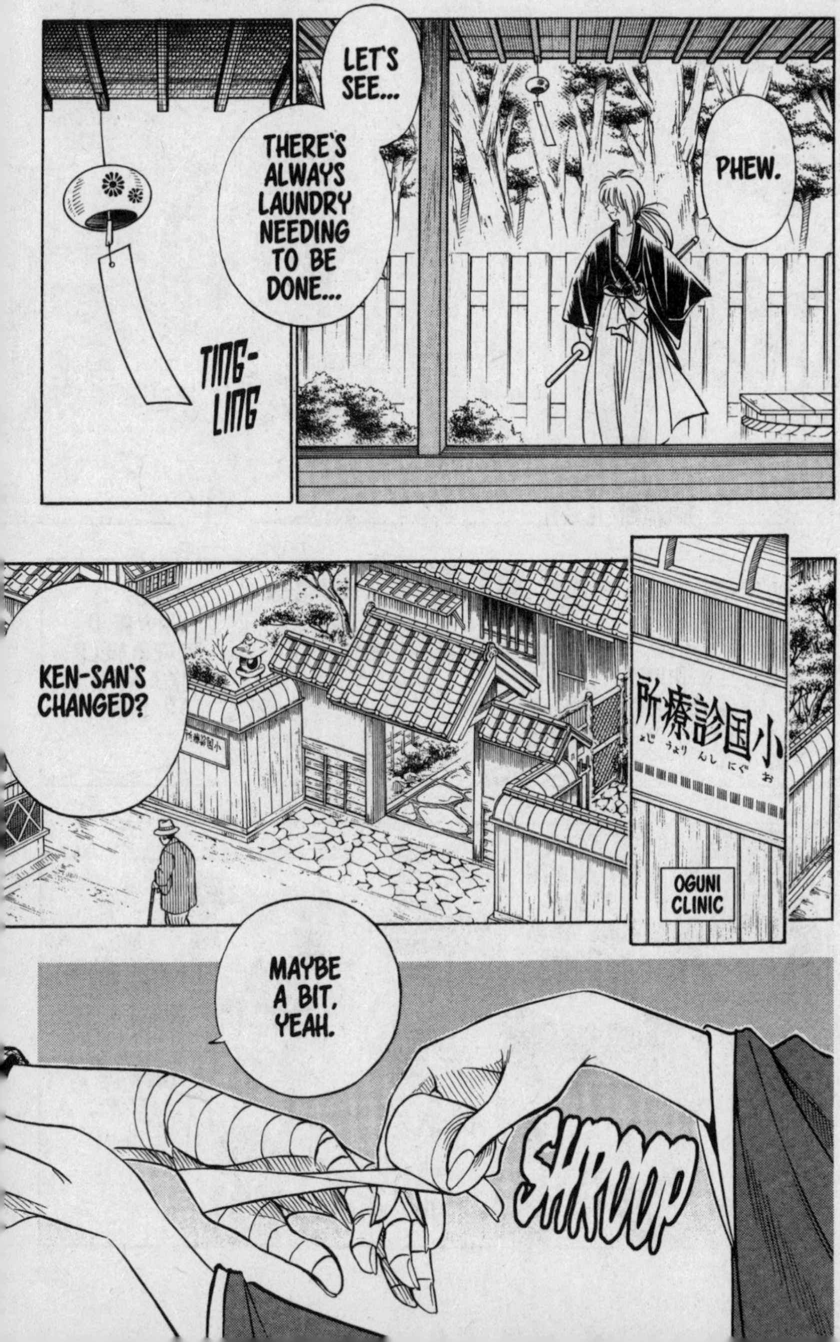
PHEW.
LET'S SEE...
THERE'S ALWAYS LAUNDRY NEEDING TO BE DONE...
TING-LING
小国診療所
OGUNI CLINIC
KEN-SAN'S CHANGED?
MAYBE A BIT, YEAH.
SHROOP

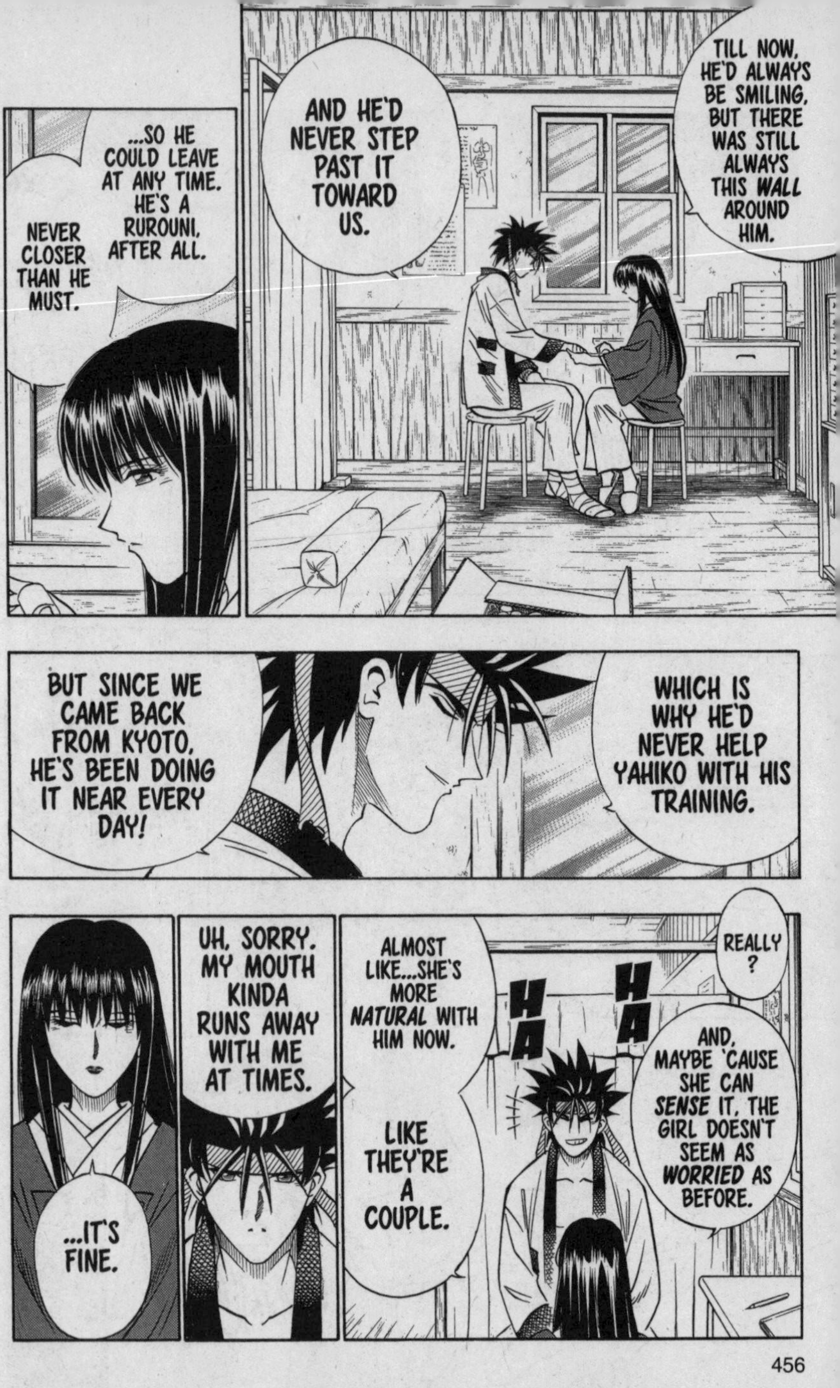
TILL NOW, HE'D ALWAYS BE SMILING, BUT THERE WAS STILL ALWAYS THIS *WALL* AROUND HIM.
AND HE'D NEVER STEP PAST IT TOWARD US.
...SO HE COULD LEAVE AT ANY TIME. HE'S A RUROUNI, AFTER ALL.
NEVER CLOSER THAN HE MUST.
WHICH IS WHY HE'D NEVER HELP YAHIKO WITH HIS TRAINING.
BUT SINCE WE CAME BACK FROM KYOTO, HE'S BEEN DOING IT NEAR EVERY DAY!
REALLY?
HA
HA
AND, MAYBE 'CAUSE SHE CAN *SENSE* IT, THE GIRL DOESN'T SEEM AS *WORRIED* AS BEFORE.
ALMOST LIKE...SHE'S MORE *NATURAL* WITH HIM NOW.
LIKE THEY'RE A COUPLE.
UH, SORRY. MY MOUTH KINDA RUNS AWAY WITH ME AT TIMES.
...IT'S FINE.

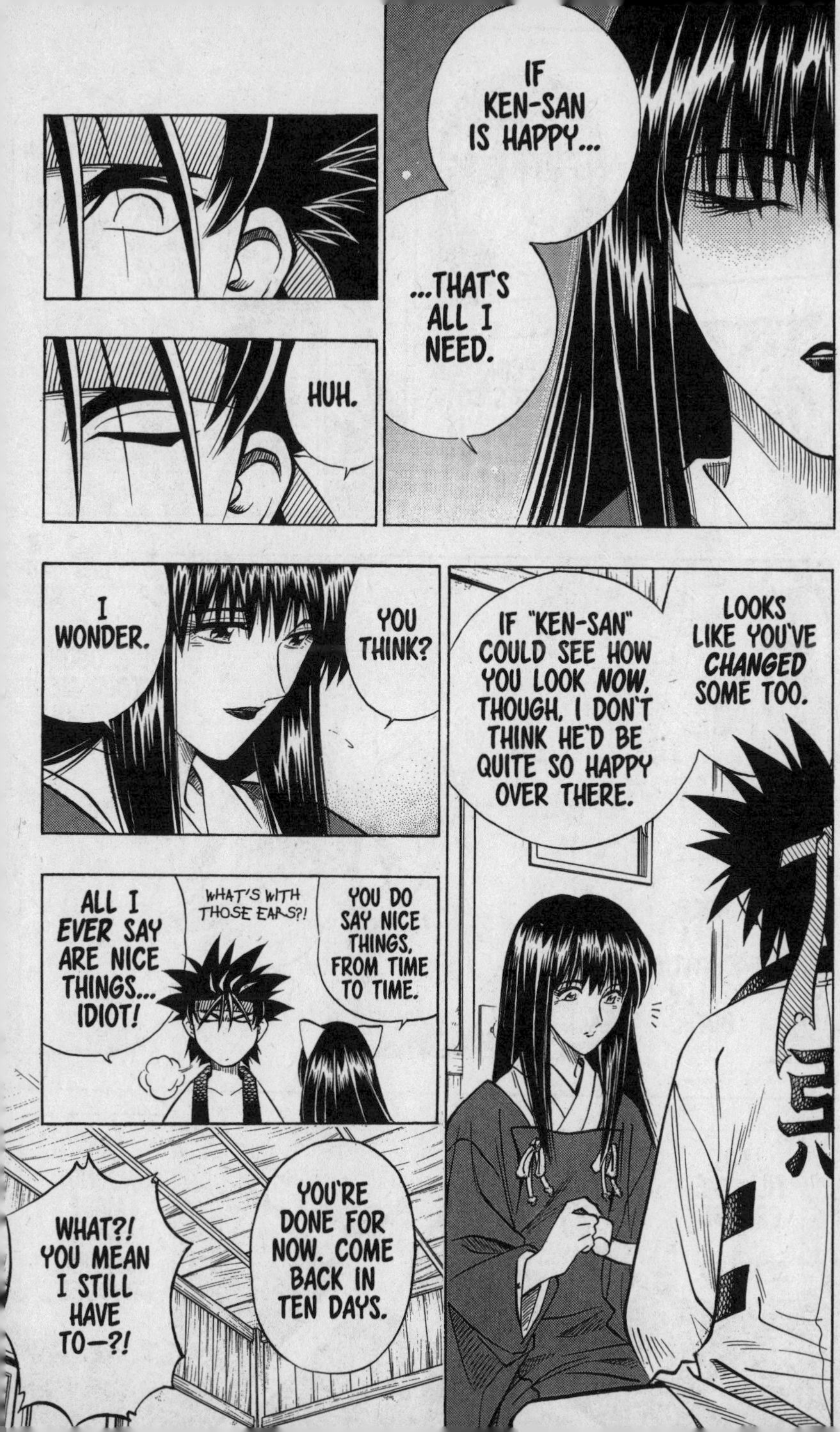
IF KEN-SAN IS HAPPY...
...THAT'S ALL I NEED.
HUH.
LOOKS LIKE YOU'VE *CHANGED* SOME TOO.
IF "KEN-SAN" COULD SEE HOW YOU LOOK *NOW*, THOUGH, I DON'T THINK HE'D BE QUITE SO HAPPY OVER THERE.
YOU THINK?
I WONDER.
YOU DO SAY NICE THINGS, FROM TIME TO TIME.
WHAT'S WITH THOSE EARS?!
ALL I EVER SAY ARE NICE THINGS... IDIOT!
YOU'RE DONE FOR NOW. COME BACK IN TEN DAYS.
WHAT?! YOU MEAN I STILL HAVE TO—?!

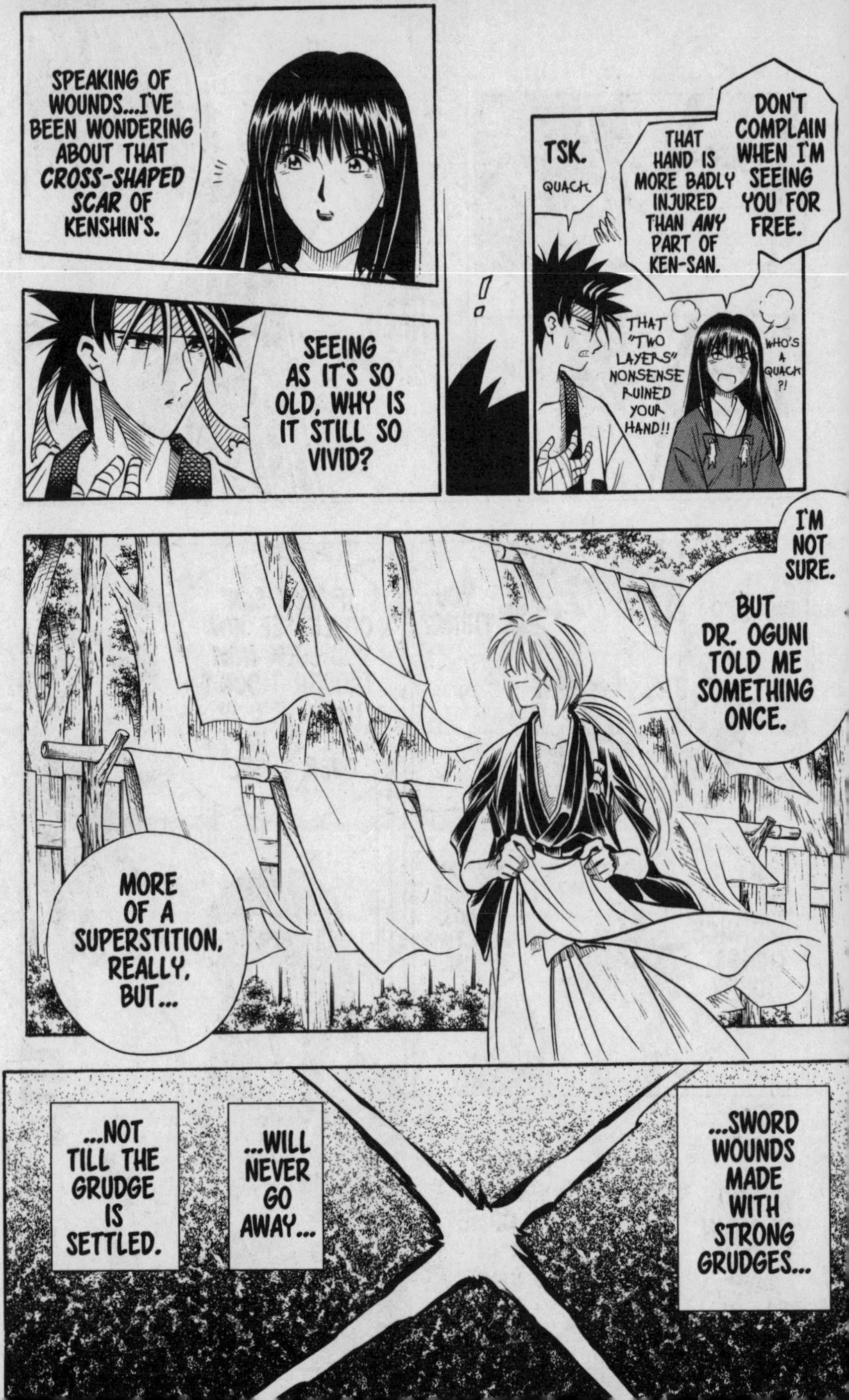
DON'T COMPLAIN WHEN I'M SEEING YOU FOR FREE.
THAT HAND IS MORE BADLY INJURED THAN ANY PART OF KEN-SAN.
TSK.
QUACK.
WHO'S A QUACK?!
THAT "TWO LAYERS" NONSENSE RUINED YOUR HAND!!
!
SPEAKING OF WOUNDS...I'VE BEEN WONDERING ABOUT THAT CROSS-SHAPED SCAR OF KENSHIN'S.
SEEING AS IT'S SO OLD, WHY IS IT STILL SO VIVID?
I'M NOT SURE.
BUT DR. OGUNI TOLD ME SOMETHING ONCE.
MORE OF A SUPERSTITION, REALLY, BUT...
...SWORD WOUNDS MADE WITH STRONG GRUDGES...
...WILL NEVER GO AWAY...
...NOT TILL THE GRUDGE IS SETTLED.

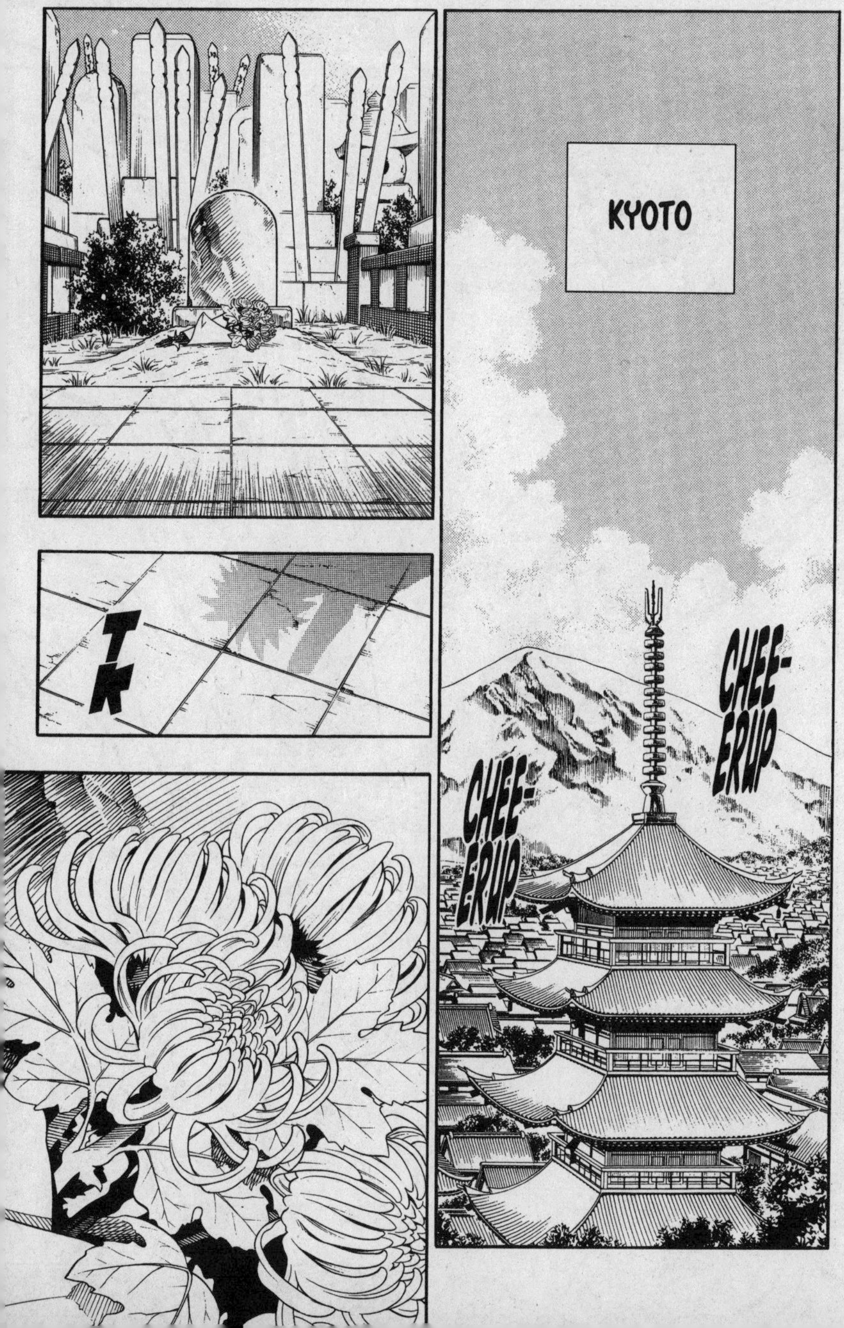
KYOTO
CHEE-ERUP
CHEE-ERUP
TK

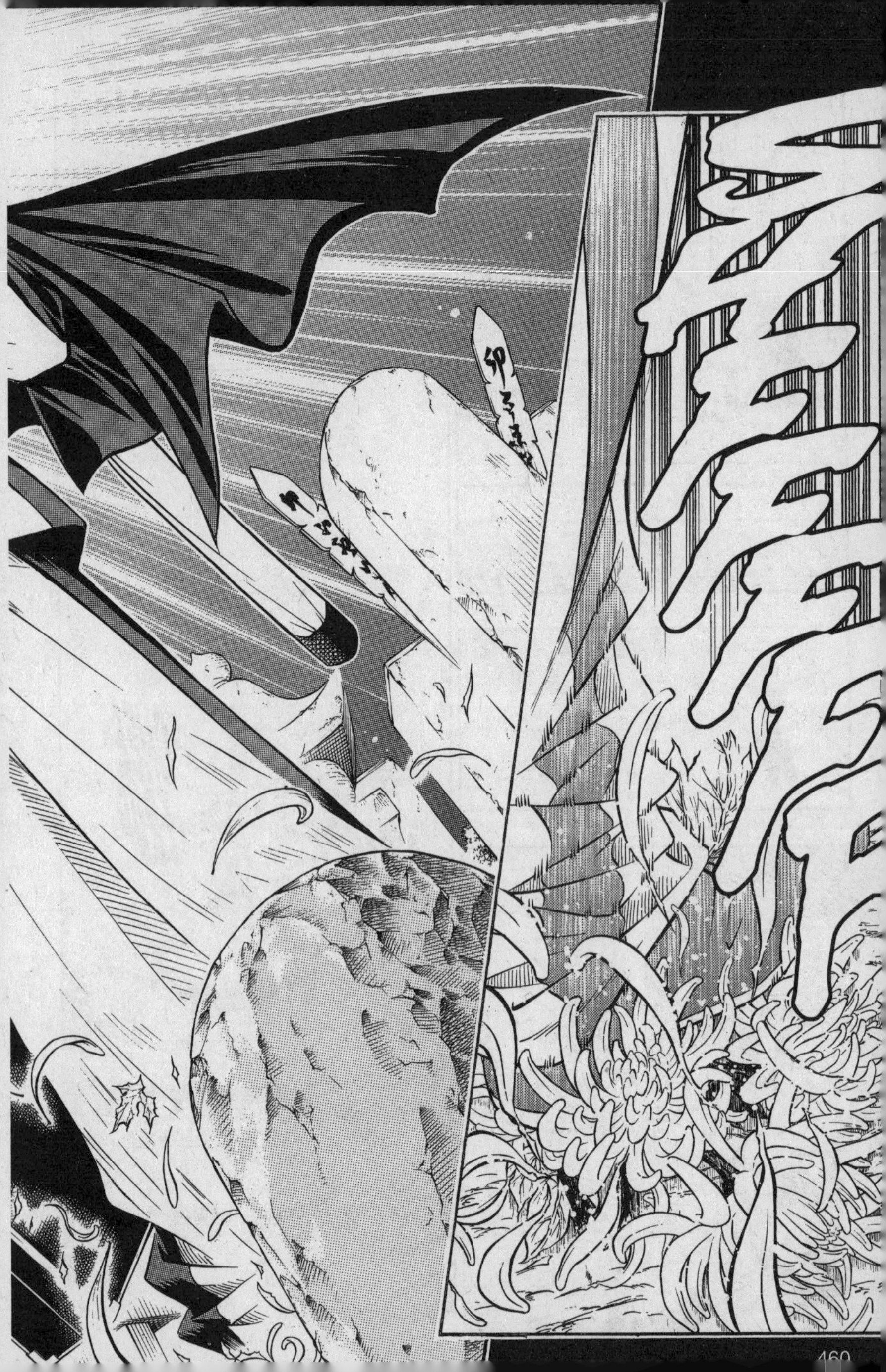

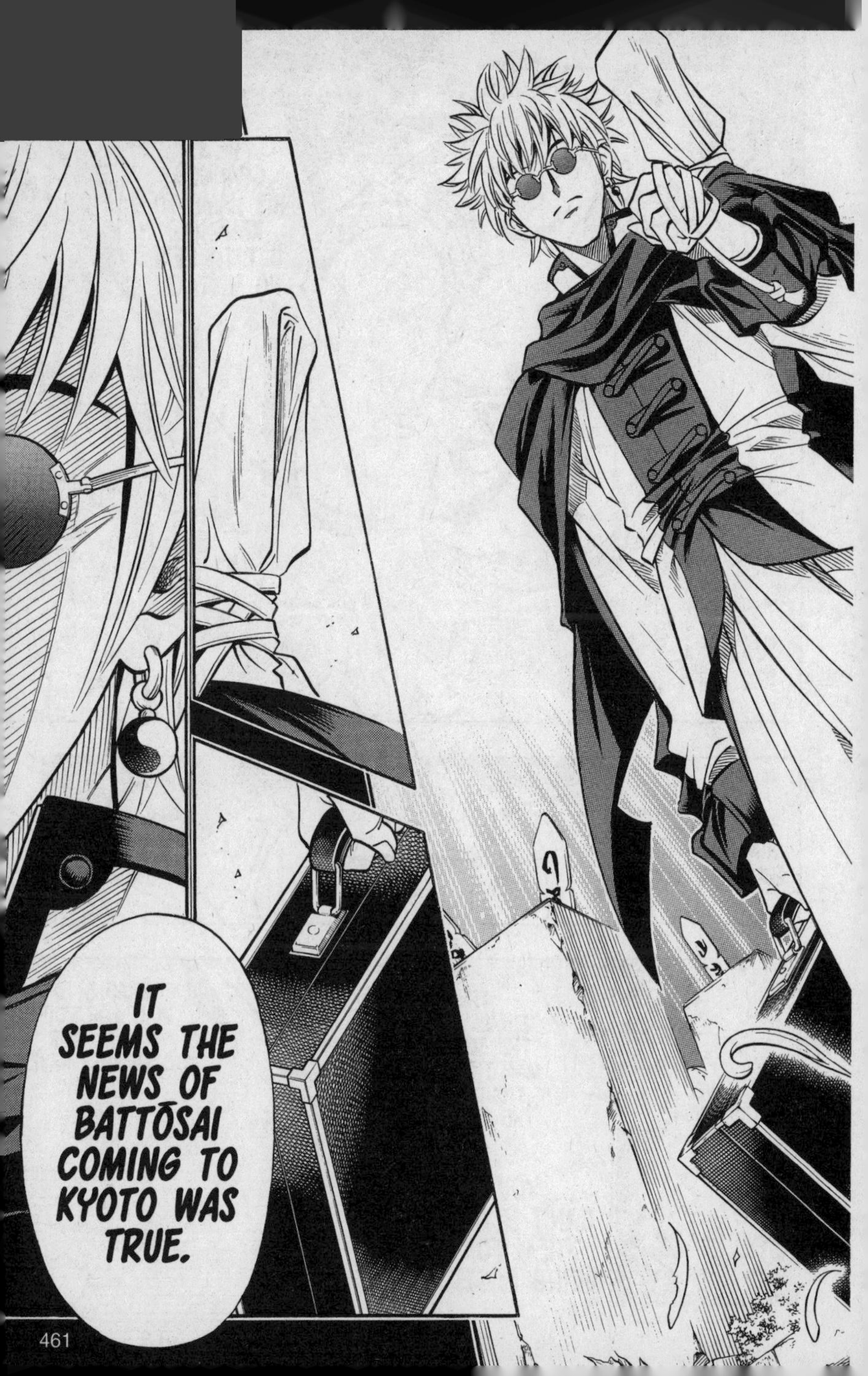
IT SEEMS THE NEWS OF BATTŌSAI COMING TO KYOTO WAS TRUE.

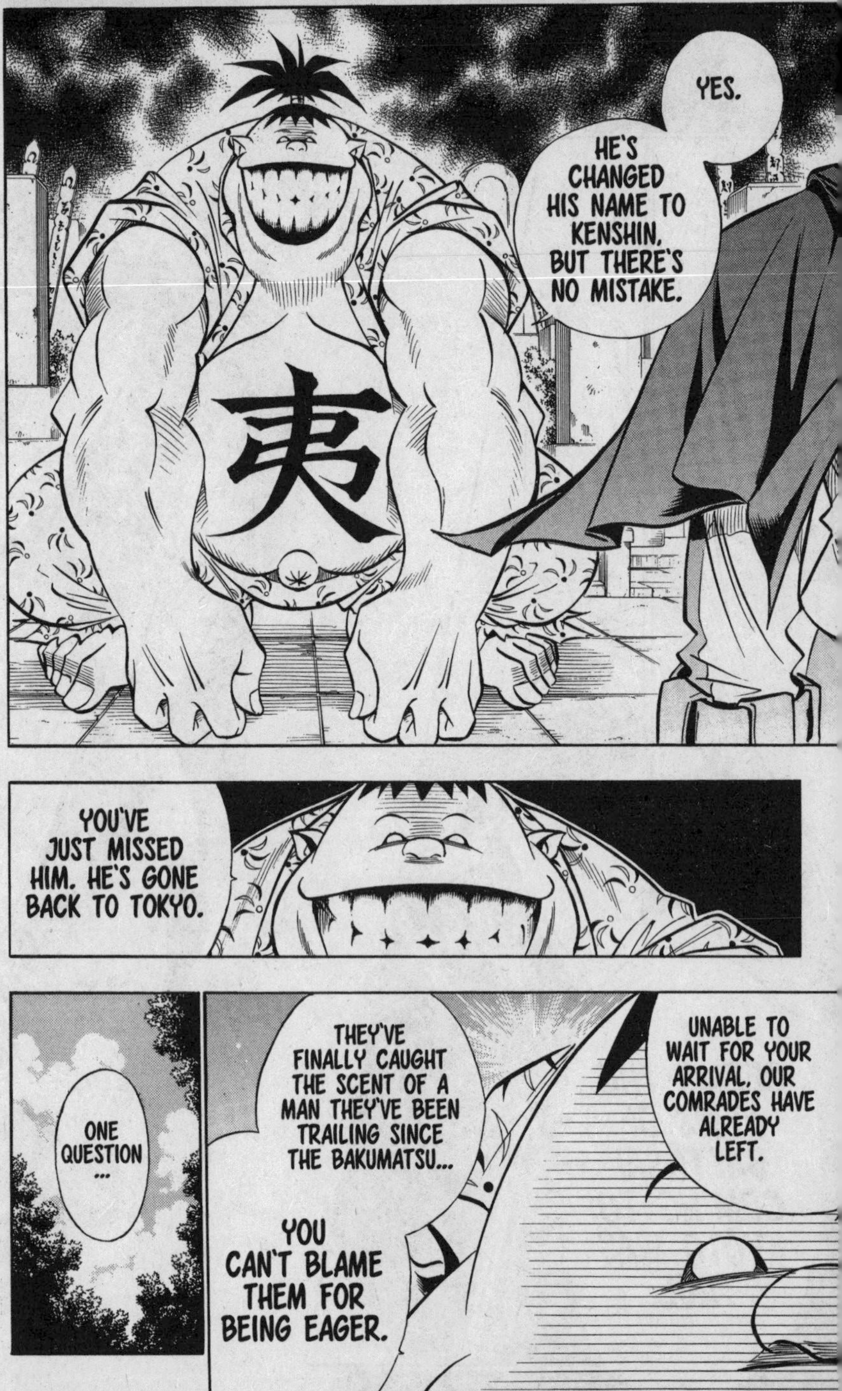
YES.
HE'S CHANGED HIS NAME TO KENSHIN, BUT THERE'S NO MISTAKE.
YOU'VE JUST MISSED HIM. HE'S GONE BACK TO TOKYO.
UNABLE TO WAIT FOR YOUR ARRIVAL, OUR COMRADES HAVE ALREADY LEFT.
THEY'VE FINALLY CAUGHT THE SCENT OF A MAN THEY'VE BEEN TRAILING SINCE THE BAKUMATSU...
YOU CAN'T BLAME THEM FOR BEING EAGER.
ONE QUESTION...

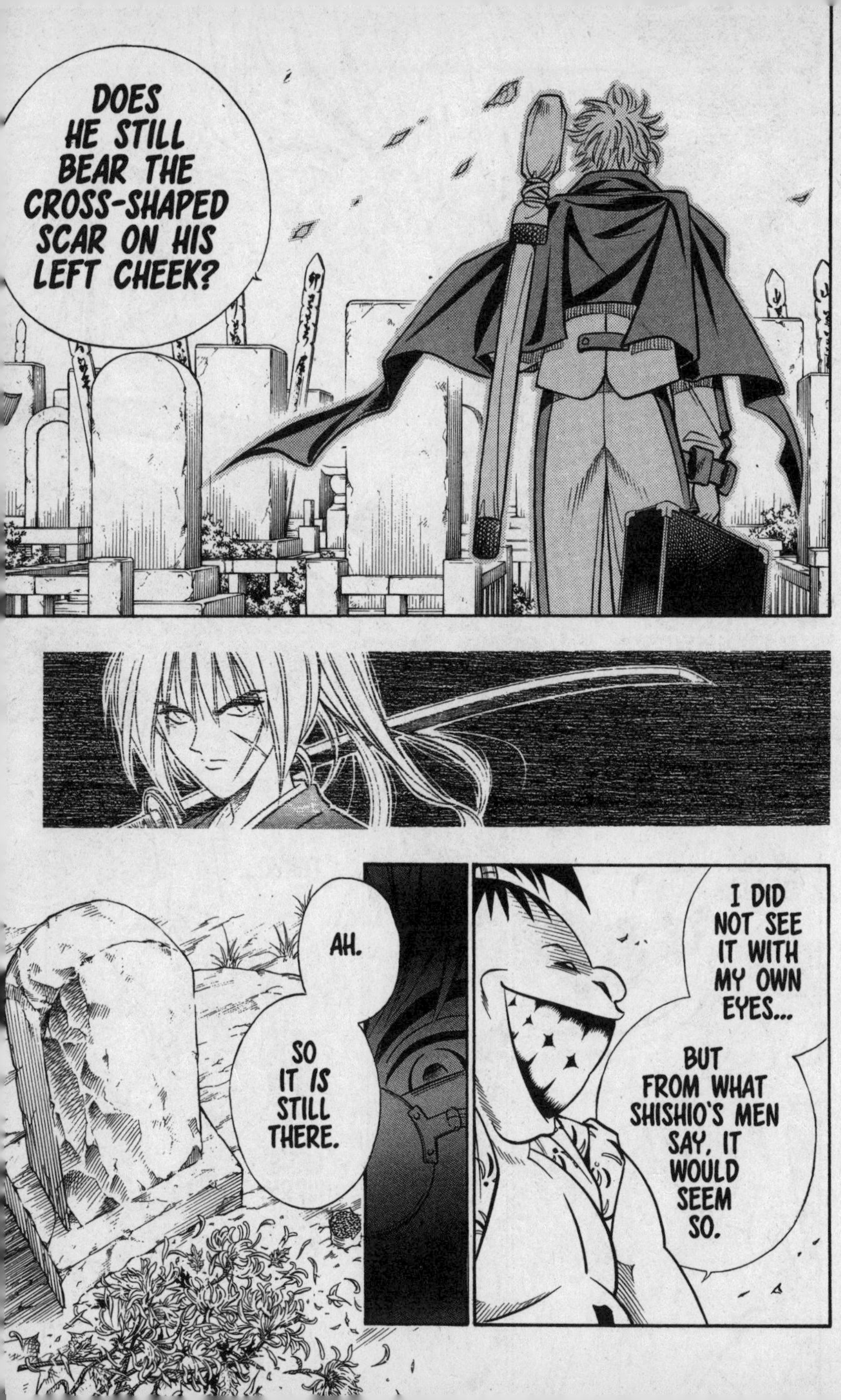
DOES HE STILL BEAR THE CROSS-SHAPED SCAR ON HIS LEFT CHEEK?
I DID NOT SEE IT WITH MY OWN EYES...
BUT FROM WHAT SHISHIO'S MEN SAY, IT WOULD SEEM SO.
AH.
SO IT IS STILL THERE.

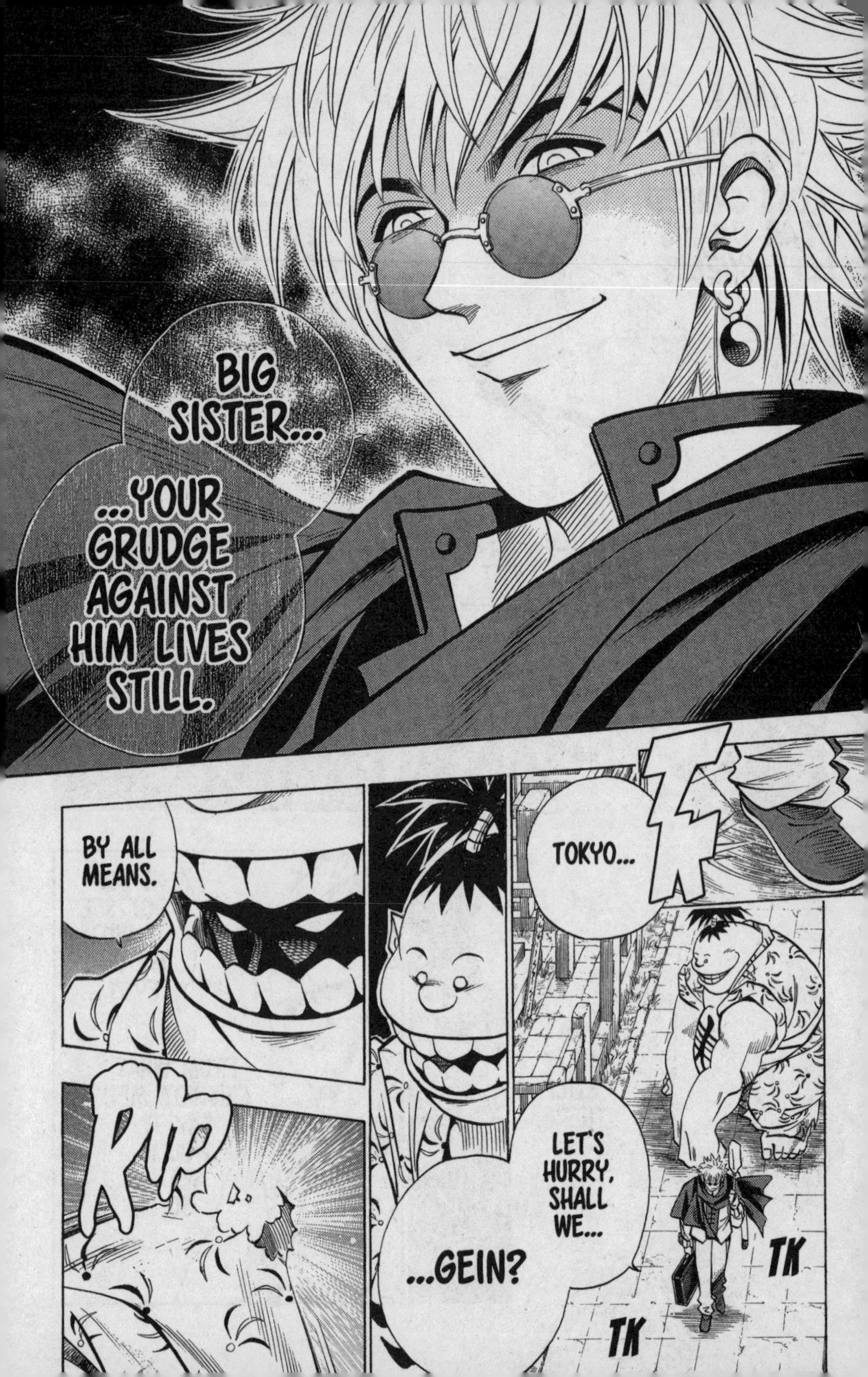
BIG SISTER...
...YOUR GRUDGE AGAINST HIM LIVES STILL.
TOKYO...
LET'S HURRY, SHALL WE...
...GEIN?
TK
TK
BY ALL MEANS.
RIP

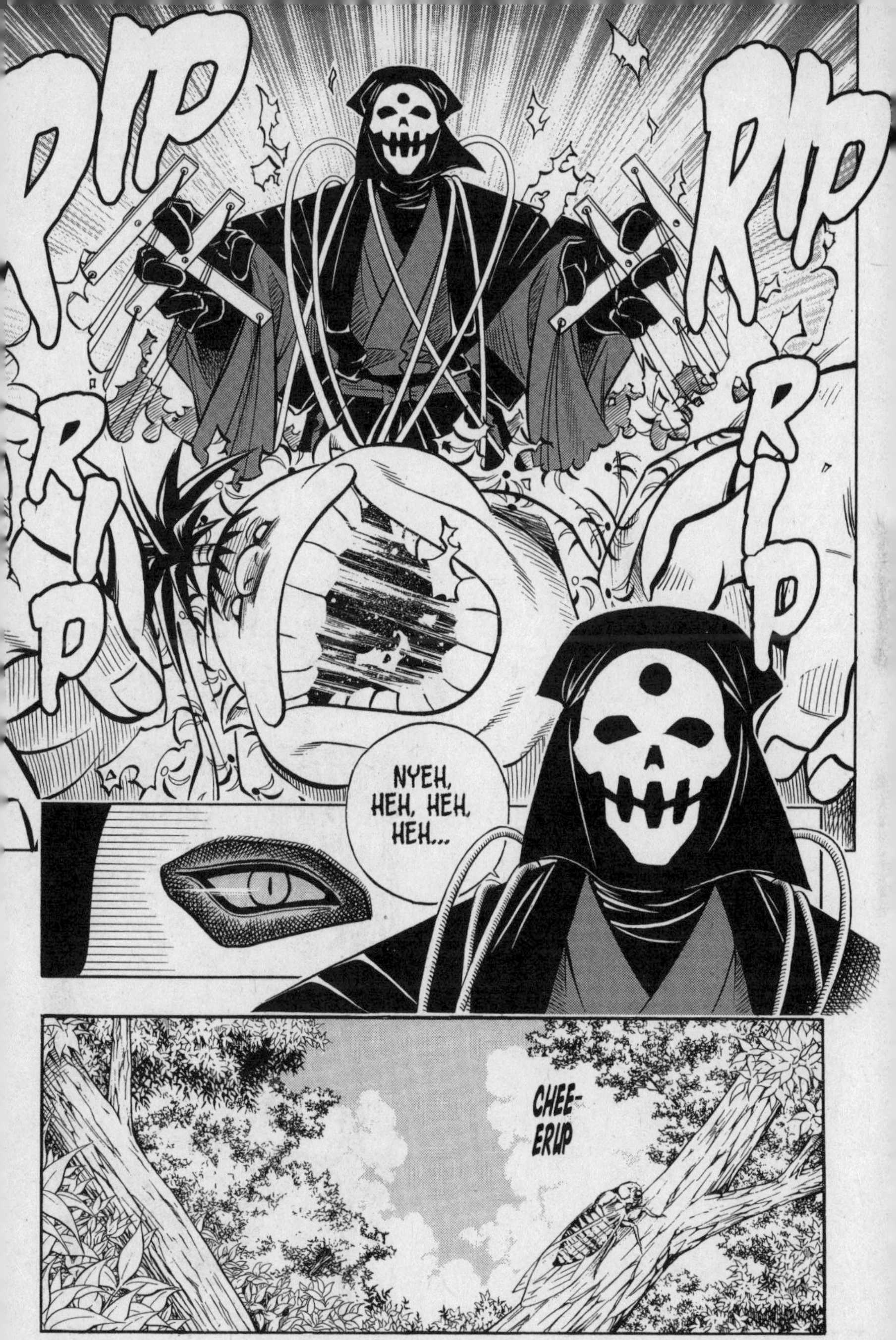
RIP
RIP
RIP
RIP
NYEH, HEH, HEH, HEH...
CHEE-ERUP

Rurouni Kenshin

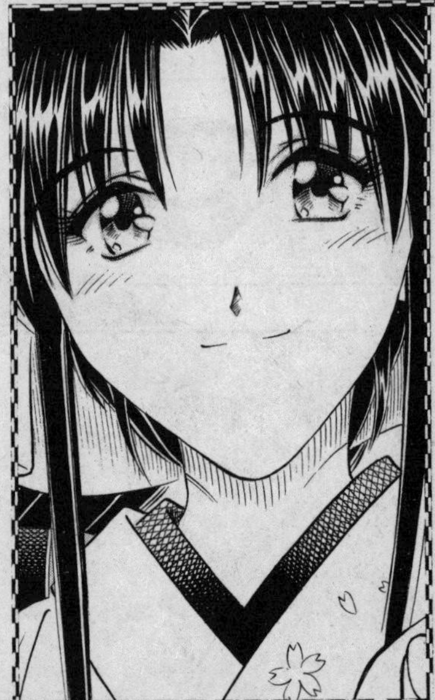

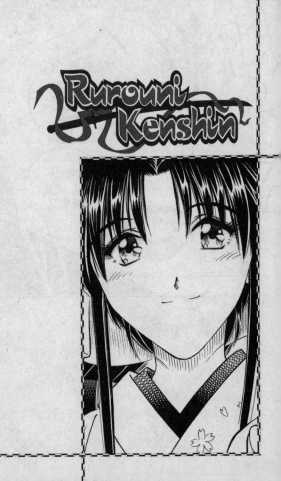

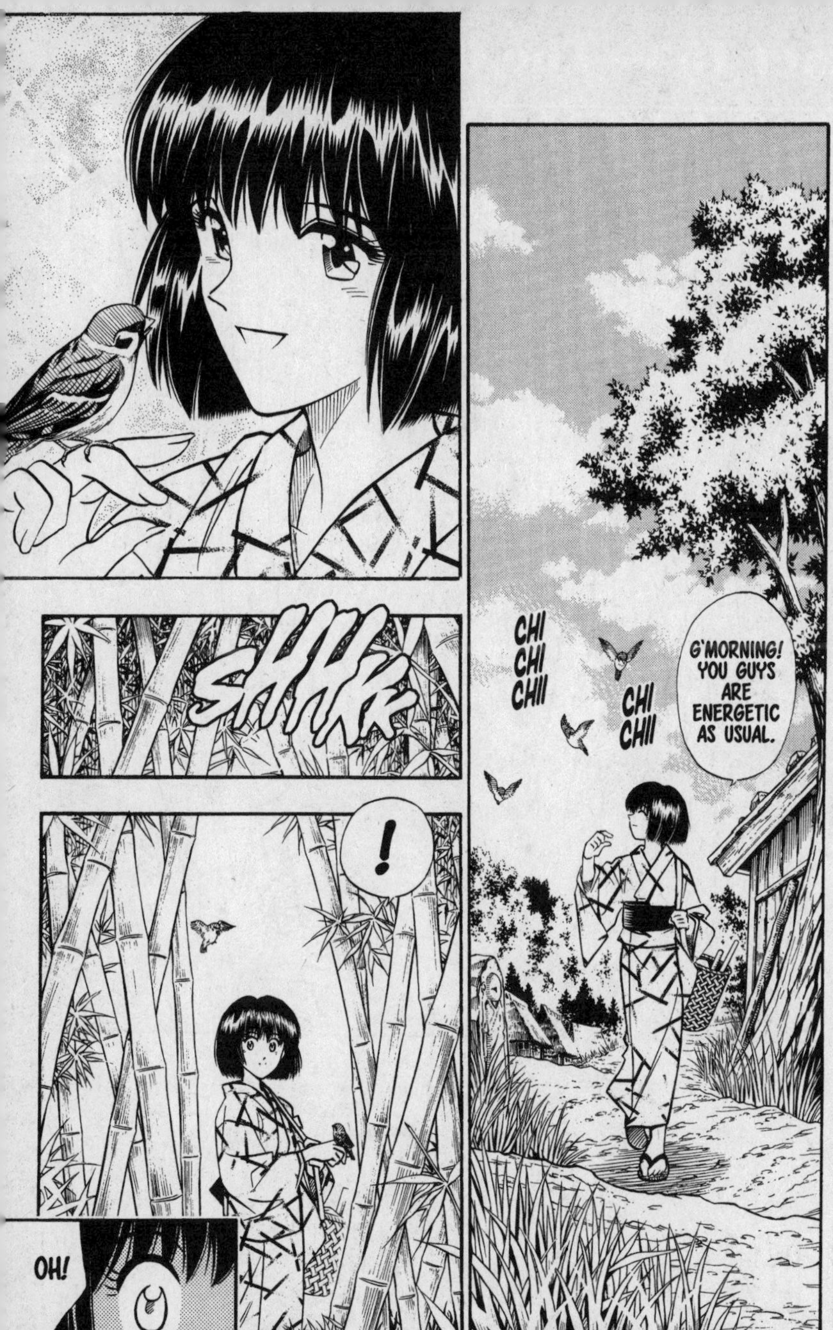
G'MORNING! YOU GUYS ARE ENERGETIC AS USUAL.
CHI CHII
CHI CHI CHII
SHHK
!
OH!

Act 153
The One-Handed Man

Act 153—The One-Handed Man

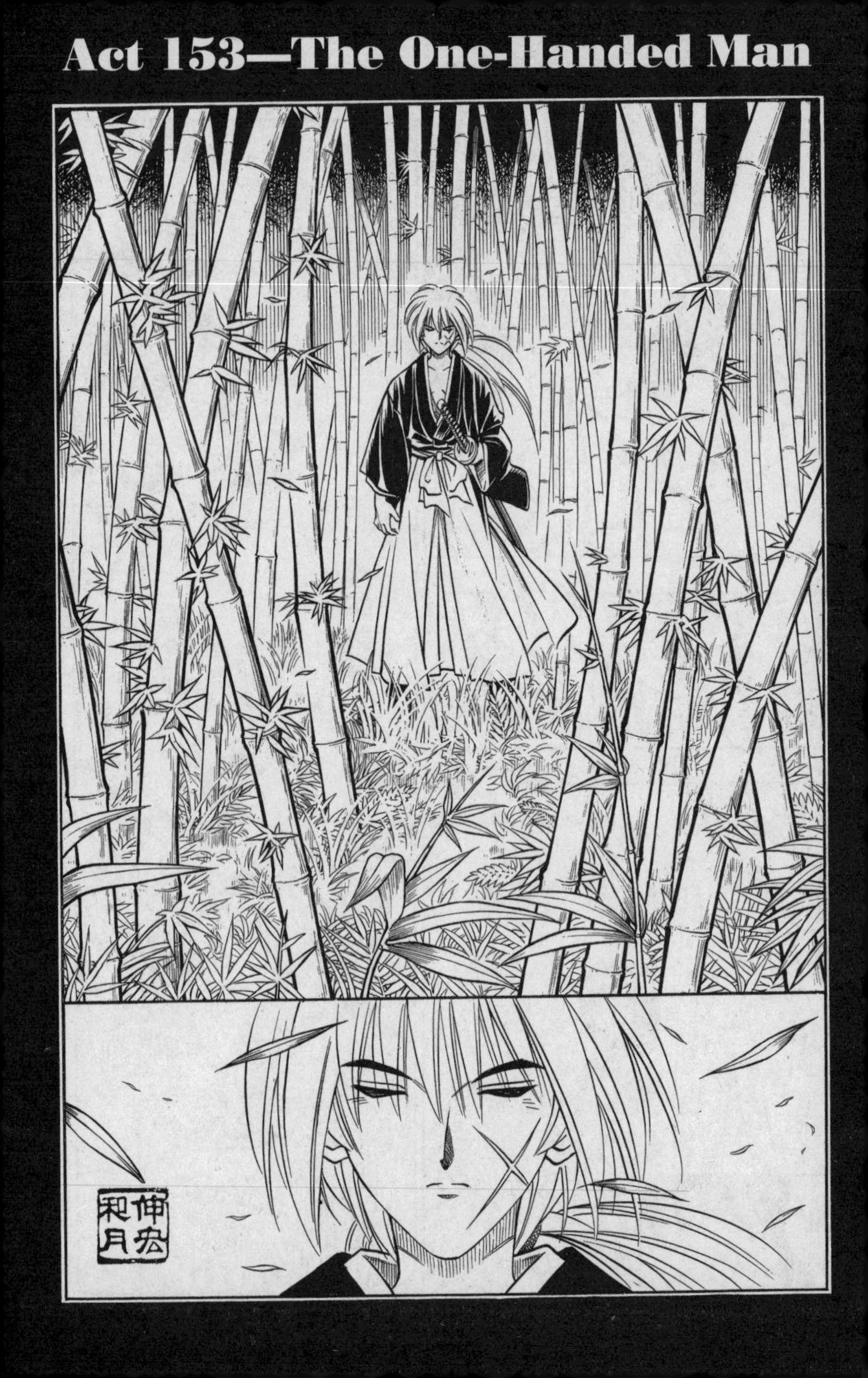
和月伸宏

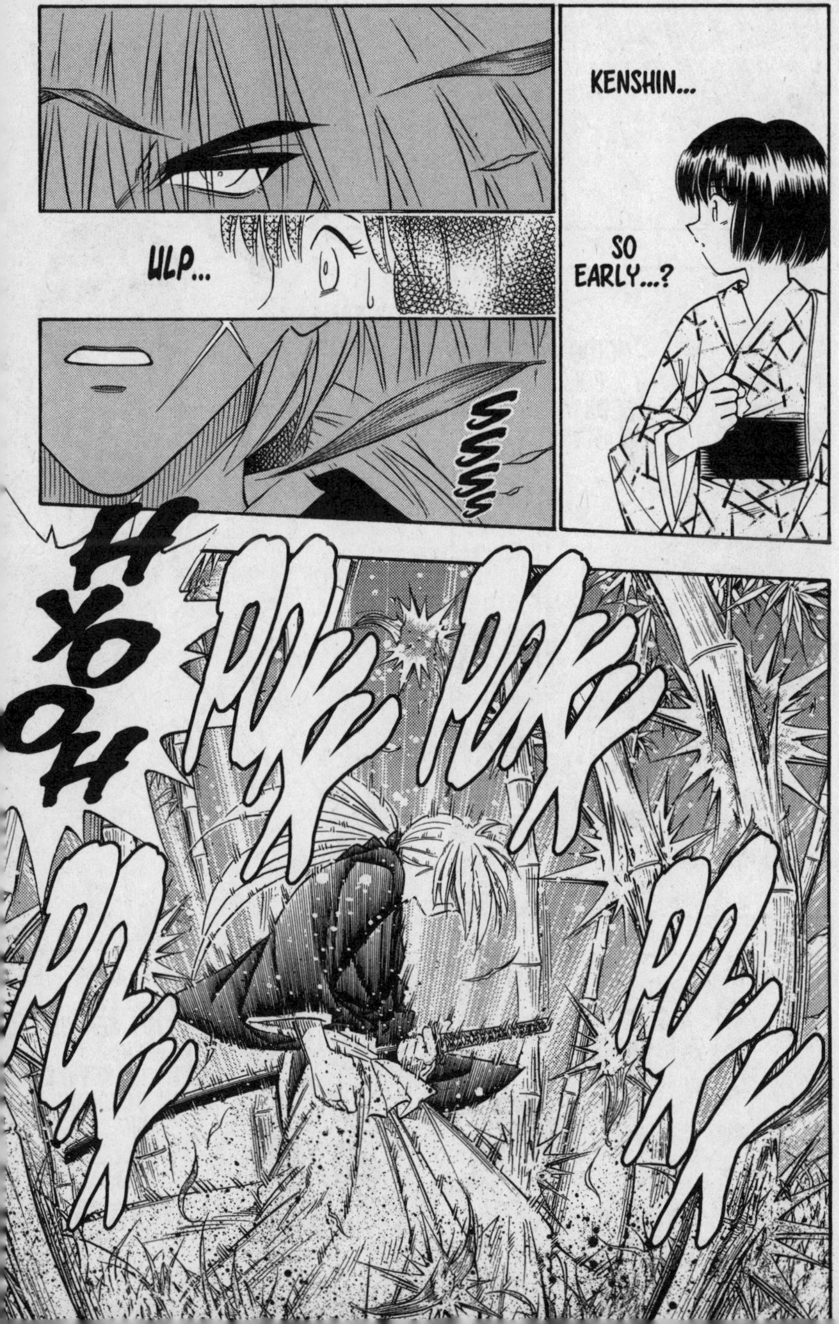
KENSHIN...
SO EARLY...?
ULP...
SSSSS
HYOOH
PLK
PLK
PLK
PLK

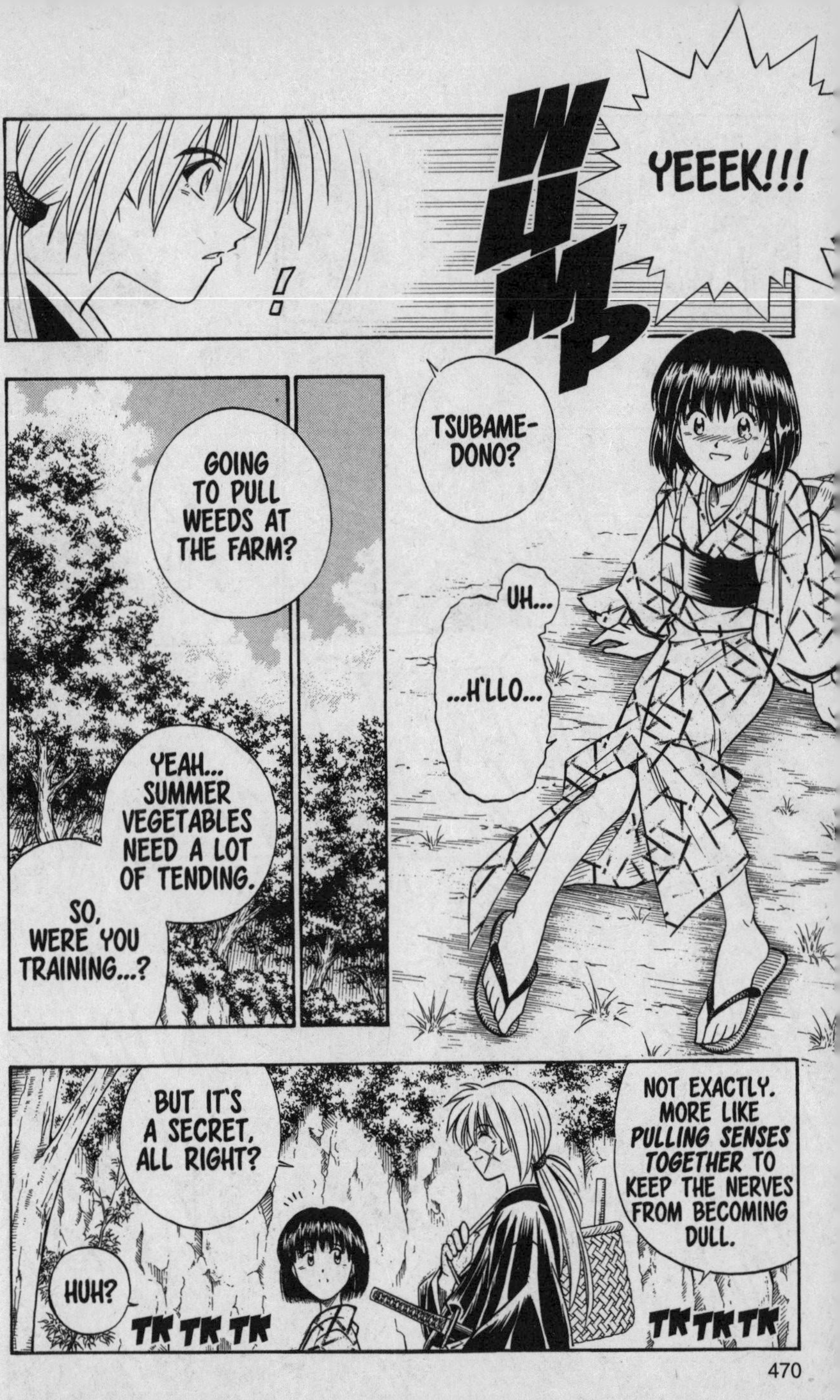
YEEEK!!!
WUMP
!
TSUBAME-DONO?
UH...
...H'LLO...
GOING TO PULL WEEDS AT THE FARM?
YEAH... SUMMER VEGETABLES NEED A LOT OF TENDING.
SO, WERE YOU TRAINING...?
NOT EXACTLY. MORE LIKE *PULLING SENSES TOGETHER* TO KEEP THE NERVES FROM BECOMING DULL.
TK TK TK
BUT IT'S A SECRET, ALL RIGHT?
HUH?
TK TK TK

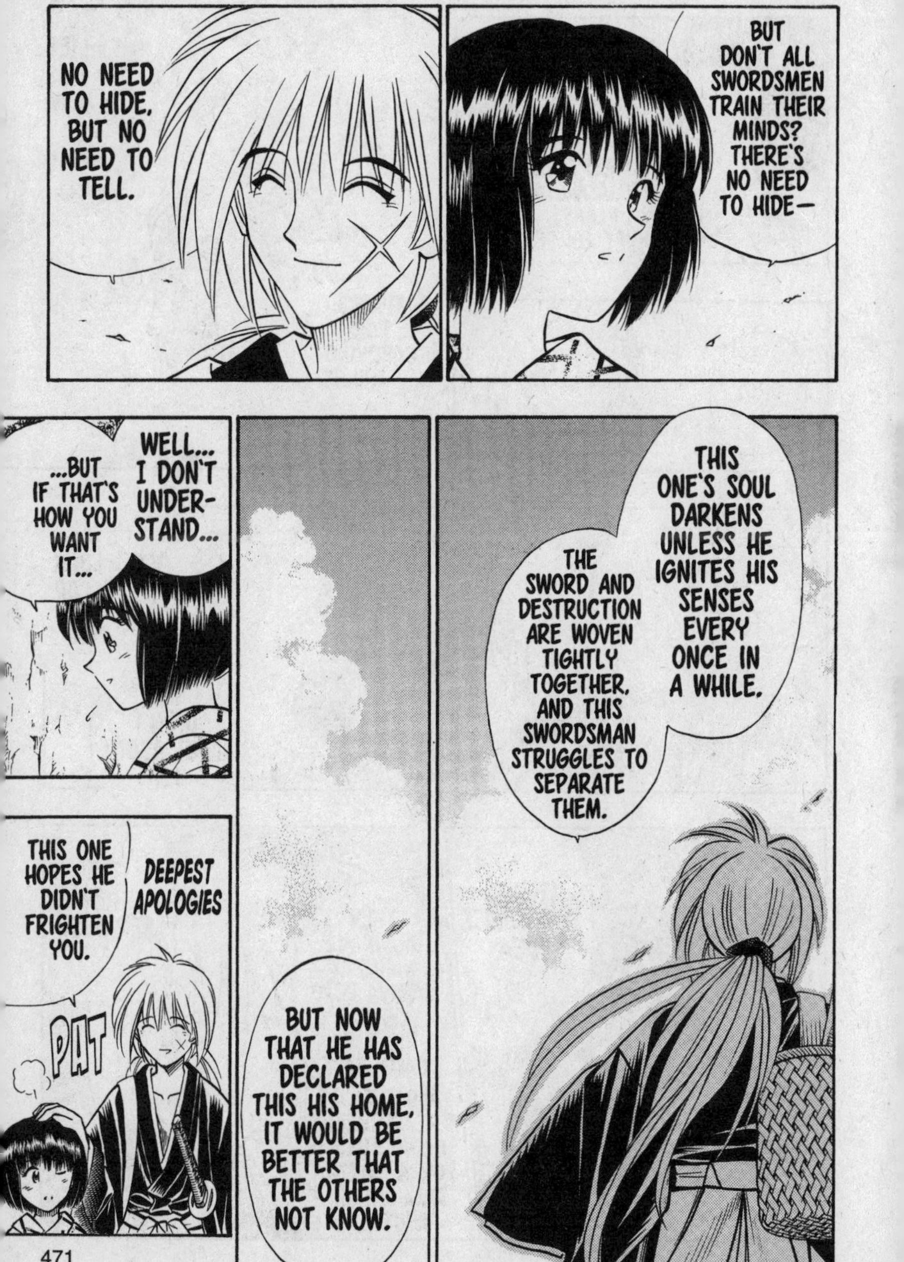
BUT DON'T ALL SWORDSMEN TRAIN THEIR MINDS? THERE'S NO NEED TO HIDE—
NO NEED TO HIDE, BUT NO NEED TO TELL.
THIS ONE'S SOUL DARKENS UNLESS HE IGNITES HIS SENSES EVERY ONCE IN A WHILE.
THE SWORD AND DESTRUCTION ARE WOVEN TIGHTLY TOGETHER, AND THIS SWORDSMAN STRUGGLES TO SEPARATE THEM.
BUT NOW THAT HE HAS DECLARED THIS HIS HOME, IT WOULD BE BETTER THAT THE OTHERS NOT KNOW.
WELL... I DON'T UNDER-STAND...
...BUT IF THAT'S HOW YOU WANT IT...
DEEPEST APOLOGIES
THIS ONE HOPES HE DIDN'T FRIGHTEN YOU.
PAT

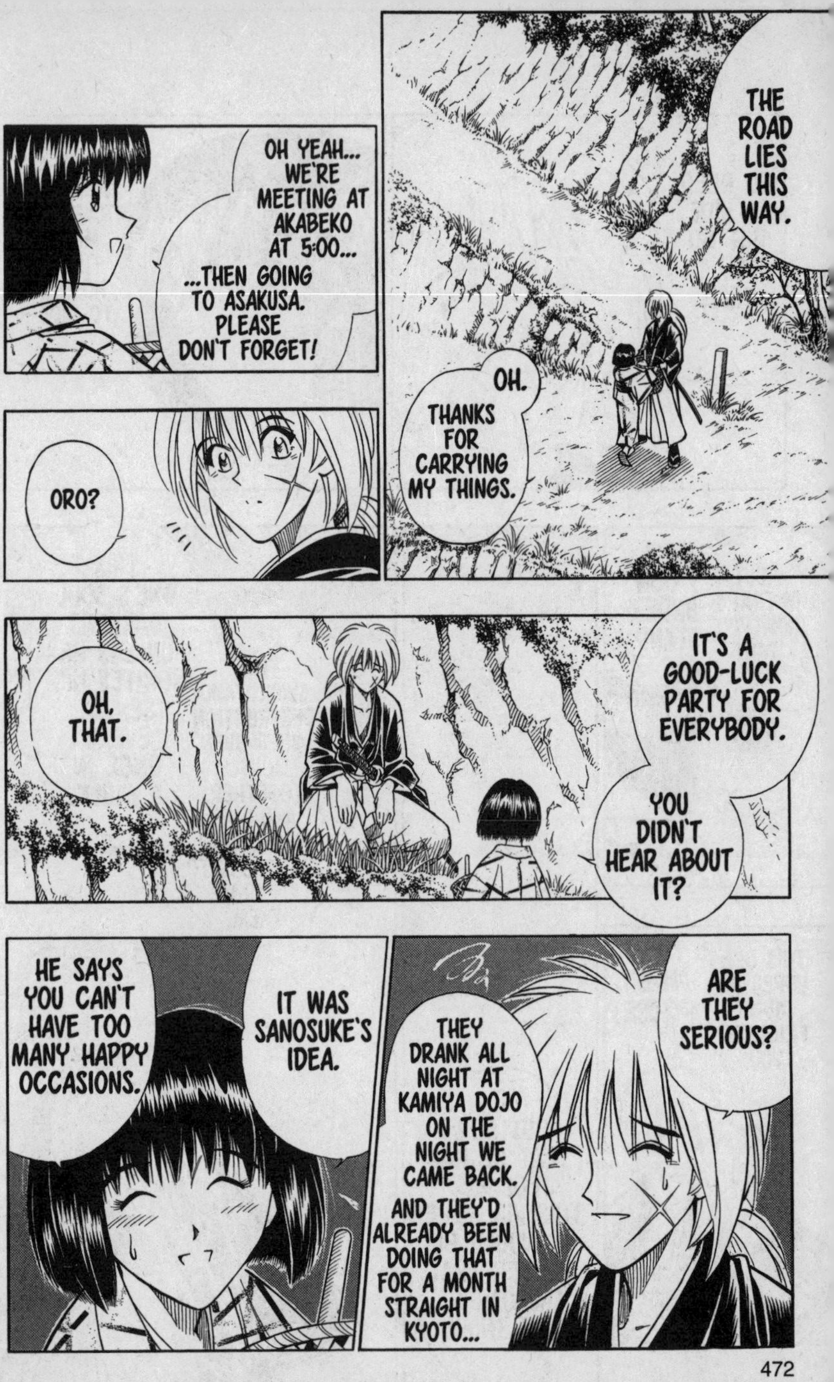
THE ROAD LIES THIS WAY.
OH.
THANKS FOR CARRYING MY THINGS.
OH YEAH... WE'RE MEETING AT AKABEKO AT 5:00...
...THEN GOING TO ASAKUSA. PLEASE DON'T FORGET!
ORO?
IT'S A GOOD-LUCK PARTY FOR EVERYBODY.
YOU DIDN'T HEAR ABOUT IT?
OH, THAT.
ARE THEY SERIOUS?
THEY DRANK ALL NIGHT AT KAMIYA DOJO ON THE NIGHT WE CAME BACK.
AND THEY'D ALREADY BEEN DOING THAT FOR A MONTH STRAIGHT IN KYOTO...
IT WAS SANOSUKE'S IDEA.
HE SAYS YOU CAN'T HAVE TOO MANY HAPPY OCCASIONS.

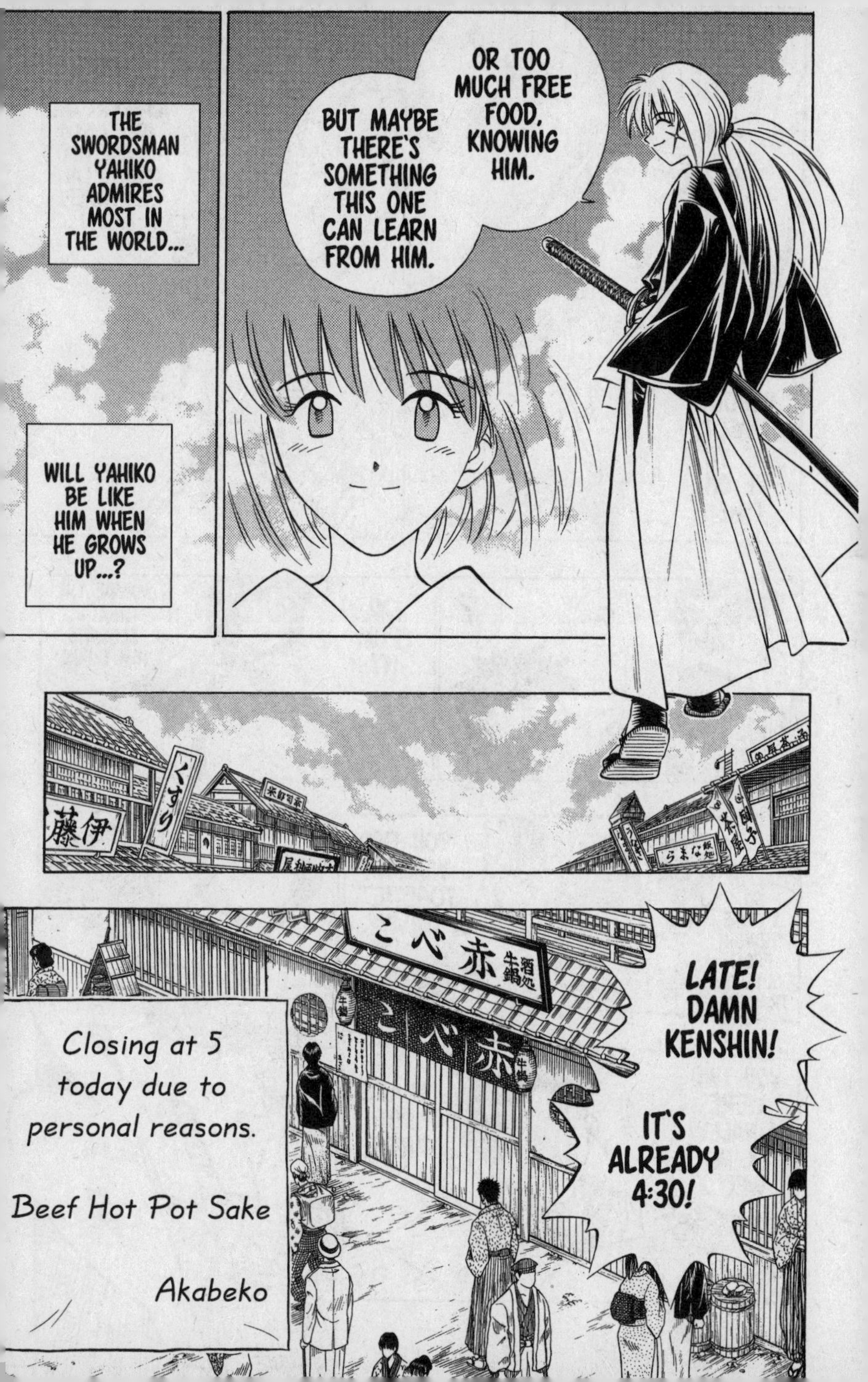
BUT MAYBE THERE'S SOMETHING THIS ONE CAN LEARN FROM HIM.
OR TOO MUCH FREE FOOD, KNOWING HIM.
THE SWORDSMAN YAHIKO ADMIRES MOST IN THE WORLD...
WILL YAHIKO BE LIKE HIM WHEN HE GROWS UP...?
LATE! DAMN KENSHIN!
IT'S ALREADY 4:30!
Closing at 5 today due to personal reasons.
Beef Hot Pot Sake
Akabeko

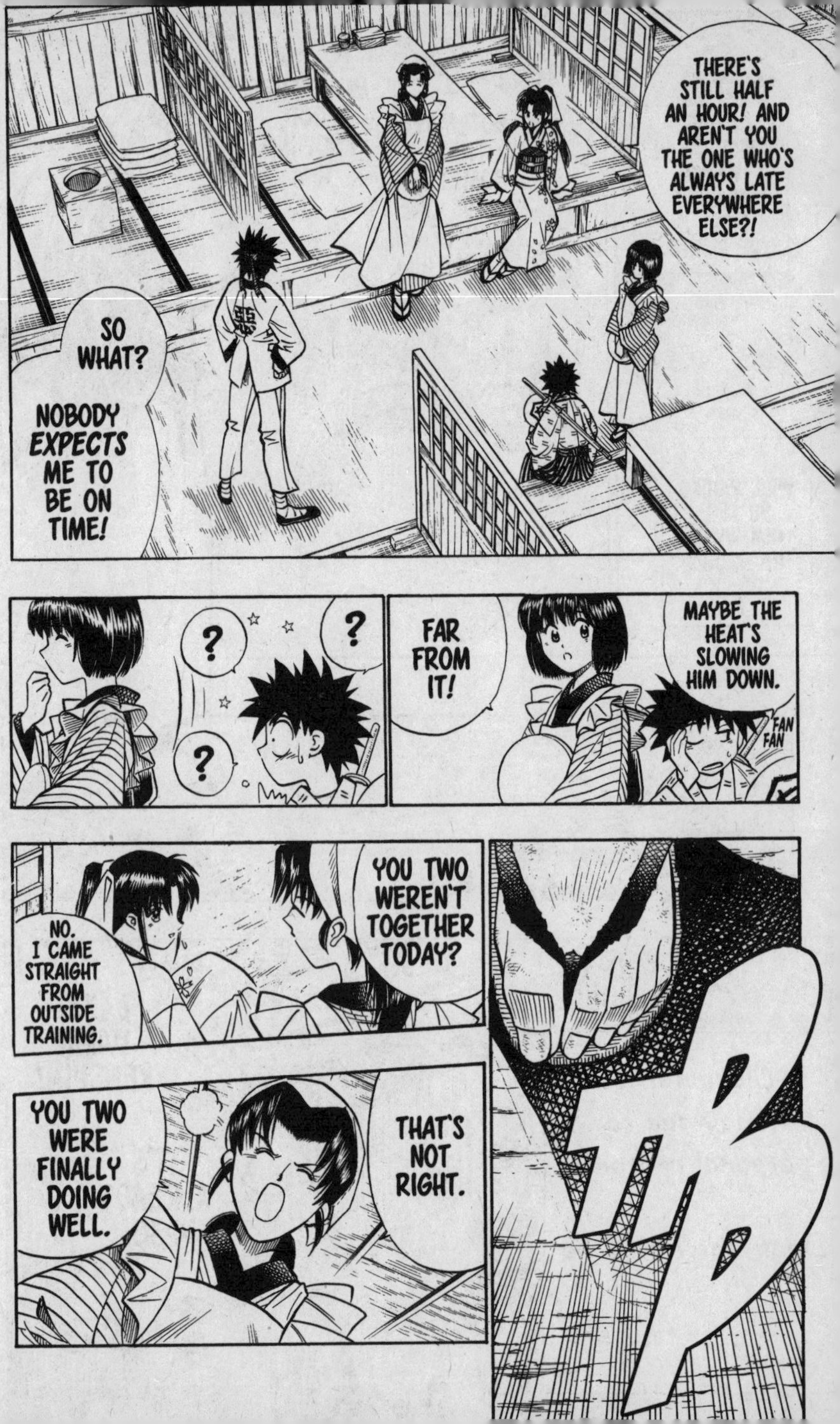
THERE'S STILL HALF AN HOUR! AND AREN'T YOU THE ONE WHO'S ALWAYS LATE EVERYWHERE ELSE?!
SO WHAT?
NOBODY EXPECTS ME TO BE ON TIME!
MAYBE THE HEAT'S SLOWING HIM DOWN.
FAN FAN
FAR FROM IT!
?
?
?
YOU TWO WEREN'T TOGETHER TODAY?
NO. I CAME STRAIGHT FROM OUTSIDE TRAINING.
THAT'S NOT RIGHT.
YOU TWO WERE FINALLY DOING WELL.

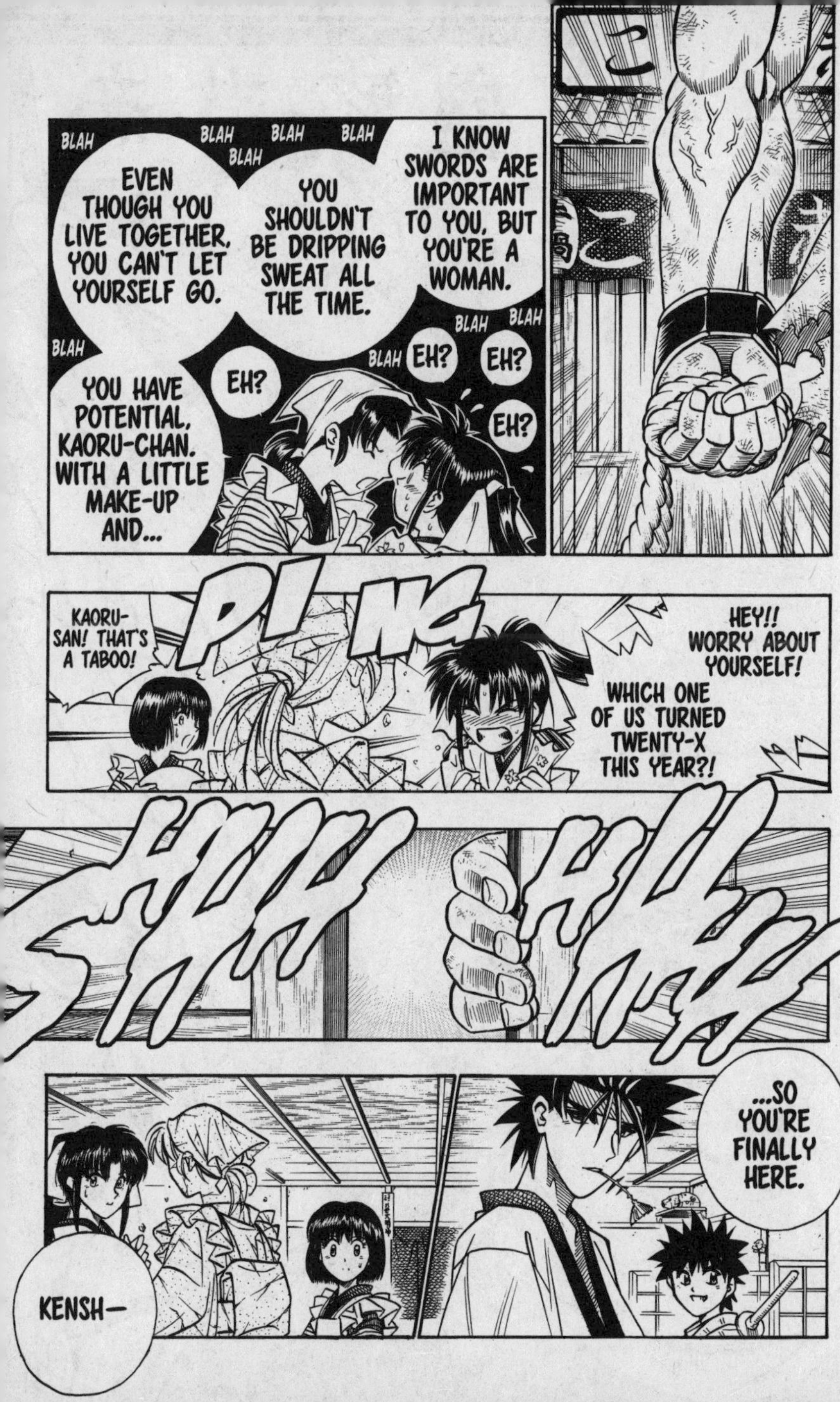
BLAH BLAH BLAH BLAH BLAH
I KNOW SWORDS ARE IMPORTANT TO YOU, BUT YOU'RE A WOMAN.
YOU SHOULDN'T BE DRIPPING SWEAT ALL THE TIME.
EVEN THOUGH YOU LIVE TOGETHER, YOU CAN'T LET YOURSELF GO.
BLAH BLAH
EH?
EH?
BLAH
EH?
BLAH
EH?
BLAH
YOU HAVE POTENTIAL, KAORU-CHAN. WITH A LITTLE MAKE-UP AND...
PING
HEY!! WORRY ABOUT YOURSELF!
WHICH ONE OF US TURNED TWENTY-X THIS YEAR?!
KAORU-SAN! THAT'S A TABOO!
...SO YOU'RE FINALLY HERE.
KENSH—

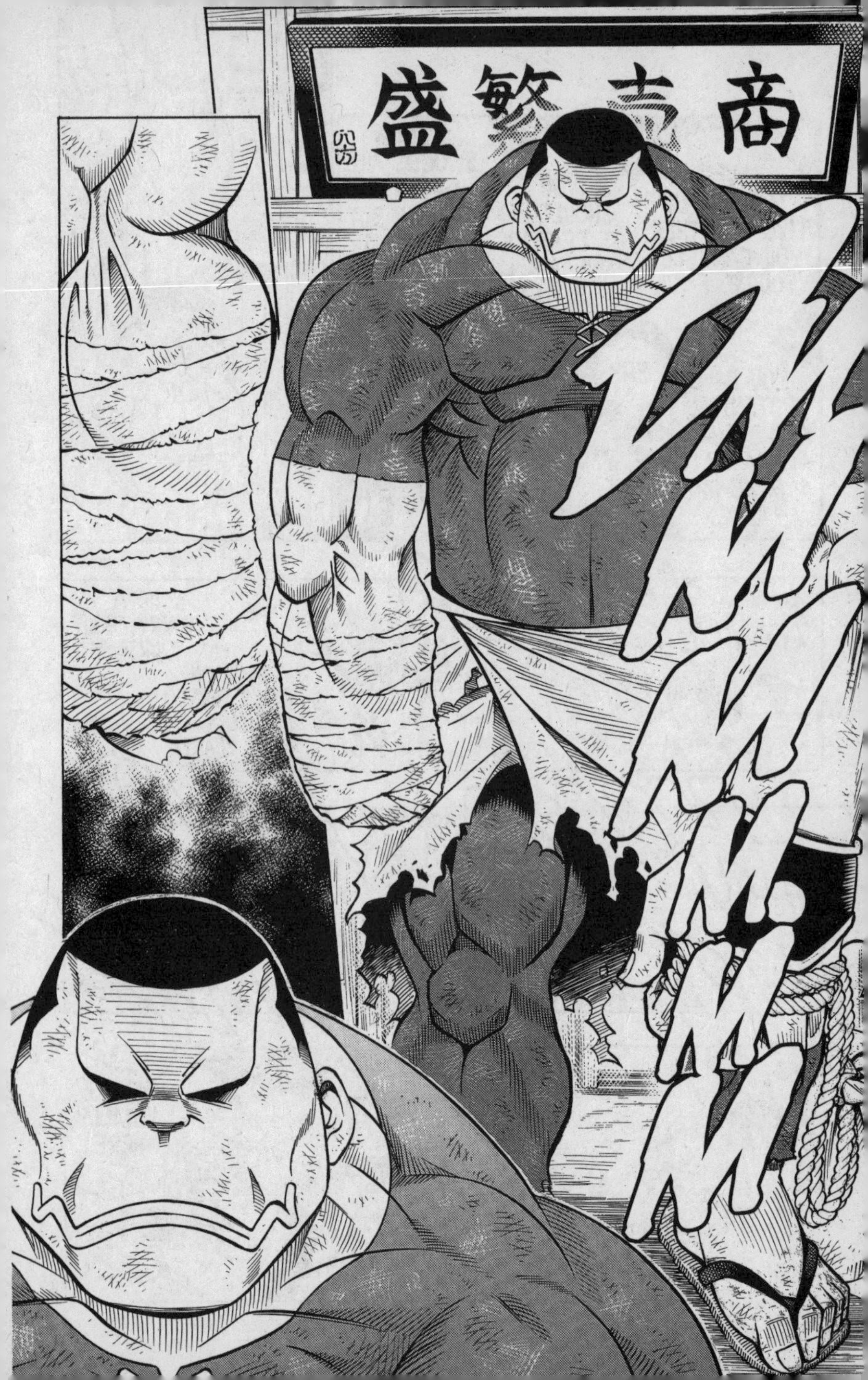
商売繁盛

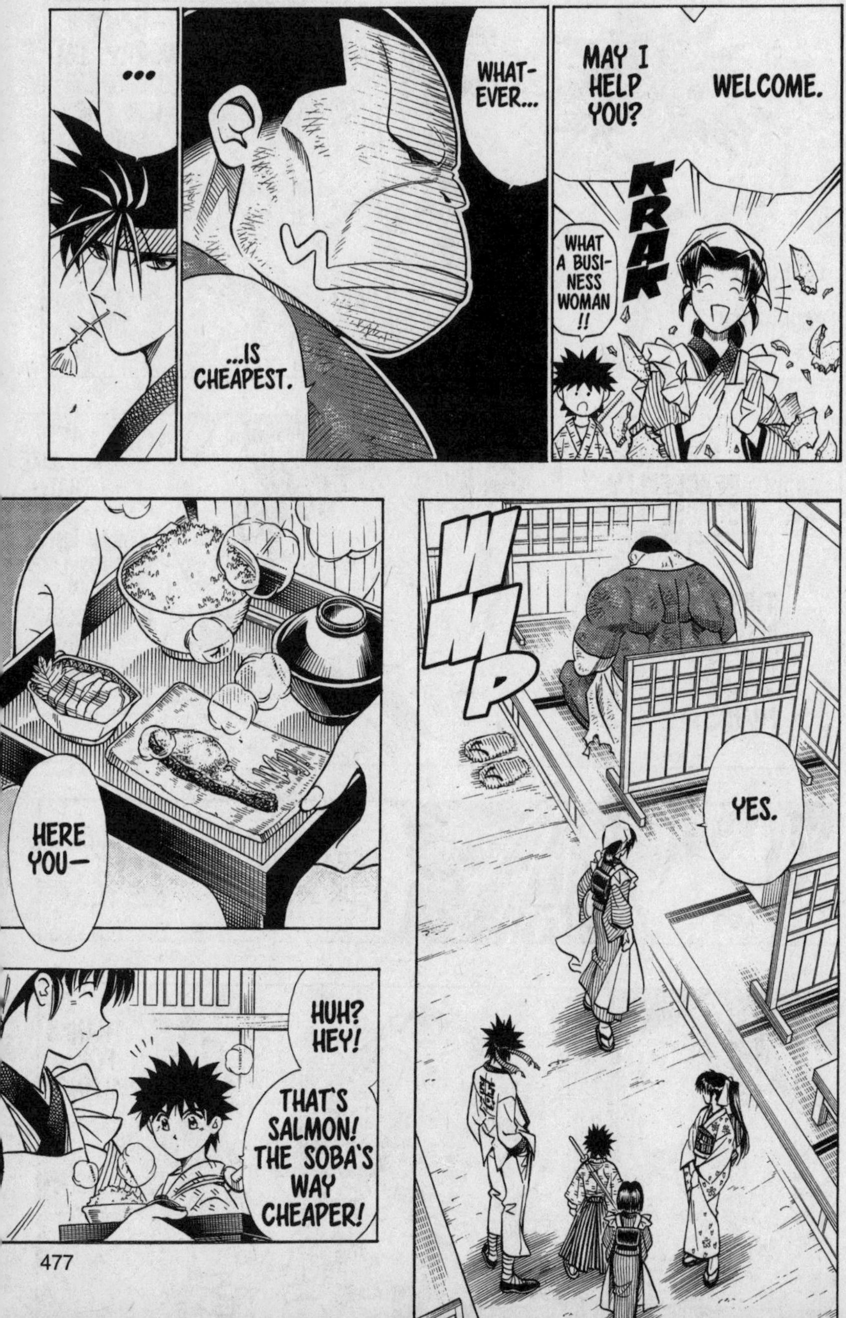
WELCOME.
MAY I HELP YOU?
KRAK
WHAT A BUSINESS WOMAN!!
WHAT-EVER...
...IS CHEAPEST.
...
WMP
YES.
HERE YOU—
HUH? HEY!
THAT'S SALMON! THE SOBA'S WAY CHEAPER!

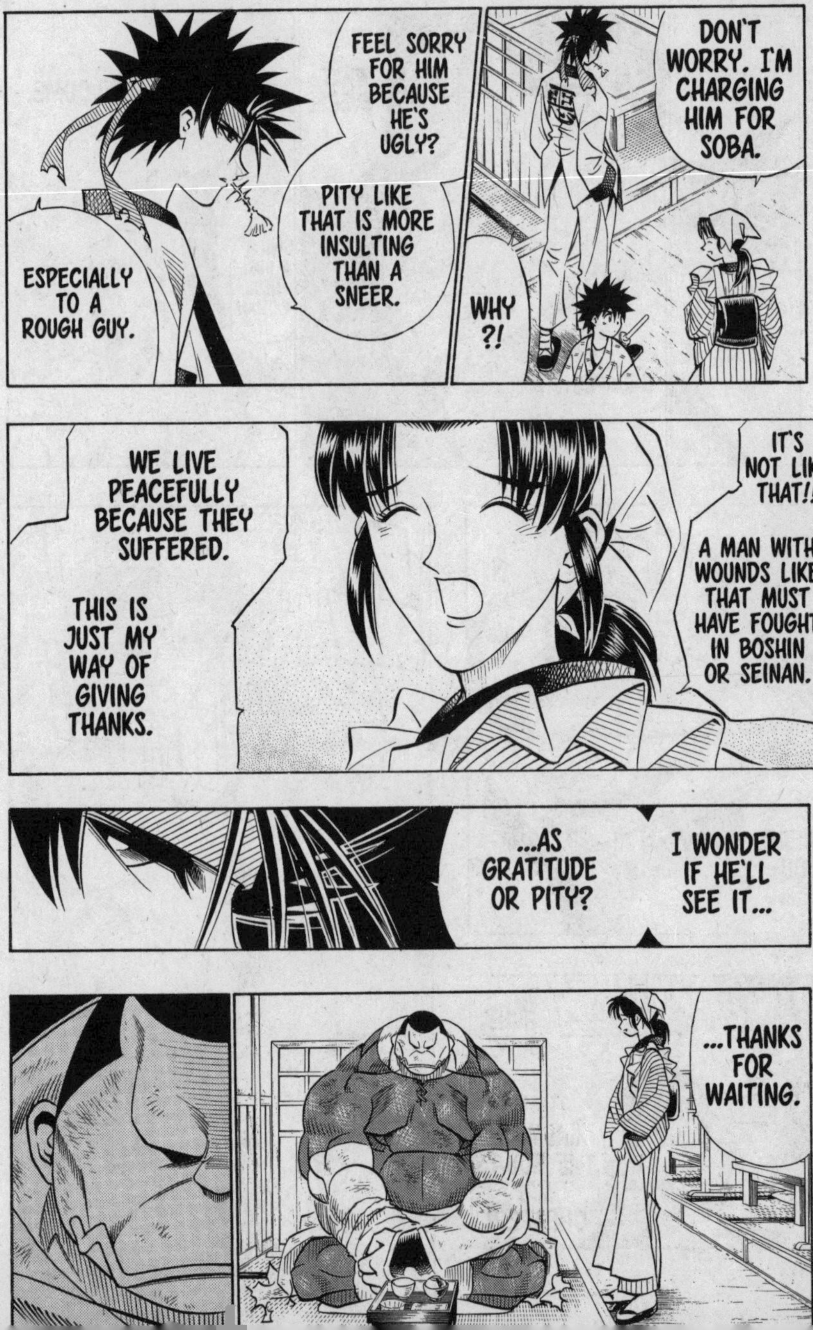
DON'T WORRY. I'M CHARGING HIM FOR SOBA.
WHY ?!
FEEL SORRY FOR HIM BECAUSE HE'S UGLY?
PITY LIKE THAT IS MORE INSULTING THAN A SNEER.
ESPECIALLY TO A ROUGH GUY.
IT'S NOT LIKE THAT!!
A MAN WITH WOUNDS LIKE THAT MUST HAVE FOUGHT IN BOSHIN OR SEINAN.
WE LIVE PEACEFULLY BECAUSE THEY SUFFERED.
THIS IS JUST MY WAY OF GIVING THANKS.
I WONDER IF HE'LL SEE IT...
...AS GRATITUDE OR PITY?
...THANKS FOR WAITING.

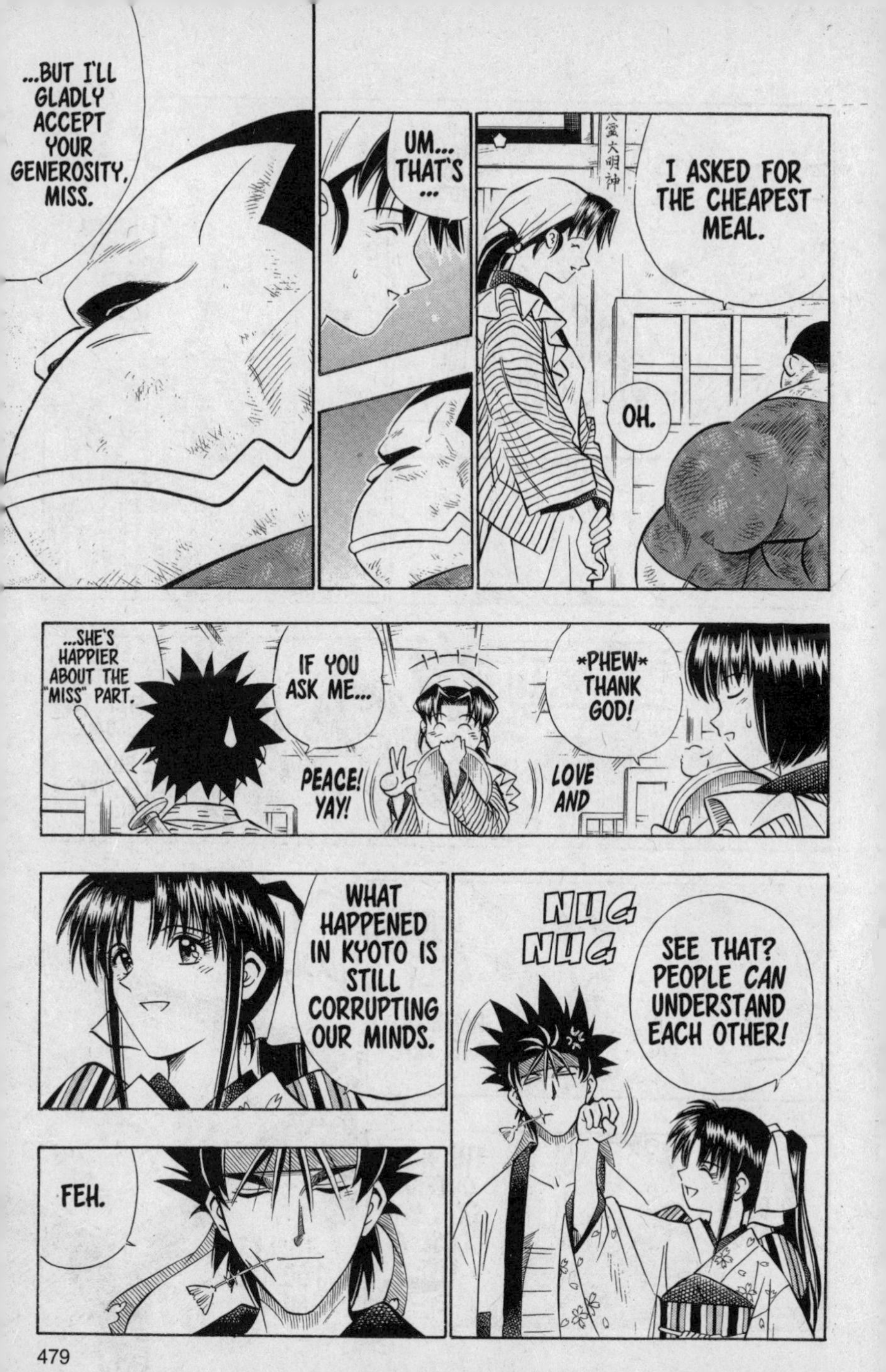
I ASKED FOR THE CHEAPEST MEAL.
OH.
UM... THAT'S ...
...BUT I'LL GLADLY ACCEPT YOUR GENEROSITY, MISS.
PHEW THANK GOD!
LOVE AND
PEACE! YAY!
IF YOU ASK ME...
...SHE'S HAPPIER ABOUT THE "MISS" PART.
NUG NUG
SEE THAT? PEOPLE CAN UNDERSTAND EACH OTHER!
WHAT HAPPENED IN KYOTO IS STILL CORRUPTING OUR MINDS.
FEH.

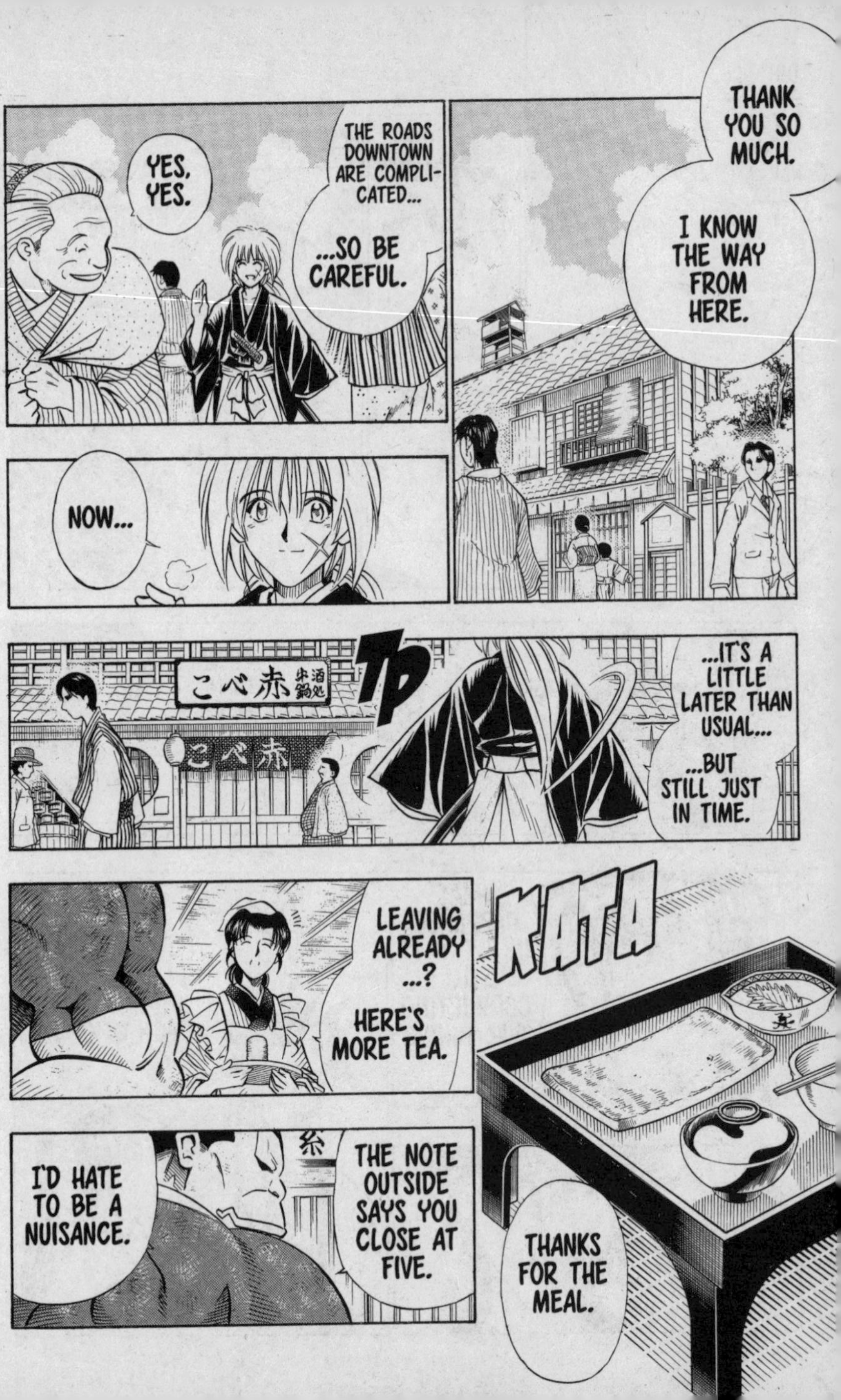
THANK YOU SO MUCH.
I KNOW THE WAY FROM HERE.
THE ROADS DOWNTOWN ARE COMPLICATED...
...SO BE CAREFUL.
YES, YES.
NOW...
...IT'S A LITTLE LATER THAN USUAL...
...BUT STILL JUST IN TIME.
TP
赤べこ
KATA
THANKS FOR THE MEAL.
LEAVING ALREADY ...?
HERE'S MORE TEA.
THE NOTE OUTSIDE SAYS YOU CLOSE AT FIVE.
I'D HATE TO BE A NUISANCE.

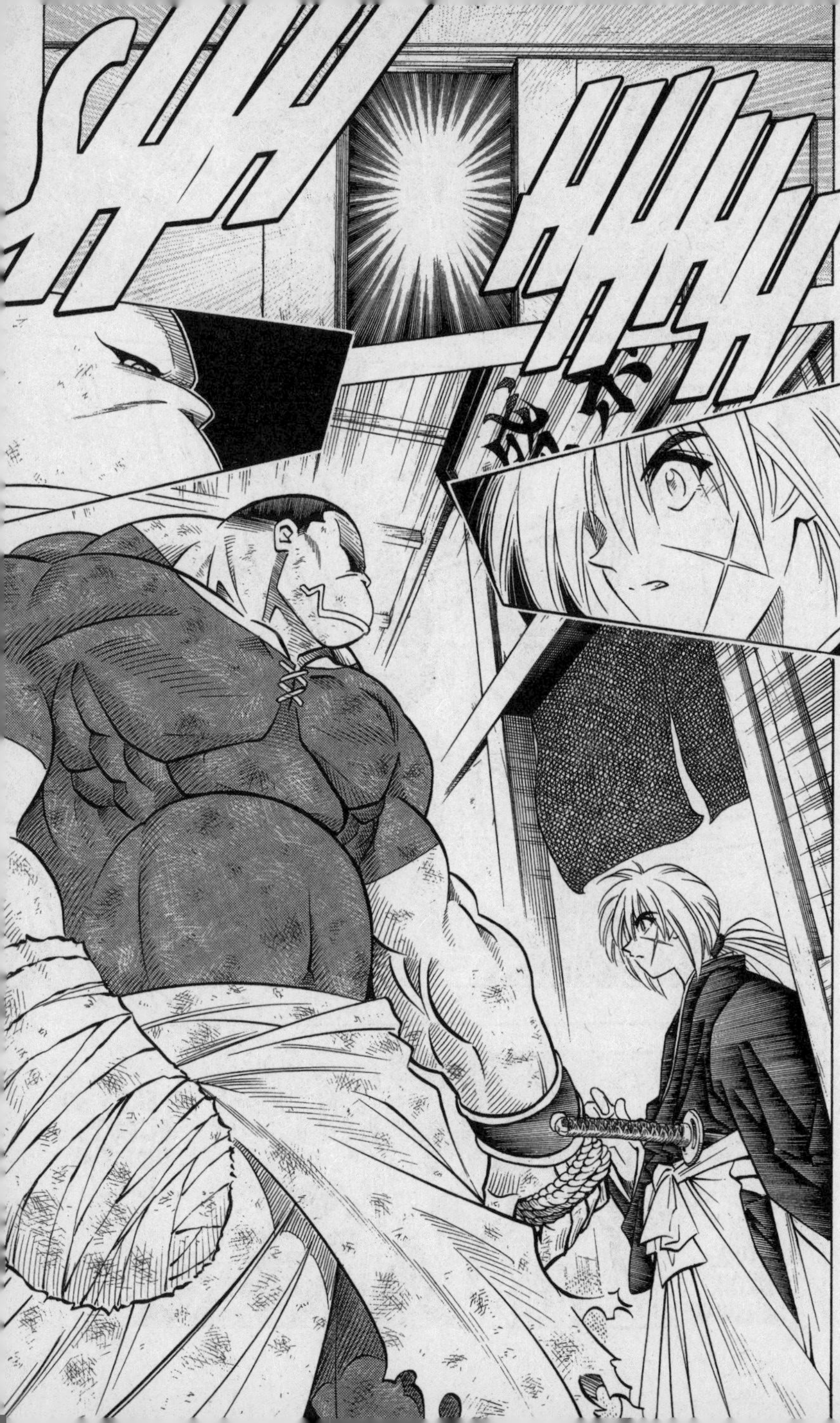
SHHHHHH

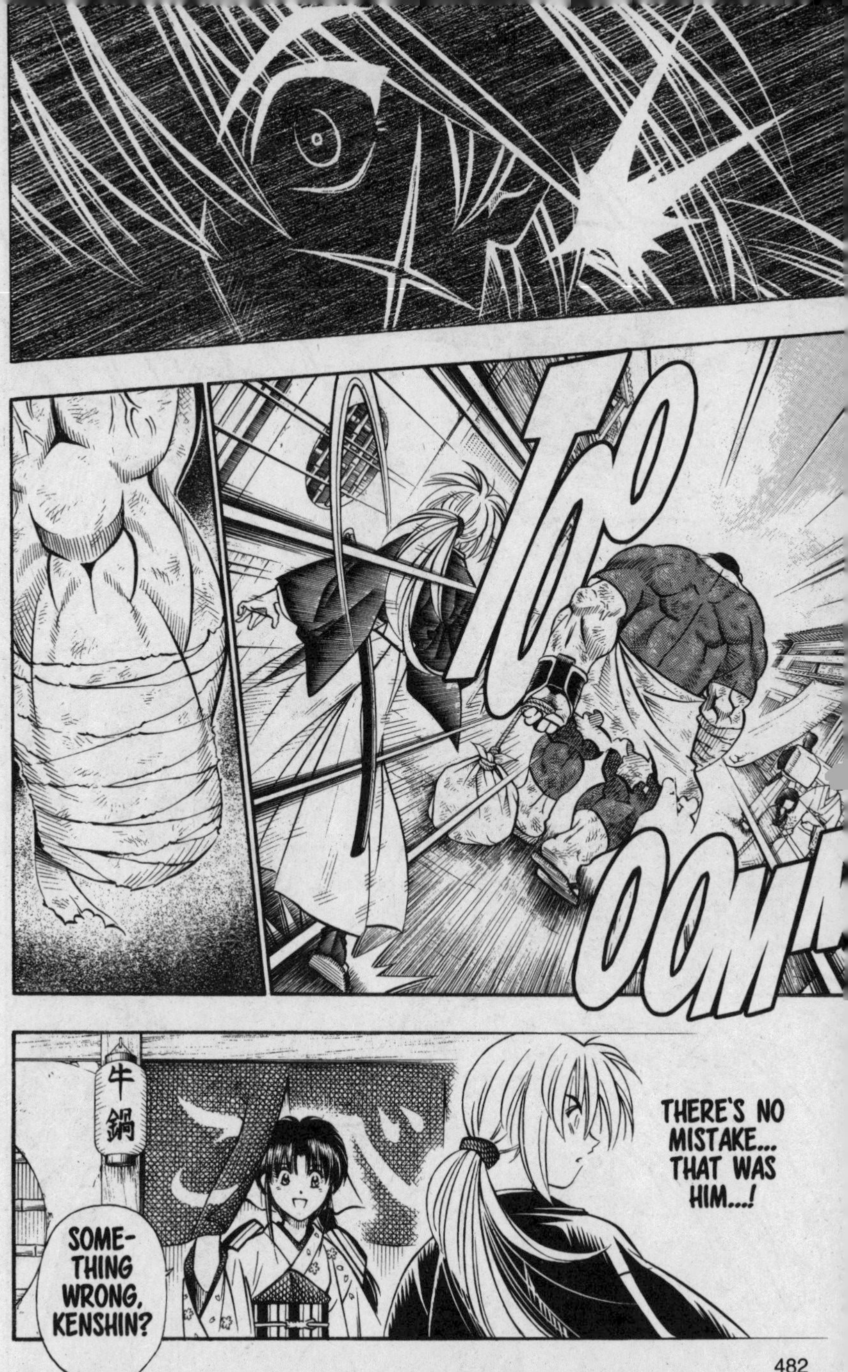
TOOOM
THERE'S NO MISTAKE... THAT WAS HIM...!
牛鍋
SOME-THING WRONG, KENSHIN?

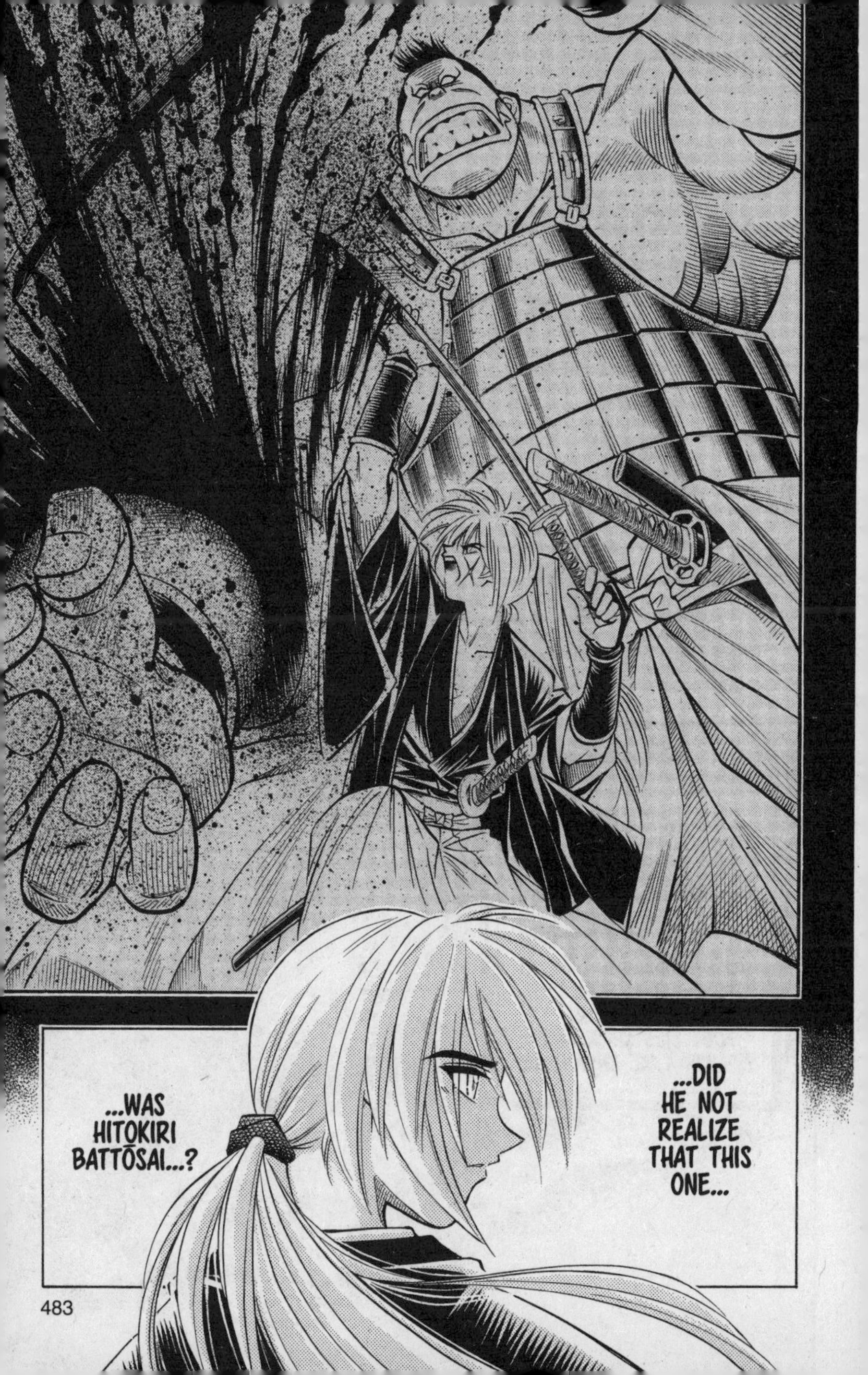
...DID HE NOT REALIZE THAT THIS ONE...
...WAS HITOKIRI BATTŌSAI...?

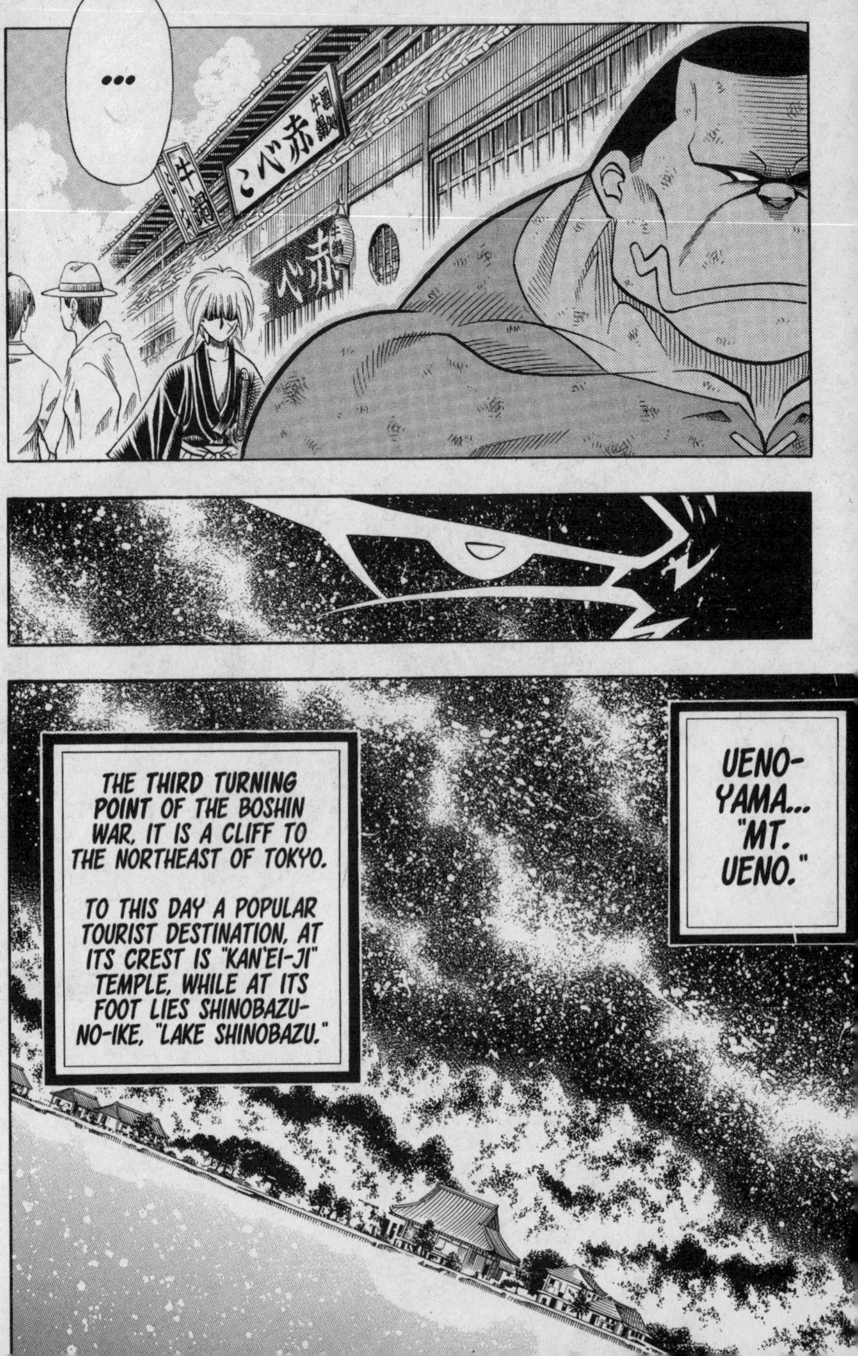
...
UENO-YAMA... "MT. UENO."
THE THIRD TURNING POINT OF THE BOSHIN WAR, IT IS A CLIFF TO THE NORTHEAST OF TOKYO.
TO THIS DAY A POPULAR TOURIST DESTINATION, AT ITS CREST IS "KAN'EI-JI" TEMPLE, WHILE AT ITS FOOT LIES SHINOBAZU-NO-IKE, "LAKE SHINOBAZU."

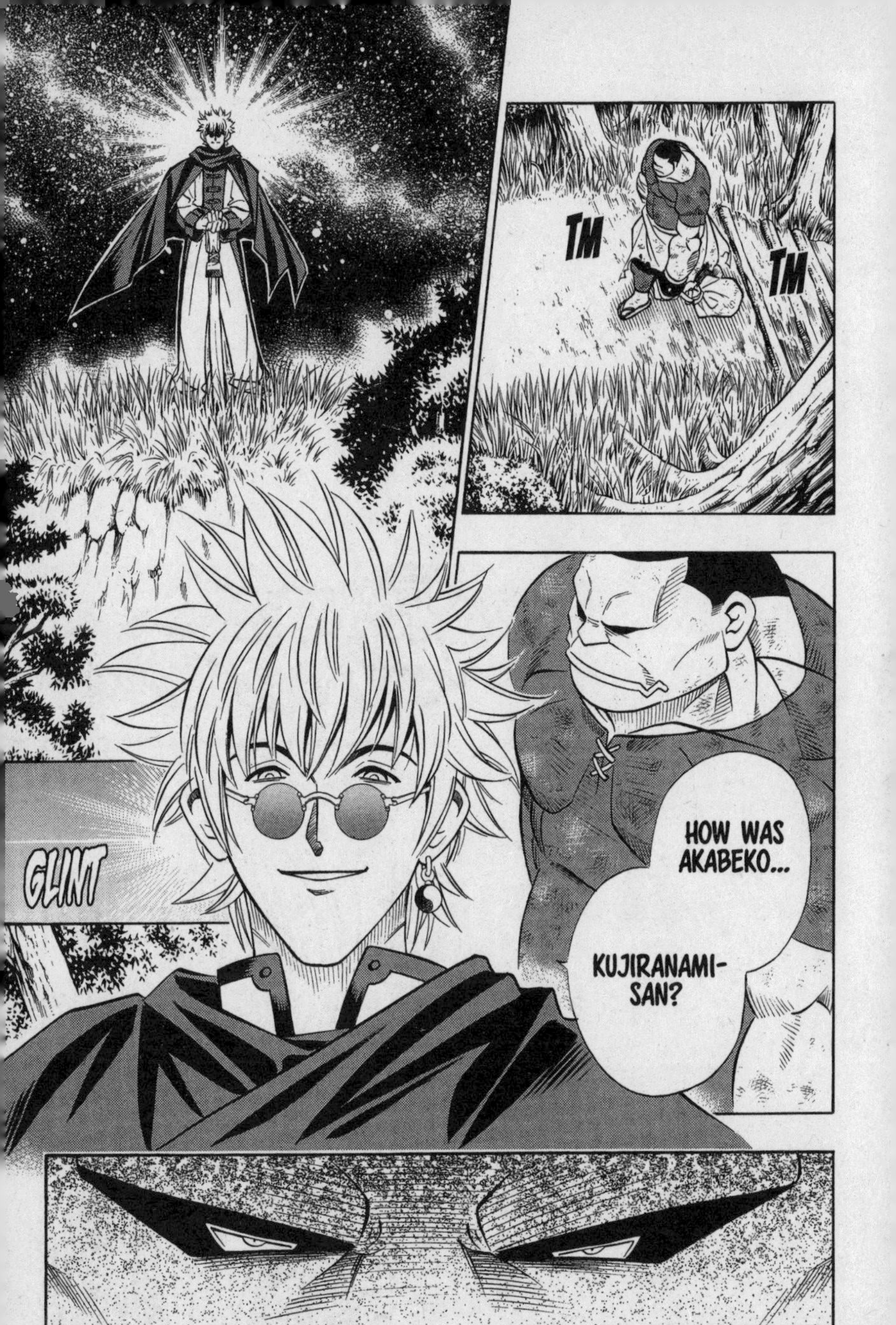
TM
TM
HOW WAS AKABEKO...
KUJIRANAMI-SAN?
GLINT

Rurouni Kenshin

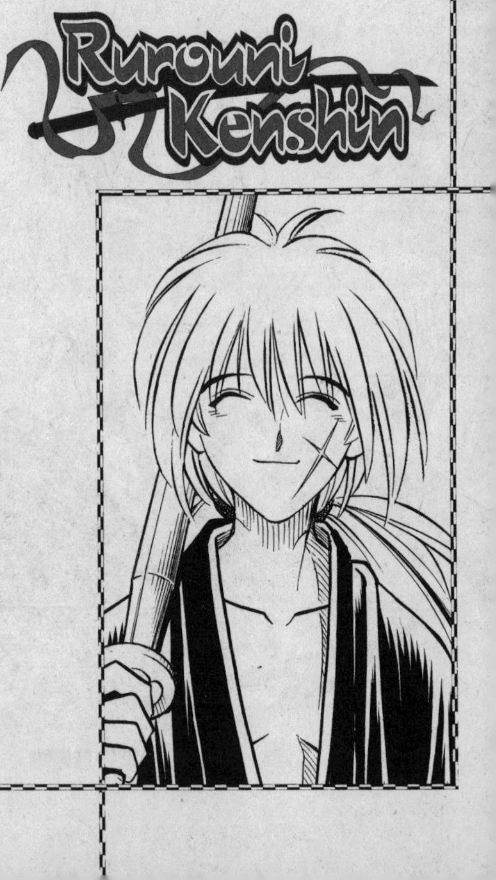

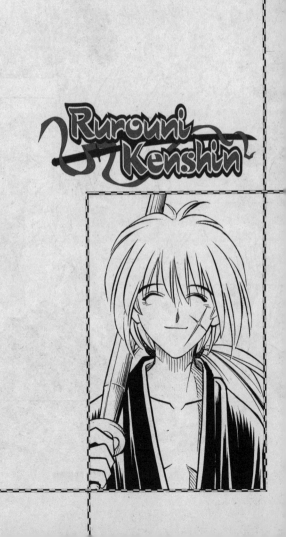

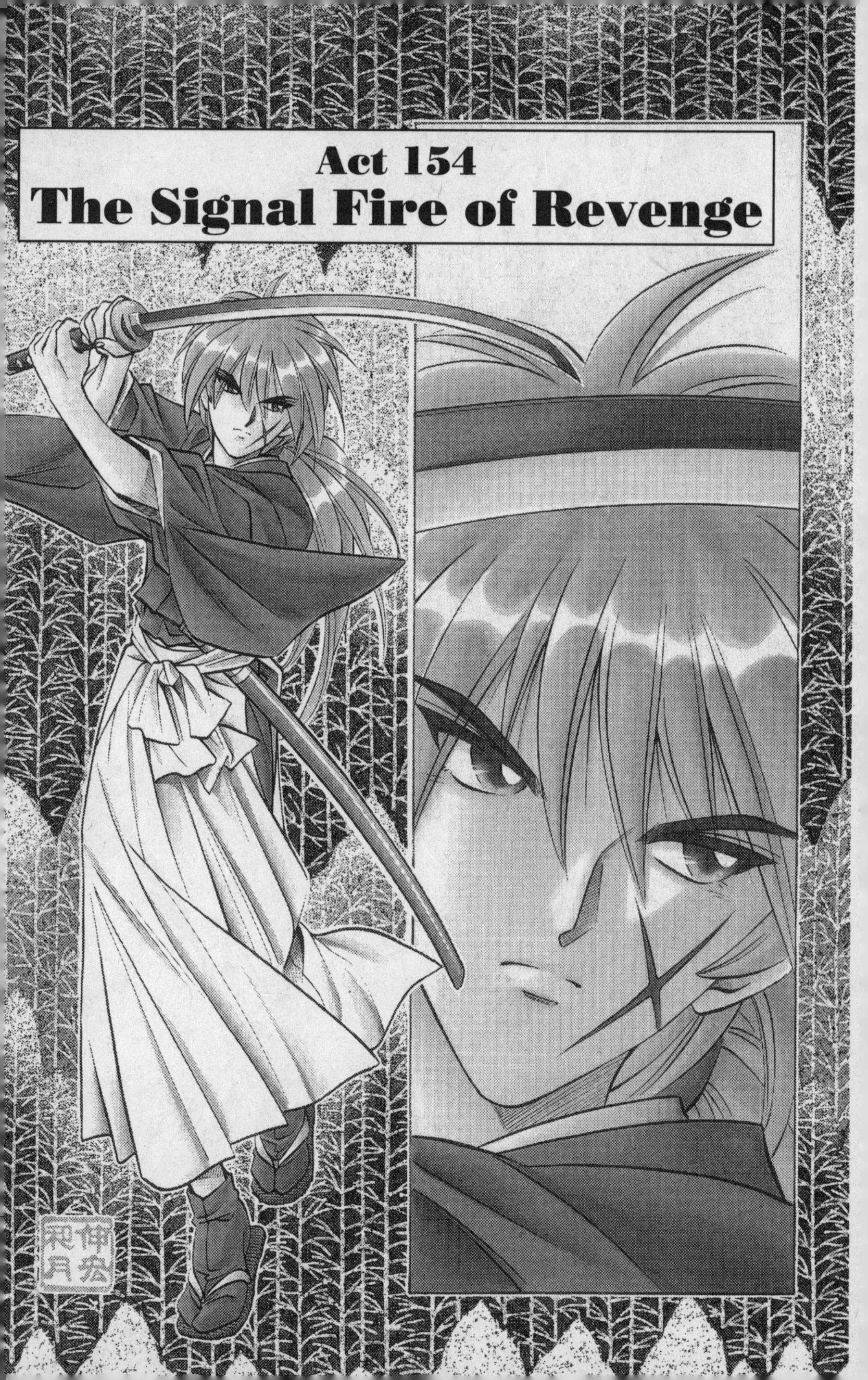
Act 154
The Signal Fire of Revenge

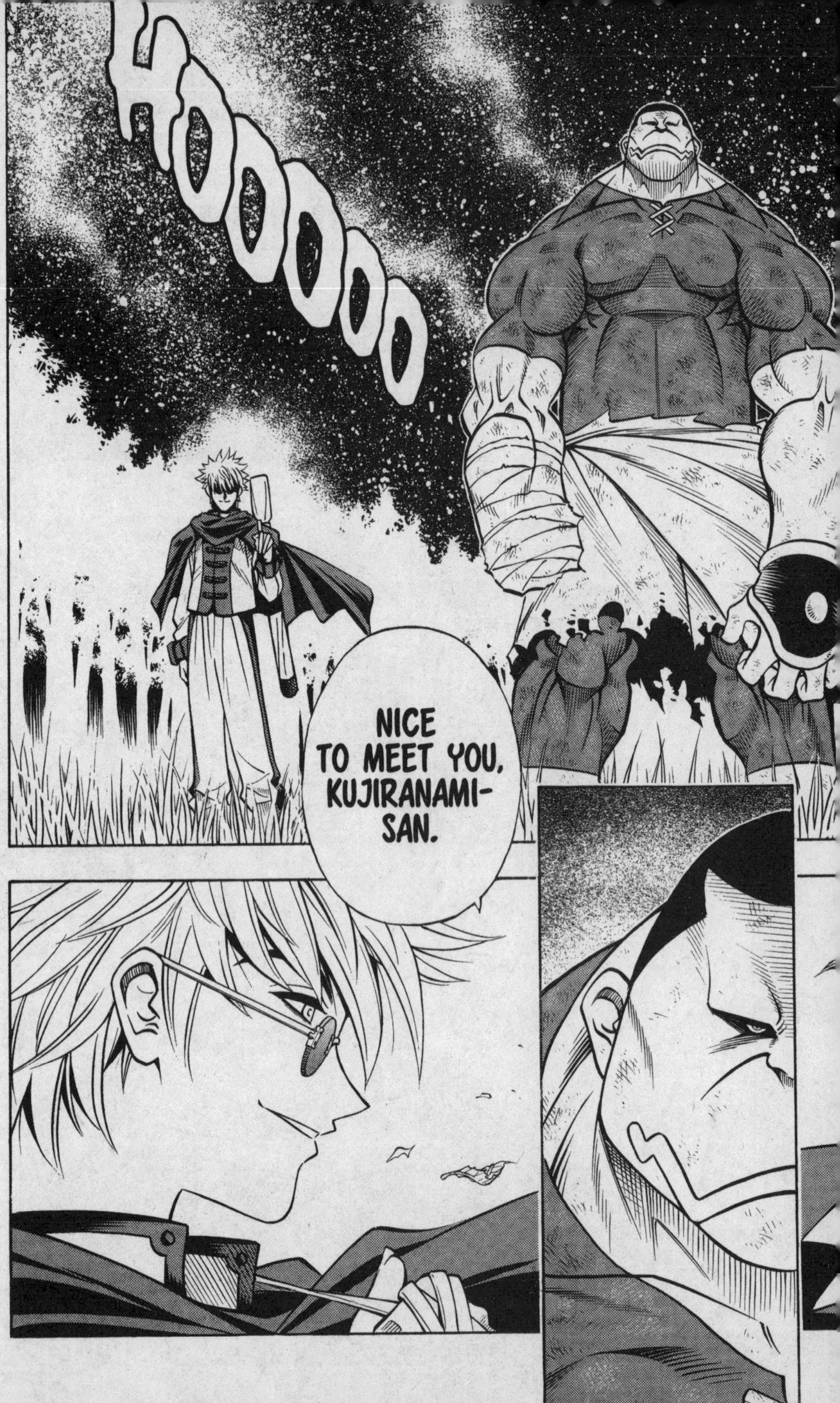
HOOOOOO
NICE TO MEET YOU, KUJIRANAMI-SAN.

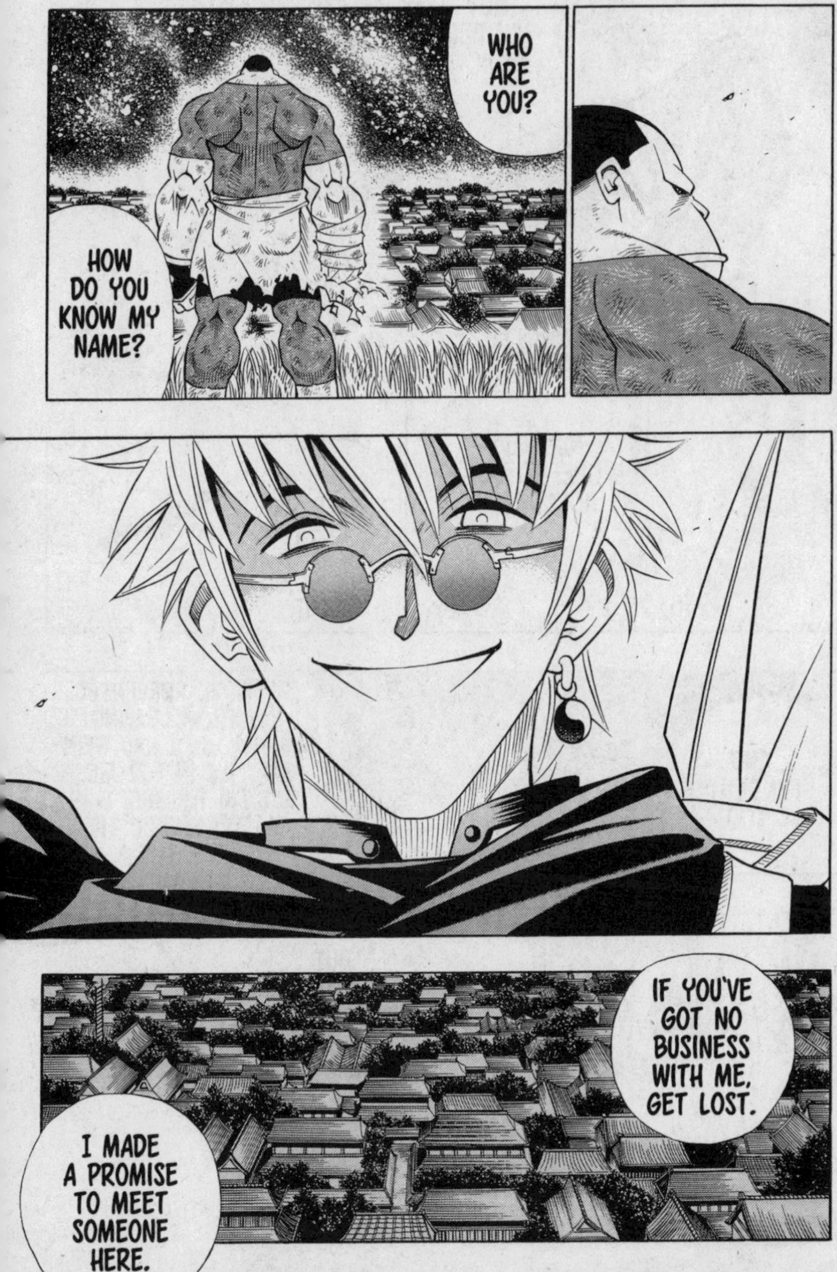
WHO ARE YOU?
HOW DO YOU KNOW MY NAME?
IF YOU'VE GOT NO BUSINESS WITH ME, GET LOST.
I MADE A PROMISE TO MEET SOMEONE HERE.

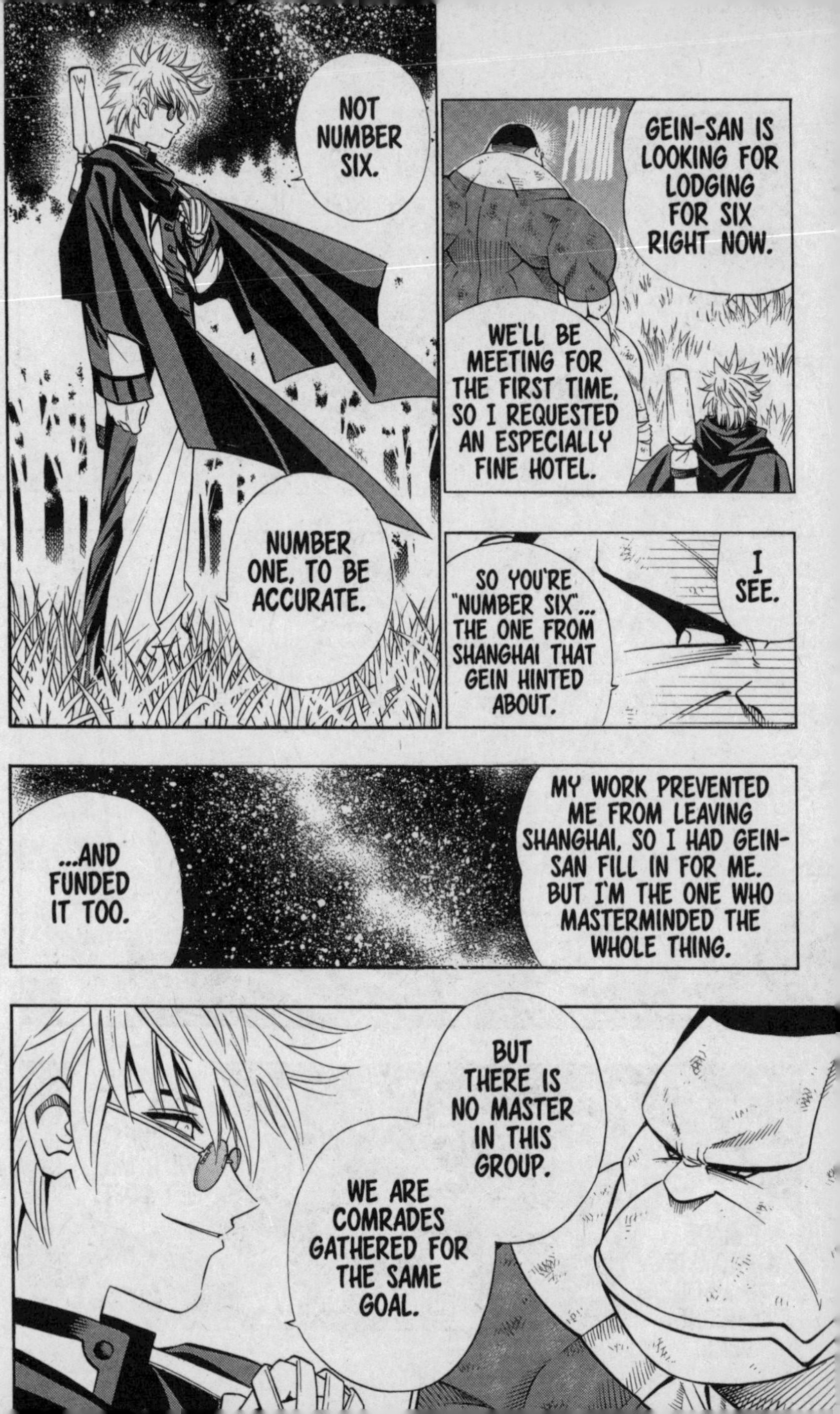
GEIN-SAN IS LOOKING FOR LODGING FOR SIX RIGHT NOW.
WE'LL BE MEETING FOR THE FIRST TIME, SO I REQUESTED AN ESPECIALLY FINE HOTEL.
I SEE.
SO YOU'RE "NUMBER SIX"... THE ONE FROM SHANGHAI THAT GEIN HINTED ABOUT.
NOT NUMBER SIX.
NUMBER ONE, TO BE ACCURATE.
MY WORK PREVENTED ME FROM LEAVING SHANGHAI, SO I HAD GEIN-SAN FILL IN FOR ME. BUT I'M THE ONE WHO MASTERMINDED THE WHOLE THING.
...AND FUNDED IT TOO.
BUT THERE IS NO MASTER IN THIS GROUP.
WE ARE COMRADES GATHERED FOR THE SAME GOAL.

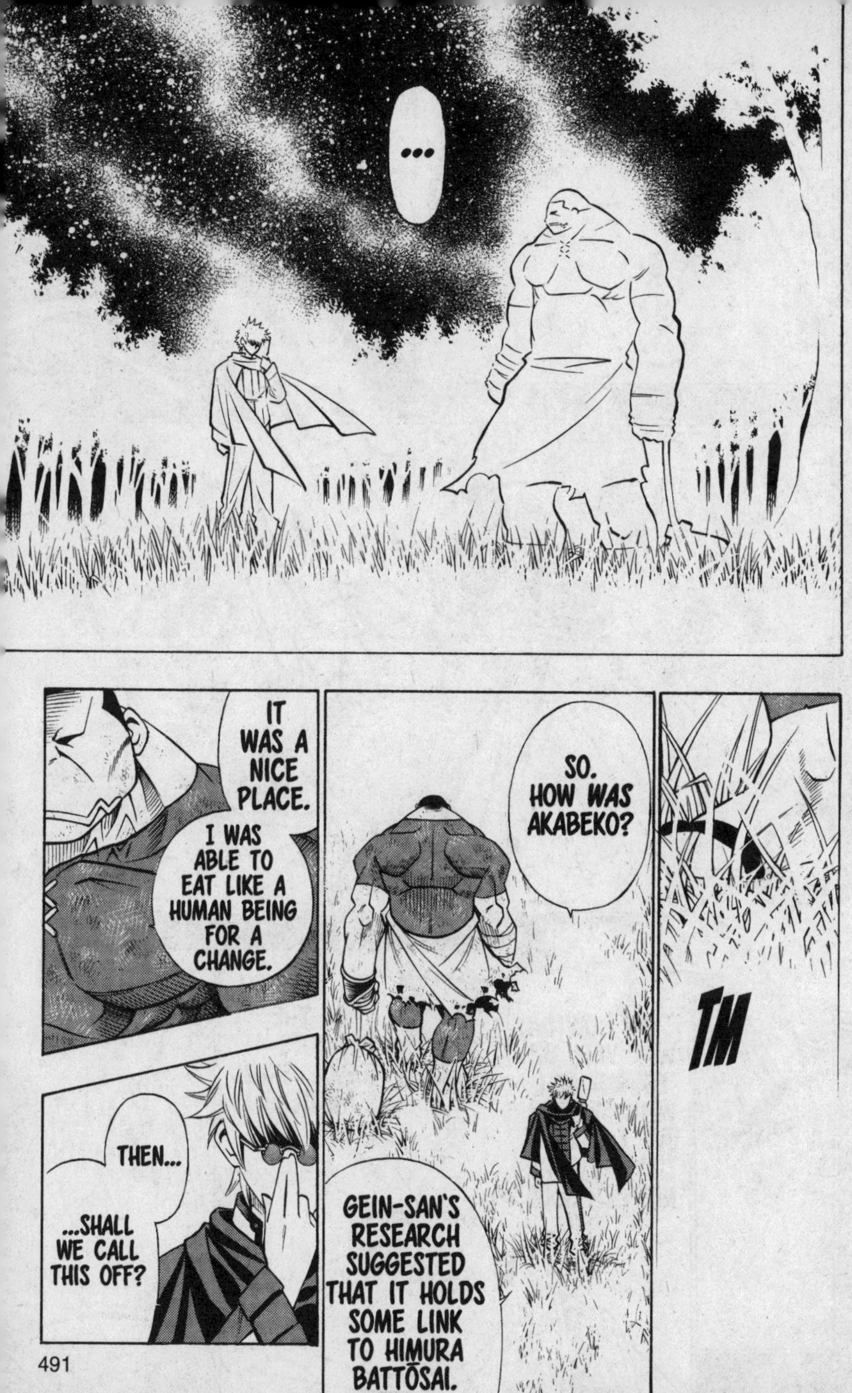
...
TM
SO. HOW WAS AKABEKO?
GEIN-SAN'S RESEARCH SUGGESTED THAT IT HOLDS SOME LINK TO HIMURA BATTŌSAI.
IT WAS A NICE PLACE.
I WAS ABLE TO EAT LIKE A HUMAN BEING FOR A CHANGE.
THEN...
...SHALL WE CALL THIS OFF?

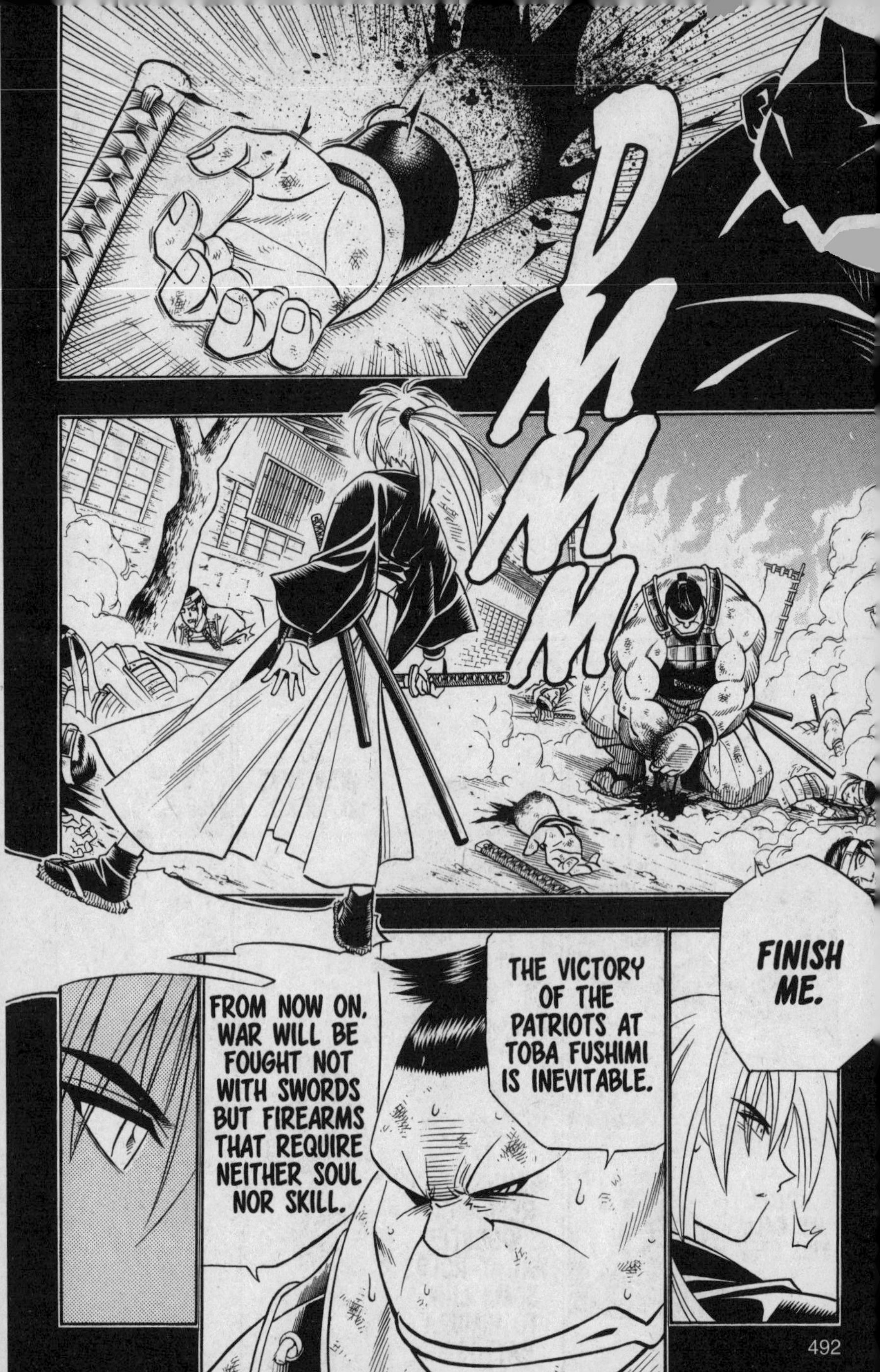
DMMM
FINISH ME.
THE VICTORY OF THE PATRIOTS AT TOBA FUSHIMI IS INEVITABLE.
FROM NOW ON, WAR WILL BE FOUGHT NOT WITH SWORDS BUT FIREARMS THAT REQUIRE NEITHER SOUL NOR SKILL.

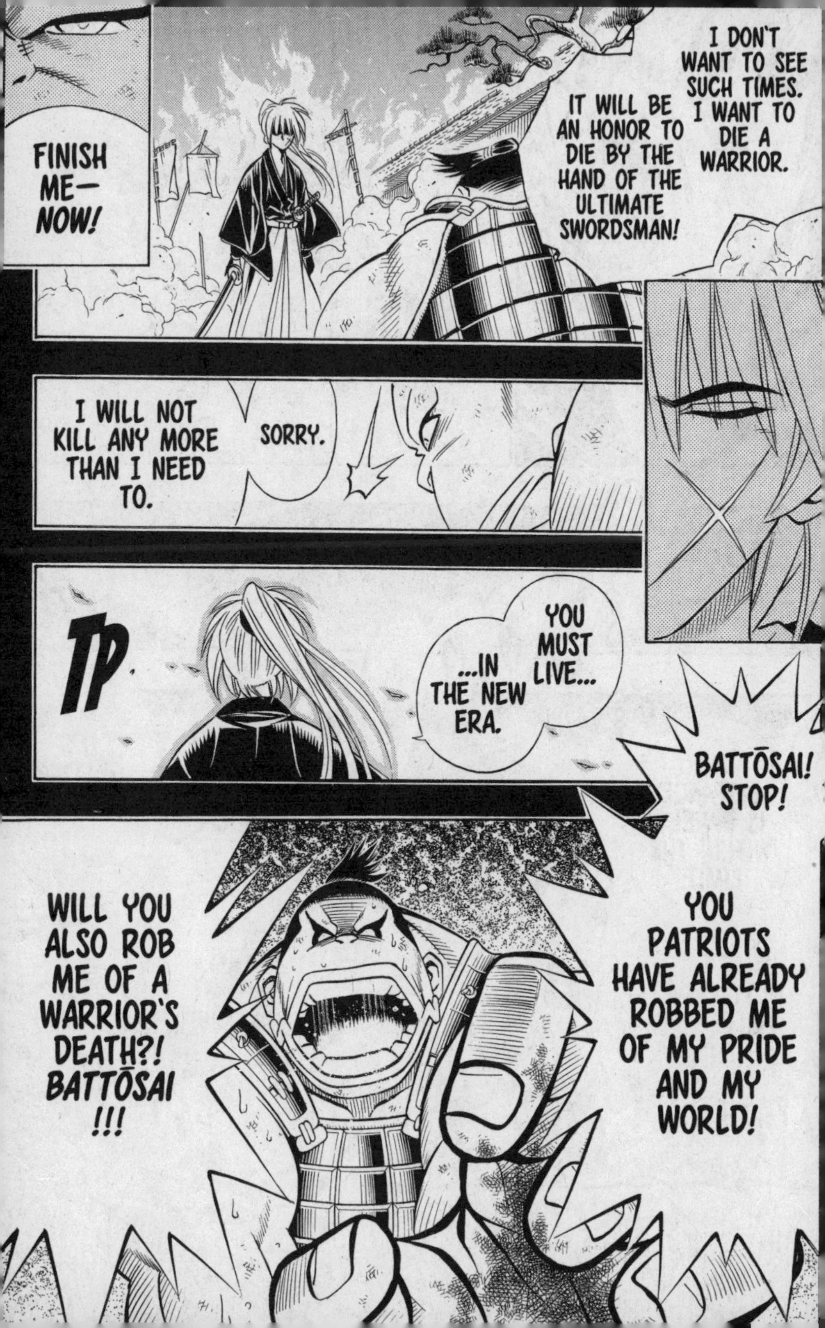
I DON'T WANT TO SEE SUCH TIMES. I WANT TO DIE A WARRIOR.
IT WILL BE AN HONOR TO DIE BY THE HAND OF THE ULTIMATE SWORDSMAN!
FINISH ME—NOW!
SORRY.
I WILL NOT KILL ANY MORE THAN I NEED TO.
YOU MUST LIVE...
...IN THE NEW ERA.
TP
BATTŌSAI! STOP!
YOU PATRIOTS HAVE ALREADY ROBBED ME OF MY PRIDE AND MY WORLD!
WILL YOU ALSO ROB ME OF A WARRIOR'S DEATH?! BATTŌSAI!!!

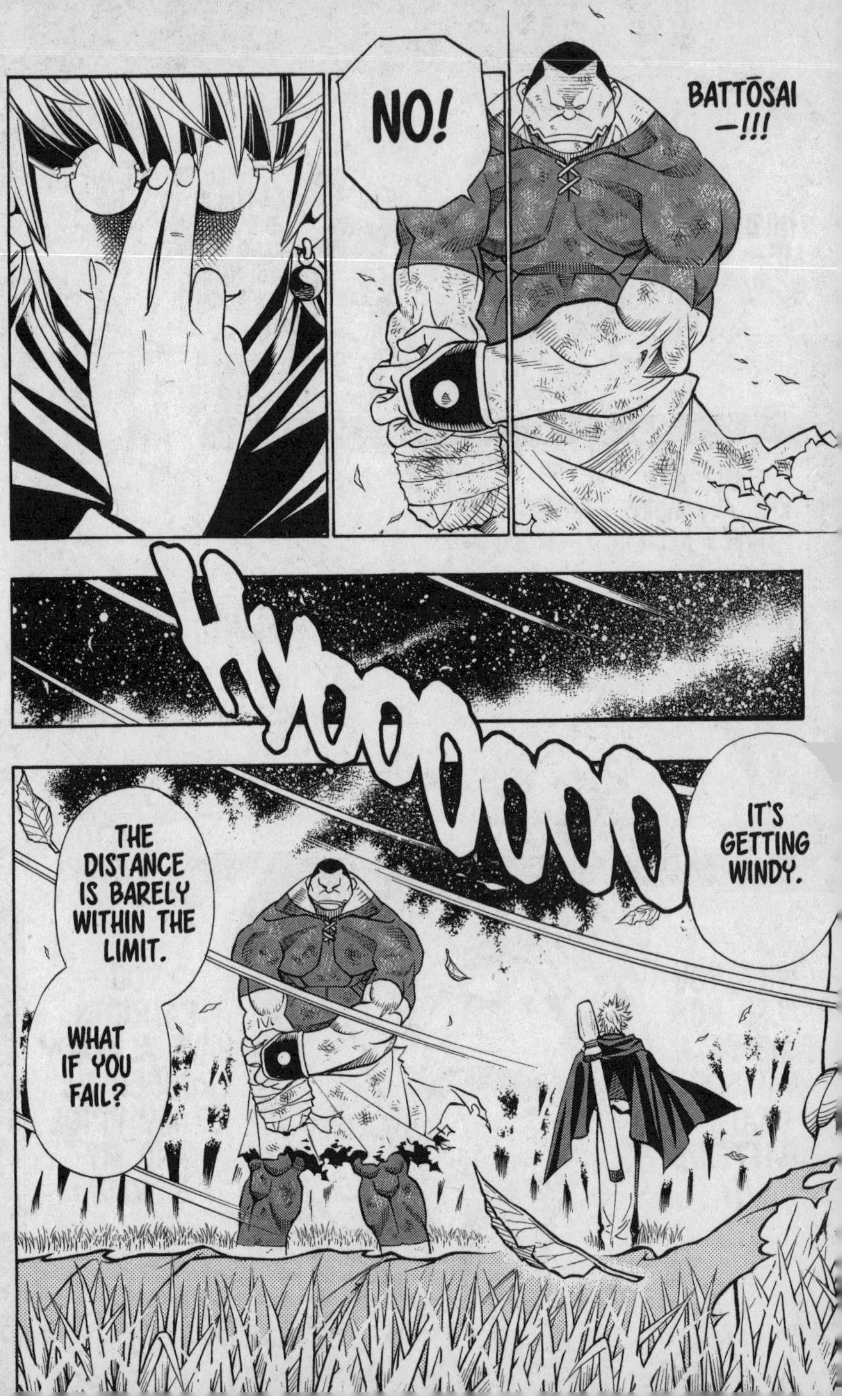
BATTŌSAI —!!!
NO!
HYOOOOOO
IT'S GETTING WINDY.
THE DISTANCE IS BARELY WITHIN THE LIMIT.
WHAT IF YOU FAIL?

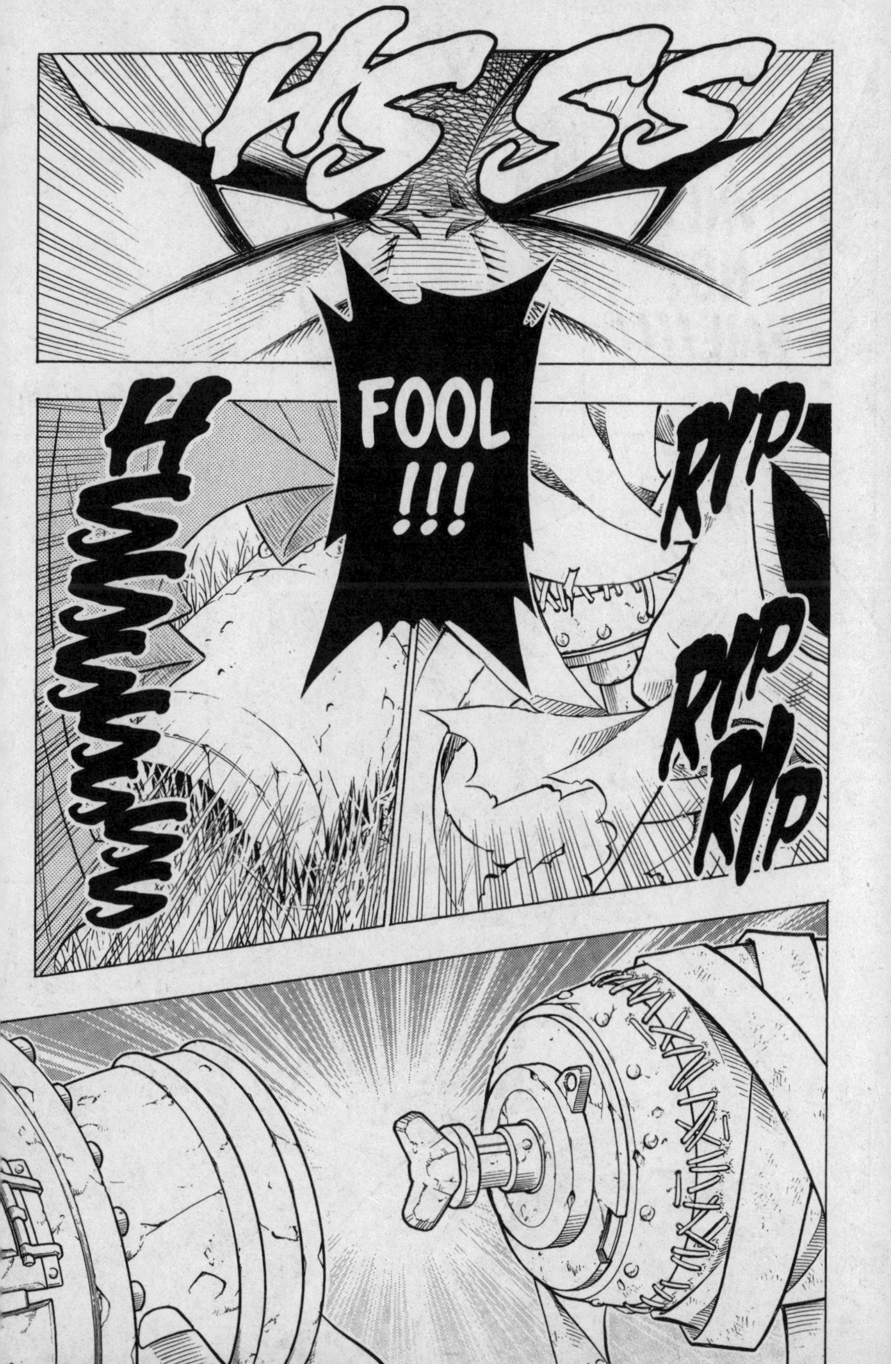
HSSS
FOOL
!!!
RIP
RIP
RIP
RIP

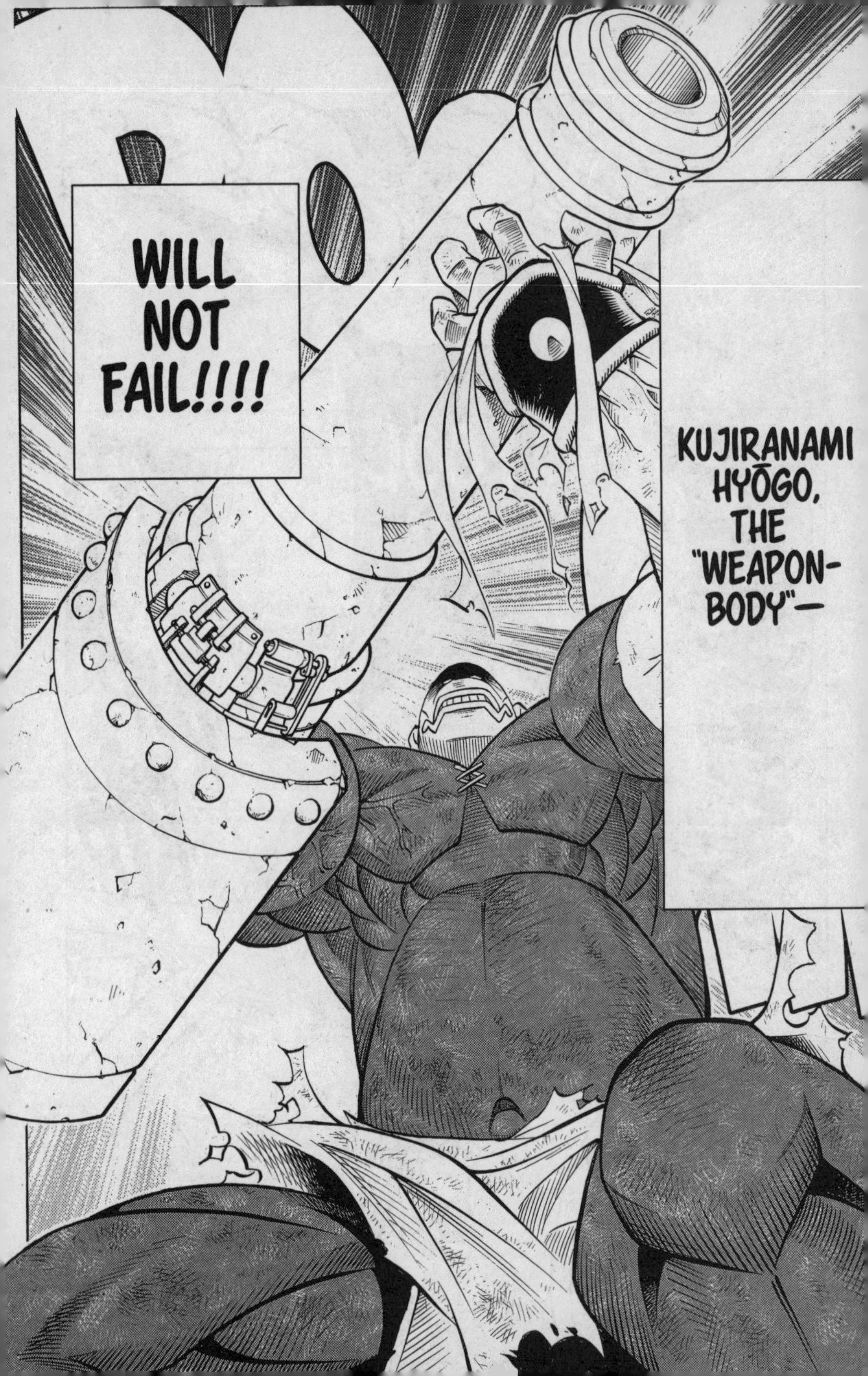
KUJIRANAMI HYŌGO, THE "WEAPON-BODY"—
WILL NOT FAIL!!!!

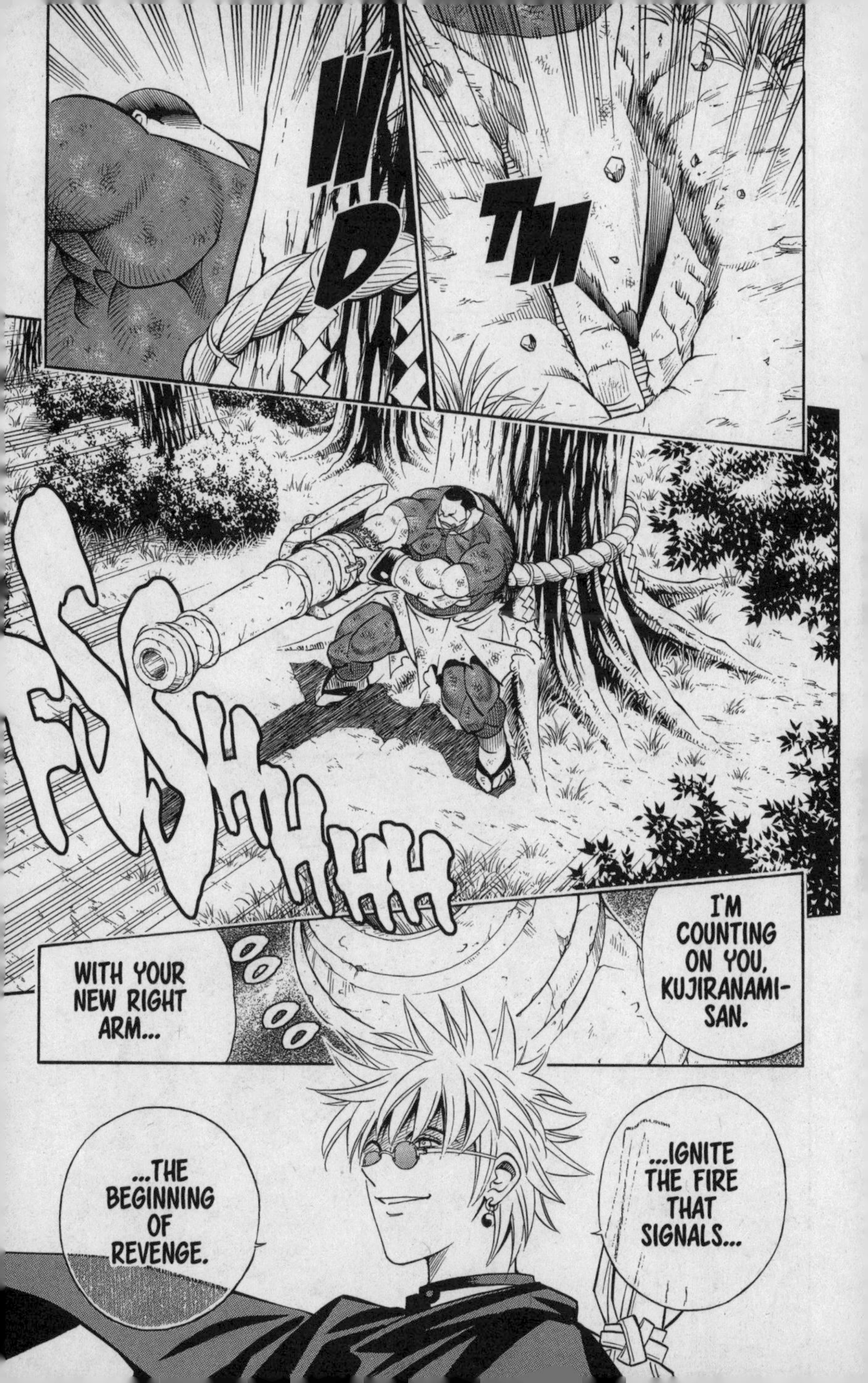

WHAD
TM
FSSHHHH
I'M COUNTING ON YOU, KUJIRANAMI-SAN.
WITH YOUR NEW RIGHT ARM...
...IGNITE THE FIRE THAT SIGNALS...
...THE BEGINNING OF REVENGE.

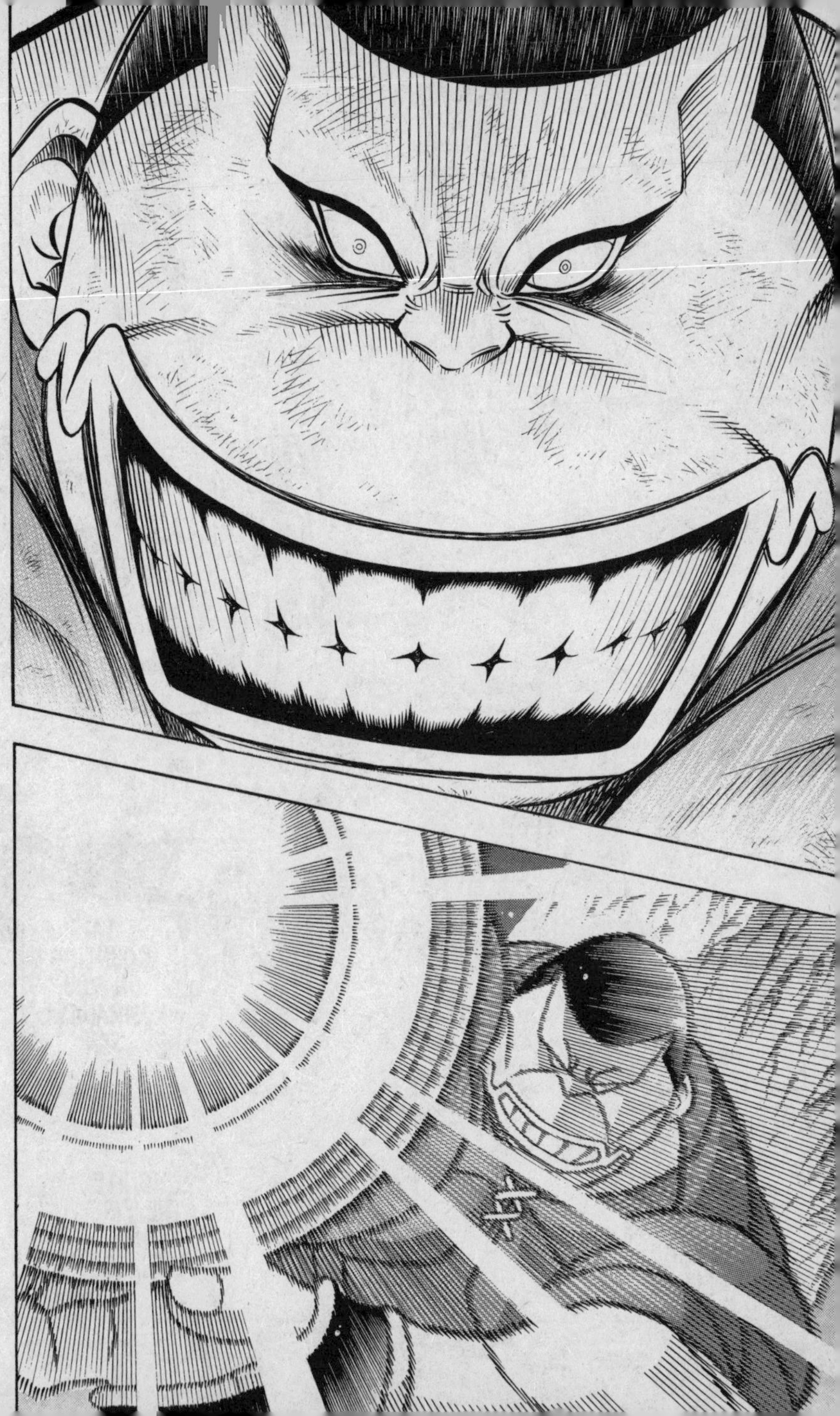

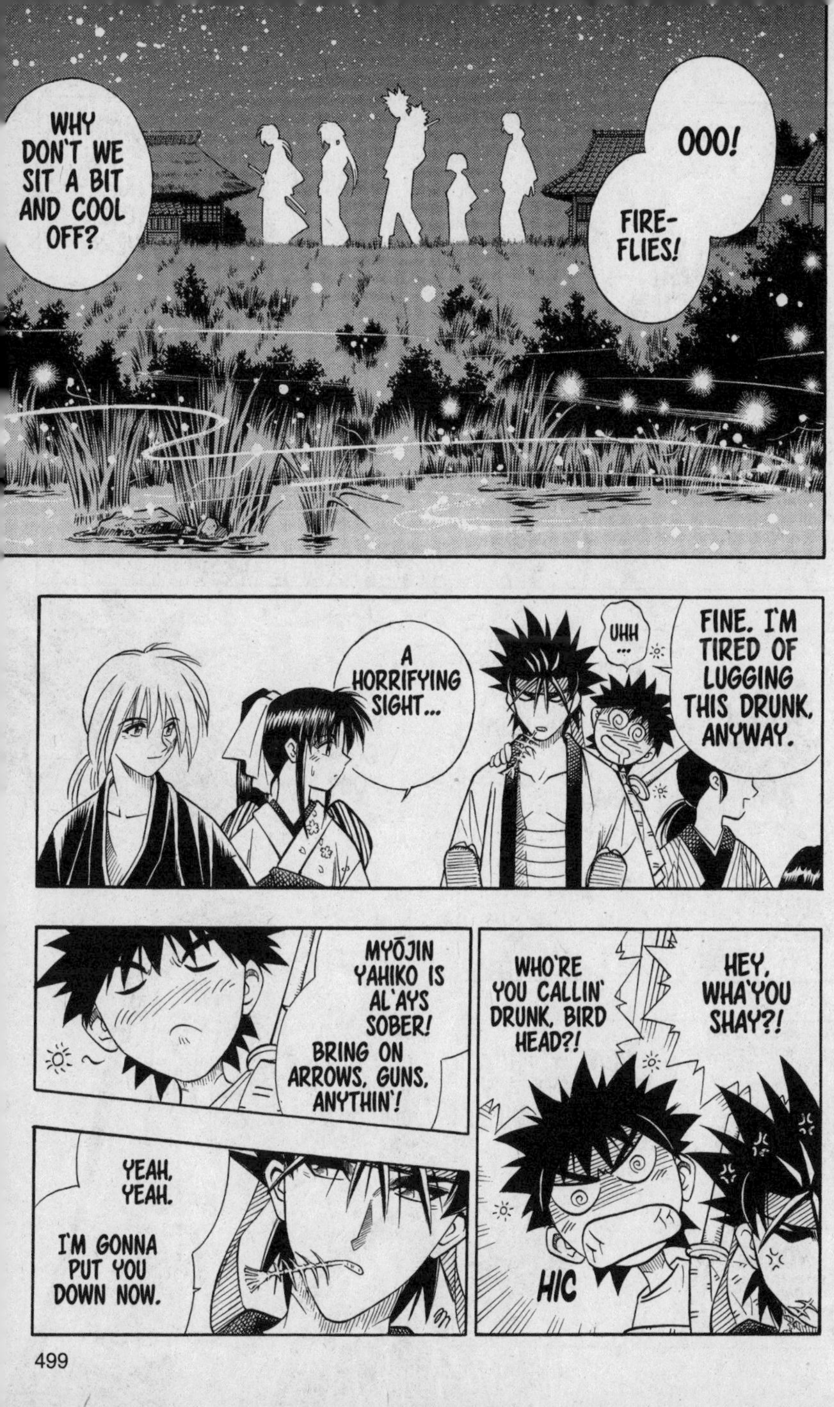
OOO!
FIRE-FLIES!
WHY DON'T WE SIT A BIT AND COOL OFF?
FINE. I'M TIRED OF LUGGING THIS DRUNK, ANYWAY.
UHH ...
A HORRIFYING SIGHT...
HEY, WHA'YOU SHAY?!
WHO'RE YOU CALLIN' DRUNK, BIRD HEAD?!
HIC
MYŌJIN YAHIKO IS AL'AYS SOBER! BRING ON ARROWS, GUNS, ANYTHIN'!
YEAH, YEAH.
I'M GONNA PUT YOU DOWN NOW.

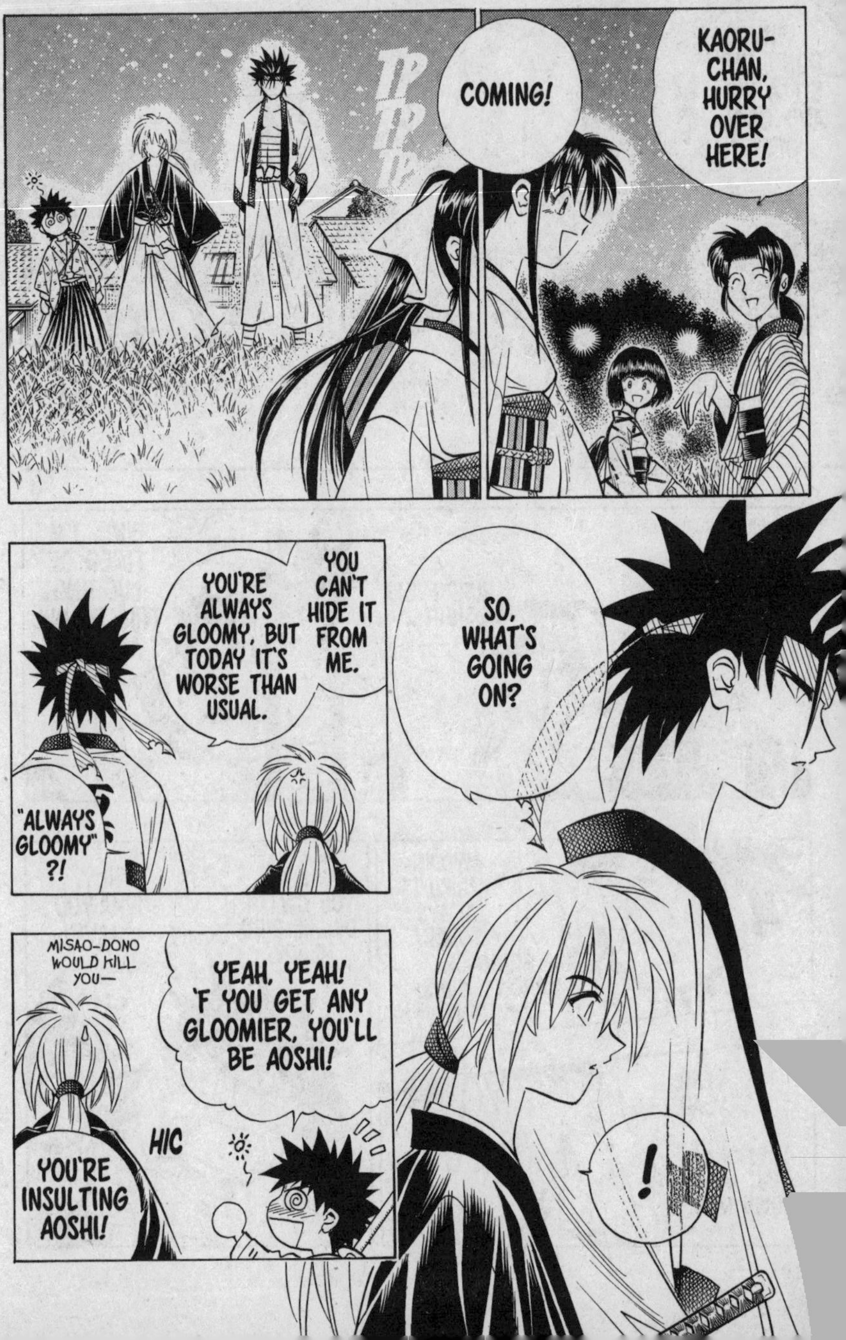
KAORU-CHAN, HURRY OVER HERE!
COMING!
TP TP TP
SO, WHAT'S GOING ON?
!
YOU CAN'T HIDE IT FROM ME.
YOU'RE ALWAYS GLOOMY, BUT TODAY IT'S WORSE THAN USUAL.
"ALWAYS GLOOMY" ?!
YEAH, YEAH! 'F YOU GET ANY GLOOMIER, YOU'LL BE AOSHI!
MISAO-DONO WOULD KILL YOU—
HIC
YOU'RE INSULTING AOSHI!

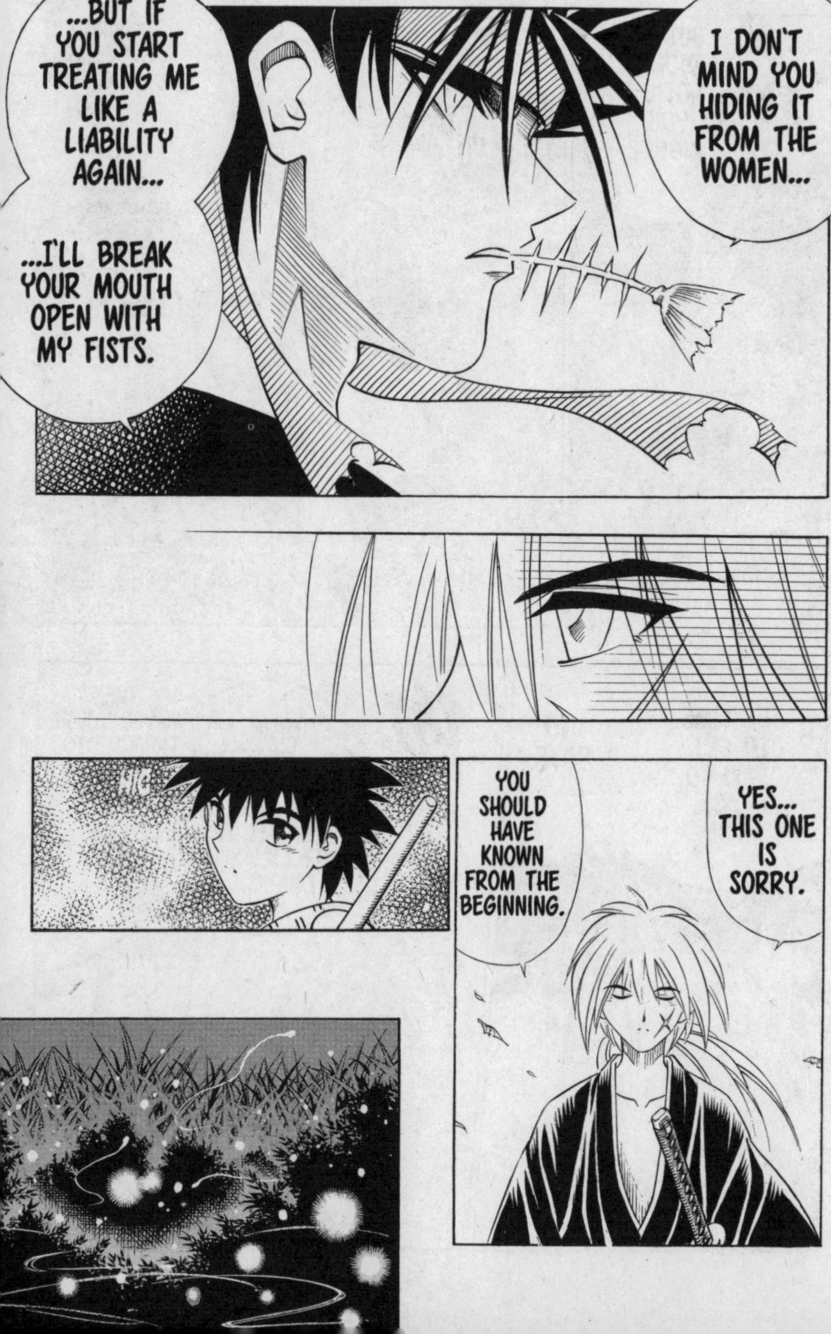
I DON'T MIND YOU HIDING IT FROM THE WOMEN...
...BUT IF YOU START TREATING ME LIKE A LIABILITY AGAIN...
...I'LL BREAK YOUR MOUTH OPEN WITH MY FISTS.
YES... THIS ONE IS SORRY.
YOU SHOULD HAVE KNOWN FROM THE BEGINNING.

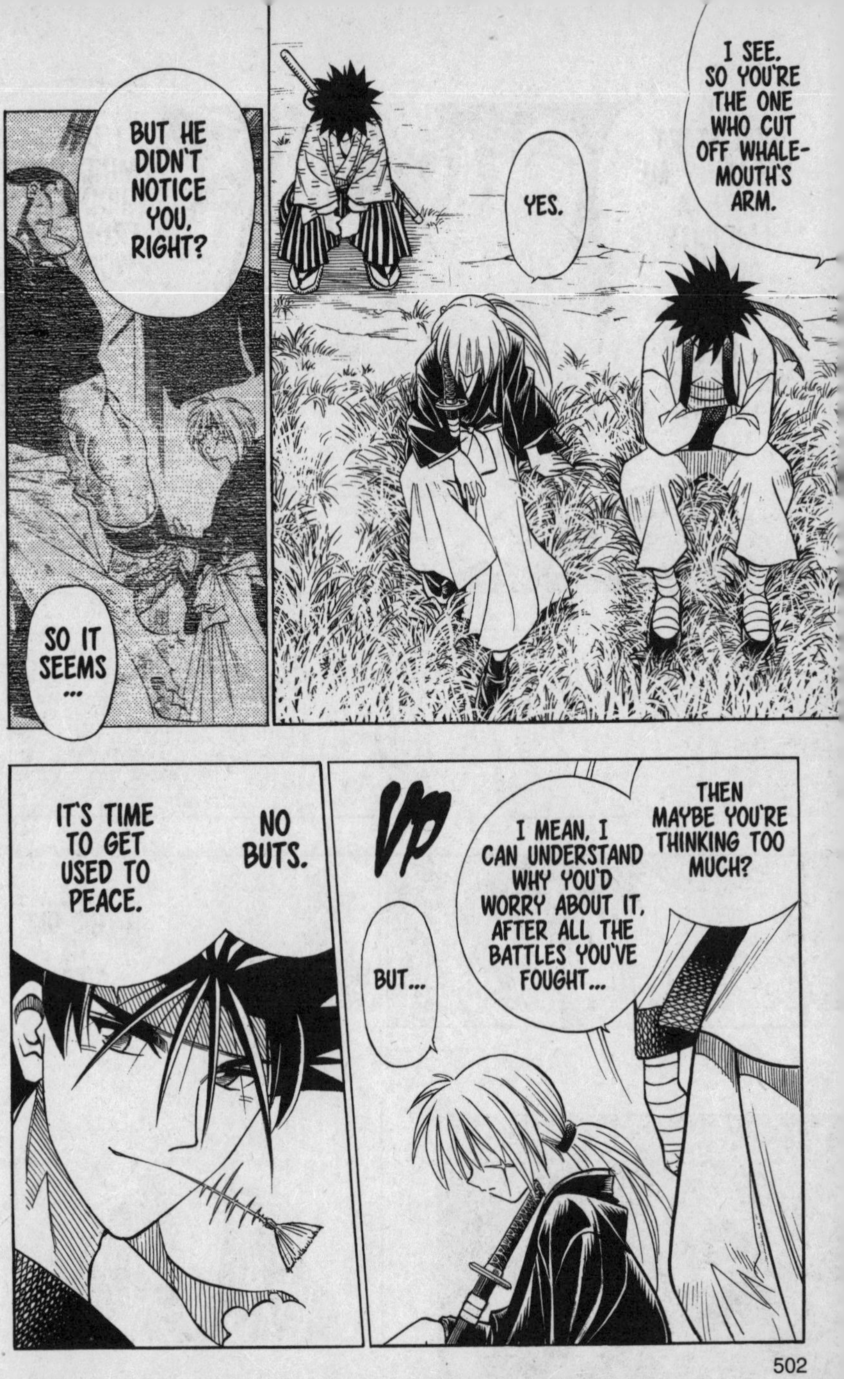
I SEE. SO YOU'RE THE ONE WHO CUT OFF WHALE-MOUTH'S ARM.
YES.
BUT HE DIDN'T NOTICE YOU, RIGHT?
SO IT SEEMS...
THEN MAYBE YOU'RE THINKING TOO MUCH?
I MEAN, I CAN UNDERSTAND WHY YOU'D WORRY ABOUT IT, AFTER ALL THE BATTLES YOU'VE FOUGHT...
BUT...
NO BUTS.
IT'S TIME TO GET USED TO PEACE.

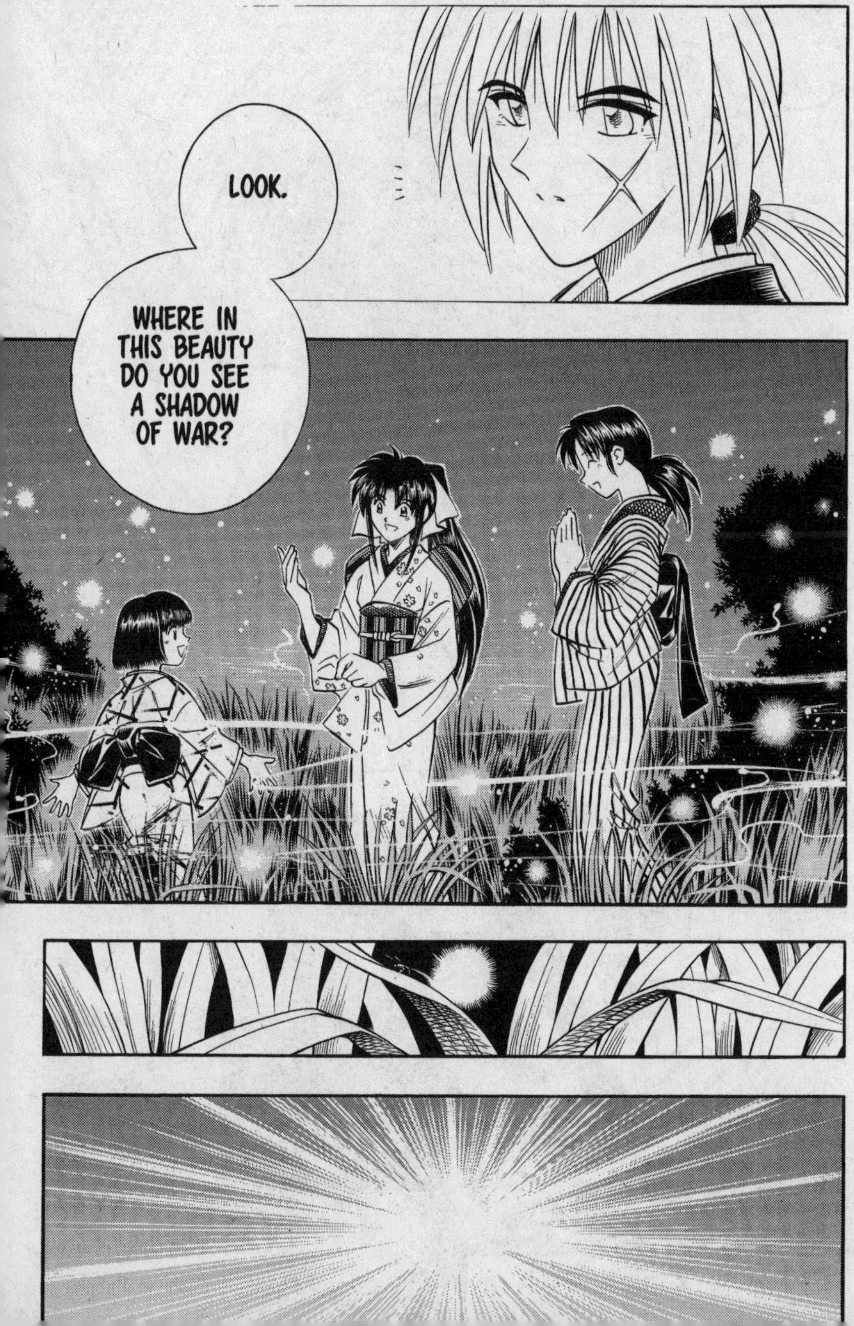
LOOK.
WHERE IN THIS BEAUTY DO YOU SEE A SHADOW OF WAR?

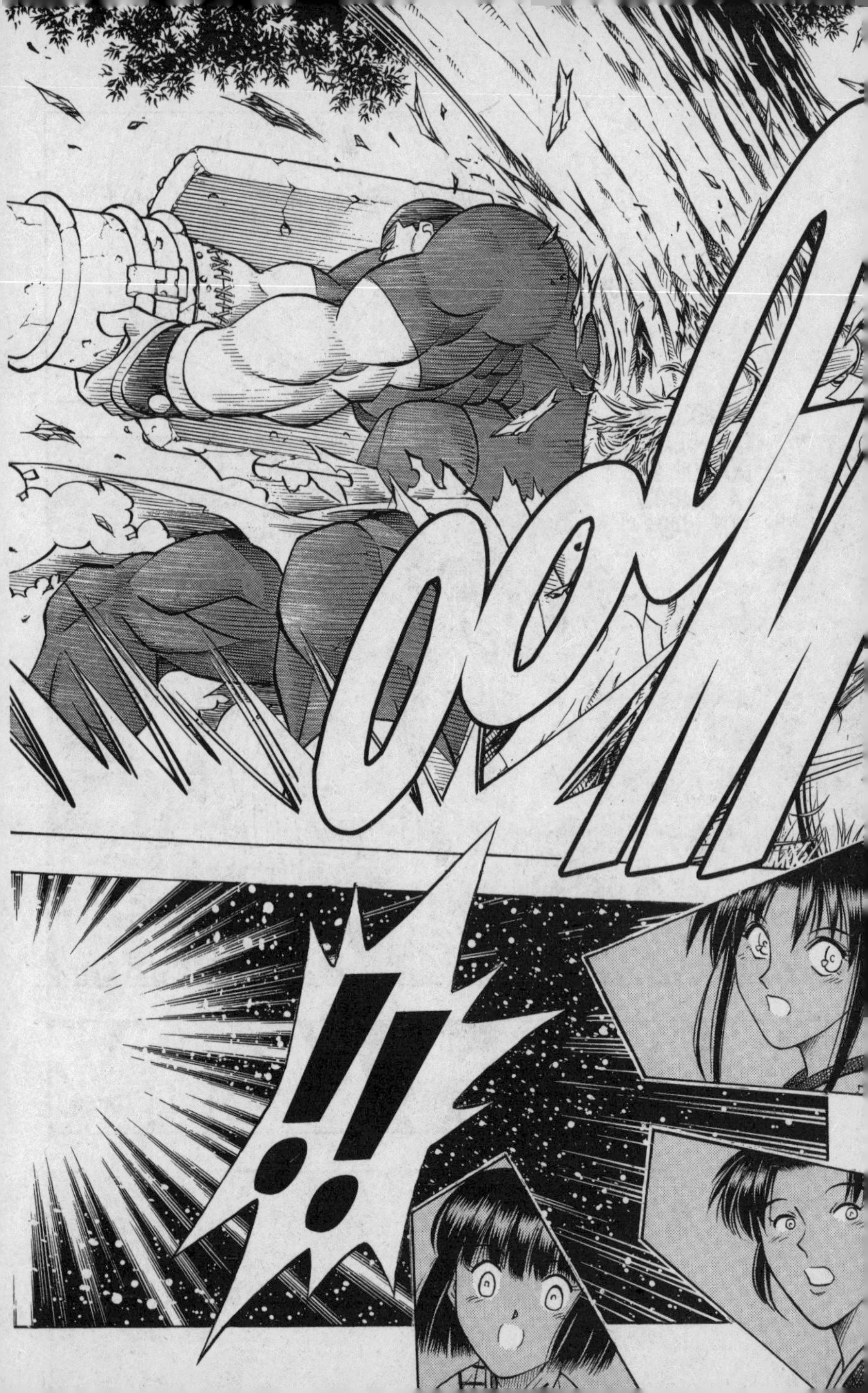
!!

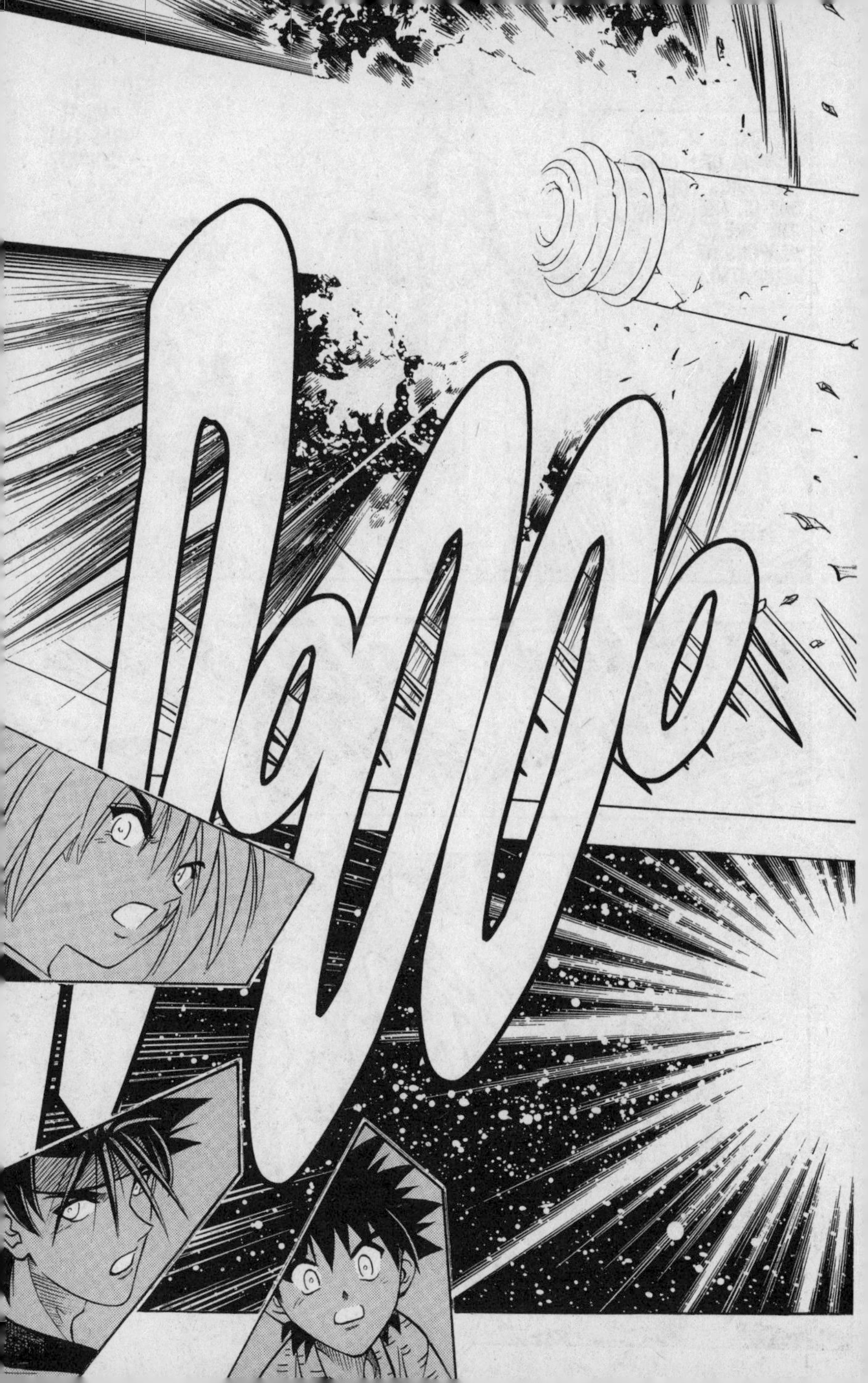

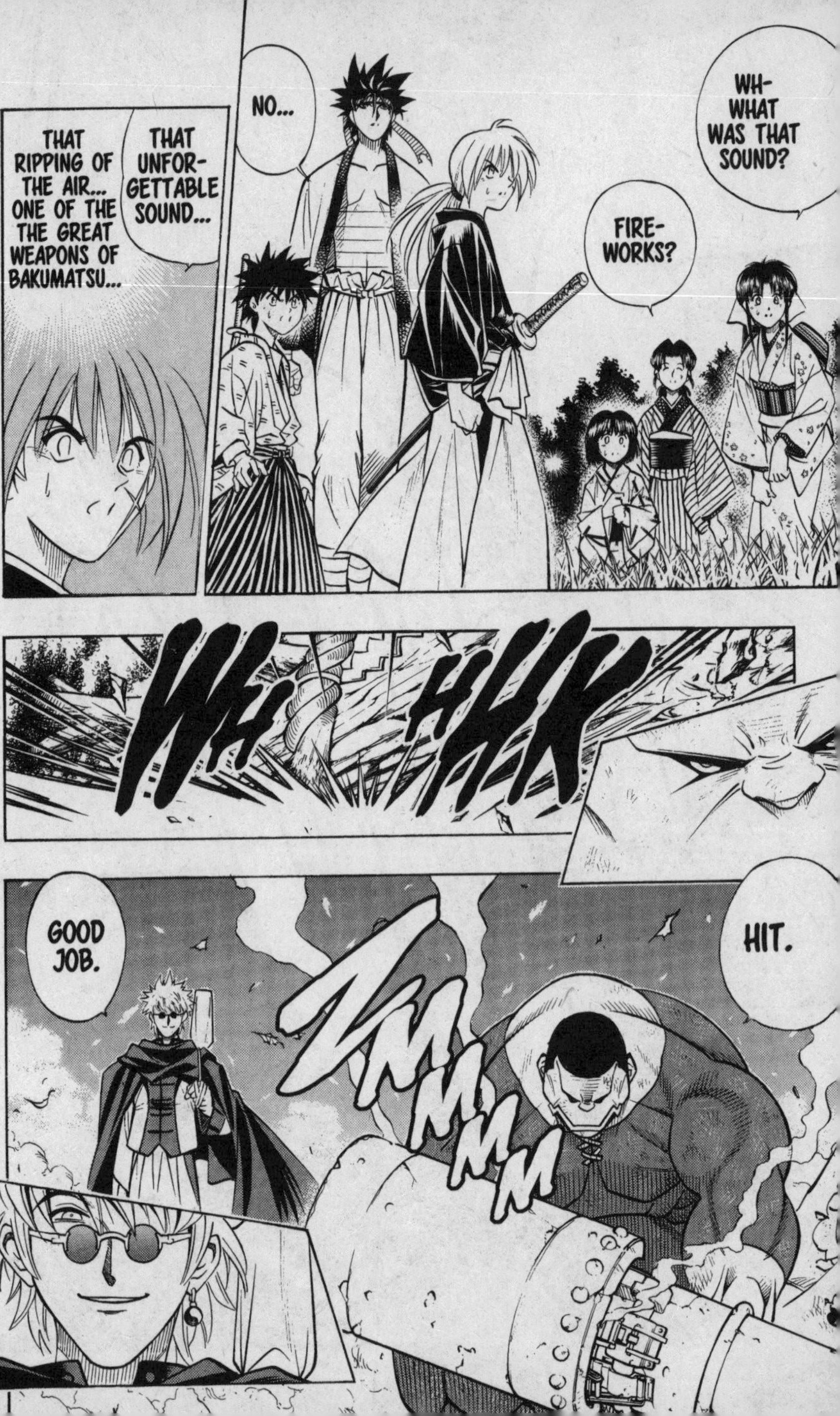
WH- WHAT WAS THAT SOUND?
FIRE-WORKS?
NO...
THAT UNFOR-GETTABLE SOUND...
THAT RIPPING OF THE AIR... ONE OF THE THE GREAT WEAPONS OF BAKUMATSU...
HIT.
GOOD JOB.

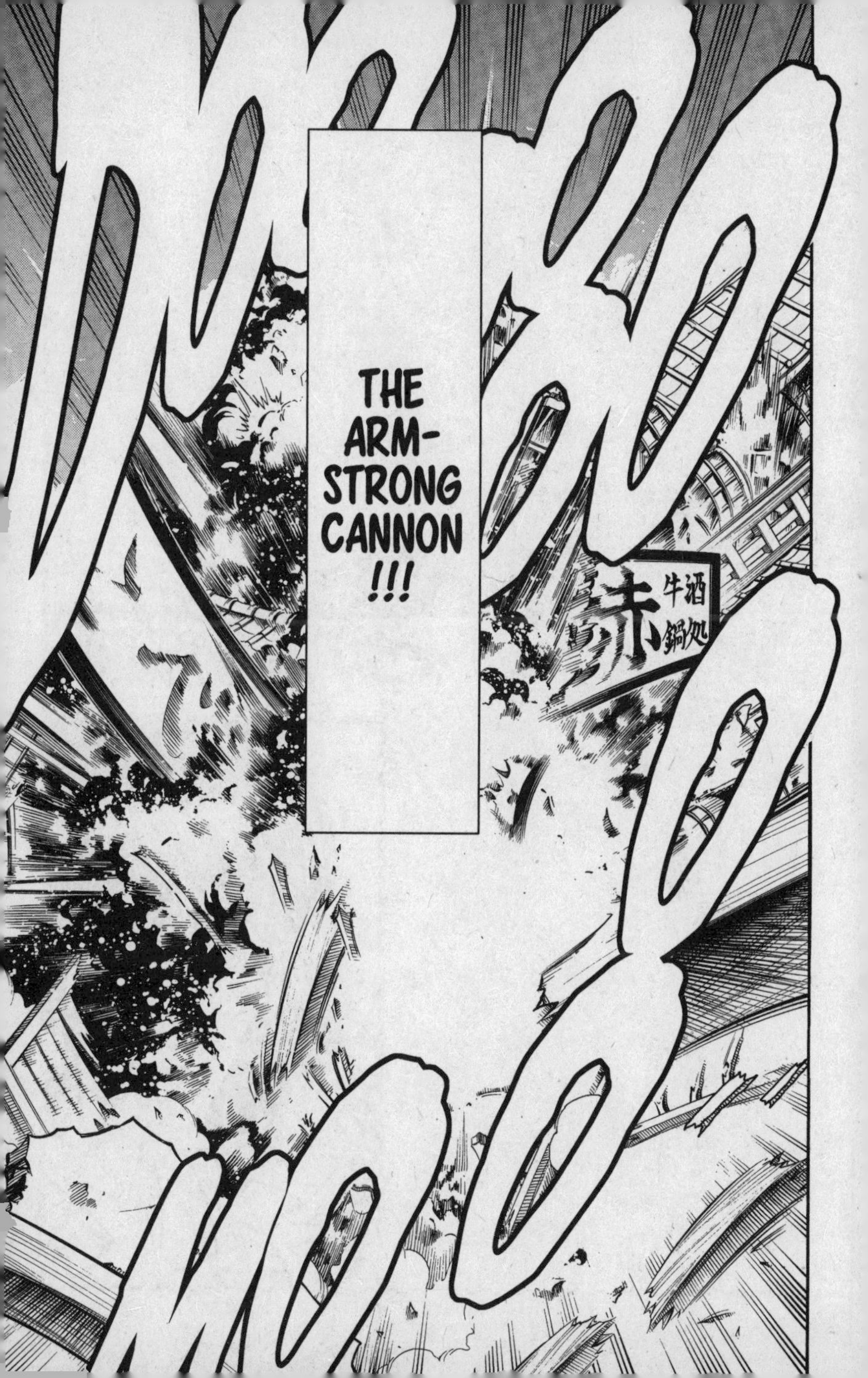
THE ARM-STRONG CANNON !!!
酒処
牛鍋

Rurouni Kenshin

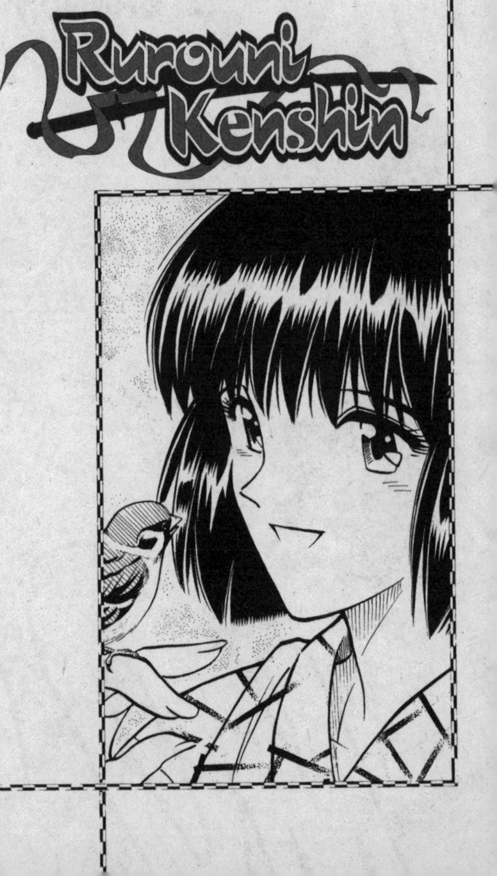

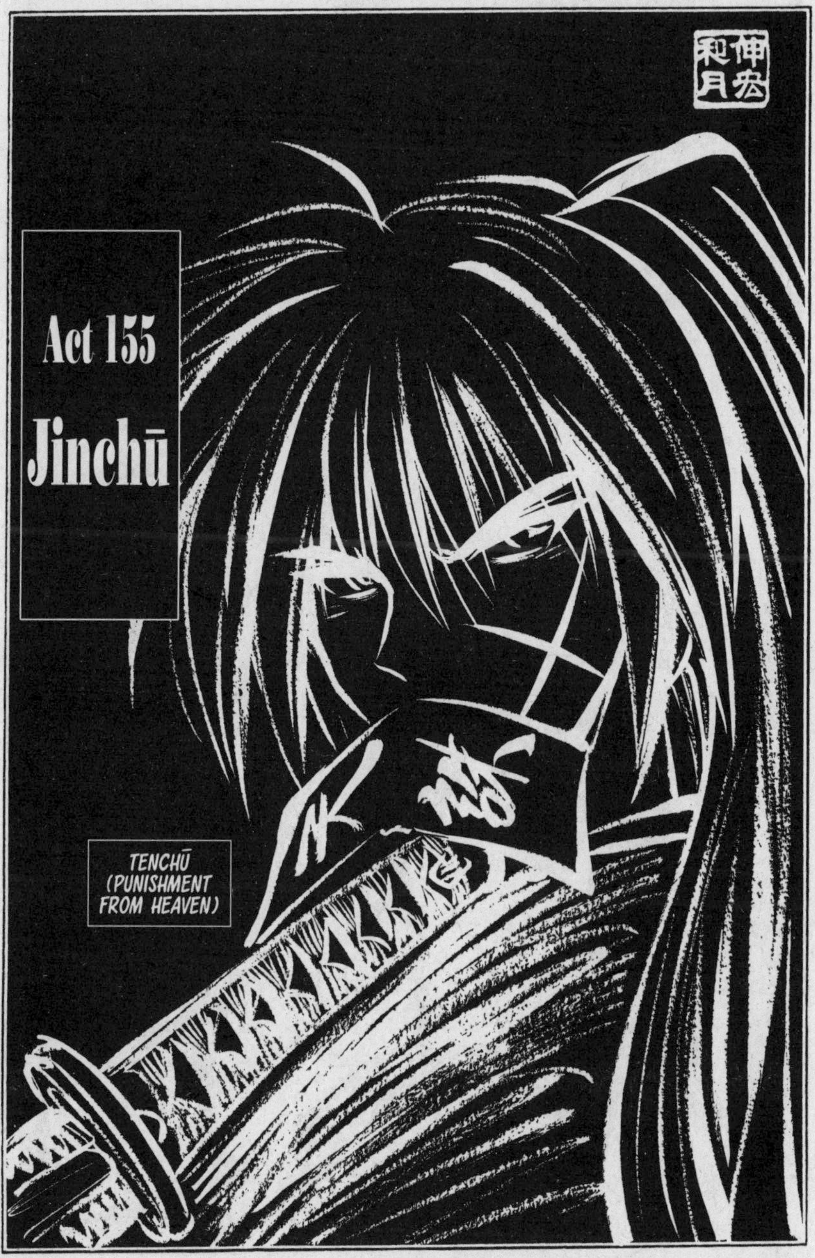
Act 155
Jinchū
TENCHŪ (PUNISHMENT FROM HEAVEN)

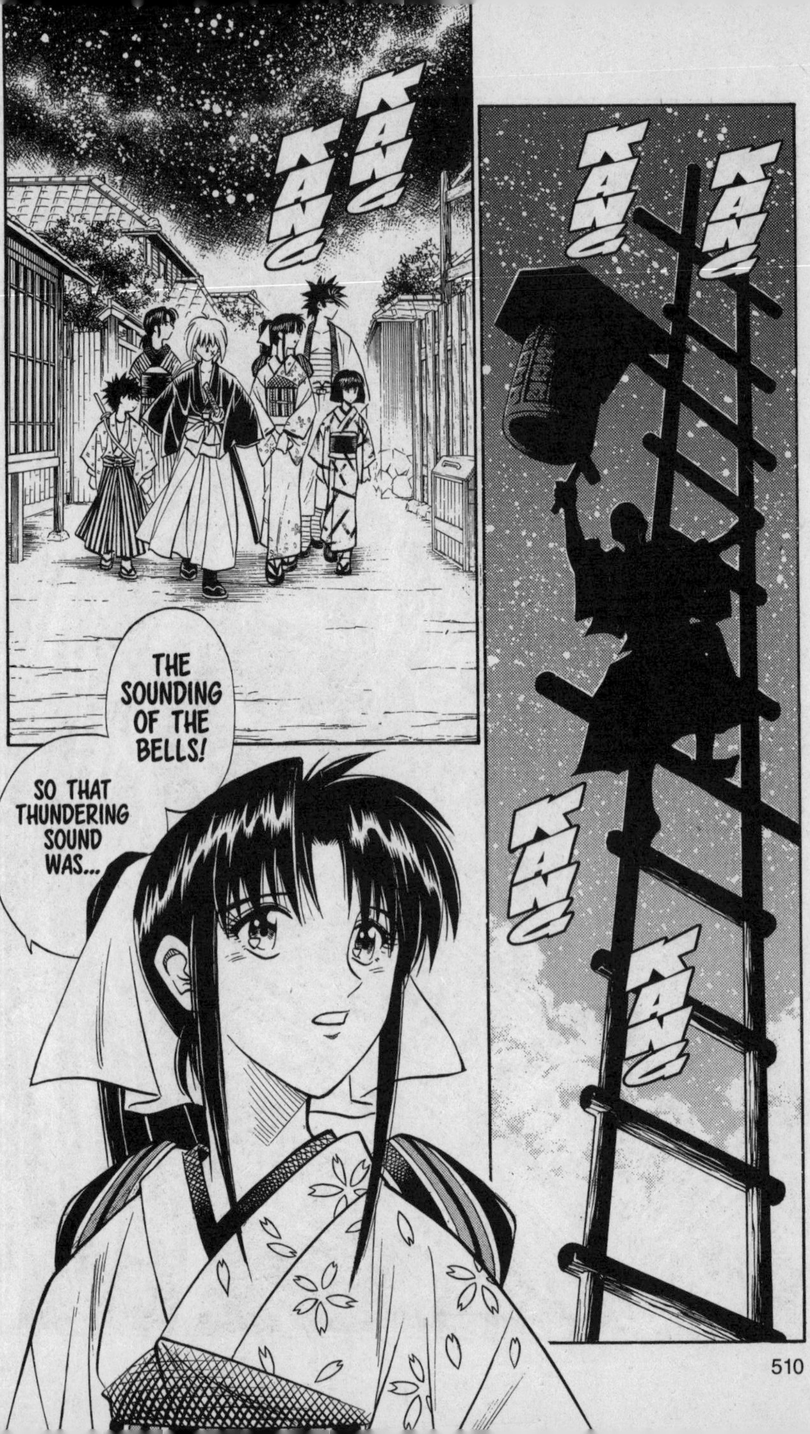
KANG
KANG
KANG
KANG
KANG
KANG
THE SOUNDING OF THE BELLS!
SO THAT THUNDERING SOUND WAS...

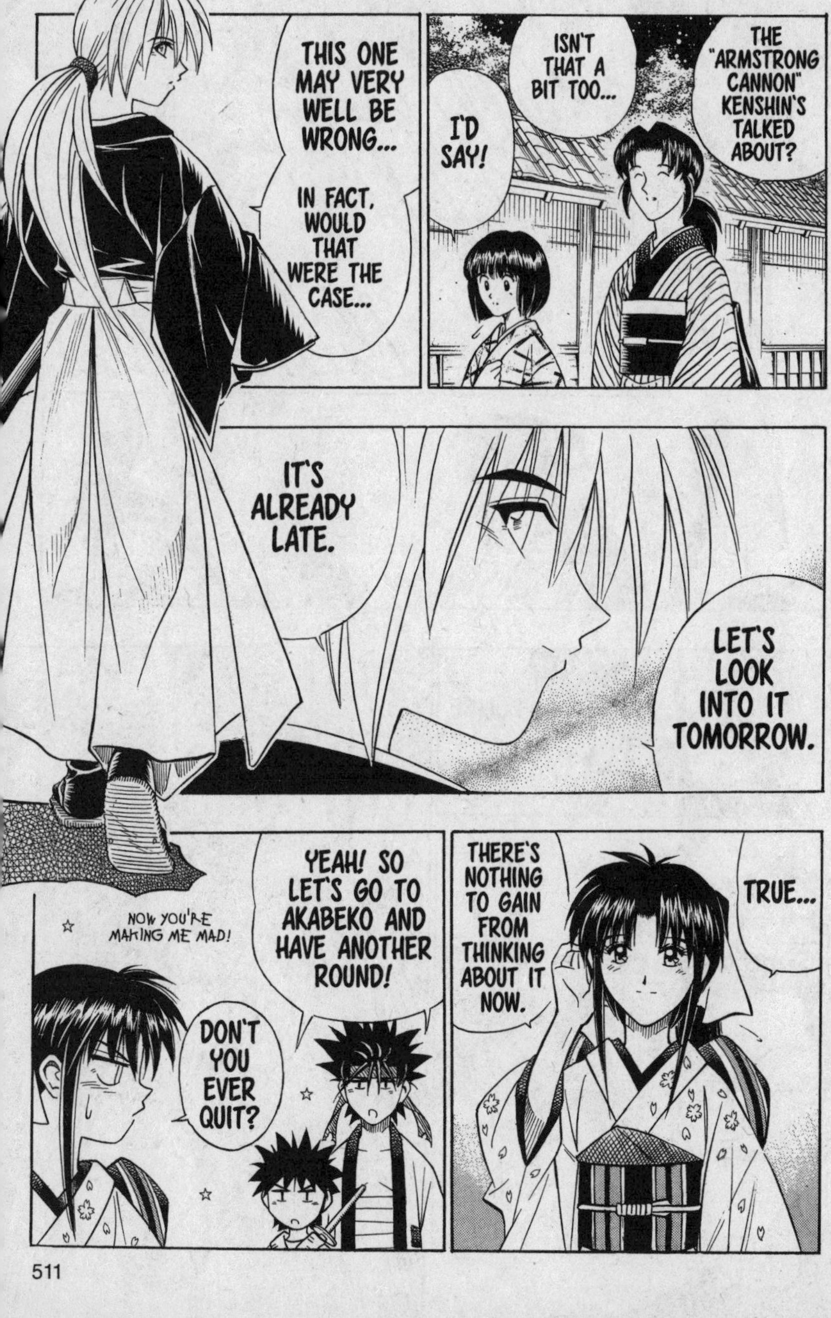
THE "ARMSTRONG CANNON" KENSHIN'S TALKED ABOUT?
ISN'T THAT A BIT TOO...
I'D SAY!
THIS ONE MAY VERY WELL BE WRONG...
IN FACT, WOULD THAT WERE THE CASE...
IT'S ALREADY LATE.
LET'S LOOK INTO IT TOMORROW.
TRUE...
THERE'S NOTHING TO GAIN FROM THINKING ABOUT IT NOW.
YEAH! SO LET'S GO TO AKABEKO AND HAVE ANOTHER ROUND!
DON'T YOU EVER QUIT?
NOW YOU'RE MAKING ME MAD!

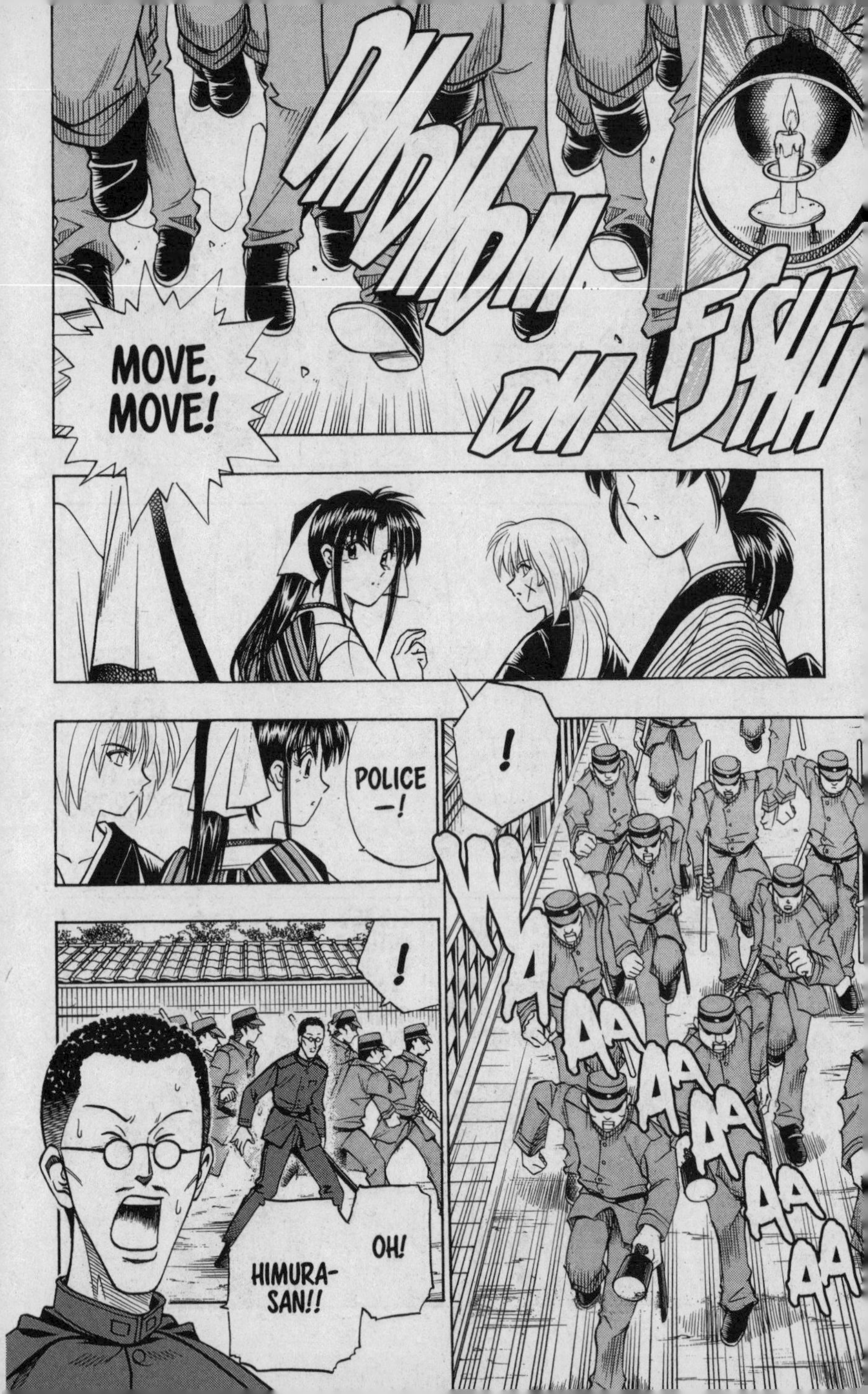
FSHH
MOVE, MOVE!
!
WAAAAAAAAAA
POLICE—!
!
OH!
HIMURA-SAN!!

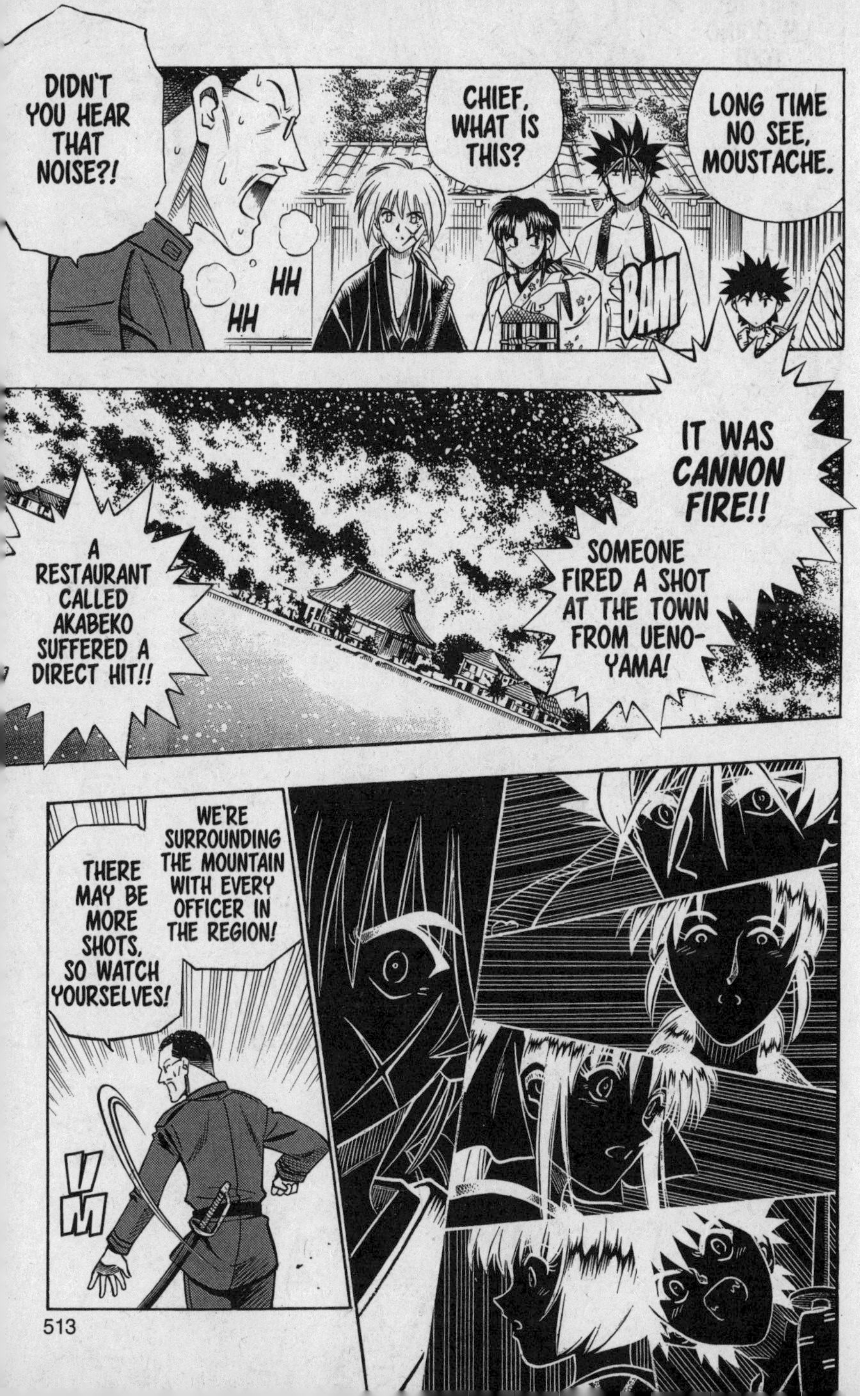
LONG TIME NO SEE, MOUSTACHE.
BAM
CHIEF, WHAT IS THIS?
HH
HH
DIDN'T YOU HEAR THAT NOISE?!
IT WAS CANNON FIRE!!
SOMEONE FIRED A SHOT AT THE TOWN FROM UENO-YAMA!
A RESTAURANT CALLED AKABEKO SUFFERED A DIRECT HIT!!
WE'RE SURROUNDING THE MOUNTAIN WITH EVERY OFFICER IN THE REGION!
THERE MAY BE MORE SHOTS, SO WATCH YOURSELVES!

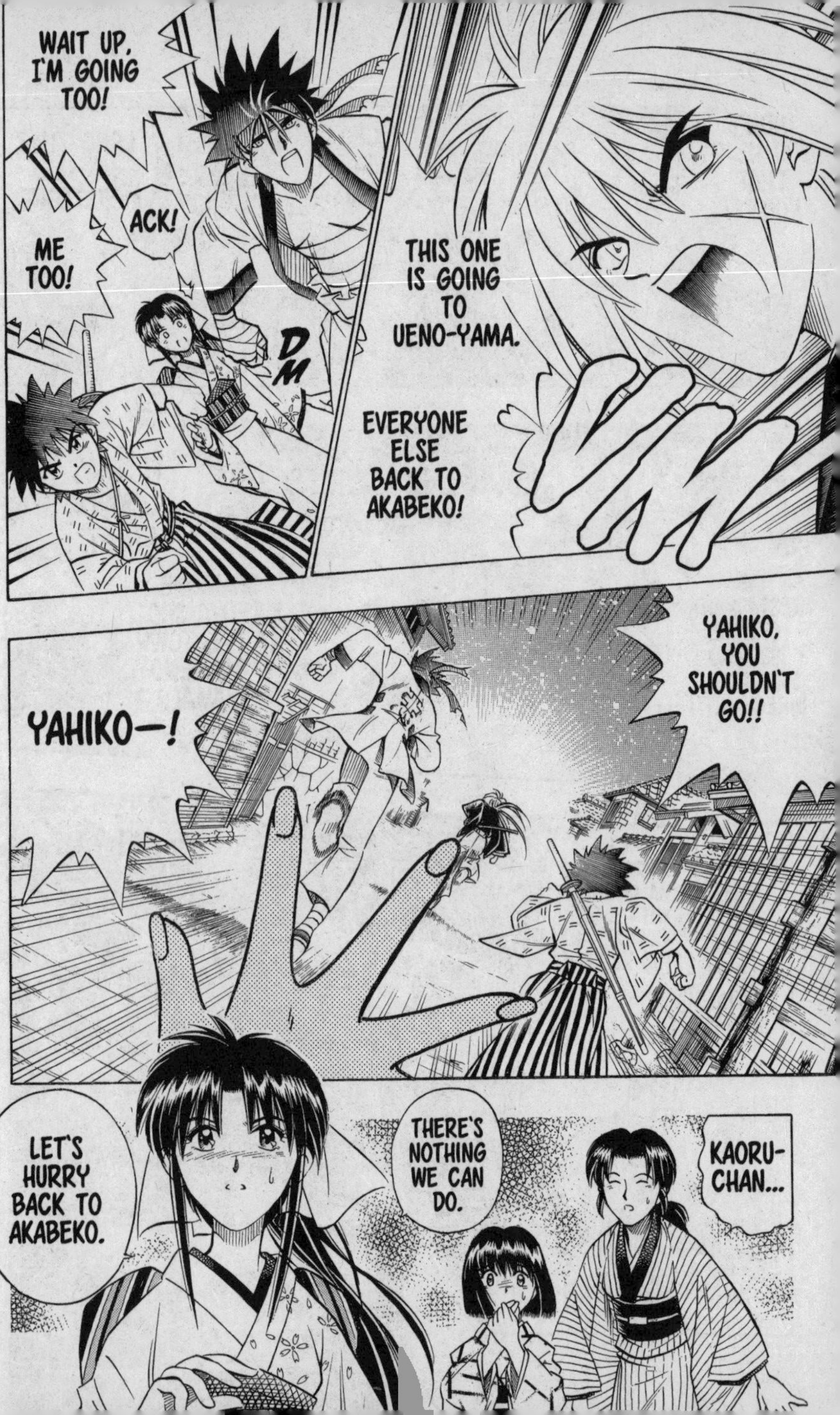
THIS ONE IS GOING TO UENO-YAMA.
EVERYONE ELSE BACK TO AKABEKO!
WAIT UP, I'M GOING TOO!
ACK!
ME TOO!
DM
YAHIKO, YOU SHOULDN'T GO!!
YAHIKO—!
KAORU-CHAN...
THERE'S NOTHING WE CAN DO.
LET'S HURRY BACK TO AKABEKO.

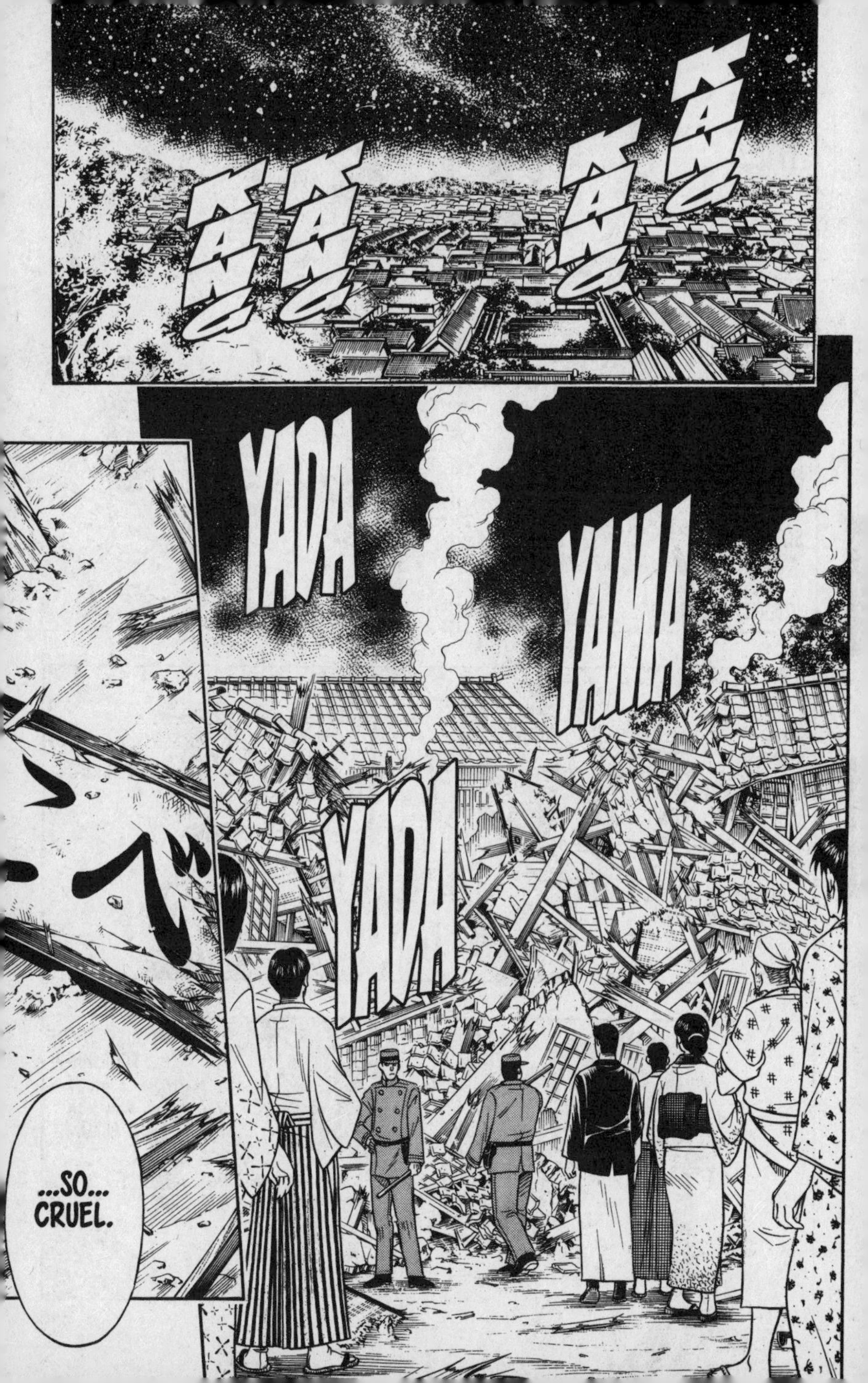
KANG
KANG
KANG
KANG
YAMA
YADA
YADA
...SO... CRUEL.

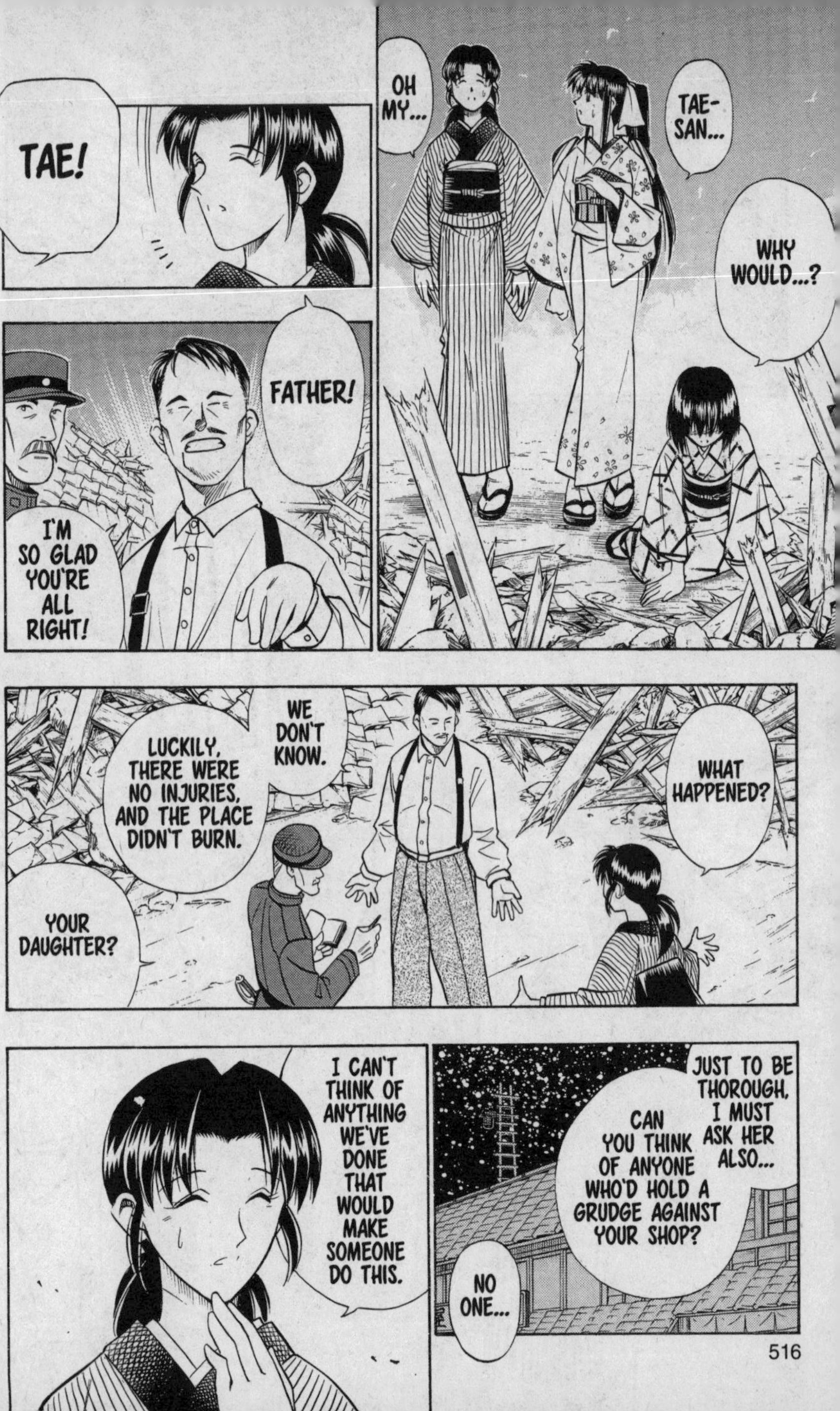
TAE-SAN...
OH MY...
WHY WOULD...?
TAE!
FATHER!
I'M SO GLAD YOU'RE ALL RIGHT!
WHAT HAPPENED?
WE DON'T KNOW.
LUCKILY, THERE WERE NO INJURIES, AND THE PLACE DIDN'T BURN.
YOUR DAUGHTER?
JUST TO BE THOROUGH, I MUST ASK HER ALSO...
CAN YOU THINK OF ANYONE WHO'D HOLD A GRUDGE AGAINST YOUR SHOP?
NO ONE...
I CAN'T THINK OF ANYTHING WE'VE DONE THAT WOULD MAKE SOMEONE DO THIS.

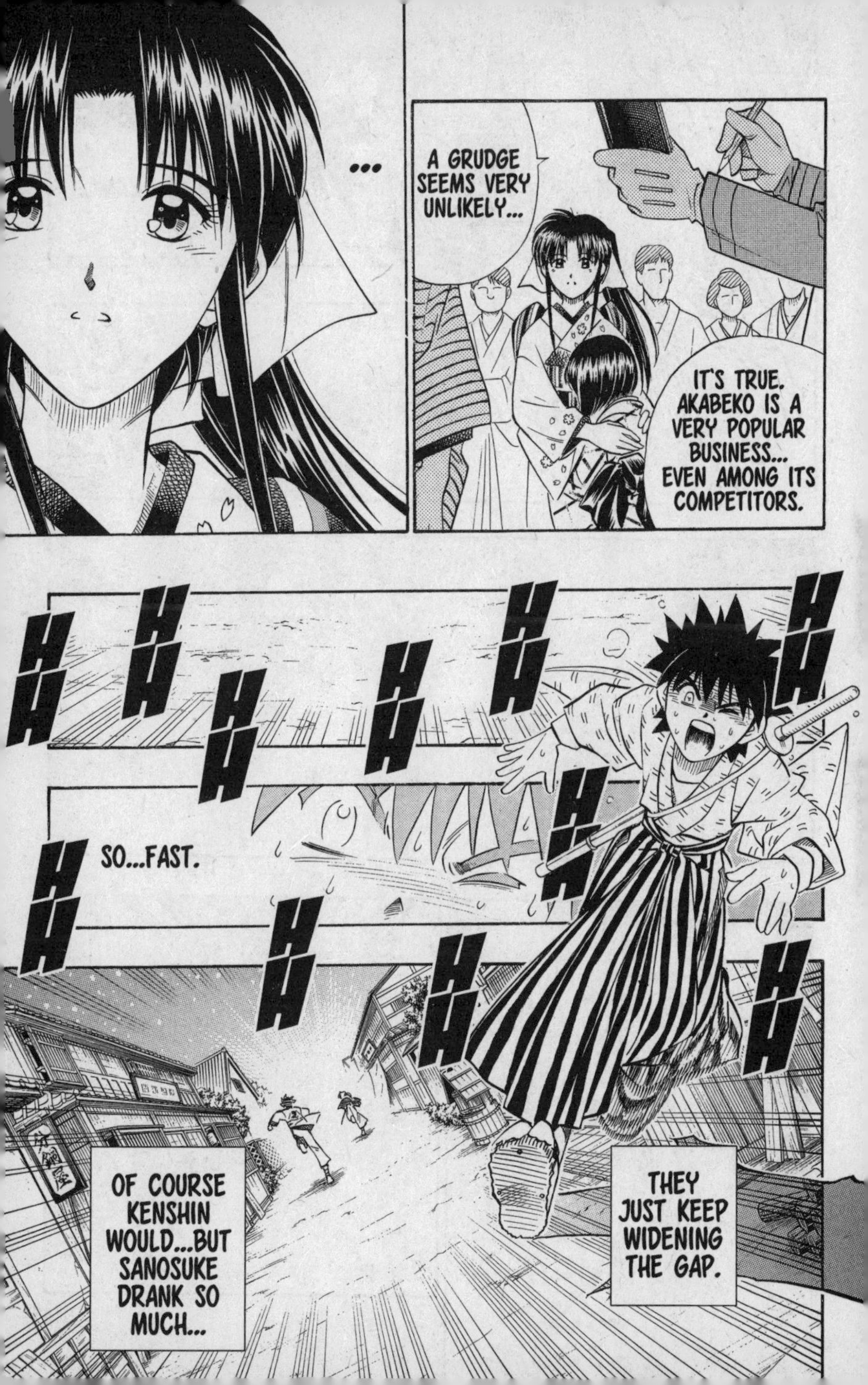
A GRUDGE SEEMS VERY UNLIKELY...
IT'S TRUE. AKABEKO IS A VERY POPULAR BUSINESS... EVEN AMONG ITS COMPETITORS.
...
SO...FAST.
THEY JUST KEEP WIDENING THE GAP.
OF COURSE KENSHIN WOULD...BUT SANOSUKE DRANK SO MUCH...

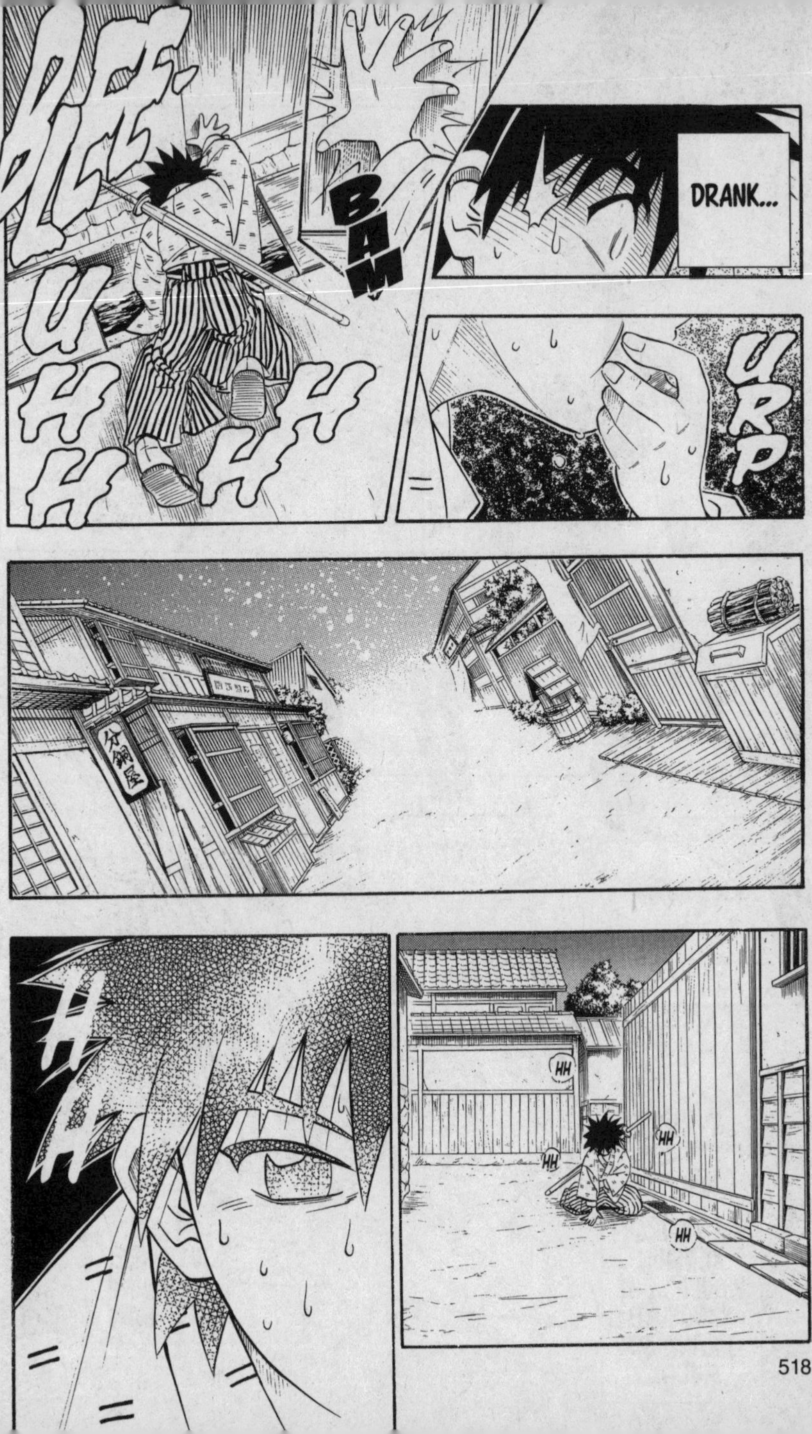
DRANK...
URP
BAM
分銅屋
HH
HH
HH
HH

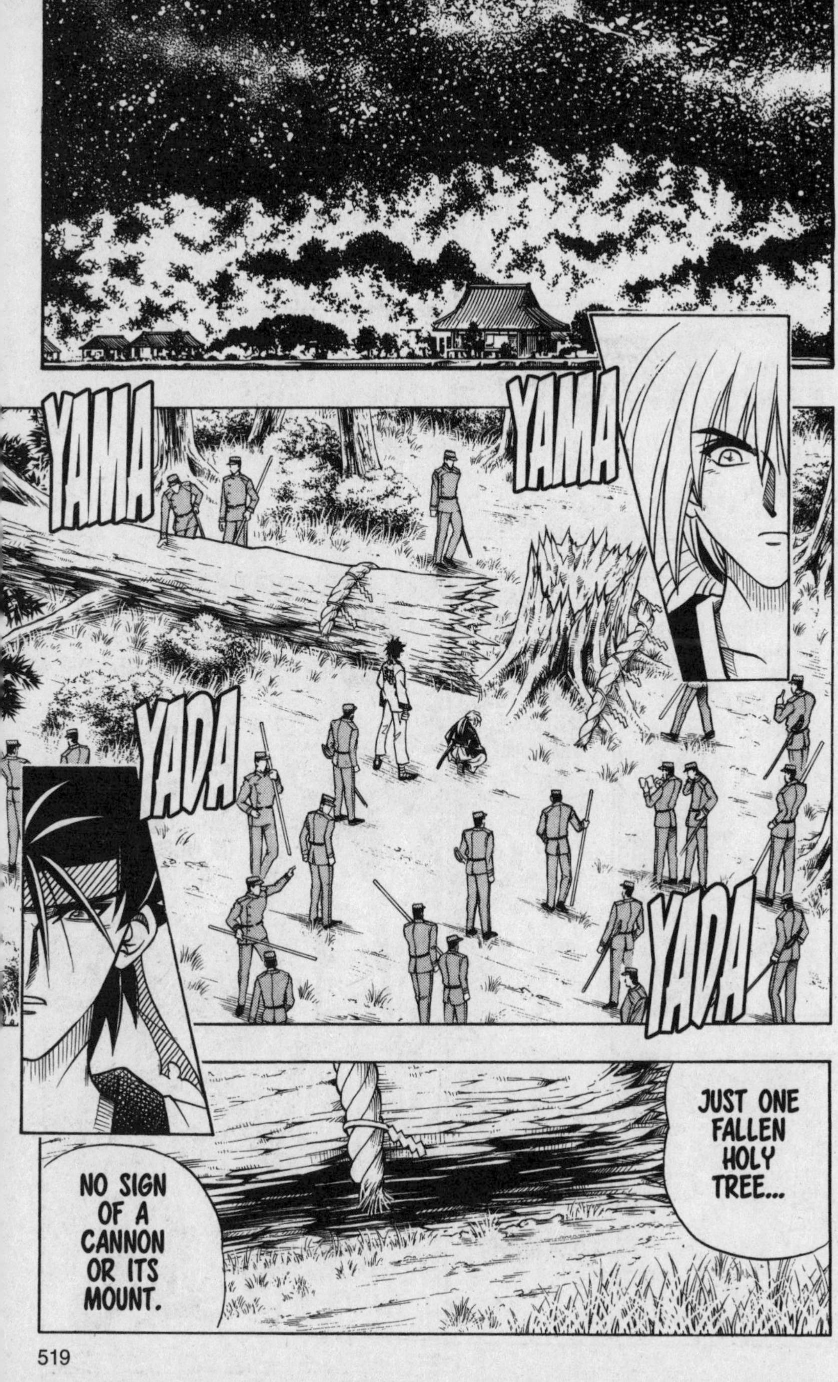
YAMA
YAMA
YADA
YADA
JUST ONE FALLEN HOLY TREE...
NO SIGN OF A CANNON OR ITS MOUNT.

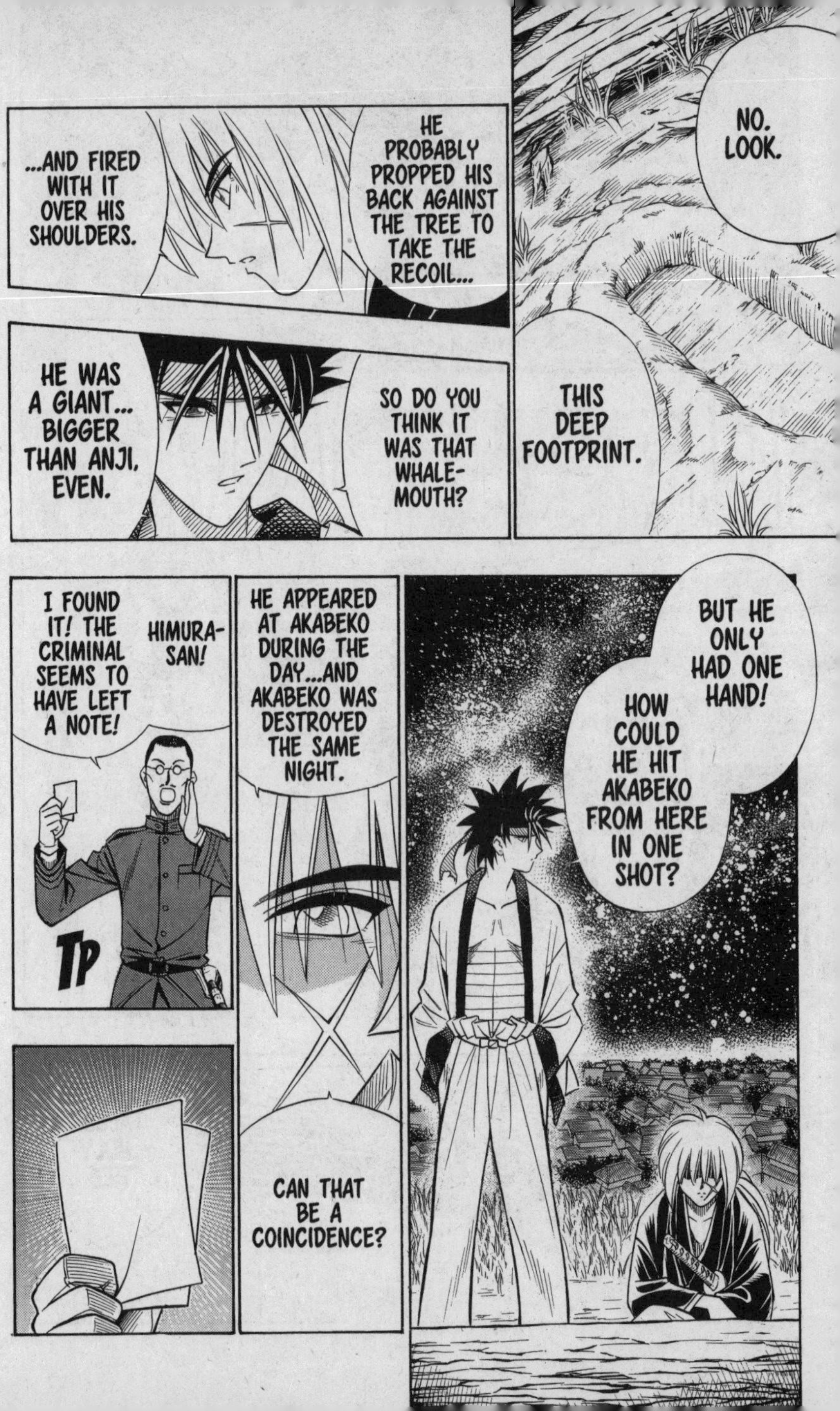
NO. LOOK.
THIS DEEP FOOTPRINT.
HE PROBABLY PROPPED HIS BACK AGAINST THE TREE TO TAKE THE RECOIL...
...AND FIRED WITH IT OVER HIS SHOULDERS.
SO DO YOU THINK IT WAS THAT WHALE-MOUTH?
HE WAS A GIANT... BIGGER THAN ANJI, EVEN.
BUT HE ONLY HAD ONE HAND!
HOW COULD HE HIT AKABEKO FROM HERE IN ONE SHOT?
HE APPEARED AT AKABEKO DURING THE DAY...AND AKABEKO WAS DESTROYED THE SAME NIGHT.
CAN THAT BE A COINCIDENCE?
HIMURA-SAN!
I FOUND IT! THE CRIMINAL SEEMS TO HAVE LEFT A NOTE!
TP

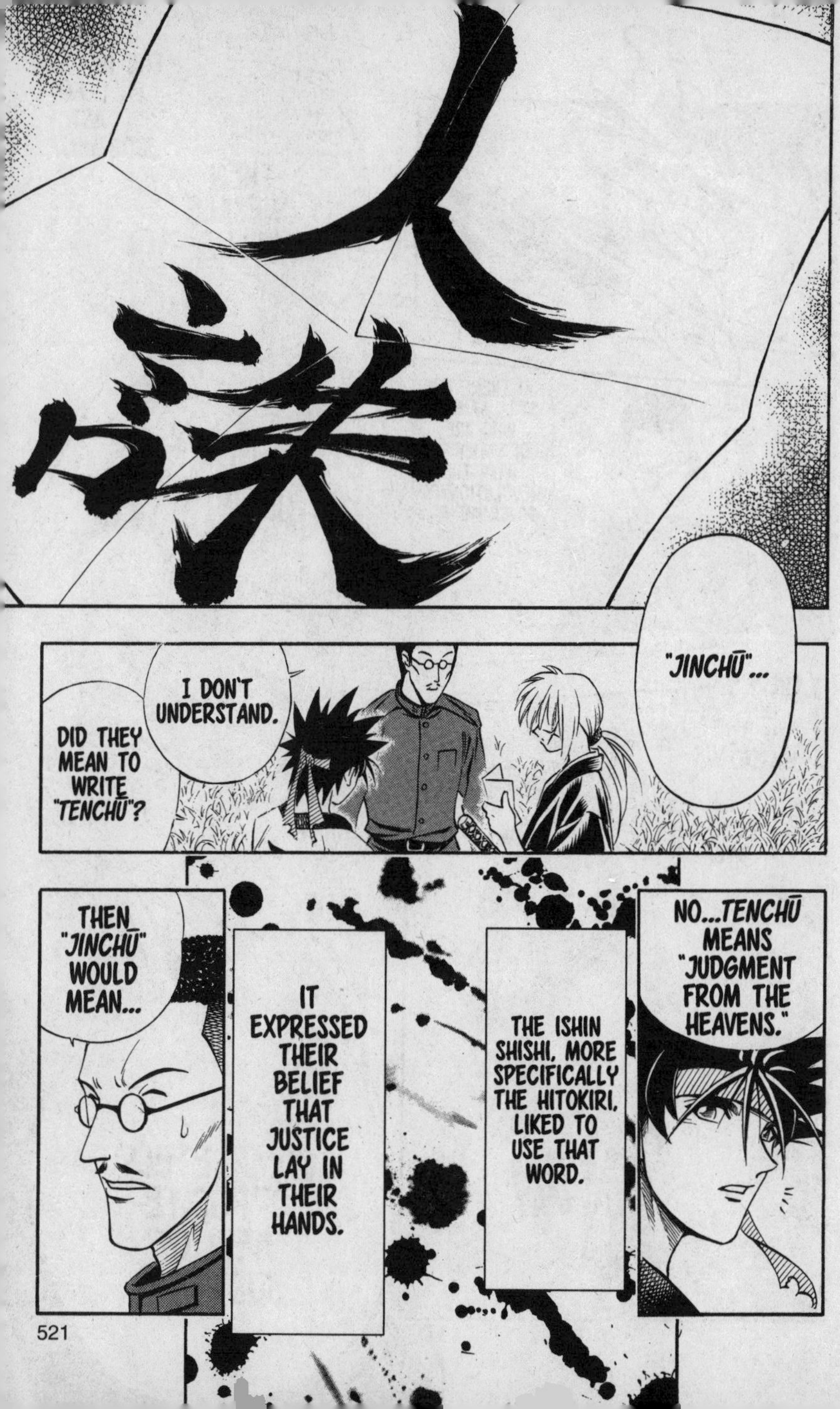
人誅
"JINCHŪ"...
I DON'T UNDERSTAND.
DID THEY MEAN TO WRITE "TENCHŪ"?
NO...TENCHŪ MEANS "JUDGMENT FROM THE HEAVENS."
THE ISHIN SHISHI, MORE SPECIFICALLY THE HITOKIRI, LIKED TO USE THAT WORD.
IT EXPRESSED THEIR BELIEF THAT JUSTICE LAY IN THEIR HANDS.
THEN "JINCHŪ" WOULD MEAN...

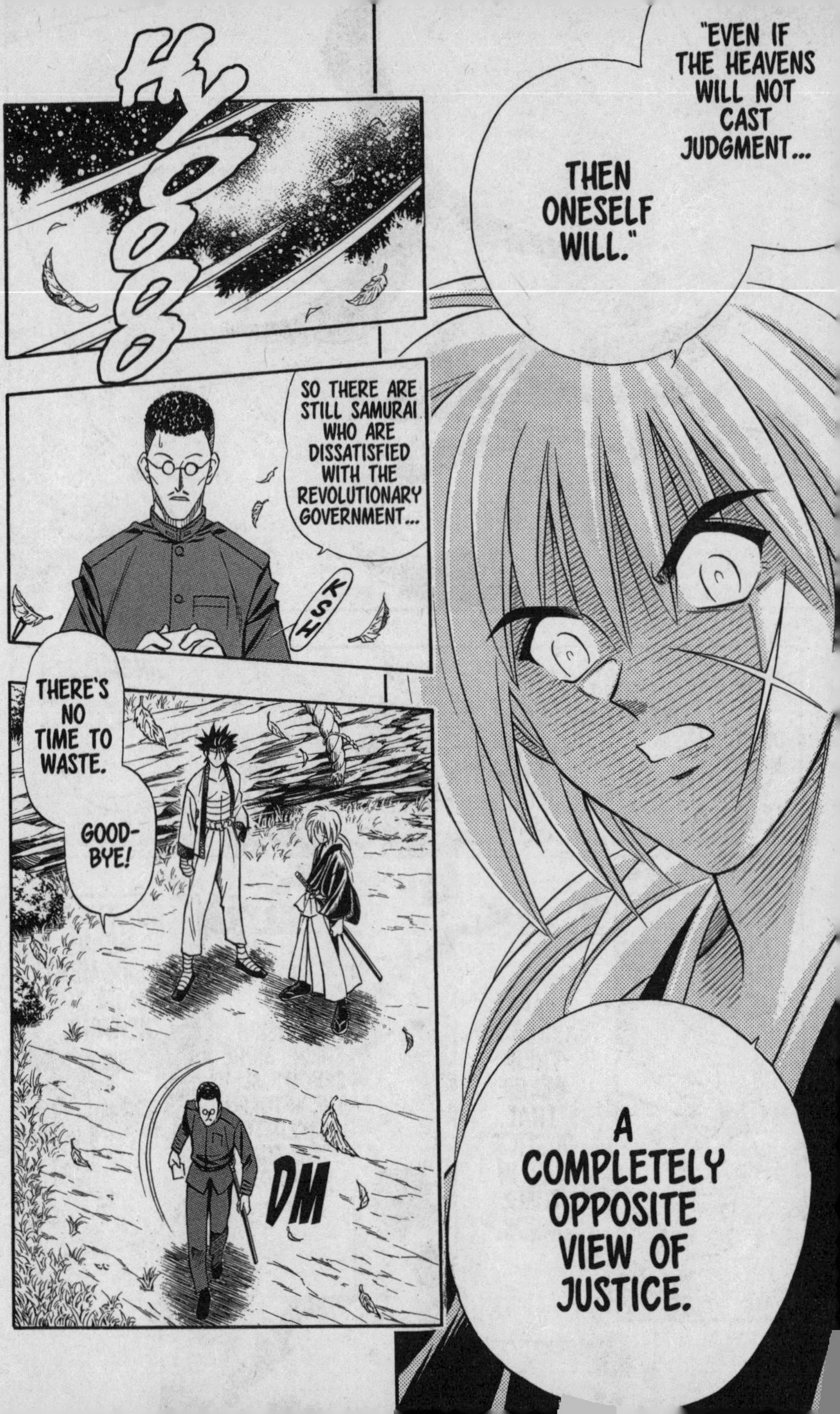
"EVEN IF THE HEAVENS WILL NOT CAST JUDGMENT...
THEN ONESELF WILL."
A COMPLETELY OPPOSITE VIEW OF JUSTICE.
HYOOOO
SO THERE ARE STILL SAMURAI WHO ARE DISSATISFIED WITH THE REVOLUTIONARY GOVERNMENT...
KSH
THERE'S NO TIME TO WASTE.
GOOD-BYE!
DM

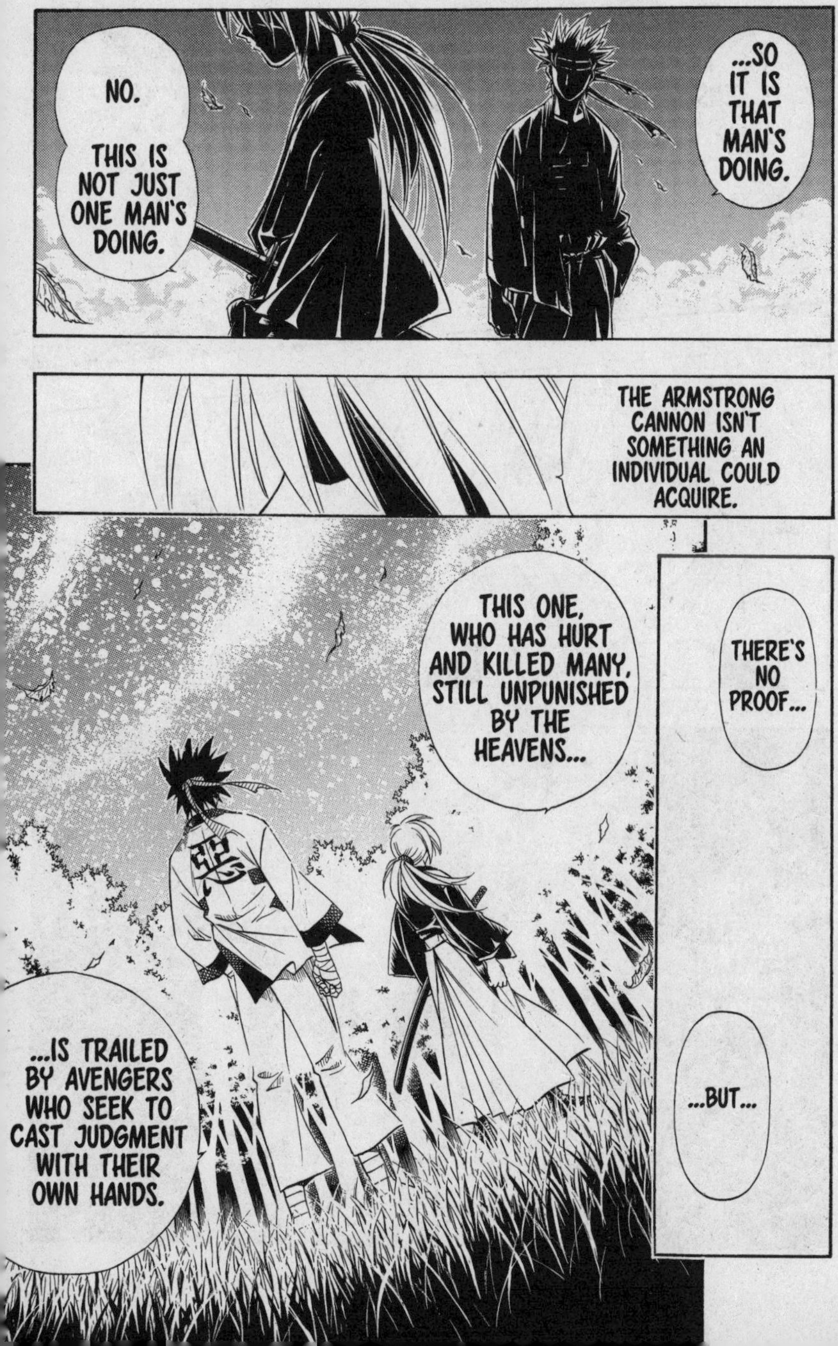
...SO IT IS THAT MAN'S DOING.
NO.
THIS IS NOT JUST ONE MAN'S DOING.
THE ARMSTRONG CANNON ISN'T SOMETHING AN INDIVIDUAL COULD ACQUIRE.
THERE'S NO PROOF...
...BUT...
THIS ONE, WHO HAS HURT AND KILLED MANY, STILL UNPUNISHED BY THE HEAVENS...
...IS TRAILED BY AVENGERS WHO SEEK TO CAST JUDGMENT WITH THEIR OWN HANDS.

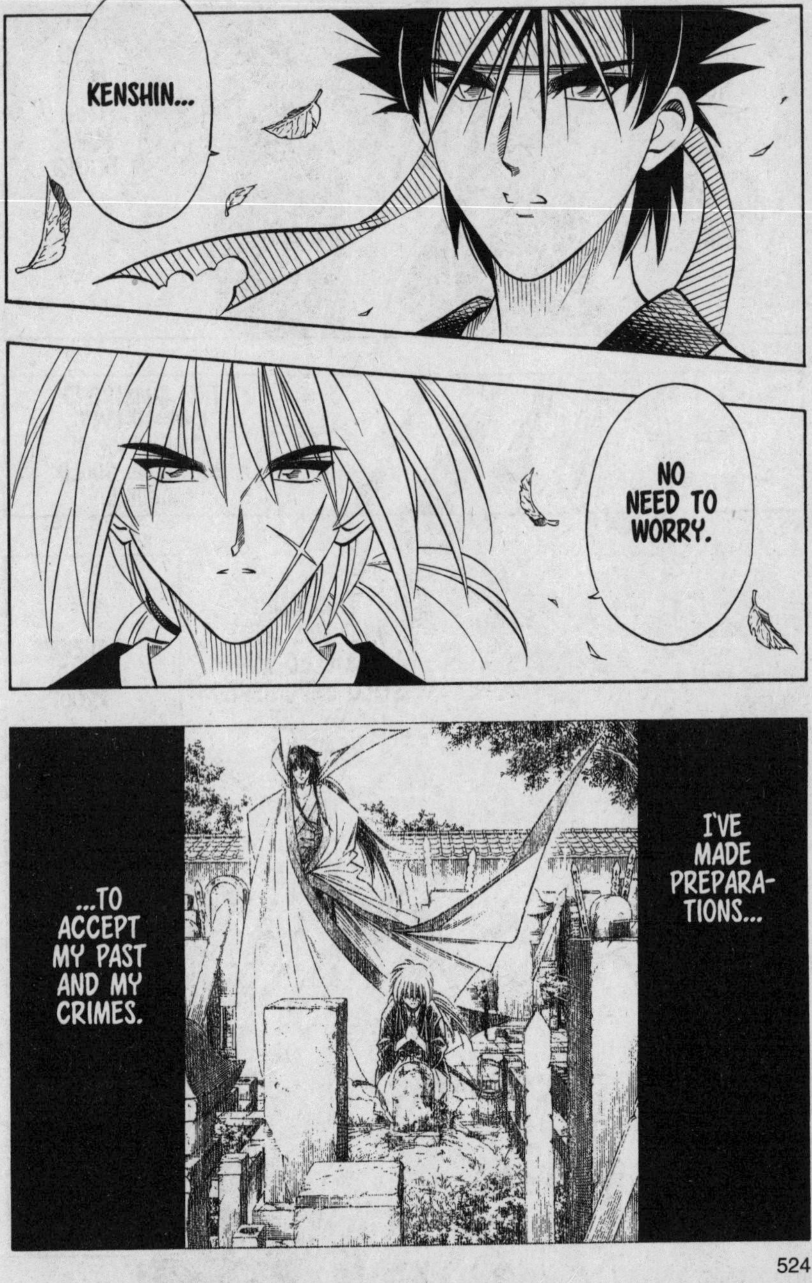
KENSHIN...
NO NEED TO WORRY.
I'VE MADE PREPARATIONS...
...TO ACCEPT MY PAST AND MY CRIMES.

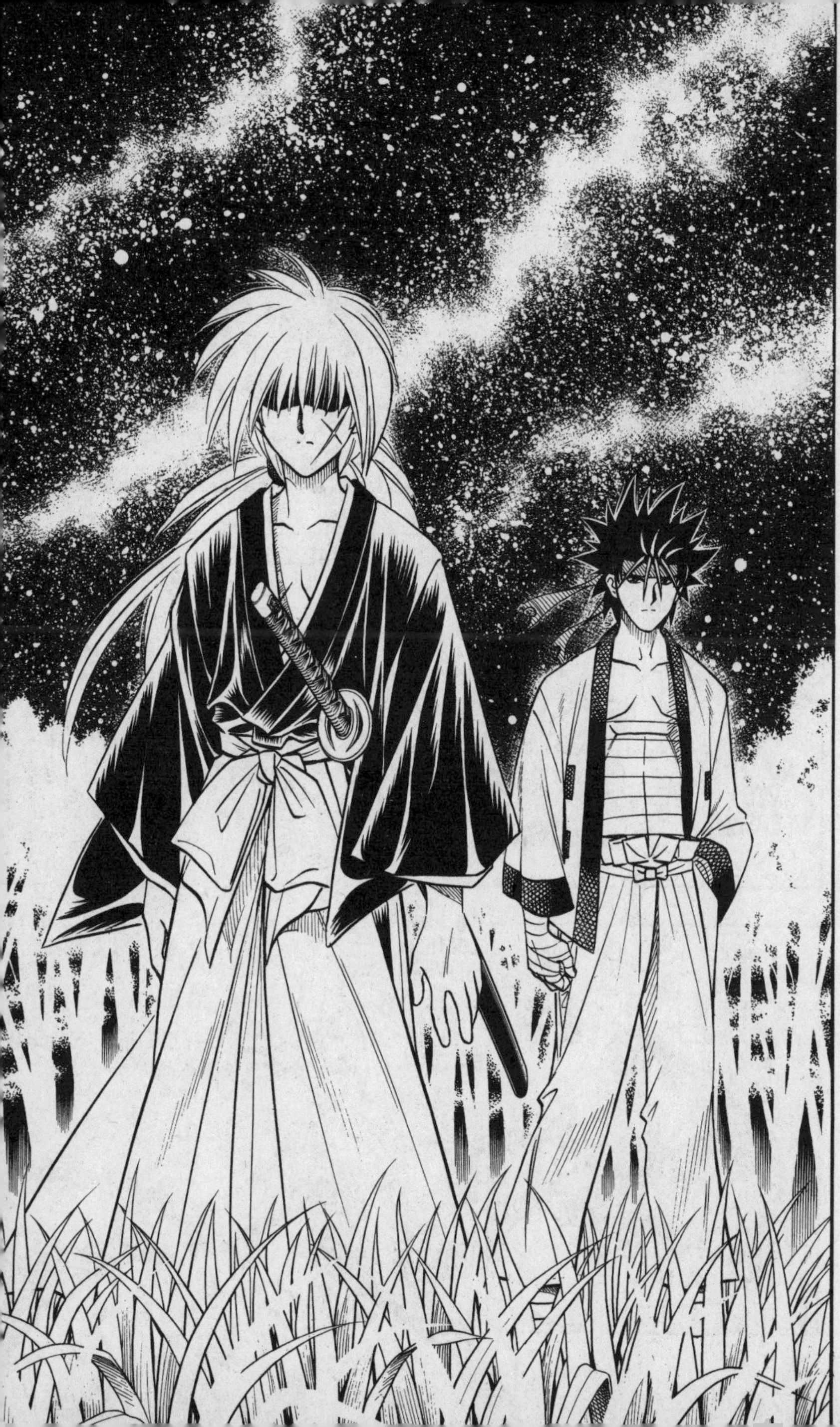

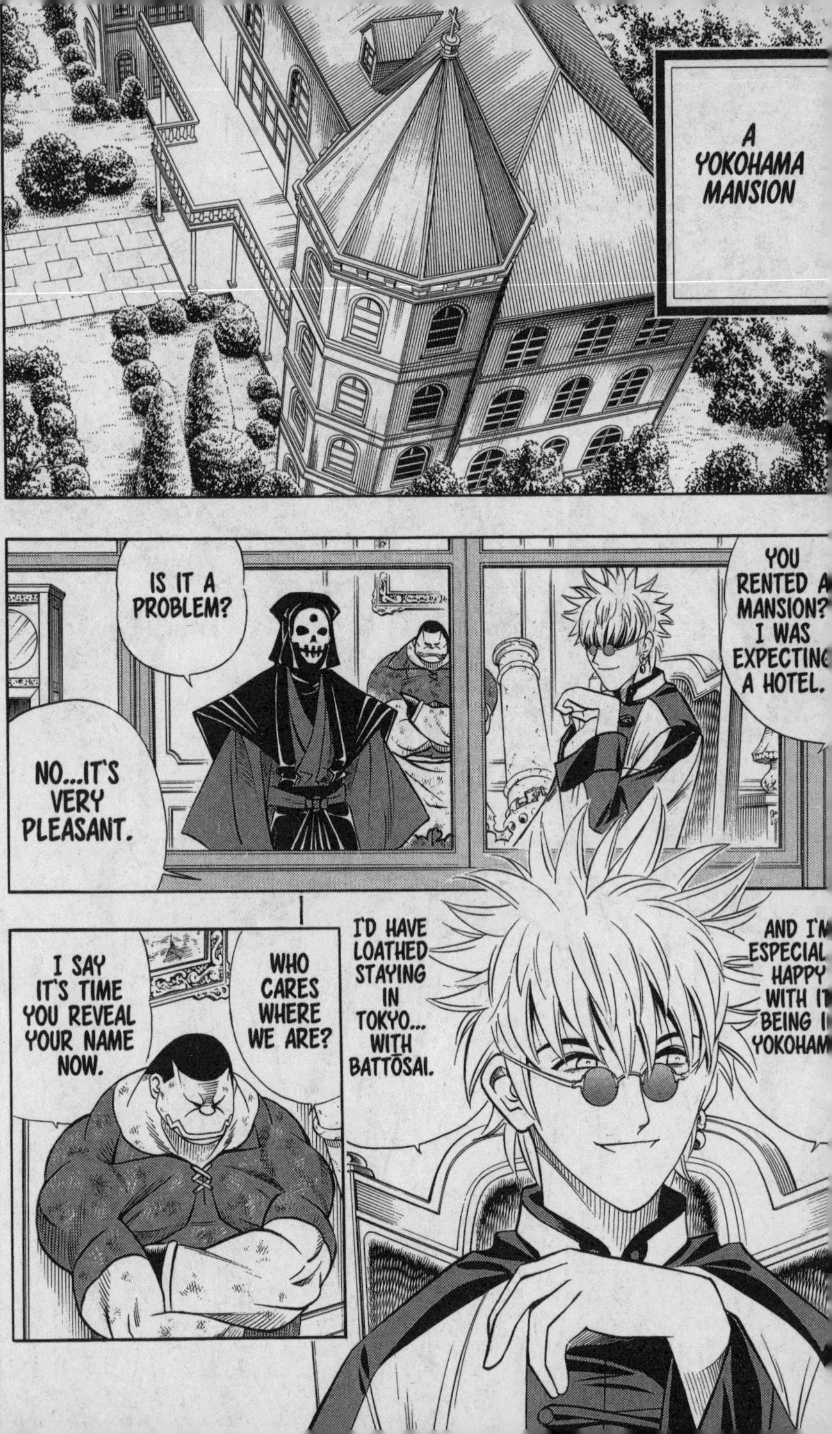
A YOKOHAMA MANSION
YOU RENTED A MANSION? I WAS EXPECTING A HOTEL.
IS IT A PROBLEM?
NO...IT'S VERY PLEASANT.
AND I'M ESPECIAL HAPPY WITH IT BEING I YOKOHAM
I'D HAVE LOATHED STAYING IN TOKYO... WITH BATTŌSAI.
WHO CARES WHERE WE ARE?
I SAY IT'S TIME YOU REVEAL YOUR NAME NOW.

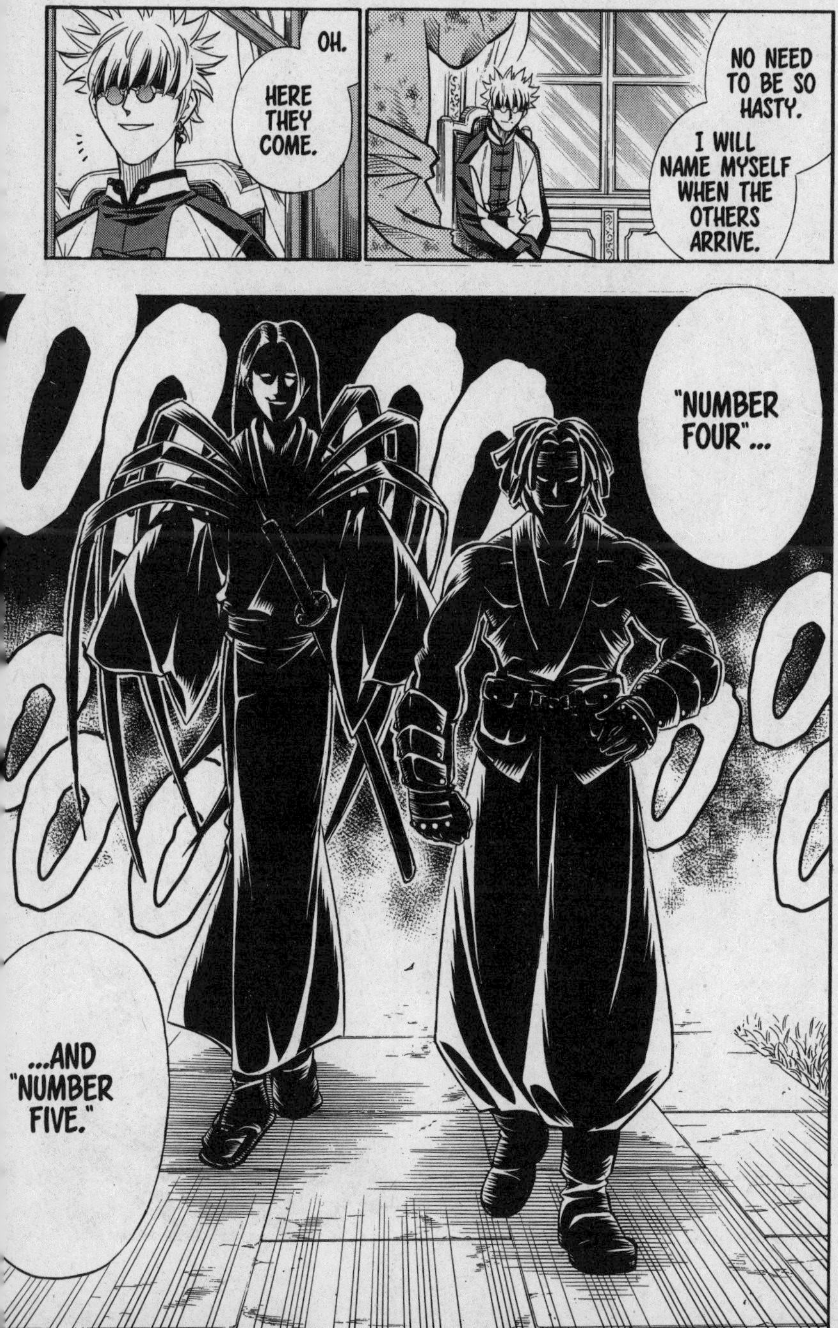
NO NEED TO BE SO HASTY.
I WILL NAME MYSELF WHEN THE OTHERS ARRIVE.
OH.
HERE THEY COME.
"NUMBER FOUR"...
...AND "NUMBER FIVE."

Rurouni Kenshin

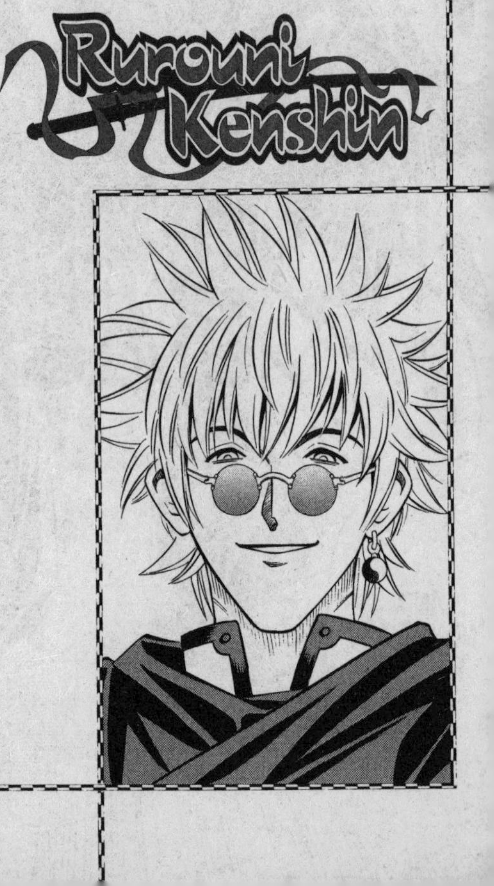

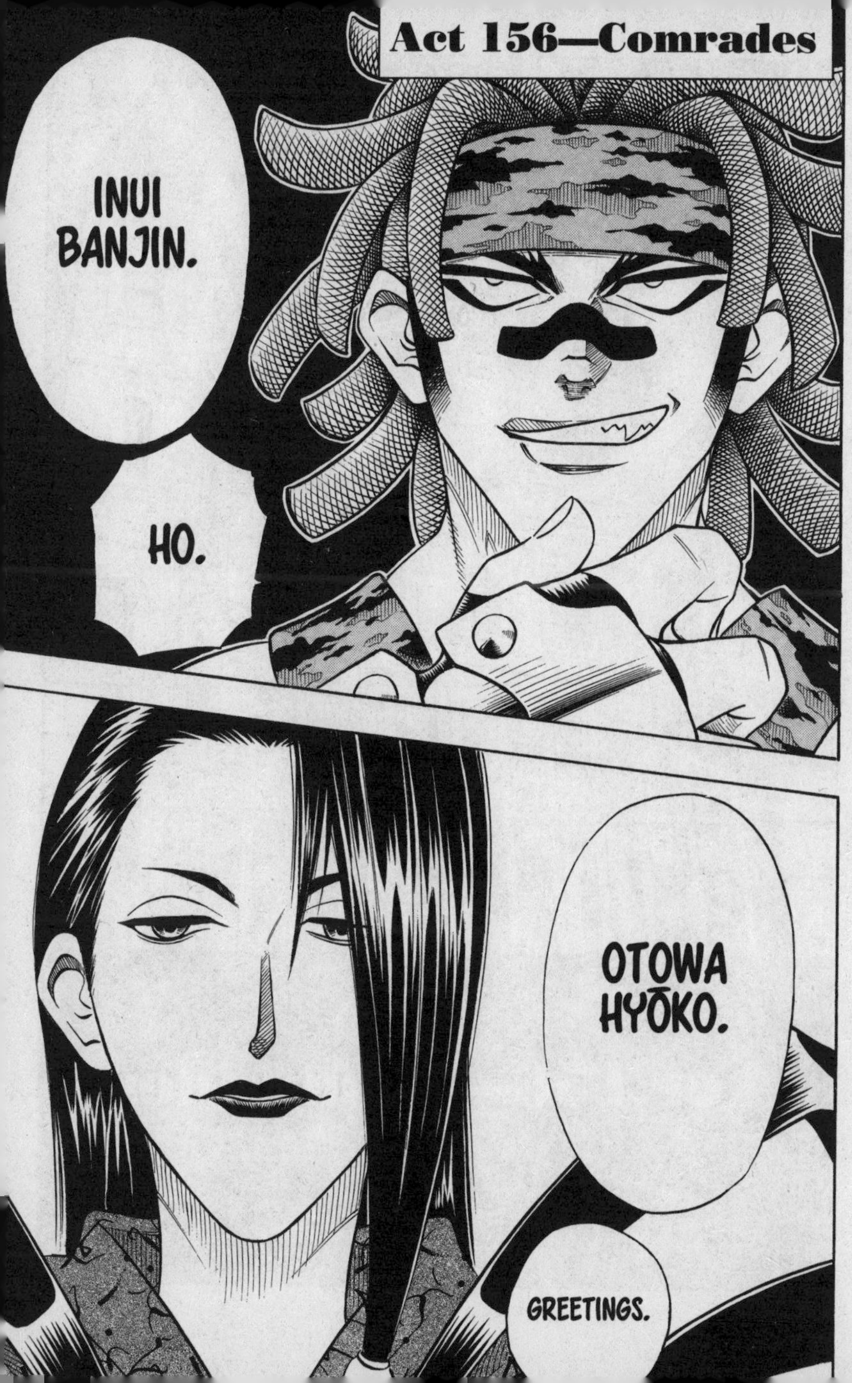
Act 156—Comrades
INUI BANJIN.
HO.
OTOWA HYŌKO.
GREETINGS.

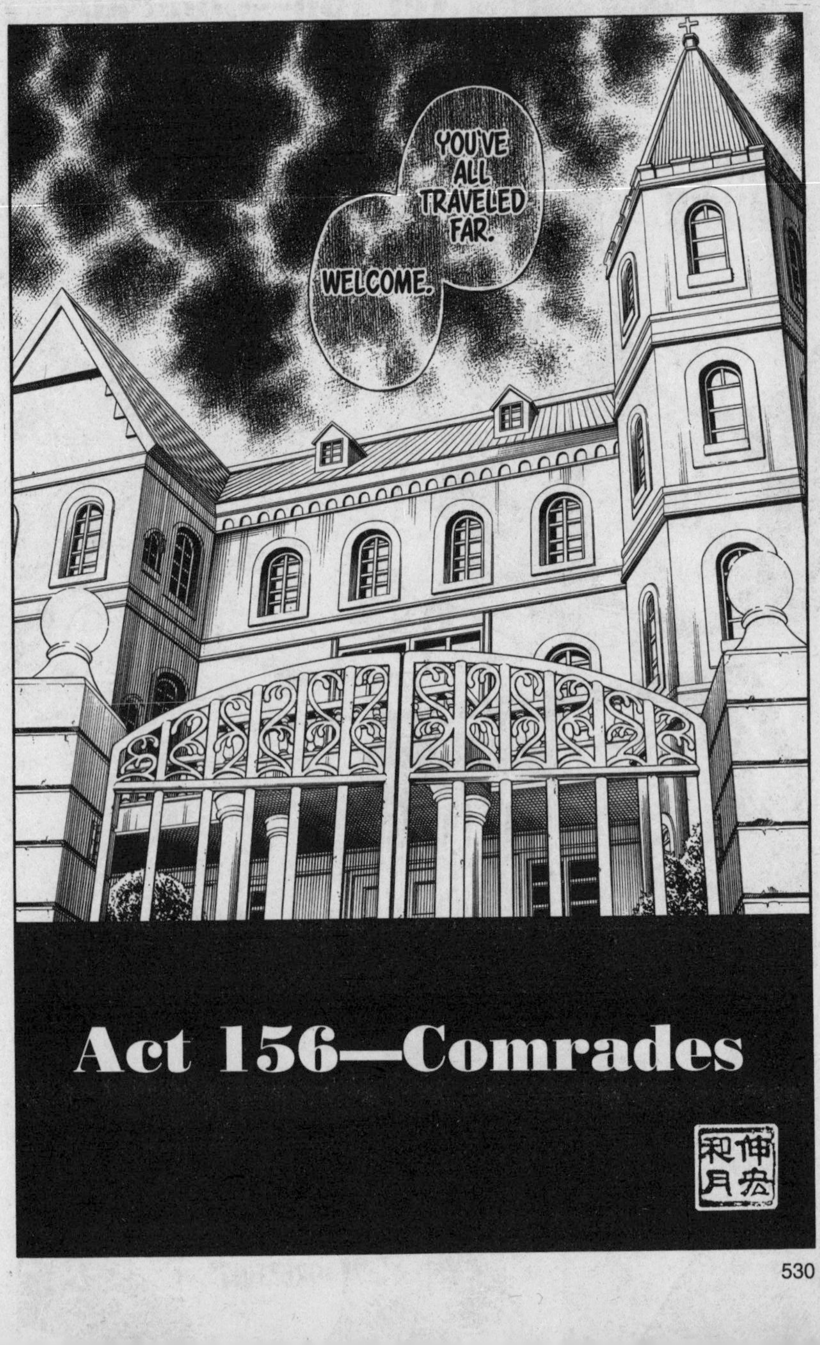
YOU'VE ALL TRAVELED FAR.
WELCOME.

Act 156—Comrades

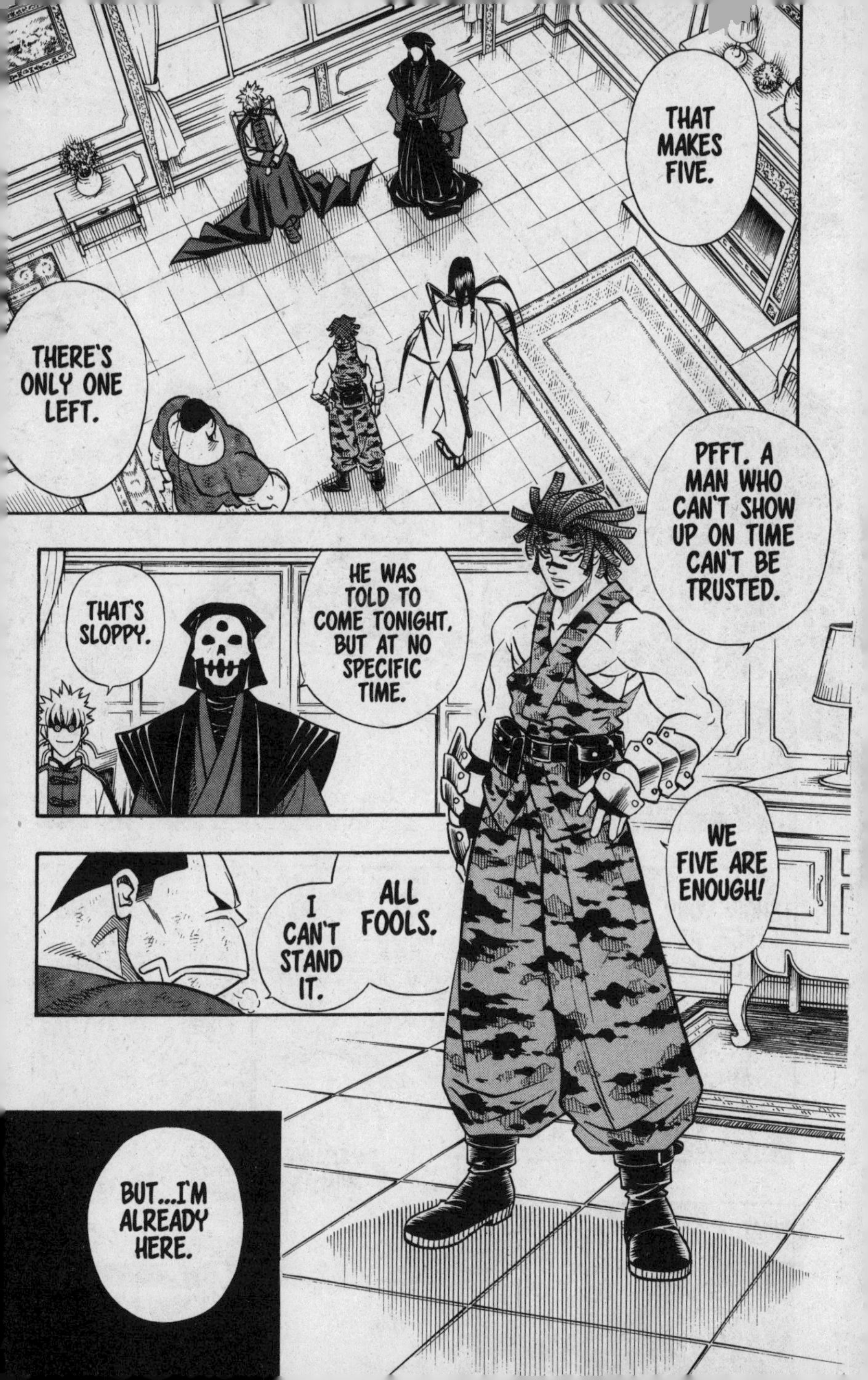
THAT MAKES FIVE.
THERE'S ONLY ONE LEFT.
PFFT. A MAN WHO CAN'T SHOW UP ON TIME CAN'T BE TRUSTED.
WE FIVE ARE ENOUGH!
HE WAS TOLD TO COME TONIGHT, BUT AT NO SPECIFIC TIME.
THAT'S SLOPPY.
ALL FOOLS.
I CAN'T STAND IT.
BUT...I'M ALREADY HERE.

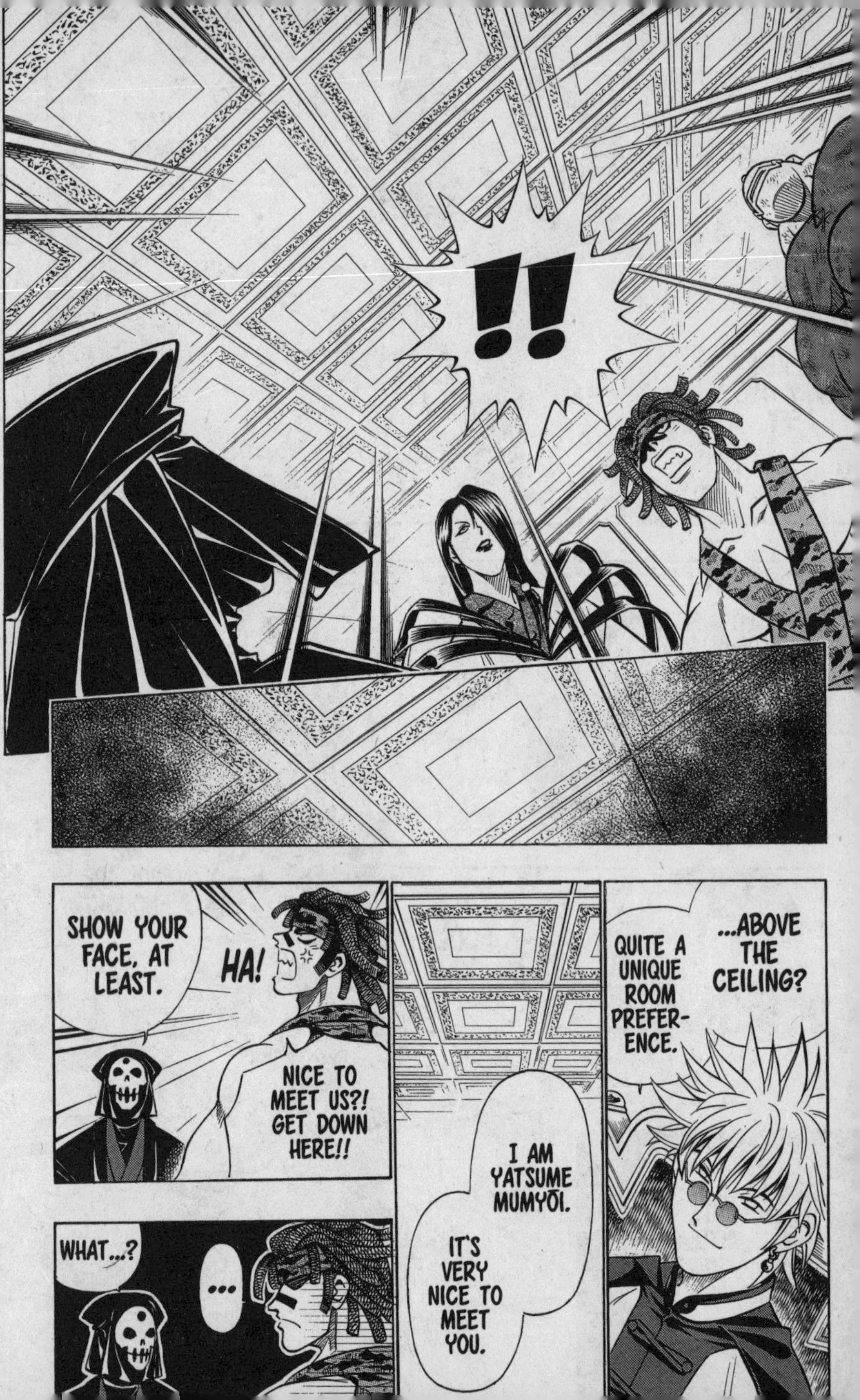
!!
...ABOVE THE CEILING?
QUITE A UNIQUE ROOM PREFERENCE.
I AM YATSUME MUMYŌI.
IT'S VERY NICE TO MEET YOU.
HA!
SHOW YOUR FACE, AT LEAST.
NICE TO MEET US?! GET DOWN HERE!!
...
WHAT...?

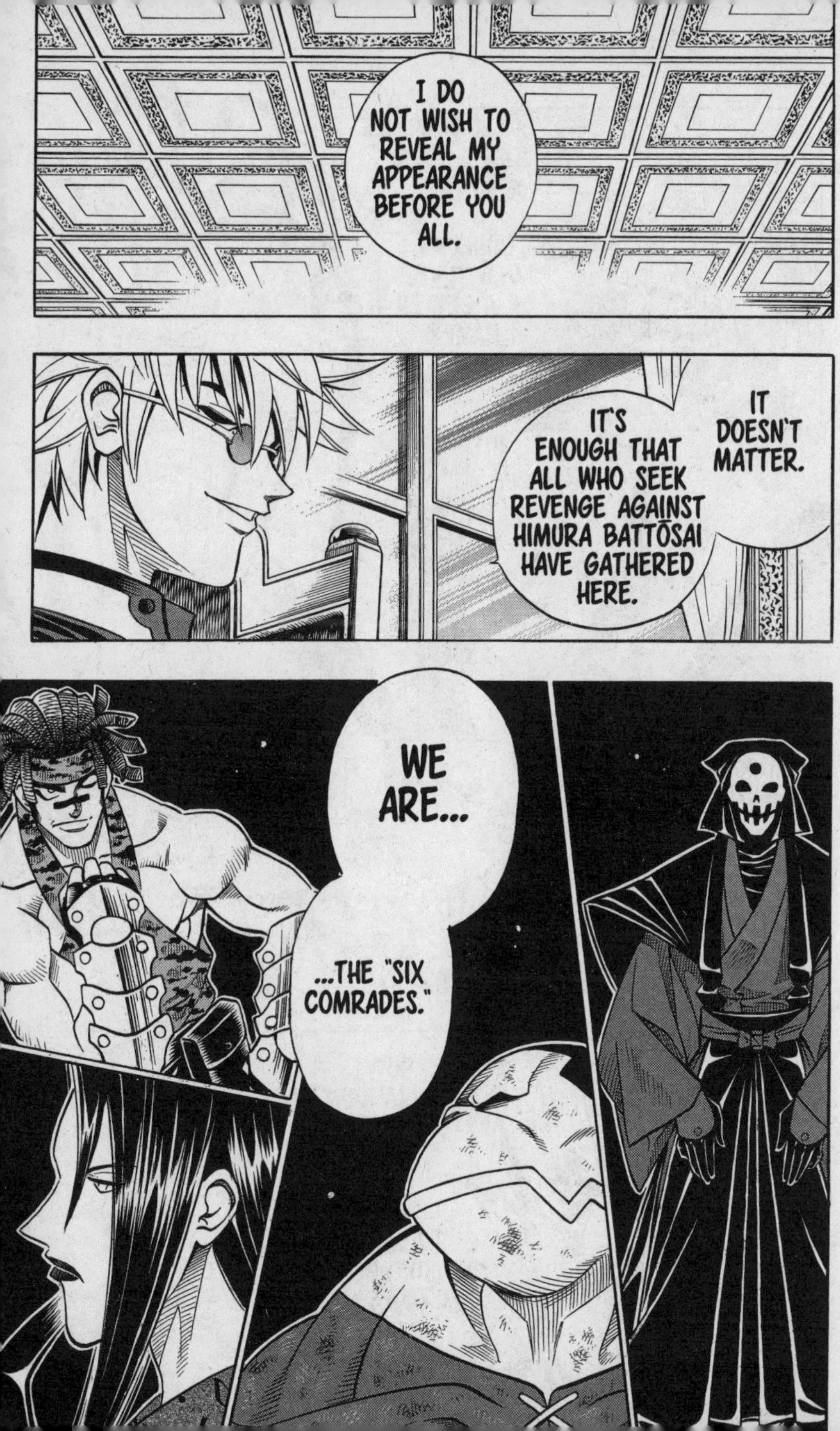
I DO NOT WISH TO REVEAL MY APPEARANCE BEFORE YOU ALL.
IT DOESN'T MATTER.
IT'S ENOUGH THAT ALL WHO SEEK REVENGE AGAINST HIMURA BATTŌSAI HAVE GATHERED HERE.
WE ARE...
...THE "SIX COMRADES."

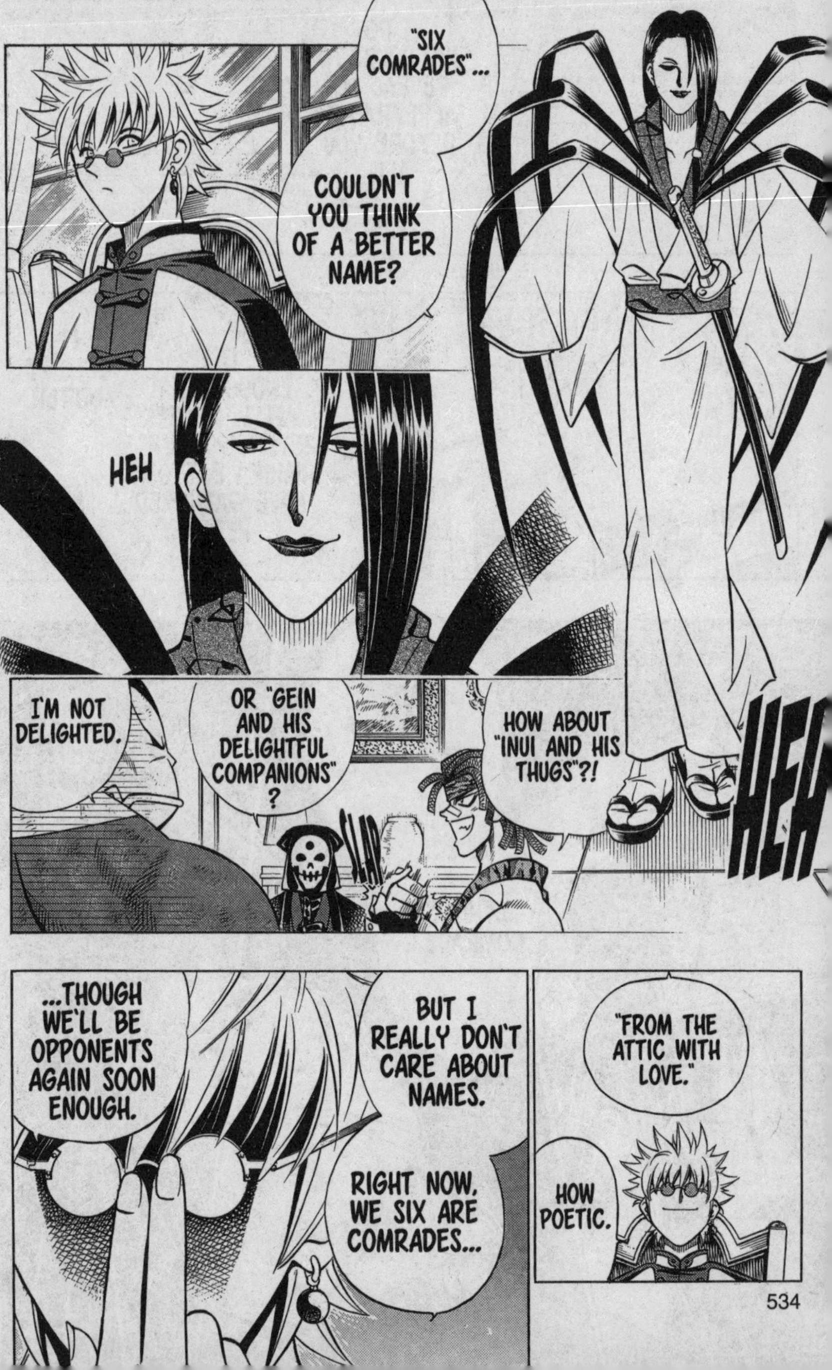
"SIX COMRADES"...
COULDN'T YOU THINK OF A BETTER NAME?
HEH
HEH
HOW ABOUT "INUI AND HIS THUGS"?!
OR "GEIN AND HIS DELIGHTFUL COMPANIONS"?
I'M NOT DELIGHTED.
SLAP
"FROM THE ATTIC WITH LOVE."
HOW POETIC.
BUT I REALLY DON'T CARE ABOUT NAMES.
RIGHT NOW, WE SIX ARE COMRADES...
...THOUGH WE'LL BE OPPONENTS AGAIN SOON ENOUGH.

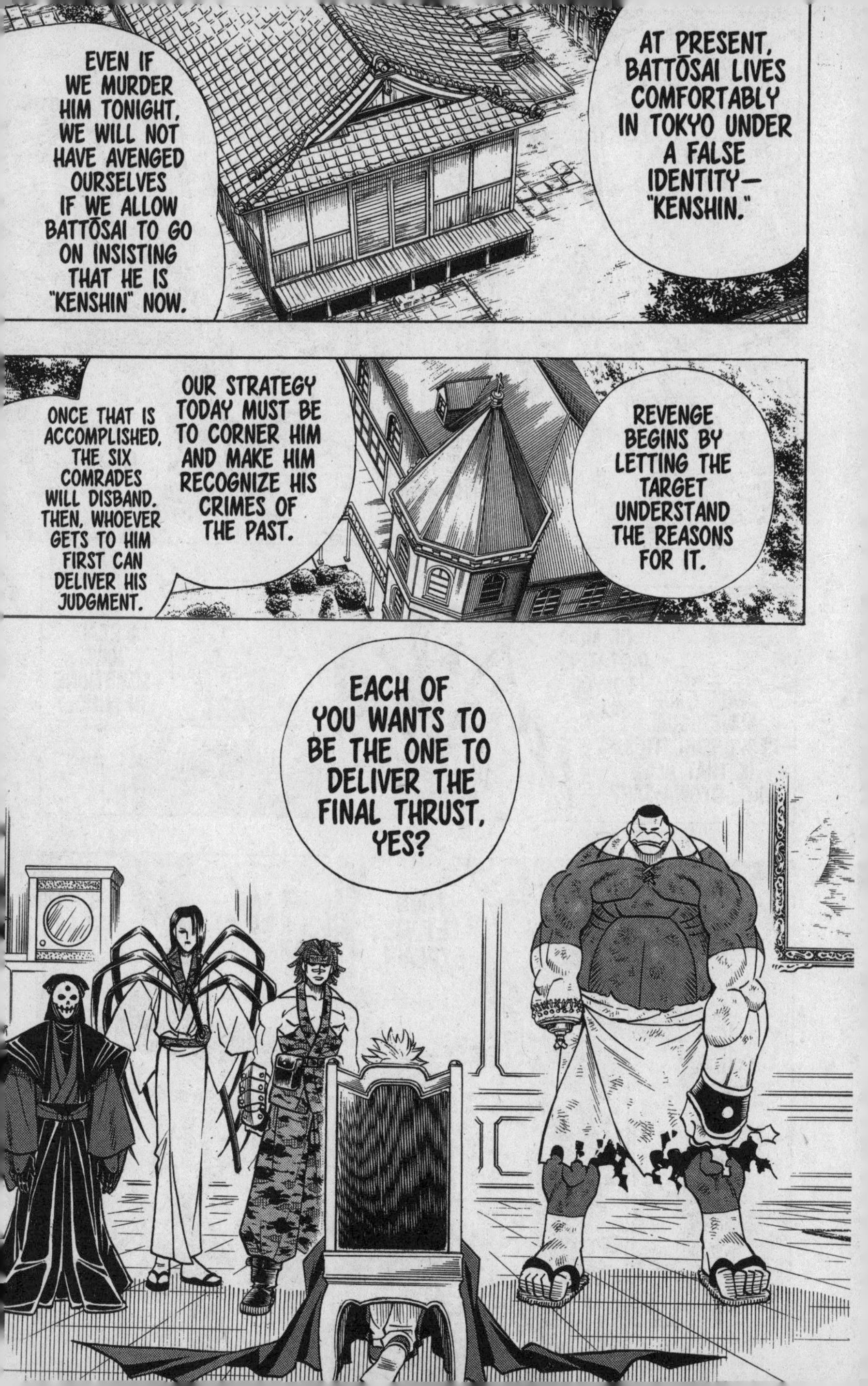
AT PRESENT, BATTŌSAI LIVES COMFORTABLY IN TOKYO UNDER A FALSE IDENTITY—"KENSHIN."
EVEN IF WE MURDER HIM TONIGHT, WE WILL NOT HAVE AVENGED OURSELVES IF WE ALLOW BATTŌSAI TO GO ON INSISTING THAT HE IS "KENSHIN" NOW.
REVENGE BEGINS BY LETTING THE TARGET UNDERSTAND THE REASONS FOR IT.
OUR STRATEGY TODAY MUST BE TO CORNER HIM AND MAKE HIM RECOGNIZE HIS CRIMES OF THE PAST.
ONCE THAT IS ACCOMPLISHED, THE SIX COMRADES WILL DISBAND. THEN, WHOEVER GETS TO HIM FIRST CAN DELIVER HIS JUDGMENT.
EACH OF YOU WANTS TO BE THE ONE TO DELIVER THE FINAL THRUST, YES?

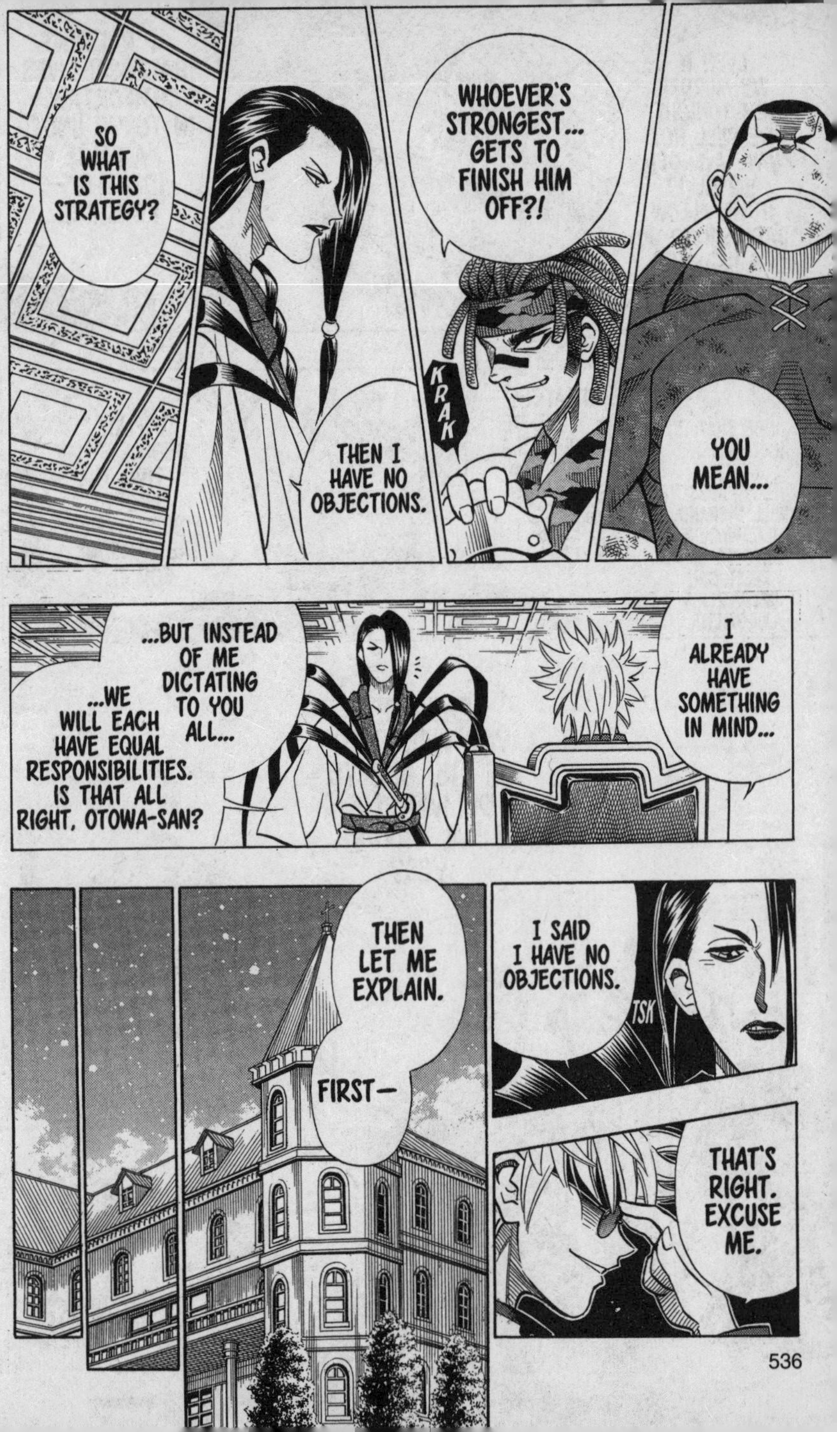

YOU MEAN...
WHOEVER'S STRONGEST... GETS TO FINISH HIM OFF?!
KRAK
THEN I HAVE NO OBJECTIONS.
SO WHAT IS THIS STRATEGY?
I ALREADY HAVE SOMETHING IN MIND...
...BUT INSTEAD OF ME DICTATING TO YOU ALL...
...WE WILL EACH HAVE EQUAL RESPONSIBILITIES. IS THAT ALL RIGHT, OTOWA-SAN?
I SAID I HAVE NO OBJECTIONS.
TSK
THAT'S RIGHT. EXCUSE ME.
THEN LET ME EXPLAIN.
FIRST—

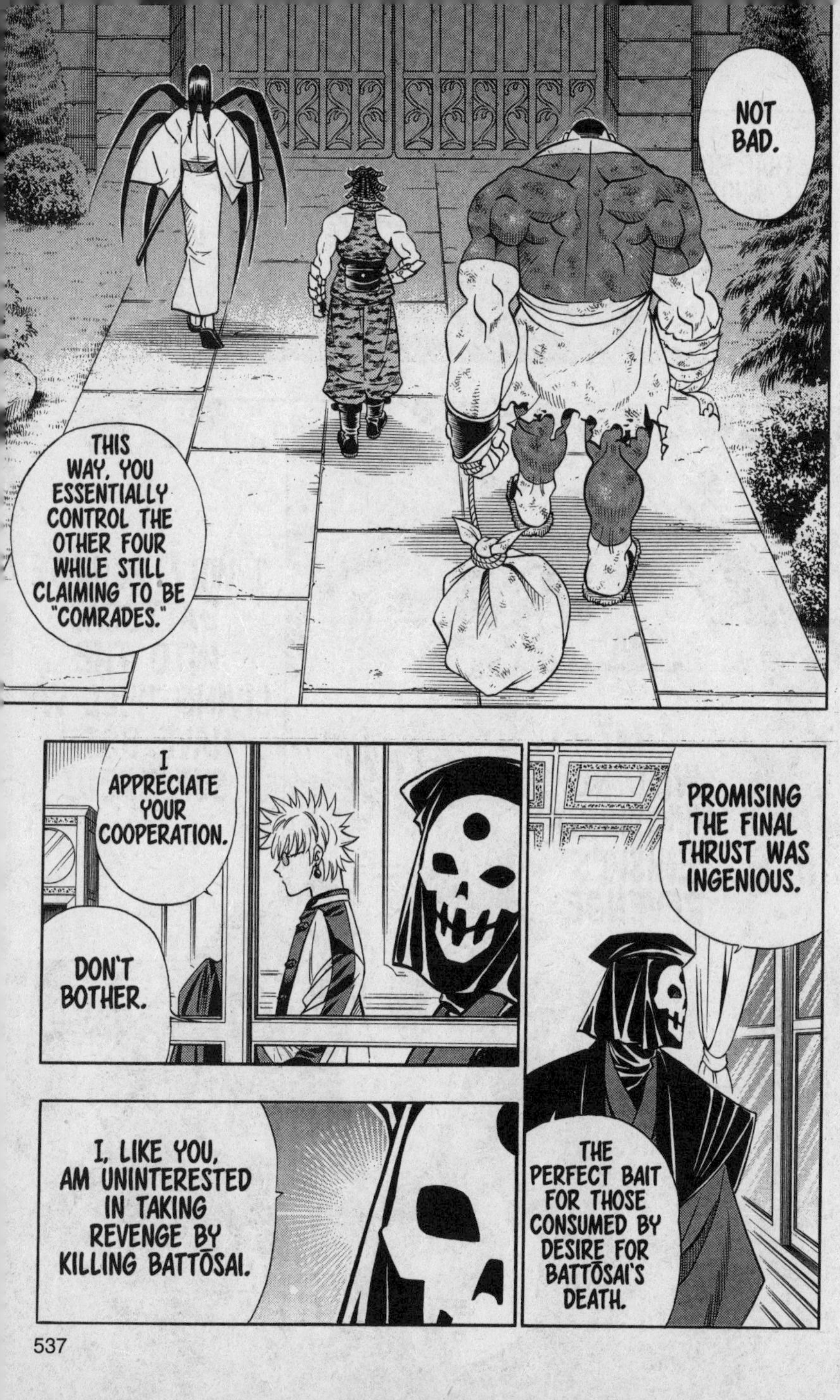
NOT BAD.
THIS WAY, YOU ESSENTIALLY CONTROL THE OTHER FOUR WHILE STILL CLAIMING TO BE "COMRADES."
PROMISING THE FINAL THRUST WAS INGENIOUS.
THE PERFECT BAIT FOR THOSE CONSUMED BY DESIRE FOR BATTŌSAI'S DEATH.
I APPRECIATE YOUR COOPERATION.
DON'T BOTHER.
I, LIKE YOU, AM UNINTERESTED IN TAKING REVENGE BY KILLING BATTŌSAI.

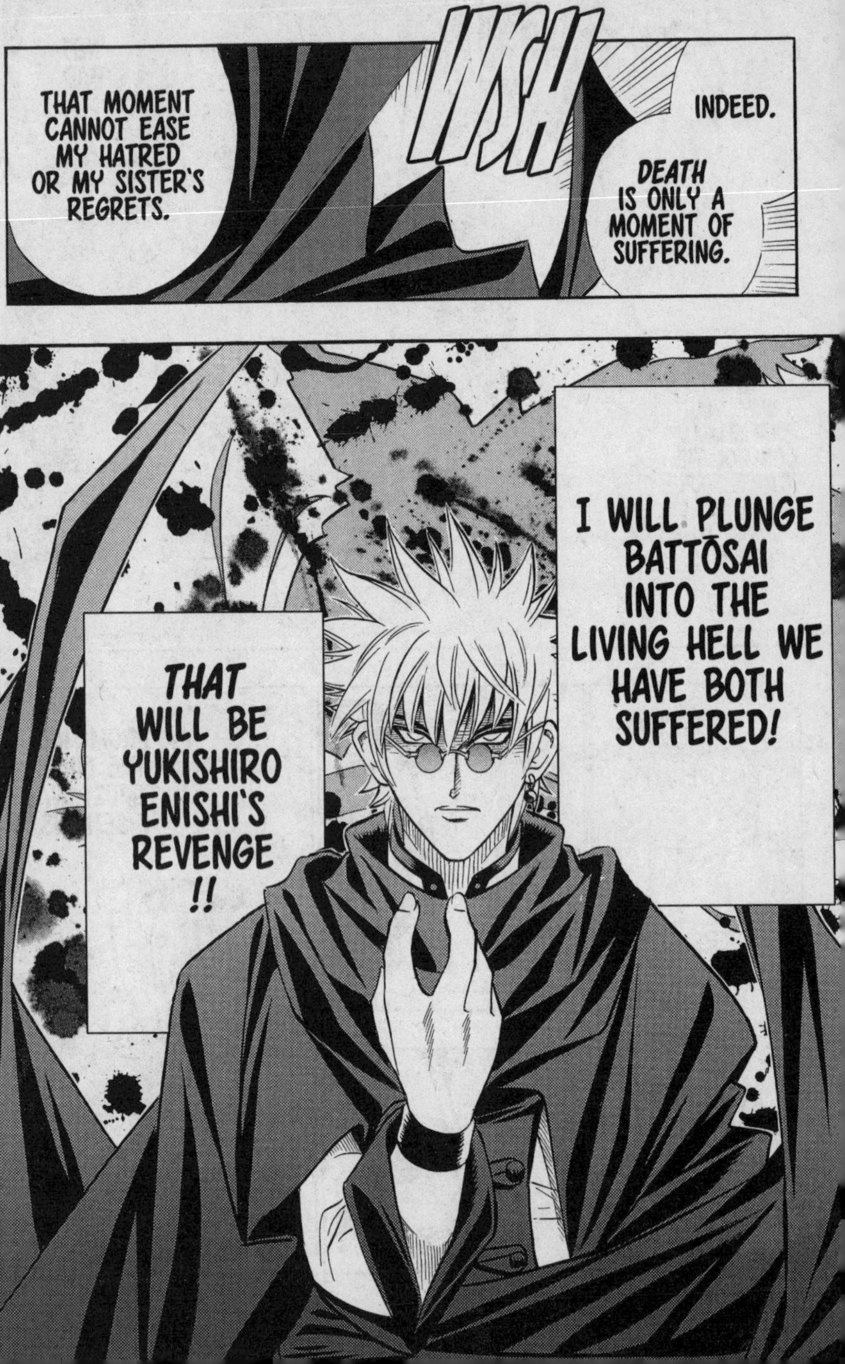
INDEED.
DEATH IS ONLY A MOMENT OF SUFFERING.
WSH
THAT MOMENT CANNOT EASE MY HATRED OR MY SISTER'S REGRETS.
I WILL PLUNGE BATTŌSAI INTO THE LIVING HELL WE HAVE BOTH SUFFERED!
THAT WILL BE YUKISHIRO ENISHI'S REVENGE !!

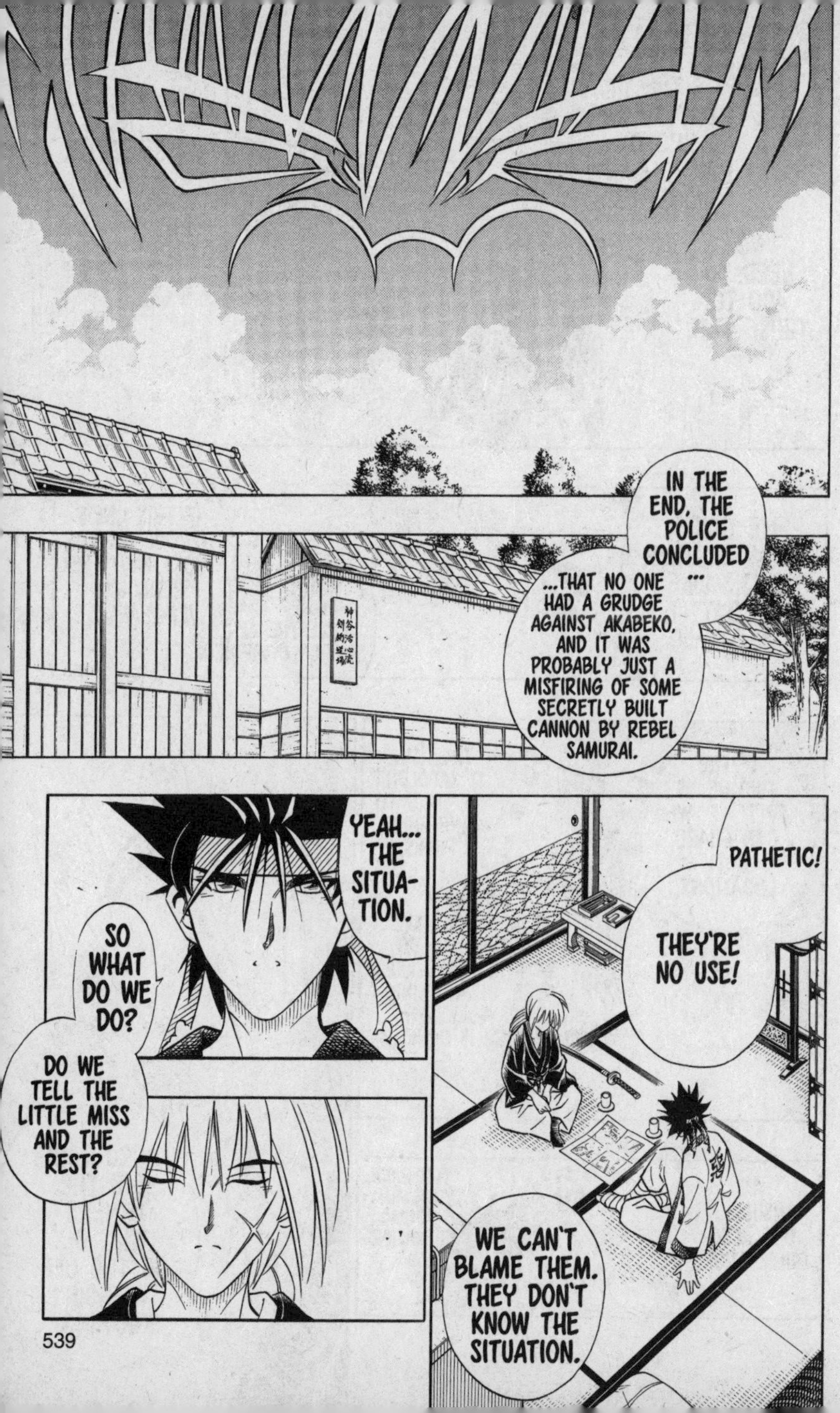
IN THE END, THE POLICE CONCLUDED...
...THAT NO ONE HAD A GRUDGE AGAINST AKABEKO, AND IT WAS PROBABLY JUST A MISFIRING OF SOME SECRETLY BUILT CANNON BY REBEL SAMURAI.
PATHETIC!
THEY'RE NO USE!
WE CAN'T BLAME THEM. THEY DON'T KNOW THE SITUATION.
YEAH... THE SITUATION.
SO WHAT DO WE DO?
DO WE TELL THE LITTLE MISS AND THE REST?

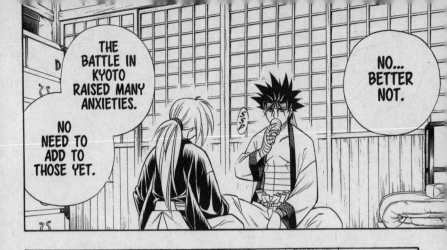

NO... BETTER NOT.
THE BATTLE IN KYOTO RAISED MANY ANXIETIES.
SSP
NO NEED TO ADD TO THOSE YET.
IF THIS ONE'S OPPONENTS ARE THOSE WHO SEEK PERSONAL VENGEANCE...
THEY'LL BE ABLE TO MUSTER MORE POWER THAN ALL THE TEN SWORDS COMBINED.
WE CAN'T ALLOW ANOTHER CRISIS LIKE THE BATTLE AT AOI-YA.
KAORU-DONO AND THE OTHERS WILL BE BETTER OFF WITHOUT KNOWING.
TRUE...AND IT SHOULDN'T BE HARD TO FIND THESE PUNKS.
THE ONLY PLACES YOU HAVE ANYTHING TO DO WITH IN TOKYO ARE HERE, OGUNI CLINIC, AND AKABEKO—WHICH IS GONE.
TI TINNG
IF THE TWO OF US SPLIT UP, WE CAN GUARD BOTH LOCATIONS.
FOR ONCE, YOUR ANTI-SOCIAL BEHAVIOR PAYS OFF.
AN INSULT... BUT ALSO QUITE TRUE.

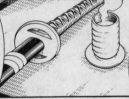

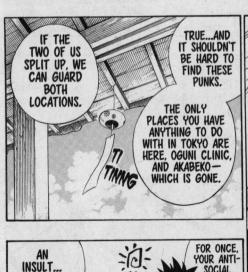

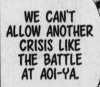

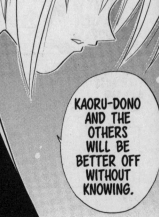

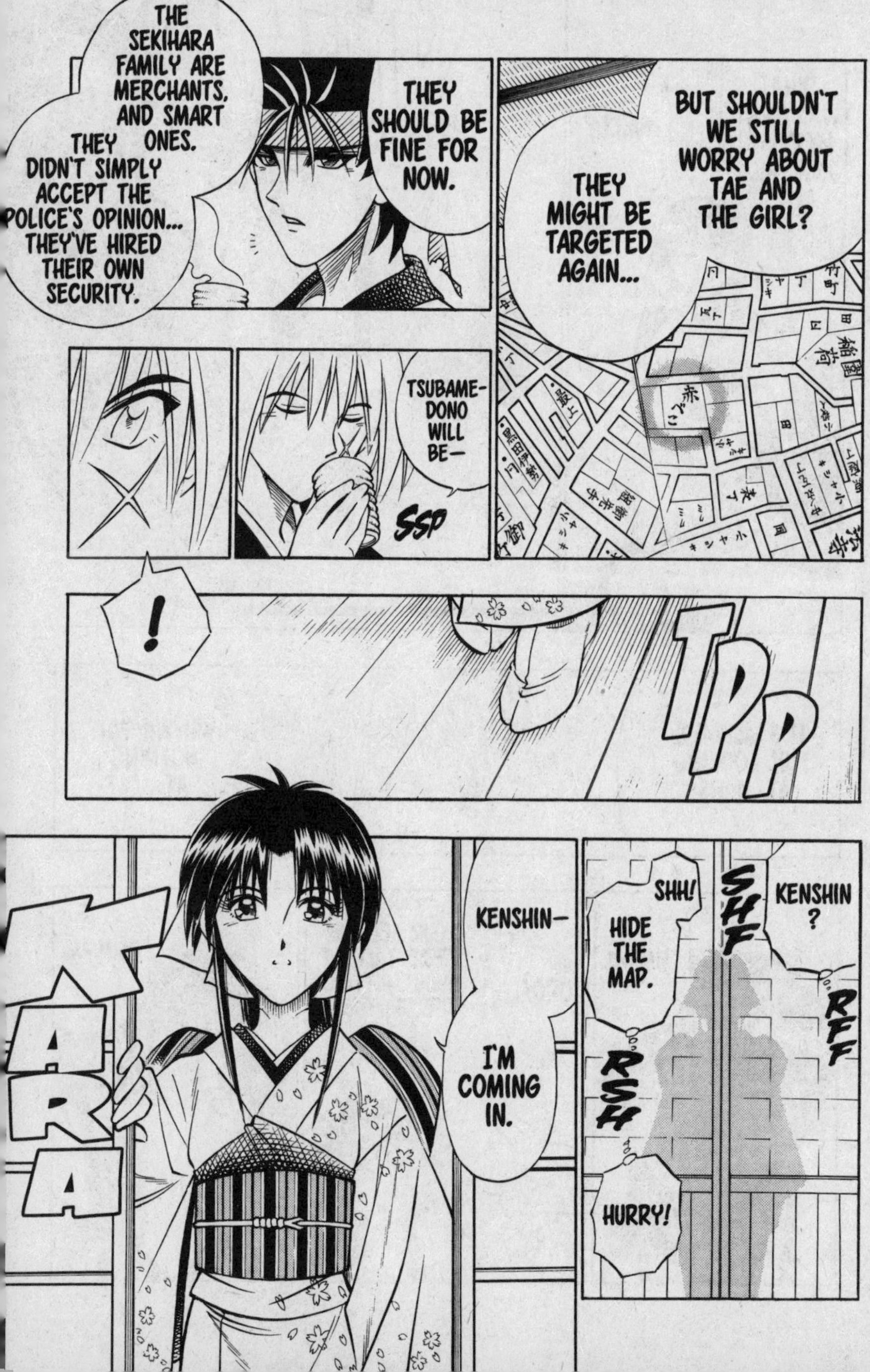
BUT SHOULDN'T WE STILL WORRY ABOUT TAE AND THE GIRL?
THEY MIGHT BE TARGETED AGAIN...
THEY SHOULD BE FINE FOR NOW.
THE SEKIHARA FAMILY ARE MERCHANTS, AND SMART ONES.
THEY DIDN'T SIMPLY ACCEPT THE POLICE'S OPINION... THEY'VE HIRED THEIR OWN SECURITY.
TSUBAME-DONO WILL BE—
SSP
TPP
!
KENSHIN?
SHF
SHH!
HIDE THE MAP.
RFF
RSH
HURRY!
KENSHIN—
I'M COMING IN.
ARA

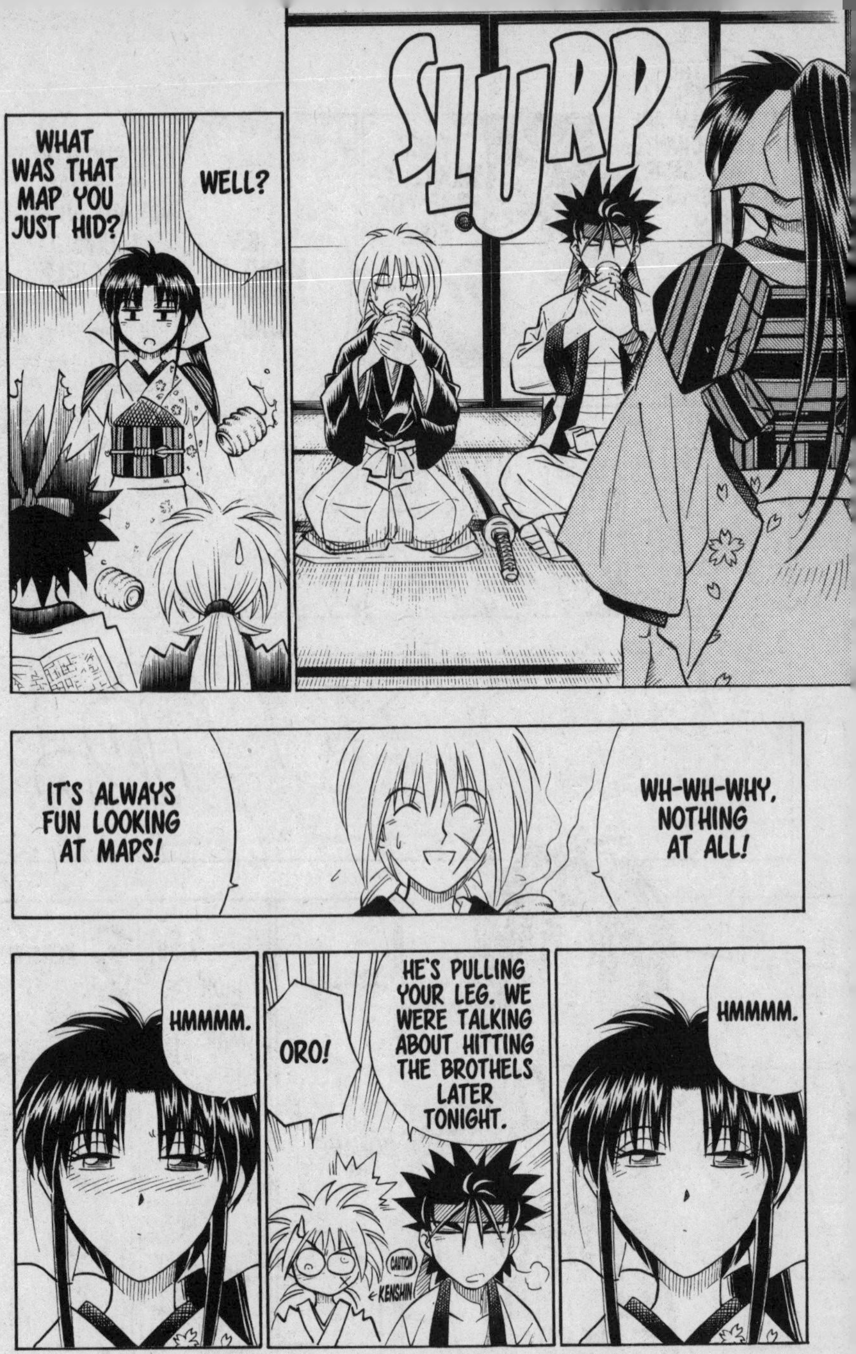
SLURP
WELL?
WHAT WAS THAT MAP YOU JUST HID?
WH-WH-WHY, NOTHING AT ALL!
IT'S ALWAYS FUN LOOKING AT MAPS!
HMMMM.
HE'S PULLING YOUR LEG. WE WERE TALKING ABOUT HITTING THE BROTHELS LATER TONIGHT.
ORO!
CAUTION
← KENSHIN
HMMMM.

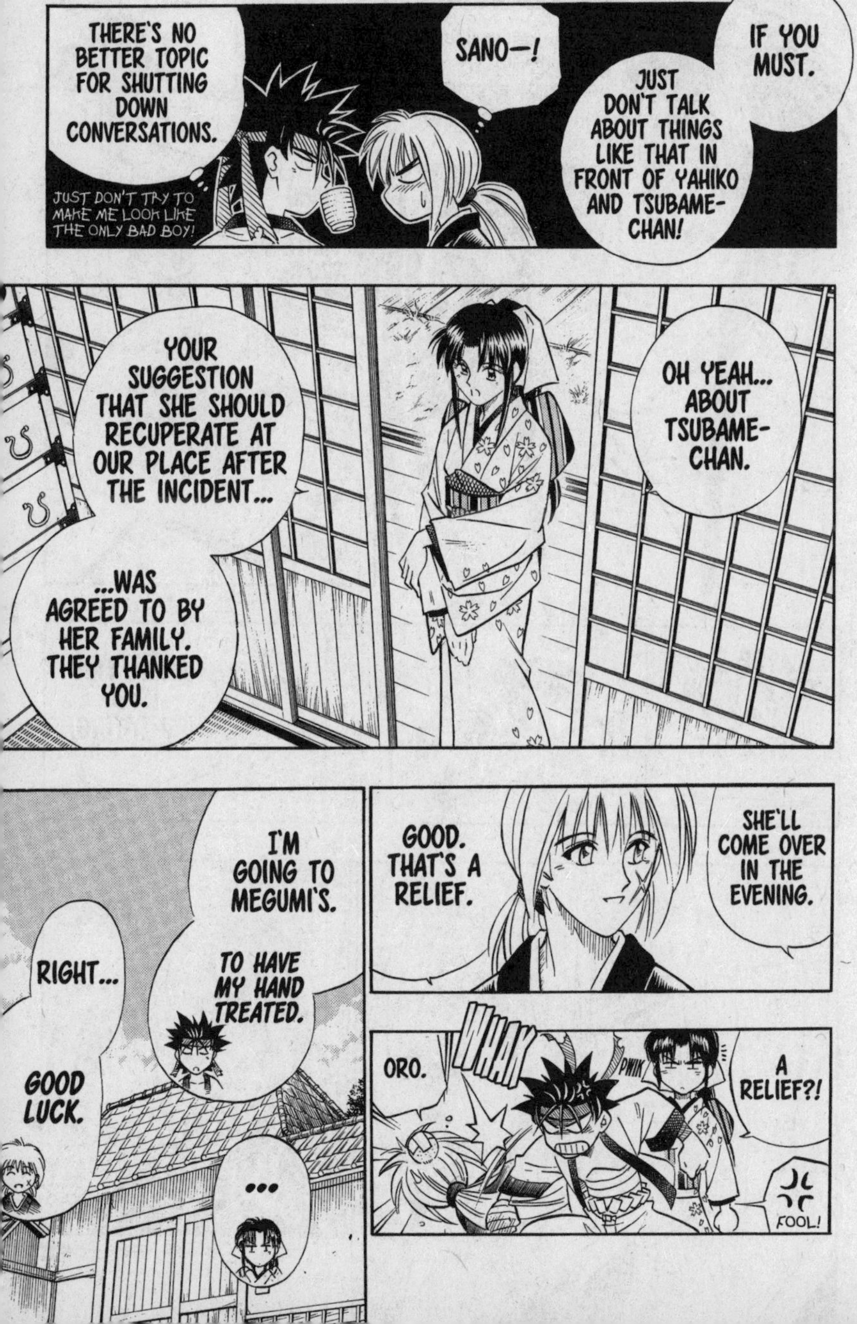
IF YOU MUST.
JUST DON'T TALK ABOUT THINGS LIKE THAT IN FRONT OF YAHIKO AND TSUBAME-CHAN!
SANO—!
THERE'S NO BETTER TOPIC FOR SHUTTING DOWN CONVERSATIONS.
JUST DON'T TRY TO MAKE ME LOOK LIKE THE ONLY BAD BOY!
OH YEAH... ABOUT TSUBAME-CHAN.
YOUR SUGGESTION THAT SHE SHOULD RECUPERATE AT OUR PLACE AFTER THE INCIDENT...
...WAS AGREED TO BY HER FAMILY. THEY THANKED YOU.
SHE'LL COME OVER IN THE EVENING.
GOOD. THAT'S A RELIEF.
A RELIEF?!
PWIK
WHAK
ORO.
FOOL!
I'M GOING TO MEGUMI'S.
TO HAVE MY HAND TREATED.
RIGHT...
GOOD LUCK.
...

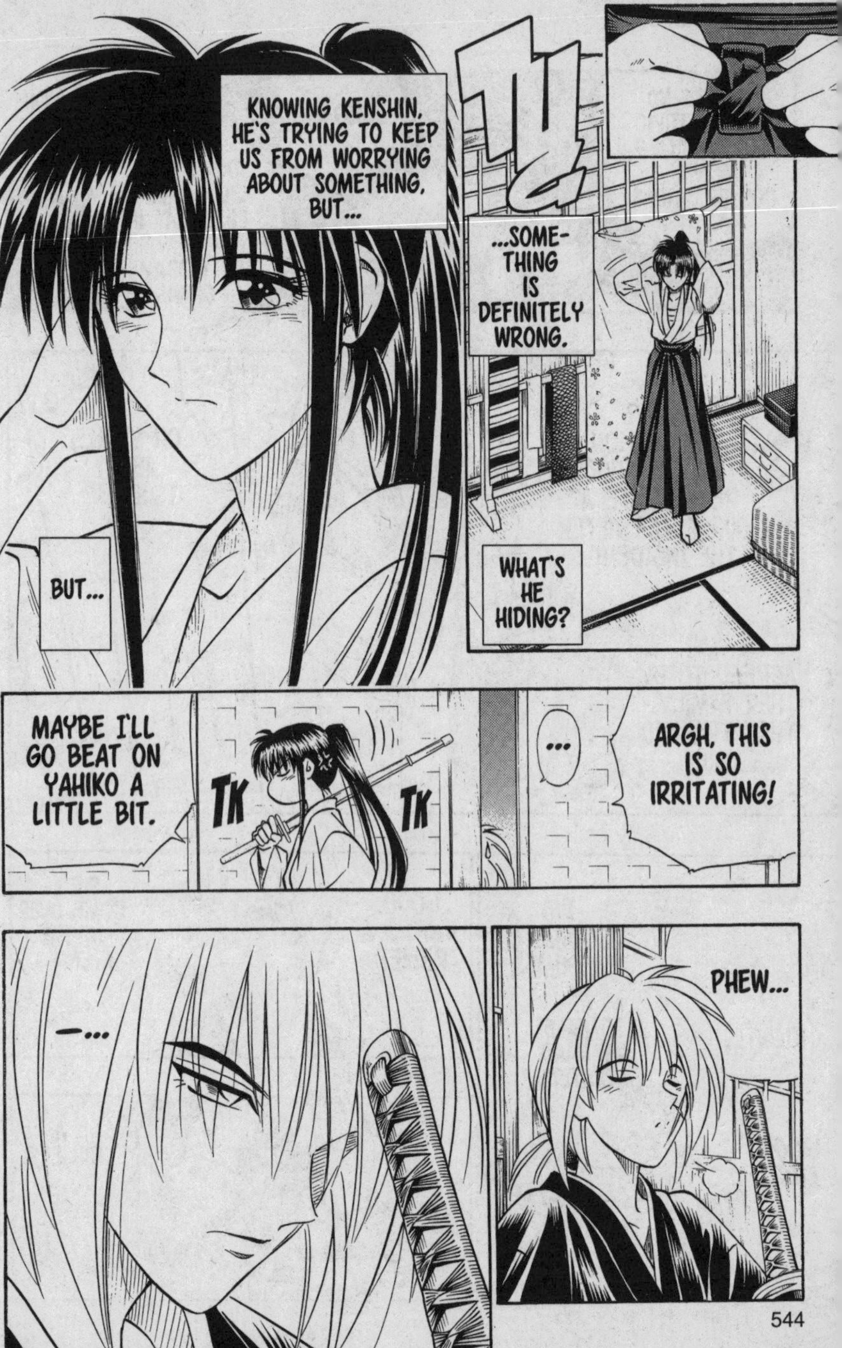
TUG
...SOME-THING IS DEFINITELY WRONG.
WHAT'S HE HIDING?
KNOWING KENSHIN, HE'S TRYING TO KEEP US FROM WORRYING ABOUT SOMETHING, BUT...
BUT...
ARGH, THIS IS SO IRRITATING!
...
TK
TK
MAYBE I'LL GO BEAT ON YAHIKO A LITTLE BIT.
PHEW...
—...

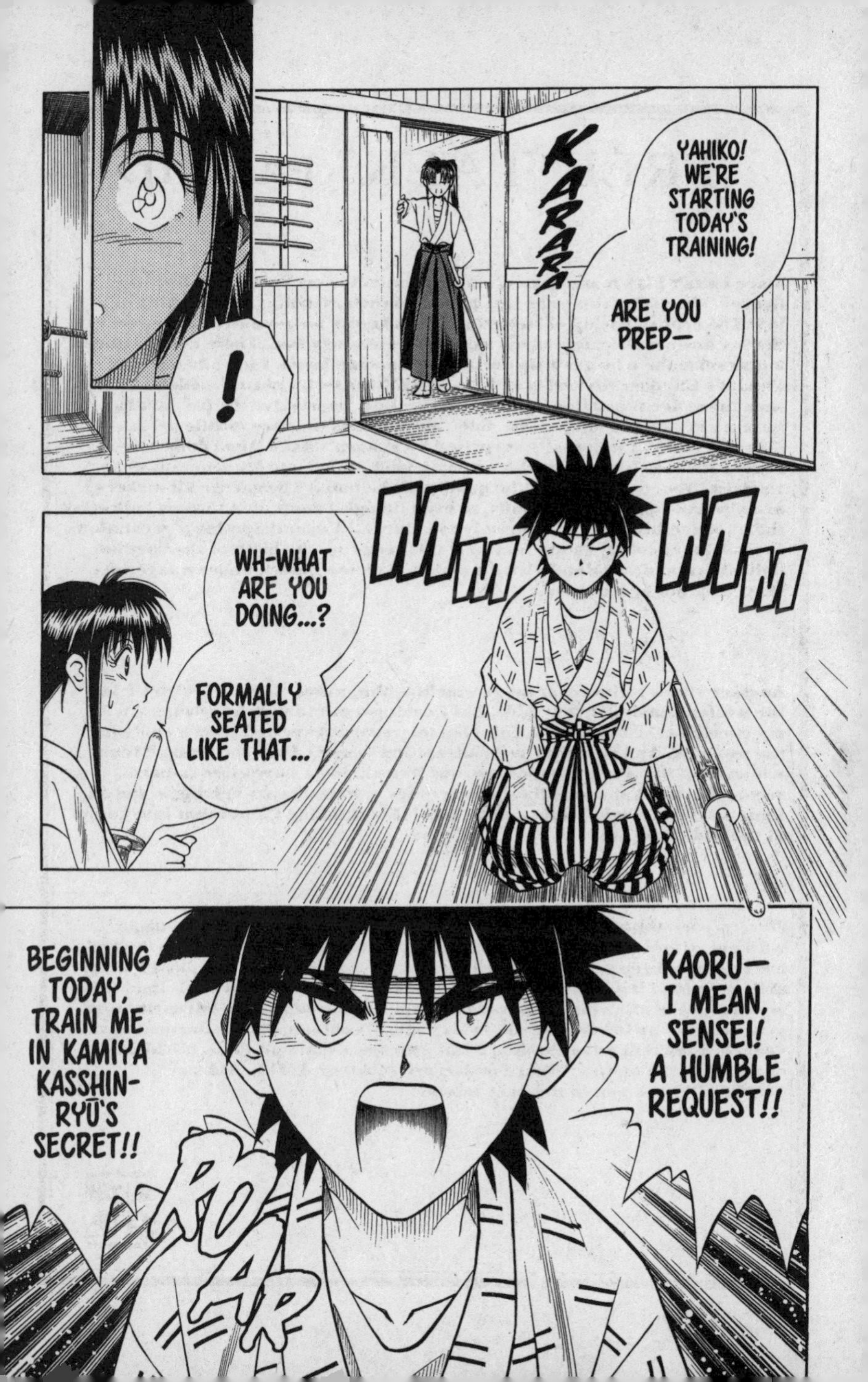
KARARA
YAHIKO! WE'RE STARTING TODAY'S TRAINING!
ARE YOU PREP—
!
MMMM
WH-WHAT ARE YOU DOING...?
FORMALLY SEATED LIKE THAT...
KAORU— I MEAN, SENSEI! A HUMBLE REQUEST!!
BEGINNING TODAY, TRAIN ME IN KAMIYA KASSHIN-RYŪ'S SECRET!!
ROAR

"FREE TALK" <PART II>

Since I can't play many games, another outlet for my stress is collecting figures. The end of this year saw a flood of them, sending me shrieking in joy! The craftsmanship of McFarlane Toys knows no bounds, and the rest of the toy business is catching up, using its technology too...These aren't figures, but as someone who grew up during the *Gundam* boom, I have to mention Bandai's *Gundam* MG series and the *Eva* LM-HG series plastic models. And then there are the action dolls. No matter how impressive the product is, I have no interest in non-mobile dolls, but the ones that are mobile are a different story. I was really surprised by Takara's *Nako-Rimu* dolls when I bought them. (This is off topic, but my friend Michimoto Munenori was surprised too, especially by the quality of the hair.) The garage kit makers are also putting out action dolls, so even though I don't plan to start collecting them (collecting Yo-toys is already too much...) I'm anticipating a revolution in model technology in the future. If this keeps up, the birth of the "action doll with seamless joints" (with a mobile skeleton hidden under a layer of skin) may not be a dream!

Another stress reliever for me is watching the sunset. The air is clearer in the winter, making it very nice. But I can't get out to watch the sunset with my current schedule, so I'm enjoying the recorded version shown early in the morning. And now they're broadcasting scenery from the train. "Train windows of the world" is nice too, but Watsuki likes more close-to-home scenes like the Yamanote line, or the roads seen from cars driving in the city. I guess I like a "lightly taken night trip." I'm thinking I'll put that into action at the end of the year.

Finally, something serious. *Rurouni Kenshin* becomes more of a struggle with every new episode. There is an overall storyline all the way to the end, but I seem to keep getting dragged into the deepness of the story, and I'm not able to control it as much as I wish I could. However, the winter is lightening my spirits and allowing me to recover some. I plan to make a full sprint next year to make up for the shortfall this year. Please support me through next year, toward that happy ending I still promise. (Again off topic, Michimoto and I share the motto, "Manga artists are DEAD or ALIVE, ALL or NOTHING.") See you in the next volume!

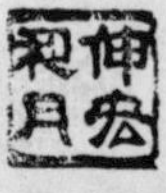
伸宏
和月

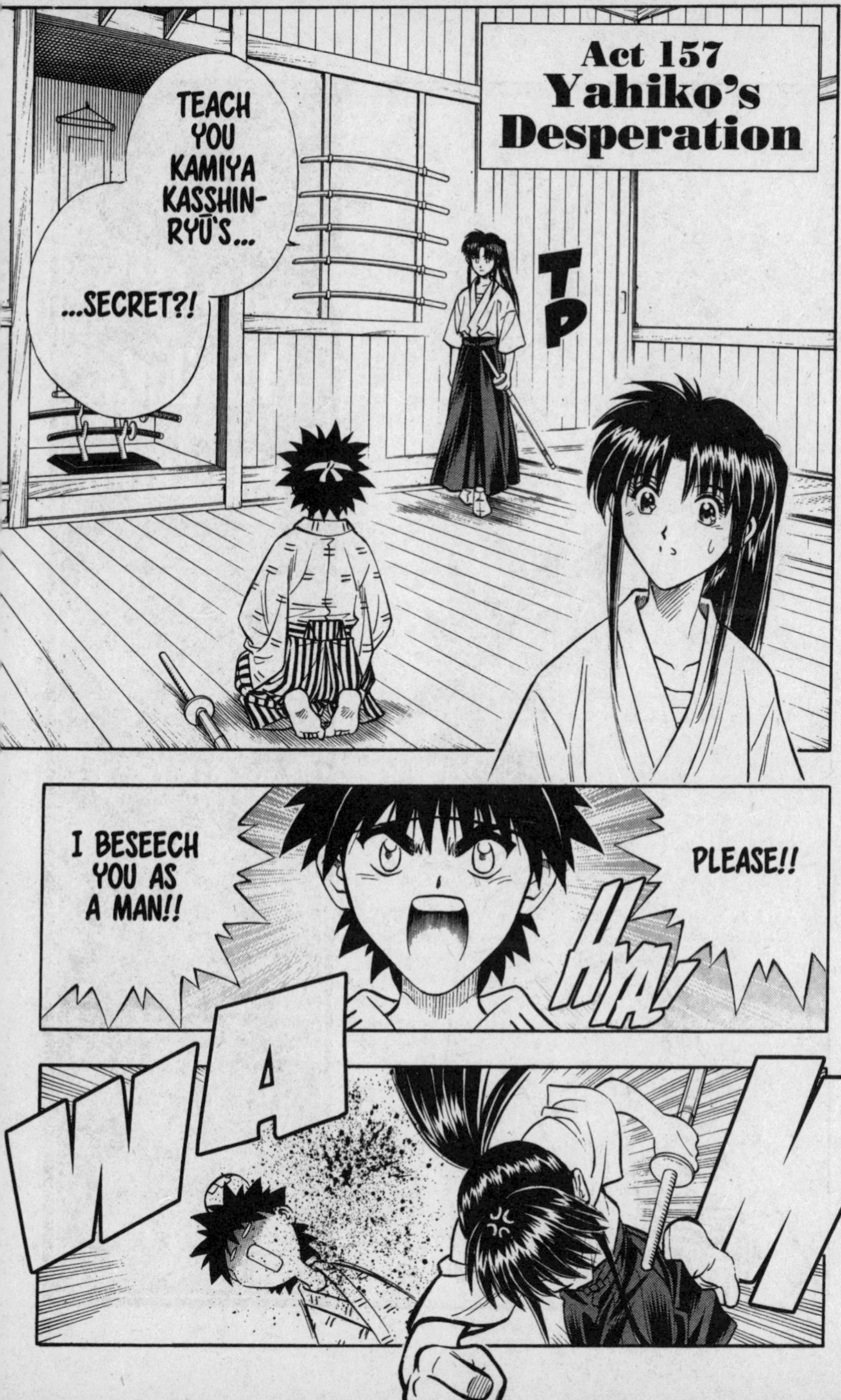
Act 157
Yahiko's Desperation
TP
TEACH YOU KAMIYA KASSHIN-RYŪ'S...
...SECRET?!
PLEASE!!
HYA!
I BESEECH YOU AS A MAN!!

Act 157
Yahiko's
Desperation

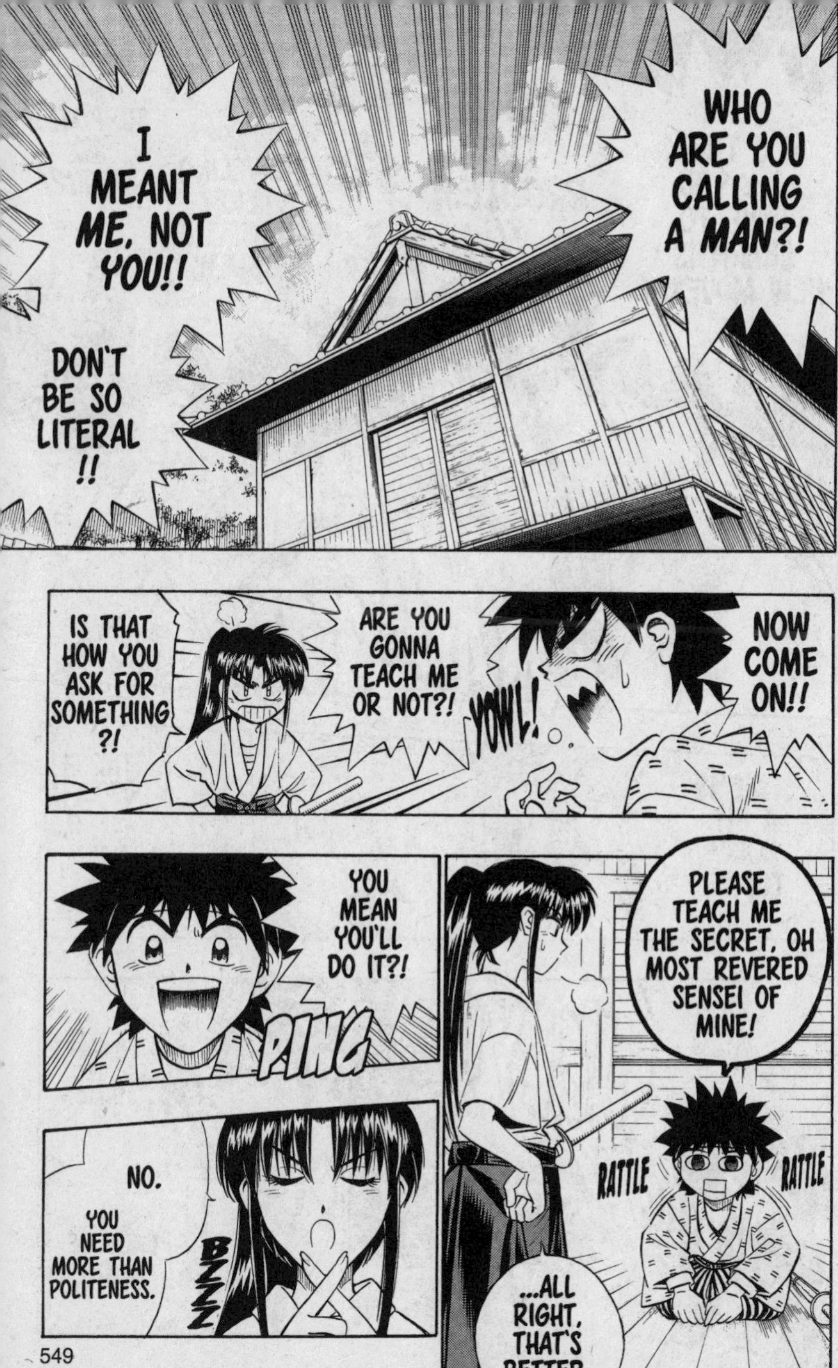
WHO ARE YOU CALLING A *MAN*?!
I MEANT *ME*, NOT *YOU*!!
DON'T BE SO LITERAL!!
NOW COME ON!!
YOWL!
ARE YOU GONNA TEACH ME OR NOT?!
IS THAT HOW YOU ASK FOR SOMETHING?!
PLEASE TEACH ME THE SECRET, OH MOST REVERED SENSEI OF MINE!
RATTLE
RATTLE
...ALL RIGHT, THAT'S BETTER.
YOU MEAN YOU'LL DO IT?!
PING
NO.
BZZZ
YOU NEED MORE THAN POLITENESS.

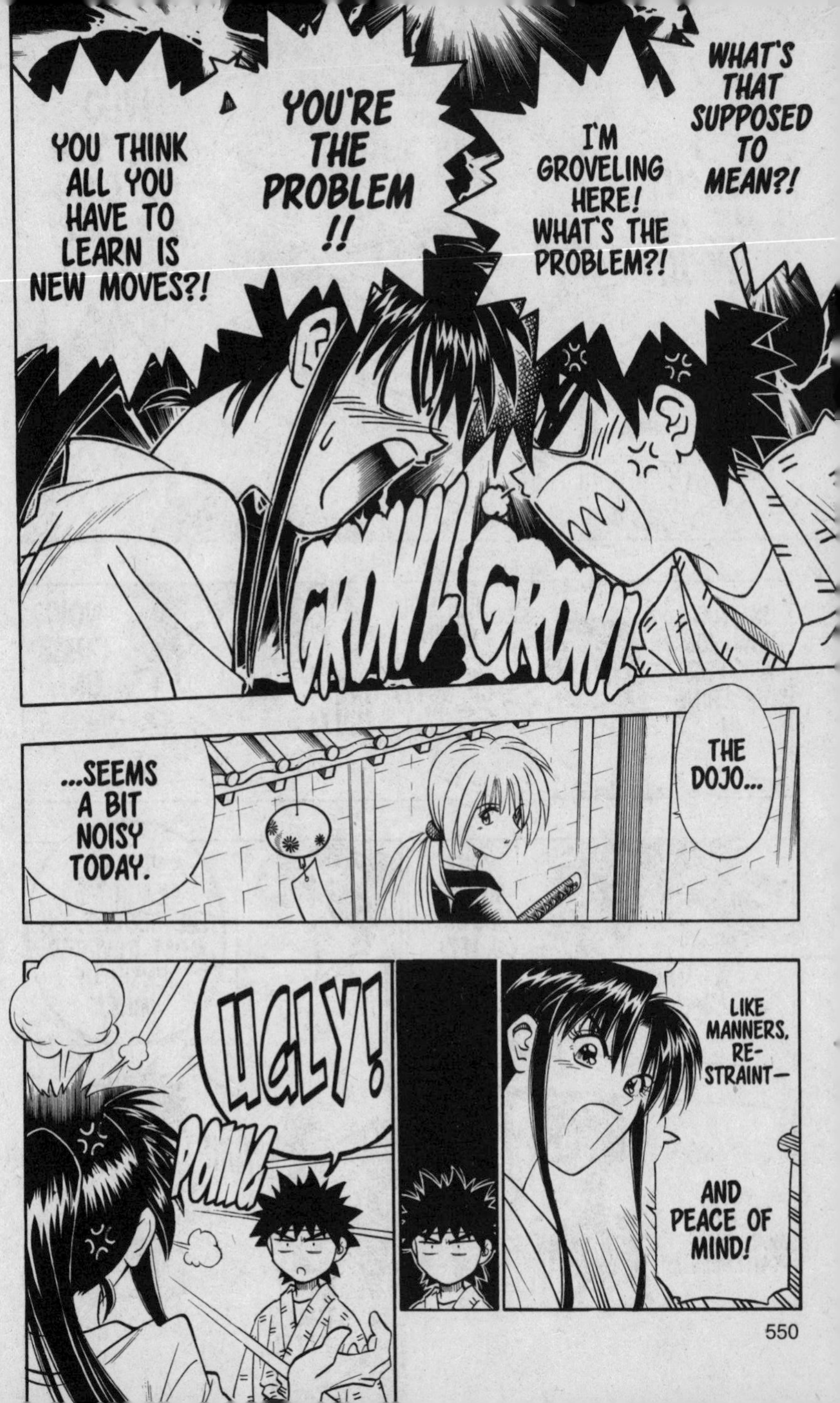
WHAT'S THAT SUPPOSED TO MEAN?!
I'M GROVELING HERE! WHAT'S THE PROBLEM?!
YOU'RE THE PROBLEM !!
YOU THINK ALL YOU HAVE TO LEARN IS NEW MOVES?!
GROWL GROWL
THE DOJO...
...SEEMS A BIT NOISY TODAY.
LIKE MANNERS, RE-STRAINT—
AND PEACE OF MIND!
UGLY!
POING

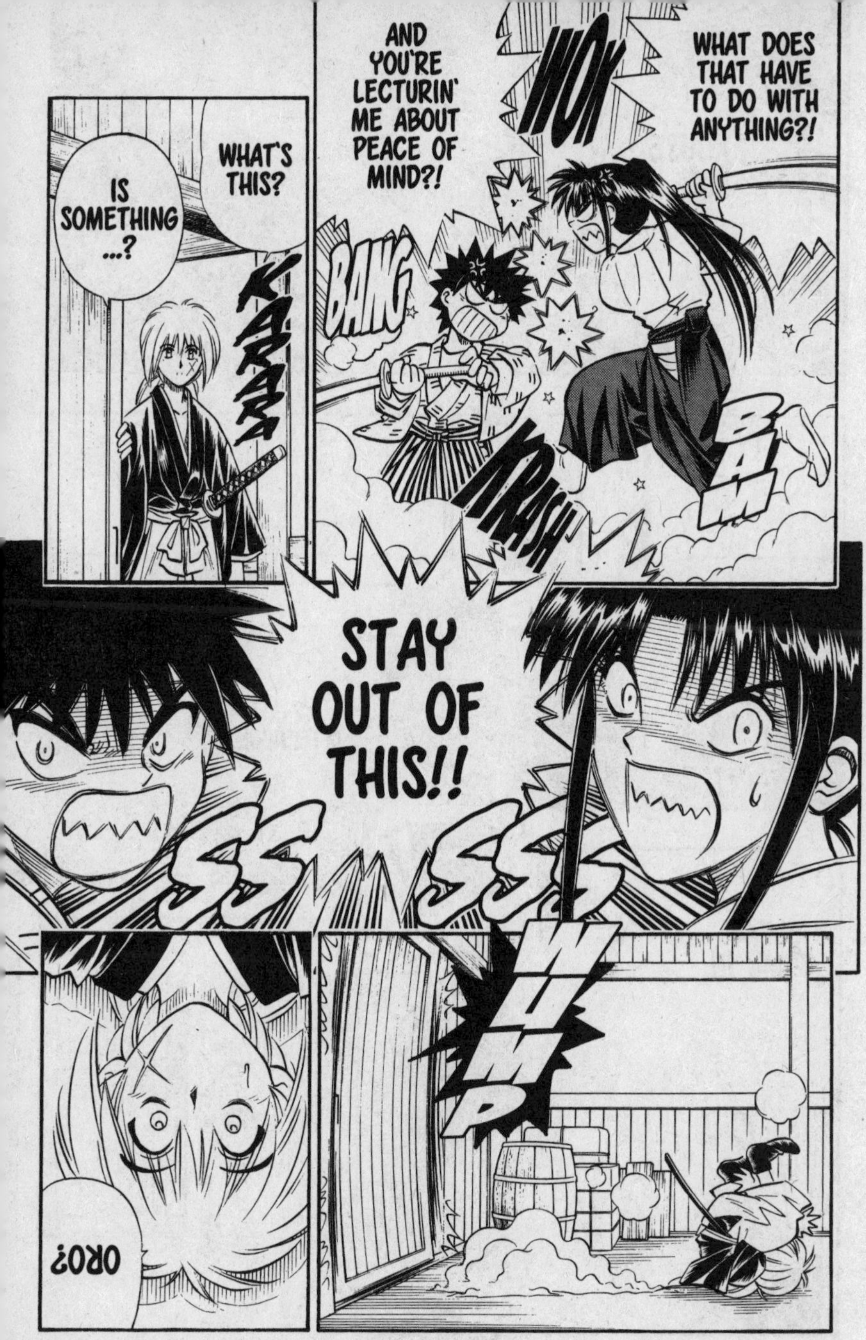
WHAT DOES THAT HAVE TO DO WITH ANYTHING?!
AND YOU'RE LECTURIN' ME ABOUT PEACE OF MIND?!
BANG
KRASH
BAM
WHAT'S THIS?
IS SOMETHING ...?
STAY OUT OF THIS!!
WHUMP
ORO?

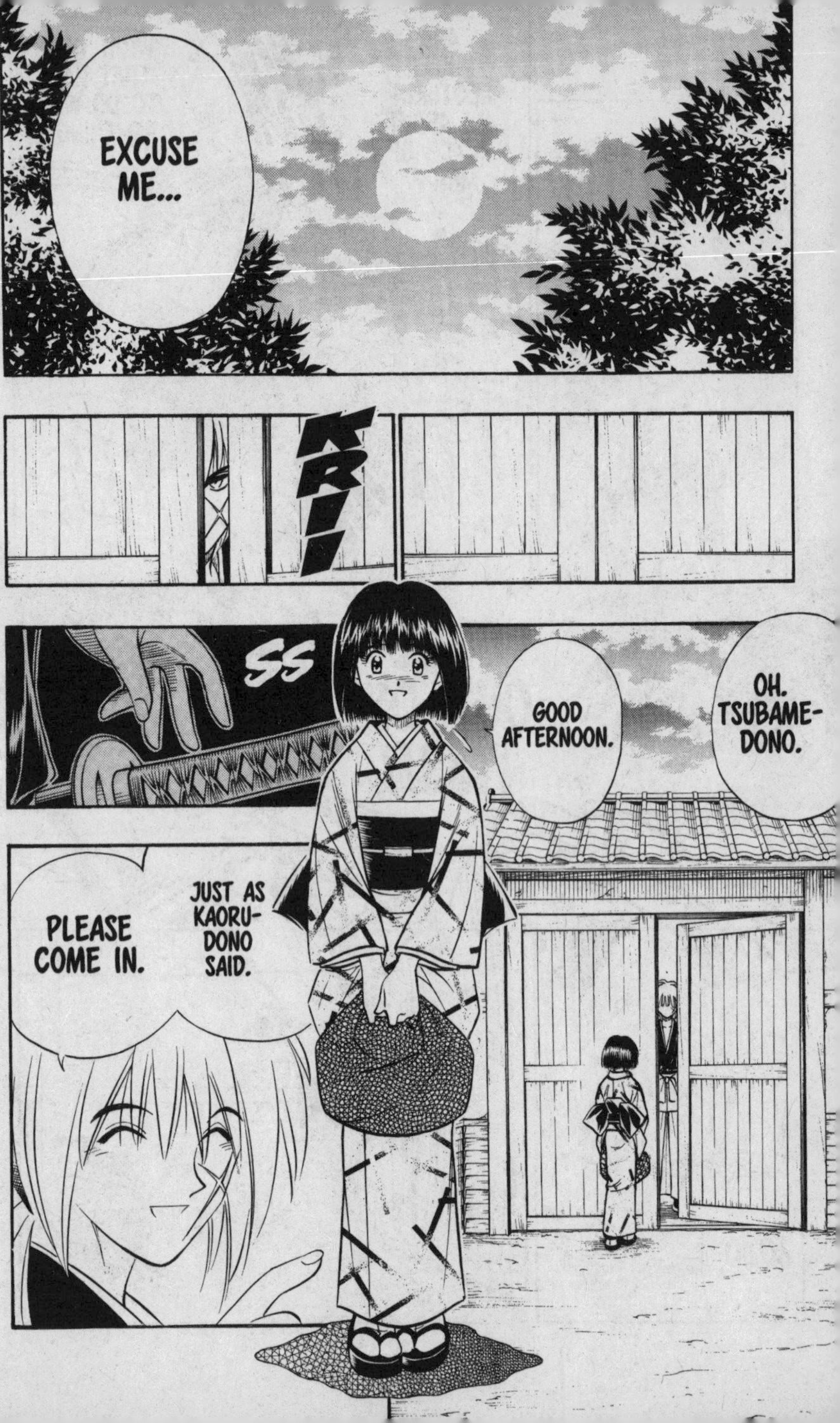
EXCUSE ME...
KRI
OH. TSUBAME-DONO.
GOOD AFTERNOON.
SS
JUST AS KAORU-DONO SAID.
PLEASE COME IN.

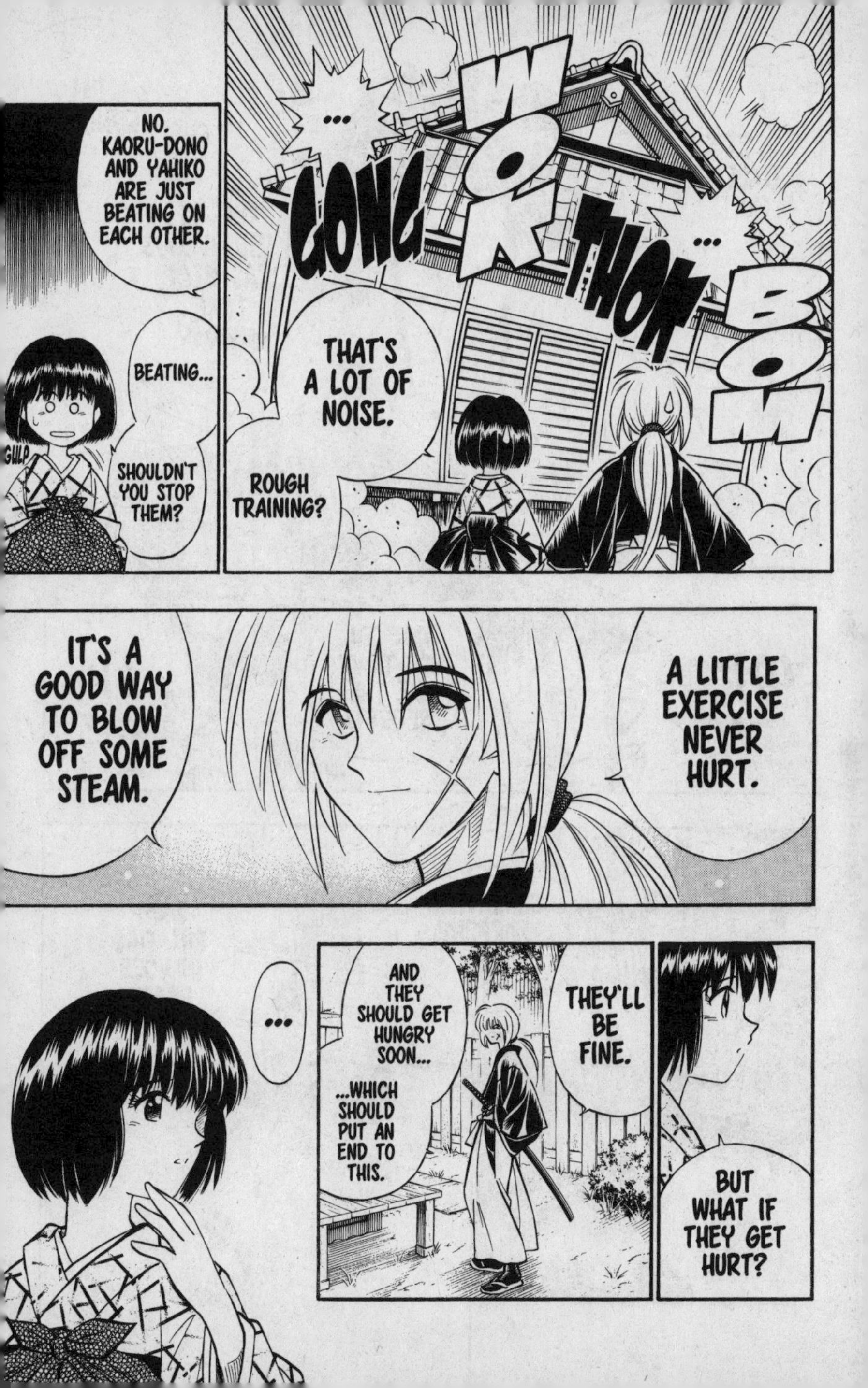
BOM
...
THOK
WOK
...
GONG
THAT'S A LOT OF NOISE.
ROUGH TRAINING?
NO. KAORU-DONO AND YAHIKO ARE JUST BEATING ON EACH OTHER.
BEATING...
SHOULDN'T YOU STOP THEM?
GULP
A LITTLE EXERCISE NEVER HURT.
IT'S A GOOD WAY TO BLOW OFF SOME STEAM.
BUT WHAT IF THEY GET HURT?
THEY'LL BE FINE.
AND THEY SHOULD GET HUNGRY SOON...
...WHICH SHOULD PUT AN END TO THIS.
...

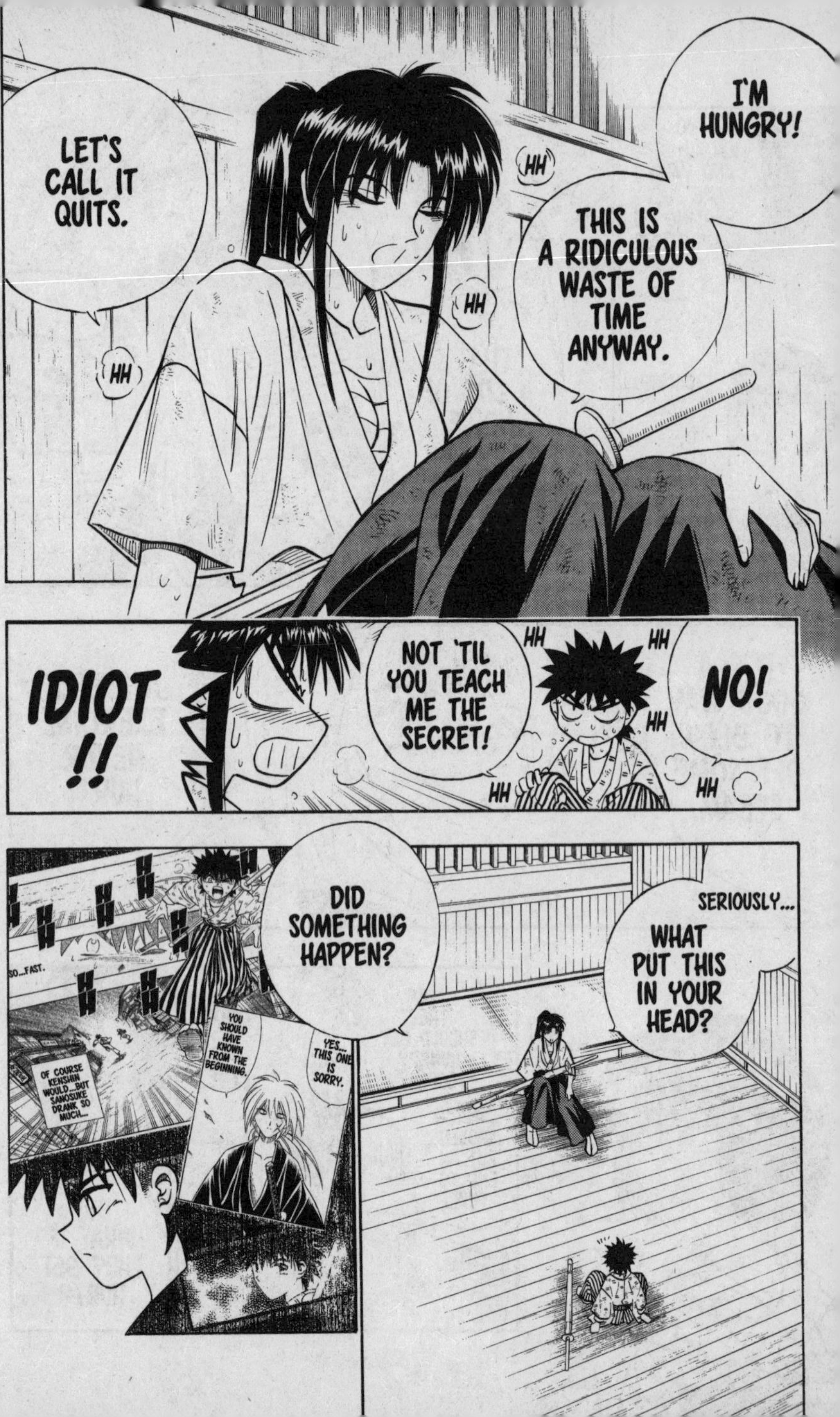
I'M HUNGRY!
THIS IS A RIDICULOUS WASTE OF TIME ANYWAY.
HH
HH
LET'S CALL IT QUITS.
HH
NO!
HH
HH
HH
HH
NOT 'TIL YOU TEACH ME THE SECRET!
HH
IDIOT!!
SERIOUSLY...
WHAT PUT THIS IN YOUR HEAD?
DID SOMETHING HAPPEN?
YES... THIS ONE IS SORRY.
YOU SHOULD HAVE KNOWN FROM THE BEGINNING.
SO...FAST.
OF COURSE KENSHIN WOULD... BUT SANOSUKE DRANK SO MUCH...

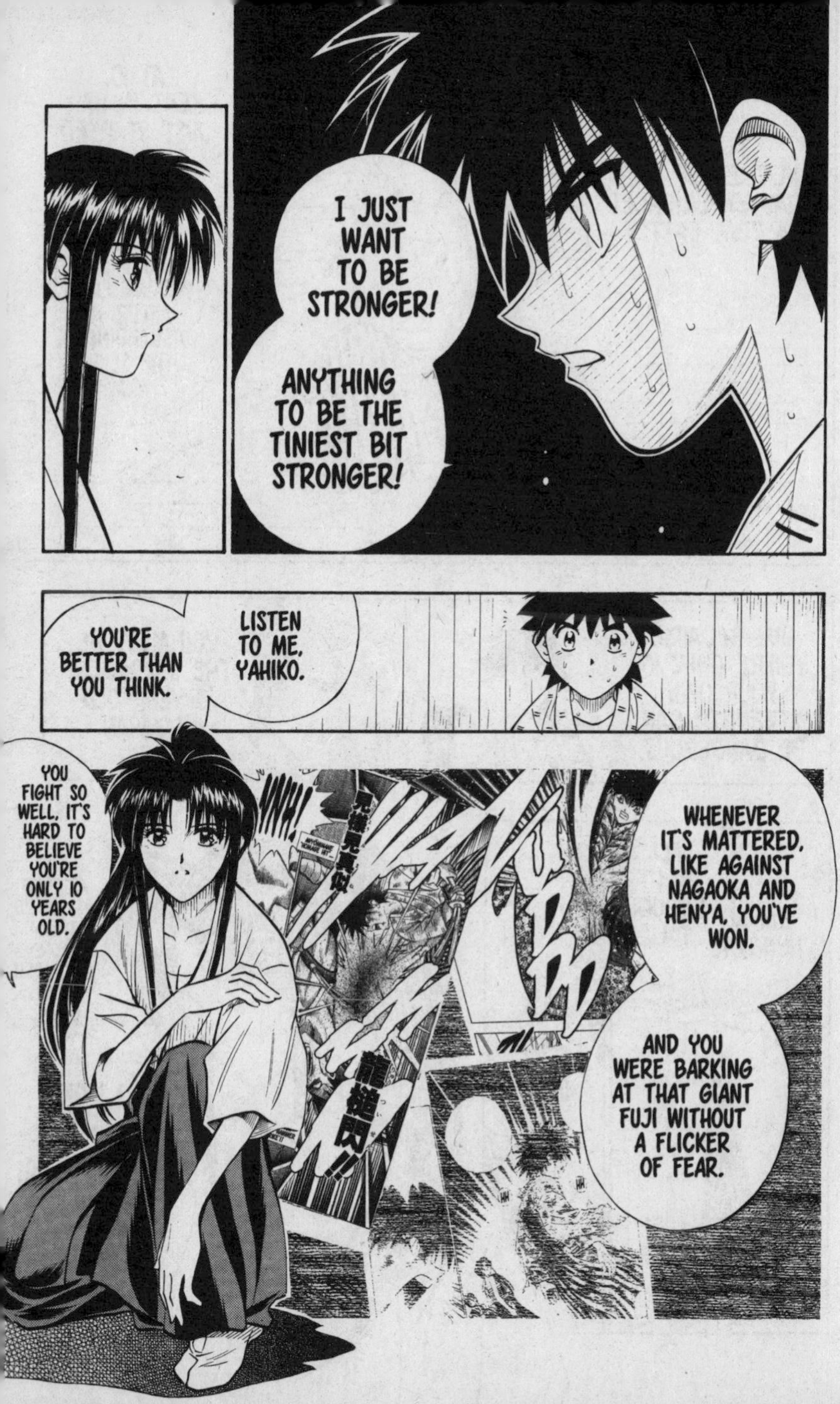
I JUST WANT TO BE STRONGER!
ANYTHING TO BE THE TINIEST BIT STRONGER!
LISTEN TO ME, YAHIKO.
YOU'RE BETTER THAN YOU THINK.
WHENEVER IT'S MATTERED, LIKE AGAINST NAGAOKA AND HENYA, YOU'VE WON.
AND YOU WERE BARKING AT THAT GIANT FUJI WITHOUT A FLICKER OF FEAR.
YOU FIGHT SO WELL, IT'S HARD TO BELIEVE YOU'RE ONLY 10 YEARS OLD.

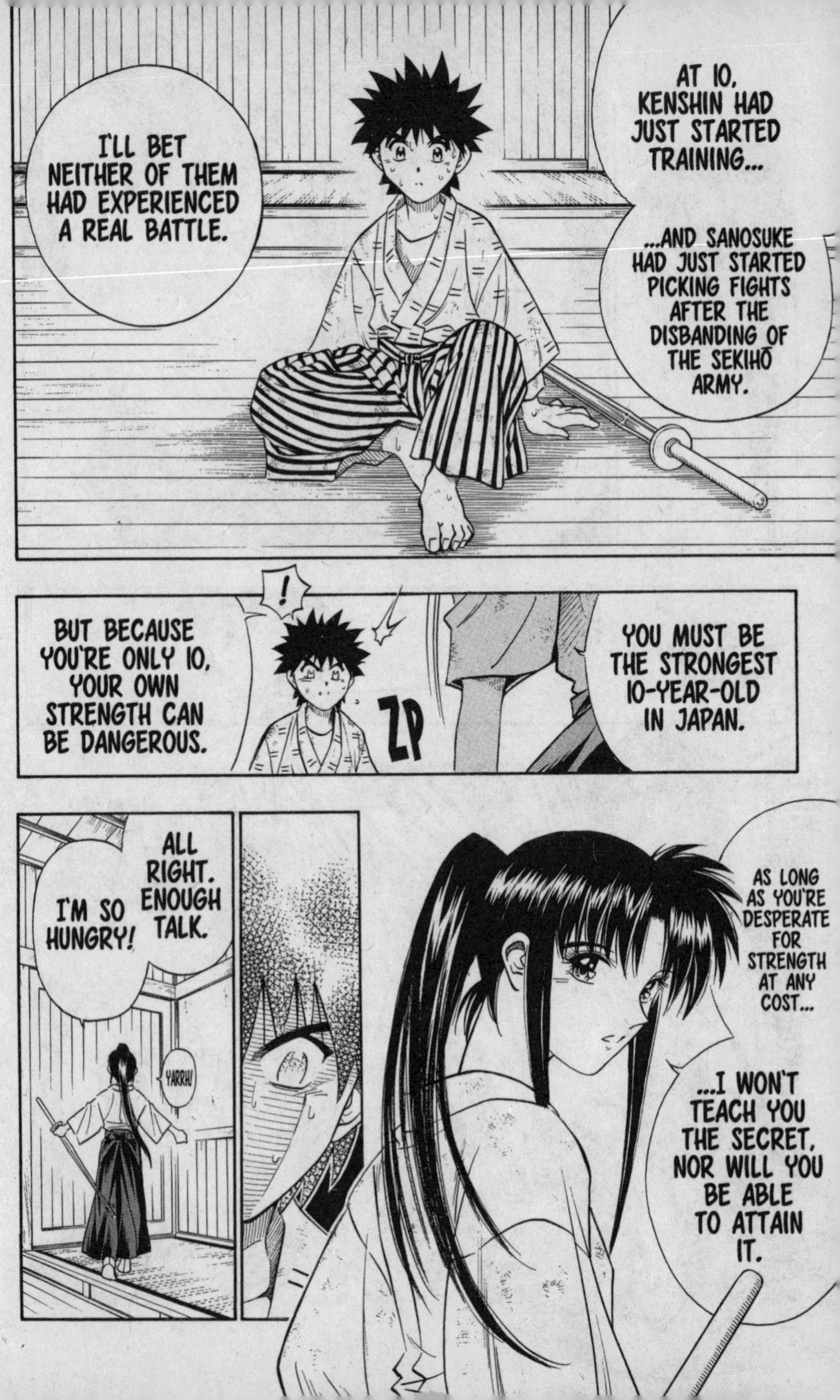
AT 10, KENSHIN HAD JUST STARTED TRAINING...
...AND SANOSUKE HAD JUST STARTED PICKING FIGHTS AFTER THE DISBANDING OF THE SEKIHŌ ARMY.
I'LL BET NEITHER OF THEM HAD EXPERIENCED A REAL BATTLE.
YOU MUST BE THE STRONGEST 10-YEAR-OLD IN JAPAN.
!
ZP
BUT BECAUSE YOU'RE ONLY 10, YOUR OWN STRENGTH CAN BE DANGEROUS.
AS LONG AS YOU'RE DESPERATE FOR STRENGTH AT ANY COST...
...I WON'T TEACH YOU THE SECRET, NOR WILL YOU BE ABLE TO ATTAIN IT.
ALL RIGHT. ENOUGH TALK.
I'M SO HUNGRY!
YARRH!

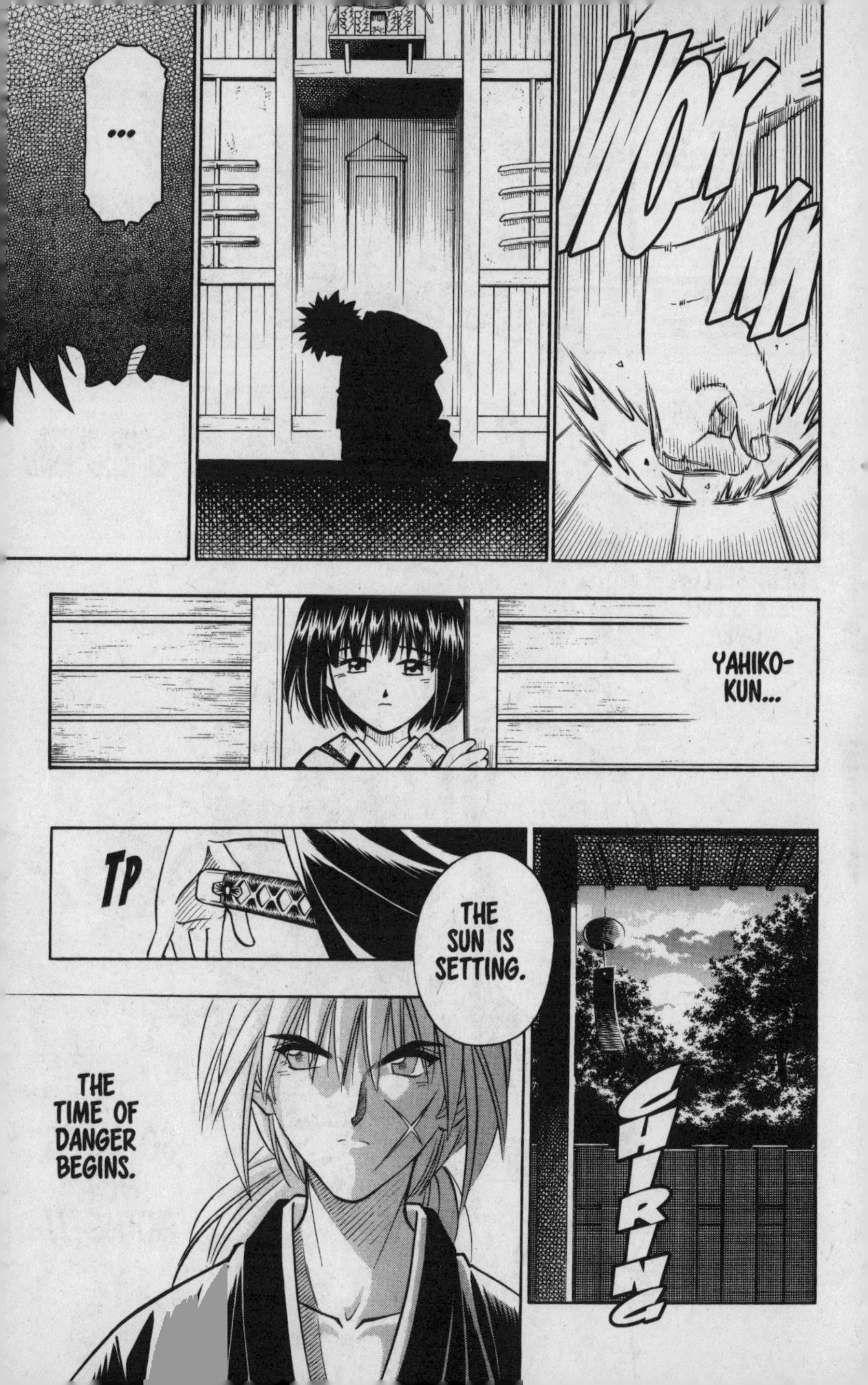
...
YAHIKO-KUN...
CHIRING
TP
THE SUN IS SETTING.
THE TIME OF DANGER BEGINS.

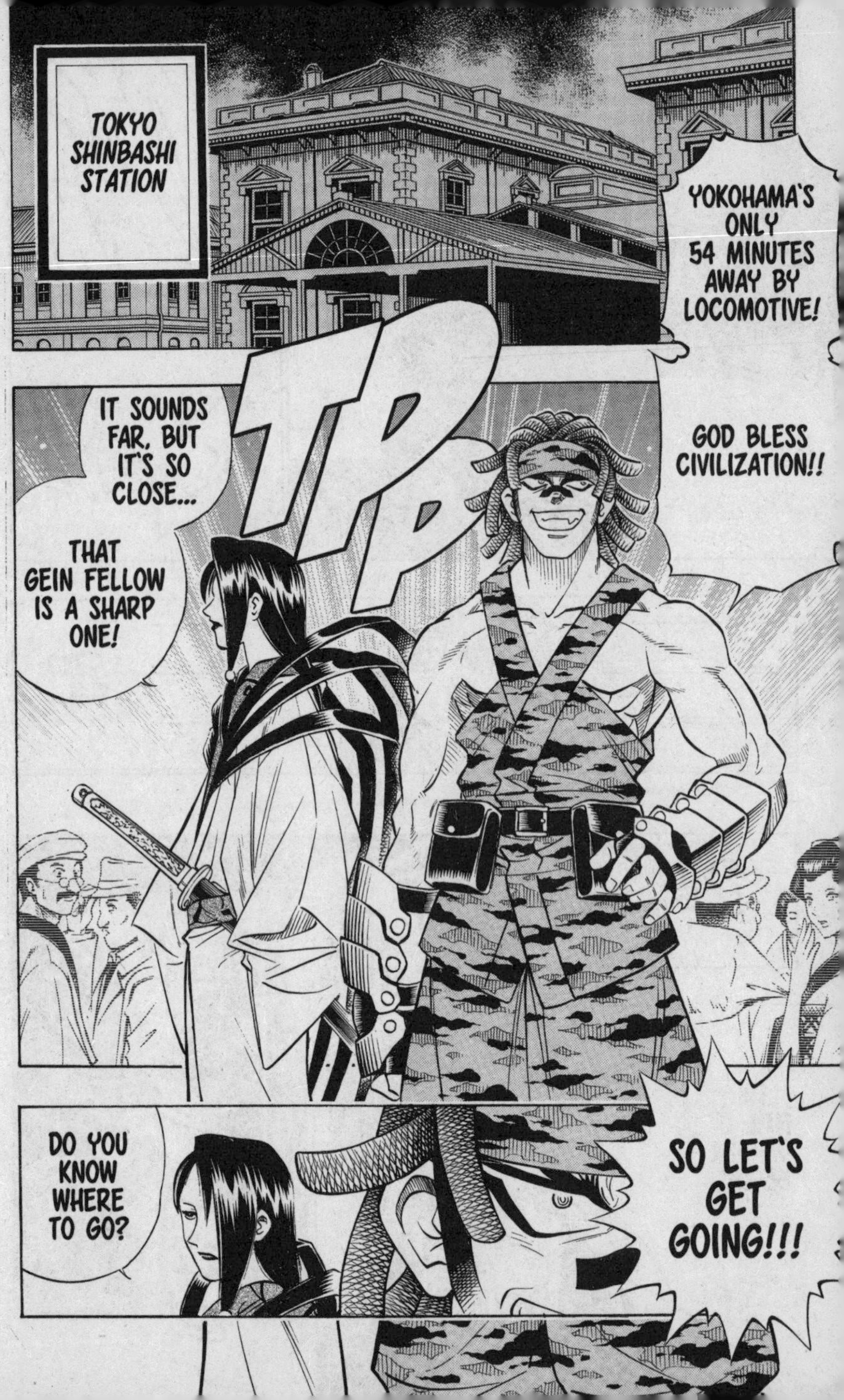
TOKYO SHINBASHI STATION
YOKOHAMA'S ONLY 54 MINUTES AWAY BY LOCOMOTIVE!
TP
GOD BLESS CIVILIZATION!!
IT SOUNDS FAR, BUT IT'S SO CLOSE...
THAT GEIN FELLOW IS A SHARP ONE!
SO LET'S GET GOING!!!
DO YOU KNOW WHERE TO GO?

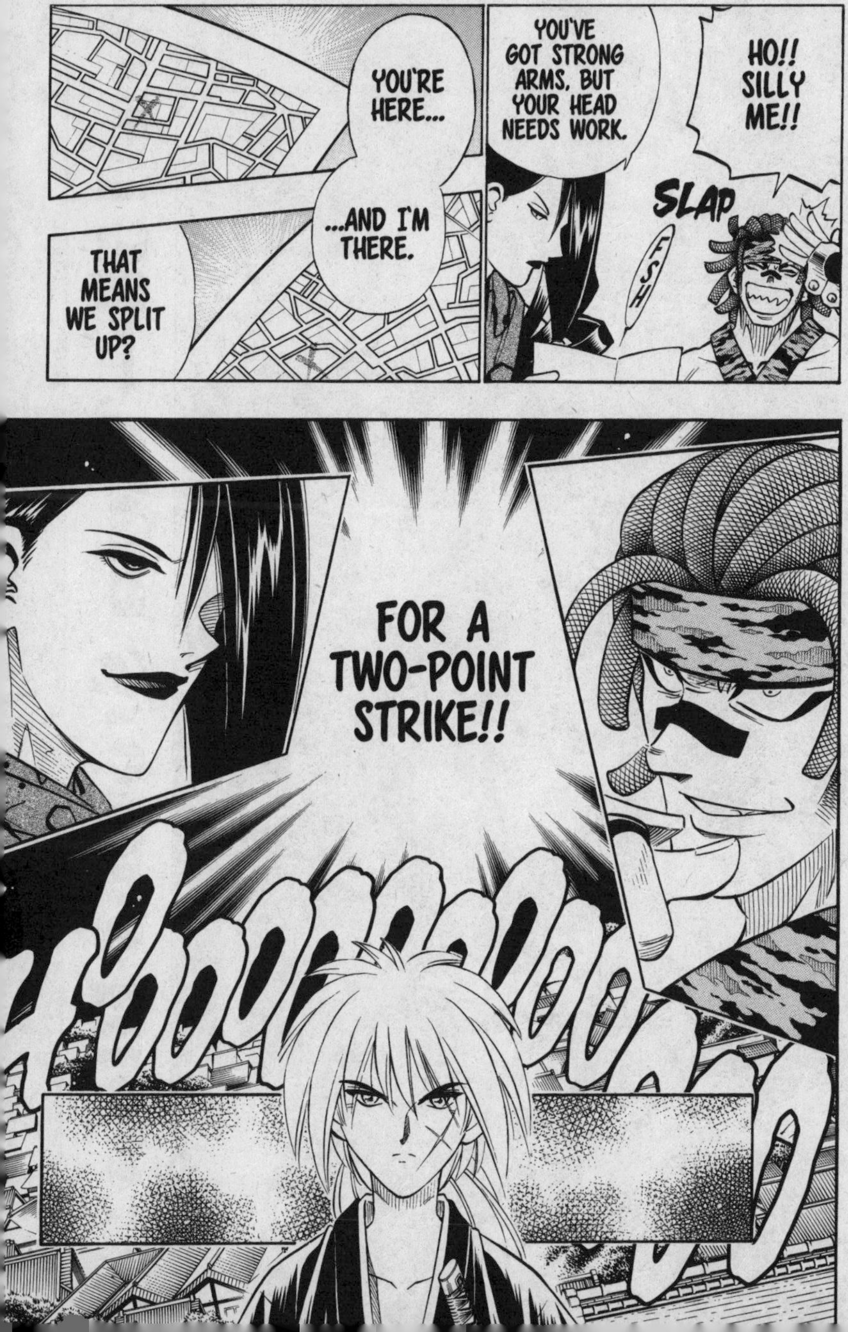
THAT MEANS WE SPLIT UP?
YOU'RE HERE...
...AND I'M THERE.
YOU'VE GOT STRONG ARMS, BUT YOUR HEAD NEEDS WORK.
FSH
SLAP
HO!! SILLY ME!!
FOR A TWO-POINT STRIKE!!

Act 158—Twin Storms Blow!

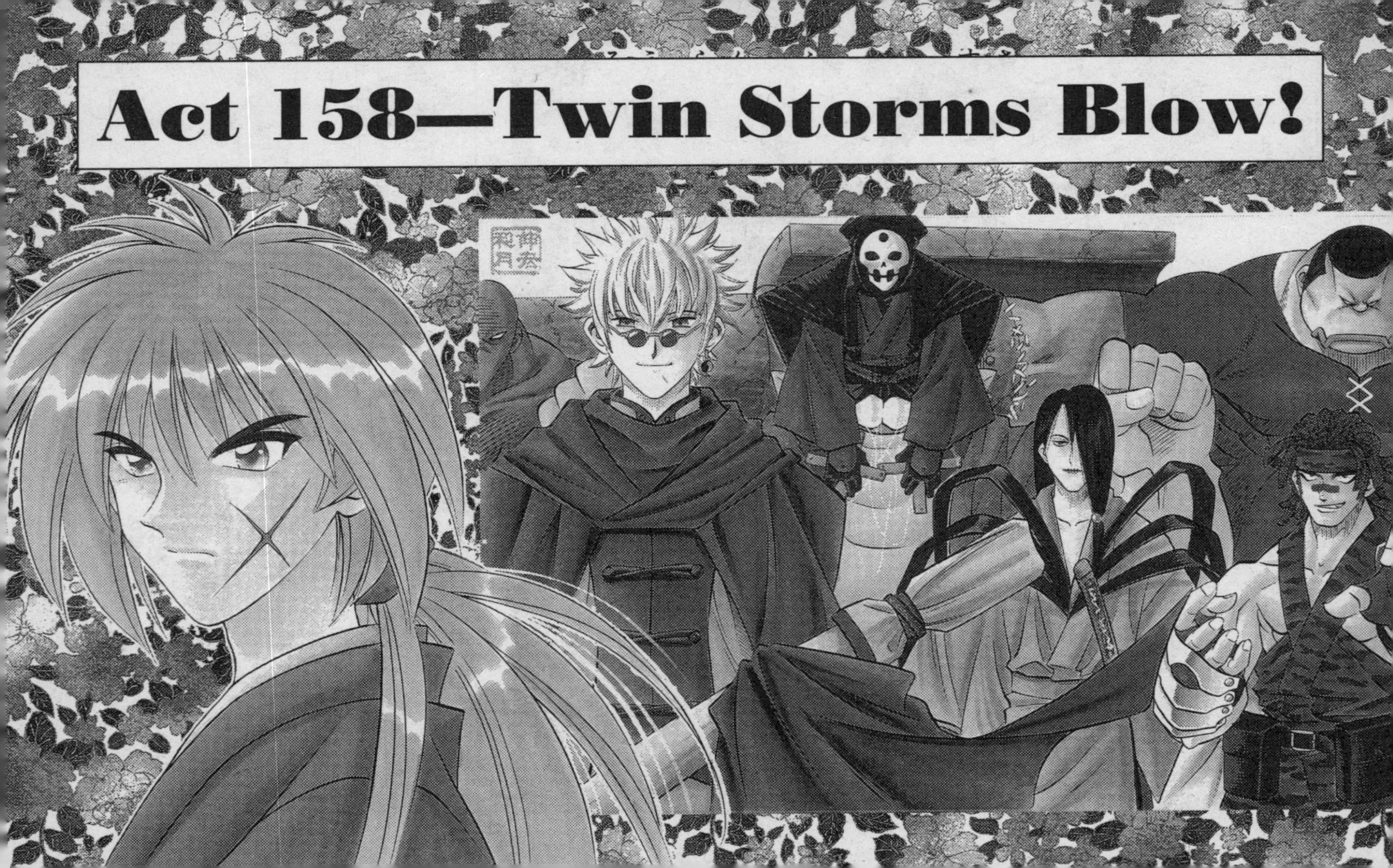

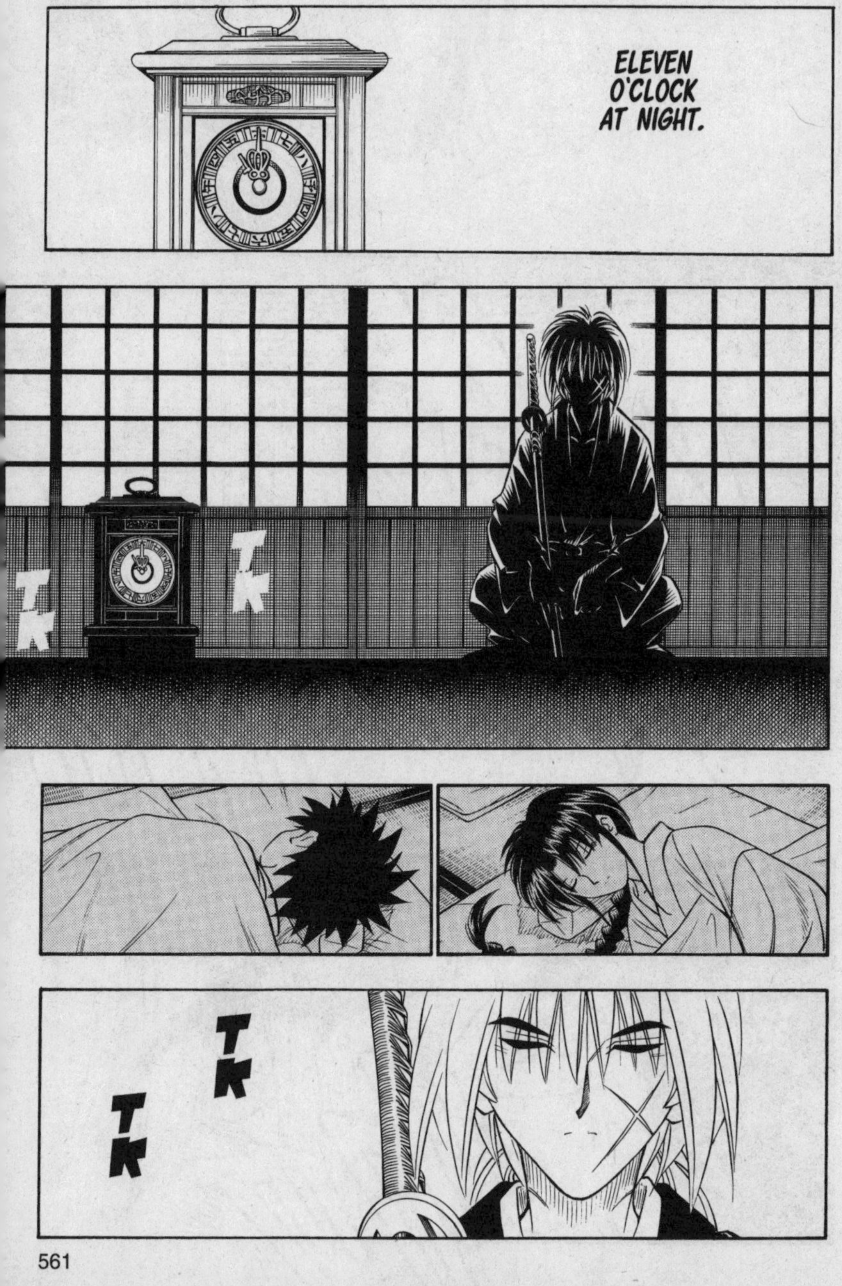
ELEVEN O'CLOCK AT NIGHT.
TK
TK
TK
TK

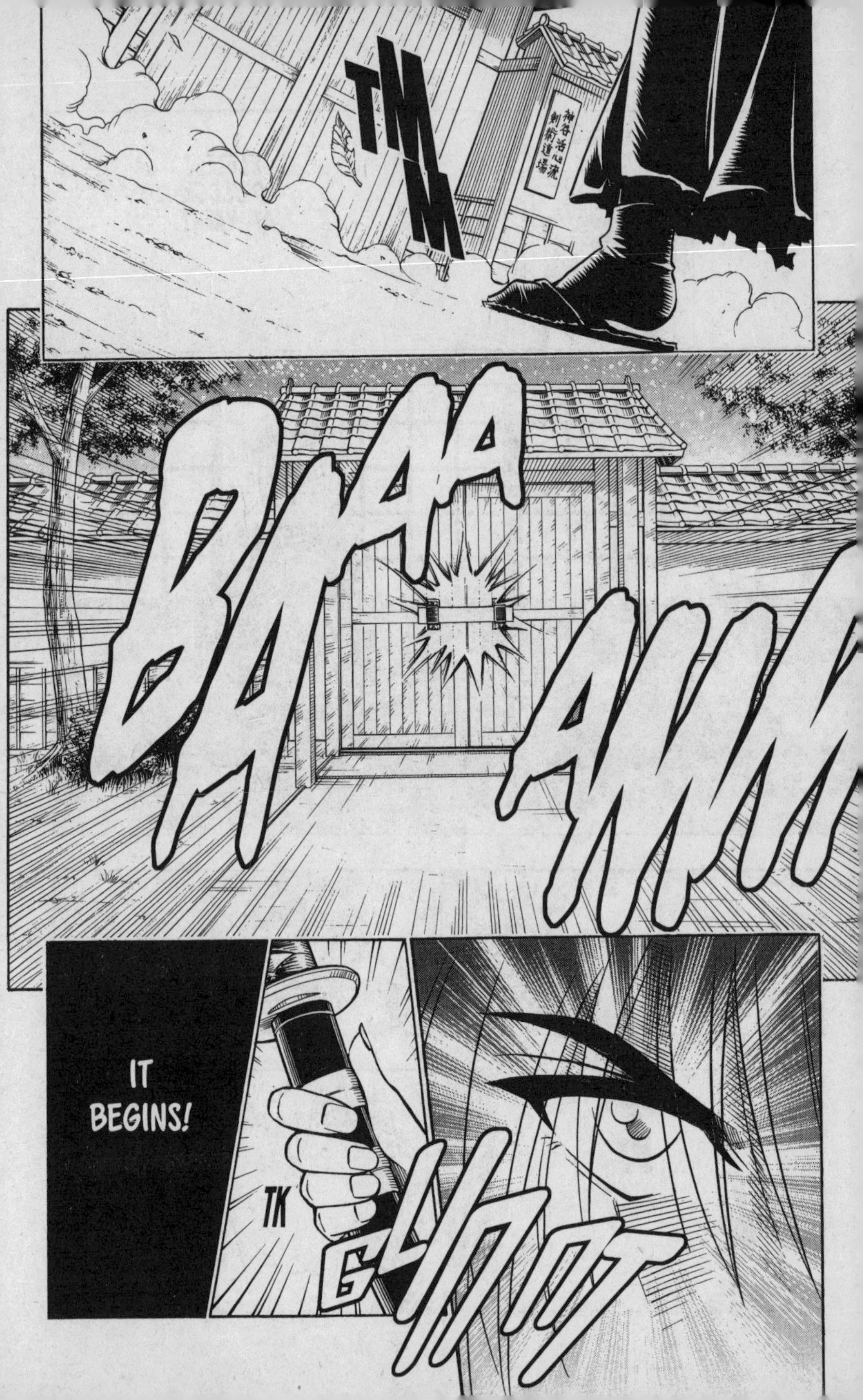
TMM
神谷活心流
剣術道場
BAAAMM
GLINT
TK
IT BEGINS!

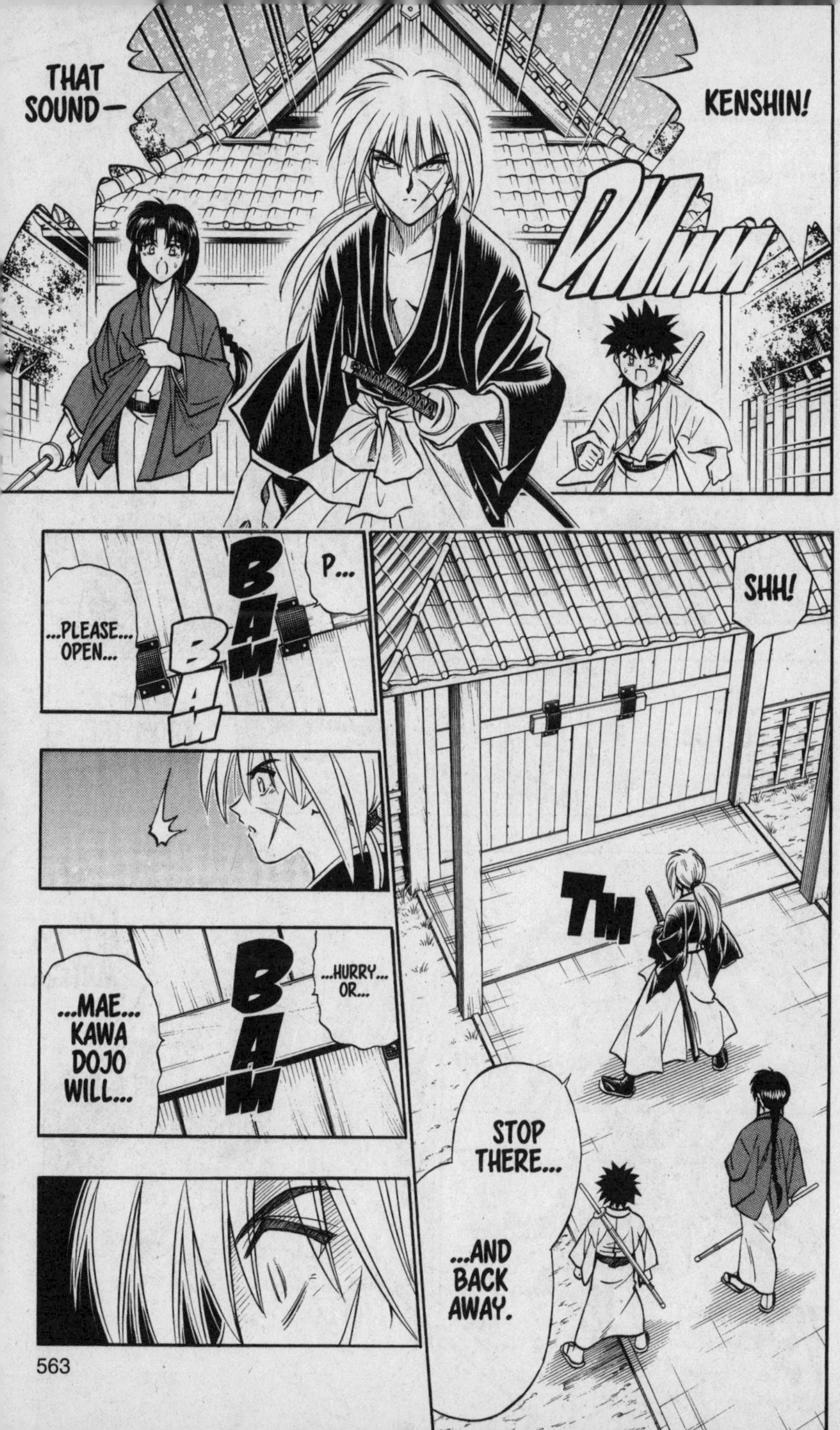
KENSHIN!
DMMMM
THAT SOUND—
SHH!
TM
STOP THERE...
...AND BACK AWAY.
P...
BAM
BAM
...PLEASE... OPEN...
...HURRY... OR...
BAM
...MAE... KAWA DOJO WILL...

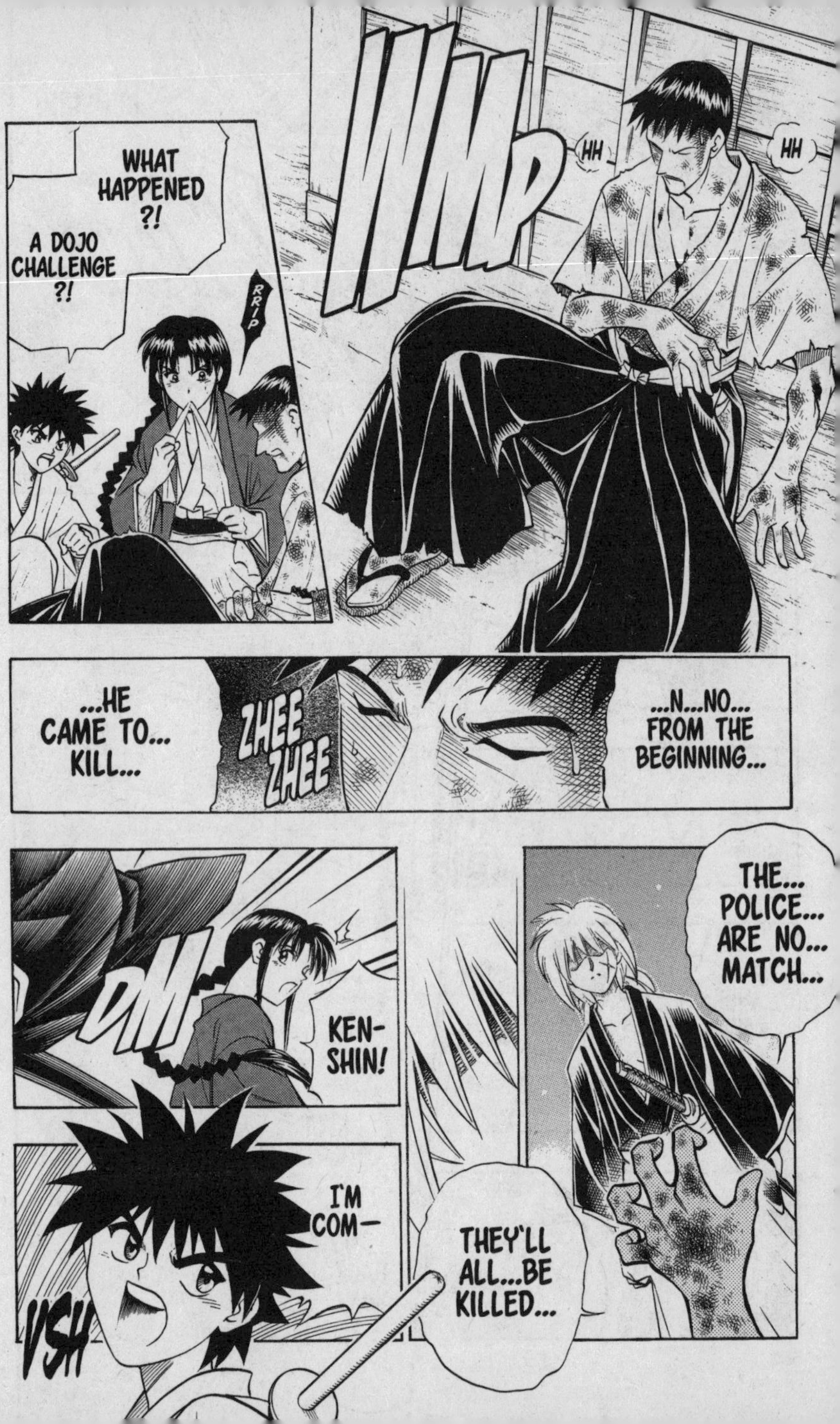
HH
HH
WMMP
WHAT HAPPENED ?!
A DOJO CHALLENGE ?!
RRIP
...N...NO... FROM THE BEGINNING...
ZHEE ZHEE
...HE CAME TO... KILL...
THE... POLICE... ARE NO... MATCH...
THEY'LL ALL...BE KILLED...
KEN-SHIN!
DM
I'M COM—
VSH

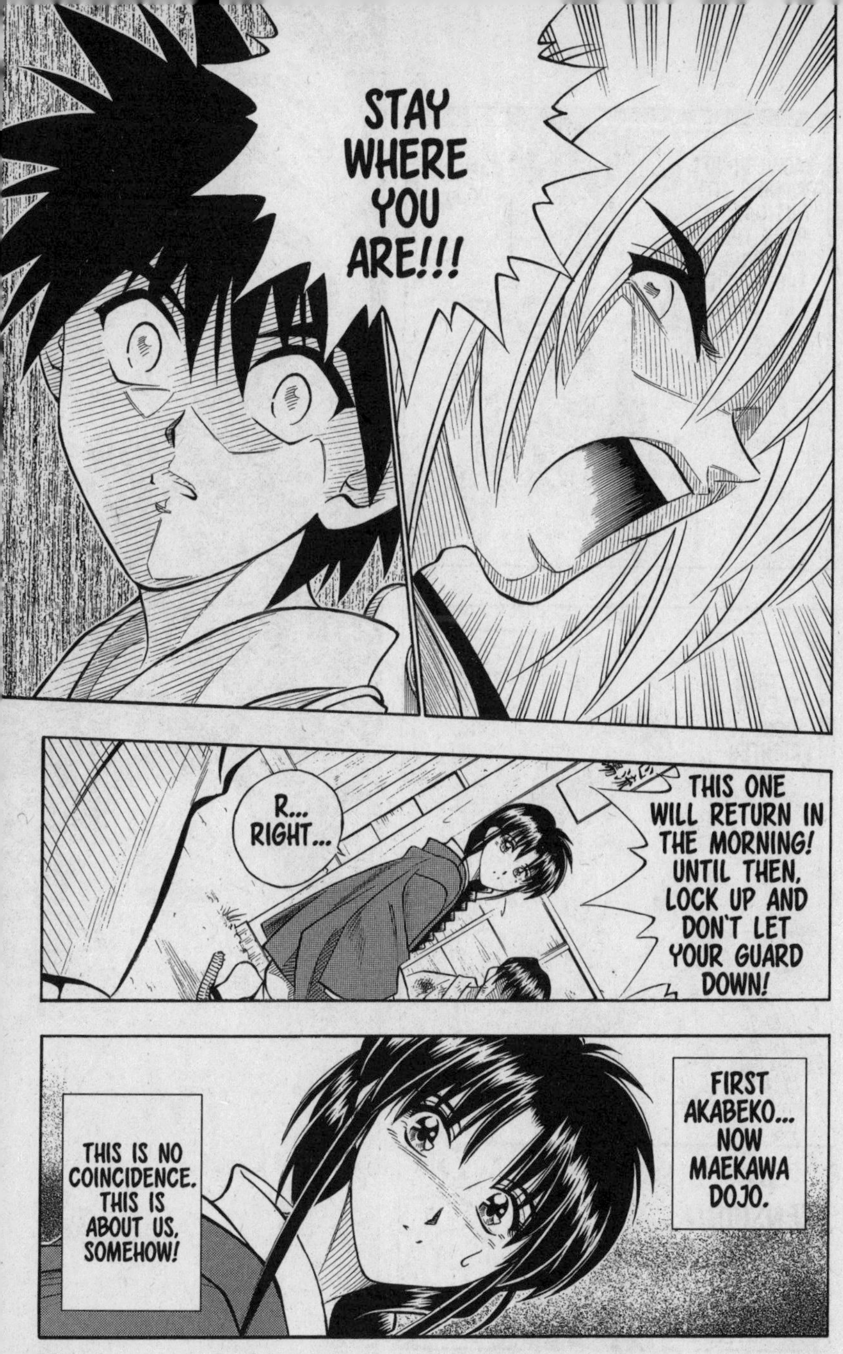
STAY WHERE YOU ARE!!!
THIS ONE WILL RETURN IN THE MORNING! UNTIL THEN, LOCK UP AND DON'T LET YOUR GUARD DOWN!
R... RIGHT...
FIRST AKABEKO... NOW MAEKAWA DOJO.
THIS IS NO COINCIDENCE. THIS IS ABOUT US, SOMEHOW!

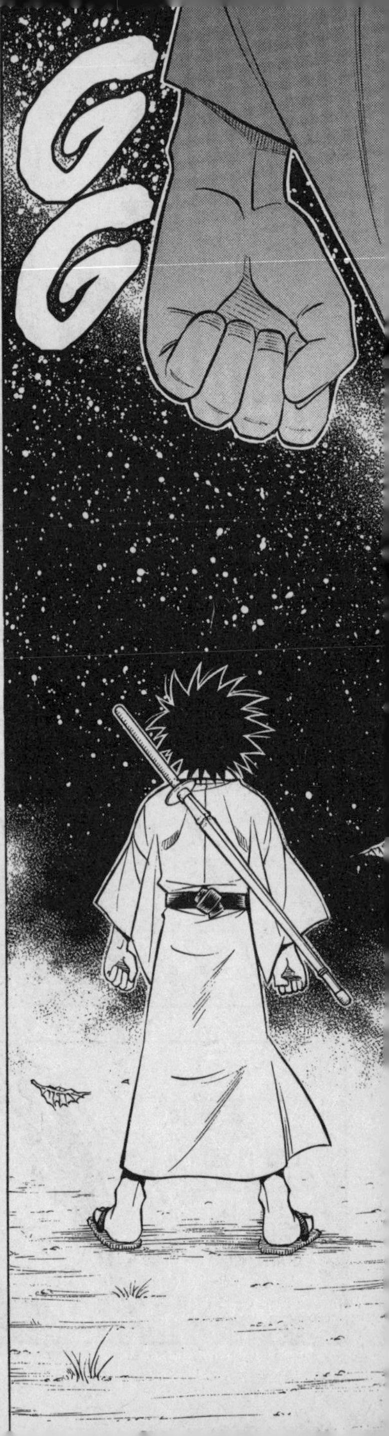
GGG

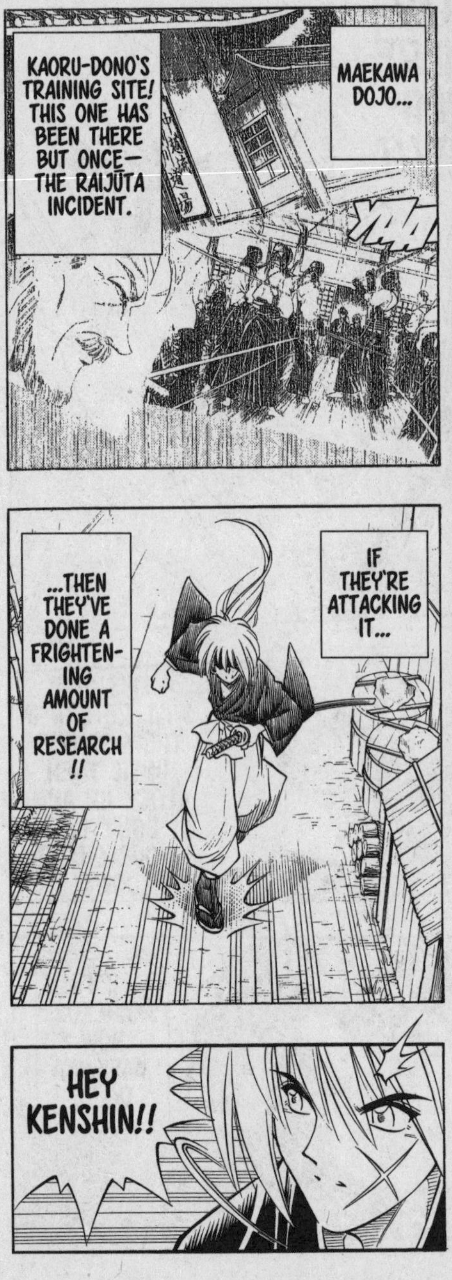
MAEKAWA DOJO...
KAORU-DONO'S TRAINING SITE! THIS ONE HAS BEEN THERE BUT ONCE—THE RAIJŪTA INCIDENT.
YAA
IF THEY'RE ATTACKING IT...
...THEN THEY'VE DONE A FRIGHTENING AMOUNT OF RESEARCH!!
HEY KENSHIN!!

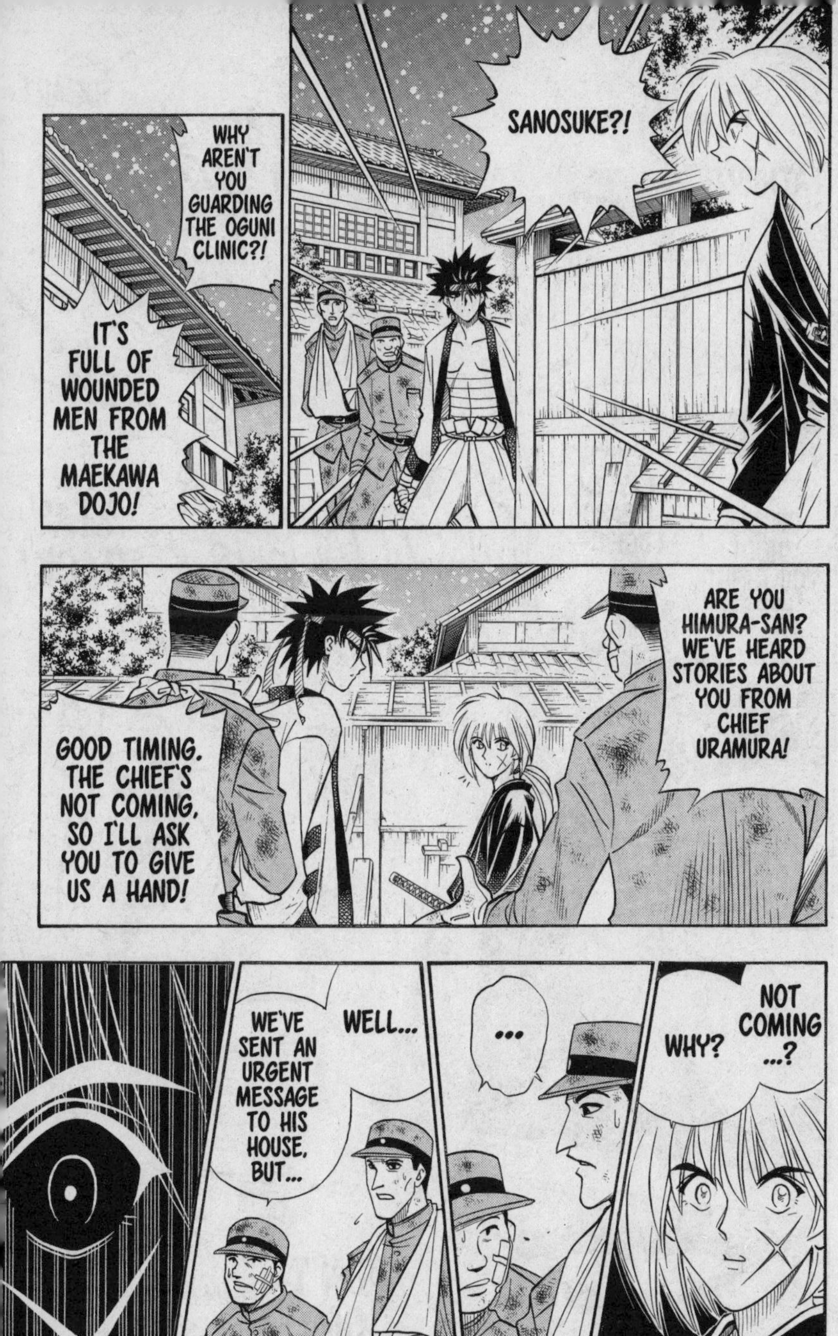
SANOSUKE?!
WHY AREN'T YOU GUARDING THE OGUNI CLINIC?!
IT'S FULL OF WOUNDED MEN FROM THE MAEKAWA DOJO!
ARE YOU HIMURA-SAN? WE'VE HEARD STORIES ABOUT YOU FROM CHIEF URAMURA!
GOOD TIMING. THE CHIEF'S NOT COMING, SO I'LL ASK YOU TO GIVE US A HAND!
NOT COMING ...?
WHY?
...
WELL...
WE'VE SENT AN URGENT MESSAGE TO HIS HOUSE, BUT...

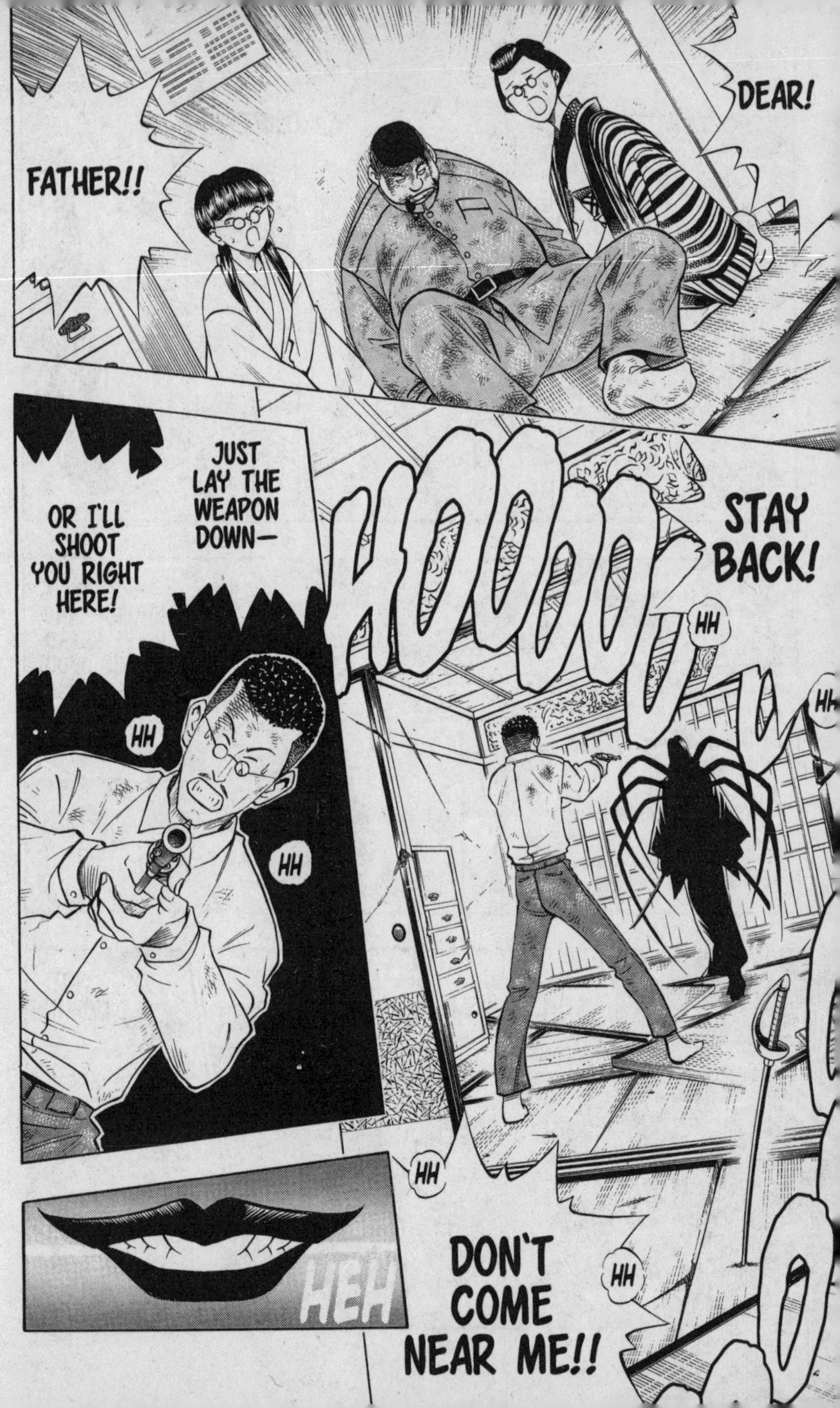
DEAR!
FATHER!!
STAY BACK!
HOOOO
HH
HH
HH
DON'T COME NEAR ME!!
HH
JUST LAY THE WEAPON DOWN—
OR I'LL SHOOT YOU RIGHT HERE!
HH
HH
HEH

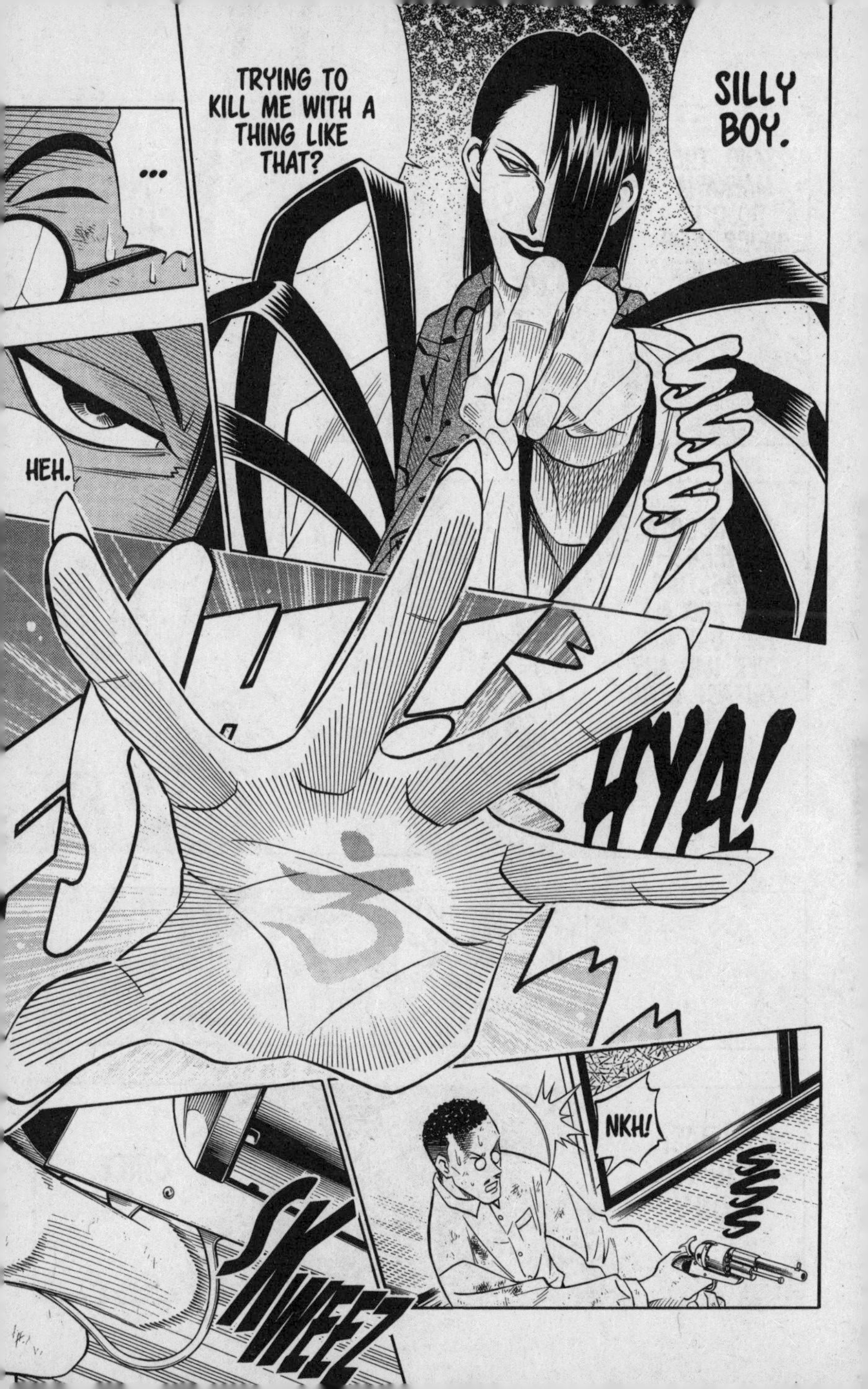
SILLY BOY.
TRYING TO KILL ME WITH A THING LIKE THAT?
...
HEH.
SSS
HYA!
NKH!
SSS
SKWEEZ

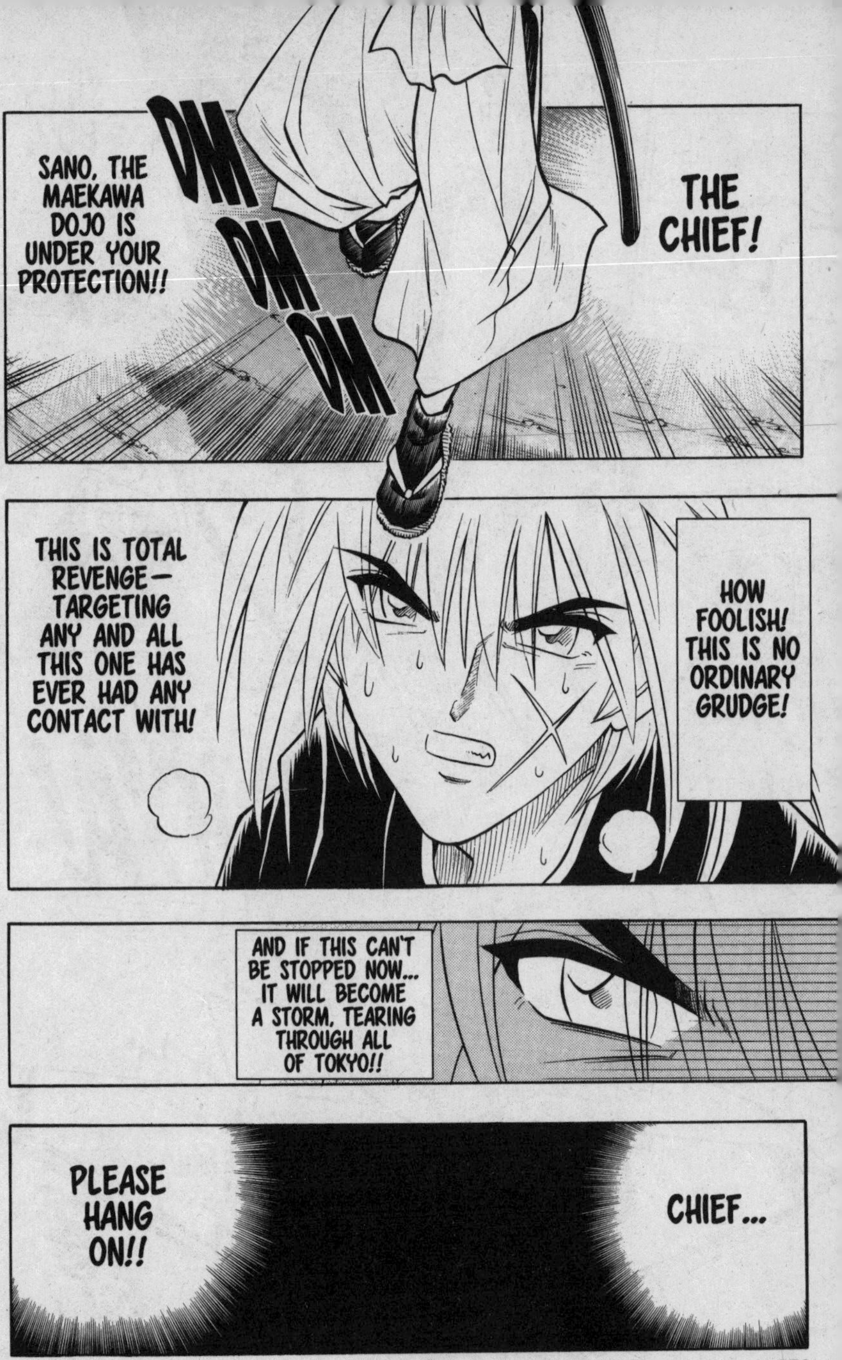
THE CHIEF!
DM DM DM
SANO, THE MAEKAWA DOJO IS UNDER YOUR PROTECTION!!
HOW FOOLISH! THIS IS NO ORDINARY GRUDGE!
THIS IS TOTAL REVENGE—TARGETING ANY AND ALL THIS ONE HAS EVER HAD ANY CONTACT WITH!
AND IF THIS CAN'T BE STOPPED NOW... IT WILL BECOME A STORM, TEARING THROUGH ALL OF TOKYO!!
CHIEF...
PLEASE HANG ON!!

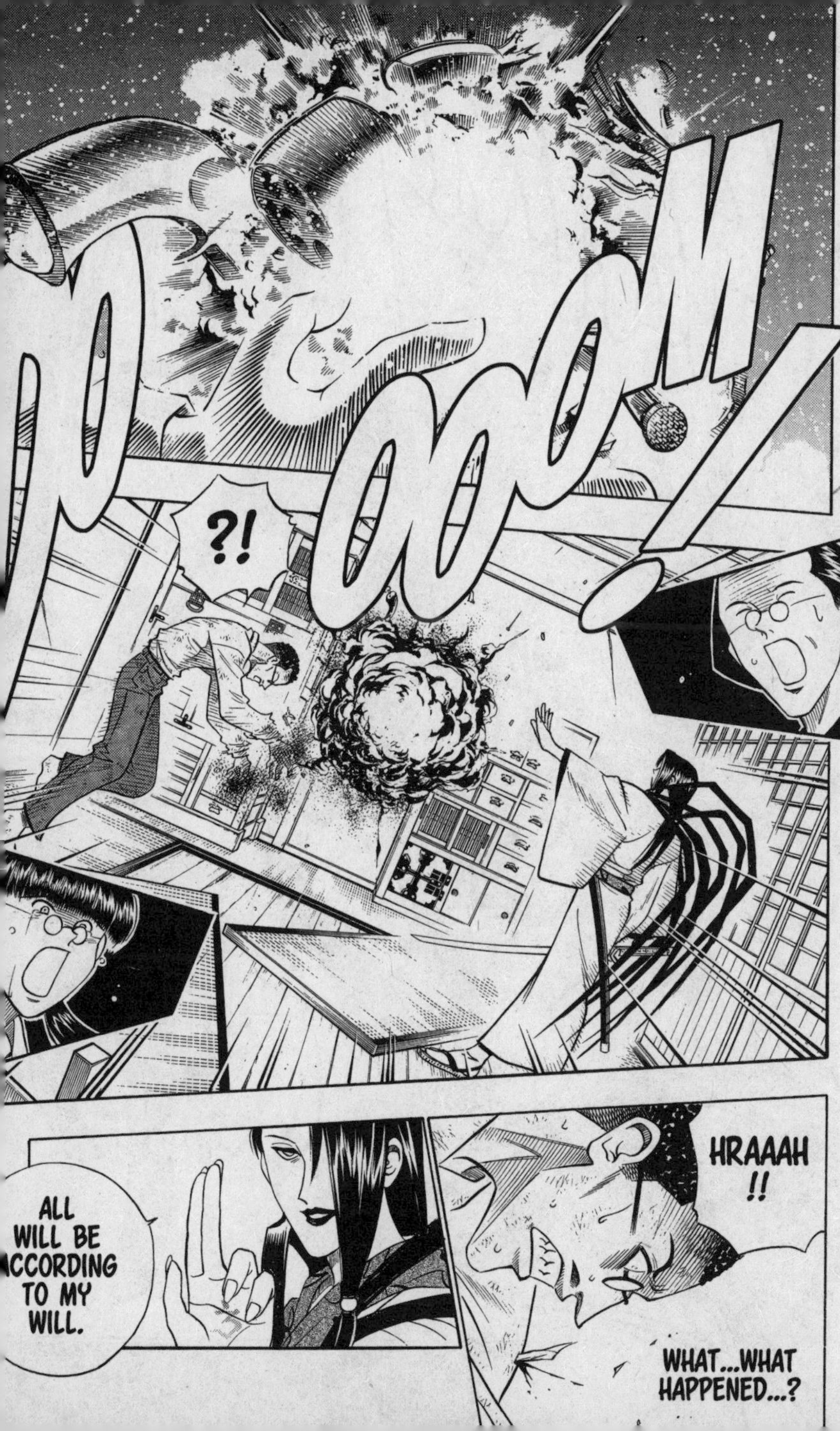
?!
HRAAAH!!
WHAT...WHAT HAPPENED...?
ALL WILL BE CCORDING TO MY WILL.

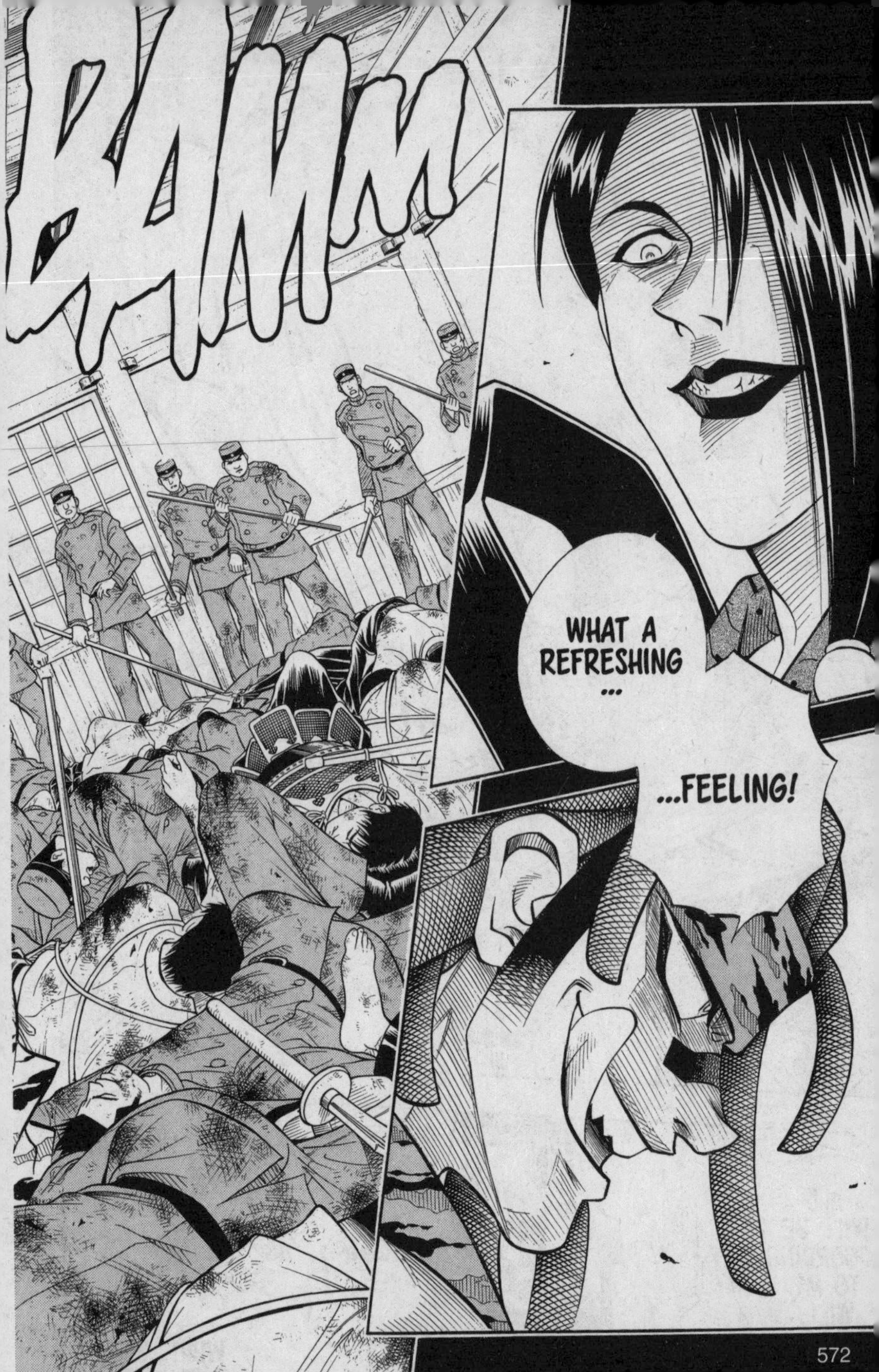
WHAT A REFRESHING ...
...FEELING!
BAMM

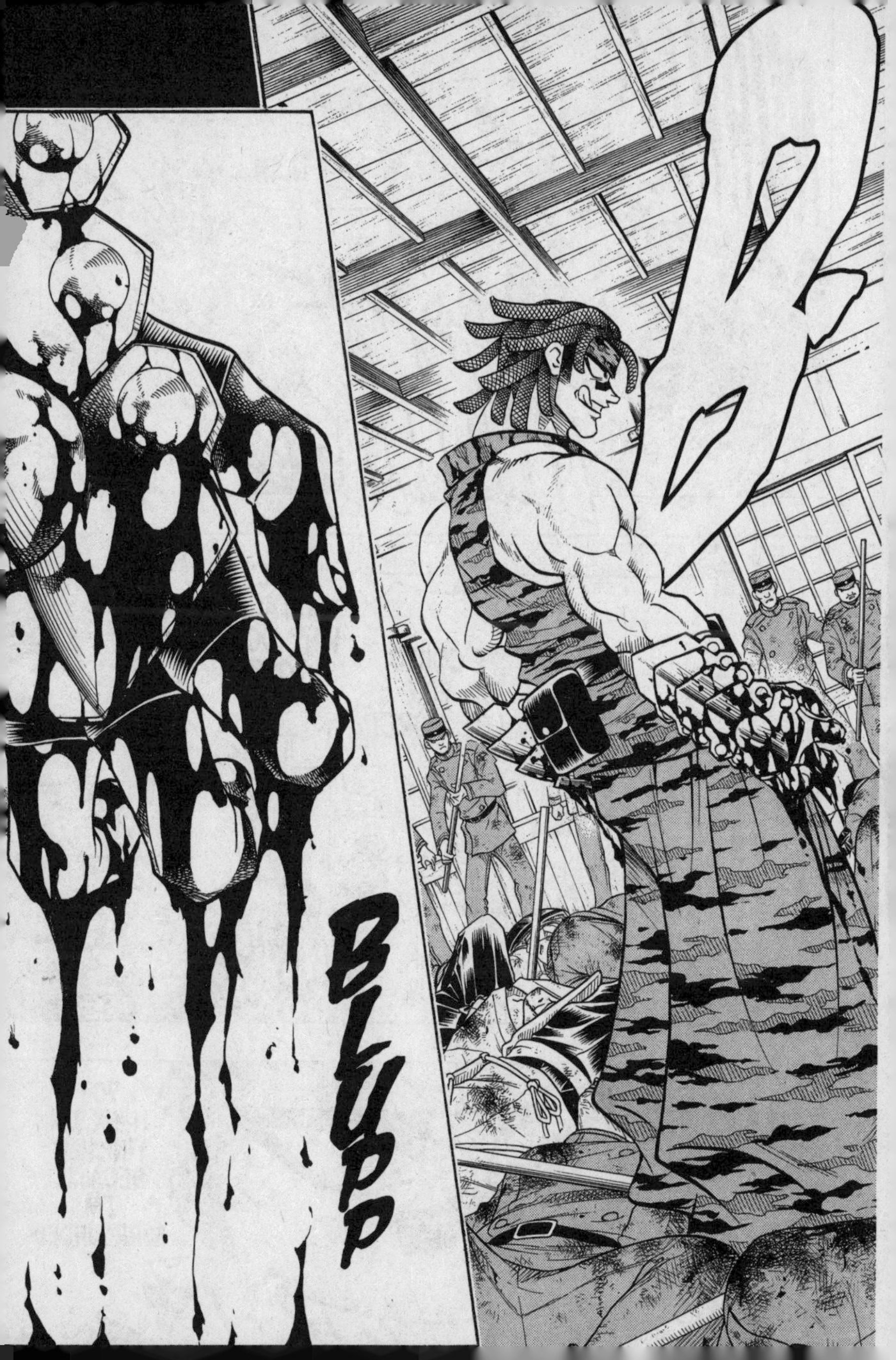
BLUPP

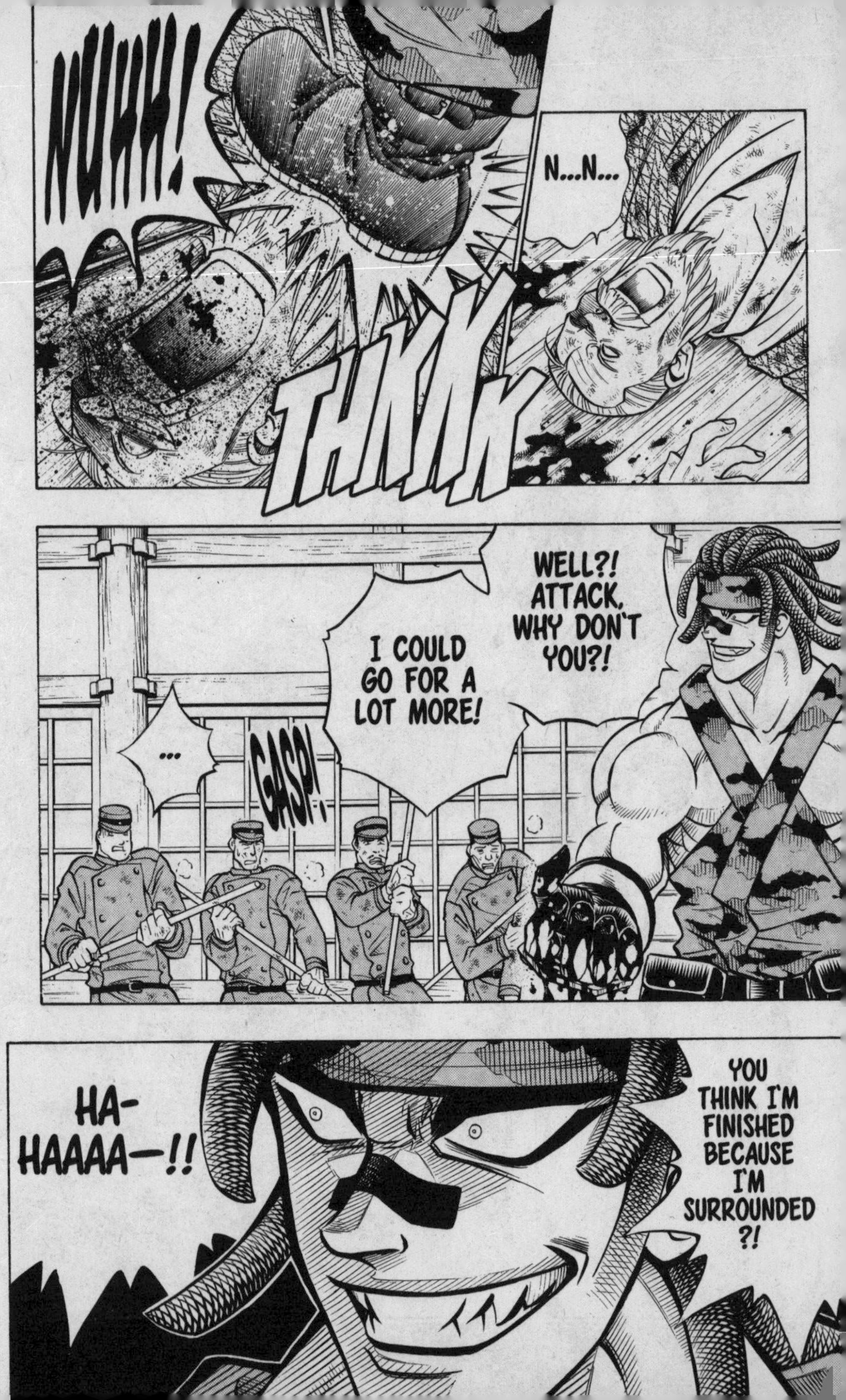
N...N...
NUHH!
THNK
WELL?! ATTACK, WHY DON'T YOU?!
I COULD GO FOR A LOT MORE!
GASP!
...
YOU THINK I'M FINISHED BECAUSE I'M SURROUNDED?!
HA-HAAAA—!!

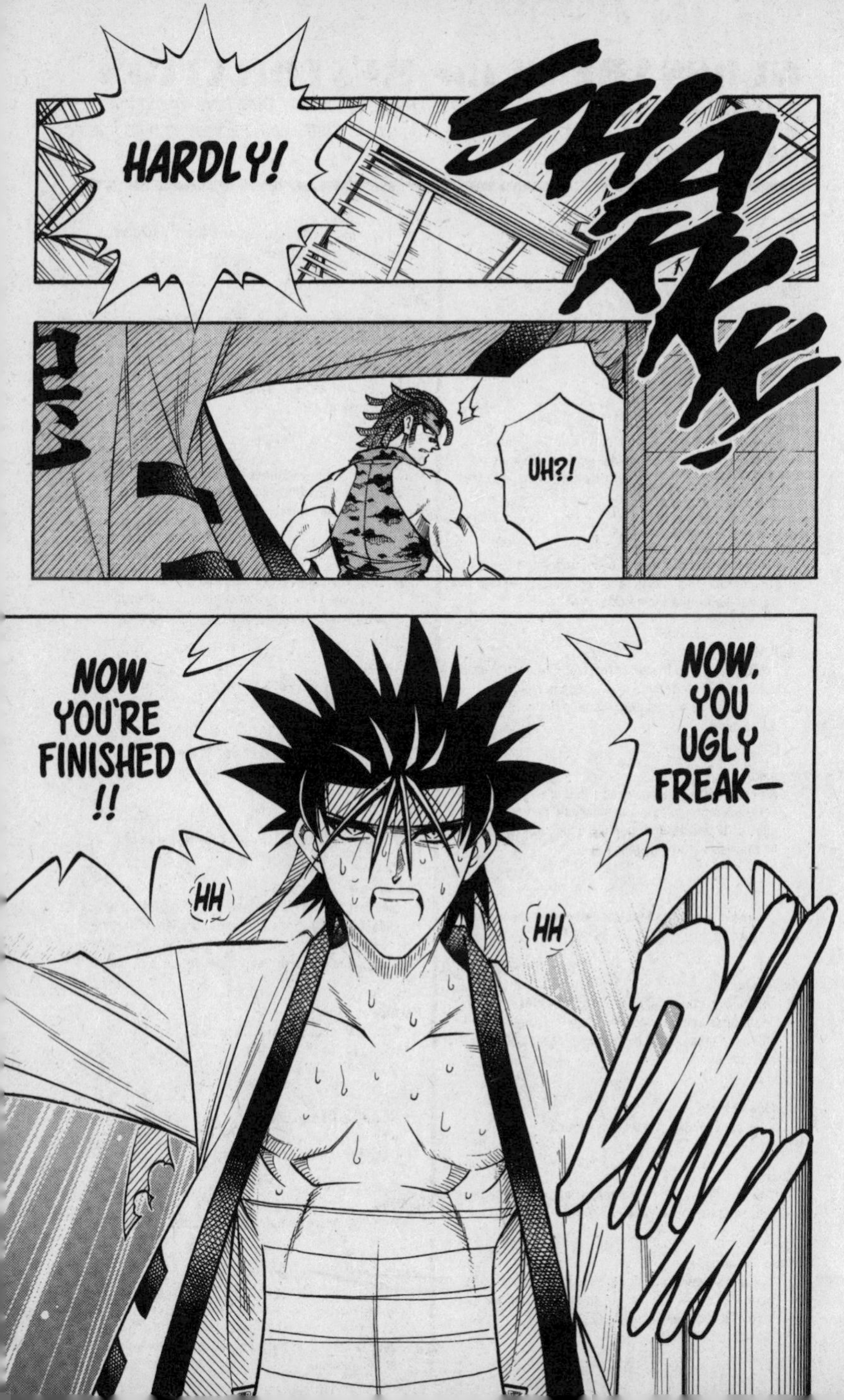
SHAKE!
HARDLY!
UH?!
NOW, YOU UGLY FREAK—
NOW YOU'RE FINISHED !!
HH
HH

GLOSSARY of the RESTORATION

A brief guide to select Japanese terms used in Rurouni Kenshin. *Both here and in the manga itself, all names are Japanese-style—i.e., last or family name first, with personal or given name following.*

dō
In kendō, a strike to the stomach.

dōgi
Karate uniform, also called a *gi*.

dojo
Martial arts training hall.

-dono
Honorific. More respectful than -*san*; the effect in modern-day Japanese would be along the lines of "Milord So-and-So." As used by Kenshin, it indicates both respect and humility.

Edo
Capital of the Tokugawa shōgunate during the era of shōgun rule (1603-1863), renamed Tokyo ("Eastern Capital") after the Meiji Restoration.

Fudō Myō-ō
In Vajrayana Buddhism, a protector and destroyer of delusions. His fearsome blue visage is typically surrounded by flames, representing the purification of the mind.

genpuku
A ceremony commemorating a young samurai's entrance into adulthood, usually held between the ages of 12 and 18. Traditionally, a samurai could not be married before his genpuku.

geta
Japanese wooden sandals, named after the noise they make.

hachimaki
Originally a charm against evil spirits, these headbands emblazoned with inspiring slogans are still worn today, often by students, as a symbol of determination.

Hijikata Toshizō
Vice-commander of the Shinsengumi.

Hirazuki
The real-life sword technique, associated with the Shinsengumi, upon which Saitō's Gatotsu is based.

Hiten Mitsurugi-ryū
Kenshin's sword technique, used more for defense than offense. An "ancient style that pits one against many," it requires exceptional speed and agility to master.

Aizu
Tokugawa-affiliated domain and site of the fourth battle of the Boshin War.

aku
Kanji character for "evil" worn by Sanosuke.

aku soku zan
"Swift death to evil," a *bushido* motto associated with the Shinsengumi.

Ashura
Often depicted with three faces and six arms, Ashura are low-ranking Buddhist deities. In Japan they're seen as supernatural guardians.

bakufu
Another word for *shōgunate*, bakufu ("tent government") refers to the samurai and other military officials who ruled Japan during the Edo period.

Bakumatsu
Final, chaotic days of the Tokugawa regime.

Bishamon
Often considered a god of war, Bishamon is usually depicted with a halo-like wheel of flames.

bokutō
Wooden kendō weapon also known as a *bokken*.

Boshin War
Civil war of 1868-69 between the failing Tokugawa shōgunate and a new movement organized to restore the Emperor to power. The pro-imperial side won, ushering in a new era of modernization.

Bushido
The "way of the warrior," a code of samurai values dating to the 17th century.

-chan
Honorific. Can be used either as a diminutive (as with a child: "Little Kentarō"), or to indicate affection ("Darling Hanako").

Chōshū
Anti-Tokugawa domain and home to many patriots.

daruma doll
Roly-poly *daruma* figures are traditionally given for good luck to those starting new ventures (a birthday, New Year's, a new business). One of the doll's blank eyes is filled in at the outset of the venture, the other at completion.

Keiō period
The era just before the Meiji era, spanning from 1865 to 1868.

kenjutsu
The art of fencing; sword arts; kendō.

Kenshin-gumi
Literally, "group of Kenshin"—translated (rather playfully) for our purposes as "Team Kenshin."

Kiheitai
Volunteer militia which, like the Shinsengumi, recruited members based on ability rather than social class. Members ranged from peasant farmers to samurai.

Kinkaku/Ginkaku Temples
Subject of a famous novel by Yukio Mishima, the Kinkaku-ji or "Temple of the Golden Pavilion" was built as a retirement home for a former shōgun and later converted to a Zen temple. Ginkaku Temple was built by another member of the shōgun's family and incorporates similar designs.

kodachi
Medium-length sword, shorter than the katana but longer than the *wakizashi*. Its easy maneuverability makes it a strong defensive weapon.

Kōgen Ittō-ryū
A real historical sword style, *Kōgen Ittō-ryū* is characterized by economy of movement.

-kun
Honorific. Nowadays it's usually a chummy form of address between male friends. When used in *Rurouni Kenshin*, however, it's more often in the older sense of superior-to-inferior, intended to express a difference in rank as well as affection.

kunoichi
Female ninja.

"ku-shaped" shuriken
Shuriken are the "throwing stars" known to lovers of samurai and ninja drama everywhere. "*Ku*-shaped" *shuriken* are shaped like the Japanese character *ku*: basically, a boomerang shape.

Kyoto
Home of the Emperor from 794 until shortly after the Meiji Restoration, when the imperial court was moved to Edo/Tokyo.

loyalists
Those who supported the return of the Emperor to power; the Ishin Shishi.

hitokiri
A skilled sword-wielding assassin, literally "person slasher."

Hitokiri Battōsai
"Sword-Wielding Manslayer," the name under which Himura Kenshin fought and killed. Swordsmen of the period sometimes adopted "professional" names to keep their birth names private.

Iba Hachirō
Famed historical swordsman (1843-1869).

Ikeda-ya Incident
An 1864 plot by a group of samurai to set fire to Kyoto and assassinate or kidnap government officials. The plot was hatched at the Ikeda-ya Inn in Kyoto.

Ishin Shishi
Famed imperialist patriots who fought to end the reign of the Tokugawa shōgunate and restore the Emperor to his ancient seat of power.

Jigen-ryū
Aggressive swordsmanship style, literally "revealed reality," which teaches practitioners to kill with a single powerful blow.

Jōdan, Chūdan, Gedan, Hassō, Wakigamae
The five basic stances of kendō. *Jōdan*: Sword lifted overhead. *Chūdan* (or *seigan*): Cut to the middle. *Gedan*: Low, sweeping block. *Hassō*: Sword held vertically, hands shoulder-level. *Wakigamae*: Horizontal guard position.

kanji
Japanese system of writing based on Chinese characters.

karakuri
Intricate mechanized dolls, *karakuri* ("mechanism" or "gimmick") are regarded today as one of Japan's great traditional crafts and a forerunner to modern robotics.

katana
The standard Japanese longsword, with a curved, single-edge blade normally positioned with the cutting side up. The name is short for *uchigatana*, "striking sword."

Katsu Kaishū
Founder of the Japanese navy. Called "the greatest man in Japan," Kaishū was born to an impoverished minor samurai family and worked his way up to the head of the Tokugawa shōgunate.

Kawakami Gensai
This infamous Edo-period assassin, known for being so fast with a sword that he could kill his targets in broad daylight, was the historical inspiration for Himura Kenshin.

patriots
Another term for Ishin Shishi, supporters of the Emperor.

rurouni
Wanderer, vagabond.

Saigō Takamori
A powerful military and political leader who oversaw the end of the Edo period, Takamori has been called "the last true samurai." Although he supported the restoration of the Emperor, he later led a revolution of disgruntled samurai opposing the rapid modernization of Japan.

sakabatō
Reversed-edge sword (the dull edge on the side the sharp should be, and vice-versa) carried by Kenshin as a symbol of his resolution never to kill again.

-sama
Very respectful honorific, used primarily to address a person of much higher rank. But it can also be used romantically: "Ah! Tsukiyama-sama…"

-san
The basic honorific, equivalent to "Mr." or "Ms." In Japanese, a name should never be spoken without an honorific.

Seinan War
Failed 1877 uprising of the samurai class against the new Meiji government and the modernization of Japan. Also known as the Satsuma Rebellion.

Seishū, Hanaoka
Japanese surgeon (1760-1835) whose use of the drug *tsusensan* during a breast cancer operation in 1805 pioneered the use of surgical anesthesia.

Sekihō Army
A pro-imperial army formed mainly of commoners; the name means "Red Vanguard." After the successful restoration of the Emperor, however, the *Sekihōtai* were scapegoated and blamed for the new regime's failed promises.

sen
Historical unit of Japanese currency, equal to one hundredth of one yen.

sensei
Teacher; master. *Sensei* is both the Japanese word for "teacher" and an honorific indicating a position of authority or expertise, including teachers, doctors, lawyers, political leaders, and renowned artists.

shinai
Wooden practice sword, traditionally constructed of well-seasoned bamboo, first used around 1750.

Meiji Restoration
Period from 1853-1868 during which the Tokugawa shōgunate was destroyed and the Emperor restored as ruler of Japan. Named after Emperor Meiji, whose chosen name was written with the characters for "culture" and "enlightenment."

Mimawarigumi
A Kyoto police force. Unlike the Shinsengumi, the Mimawarigumi were all upper-class samurai.

Mt. Hiei
Founded more than 1,200 years ago, the temple atop Mt. Hiei was built to protect Kyoto from evil spirits. Because police were barred from entering the temple grounds, criminals often took sanctuary there.

Obon
The Buddhist "Day of the Dead," Obon, or Bon, takes place in either July or August, depending on the part of the country. Today it's one of Japan's three major holiday seasons, the others being New Year's in January and "Golden Week" in May.

ohagi
Autumnal treat made from sweet rice and bean paste. The name comes from *hagi*, or bush clover, which flowers in the fall. A very similar confection called *botamochi*, or tree peony, is eaten in the spring.

okashira
Leader or boss; literally, "the head."

om
An ancient meditative symbol in both Buddhism and Hinduism, it is believed to be the sound that was spoken when the universe was created.

onigiri
These seaweed-wrapped rice balls, usually with fish or vegetable fillings, have long been a portable and convenient staple of the Japanese diet.

Ōnin War
A fifteenth-century civil war that ushered in the "Warring States Period," an era of near-constant conflict between rival lords.

oniwabanshū
Elite group of *onmitsu* ("spies") of the Edo period, now commonly called ninja.

onsen
Written with the characters for "warmth" and "springs," *onsen*, volcanic hot springs, are an important part of Japanese tradition and remain popular today. The springs are typically the star feature of an inn or other bathing facility that provides visitors with a relaxing experience.

tonfa
> A two-handed weapon, ideal for defense, often used by police during the Meiji era.

Toshimichi Ōkubo
> Samurai and political leader regarded as one of the founders of modern Japan.

wakizashi
> A sword similar to the more familiar katana, but shorter, with a blade between 12 and 24 inches.

Wolves of Mibu
> Nickname for the Shinsengumi, after the town where they were first stationed.

yakuza
> Japanese underworld; "the mob." Like organized criminals in other cultures, they're known for colorful garb (including tattoos, which are traditionally frowned on in Japan) and equally colorful speech.

Yamagata Aritomo
> Soldier, statesman and chief founder of the modern Japanese army. A samurai of Chōshū he studied military science in Europe and returned to Japan in 1870 to head the war ministry.

yatsuhashi
> A traditional sweet flavored with sugar and cinnamon. It's one of the best-known *meibutsu*, or regional delicacies, of Kyoto.

zanbatō
> A massive, single-edged sword used as an anti-cavalry weapon; the name means "horse-chopping sword."

Zipangu
> Japan was once one of the foremost mining countries of the world. Marco Polo heard rumors of *Zipangu*, the "land of gold," while in China, and it was through his writings about the marvelous golden country that Europe was introduced to Japan.

shingan
> Written with the characters *shin* ("mind," "heart," "soul") and *gan* ("eye," "insight"), *shingan* can be translated as "soul vision" or "mind's eye."

shinobi
> Another word for ninja.

Shinsengumi
> An elite police force made up of exceptionally skilled swordsmen of all social classes. The Shinsengumi ("newly selected corps") were established by the shōgunate in 1863 to suppress loyalists and restore law and order to the blood-soaked streets of Kyoto.

shizoku
> Replaced the term "samurai" in the new era. Made up of ex-samurai and military families, it came to be the gentry class.

shōgi
> Strategic board game similar to chess.

shōgun
> Feudal military leader of Japan, short for *Sei-i Taishōgun* ("Commander of Expeditionary Force Against Barbarians").

shōgunate
> Government ruled by shōguns, with even the Emperor taking orders from the ruling lords.

soba
> Buckwheat noodles, about as thick as spaghetti, served either hot or cold.

sukashi
> An evasive or defensive move in karate.

suntetsu
> Small, handheld blade designed for palming and concealment.

tachi
> A long, curved sword usually wielded on horseback.

Toba Fushimi, Battle at
> Battle near Kyoto between the forces of the new imperial government and the fallen shōgunate. Ending with an imperial victory, it was the first battle of the Boshin War.

Tokugawa Bakufu
> Military feudal government, led by powerful shōguns, that dominated Japan from 1603 to 1867.

Tokugawa Yoshinobu
> The 15th and final shōgun of Japan. His peaceful abdication in 1867 marked the end of the Edo period and the beginning of the Meiji era.

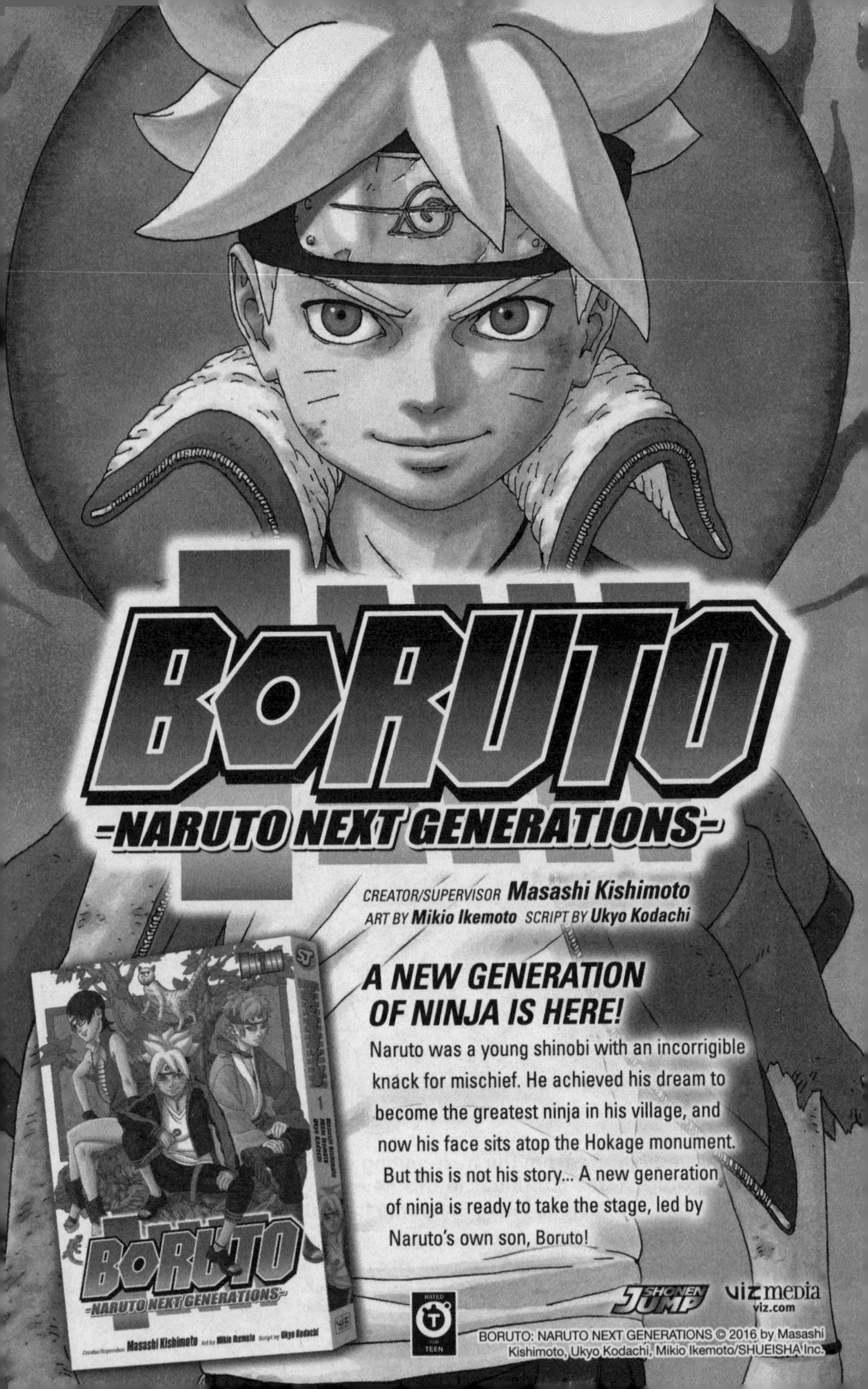
BORUTO
-NARUTO NEXT GENERATIONS-
CREATOR/SUPERVISOR Masashi Kishimoto
ART BY Mikio Ikemoto SCRIPT BY Ukyo Kodachi
A NEW GENERATION OF NINJA IS HERE!
Naruto was a young shinobi with an incorrigible knack for mischief. He achieved his dream to become the greatest ninja in his village, and now his face sits atop the Hokage monument. But this is not his story... A new generation of ninja is ready to take the stage, led by Naruto's own son, Boruto!
SHONEN JUMP
viz media
viz.com
RATED T TEEN
BORUTO: NARUTO NEXT GENERATIONS © 2016 by Masashi Kishimoto, Ukyo Kodachi, Mikio Ikemoto/SHUEISHA Inc.

Black ✦ Clover

STORY & ART BY YŪKI TABATA

Asta is a young boy who dreams of becoming the greatest mage in the kingdom. Only one problem—he can't use any magic! Luckily for Asta, he receives the incredibly rare five-leaf clover grimoire that gives him the power of anti-magic. Can someone who can't use magic really become the Wizard King? One thing's for sure—Asta will never give up!

SHONEN JUMP

VIZ media
www.viz.com

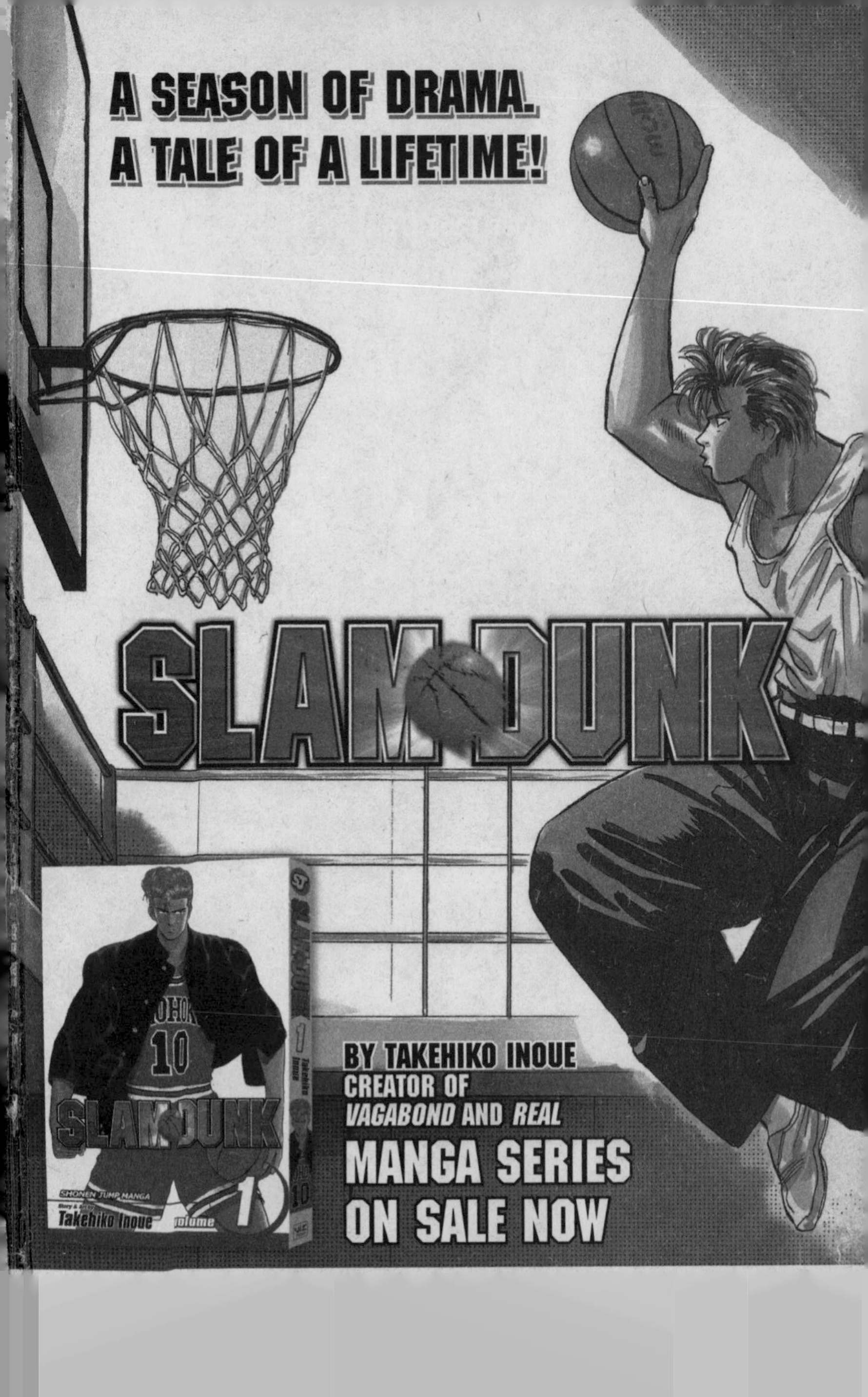
A SEASON OF DRAMA.
A TALE OF A LIFETIME!
SLAM DUNK
SLAM DUNK
SHONEN JUMP MANGA
Takehiko Inoue
volume 1
BY TAKEHIKO INOUE
CREATOR OF
VAGABOND AND REAL
MANGA SERIES
ON SALE NOW